to Maria Luisa

Roberto L. Quercetani

ATHLETICS

A HISTORY OF MODERN TRACK AND FIELD ATHLETICS
(1860 - 2000)
Men and Women

Lamine Diack
President, International Amateur Athletic Federation
President, International Athletic Foundation

Foreword

The publication of the latest work of Roberto L. Quercetani takes place, not by coincidence, with the turn of the century and of the millennium: the perfect time to look to the future, with an eye on the century we have just left.

The International Athletic Foundation was proud to support Quercetani's first edition of this important historical volume and we are equally pleased to have contributed to this new edition. Quercetani is a writer who finds his inspiration in the past. He reads between the lines of human affairs and patiently gathers every detail that he uses then to reconstruct the magnificent designs of history.

The story of Athletics is as noble as the history of humankind. It is deeply intermingled with the political, cultural and economic affairs of our different societies, just as the changes in athletic performances are a gauge of progress and the problems of humanity.

Modern athletics was born in the 19th century, mainly in Great Britain and the United States – and this was not by chance: they were two of the most highly evolved of the great nations of that period. Not far behind were France and Germany, and it was the former which had the honour of imagining the renaissance of the Olympics. With at its centre, Athletics. The history of the Olympics and of Athletics have since that time been so closely linked that, until 1983, it was impossible to separate the two.

But 1983 was the year of the first celebration of the World Championships in Athletics, which will take place for the eighth time in 2001, in Edmonton, Canada.
But the World Championships in Athletics are also the symbol of the massive growth of the movement and of the need, so clearly felt by our world, to create a solid and independent economic and organisational structure capable of promoting and channelling new passions.

For all of these things, I must thank a man who dedicated his life to the transformation of Athletics, giving it programmes and economic power that had previously been inconceivable.
That man is Primo Nebiolo, who will always remain among the great protagonists of our history and for this we are very pleased that the writer and the publisher decided to dedicate this new edition to Nebiolo's memory.

Let us look back with pride at the past, for it bears witness to how humankind's most ancient sport – Athletics – continues to possess a fascination capable of attracting new acolytes. They come from every corner of the earth and are the fruit of the labours of 210 National Federations spread among the five continents.
They are the true wealth of our organisation.

It is upon this capital that we rely to continue, in the third millennium, to write the story of our progress.

Lamine Diack

A SPECIAL TRIBUTE
by Robert J. Fasulo

Primo Nebiolo: the Consummate Explorer

*Like the great explorers of centuries past,
Primo Nebiolo was always searching for new frontiers.*

Our friend and distinguished athletics journalist Roberto Quercetani first approached the Foundation for assistance in updating this book back in November 1998. It was no surprise that the late Primo Nebiolo was one of the strongest supporters at the time.

Few true scholars of the sport other than Quercetani could better put the last century of our sport into a proper perspective and Nebiolo had always nurtured a certain pride in his compatriot's esteemed position amongst sports historians.

Forever the Tuscan gentleman, Quercetani was quick to propose that his new edition be dedicated to the memory of the late president, following Nebiolo's sudden death in November 1999. Quercetani has been in touch with the IAAF and the sport since the earliest post-war years, and understood that Nebiolo had redefined the place of the sport internationally. Modesty aside, Quercetani would confide that he was "in an ideal position to fully appreciate the enormous growth of the IAAF, mostly over the past twenty years, in terms of international prestige, influence and general impact on the world of athletics". I couldn't have agreed more.

I was therefore humbled by Quercetani's request to provide this commemoration to the late IAAF president. He would say, "Few people were as close to him as you in the last ten years, so I can't think of anyone better suited." And, modesty aside, I suppose he's right.

For people like me who had the privilege of being a daily part of Primo Nebiolo's private and public world during some of the most intense years of his IAAF presidency, we knew him as a man of absolute passion and substance. His unending dedication and commitment to athletics, the IAAF and its presidency were the sort that makes legends.

There was no such thing as 'free time' for Primo; his mind was always working and focussed, his objectives simple, but clear: grow track and field athletics to new heights of popularity, prestige and prominence and in turn, enlighten the world to the greatness of our sport.

Indeed, there was very little in Primo Nebiolo's life that could be considered typical. He had no hobbies. He didn't go to the movies or watch TV, except of course to see the occasional athletics event he couldn't attend personally or when it was to watch his football team, Juventus.
He never read best-selling novels, but his imagination was as sharp as that of any literary laureate.
He did not pay much attention to fads, but he always seemed to sense trends before they happened.

On the rare occasions when Nebiolo did have time outside the frantic pace of meetings or events or travels, he would often seek solace in the one distraction that always managed to capture his fascination: the sea.

Throughout his voracious travel schedule, he would speak nostalgically of his love for the great port cities of the world; Venice, Rio, Barcelona, Athens, Sydney, Lisbon or Los Angeles.
Whenever we had the opportunity to travel together to such places,
he would, without exception, arrange to spend half a day or more, at the sea.
He was, of course, born in a country that was not only surrounded by the sea, but also whose history was marked by some of the greatest explorers of all time.

Surely, had Nebiolo lived in the age when the frontiers of our world were being explored across the oceans, he would have been there, steadily at the helm of the great ships, firmly in command while pushing his own human limits and those around him to challenge the possibilities, to discover new worlds. Stubbornly proud of his heritage and history, he could spend hours recalling his country's contribution to the world, almost as if he had been there himself.

Nebiolo was, in many respects, the modern-day explorer of world athletics. Where he may have been limited in pushing his own capabilities as a respectable, but rather unheralded athlete, he pushed forward relentlessly as a leader from a very young age. In doing so, he inspired devotion and loyalty but also envy and antagonism.

In two short decades, his clarity of vision and strength of purpose led to remarkable changes such as the development and success of the World Championships, and their subsequent change to a biennial event. His push to transfer the IAAF Headquarters from London to Monaco was also his way of acknowledging a new commercial order in the sport. It was no surprise therefore when he led the IAAF down the path of cash awards at IAAF events, once unthinkable in the old-world amateurism of athletics. He always hoped people would understand him – especially the athletes – but usually expected that people never would.

No one more than Nebiolo understood the dire necessity of embracing, but also harnessing and controlling the commercial forces that now drive the sport. His remarkable deal-making abilities were evident when he secured the six-year, $125m renewal of the European TV rights agreement for the IAAF, which ultimately put the IAAF in the position to further reward the same athletes which he held so dear. His leadership in introducing wildcards for reigning world champions at the World Championships and the creation of the Golden League were further testimony to his vision.

Nebiolo's drive and personality may have been responsible for these innovations, but it was ultimately his keen sense of risk-taking and flair for adventure that led him to innovation and change, often in the face of enormous opposition.
By his own admission, Nebiolo made mistakes and had his faults, but in the end only history can be the judge.

Inevitably, in the moments of most intense discussion or difficulty, Nebiolo would turn to me and ask, "Is this all really worth it"? I had no answer at the time, but I have the answer now, dear president. Yes, your travails were justified.
Yes, you have taken your place in history.

For his friends and admirers who miss him, Nebiolo will remain – like the great explorers of centuries past – a larger-than-life figure whose personality and accomplishments will endure for years to come.

Robert J. Fasulo (USA) is the General Secretary of the International Athletic Foundation. He had worked with Dr Nebiolo since 1990, most recently as IAAF Chief of Staff and General Secretary of the Association of Summer Olympic International Federations (ASOIF).

ACKNOWLEDGEMENTS

We wish to thank the following authorities for their valuable contribution:
- International Amateur Athletic Federation (IAAF)
- International Athletic Foundation (IAF)
- Robert J. Fasulo
- Pierre Weiss
- Vassar College, Poughkeepsie, New York, USA
- Roger Gynn, John Manners, David Martin, Frank Zarnowski

We also wish to express our appreciation to All Sport Photographic for its important contribution.

As well as to the following authorities who offered valuable contributions for the first edition (1991):
- The Track and Field Federations of:
Ethiopia, Holland, Norway, Poland, Sweden and Trinidad;
- Mr. Pete Cava - USA, The Athletics Congress Press Information Director;
- Luciano Barra, Aldo Cambi, Ottavio Castellini, Franco Fava, Atsushi Hoshino,
Rooney Magnusson, Benigno Melzi d'Eril, Donald Potts, Mel Watman, Jon Wigley

Text: Roberto L. Quercetani
Preface: Augusto Frasca
Graphics: Diego Galbiati
Technician: Ermenegildo Chiozzotto
Photolithography: Typecolor (Cassina de Pecchi - Milan)
Printing: Garzanti Verga (Cernusco s.N. - Milan)
Produced by: SEP Editrice srl (Cernusco s.N. - Milan)
Picture acknowledgements: All Sport Photographic (UK), Roberto L. Quercetani

PRINTED IN ITALY - August 2000

© Worldwide 2000 SEP Editrice srl
Via Brescia 28 - 20063 Cernusco s.N. - Milan (ITALY)

ISBN 88-87110-23-9

CONTENTS

MEN'S ATHLETICS

Part 1: 1860-1900   Page 19
**THE BIRTH OF MODERN ATHLETICS.
REVIVAL OF THE OLYMPIC GAMES**

British and American pioneers.
From the indefatigable walkers to the earliest champions: Wefers, Myers, George.

Part 2: 1901-1920   Page 41
THE COMING OF AGE OF INTERNATIONAL COMPETITION. BIRTH OF THE I.A.A.F.

The map of the sport gains in width. The first truly representative Olympics: Stockholm 1912. Technical evolution in the various branches. The champions: Duffey, Shrubb, Horine, Kolehmainen.

Part 3: 1921-1940   Page 71
**THE EARLIEST "MYTHS":
PAAVO NURMI AND JESSE OWENS**

Birth of the British Commonwealth Games, the European Championships and other important events.

Part 4: 1941-1960   Page 127
**WORLD WAR 2 CANCELS
TWO EDITIONS OF THE OLYMPICS.
ZÁTOPEK SPEARHEADS THE REVIVAL**

The champions "who never got a chance": Davis, Warmerdam, Blozis, Hägg, Arne Andersson. The early post-war years: Zátopek, Consolini, Hary, Elliott et al. Amateurism begins to fold. USSR enters the athletic arena.

Part 5: 1961-1980   Page 195
**CHAMPIONS AND RECORDS GALORE.
POLITICAL INTERFERENCES.
AFRICA ENTERS THE PICTURE**

Athletics in a new dimension. Technique and organization evolve. Professionalism becomes the rule at high levels of performance, although not officially acknowledged as such. The champions: Hayes, Snell, Juantorena, Viren, Beamon, Brumel.

Part 6: 1981-1999   Page 277
**WORLD CHAMPIONSHIPS IN ATHLETICS.
SUPERSTARS: LEWIS AND BUBKA.
A DRAGON CALLED DOPING**

Historic barriers broken: on the track, on the field, on the road and in the philosophy of the IAAF. Even rules adapt to professionalism. TV companies and sponsors bring about major changes: the IAAF/Grand Prix and the Golden League. The champions: Carl Lewis, Moses, Michael Johnson, Bubka, Syedikh, Zelezny. Africa "rules the waves" in distance events: Morceli, El Guerrouj, Kipketer, Kiptanui, Gebrselassie.

WOMEN'S ATHLETICS

Part 1: 1900-1940   Page 355
**FROM EARLY WHISPERS
TO THE MONTECARLO "PREMIÈRE"**

From early "Field Days" at Vassar College to the advent of Eve in the Olympic arena (Amsterdam 1928). Versatile Babe Didrikson.

Part 2: 1941-1970   Page 363
**THE FIRST QUEEN
COMES FROM HOLLAND**

New powers: USSR and GDR.

Part 3: 1971-1999   Page 373
**GREAT ACHIEVEMENTS
AND SOME PROBLEMS. STARS FROM ALL
CORNERS OF THE GLOBE**

The champions: Kazankina, Koch, Griffith, Kostadinova, Joyner. A Chinese revolution in the distance events.

Flashes of lightning on the way to Sydney   Page 416
Highlights of the 2000 athletic season

Statistics   Page 419
**All-Time World Lists (Men and Women)
at the end of each period related in the text.**

Index   Page 433
All names mentioned in the text.

DEERFOOT

Lewis Bennett alias Deerfoot was an American Indian of the Seneca tribe - "Tshoti-nondawaga" (people of the mountain), as they called themselves. In the second half of the XIX century he was a prominent figure in the world of distance running and became famous on both sides of the Atlantic. The athletic skill of Indian pedestrians, invariably "swift of foot", had been admirably extolled by poet Henry Wadsworth Longfellow in his "Song of Hiawatha" (1855). I think the legendary figure of Deerfoot, the "Noble Savage" as he was sometimes called, can aptly symbolize the passion of man for speed and endurance running. In a general way his figure reflects the eternal struggle of man to excel himself and his limits. In over a century of modern athletics all continents and all races have produced champions who greatly honoured this ambition.

R. L. Q.

PREFACE

by Augusto Frasca

Nearly ten years have gone by from the appearance of Roberto Quercetani's latest book on the world history of modern athletics. This is not to say that our friend has been idle ever since. Quite the contrary: in addition to his daily commitment to sport journalism and historical research he found ways and means to realize two other books of undisputed significance, obviously faithful to his well-known methodical approach, namely "Wizards of the Middle Distances: a History of the 800 Metres", in cooperation with Nejat Kök (1993, first in Italian, then in English) and "Sfida alla distanza: I magnifici dei 5000 e 10.000 metri" (1995). On top of that he has just edited, in cooperation with Bob Phillips, a book on the Golden Jubilee of the ATFS, celebrating the 50th anniversary of that association, of which he was one of the Founder Members. Now he offers an updated version of his main work, "A History of Modern Track & Field Athletics: 1860-2000", which in its previous ventures was a remarkable success, enjoying editions in five languages (English, Finnish, Italian, Spanish and Japanese).

The last ten years have been characterized by an ever growing activity in international athletics, spearheaded by no less than five editions of the IAAF World Championships (Tokyo '91, Stuttgart '93, Göteborg '95, Athens '97 and Sevilla '99), which have proven a valuable complement to the classic quadriennal Olympics. Throughout this period of time some very great athletes have gone through the motions - suffice it to mention just two: Carl Lewis and Sergey Bubka - and the sport has seen exciting action in many stadiums of the world and on the roads as well, mostly in connection with the ever expanding "marathon planet" - from London to Rome, from New York to Beijing, from Los Angeles to Moscow, from Paris to Osaka. It would be premature and perhaps out of place to pronounce a judgment on the far-reaching effects of the most recent developments. Besides the glowing highlights provided by leading stars, I deem it advisable to single out a fact: the intensified commitment of the IAAF in acting as the driving force of athletic activity all over the world in a true perspective of "globalization", a trend now characterizing also the sphere of politics and economy. In spite of occasional errors, the international body has won quite a few battles in trying to make a growing impact on the world of sport in general and the Olympic movement in particular, as well as in setting new economic standards and establishing closer relations with international media and TV in particular. All this amounted to a new revolution that had as its main propeller Dr. Primo Nebiolo, virtually from the day he was first elected President of the IAAF during the 1981 World Cup in Rome. Athletics was to retain absolute priority in his mind up to the last day of his life in November 1999.

Athletics has gained new ground, adequate to its role as the mother of all sports. It has also acquired a new stature through the efficiency of its leadership, e.g. in opening new ways towards the study of human biology applied to sport. After emerging the victor in so many battles, the sport is now on the threshold of a new era in which it appears to be closely intertwined with the alluring but insidious world of marketing. To finally win the war and save the fruits of the revolution realized by Nebiolo and the IAAF Council the sport will have to preserve the deep-rooted values of its glorious past. This appears to be the only way to strike a lucky balance between the ever changing habits of modern civilisation and sound ethics of old. There must be a culture likely to transcend athletic prowess. Being by nature inclined towards optimistic outlooks, I hope athletics will eventually preserve its trademark as an ever youthful sport. It should in a way resemble Anton Chekhov's theatrical world which seems to have no second-rate figures as every component is the master of his own play: on the field of sport the humblest gesture of a beginner should be regarded just as significant as the most spectacular feats of a champion. In such a spirit and frame of mind we may look forward to another victorious challenge in the early years of the new Millennium. As Quercetani aptly says in his introduction, the main task facing IAAF rulers will be that of preserving the sanity of the sport.

INTRODUCTION

by Roberto L. Quercetani

The tale of track and field athletics: from prehistory to modern times.

The Greek word "athlos" stands for battle or struggle, so it is obvious that athletics reflects the competitive practice of running, jumping and throwing, rather than the mere and isolated demonstration of such gestures. On the other hand it seems reasonable to assume that even in competitive terms the history of athletics may be just as old as that of humanity itself. Many observers like to trace the origins of the sport to the necessity of primitive man to have recourse to acts of defence and offence implying such gestures. Regardless of any "contrast", however, it is a known fact that since his earliest days every human being shows a natural tendency to test his physical resources.

Traces of athletic activity can be found in Egyptian bas-reliefs dating from circa 3500 B.C., and we cannot rule out the possibility that athletic exercises may have been part and parcel of even more remote civilizations, e.g in Asia. The earliest documented news of athletic competitions in the Ancient World was at any rate located in Greece and Ireland. Classic Greek literature contains descriptions of races held in Hellas one thousand or more years before the Christian Era, generally in connection with religious festivals. Even though the origin of the Olympic Games - so called because they were held at Olympia, a town in north-western Peloponnesus - is traced by some to 1222 B.C. and by others to 884 B.C., the first "olympionikos" we know by name is Coroebus, winner of the sprint ("stadion") race in 776 B.C. He was incidentally an "enfant du pays", since he came from nearby Elis, the town that promoted the festival. The "stadion" was initially the only event on the programme. Others were added later, such as the "diaulos" (twice the length of the "stadion"), the "dolichos" (which varied from 7 to 24 "stadia") and the pentathlon (which included "stadion", long jump, discus, javelin and wrestling). Great honours were conferred on victors, whose deeds were at times extolled by famous writers and philosophers. In fact, it is through the lists compiled by such celebrities as Hippias, Aristotle and Scipio Africanus that we know most of the names of ancient Olympic victors.

Quite understandably, we have no reliable information on performances made during Antiquity, no matter if conjectures have been made by several Authors, notably about distances achieved in the long jump. Even these, however, were based on hints of dubious interpretation, apart from the fact that Greek jumpers used dumb-bells ("halteres"), swinging them forwards and backwards to supplement the action of arms and legs. Other important festivals of ancient Greece were the Pithian, Nemeian and Isthmic Games. Particularly the Pithian event, held at Delphi, had a resonance almost as great as that of the Olympics. There too notable honours were conferred on winners. As time went on, accolades became so great that their recipients inevitably became "professional".

We know in fact of an association of professional athletes which came to life circa 50 B.C. Further proof, if need be, that there is nothing new under the sun. We also know that athletes occasionally had recourse to "mysterious drinks" to enhance their performances. To the same purpose, some had their spleen removed (ancient medicine apparently failed to appreciate the real value of that organ). And prizes awarded to victors in various ways were often of considerable value in relation to the economic standard of the times. Incentives being so great, the risk of inducing corruption was far from negligible. In view of such circumstances, it may be reasonably assumed that the end of the Games, decreed by Roman Emperor Theodosius in 393 A.D., probably came as the resultant effect of several factors, not merely as the consequence of religious and political rivalries. Alongside Greek tradition one must of course recall that of the Celts.

The Lugnas Games, later called Tailteann Games (held at Tailti in County Meath, today's Teltown, north-west of Dublin) developed from local festivals. According to the "Ancient Book of Leinster", written circa 1150 B.C., they were held for the first time in 829 B.C. The programme of athletic events included high jump, pole vault, stone and javelin throw. These Games were held annually, in August. In the course of time they declined in importance and continuity, yet survived in some form or other till the XIV century.

News relevant to the Tailteann Games came from old Irish sagas in which history and legend appeared to be closely intertwined. Which could be said, to some extent, even for tales of the ancient Greek Games. In the transition from Antiquity to the Middle Ages new cultural and religious trends developed which tended to play down the importance of athletic exercises.

On the European continent the sport survived, mostly if not exclusively, in chivalrous or military tournaments. Athletic sports of a kind not far removed from that prevailing in our time began to develop in the British Isles. In the XII century London could claim several "athletic grounds" where people of different classes used to test their physical prowess in running, jumping and throwing events. In Scotland such athletic exercises played an important role in popular festivals, which to some extent have survived to this day, notably as regards weight events.

Pedestrianism flourished in Britain between the XVII and the XIX century. Under this name were bracketed walking and running events, generally over long distances and in the form of "test matches" between two or more challengers. Early in the XIX century, "Bell's Life" magazine used to have regular reports on such competitions, with times in minutes and seconds.

There is at any rate one incontrovertible fact: athletics as we know it today had its cradle in the British Isles. In one form or another, meets worthy of the name have been held in the United Kingdom and in other parts of the English-speaking world since about the middle of the XIX century. The chief merit for laying the foundations of the sport must be attributed to the English Public Schools and Universities. These pioneers adopted rules which for the most part have remained unchanged to this day.

Modern athletics virtually began when it became possible to ensure generally reliable, if not altogether "scientific", verdicts in timing races and measuring field event performances. That's where our tale really starts. What follows is a list of essential milestones in the evolution of modern athletics.

1837 - First inter-class competitions at Eton College, England.

1838 - Track meet at Hoboken, New Jersey, USA, "the first in the world to be honoured with a complete report in a newspaper", as claimed by William B. Curtis in "Early American Sports".

1839 - First track meet in Canada, held at Caer Howell Grounds near Toronto.

1849 - First athletics meet at Royal Military Academy, Sandhurst, England.

1860 - First Oxford University Sports.

1861 - First American Indoor meet, staged by the Young Men's Gymnastic Club of Cincinnati, Ohio.

1863 - First British Indoor meet, held at Ashburnam Hall in London.

1864 - First Oxford vs. Cambridge Athletics match, held at Christ Church Ground, Oxford. Eight events on the programme. Regarded by some as the "Foundational Meeting" of modern athletics.

1866 - First national championships, English, organized by the Amateur Athletic Club at Beaufort House, London.

1868 - First indoor meet in New York, organized by the New York A.C. in a buil-ding that was under construction for a skating rink.

1876 - First US Championships, organized by the New York A.C.

1880 - Foundation of the Amateur Athletic Association in Oxford, the first national body for athletics.

1883 - First track meet in Japan, organized by the Tokyo Imperial University.

1887 - "Athletics and Football", a book by Montague Shearman, published in London. First issue, 250 copies, with several reprints in subsequent years. The first comprehensive account of amateur athletics.

1888 - Foundation of the Amateur Athletic Union of the United States.

1895 - First women's track meet ("Field Day") at Vassar College, Poughkeepsie, N.Y. - First major international dual meet, New York A.C. vs. London A.C., at Manhattan Field, New York. World's best performances equalled or bettered in five events.

1896 - Inaugural edition of the Olympic Games of the modern era at Panathenaic Stadium in Athens. The idea of reviving the ancient Olympics was launched on Friday 25 November 1892 by Baron Pierre de Coubertin in the Sorbonne Amphitheatre in Paris. The International Olympic Committee was founded on 23 June 1894 in Paris, with de Coubertin as first

President. The Games were to be held at four-year intervals.

1903 - First international cross-country championship in Glasgow, with athletes from England, Scotland, Wales and Ireland. The first foreign country to enter was France in 1907.

1912 - Foundation in Stockholm of the International Amateur Athletic Federation, the body that still governs track and field athletics on a worldwide basis. Sixteen countries on original membership list, with J. Sigfrid Edström of Sweden as first President. For official purposes the birth of the IAAF was ratified at Berlin a year later. In 2000 over two hundred countries were represented in the IAAF.

1913 - First Far Eastern Games at Manila. The series came to an end with the tenth edition (Manila, 1934).

1914 - First technical rules for international competition and first list of World Records presented at the third IAAF Congress.

1917 - Foundation of "Fédération Sportive Féminine de France", the first national body for women's athletics.

1919 - First South American Championships at Montevideo.

1921 - Foundation in Paris of "Fédération Sportive Féminine Internationale". Six countries on original membership list, with Alice Milliat of France as President. The following year, FSFI organized the first Women's World Games at Stade Pershing in Paris. Women's events first appeared in the Olympic programme at Amsterdam in 1928. FSFI eventually merged into the IAAF in 1936.

1922 - A book entitled "International Athletic Annual" published in Geneva by Maurice Loesch. This was the fore-runner of statistical publications at the international level. It contained an exhaustive summary of world athletic events in 1921, with records, championship results and a World Year List. The series came to an abrupt end with the premature death of the Author, a Swiss, soon after the second edition (1923).

1923 - First International Student Games in Paris.

1926 - First Central American and Caribbean Games at Mexico City.

1930 - First British Empire (later Commonwealth) Games at Hamilton, Canada.

1931 - First Balkan Games in Sofia. - First women's international cross-country race at Douai, France.

1934 - First European Championships at Turin, Italy.

1940 - First televised track meet, the ICAAAA Indoor Championships in Madison Square Garden, New York.

1946 - Lord Burghley of England, alias Marquis of Exeter, former Olympic 400 m. hurdles champion, elected President of the IAAF.

1948 - "A Handbook on Olympic Games Track and Field Athletics" by D.H.Potts and R.L.Quercetani published at Ann Arbor, Michigan, USA. It contained the first extensive and detailed World All Time List (100-deep) in men's events, as of the end of 1947.

1950 - Foundation in Brussels of the "Association of Track and Field Statisticians". Eleven members on original list, with R.L. Quercetani of Italy as President and Fulvio Regli of Switzerland as Secretary General. Main purpose of the new organization, "propose the development and rationalizing of track and field statistics throughout the world". The "ATFS International Athletics Annual", first published in 1951, has appeared regularly ever since.

1951 - First Pan-American Games at Buenos Aires. - First Asian Games at New Delhi. - First Mediterranean Games at Alexandria.

1960 - First Ibero-American Games at Santiago de Chile.

1961 - First IAAF Walking team competition at Lugano, Switzerland (later called "Lugano Trophy").

1965 - First African Games at Brazzaville. - First European Cup (final at Stuttgart).

1966 - First European Indoor Games at Dortmund (known as European Indoor Championships from 1970 onwards).

1967 - First Europe vs. America dual meet at Montreal. The series came to an end after the second edition (Stuttgart, 1969).

1973 - The IAAF takes over jurisdiction of the International Cross-Country Championships, henceforth known as World Cross-Country Championships. - The International Track Association, a professional organization formed in 1972 by Mike O'Hara of USA, stages its first official meet at Los Angeles. ITA will fold in 1976.

1975 - Automatic suspension of athletes found to have used anabolic steroids introduced by the IAAF.

1976 - Adriaan Paulen of Holland, former 400 and 800 m. runner of international class, elected President of the IAAF.

1977 - First World Cup at Düsseldorf. - The IAAF makes automatic timing (in 100ths of a second) mandatory for World Records set at distances up to and including 400 m.

1981 - Primo Nebiolo of Italy elected President of the IAAF.

1983 - First World Championships at Helsinki.

1985 - First edition of the IAAF/Mobil Grand Prix,

a series of major invitational meets.
1986 - First World Junior Championships at Athens.
1987 - First World Indoor Championships at Indianapolis.
1989 - A new provision obliging Member federations to conduct out-of-competition doping controls introduced by the IAAF.
1998 - Six of the most important meets of the Grand Prix series elected to form the new "IAAF Golden League", offering a jackpot of $1 million - the largest prize in athletics history - to be divided among athletes (men and women) having scored victories in all such meets.
1999 - First World Youth (under 17) Championships at Bydgoszcz, Poland.
Primo Nebiolo, President of the IAAF, died of a heart attack on 7 November in Rome. Lamine Diack of Senegal as senior Vice-President became Acting President of the IAAF until its next Congress of 2001.

During the long period covered in the above list the sport has never ceased to evolve. In terms of times and distances achieved by leading athletes, progress has been great indeed. However, it would not be wise, let alone just, to compare champions of different epochs on the "face value" of their marks. Too many factors have changed in the course of time, particularly in the last fifty years. The onetime "homo ludens" has gradually developed into a highly efficient "machine". Technique and conditioning methods have undergone substantial changes through the years.
Medicine and other branches of science have influenced the situation in a serious way. Nowadays a top-class athlete is often studied and followed with scientific instruments capable of recording the reaction of his body to any type of training. Even in the most natural of sports, the material media of competition change with time. Tracks, runways and circles have changed for the better, and to a very considerable extent. So have the implements and equipment used by the athletes. Yet it seems certain that further substantial progress is possible under each of the above-mentioned factors. As a result, any speculation on the ultimates of human possibilities in athletics is just as idle and fascinating today as it was twenty-five or fifty years ago.
No matter if in the most recent years the record breaking spree at the top level has attenuated to some extent. Incentives for athletes, particularly at the highest level of competition, have become greater and greater. A tendency to regard athletic achievements as a matter of national interest first developed in Italy and Germany during the Thirties, when the totalitarian regimes then ruling in those countries discovered the importance of sport as a vehicle of political propaganda. In such a perspective, sport organizations controlled by the state began to offer their leading athletes - at a time when amateurism was still the rule - what was necessary to devote the best part of their time and energies to further their athletic potential. However, this was only the beginning. After World War II, the same pattern was resumed and perfected by Communist regimes in Eastern Europe and other parts of the world. In a "nationalized" sport no stone is left unturned to allow the best men and women to concentrate on their athletic activity.
In this respect, economic and social incentives obviously play an important role. However, such policies often evolve to the detriment of individual spontaneity and inventiveness. And when everything comes "from above" there is ample space for abuse. In liberal countries the incentives for athletes largely depended, for a long period of time, on the (usually scarce) economic resources of their clubs. Only the very best could expect to receive money "under the table" from meet promoters. In a limited number of cases these "offenders" were eventually disqualified. That is what happened to such widely publicized runners as Paavo Nurmi, Jules Ladoumègue, Gunder Hägg, Arne Andersson and Henry Kälarne, who were suspended from the amateur ranks. In USA promising athletes had a chance to land scholarships in colleges or universities, where they could train and compete for a few years under more or less favourable conditions.
Once they left school, however, they were "on their own", and in the overwhelming majority of cases they turned to "pro" sports or some other activity. Many famous athletes thus left track at the age of 22/23, with their potentialities still untapped. It was only in the Seventies that money began to flow into the world of track and field, mainly through TV companies or sponsors. The pace increased with the advent of Dr. Primo Nebiolo of Italy as President of the IAAF in 1981.
There was a marked detachment from the philosophy of amateurism, which had incidentally stemmed not so much from Pierre de Coubertin, as many historians seem to believe, but rather from Anglo-American educators of the XIX century. After thriving in hypocrisy for many years (but for occasional blasts at crypto-professionals), the IAAF decided to acknowledge the fact that modern athletes who devote the better part of their time and energies to the

sport must inevitably receive a financial reward of some sort. Prizes were first introduced officially in 1985, in the frame of the IAAF/Mobil Grand Prix, a series of invitational meets.

A ranking is established on the basis of points won in each meet, and at the end of the series the athlete who ranks no.1 in his or her event receives - officially through his national federation - a cheque for $10,000. Minor sums are awarded to place-winners, ranging from $8,000 for second place to $1,000 for eighth. There is also an overall Ranking for the highest scorers in all events: $25,000 for first place, $15,000 for second and $10,000 for third. This was a revolution vis-à-vis the past, yet "reality" continues to lie ahead of official rules by several lengths: on top of the above-mentioned prizes, star athletes can still receive appearance money over or under the table from meet promoters. The IAAF has made half-hearted attempts to put its house in order, especially in the face of bids likely to foster "inflation". But it is an uphill fight ... Sponsors, mostly representatives of multi-national companies, have offered star athletes substantial contracts, in exchange for various forms of advertizing.

Then even in liberal countries there is now a tendency to support leading athletes with money provided by national federations and/or Olympic committees. The sum total of all these "aids" is such that athletes having a "great image" can now capitalize on their talent in many different ways, to an extent which would have been unimaginable until not so long ago. Some of them can thus afford to travel around the world with a manager and receive regular advice and treatment from doctors, physiotherapists, and so on - usual practices in all "pro" sports. After courageously abandoning its former policies, the IAAF is now confronted with the task of damming up the stream.... while preserving in its name (for how long?) that 'A' which stands for amateur. For reasons explained above the overall picture of international athletics is far more complex now than it was at any time in the past.

Every country is doing its best to cope with new necessities, even to the extent of compromising with its traditions. Even Great Britain, the mother country of modern amateur athletics, now offers plenty of economic incentives to leading athletes, through official and private channels. The United States of America, who over a century ago flanked Britain in furthering the development of modern athletics, remains the no.1 power of the sport in the men's department and has recently made substantial progress in the women's section too.

The schools have remained to this day the backbone of American track power. Scholastic competition at all levels (High School, Junior College, University) is unquestionably the stiffest to be found anywhere in the world. By comparison, the club or post-graduate set-up is somewhat anaemic, in most States at least. Paradoxically enough, it was only in 1979 that a body exclusively concerned with track and field (The Athletics Congress later re-named USA Track & Field)) entered the picture.

This organization has recently introduced forms of economic support for athletes of international calibre. In actual fact, however, leading American athletes ripen the fruits of their talent, chiefly if not exclusively, in the European "summer circuit", i.e. in Grand Prix or other invitational meets. It should also be noted that the impact of black athletes, especially in the sprints, hurdles and jumps, has become greater and greater in the last three decades.

As late as 1939, USSR was a second-rate athletic power. A full scale, state-subsidized programme was only started after World War II, more or less when USSR became a member of the IAAF. The human potential of this country, embracing a large part of two continents, was obviously great. In the men's department the Soviets ranked second only to the Americans, and actually excelled them in the field events. Track events have been the Achilles Heel of the Soviet giant, with bright exceptions usually far apart in time, such as sprinter Valeriy Borzov or distance runner Vladimir Kuts. On the distaff side USSR ruled the roost for years, before giving way to the "Fräulein" of the German Democratic Republic.

The latter, with a population of 16.4 million inhabitants and an athletic movement with less than 100,000 registered athletes, made the most of its possibilities - more successfully perhaps than any other country in the world. Following in the footsteps of pre-war Germany, the GDR used sport as a major vehicle to gain a "high profile" in the eyes of the world. Every talented athlete was studied and fostered in any possible way, with the full support of science. In addition to superb results in women's athletics, the GDR was one of the world's major powers in the men's department as well.

However, the revolutionary events of 1989-90 have inevitably revealed - as it happens whenever a totalitarian regime crumbles - that "it's not all gold that glitters". In fact, the price paid for success was very high, and the methods used to achieve it rather unscrupulous. In the new economic and social set-up of unified Germany things are sure to be different. And at least for some time results are not likely to be as eye-catching as they were before. In that country a good club system and excellent technical installations provide for intense activity at all levels. It seems reasonable to assume that unified Germany will have an important role in world athletics. Britain and France have lately derived large benefits from the growing phalanx of their black citizens originating from Commonwealth or "départements d'outre-mer" (overseas) countries. Towards the end of the Eighties, Britain began to shape up as the new leader in European men's athletics, always strong in track events and better than at any previous time in the field events. Her noble tradition in the middle distance events has been upheld in recent years by men like Sebastian Coe, Steve Ovett and Steve Cram. Finland and Sweden enjoyed a privileged situation in the pioneer days of modern athletics. Nowadays they must be content with crumbs when it comes to vying for top honours in Olympic competition. The Finns still have the javelin as their parade event. Italy has had her share of champions in recent years, particularly in the long distance events. Spain seems to be gathering momentum and is now a leading force in Europe in the distance races. Portugal too has excelled in the long grind department, particularly as regards the marathon. In Europe virtually every country has at different times contributed outstanding figures to the world of athletics, were it only once and long ago as in the case of Luxemburg with Josy Barthel, winner of the 1500 m. at the Helsinki Olympics in 1952. More or less at the same time, Poland had outstanding men in several events, Hungary a superb trio of middle distance runners in Iharos, Tábori and Rózsavölgyi, and Czechoslovakia a world famous hero in Emil Zátopek. More recently, Romania and Bulgaria have offered some superlative women performers.

From 1960 onwards, Africa has had a growing impact on world athletics, chiefly but not exclusively in the middle and long distance events.

By 1990 this continent had in fact excelled Europe in this department. Kenya is the no.1 powerhouse, no matter if her organization and facilities still remain well below the quality of her leading athletes, who in many cases have risen to world class while attending US colleges. Ethiopia, Algeria, Morocco, and to a lesser extent even other African countries have all had their share of success. South Africa should also be a factor, being by now reinstated in the IAAF family.

In Asia, Japan and the Philippines were for years the dominant powers, especially the former - at the 1936 Olympics in Berlin, Japanese jumpers matched their American rivals in number of medals won (5 each).

And to this day Japan continues to show a "cult" for marathon running. Huge China has lately taken over as the continent's no.1 athletic power, approaching world class in several events, especially in the women's department. Athletically speaking, India is still sleeping. Australia and New Zealand continue to live up to their traditions. In the middle distance events both had their golden moment in the Fifties and Sixties. It should also be noted that "Down Under" the conversion from amateurism to professionalism at the top level of competition has come later than in Europe.

In Latin America only Cuba has shown remarkable progress, following methods substantially similar to those once prevalent in Eastern European countries. Other Central American countries, like Jamaica and Trinidad, have produced remarkable "speed demons" from time to time. South America is, of all continents, the one that has shown the least noticeable progress in recent decades, simply because of lack of interest and promotion. Brazil has at various times offered glimpses of its great potential. On the whole, one can predict that the number of countries vying for Olympic honours will continue to grow, slowly but steadily, first in the track events, then, with the acquisition of technical "know-how", even in the field events.

At the present time the IAAF turns a large part of its profits from major international meets and its connection with sponsors and TV companies to the benefit of underdeveloped countries to help them improve the quality of their athletic organization. With the steady advance in standards of performance and the expansion of incentives, new situations have arisen which are not easy to govern. In the first half of the XX century athletics thrived in a rarefied atmosphere, certainly not free from defects but essentially faithful to the ethical values the sport was supposed to foster. The transition to professionalism, by now a fact for most if not all athletes of international class, has obviously brought forth a lot of new problems. In the XXI century the defence of the ethical values of sport will be the most formidable task facing athletes, coaches, judges, doctors, organizers, and officials of national and international federations.

While striving to live up to the Olympic motto "citius, altius, fortius", the champions of our time, and lesser lights as well, are often urged to "do the impossible". So they sometimes supplement normal ways and means, such as training and study of technique, with something illicit, like taking drugs which in a long-range perspective can do harm to their health and spirits. As often as not, they are induced to take such "shortcuts" by coaches or by overambitious officials. Of course it seems fair to admit that the intensive,

and sometimes obsessive training methods of our time are responsible for a high number of injuries, notably "stress fractures". The German Democratic Republic, recently the most vaunted of track powers, could point in this respect to a highly significant list of "victims", some of them unable to resume competition even after repeated surgery. While admitting that modern sport medicine can successfully deal with injuries which only a few decades ago would have been incurable, it is my closely considered opinion that the price of records and medals, with the economic advantages one can derive from them, sometimes appears to be too high in the perspective of sound sport and sound ethics. Coping with the multiform problems of international athletics in the XXI century will not be an easy job. I hope that those called to perform it will first of all feel the urge to preserve the sanity of the world's most beautiful sport.
Roberto L. Quercetani

Florence, June 2000

NOTE

All times for running events are given as originally taken, e.g. with fractions of a second in halves, thirds, quarters, fifths, tenths or - for "automatic" times - in hundredths. The same applies to distances in field events, e.g. with fractions of a centimetre for marks converted from feet and inches.

THE BIRTH OF MODERN ATHLETICS. REVIVAL OF THE OLYMPIC GAMES

SPRINTS: From the mysterious "pros" to Wefers and Long

Short-distance running certainly belongs to the remotest tradition of man's athletic endeavours. The earliest event in the Olympic programme of the ancient Greeks was in fact the so-called "stadium" race (stadion), being equivalent to the length of the stadium. At Altis, theatre of the Games, such a distance was 192.27 m. Originally, the word "stadion" stood for a unity of measurement, later on it began to be identified with the race and finally with the place where the competition was held. Stone thresholds marked both start and finish.

The track was about 29 m. in width. Without attempting to pierce the clouds that still surround the "technical" conditions under which the races were run, it is perhaps interesting to note that the rules then in force recommended that corporal punishment be inflicted on competitors who took unfair advantage at the start of a race!

The athletes set off together at some word of command, though it is not known what it was.

In the early days of modern athletics the conquests of science were such as to allow a fair degree of accuracy and reliability in evaluating running feats. For example, an instrument called chronograph had been patented by Adolphe Nicole of Switzerland in 1862.

One can imagine, however, the difficult circumstances under which the times of early sprinters were recorded. Add that throughout the major part of the XIX century the most varied methods of starting a race co-existed in a rather hybrid fashion.

According to William Curtis, quoted by Archie Hahn in "How to Sprint", the inconveniences attending the start "by mutual consent" finally led to the idea of using a pistol as the best way of starting a race. Under the former method the start was sometimes

George Seward, a famous American sprinter in the Forties of the XIX century.

19

Walter George (GB) left, and Lon Myers (USA), two legendary figures in the latter part of the XIX century.

"Why wait?"

In English speaking countries "pro" athletics was in full swing for a long time, eventually dying only around 1920 with the last fireworks in South Africa and Australia. The best "pros" were at any rate excellent sprinters, and some of them had previously figured prominently in the amateur ranks.

One of these was Alfred Downer, a Scotsman of Jamaican origin. Like several others, he became a "pro" after he was ousted from the amateur family. Here is what he recalled about Scottish meets several years later in his book "Running Recollections": "No one who is on the job ever dreams of waiting for the report of the pistol, or whatever the signal may be, but is generally running some five yards (no exaggeration) when the signal is given".

delayed for a considerable time, since contenders often tried to "out-fox" each other by resorting to various stratagems.

To offset this danger, a clause was included in the articles of agreement which stated: "Start by mutual consent: if not off inside an hour (or some other specified time), then to start by pistol". Resort to the pistol turned out to be necessary in so many cases that it gradually supplanted the mutual consent system and finally became the customary way of starting sprint races.

For several decades the minimum fractions adopted in timing races were the oddest possible: halves, quarters and, only later, fifths of a second.

If one adds ignorance of the wind factor to the above considerations on starting and timing, the least one can say about the times of early sprinters is that they must be taken with a sizeable grain of salt. The fastest times were usually recorded in professional races, where the financial terms involved made all tricks possible. Under such conditions, one can hardly express any judgment on such legendary exploits as those credited to George Seward of USA (100 y. in 9 1/4, 120 y. in 11 1/2, 200 y. in 19 1/2) between 1844 and 1847 or to the Englishman Harry Hutchens (130 y. in 12 1/4, 220 y. in 21 4/5 and 300 y. in 30.0) between 1879 and 1885. No matter if, as well paid "pros", they were obviously able to devote the better part of their time and energies to the running profession. Let's consider, however, Seward's famous 100y. time. This Connecticut-born American was credited with that time at Hammersmith, England, on 30 September 1844, a few days before his 27th birthday.

According to John Cumming (author of "Runners and Walkers, a Nineteenth Century Sports Chronicle"), that performance was evoked with respect in American track circles until 1890, when the authoritative "New York Clipper", a stern observer of running feats, decided to write it off, partly on the strength of a "late"testimony by an eye-witness, who claimed that Seward had made it on a downhill road course from a 10 y. flying start, but also on the reflection that in the ensuing 46 years no amateur runner had been able to come close to that mark. Even so, Seward was generally considered by oldtimers to be a very fast mover, just like Harry Hutchens during the Eighties. William Curtis ("Father Bill") was the first amateur sprinter in USA to use spiked shoes in a major meet. This happened at New York in 1868, but the invention was supposed to have been borrowed from England. In English speaking countries the 100 y. was the sprint distance "par excellence" from the beginning. "Beat even time" (i.e. 10 seconds) was probably the first in a long series of dreams haunting track and field adepts. The earliest commonly accepted instance of a "10 dead" by a British amateur dates from 1855, when Thomas Bury of England was credited with doing just that at Cambridge. The first sprinters to record such a time in major championship races were William Wilmer at the US title meet in New York in 1878, alas with the benefit of a strong wind, and Ghana-born Arthur Wharton at the English AAA meet in London in 1886. Montague Shearman, the English historian, describes Wharton as a "coloured gentleman, flat-footed ...who manages somehow to bend his body far forward as well". Wharton later became a professional soccer player, as a goalie for Preston North End.

The crouch start ("on all fours") was probably introduced in New Zealand around 1884 by Bobby Macdonald, a Maori. Most writers, however, accept American Charles Sherrill as the earliest adept of this method in 1887, following the advice of his coach at Yale University, the famous Mike·Murphy. As Murphy relates, "When he (Sherrill) used it in his first race, he was laughed at, and the starter, thinking that Sherrill did not know how to start, held up the race to give him instructions. Finally, he was made to understand that Sherrill was simply using a new method!" Yet Sherrill (who later became a General and a diplomat) had to be content with joining the large group of 10-flat performers. First to break that barrier on an important occasion was John Owen, who at age 29 was credited with 9 4/5 at the AAU Championships held at Analostan Island, Washington, DC, on 11 October 1890. In that race he won by a foot from Luther Cary, who went on to record a surprising 9 1/2 a few weeks later at Princeton - a time which was ruled out by incredulous officials. In 1891 Cary crossed the Atlantic to record another fast time, 10 3/4 for 100 m. in Paris, but one source claimed that the start was given with a handkerchief ...

In America the 220 y. or furlong, a most exacting test for sprinters, was usually run on a straight course, which started on a line tangent to the track. The British ratified a 22 flat made under similar conditions by William Page Phillips in London in 1878. This powerful 6-foot (1.83 m.) man was to die of a heart failure only five years later. First Briton to beat 22 seconds was Charles Wood, who did 21 4/5 (from a standing start) in London in 1887. He eventually improved to 21 3/5 later in the same year. First to record a sub-22 secs. performance around a turn was the above-mentioned Luther Cary: 21 4/5 at New York in 1891.

The first major confrontation between "Kings" of the sprint from the two sides of the Atlantic took place at Manhattan Field, New York, on 21 September 1895, in connection with the historic New York AC vs London AC dual meet. The chief characters in the 100 y. play were Bernard Wefers and Charles Bradley. The former (born at Lawrence, MA., on 19 February 1873) was considered America's Fastest Human. He was a student at Georgetown University in Washington, DC. Bradley won the English 100 y.

1860
1900

Inaugural Olympic Games in Athens (1896) - 100 metres. This picture is not from the final, as stated in the previous edition, but from the second 100 metre heat. The runners, from left to right, are: L. Elliott (GB), T. Curtis (USA), winner in 12 1/5, E. Schmidt (Den), G. Marshall (GB) A. Chalkokondylis (Gre). The final was won by Thomas Burke (USA) in 12.0.

title four years in a row (1893-1896). In August 1895 at Stoke-on-Trent he was credited with 9 4/5 in a dead-heat with the above-mentioned Alfred Downer. A compact runner of medium build, he was the pre-meet favourite of most "bettors". Wefers' best years still lay ahead though. He was to score the 100/220 y. double at the AAU meet for three consecutive years (1895/97). He was a big, powerful sprinter (1.83 m./79 kg.) with plenty of staying power. The New York showdown was described in vivid fashion by William Curtis in "Outing" magazine. First, the "ambiance": "The attendance numbered 8,592 and would have been several thousand greater but for the big prices, the cheapest admission being $1.00. In addition to the crowd inside, the bluff which forms the western boundary of the grounds was black with people, and on the 155th Street viaduct, which towers high above the roofs of the stands on the southern edge of the field, the sidewalk was thronged with spectators, who stood for four hours in the scorching sun, to get far-off glimpses of the sport. Probably 12,000 people, inside and outside, saw the games. As the 100 y. runners thundered down the path, "Bradley wins" was heard more often and more loudly than "Wefers wins". But in the race the Englishman generally lagged behind. He made a desperate attempt with 40 y. to go, but Wefers answered so effectively that he finally won by about 4 feet (1.22 m.) in 9 4/5, thus equalling the world record". Wefers later won the 220 y. in 21 3/5, another record time. In 1896 he lowered the furlong mark to 21 1/5 and was credited with 30 3/5 over 300 y. He must be billed as the Fastest Human of the XIX century.

As destiny would have it, neither Wefers nor Bradley were among the athletes who competed in the inaugural Games of the modern era, held at Athens in the spring of 1896. There were no national teams and athletes were mostly recruited at the club level. The US team, chiefly put together by Prof. William M. Sloane of Princeton University, included only one national champion from 1895, quartermiler Thomas Burke. He won the 100 m. in 12 seconds flat and the 400 in 54 1/5, both times being a tribute to the slowness of the Athens track with its hairpin turns. Burke was incidentally the only one of the five 100 m. finalists to use a crouch start! He won from two good European sprinters, Fritz Hoffmann of Germany and Alajos Szokolyi of Hungary.

The 1899 AAU Championships were the occasion of the first major appearance of Arthur Duffey, who won the 100 y. title in 10.0, after recording a wind-aided 9 4/5 in a heat. In 1900 this man of medium build (born on 14 June 1879; 1.70 m./62 kg) went on to win the English AAA title, still in 10.0. He was by then considered a cinch for the Olympic 100 m. title to be awarded in Paris the following week. In fact, he led by a sound margin at the halfway point, but a muscle pull forced him to retire. Victory went to another American, Frank Jarvis, in 11.0.

While the list of America's 9 4/5 performers continued to grow in length, Europe reported its earliest sub-11 secs. men in the longer 100 m. race. Performances of 10 4/5 were credited to Emile de Ré of Belgium (1893) and Harald Andersson of Sweden (1896). By the end of the XIX century there were regular tracks only in a restricted number of countries.

English and American coaches of the time already had clear, sound concepts about the mechanics of sprinting. If read so many years later, their observations seem meticulous in matters of running form but far less demanding in terms of conditioning methods. Montague Shearman, for example, claims that a sprinter, like any athlete in general, "nascitur, non fit", no matter if "much can be done by training and practice". He goes on to say: "The best practice for a sprint race is to have continued bursts of 30 y. or so with another man, who is about as good or rather better than yourself. If practicing with a man who is inferior you should give him a short start in these spins and catch him as soon as you can. Such practice both helps a man to get into his running quickly and "pulls him out", to use a trainer's expression, i.e. leads him to do a little better than his previous best ... After half a dozen of these spins he should take a few minutes' rest and then run the full distance, or at any rate a burst of 70 or 80 y., before he goes in to have a rub down and resume his clothes".

Most revealing of the philosophy prevailing in those days is Shearman's conclusion: "For all practice it may be laid down that a man should very rarely run a trial for more than two-thirds of the distance for which he is training".

THE QUARTER MILE:
The ethereal Myers and Brown's axiom

The 400 metres race of our times has a distant predecessor in the "diaulos" of the ancient Greeks, which equalled two lengths of the "stadion", i.e. about 384 m. in the case of Olympia. However, this relationship is purely accidental, the modern one-lap event having in fact originated in the British Isles as the fourth part of a mile (= 402.34 m.).

This circumstance is of great historical importance,

1860-1900

since the quarter mile and its slightly shorter metric "child", the 400 m., were adopted as the standard lengths for foot racing tracks all over the world. It seems reasonable to assume that if modern athletics had originated on the European continent the 500 m. (i.e. half a kilometre) would have been chosen instead. The choice is perhaps difficult to explain even from an English viewpoint! Originally the quarter mile was classified as an endurance test. One of the earliest books dealing with the tactical and competitive problems of the event was in fact J.E. ("Ted") Meredith's "Middle Distance and Relay Racing". The author, who in his younger days held the world record for both 440 and 880 y., ostensibly put both events in the same category. In the early days, tactics usually consisted of a relatively fast start, with a rather long "float" midway in the race and a frenzied rush for the tape in the closing stage. As training loads were gradually intensified, faith in man's capabilities for a prolonged sprint increased accordingly and the "float" became less and less noticeable.

For many years, the 400 m. or 440 y. event was to remain the meeting point of two different types: the pure sprinter and the middle distance runner. As often as not, however, it was the former, with his tendency to run all out from the start, to assure the evolution of records. Especially in America, where the race was started at the end of a long straightaway, the initial pace was very "hot", since everybody wanted to have the pole position in negotiating the one and only turn.

Today the one-lap event is more closely related with the sprints than with the middle distances. However, there are physiological reasons which make it difficult, not to say impossible, to classify the event in the domain of pure speed. The performance of a runner is determined by the quantity of oxygen that can be conveyed into his muscles while he is in motion. At or near the 300 m. mark the maximum of "oxygen debt" is inevitably reached, at which point more oxygen is required than is in fact obtainable through respiration. At that stage the runner who has been travelling at full speed, or just about, will have to slow down considerably. Logical reflection therefore suggests even pace running throughout as the golden rule for 400 m. runners. Yet the study of splits taken during the greatest races of our time shows that this rule is seldom observed in practice.

Most records have been achieved with a "hot" pace in the early goings and consequent deceleration in the rest of the race. The "de facto" situation is well reflected in the opinion, somewhat ironic but rather axiomatic, once expressed by Godfrey Brown, Britain's greatest quartermiler in the Thirties: "The strongest man in the finish of a 400 m. race is not the one who accelerates the most, but rather the one who decelerates the least". The earliest 440 y. "match race" we know of took place at Hounslow, Middlesex, on 25 June 1849 between two famous "pros", Henry Allen Reed of England and George Seward of America. The latter has been mentioned in connection with the sprints. The race was on a road surface: after a ding-dong battle all the way, Reed (24 years old, 1.72 m./57 kg) beat his American rival, then nearly 32, by one yard. Winner's time, on a straight course, 48 1/2.

The first amateur to run the quarter inside 50 seconds was Robert Philpot, a Cambridge student, who on 7 March 1871 at Cambridge nosed out his teammate Abbot Upcher by one yard in 49 3/4. These early examples well serve a theory which has been respected ever since: at this distance, most if not all record times originate from close man-to-man tussles, and very rarely from "solo" efforts.

I do not intend to discriminate between "amateurs" and "pros" in any sort of moral way, yet it is virtually certain that the verdicts offered by amateur competitions were much more reliable than those emanating from the "pro" ranks, where corrosive elements (such as betting) were sometimes likely to cause the infringement of rules.

The first prominent figure in the annals of quartermiling as well as one of the greatest talents of the XIX century was Lawrence ("Lon") Myers of USA (born at Richmond, Virginia, on 16 February 1858).

Standing start - John Owen (USA), the first man to officially break "even time" in the 100 yards (1890).

At one time he held the US records for all distances from 50 y. to the mile! He was very slim (1.73 m./51 kg), had very long legs and "practically no body at all above the waist". After winning four AAU titles in 1880 - 100, 220, 440 and 880 y., all in one afternoon - Myers established himself as history's first consistent sub-50 secs. man in the quarter. During his career he won 15 AAU titles and three English AAA titles. In 1879 he lowered the American 440 y. record to 49 1/5. Two years later he made his first visit to England and capped a most successful tour with a splendid victory in the AAA race at Birmingham's Aston Lower Grounds in 48 3/5, which time however was not ratified as a record since the long home stretch was found to be gently sloping in the running direction. His best legal times as an amateur were 10.0 (100y), 22 1/2 (220 y), 48 4/5 (440 y), 1:22.0 (600 y), 1:55 2/5 (880 y), 2:13.0 (1000 y) and 4:27 3/5 (mile). Myers made a great impact on the sport of his time. It was almost inevitable that he should have been attracted into the "pro" ranks. He continued to run till 1885, when he decided to retire. On his return from yet another English tour, a delegation met him at New York harbour. There was a warm reception which included a parade in Manhattan and a banquet at Astor House. According to Leo Fischer, the psalm really ended in a "glory": "Myers received about $4000, which set him up in the horse-betting business". Unfortunately the great runner did not see the birth of the XX century: in 1899, pneumonia put a premature end to his life. Of lesser historical significance are the figures of two other Americans, Wendell Baker and William Downs, who earned their reputation at Beacon Park race-track in Boston, where the quarter-mile course was "nearly a straightaway". Under such conditions, Baker did 47 3/4 in 1886 and Downs was credited with 47 2/5 in 1890, both in paced efforts. Downs won the AAU title three times (1890-92), always with marks in the 50 secs. region. In the meantime, British standards had gone up considerably.

At the 1889 AAA Championships, held at Stamford Bridge, London, H.C.Lenox Tindall won a great 440/880 y. double and his time for the shorter distance was 48 1/2. In 1895 another Englishman, Edgar Bredin, achieved exactly the same performance on the same track. The first major clash between quarter-milers from the opposite sides of the Atlantic occurred later in 1895 at Manhattan Field, New York, during the historic match between the New York AC and the London AC. On that occasion the American champion, Thomas Burke, had to produce an all-out effort to beat Gilbert Jordan of England by six inches in 49.0. But Burke went on to win the 400 m. in the inaugural edition of the Olympic Games at Athens in 1896. His time on a very poor track was 54 1/5. Later in the year the same Burke did much better, 48 4/5, in annexing the AAU 440 y. crown. Another great quarter-miler emerged near the turn of the century: Maxey W. Long of USA. At the 1900 Olympics in Paris he won the 400 m. on a slow grass track in 49 3/5, after three of his teammates had withdrawn on religious grounds when they heard that the final would be run on a Sunday. A brilliant French writer, Loys Van Lee, tells an amusing story about that race. In those days Olympians competed in the colours of their own clubs or schools. Long wore the light blue and white of Columbia University, colours strikingly similar to those of Racing Club de France. At first uninitiated French spectators mistook him for one of their own boys and went out of their way to cheer him! But Long's fame is chiefly due to his achievements against the clock in the autumn of 1900. On 29 September at Travers Island, New York, he ran a quarter in 47 4/5. This remarkable mark was achieved in a handicap race on a 321.87 m. track. It is related that some of Long's helpers, once overtaken, elected to stop and enjoy history in the making as delighted spectators.

On 4 October Long chalked up an impressive 47 flat on a straight course at the Guttenberg race-track in New Jersey, helped once more by pace-setters. Here are some curious splits for the three fastest 440 y. races of the XIX century, as committed to posterity by thoughtful fans:

A semi-final of the 100 yards at the 1896 ICAAAA Championships, won by Bernard Wefers, arguably the fastest man of the XIX century. Time, 10.0.

	220 y.	440 y.
Baker (1886)	23 1/5	47 3/4
Downs (1890)	23 1/4	47 2/5
Long (1900)	22 1/2	47.0

MIDDLE DISTANCES:
The mile, a glamour event - The great George

1860–1900

There are no borderlines to delimit the so-called middle distances. At the present time, this conventional term is applied to all distances between 800 and 3000 metres. The important thing is that here, contrary to what happens in the sprints, pure speed, while remaining a fundamental requisite, is not by itself sufficient to assure success. Pace judgment and tactics also play a prominent role.

The key to championship form lies in a combination of speed, courage and intelligence. This probably explains why the top-ranking middle-distance man often has a more complex personality than his colleague from the "dashes".

In the early days of the sport, the 880 y. or half-mile (804.67 m.) was not one of the standard events as were, for example, the 440 y. or the mile. The "pros" had a more varied programme and consequently devoted more attention to the half-mile run. Yet their record times were made, as often as not, under peculiar conditions. First to duck under 2 minutes was the Englishman Henry Allen Reed with 1:58.0 at Halifax in 1854, a feat which earned him the "Champion's Belt" as well as 50 pounds. Another English "pro", James Nuttall, ran 1:55 3/4 at Manchester in 1867. Both of these were track marks, whereas the celebrated 1:53 1/2 by Frank Hewitt, an Australian "pro", was on a sloping road course at Lyttleton, New Zealand, in 1871.

In the amateur ranks, the two-minute barrier was first broken on 26 March 1873 by a Cambridge student, the Hon. Arthur Pelham, who ran the half-mile in 1:59 3/4. Here, just as in the quarter, things really began to move under the reign of the great Lon Myers, whose virtues have been extolled earlier in this chapter. Had he specialized in this event, he would no doubt have done better than 1:55 2/5, a record time he achieved in 1885. He was succeeded as unofficial world record holder by Francis Cross, an Englishman who ran the "half" in 1:54 3/5 on the Iffley Road three-lap track at Oxford in 1888. He curiously lost the record on the day of his nuptials, 21 September 1895. That was the day of the above-mentioned New York AC vs London AC match in New York.

In the half-mile race the favourites were Charles Kilpatrick for the locals and Frederick Horan for the guests. The former took the lead at the halfway mark (54 1/5) and staved off Horan's bid to win handily, 1:53 2/5 to 1:55 2/5. According to "Father Bill" Curtis, "during the race Kilpatrick had troubles noticed by only a few spectators. A furlong from the start his clothing became disarranged, and he ran the remainder of the race under such vexation and annoyance as might well have interfered with his speed". Horan, captain of the English team, sadly commented: "On 21 September we received a lesson not easy to forget".

In the early editions of the Olympic Games, 800 m. laurels were won with modest clockings: 2:11.0 by Edwin Flack of Australia at Athens in 1896, and 2:01 1/5 by Alfred Tysoe of England at Paris in 1900. Both these men belonged to the 800/1500 m. type of runner. A rival pattern was of course offered by men who alternated between the sprints and the quarter. Both types have defied time and exist even today, although the old theme "speed vs. endurance" has been recently moulded into a simple "endurance-to-speed" concept. In his excellent "Track and Field Omnibook", the famous American coach Ken Doherty discusses aerobic (with oxygen) vs. anaerobic (without oxygen) needs and suggests the following percentages:

Distance	Aerobic needs	Anaerobic needs
400 m.	25 %	75 %
800 m.	50 %	50 %
1500 m./mile	70 %	30 %

According to these figures, even pace running should be considered the ideal key to success in 1500 m./one mile running. A special halo has always surrounded the world's leading specialists at these distances. Great milers are usually written and talked of more extensively than any other species of athletic genius, no matter if the late Eighties of the current century have seen a strong revival of interest for the sprints and the marathon.

The one mile run has remote origins in British sports. Old magazines such as "Bell's Life" (first published in 1822) make reference to men who in the first half of the XIX century were able to run a mile "in about five or even four minutes". One of the earliest well documented races took place on 19 August 1865 at Manchester on a 595.27 m. grass track.

The title at stake was that of "Champion Miler of England". It was a typical "pro" race and betting was running high. Amazingly, the feud ended in a tie between William Lang, a bearded man known as the "Crowcatcher", and a darkhorse from Wales, William Richards. The time, 4:17 1/4, remained unsurpassed for sixteen years.

The Victorian Age favoured the birth of a new philosophy, that of amateurism. Maybe this ideal of the English gentleman somehow concealed a desire to keep apart from the lower classes, yet it is undeniable that it provided the grass roots of a sport governed by strict rules, hence likely to yield verdicts surely more reliable than those of the "pro" sport.

The first sub-4:30 mile by an amateur was credited to Walter Chinnery of England: 4:29 3/5 on 10 March 1868 at Cambridge. This and other later efforts were outshone by Walter Goodall George, who is unanimously considered the first of the world's great milers. George (born at Calne, Wiltshire, on 9 September 1858) was the slender type (1.80 m./61 kg) but possessed an aggregate of speed and endurance that was almost superhuman if measured on the yardstick of his time. For over five years he was the outstanding figure in British amateur ranks. He first beat 4:20 for the mile at Stamford Bridge, London, on 3 June 1882 with a 4:19 2/5 performance. Between 1880 and 1884 he won no less than ten AAA titles at distances ranging from 880 y. to 10 miles, being on occasion the only competitor in the race. His fame had by then crossed the Atlantic and the Americans were seized by a desire to match the great Englishman against their own Lon Myers. In the fall of 1882 the two running geniuses of the XIX century met in three "test matches" at New York's Polo Grounds. The global figure of fans who witnessed the series sounds almost appalling: 130,000! Myers won the first round on 4 November, beating George in the half-mile, 1:56 3/5 to 1:57.0.

On 11 November the Englishman evened the count, outpacing Myers in the mile, 4:21 2/5 to 4:27 3/5. The showdown was delayed due to Myers' indisposition and took place on 30 November, Thanksgiving Day. Over three quarters of a mile, George's superior stamina won the day, 3:10 1/2 to 3:13.0. It was a gruelling race run on a cold day, and at the end of it both runners were unconscious for a long while. For various reasons, notably including mercantile ones, it was only in the spring of 1886 that Myers and George again locked horns. In the meantime they had turned "pro" and the new series of "test matches" allowed them to cash in on laurels - for a total of $4500. The ra-ces were on consecutive weekends, on 1, 8 and 15 May. Myers won the 1000y., 2:23 2/5 to 2:24 1/5, and the three quarters of a mile, 3:15 4/5 to 3:16 4/5. Even in George's parade event, the mile, Lon emerged the winner in 4:32 2/5, with the Englishman five feet (1.52 m.) back. The following year they were pitted against each other again in Australia, and George had the upper hand, 2 to 1.

George's labours in the AAA Championships at Birmingham in 1884 were to remain memorable: on 21 June he won the mile in 4:18 2/5, his best as an amateur, the 880 y. and the 4 miles; on 23 June he won the 10 miles. After that he asked for permission to meet the famous Scottish "pro" William Cummings, who in 1881 had run a mile in 4:16 1/5. Permission was of course denied. As a result, George automatically became a "pro" the very day he met Cummings at Lillie Bridge Grounds, London, in 1885. George won hands down in 4:20 1/5. Far more famous is their second match, which took place on the same track on 23 August 1886.

After leading for the greater part of the race, George won again, in 4:12 3/4. His splits make interesting reading: 58 1/4, 63 1/2, 66.0, 65.0. Cummings challenged his rival in the last lap, stayed ahead for a while, but finally had to surrender. George was also credited with a 4:10 1/5 time trial at Surbiton in

Thomas Conneff, an American of Irish extraction, holder of the amateur 1-mile record at the end of the XIX century (4:15 3/5 in 1895).

1885, reportedly on a course which was found to be 6 y. (5.48 m) over distance! The best amateur of the XIX century was Thomas Conneff, an Irishman from County Kildare who emigrated to USA, where on 28 August 1895 at New York he ran a mile in 4:15 3/5. Almost pathetic, by comparison, is the time that earned first place for Edwin Flack of Australia in the 1500 m. of the inaugural Olympics at Athens (1896): 4:33 1/5. Charles Bennett of Britain did much better in winning at Paris four years later: 4:05.0.

Training rations used by XIX century milers look moderate, to say the least, if seen through present-time glasses. Here is a specimen for milers of that time, as offered by Montague Shearman: six daily sessions per week, at paces varying from "steady fast" to "slow", for a total of merely six kilometres. "On the seventh day, wind and weather conditions permitting, the runner would take a brisk Sunday walk of from six to ten miles, taking care not to catch a chill, and to be well rubbed down after the walk as well as after the runs". In those days man was evidently cautious in exploring his physical potentialities.

LONG DISTANCES AND MARATHON: From Deerfoot to Spiridon Louis

In the days of Pedestrianism, the long distances were the "pièce de résistance" of most "pros". A celebrated figure who aroused great interest on both sides of the Atlantic was Lewis Bennett, a Seneca Indian born in the Cattaraugus reserve near New York "around 1830". The notion that his race was particularly gifted for distance running had been spread by, among others, the poet Henry Wadsworth Longfellow, who in his "Song of Hiawatha" (1855) extols his Indian hero as being remarkably "swift of foot". Bennett became famous under the name of "Deerfoot". Well built (1.79 m./73 kg) and endowed with plenty of stamina, he emerged on the American scene in 1857, as the successor to another Seneca Indian, Albert Smith. After conquering America he went to England, where he met such standouts as Edward Mills, Jack White and William Lang, all of whom had good credentials even as one or two-mile runners. The English loved Deerfoot, especially when he appeared in his traditional custom, with "a slight red apron around his waist and a band around his head, with one eagle feather". However, some shrewd observers occasionally ventured the opinion that some of his opponents had been bribed to lose. Such a possibility cannot be ruled out altogether, but it should also be remembered that in those days a

The Airoldi story

The inaugural Olympics of the modern era (Athens 1896) assembled relatively few of the world's leading athletes of those days. Among the many who for various reasons stayed away from the feast was a prominent distance runner from Italy, Carlo Airoldi, a sturdy 27-year-old from Saronno, Lombardy. His country was among those which apparently ignored the Games, and so the self-confident Airoldi decided to go to Athens on his own - on foot. He left Milan on 28 February, after allowing himself a light "hors-d'oeuvre" in the form of a 17:17 5000 m. run. He reached Athens on 31 March. But for two boat trips (Ragusa-Corfu and Corfu-Patras), he walked for a distance of 1,338 kilometres - an average of about 50 kilometres a day. In an account he sent to the newly born Italian daily "Gazzetta dello Sport" he said: "What really held up my morale along the route was the thought that by winning the Athens race I could cash a prize of 25,000 Lire". Who was to provide that extra "fuel" is not known: certainly not the officials of the International Olympic Committee! Once in Athens, Airoldi -who among his achievements had a rather dubious 2:40:00 for 40 kilometres - was to experience a bitter disappointment. In talking to Greek officials he apparently recalled his running feats and, alas, the small prizes he had won in various Italian races. As a result of this "confession" he was inevitably barred from Olympic competition.

Carlo Airoldi (Italy), a distance runner whose story ranks among the most incredible in Olympic annals.

1860 1900

brave man from the "New World" was likely to be regarded with a grain of jealousy by English traditionalists, probably overlooking the fact that the Seneca tribe had sided with the British Army during the American War of Independence. Be as it may, Bennett's most significant feat was a one-hour record of 18,589 m. he achieved in London in 1863. This was in a twelve-mile race in which William Lang was given a 100y. handicap. At the end of a gruelling fight, Lang "won" over Bennett by merely one yard! It is also true, however, that in other races Bennett had mixed fortunes in his clashes with British runners.

Still in 1863, Lang ran two miles (3,218.69 m.) in 9:11 1/2 and ten miles (16,093.5 m.) in 52:36.0. Earlier in the same year he had to surrender to Jack White, a strong inexhaustible runner who on that occasion covered ten miles in 52:14.0, after passing the six-mile mark in 29:50.0. Still in the "pro" ranks, a remarkable feat was accomplished by Harry Watkins at Rochdale in 1899: 18,878 m. in an hour, after passing ten miles in 51:05 1/5. In doing so he broke a record of 18,839 m. set two years earlier by Fred Bacon, who in his younger days as an amateur had been a short-lived holder of the one-mile record (4:17.0 in 1895). At the turn of the century the best-on-record marks by an amateur were 14:24.0 for three miles and 30:17 4/5 for six miles, both by Sid Thomas of England, in 1893 and 1892 respectively.

Today's metric distances, the 5000 and 10,000 m., were included in the Olympic programme only in 1912. At the Paris Games (1900), however, there was a team race over 5000 m., the fastest time recorded being 15:29 1/5 by Charles Bennett of Britain, who had won the 1500 m. a week earlier.

Marathon is the name of a village in Attica, located about 40 kilometres north-east of Athens. As legend has it, the Athenians defeated the Persians there in 490 B.C. A Greek messenger, whose name is generally reported as Philippides, is said to have run all the way from the plain of Marathon to Athens to carry news of the victory to the citizens of the capital, and to have fallen dead on arriving there. The story is made all the more mythological by the fact that Herodotus, the great historian to whom we owe the greater part of the news relating to that famous battle, makes only a casual reference to the messenger, in terms quite different from those later committed to history by Lucian and Plutarch, Greek writers of the II century A.C. But then what is demanded of legends is that they be attractive, rather than true ...

At any rate, the mythical episode provided the stimulus which, at the end of the XIX century, led a French linguist and historian, Michel Bréal, to advocate the introduction of an endurance race to be named after Marathon. The first such race of modern times was to take place in connection with the 1896 Olympic Games at Athens over the distance (about 40,000 m.) supposedly covered by the mythical warrior, namely from Marathon bridge to the Athens Olympic Stadium. In preparation for that test, the Greeks allowed themselves two rehearsals, obviously on the same course.

The first one, with 12 entrants, was held on 10 March 1896 and the race was won by Charilaos Vasilakos in 3:18:00, with Spiridon Belokas second in 3:21:00. Two weeks later a similar race with 38 entrants was won by G.Lavrentis in 3:11:27, with one Spiridon Louis fifth in 3:18:27. These were in fact trial races to select the best Greek candidates for the Games. The Olympic marathon was contested by 14 Greeks and only 4 foreigners: Gyula Kellner of Hungary, Arthur Blake of USA, Edwin Flack of Australia and Albin Lermusiaux of France.

On 10 April at 2 p.m. these men lined up on Marathon bridge. The "noblest" runner in the group was Flack, a 22-year-old Aussie who had come from England on a regular leave from his job as an accountant. He ran a heat of the 800 m. on 6 April, won the 1500 m. on the 7th and the 800m. on the 9th, the eve of the marathon race! The starting gun was fired by Maj. Georgios Papadiamantopoulos, who happened to be the "mentor" of several Greek soldiers involved in the adventure - among them was

The mythical Deerfoot, a Seneca Indian who was the "Hero of two Worlds" in long distance running.

DEERFOOT,
THE SENECA INDIAN RUNNER.

a water carrier named Spiridon Louis. Track runners Flack and Lermusiaux shot their fireworks in the early going, only to fold up in the decisive stage of the race. Louis bided his time for a long while but emerged at the right moment. Although suffering from the combined effect of heat and dust, he reached the Panathinaikos Stadium as a lonely leader. The news of his arrival was brought to the large crowd and to Royalty by Maj. Papadiamantopoulos himself, who entered the arena on horseback.

The virtually unknown water carrier from Amaroussion thus won the first major marathon of modern times - in 2:58:50. His countryman Vasilakos was second (3:06:03), followed by Kellner of Hungary (3:09:35). Only nine men finished. The winner received plenty of accolades, including the privilege of a free haircut and shave for the rest of his life granted by an Athenian barber. He also received a farm from the Greek Government, as well as a horse and a cart for carrying water to Athens. Louis, who had seen the light of day on 12 January 1873, never ran again. Forty years after his triumph he appeared as a guest of honour at the Berlin Olympics. He died on 26 March 1940.

The Athens race had a loud echo in athletics circles the world over, and marathons began to crop up here and there, particularly in USA and France. The distance usually varied from 40 to 42 kilometres and in the majority of cases winners brought home high prizes. On 20 September 1896 a race of this kind was held in New York on a 40-kilometre course: it was won by John McDermott in 3:25:55 3/5. The famous Boston marathon was run for the first time on 19 April 1897, the course being just under 40 kilometres. That was Patriot's Day in Boston, commemorating the historic feat of Paul Revere 122 years earlier - a long overnight ride in that area to warn Massachusetts farmers that British troops were approaching. However, David Martin and Roger Gynn point out (in their excellent book "The Marathon Footrace") that the Boston marathon course "did not follow any portion of Revere's original ride". At any rate, linking the race with that popular holiday was certainly a useful idea. In fact, the Boston event has survived to this day and is now considered a classic.

The 1896 Olympic marathon was of course the first distance race to receive that name, but it is a fact that long races at various distances had been held long before then in several parts of the world, particularly in America, the British Isles and Scandinavia. The longer ones usually went under the name "Go-As-You-Please", meaning that competitors were free to alternate running and walking. Almost every Olympic marathon is linked with a more or less dramatic story. The 1900 race in Paris was run under intolerable weather conditions (39° C. in the shade). On a rather confused itinerary, which branched off through the streets and lanes of the French capital, home runners again took the lion's share. Michel Théato won over a distance of 40,260 m. in 2:59:45 and

1860
1900

Spiridon Louis (Greece), "chef-de-file" of modern marathon runners. Won the 1896 Olympic marathon at Athens.

Michel Théato, a French gardener who won the widely discussed 1900 Olympic marathon in Paris.

his countryman Emile Champion was second. For a long time after the race (years, in fact) some competitors from other countries continued to speak about violations allegedly committed by the French runners, who in turn counter-attacked with vigorous denials. First of the foreigners was Ernst Fast of Sweden, who finished about 40 minutes after Théato! The funny thing is that Alain Bouillé, the noted French track historian, recently cast a doubt on the nationality of the winner. He claims that Théato was actually born in 1878 as a citizen of Luxemburg! Whether or not he took the French nationality at some later date is not known.

HURDLES: From Jackson's oyster to Wyatt's camel

It is generally conceded that hurdle races have a relatively recent history. There seems to be hardly any reference to them in ancient Greek literature or even in writings of later epochs. In fact, the earliest races over hurdles governed by strict rules of some sort were held at Eton in 1843.

Originally, the three classic distances in hurdling were the 120 yards (=109.73 m.), the 220 yards (=201.17 m.) and the 440 yards (=402.34 m.), which according to the height of the barriers - always ten for each race - were commonly referred to in athletics jargon as the "highs", the "lows" and the "intermediates" respectively. In the metric world their natural offsprings were the 110, 200 and 400 metres.

The "lows", a typical American event for decades, have been recently discontinued. The hurdles for this race were only 2 ft. 6 in. high (76 cm.), and this made the event good hunting ground for sprinters. The barriers for the 110 metres or 120 yards event are 3 ft. 6in. high (1.06m.) and are placed at intervals of 10 yards (9.14 m.) from each other. Initially there is a flat course of 15 yards (13.72 m.). The slight surplus for the metric event is regained at the end, the distance from the last hurdle to the finish line being 14.02 m.

The rules now in force go back to the XIX century. The earliest barriers were solid sheep hurdles, "rigidly staked into the meadow". Under such conditions pioneers were primarily concerned with making a safe clearance, however uneconomical. In going over the barriers, the body was almost erect and the legs were raised and bent as in a standing jump. Consequently the centre of gravity remained far too high, and action over the hurdles was slow. Either leg could be used as the lead leg, and the rhythm between hurdles was all but uniform.

In view of these circumstances, one can appreciate the 16.0 performance which was credited to Clement Jackson of England at Cowley on 14 November 1865. He duplicated this time in 1867, a year after the height of the ten hurdles was standardized at 3 ft. 6 in. The career of this Indian-born pioneer came to a brisk halt when he ruptured a muscle in 1868. He later told the story in amusing terms: "I spiked a hidden oyster shell when going full bat in a hurdle handicap after the seven-leagued legs of W.G.Grace. From that date forth I have never run again, never tasted an oyster and never spoken to W.G.the Great!" In 1880, Jackson founded, along with Montague Shearman and Bernhard Wise, England's Amateur Athletic Association, the earliest example of a national body in athletics.

The "highs" began to appear in American meets during the Seventies and the honour of posting the first sub-16 secs. performance fell to Henry Williams - later known as the "Father of Minnesota Football" - who was timed in 15 4/5 over 120 y. hurdles at Berkeley Oval, New York, on 30 May 1891. In the meantime, efforts were made to devise a more practical and less dangerous kind of barrier. A stringent necessity, especially in view of the early custom of placing ropes or crossbars across the track, as recalled by Boyd Comstock in his book "How to Hurdle". Yet one had to wait till about 1900 to see the adoption of a movable, individual hurdle in the form of an inverted T.

The British attribute to Arthur Croome, an Oxford student, the introduction of the straight leg in leading over the hurdles, sometime in the late Eighties, when he was credited with 15 3/5, albeit unofficially. Yet the paternity of modern hurdling more rightfully belongs to an American, Alvin Kraenzlein (born at Milwaukee on 12 December 1876; 1.83 m./75 kg), a sort of "Owens ante-litteram" who excelled in sprin-ting, hurdling and long jumping. The straight leg form probably came natural to him, in view of his double capacity as sprinter and long jumper. On 18 June 1898 in Chicago he won the AAU 120 y. hurdles title in 15 1/5, the official American record at the turn of the century. In the same year he ran the 220 y. hurdles on a straight course in 23 3/5, another best-on-record mark. At the 1899 AAU Championships, held at Newton, MA., he won the "highs", the "lows" and the long jump, was second in the 100 y. (3 feet behind Arthur Duffey) and the high jump - all on one and the same day! At the Paris Olympics the follo-wing year he won four titles: the 110 m. hurdles (15 2/5), the 60 m. flat (7.0), the long jump (7.185 m.) and the 200 m. hurdles (25 2/5). Counting prelims and finals, he ran eight races in the space of three days. Four years earlier, at Athens, the "high hurdles" crown had been won in no better than 17 3/5 by Thomas Curtis, he too an American. The 440 yards or 400 metres hurdles has a relatively short history. This event was ignored almost completely by the modern pioneers of the sport, who admittedly thought it too uncomfortable and fatiguing, if not altogether lethal ("the man-killer event"). Even though a quarter-mile race with (twelve!) hurdles figured in the programme of the first Oxford University Sports in 1860, it was not till 1914 that this event appeared in the championship programme of such prominent athletic countries as Britain, USA and Sweden. For once we are confronted with an athletic event which since the early days was definitely more popular on the Continent than in the British Isles. In France, for example, the 400 m. hurdles had been a regular championship feature since 1893. This situation is partly reflected in the rules that govern the event. The ten hurdles, each 3 ft. (91.4 cm.) high, are laid at intervals of 35 metres. The distance from the scratch line to the first hurdle is 45 metres and the distance from the last hurdle to the finish line is 40 metres. In the corresponding English distance, the 440 y. hurdles, the surplus distance (2.34 m.) was added at the end, in the "run-in". The first sub-60 secs. performance was achieved by an Englishman, Samuel Morris: 59 4/5 in 1886. Five years later, his countryman Godfrey Shaw, who excelled even in the "highs", was credited with 57 1/5 at a distance which upon verification turned out to be 442 yards! On the eve of the Paris Olympics (1900), the favourite of many for the 400 m. hurdles crown was Henri Tauzin of France, five-time winner of the national title and credited with 58 4/5, but an American outsider, J.Walter Tewksbury, provided a major upset. Although a virtual novice in the event, he shot ahead early and was never headed. He won by a large margin from Tauzin in 57 3/5. On that occasion, the hurdles were long telephone poles laid across the track, all except the last, which was a water jump of the kind now used in the steeplechase! Several theories exist about the origins of steeplechase races in athletics. The name of the event was at any rate inherited from the horse-racing world. There is in fact an historical episode which seems to provide a useful pointer. One autumn afternoon in 1850, some members of Exeter College, Oxford, were discussing a horse race over fences and other obstacles in which they had just competed. One of the arguers, Halifax Wyatt, whose horse had fallen during the race, is said to have remarked casually: "I'd run across two miles of country on foot, rather than mount that camel again!" When somebody injected a provocative: "Well, why not?", the idea of a steeplechase race was naturally born. Later in the year, a two-mile event with 24 fences was held in a marsh at Binsey near Oxford. As poetic justice would have it, Mr. Wyatt emerged the victor.

Notwithstanding this bold start, more than a century elapsed before a strict standardization of steeplechase courses was obtained at international level! Yet a steeplechase event of sorts had appeared in the Olympics as early as in 1900: a race of 2500 m. won by George Orton of Canada in 7:34 2/5 and ... another of 4000 m. won by John Rimmer of Britain in 12:58 2/5. One of the barriers was in fact a stone fence. Even so, several competitors were bold enough to compete in both events, incidentally held on consecutive days!

HIGH JUMP:
The irrepressible Sweeney

There is no explicit reference to competitive jumping for height in Greek mythology. The Irish, however, had such an event on the programme of their Tailteann Games, first held long before the beginning of the Christian Era. In the Middle Ages, evolutions in vertical jumping were frequently linked with acrobatic feats (somersault, "wall" jump, and the like). In the British Isles the high jump remained popular through the centuries in one form or another. First to clear the magic height of 6 feet (1.829 m.) was an Englishman, Marshall Jones Brooks, who on 17 March 1876 at Marston near Oxford went over a bar

1860
1900

set at 1.831. Three weeks later, in London, the 21-year-old Brooks easily mastered 1.892. Spectators were in ecstasy as Brooks walked back under the bar! He wound up a brief but eventful season by annexing the English title with 1.829, while sporting a top hat. Quite amazing, even if seen through "modern glasses", are the feats of William Byrd Page, an American who in 1887 first mastered 1.911, then 1.930 in what was termed as an exhibition (but the mark was ratified by the AAU). Since he stood only 1.70 m., he provided history's first notable height vs. record differential: 23 centimetres. In those days high jumpers apparently showed little or no concern for the position of their centre of gravity vis-à-vis the crossbar. They simply drove all parts of the body as high as possible, generally using a slow approach, though Page exhibited what in the words of a noted American observer was "a slight backward lay-out". A good but somewhat questionable performance of 1.965 was credited to George Rowdon of England in 1890, but the record was disallowed by the AAA because of sloping ground, although a commentator of the time noted: "It is possible that the run-up to the bar was sloping, but not at the take-off place". Toward the end of the XIX century jumping form improved noticeably, chiefly thanks to the efforts of Michael Sweeney, an Irishman transplanted in USA. He was the first jumper to achieve a certain degree of proficiency with the Eastern Cut-off style, notably in the essential detail of converting horizontal speed generated in the approach run into a fair amount of vertical drive. His career spanned over 14 years, from 1888 till 1902. He broke Page's record just before turning twenty, in 1892, with 1.937. His golden year was 1895, when he gradually improved through 1.956, 1.959 and finally 1.972, a mark which he achieved in the famous New York A.C. vs London A.C. match in New York on 21 September. The following year he took the position of athletic director at Hill School, thus giving up amateur competition. However, he continued to excel as a "pro", showing great versatility: 14.60 in the triple jump and 3.09 in the pole vault. High jump results by the early Olympic winners were rather mediocre: 1.81 by Ellery Clark of USA at Athens in 1896, and 1.90 by Irving Baxter, also of USA, at Paris four years later.

POLE VAULT:
'til the frail bamboo

The pole vault is one of the most spectacular events in athletics and some experts consider it the most difficult to learn. Its origins are obviously connected with man's earliest wartime activities, since jumping with a pole over streams and fences and other obstacles was a useful medium to escape enemies or wild beasts. An event called "pole jumping" figured in the programme of the ancient Tailteann Games of Ireland. An expression such as " spear-high jump" is occasionally encountered in classic Greek literature, yet there is no trace of an athletic event of that type in writings dealing with the ancient Olympics. It is, however, interesting to note that the Germans use a strikingly similar word ("Stabhochsprung", i.e. staff-high jump) for this event in its modern version.

Under the influence of Guts Muths (author of "Gymnastik für die Jugend", 1793), pole vaulting as a gymnasium sport was practised in Germany early in the XIX century. In the British Isles the exercise probably originated in the Fen country, where poles had long been a must for negotiating ditches and canals. In the early days, pole jumping was for distance rather than for height. It fell to some members of the Ulverston (Lancashire) Cricket Club to launch pole vaulting for height as an athletic contest in England, about the middle of the XIX century. These pioneers used long, heavy poles, usually of ash or hickory, with a tripod of iron at the lower end. This was planted in the ground about three feet (91.4 cm.) in front of the crossbar. The vaulting act, made in a sitting position, came as the combined result of climbing and swinging. One of the most famous English "climbers" was Tom Ray, who enjoyed a long career before meeting a premature death at 42. He achieved a performance of 3.57 in 1888. The last record holder of the set was Richard Dickinson, who did 3.58 in 1891. By that time the event already figured in American and Japanese college meets. And the Americans soon abandoned the hand shift, thus laying the foundations of modern vaulting. Hugh Baxter, a super-athlete who dominated the scene for several years, vaulted 3.48 in 1887. It may be of interest to record that back in 1878 he had experimented with a bamboo pole, only to return to a hickory one the following year.

A long period of American domination began in 1898, when Raymond Clapp of Yale University scaled a height of 3.62. This American "reign" was to last till 1972! The first Olympic winners were William Hoyt in 1896 and Irving Baxter (not to be confused with the above-mentioned Hugh) in 1900, both with 3.30. Strange things happened on the latter occasion: to begin with, some of the best Americans stayed away from the competition on religious grounds, since the event happened to be held on a Sunday. In subsequent days, French organizers allowed them to appear in special events: in one of these, Dan Horton cleared 3.45 to win from Charles

Dvorak, 3.35. But these performances obviously had no bearing on Olympic results. Baxter, the official champion, had won the high jump an hour earlier. Not surprisingly, this feat has never been matched!

LONG JUMP:
A strange duel

This is one of the most natural events in track and field athletics. The long jumper has no implements to deal with, and invariably follows a specified direction of run. This is probably the chief reason why jumping for distance has always been a popular practice among men of all races. In fact, this was the only jumping event included in the programme of the ancient Olympic Games. The Greeks, however, used jumping weights ("halteres"), swinging them forwards and backwards while in the air to supplement the action of arms and legs. In his book "Greek Athletes and Athletics", Prof. H.A.Harris ventures the opinion that the Greeks called long jump what was in fact a double, if not triple, jump. Even in the early days of modern athletics, long jumping with dumb-bells was a popular exercise among British "pros". John Howard was credited with a mark of 9.01, apparently made with a 5 lb. (2.27 kg) dumb-bell at Chester in 1854.

The first 7-metre long jump of modern times is commonly attributed to John Lane, a sturdy little Irishman (1.73 m./70 kg): 7.05 on 7 June 1874 at College Park, Dublin, alas with suspected wind assistance (a factor which was seldom taken into consideration in the early days) and apparently on a gently sloping runway. More acceptable was perhaps a 7.06 mark which Pat Davin, another Irishman, achieved on two occasions in 1883, from grass runways. In the same year John Parsons of England joined the tiny "7-Metre Club" with 7.01. Like Davin, he also excelled as a high jumper.

America soon entered the picture and in 1886 a fast man like Malcolm Ford of New York (three-time winner of the AAU 100 y. title) brought the world record to the other side of the Atlantic with a leap of 7.08. That year incidentally saw the introduction of the take-off board. Until then, the "boundary" simply consisted of a white line marked on the ground.

The take-off board (1.21 m. in length, 20 cm. in width and 10 cm. in depth) has since been the crux of long jumpers. It is commonly felt that if the jumper could be relieved of that psychological burden while going down the runway, his distances would automatically improve by several centimetres.

Among those who took turns in breaking the world record during the Nineties was Charles Burgess Fry, a famous English all-round sportsman who jumped 7.17 at Oxford in 1893.

The struggle for world supremacy between Irish and American long jumpers reached a climax near the turn of the century. Meyer Prinstein, a student from Syracuse University, long jumped 7.23 in 1898, only to be excelled later in the season by William Newburn, a big Irishman who did 7.25, then 7.32, both times from a board take-off. The following year it was the turn of a versatile American, Alvin Kraenzlein, who improved to 7.43.

Prinstein (born in Poland in 1878) recaptured the record in the spring of 1900 at the Penn Relay Carnival in Philadelphia with an excellent leap of 7.50, easily defeating Kraenzlein (7.07) in the process. Prinstein and Kraenzlein were again pitted against each other in the 1900 Olympic final in Paris. On Saturday, 14 July (a French national holiday), Prinstein led the qualifiers with 7.175, with Kraenzlein well behind at 6.93. The final was scheduled for the following day, a Sunday, and Prinstein was among those American athletes who chose to stay away on religious grounds.

In his absence, Kraenzlein improved to 7.185, one centimetre beyond the qualifying mark of his rival, and thus won the gold medal. Rumour has it that after the qualifying rounds Prinstein and Kraenzlein agreed not to compete on Sunday. As the story goes, the former was ostensibly outraged when his companion failed to keep his word.

1860
1900

Thoughts of an athlete

In the first edition of the modern Olympics (Athens 1896) results were generally poor and the long jump was no exception. The winner, Ellery Clark of USA, then a 22-year-old Harvard student, did no better than 6.43 (although, interestingly enough, he came back three days later to annex the high jump crown as well). He recalled that day in his book "Reminiscences of an Athlete". In that event, competitors were allowed only three jumps. He fouled on the first two, then … "I shall never forget my feelings as I stood at the end of the path for my third - and last - try. Five thousand miles, I reflected, I had come; and was it to end in this? Three fouls and then five thousand miles back again, with that for my memory of the Games". Luckily enough, on that crucial last jump Clark was able to do himself justice.

TRIPLE JUMP: The "jump-as-you-please" era

The triple jump (or hop, step and jump) has been for many years one of the most neglected events. To this ostracism have largely contributed some of the major powers of the sport. In USA, for example, the event appeared on the AAU Championship programme in 1893, was dropped the following year, and resumed only in 1906. What is more, it was not incorporated in college competition till 1959. In Germany, a country usually interested in all athletic events, the triple jump was at one stage ousted from the Championship programme for several years. In Britain the event made its first appearance in the AAA Championships in 1914.

The triple jump is a deceptively easy, but in actual fact most exacting test of athletic skill, requiring as it does a high combination of strength and technique.

In few other events are the muscles subjected to such a strain as in the triple jump. Countries such as Japan and Australia in the Thirties and USSR and Poland in the Fifties have done much to popularize the triple jump, devoting full attention to the complicated technical aspects of the event.

The rules now governing the triple jump are reflected in the name which was given to it until not so long ago in the English-speaking countries: hop, step and jump. In fact the three leaps are essentially different from one another. The first leap ("hop") is made with take-off and landing on the same foot; the second leap ("step") implies landing on the other foot; the third leap ("jump") has much in common with a normal long jump. It was only recently that the definition "triple jump" supplanted the older one.

The Irish and the Scots are the acknowledged fathers of the triple jump, at least in modern times. The XIX century fashion in the Emerald Isle consisted in taking two hops and a jump, in which the best leg was used twice before the final jump. The leading Irish exponents of this form were John Daly (13.81 in 1873), John Purcell (15.11 in 1887), Daniel Shanahan (15.25 in 1888) and Matthew Roseingreve (15.26 in 1895). Two Scottish "pros" were also credited with fine marks: David Johnstone (15.39 in 1881) and Robert Hogg (15.16 in 1893).

> ### The first Olympic Champion
>
> The first title to be awarded at the Athens Olympics, on 6 April 1896, was won by James Connolly, a 30-year-old Harvard freshman. By winning the triple jump with 13.71 he became the first "olympionikos" of modern times. There are good reasons to believe that such a distinction could hardly have gone to a more deserving athlete. Historian Bill Mallon relates that "when he (Connolly) heard that several Bostonians were going to Athens (for the Games), he requested permission from his dean to leave school ... But his grades were not so good and permission was refused. Connolly then decided to drop out of school and made the trip anyway". But to achieve his end and make history he needed financial help. This was provided with money raised through a "cake sale" arranged in his parish! Connolly (born at South Boston, MA. on 28 November 1865) later became a writer of seafaring novels.

George Gray (Canada), the Father of modern shot putters.

Another Irishman, John Breshnihan, reached 15.34 in 1906, presumably the best-on-record mark with the hop, hop and jump version. With the form now in use, Shanahan did 14.50 in 1886, and Purcell reached 14.70 in 1887. However, it should be noted that the "1906 Irish Athletic Record" apparently made no distinction between different forms. This explains why Irish statisticians, e.g. Tony O'Donoghue, are still working hard to identify marks made with the now prevailing form.

Purcell's mark was excelled at the 1893 AAU Championships in Chicago, when Edward Bloss won with 14.78. This man was also credited with an interesting mark in an ultra-short indoor event: 2 4/5 over 20 yards (18.28 m.) in 1892.

At the 1896 Olympics in Athens, an American of Irish extraction, James Connolly, won with 13.71, taking two hops with his right foot and one jump. It was a "jump-as-you-please" contest, every competitor being free to use the form he liked best. Four years later, in Paris, Connolly improved to 13.97 but had to be content with second place behind Meyer Prinstein (14.47).

THROWS:
Shot Put - Horgan's unquenchable thirst

Like most of the weight events practised in the modern era, the shot put apparently originated as a test of strength within the frame of Scottish and Irish folklore. But it was only toward the middle of the XIX century that the exercise began to be moulded into its present form. The 16 lb. (7.257 kg) iron ball appeared more or less at that time and was thrown from a 7 ft. (2.13 m.) square, the boundaries of which were sunk flush with the ground. The present 7 ft. circle was introduced near the end of the century.

The first noteworthy figure in the history of the event was George Gray (born at Coldwater, Ontario, on 4 May 1865), a Canadian of medium build who in fifteen years of activity won the American AAU title ten times and raised the record from 13.38 in 1887 to 14.75 in 1898, always from a 7ft. circle. He "came of sturdy, Scots pioneer stock". As a youth he worked in the lumber camps in winter and helped his father in a drygoods store in the summer. It was not until 1886, when he became a member of the famous New York A.C., that he could afford to travel to track meets and have his expenses paid.

The Canadian was later excelled in both performance and longevity by Denis Horgan (born at Banteer, County Cork, on 18 May 1871), a sturdy Irishman who stood 1.78 m. in height. Between 1893 and 1912 he won the English AAA title thirteen times. It may be of interest to note that his weight increased from 75 kg. in 1893 to 108 kg. in 1908. By the turn of the century, however, his best mark, 14.68 in 1897, was still a bit shy of Gray's record. But more on him later. In the inaugural edition of the Olympic Games the shot was put from a 2-metre square, no matter if by then several countries had already adopted the 7 ft. circle. The Big Two, Gray and Horgan, were not there and victory went to an American, Robert Garrett, who beat Miltiades Gouskos of Greece by two centimetres with an unprepossessing 11.22. Four years later, in Paris, some of the best men were not there, and the implement was put from a 7ft. square.

Garrett improved to 12.35, yet he had to be content with third place, the winner being another American,

1860
1900

Robert Garrett (USA), who won shot and discus and placed honourably in the jumping events at the 1896 Olympics in Athens.

Richard Sheldon, at 14.10. A week earlier, at the AAA Championships in London, Sheldon had beaten Horgan, 13.98 to 13.57. The Irishman, unable to make the trip to Paris, was still thirsty for revenge.

He boldly made it a point to be present at the American AAU Championships in New York two months later. To achieve his end, "he threw up his job" and worked his passage across the Atlantic on a cattle boat, arriving in Boston on the eve of the meet. He travelled overnight to reach New York, where he thrashed Sheldon, the newly crowned Olympic champion, 14.06 to 13.61. (In between them in second place at 13.73 was Wesley Coe, an American who had not competed in Paris).

DISCUS THOW:
In the Bois, between two rows of trees ...

As the most classic of throwing events, the discus is richly illustrated in the art and literature of antiquity. The Greeks had it as part of their pentathlon contests. The exercise was also practised by the Etruscans and, to a lesser extent, by the Romans. It was a stone discus, such as can be seen in Myron's famous sculpture, Discobolus, the best replica being perhaps the one contained in Munich's Glyptothek. From fragments of early models (about 500 B.C.) it can be assumed that such discii had a diameter of about 28 cm. and a weight of about 7 kg.

For actual competition, however, the implement most commonly used was a metal one varying from 1.5 to 4 kg. in weight.

Greek throwers had a rectangular platform known as "balbis". Little is known about the rules then in force, let alone about distances achieved by leading performers. In modern times, the discus throw as we now know it was introduced by Europeans.

In 1870 the event figured in the programme of a major athletic festival held in Athens. At the inaugural Olympic celebration (1896), Greek discoboli thought they had the inside lane vis-à-vis their guests from abroad, but much to their surprise the longest throw, 29.15, was produced by an American, Robert Garrett, who won from Panagiotis Paraskevopoulos (28.95). On that occasion the competitors used a wooden discus which had a lead nucleus and an iron edge, and was thrown from a 2.50 m. square. Garrett, who was captain of Princeton's track team, had been practising with a 20 lb. (9.08 kg) steel discus for a short time, before going to Greece. Knowing that he was just a novice, he was not sure whether he should compete in that event, but he forgot about his doubts when he heard that the discus in use there was "merely" 2 kg. in weight! This detail may be curiously regarded as a fore-runner of things to come.

The philosophy now prevailing is - the harder your daily training, the lighter will seem the demand of competition. The paucity of competition anno 1896 is further reflected in the fact that Garrett not only achieved a shot/discus double, but also finished second in the long jump and third in the high jump! And he was by no means one of America's most celebrated athletes.

At the end of the century the best result achieved from a 7 ft. (2.13 m.) circle was 36.19 by Charles Henneman of USA at the 1897 AAU Championships in New York. At the Paris Olympics three years later there was a new round of the USA vs Europe feud. The event was won by Rudolf (Rezsö) Bauer of Hungary, who threw 36.04, while Frantisek Janda of Bohemia and Richard Sheldon of USA took the next positions in that order.

The battle unfolded in the Bois de Boulogne, on the grounds of Racing Club de France, namely in a lane flanked by two rows of trees. Some competitors, notably including defending champion Garrett, who finished seventh, hit the trees more than once!

HAMMER THROW:
A heritage from the Emerald Isle

The name of this event may sound misleading to the uninitiated observer watching a hammer-throwing contest for the first time. In fact, the implement used in an exercise of this type at some time in the distant past was a sledge hammer.

There is, for example, a drawing of Henry VIII in the act of throwing such a "conventional" hammer in a test of physical skill at Court. In the British Isles, throwing with an implement of this type was for centuries a pastime of the nobility and populace alike.

Hammer rules prevailing in British University Sports differed considerably from those now in force. In 1887 the Americans set the maximum length of the implement at 4 ft. (1.22 m.). It consisted of an iron ball which was connected to a handle, almost triangular in shape, by means of a steel chain (3 mm. in diameter). The implement, complete as thrown, had to weigh no less than 16 lb. (7.257 Kg). The throw was performed from a circle 7ft. (2.13 m.) in diameter. These rules were adopted at the international level only in 1908. The best results in the pioneer days of the event were achieved in USA, generally if not exclusively by Irish immigrants who in view of their large frame were to be known collectively as the "Irish Whales". The father of this illustrious family (whose latest offspring has been John Lawlor, who competing for the colours of Ireland finished fourth at the 1960 Olympics in Rome) was James Mitchel, who reigned supreme on the American scene for about ten years and eventually raised the record to 44.21 (1892).

Another boat of immigrants from the Emerald Isle brought to America the man who was to make history more than anyone else: John Flanagan (born at Kilbreedy, County Limerick, on 9 January 1873). In his native country he had earned a reputation as a fine all-rounder, with such results as 6.70 in the long jump, 14.04 in the triple jump, and his great skill in the weight events. In 1896 he won the hammer at the English AAA Championships with 40.20 and placed second to Horgan in the shot.

The following year he made his debut on the American scene (he was to remain in USA till 1911) and lost no time in raising the hammer record to 45.93. And he won the first of his seven AAU titles. On 22 July 1899, in Boston, he became the first ball-and-chain adept to break the 50-metre barrier with a throw of 50.01.

The hammer throw was first included in the Olympic programme in 1900. Flanagan led a US sweep with a 51.01 performance. A sign of the rarefied competition of those days can be found in the fact that the best non-American in the Paris event was Eric Lemming of Sweden, better known as a javelin thrower.

Before the year was out, Flanagan improved to 51.61.

JAVELIN THROW:
The Swedish Father

As a medium for war and hunting, javelins and spears must have been in use since times immemorial. As an athletic contest, the javelin throw figured in the programme of both the Olympic Games of Greece and the Tailteann Games of Ireland, in the former within the frame of a pentathlon contest.

On such an event we have stories by famous writers like Homer and Tacitus. The basic difference vis-à-vis the modern javelin lay in the use of a thong, a leather strap that formed a loop, which ancient athletes attached at the centre of gravity of the javelin, then putting their index finger, or the index and middle fingers, into the loop. The thong made the grip more secure. A rotating motion about its axis stabilized the javelin in flight and so helped it to achieve a greater distance. Even in our time there has been an attempt, made by the Spaniards in 1956, to introduce the rotation style, but the proposal was rejected by the IAAF, apparently for safety reasons. Current rules include an anti-revolutionary clause: "Non-orthodox styles are not permitted".

In the Middle Ages the javelin was generally thrown against fixed targets, and among those who distinguished themselves in this exercise were, of course, some famous sovereigns. In the second half of the XIX century, javelin throwing for distance was introduced by the Hungarians and Germans and eventually promoted on a large scale by the Scandinavians, who conceived the rules now in force. The javelin has a minimum weight of 800 grams and an overall length which may vary from 260 to 270 cm. Its diameter at the thickest point is between 25 and 30 mm. The distance from the tip of the metal head and the centre of gravity may vary from 90 to 106 cm. (the latter figure was 110 cm. until April 1986).

A cord wrapped around the centre of gravity allows a convenient grip.

At the turn of the century two different styles were used: one with the grip in the middle of the shaft, the other with a free grip, generally in the rear part of the implement. The superior practical value of the former style soon became self-evident, yet the two versions co-existed till 1908.

Also popular at the time was the javelin throw both-hands, for which the latest world record accepted by the IAAF was 114.28 (61.81 right and 52.47 left) by Yngve Häckner of Sweden in 1917.

The first major name in the modern history of the event is that of Sweden's Eric Lemming (born on 22 February 1880; 1.91 m./94 kg), a powerful man who dominated the Scandinavian picture for over a decade. He was a keen student of the event, and his style was copied by many of his contemporaries. While attributing a primary importance to the action of the throwing arm, Lemming did not underestimate the usefulness of the run-up. Equally efficient in both the free style and the modern style, he was the first man to reach 50 and 60 metres with the latter form. At the end of the century he held the world record with 49.32 (1899). The javelin throw was to appear in the Olympic programme at the "interim" Games of 1906 in Athens.

ALL-AROUND COMPETITION:
Early Attempts

The idea of an all-around "genius" has always appealed to the minds of sports-loving people. In 708 B.C. the Greeks introduced a Pentathlon in the programme of their Olympic Games. It consisted of the following events: run (probably a "stadion" length), long jump, discus, javelin, wrestling. Hellenism held versatility in

1860
1900

high esteem and this multiple competition soon became the "pièce de résistance" of the Games.

Nowadays, the pentathlon survives in various forms. There is one that includes track and field events only (long jump, javelin, 200 m., discus and 1500 m.). Such a contest was held at the Olympic Games of 1912, 1920 and 1924. More important perhaps is the "Modern Pentathlon", which includes tests in five different sports: riding, fencing, shooting, swimming and cross-country running. As far as track and field is concerned, though, the only widely known form of multiple competition is the Decathlon, which derives its name from the Greek language (deka = ten; athlos = struggle, contest) but is nevertheless an invention of modern times.

All-around competitions were held in Scotland in the early 1860's. USA and Ireland followed suit several years later. In 1884 a multiple test was included in the programme of the American AAU Championships. It consisted of ten events, in this order: 100 yards, shot put, high jump, 880 yards walk, hammer, pole vault, 120 yards hurdles, 56 lb. (25.4 kg) weight, long jump, one mile run. This Pantagruelian menu was to be devoured in a single day! Incidentally, it should be noted that contemporary "freaks" can do even better (or should I say worse). In some countries there is now the so-called one-hour decathlon, a torture for which Robert Zmelik, a Czech, holds the best-on-record score: 7897 points at Ostrava in 1992. In the regular two-day competition he could point to a personal best of 8627 points.

A great pioneer of all-around competitions was Martin Sheridan, the famous Irish-American thrower.

RELAYS: Born in Philly

Some historians of sport have attempted to establish a connection between the torch races of the ancient Greeks, which originated from a religious rite, and the relay races of our time. In the former the torch was in fact handed over from one runner to the other, and each one had to be careful not to drop it while trying to outrun the rival team. It is obvious, however, that relay racing in its present form, i.e. running with a baton, is essentially a modern creation. Two Americans from Pennsylvania University, Frank Ellis and H. Laussat Geyelin, are generally acknowledged as the inventors of the four-man race. They made their first experiment in 1893, and two years later Philadelphia acted as host to a meet which consisted mainly of relay races open to students of all classes. This was the inaugural Pennsylvania Relay Carnival, fore-runner of a series of similar meets which even today are an essential part of the American outdoor season.

The "Penn Relays" are one of the biggest mass festivals in the athletic world. Every year, in the last weekend in April, several thousand students representing hundreds of schools of every grade and order gather at the historic Franklin Field in Philadelphia for a series of hotly contested relay races. Almost equally famous are the "Drake Relays", inaugurated in 1910, and held at Des Moines, Iowa, on the same weekend as the Penn Carnival.

There can be little doubt that these relay meets, so popular in the States, have greatly stimulated and developed the well-known competitive ability of American athletes. In such races even an average performer may sometimes play a prominent role while defending the lead gained by his teammates from the attack of a superior rival. In this way every one is extended to his potential best.

The medium of relay racing is a baton made of wood, metal or any other rigid material in one piece, circular in section and hollow. It is 30 cm. in length, has a circumference of 12-to-13 cm. and weighs not less than 50 grams. It should be colored so as to be easily visible during the race. In the 4x100 m.(and 4x110 y.) relay each team must keep to their lane throughout the entire race. A closed exchange zone, 20 m. in length, the medium point of which corresponds to the scratch line, was introduced in 1926, and the outgoing baton taker had to be stationed within its boundaries. Prior to 1926, when this restriction did not exist, the outgoing runner was allowed to start before the first boundary line but still had to take the baton before reaching the second and final line. Curiously enough, a return to that situation was sanctioned in 1963. Now the members of a team, other than the lead-off man, may commence running not more than 10 m. outside the take-over zone. There is a distinctive mark in each lane to denote this extended limit.

In the currently favoured "alternated technique", the first and third men start with the baton in their right hand and use the inside of their lanes, while the second and fourth men run on the outside and take the baton with their left hand. In this procedure no man has to change the baton from hand to hand, an operation which often causes a runner to break his rhythm. The so-called "blind pass" is virtually a necessity but implies a lot of preparatory work in order to be executed with mastery.

The only other relay event included in the Olympic programme is the 4x400 m. The first leg is run in lanes to avoid clashes when most of the competitors are still closely bunched. In fact, the runners must now keep to their lanes throughout the first curve of the second lap. For obvious reasons, changes in this race are less of a decisive factor than in the sprint relay. "Blind passes" seldom occur, since the incoming man is generally tired and hence not always able to control his reflexes. Consequently, the outgoing teammate keeps his eyes on the baton until he can finally take it in his hand. As a rule, the baton is carried in the right hand but the receiving man usually takes it with the left, only to transfer it as soon as possible to the other hand.

This is the so-called "visual pass". When competition is stiff from start to finish, a 4x400m. race can be one of the most thrilling events in athletics. Both the relay events now in use were introduced in the Olympic programme at Stockholm in 1912.

The fastest time for the sprint relay at the turn of the century was 48 1/5 by A.C. Sparta Prague in 1897, a team consisting of Bohumil Pohl, Frantisek Schnepp, Karel Malecek and Jan Havel. In the longer relay the "initial" record was set by a University of Pennsylvania team made of L.Sayer, N.W.Bingham, W.F.Garcelon and S.M.Merrill: 3:25 1/5 over 4x440y. in 1893. By the end of the century the record of the mile relay was down to 3:21 2/5, thanks to a "Wonder Team" representing the New York A.C. Thoughtful chroniclers have committed to history the "splits" of this race, held at New York in 1897: Maxey Long 50.0, Harry Lyons 51 3/5, Thomas Burke 50 3/5, Bernie Wefers 49 1/5.

THE WALKS:
On the razor's edge

The term walking (same as "marche" in French or "Gehen" in German) defines one of the most fundamental of human activities, that of going about or travelling on foot. But when it comes to competitive walking, or as the British say with a somewhat contradictory term, "race walking", man is inevitably subject to the urge of breaking into a run, especially when the distance to be covered is a short one. To offset this danger, rules define race walking as "a progression of steps so taken that unbroken contact with the ground is maintained", and further state that "during the period of each step, the advancing foot of the walker must make contact with the ground before the rear foot leaves the ground". It is also stated that "the supporting leg must be straightened (i.e. not bent at the knee) for at least one moment when in the vertical upright position". Well, the history of the sport is there to tell us that the borderline between walking and running is at best a very tenuous one!

This explains why race walking, along with a large number of adepts and defenders, has always had also a fair number of detractors - people who say: "Only a mediocre runner can find solace in walking".

Both schools of thought agree at least on one point: competitive walking is at its noblest in long distance events.

The annals of English Pedestrianism are full of stories about professional walkers meeting in match races. Walking was an integral, if not exclusive, part of the "go-as-you-please" events I have alluded to in relation to long distance running. In the domain of pure walking - not guaranteed as 100% pure though - English historians give a place of honour to two legendary figures: Foster Powell and Capt. Robert Barclay Allardice.

The former, known also as a good runner, was credited with such feats as walking 100 miles (160.93 km.) in 22 hours (1789) and the 402 miles (646.95 km.) from London to York and back in 5 days 13 hours 35 minutes (1792), the latter exploit at 56 years of age. Even more renowned was Capt. Barclay, a Scotsman who in 1809 covered 1000 miles (1609.35 km.) in 1000 consecutive hours. The contract stated that he was to cover one mile in each hour, day and night.

He achieved this exploit at Newmarket Heath in the presence of a large crowd - in the space of 42 days, and thereby earned a purse of 1000 guineas. As an English commentator put it, "This was more of a sleep-denying performance than an athletic one, as a calculation will reveal".

In his book "Pedestrianism", published in 1813, Walter Thom discusses Capt. Barclay's career in profuse detail.

Among other things he relates that "at an early age, he (Barclay) showed athletic promise by walking 6 miles (9656.07m.) in an hour for 100 guineas". In his roaring years the captain would show up at major venues "dressed in a flannel shirt, flannel trousers and night cap, lamb's wool stockings and thick soled leather shoes".

America had her share of famous walkers, the most popular of all being Edward Payson Weston (born at Providence, R.I. in 1839), whose career stretched from 1861 to 1913. Historian John Cumming describes him, somewhat ironically, as "the inventor of walking". And adds that "from the start of his career he combined his ability as a walker with a special talent for winning attention and gaining publicity". In 1909 Weston celebrated his 70th birthday with a journey "from Ocean to Ocean", New York to San Francisco. The wager was to make it in 100 days, "honouring the Sunday". He needed 105 and

1860
1900

Edward Payson Weston, "the man who invented walking" in USA, as per historian John Cumming.

this failure made him so furious that he decided to try again six months later. Early in 1910 he used "a straight course" and made it to New York in 76 days 23 hours and 10 minutes.

But his feat was regarded as doubtful by some observers, "since his return trip was not carefully supervised". Cumming's final appraisal: "Not a great athlete, but an industrious and persistent one".

In terms of truly competitive walking the first milestone may be found in a 7-mile (11,265 km.) event which took place at Beaufort House, London, on 23 March 1866 in connection with the inaugural English Championships organized by the Amateur Athletic Club, a fore-runner of the AAA. Winner in 59:32 was 23-year-old John Chambers, who was to become an important figure in British sport. In the 40 years of his life this dynamic gentleman distinguished himself first as an athlete, then as a coach in several sports, and finally as an organizer of important events. A Cambridge student, as early as in 1864 he had been among the promoters of the first Oxford vs. Cambridge Sports. He had a similar role two years later in the above-mentioned English Championship meet.

The 7-mile event remained the only walking test of the Championships even when the AAA took over in 1880. Of course, or should I say unfortunately, there were athletes "who would run most of the way" and still retain the titles they had won, even when their feats were not accepted as records. At the turn of the century the fastest time on record for the 7-mile event was 51:27 by Bill Sturgess in 1895. In the "pro" ranks one J.W.Raby had been credited with 51:04 as early as 1883.

In USA the earliest championship races were in 1876 over such short distances as one and three miles, with Daniel Stern the victor in both events with 7:31 and 25:12 respectively. By the end of the century competitive walking had made its way in several European countries. In Germany, for example, such long distance grinds as Dresden-to-Berlin or Berlin-to-Vienna were very popular at the time. In France and Switzerland, walking evolved as a separate sport and this led to the formation of a body known as "Union Internationale de Marche". To see the first Olympic test in walking one had to wait till the "interim" Games of 1906 in Athens.

EDWARD PAYSON WESTON.
Walking from Portland to Chicago, Distance 1226 Miles in 26 days.

1901 1920

THE COMING OF AGE OF INTERNATIONAL COMPETITION. BIRTH OF THE I.A.A.F.

SPRINTS:
Duffey's bad luck - The "pro" circus

Arthur Duffey more than made up for his unlucky show at the Paris Olympics. Between 1901 and 1903 he dominated the sprint picture on both sides of the Atlantic and earned a reputation never before attained by an amateur sprinter. Born on 14 June 1879, he was a man of indifferent build (1.70m./62 kg). In 1901, while attending Georgetown University, he equalled the world's 100 y. record (9 4/5) several times. He had his greatest moment at the ICAAAA Championships, held at Berkeley Oval, New York, on 31 May 1902, when he thrashed some of America's best in 9 3/5. The story as told by Duffey himself was that three watches caught him in 9 3/5 while a fourth watch showed 9 2/5. With timing to one-tenth of a second Duffey would perhaps have been credited with a 9.5. On the other hand the larger fraction then in use does explain why twelve years had to elapse between the first official 9 4/5 and the first official 9 3/5. Duffey's career as an amateur ended on an abrupt note when the AAU declared him ineligible for amateur competition on charges of having cashed in on his laurels. His name was removed from all record and championship lists. Since non-winning times were not taken in those days, ICAAAA books of later years curiously carried the name of the second place finisher with no time but accompanied by a notation: "Finished second. Name of winner stricken from records".

Duffey, who won the English AAA 100 yards four years in a row (1900-03), was a fast starter, almost "too fast" in the opinion of some observers. In his book "Athletics of To-day", F.A.M. Webster tells of Duffey's experience with a North Country starter "who is said to have uttered a warning as he stood behind Duffey's curved end: "Sitha, Duffey, lad - Ah've brought shot gun for t' startin'. Ah've blank i't first barrel an't shot i't second. Tha canst guess where tha'l't get shot if tha tries any flyers". After he turned "pro", Duffey was credited with such times as 5.0 (50 y.), 7 2/5 (75 y.) and 11 2/5 (120 y.). As a keen student of sprinting he emphasized the importance of using both arms to full advantage and also "the necessity for forward action, by lifting the knees in a straight line, ... without any of the side deviation which is such a common fault with the novice sprinter". In terms of sprinting form, little or nothing has been added since then. In the first two decades of the XX century there was a definite stagnation in sprint standards, at the top if not in depth. Such legendary times as those attributed to Minoru Fujii of Japan (10 24/100 for 100 m. at the Imperial University of Tokyo on 14 November 1902) and others, defy examination because of inadequate information about the conditions under which they were made. No matter if James E. Sullivan, as president of the American AAU, received an "affidavit" from Japanese officials about the genuineness of Fujii's performance, "an electrical time recorded in hundredths of a second". Fujii, a strongly built man, was also credited with a pole vault of 3.90 (1906), then superior to the best-on-record performance.

41

Archie Hahn (USA), the first man to score a 100/200 m. double in the Olympic Games (1904).

Tempora mutantur (?)

On the subject of Duffey's disqualification there is another version which is quite different from the "official" one. It was divulged by Charles Paddock (as quoted by Kenneth Greenberg in "Track & Field News", July 1951): "In reality, the reason that Duffey was professionalized and never restored to amateur standing, even though the rules say that a man may regain his amateur status after five years, was that he deeply offended the founder of the AAU, James E. Sullivan. He (Duffey) had his (running) shoes made by an old English cobbler. Sullivan was closely associated with the A.G.Spalding & Bros. (sporting goods) Company and he gave out the story that Duffey used Spalding shoes in all of his races. Duffey vigorously denied the statement and being so much under the displeasure of Sullivan and his cohorts he was never allowed to run in amateur competition again".

At that time Sullivan was also the Editor of an excellent annual, "Spalding's Official Athletic Almanac". In the 1906 edition of that excellent book he wrote:"The Editor takes it upon himself on this occasion to act aside from all governing bodies and expunges the name of A.F.Duffey". There can be little doubt that Mr. Sullivan had a strong impact on the athletic world of those days. In the book "Irish Athletic Record 1906" one could see a page fully devoted to A.G. Spalding & Bros., London branch, advertising among other things "a shoe worn by J.W.Morton, English 100 y. champion, and another "worn by Con Leahy, Irish and Olympic champion". There was also a letter signed by John Flanagan, in which the leading hammer thrower endorsed Spalding articles. Sullivan died in 1914 and sixteen years later the AAU instituted a "James E. Sullivan Memorial Trophy", which was henceforth awarded to the American athlete "who by his example and influence as an amateur had done most during the year to promote the cause of sport". By then, however, things were beginning to take a different turn: ironically, the first recipient of the trophy in 1930 was Robert T. Jones Jr., a golfer who had just signed a motion picture contract under which he was bound to give instructions and demonstrations

In America wide publicity was given to some incredible times credited to a "pro" by the name of R.P.Williams, who between 1904 and 1906 collected four 9 1/5 marks over 100 yards, and even a 9 flat, apparently recorded by three timers at Winthrop, MA., in 1906. Williams was also credited with 47 2/5 in the quarter-mile on a course with four curves, hence over two laps! If there was a "trick" of some sort, in his case as well as in Fujii's, we obviously cannot say what it was, but these exploits certainly sound somewhat "fishy".

By the same time there were of course amateur sprinters of proven competitive ability. Outstanding among these was Archie Hahn, a little man known as "The Michigan Midget", who won three titles at the 1904 Olympics in St.Louis: 60 m. (7.0), 100 m. (11.0) and 200 m. on a straight course (21 3/5). His rivals at the longer distance - his countrymen Nathan Cartmell, William Hogenson and Fay Moulton - gave him a helping hand since they were penalized one yard for false starts. At the end, however, Hahn won by 3 yards. This detail about a strictly American rule being applied in what was supposed to be an international contest certainly tells a lot about the "parochial" nature of the St.Louis Games. Hahn confirmed his stature two years later at the "interim" Games in Athens, where he won the 100 m. in 11 1/5 (there was no 200 m. event on the programme). His career bests for the English distances were 9 4/5 and 21 3/5. Hahn stood only 1.67 m. in height and was a good starter (4 3/5 for 40 y.). He later became a coach and in 1925 he edited a precious little book ("How to Sprint"), which may be regarded as a classic. He usually indulges in many fine details about running form, much less on what we now call conditioning methods. In fact, he writes: "A six-day training week is a drawback from the oldtime professional system. Of recent years there has been a decided tendency toward underwork, and during the competitive season a three or four-day week is sufficient when finished up by hard Saturday competition". With Duffey's 9 3/5 expunged from record lists, the first official 9 3/5 was achieved by Daniel Kelly at Spokane in 1906. A newspaper from that area, the "Oregonian", later recalled a curious incident connected with that race: "The afternoon was warm and during the meet the steel tape, which had been used to measure the course, lay unrolled in the sun. After the race, a re-measurement of the track was made and the course was found to be 5in. (12.70 cm.) short of the required 100 yards. But then it was realized that the unrolled steel tape had expanded under the heat of the sun, and after it had cooled off another re-measurement showed the course to be slightly over the 100 yards". By this time there were some good sprinters in other parts of the world too. In England, Jack Morton won the AAA 100 y. title four years in a row (1904-07), beating the famous Duffey on the first occasion, and another leading American, Nathan Cartmell, on the last. Morton, who had a personal best of 9 4/5, happened to be over the hill by the time of the London Olympics: at 29 he failed to go beyond the semi-finals of the 100 m.

1901
1920

Ralph Craig (USA) winning the 100 m. at the 1912 Olympics in Stockholm.

In Scandinavia, Knut Lindberg of Sweden was credited with a nifty 10 3/5 for the 100 m. at Göteborg in 1906. In actual fact, official watches showed 10 1/5, 10 2/5 and 10 3/5. On the strength of the current IAAF rule he should have been given the intermediate time, i.e. 10 2/5, but Swedish officials apparently decided to remain on the safe side. A few months earlier, at the "interim" Olympics in Athens, Lindberg had finished no better than sixth in the 100 m. final won by Archie Hahn, but curiously enough also second in the javelin throw and sixth in the pentathlon! The Swede, who was also a good soccer player, beat Morton in a Scandinavian meet in 1907. And he finally won a medal in the official Games too: silver in the 4x100 m. at Stockholm in 1912, aged 30.

On the eve of the 1908 Olympics two sprinters from overseas starred at the AAA Championships, held in London's brand-new White City Stadium. Robert Kerr of Canada won the 100 y. (10.0) and Reggie Walker of South Africa took the 220 (22 2/5). An alarm clock which turned out to be the fore-runner of things to come. Two weeks later on the same track, both came through in splendid fashion, albeit in inverted roles. Walker (born at Durban on 16 March 1889) won the 100 m in 10 4/5 from America's James Rector, thereby becoming the youngest sprint champion in Olympic annals - a distinction he still holds. Kerr, 26, beat two other Americans, Robert Cloughen and Nathan Cartmell, to win the 200 m. in 22 3/5.

On the whole, the Americans for once suffered a major debacle.

Germany's first sterling sprinter was Richard Rau (born at Berlin on 26 August 1889), who between 1909 and 1920 won thirteen national titles, one of which over 110 m. hurdles. In a handicap race at Braunschweig in 1911, he lowered the German 100 m. record to 10.5. His fiercest rivals were Emil Ketterer and Erwin Kern.

Another excellent sprinter was William Reuben Applegarth of Britain, a medium-size runner who was at his best in the furlong.

In 1914 he ran the 220 y. around a turn first in 21 2/5, then in 21 1/5, the latter in annexing the AAA title at Stamford Bridge, London. Even though no official differentiation was made at the time vis-à-vis marks made on a straight course, Applegarth's mark was until then the fastest ever recorded under such conditions.

On the eve of the Stockholm Olympics, America's best bet appeared to be Howard Drew (born at Lexington, Virginia, on 28 June 1890), generally regarded as the first black sprinter of world calibre. A "powerhouse" of 1.71 m./ 72 kg., he was once remembered by Charles Paddock as "the smoothest piece of running machinery the world had ever seen". At the Eastern Olympic Trials Drew won the 100 m. (10 4/5) from Ralph Craig, a tall man with plenty of staying power who had twice equalled the world's best for the 220 y. on a straight course, 21 1/5 (1910-11). But in the Stockholm Games Drew strained a tendon in winning his 100 m. semi-final (10.7) and thus had to stay away from the decisive race, in which Craig came through in impressive

1924 Olympics in Paris. 200 metre final, from left to right C. Paddock (USA), 2nd; E. Liddell (GB) 3rd; J. Scholz (USA), 1st in 21.6; G. Hill (USA) 4th, partly covered; H.M. Abrahams (GB) 6th, B. Norton (USA), 5th.

1901–1920

fashion (10.8). Among those he beat was his countryman Donald Lippincott, who in his semi-final was clocked in 10.6 - incidentally the first world record ratified by the IAAF for this metric distance. Craig also won the 200 m. (21.7), with Lippincott, then not yet 19, Applegarth and Rau following in that order. It was later revealed that Craig had trained intensively to build up the stamina which allowed him to go through six rounds of competition (100/200 m.) unscathed. Many years later he was to reappear in the Olympic arena (London 1948), were it only as an alternate on the US yachting team.

It was at Stockholm that timing to the tenth of a second was used for the first time at the Games. Another innovation: lanes were no longer marked by movable cords tied to pickets but by lines of chalk on the ground. Here again the Swedes were probably considered too progressive, and as late as 1924 cords again appeared - for the last time.

The unlucky Drew fought back bravely. Later in 1912 he won the US 100 y. title (10.0) from Alvah Meyer, runner-up to Craig at Stockholm. In 1913 he won both sprint titles and the following year he tied the world records in both the 100 and 220 y., with 9 3/5 and 21 1/5 respectively. Although hailing from the East, he had his best days as a student of the University of Southern California, whose athletes (known under their battle name, "Trojans") were to remain a dominant factor in US intercollegiate athletics for many years.

Now and then, incredible times continu-ed to crop up. In 1913 a 20-year-old high school boy, Albert Robinson, was credited with 9 3/5 and 20 4/5 for the English distances. Apart from finishing second in the AAU 220 the year before, he was to remain a flash in the pan ... The above-mentioned Emil Ketterer of Germany was given times of 10.2 (heat) and 10.1 (final) for 100 m. in a meet held at Prague in 1912, apparently on a downhill course. It should be noted that starting and timing methods differed considerably from one country to the other, sometimes even within the same country; and the wind factor was often ignored.

The advent of Charles Paddock (born at Gainesville, Texas, on 11 August 1900) coincided with the end of

Fireworks of the "pro" Circus

The revival of the Olympic Games under the banner of the International Olympic Committee sanctioned the demise of professionalism, so clearly in fact that some optimistic observers came to regard it as definitive. (But the "monster" was to rise again many years later with the "Trojan Horse" method, i.e. from within amateurism itself). However, "pro" races continued to thrive here and there, at least for sometime. Between 1908 and 1914 a "pro" circus chiefly involving sprinters was a major attraction in Australia and South Africa, and to a lesser extent even in Britain, the acknowledged motherland of amateurism. Among the stars of those "match races" were Reggie Walker and William Applegarth, and two Aussies, Jack Donaldson and Arthur Postle. Applegarth defeated Donaldson, the "Blue Streak" from Down Under, in two widely heralded tests at Manchester, with 9.9 in November 1914 and 22 1/4 in April 1915. But the performances that really astounded experts were returned Down Under. Here is a summary:

- Arthur Postle - 50 y. 5 1/5 (1908); 60 y. 6.0 (1906); 70 y. 7 1/16 (1910); 80 y. 7 3/4 (1908); 100 y. 9 1/2 (1906); 150 y. 14 1/5 (1912); 200 y. 19.0 (1912).
- Jack Donaldson - 65 y. 6 1/2 (1910); 80 y. 7 15/16 (1909); 100 y. 9 3/8 (1910); 120 y. 11 1/4 (1909); 130 y. 12.0 (1911); 150 y. 14.0 (1911); 220 y. 21 1/4 (1913); 300 y. 29 61/64 (1913); 400 y. 44 3/5 (1909); 600 y. 1:12 1/5 (1909).
- Reggie Walker - 40 y. 4 2/5 (1912); 50 y. 5 1/5 (1912); 90 y. 8 4/5 (1912); 100 y. 9 2/5 (1912); 110 y. 10 2/5 (1911); 120 y. 11 2/5 (1908); 130 y. 12 2/5 (1909).

Some of these performances were to remain superior to the official amateur records for a long time. For example, Donaldson's 9 3/8 for 100 y., made at Johannesburg in 1910, was officially beaten by an amateur only in 1948 (Mel Patton, 9.3). Of course, the South African city is located 1753 m. above sea level - as we now know (even then, of course, somebody ought to have known) a rarefied atmosphere can be beneficial to short-lived efforts. Then it should be added that the rules prevailing in the "pro" ranks were definitely more flexible than those in force in amateur athletics. It is also known, for example, that the track on which Postle recorded his 9 1/2 at Kalgoorlie in 1906 dropped 3 ft. (0.91 m.) in the running direction.

World War I. In 1919 he made his international debut at the Inter-Allied Games, held in the new Stade Pershing in Paris: he won both metric sprints in 10 4/5 and 21 3/5. For about a decade Paddock was the outstanding figure of the American sprint scene - and a widely discussed one. At the 1920 Olympics in Antwerp, "Charley" won the 100 m. in 10 4/5 from his countryman Morris Kirksey, while Harry Edward, from British Guiana but competing in Britain's colours, was third. But in the 200 m. Paddock had to surrender to another American, Allen Woodring (22.0), in a close finish. Paddock had a habit of taking a leap of about 4 m. in going into the tape, a "technique" which was widely discussed by experts and laymen. Regardless of whether he really gained anything by such a stratagem, it has been sensibly suggested that he certainly "caught the eye" of the judges on the finish line.

German sprinters had to stay away from the Antwerp races. Fearing that the presence of German athletes in Belgium soon after the end of the Great War might evoke bad feelings in a wide section of the crowd, the IOC had decided not to invite Germany. This was history's first Olympic "boycott", which was to be duplicated four years later in Paris.

400 METRES:
The battle of St.Louis

A rare photo from the 1904 Olympics in St.Louis reveals that no less than 13 runners competed in the 400 m. final. They crowded the starting line in such a way that one of them was obliged to start right behind the front row! Among the front line men one can recognize George Poage of USA, the first black athlete to figure prominently in Games history. He finished sixth in that race, but two days later he was third in the 400 m. hurdles - most probably the first Olympic medal won by a man of his race. (Joseph Stadler, another American black, was second in the standing high jump on the same day, 31 August, presumably one or two hours later). The wild 400 m. battle was won by Harry Hillman in 49 1/5. This 23-year-old American later annexed two other titles, winning the 200 and the 400 m. hurdles. The Olympic 400 m. final of 1908 in London was to go down in history as the first, and to this day only "walkover" in the annals of the Games. Wyndham Halswelle, a 26-year-old London-born Scotsman, ran in splendid isolation to win comfortably in 50.0. This followed another race held two days earlier, the result of which had been annulled, as related separately.

The London incident had a beneficial aftermath: at the Stockholm Olympics four years later, the 400 m. was run in lanes for the first time. Charles Reidpath of USA, who earlier in the season had run a "quarter" in 48.0, narrowly beat Hanns Braun of Germany, 48.2 to 48.3. Another American, 20-year-old "Ted" Meredith, tried too hard too soon and dropped to fourth in the decisive stage.

But Meredith (born at Chester Heights, Pennsylvania, on 14 November 1891; 1.75m./71 kg) had won an historic 800 m. race five days earlier. He eventually lived up to expectations as a quarter-miler too. On 7 August 1915 at San Francisco he won the AAU title

---

An Anglo-American "War" in London

By 1908 the sporting rivalry between Britain and America, powerful "cousins" from the opposite sides of the Atlantic, was rather bitter. The showdown offered by the London Olympics was therefore awaited with great curiosity. By way of example, on 15 July the "Brooklyn Daily Eagle" published a vignette which showed Uncle Sam getting Olympic news from London via direct wire and saying to presidential candidates Bryan and Taft - obviously there to discuss "state matters"-: "Just a moment, please!" In a decidedly heated atmosphere there were decisions which aroused controversy. This Anglo-American "War" came to fever pitch with the 400 m. final, a four-man race which pitted Wyndham Halswelle, the British record holder (48 2/5 for 440 y.), against three "Yanks", John Taylor, John Carpenter and William Robbins. Carpenter was in the lead entering the homestretch, but then he began to run a diagonal course, giving Halswelle little or no chance to pass from the outside. The judges, apparently forgetful of traditional British coolness, invaded the track and declared the event a "no race". Carpenter, however, went on to win in times unofficially recorded as 48 3/5 (400 m.) and 49.0 (440 y.), but was disqualified. Robbins and Taylor took sides with the "outlawed" Carpenter and did not show up for the re-run, held two days later. The Americans were by no way convinced that Carpenter had impeded his British rival, let alone that their three representatives had "ganged up" on Halswelle, as claimed by some British observers. In its annual convention, the AAU "refused to recognize the disqualification of J.C.Carpenter".

in 47.0 - on a straight course and with the aid of an "excessive" wind. His closest pursuers, Frank Sloman and Binga Dismond, must have chalked up estimated times of 47.4 and 47.5 respectively. But then Sloman had won the Junior title the day before, under similar conditions, in 47.0. Meredith eventually succeeded in dislodging Maxey Long's record (47 4/5) at Cam-bridge, MA. on 27 May 1916, when he ran the quarter on a one-turn course in 47 2/5. The new mark was equalled a week later in Chicago by Binga Dismond, (whose feat was ratified by the NCAA, but not by the AAU). Then, incredibly enough, the record remained unbeaten till 1932! Meredith was certainly a great talent, even if he found it difficult to remain in form for more than a month or so. In his "high season" periods he was equally good in both the "quarter" and the "half". This circumstance led some observers to consider the two distances as being more closely related than they actually were. Such a view, shared by Meredith himself in his book "Middle Distance and Relay Racing" (1931), was generally accepted in coaching circles, and that probably explains why quarter-miling standards lagged behind for such a long period.

The no. 1 American for the Antwerp Olympics (1920) appeared to be Frank Shea, who had run a quarter in 47 3/5 in 1918. But in the Olympic 400 m. test he had to be content with fourth place. Victory went to a chain-smoker from South Africa, Bevil Rudd, in 49 3/5.

MIDDLE DISTANCES - 800 METRES:
Halcyon days of Sheppard and Meredith

The fastest halfmile time in the early years of the new century was 1:54 3/5, by Rev. Herbert Workman, an Englishman, in 1901. Interestingly enough, the Americans carried an equal time as their indoor record, by Eli Parsons in 1904 - a time registered in the last leg of a 4x880 y. relay. On that occasion, so claimed the "New York Times", "each relay (leg) was carefully timed by competent timers". Nowadays, no relay split is eligible for recognition as a record.

At the 1904 Olympics in St.Louis no less than 10 of the 13 finalists represented USA! The only European competitor, Johannes Runge of Germany, finished fifth. The winner, James Lightbody (1:56.0), had previously won the steeplechase and two days later he won the 1500 m.! More representative of the standard of those days was the field assembled at the 1906 "interim" Games in Athens. On a poor track, Lightbody narrowly lost to his countryman Paul Pilgrim (2:01 1/2).

Shortly afterwards, three great half-milers appeared on the scene: Melvin Sheppard of USA, Emilio Lunghi of Italy and Hanns Braun of Germany. The American (born at Almonesson, New Jersey, on 5 September 1883; 1.74 m./ 75 kg) was a very reliable performer who between 1906 and 1912 won the AAU 880 y. title five times, and starred in two Olympics. Lunghi (born at Genoa on 16 March 1885; 1.79 m./ 70 kg.) was Italy's first major track talent. In the spring of 1908, in the wonderful setting of Piazza di Siena in Rome, on a 370.80 m. track, he ran a kilometre in 2:31.0, a world's best for the pre-IAAF era. Braun (born in Munich on 26 October 1886; 1.80 m.) reigned supreme on German tracks for many years, at distances ranging from 400 to 1500 m. A sculptor by profession, he was to die during World War I when his plane was shot down near Cambrai (1918). These three runners were the favourites of experts on the eve of the London Olympics (1908). A week earlier, all had competed in the 1500 m., but only Sheppard had made the final (which he won in 4:03 2/5). In the 800 m. test the American took the lead after 300 m., went past the halfway mark in 53.0 - a hyperfast time in those days - and was never headed, no matter if he needed nearly a full minute to cover the second half. He went through the tape in 1:52 4/5, a new world record. Lunghi was the only one who managed to remain within striking distance, yet finished a well-beaten second in 1:54 1/5, clearly ahead of Braun (1:55

1901 1920

British milers from the first decade of the XX century. E.L. Gay-Roberts leading from Alfred Shrubb and Joe Binks.

1/5). The organizers had placed a second tape at 880 y., but Sheppard, by then on the verge of exhaustion, could do no better than 1:54.0. Lunghi, still a virtual novice at the international level, was attracted by a bid from USA and went there in 1909. In the ranks of the Irish-American A.C. he came under the tutelage of a famous coach, Lawson Robertson. In the latter part of that year the talented Italian reached his best ever form, beat Sheppard and others, and set a new world record for the half-mile, 1:52 4/5, in winning the Canadian title at Montreal on 15 September.

By 1912, however, America had regained the leadership. In addition to Sheppard, a real stalwart, there was a youngster by the name of Meredith, whose feats as a quartermiler have already been recounted. Lunghi, who in his own country never trained properly, was eliminated in a semi-final. Braun qualified for the decisive race, in which he faced six Americans and a Canadian, Melville Brock. Sheppard, the "old fox", made the following prediction: "Braun is going to win - if there is no world record". For once, Sheppard had more success as a prognosticator, because the record pace he chose to set finally killed Braun ... and Sheppard as well. In his bold attempt to "strangle" the opposition - same as in London four years earlier - the American reached the halfway mark in an unheard of 52.4, closely followed by Meredith and Braun. The German ran the race of his life, clock-wise at least, yet he was finally overrun by the "American wave". Sheppard, Meredith and Ira Davenport staged a furious battle and victory finally went to the "greenest" of them all, Meredith. The youngster from Mercersburg Academy, Pennsylvania, set a new world record of 1:51.9. Sheppard and Davenport took second and third in that order, both in 1:52.0, followed by Brock (1:52.7), Daniel Caldwell of USA (1:52.8) and Braun (1:53.1). It should be noted that official results placed Braun fourth, with Caldwell and Brock next, but a close examination of pictures available from various sources has led historians to conclude that Brock and Braun were simply placed in inverted order. Meredith went on to reach 880 y. in 1:52.5, another world record. This race offers a typical example of how a bold, strong runner can sometimes extend all his rivals to unprecedented marks.

Meredith, who incidentally had gone to Stockholm with a personal best of 1:53 4/5, was to have his best year in 1916, when in the space of two weeks he revised the record book first in the "half", then in the "quarter". The former occasion was a dual meet between Pennsylvania, his alma mater, and Cornell: he found a hard nut to crack in Vere Windnagle but finally won by three-tenths of a second in 1:52.2. At the 1920 Olympics in Antwerp the winner was 31-year-old Albert Hill of Britain, who beat Earl Eby, the American champion, by a metre in 1:53 2/5, while Bevil Rudd of South Africa was third. Hill (born on 24 March 1889; 1.78 m./ 72 kg.), a railway guard by occupation, was to annex the 1500 m. crown as well, two days later. The Great War deprived him of his best years as an athlete, yet he managed to win his first AAA title in 1910 (4 miles), his fourth and last in 1921 (1 mile). And it should be borne in mind that no Championships were held between 1915 and 1918.

1500 METRES/1 MILE: Early Wizards

Walter George's "pro" record for the mile (4:12 3/4) eluded the efforts of leading middle distance runners till 1915. Even Thomas Conneff's amateur record (4:15 3/5) withstood all assaults for a long time, up to 1911. In the meantime Bacon had lost his British record to Joe Binks, who in the AAA race of 1902 at Stamford Bridge, London, ran the distance in 4:16 4/5, beating Henry Hawtrey by 2 yards. Binks' record also had a long life and was in fact bettered only 19 years later. For a long time a prominent figure as a sports journalist and a promoter of popular events, Binks liked to recall that in his heyday he used to train "only one evening per week, winter and summer, spending about 30 minutes on each workout". The Grand Old Man of British athletics (he died at 91) would ironically add: "You will laugh at my slapdash methods of training, but I got a lot of fun out of it, which today's champions do not get".

It fell to a diminutive Briton to become the first sub-4 minute metric miler. This happened on 30 May 1908 during the British Olympic Trials at the new White City Stadium in London and the man who did the trick was 22-year-old Harold Wilson, who won the 1500 m. in 3:59 4/5. Wilson, who was only 1.62 m. tall and weighed 52 kg., went on to win the AAA one-mile title (4:20 1/5). In the Olympic 1500 m. event, however, he lost to Mel Shep-pard of USA in a tight finish - 4:03 3/5 to 4:03 2/5. Incidentally, the schedule for that event was peculiar, to say the least. There were eight heats, and only the winners were admitted to the final. It so happened that one man needed no better than 4:13 3/5 to qualify, while another, Emilio Lunghi, did 4:03 4/5 and was eliminated! In fact, Lunghi's time was bettered by only one of the eight qualifiers, Norman Hallows of Britain (4:03 2/5), precisely the man who beat Lunghi in the third heat (and went on to finish third in the final). Among other non-qualifiers were

1901–1920

defending champion James Lightbody, Jean Bouin of France, and Hanns Braun.

The years between 1908 and 1912 could be described as a period of transition during which US milers constantly grew in stature. A trio of promising young men came to the fore: John Paul Jones of Cornell University, Abel Kiviat of the Irish-American A.C., and Norman Taber of Brown University. Jones was only 20 years and 7 months when he cracked Conneff's one-mile record in the ICAAAA Meet at Cambridge, MA., in 1911 with 4:15 2/5. The following year, at the same meet, he was involved in a rare tie for first with Norman Taber (4:20 3/5), but won the half-mile in 1:53 4/5. In 1912 both were excelled by Abel Kiviat, who lowered the world's 1500 m. record to 3:55 4/5 exactly a fortnight before his twentieth birthday.

At the Stockholm Olympics, no less than 7 of the 14 finalists were from USA. This group included Kiviat, Jones, Taber, and defending champion Mel Sheppard. Britain was represented by Arnold Strode Jackson and Philip Baker. This duo had the unity of purpose which their predecessors of 1908 seemed to lack. The Stockholm race was a complete reversal of the London affair of 1908. After receiving valuable assistance from Baker in the early going, Jackson found himself in the front group around the last turn, trailing Kiviat and Taber and preceding Jones, Sheppard and Ernst Wide of Sweden. The battle that ensued in the stretch was one of extreme severity, each man doing all he knew. Sheppard soon dropped back, and so did Wide a bit later. It was not until the last 30 metres that the tall Jackson managed to pass the formidable US trio. With giant strides the Oxonian went on to win in 3:56.8, a new Olympic record. In what must be classified as one of the greatest mass finishes in the history of the Games, the following place times were recorded: Kiviat 3:56.9, Taber 3:56.9, Jones 3:57.2, Wide 3:57.6. Baker was sixth in an estimated 4:01, just ahead of another Swede, John Zander. That was unquestionably Jackson's "Day of Days". This runner of great natural ability, whose training "consisted less of running than of massages", ran the mile in a casual 4:22 3/5 in 1914, then he was enlisted in the service. In World War I he was wounded three times and eventually became, at 27, the youngest acting Brigadier General in the British Army. John Paul Jones, known as J.P. in Cornell track circles, lowered the amateur one-mile

Melvin Sheppard (USA) beating Harold Wilson (GB) in the 1500 m. of the 1908 Olympics in London.

record to 4:14 3/5 at Cambridge, MA., in 1913. His 58.3 last lap caused Norman Taber to fall behind (4:16 2/5) at the end of a gruelling fight. But the latter, probably second to Jones in sheer competitive ability, was to have the last word on the subject of records. On 16 July 1915, still on the fast Harvard track at Cambridge, he killed two birds with one stone by beating Jones' amateur record and George's twenty-nine-year-old "pro" mark. The time, 4:12 3/5, was only fractionally, if at all, faster than that of the old English champion. It was a special record attempt, and one of the handicap men finally had to give way to Taber in order to let him finish first, a condition "sine qua non" for being accepted as a record-breaker under the AAU rules of those days. Like most milers of his time, Taber ran hard and fast in the opening and closing stages but often indulged in a long "float" midway in the race. His "quarters" in the Cambridge race were: 58.0, 67.0, 68.0, 59 3/5. The first major record breaker from outside the Anglo-American sphere of influence emerged during World War I. Not surprisingly, he was a man from neutral Sweden, John Zander, who had finished seventh in the 1912 Olympic final. Between 1916 and 1918 he rewrote the newly instituted IAAF record table in four metric events (1000, 1500, 2000 and 3000 m.). On 5 August 1917 at Stockholm he ran the 1500 m. in 3:54.7. Another outstanding man of those years was Joie Ray of USA, a stocky little man who in 1919 ran 4:14 2/5 outdoors and 4:14 3/5 indoors. Yet the two dominant figures of the "lost" years, i.e. Zander and Ray, were unable to do themselves justice in the first Olympics of the post-war era. The former was suffering because of a fractured rib and gave up midway in the final; Ray, handicapped by an injury sustained in a training spin, led the field till the bell but was shunted to eighth in the closing stage. Britain scored a brilliant one-two with Albert Hill (4:01 4/5) and Philip Baker (4:02 2/5). The former had won the 800

Emilio Lunghi, Italy's first "Great" in middle distance events.

> **Olympic silver and Nobel Prize**
>
> Among those champions who have distinguished themselves also in other spheres of human endeavour one should single out Philip John Noel-Baker of Britain, an Olympic silver medallist in 1920 and winner of the Nobel Prize for Peace in 1959. Born in London on 1 November 1889 of a Quaker family, he was educated at Haverford College, Pennsylvania, and King's College, Cambridge. He was a finalist in the 1500m. in two editions of the Olympic Games - eight years apart: sixth in 1912, second to his countryman Albert Hill in 1920. In between these two races he served in ambulance units during World War I, being decorated for distinguished conduct. In 1919 he was in the British delegation at the Peace Conference. He later worked in the Secretariat of the League of Nations and was elected a Member of Parliament for the Labour Party. In post-war years he held prominent positions in Government offices. Fluent in several languages, he spent the major part of his adult life campaigning for peace and crowned his mission with an outstanding book: "The Arms Race: a Programme for World Disarmament" (1958). The following year he won the Nobel Prize for Peace. He died in London on 8 October 1982.

m. two days earlier, so he scored quite a double - at the age of 31. In 1919 he had equalled Binks' British one-mile record, 4:16 4/5. (And he was to make the record his sole property in 1921, when he ran 4:13 4/5 in the AAA Championships).

LONG DISTANCES - Finlandia docet: Kolehmainen and Nurmi

The first distance runner likely to be considered a "modern" in more than one way was the legendary Alfred Shrubb of Britain (born at Slinfold, Sussex, on 12 December 1878; 1.69 m./ 52 kg.). While in his prime, the long striding Shrubb really cornered the market, collecting world records at all distances ranging from 2 miles to one-hour running. Outstanding among the landmarks he set were the following: 9:09 3/5 (2 miles), 14:17 3/5 (3 miles), 29:59 2/5 (6 miles), 31:02 2/5 (10,000 m.) and 50:40 3/5 (10 miles). The last three were posted at Glasgow on 5 November 1904 (Guy Fawkes Day) and Shrubb called it a day only after covering 11 3/4 miles in 60:32 1/5. While en route he set a one-hour record of 18,742 m. Inspired by the sound of bagpipes and holding a sponge in his hand for perspiration, this tobacconist from Sussex "swallowed" one after the other no less than thirteen handicap men. In the same year he won the AAA one-mile title in 4:22.0. However, the AAA viewed his Herculean labours from a critical angle: following an investigation, he was suspended from the amateur ranks. Shrubb, who never appeared in the Olympics, continued to run as a "pro". He once emerged the winner in a 10-mile race in which he was opposed to a mixed relay team of men and horses! Many years later, in a contribution to Fred Wilt's book "How They Train", Shrubb supplied interesting details on his training schedule in the thirty days preceding his historic race at Glasgow in 1904. During that period he covered 286 kilometres (128.5 in the morning, 157.5 in the afternoon) for an average of 9.5 km. a day. However, if we keep in mind that he took a rest on Sundays, his average is in fact higher, almost "modern" in a moderate way. Each session consisted of a single long race at a "brisk" pace.

The 5 and 10 km. events were first included in the Olympic programme at Stockholm in 1912. In the "interim" Games of 1906 and in 1908 there had been a 5-mile (8,046.75 m.) event, won by Britons Henry Hawtrey and Emil Voigt in 26:11 4/5 and 25:11 1/5 respectively.

What ensued at Stockholm in 1912 really contributed to raise distance running standards to a new dimension, and also marked the beginning of the Finnish Era. On the eve of the Games two men stood head and shoul-

1901 1920

Arnold Strode-Jackson (GB) winning Olympic 1,500 metres from great field in Stockholm (1912). Others from left are: J.P. Jones (USA), 4th; A. Kiviat (USA), 2nd; E. Wide (Sweden), 5th; N. Taber (USA), 3rd. Times ranged from 3:56.8 for the winner to 3:57.6 for the fifth man.

ders above the rest: Johannes ("Hannes") Kolehmainen of Finland and Jean Bouin of France. The former (born at Kuopio on 9 December 1889, 1.69 m. / 60 kg.) came of a family of athletes, a species not infrequent in Finland. His elder brothers Taavetti ("Tatu") and William ("Viljami") were good marathoners, the former being also a world record holder for 20 km. (1:07:40.2 in 1913). Hannes, who like the rest of the family hailed from Karelia, ran his first marathon at the tender age of seventeen and a half: 3:06:19 over 40.2 km. in 1907, finishing third. In 1911 he began to collect national records: 8:48.5 (3000 m.), 15:28.1 (5000 m.) and 32:17.4 (10,000 m.). In the spring of 1912, at Berlin, he met Jean Bouin for the first time and beat him in a 7500 m. race. Shortly before the Stockholm Games he ran 15:16.4 (5000 m.) and 31:47.5 (10,000 m.) on consecutive days at Helsinki.

Bouin (born at Marseille on 20 December 1888; 1.68 m. / 66 kg.) tried the long distances very early, mostly in cross-country races. In 1911, in his native town, he covered 18,588.33 m. in an hour, not too far from Alf Shrubb's world record. On 16 November of the same year, at Stade de Colombes near Paris, he braved wintry weather conditions to set a magnificent 10,000 m. world record: 30:58 4/5. On that occasion he negotiated the first half in 15:11 2/5 and the second in 15:47 2/5. Curiously enough, the former split represented his best for 5000 m. up to that time! Having for years practised physical training in its most varied forms, Bouin had developed strength to such a degree that French writers liked to refer to him as the Hercules of foot racing. In the Stockholm Olympics, Kolehmainen really spread himself. In the space of nine days he took part in six races, for a total of 41 kilometres. And he won them all. His opening effort was on 7 July: a heat of the 10,000 m. (33:49.0). The following day (!) he won the final in 31:20.8, easily defeating Louis Tewanima of USA (32:06.6) and another Finn, Albin Stenroos (32:21.8). Then came the "pièce de résistance", the 5000 m., in which he was to meet Bouin. On 9 July he won his heat in 15:34.6, but in another heat the Frenchman astounded spectators with a sparkling 15:05.0, second fastest ever next to the 15:01.2 performance achieved by Arthur Robertson of Britain in 1908. The final was on 10 July. At the start of the race the ever smiling Kolehmainen looked surprisingly relaxed, while Bouin (who was so superstitious that he habitually ran with a toothpick in his mouth) appeared to be his usual earnest and absorbed self. The two champions alternated in the lead and soon got rid of their nine companions. Sven Lindhagen, the famous Swedish expert, was an eye-witness to that memorable race, and the following comes from one of his writings: "In those days no intermediate times were usually taken, or if they were, nobody cared to convey them to the public, who were by no means as knowledgeable as present-day crowds. Yet (on that day) we all felt that the two champions were travelling at a very fast pace". At the bell the Frenchman put in a devastating sprint, "the like of which no one had ever seen until then", but the Finn managed to stay in the contest. At 3 miles Bouin was still ahead of Kolehmainen (14:07.2 to 14:07.4, both well inside Shrubb's world record). The drama was resolved in the last vital stretch of "land", precisely with 20 m. to go, when the Finn inched his way ahead from the outside and finally won by a metre or so. The record times of the two champions - 14:36.6 and 14:36.7 - sounded fabulous. George Hutson of Britain was a distant third (15:07.6). Kolehmainen closed his Stockholm account triumphantly: on 12 July (i.e. after a day of rest!) he set a new world record of 8:36.9 in a heat of the 3000 m. team race (oddly enough, his teammates were below par and Finland failed to qualify for the final), and on 15 July he won a cross-country race.

Shortly after the Stockholm Games, Kolehmainen

The man who put Suomi on the map

The saga of Hannes Kolehmainen at the 1912 Olympics in Stockholm earned him a niche in Finnish history. At that time the country of the countless lakes was a Grand Duchy of the Russian Empire. Finnish sports leaders were granted permission to field a team of their own at Stockholm, but this favour did not include the use of the Finnish flag. Matti Hannus, a noted writer and historian, relates that "Kolehmainen and his teammates watched with aching hearts the Russian flag being raised as a result of their victorious efforts. Kolehmainen later noted to Philip Noel-Baker (a would-be Nobel Prize for Peace): "I would rather have lost than looked at that flag". But Noel-Baker later remarked: "Koleh-mainen was wrong. That (Russian) flag was forgotten at once, but his brilliant fight with Bouin helped Finland in her struggle for independence". In fact, the same view was aired by Prof. Lauri Pihkala, a well-known Finnish athlete, journalist and humanist. He claimed that Kolehmainen's triumph in Stockholm was one of the greatest incentives along the road that led to the establishment of Suomi (Finland) as an independent political and geographical entity in 1919.

settled in USA, where he continued to run with remarkable success for several years. He collected quite a number of AAU All Comers Records, including a 14:18 1/5 for 3 miles indoors, and a 30:20 2/5 for 6 miles outdoors, both in 1913 (His comeback in the 1920 Olympic marathon will be related later on). For many years a vegetarian, he apparently tasted meat for the first time in 1916, while a guest of Abraham L. Monteverde, an American specialist of "grand fond" racing, who in 1929 was credited with a journey of 3415 miles (about 5500 km.) from New York to San Francisco, which he accomplished in 79 days, 10 hours, 10 minutes. Bouin reached the zenith of his condition in Stockholm in 1913, when he covered 19,021 m. in one hour, a world record which stood for fifteen years. According to French statistician and historian Alain Bouillé, early in World War I Bouin "fell victim to a tragic error of the French artillery, when a howitzer put a premature end to his life". He died on 29 September 1914. Several stadia in France still bear his name.

As a footnote to the 1912 Olympics I should add that the man who finished second to Kolehmainen in the 10,000m., Louis Tewanima, was a Hopi Indian as well as a teammate of the great Jim Thorpe at Carlisle Indian School, Pennsylvania. Recalling his younger years in an interview a few years before his death (1969), he revealed that he used to train chasing rabbits, wild horses and antelopes. It is a known fact that American Indians have always worshipped physical fitness. Tewanima himself put it this way: "Body our temple".

If Kolehmainen was the first of the Finns, Paavo Johannes Nurmi was undoubtedly the greatest. Nothing that has happened in recent decades on the tracks of the world can in any way obscure, let alone efface, the grandeur of this athlete, who was the ideal example to emulate for generations of young track adepts. The "Phantom Finn" was born at Turku, a seaport in south-west Finland (Åbo in Swedish), on 13 June 1897. The son of an ebony worker, Paavo began to work for his living at an early age. He had to deliver goods by push-cart up a steep street leading to Turku Railway Station. This daily exercise probably helped him to develop muscular power. His athletic activity in the ranks of Turun Toverit ("Turku Pals") did the rest. His progress was slow at first but still sufficient to raise him to the level of Finland's best distance runners of those days. According to his biographers Paavo Karikko and Mauno Koski, he ran 1500m. in 5:43 at the age of ten and in 5:02 a year later. His official career began on 2 June 1914, when he won a junior race over 3000 m. in 10:06.9. His progression in the early years is shown in the adjoining table. While on military service at Pori (1919-20), Nurmi was able to train more intensively. And the year 1920 marked the dawn of the Nurmi Era. He began by capturing his first Finnish record: 3000 m. in 8:36.2. Then he qualified for the Antwerp Games by running 5000 m. in 15:00.5 and 1500 m. in 4:05.5 on consecutive days. After seeing that, Finnish experts rated him capable of greater deeds .... Yet in his first Olympic final, on 17 August, he was seriously challenged in the 5000 m. by Joseph Guillemot of France, who was only 1.60 m. tall and two years his junior. Nurmi was unable to respond to the last attack of his little rival, who thus took indirect revenge for Bouin's defeat against Kolehmainen eight years earlier.

The times were: 14:55 3/5 for Guillemot, 15:00.0, still a personal best, for Nurmi. Three days later, the Finn turned the tables on Guillemot in the 10,000 m. - 31:45 4/5 to 31:47 1/5. Nurmi closed his first Olympic adventure by winning the cross-country race, thus earning two golds and a silver - a collection which was to increase considerably in later years.

1901 1920

Nurmi's Early Years

Year	Age	1500 m	3000 m	5000 m	10,000 m
1914	17	-	10:06.9	-	-
1915	18	4:37.4	9:30.6	15:57.5	-
1916	19	-	-	15:52.8	34:35.0
1917	20	-	9:47.8	15:47.4	-
1918	21	4:29.2	10:10.2	15:50.7	-
1919	22	4:23.0	8:58.1	15:31.5	32:56.0
1920	23	4:05.5	8:36.2*	15:00.0*	31:45.8

* Finnish record.

THE MARATHON: Jokes in St.Louis, drama in London

St. Louis 1904. Jan Mashiani (36) and Len Tau (35), the earliest Africans in Olympic marathon annals. They probably belonged to the Tswana tribe. (For a long time they were referred to by erroneous names).

Very strange and well-documented facts occurred in the Olympic marathon at St.Louis in 1904. The race, over 40 km., was held on a hot day, mostly along dusty country roads. Leading automobiles provided an extra ration of dust: one of the competitors, William Garcia of USA, was so badly affected that he had to spend several days in hospital. Official winner in a seemingly slow 3:28:53 was another American, Thomas Hicks. While en route he had to be "revived" with strychnine sulphate served in an egg white, plus several sips of brandy. (It should be noted that under present IAAF rules the use of strychnine is forbidden). With six miles to go, Hicks was suddenly passed by another American, Fred Lorz, "who looked almost as fresh as when he left the stadium, two and a half hours earlier" and eventually went on to win unopposed. Widely acclaimed, he was about to receive a laurel from Alice Roosevelt, daughter of the President of USA, when it transpired that he had dropped out of the race at nine miles and taken a ride in an automobile - only to resume running about a mile from the stadium, "merely as a joke", as he later admitted. Officials inevitably took things more seriously. He was disqualified and the AAU banned him from any future competition. But he reappeared in 1905 and earned a valid reputation by winning the Boston marathon.

The most famous episode in Olympic history is connected with the London marathon of 1908. The chief character of the drama was Dorando Pietri of Italy (born at Mandrio in the province of Reggio Emilia on 16 October 1885; 1.59 m./ 60 kg.). This strongly built little man had begun to earn a reputation as a runner in 1904, after a short spell as a cyclist. His early official attempts were preceded by a revealing episode, related by Emanuele Carli in his book "Dorando Pietri, corridore di maratona" (1973). One day in September 1904, Carpi, the town where he resided, received the visit of Pericle Pagliani, then one of Italy's best known distance runners. Dorando seized the opportunity: "He left the pastry shop in which he worked, rolled up his apron and followed the Roman runner in his exhibition - and managed to hang on Pagliani's heels till the end!" In 1905 Pietri won a 30 km. race in Paris and the following year he qualified for the "Interim" Olympics in Athens by covering 42 km. in 2:42:00 3/5. In Athens he was in contention for over half the race, until cramp forced him to retire. In 1907 he won two events (5000 and 20,000 m) on consecutive days at the Italian track Championships. In 1908, merely 17 days before the Olympic race, he covered 40 km. in a brilliant 2:38:00 in a test at Carpi.

The London race took place on 24 July 1908, with departure from Windsor Castle and arrival at the new White City Stadium, Shepherd's Bush. The total distance, including about two-thirds of a lap on the track, was 26 miles 385 yards (42,195 m.) - an abstruse distance which for some unexplained reason was to be adopted as official for all Olympic marathons, beginning with the 1924 Games in Paris. As a result, the event so often referred to as "the classic Greek distance" actually originated from a British "convenience".

Sixteen countries were represented in the London

marathon, for a total of 56 entries. The day was hot and the time of departure (2.30 p.m.) added to the discomfort of the athletes. The leaders in the early stages were three Englishmen, Tom Jack, Fred Lord and Jack Price. One by one, however, they fell victim to their own pace and about midway in the race the lead was taken by a South African, Charles Hefferon, who with 5 miles to go had about 4 minutes on his nearest rival, Dorando Pietri. But the Italian closed the gap and caught the Springbok ace at Old Oak Common Lane. By then, Hefferon was visibly fading. Even so, Pietri had to make a big effort to draw away: he did so with success, but at a very high price. In the vicinity of the Stadium he appeared to be on the verge of collapse. The drama began to unfold after he entered the arena, where a huge crowd was awaiting the runners. Pietri first made a mistake by turning right, rather than left as was prescribed by the rules. Before he could be warned and put back on the correct track, he fell down, exhausted. Doctors and officials rushed to assist him and after a seemingly eternal time he was back on his feet. Few of those present possibly realized that such an action involved disqualification. The Italian instinctively plodded on and on, yet fell four more times before being finally assisted across the finish line. He came to the end of his Odyssey after 2:54:46 2/5. In the meantime another runner, John Hayes of USA, had entered the Stadium. He finished the race in 2:55:18 2/5. Next came the gallant Hefferon, followed by two more Americans, all inside three hours. Pietri was, of course, disqualified and Hayes (born in New York on 10 April 1886; 1.62 m./ 56 kg.) was proclaimed the winner. A study of the intermediate times shows that the London affair was in fact a "race to exhaustion". Pietri's 5-mile fractions were 27:07, 30:06, 33:15 and 35:50, on top of which it took him no less than 48:28 2/5 to cover the remaining 6 miles 385 yards - about ten minutes of which was absorbed by his gruelling experience on the White City track! In subsequent weeks, however, the Italian became the recipient of honours such as few official Olympic victors have ever had. The echo of the London marathon worldwide was such that popular interest in long grind events increased considerably. Pietri and Hayes turned professional and acted as drawing cards during the "marathon craze" that swept America in those days. The two leading characters of the Olympic race met again at New York's Madison Square Garden on 25 November 1908 in a special match race. At that time the Garden indoor track was 160.93 m. (ten laps to the mile) in circumference. On a distance exactly the same as that of the London race, the Italian won in 2:44:20 2/5, leaving Hayes nearly 45 seconds behind. Pietri beat Hayes on three more occasions, yet he had mixed fortunes with other famous "pros" such as Henri Saint-Yves, a little French waiter, and Thomas Longboat of Canada. During the hottest period of his American tour - 165 days, between 25 November 1908 and 9 May 1909 - Pietri ran 22 races at distances ranging from 10 miles to the marathon, and won 17 of them. According to Carli, in the whole of his career he entered 17 marathon races, with the following "harvest": eight victories, one second and one sixth place; he failed to finish six times and was disqualified once. The 1912 Olympic marathon in Stockholm, although contested over a distance of only 40,200 m., was modern in at least one essential aspect: it was an out-and-back course, with start and finish in the stadium. The turning point was on the high country road near the Sollentuna church. The road was swept, watered and put in good order, and all wheeled traffic was forbidden. In spite of a rather oppressive heat, times were easily the best returned in Olympic competition until then. South Africa scored a great one-two, with Kenneth McArthur in first

Carvajal, the first of the Cubans

The St.Louis Olympics of 1904 were little more than a US Inter-club Championship. Among the relatively few foreign entrants there were some Cubans, who won a fair number of medals (as many as ten in fencing, thanks to the unusual support of two US citizens, who managed to be admitted as Cubans!). In athletics, however, there was a genuine son of the island discovered by Columbus, a little man by the name of Felix Carvajal. Although he had never run a marathon before, he was sent to the Games on a public subscription, after persuading his countrymen that in him lay hidden a genius of endurance in the foot-racing department. Arriving in New Orleans, he reportedly lost all his money in a "crap game", so he had to hitch-hike to St.Louis. He appeared in the Olympic race in street shoes and clothes, yet managed to stay in contention for a long time, until he stopped to eat a couple of green apples from a nearby tree. Soon afterwards he developed cramp, and was only able to come in fourth.

Dorando Pietri (Italy) at the end of his tribulations in the 1908 Olympic marathon. The most celebrated story of the modern Games.

place (2:36:54.8) and Chris Gitsham in the runner-up position. One of the pre-race favourites, Tatu Kolehmainen of Finland, livened up the race in the initial stages but ran out of gas on the return journey and finally retired.

He was an elder brother of Hannes Kolehmainen, the man who won eternal fame in the same edition of the Games with his track victories. Eight years later, at Antwerp, Hannes himself appeared in the Olympic marathon. By then almost 31, he really began to move near the half-way point, which he reached after 1:13:10, with Gitsham, the Stockholm runner-up, in his wake. On the return journey the South African began to tire and dropped out with 2 miles to go. In the closing stage, Kolehmainen was seriously threatened by Jüri Lossman of Estonia. It was the closest finish in Olympic marathon history, and the Finn beat his Baltic "cousin" by only 12 4/5 seconds.

His time, 2:32:35 4/5, was truly remarkable in view of the fact that the course measured 42,750 m., the longest in Olympic annals. Valerio Arri of Italy came from behind in the closing stage to take third place in 2:36:32 4/5. At the end of it, Arri was fresh enough to indulge in a triple somersault, which exhilarated, among others, the Father of the modern Games, baron Pierre de Coubertin.

It goes almost without saying that in Italian track history Arri's Olympic bronze has always taken the back seat to Pietri's "lost gold".

DORANDO PIETRI, THE QUEEN'S OWN PRIZE-WINNER IN THE MARATHON RACE, WITH THE CUP HE RECEIVED FROM HER MAJESTY.

DORANDO PASSING THROUGH WEMBLEY

56

HURDLES: Smithson's Bible and Thomson's Style

The straight-leg ("sprinting") approach introduced in the "highs" by Alvin Kraenzlein was further improved by another American, Forrest Smithson, who added a delayed trail leg action of his own. He had unusual hip flexibility, which allowed him to get back to the ground with astounding speed. This tall man (1.83 m.) hailed from Portland, Oregon, so he was one of the earliest West Coast products. He achieved his best mark, 15.0, in winning the 110 m. hurdles title at the 1908 Olympics in London. The race was on a Sunday and Smithson, a student of theology, expressed his protest against Sunday competition by carrying a Bible in his left hand. In the following years several Americans matched Smithson's time, were it only over the slightly shorter 120 y. distance. The first to duck under 15 seconds, in 1916, were Earl Thomson of Canada and Fred Kelly (both 14 4/5), and Robert Simpson, who returned 14 3/5 twice within a week, first at Columbia, Missouri, then at Evanston near Chicago.

Simpson was with a tiny group of Americans who visited Sweden later in the same year. At Stockholm he ran 110 m. hurdles in 14 4/5, which time was not ratified as a world record, probably due to the fact that he knocked down several hurdles. Simpson and Thomson were responsible for introducing the "double-arm shift". The Canadian in particular, a strongly built (1.90m. / 84 kg.) but not very fast runner, is remembered for his fine form. On 29 May 1920 at Philadelphia, he ran the English distance in 14 2/5, which remained a world record for eleven years. He went on to win the Olympic 110 m. title at Antwerp in 14 4/5. By their teaching, both he and Simpson - the latter even in Scandinavia - greatly contributed to the advancement of hurdling technique. Definitely slower was the evolution in the 400 m. hurdles event. The Americans generally neglected the "intermediates", but their superior speed on the flat route largely sufficed to earn them the lion's share in international competition. Winner at St.Louis (1904) was Harry Hillman, who was clocked in 53.0, but over 76 cm. hurdles. He was still going strong by the time of the London Olympics four years later, but even though he ran an estimated 55.3 (best of his career over regulation 91 cm. hurdles) he had to be content with second place behind his countryman Charles Bacon, who set a new world record of 55.0. This event was strangely not included in the programme at the Stockholm Games (1912). A seemingly revolutionary time of 52 3/5 over 440 y. hurdles was recorded by William Meanix at the 1915 AAU Championships in San Francisco, but on a straight course and with strong wind assistance. A unique example of a race over the "intermediates" held under such conditions: spectators at the Pan-Pacific International Exposition Stadium surely "got a big kick out of it". A few weeks before the Antwerp Games (1920) John Norton ran the English distance in 54 1/5 at Pasadena, California, but shortly afterwards he lost to Frank Loomis (55.0) over the same distance at the Olympic Trials. Loomis had the upper hand in the Games as well, chalking up a new world record of 54.0 for 400m. hurdles. It was a hotly contested race, with Norton and August Desch (both USA), and Georges André of France filling the places in that order, with estimated times of 54.6,

---

"I'm the guy who won and lost his victory"

On 30 July 1908 "Corriere della Sera", Italy's best known daily, published an article from London - byline, Dorando Pietri. The champion told the tale of his London experience of the previous week. The story began with the following words: "I'm not the winner of the Olympic marathon, but as the English say, I'm the guy who won and lost his victory". Many years later, a famous British journalist, Harold M. Abrahams (the Olympic 100 m. champion of 1924) offered the following comment on the Pietri drama: "Such is the power of a "good story" that for every thousand people who have heard of Dorando, not one will be able to tell you who was the winner of the 1908 marathon race; and I always think of Dorando Pietri as the outstanding example of an athlete whose defeat brought much more recognition than ever a victory could have done". Pietri's case, aptly exploited by the press, inspired artists and writers. On the initiative of British author Arthur Conan Doyle, the inventor of Sherlock Holmes, he received from Queen Alexandra a cup which was an exact replica of the one awarded to Hayes. A young American composer, Irving Berlin, the would-be author of "White Christmas", wrote a popular song entitled, "Dorando". Italian operatic tenor Enrico Caruso supplied a cartoon on his famous countryman for an Italo-American paper. In Italy the champion was celebrated with poems and festivals. His hometown of Carpi promoted a collection in his favour which netted Lire 1,496.65.

54.7 and 54.8 respectively. André (born in Paris on 13 August 1889; 1.88 m. / 85 kg.) is still remembered as one of the greatest talents France has ever had. He excelled also in the "highs" and the high jump, having tied for second in the latter at the London Olympics of 1908, aged 19. He later became a rugby international and was nicknamed "le Bison" for his sturdiness. He died as a flyer on the Tunisian front in 1943.

STEEPLECHASE: Mixed Distances and Courses

One had to wait till 1920 and Antwerp for the adoption of the 3000 m. as the standard Olympic steeplechase distance. Prior to that, mixed distances and courses had been the rule. At St.Louis in 1904 there were "several hurdles and a 14 ft. (4.26 m.) water jump on each lap". The race was won by James Lightbody of USA, whose time for the spurious distance of 2590 m. was 7:39 3/5. He had never tried the event before, but he was known as a good middle distance runner - and in the following days he annexed two more titles, 800 and 1500 m. At the London Games (1908) the steeplechase distance was an odd 3200 m. Lightbody failed to survive the preliminary round and the title went to an Englishman, Arthur Russell, who won in 10:47 4/5, with one second to spare vis-à-vis his compatriot Arthur Robertson, the international cross-country champion. A steeplechase course similar to the one now in use was first introduced at the Antwerp Games (1920). The race, finally over 3000 m., was won by Percy Hodge of Britain, a dependable "stayer" with a fine background as a cross-country runner. Oldtimers tell us that "he used to delight crowds by running over a flight of hurdles while balancing a bottle of beer on a tray". In the Antwerp race, curiously held at 9 a.m., he won hands down in 10:00 2/5.

Hurdler Forrest Smithson (USA) purportedly holding a Bible as a protest against Sunday competition (1908 Olympics, London).

Robertson & Hillman Inc., Masters in Three-legged Racing

Lawson Robertson and Harry Hillman were prominent figures on the American track scene in the first decade of the century. The former, a good sprinter, finished second twice in the furlong at the AAU Championships (1904 and 1906) and later became a successful coach. The latter, as previously related, won three events at the St.Louis Olympics (1904): 400 m. flat, 200 and 400 m. hurdles. However, it was in a peculiar category that their names remained in the AAU record book for a long time - that of three-legged races. In this particular and somewhat dangerous game, Robertson and Hillman, harnessed to each other, were credited between 1905 and 1909 with the following records:
- 40 y. 5 1/5; 50y. 6.0; 60 y. 7 1/5; 75 y. 8 4/5; 100 y. 11.0; 110 y. 12 3/5; 120 y. 14.0.

Not surprisingly, they were rather similar in build: Robertson 1.83 m / 68 kg.; Hillman 1.80 m. / 65 kg.

JUMPS - High Jump: Horine, a smart inventor

In the first decade of the new century Olympic laurels in the high jump were won with relatively unimpressive performances. Sam Jones of USA won at St.Louis (1904) with 1.80, and Con Leahy of Ireland needed nothing better than 1.775 to win at the "Interim" Games in Athens (1906). Among place winners on both occasions was Lajos Gönczy of Hungary, one of the first "continentals" to emerge in this event, with a best of 1.82 in 1904. A good overall standard was first attained in the London

Olympics (1908), with seven men mastering the 6 ft. (1.829 m.) barrier. Harry Porter of USA won with 1.905, while three Europeans, Con Leahy, István Somodi of Hungary and Georges André of France tied for second at 1.88. The first man who really made history in the event was George Horine of USA (born at Escondido, California, on 3 February 1890; 1.80 m. / 73 kg.). Like most jumpers of his day, Horine began with the scissors style, i.e. approaching the bar from the right side and jumping off the left foot. His best with this form, while a high school boy, was 1.549. The story of his subsequent experiences is best told by H.Archie Richardson in his "Little Black Book": "Moving with his family to Palo Alto, and still wishing to continue high jumping, the youngster was disappointed to find that the backyard of their new home was so constructed that in order to practise jumping he had to set the standards in such a manner that he was forced to run from the left side instead of from the right, as formerly. As it was necessary for him to jump from his left foot, he was compelled to figure out a new method and the Horine variant of the Western Roll technique of high jumping was the result". In rolling over the bar, his body was virtually parallel with the ground, and his centre of gravity lay much lower than in previous styles of jumping - hence the economy of the operation. The smart inventor hailed from the West Coast, and so the new form was aptly named "Western Roll". Within a short time, while still using the new form in a rudimentary manner, he improved to 1.753 in 1909. After enrolling at Stanford University, however, he was induced to abandon his unorthodox form in favour of a straight-on jump. Even so, he continued to improve: 1.87 in 1910, 1.93 in 1911. It looked as if his "reactionary" coach was right after all. But Horine had different views and eventually returned to his self-developed form. From then on he really scaled the heights. Early in 1912 he set a new American Collegiate record of 1.949 and on 29 March, at Palo Alto, he did 1.984 for a new world record. A few weeks later, on 18 May, still on the Stanford campus at Palo Alto, he went over a crossbar set at 6 ft. 7 in. (2.007 m.), after a hard fight with his teammate Edward Beeson, who was second at 1.943. As Horine himself candidly admitted in one of his writings, "My jump at 6-7 was not clean", inasmuch as he touched the bar in going over (which is, of course, all but rare in record efforts). On the other hand, he claimed that he had "one-to-two inches (2.5-to-5 cm.) to spare" in his previous record jump at 1.984. Be as it may, he became history's first 2-metre jumper. (Whether he "knew" or not, that is another question). The American inventor was awaited at the Olympic Games in Stockholm with mixed feelings of anxiety and incredulity. Unluckily enough, he was apparently past his peak when he faced the élite of the world, barely two months after his greatest achievement. He had to be content with a bronze medal at 1.89. Another American, the tall Alma Richards, won at 1.93 after a great battle with the lithe and nervous Hans Liesche of Germany (1.91). Among other place winners was Jim Thorpe, the famous all-rounder, who cleared 1.87. It should be noted that only four weeks earlier, at New York, Thorpe had mastered 1.956, beating Richards (1.93) and Horine (1.905).

Horine's contribution to the event was certainly great, no matter if critics of the time regarded his style of jumping as a bit difficult to learn. The advantages in clearance form were so obvious, however, that the new form gradually caught on, first in the States, and much later in the rest of the world. A curious detail: Horine won the AAU title just once, in

1901
1920

Hannes Kolehmainen (Finland) winning the 10,000 metres at the 1912 Olympics in Stockholm. He inaugurated the Finnish Era in long distance running.

59

1915, with no better than 1.848. In the six-year span of his career, however, he won 59 of his 64 competitions and mastered 6 ft. 3 in. (1.905 m.) or higher on seventeen occasions. He once cleared 2.038 in practice. Another Californian, Edward Beeson, was the next record-breaker. Using a variant of the Western Roll and reportedly taking advice from .... shotputter Ralph Rose, in 1914 at Berkeley he cleared 2.014. On that occasion he and Horine began by mastering 1.84, then they chose to try the new record height: Beeson "made" it on his second attempt, while Horine failed three times. Next to appear on the American scene was a truly amazing jumper hailing from the Rocky Mountains: Clinton Larson. In a way he can be credited with using a "Fosbury Flop" ante litteram, with a face-upward, back-to-the-bar position resulting in a complete layout. Indifferent in height (1.76 m.) but capable of running the 100 y. in 10 1/5, he laid the stress on the approach run. In 1917 he won the AAU title (1.892) and cleared 2.029 in an unsanctioned meet at Provo, Utah. In 1919 he came to Europe and won his event at the Inter-Allied Games in Paris with 1.864. In 1924, when he was nearly 32, he went over a bar set at 2.07 in the course of an exhibition at Magna, Utah. In 1920 the Olympic title was won by Richmond Landon of USA with a jump of 1.94. Third in the event was Bo Ekelund of Sweden, who in later years was to become one of his country's leading athletic personalities.

POLE VAULT:
Lex Americana
(with a French interference)

America's domination in pole vaulting was to continue for nearly ... three-quarters of the new century, with rare interferences by specialists from other countries. The first record-breaker of the XX century was Norman Dole, who vaulted 3.69 in 1904. He was not present at the St.Louis Olympics though, and the title was won by another American, Charles Dvorak (3.50). Another famous absentee on that occasion was Fernand Gonder, a distant fore-runner of the French vaulting school of our days. This man of medium build (1.70 m. / 56 kg.) was born at Rochefort on 12 June 1883. He first became acquainted with pole vaulting while in military service at Bordeaux in the spring of 1904. A few weeks later he set his first French record with 3.38. Then he went on to win the national title in Paris with 3.69, thereby equalling Norman Dole's world record, set only a few weeks earlier. On 4 June 1905, at Gradignan, Gonder improved to 3.74 to become the only owner of the record. In the same year he reportedly cleared 4.00 during an exhibition. Contrary to what was said and written in other countries, Gonder was not a "pole climber": his form conformed with present-day rules. He became internationally known in 1906, when he won at the "Interim" Games in Athens with 3.50, beating among others Bruno Söderström of Sweden and Edward Glover of USA, runner-up at the AAU Championships in 1905. Gonder turned to rugby shortly afterwards and thus missed the 1908 Olympics in London, where Edward Cook and Alfred Gilbert, both of USA, were bracketed in an unusual tie for first at 3.71, each earning a gold medal! In the meantime, Americans had regained the pole position even in the record department: by the end of 1908 the new "ceiling" was 3.90, by Walter Dray. The above-mentioned Alfred Gilbert cleared a bar set at 4 metres during an exhibition at Westville in 1909. When his career was over he turned to business and eventually made a fortune as president of a toy factory. History's first official 13-footer was a Yale man, Robert Gardner, who did 13 ft. 1 in. (3.98) at Philadelphia on 1 June 1912. Exactly a week later the metric minded world received a more intelligible message when Marc Wright, a left-hander of medium build (born at Chicago on 21 April 1890), cleared 4.02 in the Olympic Trials at Cambridge, MA. Wright's form included some of the vital elements of modern vaulting technique, like a run of about 30 m., a prolonged "swing", a single-hand release, first with the lower (left) hand, then with the upper one (right), and an arch position in going over the bar. Same as high jumper George Horine, however, he failed to do himself justice at the 1912 Olympics in Stockholm. In a hotly contested event, six men went over 3.80 and victory went to Harry Babcock of USA at 3.95, while his compatriots Wright and Frank Nelson tied for second at 3.85. First of the great post-war vaulters was Frank Foss of USA, who perfected the "jackknife" clearance form, so called after the figure described by the body in going over the bar. In 1919 at Chicago he bettered Wright's record with a 4.05 vault. The following year he improved to 4.09 in winning the Olympic title at Antwerp. He was to remain for many years (till 1980) the only vaulter to have won both honours simultaneously. Foss achieved the record height in what we may call a "modern" way: after failing in his first attempt at 4.00, he asked to take the remaining trials at 4.09 - and succeeded. Of course he had previously secured his victory at a lower height. Henry Petersen of Denmark was second with no better than 3.70.

LONG JUMP: O'Connor, a heavy pipe smoker

At the dawn of the new century Ireland had a man who was seemingly in a class with the American duo Kraenzlein-Prinstein. He was Peter O'Connor (born in County Wicklow on 18 October 1874). Like other leading athletes of his time, he missed the Paris Olympics (1900), but a few weeks later he exceeded Prinstein's world record with a 7.51 effort. It should be noted, however, that shortly before the Paris Games the man from the Emerald Isle had lost to Kraenzlein in the AAA Championships in London - 6.81 to 6.96. The slender O'Connor had his vintage year in 1901, when he improved to 7.54, and finally, on 5 August at Ballsbridge, Dublin, to 7.61. These marks were made from a hard board take-off. In the same year O'Connor also did 7.63 at Portlaoise, but on a downhill runway. His marks outside of Ireland were not so impressive, yet he won the English AAA title for six years in a row (1901-06), his best mark of the series being 7.25. In 1904 he missed the Olympics again, but two years later he took part in the "Interim" Games at Athens, where he lost to Prinstein in the long jump, 7.025 to 7.20, but evened the count with the American in the triple jump, after Prinstein called it a day due to an ankle injury. O'Connor, who was also a leading high jumper (1.88), had a technique of his own: "he drew the knees up towards the chin and relied on his initial velocity to carry him sailing through the air". He jumped, mainly if not exclusively, on nervous energy. So bad were the conditions prevailing in those days that during his long career he sprained his take-off (left) foot on seven occasions. He once admitted: "I never had a trainer, and I was a heavy pipe smoker".

Prinstein made amends for his bad luck at the Paris Games by scoring a fine double four years later in St.Louis (1904). He won the long jump with 7.34 and the triple jump with 14.35 - a feat no one has been able to duplicate as of today. In both events he achieved his best distance on the last trial. O'Connor's record was threatened for the first time in 1908, when his countryman Tim Ahearne did 7.57 at Kanturk, barely two weeks after finishing no better than eighth (at 6.72) in the Olympic final in London, which was won by Frank Irons of USA with 7.48. America's lucky streak remained unbroken four years later in Stockholm, when Albert Gutterson improved on his previous best by almost a foot with a 7.60 effort. The great tradition of black long jumpers was inaugurated in the early postwar days by Sol Butler, an American who distinguished himself on both sides of the Atlantic. In 1919, at the Inter-Allied Games in Paris, he won with 7.557, a mark curiously accompanied in press reports by a previously unheard of verdict: "wind assisted". In 1920 Butler earned a berth on the US Olympic team with a 7.51 effort, leaving his nearest rival 38 cm. behind. But at the Antwerp Games the strongly built Butler was unlucky enough to injure himself in the qualifying round. He wound up seventh at 6.60. This opened the door to Europe's first victory in the event: William Petersson of Sweden (who later changed his name to Björneman) clinched the gold medal with 7.15.

1901 1920

Ray Ewry (USA), "the Human Frog", a dominant figure in the standing jumps in the early days of the century.

61

TRIPLE JUMP:
Ahearne & Ahearn Ltd.

The first man to achieve notable distances in international competition was Meyer Prinstein of USA, no matter if his winning efforts in the Olympics - 14.47 in 1900, 14.35 in 1904 - appear rather irrelevant if compared with his known potential as a long jumper. The programme of the 1900 and 1904 Olympics also included a standing hop, step and jump, which was won on both occasions by Ray Ewry of USA. This legendary athlete (born at Lafayette, Indiana, on 14 October 1873, 1.85 m. / 73 kg.) is remembered as the greatest specialist of all time in the standing jumps. During his career, which lasted nearly twenty years, he amassed a huge number of championship titles, including eight Olympic gold medals (plus two at the "Interim" Games of 1906). His best Olympic marks were: St.high jump, 1.65 (1900); St.long jump, 3.47 (1904); St.hop, step and jump, 10.58 (1900).

The last internationally visible sparks of Irish tradition - apart from Eamonn Fitzgerald's unheralded fourth place at the Los Angeles Olympics of 1932 - were offered by the Ahearne brothers of County Limerick, Timothy and Daniel. The former won the triple jump in the colours of Great Britain at the 1908 Olympics in London, at the age of twenty-two, with 14.91. His younger brother Daniel (born in County Limerick on 2 April 1888; 1.78 m. / 72 Kg.) soon emigrated to America, where he dropped the final 'e' of his family name. He was probably the first of the great triple jumpers. Between 1910 and 1918 he won the AAU title eight times, that is every

The American trio who made a clean sweep in the shot put at the 1912 Olympics. From left: Pat McDonald, first; Whitney, third; and Rose, second.

year except once, in 1912, when victory went to Platt Adams, a famous all-round jumper. As a record-breaker, Daniel did 15.12 in 1910 and 15.52 in 1911, both times at Celtic Park, Long Island, New York. The latter mark consisted of a 6.10 hop, a 3.50 step and a 5.92 jump. But he was to join that legion of athletes who just could not do themselves justice in the Olympic Games: he did not compete at Stockholm in 1912, and eight years later, at Antwerp, he was past his peak and had to be content with a sixth place (14.08). Winner at Stockholm was Gustaf ("Topsy") Lindblom of Sweden with 14.76. Incidentally, Lindblom shared with the famous Torsten Tegnér (for many years Editor and Publisher of "Idrottsbladet", Stockholm) the honour of pioneering Swedish sports journalism. The Olympic final of 1920, held under poor conditions, was won by a Finn, Vilho Tuulos, with 14.505. By then the heyday of Irish and American triple jumpers was over.

THROWS - SHOT PUT:
The massive Rose

In the shot put the circular platform (7 ft. or 2.13 m. in diameter) was introduced in international competition at the St.Louis Olympics (1904). In the absence of Ireland's Denis Horgan, the event turned out to be a test of strength between two Americans, the mammoth-like Ralph Rose and the squat Wesley Coe. The former won with 14.81, a new world record, while Coe was second with 14.40. A prompt reply came from the other side of the Atlantic a few weeks later, when Horgan reached his lifetime best, 14.88, at Mallow. Coe fought back successfully the following year with a 15.09 toss in winning the AAU title at Portland, OR. In later years, Rose eventually proved the strongest of the trio and gradually built up a substantial lead on all his contemporaries, winding up with a 15.54 effort in a triangular meet at San Francisco on 21 August 1909. As for Horgan, he went back to America in 1907 and found a job with the New York police, just like other strong men from Ireland who had earlier emigrated to USA. Later in the same year, however, he was involved in a brawl among immigrants from different countries and received a blow on the head with a shovel. His skull was fractured, but he survived and eventually returned to the athletic "warpath" in 1908, when he won the English AAA title and finished second to Rose in the London Olympics, 13.62 to 14.21. The massive Rose (born at Healdsburg, CA., on 17 March 1884) was all set to win the Olympic event for the third time at Stockholm in 1912, but his best throw on that occasion, 15.25, only sufficed to earn him a second place behind his countryman Pat McDonald, who reached 15.34.

Rose had begun at 15, when his weight was a remarkable 95 kg. At the peak of his career he had a portly build: 1.97m. / 127 kg. He impersonated the archetype of the shot put champion, of whom only strength, and then more strength, was demanded. His action in the ring may have been far less dynamic than that of present-day greats, but the following passage about the toss that won first place for Rose from Charles Lucas' brilliant account of the St.Louis final may be of interest: "Carefully poising the weight in the palm of his high-lifted hand, where it fitted like a marble in the hand of a small boy, leaning back as far as he could without losing his balance, and lifting his leg up to his waist, Rose made one mighty move, throwing his body forward, and the shot flew from his hand ..." (to 14.81, as related above). The uncultivated potential of this giant must have been tremendous, even if the famous 16.56 effort allegedly credited to him during an unsanctioned meet in his native town of Healdsburg in 1909 seems to lack the support of convincing evidence.

But then even his official best (15.54) was good enough to resist all attacks for nineteen years. One should also remember that the leading shot putters of those days were primarily all-round throwers who cared little

1901
1920

Martin Sheridan (USA), a twotime Olympic winner in the discus (1904 and 1908).

for specialization. At the 1909 AAU Cham-pionships, Rose won shot, discus and javelin, and finished second in the hammer! The chain of American victories in the Olympics was finally broken at Antwerp in 1920, when Ville Pörhölä of Finland, he too a fine all-round thrower, won the shot with 14.81.

DISCUS:
"Father" Järvinen

Present discus rules came into force at the international level in 1908, when the weight of the wooden implement was set at 2 kg., presumably after a bronze discus found at Olympia during excavations conducted there in the 1870's by a German crew led by archaeologist Ernst Curtius. The throw was to be made from a circle of 2.50 m. in diameter.

Prior to that, Americans Martin Sheridan and Ralph Rose had achieved the same distance, 39.28, at the St.Louis Olympics (1904), with the former winning the title in a throw-off. By the same time there was also a Greek style event, which appeared on the Olympic programme at the "Interim" Games (1906) and again in 1908 in London. This exercise, believed to be a faithful reconstruction of the classic event, had rather complicated rules and called for somewhat unnatural movements. For these reasons it was abandoned shortly afterwards. Sheridan (born at Bohola, County Mayo, on 28 March 1881) was yet another stalwart from Irish stock who scaled the heights while residing in USA. He was a great all-round thrower, with the discus as his parade event. He first captured the world record in 1901 with 36.77, then continued to improve, eventually reaching 43.69 in 1905. He won Olympic gold in 1904, as previously related, and again in 1908, when he also annexed the "Greek style" event and finished third in the standing long jump! One of his European contemporaries, Verner Järvinen of Finland, did 44.84 in 1909, but from a 2.70 m. circle. This man (born at Juupajoki on 4 March 1870) is

John Flanagan, an American of Irish extraction, threetime Olympic winner in the hammer (1900, 1904 and 1908).

remembered in Finnish circles as "Isä"(father)-Järvinen. He was the head of one of the greatest athletic families the world has ever known. The first of his four sons, Yrjö, was a javelin thrower of national class (58.50); the second, Kalle, was a shot putter of world calibre (15.92 in 1932); the third, Akilles, and the fourth, Matti, were athletes of historical stature. (Their feats are related in the sections devoted to the decathlon and javelin respectively). Järvinen the Elder had a very long career: at the age of 54 he still managed to hurl the discus over 38 m.

The first world record to be ratified by the IAAF, achieved from an "Olympic" (2.50 m.) circle, was 47.58 by James Duncan of USA in 1912. At the Stockholm Games of the same year, however, Duncan was no luckier than other newly crowned world record holders such as George Horine and Marc Wright: he had to be content with third place in an event won by Armas Taipale of Finland at 45.21. In those pioneering days, the stress was primarily laid on the arm action, little attention being paid to the movements of the trunk and legs.

Taipale was one of the first throwers who corrected this, using legs and hips to good if not full advantage. Spurred on by his countryman Elmer Niklander, Taipale improved to 48.27 at Copenhagen in 1913 and 48.90 at Tallinn in 1914. Although these marks never received IAAF recognition, the Finn convinced many a doubter that the 50-metre barrier was well within the limits of human possibilities.

HAMMER THROW:
The roaring years of the "Irish Whales"

John Flanagan remained a dominant figure in hammer circles throughout the first decade of the new century. After his victory at the Paris Olympics (1900), he won two more gold medals (1904 and 1908), thereby setting a record streak that was to remain unsurpassed till the advent of discus genius Al Oerter.

A massive medium height man (1.78 m. / 100 kg.), Flanagan continued to improve till the age of 36, when he achieved a lifetime best of 56.18 at Newhaven, Connecticut, on 24 July 1909. He was the first hammer champion to master the three-turn technique.

Next in the line of great Irish-American hammer throwers were Matthew McGrath (born at Nenagh, County Tipperary, on 20 December 1876; 1.82 m. / 112 kg.) and Patrick Ryan (born at Pallasgreen, County Limerick, on 4 January 1887; 1.88 m. / 113 kg.). The former had a very long career and represented USA in four editions of the Olympic Games.

In 1928, aged 52, he tried to qualify for the fifth time but fell 78 cm. short of his goal at the US Olympic Trials. In 1933, aged 57, he still managed to reach 45.98. In his younger days he finished second in London (1908), struck gold in Stockholm (1912) with 54.74, was fifth at Antwerp (1920) and again second at Paris (1924).

Ryan, who arrived in the States from Ireland in 1910, was not eligible to represent USA at the Stockholm Games, so he had to wait another eight years for his first, and last, Olympic chance. At Antwerp (1920) he seized the opportunity in superb style, winning with 52.875 and leaving his nearest opponent, Carl Johan ("Massa") Lind of Sweden, over 4 metres behind.

McGrath and Ryan battled for years at distances which were far ahead of their contemporaries. Their favourite "playing ground" was at Celtic Park on Long Island, New York. It was there that McGrath succeeded Flanagan as world record holder with a 57.10 throw on 29 October 1911. Ryan's reply came on 17 August 1913 on the same site.

On that occasion the "New York Times" committed to history the complete series of Ryan's throws: 51.28, 52.60, 54.99, foul, 54.23, 57.77. The record throw was unsurpassed for almost a quarter of a century.

And only four days earlier McGrath had made a throw of 58.17 in the course of an exhibition at College Point, New York.

In their roaring years, Ryan and McGrath had the seasonal records listed nearby.

1901
1920

	Ryan	McGrath		Ryan	McGrath
1910	50.39	51.32	1916	56.86	56.79
1911	54.58	57.10	1917	52.77	-
1912	55.77	54.97	1918	-	53.87
1913	57.77	56.56	1919	53.48	53.20
1914	56.74	55.65	1920	52.875	51.79
1915	57.10	53.20			

(McGrath: 54.10 in 1925, 45.98 in 1933)

The driving force behind these pioneers was a spirit of emulation which arises only between congenial souls. At the death of his great predecessor John Flanagan, in 1938, McGrath paid a tribute to his old rival and friend in "The Amateur Athlete":"His (Flanagan's) skill and form was cultivated from early youth and while he was not only of the average size, I had an advantage of height and weight over him, still his form was more to perfection than mine. While on the subject of form, we threw the hammer with legs, body and arms which our successors of today do not, they use only their arms".

With the inevitable decline of Ryan and McGrath, the clock was put back several years.

JAVELIN THROW: Finland takes over

Eric Lemming of Sweden continued to be the undisputed master of the tiny javelin fraternity for many years to come. He bettered the world record several times, from 53.79 in 1903 to 58.27 in 1911. The event was included in the Olympic programme at the "Interim" Games of 1906 in Athens, where Lemming imparted a lesson to his contemporaries, winning the event at 53.90, with almost nine metres to spare! Scandinavians made a clean sweep of the top seven positions. Two years later, in London, Lemming won both the modern style (54.83) and the free style (54.44) event. Record books also credit him with history's first 60-m. throw, but in reality this barrier was first broken by Mór Kóczán-Kovács of Hungary in 1911 with a 60.64 throw, which was however achieved with the free style. First to better 60 m. with the modern style was Julius ("Juho") Saaristo of Finland, who in the course of a two-hands event at Helsinki on 25 May 1912 reached 61.45 with his best (right) arm. But he was aided by a strong wind, and that explains why the role of history's first conqueror of that barrier is commonly attributed to Lemming, who "chose" the noblest occasion for his 60.64 of 6 July 1912 in Stockholm: the eagerly awaited Olympic final, in which he beat Saaristo (58.66) and Kóczán (55.50). Only three days later, in the two-hands event, Saaristo took revenge with a right-hand throw of 61.00.

The Swede, however, was to have the last word for that momentous season: late in September, still at Stockholm, he reached 62.32.

It should be added that the two-hands event, very popular in Scandinavia in the early days, remained on the IAAF record book till 1938. By then the official record was 114.28 (61.81 right, 52.47 left) by Yngve Häckner of Sweden in 1917. Olav Sunde of Norway had a better performance which was never ratified: 117.21 (66.86 right, 50.35 left) in 1930.

Lemming, who in the latter part of his career competed under the pseudonym of Erik Otto, had another good season in 1913 (62.16), then he began to decline. Yet, as late as in 1917, he was able to annex one more Swedish title, his last, in the two-hands shot put.

By that time the Finns had taken the javelin ("keihäs" in Finnish) to their hearts, electing it as their "national" event. Light implements were introduced to help teenagers who wanted to become familiar with the exercise. Good results followed and within a short time the Finns wrested the javelin monopoly from the hands of their Swedish "cousins". The innate interest of the Finns in javelin throwing was probably linked with an ancient wartime tradition of the Ugro-Finnic peoples.

The first of the great Finns was Jonni Myyrä (born at Savitaipale on 13 July 1892; 1.84 m. / 83 kg.), who added dynamic force to Lemming's copy-book style. He exceeded Lemming's record with a 63.29 throw at Malmö in 1914, but Swedish officials ruled the effort wind-assisted. Later in the same year he did 62.58 under normal conditions, then improved to

Eric Lemming (Sweden), the Father of modern javelin throwing.

64.81 in 1915 and 65.55 in 1919. But only the last of his records - 66.10 on 25 August 1919 at Stockholm - was ratified by the IAAF. Myyrä won his first Olympic title at Antwerp (1920) with 65.78. Three other Finns monopolized positions 2-to-4, thus giving Suomi a memorable sweep.

DECATHLON:
The waltz of Scoring Tables - "Bright Path"

The decathlon in its present form was put on the map of athletics by the Swedes. After experimenting for years, the Northerners finally chose the following sequence of events: 100 m., long jump, shot put, high jump, 400 m., 110 m. hurdles, discus, pole vault, javelin, 1500 m. As a medium for ranking the competitors they devised a scoring table, the basis for which was provided by the Olympic records of the time. After the 1912 Olympics in Stockholm, during which such records fell like autumn leaves, the scoring was changed in accordance with the new marks.

Since then, the waltz of scoring tables has never come to a halt. Every fifteen years or so, a new table was devised to replace the "rotten" one. But progress in all branches of the sport continued unabated and every new table invariably failed to resist the ravages of times and distances for long. The Finnish Table introduced in 1934 was probably one of the best, yet it was "blown up" during the Fifties, when records and overall standards soared to generally unexpected heights. After many bold attempts made by "experts" from different countries, nobody can say how long any present or future scoring table is going to last, because it is well-nigh impossible to forecast the oscillations which are likely to occur in the ratio among the various events, let alone to predict if and when a certain crystallization will ever be achieved. Some track statisticians tend to widen the scope of the tables, which were primarily conceived as a medium for ranking competitors in the decathlon and not for weighing the absolute and relative value of performances in all events of track and field. No matter how careful the study of the mathematical and statistical factors contributing to the establishment of such tables, any further attempt to provide a scoring system likely to stand up for more than a few years will be an act of great courage, resembling a Sisyphean, rather than Herculean, labour.

The Swedes staged a "rehearsal" which took place at Göteborg on 15 October 1911. Winner of the one-day event was Hugo Wieslander, who amassed 6903.92 points. If converted to the current (1985) table, his results would now be worth 5386 points. For the

1901
1920

Jim Thorpe (USA), the first famous "Jack of all trades" in modern athletics. Won pentathlon and decathlon at the 1912 Olympics in Stockholm.

67

Olympic decathlon to be held at Stockholm (1912), experts deemed it advisable to adopt a three-day schedule. The historic competition thus took place on 13-14-15 July. Great lustre to this inaugural contest was given by the presence of America's famous all-rounder Jim Thorpe. He was born at Bellemont, OK., in a one-room log cabin on the banks of the North Canadian river, on 28 May 1888. Although often referred to as a full-blooded Indian, Thorpe was - according to his biographer Maxwell Stiles, noted California columnist - "three-eighths Pottowatomie and one eighth French on his mother's side, one-fourth Sac and Fox and one-fourth Irish on the side of his father." His parents, Hiram and Charlotte, were tall, massive people, both around 100 kg. in weight. As the tale goes, "the first thing Mrs. Thorpe saw after the birth of Jim and his twin brother Charlie was the bright, sunlit path leading up to the cabin". And so Jim was given the Indian name of Wa-Tho-Huck, which means Bright Path. He eventually had a better lot than Charlie, who was to die of spinal meningitis at the age of eight. Jim spent the early years of his life working with his father - racing, hunting and fishing as a child of nature, probably the best type of "conditioning" for any would-be athlete! He began his sports career at Carlisle Indian School in Pennsylvania. Football, American version, was his first love, but one day his athletic skill caught the eye of a famous coach, "Pop" Warner, who won Jim to track and took him under his wing. In spite of his aversion for hard, systematic training, Thorpe quickly became a good athlete and emerged as an all-round talent. As a one-man team for Carlisle he was supplemented in the long distance department by another famous Indian, Louis Tewanima.

The 1912 Olympics in Stockholm were to be the decisive test of Thorpe's athletic ability, and he passed it with the highest possible marks. There was also a pentathlon on the programme, and Jim won easily, with first places in four of the five events. His marks in this competition (7 July) were: 7.07 in the long jump, 46.41 in the javelin, 22.9 in the 200 m., 35.57 in the discus, and 4:44.8 in the 1500 m. Six days later he tackled the decathlon, in which he had the following marks:
- 13 July: 11.2 (100 m.), 6.79 (long jump), 12.89 (shot put);
- 14 July: 1.87 (high jump), 52.2 (400 m.), 36.98 (discus), 15.6 (110 m. hurdles), the last two being in inverted order vis-à-vis the present-day schedule;
- 15 July: 3.25 (pole vault), 45.70 (javelin), 4:40.1 (1500 m.).

Even allowing for the fact that the competition was spread over three days (a cautious experiment never to be repeated in the Olympics), Thorpe's final score of 8412.955 points (equivalent to 6564 under the present scoring table) must be considered excellent in relation to the time in which it was achieved. Thorpe literally won "hands down", since second place man Hugo Wieslander of Sweden amassed no more than 7724.495 points (still a personal best). It should be noted that Thorpe also tied for fourth in the individual high jump event at 1.87. In complimenting him, King Gustaf V of Sweden reportedly said: "Sir, you are the most wonderful athlete in the world".

However, Thorpe's epic had a sad tailpiece. In January 1913 an American newsman discovered that the double Olympic champion had played "pro" baseball in the summer of 1909, earning $60-to-$100 a month. Following an investigation, the AAU deprived Thorpe of his amateur status. And the International Olympic Committee decided to deprive him of his medals. The name of the great athlete thus disappeared from record books. Thorpe later tried his luck in other sports, and had great success in football. Then, almost inevitably, he sank into oblivion till his death in 1953.

But as late as in 1982, possibly in accordance with the dictum, "tempora mutantur", the IOC decided to reinstate him as double Olympic champion ...

At the Antwerp Olympics (1920) the decathlon, held over two days, was won by Helge Lövland of Norway with 6804.35 points. In the meantime the 1912 table had been revised on the basis of the records set during the Stockholm Games.

RELAYS:
Early "Traffic Accidents"

A relay event appeared for the first time in the Olympic programme in 1908. The distance was 1600 m., with legs of 200, 200, 400 and 800 m. A US team consisting of William Hamilton, Nathan Cartmell, John Taylor and Melvin Sheppard won in 3:29 2/5. Taylor, still under 20 at the time and a student at the University of Pennsylvania, became the first black to win an Olympic gold medal. He was to die of typhoid fever before the year was out.

Relay events as we know them today were contested for the first time at Stockholm in 1912. An American quartet ran 42.2 in a semi-final of the 4x100 m., only to be disqualified for passing the baton out of zone. Britain won the final in 42.4 with David Jacobs, Harold Macintosh, Victor d'Arcy and William Applegarth. Here too there was an "accident": Germany finished second but was disqualified for passing out of zone.

German officials later disputed the verdict on the

The 10,000 m. walk at the 1912 Olympics in Stockholm. An eagle-eyed judge is about to disqualify Norman (South Africa), first from right. Goulding (Canada), centre, will go on to win.

strength of a picture published in "Aftonbladet", which seemed to prove the "innocence" of their runners. But their plea was rejected.

It should be noted that the German quartet had earlier won their semi-final in 42.3, incidentally the first mark to be ratified as a world record by the IAAF.

The Americans took partial revenge by winning the 4x400 m. relay in world record time, 3:16.6, with Melvin Sheppard, Edward Lindberg, "Ted" Meredith and Charles Reidpath.

The 29-year-old Sheppard crowned a splendid career with his fourth Olympic gold medal.

At the Antwerp Olympics (1920) the American short relay team consisted of such fine sprinters as Charles Paddock, Jackson Scholz, Loren Murchison and Morris Kirksey. They went home the winners in 42 1/5, a new world record.

In the 4x400 m. "traffic accidents" turned out to be the rule: in the preliminary round, collisions affecting USA, Sweden, France and South Africa took much off the glamour of the final, which was won by a British team in 3:22 1/5.

1901
1920

WALKS:
A turbulent overture

Walking events first appeared in the Olympic programme at the "Interim" Games of 1906 in Athens.
It was a debut characterized by strong differences of opinion on the relative fairness of walking styles.
There were two events, 1500 and 3000 m., held on consecutive days. The former, obviously too short, hence risky as a test of fair walking, gave rise to bitter controversy when the first two finishers, Richard Wilkinson of Britain and Eugen Spiegler of Austria, were disqualified, and the third, George Bonhag of USA, barely escaped a similar verdict: two judges out of four ruled his form illegal, but Prince George of Greece, president of the jury, cast his decisive vote in Bonhag's favour.
The 24-year-old American was actually a middle distance runner, but he had done much worse than expected in his events, so he turned to the short walk, an entirely new test for him, for partial consolation.
The 3000 m. event was won by György Sztantics of Hungary. Here again, Wilkinson and Spiegler had finished first and second in that order, just to be disqualified exactly as in the 1500 m. the day before!
At the London Olympics (1908) Britain had a remarkable double winner in 33-year-old George Larner, a Brighton policeman who beat everybody in both 3500 m. and 10 miles. Here at last we had an Olympian of bright fame, credited with record performances at various distances.
There was only one walking test at the Stockholm Olympics (1912), over 10,000 m. Severe, eagle-eyed judges allowed only four competitors to finish unscathed. James Goulding of Canada won in 46:28.4 from Ernest Webb of Britain and 19-year-old Fernando Altimani of Italy, who thereby inaugurated a national tradition which has been honoured ever since.
This youngster had taken to race walking in his free hours at the end of his day's work in a printing house.
At Milan in 1913 he covered 11,403 m. in one hour, after clocking 44:34 2/5 for 10,000 m. enroute, but his performances were not ratified as world records because of insufficient registered timers.
A wound suffered in World War I prevented him from taking part in the Antwerp Olympics (1920). By then, however, Italy had a new emerging force in Ugo Frigerio (born at Milan on 16 September 1901). He too a printer (at "La Gazzetta dello Sport", Italy's sports daily), Frigerio made a sensational Olympic debut as a junior at Antwerp, winning the 10,000 m. in 48:06 1/5 and the 3000 m. in 13:14 1/5. In race walking, more perhaps than in most other athletic events, honours won in major international competition easily outweigh record performances made in "solo" efforts.
Even so, I wish to mention the best-on-record performance for the 20,000 m. at the end of 1920: 1:39:22.0 by Niels Pedersen of Denmark at Copenhagen in 1918.

1921 1940

THE EARLIEST "MYTHS": PAAVO NURMI AND JESSE OWENS

SPRINTS:
The incomparable J.C.Owens

As a "speed merchant" Charles Paddock had his greatest year in 1921. Thriving in the balmy weather of California, he rewrote the record book for the sprint distances. He began on 26 March at Berkeley with a record-tying 9 3/5 and a record-smashing 20 4/5 (straight course) over the English distances; then he continued on 23 April at Redlands with three more records: 10 2/5 (100 m.), 30 1/5 (300 y.) and 33 1/5 (300 m.). On 18 June two record attempts were organized for him at Pasadena by the Southern Pacific AAU. Official timers were stationed at intermediate distances too, and Paddock was credited with the following times:
 - 1st race: 8 4/5 (90 y.), 9 3/5 (100 y.), 10 1/5 (110 y.); 2nd race: 12 2/5 (130 y.), 14 1/5 (150 y.), 19.0 (200 y).

The shorter race was, of course, the big event. Under AAU rules of the time, records could only be accepted for the full distance at which a race was run. For that reason, Paddock's 10 1/5 for 110 y. (=100.58 m.) could not be accepted as an American 100 m. record! Apart from the absurdity of such a rule, it seems fair to say that the times given for Paddock in that race leave room for doubt. Of course one must not forget that timing to the fifth of a second implies a great deal of approximation. If the timing had been to the tenth of a second, those intervals would surely have looked different. In later years Paddock returned to top form on two or three occasions, e.g. at West Orange, NJ, in 1924, when he annexed the AAU titles with 9 3/5 and 20 4/5; and particularly at Los Angeles on 15 May 1926, when in a very close duel with Charles Borah he ran the century in 9.5, a time which was ratified by the IAAF as 9 3/5. Paddock competed in two more editions of the Olympic Games. He was fifth in the 100 m. and second in the 200 m. at Paris (1924), and was a semi-finalist in the 200 m. at Amsterdam (1928). He won five AAU titles in outdoor competition. He was the type of colourful and controversial athletic figure who makes good copy, and newsmen were lavish in commenting on his achievements as well as his personal tricks. He later appeared in several films, including one aptly entitled "Nine and three-fifths seconds". He died in an air crash over Alaska in 1943, while serving as a captain in the Marines. A US ship was named after him. Paddock's most serious rival was his countryman Jackson Scholz, who scored a great trick - to make sprint finals in three successive Olympic Games. After a fourth place in the 100 m. at Antwerp, he continued with a second place in the 100 m. and a win in the 200 m. (21 3/5) in Paris, and closed with a fourth place in the 200 m. at Amsterdam. He had mixed fortunes in his duels with Paddock. Clockwise he was credited with an official 20.9 for 200 m. in 1924 and had an unaccepted 9.5 for 100 y. the following year. At the Paris Olympics, however, both Americans were upset by Harold Abrahams of Britain (born at Bedford on 15 December 1899), who only a few weeks earlier had run the 100 y. in 9 3/5, a time not ratified by

A rudimentary Olympic Village at the 1924 Games in Paris. The first full-fledged one will appear at Los Angeles in 1932.

the AAA due to a slight declivity of the track in the running direction. Abrahams became the first European to win an Olympic 100 m. crown. He hit the right form at the right time, running the distance in 10 3/5 three times - quarter-final, semi-final and final. In the decisive race he won from Scholz and Arthur Porritt of New Zealand, like Abrahams an Achilles Club man. Shortly after his death in 1978, Abrahams was featured (by actor Ben Cross) as one of the leading characters in the Oscar winning film "Chariots of Fire" (1981). An interesting entry among record performers from the early Twenties was Cyril Coaffee of Canada, who chalked up a record-tying 9 3/5 for 100 y. in the 1922 Canadian Championships, held at Calgary (altitude, 1048 m.). This was the first record performance presumably influenced by reduced air pressure. German sprinters had to bypass the Olympics twice (1920 and 1924). That was a serious blow for a country which probably ranked second only to USA as a sprinting power. Hubert Houben was a prominent figure for several years. Although none of his many clockings in the range 10.3/10.5 for 100 m. was accepted as a German record, he scored important victories against leading foreign sprinters, e.g. over Paddock and his countryman Loren Murchison at Berlin in 1924, and in the AAA Championships (220 y.) in 1927. His successor as Germany's sprint king was Helmut Körnig, a temperamental but brilliant performer. In the 1926 German Championships at Leipzig he won the 100 m. in 10.3, which was ratified as a national record as 10 2/5, even though it was aided by a wind of about 4 metres per second. Of course there was no international wind rule at the time. In USA, however, there was a maximum allowance of 5 miles per hour (2.2 m/s) for the ratification of marks made on straight courses. The man who first managed to break the Paddock monopoly in the record book was a slim Nebraskan, Roland Locke. Usually at his best in the furlong, he had his peak year in 1926, when he did 20.5, then 20.7 twice, and 20.9 in the 220 y. In his fastest race (the time was ratified by the IAAF as 20 3/5) he ran the first 96 y. around a turn and the remaining 124 y. on the straight. Another prominent sprinter in the mid-Twenties was William DeHart Hubbard, then holder of the world's long jump record, who was credited with an official 9 3/5 for 100 y. in 1926.

A few weeks before the Amsterdam Olympics, America found a new star sprinter in Frank Wykoff (born at Des Moines, Iowa, on 29 October 1909; 1.75 m./ 66 kg.). He made the nation's headlines as a schoolboy in 1928, when he beat the declining Paddock and other good sprinters with eye-catching "metric" times of 10 3/5 and 20 4/5. In the Olympic arena, however, Wykoff was unrecognizable. Somebody suggested that he probably lost his form on the long boat trip. Lack of experience and strong competition probably explain his failure more plausibly. In the 100 m. he had to be content with fourth place in a race won by Percy Williams of Canada in 10 4/5. Although depicted in European papers as an outsider, Williams could point to a nice 10 3/5, achieved at the Canadian Trials. Jack London, a powerful man representing Great Britain, was second, and Georg Lammers of Germany was third. Williams (born at Vancouver, B.C., on 19 May 1908; 1.78m./ 58 kg.) made the surprise even greater by annexing the 200 m. crown in 21 4/5. Runner-up was Walter Rangeley of Britain, who left behind such men as Körnig and Scholz. The preliminaries and the "dead" track had taken a lot out of the runners. In fact, the fastest times were recorded in the early rounds: 10 3/5 by Williams, Robert McAllister (USA) and London in the 100 m.; 21 3/5 by Körnig in the 200 m. Williams was coached by Bob Granger, who on a cold day before a race would rub Percy's body with coconut butter and dress him in three or four track suits and sweaters to prevent loss of valuable body heat.

Körnig found partial consolation in post-Olympic meets. On 19 August at Grunewald Stadion in Berlin (600 m. track) he sped over a 200 m. course with only a slight turn in 20.9, beating Henry Russell of USA (21.1), Jakob Schüller and Houben of Germany, and Locke of USA. It was stated in an account of the race that "the wind began to blow as soon as the race was over". An electric timer, the Löbner apparatus, caught Körnig in 20.82. A week later at Bochum, the German ran the same distance in 21.0 on a course with a near complete turn, with Houben, Schüller (both 21.1) and Locke following in that order.

In the years between Amsterdam and Los Angeles the dominant figures of the sprints were Wykoff, George Simpson and Eddie Tolan in USA, Williams in Canada, Körnig in Germany and Daniel Joubert in South Africa. One by one all Paddock's world records were removed from the tables, while standards went up in practically every corner of the globe. Tolan (born at Denver on 29 September 1908; 1.70 m. / 65 kg.), a compact sprinter who used to run with spectacles taped to his temples, was the first stet to be officially credited with 9.5 for the 100 y. This was at Evanston, Illinois, on 25 May 1929, when Tolan won by a scant margin from his arch rival, George Simpson (born at Columbus, Ohio, on 21 September 1908; 1.80 m./ 75 kg.). The latter evened the count on the same occasion, beating Tolan in the 220 y. with a classy 20.6. Simpson, tall and slender, had a very long stride and a uniform running action, while Tolan, a natural talent refined in years of assiduous coaching, had extra speedy leg work. The year 1929 was especially memorable for the introduction of a new device in major championship competitions: starting-blocks. These turned out to be an obvious advantage compared to man-made starting-holes. The invention was perfected by two knowledgeable students of athletics, George Bresnahan and William Tuttle, in 1927.

1921
1940

Carlton, a mystical aftermath

One of the most peculiar episodes in the history of sprinting concerns Aussie star James Andrew Carlton (born at Lismore, NSW, on 10 February 1908). He first revealed his talent by running the English distances in 10.0 and 21.8 as a junior in 1927. The following year he was good enough to reach the quarter-finals at the Amsterdam Olympics in both 100 and 200 m. By 1930 he was capable of 9.6 in the 100 y. and 21.3 in the 220 y. around a turn. His next (and last) clash with a top class international sprinter occurred in New Zealand in 1931, when he beat the famous George Simpson of USA on two occasions. Before the year was out, Carlton was credited with a wind-assisted 9.4 in the 100 y. and with 21.0 in the 220 y.
What happened at the Sydney Cricket Ground on 18 January 1932 is still a matter of controversy among Australian oldtimers.
The 220 y. was run around a full turn of the oval track. Carlton, in lane 2, soon pulled away from the rest and won with eight yards to spare on Ewan Davidson, a sprinter of national class.
Timers caught Carlton in a surprising 20.6, easily and by far the fastest time ever recorded on a full-turn course. No wind gauge was available, and so referee Laurie Drake used a piece of wool to test the "feelings" of the air - and finally decided to rule the effort wind-assisted. In doing so, he sparked an Australia-wide furore, since many eye-witnesses disputed his verdict. The argument subsided somewhat five days later, when it was announced that Carlton "had run his last race". On that very day, the fastest man from Down Under entered a training centre for Sacred Heart Missionaries, a Catholic seminary. As Father Carlton he was ordained in 1939 and for a further six years he remained out of the public eye - only to re-emerge in 1945, when he left the priesthood to marry. This great sprinter - in the words of an Aussie commentator, "almost too fast for his own good" - thus remained a virtual unknown to the outside world. He died at the age of 43 in 1951. In the opinion of former Australian sprint star "Slip" Carr, he "set standards of achievement and conduct that came as close as possible to the ideal".

Harold Abrahams (GB) no.419, winning the 100 metres at the 1924 Olympics in Paris. Time, 10.6. Others from left to right are: A. Porritt (N.Z.), 3rd; C. Bowman (USA), 4th; L. Murchison (USA) 6th; J. Scholz (USA) 2nd; C. Paddock (USA) 5th.

From experiments conducted on a large scale, they came to the conclusion that the normal gain derived by a sprinter in a 100 y. race could be valued at an average of 34 thousandths of a second, i.e. about one foot (30 cm.) in actual running distance. Equally if not more important is the psychological advantage of having a firm foothold for a fast getaway. In the 1929 NCAA Championships at Chicago the new device apparently paid dividends: Simpson beat Tolan in the 100 y. final in 9.4. Starting-blocks being still illegal at the time, the mark could only be accepted as an NCAA record. Tolan came to Europe in the summer of 1929 and made a big impression wherever he ran. He equalled Paddock's 100 m. record (10.4) several times and was beaten only once, in a tight finish by Georg Lammers of Germany, the Amsterdam bronze medallist. Wykoff gradually made amends for his poor show at Amsterdam. He had his greatest year in 1930. On 10 May at Los Angeles he became history's first official 9.4 man for the 100 y., using normal starting-holes. A month later he duplicated his record time in the NCAA race, beating Simpson and Tolan among others.

Wykoff did not like the furlong, although he was once timed in 20.5 over a 218 y. straight course in 1931. Williams confirmed his class on several occasions. In 1929 he beat Tolan by inches in a 100 y. race (9.6). On 1 July 1930 at Vancouver he was beaten by Tolan and Simpson in the 100 m. The winner's time, 10.2, never gained approval. On 9 August of the same year Williams ran a legitimate 10.3 in the Canadian Championships at Toronto, thus removing Paddock's world record.

The Canadian also won the 100 y. title at the inaugural British Empire and Commonwealth Games held at Hamilton, Ontario, in 1930. Then he gradually lost form and was past his peak by the time of the Los Angeles Olympics (1932).

Daniel Joubert is still regarded as one of the greatest sprinters ever produced by South Africa. In the Inter-Varsity Championships at Grahamstown in 1931 he amazed Springbok experts with two sterling 100 y. performances: a wind-assisted 9.3 (heat) and a legitimate 9.4 (final), and with 21.3 for 220 y. around a turn. Strangely enough, his century mark was only submitted to the IAAF fifteen years later and it was ratified shortly before the first official 9.3 was run! In Europe, the fastest times continued to be returned by Germans. During a tournée in the Far East in 1929, Eugen Eldracher ran a wind-assisted 10.3 for the 100 m. at Keijo (Seoul). In view of the Los Angeles Games attention began to be centred on a rising star, Arthur Jonath (born at Bentrop on 9 September 1909; 1.79 m./ 73 kg.), who on 5 June 1932 at Bochum became the first European to clock an official 10.3 for the metric century.

In 1932 the American pre-Olympic season was dominated by a rising star, Ralph Metcalfe (born at Atlanta, Georgia, on 29 May 1910; 1.80m./ 83 kg.). This magnificent athlete first attained national prominence as a High School boy in 1928. Three years later, while a freshman at Marquette University, he was fifth in the 100 y. and second to Tolan in the 220 y. at the AAU Championships. In May 1932 he started in high gear with a wind-assisted 20.4 for 220 y. straightaway. At the NCAA Championships, held at Chicago on 11 June, he scored a great double with 10.2 in the 100 m. and 20.5 in the 220 y. straight, and intermediate times of 9.5 (100 y.) and 20.3 (200 m.). Like several other records made in NCAA competitions, Metcalfe's marks were ratified by the collegiate body, but for some unexplained reason never

1921
1940

gained AAU (nor, for that matter, IAAF) approval. At the US Final Olympic Tryouts in Palo Alto, Metcalfe beat Tolan in both the 100 and 200 m. Third in both races was George Simpson, while Frank Wykoff, just recovering from an early-season injury, only qualified for the relay team.

In the Olympic arena, Metcalfe appeared to be slightly past his peak for the season, while Tolan was visibly gathering momentum. In the second round of the 100 m., Tolan set a new Olympic record of 10.4. The first semi-final saw the elimination of the defending champion, Williams of Canada. The final on 1 August put together, from the second to the seventh lane, Takayoshi Yoshioka of Japan, the Asian record holder (10.5), Joubert of South Africa, Metcalfe, Simpson, Jonath of Germany and Tolan. Little Yoshioka, who used to run with a handkerchief round his head, lived up to his reputation as a superlative starter and led the field in the early part of the race, only to be overtaken near the halfway mark, when first Tolan, then Metcalfe, decisively shot ahead. The two Americans went through the tape virtually even. As revealed later by the photo-finish apparatus, Tolan crossed the finish line with his torso an inch (2.5 cm.) or so ahead of Metcalfe, who used a body lean.

Under the rule then in force Tolan was rightly declared the winner. Under the present rule (which states that "the competitors shall be placed in the order in which any part of their bodies, i.e. torso, reaches the nearer edge of the finish line"), Metcalfe would have probably earned a dead-heat. The Kirby Photo-electric Camera actually gave the same time, 10.38, for both runners. Hand timers credited the two men with a record-equalling 10.3. Jonath was third in 10.4 (electric time, 10.54) just ahead of Simpson, while Joubert and Yoshioka closed up the rear.

In the 200 m., Tolan more than confirmed his superb condition and won easily in 21.2 (electric time 21.12), while Simpson (21.4) and Metcalfe (21.5) shunted Jonath to fourth place. Later, news filtered through to the effect that Metcalfe had been given a handicap of about a metre because of an error in the measurement of his lane. To his credit it must be said that he refused to ask for a re-run, since he did not wish to jeopardize Uncle Sam's clean sweep.

But Metcalfe's best work still lay ahead. He closed the Olympic year with a sizzling 19.8 for 220 y. straight in a handicap race at Toronto, an effort which was apparently nullified by a wind of unspecified velocity. In 1933-34 Metcalfe proved to be the World's Fastest Human in no uncertain way. During that period he had only one possible "scare", namely in the 100 m. of the 1934 AAU when he had to come from behind to nip one Jesse Owens at the tape (time for both, 10.4).In 1933 Metcalfe came to Europe and made men like Berger of Holland and Borchmeyer and Jonath of Germany look like "pikers". In 1934 he visited Japan and treated Yoshioka in a like manner. Clockwise he had one of his greatest days on 17 June 1933 in the NCAA Championships at Chicago, when he ran the English distances in 9.4 and 20.4. Once again his times were not ratified by the AAU. During his tournées abroad he ran the 100 m. in 10.3 several times and at Budapest on 12 August 1933 he sped over a 200 m. course with a partial turn in 20.6 (handicap race), which time was accepted as a world record. In 1934 he did 20.2 for the same distance but on straight courses, first at Tokyo, then at Dairen, with a wind at his back on both occasions. Metcalfe is recalled as one of the fastest finishers in the annals of sprinting. He was somewhat slow in rounding into top gear,

Percy Williams (Canada), arms flung wide, winning the 100 metres at the 1928 Olympics in Amsterdam. Time, 10.8. Others from left to right are: F. Wykoff (USA), 4th; R. McAllister (USA), 6th; J. London (GB), 2nd; G. Lammers (Germany), 3rd; W. Legg (S.A.), 5th.

apparently due to his faulty form in the early stages. But once he got into his real 8 ft. 6 in. (2.59 m.) stride he was well-nigh invincible. Metcalfe was still in his prime when two other "Greats" appeared on the American scene. Both came from the Deep South. One was Eulace Peacock (born at Dothan, Alabama, on 27 August 1914; 1.82 m./ 82 kg.), a heavily muscled man who in 1934-35 competed with great success in European meets, recording two legitimate 10.3 marks for the metric century, and losing only two races. The other rising star was J.C.Owens (born at Oakville, Alabama, on 12 September 1913; 1.78 m./ 71 kg.), possibly less impressive than Metcalfe and Peacock in sheer muscular power, but built on well-proportioned, statuesque lines. Owens combined the agility and strength of a panther. Known as Jesse since his schoolboy days, he reached athletic greatness in the Middle West, after his family left the Deep South to settle down in Cleveland. In 1932, while a student at the East Technical High School, he ran 100 m. in 10.3, with the aid of a wind. Subsequent pre-Olympic tests proved that he was not yet ripe for championship races. In his own admission, " I tightened up under the pressure of competition against older, more mature athletes". Then maybe his interest in those days lay elsewhere. In July he married his longtime girl friend Ruth Solomon. Both were minors at the time, and so they had to elope to Erie, Pennsylvania (a state with more lax marriage requirements) to be declared husband and wife by a Justice of the Peace. Early in August, Jesse and Ruth had their first child, a girl. Father celebrated with two wins and a second place in a post-Olympic meet in Cleveland, notably running 100 y. around a turn in 9.6! In 1933, his last year at East Technical High School, Owens had his real breakthrough. In the Interscholastic Championships at Chicago, on 17 June, he ran the sprints in 9.4 and 20.7, and long jumped 7.56. His time for the century was unmatched as an American interscholastic record until 1954. Years later, he was asked about the difference, if any, between his 9.4 in High School competition and his 9.4's of later years in college. He replied: "About six yards" (5.48 m.). This was probably underestimating his ability as a youth, yet the anecdote serves to convey the useful idea that times of seemingly equal face value, made in different grades of competition, can often differ strongly in intrinsic value. In 1934, while a freshman at Ohio State University, Owens had a limited athletic activity, yet he closed the season on a high note by coming second to Metcalfe in the AAU 100 m. He really began to make history in 1935. Incidentally, it was chiefly thanks to his High School coach Frank Riley (who had helped him "on and off the track" for years) that Jesse made it to Ohio State. Once there, he came under the tutelage of Larry Snyder, one of America's best known coaches. The results of Snyder's refining work became apparent in the spring of 1935. Competing in three or four events virtually every weekend, Jesse chalked up times of 9.5 and 9.4 in the 100 y. as well as 20.9 and 20.7 in the furlong. His Day of Days fell on 25 May at Ferry Field, Ann Arbor, Michigan, at the Western Conference ("Big Ten") Championships. A few days earlier, while indulging in the innocent game of touch football with some of his teammates, Owens had sustained a back injury. On the eve of the big meet he and his coach were uncertain whether he would be able to contribute an all-out effort for the benefit of his Ohio State team ("The Buckeyes"). They finally decided that he would try the first event, and then see .... He started at 2.45 p.m., running the 100 y. in a record-equalling time, 9.4, after which he felt much better. In the 75 minutes that followed, he gathered three more world records: 8.13 in the long jump, 20.3 in the 220 y. and 22.6 in the 220 y. hurdles, the last two being on a straight course. He was up against good competition: Robert Grieve was second in the century in 9.5, and Andrew Dooley trailed him in the furlong in 20.7. Even so, he was never seriously challenged. Under a new IAAF rule, his furlong marks were also acceptable as world records for the slightly shorter metric distance, so he did in fact break five world records and equalled another. On that occasion Owens started from holes, since he did not have the benefit of starting-blocks. J.Kenneth Doherty, a former decathlon ace and now

Eddie Tolan (USA), nearest camera, winning the 100 metres by a hair's breadth from Ralph Metcalfe (USA) at the 1932 Olympics in Los Angeles. Both were given the same time, 10.3. Others from left to right are: T. Yoshioka (Japan), 6th; D. Joubert (S.A.) 5th; G. Simpson (USA) 4th; A. Jonath (Germany) 3rd.

1921 1940

one of America's most famous track scholars, was among the lucky spectators (about 10,000) at Ferry Field. He acted as Meet Director. In his book "Modern Track and Field" he gives enlightening details on timing conditions: ".... large dialed tenth-second watches were used, with hands that move in tiny segments and therefore stop between as well as on the tenth-second markers. The hands of all three official watches (in the 100 y. final) were actually closer to 9.3 than to 9.4, but of course the slower time had to be recorded officially. Further, the starter for the race was W.J.Monilaw, who was insistent in his starting that the "set" should be held at least two seconds so that the chances of a "flyer" would be minimized". There was no international wind rule at the time, yet Owens' efforts were measured also along that line. Readings were as follows: +1.55 m/s in the 100 y.; +0.83 m/s in the 220 y.; and +0.46 m/s in the 220 y. hurdles, i.e. all within the maximum wind assistance (+2.0 m/s) allowed under present rules. In June Owens continued to sweep the board in college meets and won the esteem of West Coast fans with four wins at the NCAA Championships in Berkeley. This hard schedule caused him to lose part of his springtime sparkle, and defeat finally came to him - in the biggest test of the season, the AAU Championships. On 4 July, Independence Day, 15,000 spectators gathered at the University of Nebraska Memorial Stadium in Lincoln to see what was possibly the greatest trio of sprinters ever assembled in a 100 m. race: Jesse Owens, the newly crowned recordman, Ralph Metcalfe, the defending champion, and Eulace Peacock, a redoubtable challenger. The latter showed what he could do by beating Owens in a sizzling 10.2 heat. The record time was nullified by an assisting wind of 2.3 m/s. In the final the only white man who, according to the experts, seemed to have the ghost of a chance against the formidable black trio was George Anderson. A few weeks earlier, in California, he had run what could be described as the fastest 9.5 in the history of the 100 y. Incredible as it may sound, no less than seven timers out of eight caught Anderson in .... 9.2, and only one in 9.5. Although this one admitted that his visual attention had been diverted by the flash of a photographer, the 9.5 version was accepted as official! In the Lincoln final, Anderson managed to stay the course in the early going, after which he had to give way to his great rivals. Peacock pulled away near the 50 m. point. Once again, Metcalfe came up with his devastating finish, passed Owens but fell 60 cm. short of Peacock at the tape. The winner's time was again 10.2, but a following wind of 3.5 m/s nullified it for record purposes. Metcalfe and Owens finished in that order with estimated times of 10.3 and 10.4 respectively. In the same meet Peacock also beat Owens in the long jump, while Metcalfe won the 200 m. from lesser opponents. Peacock defeated Owens in two more races before the end of the season, and thus closed his 1935 outdoor account having won three out of five sprint clashes with the Ohio State flash.

In the years between Los Angeles and Berlin, the leading European sprinters were Christiaan Berger of Holland, Erich Borchmeyer of Germany, Paul Hänni of Switzerland, and József Sir of Hungary. Berger had his best season in 1934, when he beat Peacock in the 100 m. at Amsterdam (10.5 to 10.6), equalled Jonath's continental record (10.3) and finally won both sprints at the first European Championships in Turin (10.6 and 21.5). Borchmeyer, the heavy type of sprinter, ran 10.3 on several occasions (but never got IAAF recognition) and was second to Berger in the 100 m. at Turin. Hänni traded wins with Peacock at Basel in 1935 with times of 10.4 and 21.2. Sir scored a double in the Seventh World Student Games at Budapest in 1935.

In 1936 Owens made no mistakes. Although not visibly faster than the year before, he appeared to have gained in staying power. Still alternating his sprint labours with hurdling and long jumping chores, he went through the exacting season practically unscathed. He tried the furlong around a turn and by the end of May was down to 21.1. He also had a 20.5 for the 220 y. straightaway, a wind-aided 9.3 and a legal 9.4 for the 100 y. On the first day (19 June) of the NCAA Championships in Chicago, he clocked 11.2 over a course which on remeasurement was found to be 10 m. in excess of the supposed 100 m. ! The following day, under perfect conditions (aiding wind, 1.2 m/s) he won the final in 10.2, after being officially timed in 9.4 at the 100 y. mark. In doing so, he whipped a fine field of sprinters: 2.Foy Draper 10.3, 3.Sam Stoller 10.3, 4.Adrian Talley 10.4, 5.Harvey Wallender 10.4, 6.George Boone 10.4, 7.Donald Dunn 10.5, 8.Perrin Walker 10.5, 9.Morris Pollock 10.6. However, upon remeasurement the course was found to be 99.985 m. ! (In 1938, after considering all the factors involved, the IAAF decided to ratify Owens' mark as a world record). At the AAU Championships, held in early July at Princeton, N.J., Owens won the 100 m. in 10.4 and left the way free for Metcalfe in the 200 m. A week later, in the US Final Olympic Tryouts in New York, Owens won the 100 m. on the first day, again in 10.4, with Metcalfe second and Frank Wykoff third in a brilliant comeback. Peacock, still nursing an early-season injury, had been eliminated

Jesse Owens winning the 200 metres at the 1936 Olympics in Berlin. Time 20.7. Right behind him is Mack Robinson (USA), 21.1, who passed away early in 2000. Only other visible finalist is L.Orr (Canada), 5th.

in the first round. The next day Owens won the 200 m. around a turn in 21.0 from Mack Robinson and Robert Packard, while the usually dependable Metcalfe ran one of the poorest races of his career and finished fourth.

Owens' legendary "Week of Weeks" at the Berlin Olympics is best related by a chronological list of his achievements:

- 2 August: 11.29 a.m., 100 m. heat, 1st in 10.3 (wind +1.7 m/s); 3.04 p.m., 100 m. quarter-final, 1st in 10.2 (+2.3m/s).
- 3 August: 3.30 p.m., 100 m. semi-final, 1st in 10.4 (+2.7 m/s); 5 p.m., 100 m. final, 1st in 10.3 (+2.7 m/s).
- 4 August: 10.30 a.m., long jump, qualifying round: achieved the qualifying distance, 7.15, on his third and last try; 10.45 a.m., 200 m. heat, 1st in 21.1 (adverse wind); 3.44 p.m., 200 m. quarter-final, 1st in 21.1 (aiding wind); 4.30 p.m., long jump, final, 1st with 8.06 (aiding wind).
- 5 August: 3.05 p.m., 200 m. semi-final, 1st in 21.3 (aiding wind); 6 p.m., 200 m. final, 1st in 20.7 (allowable wind assistance).
- 8 August: 3 p.m., 4x100 m. relay heat, time 40.0 (tying world record), first leg.
- 9 August: 3.15 p.m., 4x100 m. relay final, time 39.8 (world record), first leg.

In all the above-mentioned events, Owens invariably emerged as the undisputed winner. He collected four gold medals without ever being challenged seriously, save perhaps in the long jump, as will be related later on. In the 100 m. Metcalfe had a poor getaway and a strong finish and wound up second (10.4), ahead of twenty-year-old Martinus Osendarp of Holland (10.5), who nosed out veteran Wykoff in the battle for bronze. In the 200 m., which was run in a drizzle, Owens appeared to be trying hard near the end, yet he won from Mack Robinson (21.1) and Osendarp (21.3) by a wide margin. Quite understandably, Owens did not take the post-Olympic meets too seriously. On 10 August at Cologne he was second to Metcalfe in a 100m. race, the story of which can in no way detract from Jesse's fame. With only 20 m. to go, Owens was leading Metcalfe by almost 2 m.,then he suddenly decided to ease up in order to give way to his rival and friend Metcalfe. The latter went on to win in 10.3. On hearing the winner's time, Owens (second in 10.4) probably realized that he had thrown away the chance of his lifetime!But then that was not the only day on which he appeared to have no undue affection for records. Even today some oldtimers maintain that he could have done better in this or that event if he had shown a greater singleness of purpose. This is of course idle speculation.

Owens was attracted toward professional activities soon after the Berlin Olympics. His last appearance as an amateur was at White City Stadium, London, on 15 August 1936, when he ran the third leg in a 4x100 y. relay which was won by the US national team over a Commonwealth foursome in 37.4. Metcalfe closed his long career at the same time, after his second European campaign. He had the rare distinction of twice finishing second in an Olympic 100 m. final. Even more remarkable perhaps was his record in AAU competition: between 1932 and 1936 he won eight titles (three in the 100 m., five in the 200 m.). Peacock continued for many more years. He never regained his 1935 form but he distinguished himself as a fine all-rounder in pentathlon competition.

Martinus Osendarp of Holland (born at Delft on 21 May 1916) was Europe's Fastest Human for several years. He would suffer an occasional defeat now and then, e.g. to Lennart Strandberg of Sweden over 100 m. in a post-Olympic meet at Malmö in 1936 (10.6 to 10.3), but on the whole he was a most dependable performer.In 1938 he scored a double at the European Championships in Paris (10.5 and 21.2). Possibly the only man who could have challenged him if he had been present on that occasion was Cyril Holmes of Britain, who earlier in the year had scored a similar double over the English distances (9.7 and 21.2) at the British Empire and Commonwealth Games in Sydney. A solid sprinter with no weak points, Osendarp never did better than 10.4 or 21.1 officially (although he once did 10.3 with a following wind), but his competitive ability stamped him as possibly the greatest European sprinter up to that time. Other fine speedsters of the late Thirties were Orazio Mariani of Italy, Jakob Scheuring and Karl Neckermann of Germany. Even after the departure of Owens and Metcalfe, good sprinters continued to be a dime a dozen on the American market. At the 1939 AAU Championships in Lincoln, Nebraska, a classy 100 m. final was assembled. After a furious battle, Clyde Jeffrey emerged the winner in a wind-aided 10.2. Among the place winners were Ben Johnson, a man with a Blitz start - at the 1938 Millrose Games in New York he ran the 60 y. in 6 seconds flat, a time the AAU refused to ratify; and tall, long striding Perrin Walker, a poor starter with an excellent pick-up. Both competed with great success even in Europe. Jeffrey equalled Owens' 100 y. record (9.4) in 1940, but like other champions of the time he was deprived of his Olympic chance by World War II.

400 METRES - Memorable Duels: Carr vs Eastman, Harbig vs Lanzi

We have already mentioned the fact that "Ted" Meredith and many of his contemporaries considered the "quarter" as being more closely related to the "half" than to the sprints. Among those who, by way of practice rather than theory, took exception to that habit of mind was Eric Liddell of Britain. This great Scotsman was for many years the holder of the British 100 y. record with 9.7. He thus possessed speed to an extent probably unknown to most quarter-milers of his time. Although not a copybook stylist, he was able to generate tremendous power, which some observers liked to consider as an emanation of his well-known spiritual fervour. In view of the 1924 Olympics in Paris he decided to forget about the 100 m. and concentrated on 200 and 400 m. His fastest "quarter" prior to the Games was 49 3/5, not very impressive in the eyes of international observers. The Colombes track then measured 500 m., so the runners had to negotiate only one turn. In the preliminaries, Joseph Imbach of Switzerland, a 10.6 100 m. man, lowered the Olympic record to 48.0. The semifinals were won by Horatio Fitch of USA (47 4/5) and Liddell (48 1/5). In the decisive race, the following day, Liddell drew the outside lane and went out extremely fast. He astounded watch-holding onlookers by passing the half-way mark in 22 1/5. In the second half, although visibly suffering, he stood up to the challenge of his main pursuer, Horatio Fitch of USA, and won by a comfortable margin in 47 3/5. Close behind Fitch (48 2/5), in third place, was Guy Butler (48 3/5), another Briton with a pronounced sprinting ability.

Liddell was born at Tientsin, China, on 16 January 1902 as the second child of evangelistic parents. After his Paris triumph he had another track season (1925) during which he lowered his best for the "quarter" to 49 1/5. A few days after that he went back to his native country as a missionary. While in the Far East he occasionally returned to his athletic

1921
1940

Birth of a name

More than half a century has elapsed since Jesse Owens' heyday, yet it would be difficult even today to find any other "name" more universally known in track and field sport. Still regarded by many as the perfect natural talent, if ever there was one, Owens has inspired generations of young athletes all over the world. Among those few who have endeavoured to delve into Owens the man, no one seems to have gone deeper than William J. Baker, a professor of history at the University of Maine and author of the book "Jesse Owens, an American Life". He reveals, among other things, that Jesse, thirteenth and last in a long line of children generated by Henry and Emma Owens (three of which died at birth), was actually christened James Cleveland. His was a poor family living in an atmosphere of racial bigotry. Their Baptist faith made them more similar to the chief character of H.B.Stowe's "Uncle Tom's Cabin" than to Black Power militants of the present century. Owens' future as regards his name was moulded the day he entered Bolton Elementary School. Here is how Baker tells the story: "In response to his teacher's asking him his name, he reportedly replied: J.C.Owens, in a thick Southern drawl. The teacher understood him to say Jesse and asked if that was correct. J.C. ma'am, he timidly mumbled. Once more she misunderstood and again asked him if he had said: Jesse. Eager to please, he gave up: Yes, ma'am, Jesse Owens". That is how Jesse for ever replaced James Cleveland in the eyes of the world.

79

love, e.g. in 1929, when he beat a famous German visitor, Otto Peltzer, in a 400 m. race at Tientsin, 49.1 to 49.3. Liddell died in a Japanese internment camp at Weihsien on 21 February 1945. Many years later he was featured - alongside his onetime rival for sprinting supremacy in Britain, Harold Abrahams - as one of the main characters in the Oscar winning film "Chariots of Fire" (1981). In this movie, actor Ian Charleston offers a delightful portrait of the onetime Scottish sport idol. But fiction obviously claims its rights, and some details do not coincide with reality. For example, Liddell learnt about the 1924 Olympic time schedule (with the 100 m. heats being on a Sunday) long before he embarked for France - not at the last moment as related in the film. Furthermore, the screen play shows Liddell while receiving a note from an American athlete shortly before the start of the Olympic 400 m. final. In reality, that note had been given to him early in the morning by a British masseur. Liddell opened it at the Stadium. The note carried a quotation from Samuel: "In the old book it says, He that honours me I will honour". By his own admission, Liddell was deeply touched and inspired by those words.

The other side of the medal

Incredible as it may sound, Jesse Owens, the most widely acclaimed athlete of the XX century, hung up his spikes a few weeks before turning 23. After his triumphs in Berlin and a parade in his honour in Cleveland, he soon discovered the ephemeral side of his glory. In the Thirties no champion could expect to derive more than medals and records from his athletic ability. Having a family to support, he decided to leave Ohio State University to concentrate on earning a decent living. He was soon absorbed in "pro" shows of various kinds, like running against a horse. Later on, as a businessman, he had ups and downs. Baker describes him as "a man of heart, who eventually became a polished speaker and promoter, even though he never managed to write fluently". In his old age, Owens was employed by the American Olympic Committee as a popular PR man, ever ready to voice age-old American beliefs such as: "In America, anyone can still become somebody... It happened to me, a kid who had come from the worst poverty to be thrown wildly to the top of the tallest mountain, and somehow had landed on his feet".

Progress in the one-lap circuit during the Twenties was generally slow, and times under 48 seconds were a rarity even in the States, although many races there were on courses with only one turn. The fastest 400 m. clocking of the decade was, however, a record-shattering 47.0, achieved at Palo Alto on 12 May 1928 by Emerson "Bud" Spencer, a 6-footer from Stanford University. Two weeks later, much to the surprise of West Coast fans, Spencer was beaten by Ray Barbuti, a stocky Easterner, in a 48.8 "quarter" at the ICAAAA Championships. Then Spencer failed badly at the US Olympic Trials and was selected only for the 4x400 m. relay. Barbuti continued his winning ways: at the Amsterdam Games he was the one and only American to win a track event. In a hectic finish he beat Jim Ball of Canada for the 400 m. crown, 47 4/5 to 48.0. In post-Olympic meets, Spencer beat 48 seconds fleetingly. The year 1931 marked the eve of a new era in quarter-miling. First Ben Eastman, then Victor Williams, both Californians, tied Meredith's fifteen-year-old world record (47 2/5). Eastman (born at Burlingame, California, on 9 July 1911; 1.85 m./ 70 kg.) was a blond, bespectacled student from Stanford University. He "exploded" in a dual meet on his home track at Palo Alto on 26 March 1932, when he clipped one full second off the world 440 y. mark with an amazing 46.4 performance. His coach, former Olympian "Dink" Templeton, was in hospital on that day, but he kept in touch with his pupil by long distance telephone. His pre-race instructions were peremptory: "Go right out from the gun and run just as fast as you can. Run easily, without effort, but run like hell". That is what "Blazing Ben" did. At the halfway mark he was timed in a hyper-fast 21.3, after which he survived, painfully but gallantly, for a 25.1 second half and a new world record. James Gordon finished a distant second in 47.8. Strangely enough, Eastman was considered the 440/880 type of runner, but in the Palo Alto race he obviously ignored his origin and ran like a full-blooded sprinter. He concluded his day's work with a scorching leg in the 4x440 y. relay: 45.9! To convince the incredulous, Eastman ran another fast "quarter" at Berkeley a few weeks later: 46.5. By then he was unanimously regarded as an odds-on favourite for the Olympic 400 m. title. However, a shocking surprise awaited him and his California admirers: on 2 July, at the ICAAAA Championships, exceptionally held in a West Coast town (Berkeley), he lost to a relatively little known Easterner, Bill Carr of Pennsylvania University, in a thrilling 440 y. race - 47.2 to 47.0. This was the first chapter of an East vs West feud that kept American fans agape for several weeks. It was also, if not primarily, a rivalry between two of America's most famous coaches, "Dink" Templeton of Stanford and Lawson Robertson of Penn. Carr (born at Pine Bluff, Arkansas, on 24 October 1909; 1.75m./ 70 kg.) was a dark-haired, compact man known in Eastern circles as an excellent relay runner, a better-than-average sprinter and a fair 7 m. long jumper. His fastest "quarter" prior to the Berkeley race was only 48.4 though. Eastman, who was more on the lanky side, had been spreading his talent on both the "quarter" and the "half", and had in fact become the world record holder for the longer distance (1:50.9) as well. The two great runners met again in the US Olympic Tryouts at Palo Alto on 16 July. Although competing in the lion's den, the irrepressible Carr came from behind (as he had done at Berkeley) to nip his opponent in the closing stage, this time over 400 m., 46.9 to 47.1. The third and final round was played at Los Angeles on 5 August, the prize at stake being nothing less than an Olympic crown. Two hours earlier, Carr had won his semi-final in 47.2, and Eastman took the other "semi" in 47.6. In the decisive race, Carr drew lane 4, while Eastman had a strategically favourable position in lane 2. It was a memorable ding-dong battle all the way. The intermediate times aptly tell the story of the race, which was run on a two-turn course (Eastman's 46.4 and 46.5 "quarters" early in the season were both made around a turn):

	100 m.	200 m.	300 m.	400 m.
Carr	10.9	22.1	33.8	46.2
Eastman	10.8	21.9	33.7	46.4

Carr was thus rewarded with a new "metric" record. He had shown better pace judgment than the man who was regarded as the middle-distance type of runner. Alex Wilson of Canada, he too an excellent 880 y. man, was third in 47.4. Much to the disgust of rabid track fans from coast to coast, the Carr vs Eastman epic lasted only one summer. The Olympic champion, by then known as "the fastest Car(r) in America", was seriously injured in a traffic accident early in 1933 and never ran again. Eastman concentrated chiefly, if not exclusively, on the half-mile for the rest of his career. In the meantime European one-lap specialists continued to lag behind their American counterparts. On this side of the Atlantic the event was always run in lanes, which probably made for less aggressive tactics. There were two important events in 1934: Godfrey Rampling of Britain won the Commonwealth 440 y. title in 48.0, and Adolf Metzner of Germany annexed the first European 400 m. crown in 47.9. Liddell's European

1921
1940

Eric Liddell (GB) stayed away from the 100 m. of the 1924 Olympics (to be started on a Sunday), but won the 400 m.

record for the metric distance (47 3/5) had been equalled twice, first by Hermann Engelhard of Germany in 1928, then by Raymond Boisset of France in 1934, both times on the site of Liddell's performance, i.e. at Stade de Colombes near Paris.
First black runner to join the top ranks since Binga Dismond's days was Archie Williams (born at Oakland, California, on 1 May 1915; 1.83 m./80 kg.). His quotation in 1935 was that of a promising 49 seconds youngster, no more. But in 1936 he really scaled the heights. In April he ran the 440 y. in 47.4, and in May he improved to 46.8. He really let himself go in a heat of the NCAA Championships at Chicago on 19 June when he clocked 46.5 around one turn, after being officially timed in a record-shattering 46.1 at the 400 m. post. On that occasion he ran the first "half" in 21.6. Second at the metric distance - the one officially included in the programme - was Harold Smallwood (46.4), a Californian who was to be a stand-in to movie actor Robert Taylor in the film "A Yank at Oxford" (1938), namely in a sequence in which the actor was to tear past a bunch of runners in a quarter-mile race at Oxford's Iffley Road track. A week after Williams' record run at Chicago (where he won the 400 m. final in 47.0), Jimmy LuValle ran 400 m. around two turns in 46.3. At the Olympic Tryouts in New York, Williams (46.6) won from Smallwood and LuValle. The US trio naturally came to Europe with visions of a clean sweep. Britain, however, was by then ready to add new lustre to her traditions. Godfrey Brown in particular looked very promising, even though his best time for the "quarter" was only 48.1. Bill Roberts had a "metric" 47.7 to his credit. In the Olympic final, both Britons rose to the stature of their US rivals. LuValle (lane 2) and Williams (lane 5) ran hard and fast in the early stages, while Roberts (lane 3) and Brown (lane 6) appeared to be biding their time. The two Britons started their counter-offensive round the last curve. Brown collared LuValle with 40 m. to go, then closed in on Williams, failing to catch him by inches. Roberts too finished strongly, just failing to catch LuValle. The official timing (which gave 46.5, 46.7, 46.8, 46.8 for the four men, in the order of finish mentioned above) was obviously errratic. The "Zielbildkamera" (photo-finish camera) told the story in more truthful terms: Williams 46.66, Brown 46.68, LuValle 46.84, Roberts 46.87. Excellent performances on a two-turns course, especially if one considers that the final was run only two hours after the semi-finals. Brown (born at Bankura, Bengal, on 21 February 1915; 1.83 m./70 kg.) was probably the world's best quarter-miler in the years 1937-38.His habit of running just fast enough to win possibly prevented him from exploring the depths of his potential. Although a very good sprinter (9.7 for 100 y. on a slightly sloping course), he liked running the "quarter" at an even pace throughout.In fact he showed great promise in the two-lap department as well, with a casual 1:52.2 during a tournée in America, and in London, in 1937, with a superlative relay leg against Rudolf Harbig of Germany. In 1938 he won the European title on the new (400 m.) Colombes track in 47.4. A week later, in Milan, he beat Ray Malott, the American champion, 47.1 to 48.4. In fairness to the latter, however, it should be added that he was by then at the end of a long European campaign, which came on top of an exacting US season. Malott ducked under 47 seconds several times in 1938, his greatest feat consisting in two fast "quarters", 46.7 and 46.6, within one hour at Palo Alto on 3 June.
In Europe, the sceptre of Brown and Roberts was taken over by Rudolf Harbig of Germany and Mario Lanzi of Italy. The former (born at Dresden on 8 November 1913; 1.74 m./ 68 kg.) began as a distance runner in 1932, and later settled on the double track of 400 and 800 m. He beat 47 seconds for the first time in vanquishing Harley Howells of USA, 46.8 to 47.4, at Dortmund in 1938, but only a few days later he bowed to Malott, 47.3 to 46.9, in the Germany vs USA dual meet at Berlin.
Lanzi (born at Castelletto Ticino, Novara, on 10 October 1914; 1.80 m./76 kg.) first emerged as a "metric miler", then turned to the 800m., and finally moved to the 400 m. "in search of speed" in 1936 and almost made the Olympic one-lap final. The strongly built Italian first beat 48 seconds in June 1939 and had a best of 47.2 when he met Harbig at Milan on 16 July. That was the day after their historic clash in the 800 m. At the shorter distance, which was run around one turn, Lanzi led Harbig by several metres (22.2 to 22.8) at the half-way point. The German, even if less brilliant than the day before, gradually closed the gap and finally won by a very scant margin. Both were timed in 46.7, thus equalling Brown's European record. Harbig felt that he could do better in fresh condition, and he proved it on 12 August at Frankfort/Main, on another 500 m. track. Lanzi was again his chief opponent, or should I say his involuntary "hare": The Italian, in lane 6, acted as a useful reference point for Harbig in lane 3, but folded up rather seriously in the conclusive stages. The film of the race is reflected in the 100 m. splits:

	100 m.	200 m.	300 m.	400 m.
Harbig	11.3	22.0	33.6	46.0
Lanzi	11.2	21.7	33.5	47.2

Harbig thus shaved one-tenth off Archie Williams' world record. Later in the season both Harbig and Lanzi scored victories over Brown, who appeared to be past his peak by then. In 1940 Lanzi equalled his own record (46.7) in the Italy vs Germany dual meet at Turin, but Harbig was not in the race.

Possibly the greatest of all American prospects in the late Thirties was John Woodruff, the Olympic 800 m. champion of 1936. For three consecutive years (1937-39) he won the "quarter"at the ICAAAA Championships, always in 47.0. On all three occasions he ran and won both 440 and 880 y. on the same day. If the 1940 Olympics had not been cancelled because of World War II, Harbig, Lanzi and Woodruff would have been confronted with a major problem in choosing between 400 and 800 m. In the shorter race they might have encountered stiff competition from two Commonwealth athletes, Lee Orr of Canada and Denis Shore of South Africa. The former had times of 9.5, 20.8 (straight course) and 46.8 for the English distances. The Springbok had a long career, during which he amassed a huge number of victories and titles in home competition, with best times of 9.5, 21.2, 47.0 at the standard distances, as well as a best-on-record 29.8 for 300 y. and a remarkable 1:09.5 for 600 y. But he did not fare so well in his rare appearances abroad.

MIDDLE DISTANCES - 800 METRES:
From Hampson's tactical masterpiece to Harbig's memorable exploit

The outstanding figures in the 800 m. department during the Twenties were Douglas Lowe, a British lawyer, and Otto Peltzer, a German doctor. The former (born at Manchester on 17 August 1902) was a runner of multiform qualities, not the least of which being a pronounced tactical acumen. He had the rare privilege of winning the 800 m. in two consecutive editions of the Olympics. In 1924, at Colombes, he was no better than sixth in a nine-man field at the half-way mark, started his bid 200 m. from home and eventually won after a great ding-dong battle with Dr. Paul Martin of Switzerland. Lowe was clocked in 1:52 2/5, easily his best up to that time. Martin was second (1:52 3/5), ahead of Schuyler Enck of USA and H.B.Stallard of Britain (both 1:53.0). Lowe also finished fourth in the 1500 m. (3:57.0). True to the spirit of his generation, Lowe ran merely to win. Only once during his career did he find himself in a record race, and on that occasion he was shunted to second by Otto Peltzer of Germany. This happened on 3 July 1926 at Stamford Bridge, London, in the AAA Championships. The German (born at Ellernbrook, Holstein, on 8 March 1900; 1.86 m./ 72 kg.) was known and feared for his strong finishing kick. Possibly in the hope of taking the sting out of his rival, Lowe ran unusually hard for the greater part of the race, passed the 440 y. mark in 54 3/5 and managed to hold off Peltzer down the backstretch and round the last curve. But the German had enough left for one more assault and finally drew away to win by about 3 y. in the record time of 1:51 3/5. Apparently no time was taken for Lowe, although he must have himself equalled or bettered the previous world record (1:52 1/5). Cecil Griffiths was third, 6 y. farther back. Apart from any consideration on his own tactics, Lowe was strongly impressed by Peltzer's finishing speed. This lesson led the Briton to intensify his speed work. In 1927 he ran the "quarter" in 48 4/5, an achievement that gave him full confidence for the Olympic test at Amsterdam the following year. There was a marked upward trend in 800 m./880 y. performances in 1928. USA had a strong contender in Lloyd Hahn, a Nebraska-born talent who had started his racing career as a sprinter and had later reached national prominence as a miler. In March 1928 he ran the half-mile in 1:51 2/5 on a 4-lap armoury (board) track in New York for a US indoor record. On 7 July he won the AAU 800 m. title at Harvard University Stadium in Cambridge with exactly the same time, a new world record for the metric distance, and went on to break a second tape at 880 y. in 1:52 2/5.

France entered the picture just a few days later, exactly on her national holiday, 14 July, when little Séra Martin ran 800 m. in 1:50 3/5 at Colombes. A good solo runner with practically no finishing kick, Martin had 400 m. fractions of 53.0 and 57 3/5.

At Amsterdam, Lloyd Hahn ran his semi-final in 1:52 3/5, with Phil Edwards, a Canadian, and Séra Martin close on his heels. Peltzer was eliminated in the other "semi", a slower affair in which Lowe was content to qualify in second place. The following day, in the final, Hahn led the field in a virtually slow first half (55 1/5). Lowe launched his attack in the backstretch of the last lap and irresistibly drew away to win in 1:51 4/5, his best up to that time and a new Olympic record. While the other favourites folded under the pressure of the occasion, Erik Byléhn of Sweden came up fast to take second in 1:52 4/5. Hermann Engelhard of Germany was third (1:53 1/5). Next came Edwards (1:54.0), Hahn (1:54 1/5)

1921
1940

Douglas Lowe (GB) beats Paul Martin (SWZ) in the 800 metres at the 1924 Olympics in Paris. Winner's time, 1:52.4.

and Martin (1:54 3/5). The débacle of the last two caused commentators in America and in France to spend countless words in an effort to find a suitable explanation. Lowe ran his last major race at Berlin a few weeks later, downing his old rival Otto Peltzer in no uncertain fashion, 1:51 1/5 (his best ever) to 1:52 1/5, while Séra Martin could do no better than fourth. Lowe made his impact strongly felt also as a track scholar. His teachings well reflect the mentality prevalent in his time. Some of his hints on training and racing may seem too cautious to present-day observers, but one should bear in mind that in Lowe's days athletics was, generally if not always, just a form of recreation - even for the champion runner. Shortly before the 1932 Olympics in Los Angeles, USA found a man who looked capable of putting an end to British domination in the two-lap business. The man in question was Ben Eastman, the great quarter-miler, who on 4 June of that year, at San Francisco, ran 880 y.in 1:50.9, after passing an 800 m. post in 1:50.0, both new world records. But, as has been related previously, his rivalry with Bill Carr in the one-lap department induced him to choose the 400 m. for the Games. Of course no one can tell what the blond American would have done in the 800 m. As it was, the Los Angeles final offered great competition and unexpected record times. And Great Britain once again provided the winner with Thomas Hampson (born at Clapham, South London, on 28 October 1907; 1.84 m./ 69 kg.).He was the reigning British Empire half-mile champion, having won the title in 1930 with 1:52 2/5, which was still his personal best when he entered the Los Angeles arena two years later. In the Olympics he ran a masterful race. He kept away from the hot pace set by Phil Edwards of Canada (400 m. in 52.3) and was a distant fifth at the bell, while veterans Peltzer and Séra Martin, farther back, looked hopelessly out of it. In the second lap, Hampson gradually made up lost ground and passed one runner after the other, including the by then fading Edwards. Near the end, however, the English teacher met stiff competition from another Canadian, Alex Wilson, who like Edwards had made the grade while a student in the States. Wilson was known as a first-rate quarter-miler, yet Hampson, rallying his last resources, drew

1921–1940

away a few metres from home and won in 1:49.7 (which according to the rule then in force was officially rounded off to 1:49.8). It was 2 August 1932, the day of history's first sub-1:50 performance. The gallant Wilson was a close second in 1:49.9, well ahead of Edwards (1:51.5). The Americans monopolized positions from four to six, a meagre consolation for West Coast fans, who would have liked to see the bespectacled Eastman in the historic race. Hampson, who was also wearing spectacles by the way, reached the peak of his condition on the day that counted most, and did so with a touch of wisdom, as evidenced by his 400 m. fractions - 54.8 plus 54.9. Eastman had his best year as a half-miler in 1934, when he proved consistently capable of times around 1:50. In his Eastern début, at Princeton's Palmer Stadium on 16 June, he led from gun to tape and set a new half-mile record of 1:49.8, with 440 y. fractions of 54.0 and 55.8. Runner-up in that race was another American, Charles Hornbostel (1:50.7). Eastman went on to capture the AAU 800 m. title in 1:50.8, then made a successful European tournée, downing among others the Swedish champion Eric Ny in a race at Stockholm with an impressive 1:50.0. Curiously enough, "Blazing Ben", who had by then abandoned the "quarter", was to remain the "runner of even years". He returned to action in 1936, ran the 800 m. in 1:50.1, then failed in his bid to make the Olympic team. In 1933 the leading two-lap runners were Hornbostel and Glenn Cunningham of USA, both 1:50.9 in finishing in that order in the NCAA 880 y. race, and Luigi Beccali of Italy, the Olympic 1500 m. champion, who lowered his country's 800 m. record to 1:50.6 in a handicap race at Florence. Cunningham and Beccali represented the 880/mile type of runner, and their consistency was such that they would have probably beaten Hampson's record if they had met while Cunningham was in Europe. In 1934 Italy discovered a new talent in broad-shouldered, twenty-year-old Mario Lanzi. At the inaugural European Championships in Turin, this powerful youngster finished a close second to Miklós Szabó of Hungary (both 1:52.0). It should be noted that Lanzi had run an unduly fast 1:51.8 in a heat the day before, after following the crazy pace set by Eric Ny, who only a week earlier in Stockholm had lowered the Swedish record to 1:50.4. By 1936 the Americans had found a great Olympic prospect in John Youie Woodruff (born at Connellsville, Pennsylvania, on 5 July 1915; 1.89 m./ 75 kg.), a thoroughbred who had emerged in 1935 with a metric 1:55.1 and a second place in the AAU Junior Championships. In 1936, as a freshman at the University of Pittsburgh, he made the headlines when he beat Hornbostel in the 800 m. with 1:51.3. In the AAU Championships at Princeton the novice foolishly toyed with his rivals and was finally outfoxed by Charles Beetham, 1:50.4 to 1:50.3. The Final Olympic Tryouts were held in New York on 11/12 July. In the 800 m. heats, run on the first day, Woodruff produced a sensational 1:49.9. Among the other qualifiers was Ben Eastman. The final was run on the second day, a Sunday. Tragedy struck national champion Beetham, who fell with 300 m. to go. Woodruff had no trouble in holding off Hornbostel and Harry Williamson in a 1:51.0 finish. Eastman, short on condition after a twenty-months layoff, found himself dead last in the initial stage and could finish no better than sixth.

The thorny side

Otto Peltzer passed away a few minutes after attending the nth track meeting of his life at Eutin in his native Schleswig-Holstein on 11 August 1970, aged 70. Although one of the greatest German athletes of the first half of the 20th century, Peltzer was for years something of an unsung hero in his own country. In celebrating his 70th birthday a few months earlier, "Leichtathletik" casually remarked that his life was "spattered with thorns at times". The full significance of these words was explained as late as in 1998 during the celebration of the 100th anniversary of German athletics by an erudite speaker, Prof. Walter Jens, president of the German Academy of Arts, "a political thinker with a philosophical spirit". Peltzer, he said, was a man endowed with a liberal and versatile mind who happened to live part of his adult life in a period of obscurantism for his country. Often at odds with sport authorities, his position became more and more uncomfortable after the advent of the Hitler regime. He found temporary refuge in Sweden, where he worked as a sport writer and coach. When he returned to Germany he was arrested and finally doomed to forced labor in the Mauthausen concentration camp. He went through very hard times till 1945, when the Americans finally set him free. Although beset by health problems, he had enough élan left for a new life. He emigrated to India, where he earned his living as a coach and medical advisor. He regained the "Abendland" (West) in the latter part of his life.

Rudolf Harbig (Germany), centre, seen in one of his rare defeats: second to Ray Malott (USA) in the 400 metres of an international dual meet at Berlin in 1938. Times, 46.9 and 47.3. Jimmy Herbert (USA), left, was third.

The unlucky Beetham, a cunning tactician if ever there was one, felt that he could beat the times of the men who had secured a berth on the Berlin-bound ship and offered to prove it in a solo time trial. Quite predictably, the powers that be refused to listen to him. (Two years later, in a race at Dresden, Beetham finished a close second to one Rudolf Harbig). The Olympic final was run on 4 August. Phil Edwards of Canada, running in his third Olympiad, led the field for the major part of the first lap. The pace was slow, yet Mario Lanzi managed to get himself into a "box". At the half-way mark he lagged far behind leaders Edwards and Woodruff (57.4). The tall American tore away round the last turn and majestically entered the short final stretch, heading for home as the most likely winner. Lanzi, still fourth with 200 m. to go, gained on everybody in the final stages but had to be content with second place. The American won in 1:52.9 from Lanzi (1:53.3) and Edwards (1:53.6), while Kazimierz Kucharski of Poland took fourth place, ahead of the American duo Hornbostel-Williamson. Woodruff was the class of the field, yet Lanzi (whose 400 m. fractions were estimated at 58.4 and 54.9) could have been a more serious threat with more skilled tactics. This Berlin experience led the Italian to adopt an entirely different line in subsequent meets: front running throughout. For one reason or another, though, he never struck the right measure. A few days after the Games, at Malmö, he equalled Beccali's Italian record (1:50.6) but on 20 August, at Stockholm, he was again defeated. On this occasion he led the field in the first lap (53.4) but finally had to be content with third place (1:51.4). Glenn Cunningham, runner-up in the Olympic 1500 m., won in world record time, 1:49.7, from John Powell of Britain (1:50.8). In the despair of defeat, Lanzi probably failed to realize that he had at least beaten the man who in later years was to become his "bête noire" - Rudolf Harbig of Germany, sixth in that race in 1:55.3. Maybe the two future rivals met for the first time without noticing each other. Eastman's half-mile record was beaten in 1937 at New York by Elroy Robinson, a West Coast runner who had by-passed the Olympic season on account of an injury. Robinson finished in 1:49.6, after leading from start to finish (440 y. fractions: 53.5 and 56.1). Howard Borck was second in 1:50.7. Europe's turn came the following year when Britain's fastest miler, Sydney Wooderson, decided to try his hand at the shorter distance. Indifferent in physical appearance but endowed with plenty of stamina and, above all, with tremendous will power, Wooderson revealed his potential as a two-lap runner when he beat Mario Lanzi in an 880 y. race in London, 1:50.9 to 1:51.1. Less than three weeks later, on 20 August, a record attempt was staged for him at Motspur Park. Running in a framed handicap from scratch, the diminutive Briton was forced into a swift early pace (440 y. in 52.6) that did not suit his racing habits. Even so, he managed to finish in 1:48.4 (800 m.) and 1:49.2 (880 y.), thus conquering two world records with a single stroke. The slowest of his 110 y. fractions was the last (14.8), while the fastest was the second (12.5). However, he continued to regard the mile as his best distance and opted for the 1500 m. in view of the European Championships. So he did not meet Rudolf Harbig. On account of his decision, middle-distance annals lack the lustre of what would have been one of the greatest clashes of all time between the 800/1500 m. type of runner and his opposite number, the 400/800 m. variety. Harbig first beat 2 minutes for the 800 m. in 1934, improved to 1:54.1 the following year, and to 1:52.2 in 1936. He joined the élite in 1937 with a consistent competitive record and a best of 1:50.9. Shortly before the 1938 European Championships in Paris he lowered his 400 m. best to 46.8. His chief rival for the continental title was Mario Lanzi, who in 1937 had lowered his 800 m. record to 1:50.5. At Stade de Colombes, Lanzi again led the field at the half-way point (53.3) but had no answer when Harbig launched his attack. The German drew away with astounding ease to win the European title in 1:50.6. Jacques Levêque of France came from behind to beat Lanzi for second place, 1:51.8 to 1:52.0. Harbig and Lanzi met for the third time at Milan a week later and the newly crowned European champion was again the winner, 1:52.6 to 1:53.2. The year 1938 had been one of intensive training and competition for Harbig. In the summer he averaged ten practice sessions and ten competitive races per month. His coach Woldemar Gerschler made it a point that each session should be one of hard work, including a series of severe tests at various distances and short intervals for jogging after each run. Maybe a similar method had been followed by others long before then, yet Gerschler was first to find a name for it: "Intervall-Training".

The Harbig-Lanzi epic reached its climax in 1939. The Italian was by then putting the stress on speed. Early in the season at Pisa he ran 1:49.5 (800m.) and 47.4 (400 m.) on consecutive days and early in July he lowered his 400 m. best to 47.2. Harbig too continued to progress and by the same time he could point to such times as 21.5 (200 m.) and a new German record of 1:49.4 (800 m.). The stage was set for the fourth and most famous clash between the two champions. The duel took place in the Italy vs Germany match on 15 July. The scene of the struggle was the Milan Arena, an old elliptic construction described in the guide books as a compromise between a circus and a theatre Roman style, and in which Napoleon I once paraded the élite of his army. The track, 500 m. in circumference, was fast and well conducive to top performances. A comparatively small crowd watched the race, which was started on the backstretch, so that the runners had to negotiate only three turns. Lanzi was nearest the curb, while Harbig started in lane 3. In between the two champions were Hans Brandscheit of Germany and Mario Bellini of Italy. All runners took a crouch start, and Lanzi got off the marks like a bullet. He passed the 200 m. in 24.6. Harbig was an unworried second, a few metres back. At the half-way point the big Italian was timed in 52.5, while Harbig (52.8) still appeared to be following rather than chasing his rival. At 600

1921
1940

Mario Lanzi, right, and Rudolf Harbig, after one of their memorable duels.

m. Lanzi was still in the lead (1:19.8), but by then the self-confident German was drawing close. Lanzi kept going strong till 700 m. (1:33.4). But that was all he could offer for the day: at that point he collapsed in no uncertain fashion and had to give way to his rival. Harbig, incredibly full of running, was not content to win. In his determined quest for the record he chopped his stride and went on at relentless speed. He reached the finish line in 1:46.6, i.e. 1.8 seconds under Wooderson's world record. The other runners also achieved personal bests: Lanzi 1:49.0 (he eased up ostensibly near the end), Brandscheit 1:50.3, Bellini 1:52.6. With more cautious behaviour, Lanzi would have probably achieved a faster time, yet his temerity was certainly paramount in extending Harbig to his potential best. On the other hand, the German deserved the highest praise for his determination in pursuing the record far beyond the necessity of winning the race.

The fifth round between the two champions took place at Berlin, two weeks after the historic Milan race. The tactical pattern was virtually the same, except that this time Harbig won economically, 1:48.7 to 1:49.2. On the other side of the Atlantic, John Woodruff continued to rule the roost for several years after his Olympic victory. In the opinion of most experts he never came close to realizing his enormous potential. Even so, his class was so great that he often gave the impression of toying with the opposition. His major exploits are worth a detailed mention:

(1) On 17 July 1937 at Dallas, Texas, he met Elroy Robinson, freshly crowned half-mile record holder, in the 800 m. The race was run at night, under floodlights, but with a temperature of about 32 C. Robinson was in the lead at 400 m. (52.5), with Woodruff fairly close behind (52.8). In the backstretch of the final lap the Olympic champion easily forged ahead and won by about 6 m. in 1:47.8. On remeasurement of the course, the distance turned out to be 5 ft. (1.52 m.) short. Woodruff was thus robbed of a well-deserved world record. He ran the equivalent of 1:48.0 for the full distance - at a time when the mark stood at 1:49.6. And he did so on a small five-lap (321.87 m.) track, in decisively beating the official record holder.

(2) On 14 March 1940 at Hanover, N.H., he covered 800 m. in 1:47.0 and 880 y. in 1:47.7, well below any indoor mark registered up to that time. This was in a handicap race on a large, banked board track (239 m.) and Woodruff probably ran the wisest race of his life, with "quarters" in 54.0 and 53.7.

(3) On 7 June 1940 at Compton, California, he lowered the US 800 m. record to 1:48.6, virtually after leading from start to finish (400 m. fractions: 52.0 and 56.6). The race was around four turns and Paul Moore was a fairly close second in 1:49.0.

From July 1936 to the end of his career, four years later, Woodruff never lost a major race, although he was occasionally beaten in low-fire competitions. In 1939 he ran the mile in 4:12.8. Harbig and Lanzi met for the sixth time at Stuttgart in 1940, with the Italian leading as usual in the early stages (400 m. in 53.0) and Harbig eventually turning the tables on him at the decisive moment, 1:47.8 to 1:49.3. Lanzi chose to play the cautious way at Como the following month and finally nipped his rival, 1:54.2 to 1:54.7.

1500 METRES/1 MILE: The Days of Beccali and Lovelock

A closer adherence to the canons of even pace running in the 1500 m./mile department could only be introduced by a born distance runner. The man ideally suited for the purpose was Paavo Nurmi of Finland. In 1921 the "Phantom Finn" ran the English distance in 4:13.9 and two years later, exactly on 23 August 1923 at Stockholm, he captured the world record with a time of 4:10.4, after passing 1500 m. in 3:53.0. (For some reason, the latter was not ratified as a record by the IAAF). In this race he was spurred on by his Swedish rival Edvin Wide (4:13.1). Nurmi's "quarters" were 60.3, 62.9, 63.5 and 63.7.

On 19 June 1924, at Helsinki, Nurmi lowered his 1500 m. best to 3:52 3/5. The following month, in Paris, he won the Olympic title hands down in 3:53 3/5. These were by no means all-out efforts, because on each occasion he had a 5000 m. race awaiting him later in the same afternoon! In Paris he beat Willy Schaerer of Switzerland (3:55.0), H.B.Stallard (3:55 3/5) and Douglas Lowe (3:57.0) of Britain. During his 1925 tournée in USA, the Finn lowered the indoor record for the mile to 4:12.0, a time which was equalled ten days later by Joie Ray of USA.

On 11 September 1926 Nurmi witnessed the fall of his 1500 m. record. The race was at Berlin, on the new track of the Sport Club Charlottenburg, in the presence of a capacity crowd (20,000). His opponents were Dr.Otto Peltzer of Germany, holder of the world's half-mile record (1:51 3/5) and Edvin Wide, the Finnish-born Swede. It was a dramatic race, which proved that even the great Nurmi was, after all, a human being, and as such not invincible. A moment before the start, a small boy, climbing a pole for a better view, caused the Finnish flag to fall. Nurmi, believed to be a superstitious man, was too intent on the race to witness this bad omen ...

1921 1940

The Finn led for two-thirds of the way (400 m. in 61,0, 800 m. 2:02.2, 1000 m. 2:34.8). Wide and Peltzer went past him in the closing stage, and the German, a highly-strung, nervous athlete, won the stretch battle with his superior "kick". The times were truly historic: Peltzer 3:51.0, Wide 3:51.8, Nurmi 3:52.8. A picture of the finish would suggest that Wide and Nurmi were not so far behind the winner: they must have slowed down rather abruptly at the end, or (more probably) the times given for them were inaccurate. Possibly for the first time in history, the 1500 m. record was intrinsically better than the one-mile mark. Peltzer's moment of glory as a 1500 m. specialist was ephe-meral. The next Great in the history of the event was Jules Ladoumègue of France (born at Bordeaux on 10 December 1906; 1.71 m. / 59 kg.). A highly emotional runner with a galloping stride, "Julot" was for years the pride of French athletics. He lost his parents very early and the hard life he was confronted with as a boy probably made an imprint on his character. He turned out to be a temperamental runner - with plenty of talent. He emerged as a distance runner in 1926, but the following year he turned his attention to the 1500 m. He was down to 4:03 3/5 in little or no time and also ran a more revealing 8:40 4/5 for 3000 m., a new French record. He eventually made the grade as a 'Class A' 1500 m. runner in 1928. From 3:58.0 to 3:55 1/5 in June (in the latter race beating Luigi Beccali of Italy, 3:59 3/5), he improved to 3:54 3/5 and 3:52 1/5 in July, this last in winning the French Championship title. He thus went to the Amsterdam Olympics as a world leader. However, the Finns had by then found successors for Paavo Nurmi. At the Olympic Trials in Helsinki, Harri Larva beat Eino Purje after a gruelling fight, 3:52.6 to 3:53.1. At Amsterdam, on 2 August, a cold shower awaited Ladoumègue and his fans. He took the lead in the backstretch of the last lap but was outsprinted by the tall Larva in the closing stage. The Finn won rather comfortably, 3:53 1/5 to 3:53 4/5. Purje was third in 3:56 2/5. In post-Olympic meets, Ladoumègue ran 3:52 4/5 and did 1:52.0 in the 800 m., while Larva came close to the one-mile record with 4:11.0 and lowered his 1500 m. best to 3:52.0. Ladoumègue reached the zenith of his form in 1930-31, when he set the following world records:

3:49 1/5, 1500 m. (Paris, 5-10-1930)
2:23 3/5, 1000 m. (Paris, 19-10-1930)
5:21 4/5, 2000 m. (Paris, 2-7-1931)
3:00 3/5, 3/4 mile (Colombes, 13-9-1931)
4:09 1/5, 1 mile (Paris, 4-10-1931)

All these marks except one were made at Stade Jean-Bouin, which had a circumference of 450 m. The three-quarter mile record was made at Colombes, on the track of the 1924 Olympics, and this was the only occasion on which "Julot" really had to fight: he beat Eino Purje by a few centimetres, and both runners were given the same time, 3:00 3/5. All the other races were special record attempts, in which Ladoumègue was aided by other runners. In his 1500 m. effort in 1930 he received valuable assistance from such "de luxe" hares as Séra Martin and Jean Keller, and took the lead with 500 m. to go. His splits were estimated as 58.6, 62.0, 63.8 and, for the last 300 m., 44.8. Second in this race was Luigi Beccali in 3:57 4/5. In his one-mile record attempt, Ladoumègue remained in the shadow of René Morel, a 1:54 two-lap runner, for about two-thirds of the race, then shot ahead, passed the 1500 m. mark in 3:52 2/5 and covered the last 109.35 m. in 16 4/5. His "quarters" were: 60.8, 63.4, 63.8, 61.2. It is perhaps relevant to add that Ladoumègue's 3:52 1/5 in the 1928 French title meet was to remain his best ever time in a competitive race over the "metric mile". Unfortunately he was ousted from the amateur ranks in the spring of 1932 for accepting under-the-table money in connection with some appearances in Northern France. He was thus precluded from giving the true measure of his ability in the Los Angeles Olympics. Prior to the advent of Luigi Beccali, Italy had never had a 1500 m. runner of world class (Emilio Lunghi could have been one, but he only ran the distance sporadically). The stoutly built Beccali (born at Milan on 19 November 1907; 1.69 m./ 63 kg.) remedied the situation in brilliant fashion. He made his début as a runner at age fourteen, in a 5000 m. race. As might be expected, the result was disastrous, and "Nini" decided to give up track in favour of cycling. Luckily for Italy, who did not lack good cyclists, his showing on wheels left something to be desired. He eventually returned to his first love, but it was only in 1926 that he began to distinguish himself. He first ducked under 4 minutes for the 1500 m. in 1928, in losing to Ladoumègue. As related above, his time on that occasion was 3:59 3/5. At the Amsterdam Olympics, his inexperience cost him dearly and he was eliminated in a heat. In fact his road to success was a long one. Between 1928 and 1931 he continued to improve slowly but steadily, and learned much from those who defeated him. By 1931 he had sharpened his finishing "kick", but it may be interesting to record that during that year he lost, always by a very narrow margin, to László Barsi in Budapest (800 m.), to Thomas Hampson in London (880 y.), to Janusz Kusocinski in Poznan (1500 m.) and to Ettore Tavernari in Milan (800 m.). In preparation for the Los Angeles rendezvous Beccali intensified his training, under the tutelage of a perceptive coach, Dr. Dino Nai. When the 1932 Olympic season got under way he was literally a new man. On 15 May, at Milan's Arena, he lowered his 1500 m. best from 3:57 1/5 (1930) to 3:52 1/5, which was to remain the world's fastest time in pre-Olympic weeks. Yet he was not considered a favourite by the majority of experts. Quite a few things had happened elsewhere. At the US Final Tryouts in Palo Alto, a young trio - Norwood Hallowell (3:52.7), Frank Crowley and Glenn Cunningham - qualified for the Games by shunting into fourth place the highly touted Gene Venzke. This athlete, a very popular figure in Eastern track circles, had set a remarkable one-mile indoor record of 4:10.0 in February and had run the 1500 m. in 3:52.6 for a US outdoor record in June. Among other leading contenders were the Finnish veterans Larva and Purje, Phil Edwards of Canada, Jerry Cornes of Britain, AAA one-mile champion (4:14 1/5), and a young New Zealander, Jack Lovelock, who as a student at Oxford had set a new British one-mile record of 4:12.0 in May. The Los Angeles final was on 4 August. Mid-way in the race, nobody wanted to set the pace. Edwards broke the ice going into the third lap and shot out of the bunched field, with Cunningham in his wake. The North American duo soon opened up a mighty gap, which must have been about 20 m. with 300 to go (3:07.0). But exactly at that stage Cornes and Beccali began to close in on the two fugitives. The European duo, still full of running, inexorably drew closer and closer. Round the last curve, Beccali ran away from Cornes. Then, in the homestretch, the Italian collared Cunningham and finally passed Edwards, to win by a comfortable margin in 3:51.2, a new Olympic record and third fastest time ever. He covered the last 300 m. in an estimated 41.7, which was a killing pace in those days. Cornes caught Edwards in the last few metres and finished second in 3:52.6. He was followed by the Canadian (3:52.8), then by Cunningham (3:53.4). The Finns never came into their own, and the green Lovelock was in their company as an "also ran". Yet Lovelock was the man of the future. The Kiwi ace (born at Greymouth on 5 January 1910; 1.69 m./ 60 kg.) had come to Oxford from Down Under in the fall of 1931 as a 4:26 miler. Consequently, his 4:12.0 in the spring of 1932 had created quite a stir in British track circles. This pink-faced, light-footed man was said to run on his nerves. But he was wise enough to concentrate on no more than one or two major commitments per season. He reached world prominence less than a year after his Olympic experience, namely on 15 July 1933 at Princeton, New Jersey, when he conquered the world's one-mile record with 4:07.6, at the end of a gruelling fight with Bill Bonthron of USA (4:08.7, second fastest ever). A tremendous improvement for two runners who only a few months earlier were regarded as "green". Lovelock's lap times were: 61.4, 62.2, 65.1, 58.9. I may add that one of the shoes worn by "Bonny" Bonthron in that historic race is still preserved, in a gold coating, at Princeton University. Beccali had started his 1933 campaign late and in low gear, improving on his 800 m.best slightly, to 1:53.2. But he was ready when Lovelock came to Italy for the World Student Games. The encounter took place in Turin on 9 September, over 1500 m. Beccali boldly went into the lead near

Luigi Beccali (Italy), one of the two men to have won the 1500 m. in both Olympic Games and European Championships.

the one-kilometre mark. He ran hard and fast, with Lovelock on his heels. Entering the homestretch, the New Zealander tried to pull even, but Beccali held on bravely and the end of the fierce struggle found him first by a safe margin - 3:49.2 to 3:49.8. Ladoumègue had been matched "under competitive conditions", as one Italian commentator wilfully hastened to add. Eight days later Beccali tried again, in the Italy vs Great Britain dual meet at Milan's Arena, on a 500-metre track. He was opposed to Reginald Thomas, a solid 4:13 2/5 miler and a three-time AAA champion. Beccali again launched his attack early in the third lap. He drew away from Thomas and reached the finish line in 3:49.0, a new world record. Thomas was second in 3:53.6. Beccali's splits were: 60.0 (400 m.), 2:04.2 (800 m.), 3:06.0 (1200 m.).

French and Italian commentators were by then engaged in a heated discussion on the relative merits of "Julot" Ladoumègue and "Nini" Beccali. The French runner, then a professional, wanted to outshine the fame of his rival from across the Alps: in specially arranged record attempts at Stade Jean-Bouin, Paris, he did 3:50.8 (14 October), 3:51.4 (18 October) and 3:50.4 (21 October). At the same time Beccali succeeded Emilio Lunghi as holder of the Italian 800 m. record with 1:50.6, and ran his third sub-3:50 "metric mile" (3:49.6). This was to remain a rare example of an "amateur" and a "pro" trying to outdo each other in different theatres of operation at the same time in a not-too-distant epoch. It should also be mentioned that Ladoumègue and Eino Purje of Finland were the first European athletic notables to compete in USSR (1934), a country then not affiliated to the IAAF. The Frenchman was later "requalified" and in 1943, at nearly 37 years of age, he ran the 1500 m. in 3:58.4 ! American milers counter-attacked in 1934. That was the year of the famous feud between Glenn Cunningham, the "Iron Man of Kansas", and Bill Bonthron. The former (born at Atlanta,, Kansas, on 4 August 1909; 1.75 m./ 75 kg.) was America's most durable middle-distance runner during the Thirties. At the age of eight his legs were badly burnt, yet he overcame this great handicap and by 1930 he was one of the nation's leading High School milers with 4:24.7. After his fourth place in the 1500 m. at the Los Angeles Olympics, in 1933 he won a great one-day double at the AAU Championships (1:51.8 and 3:52.3), then had a successful European tour. In March 1934 he lowered the indoor one-mile record to 4:08.4. On 16 June, at the Princeton Invitational Meet, he soundly thrashed Bonthron and set a new world record of 4:06.7, with "quarters" of 61.8, 64.0, 61.8 and 59.1, while his arch rival struggled home a distant second in 4:12.5. Yet "Bonny" fought back and a week later he turned the tables on Cunningham at the NCAA Championships in Los Angeles, 4:08.9 to 4:10.6. Counting indoor races, the two champions were by then 2-to-2 for the season. Bonthron, a "big kicker", won the rubber race over the 1500 m. at the AAU Championships in Milwaukee on 30 June, no matter if narrowly - 3:48.8 to 3:48.9. For the first time since Abel Kiviat's days, the world record for the "metric mile" was in American hands. The lap times were: 61.3, 60.5, 64.2 and, for the last 300 m., 42.8. Gene Venzke was third in 3:50.5. Beccali did little running in 1934-35. After suffering a bitter defeat against Eric Ny of Sweden at Malmö in 1934 (3:54.3 to 3:50.4), he was back in stride for the European Championships in Turin, where he won in

1921
1940

The most famous clash between Bill Bonthron and Glenn Cunningham: the AAU 1500 metres at Milwaukee in 1934. "Bonny", left, won in 3:48.8, with Cunningham just 0.1 behind, both under the listed world record. (Courtesy "Track & Field News").

Otto Peltzer (Germany) in his banner year, 1926, beating Edvin Wide (Sweden) and Paavo Nurmi (Finland) in the 1500 metres at Berlin. Time, 3:51.0, a new world record.

3:54.6 from Miklós Szabó of Hungary (3:55.2). Early in 1936 he thought that his best Olympic chance would be in the 5000 m. and began to train accordingly. Shortly afterwards he gave up the idea and in June he ran the 1500 m. at Budapest in 3:50.6. On that occasion his last 300 m. took no less than 46.3, and observers began to wonder if long-distance training had not taken the zip out of him. In England, Lovelock had a serious opponent in little Sydney Wooderson, who did in fact win four out of six mile races from the New Zealander in 1934-36. It is true, however, that one of Lovelock's successes was in a very important meet, the 1934 British Empire Games in London - 4:12.8 to 4:13.4. And Lovelock again beat the American élite in the Princeton mile in 1935 (4:11.2). In pre-Berlin weeks he posted such times as 1:55.0 (880 y.) and 14:20.2 (3 miles). At the same time Wooderson seemed ready for virtually every major task, so it was tragedy indeed when shortly before the Games he sustained an ankle injury. He went to Berlin all the same, but found himself unable to produce an all-out effort and consequently had to give up in a heat. At the US Olympic Tryouts in New York on 12 July, Cunningham won the 1500 m. by a narrow margin from a new star, Archie San Romani. Both returned the same time, 3:49.9. Gene Venzke was third (3:52.2), shunting Bill Bonthron (3:53.7) out of the Olympic team.

The Berlin 1500 m. final (6 August) is still remembered as a classic in the history of the event, were it only for the tactical skill displayed in it by a man who had keyed himself up for the occasion with unsurpassed precision. This man was Jack Lovelock, and he launched his attack with 400 m. to go. Prior to that stage, Cunningham and Ny had set the pace (400 m. in 61.5, 800 m. in 2:05.2). The American tried to run away in the third lap, but Lovelock was quick to follow him, and when he made his bid even the powerful Cunningham was unable to answer. Lovelock ran the last 400 m. in 56.8 and the last 300 m. in 42.4. He came home an exhausted but glorious winner in 3:47.8 - one full second under Bill

Bonthron's world record. Cunningham was second in 3:48.4. Defending champion Beccali, who had been spiked early in the race, never appeared to be in the hunt, yet he finished third in 3:49.2. San Romani was fourth (3:50.0), followed by veteran Phil Edwards of Canada (3:50.4) and Jerry Cornes of Britain (3:51.4). Four of the first six improved on their previous best. Beccali and San Romani missed their own by 0.2 and 0.1 sec. respectively! Edwards, who hailed from British Guiana, represented Canada in three editions of the Games. He figured prominently in five individual finals (800 m., fourth in 1928, third in 1932 and 1936; 1500 m., third in 1932, fifth in 1936) and three relay finals (4x400 m., third in 1928 and 1932, fourth in 1936). After peaking so well at the right time, Lovelock ran just one more race, a half-hearted effort in the Princeton mile on 3 October. He lost to San Romani, 4:10.1 to 4:09.0. Cunningham was third in 4:13.0. The Kiwi ace was an amateur in the truest sense of the word. When his immediate pleasure for the Olympic event wore off, he said: "It isn't the fun it used to be. I think it's about time to hang up my shoes". And so he retired. One day in December 1949 newspapers around the world carried the sad news that Dr. John Lovelock, for nine years the victim of double vision from a riding accident, had fallen to his death under a subway car in New York. Beccali continued to run for several more years. Strangely enough, he had never seriously tried the English mile in his best years. He partly remedied this during his American tournée in 1937, doing 4:09.0 indoors and 4:09.6 outdoors, both in losing efforts though. He never again found his winning ways, at least against the world's best. He later settled in the States. He is still the only 1500 m. man who can claim victories in both Olympic and European Championships. He died in Italy in 1990. Cunningham had his best years after the Berlin Olympics. He amassed a high number of classy performances and established himself as the most consistent miler of his time. In February 1938 he ran the 1500 m. indoors in 3:48.4, matching his Berlin time on an eleven-lap (to the mile) banked board track. On 3 March of the same year, on a 239 m. banked board track at Hanover, N.H., he ran the mile in 4:04.4. His last major race was also his fastest ever, at least in the "metric mile": in the 1940 AAU Championships at Fresno, California, he did 3:48.2 in finishing second to Walter Mehl (3:47.9). The latter thus missed Lovelock's world record by 0.1 sec. Third in this race was Paul Moore (3:48.7), a promising runner who like many others was to have his career badly curtailed by World War II. Wooderson reigned supreme as Europe's best in 1937-39. In a specially framed handicap at Motspur Park on 28 August 1937 he captured the world's one-mile record with 4:06.4 (lap times: 58.6, 64.0, 64.6, 59.2), after passing the 1500 m. mark in 3:50.3. This tough little runner (born in London on 30 August 1914; 1.67 m./ 56 kg.) was a great competitor. In 1938 he easily won the European 1500 m. title in 3:53.6 from Joseph Mostert of Belgium (3:54.5) and veteran Luigi Beccali (3:55.2). A week later, in Milan, he won a slow tactical affair in 3:58.4 from Beccali (3:58.8) and Charles Fenske of USA (3:59.0). Fenske, then one of America's leading milers, was to be responsible for the only major defeat suffered by Wooderson in that period: it was in the famous Princeton mile of 1939 that the Briton was shunted to fifth place (4:13.0) in a rough affair won by Fenske in 4:11.0. British observers claimed that Wooderson was fouled by Blaine Rideout with 160 m. to go, but pictures failed to bear out such a claim in a convincing manner, although Rideout himself (who finished fourth) admitted: "I cut in (on him) too quickly, I'm sorry. That's the last thing I'd want to do to a beaten runner". Sweden, always a good international quantity in this event, saw the dawn of its "boom" in 1939, when young Arne Andersson came practically from nowhere to create a new national 1500 m. record of 3:48.8 in the match against Finland at Stockholm, after a fierce duel with his countryman Åke Jansson, 3:49.2. (The latter changed his last name to Spångert in 1940). Two other Swedes, Henry Kälarne and Gunder Hägg, passed through the breach in a race at Göteborg in 1940 and joined the world class, with times of 3:48.7 and 3:48.8 respectively.

LONG DISTANCES - 5000 and 10,000 metres: the Finnish Era

After analyzing his defeat by Joseph Guillemot in the 5000 m. of the Antwerp Olympics, Paavo Nurmi came to the conclusion that it had probably come as a result of his faulty pace judgment. He went to work on that detail most seriously, and to check his progress he developed a habit of holding a watch in his hand in both training and competition. He set his first world record at Stockholm in 1921: 10,000 m. in 30:40.2. This inaugurated a fabulous series which was completed ten years later at Helsinki when he set his twentieth world record: 2 miles in 8:59.5. The most significant year of the Nurmi era was 1924. Outstanding among his achievements during that season were two famous one-day "doubles".

On 19 June at Helsinki he ran 1500 m. in 3:52.6, took an hour's rest and then covered 5000 m. in 14:28.2 - new world records both! This was meant as a rehearsal for the Paris Olympics. The second "double" thus followed at Stade de Colombes on 10 July (that day incidentally marked the twelfth anniversary of the memorable Kolehmainen vs. Bouin duel in the Stockholm Olympics). Nurmi began by annexing the 1500 m. crown "sans coup férir" (i.e. hands down), as a French commentator put it. Time, 3:53 3/5. Only 42 minutes later he was at the start of the 5000 m., in which he faced the only men in the world who could possibly give him something to think about, Ville Ritola of Finland and Edvin Wide of Sweden. Wide lost contact mid-way in the race, but Ritola fought bravely and succumbed to Nurmi only by a scant margin, 14:31 2/5 to 14:31 1/5. Two more victories, one in the cross-country race (12 July) and the other in the 3000 m. team race (13 July), aptly completed Nurmi's golden adventure in Paris. He did not run the 10,000 m., and Ritola seized the opportunity to win the race in world record time, 30:23 1/5. In his 1924 mood, however, Nurmi did not accept "back talk" from anybody, and on 31 August at Kuopio he eclipsed Ritola's effort with a scintillating 30:06.1. This mark, which was officially ratified as 30:06 1/5, stood longer than any of his other records at standard distances. In 1925 Nurmi visited the United States. In the space of five months he ran 55 races (45 indoors and 10 outdoors) and was only beaten twice. On one occasion, in an indoor 5000 m. race, indigestion forced him to retire and Ritola went on to win in 14:33 3/5. Another time, he lost to Alan Helffrich of USA over 880 y. It should be noted that Nurmi never cared to run anything faster than 1:56.3 in a regular 800 m. race. In all his other appearances, Nurmi annihilated practically every man that was opposed to him. He set many American records, including one of 8:58 1/5 for two miles indoors - history's first sub-9 minutes clocking. Huge crowds turned out to see the "Phantom Finn", and thousands of would-be spectators had to be turned away. Ritola set a great indoor record of 14:23 1/5 for the 5000 m. (with Nurmi not in the race).

In later years, Nurmi took things relatively easily, except for occasional outbursts. Lack of major incentives and recurrent rheumatism may explain his fading furore. Even so, he went on winning. Between 1926 and 1931 he lost only three important races. Two of these were on consecutive days at Berlin in the fall of 1926: against Peltzer and Wide in the 1500 m. (as previously related) and against Wide in the 2 miles. The third major loss came in the 1928 Olympics at Amsterdam, when Ritola defeated him in the 5000 m., 14:38.0 to 14:40.0. A few days earlier, Nurmi had beaten Ritola in the 10,000m., 30:18 4/5 to 30:19 2/5. By then, Nurmi's Olympic tally amounted to twelve medals (nine gold, three silver) - as opposed to Ritola's eight (five gold, three silver). In both training and competition Ritola (born at Peräseinäjoki on 18 January 1896; 1.77 m./ 62 kg.) was probably less "rational" than his great rival, yet he knew how to rise to the occasion when high honours were at stake. He may be considered the most underrated of distance champions. It was Nurmi's secret wish to close his career with a smashing victory in the 1932 Olympic marathon at Los Angeles. In fact he was on the spot and ready to set the world on fire for the last time, when on the eve of the Games he was suspended from the amateur ranks "on good and sufficient grounds". Nurmi continued to compete in Finland as a "national amateur" with the "nihil obstat" of SUL (the Finnish Athletics Federation), whose president at the time was Urho Kaleva Kekkonen, a former national high jump champion (1.85 m. in 1924) and future President of the Finnish Republic. Nurmi scored one of his most surprising victories in 1933, when he won the 1500 m. at the Finnish Championships in 3:55.8, outsprinting the likes of Paavo Mickelsson, Eino Purje and Lauri Lehtinen. He was then thirty-six. During his long career Nurmi set twenty official world records. Here are the ones not previously mentioned:
- 2000 m., 5:26.3 (1922) and 5:24.6 (1927); 3000

Paavo Nurmi as a shop-keeper in Helsinki, 1962. His customer is Herb Elliott, the great Australian miler.

m., 8:28.6 (1922), 8:25.4 and 8:20.4 (both 1926); 3 miles, 14:11.2 (1923); 5000 m., 14:35.3 (1922); 6 miles, 29:36.4 (1930); 10 miles, 50:15.0; 1 hour running, 19,210 m.: (both 1928); 20,000 m., 1:04:38.4 (1930). Plus three more records at distances which are no longer recognized by the IAAF. In later years Nurmi supplied a critical analysis of his training methods. His daily schedule, more than adequate to the needs of his time, consisted for the most part in long and relatively slow runs, usually preceded by equally long walks. If compared with the often oppressive training methods of present-day runners, Nurmi's onetime ration naturally seems insufficient, notably as regards quality. In his own admission, speed work really entered his mind only in the later years of his career. Although he had the great merit of perceiving the importance of even-pace running, it may be argued that by this constant thought he obviously limited himself and probably left his potentialities untapped. Seen in their proper historic perspective, however, Nurmi's feats can only be described as fantastic. He was honoured in his mother country as few athletes, if any, have ever been honoured. A statue of the great champion, commissioned by the Finnish Government to sculptor Wäinö Aaltonen in 1924, is to be seen in front of the Helsinki Olympic Stadium. Nurmi passed away on 2 October 1973 in Helsinki. He was given a state funeral which was attended by President Kekkonen and several other Finnish champions of different generations. Even after Nurmi's retirement from big-time competition, Finland continued to rule the roost in distance running. In the Olympic Games of 1932 and 1936 the sons of Suomi won no less than twelve of the eighteen medals awarded in the 5000, 10,000 m. and 3000 m. steeplechase! On 19 June 1932 two Nurmi records were broken - at different venues! Here was the first indication that even the greatest of champions cannot stop the clock of history. At Antwerp, Janusz Kusocinski of Poland ran 3000 m. in 8:18.8, eclipsing Nurmi's 8:20.4 of 1926. More or less by the same time, in Helsinki, Lauri Lehtinen and Volmari Iso-Hollo finished in that order in a "hot" 5000 m. race, both well under Paavo's record (14:28.2) with times of 14:16.9 and 14:18.3 respectively. At the Olympic Games in Los Angeles, the Finns learnt to their cost that the small, slightly hunch-backed Kusocinski (who was incidentally the Polish 800 m. champion in 1:56.6) was a very tough nut to crack. In the 10,000 m. (31 July) the twenty-five-year old Pole led for the greater part of the distance and ran away from Iso-Hollo with 200 m. to go. Although dropping to a dog trot in the last few metres, he won comfortably in 30:11.4, a new Olympic record and more than 20 secs. under his previous best. "Iso" (Finnish for great) was second in 30:12.6, with his countryman Lauri Virtanen in third place (30:35.0). After that cold shower, the Finns

1921
1940

Little Kohei Murakoso (Japan) leading Finnish trio Askola-Salminen-Isohollo in the 10,000 metres at the 1936 Olympics in Berlin. The Japanese failed in his gallant attempt to break the Finnish hegemony and finished fourth behind his Nordic rivals. Salminen won in 30:15.4.

awaited the 5000 m.in a revengeful spirit. Kusocinski stayed away from the race, but another "stranger" filled the gap and played the "trouble-fête".This dark horse was Ralph Hill of USA, a 4:12.4 miler in 1930 (when the world record stood at 4:10.4) who had earned a place in Uncle Sam's team with an easy 14:55.7 effort at the Olympic Tryouts in Palo Alto. In the Los Angeles final (5 August) Hill was pitted against Lehtinen, the world record holder, and Virtanen. The latter was outpaced though, and in the closing stage Lehtinen was left alone to battle it out with the man "who was not supposed to be there". When they entered the homestretch, amidst the pandemonium of the large attendance, the American gathered himself together and tried to pass his rival, first from the outside, then from the inside. Lehtinen held him off, but not without first swinging wide and then closing in. Hill was thus obliged to cut his stride, and when he got back into high gear it was too late. Lehtinen won by half a metre, and the time for both was 14:30.0. Virtanen was again third (14:44.0). The judges finally decided that the Finn had not wilfully interfered with his rival. The crowd, who in such cases are not apt to think twice, gave way to their feelings with loud boos. Announcer Bill Henry (a well-known sports writer, who in 1948 was to edit an enlightening "History of the Olympic Games") rose to the occasion and quietened the masses with the words: "Remember, please, these people are our guests". As a matter of fact, the film of the race leaves little doubt that Lehtinen did hinder his rival to some extent. Hill offered a supreme example of sportsmanship when he said: "Lehtinen was so exhausted that he was merely steering a blind course". In fact, the last lap took 69.2 secs. Lehtinen and Hill were to meet again at Chicago two weeks later in a widely heralded "rematch". Janusz Kusocinski was also in this race. Lehtinen, possibly affected by the ballyhoo made about the Los Angeles affair, was a shadow of his former self and did not finish. Kusocinski finally edged Hill, 14:59.9 to 15:02.0. In subsequent years the Pole was handicapped by recurrent injuries. Even so he managed to finish second to Roger Rochard of France, 14:41.2 to 14:36.8, in the 5000 m. of the first European Championships in Turin (1934). In 1939 "Kuso" offered a final glimpse of his potential when he ran the distance in 14:24.2, his best ever. He died in World War II as a fighter in the Polish "résistance". The most important meet of the Polish track calendar is named after him.

The 1936 Olympics in Berlin marked the climax of the Finnish Era. In the 10,000 m. (2 August) a Finnish trio consisting of Ilmari Salminen, Arvo Askola and Volmari Iso-Hollo made a clean sweep, finishing in that order with times of 30:15.4, 30:15.6 and 30:20.2 respectively. They were put to a hard test by a little, stubborn Japanese, Kohei Murakoso (fourth in 30:25.0), who was outpaced only in the last of the twenty-five laps. Murakoso, by then 31, was Asia's first great distance runner. Five days later, in the 5000 m., the Finns were out for another clean sweep, but in addition to Murakoso they had a dangerous "cousin" to reckon with, Henry Jonsson (later Kälarne) of Sweden. In the last kilometre Salminen collided with Lehtinen, fell and lost valuable ground. Lehtinen was quick to regain his stride but he had no answer to the bid of his compatriot Gunnar Höckert, who went on to win in 14:22.2. Lehtinen was second (14:25.8), while Jonsson (14:29.0) shunted Murakoso to fourth (14:30.0). All the first four except Lehtinen improved on their personal best. The Japanese again surpassed his previous efforts by a wide margin, yet remained without a medal. Höckert closed his brilliant season with two world records: 8:14.8 for 3000 m. and 8:57.4 for 2 miles. He was probably the most talented of Nurmi's "sons", but ill health prevented him from maximizing his potential in later years. He died on a battlefield in Karelia in February 1940, one day before his 30th birthday. The last of Nurmi's major records (30:06.1 for 10,000 m.) fell in 1937 at Kouvola, when Ilmari Salminen, the metronome type of runner, covered the distance in 30:05.5. This reliable performer was European 10,000 m. champion twice, with 31:02.6 in Turin (1934) and 30:52.4 in Paris (1938). The greatest collector of world records among Nurmi's heirs was Taisto Mäki (born at Rekola on 2 December 1910; 1.73 m./ 64 kg.).Clearly less vulnerable than any of his predecessors on the double account of speed and endurance, Mäki was European 5000 m. champion in 1938 (14:26.8) and had his greatest year in 1939, when he set the following world records, all at Helsinki's new Olympic Stadium: - 16 June: 14:08.8 (5000 m.), with 13:42.4 (3 miles) en route; 7 July: 8:53.2 (2 miles); 17 September: 29:52.6 (10,000 m.), with 28:55.6 (6 miles) en route. Mäki, who late in 1938 had bettered Salminen's 10,000 m. record with a 30:02.0 effort, became history's first sub-30 minutes performer a year later, after covering the first half in 14:58.2 and the second in 14:54.4. In most of his fastest races he had a useful rival and partner in Kauko Pekuri. Decades of popularity for distance running had created among Finland's "long grind" specialists an unwritten but universally accepted code, under which every champion runner felt bound to contribute, within the limits of his possibilities, to every record attempt, by doing his share of the donkey (i.e. pacesetting) work.

MARATHON - New Blood from South America, Africa and Asia

At a time when Nurmi and Ritola were beginning to corner the market in the long track events, Finland could naturally afford the luxury of sending other distance runners of better-than-average ability to the road events. At the 1924 Olympics in Paris, the colours of Suomi were again carried to victory, this time by 35-year-old Albin Stenroos, who had finished third in the 10,000 m. at Stockholm twelve years earlier! In Paris he covered the standard distance (42,195 m.) in 2:41:22 3/5, beating runner-up Romeo Bertini of Italy by nearly six minutes. The story of the man who finished third in that race, Clarence DeMar of USA, is related separately. The "marathon bug" was beginning to infect practically every area of the globe. Outstanding among "new" countries on the marathon map were Japan and Argentina. At the 1928 Olympics in Amsterdam two Japanese runners, Kanematsu Yamada and Seiichiro Tsuda, finished fourth and sixth respectively. Winner was an Algerian representing France, Boughera El Ouafi, who covered the standard distance in 2:32:57. Miguel Plaza of Chile, the king of South American distance runners, was second, only 26 seconds back. The best Finn, Martti Marttelin, had to be content with a bronze medal. An interesting entry was Joie Ray, America's fastest miler during the early Twenties (4:12.0 indoors in 1925), who finished a brilliant fifth. Later on he earned a reputation in "dance marathons" as well. The 1932 Olympic marathon at Los Angeles took place in the shadow of a great absentee - Paavo Nurmi. The "Phantom Finn" had won a trial race over a 40,200 m. course earlier in the season in the promising time of 2:22:03.8. As previously related, he was barred from the Los Angeles Games at the last moment by the IAAF, on charges of having cashed in on his track fame. Whether Nurmi, who had a bad leg at the time, could have won the Olympic marathon is, of course, open to question.

The actual winner, Juan Carlos Zabala of Argentina, covered the distance in 2:31:36, a new Olympic record. Zabala had spent the early years of his life in an orphanage, until he was adopted by Alexander Stirling, a physical training instructor. Under the influence of his protector, young Juan Carlos eventually developed into a great runner. At twenty years of age, in 1931, he won the 10,000 m. at the South American Championships in 31:19.0 (fourth best in the world for that year) and was second in the 5000 m. Later in 1931, he came to Europe and made a great marathon debut at Kosice.

In driving rain, he left some of Europe's best "long grind" specialists far behind, winning with nearly 15 minutes to spare in 2:33:19. In the 1932 Olympic race he was in the lead for the greater part of the race. He reached the turning point in 1:20, followed by Lauri Virtanen of Finland. On the return journey, first Virtanen and then Duncan McLeod Wright, a Scotsman, wrested the lead from Zabala, but the Argentinian always fought back bravely and regained his position. While the Finn dropped out, Sam Ferris of Britain came up from behind with an impressive run. At the end of it, he failed to catch Zabala by merely 19 seconds. Ferris was then a stout veteran of 31. His fame in the British Isles was chiefly due to his phenomenal string of successes in the "Sporting Life" marathon, one of the world's most renowned endurance tests. This event, jointly promoted by the newspaper and Polytechnic Harriers, was first held in 1909, on the course of the Olympic marathon of the previous year. Ferris won the event eight times (1925-29 and 1931-33). At Los Angeles he was making his third Olympic appearance, after finishing fifth in 1924 and eighth in 1928. In 1936 Zabala came to Europe several months before the Berlin

1921 1940

Taisto Mäki nips Henry Jonsson Kälarne, 14:17.8 to 14:18.8, in the 5000 metres of the Sverige vs Suomi dual meet in Stockholm in 1939. (Courtesy Svenska Fri-Idrottsförbundet).

Olympics. He tuned up with a number of track and road races in Germany and lowered the South American 10,000 m. record to 30:56.2, which was then a truly "Finnish" achievement. He also set a new world record for 20,000 m.: 1:04:00.2. In the meantime, however, new men had come to the fore - especially in Japan. In 1935 Europeans were shocked by a couple of news items emanating from the islands of the Rising Sun. On 3 April at Tokyo, Yasuo Ikenaka was credited with a time of 2:26:44 for the standard distance. Discussions on this amazing achievement were still going on when later in the same year, namely on 3 November at Tokyo, a fractionally faster time, 2:26:42, was credited to Kitei Son.

Kee-Chung Sohn (Korea), who won the 1936 Olympic marathon in the colours of Japan, under the name of Kitei Son.

This redoubtable little man (born at Sinuiju, Korea, on 29 August 1914 as Kee-Chung Sohn; 1.65 m. / 58 kg.) went on to conquer the world in the 1936 Olympic marathon, while Ikenaka failed to do himself justice in the Trials race.

In the early stages of the Berlin event, Juan Carlos Zabala was again the prominent figure. At the half-way point he was in the lead, with Son 50 seconds behind. But at the twenty-eighth kilometre the Argentinian was caught by Son and Ernest Harper of Britain and had to give way to both. The defending champion plodded on till the thirty-second kilometre, when a major crisis forced him to retire. Son drew away from Harper in the conclusive stage and kept gaining ground till the end. He won in 2:29:19.2, more than two minutes under Zabala's Olympic record. Harper was second (2:31:23.2) and another Japanese, Shoryu Nan, was third (2:31:42.0). Then came the Finns Erkki Tamila and Väinö Muinonen, who had been tipped as the most likely winners by conservative European observers.

No murmur, thank you

America's most famous marathon runner during the "Roaring Twenties" was Clarence DeMar (born at Madeira, Ohio, on 7 June 1888; 1.73 m./ 63 kg.).Although he reached his peak in that decade, his fabulous career spread over a period of forty-five years, from 1909 to 1954, by which time his marathon tally had surpassed the one-hundred mark! He was the king of the Boston marathon, a classic in which he scored seven victories (1911, 1922, 1923, 1924, 1927, 1928 and 1930), besides finishing among the top ten on eight more occasions. He represented USA in three editions of the Olympic Games, always in his parade event, placing twelfth at Stockholm (1912), third at Paris (1924) and twenty-seventh at Amsterdam (1928). His fastest time on a standard course was 2:31:07 4/5 in finishing second to another American, Albert "Whitey" Michelsen (2:29:01 4/5), at Port Chester in 1925. What really amazed experts was the fact that while in his prime DeMar stayed away from the running path for nearly five years, up to 1917, due - partly if not entirely - to persistent rumours about a suspected heart murmur. However, exhaustive medical research conducted in the Twenties at the Harvard Fatigue Laboratory showed such early diagnosis to be completely wrong. In fact, his cardiovascular stamina was then described as "incredible". DeMar died from cancer at the age of seventy.

HURDLES - 110 METRES HURDLES: Towns and Wolcott, pearls of an American dynasty

Earl Thomson of Canada duplicated his 14 2/5 for 120 y. hurdles in 1921. But at the end of his reign the Americans again emerged as the dominant power. During the Twenties, however, they were seriously challenged on more than one occasion. At the 1924 Olympics in Paris, Dan Kinsey, an American who used to practice hurdling over park benches in St.Louis, won in 15.0, beating Sydney Atkinson of South Africa by merely 20 cm. The Springbok was a versatile talent: in 1925 he long jumped 7.34, at a time when only half a dozen men in the world could master that distance. And he was clever enough to renew his challenge at Amsterdam in 1928. After another ding-dong battle all the way, he won in 14 4/5, beating Stephen Anderson of USA by the proverbial whisker. Atkinson was to remain the last non-American to win the "highs" till 1976! At Amsterdam another South African, George Weightman-Smith, had done 14 3/5 in a semi-final, a new world record for the metric distance. Scandinavians were by then taking full advantage of Robert Simpson's teachings. Sten Pettersson, a big name in Swedish athletics history, was at different times holder of the world record for the "highs" (14.7 for 110 m. in 1927) and the "intermediates"(53 4/5 for 400 m. in 1925). To this day the last man to figure in IAAF books in such double capacity. "Sten-Pelle" was for many years a stalwart of the yellow-and-blue team in international matches. In 1930 he lowered his best for the "highs" to 14.6. In the meantime, however, the world record had been captured by another Swede. On 25 August 1929, during the Sweden vs. Norway match at Stockholm, twenty-year-old Eric Wennström clipped three-tenths off his previous best with a surprising 14.4.The Swedes, traditionally sceptical about records made in the short distances, found it hard to believe in the authenticity of Wennström's mark, which was, however, accepted as a national and world record. Wennström ran 14.6 under unfavourable conditions later in the season. In subsequent years he was hampered by poor health and never again rose to world prominence. His record was equalled in 1931 at Helsinki by Bengt Sjöstedt of Finland. However, not one of these men matched the brilliance of the Amsterdam runner-up, Stephen Anderson of USA, who between 1928 and 1930 amassed five 14.4 clockings, only the last of which, made in the 1930 AAU Championships at Pittsburgh (over 120 y.), was ratified by the IAAF. Anderson was very successful in his duels with Pettersson and other leading Europeans. A solid career record was later shown by Percy Beard, one of the tallest men seen until then in the high-hurdles ranks. Unlike the majority of his coun-trymen, Beard (born at Hardinsburg, Kentucky, on 26 January 1908; 1.93 m./ 84 kg.) emerged after leaving college. He improved from 14.8 in 1930, his last year in school, to 14.2 in 1931, a time he duplicated in 1932 and in 1934, the last time over the metric distance at Oslo. At the Los Angeles Olympics he hit the sixth hurdle while leading, lost his rhythm and despite a gallant recovery he finally lost to his countryman George Saling, 14.7 to 14.6. Third place went to Don Finlay of Britain (14.8), not

1921 1940

Earl Thomson (Canada), Olympic 110 metre hurdles champion in 1920.

99

without an intermezzo which is related separately. At Los Angeles, particularly in the final, hurdles (then in the shape of an inverted T) fell like autumn leaves, although less gently. This pattern, prevalent in those days, was aggravating in more than one way, since a rule passed after World War I called for the disqualification of any runner who knocked down three or more hurdles - not to mention the fact that it was sufficient to knock down one to be deprived of a record! A new type of hurdle, in the shape of an L, was introduced in 1935. The base was furnished with weights and the overturning force thus required was 8 lb. (3.63 Kg.). This change offered substantial advantages, since it lessened the chance of injury and consequently freed the athletes of a psychological hindrance. No wonder then that times close to 14 seconds became more and more frequent. Between 1932 and 1936, America produced quite a number of 14.2/14.3 performers. Olympic champion George Saling was probably the most versatile of them all: in his best year, 1932, he ran the "highs" in 14.2 and the "intermediates" in 52.1. Less than a year later he met an untimely death in an automobile accident. Other prominent hurdlers of that period were Jack Keller (who had an unratified 14.1 in 1933), John Morriss, Gus Meier, Tom Moore, Leroy Kirkpatrick, Alvin Moreau (credited with an unofficial and somewhat doubtful 13.9 in 1935), Phil Cope, Roy Staley, Sam Allen and Forrest Towns. It fell to the last-named to achieve history's first official sub-14 secs. mark.

Fair Play, Vintage 1932

Possibly the first case of an Olympic medal that changed owner as a result of a photo finish verdict occurred at the 1932 Games in Los Angeles. In the final of the 110 m. hurdles, finish judges first awarded third place to Jack Keller of USA, with Don Finlay of Britain in fourth. But evidence later supplied by the Kirby Photo-electric Camera proved that the 23-year-old RAF flyer was entitled to the bronze medal, having in fact finished barely ahead of Keller. British chroniclers relate that following this reversal "Keller elected to visit the quarters of the British team personally, for the purpose of handing over the third medal, which he had already received, to the Englishman". A very nice story, vintage 1932 - a time when Olympic medals did not weigh so heavily as at the present time.

Forrest "Spec" Towns (born at Fitzgerald, Georgia, on 6 February 1914; 1.88 m./ 78 kg.) was superior to most if not all his contemporaries in basic speed: 9.7 over 100 y., (as opposed to Beard's 10.2). In 1935 he won the AAU Junior title with a wind-assisted 14.4. The following year he was consistently head and shoulders above his rivals, both at home and abroad. He went to Berlin as the new world record holder with a 14.1 for the metric distance. In the Olympics he offered a fine display of hurdling technique, clinching the title in 14.2, after a 14.1 "semi" earlier on the same day. Durable Don Finlay of Britain won the silver medal in 14.4, in a close finish with Fred Pollard, an American, and Håkan Lidman of Sweden, who finished third and fourth respectively, both in 14.4.

Towns had his Day of Days on 27 August 1936 at Oslo, when he linked his name with one of the most talked-of performances in track history. Prior to that meet he had returned no less than five 14.1 clockings, naturally under the most varied conditions. His consistency stamped him as a 13.9 prospect if and when he would put "all his pieces together". But on the fast Bislett track he far exceeded the brightest expectations. Making shambles of the opposition, he ran an inspired race, at the end of which the official timers caught him in 13.7, 13.7 and 13.8, while two alternates showed 13.6 and 13.7. He was consequently credited with 13.7. (Olympic finalist Larry O'Connor of Canada was a distant second in 14.6). When the verdict of the watches was made public, Towns himself was among the incredulous. Yet the course was found to be marginally over distance (110.03 m.), and there was no wind. The IAAF records committee went to the trouble of studying a film of the race. Then, almost two years later, the mark was ratified as a world record. Towns closed his superlative 1936 campaign with four more 14.1 clockings. He may have been helped by some invisible factor in his Day of Days. But there is no doubt that by 1936 standards he was clearly the perfect hurdler. He continued through the 1938 indoor season, but with declining interest.

Before the ratification of Towns' 13.7, another American, Bob Osgood, ran the 120 y. hurdles in 14 flat (1937). This time was equalled in 1938 at the British Empire Games in Sydney by Thomas Lavery of South Africa, but the mark was refused recognition because of suspected wind assistance, a ruling which was disputed by several observers. In contrast with an IAAF rule passed in 1936, there was no anemometer during the race. At any rate Lavery turned out to be a durable hurdler: in 1950, aged thirty-nine, he was still capable of 14.2/14.3. Undeniably the first man to prove sub-14 secs. class was Fred Wolcott of USA (born at Snyder, Texas, on 18 November 1917). Possibly less impressive than Towns in technique and physical structure, although he stood 1.81 m. and weighed 77 kg., Wolcott reminded experts that speed between the hurdles was, after all, the prime requisite for any would-be record performer. This blond Texan, who ran the 100 y. in 9.5 several times, was above all a great competitor. His breakthrough occurred in 1937, when he ran 14.3. The following year he ducked under 14 secs. for the first time at the Texas Relays in Austin, with 13.9 for the English distance, a time he duplicated later in the year at Stockholm over 110 m. hurdles. In a triangular meet at Austin in 1940 he was extended by Boyce Gatewood to a sterling performance: 13.7 for the 120 y. hurdles, a time which was accepted as a college record only. Gatewood, who played second fiddle to Wolcott in countless races, had his best day right then and there, finishing second in 13.8. Later in the year, at Princeton, Wolcott succeeded Jesse Owens as holder of the world record for the "lows", with 22.3 (200 m.) and 22.5 (220 y.). His form over the hurdles was not so polished as Towns' (the latter was said to have gone through the 1936 season "virtually without knocking down a hurdle"). In fact his rare defeats occurred when he happened to make a mistake in clearing the barriers.

For over a decade, Europe had only two hurdlers who could vie with America's ever-changing phalanx of "timber-toppers". These men were Donald Finlay of Britain and Håkan Lidman of Sweden. The Englishman (born at Christchurch, Hampshire, on 27 May 1909; 1.82 m./ 77 kg.) stands in the history of the event as a unique example of longevity. He joined the European élite in 1931 when he did 14.8 and was still in the select group in 1951, when he could still do 14.8! In addition to winning medals in two Olympic Games (bronze at Los Angeles, silver at Berlin), he was European 110 m. hurdles champion in 1938 with his best legitimate mark, 14.3. In 1937, possibly his best year, he ran the metric distance in 14.2 at Colombes and 14.1 at Stockholm only to see his marks rejected because of suspected wind assistance. Lidman (born at Göteborg on 31 January 1915; 1.89 m./) also had a very long career, during which he competed in an estimated 500 hurdle races. Twice an Olympic finalist (fourth in Berlin, sixth in London twelve years later), he won the European title in 1946 (14.6). On 22 September 1940 at Milan he lowered the continental 110 m. hurdles record to 14.0, a time he was to duplicate seven years later at Buenos Aires in barely losing to Argentina's Alberto Triulzi, also timed in 14.0. The bespectacled Lidman had a most efficient and economical clearance.

400 METRES HURDLES - A super record for "Slats" Hardin

1921 1940

The most brilliant performer in the "intermediates" during the Twenties was Frederick Morgan Taylor (born at Sioux City, Iowa, on 17 April 1903; 1.86 m./ 75 kg.). This great competitor reached the Olympic final on three occasions and won a medal every time. In 1924 he won the title in 52 3/5, equalling a world record he had set earlier in the year at the US Olympic Tryouts in Cambridge,

F. Morgan Taylor (USA), Olympic 400 metre hurdles champion in 1924.

Massachusetts. In Paris, however, he knocked down a hurdle and his performance could not be submitted to the IAAF. And his earlier mark was ratified only as a US record. In 1928 he finally "made" the IAAF record book with a nifty 52.0 performance at the US Olympic Tryouts in Philadelphia on 4 July. He seemed all set for another Olympic victory, but on the poor Amsterdam track he was upset by a most obstinate, even if somewhat unorthodox, hurdler from Great Britain: David George Brownlow Cecil, better known as Lord Burghley. A supreme effort carried the Briton across the tape in 53 2/5, ahead of Frank Cuhel of USA (who had been timed in 52 1/5 in finishing second to Taylor at Philadelphia) and defending champion Taylor, who were both clocked in 53 3/5. Taylor returned to the warpath in 1932 and won a bronze medal at the Los Angeles Olympics. This great athlete is said to have run no more than about thirty races at this distance in the whole of his long career. On the flat he was one of the fastest quarter-milers of his time (48 1/5), and he was also a better-than-average long jumper with a wind-assisted effort of 7.67, which stood as a family record till 1952, when his son "Buzz" leaped 7.77.

Lord Burghley (born at Stamford, Lincolnshire, on 9 February 1905; 1.80 m./ 70 kg.) was the outstanding all-round hurdler in Britain for many years. By his athletic prowess and personality he made a great impact on the sport of his time, first as a competitor, then as a political figure, till he finally became president of the IAAF in 1946, an office he held for thirty years. The only European hurdlers who could measure up to his class were Luigi Facelli of Italy and Sten Pettersson of Sweden. Particularly famous are the duels between the English Lord and his arch rival and friend Facelli, who was by profession a glassblower. Italian papers liked to refer to their rivalry, somewhat emphatically, as a token of the virtues of sport in pitting against each other, on equal terms, two men of entirely different social extraction. Facelli and Lord Burghley met eleven times: at the end of their feud the Italian led 6 to 5 (or 5 to 4, if we count finals only). However, the Englishman had the upper hand in the Olympic finals of 1928 and 1932. Facelli represented his country in four editions of the Olympics (Paris, Amsterdam, Los Angeles and Berlin) and reached the final of the 400 m. hurdles twice: sixth in 1928 and fifth in 1932. He ranked among the world's top ten for over a decade (1924-35). At the age of 41 he still managed to run the distance in 57.0. He reached his peak in 1929, when he did 52 2/5, equalling the European record set by Sten Pettersson the year before. He also ran 52.5 in beating F.Morgan Taylor in a post-Olympic

When history reads like a fairy tale

Relatively speaking, i.e. in relation to the size of its team, it is doubtful if any country has ever enjoyed in the Olympics a measure of success comparable to that of Ireland at the 1932 Games in Los Angeles. On that occasion, a four-man team from the Emerald Isle brought home two gold medals , incidentally won on the same day (Bob Tisdall in the 400 m. hurdles and Dr. Pat O'Callaghan in the hammer throw) plus a fourth place (Eamonn Fitzgerald in the triple jump). The most amazing character of the tale was Robert Morton Newburgh Tisdall, a man from Tipperary who first surpassed himself in winning the "intermediates" from a crack field, then finished eighth in the decathlon. In what was supposed to be his parade event, the 400 m. hurdles, he had to his credit only three previous tries! His debut dated from a visit to Greece in 1930, when he ran 55.0. In pre-Olympic weeks he ran 56 1/5, then 54 1/5, both over 440 y. As a student at Cambridge he had certainly shown remarkable versatility, yet his pre-Games efforts were hardly indicative of things to come. While nursing an ankle injury from the previous year, he had scarce opportunities for proper training. As the tale goes, during the long trip to LA, by sea and by rail, he slept badly and lost five pounds (just over 2 kg.). Once in the Olympic Village, he thought it advisable to recover with a different schedule, spending 15 out of every 24 hours in bed for eight days! He "woke up" to gentle training only three days before the first round of his event. In view of these circumstances, his performance at the Los Angeles Coliseum on 1 August 1932 may well be rated as one of the most surprising in track history. Irish sources claim that part of the secret lay in the fact that in his rare training sessions Bob usually ran over a longer distance, on a course that was entirely flat ... except for three hurdles placed near the end of the journey. For sure, speed was not the least of Tisdall's "atouts": in this respect, his 49.0 over 400 m. flat (last event of the first day) in the Olympic decathlon was highly enlightening. Shortly after his Olympic triumph, Tisdall settled down in South Africa (where he occasionally competed "just for the fun of it"). He was to remain the typical example of an athlete who won perennial fame in a single day of glory.

meet at Chicago in 1932 (that was Taylor's last appearance in a major meet).

Pettersson also had a long career, during which he won no less than twenty-two national titles. He was a fairly close fourth (53 4/5) in the 1928 Olympic final. However, Lord Burghley was the most brilliant of the three by the clock: he could point to such marks as 14.5 in the "highs", 24.3 in the "lows" (both at the English distances), and 52.2 in the 400 m. hurdles. Facelli had "metric" times of 14.8, 24.8 and 52.4; Pettersson did 14.6, 25.2 and 52.4. In the 1932 Olympics in Los Angeles, the "man-killer event" was one of the highlights of the Games. On the fast Coliseum track (then the only one in America with a circumference of exactly 400 m.), veterans Taylor, Burghley and Facelli were again redoubtable, yet they could not counter the attack of a young duo, Robert Tisdall of Ireland and Glenn Hardin of USA. The former (born at Nuwara Eliya, Ceylon, on 16 May 1907; 1.86 m./ 74 kg.) was a Cambridge student who had come to Los Angeles with a personal best of 54 1/5 (440 y., grass track). In the Olympic arena he revealed unsuspected potential by winning his semi-final in 52.8. And he rose to spectacular heights in the final the next day (1 August). Drawn in lane 4, the tall Irishman ran well from the start, held his form throughout the race, and finally won in world record time, 51.7. The supposedly "green" Hardin (lane 7) finished strongly to take second place in 51.9, ahead of Taylor (52.0), Lord Burghley (52.2) and Facelli (53.0). In accordance with the rule then in force, the times for the first two were officially rounded off to the nearest fifth, and by way of compromise Taylor, the third man, was given an ungenerous 52.2. Still in compliance with another rule of those days, Tisdall, having knocked down the last hurdle, lost his right to become the new world record holder. It so happened that Hardin, the runner-up, lost the race but won the record, with 52.0. The Kirby Photo-electric Camera supplied a more faithful version of the times: Tisdall 51.67, Hardin 51.85, Taylor 51.96, Burghley 52.01 - new personal records for all four.

Glenn ("Slats") Hardin (born at Derma, Mississippi, on 1 July 1910; 1.88 m./ 77 kg.) was Taylor's rightful successor. He possessed to a great extent that natural gift which is so essential in all athletic events: speed. He ranked among the fastest quarter-milers in the States and in 1934 he ran the distance in 46.8, until then the second fastest time on record. In the same year he won the AAU 400 m. hurdles title at Milwaukee in 51.8, a new world record.

Then he came to Europe and things really began to happen. On 26 July, in the time-honoured Stockholm Olympic Stadium, he produced an inspired performance, negotiating one lap (383 m.) plus 17 m. in 50.6, a time which understandably sounded unbelievable to his contemporaries.

While en route he slightly dislodged a hurdle: at first this incident gave rise to a rather heated debate, which was soon quelled, however, since the rules held no sanction in such a case. A distant second (55.8) in that historic race was Jacob Lindahl of Sweden, who was to become one of Scandinavia's best-known athletics administrators.

Experts obviously expressed amazement over the fact

1921
1940

Robert Tisdall (Ireland) winning the 400 metre hurdles at the 1932 Olympics in Los Angeles from Glenn Hardin, nearest camera, F. Morgan Taylor (both of USA) and Lord Burghley (GB). The winner's time, 51.7, was not ratified as he had knocked down the last hurdle.

Stockholm 1934: Dan Ferris (white cap), Secretary General of the AAU, discussing with Swedish officials after Glenn Hardin (USA) broke the world 400 metres hurdles record by 1.2 with an unheard of 50.6. The debate was about a slightly dislodged hurdle, but the rules held no sanction in such a case and so the time was ratified by the IAAF.

that the record was bettered by 1.2 secs. in one stroke. But it is doubtful whether Hardin was substantially a better hurdler than Taylor. In fact, the "flat-hurdles" differential of the two athletes was identical: 4.1 (Hardin 46.5* and 50.6, Taylor 47.9* and 52.0, where the asterisk stands for a 440 y. time less 0.3). But Hardin had a definite edge in terms of pure blazing speed.

In the latter part of his 1934 European tournée he twice did 51.4, still without being extended. In 1936 he qualified for the Berlin Olympics with 51.4, winning from Joseph Patterson (51.6) and Dale Schofield (51.7). At Berlin, the world record holder could not help obliging with an Olympic victory: he did so with 52.4, ahead of John Loaring of Canada (52.7) and Miguel White of the Philippines (52.8). Patterson, fourth in 53.0, was to die a hero's death three years later, entrapped in the sunken submarine "Squalus".

Up to then, and for many more years to come, Europeans and Americans followed two different patterns in this event, the former concentrating on technique and rhythm, the latter relying primarily, if not entirely, on speed. In the Thirties, men like Hans Scheele of Germany and Prudent Joye of France, both hardly capable of beating 49 secs. on the flat route, managed to become champions of Europe in the "intermediates" with times of 53.2 and 53.1 respectively.

Even in those days, however, there was a European who appeared to have "American potential": versatile József Kovács of Hungary, who could point to the following set of times: 10.5, a somewhat doubtful 21.0, 33.3 and 47.7 on the flat; a wind-assisted 14.4, 23.7 and 52.9 over the hurdles. Like other Magyar athletes of his time, Kovács had a carefree attitude and never took the trouble of working hard in any event.

At the 1939 German Championships in Berlin, 24-year-old Friedrich-Wilhelm Hölling, a lean athlete with good technique and moderate speed, pressed the European metric record down to 51.6. In his wake, Georg Glaw was timed in 52.0. These were two of the many athletes from Europe and other continents whose career was brought to an abrupt end by World War II.

But America luckily found a man who managed to beat 52 secs. both before and after the conflict: Leroy ("Roy") Braxton Cochran (born at Richton, Mississippi, on 6 January 1919; 1.77 m./ 70 kg.).

At the 1939 AAU Championships in Lincoln, in what was virtually his debut in big-time competition, he accomplished a commendable workmanlike job and won the 400 m. hurdles in 51.9, barely ahead of Bob Simmons (52.0), son of the Chief Justice of the Nebraska Supreme Court. Cochran came to Europe later in the year and in a 440 y. hurdles race at London's White City edged the newly crowned European record holder, F.W.Hölling, 52.7 to 53.1.

The following year, Cochran suffered the only major defeat of his career in the 400 m. hurdles when he lost to a tall Californian, Carl McBain, 52.1 to 51.6, in the AAU Championships at Fresno.

STEEPLECHASE:
Finnish Domination

The decisive turn came in the Twenties, when the Scandinavians, undisputed masters of the long distances, began to take real interest in the steeplechase.

At the 1924 Olympics in Paris the event was won by Ville Ritola of Finland, Nurmi's arch rival, in 9:33 3/5. However, lack of interest in most of the other areas of the world left Northern Europeans with little or no incentive, and consequently progress was slow. In 1928 at Amsterdam, the Finns went to work more seriously, aiming for a grand slam through unselfish team-work. Toivo Loukola, acknowledged to be the most refined steeplechaser in the Finnish camp, soon built up a decisive lead, while his team-mates Nurmi and Ove Andersen ostensibly bided their time in "towing" the pursuers' group. In those days it was almost axiomatic that no one running on Nurmi's watch could incur faulty pace judgment.

For that reason, perhaps, foreign opponents allowed themselves to be held back, and Loukola won by a block in 9:21 4/5. Nurmi and Andersen made it a clean sweep for Suomi by outsprinting their rivals in the closing stage. Nurmi, by no means a specialist in the event, was second in 9:31 1/5.

Defending champion Ritola had dropped out in the early stages.

The greatest steeplechaser in the Thirties was unquestionably Volmari Iso-Hollo (born at Ylöjärvi on 1 May 1907; 1.76 m./ 64 kg.). A gifted runner, but somewhat reluctant to train systematically, "Iso" not only won two Olympic gold medals in the steeplechase but also achieved an impressive series of times over flat distances ranging from 3 to 15 kilometres. At the 1932 Olympics in Los Angeles his time was 10:33.4, which was obviously disappointing in view of the fact that he had earlier won his heat in 9:14.6. On verification, it turned out that due to a "lapsus" on the part of the lap counter (actually a substitute), the runners had negotiated 3 kilometres plus 460 m. By mutual consent, the competitors decided not to ask for a re-run. Iso-Hollo successfully "repeated" four years later in Berlin, whipping a strong field in 9:03.8, easily the best time on record until then.

His countryman Kaarlo Tuominen took second place (9:06.8) ahead of Alfred Dompert of Germany (9:07.2). Iso-Hollo, the happy-go-lucky type of runner, could have beaten 9 minutes in his hey-day if he had been spurred on by stiffer competition.

JUMPS - High Jump: the advent of the Straddle

The outstanding figure of the Twenties in the high jump was Harold Osborn (born at Butler, Illinois, on 13 April 1899; 1.81 m./ 78 kg.).

A keen student of form, he developed a very efficient side-to-the-bar clearance and outshone all his predecessors in brilliance and consistency of performance.

As a great all-round man, he holds a unique record, being the only athlete to this day to have coupled an Olympic victory in an individual event with a victory in the decathlon. This happened at Paris in 1924: first he annexed the high jump crown at 1.98, then he won the ten-event grind with a record score. His best official mark in the high jump was 2.038 at Urbana, Illinois, on 27 May 1924.

The following year, at the Texas Relays in Austin, he did 2.056 in an exhibition. He was the first American to master the classic 2-metre barrier, on several occasions, under the eyes of European crowds. It was as a result of his trick of pressing the bar back in toward the uprights with his hand that the IAAF introduced a new rule to the effect that the bar should be able to fall on either side. Osborn married his female counterpart Ethel Catherwood of Canada, who won the women's title in the high jump at the Amsterdam Olympics (1928).

This bespectacled American, who was to become a doctor of osteopathy, had a long career: he managed to clear 1.981 at the age of 37 and in the same year, 1936, he set a world record of 1.676 in the standing high jump. Third in the 1924 Olympic final in Paris was Pierre Lewden of France, whose name was to symbolize a modified scissors style which practically cornered the market in continental Europe for many years.

Lewden's best, 1.95 in 1925, was fractionally inferior to the best-on-record for Europe, jointly held at 1.956 by Tim Carroll of Ireland (1913) and Benjamin Howard Baker of Britain (1921).

By the end of 1932, i.e. twenty years after Horine's historic record (2.007), only ten men had jumped 2 metres or higher. The only non-American in that

H.M.'s Splash

A funny and vaguely chivalrous interlude occurred at the Amsterdam Olympics (1928) during a heat of the 3000 m. steeplechase. The characters in the play were Paavo Nurmi of Finland and Lucien Duquesne of France. Spectators were treated to a rare sight when the great Paavo, in trying to negotiate the first water jump, fell headlong into it.

The oncoming Duquesne stopped and helped his colleague out of that position - unbecoming for any athlete, let alone the King of Runners. Nurmi, visibly touched, broke his legendary silence and briefly thanked Duquesne, then felt morally bound to "tow" his saviour for the rest of the race. Toward the end of the journey Nurmi tacitly invited the Frenchman to go out in front and break the tape, but Duquesne, knowing himself inferior to the great Finn, refused to consent and chose to retain his (second) place.

1921
1940

group was Simeon Toribio of the Philippines, who cleared exactly that height in the Ninth Far Eastern Games at Tokyo in 1930. In the Olympics, however, long drawn competitions made it difficult for anyone to reach record heights.

So at Amsterdam, in 1928, Robert King of USA won the Olympic title with 1.94, while Osborn finished fifth. Four years later, at Los Angeles, Duncan McNaughton of Canada broke the long chain of American victories by defeating Robert Van Osdel, Toribio and Cornelius Johnson in a jump-off, after all four had cleared 1.97 in the competition proper. The Canadian, who chose that occasion to make the best jump of his career, had matured as a star athlete while a student at the University of Southern California.

One of his team-mates was Van Osdel, the American who took second place in the Olympic event. Dean Cromwell, famous coach of the "Trojans", had been teaching his two pupils how to beat each other while beating all others. Seldom, if ever, did two men learn the same lesson so well! A P.S. seems to be in order: if the fewer trials-and-misses rule had been in force then, Van Osdel would have won, having cleared 1.97 on his first attempt. Johnson, McNaughton and Toribio would have followed in that order.

Europe had to wait till 1934 to welcome her first 2-metre jumper. This was Kalevi Kotkas (born at Reval - now Tallinn - on 28 July 1913; 1.94 m./ 96 kg.). This Estonian-born athlete opted for the Finnish nationality in 1932. His first clearance of the magic height occurred in South America during a night meet at Rio de Janeiro on 7 March 1934, when he mastered a bar set at 2.01. Later in the year he won the European Championship title at Turin with 2.00. Even a modern observer is astonished to learn that Kotkas could lift his massive frame rather consistently over 1.98 while using a modified version of the scissors. More understandably, perhaps, he was also a first class discus thrower (51.27 in 1937) and a good shot putter (15.55 in 1938). Later in 1934, two other Europeans quickly followed in Kotkas' footsteps: Mihály Bodosi of Hungary and Veikko Peräsalo of Finland did 2.005. In 1935 two Japanese jumpers, Hiroshi Tanaka and Yoshiro Asakuma, raised the Asian record to 2.01.

All these men used the Eastern cut-off, or slight variations of it. In USA the last major exponent of this jumping form was George Spitz, appropriately enough an Easterner, who flirted with the record heights in the early Thirties, with top marks of 2.045 indoors (1932) and 2.032 outdoors (1934).

The forgotten record

One of the earliest European adepts of the Straddle was Nikolay Kovtun of USSR, who in a meet attended by 50,000 spectators in Moscow on 17 June 1937 cleared 2.01, second best ever by a European up to that time. He was Russia's first 2-metre man and his record remained unmatched in the large Euro-Asian country for 18 years. In the intervening time, however, his mark had been removed from the USSR record list for other reasons ... This sad story, for a long time unknown to the majority of Russian sport fans, was brought to light by Yevgeniy Malkov in the daily paper "Sovyetskiy Sport" on 24 June 1988. The article, titled "A Jump in the Unknown" and subtitled "Truth from Distant Years", revealed that after his record performance Kovtun had little time to rejoice. Before the year was out "some people in uniform came to his training camp and took him aside. After that, he was never seen again.

Those were the days when thousands of guiltless individuals were branded as enemies of the people. And nobody was given further explanations". Kovtun was sentenced to ten years in jail, a time he spent in the North under hard circumstances. He was freed in 1947, but only three years later he was arrested once more and sentenced to another five years, a time he spent in the Urals. Meanwhile, Soviet statisticians had been given lessons in putting back the clock of history: Kovtun's name and records (he also held the USSR triple jump mark, 14.66 in 1936) were expunged from all books. In early post-war years Yuriy Ilyasov was credited with a new national record of ... 1.99. As destiny would have it, Kovtun was set free in 1955, the year in which Yuriy Styepanov improved on his record with 2.02.

Another jumper of his generation, Edmund Rokhlin, recalls meeting Kovtun after the liberation: "He in no way resembled the strong young man I knew from pre-war days. Silent, reserved, he hardly spoke with anybody. And he no longer had any interest in sport." Kovtun died of a heart attack in 1981. In 1988 the monthly magazine "Lyogkaya Atletika" published revised summaries of the USSR Championships for the period 1920-40. The names of once expunged athletes appeared in bold type. In addition to Kovtun's, I counted 38 such entries!

The man who succeeded Osborn as world record holder was a Western Roll jumper from California, Walter Marty, who did 2.048 in 1933 and 2.061 in 1934. Still in '34, he cleared 2.07 in an unsanctioned meet. The tradition of great black high jumpers was inaugurated by Cornelius Johnson (born at Los Angeles on 21 August 1913; 1.91 m./ 78 kg.), who is remembered as one of the most invincible performers in the annals of the event. As previously related, this precocious Western Roller finished fourth at the Los Angeles Olympics at the age of nineteen. He had improved from 1.828 in 1930 through 1.93 in '31 till 1.997 in the Olympic year. "Corny", whose legs accounted for 49 per cent of his height, first mastered a record height in the AAU Indoor Championships at New York's Madison Square Garden on 22 February 1936, when he cleared 2.055 from a board take-off. Rather unexpectedly, he got company at that height from another American jumper, Edward Burke, who eventually won the title in a jump-off.

Exactly on the same day, possibly a few hours later, at Fort Collins, Colorado, Gilbert Cruter cleared 2.054 from a dirt take-off in another indoor meet. Both Burke and Cruter were only 21 at the time.

Johnson conquered the official world record, i.e. the outdoor one, at the US Olympic Tryouts on 12 July, still in New York. On that occasion several good jumpers folded up under the pressure of the occasion. Marty, Spitz, Burke and Mel Walker (who had done 2.032 at the AAU Championships a week earlier) were unable to clear 1.981. Delos Thurber, a Californian, secured the vital third place and a berth on the Olympic team by going over that height, leaving Johnson and Dave Albritton alone to fight it out between themselves after that. Having by then got the tickets they wanted so much, the two men mastered 2.032 and had the bar raised to 2.076. Both "made" the record height on their second try, first Johnson, then Albritton. By then, however, Johnson had enough of co-ownerships. At the Berlin Olympics he was all alone over 2.03, thus winning the most coveted of titles. Albritton, Thurber and Kotkas followed in that order, all with 2.00. All the first four thus broke Osborn's twelve-year-old Olympic record (1.98). And Kotkas became the first man in history to jump 2 metres and go unrewarded by a medal.

In the four-year period between Los Angeles and Berlin, Johnson was outjumped only once, by Al Threadgill in an indoor meet in 1936. He continued through the 1938 indoor season. Johnson died under tragic conditions in 1946.

Kotkas had his greatest day at Göteborg on 1 September 1936, when he raised the European record to 2.04, beating Olympic runner-up Albritton (2.02). In subsequent seasons, the Finn put on further weight, and his standard as a high jumper went down slowly but steadily.

Albritton (born at Danville, Alabama, on 13 April 1913; 1.905 m./ 79 kg.) was then only at the beginning of a fabulous career. Between 1936 and 1950 he won the AAU title five times and matched the height of the eventual winner on two other occasions. He was also the first jumper of international renown to adopt a prone position over the crossbar, thus introducing what came to be known as the "belly roll", or straddle style of jumping. This form was used in championship competition for the first time as early as in 1930 by a Cromwell protégé, Jim Stewart of the University of Southern California, who in that year cleared 1.988. This most economical of all clearance forms calls for great co-ordination and perfect timing. Another early exponent of the belly roll was Gilbert Cruter, a tall man from Colorado, mentioned earlier in this section.

Last in the chain of prominent American jumpers of those days was Melvin Walker, who cleared 2.076 from a dirt take-off indoors in 1937, then came to Europe later in the same year and twice bettered the official world record, first with 2.08 at Stockholm, then with 2.09 at Malmö on 12 August. Walker used the Western Roll.

POLE VAULT:
American Symphony

Early in the Twenties, Europeans in general and Scandinavians in particular were becoming familiar with the art of pole-vaulting. Henry Petersen, a Danish gymnast, was an Olympic finalist on two occasions (second in 1920, fourth in 1924). He emerged at eighteen with a national record of 3.69 (1918), a great achievement for a junior in those days. Seven years later he wound up with 4.038. In the meantime, however, another Scandinavian had risen to more spectacular heights.

Charles Hoff of Norway (born at Fredrikstad on 9 May 1902; 1.88 m./ 76 kg.) came to athletics through cross-country running. He took up vaulting in 1920. The following year he captured the Norwegian record at 3.545 and brought it to 3.87 before the season was out. The latter mark was good enough to earn him a third place in the 1921 World List! Such a detail certainly points to the relative paucity of competition in those days. In 1922 Hoff became Europe's first 4-metre man with a 4.02 clearance and later in the season he set a new world record of 4.12. In subsequent years he built up a substantial

Harold Osborn (USA), double Olympic champion in 1924 (high jump & decathlon). In 1925 he showed Europeans how 2 metres heights, or just about, could be mastered, even in a queer setting.

lead over his American and European opponents by achieving record marks of 4.21 in 1923, 4.23 and 4.252 in 1925. The last performance, made at Turku, Finland, on 27 September, remained unsurpassed as a European record till 1937. Hoff was, however, denied the supreme satisfaction of winning Olympic laurels. In 1924 an injured ankle forced him to give up vaulting in the weeks preceding the Paris Olympics, but apparently allowed him to do a fair amount of running.

So the world's no.1 vaulter appeared at Stade de Colombes only as a runner: he reached the semi-finals of the 400 m. and earned eighth place in the 800 m. final! His absence from the pole vault competition was historically important, in that it allowed America's winning streak to continue. (It was finally broken in ....1972). The title went to Lee Barnes, a High School boy who won at 3.95, after a jump-off with Glenn Graham. The winner was one week short of his eighteenth birthday. He has remained to this day the youngest Olympic champion in vaulting history.

Maybe Hoff could have vied for a gold medal also in 1928, if in the meantime he had not been ousted from international competition for infringing the amateur code. Before then, in 1926, he had given lessons to his American rivals during a memorable US tour, which curiously coincided with his honeymoon trip. While there, he improved on the US record many times, with bests of 4.17 indoors and 4.19 outdoors. Hoff, the first major exponent of the "flyaway" style, continued to perform as a "pro". In 1931 he vaulted 4.32 (a mark superior to the official world record) and in '30 he amassed 7,629.215 points in the decathlon. As an amateur he had shown his versatility with such marks as 10.8, 21.8, 49.2 and 1:55.9 in the flat races, 16.2 in the 110 m. hurdles, 7.41 in the long jump and 14.38 in the triple jump. In Norway he was re-qualified as a "national amateur" and in 1933 he won his last championship title with 3.80. He must be considered one of the greatest talents ever to come out of Europe. When he disappeared from the amateur scene, no continental vaulter was able to match or even remotely approach his feats. The Americans therefore lost no time in regaining full control of the situation.

1921 1940

Only one year after Hoff's American visit, the 14-foot (4.26 m.) barrier was broken for the first time by a twenty-three-year-old Yale man, Sabin Carr. This well built athlete had improved from 3.96 in 1925 to 4.04 in 1926. He captured the world record at Philadelphia on 27 May 1927 with a 14-foot clearance and the following year he vaulted 4.29 from a board runway indoors.

The Paris Olympic champion, Lee Barnes, fought back in 1928, when he raised the world mark to 4.31 in a spring meet at Fresno, California, with Ward Edmonds second at 4.26. Both represented California schools. At the Amsterdam Olympics, however, Carr had the upper hand and won with 4.20, while Barnes, the tiny type of vaulter, finished no better than fifth, ironically enough with the same mark (3.95) that had earned him a gold medal four years earlier in Paris.

Sixth in the Amsterdam final, ahead of the best Europeans, was a man from the country of the Rising Sun, Yenataro Nakazawa. The following year another Japanese, Shuhei Nishida, raised the national record over the 4-metre barrier to 4.10. In 1932 Nishida went to the Los Angeles Olympics with a personal best of 4.15, seemingly not good enough to stamp him as a potential danger to the all conquering Americans.

In fact, US vaulters had gone wild at their Olympic Trials in Palo Alto, with Bill Graber raising the world record to 4.37 and Bill Miller clearing 4.30 to take second place. In the Olympic battle, however, Graber failed to live up to expectations. After clearing 4.15, he passed the next height (4.20), then failed at 4.25. He even lost the bronze medal, which went to his countryman George Jefferson at 4.20. Miller was left alone to battle it out with Nishida. The Japanese, a light vaulter of medium build endowed with great stamina, amazingly improved on his personal best three times, finally clearing 4.30. But Miller stood the challenge bravely and won the day by going over 4.315 at his third attempt. The bar jiggled but stayed on, and Uncle Sam was again the master of the vaulting fraternity.

Even in later years Nishida continued to achieve his best marks in "hot" competition. During a European tournée in 1935 he twice equalled his personal best (4.30), first at the World University Games in Budapest, then in a Five-Nations (Sweden, Germany, Hungary, Japan, Italy) match in Berlin. His travel companion was Sueo Oe, who had previously beaten Nishida at Tokyo with a 4.25 vault. But during their European visit they were defeated by the leading Americans of that year, Keith Brown and Bill Sefton. Brown, the last major exponent of the Yale tradition, had raised the world record to 4.39 in a spring meet at Cambridge, Massachusetts. Besides being a very consistent vaulter, he was also a 1.984 high jumper. Much to the regret of his Eastern fans he was sidelined with an injury in 1936 and had to give up his Olympic hope.

The USA vs. Japan feud reached its acme in 1936. Shortly before leaving for Europe, Oe upped the Japanese and Asian record to 4.34. At the same time American vaulters were fighting hard to secure tickets for the Berlin Olympics. In the AAU Championships at Princeton on 4 July, 22-year-old George Varoff topped a fine field with a new world record of 4.43. Only a few months earlier he was a virtual unknown, lost in the cohort of America's 13-foot-plus men. Now he seemed to have the inside lane in the race to Berlin. Had he been superstitious, he might have been worried in remembering what had happened to other world record holders - Dray, Wright, Hoff, Barnes, Graber - before or during previous Olympics. In the Final Tryouts event, held on 12 July in New York, Varoff ran into unexpected trouble. When the bar was raised to 4.34 he was still in the game, but so were three California vaulters, Bill Sefton, Earle Meadows and Bill Graber. A few minutes later Graber and Meadows (both on first try) and Sefton (on third try) had mastered the height, while Varoff was at the end of the runway, facing his last chance. At the decisive moment, pressure got the best of him - and he failed.

A newly crowned world record holder thus had to bypass the Games. Such a thing could only happen in America: that was the favourite comment of foreign observers. A few moments after the drama had come to an end, Varoff was at the "mike" wishing good luck to his conquerors, all of whom incidentally were (or had been) pupils of Dean Cromwell at the University of Southern California.

In the Olympic final at Berlin, Graber duplicated his mark of 1932 in Los Angeles (4.15) and had to be content with fifth place. The America vs. Japan battle finally involved four men: Meadows and Sefton on one side, Oe and Nishida on the other. All four cleared 4.25, after which the bar was raised to 4.35. The competition had been going on for nearly five hours. Performing under floodlights, amid the cheers of their respective supporters, the four men offered the last measure of their resources. Sefton, Oe and Nishida all came close at least once, but failed. Only Meadows, who had a personal best of 4.37, made it, on his second attempt. The two Japanese beat Sefton in a jump-off and were bracketed in a tie for second place. The leader of the Japanese team, in an ante-litteram application of the fewer misses rule, thought Nishida should have the silver medal (he had gone over 4.25 on his first try, while Oe needed two), but the two athletes finally decided to cut the medals in two parts, so that each had his share of both silver and bronze! (P.S. A few days later, George Varoff vaulted 4.38 in a "consolation" meet held in New York!).

Early in 1937 Oe competed successfully in American indoor meets. In his first appearance on boards, at New York's Madison Square Garden, he had to use a borrowed pole (his own implements were badly damaged during the long trip by sea and land), yet he managed to beat Olympic champion Earle Meadows, 4.34 to 4.26. At the end of his US tour, the medium built (1.75 m./ 60 kg.) Keio University student was 2-to-2 vs his American rival (plus a tie).

The 1937 outdoor season was marked by the duel between Bill Sefton and Earle Meadows. The former (born at Los Angeles on 21 January 1915; 1.90 m./ 82 kg.) got the ball rolling with a new world record of 4.45 at Los Angeles in April. But Meadows (born at Corinth, Mississippi, on 29 June 1913; 1.85 m./ 72 kg.) lost little time in joining the parade. Early in May at Palo Alto both cleared 4.48. In the Pacific Coast Conference meet, held at Los Angeles on 29 May, the "Heavenly Twins" (as they were by then called) faced a crossbar set at 4.54: Sefton made it on his first try and was declared Conference champion. Meadows needed three tries to master the record height, thus becoming the most illustrious "non-winner" in vaulting annals. In June the consistent Sefton won the NCAA title with 4.49. The AAU Championships at Milwaukee on 3 July offered a gigantic four-way battle, in which the two record holders were matched at 4.46 by George Varoff and Cornelius Warmerdam. For once, the fewer misses count was used to decide positions: 1.Sefton, 2.Warmerdam, 3.Meadows, 4.Varoff. About two months later Sefton and Meadows visited Japan. By then they were past their peak for the season and the reliable Sueo Oe won the first round at Tokyo with 4.30, with Sefton second (4.20).

Meadows injured a shoulder and could do no better than 4.10. The Olympic champion was out for the rest of the tour. Sefton lost one more before finally winning at 4.35 in the last meet of the tour. Before the year was out, Oe achieved his lifetime best: 4.35. He died in the Philippines during World War II. Sefton called it a day after his brilliant 1937 campaign. He thus retired at 22, his potentialities still untapped. Not the last of his admirers was Meadows, who for his part remained in action for many more years. In 1948, at thirty-five years of age, he mastered 4.42 in two different indoor meets!

Hoff's European record was finally shattered on 17 June 1937 at Moscow, when Nikolay Ozolin, the first world class athlete produced in the USSR, vaulted 4.26. Ozolin reached the major heights after many years of hard work, thereby setting a pattern which was to be followed in later years by many of Russia's best athletes. He captured the USSR record for the first time in 1927 with a 3.435 vault, at the age of twenty-one. To establish himself as Russia's best, however, he had to battle first with Vladimir Dyachkov, then with Gavriil Rayevskiy. Ozolin improved on his European record twice, with 4.29 in 1938 and 4.30 at Moscow on 31 July 1939. Much to his dismay, USSR was not a member of the IAAF at the time, and his record efforts could not be ratified at the international level. When this was remedied, after the end of World War II, Ozolin finally got a chance to vie for a European title: but at the ripe age of 40, in 1946, he had to be content with second place (4.10) at the European Championships in Oslo, behind Sweden's Allan Lindberg (4.17). The pole vault was in any case Russia's first parade event: Dyachkov cleared 4.20 in 1939 and Rayevskiy did 4.23 in 1940. At the end of their career, both Ozolin and Dyachkov earned an international reputation as coaches of the jumping events.

The first European vaulter to receive international recognition for a mark over Charles Hoff's old record was Erling Kaas of Norway, who did 4.27 in 1939. It should be noted that in the early editions of the European Championships (1934 and 1938), with USSR not taking part, marks of 4 metres or slightly superior were good enough to give first place. In 1946, at Oslo, Kaas was in the game but just like Ozolin he could do no better than 4.10 and finished fourth.

Few athletes, if any, ever made so much history in any event as Cornelius Warmerdam did in the pole vault during the early Forties. "Dutch" (as he was known, because of his Dutch origin) was born at Long Beach, California, on 22 June 1915. In his prime he stood 1.83 m. and weighed 72 kg. He took up vaulting at fourteen, while at Hanford High School. From 1929 to 1932 his annual progress was steady: 2.74, 3.04, 3.32, 3.73. Then, as related by Cordner Nelson in his book "Track's Greatest Champions", "he chose to work on his father's ranch, 40 acres of peaches and apricots", instead of going to college. Now and then, however, he would continue to practice vaulting, "on their fruit drying field". Until, one day in 1933, he caught the eye of a curious observer, who felt bound to approach Fresno State coach Flint Hanner and told him: "I just saw a kid jumping well over 13 feet (3.96) ... in a spinach patch". Hanner casually observed: "That's not much of a broad jump". By the time the coach realized his mistake, Warmerdam was bound to more remarkable: 4.11 in 1934, 4.28 in 1935, 4.31 in 1936 and 4.46 in 1937, his last year in college. By then he was one of America's premier vaulters, but if he had called it a day at that stage (as did most of his compatriots after leaving college) he would now be remembered only by a select group of statisticians. But he chose to go on, combining sport with his job, and joined the San Francisco Olympic Club. In 1938 he raised his best to 4.42, won the AAU title at 4.40 and was first in the Germany vs. USA dual meet at Berlin. The following year he set a US and world indoor record of 4.42 but was content with 4.40 outdoors and lost to George Varoff in the AAU Meet. In the meantime he had raised his grip on the pole to 13 feet (3.96). His rise to heights then rightly regarded as stratospheric began in 1940, by which time he was teaching history and geometry in a mountain high school. On 13 April of that year, at Berkeley, he delighted a small crowd with history's first 15-foot (4.57) vault, a height he cleared on his second attempt. After breaking that psychological barrier he went from strength to strength. He closed his 1940 account with a new record, 4.60, at the AAU Championships in Fresno. And that was by no means the end.

LONG JUMP - Owens breaks the 8-metre barrier

Peter O'Connor's long awaited successor as world record holder finally appeared in the person of Edwin Gourdin, an American from Harvard University, who in 1921 climaxed a season of consistent long-jumping with a 7.69 effort during an Anglo-American Inter-Varsity meet at Cambridge, Massachusetts. He was a better-than-average sprinter and on that same occasion he beat Harold Abrahams of Britain in the 100 y. (as well as in the long jump). Unfortunately Gourdin was to join that group of athletes who had reached their peak in non-Olympic years.

By 1924 a new man had appeared on the scene: William DeHart Hubbard (born at Cincinnati on 25 November 1903). A man of medium build endowed with great speed and stamina, Hubbard was to prove the outstanding long jumper of the pre-Owens era. He won the AAU title for six consecutive years (1922-27), an astounding achievement in such a nerve-wrecking event as the long jump. His style included a run of less than 30 m., a remarkable acceleration and a single, fast kick of the lead leg.

**1921
1940**

Dave Albritton (USA) tying an ultra-fresh world record in the high jump (2.076) at the 1936 Olympic Tryouts in New York. First to master that height, a few minutes earlier, was Cornelius Johnson, here lying on the grass.

He was at one time co-holder of the world's 100 y. record (9 3/5 in 1926) and won that event at the 1925 NCAA Championships. On the same occasion (Chicago, 13 June) he achieved his best official mark, a new world record of 7.89, winning from F.Morgan Taylor (7.37), the great 400 m. hurdles specialist. Two years later, at Cincinnati, Hubbard reached 7.98, a mark which was not accepted because the landing pit was one inch (2.54 cm.) lower than the take-off board. He was the first long jumper to show consistency in the 25-foot (7.62) range. He won the 1924 Olympic title with 7.445 - and on that jump he fell back, thus losing vital centimetres. The day before, spectators had been treated to an even greater display of long-jumping ability, when another American, Robert LeGendre, was credited with an amazing 7.765 during the pentathlon. This record effort came as a surprise. In fact, it transcended the known ability of the 26-year-old LeGendre, who in the States had always played second fiddle to Hubbard.

In 1928, with Hubbard injured and probably past his peak, two men engaged in a fierce battle for the conquest of that elusive 26-foot (7.92) barrier. They were Edward Hamm, an American, and Silvio Cator, who was from Haiti. The former succeeded Hubbard as world record holder with a jump of 7.90 in the US Olympic Tryouts at Cambridge, Massachusetts, on 7 July. He went on to win the Olympic title from Cator, 7.73 to 7.58. But the Haitian, who at one time was captain of his country's national soccer team, got partial revenge when he became history's first official 26-footer at Colombes on 9 September, reaching 7.93 on his sixth and last try.

A prominent figure in the world long-jumping picture in the fall of 1931 was Chuhei Nambu, a stocky little man from Japan, who on 27 October at Tokyo achieved a surprising leap of 7.98. A good sprinter (10.5 for 100 m. in 1933), Nambu was equally proficient in both long jump and triple jump, two events which in reality are not so closely related as one might think. This double capacity enabled him to win two medals in the 1932 Olympics at Los Angeles: bronze in the long jump (7.45) and gold in the triple jump with a new world record of 15.72. The former event was won by Edward Gordon of USA with 7.64. This athlete was to enjoy a long career, no matter if he performed at generally inferior levels in subsequent years.

In the Thirties the long jump fraternity was gratified by the appearance of a man who was to outshine all his predecessors by no mean margin. This super athlete was J.C. ("Jesse") Owens, whose debut in athletics has been recounted earlier in this chapter. The "Ebony Antelope" was such a born talent that he lost no time in joining the top ranks: from 7.35 in 1932 he improved to 7.60 the following year, and to 7.81 in 1934, by which time he was firmly established as the no.1 master of the art. In 1935, his sophomore year at Ohio State University, Owens began to set his eyes on Nambu's world record. At the Drake Relays in April he missed the target by a fractional margin with a 7.97 jump, on which he fell back in landing, thereby losing something like 15 cm. ! But on his Day of Days, 25 May 1935 at Ann Arbor, Michigan, he found the time to capture the long jump mark as well. In between his record breaking chores on the track, he paid a visit to the long jump pit, a newly laid grass runway, placed directly in front of the stands. The announcer had the delightful

Eulace Peacock (USA), the sprinter/long jumper Jesse Owens feared most.

1921–1940

effrontery to suggest that Owens would try for a new world record. After a run of about 30 m. he took off, and after a simple kick, more of a swing perhaps, he landed at 26 feet 8 1/4 inches (8.13). That was to remain his only jump for the day, but it went down in history as man's first official 8-metre leap. (Claims that Silvio Cator reached 8 metres even in his native country in the spring of 1929 have never been substantiated). And Owens' record was to remain unbeaten for 25 years. Even though there was no international wind rule at the time, careful officials recorded the wind in Jesse's favour as 1.49 m/s, which would be legal even in relation to the present rule. Second in that memorable event at 7.66 was Willis Ward, a 2.01 high jumper.

To everybody's surprise, Owens learned the taste of defeat only a few days after his Ann Arbor triumph. It happened at the AAU Meet in Lincoln, Nebraska, on 4 July, and his conqueror was muscular, Eulace Peacock, who chose the occasion to reach a personal best of exactly 8 metres. Owens came close to that distance twice but could go no farther than 7.98. Peacock, who as previously related was a great sprinter, did not possess Owens' floating style, but was endowed with tremendous power. Unfortunately, a muscular ailment forced him down early in 1936. At the US Olympic Tryouts (to which he was exceptionally admitted by the AAU even though he did not have a qualifying mark) he made a desperate attempt but his condition did not carry him beyond a pitiful (for him) 7.08.

In the meantime, Europeans were showing improved form. O'Connor's time honoured continental record was finally surpassed in 1928, when Rudolf Dobermann of Germany reached 7.645, an achievement which was virtually matched later in the year by another German, Erich Köchermann, with 7.64. Not surprisingly, the country with the richest reservoir of good sprinters was taking the leadership in the European long jump department. One should however mention a great might-have-been, Harold Abrahams of Britain, a first class sprinter who reached 7.38 in 1924 but was for ever barred from further progress the following year when he sustained a serious injury.

In the Thirties Germany had two excellent specialists, Luz Long and Wilhelm Leichum. The former eventually wound up with superior marks, best of which was a 7.90 effort in 1937. The latter, a 10.4 metric sprinter, was twice European champion (1934 and 1938) and won the event in the dual meet with USA in 1938. In the 1936 Berlin Olympics Long rose to the challenge of the great Owens, drawing level with the American at 7.87 mid-way in the competition. But Owens quickly reacted with jumps of 7.94 and 8.06 in the conclusive rounds. That was the "hottest" long jump event of pre-war days, no matter if marks benefited from a favourable wind. Naoto Tajima of Japan was third at 7.74, followed by Arturo Maffei of Italy and Leichum, both at 7.73, while decathlon man Robert Clark of USA had to be content with sixth place (7.67). Long made up for his unimpressi-

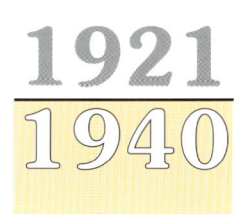

Luz Long, European record holder in the long Jump (7.90 in 1937), exhibits his "hang" style.

113

Charles Hoff (Norway) in one of his world record efforts in the pole vault: 4.235 at Oslo in 1925.

ve speed with a well synchronized, polished "hang" style of jumping. On the other hand, it is generally admitted that Owens did not contribute anything new to the technique of the event. Yet no one until then had been able to perform the exercise with the supreme confidence and the unparalleled smoothness of action that were characteristic of the American. Posterity is obviously inclined to regret that such a unique talent quit the arena at the age of twenty-three.

TRIPLE JUMP - Oda opens Japan's vintage season

Europe's most proficient triple jumper during the Twenties was Vilho Tuulos of Finland (born at Tampere on 26 March 1895; 1.83 m./ 77 kg.). His active career spread over twenty years but he reached the zenith of his condition in 1923, when he scored a fine double at the International Games in Göteborg with 7.31 in the long jump and 15.39 in the triple jump. A few days later, namely on 6 July at Borås, Sweden, he reached 15.48, which was to stand as a European triple jump record for sixteen years. He was one of the first specialists to lay adequate stress on the "step", in which he maintained a good elevation, thereby achieving a remarkable degree of uniformity throughout the three leaps.

The 1924 Olympic final produced startling results. The event was on 12 July. Luis Brunetto of Argentina, the South American champion, took an early lead with 15.425, far better than anything he had done at home. Anthony ("Nick") Winter, a 30-year-old Australian, led the other series of qualifiers with 15.18, three centimetres beyond his personal best. On his last try of the final Winter went wild with a feat of sheer strength and reached 15.525, dislodging Dan Ahearn's world record by a fractional margin. His leaps were as follows: 6.11, 5.09, 4.32. In such company, Tuulos had to be content with a bronze medal with 15.37. However, Finnish historians still rave about a hairline foul in which Tuulos was said to have landed at 15.72. The pit was by then in such a poor state that it was virtually impossible to clearly identify the "foul line".

A young Japanese finished a hardly noticed sixth in that memorable event with 14.35. He was Mikio Oda (born at Hiroshima on 30 March 1905; 1.67 m./ 65 kg.) and in the course of that battle he gathered many useful hints. After returning home, he worked more and more assiduously to develop his potential. In doing so he acted as an eye-opener in making his countrymen realize fully their natural vocation for the jumping events. While waiting to see "the Rest of the World" again at Amsterdam (1928), he showed steady improvement: 14.805 in 1925, 15.343 and 15.355 in 1927, 15.41 in 1928. Encouraged by these achievements and the titles won at the Far Eastern Games, he came back to Europe with plenty of self-confidence. At Amsterdam in 1928 he won Asia's first Olympic gold medal with 15.21, after a fierce battle with Levi Casey of USA (15.17). Veteran Tuulos, who shortly before the

Games had reached 15.58 with the aid of a breeze, won his third Olympic medal, finishing third with 15.11. Fourth place went to another Japanese, Chuhei Nambu (15.01).

That was the dawn of a brilliant era for Japan's triple jumpers. Oda, an excellent all-round jumper (personal bests of 7.52 in the long jump, 1.92 in the high jump and 3.80 in the pole vault) set a new world record of 15.58 at Tokyo on 27 October 1931, when he was extended by a new challenger, Kenkichi Oshima (15.44). That was a historic day for Japanese athletics: in the same meet Nambu captured the world's long jump record with 7.98. Early in 1932 Oda was sidelined with an injury after a promising start (15.55) and was thus prevented from performing at his best in the Los Angeles Olympics. Few athletes, if any, have made a greater contribution to the advancement of athletics in their own country.

Chuhei Nambu, who had been Oda's chief rival in Japan for several years, filled the gap more than adequately in Los Angeles. He used a very long hop of 6.40, a step of 4.39 and a jump of 4.93 to achieve a new world record of 15.72. Consistent Eric ("Spänst") Svensson of Sweden (15.32) took second place ahead of Kenkichi Oshima (15.12).

The Japanese continued to dominate the event throughout the Thirties. Next in the line of world class jumpers were Oshima and Masao Harada, who had their field day at Koshien Grounds, Osaka, on 16 September 1934, during a Japan vs USA match. Each had five valid efforts over 15 m. On his second try Harada reached 15.75, but in the last round Oshima rose to the occasion with 15.82, a feat in which he was aided by a wind of 2.2 m/s. The mark was ratified as a Japanese record but never made the IAAF book (nor did, for that matter, Harada's 15.75) even though the "wind rule" in force nowadays was not introduced until 1936.

Of all countries in the world, Australia was then the only one capable of challenging Japan. Jack Metcalfe, a fine all-rounder, had won the 1934 British Empire Games event in London with 15.63. He really let himself go in December of the following year at Sydney, when he broke Nambu's world record with 15.78. On that occasion he was spurred on by Basil Dickinson (15.64). At the end of his career Metcalfe could point to marks of 1.988 in the high jump and 7.42 in the long jump. At the 1936 Olympics in Berlin he managed a triple jump of 15.50 but had to be content with third place behind two Japanese jumpers. The event, held on 6 August, was featured by the "explosion" of Naoto Tajima, who began with 15.76 in the first round of the final, and then sailed for an unprecedented 16.00 on his fourth attempt.

1921
1940

Mikio Oda (Japan), winner of the triple jump at the 1928 Olympics - Asia's first gold medal in the annals of the Games.

Naoto Tajima (Japan) in his winning effort in the triple jump at the Berlin Olympics (1936): a new world record of 16.00.

Clarence "Bud" Houser (USA), the last thrower to win shot and discus in the Olympics (1924). Won the discus again in 1928.

The new world record was achieved with a hop of 6.20, a step of 4.80 and a jump of 5.00. Masao Harada was second at 15.66. Tajima (born at Iwakuni on 15 August 1912; 1.78 m./ 67 kg.) was better known as a long jumper, an event in which he had done 7.74 in 1935 and again at Berlin in finishing third in the Olympic final. His best triple jump effort prior to the Games was only 15.40, but his great comethrough performance did not surprise those who had watched him in training spins.

Most of the Japanese triple jumpers of pre-war days were primarily good long jumpers, with marks ranging from Oshima's 7.47 to Nambu's 7.98. They generally used a long hop, and consequently had to apply the principle of progressive elevation in the remaining leaps. In post-war years, however, interest for what was once considered a national event began to fade considerably.

In Europe, interest in the triple jump had been kept alive by the Scandinavians. Nordic specialists generally had a good technique and relied on elasticity (Swedish: "spänst") to make up for their insufficient speed. After Tuulos and Svensson, the leading exponent was Onni Rajasaari of Finland, who in the summer of 1939 succeeded Tuulos as European record holder with 15.52. In the same year Kaare Ström of Norway had a mark of 15.82 nullified (at least for record purposes) by an aiding wind.

THROWS - SHOT PUT: Elephant Baby's greatest day

A thrower of multiform capabilities in the Twenties was Clarence ("Bud") Houser of USA (born at Winnigan, Missouri, on 25 September 1901; 1.85m./ 85 kg.). He laid a particular stress on speed, a trend which was by then catching on slowly but steadily. At the 1924 Olympics in Paris he scored a shot/discus double (14.995 and 46.155) which has since remained unmatched. His best with the shot was 15.42 (1926), and so Rose's old record remained untouched.

At the end of 1927 only nine other men had bettered 15 metres. This incredible torpor ceased in the Olympic year 1928. The man who broke the ice was John Kuck of USA, who did 15.55 and 15.59 in early season meets, only to be momentarily outshone by Emil Hirschfeld of Germany, who went to the Amsterdam Olympics as the new record holder with 15.79. In the "meet of the year" the German had an excellent 15.72 but much to his regret he had to be content with a bronze medal. Kuck and his compatriot Herman Brix rose to the occasion with 15.87 (a new world record) and 15.75 respectively.

Hirschfeld staged a consolatory comeback shortly after the Games at Bochum when he recaptured the record with a 16.045 toss.

Between 1929 and 1938 USA and Europe battled for supremacy with mixed fortunes. The Old Continent was represented at the Los Angeles Olympics (1932) by three 16-metre men: Frantisek Douda of Czechoslovakia (16.04 in 1931), Zygmunt

1921 1940

Heljasz of Poland (16.05 early in 1932) and Hirschfeld. But at the Memorial Coliseum the Americans again finished one-two when the consistent and well-proportioned Leo Sexton won at 16.005 from Harlow Rothert (15.67). Douda (15.61) and Hirschfeld (15.56) filled the next positions. Before the season was out, the world record was revised on two occasions, first by Sexton (16.16), and then by Douda (16.20). The "modern shot putter" was by then beginning to shape up. Sexton, for example, had enough spring to manage 1.93 in the high jump.

The balance between the two continents was momentarily broken in 1934. First by John Lyman, who produced an early season record of 16.48 in California, then by Jack Torrance, a giant who really made history. The latter (born at Weathersby, Mississippi, on 20 June 1912) was nicknamed "Elephant Baby" on account of his large frame. He had emerged from virtual obscurity in 1933 with 16.10. Early in 1934 he quickly replied to Lyman's opener with a new record, 16.80. At the AAU Championships in Milwaukee he beat Lyman in a torrid battle, 16.89 to 16.70, while a man of Greek extraction, George Theodoratus, was third with 16.30. Torrance and Lyman spent part of the summer in Europe, where the former really went wild. Torrance's big day was at Oslo on 5 August. Bislett has always been known as a "miracle" venue for world shattering events, and on that occasion spectators were indeed treated to a memorable feat. After a series of throws in the 16.07-16.84 range, on his penultimate attempt Torrance got one off to 17.40, over half a metre beyond his most recent record! That phenomenal toss obviously caused a great deal of excitement, in the field as well as in the stands. Torrance was invited to negotiate a Lap of Honour. To indulge in this typically European celebration he passed up his sixth try.

On the spur of the moment, some observers saluted Torrance's exploit as the last word in putting the 16-lb. shot. Amidst the general excitement, one comment passed almost unnoticed, namely that made to a Norwegian newsman by John Lyman, who was a distant second in the Oslo event with 15.80. The former world record holder was quoted as saying that Torrance's speed in that momentous fifth put had been anything but impressive. This is well credible, since the vital statistics on the "Elephant Baby" (as taken in the office of the Stockholm "Idrottsbladet" a few days later) told the following tale: height, 1.90 m., weight 138 kg. Torrance wound up his European tournée with marks of lesser value, best of which was a 16.85 toss in Paris, where he also threw the discus 48.11. In an exhibition in the States he did 17.19.

After leaving Louisiana State University, however, Torrance gradually lost his enthusiasm. Being attracted by exercises that called for more brute strength, he lost form and declined rapidly. After his great 1934 season he never again exceeded, or even approached, the 17-metre line, save for a 16.98 in an exhibition in 1935.

He eventually fell flat in 1936 and went to the Berlin Olympics as a shadow of his former self.

The "mountain man" wound up an unhappy fifth with a pathetic (for him) 15.38. Europe won the day with Hans Woellke, a German police officer, who edged Sulo Bärlund of Finland after a close duel, 16.20 to 16.12. Another German, Gerhard Stöck - who was to win the javelin a few days later - was third ahead of the best American, Sam Francis.

That was one of the severest debacles ever suffered by Uncle Sam in one of the so-called American events. Woellke raised the European record to 16.60 in a post-Olympic meet. In subsequent years he traded wins with his compatriots Stöck and Heinrich Trippe as well as with a consistent Estonian, Aleksander Kreek, who was crowned European champion in 1938. All of these men had marks in the range 16.40/16.60.

In the meantime, however, American coaches were devoting more and more attention to the dynamic aspects of the event. The shape of things to come was evident by 1939, when Elmer Hackney produced two 17-metre efforts, 17.04 and 17.02, the latter in winning the NCAA title at Los Angeles.

That was a historic event in terms of overall standards: Bill Watson, a great all-rounder, was second at 16.62, and the fourth man did 16.20. Watson was an unusual combination of jumper/thrower, with marks of 7.76 in the long jump and 49.84 in the discus. In 1940 he won the AAU decathlon title with 7523 points.

Here was perhaps the fore-runner of the ultra-dynamic putters of the present time.

DISCUS - American music (with European intermezzi)

"Bud" Houser actually had his best days as a discus thrower. He won the event twice in Olympic competition, with 46.155 in 1924 and 47.32 in 1928. On the latter occasion he earned a "photo finish" decision: Antero Kivi of Finland was second at 47.23 and James Corson of USA took third place at 47.10. Mark-wise, Houser had his greatest day at Palo Alto in 1926, when he set a world record of 48.20. In the ring he took one and one-half turns, with a series of very quick steps.

The 50-metre line was first surpassed by Eric Krenz of USA (born on 7 May 1906; 1.85 m./ 95 kg.). He finished fourth in the shot put at Amsterdam in 1928 and the following year he captured the world's discus record with 49.90. He made history at Palo Alto on 17 May 1930 when he got one off to 51.03. His form consisted in dropping very low at the back of the circle and hopping high up and then down for the final pull. During the middle of the turn, both his feet were for a short while off the ground together. In this he differed from Armas Taipale and other throwers who used the "pivot" style, with at least one foot on the ground at all times. Krenz's distance was excelled later in 1930 by Paul Jessup, a big man (1.98 m. / 98 kg.) who reached 51.73 in winning the AAU title at Pittsburgh. Krenz had little or no time to reply: in 1931 he met premature death at Lake Tahoe, while trying to save the life of a child. Meanwhile, European throwers did not want to be left behind. In the Twenties the leading continental powers in the discus were Finland with Vilho Niittymaa and Antero Kivi, and Germany with Hans Hoffmeister and the gigantic Ernst Paulus. Hoffmeister threw 48.77 in 1928, but his mark only made the books as a German record. On the subject of unratified marks I may also mention a 48.18 effort by Glenn Hartranft of USA in 1924, which was disallowed "because of a high wind". In fact, there can be little or no doubt that wind can play an important role in discus throwing, no matter if IAAF rules fail to contemplate such an occurrence. Insiders claim that most if not all discus records have been influenced by Aeolus, particularly by quartering winds that keep the implement high and thus prolong its trajectory.

By 1930 Europe's leading discus power was Hungary, and it fell to a Magyar athlete, József Remecz, to become Europe's first 50-metre man in 1932 with a mark of 50.73. He was closely joined beyond the once magic line by Paul Winter of France (50.71). Another Frenchman, big Jules Noël, did 49.44 in the same year. But the Los Angeles Olympic rendez-vous again saw an American on top: John Anderson, fifth at Amsterdam in 1928, struck gold with 49.49, while his countryman Henri Laborde (48.47) finished second ahead of Winter and Noël. (World record holder Paul Jessup finished no better than eighth). The two Frenchmen were for many years useful point-winners for the Tricolore in international dual meets.

The first thrower of any country to become familiar with the 50-metre line was Harald Andersson of Sweden (born in Michigan, USA, on 2 April 1907; 1.90 m./ 99 kg.), who combined power and speed to a remarkable extent. In a dual meet with Norway at Oslo on 25 August 1934 he brought the world record back to Europe with a heave of 52.42. Even though not all his throws were officially measured, the average of his six valid efforts was estimated as an unprecedented 51.30! Later in the same year he won the European title at Turin with 50.38. But in the spring of 1935 international experts were stunned by a news item from Magdeburg: during a local meet there, a virtual unknown by the name of Willi Schröder had hurled a discus 53.10. The previous year he had done no better than 44.00 in official competition, but had shown promise with a 51.29

Official negligence

It happened at the Los Angeles Memorial Coliseum on 3 August 1932, during the Olympic discus final. Jules Noël, a big, consistent Frenchman, was regarded as a good medal prospect. On his fourth attempt he lived up to expectations with a throw which in the eyes of several European onlookers was well beyond 48 m. Incredible as it may seem, at that very moment the judges had their minds and eyes on the dramatic pole vault battle which was unfolding not far from there between local favourite Bill Miller and Japan's Shuhei Nishida. And no one could safely trace the spot where Noël's discus first hit the ground. Negligence induced by patriotic feelings, no doubt. The announcer regretfully but honestly admitted that Noël's throw was not measured. When the event was over, Noël was in fourth place with no better than 47.74, close behind his countryman Paul Winter (47.85). The judges felt bound to allow the unlucky Frenchman an extra throw, but he failed to do himself justice. Of course there is nothing really new under the sun. American sources claim that at the 1928 US Olympic Tryouts, held at Cambridge, Massachusetts, judges "did not see"a throw by Eric Krenz which by most accounts would have qualified the would-be world record holder for the Olympic event. (As it was, Krenz managed to go to Amsterdam as a shot putter). At the 1980 Olympics in Moscow, Luis Mariano Delis of Cuba was ostensibly "penalized" by Soviet judges in the measurement of a throw which according to neutral eye-witnesses would have probably earned him a gold medal (the Cuban had to be content with third place).

effort in an unsanctioned event late in the year. An unusual detail, Schröder's record throw was achieved before noon.

The German, then 23, was 1.84 m. tall and weighed 87 kg. He was able to generate great speed, so much in fact that he often found it hard to stay in the ring, hence his inconsistency. He was once reported at 55 m. in training, but never managed to hit 51 m. in important competitions. Andersson, who had more power and co-ordination than his German rival, responded with a throw of 53.02 later in 1935, and continued to perform with amazing consistency. But in 1936 an injured hand put him off balance in the race for Olympic honours, and Europe was thus deprived of its best card.

At Berlin, world record holder Schröder was unable to fulfil the expectations of the huge crowd: he won access to the final round only after a throw-off with another competitor, finally finishing a disappointing fifth. America again scored a one-two, with Kenneth Carpenter the winner at 50.48 and big Gordon Dunn second at 49.36. Third man and best of the Europeans was Giorgio Oberweger of Italy (49.23). The winner, a reliable competitor, closed his best season with a near-record performance (53.08) in a post-Olympic meet at Prague. The gifted but inconsistent Schröder had his best year as a competitor in 1938, when he first beat the Americans Phil Levy and Pete Zagar in the Germany vs. USA dual meet at Berlin with 50.19, and then edged Oberweger at the European Championships in Paris, 49.70 to 49.48. Another Italian, 21-year-old Adolfo Consolini, was fifth in the latter meet with 48.02. He passed almost unnoticed, yet here was the man who in the course of his career was to reach the highest peaks and beat all longevity records.

HAMMER THROW - The Christmann School

In the first two decades of the century the Irish hammer tradition had been given great lustre: five Olympic victories, all by natives of the Emerald Isle representing USA. The chain was broken in 1924, when a native-born American, Fred Tootell, used his excellent technique to good advantage and won in Paris with 53.295. Matt McGrath, then a portly 48-year-old veteran, was second, more than two metres behind - to this day the oldest man to mount the Olympic dais in a throwing event.

Europeans were becoming more conscious of their possibilities in the ball-and-chain event. Particularly in Scandinavia there were big men who made it a practice to throw a hammer to "near-Irish" distances. Carl Johan ("Massa") Lind of Sweden, who won the English AAA title in 1922 with 52.51 at thirty-nine years of age, was a legendary figure, and so was his compatriot Ossian Skiöld, who did 53.85 aged thirty-eight, in 1927. In the British Isles the outstanding men were Tom Nicolson and Malcolm Nokes. The ultimate record set by the latter, 52.76 in 1923, was unsurpassed as a British best for twenty-four years.

Ireland did, however, produce another outstanding figure: Patrick O'Callaghan (born at Kanturk, County Cork, on 15 September 1905; 1.86 m./ 86 kg.), who after indulging in practically every event on the athletic programme finally chose to concentrate on the hammer in 1927. His first official competition produced a startling result: 41.49. By the end of the season he was up to 46.17, which mark was good enough to secure him a place among the world's top twenty hammer men of the year. In 1928 he went

1921
1940

Pat O'Callaghan (Ireland) at the time of his second victory in the Olympic hammer throw (1932).

119

Karl Hein, Olympic and European champion in the hammer throw. (Courtesy FIDAL, Roma).

to Amsterdam, where he met the cream of the ball-and-chain fraternity in the Olympic contest. Skiöld, the Swedish veteran, led through the fourth round with 51.29, but then O'Callaghan got one off to 51.39 and that was good enough to win the gold medal for the Irish "newcomer". Four years later, at Los Angeles, it was the same story: another veteran, Ville Pörhölä of Finland (who had won the Olympic shot put title at Antwerp twelve years earlier!), led through the penultimate round with 52.27, but on his sixth and last trial the defending champion came up with a throw of 53.92 and again struck gold! Being the type of athlete who loves competition because of its challenging aspects, O'Callaghan had only a moderate interest for records set in "cold" meets. Even so he twice managed to improve on the European record, first with 56.06 in 1931, then with 56.94 in 1933. By 1936 "Doc Pat" had entered the medical profession. Furthermore he lacked incentive, since the federation of which he was then a member (NACA) was no longer recognized by the IAAF, which automatically barred him from international competition. As a result he went to the Berlin Olympics merely as a spectator. But on 22 August 1937 he hit the headlines again - with a bang: competing in the Cork County Championships at Fermoy, on his fourth try he threw the hammer 59.56! In actual fact the record throw was first announced as 60.56, but sometime later it was revealed that the throw had been measured ... from the centre of the circle and not, as prescribed by IAAF rules, from its inner edge! It was also learned that the circle was only 2.00 m. in diameter, instead of the prescribed 7 feet (2.13 m.). As a result, the actual measurement from the inner edge of the circle would have given 59.56 - still beyond anything recorded up to that time. To add further irony to this incredible affair, the hammer turned out to be 6 ounces (about 170 grams) overweight! The correct distance was accepted as an NACA record. Given the peculiar circumstances under which the mark was made, one may doubt whether it would hold water if submitted to the IAAF. In his book "Great Moments in Athletics", F.A.M.Webster tells an amusing story. In 1938 Erwin Blask of Germany visited Ireland and while there he tried to better O'Callaghan's mark - without success. Before the contest got underway he was given a glass of stout. "That's what Dr. Pat had drunk before making his great throw", insiders told him. To which Blask retorted: "I don't believe that. I think that is what you gave to the judges before they measured that big throw of his". O'Callaghan never competed in the European Championships. Winner of the first continental title at Turin in 1934 was Ville Pörhölä of Finland, then thirty-seven years of age, with 50.34. Longevity was the rule among hammer throwers in those days: the first six of the Turin event averaged thirty-six! Germany had neglected the hammer throw almost completely until then. In 1920 the country's record was still under 40 metres and fifteen years elapsed before it was brought over 50 metres (Erwin Blask, 51.66). By then, however, the Germans had decided that something should and could be done to take advantage of the general lack of interest for this highly technical event prevailing in most other countries. Under the guidance of coach Sepp Christmann, German hammer throwers got down to work, and in a short time they achieved surprising results. In 1935-36 the national record was revised many times and on the eve of the Berlin Olympics the country had two men capable of vying for top honours.

These men were Erwin Blask (born at Friedrichsheide, East Prussia, on 20 March 1910; 1.80 m./97 kg.) and Karl Hein (born at Hamburg on 11 June 1908; 1.82 m./ 98 kg.). The latter, a virtual unknown in 1935 when his best was 47.31, went to the Olympics as German champion and record holder with a mark of 54.29. By the same time, Blask reached 53.51. In the absence of Dr. O'Callaghan, the most serious rival of the German duo was Fred Warngård of Sweden. The Berlin final (3 August) outshone all previous competitions in the event. Blask raised the German record to 55.04 in the second round and Warngård counteracted by beating the Swedish record twice, with a best of 54.83 in the fourth round. Hein moved up to second in the fifth round and grabbed the title on his last try with a throw of 56.49.

That marked the beginning of the German era in hammer throwing. Hein and Blask seemed to excel their Irish predecessors in terms of speed. A most important detail of their form, still valid nowadays, was that the left foot, used as a pivot, would roll alternately on the heel for 180°, then on the ball-toe for another 180°, generating a highly progressive acceleration.

The rivalry between Hein and Blask was particularly "hot" in 1938. The former beat Ryan's time honoured world record with a throw of 58.24 at Osnabrück on 21 August. Only six days later, in the Sweden vs. Germany dual meet at Stockholm, Blask crowned a phenomenal series with a top effort of 59.00. But in the most important test of the year, the European Championships in Paris, Hein turned the tables on his arch rival, 58.77 to 57.34. Each had an average for the season that lay around 56 metres! In 1939 they were joined by another standout, Karl Storch, who was destined to have a long career.

On the eve of World War II Germany had fifteen men over 50 metres, about one third of the world's total.

JAVELIN THROW - Järvinen and his heirs

Jonny Myyrä of Finland won the Olympic title again at Paris in 1924, with a 62.96 effort - a double no one has been able to duplicate since then. Second place went to Gunnar Lindström of Sweden, who conquered the world record three months later with 66.62. Myyrä then settled down in the States, where he was credited with an impressive 68.56 in an unsanctioned meet held at Richmond, California, in the fall of 1925. The following year, under similar circumstances, he threw the discus 46.76.

One of the first throwers to exhibit a high combination of speed and technique was Eino Penttilä of Finland, who was only twenty-two when he raised the world record to 69.88. This was at Viipuri (now Viborg in the USSR) in 1927, and the Finn appeared to be an odds-on favourite for the Olympic title to be awarded at Amsterdam the following year. At the decisive moment, however, he was hampered by an injured foot and had to be content with sixth place. The winner, Erik Lundqvist of Sweden, did 66.60.

On 15 August of the same year, at Stockholm, the Swede became history's first 70-metre man at the age of twenty with a brilliant effort of 71.01. His series on that occasion was: 66.25 - 67.60 - 67.50 - 71.01 - 69.10 - 70.10. He had improved by more than eight metres in one year, and there was no telling what he would do in the end. Unfortunately a mental disease gradually conquered him and he was obliged to retire all too soon. He staged a comeback in 1936 and amazed experts by reaching a new per-

1921
1940

Matti Järvinen, the most famous of Finland's many javelin aces. Under his reign the world record advanced more than 6 m.

sonal best of 71.16 with his powerful thrust of old.

In the meantime, however, the Finns had taken adequate steps to ensure that Lundqvist would be the last "interruptor", at least for a long time to come. From 1930 to 1950 they held the leadership almost without a break. The greatest figure of the Finnish era was Matti H.Järvinen (born at Tampere on 18 February 1909; 1.86 m./ 84 kg.), the youngest offspring of Verner Järvinen, whose contribution to athletic history has been dealt with in Part II. Matti was brought up in a great athletic atmosphere and became a gymnast at the age of three.Through many years of conditioning exercises he developed far beyond family expectations. Maybe it was not by mere chance that father Järvinen saw each of his sons excel his elder brothers in athletic skill.

Matti made his official debut as a javelin thrower in 1926 and his very first result was amazing: 54.26. By the same time, however, he developed a "javelin elbow", a condition which made him stop for a long time. His solitary effort was at any rate good enough to earn him a place among Finland's fifty best javelin throwers of 1926. Once healed, the slightly dislocated right arm turned out to be an advantage because of its greater flexibility. In 1929, his first year of full activity, Matti broke through in no uncertain manner: Finnish champion with 66.18 and no.1 in the World Year List with 66.75! It would be difficult to find another field event man who had such a Blitz start. Of course, one should not forget that Järvinen was an extremely well-conditioned athlete, having practised various sports, notably including baseball, from childhood.

Matti Järvinen's great career can be summarized as follows:

(1) After his first world record throw (72.38 in 1930), which was to remain unofficial, he wrote his name in the IAAF record book ten times: 71.57, 71.70, 71.88 and 72.93 in 1930; 74.02 in 1932; 74.28, 74.61 and 76.10 in 1933; 76.66 in 1934; 77.23 on 18 June 1936 at the Eläintarha (Zoological Garden) Grounds in Helsinki.

(2) Won the Olympic title at Los Angeles (1932) with 72.71, exceeding 70 metres in five of his six throws, while the runner-up, Martti Sippala of Finland, did no better than 69.80. (Penttilä, third at 68.70, made it a clean sweep for Suomi). Incidentally, a widely spread story claims that Järvinen's winning distance at Los Angeles (which was to stand as Olympic record till 1952) was "adopted" as the height of the Marathon tower of the Helsinki Olympic Stadium, inaugurated in 1938. (Although a Finnish expert once commented, somewhat ironically: "If so, that was at best a lucky coincidence").

In 1936, on the eve of the Berlin Olympics, Järvinen looked like a certainty for a "repeat", but a back injury stopped him in the crucial pre-Olympic weeks. Lacking condition, he managed no higher than fifth at 69.18, in an event won by Gerhard Stöck of Germany at 71.84. For once, Finland had to be content with "lesser" medals: Yrjö Nikkanen second (70.76) and Kalervo Toivonen third (70.72).

(3) Was European champion twice, with 76.66 at Turin in 1934, and 76.87 at Paris in 1938, marks which were to remain his best ever, next to his ultimate record of 77.23 in 1936. A further proof of his competitive élan.

Järvinen's contribution to the advancement of javelin standards was great in more than one way. From a technical standpoint he differed from most if not all his predecessors in that he made the various phases of the exercise look like one continuous movement, in which smoothness of action and driving force melted into an ideal mixture.

In the latter part of his career the bespectacled Matti had a most serious opponent in his compatriot Yrjö Nikkanen (born at Kanneljärvi on 31 December 1914; 1.79m./ 77 kg.). Here was another precocious talent who beat 70 metres in the third year of his career (71.30 in 1935). After winning a silver medal in the Berlin Olympics, Nikkanen rose to Järvinen's stature in 1938. During that season, in fact, he won 8 out of 12 from his arch rival, twice bettering the world record: 77.87 at Karhula, then 78.70 at Kotka. The latter event took place on the threshold of the Finnish winter, on 16 October. The temperature was only 6° C. and there had been plenty of rain in the preceding days. To allow the two champions to get one last try at the record, gasoline was used to dry the rain-soaked runway. Järvinen opened with a normal 69.30. Then came Nikkanen with a real killer: 78.70. An effort which cost him a slight muscle injury - an equitable price to pay for a world record that remained unbeaten till 1953! After that great achievement, the excitement in and around the field was such that even the old warrior Järvinen for once folded under pressure. He completed a mediocre series with a 69.32 throw.Nikkanen had a most powerful thrust, but generally lacked the competitive ability of his great rival. In fact, at the European Championships in Paris a few weeks earlier, Järvinen had confounded experts with his best ever series and a clear victory over Nikkanen, 76.87 to 75.00.

At forty years of age, Järvinen still managed to beat 67 metres. A fair all-round thrower, he was also a good long jumper (7.26) and an 11.1 metric sprinter. Finnish experts maintained that if he had concentrated on the decathlon he would have possibly excelled his brother Aki, twice a silver medallist in the Olympic ten-event grind.

The Finnish era reached the zenith in 1939, with seven throwers in the 70-metre-plus region, exactly 50 % of the world's "output". Among the other good javelin throwers of the late Thirties I may single out Gustav Sule of Estonia (75.935 in 1938), Lennart Atterwall of Sweden (75.10 in 1937, albeit "wind-assisted", and as such not ratified as a national record) and Olympic champion Gerhard Stöck of Germany (73.96 in 1935, in losing to Järvinen, 74.30).

DECATHLON - Bausch and Morris: one year is enough for glory

After the experiment of 1912 in Stockholm, the schedule of the decathlon was changed to make it a two-day competition, with five events each day.

This obviously made it more difficult to match Jim Thorpe's (unofficial) record. Of course, the number of active decathlon men was scarce in those days and slipshod methods of training were the rule for most of those who tried their hand at the ten-event grind. Early in the Twenties, Northern Europe had an excellent all-round man in Aleksander Klumberg (Kolmpere) of Estonia, whose score of 7485.61 points at Helsinki in 1922 (with marks which would be worth just over 6000 under the present scoring table) was the first to be ratified as a world record by the IAAF. At the Antwerp Olympics (1920) the Estonian was forced to retire after eight events. He excelled in the javelin (63.60), the long jump (7.20) and the triple jump (14.33).

Winner of the decathlon at the 1924 Olympics in Paris was Harold Osborn of USA (who only a few days earlier had won the high jump). He beat, among others, Aleksander Klumberg, who finished third. The winner chalked up a record score of 7710.775 points (6476 under the present table). From the earliest days of all-round competitions, Americans tended to capitalize on the so-called natural events, making maximum points in the short distances, the high jump, and the long jump. Scandinavians, being generally less gifted in that department, tended to specialize in the technical (field) events. Two Finns, Paavo Yrjölä and Aki Järvinen, were probably the first men who really took all the ten events to their hearts without apparent discrimination. Yrjölä had his best score in 1930 at Aalborg, Denmark, with 8117.300 points (6703 under the present table). And he won the 1928 Olympic title ahead of Järvinen. The latter (born at Jyväskylä on 19 September 1905; 1.87 m./ 84 kg.) was, of course, an offspring of the famous Järvinen mentioned in Part II. He finished second also at Los Angeles in 1932, losing to a record-smashing rival, James Bausch of USA, who amassed 8462.235 points (6735 under the present table).

When the scoring system was changed in 1934, Järvinen discovered much to his surprise that under the new system he would have won the Olympic title not once but both times! Bausch was at any rate a remarkable athlete. His strong events were the pole vault (4.05), the shot put (15.33) and the javelin (61.61). The last result was achieved in the Olympic competition at Los Angeles and eventually won the day for him, since Järvinen, a Finn, could manage no more than 61.00. To add further irony to the situation, the Finn had earlier outshone the American in the 100 m., 11.1 to 11.7! Järvinen's forte was in fact a track event, the 400 m. hurdles, in which he finished second at the 1934 European Championships in Turin with 53.7.

Those were the days when the Americans would remember the decathlon only in Olympic years. Even so, they captured each and every Olympic title contested between 1932 and 1960! Europe had its share in the advancement of records though, thanks to Hans-Heinrich Sievert of Germany (born at Eutin, Schleswig-Holstein, on 1 December 1909; 1.88 m./ 88 kg.). He succeeded Bausch as official world record holder in 1934 at Hamburg with 8790.46 points (7147 under the present table).

He was very good in the shot put (15.89) and the discus (49.32), but also managed a long jump of 7.48 in connection with his highest score. He won the 1934 European title but two years later an injury forced him to bypass the Berlin Olympics. By then USA obviously had a worthy candidate, in the person of Glenn Morris. Mainly known as a runner (54.4 for 400 m. hurdles in 1934), he turned to the decathlon early in the Olympic year and on his second attempt he broke Sievert's world record with 7884 points as per new "Finnish Table" adopted in 1934 (7213 under the present table). Morris went on to win the Olympic title at Berlin with a higher score, 7900 points (7254 under the present table).

Experts obviously wondered what Bausch and Morris could have achieved if they had devoted their attention to the decathlon for more than one year.

RELAYS - 4x100 METRES: Wykoff's golden triple

Times changed for the better in the 1924 Olympics. The Britons, with Olympic 100 m. champion Harold Abrahams in the lead-off leg, fought bravely all the

1921
1940

way against their rivals from America, who finally won in 41.0, equalling the world record they had set in a semi-final earlier in the day. The four Americans were Frank Hussey, Louis Clarke, Loren Murchison and Alfred Leconey. Britain was second in 41 1/5.

Club teams began to have a say in 1927 when a Newark A.C. quartet posted a creditable 41.0 for the 4x110 y. relay during the AAU Championships at Lincoln, Nebraska. It was in the late Twenties that Germany took over from Britain as the leader in European sprint relay racing. In June 1928 the Germans were clocked in 40.8 on three different occasions, but for some reason not one of these marks was ratified by the IAAF. At the Amsterdam Olympics the Americans had to go all out to beat a German team (which consisted of four 10.4 metric men), 41.0 to 41 1/5. The lead-off runner for the winning team was young Frank Wykoff, who was to turn the trick twice more, at Los Angeles (1932) and Berlin (1936). He is to this day the only runner to have been in a victorious relay team in three different Olympics. The rarity of Wykoff's feat lies not so much in his winning three gold medals over a period of eight years (1928-36), but rather in qualifying among America's top four 100 m. men in three editions of the Olym-pic Tryouts. In a post-Olympic meet at Berlin on 2 September, the Germans found partial consolation for their Olympic defeat by posting another 40.8 for the metric relay, which time was ratified by the IAAF. The foursome consisted of Arthur Jonath, Richards Corts, Hubert Houben and Helmut Körnig. The following year two German club teams bettered 41 seconds: Sport Club Charlottenburg, Berlin (40.8) and Eintracht Frankfurt (40.9). An adequate reply came from America only in 1931 when a University of Southern California quartet with Wykoff in the anchor leg lowered the world's 4x110 y. relay record to 40.8. Considering the distance involved (402.34 m.), this could be rated as the equivalent of 40.6 for the 4x100 m. relay.

At the 1932 Olympics in Los Angeles the Americans decided to do without the services of such standouts as Eddie Tolan and Ralph Metcalfe, who had finished one-two in the individual 100 m. event. Even so, their quartet of Robert Kiesel, Emmett Toppino, Hector Dyer and Frank Wykoff first clocked 40.6 in a heat, then won the final in 40.0, a new world record, leaving Germany far behind (40.9).

In 1936 Wykoff emerged from virtual retirement a few weeks before the Berlin Olympics and again managed to make Uncle Sam's team. In the Games the initial legs were assigned to Jesse Owens and Ralph Metcalfe, while Foy Draper and Wykoff were to carry the baton in the closing stages. The team warmed up by equalling the world and Olympic record, 40.0, in a heat. In the decisive race the great Owens settled the issue at the start, gaining at least 5 m. on his nearest opponent. His teammates increased the lead further and Wykoff, then a veteran of 27, broke the tape in world record time, 39.8. Italy was a surprising but distant second (41.1), ahead of Germany (41.2). Holland's anchor man, Martinus Osendarp, dropped the baton about 25 m. from home, then finished a shade ahead of his German opponent, only to see his team disqualified.

The Germans, bitterly disappointed at Berlin, were back in their stride some years later: on 29 July 1939, on the same track, a team consisting of Erich Borchmeyer, Gerd Hornberger, Karl Neckermann and Jakob Scheuring ran the metric relay in 40.1 for a brilliant European record. Italy was runner-up in 40.8. Meanwhile, the 4x110 y. record lagged somewhat behind, namely at 40.5 - a time returned in 1938 by a University of Southern California team which notably included Payton Jordan, who was to become one of America's most successful coaches.

4x400 METRES: Anglo-American battles

Competition is the key to record times in the 4x400 m. relay. As a result, Olympic finals invariably yielded the best clockings. At the Paris Games (1924) the rule was respected thanks to a US quartet consisting of Commodore Cochran, William Stevenson, Oliver MacDonald and Alan Helffrich. They won in 3:16.0, a new world record, while a Swedish team anchored by Nils Engdahl was a fairly close second (3:17.0). Four years later, at Amsterdam, the Americans were extended by a strong German quartet, yet they won again and lowered the record to 3:14 1/5.

The team consisted of George Baird, Emerson Spencer, Fred Alderman and Ray Barbuti, all capable of 47/48 secs. in the individual 400 m. event. Germany was second in 3:14 4/5.

A few days later the American team - with hurdler Morgan Taylor replacing Alderman - did even better in the 4x440 y. relay. Pitted against a British Empire quartet in London, they chalked up an impressive 3:13 2/5, which was worth about 3:12 1/5 for the metric relay. In 1931 a Stanford University team ran the English distance in 3:12.6, with Ben Eastman in the anchor leg. The first time under 3:10 was registered in the Los Angeles Olympics on 7 August 1932 by an American foursome - Ivan Fuqua (47.1), Edgar Ablowich (47.6), Karl Warner (47.3) and Bill Carr (46.2) - with a new world record of 3:08.2, despite the fact that America's second best man, Ben

Eastman, was not in the race. Britain was second in 3:11.2. On that occasion Lord Burghley ran the third leg in 46.7, the fastest lap of his brilliant career. British tradition in the 4x400 m. relay is a bright one indeed. In Olympic competition, the Union Jack was again brought to victory at Berlin in 1936.

On that occasion the American leadership decided to do without the services of Archie Williams, Jimmy LuValle and Harold Smallwood, the trio that had represented Uncle Sam in the individual race, and fielded instead a fresh quartet with Harold Cagle, Robert Young, Edward O'Brien and Al Fitch. Britain presented a magnificent foursome: Frederick Wolff, Godfrey Rampling, William Roberts and Godfrey Brown. The Britons took the lead in the second leg and were never headed. They won in 3:09.0, second best on record. Their respective splits were: 49.2, 46.7, 46.4, 46.7. The Americans had to be content with second place in 3:11.0, ahead of Germany and Canada (both 3:11.8). Anchor man for the German team was Rudolf Harbig (47.6). Two weeks later, at London's White City Stadium, the cream of quarter-milers from the British Empire and USA met in a 4x440 y. relay. This time the Americans fielded just about their best team, with Williams, Fitch, Glenn Hardin and LuValle. The British Empire team consisted of Roberts, Rampling, William Fritz of Canada, and Brown. After a hectic ding-dong battle all the way, Brown overtook LuValle in the decisive leg and won by a few centimetres. The time for the winning team was a record-shattering 3:10.6. Brown was timed in a blistering 45.9.

The presence of Fritz, a Canadian, prevented the record from being recognized by the IAAF. Be as it may, the following year a slightly better mark, 3:10.5, was chalked up at Palo Alto, California, by a Stanford University team consisting of Charles Shaw, Ernest Clark, Craig Williamson and Clyde Jeffrey. This was an unusual feat made in a virtual "solo" race - the runner-up finished over 100 y. behind.

WALKS
The impeccable Frigerio

The walking events had a decidedly hard life in the period 1921-40, still in connection with the debatable matter of racing styles. To dampen controversy it was decided ... to reduce the Olympic events to a minimum: between 1924 and 1936 there were just three such competitions.

At the Paris Games (1924) the 10 km. was the only walking event on the programme. Ugo Frigerio of Italy duplicated his Antwerp win in 47:49.0, leaving Britain's Gordon Goodwin some 200 m. behind.

Frigerio was acclaimed in his heyday as an impeccable stylist and a "man full of colour". Italian commentators seemed to appreciate the latter quality even more than the former. In 1925 he was invited to USA. Throughout the American indoor circuit he shared the limelight with the great Nurmi, the running marvel, and set several walking records, notably including a mark of 44:38 for 10 km. (and 43:09 4/5 for 6 miles en route). He would have probably added to his collection of Olympic medals if the IAAF had not decided to do without the walking events for the Amsterdam Olympics (1928). This ban was luckily lifted four years later. The only walking event at Los Angeles was the 50 km. Frigerio, by then thirty-one, made a comeback and again faced the world's élite - alas at a distance he was not familiar with. He shared the lead for a long time with Janis Dalins of Latvia and Tommy Green of Britain. Green had a bad time from the sun at the three-quarter distance and lost nearly a minute. But he was put back in stride by a cold douche and quickly made up for the ground lost. The Briton, a 38-year-old railway man and the father of four, eventually pulled away from his rivals and won by a solid margin in 4:50:10 from Dalins (4:57:20) and Frigerio (4:59:06). The Italian collapsed across the finish line in winning his fourth Olympic medal.

1921
1940

Paavo Yrjölä (Finland), Olympic decathlon champion in 1928.

Britain once again supplied the winner of the 50 km. event at Berlin in 1936, this time with Harold Whitlock, who won in a nifty 4:30:42. Just like Green four years earlier at Los Angeles, Whitlock had a crisis but he fought back bravely and won comfortably from Arthur Tell Schwab, a 40-year-old Swiss (4:32:10). Many things can happen in the course of such a soul searing long distance grind: to cope with them one needs, above all, strong mental qualities.

The above-mentioned Dalins had won the first European title at 50 km. at Turin in 1934. He also held the world record for the 20 km. track event with 1:34:26.0 (1933). Whitlock, a motor mechanic by profession, had won international renown as early as in 1935 when he became the first man to cover the London to Brighton course in less than 8 hours. In 1938, aged thirty-five, he won the European title for the 50 km. in Paris.

1941-1960

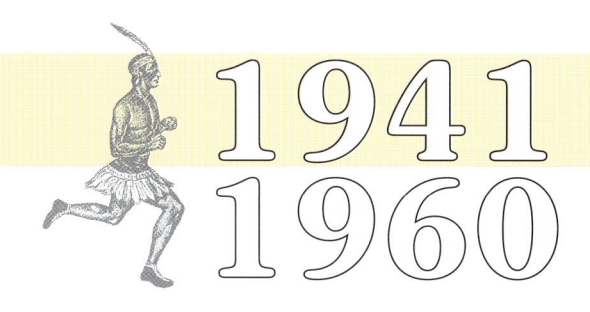

WORLD WAR 2 CANCELS TWO EDITIONS OF THE OLYMPICS. ZÁTOPEK SPEARHEADS THE REVIVAL

SPRINTS - 100 & 200 METRES:
Occasional European clouds in America's sky

World War II with its implications far and wide caused the cancellation of two Olympics, 1940 and 1944. Among those who suffered most because of this sad state of affairs was Harold Davis, the "California Comet", the man who ruled the roost in American sprint circles during the early Forties. Davis (born at Salinas, California, on 5 January 1921; 1.78 m./ 72 kg.) was one of those tremendously gifted athletes who can do marvellous things practically from the beginning. In 1938, as a 17-year-old High School boy, he ran the English distances in 9.7 and 21.0 (straight course). He began to give the full measure of his greatness in 1940. Dr. Donald H. Potts, a keen and astute student of sprinting history, recalls the unusual circumstances of Davis' breakthrough as a top-ranking sprinter as follows (at Los Angeles, on 17 May 1940): "They had lined up a crack field in the 100 y. dash, including Mozelle Ellerbe of Tuskegee, twice NCAA 100 y. champion. It was Ellerbe who won the race (9.7), but the man who finished fourth attracted much attention. He stumbled at the start, fell on all fours, recovered and then made up 4 to 7 m. on some of the nation's crack sprinters in the last 65 m. The runner was young Harold Davis from Salinas Junior College".

Even apart from falls, Davis never rose above the average in starting ability. But he went on to impress observers more and more with his amazing "finishing kick". In the four years of his reign as king of American sprinters (1940-43), he never lost a race in the furlong and was beaten on only one important occasion in the century, namely by Norwood "Barney" Ewell in the 1941 AAU 100 m. at Philadelphia. And Davis probably ran one of his greatest races on that very occasion: an atrocious start caused him to lag 3 m. behind Ewell at the half-way mark, but a fantastic rush in the closing stage brought him within centimetres of his great rival at the tape. If I add that both were timed in 10.3, it seems reasonable to assume that Davis must have come very close to the maximum of known human potential in the second half of that incredible race. "Bud" Winter, who was Davis' coach at Salinas, has committed to history some interesting splits for Davis' fastest races. On 6 June 1941 at Compton, when he equalled Owens' world record for the 100 m. (10.2), Davis covered the first half in 5.7 and the second half in 4.5. In his two 20.2 straightaway races, aided on both occasions by a wind over the limit, Davis ran halves of 10.3 and 9.9, namely at Fresno, 17 May 1941 (220 y.) and in New York, 20 June 1943 (200 m.). Between 1940 and 1943, Davis won seven AAU outdoor titles (three at 100 m., four at 200 m.). He also equalled the world's 100 y. record, 9.4, and in the same year, 1942, he achieved his best legitimate time for the furlong, 20.4. Had the Olympics taken place in 1940 and 1944, only one man could have made things a bit

127

difficult for him, the above-mentioned Ewell, one of the most durable sprinters the world has ever seen. Ewell (born at Harrisburg, PA., on 25 February 1918; 1.80 m./ 71 kg.) figured among the fastest sprinters in America, and for that matter in the world, from 1937 to 1948, apart from a spell during the war when he was in the Services. In 1941 he traded wins with Davis at the AAU Championships, winning the 100 m. by a whisker in 10.3 as related above, and finishing second to the "California Comet", 20.5 to 20.4, in the 200 m. straightaway. He won six AAU outdoor titles, the first in 1939, the last in 1948 - and he was AAU Junior champion as early as in 1936. He was also a leading long jumper: 7.68 indoors in 1942.

In the early post-war years two excellent sprinters developed in North America, Melvin Patton of USA and Lloyd LaBeach of Panama. The former (born at Los Angeles on 16 November 1924; 1.85 m./ 72 kg.), a dashman with a silken stride, came to the fore in 1942 with times of 9.9 and 21.4 for the English distances. The following year he improved to 9.8 and 21.2. Then the war put a brisk halt to his promising career, and it was only in 1946 that he resumed his athletic activity, as a freshman at the University of Southern California. In 1947 he equalled the world's 100 y. record, 9.4, and ran the furlong in 20.4. For some curious reason, however, he failed to appear in AAU meets. His fiercest rival by then was Lloyd LaBeach (born at Panama City on 28 June 1923; 1.85 m./ 73 kg.), a Panamanian who was educated first in Jamaica, then in USA.

Being on the whole a self-taught and self-advised athlete, he compiled a superb series of fast times but was not always at his best on big occasions. The first major clash between him and Patton occurred at the Pasadena Games in 1947 and resulted in a tie, with the Californian first in the 100 m. (10.5) and LaBeach winning the 220 y. (20.8). The most memorable chapter of their feud unfolded at Fresno on 15 May 1948. In the 100 y., after a number of false starts, Patton was off fast and soon appeared to have a decisive lead on LaBeach. Even though Patton's pick-up was considered nonpareil, LaBeach

Start and finish of the 100 metres final at the 1948 Olympics in London. The winner is hurdler Harrison Dillard (USA), extreme left, time 10.3. Others from left are: A. McCorquodale (GB), 4th; E. McDonald Bailey (GB) 6th; L. LaBeach (Panama), 3rd; N. Ewell (USA) 2nd; and M. Patton (USA), 5th.

128

managed to close the gap almost entirely and finished only 30 cm. back at the end. The winner was rewarded with a new world record, 9.3, while LaBeach was given 9.4. As one keen observer pointed out, chance had a large part in awarding the first official 9.3 to Patton and not, say, to Simpson or Owens. In fact, the three official watches on Patton read 9.3, 9.3, 9.4, while two alternates showed 9.3 and 9.4. Both Simpson at Chicago in 1929 and Owens at Ann Arbor in 1935 were timed alternatively in 9.3 or 9.4, except that the majority of timers designated as official before the races were on the 9.4 side. In the days of manual timing it took three watches to make a verdict official, yet records were not infrequently determined by one timepiece - operated, like all others, by the fallible human element - going this way or that way. Later in the same afternoon at Fresno, LaBeach ran the 100 m. in 10.2, with Patton not in the race. On 4 June at Compton, the Panamanian ace posted another 10.2 and ran the 220 y. straightaway in 20.3 (time at 200 m., 20.2). Although the wind on these occasions was within the permissible limit, for some obscure reason the marks were never ratified by the IAAF. A few weeks before the London Olympics, Patton and LaBeach reigned supreme in the thoughts of (amateur) prognosticators, who at best gave an outsider's chance to veteran "Barney" Ewell. But to make things difficult for both athletes and tipsters, there came a trouble-maker: hurdler Harrison Dillard of USA. The holder of the world record for the 120 y. hurdles (13.6 early in 1948) had, in 1947, sped over 100 m. flat in 10.3. At the US Final Olympic Tryouts at Evanston, on 9 July, Dillard secured a berth on the Olympic team by placing third (10.4) in the 100 m. behind Ewell, who ran the race of his life (10.2), and Patton (10.3).

The great hurdler just sneaked into the team, centimetres ahead of Eddie Conwell, a wizard of the start if ever there was one.

Ewell thus became a co-holder of the world record at the age of thirty. A Bulova Photo-Timer used as a reserve told the story in more exact terms: 10.33, 10.44, 10.50 and 10.53 for the first four. On the following day Patton won the 200 m. around a turn in 20.7, with Ewell receiving the same time in second place. Both equalled Owens' best-on-record mark, set in the Berlin Olympics in 1936. Cliff Bourland, better known as a quarter-miler, was third in 21.0.

On the eve of the London rendezvous, the European armour appeared to be weaker than usual. With Osendarp serving a prison term for collaborating with the Germans and Strandberg well past his peak, none of the sprinters from the Old Continent loomed as a threat to America's representatives. Two years earlier, at the European Championships in Oslo, Jack Archer of Britain had won the 100 m. in 10.6. Yet he was not even the fastest man in the British Isles, because that title rightfully belonged to Emmanuel McDonald Bailey, a copybook stylist hailing from the Caribbean area (born at Williamsville, Trinidad, on 8 December 1920; 1.80 m./ 65 kg.) "Mac" was for many years one of the dominant figures in British athletics circles. Between 1946 and 1953 he collected no less than fourteen AAA titles. Just a few weeks before the London Olympics, a home-made British sprinter, Alistair McCorquodale, came to the fore in meteoric fashion and began to talk on even terms with the great "Mac". The Wembley track (specially laid for the Olympics: it was in fact dismantled as soon as the Games were over!) turned out to be the fas-test surface in the history of British athletics. On 31 July, 84,000 spectators saw the final of the 100 m. Patton drew the inside lane, then came Ewell, LaBeach, McCorquodale, McDonald Bailey and Dillard. It must be said that Patton and "Mac" practically lost the race at the start and never looked like their real selves. Dillard, who had gone through the prelims with times of 10.4, 10.4 and 10.5, held a narrow but decisive lead from gun to tape. At the other end of the track, Ewell looked dangerous as he closed the gap gradually. The 30-year-old veteran actually thought he had won and, after having waited for that moment many years, he indulged in an impromptu dance to celebrate. The official verdict which awarded the victory to Dillard thus came as a bitter pill for the durable Ewell. LaBeach, although not as good as in his best days, was third, just ahead of McCorquodale, a squat-shouldered rugby player, while Patton and McDonald Bailey closed up the rear in that order. The official times for the first three were 10.3, 10.4 and 10.6, but it was apparent that they bore no relation to the actual intervals. According to an electric timer, only 11 hundredths of a second covered the first four, which means that McCorquodale in fourth place should have been credited with 10.4! Patton was burnt by a strong desire to make amends for his poor show in the century and on 3 August he went to the starting line of the 200 m. final fully determined to prove his greatness to the big international audience. Ewell, by then in the twilight of his career, was moved by an even more stringent necessity: for him it was obviously a case of now or never. Ewell was off faster than Patton, but the latter had an early pick-up, collared his rival in the final part of the turn, and shot into the lead on entering the homestretch. Ewell fought back with dogged determination, but Patton

1941
1960

held on gamely and won by half a metre. Both were timed in 21.1, while LaBeach was again third (21.2). That victory gave Patton the incentive he needed for another season of full action on the cinder path. His greatest moments in the struggle against time came on 7 May 1949 at Westwood, Los Angeles, during a dual meet between UCLA and their cross-town rivals, USC, Mel's university. Running as only a great champion does in his most inspired moments, Patton offered an uninhibited yet smooth display of sprinting ability. He began with a splendid 9.1 in the 100 y., alas assisted by a wind of 2.90 m/s, then continued with a legal 20.2 in the 220 y. straightaway. In the latter race the wind in his favour was 1.50 m/s. In the century the three official watches gave 9.1, 9.1 and 9.0: had the wind stayed within the limit, he would have probably earned a legal 9.2. In the furlong two watches gave 20.2 and one showed 20.1. Patton won both races by a "block". He was second to none of his contemporaries in pure blazing speed, but his habit of by-passing the AAU Championships probably cost him a few points in the eyes of experts, more in fact than his actual defeats (two in the 100, one in the furlong) in the three-year period 1947-49.

In his last major race, the 220 y. final of the 1949 NCAA Championships, Patton (20.4) was extended by a newcomer, Andy Stanfield, who finished a close second in 20.5. This statuesque runner (born in Washington, D.C. on 29 December 1927; 1.85 m./77 kg.) went on to score a double over the metric distances at the AAU Championships (10.3 and 20.4, the latter wind-assisted) and thus established himself as the new king of American sprinters. In later years, recurrent muscle injuries prevented him from showing a consistency equal to his class. On 26 May 1951 at Philadelphia he ran the 220 y. around a full turn in 20.6. By then the IAAF had finally decided to distinguish between marks made on a straight track and those made around a turn. Stanfield's mark thus became the first official world record for the latter category. In USA the straightaway event was discontinued only in the late Sixties. Lloyd LaBeach had his best year as a record-breaker and globe-trotter in 1950. In Europe he twice clocked 20.7 for the 200 m. around a turn, beating among others Herb McKenley of Jamaica and Emmanuel McDonald Bailey of Trinidad. Then, on 7 October at Guayaquil, Ecuador, he was credited with a sensational 10.1 for the metric century. There was no anemometer though and this obviously prevented ratification by the IAAF. The time of the runner-up, Andres Fernandes Salvador, 10.3, was ratified as an Ecuadorian record though. However, the timing was regarded as doubtful by some observers. At the same time, McDonald Bailey continued to rule the roost on British tracks. As often as not, however, he had to go abroad to post his fastest times. On 25 August 1951 at Belgrade he ran the 100 m. in 10.2, thus equalling the world record. His mark was also accepted as a European record, since the Trinidad speedster had been a resident of Britain for more than the required five years. In 1950, however, he had not been admitted to the European Championships, and the continental titles, contested by a mediocre lot, had gone to

---

The luck of the game

In discussing sport results, fans sometimes fail to fully appreciate how infinitesimal can be the difference that separates victory from defeat. The luck of the game, that is. On occasion even such an important laurel as an Olympic title may come as the result of a long series of close decisions, or "lucky" cards. Typical in this respect is the case of Lindy Remigino, winner of the 100 m. at the Helsinki Olympics. In the States he was regarded merely as a good sprinter - one of many - with a fierce competitive spirit. In the spring of 1952 there were at least three Americans who clearly excelled him as 100 m. aces: Jim Golliday, the strongest of them all, was sidelined with a muscle injury on the eve of the Olympic Trials; Andy Stanfield, another injury-prone sprinter, decided to put all his eggs in one basket, the 200 m.; Art Bragg, winner of the 100 m. at the Trials in 10.5, was stopped by injury in one of the Olympic semi-finals. Remigino, a 21-year-old medium-size sprinter of Italian (Piedmontese) extraction, went through the ordeal of the selection process almost unnoticed: fifth in the NCAA meet in 10.8 (Golliday first in 10.4); eliminated in a semi-final (10.8) at the AAU meet; second in the all-important race of the Olympic Trials in 10.6 - the same time credited to three others who finished close behind him! At Helsinki he won Olympic gold in 10.4, actually with one hundredth of a second to spare vis-à-vis runner-up Herb McKenley. However, it must be conceded that Remigino was at his best at the right time. After all, even luck needs assistance (from man) in order to be effective .... The story has a worthy P.S. A few days after the Games, at Oslo, Remigino ran the 100 m. in 10.2, aided by a wind of 2.08 m/s., hence barely above the permissible limit.

1941–1960

Etienne Bally of France in the 100 m. (10.6) and to Brian Shenton of Britain in the 200 m. (21.5). Holland seemed to have exhausted her vein, and Germany was not yet ready to return to her tradition.

Early in 1952 the leading American candidates for Olympic honours were Stanfield, agile and consistent Art Bragg, and powerful Jim Golliday. This last (born at Sacramento, California, on 23 April 1931; 1.76 m./ 76 kg.) looked like the class of the nation when he downed a crack field at the NCAA Championships, running the 100 m. against a stiff wind in 10.4. But a muscular ailment prematurely put paid to his Helsinki chances. In his absence, Bragg won the 100 m. at the Final Olympic Trials in 10.5, the other qualifiers being Lindy Remigino and Dean Smith. It should be added that Smith actually tied for third with Jim Gathers, but was given the nod on the opinion of Olympic coaches. Stanfield elected to concentrate on the 200 m. and won in splendid fashion in 20.6, with Thane Baker and Gathers following in that order, both in 20.9.

At Helsinki, Bragg too fell the victim of muscular trouble. After many years, the throne of American sprinters seemed likely to be overturned. McKenley, the great Jamaican quarter-miler, chose to run the 100 m. at the last moment, supposedly to warm up for the 400 m. In the final the field, although not in a class with those of the three previous editions of the Games, was such as to offer a close, fascinating race. In fact, first and last man were never more than a metre apart. Remigino was in the lead at the half-way point, but McKenley was coming on like a whirlwind. With a driving finish he caught Remigino at the tape and actually shot ahead just after crossing the finish line. This circumstance probably led some onlookers to believe that McKenley had won. The finish was the closest possible, and the photo finish had to be supplemented by a set-square, through which it was possible to determine that Remigino's right shoulder was fractionally ahead of McKenley's torso at the tape. "Mac" was a close third, with Smith centimetres further back. The first four were all credited with 10.4. A photo-timer used as unofficial "supplementary evidence" gave a more exact and far less generous set of times: 10.79, 10.80, 10.83 and 10.84. The 200 m. title was won, as expected, by Andy Stanfield, who equalled Owens' Olympic record (20.7) in beating his countrymen Baker and Gathers (both 20.8). McDonald Bailey was fourth in 21.0.

Patton, no.71, took revenge in the 200 metres (1948 Olympics), winning from veteran "Barney" Ewell, no.70. Time for both, 21.1. Others from left: C. Bourland (USA) 5th; L. LaBeach (Panama) 3rd; H. McKenley (Jamaica) 4th. Not visible, in lane 6, L. Laing (Jamaica) 6th.

Bobby Morrow (USA) winning the 200 metres at the Melbourne Olympics (1956) from A. Stanfield (USA), no.88. Others from left: J.T. de Conceição (Brazil) 6th; T. Baker (USA) 3rd; B. Tokaryev (USSR) 5th and M. Agostini (Trinidad) 4th. Winner's time, 20.6.

In the four-year period between Helsinki and Melbourne the select group of leading "speed merchants" also included three non-Americans: Mike Agostini of Trinidad, Hector Hogan of Australia, and Heinz Fütterer of Germany. Agostini, the offspring of a sports-minded family of Portuguese descent, was a most precocious talent. At eighteen he ran the English distances in 9.4 and 21.1 (turn). An excellent starter, despite - or perhaps, because of - his not so good hearing, he played a prominent role for many years. A first-rate globe-trotter with an amusing personality, at the end of his career he could match anybody's knowledge about athletes, starters and tracks from practically every corner of the world.

Hogan, known as the "Queensland Hurricane", was an "Aussie" of medium build who got off the marks like a bullet and used a very long stride while in high gear. Clockwise, he had his greatest day on 13 March 1954 at Sydney, when he tied Mel Patton's 100 y. record (9.3). Later in the day he also ran the 100 m. in 10.2. The latter mark, however, could not be submitted to the IAAF since it was made in a "mixed" handicap with three males pitted against three women, the men running 100 m. and the distaff side only 100 y. (Best of the latter group was Marlene Mathews, who did 10.5). Later in the season, however, Hogan was soundly beaten in both sprints at the British Empire Games in Vancouver. Winner of the 100 y. was Agostini (9.6). Hogan also excelled as a long jumper (7.65).

1941 1960

The first European native who proved a consistent world-class sprinter in post-war years was Heinz Fütterer of Germany (born at Illingen-am-Rhein on 14 October 1931; 1.64 m./ 72 kg.). A former soccer player, on the small side but very compact, he first gave the measure of his ability at the international level in 1953, when he had some close tussles with Art Bragg. In 1954 he won a double (10.5 and 20.9) at the European Championships in Bern, then went to Japan and brought a perfect season to a climax with two 10.2 clockings in the 100 m. and 20.8 in the 200 m. (full turn). His second 10.2 (Yokohama, 31 October) was accepted as a world record. Still strong in 1955, when he did 20.6 at Köln on a course with a slight turn, Fütterer began to fade in 1956.

Meanwhile, Bragg, Golliday and Stanfield continued to dominate the picture in the States. On 14 May 1955 at Evanston, Illinois, the powerful Golliday equalled the world's 100 y. record (9.3). With three official watches showing 9.2, 9.3 and 9.3 and two alternates showing 9.2 and 9.4, his actual time was a "fast" 9.3, if not a "slow" 9.2. The wind in his favour was 1.5 m/s. American experts still wonder what Golliday might have achieved if his muscles had not failed him now and then. At his best he looked very much like the perfect sprinter. Still in 1955 a new star appeared on the American firmament: Bobby Morrow (born at Harlingen, Texas, on 15 October 1935; 1.85 m./ 75 kg.). He proved wellnigh invincible in interscholastic competition, with best times of 9.6 and 21.1 in 1954. It may be regarded as typical of the vagaries of hand timing that he was credited with some of the fastest times of his career before his actual breakthrough on the national scene. It happened on 3/4 June 1955 at Abilene: on the first day he ran the English distances in 9.4 and 20.6 (around a turn) in the prelims; on the following day he won the finals in 9.1 and 20.9. All these times, except the 9.4 mark in the century, were made with a wind well exceeding the permissible limit. Even so, his 9.1 (wind 3.12 m/s) equalled Patton's fastest wind-aided effort. It is true that over the years the wind of Texas had produced an incredible number of fast times, but here was a man who wanted to prove that the Lone Star State had sprinters who could beat the world under any circumstance. He began to prove this later in the same year at the AAU Championships in Boulder, Colorado (altitude, 1655 m.), where he won the 100 y. in 9.5, beating among others Rod Richard, who earlier in the year had scored a "metric" double at the Pan-American Games in Mexico City (10.3 and 20.7).

The year 1956 was to be one of the most eventful in the annals of sprinting. Mike Agostini started the fireworks in March, when he sped over a new, lightning-fast track at Bakersfield, California, to clock 20.1 for the 220 y. straightaway. But his record lasted less than three months.It fell under the assaults of a thoroughbred from Duke University, Dave Sime (born at Paterson, New Jersey, on 25 July 1936; 1.88 m./ 81 kg.). Hardly known prior to 1956 (the year before his best in the century was 9.6), Sime got started in the new season with an American indoor record of 9.5, leaving Stanfield 2 m. behind. Then, in outdoor meets, he really let himself go. Between 26 March and 9 June, counting legal marks only, he did 9.3 twice and 9.4 six times for the 100 y.; and 20.0, 20.1, 20.2, 20.3 twice, and 20.4 for the 220 y. straightaway! Most of these were in "cold" races in the warm Southern climate, yet he had his greatest day at Sanger, California, on 9 June, when he beat Agostini twice, 9.3 to 9.4 in the 100 y. and 20.0 to 20.4 in the 220 y. In the latter race, Sime had an ordinary start and Agostini managed to hold him back till 120 y. The wind was a legal 1.35 m/s.

With the US Final Olympic Trials only three weeks away, nobody would have dared to predict the exclusion of the new speedball from the Melbourne-bound team. Yet the "Blue Devil of Duke" met defeat and disaster in the meets that mattered most. At the NCAA Championships in Berkeley he was pitted against Morrow, whom he had beaten at the Drake Relays in April (9.4 to 9.5), not without the benefit of a dubious start. At Berkeley, however, the reliable Morrow won the 100 m. from a crack field in 10.4, leaving behind Sime (10.54), Agostini (10.55) and Leamon King (10.63), who had been credited with a record-equalling 9.3 for the 100 y. at Fresno a few weeks earlier. A bitter surprise awaited Sime in the 200 m. around a turn. Until then he had never run the curve in competition, and whether or not this had anything to do with what followed, he did in fact pull a muscle just as he was going round the turn. Morrow won in 20.6.

That was the end of Sime's Olympic dream. True, the Melbourne Games were more than four months away, but under the rigid American system the tickets for the trip Down Under were to be assigned at the Final Trials two weeks later. In the absence of his great rival, Morrow was again a double winner, with 10.3 and 20.6. The other Olympic berths went to Murchison and Baker (both 10.4) in the 100 m., to Baker (20.7) and Stanfield (20.9) in the 200 m. The last two thus qualified for their second trip to the Olympics.

Even after the demise of the unlucky Sime, further circumstances occurred which showed up the negati-

133

ve side of the AAU selective system. Early in August, the Berlin Olympic Stadium was the theatre of the CISM (Conseil International du Sport Militaire) Championships. Among the entries in the 100 m. were two Americans, stocky Willie Williams and little Ira Murchison. The former had failed at the Trials, not without the excuse of a muscle injury. In the heats (3 August) Williams created quite a stir with a 10.1 clocking. The next day, in a semi-final, Murchison (who stood only 1.62 m. but weighed 65 kg.) returned the same time. Quite understandably, the outcome of the final was awaited with great curiosity in metric-minded Europe.

The two characters in the play had dreams of a 10-flat performance .... But on 5 August the famous track was washed by the rains, which let up just one hour before the race. Murchison, an explosive starter, held a minor lead in the initial stage, but Williams had a good pick-up and finally won by about 30 cm. The winner's time was again 10.1, while Murchison was given 10.2. In none of the three 10.1 races did the wind creep over 1 m/s. The times were therefore ratified as world records by the IAAF. Williams was by no means an unknown. He had won the NCAA 100 y. title twice (1953-54). He was to be heard of again in 1957, when he had wind-aided times of 9.3 and 20.3 for the English distances. One month before the Olympics, the new 100 m. record, 10.1, was twice equalled by another American, Leamon King, a smooth-striding dashman who could sometimes produce a terrific lift in the final stages. But just like Williams, he had failed at the Trials .... Morrow had a virus infection in the fall, yet he managed to recover in time for the big test. In all his appearances at the Melbourne Cricket Ground he proved as great a sprinter as any in Olympic history. He went through the 100 m. series without a loss, with times of 10.4 (heat), 10.3 (quarter-final), 10.3 (semi-final) and 10.5 (final). In all these races except the first he ran against the wind. In the decisive race he battled a cold adverse wind of 5 m/s and won by a good metre from his compatriot Thane Baker, who was also timed in 10.5. Hector Hogan of Australia finally proved his 9.3 (100 y.) potential and finished a very close third in 10.6, ahead of Murchison, Manfred Germar of Germany and Agostini. The automatic but unofficial photo-timer caught the first three in 10.62, 10.77 and 10.77. In the 200 m. Morrow ran with a bandaged thigh and ostensibly saved his energies for the last round, in which he produced the third legitimate 20.6 of his career and won from Stanfield (20.7), while Baker easily held off Agostini for third place, 20.9 to 21.1.

Baker, a sprinter with a great competitive heart and supreme ability as a curve runner, brought his tally of Olympic medals to three (two silver, one bronze). He had to wait for the relay to hit gold at last.

The rising star of Europe was Manfred Germar of Germany (born at Köln on 10 March 1935, 1.82 m./ 72 kg.), who in 1957-58 rose to heights previously unknown in European-born sprinters.

His class was especially evident in the 200 m., at which distance he remained undefeated from 1956 till July 1960. His best times were 10.2 in the 100 m., 20.6 (full turn) and 20.4 (slight turn) in the 200 m. Unfortunately for him, the Melbourne Games found him not yet ripe, and the Rome Games four years later came when he was clearly past his peak. At the 1958 European Championships in Stockholm he won the 200 m. (21.0) but suffered a bitter and partly unexpected defeat in the century. Making his first major international appearance in that race was a new sprint phenomenon, Armin Hary (born at Quierschied, Saarland, on 22 March 1937; 1.82 m./ 71 kg.), a German citizen since 1957, when the Saar became the tenth Land (state) of the Federal Republic. Already a 10.4 man the year before, Hary had made the grade at the German Championships in July, when he finished a close second to Germar in the 100 m., the time for both being 10.2. At Stockholm the powerful Hary, known as an explosive starter, took what in the opinion of most onlookers was a blatant flyer and was never headed. Germar and a new British star, Peter Radford, chased him all the way and both had a strong finish, yet failed to catch Hary, who won in 10.3, with Germar and Radford following in that order, both in 10.4. The debate on Hary's "Blitz-start" was still raging when the news was flashed to the athletic world on the evening of 6 September that the 21-year-old German had run the metric century in the startling time of 10 seconds flat. This happened in the afternoon of that day at Friedrichshafen, a town on Lake Constance. However, Hary's high-sounding time was made in an unsanctioned race, which was run at the request of Hary and other sprinters, after the European champion had done 10.3 in the official event. Apart from technicalities, it was found that the track was sloping gently in the running direction.

Germar and Hary found a worthy opponent in Peter Radford, a would-be schoolmaster from England who later in 1958 ran the metric distances in 10.3 and 20.8, a week before his nineteenth birthday. Radford had his best year in 1960: on 28 May at Wolverhampton, running on one of Britain's fastest tracks, he did 9.4 (heat) and 9.3 (final) in the 100 y., and 20.5 in the 220 y. around a turn. In all these races he was aided by a slight wind, which crept over the allowable limit only during the 9.3 century. His furlong time was accepted as a world record by the IAAF. This mark occurred in what was virtually a solo effort (the runner-up did 22.4), a rare example in the annals of sprinting.

France had by then two sprinters of international calibre in Jocelyn Delecour (10.3 and 20.9 in 1958) and Abdoulaye Seye, from Senegal who in the pre-Olympic weeks of 1960 posted such times as 10.2 and 20.7, plus a remarkable 45.9 in the 400 m.

Italy, another country with relatively modest traditions in sprinting, joined the debate shortly before the Rome Games with Livio Berruti (born at Turin on 19 May 1939; 1.80 m./ 66 kg.), a natural talent with the silken stride of a gazelle. He equalled the Italian 100 m. record, 10.4, at the age of eighteen. Two years later, in 1959, he was good enough to beat Hary in the 100 m. and Seye in the 200 m. during a hexagonal match at Duisburg.

Later in the same year he took some lessons from Ray Norton of USA in Sweden but ran the 200 m. around a turn in 20.8, the only time he managed to beat his American rival.

In the States Bobby Morrow continued to reign supreme for two more years (1957-58), but in 1959 muscular ailments began to slow him down. Yet most international experts agree, even today, that the competitive record compiled by Morrow between 1955 and 1958 suffices to stamp him as one of the greatest sprinters of all time. In that four-year period he won all the major championship titles for which he competed, with only one exception, the AAU 220 y. in 1955, the year of his debut in big-time competition. Counting legitimate marks only, he ran the 100 y. in 9.3 once (Austin, 14 June 1957) and in 9.4 sixteen times; the 100 m. in 10.2 seven times, the 200 m. around a turn in 20.6 three times, and the 220 y. straightaway in 20.4.

Morrow's arch rival, Dave Sime, potentially second to none of the great sprinters in pure blazing speed, had an uneven record. But he managed to make a nice comeback in 1960. However, on the eve of the Games the no.1 American was Ray Norton, a tall, powerful man who between 1958 and 1960 compiled a fine set of marks: 9.3 in the 100 y. three times, 10.1 in the 100 m., 20.6 in the 220 y. around a turn, and 20.1 on a straight course (with 19.9 for 200 m. en route). Other strong candidates were Charles Tidwell and Stone Johnson. The former was credited with a nifty 20.2 for the 220 y. around a turn at Abilene on 16 April 1960, on a course which turned out to be 1.57 m. short. He also ran the 100 m. in 10.1, but an injury stopped him on the threshold of the Olympic Trials, which were held at Palo Alto, California. In this crucial meet Norton won the 100 m. from Frank Budd, Sime and Paul Winder as all four were credited with 10.4. Sime actually got a tie for third with Winder, but later in the summer he posted a fast 10.1 and thus earned the coveted berth. Norton also won the 200 m. in a record-tying 20.5 from Stone Johnson (20.8) and Les Carney (20.9), who shut out the great Bobby Morrow (21.1). It should be added that Johnson too had a legal 20.5 in the prelims.

Yet the most sensational of all pre-Olympic marks were returned in Switzerland and Canada. On 21 June 1960, running on the magic Letzigrund track in Zurich, Armin Hary was credited with 10.0 for the 100 m. not once, but twice! The duplicate was necessary, though, because only the later performance was made under acceptable conditions. In the first race Hary took a "flyer" à la Hary. The starter had a pistol for recall in his left hand but somehow failed to use it. He later admitted his mistake and the race was annulled. Hary, who had won from Abdoulaye Seye (10.3), protested at first, then he calmed down and went back to his marks, fully determined to "show 'em". There was a new starter for the re-run, incidentally the same man who had sent Martin Lauer off to a happy 13.2 record journey over 110 m. hurdles on the same track in 1959. Only two contestants from the former race lined up alongside Hary at the start: Jürgen Schüttler of Germany and Heinz Müller of Switzerland. This time Hary was off correctly. With his characteristic early pick-up he soon put daylight between himself and the opposition, and then continued to run hard till the end. He was rewarded with another "even time" clocking, his third since 1958, but for official purposes the first in the history of the metric century. Müller (10.3) and Schüttler (10.4) respectively equalled and bettered their previous bests. The three official watches on Hary showed 10.0, 10.0 and 10.1. The wind was blowing at a moderate velocity (0.9 m/s) and the Longines electric timer showed 10.25 (In the preceding race the reading was 10.16).

History's second official "10 flat" for the 100 m. came a few weeks later, on 15 July at Saskatoon, Canada, and was achieved by a Canadian, Harry Jerome (born at Prince Albert, Saskatchewan, on 30 September 1940; 1.80 m./ 77 kg.). He had previously shown his class in several US meets, yet his 10.0 in the Canadian Olympic Trials caused quite a stir. Conditions were checked and found correct: a legal wind of 1.8 m/s and a distance which turned out to be 5 cm.long.

The Rome Olympics came at the right time to show who was the World's Fastest Human anno 1960. When the chips were down,Hary was the name. His early acceleration impressed experienced American observers as truly phenomenal.

1941
1960

135

Furthermore, Hary displayed a combination of arrogance and coolness such as only few sprint "demons" can command. One of his two "breaks" occurred in the 100 m. final, yet when the gun was fired again he went off as well as anyone else, and possibly better. Rumour has it that starter Primo Pedrazzini spent a sleepless night, anticipating the task facing him in connection with Hary's Blitz-start. At any rate, the interval between "pronti" (set) and the gun was a normal 1.9 secs. The German built up a sizeable lead in the early part of the race. Even the great Sime appeared to be hopelessly out of it at the half-way mark. But in the closing stage the "Blue Devil of Duke" came back like a whirlwind and made up valuable ground on Hary. At the tape, however, the German was still ahead by a narrow but visible margin. Officially both were timed in 10.2, but the automatic timer gave 10.32 for Hary and 10.35 for Sime. (Hary had first done 10.2, a new Olympic record, in a quarter-final). Peter Radford of Britain also had an unimpressive getaway and a grand finish: he wound up a close third, just ahead of Enrique Figuerola of Cuba and Frank Budd of USA, as all three were timed in 10.3. (The automatic timer was more discerning: 10.42, 10.44 and 10.46). Ray Norton was a disappointing sixth in 10.4. An illustrious victim in the semi-finals was Jerome, who pulled a muscle while in a good position to qualify for the decisive round. Sime, who had never won a major title at home, certainly closed his career on a high note. Hary did not run the 200 m., a distance he had often by-passed in German meets too, even though he had marks of 20.5 (slight turn) and 20.9 (full turn). Livio Berruti, the Italian hope, had finally chosen to concentrate on the 200 m. He came to the Olympic rendezvous in the form of his lifetime, with a fresh personal best of 20.7 (plus an earlier 10.2 in the 100 m.) and plenty of self-confidence. He sped round the half-lap circuit in 21.0 (heat) and 20.8 (quarter-final) on 2 September.

The following day, on a windless afternoon, he offered a superlative display of his ability as a curve runner. In the semi-final the 21-year-old Italian, wearing his customary sun glasses, was pitted against Norton, Johnson and Radford, i.e. the three men who held the official world record (20.5). That could hardly be regarded as a piece of good seeding. Berruti was thus confronted with the task of beating at least one of the three record holders in order to make the final. He ran such an inspired race that he beat them all! He came off the turn with a decisive lead and went home in 20.5, equalling the world record. Norton (20.7) was second ahead of Johnson (20.8). Radford put on a game effort but could do no better than fourth (20.9) and was eliminated. The other "semi" was not so hectic: Seye won in 20.8 from Marian Foik of Poland (21.0) and Les Carney (21.1), believed to be America's third string. Less than two hours later the six finalists lined up in the following order: Foik in the pole lane, then Seye, Johnson, Berruti, Norton and Carney. After a false start, Berruti was off well and ran the curve in a "divine" fashion. He entered the homestretch well ahead of his opponents, and being by then an elated man he was not to be headed. He won comfortably (although not as relaxed as in the "semi") and again equalled the world record (20.5). Carney, in the outside lane, ran the race of his life and closed slightly on Berruti in the final stage, clocking 20.6. Seye was perhaps the strongest finisher but had to be content with third place (20.7), while Foik, fourth (20.8), upset two of the pre-race favourites, Johnson (20.8) and Norton (20.9). Berruti thus became the first non-American to win the Olympic 200 m. title since 1928. The electric timer caught him in 20.62 (as opposed to 20.65 in the semi-final) and Carney in 20.69. American experts were at a loss for explanations in discussing Norton's disappointing show.

Among those who failed to reach the 200 m. final was Edward Jefferys of South Africa, who in March at Pretoria (altitude, 1333 m.) had run 220 y. on a straight course in 20.2 (200 m. time, 20.1). The Rome events certainly raised the stock of European sprinters as no previous Olympics had ever done. Hary had emulated Harold Abrahams in the century, and Berruti was the first European to strike gold in the 200 m. Yet the Americans, although deprived of a man like Tidwell, had placed three men in each of the two sprint finals.

400 METRES - Jamaica's Halcyon Days

In 1941 another keen rivalry blossomed in the States, more precisely in California. The characters of the feud were Grover Klemmer and Hubie Kerns, both sons of the Golden State. The former (born at San Francisco on 16 March 1921; 1.88 m./ 77 kg.) was the prize picture of an athlete and had done 46.8 (400 m.) and 47.0 (440 y.) at the age of nineteen. On 31 May 1941 at Berkeley he tied Eastman's quarter-mile record (46.4) in beating Kerns (47.1). The latter evened the count three weeks later in the NCAA Championships at Palo Alto, over the same distance, in 46.6. This was a close finish and Klemmer had to be content with

1941 1960

third place, just behind Harold Bogrow (both 46.8). The "rubber race" took place in the AAU Championships at Philadelphia on 29 June. It was over 400 m., on a one-turn course. Klemmer made his move at the head of the homestretch and won by 30 cm. from Kerns, who just held off a fast-closing Cliff Bourland. All six place-winners were clocked under 47 seconds, the order of finish being as follows: Klemmer 46.0 (equal to Harbig's world record), Kerns 46.1, Bourland 46.1, Al Diebolt 46.4, Jim Herbert 46.8, Jack Campbell 46.9. The event was not run in lanes, and Klemmer finished in the outer section of the track, close to the wall encircling the Franklin Field surface. It should be noted that Klemmer, Kerns and Bourland averaged just over twenty in age. Unfortunately World War II meant a brisk halt in the rise of these young men. Only Bourland was able to rise again in 1948, placing fifth in the 200 m. at the London Olympics.

In Europe, Harbig and Lanzi met twice in 1940-41, with the Italian winning the last tussle. At the end of their feud in the one-lap event (1939-41), the German still led, 3 to 1. Harbig was killed on the Eastern front in 1944.

Yet it was during the war years that a new talent, probably the greatest of all up to that time, gradually reached athletic maturity - a tall and lean sprinter from Jamaica, Herbert McKenley (born at Clarendon, Jamaica, on 10 July 1922; 1.85m. /72 kg.). He went to study in USA, and while at Boston College in 1943 he was credited with 21.4 (220 y.) and 47.7 (400 m.). Later he moved to Illinois University and by 1946 he was beginning to ascend the Olympus of track "Greats". In May he ran the "quarter" in 46.9. This was merely a prelude to the first major day of his career, 1 June 1946, when on his home track at Champaign, Illinois, he chalked up a record-breaking 46.2 for the quarter-mile, then ran the furlong straightaway in 20.6, and rounded off a big day with a fast anchor leg in the mile relay. In the record race, he covered the first 220 y. in a sizzling 20.9, then "survived" for a 25.3 second half.

From then on, McKenley was to remain for years the most authoritative advocate of suicidal tactics in quarter-mile running. Even so, in the period 1946-52 he amassed a great tally of sixty-three clockings under 47 seconds for the 400 m. (or under 47.3 for the 440 y.), outshining in quality and quantity of performances all his predecessors. During his career, "Hustling Herb" travelled extensively throughout the world and practically set a new training pattern: "keep fit through non-stop competition". A study of his greatest achievements against the watch confirms that he invariably gave too much too soon.

Unofficial yet reliable splits read as follows: 20.8 + 25.4 = 46.2 (440 y.) at Salt Lake City (altitude, 1338 m.) on 21 June 1947; 21.2 + 24.8 = 46.0 (440 y.) at Berkeley, 5 June 1948; 20.9 +25.0 = 45.9 (400 m.) in a heat of the AAU Championships at Milwaukee on 2 July 1948. One still wonders what times would have come within his reach if he had planned his races a little more cautiously when he was at the peak of his condition. On 23 August 1947, running on a boardwalk straightaway at Long Branch, N.J., he took advantage of an aiding breeze to clock 45.0 for the 440 y. Inevitably, though, his break-neck speed in the early stages was to cost him dearly in the final count of several important races.

In his career, Herb met three "bêtes noires". The earliest of these was Elmore Harris of USA, a Bronx tailor who in the years 1944-46 took the measure of McKenley on several occasions, notably in the 1946 AAU 400 m. race at San Antonio, Texas (46.3 to 46.6). Unfortunately, Harris was to disappear from the scene all too soon.

Herb's other "bêtes noires" came from Jamaica, of all countries. One was gigantic Arthur Wint (born at Manchester, Jamaica, on 25 May 1920; 1.94 m./ 77 kg.), who had reached athletic prominence on his native island long before McKenley.

As early as in 1938, at the Central American and Caribbean Games at Panama City, Wint won the 800 m. in 1:56.3 and finished third in the 400 m. hurdles (after clocking 55.4 in a heat). In the 1946 edition of the same meet, at Barranquilla, Colombia, Wint beat McKenley in the 400 m., 48.0 to 48.5. By

Armin Hary (Germany) at the tape of history's first official "10 flat" for 100 meters (Zurich, 21 June 1960).

137

then, Wint was stationed in England with an assignment in the RAF. On the eve of the London Olympics (1948) his best for the "quarter" was 47.4 - not good enough to scare McKenley, who by the same time was having a record-breaking spree in USA, as related above. At Wembley, prior to their tussle in the 400m., both McKenley and Wint had run other distances, with the former finishing fourth in the 200 m. and the latter placing second to Mal Whitfield in the 800 m. The long-striding Wint began to reveal his hidden potential for the one-lap event on 5 August, when he won a semi-final in 46.3, missing Bill Carr's Olympic record by one-tenth of a second. The final was run later in the same afternoon, with McKenley in lane 2 and Wint in lane 3. True to his habit, "Hustling Herb" ran very fast in the initial stages, while Wint, the 400/800 m. type of runner, showed a more careful approach. At the half-way mark, Herb led his compatriot by several metres, 21.4 to 22.2. McKenley began to fade in the second half of the race - even more visibly than usual, an impression which was probably generated by Wint's simultaneous recovery. Coming along in his "seven-league boots", Wint inexorably closed the gap, shot ahead of his rival with 20 m. to go and won rather comfortably, 46.2 to 46.4. Mal Whitfield of USA was a brilliant third in 46.6.

McKenley's unexpected débacle, certainly more surprising than that of Eastman against Carr in 1932, was rather difficult to explain. Wint timed his peak condition for the Games in a masterly way. Herb again went out too fast too soon, and this cost him dearly in the smoky and humid London atmosphere. The relatively soft track probably disconcerted him quite a bit. Not surprisingly, he returned to his winning ways in post-Olympic meets, beating Wint three times in as many clashes.

Emulation can certainly work wonders: in the wake of McKenley and Wint, a third "Great" came out of Jamaica in the person of George Rhoden (born at Kingston on 13 December 1926; 1.78 m./ 68 kg.). This agile, panther-like runner played second fiddle to his great compatriots for a long time. At the Central American and Caribbean Games in Barranquilla, 1946, he was third in 49.3; in the London Olympics, two years later, he reached the semi-final (47.6). His turn came in 1949, when he

George Rhoden (Jamaica) beats his countryman Herb McKenley in the 400 metres at the 1952 Olympics in Helsinki. Official time for both, 45.9, but electric timing "saw" a difference of 0.11 between them. Others from left to right: O. Matson (USA), 3rd; K-F. Haas (Germany), 4th; A. Wint (Jamaica), 5th; M. Whitfield (USA), 6th.

138

1941
1960

was a freshman at Morgan State College in America. In the AAU 400 m. race at Fresno, he "outkicked" McKenley for the first time, 46.4 to 46.8.

The following year the two Jamaicans met ten times, and Herb led his rival at the end of the series, 6 to 4. Yet Rhoden won on key occasions such as the AAU 400 m. race (46.5 to 47.2) and in an epic battle at Stockholm (46.0 to 46.1). Rhoden produced a great solo performance at Eskilstuna, on 22 August. Running on one of Sweden's fastest tracks, 426 m. in perimeter, he passed the 200 m. mark in a scorching 20.9, then "survived" well enough to clip one-tenth off McKenley's 400 m. record with 45.8. Rhoden and McKenley had at least one trait in common: both were very good also as "pure" sprinters. In fact they were co-holders of the Jamaican 100 m. record at 10.3. During the late Forties European 400m. standards were not up to the tradition of Brown, Roberts, Harbig and Lanzi. In 1946, Niels Holst Sörensen of Denmark, the 400/800 m. type of runner, won the European title in 47.9. Four years later the continental laurel went to Derek Pugh of Britain in 47.3. The Germans, who had to by-pass the European rendezvous, showed two Olympic hopefuls in Karl-Friedrich Haas and Hans Geister. The former (born in Berlin on 28 July 1931; 1.86 m. / 72 kg.) ran 47.5 at nineteen and in 1952, on the eve of the Helsinki Olympics, he won the German Championship title in 47.0.

But 1952 was to be the vintage year of Jamaica's quarter-milers. McKenley did not spread himself thin in pre-Olympic meets. Being out of college by then, he was able to plan things more carefully. Rhoden also rounded into form slowly, after losing to Mal Whitfield in the AAU 400 m. race (46.7 to 46.4). Wint, well in his thirties and still showing a certain preference for the 800 m., was ready to defend his Olympic title, however.

At Helsinki, semi-finals and final of the 400 m. were again contested in the same afternoon (25 July). In the first "semi" Wint was obliged to produce a major effort in order to qualify: he won in 46.3 from Haas and Whitfield (both 46.4), while Eugene Cole of USA (46.8) became the first man in Olympic history to miss the final with a sub-47 seconds effort. McKenley won the second "semi" in 46.4 from Rhoden (46.5) and Ollie Matson of USA (46.7), who cut out Hans Geister of Germany (46.7). In the final Wint drew lane 2, McKenley lane 4, and Rhoden lane 6. The 32-year-old defending champion amazed experts and friends by running the first 200 m. in 21.7, possibly the fastest time of his career at the distance! Rhoden (22.2) and particularly McKenley (22.7) were in the meantime showing signs of wisdom.

The ebb obviously found Wint in a state of insolvency, i.e. unable to pay his major (oxygen) debt. He practically disappeared from the hunt as they went into the homestretch. Exhibiting the most phenomenal pick-up of his career, McKenley collared Rhoden a few metres from the tape, but in the last strip of vital land Rhoden, assuming the shape of an arc, rallied his innermost energies and edged his rival by the better part of a metre. The manual time for both was 45.9, truly exceptional coming as it did on top of another major effort only two hours earlier. An automatic timing device caught Rhoden in 46.09 and McKenley in 46.20. Matson was a surprise third in 46.8, followed by Haas (47.0), Wint (47.0) and Whitfield (47.1). Ironically enough, McKenley ran the wisest race of his career, but Rhoden certainly met the challenge in a manner well befitting a world champion. It should be added that McKenley had finished a very close second in the 100 m. four days earlier. To this day, no runner of the "modern era" has been able to shine in such a way at distances as far apart as the 100 and 400 m. Haas too was an excellent all-round sprinter, with 10.4 and 20.7 (slight curve) at the shorter distances. The Helsinki Olympics also put in orbit the first great 400 m. man ever to come out of the USSR: Ardalion Ignatyev (born at Teideryakovo, Chuvash, on 22 December 1930; 1.73 m./ 73 kg.). At Helsinki he had reached the semi-final, in which he was eliminated with 47.4, a new personal best. The Russian was the compact type of runner, while the tall Haas was definitely on the lanky side. In 1953 the German lowered his personal record to 46.3 at Milan on a one-turn course. In the same year, Ignatyev improved to 46.8. The two crossed swords for the first time in the 1954 European Championships at Bern. And Ignatyev won an easy victory in 46.6 from Voitto Hellsten of Finland (47.0), while Haas, very disappointing and probably not in the best physical condition, was only fourth (47.6). Later in the season, at Kiev, Ignatyev barely missed Harbig's European record with a 46.1 performance.

He finally hit the target on 25 June 1955 at the Znamenskiy Memorial meet in Moscow, his 46.0 around two turns being made up of 200 m. fractions of 21.5 and 24.5.

Early in 1955 the athletic world had been shocked by a news item from Mexico City. During the second Pan-American Games there, on 18 March, two Americans chalked up sensational times: 45.4 and 45.6! Lou Jones was the winner, and Jim Lea was the runner-up - both well inside Rhoden's 400 m. record (45.8). To be sure, the two record-breakers were no unknowns. Lea had won the AAU 440 y.

139

title in 1954, beating Jones in a close race, 46.6 to 46.7. Yet their improvement in one single stroke was so great that track "nuts" at first found the new record figures hard to believe. But astute observers took into account the rarefied atmosphere of the Mexican capital (2200 m. above sea level). Lowered air resistance undoubtedly favoured the athletes, particularly those engaging in short-lived efforts falling in the so-called anaerobic sphere. In his record race, Jones covered the first 200 m. in 21.1, then bravely held off a resurging Lea in the homestretch. Another American, J.W.Mashburn, was third in 46.3. The winner lost consciousness once the race was over, but recovered shortly afterwards. D.H.Potts, an eyewitness at this incredible race, reported the following impromptu reactions by interested observers Jones and Lea: "When was the last time they measured this track?" Herb McKenley, watching from the stands, said: "Now I've seen everything". (Happily enough, he was to see a lot more in years to come).

Notwithstanding these early impressions, Jones and Lea later managed to improve upon their Mexico marks in normal atmospheric conditions. In 1956 at Modesto, Lea lowered the world's 440 y. record to 45.8 in an evenly-paced effort (22.8 + 23.0). Later in the same year, namely on 30 June at Los Angeles, Jones ran the race of his life, decisively beating Lea, 45.2 to 45.7, in the 400 m. of the US Olympic Trials. Jones (born at New Rochelle, New York, on 15 January 1932; 1.83 m./ 76 kg.) copied McKenley's form with 200 m. fractions of 21.3 and 23.9. He ran in lane 8 (Lea was in lane 7) and thus had the advantage of sweeping turns.

Five months later, in the Melbourne Olympic arena, the highly touted American duo met disappointment and disaster. Lea was indisposed and had to surrender in the second round. With semi-finals and final still crowding in the same afternoon, Jones was lucky to qualify for the decisive race in 47.3, while in the other "semi" Charles Jenkins, believed to be America's third string, needed 46.1 to edge stocky Voitto Hellsten of Finland (46.1) and a revived Haas (46.2) by a narrow margin. Jenkins equalled his personal best, while the Finn and the German ran faster than they had ever done before. So did fourth place man Kevan Gosper of Australia, only to find that his 46.2, a new national record, was not good enough to make the final. The other finalists were Ignatyev and 19-year-old Malcolm Spence of South Africa. In the final Jones ran the first half in 21.8 and hit the 300 m. mark in 33.4, at which stage he saw, much to his surprise, that Ignatyev (33.5) was still in contention,

Glenn Davis (USA), first from left, setting a 440 yards world record of 45.7 at Berkeley, California, in 1958. Runner-up in lane 4 is his arch rival Eddie Southern. Both were equally outstanding in the one-lap event, with or without hurdles.

while Jenkins (33.9), Hellsten, and Haas (34.3) appeared to be gathering momentum. From then on, Jones looked like a shadow of his June self: he folded badly in the crucial stage, leaving the other four free to battle furiously for the honour he had dreamt of for himself. Jenkins, who had a good reputation as an indoor performer, miraculously saved Uncle Sam from a complete wreck, winning the day in 46.7, just ahead of Haas (46.8), who finished stronger than anyone else, while Ignatyev and Hellsten were bracketed in an unusual tie for third place (47.0), and Jones strolled home a dejected fifth (48.1). As in Los Angeles (1932) and London (1948), the holder of the world record had been defeated in the Olympic final. The well built Jenkins owed his victory to the stamina he had acquired in many hard relay and indoor races - exactly like Bill Carr in 1932. Hellsten is still remembered as the finest "all-round sprinter" in Nordic history, with times of 10.6, 21.3, and 46.1. (No matter if one or two others have recently done better, clock-wise at least). And he also tried the 800 m. with remarkable success: 1:50.1. Shortly afterwards, something unusual happened in the high spheres of the one-lap department. Glenn Davis and Eddie Southern, the Americans who had finished one-two in the Olympic 400 m. hurdles at Melbourne, decidedly turned to the "flat route" and quickly proved "tops" there too. Davis (born at Wellsburg, West Virginia, on 12 September 1934; 1.83 m./ 77 kg.) was coached at Ohio State University by Jesse Owens' tutor, former intermediate hurdler Larry Snyder (52.4 in 1924). In fact this famous coach was once quoted as saying that Glenn was possibly a greater talent than Jesse himself. The true iron-man type of runner, Davis first beat 47 seconds in 1957 (46.8 for the 440 y.). The following year he topped a great field in the NCAA quarter-mile race at Berkeley in 45.7 (22.0 + 23.7). Later in the year he ducked under 46 seconds for the metric distance in four consecutive European meets, with times of 45.6 (Oslo), 45.6 (Moscow), 45.5 (Warsaw) and 45.6 (Budapest)! Especially remarkable was the fact that at the same time he was consolidating his position as the world's no.1 intermediate hurdler. As for his basic speed, suffice it to say that in 1958 he was second to Bobby Morrow in the AAU 220 y. race, 21.1 to 20.9.

Southern, who came from the Lone Star State, looked even more impressive than Davis in physical appearance, being in fact 1.85 m. tall and 81 kg. in weight. But the big Texan apparently lacked the solidity, psychological if not physical, of his arch rival. He ran the English distances in 20.7 and 47.2 in interscholastic competition at the age of seventeen. He made further progress in later years, yet lost to Davis regularly in all big meets - with or without hurdles. He achieved his fastest ever time for the 440 y. flat in 1958, winning the AAU title (in the absence of Davis) in 45.8. On the eve of the 1960 Olympics there were unmistakable signs of an oncoming earthquake in the 400 m. department. In Europe the most interesting figure was Karl Kaufmann of Germany (born in New York on 25 March 1936; 1.83 m./ 76 kg.). Originally a good but not exceptional sprinter (10.5 and 21.0), and barred as such in his own country by Fütterer and Germar, he began to concentrate on the 400 m. in 1958 and got started in the new event with a bang, finishing fourth in the European Championship race at Stockholm. He improved from 46.9 in 1958 to a new European record of 45.8 (fractions of 22.3 and 23.5) on a one-turn course at Köln on 19 September 1959. In the Olympic year he did even better with a scintillating 45.4 (21.9 + 23.5) around two turns in the German title race at Berlin on 24 July. Another fine prospect was Abdoulaye Seye, a Senegalese representing France, who in pre-Olympic weeks chalked up a creditable 45.9. He was, however, a "pure" sprinter, and as such he chose to concentrate on the 200 m. for the Games. Malcolm Spence of South Africa, an Olympic finalist as a teen-ager in 1956, lowered his best for the "quarter" to 45.9 early in 1960.

Even more surprising was the rise to fame of the compact Milkha Singh of India (born at Lyallpur on 17 October 1935; 1.73 m./ 66 kg.), who acted as an ice-breaker in a country of untapped athletic potentialities. In 1958 he had won the Empire Games 440 y. title at Cardiff in 46.6, beating Spence among others. In 1960 he came to Europe early, having by then times of 20.7 and 46.1 to his credit. Just before the Games he improved to 45.9 - an outstanding achievement at a time when hardly another man in the whole Asian continent could beat 48 seconds.

In USA the struggle for berths on the Olympic team was raging more furious than ever before. There were newcomers galore, and one of them, Otis Davis (born at Tuscaloosa, Alabama, on 12 July 1932; 1.85 m./ 74 kg.), had come up from nowhere the year before with a 46.2 "quarter". He gained a vital third place at the US Olympic Trials, just behind Jack Yerman (46.3) and Earl Young, and barely ahead of Ted Woods, another novice who had previously caused quite a stir with a 45.7 clocking at the metric distance. In Europe, shortly before coming down to Rome, Davis lowered his personal best to 45.6, thus giving unmistakable evidence that he was ready to sting. In Rome the greatest array of 400 m. men ever assembled was given the benefit of semi-finals and final on separate days. The fireworks began in

1941
1960

the quarter-finals, when Otis Davis equalled the Olympic record (45.9). He went on to win the first "semi" in 45.5 (22.5 + 23.0), followed by Milkha Singh (45.9) and Manfred Kinder of Germany (46.0), while 21-year-old Robbie Brightwell lowered the British record to 46.2 but was eliminated. In the second "semi" Kaufmann came through with astonishing ease (45.7), while Spence (45.8) and Young (46.1) were the other qualifiers. In the final (6 September) Spence was not feeling well, yet he chose to act as trail-blazer and covered the first 200 m. in 21.2, while Davis and Kaufmann (both 21.8) were intentionally lagging behind. The American made his greatest effort round the last turn and shot into the lead at 300 m. (32.6), after a wondrous 100 m. fraction (10.8). While Spence was fading, Kaufmann passed the 300 m. in 33.3, after which he offered what must have been the fastest finish in the history of the event. He began to close the gap that separated him from Davis. A few metres from home, the two were almost level, but then Davis miraculously found resources enough to save the last few centimetres of his once big lead. Kaufmann tried a leap à la Paddock in going into the tape but just failed to catch his rival. The verdict of hand timers was sensational: 44.9 for both.

The electric photo-timer saw a slight difference though: Davis 45.07, Kaufmann 45.08. Spence managed to finish third ahead of Milkha Singh, 45.5 to 45.6 (new personal bests). Kinder and Young closed up the rear in that order, both in 45.9 - which time equalled the pre-Rome Olympic record! The advantage of running semi-finals and final on separate days thus became crystal clear.

After the Games, Davis and Kaufmann met on two more occasions: they were bracketed in a tie at Köln (both 45.7), then the German finally edged his rival at Wuppertal, 46.5 to 46.7. By then the pressure was off and times suffered accordingly.

MIDDLE DISTANCES - 800 METRES: From "Marvelous Mal" to Harbig's successor

The last clash between Mario Lanzi and Rudolf Harbig took place in the Italy vs Germany dual meet at Bologna in 1941. Running on a soft track, the Italian for once chose to play the waiting game. He came on near the end of the last turn and finally won, 1:49.0 (equalling his Italian record) to 1:49.2. It should be added that Harbig and his teammates had just reached Bologna from Bucharest after a 47-hour rail journey across war-torn Europe (hostilities on the Eastern front had begun a few days earlier). The end of their famous feud found Harbig in the lead, 8 to 4 (3 to 1 in the 400 m., 5 to 3 in the 800 m.).

The best Europe was able to offer between 1943 and 1948 came from three Nordic runners: Niels Holst Sörensen of Denmark, Bertel ("Bebbe") Storskrubb of Finland and Hans ("Bulldog") Liljekvist of Sweden. The Dane in particular was a hard man to beat, and very fast (47.6 for the 400 m.). In the Sweden vs. Denmark dual meet at Stockholm in 1943 he beat Liljekvist after a bitter fight, 1:48.9 to 1:49.2. (In later years, Sörensen was to become a Major General of the Danish Army). Storskrubb alternated the 800 m. (1:49.3 in 1945) with the 400 m. hurdles (European champion in 1946 with 52.2).

France was back in the picture by the end of the war with a temperamental but dedicated Parisian who had developed gradually: Marcel Hansenne. At the 1946 European Championships in Oslo, Sörensen and Hansenne were upset by tall Rune Gustafsson of Sweden (1:51.0) in a close finish. The Frenchman reached his peak shortly before the London Olympics, when he ran the 800 m. in 1:48.3 in ... a heat of the Paris Championships, after a well-judged race (54.0 + 54.3). It is perhaps interesting to add that he never bettered 49 seconds in the 400 m. Another great prospect for the London Games was Douglas Harris of New Zealand, who in 1947 at Wanganui missed the world's half-mile record by a fifth of a second with a 1:49.4 performance, after a fantastic battle with John Fulton, a versatile American runner who finished a close second in an estimated 1:49.5. Unfortunately, the Kiwi ace met disaster in one of the Olympic semi-finals: he snapped the Achilles tendon of his left leg and had to be carried away on a stretcher. At Wembley in 1948 and again at Helsinki in 1952 the dominant figures in the 800 m. were Malvin Whitfield of USA and Arthur Wint of Jamaica. The final at Wembley was not, strictly speaking, a race of great emotions. The American took the lead at the bell (54.2), then staved off Wint's challenge and won comfortably from the tall Jamaican, 1:49.2 to 1:49.5. Hansenne got himself into a "box" initially, then poured it on all the way and finished third in 1:49.8, a remarkable achievement for a man who obviously lacked the phenomenal speed of either Whitfield or Wint. Sörensen, by then a shadow of his former self, was a distant eighth. The picture was essentially the same at Helsinki four years later, except that this time the leader at the half-way mark was Wint (54.0). Curiously enough, "Marvelous Mal"

1941 1960

faithfully duplicated his pace and his final time of four years earlier (54.2 + 55.0 = 1:49.2), passing his rival in the backstretch and gliding home the winner by 2 tenths of a second.

In a furious battle for third place, Heinz Ulzheimer of Germany barely held off Gunnar Nielsen of Denmark (both 1:49.7).

Whitfield (born at Bay City, Texas, on 11 October 1924; 1.85 m. /76 kg.) was, literally speaking, the prize picture of an athlete. He had the smoothest running action one can possibly imagine. He always ran to win and seldom, if ever, to break records. An outstanding American observer, Cordner Nelson, once wrote: "Whitfield has no superior as a tactician. Cool and poised, he can jockey through any field, follow any pace, and hold his own in any stretch drive". Whitfield was the world's leading two-lap runner for six years (1948-53). Between June 1948 and June 1954 he suffered only two defeats of some consequence, both in early season meets. As he glided along and ran away from his rivals, usually in the backstretch of the last lap, he seemed to be going downhill. But his temperament led him to relax once victory was assured. He was like a matador in that he liked to invite his opponent to fight back. This probably explains why he never approached Harbig's 800 m. record. His best at this distance was 1:47.9 at Turku, Finland, in 1953, on his way to breaking the (softer) half-mile record with a 1:48.6 clocking. His metric fractions on that occasion were 53.2 and 54.7. Accustomed often to double 400 and 800 m. in the same meet, he gave the full measure of his stamina at Köln in 1953, when in the space of 45 minutes he ran 1:48.4 and 46.2, and again at Eskilstuna, Sweden, later in the same year, when in the space of an hour he ran the kilometre in 2:20.8, a new world record, and the 440 y. in 46.2 (time at 400 m.: 45.9, his best ever). He had probably missed the chance of his lifetime at Berea, Ohio, in 1950, when he was crazy enough to follow a hustling "hare" with fractions of 21.6 (220 y.) and 50.5 (440 y.). Not surprisingly, he faded badly in the second lap, yet managed to finish in 1:49.2, equalling the world record, then held by Sydney Wooderson! It fell to a Belgian to succeed where the great Whitfield had failed, namely in erasing the name of Rudolf Harbig from the list of world record holders. The man in question was Roger Moens (born at Erembodegem, Eastern Flanders, on 26 April 1930; 1.75 m. /70 kg.). This compact runner had a methodical approach. Advised by Harbig's coach, Woldemar Gerschler, he proved his ability at all distances ranging from 400 m. (47.3 in 1955) to the mile (3:58.9 in 1957). Almost unbeatable when he could concentrate on one or two major rivals, this racing genius occasionally fell victim to nervous tension when running in large fields. He began at seventeen but refrained from excessive training loads until he was in his twenties. At the 1952 Olympics in Helsinki he ran the 400 m. but was eliminated in a heat. In the 800 m., his parade event, he improved from 1:52.6 in 1952 to 1:48.8 in 1953. On the eve of the 1954 European Championships he loomed as an odds-on favourite for the continental crown on the strength of his 1:47.5 at the Belgian title meet early in August. But things took a different turn on the Neufeld track at Bern on 28 August. Audun Boysen of Norway set the stage for a magnificent five-man struggle by leading the field through a 52.4 400 m. At the end of a gruelling stretch battle, little Lajos Szentgáli of Hungary emerged the winner in 1:47.1 (52.8 + 54.3) - almost two seconds under his previous best! In the fastest two-lap race ever, Lucien DeMuynck of Belgium was second (1:47.3), followed by Boysen and Derek Johnson of Britain (both 1:47.4), while Moens had to be content with fifth place (1:47.8), after fading in the torrid stretch battle. At any rate, later developments showed that Moens had something in store which his Bern conquerors apparently had not. In 1955 he made Harbig's 800 m. record (1:46.6) his chief target.

In June he "warmed up" with 1:47.5 at Brussels and 1:47.0 at Nuremberg, and in July, still at Brussels, he defeated a coming "Great" from USA, Tom Courtney, 1:48.1 to 1:49.0. To beat Harbig's record, however, the Belgian needed a Lanzi. He found an essentially similar stimulant in Audun Boysen of Norway. The two rivals and friends planned an all-out attack on the world record.

Scene of the plot was the "miraculous" Bislett track in Oslo, on 4 August 1955. However, the pattern of the race was different from that of the Harbig-Lanzi affair of 1939 in at least one detail: neither of the two champions did the "donkey" work in the early stages. Acting as a hare for the two gentlemen was a virtual unknown, Finn Larsen of Norway, who covered the first 400 m. in 52.0, with Moens hot on his heels, and Boysen a few metres farther back. The Belgian forged ahead in the second lap and Boysen, usually a front runner, was for once obliged to make his bid starting from behind. A long, sustained sprint carried him a bit closer to Moens, who never faltered and finally won by a long metre in 1:45.7 (estimated halves: 52.0 and 53.7), while Boysen was second in 1:45.9 (52.6 + 53.3). Times which obviously made history.

The star of the great Whitfield was by then declining, but a new generation of excellent two-lap runners was coming up in USA.

At Berkeley, on 26 March 1955, Lonnie Spurrier lowered the world's half-mile record to 1:47.5 in an unusual solo effort (51.6 + 55.9). At the AAU Championships of the same year in Boulder, Colorado (altitude, 1655 m.), the 880y. event produced a set of times that compared on even terms with that of the 1954 European Championship race. Arnie Sowell, a bouncing rubber ball, led the field from start to finish and won in 1:47.6 (51.7 + 55.9) from Courtney (1:48.0), Billy Tidwell (1:48.1), Lang Stanley (1:48.6) and Spurrier (1:48.7). The winner, a slim, graceful athlete, was on the verge of collapse after such a phenomenal effort.

Courtney (born at Newark, New Jersey, on 17 August 1933; 1.88 m./ 82 kg.) was the heavy type of runner as middle distance men go. He remained in the shadow of Sowell for a considerable time, but never ceased to improve. By 1956 he could hold his own with the best quarter-milers and in fact won the AAU 400 m. title in 45.8. The year before he had learned something vital about tactics on a successful European tour, losing on only two occasions: to Moens in Brussels, as related above, and to Gunnar Nielsen in Copenhagen over 880 y., when the Dane of the flowing hair nosed him out in a tight finish (both 1:48.2).

Courtney chose a very important occasion for his first major victory over Sowell: the US Final Olympic Tryouts at Los Angeles, on 30 June 1956. That race (in which both champions used starting blocks!) was Whitfield's swan song. Sowell set a hot pace and passed 400 m. in 51.7, with the self-confident Whitfield in his wake and Courtney about 7 m. back. In the backstretch of the final lap the 32-year-old Whitfield launched his usual attack - only to find that he lacked the strength required to last that pace. While he disappeared from the hunt, Courtney came up like a tornado, collared Sowell and beat him in the race to the tape, 1:46.4 to 1:46.9, while the gallant Whitfield was sixth in 1:49.3, just one-tenth short of the time which had won for him two Olympic gold medals! It was certainly a great psychological advantage for Courtney to have turned the tables on Sowell just a few months before the Olympics.

Shortly before the Melbourne rendezvous, tragedy struck Moens in the form of a severe foot injury sustained in an impromptu training session at night while in Athens. Even if deprived of the world record holder, the Olympic final was impressive in more than one way. Sowell led the parade through the first lap (52.8), followed by Courtney, Boysen and Derek Johnson of Britain. In the homestretch the runners faced a strong wind. While Sowell faded, Courtney and Johnson engaged in a bitter fight for victory. The American, taller and squarer than his British rival, finally won, 1:47.7 to 1:47.8. Boysen took third place (1:48.1) ahead of Sowell (1:48.3).

Courtney had mixed fortunes in his duels with Moens. The American had won a close tussle with the world record holder in a half-mile race at Compton in June 1956 (both 1:49.0), but the Belgian turned the tables on him in an 800 m. affair at Oslo in July 1957, 1:46.0 to 1:46.2. Meanwhile, the American had captured the softer 880 y. record in a night race at Los Angeles on 24 May 1957, with 1:46.8 (52.2 + 54.6). In the summer of the same year, Courtney came dangerously close to Moens' metric record at Oslo on 9 August. He allowed himself to be misled by the deceptively slow pace of a "de-luxe hare", former Olympian Reggie Pearman of USA, and hurried over the first 400 m. in 50.7. Even so, he survived for a second lap in 55.1 and a final time of 1:45.8, one tenth off Moens' mark. Derek Johnson was second with a British all time best of 1:46.6, while Boysen finished third in 1:47.3. Courtney had another great season in 1958, when he again proved that he was capable of carrying on his broad shoulders the entire load of a race against time and opponents of class. In the space of a month he amassed four 800 m. clockings in the range 1:46.8/1:47.1! Yet the finest two-lap effort of that year was offered by Herbert Elliott of Australia. Although only 20 at the time, he had already established himself as the King of Milers. In the British Empire Games at Cardiff he scored a superlative double, with 1:49.3 in the 880 y. (58.8 + 50.5 !) and, four days later, 3:59.0 in the mile. The following week, in London, he chalked up a fine 1:47.3 for the half-mile. The European 800 m. title, contested in the same year at Stockholm, went to Michael Rawson of Britain, who emerged the winner in a tight finish in 1:47.8, barely ahead of the ever present Boysen and Paul Schmidt of Germany (both 1:47.9). Like many other races of recent years, the Stockholm final was characterized by more or less serious "elbowing" among contenders in the all-too-short distance separating the curved starting line from the first turn. As a result of this, the IAAF ruled that in major international meets the first 100 m. of the race should henceforth be run in lanes.

There were some notable changes in the balance of powers during the months preceding the Rome Olympics. In Europe, Boysen and Johnson were no longer in the game, and Rawson seemed unable to reproduce his 1958 form. In Germany, Harbig's old national record had been beaten in 1959 by Paul Schmidt, a sturdy little runner with a strong finish, with 1:46.2. By the same time, Jamaica took pride in the achievements of George Kerr, a McKenley protégé and like his tutor a student at the University of Illinois. He was just as good in the "quarter" (46.0) as in the 800 m. (1:46.4). The latter mark was posted in winning the 1960 NCAA title, and that apparently led Kerr to put all his Olympic eggs in the two-lap basket. USA, following the retirement of Courtney and Sowell, had a bunch of fine but relatively inexperienced runners. Tom Murphy, winner at the Trials in 1:46.7, was believed to be the best bet. On the eve of the Games, Moens was on the war-path, grimly determined to make his last bid. He had run a mile in 3:58.9 in 1957, and a couple of months before Rome he lowered the Belgian 1500 m. record to 3:41.4. Even so, he still considered the 800 m. his best bet. In Rome, the event was contested in four rounds which were run off in the space of 53 hours! Such a Herculean task seemed well calculated to separate the men from the boys, yet the big surprise was provided by a "boy" who on paper form was at best considered a long-shot prospect: Peter Snell of New Zealand (born at Opunake, Taranaki, on 17 December 1938; 1.79 m. /80 kg.). His pre-Rome carnet included a national 880 y. record of 1:49.2 and little-noted victories over Herb Elliott at 800 m. and over Murray Halberg, another Kiwi, at 2000 m. Still, he opened his Olympic saga with a personal best of 1:48.1 in the first round. Then he finished on Moens' heels in a quarter-final (1:48.6 to 1:48.5) and stayed ahead of the Belgian in a "semi" (1:47.2 to 1:47.4). George Kerr also looked very impressive, winning the other "semi" in 1:47.1. In the final (2 September) Christian Wägli of Switzerland led the operations and reached the half-way mark in 51.9, followed by Schmidt, Kerr, Moens and Snell. The battle began to flare up as the runners went round the last turn. Wägli had by then given all he had. Moens shot ahead entering the homestretch. The master tactician was unwise enough to look round, not once but three times, to see where the opposition lay. The challenge came, not from Kerr as Moens probably expected, but from Snell, who sneaked through on the inside. Moens naturally began to pour it on, but Snell, pounding the ground with his powerful legs reminiscent of a shot-putter's, inexorably closed the gap, then inched his way ahead. Moens' last ditch counterattack was of no avail. The young Kiwi won,

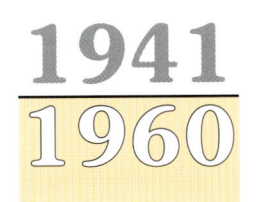

1941
1960

Swedish middle distance saga from the Forties: Gunder Hägg leading Arne Andersson.

1:46.3 to 1:46.5 (the electric timer saw a closer finish: 1:46.48 to 1:46.55). Kerr was third (1:47.1), followed by Schmidt (1:47.6), Wägli (1:48.1) and Manfred Matuschewski of Germany (1:52.0). Postrace comments and interviews revealed how the "green" Snell had prepared for the Olympic rendezvous. While his famous rival from Belgium remained faithful to the fundamental principles of Interval Training, Snell followed a different school of thought, that of Arthur Lydiard, the "apostle" of Endurance Training. This essentially consisted of long runs at a sustained pace, intended to develop a high degree of "resistance to speed". Snell would usually train on undulating courses, mostly in the country. In his autobiography "No bugles, no drums" (written with Garth Gilmour and published in 1965), he later recalled his early experiences with a group of Lydiard-inspired die-hards on the Waiatarua course, "a soul-searing 22-miler (35.40 km.) through the steep and densely bushed Waitakere Ranges", and other training "chores", up to the conquest of the 100-miles (160.93 km.) per week ration. Only in the vicinity of the Games did he return to the track for a series of speed tests. In all probability, Lydiard simply emphasized methods previously followed by others, at various times and in a different measure.

At the International Convention of Coaches held at Duisburg in 1964, Roger Moens recalled his Rome experience as follows: "The tour de force to which we were exposed in the Games finally killed my basic speed and glorified the exceptional stamina of Peter Snell, who had been training like a marathon runner".

1500 METRES/1 MILE - Magic feuds: Hägg vs. Andersson, Bannister vs. Landy - The incomparable Elliott.

In the years of World War II the 1500 m./one mile scene was dominated by two Swedes, Gunder Hägg and Arne Andersson. They simply re-wrote the record book, and in their wake other Swedes also reached world class. This Swedish boom was partly favoured by the virtual absence from the athletic scene of several important powers then engaged in the fields of unfriendly strife. But this was at best indirect help, and it is only fair to admit that other factors played an important role in promoting such a growth of brilliant middle-distance talents. A sports loving man by the name of Gösta Olander, a humanist rather than a coach in the common sense of the word, had established a tourist and training centre in the idyllic setting of Vålådalen (Jämtland), and it was there that Hägg, Kälarne and others found the inspiration for their superlative efforts. At a time when many of the world's leading runners were gradually becoming slaves to the cinder track and the stopwatch, Olander preached a "return to nature", i.e. running without what he considered the artificial limitations of time or distance. His idea of "Fartlek" (speed play) could only have originated in an unique atmosphere such as that of Vålådalen (which in later years was to attract runners from other countries as well). In winter and summer, the running guests of that resort (600 m. above sea level) would train down at the lakes and through the forests, mostly on undulating ground, never departing from the canons of "löpargladje" (joy of running). Thus they would sound out their possibilities. As time went on and their stamina increased, they would set themselves a goal and then go for it with ever growing intensity. Quality, however, would always prevail over quantity. In actual fact, however, only one of the two paramount figures of the Swedish Era, namely Hägg, could properly be considered a product of the Olander school of thought. Andersson, as we shall see later, trained along conventional lines for the better part of his career. Gunder Hägg (born at Sörbygden, Jämtland, on 31 December 1918; 1.80 m./68 kg.) began to take interest in running at the age of seventeen. His first adviser was Fridolf Westman, a farmer who had previously "made" Henry Jonsson, a bronze medallist in the 5000 m. at the Berlin Olympics (who in 1939 changed his name to Kälarne to honour the village by the same name in which he had emerged to athletic renown). Gunder, the ideal physical specimen for the middle-distance events, soon showed great natural inclination for running. He became a known quantity in Sweden in 1937, when he ran the 3000 m. in 8:36.8. The following year he did 15:00.7 in the 5000 m. and 9:23.0 in the steeplechase, and created a mild sensation by placing second in the latter event (9:28.4) at the national championships. An illness and then military service put a halt to his athletic endeavours. But it was in fact during that period that he began to visit Vålådalen, where he discovered a new form of "löpargladje". He rose to greatness in 1940, in a series of duels with Henry Kälarne. In the 1500 m. he did 3:51.8, then 3:48.8 in finishing a close second to Kälarne (3:48.7) at Göteborg on 7 August; in the 3000 m. he did 8:11.8, again in the wake of Kälarne (8:09.0, a new world record) at Stockholm on 14 August. A fantastic improvement

1941 1960

vis-à-vis his pre-1940 bests at these distances, 4:04.6 (1938) and 8:36.8 (1937) respectively. In 1941 he began to establish himself as the undisputed master of Swedish middle-distance runners. On 10 August at Stockholm he won the national 1500 m. title in 3:47.6, his first world record. In this race he led for over two-thirds of the distance, finally trouncing Arne Andersson (3:48.6) and Kälarne (3:49.2). Shortly afterwards, Hägg ran into trouble with Svenska Idrottsförbundet (Swedish Athletics Federation) and was suspended from competitive activity for ten months. On 1 July 1942 he celebrated "regained freedom" with a new world record, which turned out to be merely an "hors-d'oeuvre" to the Gargantuan feast which was to follow. In the adjoining table I give the imposing list of his world records - ten in the space of 82 days! - during that memorable summer.

In his golden summer Hägg set a virtually new pattern: very frequent competitions, interspersed with training sessions of moderate intensity in the Paradise of Vålådalen. Despite the global war, his fame had expanded well beyond the boundaries of Sweden and in 1943 he was invited by the AAU to make a tour of the States. Hägg crossed the Atlantic on a small ship. He came, saw and conquered - from coast to coast, beating the likes of Greg Rice, Gil Dodds and Bill Hulse, who were certainly no slouches. The atmosphere, however, was not that of the idyllic summer evenings in Sweden, and times were good but not exceptional. Gunder's best performances while there were 4:05.3 (1 mile) and 8:51.3 (2 miles). He extended Hulse (4:06.0) and Dodds (4:06.1) to meritorious achievements, both under Glenn Cunningham's nine-year-old US 1-mile record.

While the "cat" was away from Sweden, "mouse" Arne Andersson reached new, unexpected heights.

Andersson (born at Trollhättan on 27 October 1917; 1.78 m./71 kg.) personified the runner "who made himself great". Admittedly not a born great as was his rival, Arne was above all a fighter. After playing second fiddle to the placid Jämtland lumberjack for two years (1941-42), schoolmaster Andersson managed to bridge the gulf almost completely. Essentially a power runner, he gradually developed a more economical running action. In 1943, while Hägg was in the States, he set two world records, both in his hometown of Göteborg: 4:02.6 for the mile on 1 July and 3:45.0 (actually 3:44.9) for the 1500 m. on 17 August. By then he was ready to talk with Hägg on even terms, and in 1944-45 the two battled as never before - and with mixed fortunes. An epic which marked the Golden Age of Swedish athletics.

Andersson knew that he could never match Hägg as a front runner, so he would generally trail his rival for the greater part of the race and would then try to beat him with his strong finishing "kick". Hägg would usually rely on a long, sustained drive to take the sting out of Andersson. In 1944-45 Andersson's tactics paid dividends on several occasions. The Swedish public was rather hostile to Arne for it. Hägg, a tremendously gifted athlete, had always been the favourite of the crowd, who greatly admired his smooth and powerful front running. On the other hand it is obvious that a champion runner, like any runner in general, must first know his resources and then plan his racing tactics accordingly. And that is what Andersson did.

The three major 1944-45 races between Hägg and Andersson are briefly summarized as follows: Göteborg, 7 July 1944 - 1500 m.: 1.Hägg 3:43.0 (world record), 2.Andersson 3:44.0, 3.Rune Gustafsson 3:48.2, 4.Rune Persson 3:51.8. A young "hare" by the name of Lennart Strand set the pace in the first half of the race, followed by Hägg (56.7,

Hägg's Golden Streak (1942)

Göteborg	1 July	1 mile	4:06.2*
Stockholm	3 July	2 miles	8:47.8
Stockholm	17 July	1500 m.	3:45.8
Malmö	21 July	2000 m.	5:16.4*
Oestersund	23 August	2000 m.	5:11.8*
Stockholm	28 August	3000 m.	8:01.2
Stockholm	4 September	1 mile	4:04.6
Stockholm	11 September	3 miles	13:35.4
Göteborg	20 September	5000 m.	13:58.2*
		(enroute: 3 miles	13:32.4)

(* Actual time one tenth faster, but rounded off to nearest fifth in accordance with IAAF rule then in force)

Sir Roger Bannister, later a London neurologist. Made history in 1954 with the first sub-4 min. mile.

Bannister winning the "Mile of the Century" from John Landy, 3:58.8 to 3:59.6 (1954 Commonwealth Games).

1:56.5), with Andersson farther back. Hägg forged ahead in the third lap and passed the 1200 m. in 2:58.0. Arne was on his heels, but suddenly his legs "felt like lead" (possibly as a result of a record race at Stockholm two days earlier: 2:56.6 for three-quarters of a mile) and in the end he had to give way to his rival. Malmö, 18 July 1944 - 1 Mile: 1.Andersson 4:01.6 (world record), 2. Hägg 4:02.0, 3.Gustafsson 4:05.6, 4.Persson 4:06.8. Strand again acted as "hare", with the Big Two in his wake. When Hägg forged ahead, he tried to force the pace as usual but found himself unable to "kill" Andersson, whose dreadful finishing "kick" won the day. Estimated "quarters" for the winner were as follows: 57.1, 59.6 (1:56.7), 62.9 (2:59.6), 62.0 (4:01.6).

Malmö, 17 July 1945 - 1 Mile: 1.Hägg 4:01.4 (world record, actually 4:01.3), 2.Andersson 4:02.2, 3.Persson 4:03.8, 4.Strand 4:09.2. The "donkey" work in the early going was done by Åke Pettersson, Hägg's teammate. Gunder again took the lead in the crucial stage and effectively "stung" his great rival Arne, finally drawing away from him with 70 m. to go. Hägg's estimated "quarters": 56.7, 62.7 (1:59.4), 62.0 (3:01.4), 59.9 (4:01.3).

The two giants were thus responsible for the biggest advance ever registered in the history of the 1500 m. and one mile. Hägg finally had the last word at both distances. Progress vis-à-vis pre-war world records was remarkable: 4.8 secs. in the 1500 m., and 5.1 secs. in the mile! Throughout those hectic years the two champions went out of their way to appear in meets, big and small, all over Sweden. Promoters more than seconded them in that direction and, almost inevitably, both sides committed abuses. "Svenska Idrottsförbundet" could no longer tolerate the continuous infringements to the amateur code and early in 1946 Hägg, Andersson and Kälarne fell victims to a disqualification "sine die". Hägg, well satisfied with his accomplishments from whatever angle he looked at them, did not take his adverse fate too dramatically, but Andersson, who probably felt he still had something to say, remained inconsolable for years and found a partial outlet for his frustrated love by taking part in cycling, and sulky competitions. It is quite possible that another full season of joint efforts on the track would have brought either or both under the magic four-minute mile.

The "Big Two" disappeared from the scene when one of their opponents seemed ready to challenge them. This man was Lennart Strand (born at Malmö on 13 June 1921; 1.73 m./61 kg.). After playing the role of "de luxe hare" to Gunder and Arne in quite a few races, Strand suddenly realized his potential and began to build his own house. In the fall of 1945 he beat both his former masters in a 4:04.8 mile, but one must add that Andersson, and particularly Hägg, already sensed their forthcoming "death" and were therefore in a state of moral disarmament.

Strand, a great natural talent endowed with unique suppleness, was capable of following any pace and had an excellent finish. Nerves were his Achilles Heel: few runners would be as tense as he before any major commitment. Even so, he was for several years the world's outstanding 1500 m. man. In 1946 he won the European title at Oslo in 3:48.0, with his countryman Henry Eriksson second (3:48.8). In 1947 he improved to 3:44.8 at Gävle, then on 15 July at Malmö he equalled Hägg's world record with 3:43.0. In the latter race a "hare" dictated the pace for over half the distance, then Henry Eriksson took over and led till the homestretch. Strand's patented finish won the day. Intermediate times: 57.8, 1:59.3, 2:59.6, last 300 m. in 43.4. Eriksson was a brilliant second in 3:44.4. This race curiously looked like a replica of the latest Hägg vs. Andersson duels, with Eriksson in the role of pacesetter and Strand in that of the "big kicker".

As destiny and Strand's nerves would have it, Eriksson the "eternal second" chose a most important occasion to finally turn the tables on his conqueror: the Olympic 1500 m. final at Wembley on 6 August 1948. The race was run in a downpour. Eriksson, the compact type of runner, was better equipped, physically and psychologically, for such a test of sheer strength and beat Strand for the first time in 3:49.8, a remarkable time in view of the conditions. Strand barely salvaged second place from the last-ditch assault of Wim Slykhuis of Holland (3:50.4 for both).

After his great Olympic victory, Eriksson ceased to be just one of Sweden's countless Eriksson's and was nicknamed "Guld-Eriksson" (guld, Swedish for gold). Strand, the hypersensitive type, was shocked by his failure to dominate a perennial underdog in the race that counted most.

In later years he offered occasional glimpses of his greatness, but his psychological set-up became weaker and weaker. His demise became apparent the day he dropped out of the European title race at Brussels in 1950, after 350 m. of a lifeless effort. The title was won by Slykhuis, a cunning tactician, in 3:47.2, with Patrick El Mabrouk of France second (3:47.8) and Bill Nankeville of Britain third (3:48.0). By the time the 1952 Olympics came round the number of outstanding 1500 m. men was higher than ever before. At the German Championships in Berlin on 29 June, Werner Lueg equalled the world record with a 3:43.0 effort. The German, then twenty years and nine months of age, was extended by his countryman Günther Dohrow, who finished second in 3:44.8.

This impressive performance obviously made Lueg the "logical" favourite of many for the Olympic crown. Few experts, if any, paid attention to a more mature performer, Josy Barthel of Luxemburg (born at Mamer on 24 April 1947; 1.73 m./ 66 kg.), who under the guidance of Harbig's coach Woldemar Gerschler had silently keyed himself up for a major "explosion". After showing early promise (3:51.0 at twenty), he had finished ninth in the 1948 Olympics. Then he showed no apparent progress till June 1952, when he lowered his best to 3:48.5. It is related that during a dinner attended by German and Luxemburg officials and athletes shortly before the Helsinki Games, one of the German guests, after wishing good luck to Luxemburg Olympians, said: "We all know that Luxemburg does not expect to win any gold medal at Helsinki. Even Monsieur Barthel will be no Olympic champion, but, as you know, the important thing in the Olympic Games is not so much winning but taking part". Barthel is said to have listened to this uncalled for opinion not without an ironical smile.

The 1500 m. schedule at Helsinki was an exacting one. Due to the high number of entrants, it had been changed at the last moment to include not two but three rounds, to be run off within fifty hours or so. Among those most irritated by this change was Roger Bannister of Britain, who had been counting on a day of rest between heats and final. In the decisive race (26 July) Lueg jumped into the lead in the third lap and had a 3-metre lead on Barthel as they went into the last curve. But he was beginning to tire and Barthel, still full of running, collared him with 50 m. to go, then pulled away. By then, however, an outsider from USA, Bob McMillen, came up with a belated but devastating burst of speed and failed to catch Barthel by only half a metre. Both runners were officially credited with 3:45.2, but the Luxemburg ace was actually clocked in 3:45.1. (The electric timer caught the first two in 3:45.28 and 3:45.39). Lueg was a close third (3:45.4), while Bannister barely took fourth place ahead of El Mabrouk (both 3:46.0). Next came Rolf Lamers of Germany (3:46.8), Olle Åberg (3:47.0) and Ingvar Ericsson (3:47.6), both of Sweden, who thus brought to eight the number of men who ducked under Lovelock's 16-year-old Olympic record (3:47.8). McMillen ran the last 300 m. in 41.3 (Barthel 41.7), finally improving on his previous best by 4.1 secs.! In post-Olympic meets Barthel confirmed that he was the best miler of the 1952 lot. He again beat Lueg, McMillen and even Gaston Reiff of Belgium, a 4:02.8 miler, and finally lowered his personal best to 3:44.1. In following years he was absorbed by other interests and never returned to his superb 1952 form.

The possibility of a mile being run in less than 4 minutes had never ceased to capture the imagination of track enthusiasts in English speaking countries. In 1953 both Bannister and John Landy of Australia were timed in 4:02.0, thousands of miles apart. By the same time a young American, Wes Santee, lowered the US record to 4:02.4.

The decisive race for the elusive target was on and the honour of running the first 3-minute plus mile fell to a son of Britain, the mother country of miling. The man who did the wonderful trick was Roger Gilbert Bannister (born at Harrow on 23 March 1929; 1.87 m./ 70 kg.), a man endowed with above-average qualities, both physically and intellectually. He used his talent and good judgment in developing from a 4:53 miler in his first race in 1946 to a 4:09.9 world-class man in 1950, the year in which he finished third in the 800 m. (1:50.7) at the European Championships in Brussels. After his somewhat frustrating experience at the Helsinki Olympics, he improved to 4:02.0 for the mile in 1953, a time which was not ratified as a British record on the grounds that he had been paced by a lapped runner in the latter part of the race. In preparing for his final assault on the 4-minute barrier, Bannister planned every detail with scrupulous care. He received valuable advice from Franz Stampfl, an Austrian coach who later settled down in Australia. Bannister's schedule followed the general lines of "interval training", with the stress on quality rather than quantity. Being the type of athlete who would not allow his running to interfere too heavily with his other interests in life, he carefully rationed his appearances. By 1954 he had built up sufficient stamina for a major effort over the entire one-mile distance, yet he felt that he needed assistance from others in the early going if he was to preserve intact his patented turn of speed for the all-important last lap. The young Oxonian had his rendezvous with destiny on 6 May 1954 at Oxford. Before relating the circumstances of his record race, however, I deem it advisable to give here his training schedule in the three preceding weeks, as related by Ross McWhirter in "Athletics World":

- 12 April - 7x880 y. in 33 minutes, with 3 min. rests;
- 14 April - 3/4 mile solo in 3:02.0 (laps 61, 61 and 60);
- 15 April - 880 y. in 1:53.0 solo;
- 16/19 April - Rock climbing in Scotland;
- 22 April - 10x440 y. (average 58.9), first 56.3, last 56.3;
- 24 April - 3/4 mile in 3:00.0 in company with Chataway;
- 26 April - 3/4 mile in 3:14; 8 min. rest; 3/4 mile in 3:08.6
- 28 April - 3/4 mile solo in 2:59.9 in high wind;
- 30 April - Final two-lap time trial, 1:54 1/5 May - Rest.

In the early afternoon hours of that memorable day (6 May), Bannister still was not sure if he should make the attempt he had planned with his Achilles Club teammates and friends Chris Chataway and Chris Brasher. A strong wind was blowing across the Iffley Road track. That was the opponent he feared most ...

Fortunately, Aeolus kindly disappeared from the scene shortly before the six-man field went to the starting line at 6 p.m. "Alea jacta est", and the race was on. Brasher led for about two and a half laps, with Bannister and Chataway in his trail. Then Chataway took over, with Bannister on his heels. The would-be record breaker shot ahead with about 210 m. to go and punished himself down to the sweet end, which was reached in - 3:59.4. His lap times were: 57.5, 60.7 (1:58.2), 62.3 (3:00.5), 58.9. Hägg's mark was thus bettered by two seconds.

A superb effort, no matter if imperfect in pace judgment. Chataway, a distant second, lowered his personal best to 4:07.2.

Quite understandably, Bannister's feat received tremendous publicity, clearly more than most other famous athletic deeds before and after. Other great milers were burning to follow in Bannister's footsteps and possibly beat his record. Australia had a serious challenger in John Michael Landy (born in Melbourne on 12 April 1930; 1.82 m./69 kg.). He was coached by Percy Cerutty, an eccentric and intelligent man who in his fifties had suddenly run away from conformist town life to return to Nature, which he found at Portsea, Victoria. There, in addition to strengthening his body with a bold programme of physical exercises, he tried to instil in young people his own love for running by showing them what tremendous possibilities lay hidden in their bodies, only waiting to be developed.

Distant Prophecy

Predicting a world record in athletics is an extremely hazardous endeavour. Yet we know that Roger Bannister had been "identified" as a likely 4-minute miler as early as in 1949, i.e. five years before his historic race at Iffley Road. On 7 June of that year the Swedish "Idrottsbladet" carried an article by its London correspondent Erik Rydbeck, which bore the title: "Drömmil av Bannister ?!" (Dreammile by Bannister ?!). The writer said: "The name of young Bannister is in everybody's mouth. Quite a few experts regard him as the man most likely to break the 4-minute barrier in the mile. To this day he has done no better than 4:16.2, yet he looks very impressive, though not like the type of runner who can go out alone after a record". The prophecy turned out to be exact - even in the perception of Bannister's racing tactics.

The Portsea atmosphere was in some ways reminiscent of Vålådalen's, except that the Cerutty set seemed to lay the stress on quantity as well as on quality. Landy was probably the first above-average human specimen to come under Cerutty's wings. He improved in a dramatic fashion, from 4:14.6 in 1951 to 4:02.1 in 1952. Then things apparently became more difficult and further progress was minimal, with 4:02.0 near the end of 1953. Cerutty always advised his pupils to go out in front and set their own pace. Landy thus became the greatest front runner the world had ever seen. To join Bannister in sub-4 minute territory, however, he needed the help of a balmy Nordic evening and a fast track. He found both at Turku, Finland, on 21 June 1954. In a mile race he took the lead after 700 m., then poured it on all the rest of the way and finished surprisingly fresh - in 3:58.0 (actual time 3:57.9), thus smashing Bannister's world record. His 440 y. fractions were: 58.5, 60.2 (1:58.7), 58.5 (2:57.2), 60.7. In the meantime the 1500 m. world record had been revised too. In his one-mile race at Oxford, Bannister was unofficially timed in 3:43.0. A few weeks later at Compton, California, Wes Santee ran the metric distance in 3:42.8. But Landy excelled these marks with an official 3:41.8, enroute to his one-mile record at Turku. The stage was set for the "clou" of the season, the Landy vs. Bannister clash in the one-mile race of the British Empire Games at Vancouver (7 August). Never, until then, had a duel between athletic "Greats" been covered with similar intensity - by press, radio and TV. And it was chiefly Landy's merit if this eagerly awaited Mile of the Century lived up to its name. Eight men lined up at the start of the race, with Landy nearest the pole. True to his custom, he took the lead after no more than 275 m. What followed was reminiscent of the Harbig-Lanzi 800 m. classic at Milan in 1939. Just like Harbig, Bannister followed but did not chase his rival. At times Landy had a lead of several metres, but Bannister would always remain in contention. Entering the homestretch, Landy cast a nervous glance over his left (inside) shoulder. Right then and there, Bannister started his bid. His finish practically left the great Landy sitting, and that was the end of one of the greatest battles in miling history. Rich Ferguson of Canada was an unheralded third in 4:04.6, still a personal best. The intermediate times tell the story in precise terms:

Bannister		Landy
58.8	440 y.	58.2
(60.6) 1:59.4	880 y.	1:58.2 (60.0)
(59.3) 2:58.7	1320 y.	2:58.4 (60.2)
3:42.2	1500 m.	3:41.9
(60.1) 3:58.8	1 mile	3:59.6 (61.2)

Bannister obviously owed his victory to his superior finish :16.6 vs Landy's 17.7 over the last 109.35 m., just short of 120 y. It should perhaps be remembered that in his relatively quiet record run at Turku six weeks earlier Landy had covered the same stretch of track in 16.1. This probably serves to remind us that the stress of competition is mental as well as physical, which explains the difference between a "cold" and a "hot" race. Several days later it transpired that Landy had cut a foot rather badly during an early morning stroll on the eve of the race. He was generous enough to minimize the importance of that mishap. In this, as in similar cases, I think that no man in anything but perfect condition could have run as superbly as Landy did in that memorable race.

Bannister crowned a perfect season with a victory in the 1500 m. at the European Championships in Bern. Once again he resorted to his excellent turn of speed (54.7 for the last 400 m.) to go home the winner in 3:43.8, ahead of Gunnar Nielsen of Denmark (3:44.4) and Stanislav Jungwirth of Czechoslovakia (3:45.4). Sándor Iharos of Hungary, who on 3 August in Oslo had set a new European record of 3:42.4, finished a disappointing sixth in 3:47.0. Bannister was well satisfied with his perfect 1954 record - one historic "mile"-stone and two brilliant victories in major international games - and therefore decided to retire from the athletic scene. He was the typical amateur who loved the sport but was not prepared to make it the one and only ambition of his youth. He generally had a rather detached approach,

1941
1960

Herb Elliott (Australia) winning the Olympic 1500 metre title in Rome, 1960. Time: 3:35.6, a new world record. The runner-up was 2.8 behind.

old Oxford-style, yet he could also show a great singleness of purpose when major honours were at stake. As a follower of Aesculapius, he later became a distinguished neurologist.

America's leading miler, Wes Santee, continued to amass a string of great performances, finally ranging from 1:47.8 (800 m.) to 4:00.5 (1 mile), both in 1955, in addition to the above-mentioned 3:42.8 for the 1500 m. (1954), a short-lived world record. However, excessive publicity was made about his name and achievements, and this inevitably led to abuses. Late in 1955, when only twenty-three, he was ousted from the amateur ranks by the AAU. In 1955 other milers passed through the breach opened by Bannister and Landy. In a race in London, three men broke the once magic 4-minute barrier, with László Tábori of Hungary winning in 3:59.0 from two Britons, Chris Chataway and Brian Hewson (both 3:59.8). The 1500 m. record had been lagging behind for a while, but still in 1955 three Europeans were thoughtful enough to do something about it: first Sándor Iharos at Helsinki on 28 July, then Tábori and Gunnar Nielsen of Denmark at Oslo on 6 September, all achieved the same time, 3:40.8, a new world record. In the latter race Tábori barely nipped his Danish rival, after covering the last 300 m. in a sizzling 40.8.

By 1956 good 1500 m./one mile runners really were ten a dime. The group included, among others, István Rózsavölgyi of Hungary and Ron Delany of Ireland. The former (born at Budapest on 30 March 1929; 1.77 m./58 kg.) was a teammate of Iharos and Tábori in the Honvéd (Army) club. The trio was coached by Mihály Iglói, himself a former middle distance runner (3:52.2 for the 1500 m. in 1937) who later emigrated to USA, where he developed other sub-4 minute men. Rózsavölgyi was to prove the most durable of the three Magyar "musketeers", at least as a 1500 m. man. Over a number of years he amassed a high tally of excellent marks, but for one reason or another he failed to do himself full justice in major championship meets. Delany (born at Arklow, County Wicklow, on 6 March 1935; 1.84 m./75 kg.) was quite a different type: a match winner if ever there was one in athletics, he relied on his supersonic finishing speed to settle the issue, but being generally unwilling to punish himself in training he sometimes lacked the endurance which was required to follow a record pace. In June 1956 at Compton, California, he ran a mile in 3:59.0, barely beating another strong finisher, Gunnar Nielsen (3:59.1).

John Landy had virtually retired after losing to Bannister in the Mile of the Century, but by 1956 he was again ready to sting. By then Australia had another great prospect in Jim Bailey, who at Los Angeles in May 1956 created a sensation by edging Landy in a close finish, 3:58.6 to 3:58.7. Landy forced the pace for the major part of the race and was directly responsible for the "death" of Ron Delany, who dropped back early and finished a distant third in 4:05.5. Bailey, 27, used a 55.5 last lap to nip Landy at the tape. It was apparent, however, that Landy was no longer the "restricted runner" (his own words) of 1954: his work on speed was paying dividends. Unfortunately, Bailey was taken ill on the eve of the Games and thus lost the chance of his lifetime. Rózsavölgyi and Tábori went to Melbourne in subpar condition, especially the former: political events in their mother country had left a severe mark and

> **"Remove artificial, harmful, civilizing mediums"**
>
> Herb Elliott was a tremendously gifted athlete, both physically and mentally, yet it is doubtful if he would have ever realized his potential if he had not been lucky enough to catch the eye of Percy Cerutty. Certain European critics claim that Cerutty has said little or nothing new on the technical aspects of running, but this opinion apparently ignores the very core of Cerutty's message - in fact he worked chiefly, if not exclusively, on the psychology of his protégés. Here is an excerpt from his book "Running with Cerutty" (published by "Track & Field News" in 1959): "Man is an animal. Naturalistically he fluctuates from day to day - his feelings, strength, abilities, desires. Capacities vary from day to day, hour to hour. His strength ebbs and flows. Civilization, the daily routine of school and work, disciplines him, conditions him, and mostly reduces him to an automaton, a robot. How futile to add to such a regime his athleticism. How much better to use his training, conditioning and racing as a means, as it should be, to at least temporarily remove him from these artificial, and harmful, civilizing mediums that result from normal school and work." First of all, Cerutty tried to remove from the mind of his athletes every preconception on the supposed limits of human possibilities. He used to say: "Nobody knows where these limits lie - if they really exist". He thought his athletes should merely be concerned with improving their potential through "intensive and joyful" daily training.

their preparation, both moral and physical, surely left something to be desired. Even so, the Olympic final (1 December) did not fall below expectations. Landy, made more cautious as a result of his losses to Bannister and Bailey, did for once play the waiting game while others were livening up the race. Also biding his time, much more than Landy in fact, was Delany. Still tenth with one lap to go, the Irishman began to move with 300 m. to go. He put up the most devastating burst of speed ever seen in big-time competition. Covering the last 300 m. in an unheard of 38.8, he passed one rival after another and came home the winner in 3:41.2. Few runners, if any, had ever shown such a tremendous self-confidence in an Olympic final. Yet figures revealed that he had run a wise race, with 400 m. fractions of 60.0, 61.4 and 61.0, before unleashing his "corker". The idol of the home crowd, Landy, finished stronger than in any of his previous efforts, yet he just failed to catch Klaus Richzenhain of Germany, who ran the race of his life in shunting the Aussie to third place (both 3:42.0). Tábori (3:42.4), Hewson and Jungwirth (3:42.6) followed in that order. Eight men officially broke the Olympic record (3:45.2) and Ken Wood of Britain, ninth, probably became the first man in history to break an Olympic record without getting credit for it, since he was timed only on private watches! The event thus entered a new era. The Melbourne race was Landy's swan song, since he retired shortly afterwards - this time for good. His contribution to the advancement of miling standards was invaluable, yet in the opinion of some observers he could have been an even greater three-miler. In a casual attempt at that distance in 1956 he posted a significant 13:27.4. But he admitted that he had no flair for the longer distance.

Among the crowd at Melbourne's Cricket Ground the day of Delany's Olympic victory was an 18-year-old Australian boy, Herb Elliott, the latest find from Percy Cerutty's stable. His best for the mile was 4:20.4, dating from 1955. A severe foot injury had subsequently cost him a lay-off of about a year. This great natural talent (born at Subiaco, Perth, on 25 February 1938; 1.81 m./68 kg.) celebrated his 19th

1941
1960

A view from the back
by Tony O'Donoghue

The race in 1958 was the climax of a series of "match" races in Dublin over the period from 1954 pitting Ron Delany against a succession of world-class visitors. There had been a couple of great half-mile races in 1955 against Derek Johnson (GB) whilst in 1956 the protagonist was Brian Hewson (GB) at 1 mile. The following year saw a winning return match in Dublin against Derek Ibbotson shortly after the latter's 3:57.2 WR in London where Delany had been second. The 1956 and 1957 meets had played to attendances of 40,000 or more on a five-lap grass track at the Rugby Union headquarters, Lansdowne Road, and had generated the revenue to fund the construction of a quality track at Santry, which opened in early 1958.

The Australians (and New Zealand's Murray Halberg) were in Europe primarily for the Commonwealth Games in Cardiff; Albert Thomas had made an earlier foray to Dublin in July setting a world 3 Mile record (13:10.8) and had enthused about the new lay-out to Elliott. Delany had climaxed a golden Collegiate career in the USA with a unique 880-Mile double in the space of 45 minutes at the NCAA Championships so that there was massive public interest locally at the prospect of a meeting between the Olympic champ and the Commonwealth winner Elliott, and with the highly-regarded Mervyn Lincoln as a supporting player. The overflow crowd at Santry was immense and the event caused city-wide congestion with access to Dublin Airport being effectively blocked for several hours.

I saw most of the race from the back of the field though I sustained an early war-wound...an elbow in the ribs from Elliott on the first bend! Afterwards we were in near shock! Remember that it was only 4 years since Iffley Road and, since Ibbotson's mark had not yet been formally ratified, that technically the World Record had been eclipsed by a margin of 3.5 seconds... and by four athletes!

Afterwards, standing beside Elliott in the showers, I compared a 59 kg., 21 year-old frame with his superbly developed 19 year-old physique and lost all delusions.. I realised that any significant contribution to Track & Field would have to be in some area other than active participation.

(Note: Tony O'Donoghue finished the race in 4:19.7, a personal best. He is now a member of the Fourth Estate as well as an active statistician in the ranks of the ATFS).

birthday with an impressive double at the 1957 Australian Championships: one mile in 4:00.4 and 880 y. in 1:49.3, in the space of forty-eight hours. Over the longer distance he soundly beat Mervyn Lincoln (twelfth in the 1956 Olympic final, after dropping back in the third lap due to a pain in his leg). Lincoln was a protégé of Franz Stampfl, Bannister's onetime coach. This was the inaugural chapter of a keen rivalry between two great milers and, more specifically perhaps, between two great coaches, Cerutty and Stampfl. In a way, this was also a replica of the Landy-Bannister feud, but in inverted roles, because in this case the Stampfl protégé was to play the part of the "eternal second".

Elliott never bothered, as did most European runners, about the relative merits of speed and endurance: he simply considered the two factors as one. In his racing tactics he followed Landy's example, with more confidence and ability. In other words he would try to reap the fruits of victory over the entire distance, not necessarily over one particular section of it. Only two men, Lincoln in 1958 and Dan Waern of Sweden in 1960, occasionally managed to stay with him till the homestretch. In all other races he took the sting out of his opponents long before the end.

Apart from a loss to an elder runner as a junior, Elliott was never beaten at 1500 m. or one mile during his career. An idea of his wide range can be gathered from the fact that in 1958 he also topped the World Year List for the two-lap event, with a time of 1:47.3 (880 y.), and in 1960, in a casual attempt over 5000 m., he was timed in 14:09.9. On one occasion he was said to have run 30 miles (48 km.) without a break in a single training spin - in the midst of the Australian summer.

Elliott set his first world record on 6 August 1958 at Santry Stadium, Dublin, in one of the most memorable races in miling annals. Pitted against his countrymen Lincoln and Albie Thomas, New Zealand's Murray Halberg and Olympic champion Ron Delany, he thrashed them all and came home in 3:54.5 - 2.7 secs. under the record set by Britain's Derek Ibbotson the year before, the greatest improvement in the history of the mile. His "quarters" were: 56.4, 61.8 (1:58.2), 61.0 (2:59.2), 55.3 (3:54.5). At 1500 m. he was unofficially timed in 3:39.6, so he covered the last 109.35 m. in 14.9. Lincoln (3:55.9), Delany and Halberg (both 3:57.5), and Thomas (3:58.6) all ran faster than they had ever done before, yet they could make no impression on the flying Elliott. But it should be noted that Lincoln, departing for once from his usual tactics, went into the lead in the third lap, indirectly alleviating Elliott's task before the final rush for the tape.

On 28 August 1958, at Göteborg, Elliott was pitted against the cream of Europe over 1500 m. He outclassed all his opponents, leaving Stanislav Jungwirth, the reigning world record holder (3:38.1 in 1957), three full seconds behind! Elliott led for nearly half the distance and finished in 3:36.0. His 400 m. fractions were 57.5, 60.0 and 58.0, his last 300 m. 40.5. Jungwirth was second (3:39.0), followed by Halberg (3:39.4), Rózsavölgyi (3:40.0) and Waern (3:40.9).

Elliott gave the full measure of his greatness in the Olympic 1500 m. final of 1960 in Rome. This race can be considered Elliott's greatest as well as the most impressive one-man show in Olympic middle distance annals. The pace in the first 700 m. (1:42.8) was not to his liking, so he took over right there and then and covered the remaining 800 m. in a hair raising 1:52.8, incidentally the time that in 1908 had earned a gold medal for Mel Sheppard in the 800 m. of the London Olympics! Elliott's 400 m. fractions were: 58.8, 59.3, 55.9, and his last 300 m. 41.6. He thus reaped a final time of 3:35.6, a new world record. His scorching pace in the third lap left his rivals standing.

The race for second place was won by 24-year-old Michel Jazy of France (3:38.4), while veteran Rózsavölgyi won a well-deserved bronze medal (3:39.2). Dan Waern was fourth in 3:40.0. Elliott's winning margin, 2.8 secs., was to be regarded as phenomenal for a race of this calibre.

Even if clearly outshone by Elliott, Europeans had not ceased to improve. In a 1500 m. race at Turku on 11 July 1957, hence shortly before the advent of the Aussie star, Olavi Salsola of Finland won an all-Nordic affair with a record time of 3:40.2. In a tight finish he beat two other Finns, Olavi Salonen and Olavi Vuorisalo, and Sweden's Dan Waern, who finished in that order in 3:40.2, 3:40.3 and 3:40.8 respectively. After the race, the happy winner made a prediction: "Somebody will run under 3:40 soon". He proved an excellent prophet: the very next day, on a 364-metre track at Stará Boleslav Houstka, Stanislav Jungwirth of Czechoslovakia cut 2.1 sec. off the fresh record! In terms of pace judgment, however, this race was simply abnormal: after following some "hares" through a 1:54.2 800m., Jungwirth took over with 600 m. to go, suffered more than a bit the rest of the way, yet managed to finish in 3:38.1. Still in 1957, British tradition gained new lustre when 25-year-old Derek Ibbotson recaptured the mile record for the mother country with a scintillating 3:57.2, beating the likes of Delany (3:58.8) and Jungwirth (3:59.1). This was in London on 19 July and Ibbotson's "quarters" were 56.0, 60.4, 63.9 and 56.9. The following year another

Zátopek: his early years				
Year	Age	1500 m.	3000 m.	5000 m.
1941	19	4:20.3	—	—
1942	20	4:13.9	9:12.2	16:25.0
1943	21	4:01.6	8:56.0	15:26.6
1944	22	3:59.5	8:34.8	14:55.0
1945	23	4:01.4	8:33.4	14:50.8
1946	24	3:57.6	8:21.0	14:25.8
1947	25	3:52.8	8:08.8	14:08.2

1941 1960

Briton, Brian Hewson, won the European 1500 m. title in Stockholm in 3:41.9. Another middle distance runner who, like Jungwirth, was at his best in prefabricated, "cold" record attempts, was Siegfried Valentin of Germany, who set a European one-mile record of 3:56.5 in a race of that sort at Potsdam in 1959, but was eliminated in a heat of the 1500 m. in the 1960 Olympics.

LONG DISTANCES - 5000 and 10,000 m.: Zátopek and Kuts, the leading lights

The Finnish hegemony in the long distances was broken in the early Forties by a man from nearby Sweden, Gunder Hägg. "Gunder the Wonder" (whose rise to greatness has been charted in the preceding chapter) made only two notable inroads in the proper long-distance department, but those were memorable ones. Prior to 1942 he had tried the 5000 m. on rare occasions, once beating the great Kälarne at Helsinki in 1940, 14:38.2 to 14:38.4. In his Year of Years, 1942, he tried the 3 miles at Stockholm on 11 September and stunned experts with a new world record of 13:35.4. He did even better over 5000 m. at Göteborg on 20 September. On a track that was not at its best due to earlier rain he led from 1400 m.to the end and knocked 10.6 seconds off Mäki's world record with a startling 13:58.2 (actual time 13:58.1), after collecting a new global standard for 3 miles enroute (13:32.4). His kilometre fractions were: 2:40.0, 2:47.0, 2:51.5, 2:50.5, 2:49.2. Bror Hellström, a distinguished distance runner, finished a distant second in 14:41.4. This superlative effort proved that a great miler with plenty of stamina could quietly move up to the longer distances and discover new horizons. Hägg confirmed his great potential in 1944, when he beat Viljo Heino of Finland at Helsinki, 14:24.4 to 14:24.8. And Heino was in fact the last of the great Finns, for a long time to come. Earlier in 1944 he had lowered the world's 10.000 m. record to 29:35.4 (during a half-hour race) and run the 5000 m. in 14:09.6. At the end of World War II another great miler followed in Hägg's footsteps, i.e. moved successfully to the longer distances. This man was veteran Sydney Wooderson of Britain, who astonished his sup-

Emil Zátopek (Czechoslovakia) on his way to victory in the marathon of the 1952 Olympics in Helsinki, his third gold medal in those Games.

155

porters towards the end of his career with some superlative efforts outside of his normal sphere of influence. In 1946, that is a year after achieving his best one-mile time (4:04.2, in losing to Arne Andersson, 4:03.8), the little Englishman won the AAA 3-mile title in 13:53.2 from up-and-coming Wim Slykhuis of Holland (13:54.2). Then he went on to capture the European 5000 m. title at Oslo with 14:08.6, the second fastest time on record. With an all-out effort in the truest sense of the word the 32-year-old Wooderson beat a star-studded field, the place winners being Slykhuis (14:14.0), Evert Nyberg of Sweden (14:23.2), Heino (14:24.4), Emil Zátopek of Czechoslovakia (14:25.8) and Gaston Reiff of Belgium (14:45.8).

Vladimir Kuts (USSR) won 5000 and 10,000 m. at the 1956 Olympics in Melbourne.

Emil Zátopek (born at Koprivnice, Northern Moravia, on 19 September 1922; 1.74 m./67 kg.), then a virtual unknown in international circles, was silently laying the foundation of a new era in distance running - the Zátopek Era. Not the least of his achievements was that of putting Czechoslovakia on the map of distance running. Prior to his advent, the Czech national records for the 5000 and 10,000 m. were no better than 15:14.8 and 32:15.8 respectively. Zátopek had no easy passage in his younger days. He found time and opportunity for training and racing only when he moved to Zlín, where he worked as an apprentice in a shoe factory. His first race was on 27 April 1941: second over a 1400 m. course in 4:24.5. He tasted victory only on his fifth attempt, in 1942, when still over 1400 m. he was timed in 4:08.9. His progression in the early period of his career is given in the adjoining table.

The turning point in his career probably occurred in the fall of 1945, when the famous Swede Arne Andersson paid a short visit to Czechoslovakia. Emil was greatly impressed by the superb physical condition of Hägg's chief rival, and came to the conclusion that he himself had not trained hard enough up to then. Yet he was to follow Swedish methods only to a certain extent. From then on he subjected himself to a schedule which went far beyond the usual norms of "Fartlek". Running over a fixed distance - usually 200 or 400 m. - many times, he would slow down to a dog trot during intervals. Over 200 m., for example, his normal running time would be 34 seconds, his jogging time 60 seconds. Over 400 m., his times would be 60 and 90 seconds respectively. He often wore heavy basketball shoes in training, and on rainy days even soldier's boots. His daily running ration was increased gradually through the years, and intervals became shorter. At the peak of his career he averaged over 1000 hours of running per year, 800 km. per month - i.e. well over half a marathon per day! His basic principle was to make his training so hard that competitive racing would by comparison come as a light matter to him. Great courage and an unlimited ability to endure: this, in a nutshell, was the message that Zátopek conveyed to the would-be distance runners of the world.

His fifth place in the 5000 m. at the 1946 European Championships (accompanied by a new national record of 14:25.8), was the starting point of his international career. He made his competitive debut over 10,000 m. in May 1948 and surprised a lot of people, who obviously knew little or nothing about his hard training schedule, with an excellent 30:28.4. In his second try, three weeks later, he came dangerously close to Viljo Heino's world record with an astonishing 29:37.0. His third try occurred in the

London Olympics, on 30 July. For about fifteen laps Heino managed to stay in contention, but then Zátopek released one of his characteristic bursts, and that was the beginning of the end for the world record holder, who collapsed under the combined effect of heat and racing pace, and soon dropped out. The Czech thus won his first Olympic gold medal in 29:59.6. Well behind him, Algerian-born Alain Mimoun of France won his first Olympic silver medal in 30:47.4. Three days later, in the 5000 m. final, Zátopek met Gaston Reiff of Belgium, a middle-distance runner with a copy-book style and a keen sense of racing. The race was marred by the rain, and conditions made the duel truly dramatic. Zátopek lost contact in the next-to-last kilometre, and the Belgian built up a substantial lead. At the bell he had nearly 40 m. on Zátopek, and halfway between the two was Wim Slykhuis of Holland. By then, however, Zátopek was charging back with fury. He caught Slykhuis and left him standing, then kept making up ground on Reiff. But the remaining distance was too short and fatigue too great: the Czech failed to catch Reiff by a metre or so. The times, 14:17.6 and 14:17.8. Slykhuis was third in 14:26.8. Reiff and Zátopek were re-matched at Prague later in the season, and Reiff was again the winner, 14:19.0 to 14:21.0. In pre-Olympic meets, Zátopek had set new national records of 8:07.8 (3000 m.) and 14:10.0 (5000 m.). The former was to remain his fastest ever. What Zátopek did in his best years (1948-55) can be summarized as follows:

(1) Four times Olympic champion (10,000 m. in 1948, 5000, 10,000 and marathon in 1952);

(2) Three times European champion (5000 and 10,000 m. in 1950, 10,000 m. in 1954);

(3) Undefeated over 5000 and 10,000 m. from October 1948 to June 1952;

(4) Undefeated over 10,000 m. from May 1948 to July 1954 for a total of 38 consecutive wins.
In 1949 he ran this distance 11 times in competition;

(5) Between 1949 and 1955 he set 18 world records for distances ranging from 5000 to 30,000 m. His ultimates: 13:57.2 (5000 m), 27:59.2 (6 miles), 28:54.2 (10,000 m.), all in 1954; 48:12.0 (10 miles), 59:51.6 (20,000 m.), 20,052 m. (1 hour), all at Stará Boleslav Houstka on 29 September 1951; 1:14:01.0 (15 miles), 1:16:36.4 (25,000 m.) in 1955; 1:35:23.8 (30,000 m.) in 1952.

For five years (1949 through 1953) Zátopek was the undisputed king of distance runners. At the 1950 European Championships in Brussels he won the 10,000 m. hands down in 29:12.0, leaving his nearest rival, Mimoun, sixty-nine seconds behind! Three days later he knocked out his old rival Reiff in the 5000 m. after a fabulous ding-dong battle. To the dismay of a huge Belgian crowd, Reiff had to give way to the Czech in the last lap. While Zátopek went on to win in 14:03.0 (last 400 m. in 62.4), Reiff was so exhausted that he finally lost second place to Mimoun, 14:26.2 to 14:26.0. Towards the end of the epic race, the crowd's dismay turned into applause for the famous guest.

The Helsinki Olympics (1952) were the "chef-d'oeuvre" in Zátopek's unique collection of great achievements. In the week from 20 to 27 July he outshone the feats of Kolehmainen and Nurmi, coupling his victories in the 5000 and 10,000 m. with a triumph in the marathon. That unthinkable triple showed the full measure of Zátopek's greatness. He began with an easy win in the 10,000 m. (20 July) over Mimoun, the "Eternal Second" - 29:17.0 to 29:32.8. Two days later he went through a heat of the 5000 m. unruffled. His severest test was in the final (24 July), which is still

1941
1960

Zdzislaw Krzyszkowiak (Poland) winning the European 5000 metre title under adverse weather conditions at Stockholm in 1958.

remembered as one of the greatest battles in Olympic annals. At the bell four men were in the lead: Zátopek, young Chris Chataway of Britain, bespectacled Herbert Schade of Germany, and Mimoun. Somebody feared that Zátopek's heavy training mileage in preparation for his marathon debut might have taken something out of his finishing zip, but he lost no time in proving doubters wrong. Chataway made a courageous bid in the backstretch, but as they went round the last curve he stepped on the curb and fell, possibly as a result of incoming fatigue. Zátopek took a decisive lead and from then on his rivals really had no chance. After covering the last lap in 58.1, he came home the winner in 14:06.6, followed by Mimoun (14:07.4), Schade (14:08.6), Gordon Pirie of Britain, and the unlucky Chataway (both 14:18.0). In the final stage of that memorable battle, Zátopek embodied the truest expression of aggressiveness I have ever seen on a running track. What he did in the marathon on 27 July will be recounted in a later chapter. As a champion distance runner Zátopek had no weaknesses. A superlative solo runner (he received little or no help from others in his record attempts), he was also a clever tactician, and an almost unbeatable finisher. He never revealed great potentialities as a middle-distance runner (apart from a 3:52.8 in the 1500 m. in 1947), yet his sudden bursts of speed made countless victims. Last but not least, he was supreme as a fighter. The year 1954 marked the beginning of the end for this fantastic human machine. He had shown the way, and others quickly followed in his footsteps, taking upon themselves a similar burden of daily sacrifices. But it is interesting to note that Zátopek, then thirty-two, rose to the challenge magnificently and ran faster than ever before over both 5000 and 10,000 m. This most crucial stage in his career coincided with the rise of a new star, to whom the old champion finally had to give way. This man was Vladimir Kuts of USSR. In such cases it is virtually impossible to determine to what extent the rise of one man causes the decline of another, or vice versa.

Kuts (born at Aleksino, Ukraine, on 7 February 1927; 1.72 m./72 kg.) came to athletics even later than Zátopek. In his youth he practised other sports, including boxing. He became a distance man of national calibre in 1952, with times of 14:32.2 (5000 m.) and 31:02.4 (10,000 m.). The following year he entered bigtime competition with a bang by threatening the great Zátopek in the Youth Festival of the Eastern Bloc at Bucharest. In the 5000 m., he drew away from the Czech at the start (sic) and stayed in the lead till the closing stage of the race, when Zátopek reversed positions to win, 14:03.0 to 14:04.0. In later years, Kuts remained faithful to the cliché he had exhibited in that race. On 3 July 1954 at Budapest, a diminutive (1.63 m.) Hungarian runner, József Kovács, broke the chain of Zátopek's victories in the 10,000 m., beating the Czech in a frenzied sprint, 29:09.0 to 29:09.8. Meanwhile Chataway, the hard-luck kid of the Helsinki Olympics, had established himself as a mature distance runner with 3-mile times of 13:32.2 and 13:35.2, the latter in winning the Empire Games title at Vancouver. In the European Championships at Bern, Zátopek showed a quick return to form, winning the 10,000 m. from Kovács with astounding ease, 28:58.0 to 29:25.8. But his hardest task was yet to come, namely in the 5000 m., where he was pitted against a fresh duo, Kuts-Chataway. The Czech was still the favourite of many, having beaten Hägg's world record early in the season with a 13:57.2 effort. As in Bucharest the previous year, Kuts boldly decided to settle the issue at the start. He soon built up a big lead. In failing to react, Zátopek and Chataway possibly underestimated Kuts's strength, or maybe they overestimated their own. When they finally rose to the challenge, they had no time to remedy the situation. Kuts won in 13:56.6, a new world record. Chataway nipped Zátopek for second place, 14:08.8 to 14:10.2. Maybe the last two could have come closer to threatening the Soviet with more alert tactics, but it is salutary to record that Kuts's last kilometre (2:44.3) was as fast as his first (2:44.0). The winner also set a new 3-mile record of 13:27.4. A few days later, at Stockholm, Zátopek came close to Kuts's fresh world record with 13:57.0. And on 13 October Kuts and Chataway met again during a floodlight meet at London's White City. Kuts maintained the lead throughout most of the race, as far as the 3-mile mark (13:27.0, a new world record) and farther, but Chataway never let him go and finally won the night, 13:51.6 to 13:51.8, bringing the crowd of 50,000 to its feet. The untiring Ukrainian, however, had the last word for the year: at Prague on 23 October he recaptured the world record with a magnificent solo effort: 13:51.2 (3 miles in 13:26.4).

Kuts reached the peak of his condition in 1956. Early in the season he found a worthy rival in Gordon Pirie, a filiform Englishman who in 1953, aged twenty-two, had run the 5000 m. in 14:02.6 and the 10,000 m. in 29:17.2. On 19 June 1956, at Bergen, Norway, he was opposed to Kuts in the 5000 m. Playing the waiting game that had occasionally paid dividends for Chataway, Pirie stayed in Kuts's wake throughout the entire race, then used his finishing kick to run away from his rival in the last lap. He was rewarded with a new world record, 13:36.8, while Kuts finished in 13:39.6. But five months later, in the Melbourne Olympics, Kuts was to reverse the decision in no uncertain manner. Prior to going Down Under, he captured the world's 10,000 m. record in Moscow with a 28:30.4 effort. In Melbourne he literally K.O.'d his rivals in the 10,000 m., winning in 28:45.6 from Kovács of Hungary (28:52.4) and Allan Lawrence of Australia (28:53.6), while Pirie finished a disappointing eighth. Five days later, in the 5000 m., Pirie offered a better fight, but Kuts was not to be denied: he won again, by a decisive margin - 13:39.6 to 13:50.6. Another Englishman, Derek Ibbotson, was third in 13:54.4. Although not as cunning as Zátopek as a tactician, Kuts was superior to his great predecessor in sheer strength. In his training he attributed more importance to speed work. His "killing" tactics made countless victims. Among those he destroyed in the Melbourne Games was Dave Stephens of Australia, who had set a world 6-mile record of 27:54.0 in January. The Aussie ace finished no better than twentieth in the Olympic 10,000 m. It must be said, however, that Stephens was not in good physical condition on that momentous occasion. Of course, Kuts's schedule between 1952 and 1956 had been frightening. This became apparent in 1957, when a stomach ailment obliged him to cut his training and racing ration. He narrowly lost to his countryman Pyotr Bolotnikov in the 10,000 m. at the USSR title meet in Moscow, 29:10.0 to 29:09.8, but fought back bravely in a 5000 m. at Rome's Stadio Olimpico on 13 October. His scorching pace forced Bolotnikov to drop back after less than 2000 m. In a magnificent solo effort, Kuts lowered the world record to 13:35.0. His kilometre fractions were: 2:37.8, 2:46.5, 2:44.4, 2:44.2, 2:42.1. That was his swan song. "Sputnik", as the Rome crowd called him during that record journey, later faced several health problems which put an end to his racing career. He died at 48, in 1975. Further details on the good Britons of that period seem to be in order. Pirie alternated splendid days with sombre ones. In addition to his 5000 m. world record, he set a global mark of 7:52.8 (actual time, 7:52.7) for 3000 m. at Malmö in 1956, beating the likes of Rózsavölgyi, Iharos and Tábori. Chataway, the red-haired Oxonian, was more solid both physically and morally, but also less likely to subject himself to hard training. Like Pirie, he joined the sub-4 minute mile Club. He later became a Member of Parliament and a Minister in the British Government. Another great distance runner of that period was Sándor Iharos of Hungary (born at Budapest on 10 March 1930; 1.80m./65 kg.), who in addition to his 3:40.8 world record for the 1500 m. set global standards also in the 5000 (13:40.6 in 1955) and 10,000 m. (28:42.8 in 1956). The Hungarian insurrection of 1956 with its repercussions far and wide caused him to miss the Melbourne Olympics. In view of his previous not-so-brilliant record in major competitions, however, I doubt if he could have ever risen to the stature of Kuts in the Olympic arena. After parting from his coach Mihály Iglói, still in 1956, he was never the same athlete again.

By the same time, Australasia came into the long-distance picture with several fine specimens. In addition to the above-mentioned Dave Stephens, who was unlucky enough to be sidelined with a serious injury when at the peak of his form, there was little Albie Thomas, another "Aussie" who in 1958 lowered the world's 3-mile record to 13:10.8. But the best of the men from Down Under was Murray Halberg of New Zealand (born at Eketahuna on 7 July 1933; 1.80 m./62 kg.). Severely injured while playing rugby football at seventeen, it was thought that he would remain an invalid for the rest of his life. However, his dedication in trying to overcome his condition was such that not only was he restored to normal health, except for a

1941
1960

Abebe Bikila (Ethiopia) leading Rhadi (Morocco) in the closing stage of the 1960 Olympic marathon in Rome.

159

withered arm, but also attained the highest honours one can hope for in athletics! His breakthrough as a class runner came in 1954, when he did 4:04.4 for the mile and finished fifth in the same event at the Empire Games at Vancouver. In later years he concentrated on the longer distances and in 1958 he won the 3 miles at the Empire Games in Cardiff in 13:15.0, with a blistering 3:11.4 over the last 3/4 mile. Thomas was second in this race with 13:24.4. Halberg's greatest triumph was in the 1960 Olympics in Rome, when he downed the world's best distance runners in the 5000 m. After staying with the leaders for nine laps, he launched a bold surprise attack and soon found himself alone. His courage eventually won the day, no matter if he faded a little near the end. He won in 13:43.4 from Hans Grodotzki, a compact German (13:44.6) and Kazimierz Zimny of Poland (13:44.8). Six days later, in the 10,000 m., Halberg was not so brilliant and had to be content with fifth place. The race was won by 30-year-old Pyotr Bolotnikov of USSR, who like his great countryman Vladimir Kuts had gradually matured after a late start. As reported earlier in this chapter, he first made the headlines in 1957, beating Kuts himself in the 10,000 m. That was in fact the distance he elected to run in Rome. He threw away his mask with 700 m. to go, and what the track world saw was a new Kuts. He covered the last kilometre in 2:38.6 and the last 400 m. in 57.4 for a final time of 28:32.2, a solid 26 seconds under his previous best. Grodotzki was again second (28:37.0) and Dave Power of Australia was third (28:38.2). Bolotnikov closed his great season with a fast 13:38.1 in the 5000 m. and a world record 28:18.8 in the 10,000 m. The latter was at Kiev on 15 October, and Bolotnikov showed excellent pace judgment, with 5000 m. fractions of 14:07.0 and 14:11.8. Among other leading European distance men of those years I wish to mention Zdzislaw Krzyszkowiak of Poland, who scored a fine double at the 1958 European Championships in Stockholm, with 28:56.0 in the 10,000 m. and, four days later, 13:53.4 in the 5000 m. He was primarily a steeplechaser (Olympic champion in 1960), just like his countryman Jerzy Chromik, another strong distance runner.

MARATHON:
Africa's coming-of-age

During World War II international marathon activity was obviously at a low ebb. The best results were offered by the Boston classic, in which Gérard Coté of Canada, who had first won the event in 1940, was able to come through the winner on three more occasions (1943, '44 and '48). Clock-wise, the most notable performance was registered in the 1947 edition, won by Yun Bok Suh, a diminutive (1.55 m.) Korean, in 2:25:39, fastest time on record up to then. In 1948, i.e. forty years after the Dorando Pietri saga, London was again the scene of a dramatic Olympic marathon. An unprecedented mass finish saw three men closely bunched at the entrance to the stadium. Etienne Gailly of Belgium, a leader for the major part of the race, fell victim to exhaustion a few hundred metres from the tape and was overtaken, in quick succession, first by Delfo Cabrera of Argentina, then by Tom Richards of Britain. Zabala's compatriot, an ultra-solid, heavily moustached veteran never led the parade until he passed Gailly inside Wembley Stadium! He won in 2:34:51.6. Richards finished 16 seconds later, and Gailly was third, 26 seconds farther back. That was Cabrera's first marathon, officially at least. As a trackman the Argentinian had been prominent for years, his best credential being a 14:44.3 in the 5000 m. in 1941. No marathon "Great" had ever been speedy enough to prove just as great, simultaneously, on the shorter track routes. Hannes Kolehmainen had indeed won Olympic titles on the track and in the marathon, but not at the same time. The first and to this day sole example of ubiquity in this respect is that offered by Emil Zátopek in the 1952 Olympics at Helsinki. After winning the 10,000 m. (20 July) and the 5000 m. (24 July), the inimitable Czech decided to add luster to the marathon field and on 27 July lined up with sixty-seven long-grind specialists at the start of the classic event. Officially that was the first marathon of his career. However, his daily "running ration" for several years past had made him thoroughly familiar with the labours which await a would-be marathon runner. The early pace, no matter if fairly fast (first 10,000 m. fractions in 32:12 and 32:15), was not exactly "Zátopekian". When the pace slackened (next 10,000 m. fractions in 34:15 and 36:28), the true specialists dropped back and Zátopek found himself in the role of lone leader. Jim Peters of Britain, the pre-race favourite of several experts on the strength of his record time (2:20:41.2) in the Polytechnic Harriers event earlier in the year, developed cramps and was forced to retire after 32 km. Upon entering the Olympic Stadium, Zátopek received a standing ovation from the knowledgeable Finnish crowd. He finished in 2:23:03.2. Reynaldo Gorno of Argentina was second, about two and a half minutes farther back. Defending champion Cabrera had a much faster time than four years earlier in London, yet he had to be content with a sixth place. In the meantime, marathon races continued to grow in number. The above-mentioned Jim Peters (born in Homerton, London, on 24 October 1918; 1.70m./57 kg.) made amends for his unlucky show at Helsinki with a string of brilliant performances. On 13 June 1953, in the Polytechnic Harriers event from Windsor to Chiswick, he broke the 2:20 barrier with a sparkling 2:18:40.2. In the same year, on 4 October at Turku, he did even better with 2:18:34.8. His greatest feat was on 26 June 1954, once again on the Windsor-to-Chiswick course, which he negotiated in 2:17:39.4. But the race that earned him a niche in the hall of track immortals was the British Empire marathon at Vancouver later in 1954. The race was run on a difficult course and in sweltering heat. Peters, who started as an odds-on favourite, was not content to win, and generously gave himself in an effort to complete his journey in remarkable time. Some 2 hours 19 minutes after the start, the announcer informed spectators packing the stadium on that 7th of August (earlier in the afternoon they had witnessed the Bannister vs. Landy "Mile of the Century") that Peters, the leader of the marathon, had reached the hill just outside the stadium but appeared to be in trouble. Several minutes passed before he entered the arena, a staggering and wobbling figure. In a true repetition of the Pietri drama of 1908 (oddly enough, Peters appears to be the English translation of the Italian family name Pietri), the Englishman fell eleven times during that tantalizing last lap, until the manager of the English team decided to put an end to his Odyssey. He was borne off the track while some 200 yards away from the appointed finish. The official winner of the race was Joe McGhee of Scotland (2:39:36). The psychological and physical reactions in Peters were such that he was advised by his doctors to retire from full athletic activity.

The 1956 Olympic marathon in Melbourne crowned an athlete who for many years had remained in the shadow of Emil Zátopek. This man was Algerian-born Alain Mimoun O'Kacha of France, who at the time was near his thirty-sixth birthday. At ease in a warm climate, he ran his first official marathon in 2:25:00, leaving the runner-up, Franjo Mihalic of Yugoslavia, over 1 1/2 minutes back. Veikko Karvonen of Finland took third place: here perhaps was the best example of a "pure" marathoner who could point to an impressive series of consistent performances at the classic distance, notably including a victory in the 1954 European Championship event. Sixth in the Melbourne race was defending champion Zátopek, then 34 and just recovering from an operation. Shortly afterwards the world saluted the USSR's first great marathon runner, Sergey Popov. At the 1958 European Championships in Stockholm, this little Siberian won in 2:15:17.0, easily the best-on-record performance up to that time. In doing so he left his nearest rival over 5 minutes behind. So great was the sensation created by Popov's inexorable mastery that he was henceforth considered as the man to beat for the 1960 Olympic title.

However, if there is an event in athletics that has no sure fire favourite, that event is certainly the marathon. The winner of the Olympic marathon in the Eternal City was a man previously unknown to

1941
1960

No answer

I am among the lucky track fans who saw Emil Zátopek in his Week of Weeks at the Helsinki Olympics in 1952. And about a quarter century later I had a chat with him during the European Championships at Prague in 1978. I found him as kind and humorous as ever, even though he had gone through troubled years for siding with those who turned out to be the (temporary) losers during the Prague Spring of 1968. I invited him to give me his retrospective views on his track career. What he said in reply was in fact a monument to his proverbial modesty. In sharp contrast with the type of champion from yesteryear who likes to take refuge in the ivory tower of his "old days", he candidly told me: "I think I had a fair amount of luck. That was a time when track thrived at a low-fire temperature. Most countries still had to heal the wounds caused by World War II and the turnover in talent was understandably slow. Finland's great pre-war runners had disappeared, apart from Viljo Heino who was near the end of his career". Recalling the 1952 Olympic marathon, he said: "In a way, that was probably my easiest victory. It was not the "new" distance that frightened me, but rather the possibility of certain paces - which nobody chose to impose." This checks pretty well with a story I heard at Helsinki shortly after the race. While sharing the lead with Gustaf Jansson of Sweden and Jim Peters of Britain, Zátopek the novice was said to have addressed his companions in English with the following words: "I know virtually nothing about marathon running, but don't you think we ought to go a little faster?" Receiving no answer, the Czech sped up anyway - and ran away from his rivals.

the overwhelming majority of experts. His name: Abebe Bikila. He came from Ethiopia and had a Scandinavian coach, Olli Niskanen. Before coming to Rome, the 27-year-old Bikila had tried the marathon twice in competition, with times of 2:39:50 and 2:21:23. The latter in particular was worthy of note, since it was made at Addis Ababa, a city located 2400 m. above sea level.

The Rome race (10 September) was run entirely outside the stadium, with departure from Capitol Hill and arrival under the Arch of Constantine. The itinerary unfolded, broadly speaking, along the ancient Appian Way. Luckily enough, the start was at 5.30 p.m., so that the competitors did not have to suffer unduly from the Roman heat. Abebe Bikila, who ran bare-footed, was in the front row from the start. His sole companion in the latter part of the race was another African, Rhadi ben Abdesselem of Morocco. They went through fast 10 km. fractions of 31:07, 31:32, 31:50, then slowed down to 34:04. The Ethiopian drew away from his rival with less than one mile to go and won in 2:15:16.2, shaving 0.8 secs. off Popov's best-on-record time. Rhadi was a brilliant second in 2:15:41.6, followed by Barry Magee of New Zealand (2:17:18.2). The first fifteen finishers broke Zátopek's Olympic record and pre-race favourite Popov had to settle for a fifth place.

History reread

For many years the world of athletics took it for granted that Abebe Bikila was born at Mout on 7 August 1932, as indicated in the official entry list of the 1960 Olympics in Rome. But the birthdates of African athletes are often controversial, especially if dating from pre-independence days. In Bikila's case a different version, presumably the definitive one, arose only after his death (1973), when the Ethiopian Government erected a monumental tomb in his memory at Addis Ababa. On it one can read:
Here lies the hero Capt. Abebe Bikila.
Born at Jatto, Debre Birhan, in 1933.
Died at Addis Ababa in 1973.
The inscription, with the dates of his victorious Olympic marathons (Rome '60 and Tokyo '64), is in four languages: Amharic, English, Italian and Japanese, each carved on the half of a concrete ball. In the middle of the monument is a bronze bust of Abebe Bikila (which means "budding flower" in Amharic).

HURDLES - 110 METRES: Dillard's incredible adventure

The great Fred Wolcott crowned an almost flawless career by equalling Towns' world record for the 110 m. hurdles (13.7) at the AAU Championships in Philadelphia on 29 June 1941. In a windless race, he won from Joe Batiste (13.9). That was his last season in bigtime competition, even though he returned for a casual 14.1 in the classic "Sugar Bowl" meet at New Orleans on the last day of 1942. The world's greatest "high" hurdler in the early post-war years was another American, William Harrison Dillard (born at Cleveland on 8 July 1923; 1.78 m./70kg.). As a teen-ager, in 1936, he witnessed a parade in his native town in honour of Jesse Owens, coming home from his victorious Berlin campaign. As the story goes, right then and there the boy decided to emulate the athletic feats of the "Ebony Antelope". "Bones", as he was called on account of his skinny physique, rose to national prominence at the 1942 AAU Championships in New York: after finishing a close second in the "lows" and third in the "highs" in the Junior meet, he made his début in the Senior meet the following day, coming fifth in the 400 m. hurdles in 53.7. In later years he virtually forgot about the "intermediates" and concentrated on the short distances, with and without hurdles. During World War II he competed with success as a serviceman in Italy and Germany (10.6 and 14.6 in 1945). Back in the States, he improved rapidly: 13.9 in 1947, then a record breaking 13.6 over 120 y. hurdles at Lawrence on 17 April 1948, a race he won with 8 m. to spare from Clyde Scott, who a few months later was to win a silver medal in the Olympics. In the meantime he had set new standards in the "lows" as well, with a new world record of 22.3 (1947). By the end of June 1948 Dillard could point to a fabulous string of 82 consecutive wins on the flat and over the hurdles, indoors and out. The chain was broken at the AAU Championships in Milwaukee. Four races (prelims and finals of 100 m. and 110 m. hurdles) within 67 minutes proved his undoing: in the hurdles final he lost to Bill Porter, 14.3 to 14.1. The following week he was at Evanston, Illinois, for the US Final Tryouts, and again chose to play at two tables. A wise decision ... because after securing a berth on the team in the 100 m., the following day he met disaster in his parade event, the "highs". After hitting three hurdles badly, he dropped out, while Porter (13.9), Craig Dixon and

Scott went on to win the three berths for the Olympics. (In what incredible way Dillard made amends for his failure - that is a story I have told in the "Sprints"chapter). Some critics maintained that Dillard was partly handicapped by his indifferent height and his consequently low centre of gravity, which made his action over the hurdles somewhat perilous. In his best days, however, he was as clean a "timber-topper" as any of the other Greats - and faster than most if not all of them. In the Olympic 110 m. hurdles final, the consistent Porter - who had first beaten Dillard in the "lows" in 1947 - won in brilliant style, equalling his personal best (13.9), while Scott and Dixon (both 14.1) made it a clean sweep for USA. Fourth place went to Alberto Triulzi (14.6), an Argentinian who in the fall of 1947 at Buenos Aires had won by a few centimetres from Håkan Lidman of Sweden, with both returning a fast 14.0. In London the bespectacled Swede, by then 33, finished sixth. Another great European hurdler from pre-war days, Don Finlay of Britain, failed in his bid for a third Olympic final (sixteen years after his first) when he fell in one of the preliminary heats. In 1949, at the age of forty, the indestructible Finlay ran the 120 y. hurdles in 14.4 at London's White City, his best legal mark on English soil. Porter retired after his London triumph, aged twenty-two, but Dillard stayed in competition even after leaving college, with a not-so-secret dream: do himself justice in the "highs" at Helsinki in 1952. In the intervening time he continued to be almost invincible in the short indoor tussles, in which his "Blitz" start paid dividends, but was outshone outdoors, in 1949-51, first by Craig Dixon, then by Dick Attlesey. Attlesey (born at Compton, California, on 10 May 1929; 1.92 m./81 kg.) was not as great as Dillard in terms of speed, but his statuesque build and his excellent technique largely sufficed to bring him to the top. He reached national prominence in 1949 with a time of 14.0. That was still his personal best when he went to Fresno on 13 May 1950 for the annual West Coast Relays. In that meet he astounded experts by clipping half a second off that mark, thus succeeding Dillard with a new 120 y. hurdles record of 13.5. This rash improvement seemed to offer a replica of the 1936 Towns story, but any resemblance was soon dispelled when he won the AAU 110 m. hurdles title in 13.6. Then he came to Europe and on 10 July, at the Eläintarha (Zoological Garden) ground in Helsinki he ran another 13.5, this time over 110 m. hurdles. Attlesey was still on top in 1951 (13.6), but then injuries caused him to lose form and, like other world record holders, he disappeared from the front ranks on the eve of the 1952 Olympics. Dillard was by then returning to his first love, the hurdles, with élan. And in 1952 he laid all his eggs in that basket. Throughout the Olympic season, "Bones" had a formidable rival in Jack Davis. At the US Olympic Tryouts, Dillard prevailed, 14.0 to 14.1. So he did in the Games final, building up a lead in the early stages, then staving off Davis' counter-attack. Both were officially timed in 13.7, but the automatic timer showed 13.91 for Dillard and 14.00 for Davis. Art Barnard, third in 14.1, gave USA another grand slam, while Yevgeniy Bulanchik of USSR was fourth in 14.5. In Helsinki, as in London four years earlier, Dillard contributed to the success of the US sprint relay team. With a total of four Olympic gold medals (1948-52) he thus matched the tally of his boyhood hero, Jesse Owens. The Helsinki runner-up, Jack Davis (born at Amarillo, Texas, on 11 September

1941
1960

Alain Mimoun (France), left, marathon winner in the Melbourne Olympics (1956), and Emil Zátopek, sixth in same race. (Courtesy "Track & Field News").

1930; 1.90 m./81 kg.) was next in the line of America's great high hurdlers. Very strong and endowed with good speed (21.1 in the 200 m.), he worked for several years an average of four hours a day, a rather abundant ration for a hurdler. He improved from 14.6 in 1950 to 13.7 in 1951, then to 13.6 in 1953. He eventually reached the zenith of his form in 1956. Like Dillard, he thus waited (impatiently, I presume) four years to have another crack at the Olympics. But unlike Dillard, at the decisive moment he was to fall centimetres short of his goal. On 22 June 1956, in a heat of the AAU Championships at Bakersfield, California, Davis found the ideal conditions for a faultless race and clocked 13.4 for the 110 m. hurdles, eclipsing Attlesey's world record. Maybe that long-sought success put him off balance for a while, because he dropped to third in the final, behind Lee Calhoun (13.6) and Joel Shankle. Calhoun (born at Laurel, Mississippi, on 23 February 1933; 1.85 m./75 kg.) turned out to be no fluke, and Davis saw much, perhaps too much, of him in subsequent weeks. At the US Olympic Tryouts they dead-heated for first (13.8), while Shankle took third place. In a pre-Olympic meet at Bendigo, Victoria, on 17 November, Davis showed some fireworks: at the end of a 120 y. hurdles race he was timed in a nifty 13.3. Chief judge Ray Weinberg (Australian record holder at 14.0) used a "handkerchief anemometer" and ruled that there was no wind assistance. The Australian AAU accepted Davis' effort as an All Comers record as 13.4, just to be on the safe side. To be even safer, the IAAF simply ignored the Bendigo affair. Calhoun finished second in this race in 13.5. But the roles were reversed in the Olympic final at Melbourne (28 November): here Calhoun, was off faster and ran a steady race throughout. Davis again finished strongly but had to surrender. The time for both was 13.5 - quite impressive in view of the adverse wind (1.9 m/s). The automatic timer gave 13.70 for Calhoun and 13.73 for Davis. Once again, the man from Amarillo had been nosed out by a team-mate who was his master in getting off the marks. Davis thus had the rare fortune - or was it a misfortune? - of twice sharing an Olympic record, both times as a runner-up. With Shankle third in 14.1, USA scored another clean sweep. Martin Lauer of Germany was fourth in 14.5. Lauer (born at Köln on 2 January 1957; 1.86 m./75 kg.) loomed as a superlative talent since his earliest years in athletics. He took up the senior (1.06 m.) hurdles early in 1956 and crowned a meteoric rise on 22 September of that year at Hamburg with a nifty 13.9 for the metric distance, aided by the maximum permissible wind (2.0 m/s). He thus became the first non-American to duck under 14 seconds under legal circumstances. In early post-war years, European high hurdlers had been lagging far behind their American colleagues. Continental championship titles were won with such times as 14.6 (Lidman in 1946 and André-Jacques Marie of France in 1950) and 14.4 (Bulanchik in 1954). In 1957-58 Lauer rose to "American heights", running the 110 m. hurdles in 13.7 on six occasions, and winning the 1958 European title at Stockholm in one of them. He was to reach his peak in 1959, when he was offered the chance of his lifetime (as a record breaker that is) not once but twice, and both times on the Letzigrund track at Zurich, fast as lightning. On 16 May he lowered his European record to 13.5 and on 7 July he shattered Davis' world record with an incredible 13.2. In the latter race he won from Willie May of USA (13.6), while no less than five of the seven

Roy Cochran (USA) emerged as a world class 400 m. hurdler in 1939 but had to wait till 1948 to earn an Olympic crown.

entries equalled or bettered their previous bests. This detail, coupled with the fact that the starter of the race was known as a "fast gun", seemed to suggest the idea that the new record exaggerated the ability of the German champion. The wind in his favour was 1.9 m/s and an automatic timer caught Lauer in 13.56. Later in the year, at Wuppertal, Lauer beat Olympic champion Lee Calhoun, 13.9 to 14.0. The newly crowned world record holder (the first non-American to do the trick since 1931!) sustained an injury early in 1960. By early August, however, he had recovered to the point of doing 13.6, besides equalling his personal best for the 100 m. flat, 10.4. His main rivals in Rome were, of course, the three American entries - Calhoun, May and Hayes Jones. At the US Olympic Tryouts, Calhoun won in 13.4 from May and Jones (both 13.5). On 21 August, at Bern, Calhoun equalled Lauer's world record with a smooth and windless 13.2 effort, leaving Jones far behind (13.7). In the Rome Olympic final, Lauer fought bravely all the way but could not prevent another US sweep - the fourth in a row since 1948! Calhoun and May lunged at the tape simultaneously, and the former won by the proverbial whisker. The times (with the unofficial automatic readings in parentheses): Calhoun 13.8 (13.98), May 13.8 (13.99), Jones 14.0 (14.17), Lauer 14.0 (14.20). The German hit no less than three hurdles. The case of Calhoun, twice an Olympic champion by the narrowest of margins, contrasts neatly with that of Jack Davis, twice a runner-up (1952-56) by a similarly infinitesimal margin. But in the eyes of many casual observers the difference between "winner" and "loser" is al-ways an abnormally great one. In June 1961 Lauer was the victim of a serious foot infection and had to undergo a series of operations. This put an end to his career when he was only 24. In later years, he was to attain a certain degree of popularity as a singer of folk and Western music. Other leading Europeans of that period were Peter Hildreth of Britain, Stanko Lorger of Yugoslavia and Anatoliy Mikhailov of the USSR. The last two also had a personal best of 10.4 in the 100 m. flat, just like Lauer (who once did 10.2 with an aiding wind of 2.8 m/s).

1941
1960

Don Finlay (GB), twice an Olympic medallist in the "high hurdles" (1932 and '36), here winning a race at Chiswick in 1948, at the age of 39.

165

400 METRES HURDLES:
An indestructible "Jeep"

The world record for the 440 y. hurdles, definitely soft (52.6) if compared with Hardin's mark for the metric distance (50.6), was broken by Roy Cochran at Des Moines in 1942 with a 52.2 effort. The big difference between the two standards could partly be explained by the fact that in America the distance between hurdles in the 440 y. event was 40 y. (36.57 m.). Later on it was reduced to 35 m., to comply with that used for the 400 m. event. After serving with the US Navy during the war, Cochran returned to the track in 1946 and in the AAU Championships of that year, at San Antonio, Texas, he finished third in the 400 m. flat with a strong 46.7. He had his best season in 1948, aged 29. At the US Olympic Tryouts he had to work hard to emerge the winner in 51.7, barely ahead of Dick Ault (51.8), while Jeffrey Kirk nosed out George Walker (both 51.9) for the coveted third place. In the Olympic final at Wembley, Cochran stood head and shoulders above his rivals and won with a new personal record, 51.1. Duncan White, a 30-year-old veteran from Ceylon, was a fine second in 51.8, ahead of Rune Larsson of Sweden (52.2). Among those who just failed to make the final were Bertel ("Bebbe") Storskrubb of Finland, the 1946 European champion (52.2) and a 1:49.3 two-lap runner, and Jean-Claude ("Kiki") Arifon of France, who only a few weeks later at Stade Jean-Bouin in Paris was to equal Hölling's European record (51.6). Shortly afterwards, the 22-year-old "Kiki" ran into trouble over an affair of love and kleptomania, which eventually put paid to his promising career.

By 1950 Italy had found a man capable of reviving the tradition of Luigi Facelli in the person of Armando Filiput, who improved from 53.4 in 1949 to 51.9 in winning the European title at Brussels the following year. A few weeks later, at Milan's Arena, he lowered the world record for the 440 y. hurdles to 51.9, after equalling the European metric record (51.6) enroute. In his best races the tall (1.86 m.) Italian usually strode "seventeens" all the way between hurdles. But he was to be one of those athletes for whom the Olympics came when they were past their peak. In the 1952 Games at Helsinki he finished an undistinguished sixth.

Second to Filiput in the 1950 European Championships with 52.4 was Yuriy Lituyev of the USSR (born at Irbit near Sverdlovsk on 11 April 1925; 1.83 m./78 kg.), who was to become one of the most durable performers in the history of the event. Through years of assiduous application he showed what a relatively mediocre one-lap runner (his best for the 400 m. flat was 48.0 in 1958) could achieve over the "intermediates". He began with 53.1 in 1949 and by the same time he scored 6880 points (1934 Table) in the decathlon. His progress in subsequent years was steady: 52.4 (1950), 51.7 ('51), 51.2 ('52), by which time he was firmly established as Europe's no.1. In the 1952 Olympics he won the silver medal (more on this race later). In 1953 he ducked under 51 seconds for the first time in winning a close tussle with Anatoliy Yulin, 50.7 to 50.9, at the USSR Championships in Moscow. On 20 September of that year he used the fast Népstadion track in Budapest for an all-out effort. The split taken for him at the half-way mark (23.5) was fantastic for a man of limited possibilities in the domain of pure speed, yet he had enough left for a 26.9 effort in the second half. His final time, 50.4, thus broke Hardin's 19-year-old world record. In this race Lituyev strode "thirteens" up to the eighth hurdle, then "fifteens" the rest of the way. Yulin was a well beaten second in 51.4.

In 1954 Lituyev obstinately tried to stick to the "thirteen-all-the-way" schedule, but with little success. The tendency to insist in over-striding cost him dearly at the European Championships in Bern, where his perennial underdog Anatoliy Yulin shot ahead of him in the closing stage to win, 50.5 to 50.8. Yulin too was a product of hard work. He had a deceptively slow 49.0 as his best time on the flat route, hence a differential of merely 1.5 secs. Lituyev, no matter if bitterly disappointed, continued with dogged determination: after a fourth place in the 1956 Olympics, he finally struck gold at the 1958 European Championships in Stockholm, aged 33, with a 51.1 effort. In the meantime, the Americans continued to show little interest for the "intermediates". But they invariably fired up in time for the Olympics. In 1952 the man for the occasion was stocky Charles Moore (born at Coatesville, Pennsylvania, on 12 August 1929; 1.83 m./77 kg.), a 47.0 quarter-miler and, like Hardin, NCAA champion on the flat route. On the eve of the Helsinki Olympics he could point to four seasons of world leadership in the "intermediates", with times of 51.1 (1949), 51.5 ('50), 51.4 ('51) and 50.7 in the US Olympic Tryouts at Los Angeles in June 1952. On the fast Helsinki track he fully confirmed his competitive ability: he ran 51.8 (heat) and 50.8 (quarter-final) on 20 July, 52.0 (semi-final) and again 50.8 (final) on 21 July. In the decisive race he won from Lituyev (51.3) and John Holland of New Zealand (52.2). One cannot help noticing how great Moore was in his début at the distance, and how little he progressed (0.4 in three years) in the following seasons. Sporadic activity in the States (he ran the distance no more than 24 times in 1949-52) was probably the chief deterrent. Notwithstanding this monotonous trend, by 1956 America was able to field two super-athletes, Glenn Davis and Eddie Southern. I have referred to their meteoric rise in connection with the 400 m. flat. These great specimens of physical prowess needed little routine to reach the very top in the "intermediates". Davis, a Jack-of-all-trades in high-school competition, continued to show versatility as a student at Ohio State University (Owens' Alma Mater). He was excellent in the sprints, as well as in the "highs", the "lows" and the long jump (7.32). For his stamina and suppleness he was given the nickname "Jeep". In the spring of 1956 he made his début in the "intermediates" with 54.4. By his third try he was down to a sensational 50.8! Southern blossomed more or less by the same time. He could point to an early effort of 53.4 in 1955, when he was barely seventeen. In the Olympic year the tall Texan opened his account with a 51.6 for the metric distance, soon followed by a 51.5 for the 440 y. hurdles. He met Davis for the first time at the AAU Championships at Bakersfield, California, when Davis began to impose his rule by a decisive margin, 50.9 to 51.5. It was noted that Davis used the left, or inside, leg as his lead leg in going over the hurdles, thus respecting that rule (a golden one in turn running, according to experts) which Hardin and Cochran, among others, had neglected to observe. The next duel between Davis and Southern took place a week later at the US Olympic Tryouts in Los Angeles. The final of the 400 m. hurdles was run on 29 June at 9.30 p.m., some 90 minutes after the heats. Southern, in lane 5, was in an ideal position vis-à-vis Davis, lane 6. From the third to the last hurdle the two were never more than centimetres apart. When fatigue began to tell they were obliged to shorten their stride, and it was in that crucial stage that Davis proved what a great competitor he was. He won the historic race, 49.5 to 49.7. The 50-seconds barrier was finally broken, and by two men in the same race. Third in 50.6 was Josh Culbreath, who had been for three years (1953-55) the best, and perhaps the only real specialist of the "intermediates" in the States. He lost his supremacy for ever on that occasion. Davis used thirteen strides

1941
1960

Harrison Dillard, centre, on his way to victory in the 110 metre hurdles of the 1952 USA Olympic Trials in Los Angeles. Jack Davis, left, was second. Billy Anderson, right, lost the vital third place to Art Barnard, not visible in the picture. Dejected man kneeling on the ground is Craig Dixon, who fell and saw his Olympic dream go down in tubes.

between hurdles up to the seventh barrier, and seventeen thereafter. A few months later, in the Melbourne Olympics, he crowned a fantastic season in splendid fashion. There was an interval of two and a half hours between semi-finals and final. In the penultimate round Southern unnecessarily ran strongly throughout and won in 50.1, with Davis second in 50.7. In the final, Southern led Davis in the early going (22.5 to 22.7 at the fifth hurdle, i.e. at 185 m.), but ran out of gas in the crucial stage, and Davis was once again the winner by a decisive margin, 50.1 to 50.8. Gert Potgieter of South Africa was lying third with 50 m. to go but hit the last hurdle ("Heartbreak Hill") very badly, fell, and finished last. Consistent Josh Culbreath was third in 51.6, ahead of veteran Yuriy Lituyev (51.7) and David Lean of Australia (51.8). Davis was to reach the zenith of his form during his European "tournée" of 1958, after capturing the world record for the 440 y. hurdles at the AAU Championships with a 49.9 clocking. He ran the metric distance in 49.8 twice, in Oslo and Warsaw. On 6 August at Budapest, on the track where Lituyev had made history five years earlier, Davis strode "fifteens" all the way, hit the last hurdle and yet managed to finish in 49.2, a new world record. The persistent Culbreath was second in 50.5.

Almost at the same time a Springbok was rising to similarly spectacular hieghts: Gerhardus ("Gert") Potgieter. In the Empire Games at Cardiff in 1958 he lowered the world's 440 y. hurdles record to 49.7, winning from David Lean of Australia (50.6). The South African, a thick-set athlete seemingly made "à propos" for the "man-killer" event, had emerged with a significant 52.5 in 1955, after a short practice over the distance. In the 1956 Olympics he ran 51.3 in a semi-final, before meeting ill fate (as related above) in the final. This versatile performer hit the form of his lifetime early in 1960, twice beating his compatriot Mal Spence over 440 y. flat, clocking 46.3 on one of these occasions. On 16 April he celebrated his twenty-third birthday in the South African Championships at Bloemfontein with a superb 49.3 over 440 y. hurdles. In this race he strode "thirteens" only till the third hurdle and "fourteens" thereafter, thus changing his lead leg for the major part of the journey. The large circumference of the track (502.92 m.) and the altitude of Bloemfontein (1426 m.) may have favoured him to some extent. His long-awaited clash with Glenn Davis in the Rome Olympics did not materialize though: a few weeks before D-Day, Potgieter was involved in a car accident in Germany. He sustained major injuries, ultimately losing his left eye. Despite this grave handicap, he returned to the track a couple of years later and ran the 400 m. hurdles in 52.1, an almost unbelievable feat for a man in his condition. Davis, bothered by injuries in 1959, was back in stride for the Rome Olympics. At the Stadio Olimpico he became the first man in history to win the "intermediates" in two editions of the Games. He achieved his goal with a workmanlike effort in which his fighting spirit was definitely more in evidence than his rhythm. He had 200 m- fractions of 24.0 and 25.3 for a final time of 49.3. For once semi-finals and final were held on different days, and this obviously allowed the top men to run at their best when most needed. USA had another clean sweep, with Clifton Cushman second (49.6) and Dick Howard third (49.7). Helmut Janz of Germany was an unlucky fourth in 49.9 (23.9 + 26.0), but he became Europe's first sub-50 secs. performer. It should be noted that Janz, 26, had a differential of 2.1, clearly inferior to that of "Jeep" Davis (3.8). Two of the three triumphant Americans were to meet untimely deaths a few years later: Cushman in the Vietnam war (1966) and Howard because of an overdose of heroin (1967). Salvatore Morale of Italy, who had missed the Olympic final by the proverbial whisker, was the world's outstanding performer in 1961-62. A copybook stylist with an average pure speed quotient (47.6 for 400 m.), he emerged in 1957 with a scintillating 51.7, a European Junior (under 20) record, and second in the world only to Eddie Southern's 49.7 at the age of eighteen. It was at that time that I tipped him as "a Southern European who could become a European Southern". In fact, the Italian first matched and then surpassed his American colleague, clock-wise at least. On 15 October 1961 in Rome he lowered the European record to 49.7, going on to break a 440 y. tape in 50.1. The following year he had his Day of Days on 14 September at Belgrade, when he won the European title in 49.2 (200 m. fractions, 23.9 and 25.3), thereby equalling Davis' world record. In this race Morale strode "fifteens" all the way, as Davis had done in Budapest four years earlier. Jörg Neumann of Germany was second (50.3), upsetting his older compatriot Helmut Janz (50.5).

STEEPLECHASE:
Codified, at last

The Swedish boom in the distance events during the early Forties inevitably had bearing on steeplechase standards too. History's first sub-9 minute clocking was in fact registered at Stockholm on 4 August 1944, when Erik Elmsäter negotiated 3000 m. on a course including 37 hurdles - then the norm in advanced track countries - in 8:59.6. Born as Erik Pettersson in 1919, he had changed his last name to Elmsäter in 1940. Barely above average as a flat runner, he had mastered the hurdling technique to a notable extent. In the 1948 Olympics in London the Swedes monopolized honours with Thore Sjöstrand, Elmsäter and Göte Hagström, who finished 1-to-3 in that order. A dead track kept the winner's time (9:04.6) over Iso-Hollo's Olympic record. The menace to Swedish supremacy was expected to come from Raphaël Pujazon of France, the 1946 European champion (9:01.4), but the Frenchman was assailed by stomach trouble early in the race and had to retire.

The 1950 European Championships in Brussels provided the biggest upset in the history of the event. A virtually unknown Czech, Jindrich Roudny, whose best prior to that meet was an unimpressive 9:25.0, confounded experts with a runaway victory in 9:05.4. At the same time, a decisive step forward in the popularization of the steeplechase came from Russia. The first sub-10 minute clocking in the large Euro-Asian country was registered as late as in 1937, but in 1950 the number of Soviet steeplechasers capable of beating 10 minutes was sixty-two. By virtue of their methodical approach, the Russians reached the top in a relatively short time. Vladimir Kazantsev was probably the first "metronome" in the annals of the barrier event. Barely superior to Iso-Hollo in basic speed (8:18.4 vs. 8:19.6 in the 3000 m. flat), he worked assiduously on technical points and showed how much could be gained on that ground. In 1951 he ran the distance in 8:49.8, history's first sub-8:50 effort, and on 12 June 1952 at Kiev he improved to 8:48.6. Despite these brilliant performances, Kazantsev was to add his name to the long list of hot pre-Olympic favourites who were upset by dark-horses on the decisive day. His "bête noire" at Helsinki was an American, Horace Ashenfelter.

The steeplechase had never really caught on in the States. Opportunities for competition in the event were so rare that only a bright self-made man could break the ice. "Nip" Ashenfelter was such a man, even if he received help from coach "Chic" Werner while in college and was later inspired by his rival and friend Fred Wilt, whose contribution to the advancement of distance running in America was to become monumental. Ashenfelter had developed as a competitor in the heated "carrousel" of indoor tracks.

He went to Helsinki, aged 29, with a steeplechase best of 9:06.4. More significant was his time of 8:51.4 for 2 miles (without hurdles) indoors. On the fast Helsinki track he showed a complete lack of respect for the world's most renowned steeplechasers by winning his heat in a surprising 8:51.0. In the final, two days later, the early pace-setter was Mikhail Saltikov, Russia's second string (1000 m. in 2:49.8). Then Ashenfelter and Kazantsev were left alone to battle it out till the bitter end. Alternating in the lead, they reached 2000 m. in 5:47.4. The feud hit dramatic notes in the last lap. After a prolonged ding-dong battle, Kazantsev faltered in going over the last water jump and Ashenfelter drew away to win in 8:45.4, a new world's best and an improvement of 21 seconds over his pre-Games record! The real nip-and-tuck battle in the closing stage was between Kazantsev and John Disley of Britain, the Russian barely salvaging second place from the assault of the strong finishing Welshman, 8:51.6 to 8:51.8. The appreciative crowd lavishly cheered the heroes of the battle and had a specially warm applause for Olavi Rinteenpää, not only because he was a Finn but rather because he put up a personal best of 8:55.2 in finishing fifth. A year later, on the same track, Rinteenpää improved to a world's best of 8:44.4.

At the 1954 IAAF Congress in Bern, definite rules for the 3000 m. steeplechase were finally adopted and the event was added to the list of official world records. Such rules, still in force at the present time, required the inclusion of five hurdles for every lap. One of these, namely the fourth, projects into a water jump, which as a permanent feature obviously has to be placed inside the normal track. Because of this anomaly, a steeplechase lap is usually 390 m. in circumference. The course is flat in the initial 280 m., then comprises a total of 28 hurdle jumps and 7 water jumps, and turns flat again for the final 68 m. The water jump is a 3.66 m. square with a depth of 70 cm. Following the introduction of these rules, even in English speaking countries the 3000 m. supplanted the original 2-mile distance.

No retro-active ratification of records was considered, and so the inaugural world record was naturally provided by the 1954 European Championships in Bern. Sándor Rozsnyói of Hungary earned title and record with 8:49.6. The codification of the event obviously produced increasing interest, and a growing number of better-than-average middle-distance men turned their attention to the steeplechase. Among them was Jerzy Chromik of Poland, who in 1955 twice bettered the world record, finally with an 8:40.2 clocking at Budapest on 11 September, in a victorious duel with Rozsnyói (8:45.2). In the same year the Pole ran 1500 m. on the flat in 3:44.8. He was later hampered by poor health and his further activity was sporadic.

The year 1956 saw increased activity at the top level,

1941
1960

and prior to the Melbourne Olympics the world record was bettered twice, first by Semyon Rzhishchin of USSR in Moscow with 8:39.8, then by European champion Rozsnyói in Budapest with 8:35.6 (actual time 8:35.5). But the Olympic title went to an outsider, Christopher Brasher, a 28-year-old Briton born in British Guiana. A couple of years earlier, Brasher had enjoyed indirect fame as one of the main characters in the play of Roger Bannister's historic sub-4 minute mile at Oxford. He went to Australia with a personal best of 8:47.2. In the decisive race he literally surpassed himself: he killed the opposition with a last kilometre in 2:47.2 and won in 8:41.2. At first he was disqualified on charges of having hindered an opponent, Ernst Larsen of Norway. But the Jury of Appeal, after hearing the parties involved, came to the conclusion that the foul had been unintentional and not a determining factor in the outcome of the race. Brasher was consequently reinstated as winner of the gold medal. Sándor Rozsnyói was second (8:43.6) and Larsen was third (8:44.0).

Chromik, who earlier in the season had run the 3000 m. flat in an eye-catching 7:56.4, could not compete in the Olympics because of illness. He made a brilliant comeback in 1958. On 2 August of that year, at Warsaw, he lowered the world record to 8:32.0, after a hot battle with his countryman Zdzislaw Krzyszkowiak, who finished second in 8:33.6. In this race Chromik covered the first half in 4:19.5 and the second in a startling 4:12.5. Later in the month, at Stockholm, Chromik won the European title in 8:38.2, after outsprinting former world record holder Rzhishchin (8:38.8). Here the theme of the race was technique (Rzhishchin) vs. speed (Chromik), and the latter won the day. The above-mentioned Krzyszkowiak (born at Wielichowo on 3 August 1929; 1.72 m./59 kg.) was a great distance runner on the flat as well as over hurdles. He too was hampered by poor health at times, but managed to earn a solid reputation with a series of brilliant performances. In the 1958 European Championships he left the steeplechase to the care of his compatriot Jerzy Chromik, in order to concentrate on the 5000 and 10,000 m., and, as previously related, he won both events in impressive fashion. In 1960, his tenth season as an active steeplechaser, "Krzys" really cornered the market. On 26 June at Tula he won a hot duel from Nikolay Sokolov of USSR, 8:31.4 to 8:32.4, his new world record resulting from kilometre fractions in 2:49.0, 2:53.5 and 2:48.9. The Pole went on to score a smashing victory in the Rome Olympics, braving the heat and redoubtable opposition with a remarkable 8:34.2 effort. Sokolov was again the runner-up (8:36.4).

JUMPS - High Jump: Russians upset Thomas

American jumpers broke into the world record department again in 1941. It all started with a most unusual coincidence: on 26 April 1941, Walker's world record (2.09) was exceeded twice within a few hours - at different sites. First Bill Stewart jumped 2.092 at Provo, Utah; then Les Steers went over a crossbar set at 2.102 at Seattle, Washington. The latter showed great consistency throughout the entire season and crowned an unprecedented series with a jump of 2.108 at Los Angeles on 17 June. (Strangely enough, the IAAF ratified the mark as 2.11). Lester Steers (born at Eureka, California, on 16 June 1917; 1.87 m./88 kg.) perfected the straddle to a most remarkable degree. His body sometimes appeared to be draped around the crossbar. The heavy type of jumper, he was a precision instrument the like of which the world had never seen before. One day, during a training session, he jumped at 6 ft. 6 in. (1.981) thirteen times, just one after another, and made twelve of them. Early in 1941, during an indoor exhibition at Eugene, he went over a bar set at 2.146 - the first known effort over 7 feet (2.134), no matter if unofficial. Steers had emerged as a High School boy in 1936 with 1.965. He continued to progress regularly: 1.981 in 1937 and 1938, 2.038 in 1939, and 2.067 in 1940, when he also mastered 2.086 in an exhibition. He was AAU champion twice (1939-40), but strangely lost to Bill Stewart on the fewer misses count in the 1941 meet, after both had cleared 2.076. World War II obviously put a premature end to his career, but for many years to come he was recalled by coaches and athletes as a steady reference point in terms of technique. At a Coaches Clinic in 1941, Steers revealed that his weight had increased from 80 kg. in 1940 to 88 kg. in 1941. His best with the Western Roll was 2.038.

The crisis brought about by years of limited activity was well reflected in the result of the 1948 Olympics in London. John Winter of Australia, who could point to a personal best of 2.013, won the gold medal at 1.98. He had a wrenched back and made the winning height in a gallant effort, after which he had to call it a day. Fortunately for him, not one of his rivals was able to fight back successfully. For once the Americans had to be content with third and fourth place. Steers' successor appeared in the early Fifties in the person of Walter Davis, an American who was a victim of polio in the early years of his life. He gamely recovered and, like other great athletes, used sport as a vehicle towards complete physical rehabilitation. In 1952 he won the Olympic title at Helsinki with a 2.04 jump that matched his own height. On 27 June 1953, at the AAU Championships in Dayton, Ohio, he raised the world record to 2.124. He even went over 7 feet in unofficial tries. Davis had a relatively short career and left the athletic arena without having explored his full potential. At the Helsinki Olympics, third place went to José Telles da Conceição of Brazil with 1.98. To this day one of the greatest talents to come out of South America, Telles became in 1954 the first 2-metre jumper from that continent and in 1956 he finished sixth in the 200 m. at the Melbourne Olympics. At the end of his career he could point to such marks as 10.2 (100 m.), 20.8 (200 m.), 7.40 (long jump) and 6173 pts. (decathlon, 1950 Scoring Table). In athletics, conventional limits likely to give food for thought often amount to a psychological barrier. The 7-foot (2.134 m.) high jump had been a most elusive target for leading English speaking jumpers for decades. The trouble lies in the fact that the athlete knows exactly what he is up against, and that often makes him "sick". A typical example was Ernie Shelton, a very consistent Californian, who in 1953-55 collected no less than 21 competitive marks in the range 2.08/2.115. He was probably the first among top-class jumpers to effectively combine the straddle with a dive. The rule under which at least one of the competitor's feet should clearly precede the head over the bar had been repealed late in the Thirties, and as time went by the advantages offered by the new situation were being grasped by an ever growing number of jumpers. Shelton flirted with the 7-foot barrier for years, repeatedly failing to make it by infinitesimal margins. In few events, if any, can the difference between a failure by a hair's breadth and a lucky clearance (with the bar quivering) be as little as in the high jump. But athletics history, like all history, does not consider near failures. A worthy "pendant" to Shelton in form and consistency was Bengt Nilsson of Sweden (born at Härnösand on 17 February 1934; 1.81 m./67 kg.), who put Europe back on the world high jump map. For years, results at the European Championships had been indicative of a low ebb. Anton Bolinder of Sweden won at Oslo in 1946 with 1.99, a personal best. Four years later, at Brussels, Alan Paterson, a Scotsman who held the British record with 2.019 (1947), topped the field with 1.96. Incidentally, Paterson was only 19 when he achieved his record mark. Nilsson used a polished version of the dive straddle and eventually became Sweden's most popular athlete since the days of Hägg and Andersson. He first mastered 2 metres in 1953 with a 2.01 effort. He had his best year in 1954. After breaking Kotkas' European record at Halmstad with a 2.05 clearance, he really went wild at Göteborg on 15 July: jumping from the same take-off that had yielded Kotkas' record (2.04) in 1936, he improved on his fresh record three times in the space of 14 minutes, clearing 2.06, 2.08 and 2.10 - a true masterpiece in the art of concentration. Following an easy win in the European Championships at Bern (2.02), Nilsson closed his 1954 account with a 2.114 jump on 19 September, still at Göteborg. That was an improvement of 10 cm. over his 1953 best.

Between 1953 and 1955, Nilsson and Shelton met several times in Scandinavian meets and each had his share of victories. After collecting ten marks at 2.08 or higher in 1954-56, Nilsson was unlucky enough to be hit by injury on the eve of the 1956 Olympics, in which he competed as a severely handicapped man. After that bitter experience, he lost interest and consequently disappeared from the picture. Curiously enough, the year 1956 also proved to be the swan song of Ernie Shelton. Either or both of them may have run out of nervous energy as a result of their most exacting schedule in the preceding years.

The decline of Shelton and Nilsson curiously coincided with the arrival of history's first (official) 7-foot jumper. This was Charles Dumas (born at Tulsa, Oklahoma, on 12 February 1937; 1.87 m./81 kg.). He used a surprisingly slow run, but had a tremendous lift. He matured to athletic greatness in the favourable California climate and progressed from 1.969 in 1954 to 2.089 in 1955. He was crowned world record holder on a most significant occasion - the US Olympic Tryouts at Los Angeles on 29 June 1956.

This agile athlete straddled over a bar set at 2.15 on his second attempt and thus broke by a clear margin one of the toughest mental barriers. Shelton, fifth with 2.045, failed to qualify for Melbourne. The ever turning wheel of life: an old champion was dead, a new champion was born. In Australia Dumas, who had not turned 20 yet, found a hard nut to crack in Charles ("Chilla") Porter of Brisbane, his senior by only one year. Inspired by the familiar atmosphere, the Australian made the day of the Olympic final the greatest of his athletic career. During the competition he managed to improve on his previous best (2.038) three times, a fantastic achievement in such a long drawn event as an Olympic final. Finally he sailed over 2.10. Dumas, who appeared to have no nerves, gathered himself together and clinched the gold medal by going over 2.12 on his third attempt. Igor Kashkarov of USSR was third (2.08), while Stig Pettersson of Sweden, Nilsson's heir apparent, took fourth place at

1941
1960

2.06. Experts were greatly impressed by the excellent co-ordination of Kashkarov, a heavy jumper weighing 88 kg. That was the earliest sign of Russia's coming of age as a new high jump power. In 1954 Yuriy Styepanov had placed fifth in the European Championships with an unprepossessing 1.93, but the following year he raised the USSR record to 2.02, thus improving by one centimetre the pre-war mark of Nikolay Kovtun, a man whose incredible vicissitudes have been related in a previous chapter.

By 1956 Styepanov had changed from the Eastern cut-off to the dive straddle, improving to 2.04. In June 1957 he upped his best to 2.09 and on 13 July of the same year at Leningrad, his native town, he sailed over 2.11, and then raised the world record to 2.16 (actual height, 2.162). Quite obviously, the spectacular feat of the 25-year-old Russian aroused a great deal of curiosity, which increased further when later in 1957 two other Russians, Vladimir Sitkin and Igor Kashkarov, came up with marks of 2.15 and 2.14 respectively. No matter how good the technique of these men, their progress seemed somewhat unreal to certain observers. Very soon it transpired that these and other Russian jumpers were using a thick (2 to 4 cm.) sole in the shoe of their take-off foot. Such a device, which offered obvious advantages, was not a Russian invention though. Experiments along that line had been made in other countries long before then, e.g. by Bengt Nilsson, even though he was once quoted as saying that he had never used a built-up shoe in any of the major meets. At any rate, the new fashion quickly caught on, and very soon every top class jumper in Europe had a built-up shoe of his own. Marks well over 2 metres became commonplace. The IAAF, reacting to urges from several quarters, finally banned the "orthopaedic shoe" and set the maximum permissible thickness of soles at 13 millimetres.

But the stable door was closed in 1958, with no retro-active measures, and in the meantime Styepanov's 2.16 had been ratified as a world record. At the 1958 European Championships in Stockholm, Styepanov did 2.06 and had to be content with sixth place. The event was a real thriller and victory finally went to a Swedish outsider, Rickard Dahl, who came through with 2.12, his best ever. Jirí Lánsky of Czechoslovakia and Stig Pettersson of Sweden were second and third respectively (both 2.10). Russia's spectacular rise as a major high jump power continued well beyond the interlude

John Thomas (USA), a great high jumper in the early Sixties.

of the built-up shoe. In the two earliest USA vs USSR dual meets (1958-59), former world record holder Charles Dumas was bea-ten, first by Styepanov, then by Robert Shavlakadze. Early in 1960, however, the appearance of a new and truly gigantic American prospect seemed likely to shift the balance in favour of USA again. John Curtis Thomas (born at Boston on 3 March 1941; 1.96 m./88 kg.) was the prototype of what technicians call a natural talent. This powerfully built man improved from 1.73 in 1956 to 1.95 in 1957, then 2.10 during a "tournée" in Japan in 1958. He mastered 7 feet (2.134) for the first time indoors, in 1959, and a few weeks later he improved to 2.165, still from boards. On the eve of the outdoor season he caught his left (take-off) foot in an elevator shaft. The injury was so serious that he only returned to action towards the end of the year. But in 1960 he resumed his ascension. First he raised the indoor record to 2.197, then he moved outdoors and in the space of two months he bettered the official world record time and again, with 2.171, 2.178, 2.184 and finally 2.229. This last effort (actually measured as 2.232 but later rounded down to the nearest quarter of an inch) occurred in the US Olympic Tryouts at Palo Alto, California, on 1 July. The other two qualifiers for the trip to Rome, 18-year-old Joe Faust and Dumas, were left far behind, with 2.134 and 2.108 respectively. The amazing consistency of the new world record holder stamped him as an odds-on favourite for the Olympic crown. In the meantime, however, the Russians were working really hard to make up for lost ground. The trio they selected for Rome was a redoubtable one. It consisted of Robert Shavlakadze, a moustached Georgian with a personal best of 2.13; Viktor Bolshov, a 21-year-old talent who had improved in two years from 1.95 to 2.15; and Valeriy Brumel, then eighteen, who had been picked at the last moment: after placing no better than sixth at the USSR Championships, he suddenly rose to a spectacular European record of 2.17 in mid-August. Yet few international experts, if any, interpreted the latest Russian pre-Olympic news as an alarm signal for John Thomas.

But on 1 September, at Rome's Stadio Olimpico, things took an unexpected turn. Thomas, who until then had been fighting mainly against records rather than opponents, found himself confronted with a different challenge. As the contest unfolded, his mood changed from over-confidence to fear. At first he neglected to warm up between jumps, and by the time he rose to the challenge mentally, nervous tension did the rest. Best he could do for the day was a second-time clearance at 2.14, but so did Brumel and Bolshov, while Shavlakadze needed only one jump to clear that height. At 2.16 the 27-year-old Georgian was over on his first attempt, Brumel on his second, while Thomas and Bolshov failed three times. On the fewer trials and misses rule, Thomas barely salvaged third place, ahead of Bolshov, while veteran Shavlakadze edged Brumel for the gold medal. Stig Pettersson was fifth (2.09) and defending champion Dumas was sixth (2.03).

The three Soviets were athletes of strong but not exceptional build: Shavlakadze 1.86m./ 82 kg; Brumel 1.85 m./77 kg.; Bolshov 1.83 m./80 kg. Their splendid co-ordination in every phase of the exercise allowed them to make up for their physical inferiority vis-à-vis Thomas. They came to Rome "oiled" to perfection and fully determined to make things difficult for the fresh world record holder. Shavlakadze, a smooth belly-roller, was by Rome time the most experienced of the trio, but Brumel was the rising star and on 25 October, at Uzhgorod, he raised the European record to 2.20 (actual height, 2.203). Born at Tolbuzhino, Siberia, on 14 April 1942, as a youth he had hardly shown a particular vocation for high jumping: his best at 14 was 1.40. The next two years were of decisive importance for his future career: between 1957 and 1958 he improved from 1.75 to 1.95. His first coach was Pyotr Stein, who introduced him to weight training, by then considered as one of the most effective media for the conditioning of an athlete. In 1959 Brumel upped his best to 2.01. Early in 1960 he came under the wing of Vladimir Dyachkov, a former pole vaulter (4.20 in 1939), then regarded as the most knowledgeable high jump coach in Russia and possibly in the world. More on Brumel and his major deeds in the chapter devoted to the period 1961-1980.

POLE VAULT - From the incomparable "Dutch" to the Metal Era

After breaking the 15-foot (4.57) barrier in 1940, Cornelius Warmerdam went from strength to strength. From then on his ability practically knew no bounds. With unmatched perseverance he went higher and higher: 4.64 and 4.71 in 1941, 4.74 and 4.77 in 1942. The last mark occurred at Modesto, California, on 23 May, and his clearance of the record height was so ample that one official estimated his effort as worth 4.82. Spectators broke the crossbar into bits for souvenirs! From board runways, indoors, Warmerdam did 4.58 and 4.75 in 1942, and finally 4.78 at Chicago on 20 March 1943. He achieved the last of his forty-three vaults over 15 feet (4.57) in winning the 1944 AAU outdoor title at New York. He was then a naval lieutenant, and that was to remain his last appearance in big-time competition. Eight years later, at the age of thirty-seven, he cleared 4.37 in an exhibition. With the war draining the ranks of America'a active vaulters, Warmerdam had no competition to spur him on during his best years. All the greater, therefore, was his merit for conquering previously unexplored heights the way he did. At the end of 1944 his lead vis-à-vis history's second best performer was as great as 23 cm.! Yet in the opinion of American technicians he contributed little new, if anything, to the art of pole vaulting. As Ken Doherty once put it, "he simply did everything right that others had been trying to do for years". Above all, "Dutch" maintained that all phases of the exercise should unfold as one continuous movement, with no pauses or hitches of any kind. In his vaults at the major heights he would use a grip of 4.03 m., measured from the lower part of the upper hand to the ground. Remarkably enough, in training he would never try anything above 14 feet (4.26). After the retirement of this phenomenon, the debate among the world's leading vaulters was resumed at pre-Warmerdam heights. It was as if someone had put the clock of history back several years. At the 1948 Olympics in London, Guinn Smith of USA won the title of world champion with a 4.30 vault. After doing 4.43 as early as in 1941, aged twenty-one, he had lost his best athletic years because of the war. He qualified for the Games with a 4.47 effort, and in London he braved the risk of a water-logged runway and the pain of a tightly strapped knee to win the title from Erkki Kataja of Finland and Bob Richards of USA, who finished in that order, both with 4.20. By this time, however, the bamboo pole was being replaced with a metal pole of carefully blended alloys. Whether the new material represented a definite improvement over the best bamboo types is still a matter of debate. The metal pole was generally conceded to be slightly less flexible, but safer than the bamboo pole. Be as it may, the "fashion" of 15-foot vaults introduced by Wamerdam did not catch on until 1951. The ice was broken in an indoor meet early in the year, when Bob Richards, the London bronze medallist, slipped over a bar set at 4.59. Less than two months later he was up to 4.69, still indoors. Meanwhile another vaulter, Don Laz, had mastered 4.59 under similar conditions. It is generally conceded that boards provide some additional spring. On 21 April there were two 15-foot efforts outdoors too, at different sites and within a few hours of each other: first by Don Cooper with 4.57 at Lawrence, Kansas, then by Laz with 4.61 at Los Angeles. Laz in particular was acknowledged to have a great potential, but for some reason he fell somewhat below expectations. By the end of his career his best was 4.62, and he went 2 cm. higher indoors. Cooper, who was a 9.7 100 y. man, had a somewhat sporadic career and failed to improve

The deceptive side of progress

Bob Richards and Don Laz, two great vaulters who won gold and silver respectively at the 1952 Olympics, both had sons who aimed at surpassing their parents in the same art. Markwise, Bob Richards Jr. and Doug Laz can be said to have been successful: in fact, they scaled heights of 5.33 (1973) and 5.30 (1976) respectively, i.e. well beyond their fathers' marks (4.72 for the Reverend Richards, 4.64 for Laz). Apart from the fact that "juniors" had the advantage of using fibre-glass poles, it is however a fact that neither managed to make an impact on the vaulting élite of the Seventies. Doug Laz had to be content with fifth place at the 1976 US Olympic Trials, and Richards Jr. never made the grade in top-class competition. In the meantime there had been a revolution in vaulting standards and the "price of glory" had risen to spectacular heights. Hence the deceptive side of progress. Something similar had previously happened to the offspring of other famous champions, e.g. to Morgan ("Buzz") Taylor Jr., a son of the 1924 Olympic 400 m. hurdles champion. "Buzz" elected to specialize in what had been his father's second love, the long jump. He excelled daddy's best with a 7.77 effort but did not go beyond a fourth place at the 1952 US Olympic Tryouts. A better achievement was that of Billy Hardin, a son of the 1936 Olympic 400 m. hurdles champion. In 1964 he ran the distance in 49.8, bettering his father's onetime world record (50.6), and in so doing he qualified for the Tokyo Olympics. But in the Games he was eliminated in the penultimate round. Athletic annals show at least one chain connecting father and son in the happiest possible way. That belongs to a Hungarian family and I will tell the story in connection with the period 1961-1980.

further. Robert Richards (born at Champaign, Illinois, on 20 February 1926; 1.78 m./74 kg.) was the first vaulter who managed to lift himself to heights in the "Warmerdam region". Like "Dutch", he was a good but not exceptional performer in his early years. By 1947, his last year in college, his best was 4.30. But he had plenty of strength and determination, and by dint of hard work he eventually managed to reach the top. At the end of his long career he could point to personal records of 4.70 outdoors (1956) and 4.72 indoors (1957). This dedicated athlete, who as a youth had known some of the difficult sides of life, failed in his repeated attempts to surpass Warmerdam, whom he once described as "part sprinter, part shock-absorber, part acrobat, and part strong man - simply not human". Even so, Richards had great success as a competitor. He became the first vaulter in history to win the Olympic title twice. At Helsinki in 1952 he won from Don Laz, 4.55 to 4.50, and at Melbourne in 1956 he won from Bob Gutowski, 4.56 to 4.53, each time at the end of a long-drawn contest. Richards won nine outdoor and eight indoor pole vault titles in AAU competition. And he exceeded Warmerdam in quantity, if not in quality, amassing a tally of 126 vaults over 15 feet (4.57). As a minister of religion, he once apologized for having done no better than 4.67 in a big night meet, to which he had gone after making five sermons in as many different cities over the preceding five days! As a decathlon man, far from polished in some events, he was good enough to win the AAU title three times. His best under the 1950 scoring table was 7313 pts (1954).

In the early Fifties, European vaulting standards showed an encouraging upward trend. For many years in the past, several of the best vaulters from Europe had been good gymnasts with little basic speed. This situation was now being remedied, and the two men who dominated the continental picture in those years were both capable of 14.7 in the "high" hurdles. They were Ragnar ("Ragge") Lundberg of Sweden and Pyotr Denisenko of USSR. The former was European champion in 1950 with a 4.30 vault and figured prominently in three editions of the Olympics: fifth in 1948 and 1956, third in 1952. He held the European record for several years and wound up with a lifetime best of 4.46 in 1956. Denisenko was fourth at the 1952 Olympics and achieved his best, 4.46, in 1954, when he was thirty-four. In terms of longevity, he nearly matched his predecessor Nikolay Ozolin, in that he still managed 4.30 at thirty-nine. Denisenko also amassed 6680 pts in the decathlon (under the 1950 scoring table). Further progress towards American heights was achieved by Eeles Landström of Finland and Georgios Roubanis of Greece, both of whom, however, learned some of the finer points as students in American universities. Landström was European champion twice, with 4.40 in 1954 and 4.50 in 1958. Roubanis mastered 4.60 in 1958 and was probably the first man to use a fibre-glass pole in a major meet: it happened at the 1956 Olympics in Melbourne, where he won a bronze medal with 4.50. By that time the advancement in overall standards in the States was such as to suggest that Warmerdam's record (4.77) would be beaten quite soon. The long-awaited successor was Bob Gutowski (born at San Pedro, California, on 25 April 1935; 1.83 m./68 kg.). After a rather unimpressive start, this light-footed American made the big jump between nineteen and twenty-one: 4.00 in 1954, 4.43 in 1955, 4.70 in 1956. The last mark came several weeks after the US Olympic Tryouts, in which Gutowski had finished fourth, thus failing to make the team under the rigid selective system followed by the AAU. Later in the summer, the man who had shunted Gutowski to the unpleasant fourth place, Jim Graham, dislocated an ankle. On the eve of the Melbourne Games, Graham was still struggling to regain top form, just when Gutowski was beginning to reveal his great potential. In this peculiar situation, Graham generously gave up his right to compete in the Olympics so that a better man could represent the States. As an outstanding commentator put it, "Gutowski's 4.70 convinced Graham that America needed Gutowski more than Graham needed the very great honour of competing in the Olympics". Incidentally, Jim was a son of Glenn Graham, the man who lost the 1924 Olympic pole vault title in a jump-off. As related above, Gutowski proved worthy of the sensitive choice of his companion by finishing second at Melbourne. But his greatest hour came on 27 April 1957 at Palo Alto, California, when he succeeded Warmerdam as world record holder with a 4.78 clearance. Gutowski, a 9.9 100 y. sprinter, made his record with an aluminium pole. On 15 June of the same year, at Austin, Texas, he improved to 4.82, but owing to a difference of opinion over a technicality the mark was accepted by the AAU and not by the IAAF. It may be of interest to record that Gutowski long jumped 7.39 some forty minutes before beating Warmerdam's record for the first time. In 1960 he raised his best for the horizontal jump to 7.54. At the same time, however, he slipped to seventh in the pole vault at the US Olympic Tryouts Later in the summer he died in a car accident. Last of the great metal pole vaulters was Don Bragg.

This powerful acrobat, aptly nicknamed "Tarzan", was a precocious talent. He managed 4.19 at eighteen and mastered 15 feet (4.57) for the first time at twenty. In 1959 he raised the indoor record to 4.81 and on 2 July 1960 at Palo Alto, California, he won the event at the US Olympic Tryouts with a new world outdoor record of 4.80, which mark was curiously inferior to Gutowski's American record. Bragg, one of the biggest (1.90 m./89 kg.) men in the annals of the event up to that time, went on to capture the Olympic title in Rome with a 4.70 clearance, a remarkable achievement after nearly six hours of a tantalizing contest. His compatriot Ron Morris was second at 4.60, while two "American-educated" vaulters, Eeles Landström of Finland and Rolando Cruz of Puerto Rico, took third and fourth respectively, both with 4.55. Among those who fell below expectations were two Europeans, Janis Krasovskis of USSR and Manfred Preussger of Germany, who held the continental record at 4.65. Vladimir Bulatov of USSR, a Siberian who in 1959 had matched Bragg at Philadelphia with a 4.64 vault, sustained a severe ankle injury in a practice vault and could not compete. Bragg retired after a low-key season in 1961.

LONG JUMP: Owens' successor finally arrives

Not surprisingly, the post-Owens era was marked by a definite regress in top performances. It was only in the Forties that a real menace to Owens' record (8.13) appeared in the person of Willie Steele, an American who had the muscular power of Eulace Peacock. In the spring of 1942, just before turning nineteen, Steele reached 7.80. Then the war put a halt to his development. After serving with the US Army in the Mediterranean area, Steele returned to civilian life and athletics and in 1947 he came dangerously close to Owens' mark with a leap of 8.07. This occurred at Salt Lake City (altitude, 1338 m.). He qualified for the 1948 Olympics with 7.97 and on that occasion he had a hairline foul of 8.18. In London, not even a bad leg could prevent him from clinching the gold medal with 7.825. A man whose potentialities were never fully tapped was Andy Stanfield, the Olympic 200 m. champion of 1952. In one of his relatively rare attempts, in 1951, he reached 7.85. At the 1952 Olympics in Helsinki the event was dominated by two Americans, Jerome Biffle and Meredith Gourdine, who finished one-two in that order, with 7.57 and 7.53 respectively. The first white jumper beyond the 8 m. line did not appear until 1955. This man was John Bennett of USA, whose 8.01 at the Pan American Games in Mexico City was not good enough for victory, since his compatriot Ross Range sailed 8.03 on the same occasion.

A man who chased Owens' record for years was Greg Bell, who over a period of four years (1956-59) had three competitive efforts between 8.09 and 8.10. He won the Olympic title at Melbourne in 1956. That competition provided a typical example of how athletic performances can be influenced by atmospheric conditions. During the long jump final the wind ranged from 14 m/s adverse to 9 m/s favourable! Bell and Bennett finished one-two and achieved their best marks in the face of the wind: 7.83 and 7.68 respectively. The bronze medal went to consistent Jorma Valkama of Finland (7.48). As time went on, Owens' record tended to become a myth. But even in the so-called natural events, progress cannot be delayed indefinitely. In Europe, Long's continental record from pre-war days (7.90) was finally beaten at Bucharest in 1956 by a Dutchman hailing from Curaçao, Henk Visser, who reached 7.98. A great stylist but rather nervous and prone to injuries, Visser probably missed the chance of his lifetime later in the same year, when the Dutch team withdrew from the Melbourne Olympics.

Europe's first 8 m. man was Igor Ter-Ovanesyan (born at Kiev on 19 May 1938; 1.86 m./78 kg.), a man of Armenian extraction whose father Aram had been USSR record holder in the discus (42.595 in 1933). Acknowledged to possess great natural gifts, Ter-Ovanesyan showed remarkable versatility: 10.4 (100 m.), 2.00 (high jump) and 7184 pts (decathlon, 1950 scoring table). With his high aggregate of speed and elevation, he was obviously attracted by the long jump. At eighteen, in 1956, he made the headlines with a jump of 7.74, but the Melbourne Olympics found him too "green" and he did not go beyond the qualifying round.

Two years later he was crowned European champion in Stockholm with 7.81. On 16 May 1959, in Moscow, he bettered the continental record with 8.01, even though he fell back in landing. Europe finally had a man capable of threatening America's best. By 1960 Germany had an excellent prospect in Manfred Steinbach, who had emerged as a good sprinter (10.4 and 21.2) while living in East Germany. After taking up residence in the Federal Republic, he concentrated on the long jump. He "exploded" on 24 July 1960 in Berlin: after breaking Long's German record with 7.93, he took advantage of a gust of wind (3.2 m/s) to reach 8.14. This mark was fractionally superior to Owens' world record, but conditions obviously made it unacceptable. That was the lightning. The thunder came on 12 August 1960 at Walnut, California, when a lean American by the name of Ralph Boston made a tremendous leap of 8.21 in windless conditions. This phenomenal effort capped a brilliant series: 7.26 (he sat back in the pit!) - 7.94 - 8.07 - 7.96 - 8.21 - pass. He took a 37 m. run for his record jump. Boston (born at Laurel, Mississippi, on 9 May 1939; 1.87 m./74 kg.) had come to the fore at twenty with an excellent 7.69. In his junior days he was, like Owens, a 24-foot (7.31) jumper. At the peak of his career he could point to the following marks: 13.7 (120 y. hurdles), 22.4 (220 y. hurdles, straightaway), 2.057 (high jump) and 15.45 (triple jump). He had fair speed and could do a 9.7 100 y.

With three 8 m. men in the field, the Rome Olympic final (2 September) not surprisingly outshone even the great Berlin event of 1936. Boston won, as expected, with a new Olympic record of 8.12, achieved on his third attempt. But the next three place winners were close on his heels. The most serious challenger was his compatriot Irvin ("Bo") Roberson, a tall, muscular man who produced the finest leap of his career, 8.11, on the very last jump of the competition. Ter-Ovanesyan was third with a new European record of 8.04 and Manfred Steinbach fourth with 8.00, a new German record. Jorma Valkama took fifth with 7.69: this consistent Finn was to die only two years later.

TRIPLE JUMP -
A soloist from Brazil:
A.F. da Silva

Last of the great Japanese triple jumpers was Genken Kim, actually a Korean who in the geopolitical situation of the early Forties represented the land of the Rising Sun. He was born in Korea on 13 December 1918 as Won Kwon-kim. As a junior, in 1937, he reached 15.23, and two years later he had a successful European "tournée". He was the world leader for several years, with top marks of 15.82 in 1941 and 15.86 in 1943, and also did 7.66 in the long jump. In the early years of his career he was apparently criticized by some experts for using a "hop" definitely shorter than that prevalent in the Oda school. But later on he was acknowledged to possess a fine balance in the various phases of the exercise. He is said to have bettered Tajima's world record (16.00) in training. After World War II he was able to represent his native country at the 1948 Olympics in London: by then past his peak, he finished an undistinguished twelfth with 14.25, six centi-

metres behind one A.F. da Silva (more about him later in this chapter). The winner in London was Arne Åhman of Sweden, who beat George Avery of Australia in a tight duel, 15.40 to 15.365. Ruhi Sarialp of Turkey was third with 15.025. Åhman was to excel also as a high jumper (1.99).

The first phenomenon of the post-Japan era came from a country hitherto undistinguished in athletics - Brazil. This was Adhemar Ferreira da Silva (born at São Paulo on 29 September 1927; 1.77 m./69 kg.). Prior to his appearance on the scene, Brazil had had a couple of 15 m. triple jumpers, but it is generally conceded that Adhemar's rise to fame was that of a solitary genius. The natural talent of this magnificent athlete was adequately exploited through the methodical approach of his European coach, Dietrich Gerner of Germany (a 55.1 "intermediate" hurdler in 1927).

1941
1960

Adhemar Ferreira da Silva (Brazil), a twotime triple jump winner in the Olympics (1952 and 1956), the first great field event man produced by Latin America.

177

Józef Schmidt (Poland), twotime triple jump champion in the Olympics (1960 and 1964).

From 13.05 in his first competition in 1947, Adhemar improved to 16.56 in his 100th competition in 1955. As a record breaker he first entered the picture on 3 December 1950 at São Paulo, when he equalled Tajima's fourteen-year-old mark (16.00). The following year, namely on 30 September at Rio de Janeiro, he became the sole owner of the record with a 16.01 effort. A menace to the throne of this "Paulista" was by then looming in the person of his compatriot Helio Coutinho da Silva, a "Carioca" (i.e. a native of Rio de Janeiro) who late in 1951 did 15.99. Unfortunately, a serious injury put paid to the chances of the talented Helio, who was a 10.4 metric sprinter.

Adhemar continued to improve and his ability as a big-time jumper came in full evidence at the 1952 Olympics in Helsinki, when he beat his own world record in four of his six trials and won the gold medal with 16.22. Trailing him in that memorable event were Leonid Shcherbakov of USSR (15.98) and Arnoldo Devonish of Venezuela (15.52).

Shcherbakov was the "chef de file" of a new dynasty of triple jumpers. Soviet technicians had spotted the triple jump as one of the weakest points in the armour of rival countries in Europe and North America. So they began to work hard to take full advantage of the situation. Shcherbakov (born at Olyebino on 7 April 1927; 1.78 m./73 kg.) broke the ice at the 1950 European Championships in Brussels, annexing the continental title at 15.39. After his brilliant second place in the 1952 Olympics, he continued to improve. He worked assiduously to strengthen his leg muscles, using weights around his waist in training sessions. After reaching maximum height in the "hop", he would take advantage of his hyper-strong ankles for a low and long "step", and would finally regain height in the "jump". Being a man of mediocre speed, however, he needed eight seasons to improve from 15.43 in 1949 to 16.46 in 1956. He won his second European title at Bern in 1954 with 15.90 and wrested the world record from A.F. da Silva on 19 July 1953 in Moscow with 16.235. The Brazilian took up the gauntlet, and again chose a major competition as the occasion for his reply. At the Pan American Games in Mexico City on 16 March 1955 he topped all his previous efforts with a magnificent 16.56. This record performance was achieved with an aiding wind of merely 0.2 m/s. and with a ratio of 6.28 ("hop"), 4.95 ("step") and 5.33 ("jump"). Arnoldo Devonish was second at 16.13. At the 1956 Olympics in Melbourne (27 November) Adhemar Ferreira da Silva became the first triple jumper since Prinstein's pioneer days to successfully defend his title of world champion. His chief opponent was Vilhjálmur Einarsson, a strong man from Iceland who took the lead in the second round with 16.26. The Brazilian rose to the challenge with 16.35 in the fourth round - and that was the winning jump. Vitold Kreer of USSR was third (16.02), while former world record holder Shcherbakov had to be content with sixth place (15.80). Adhemar was a man of moderate speed and his ability as a long jumper was just fair (7.33). Even so he became the greatest athlete in South American history. He had first appeared in the Olympics in 1948: eleventh. He made his fourth appearance in 1960 in Rome: fourteenth.

The Russians recaptured the world record during

the inaugural USSR vs USA dual meet in Moscow in July 1958, when Olyeg Ryakhovskiy jumped 16.59, mainly by virtue of a 6.46 "hop".
The following month, at the European Championships in Stockholm, he was decisively beaten by József Schmidt of Poland, who braved the adverse elements and a poor runway to reach a personal best of 16.43. Ryakhovskiy, who was actually an Asian, barely held off Einarsson of Iceland in a close fight for second place, 16.02 to 16.00. USSR fought back in 1959, when Olyeg Fyedoseyev used his potential as a long jumper (7.77) to reach 16.70 for a new world mark at Nalchik (Caucasus). But Schmidt was to top them all in the Olympic year 1960. The Pole (born at Michalkowice on 28 March 1935; 1.84 m./77 kg.) was regarded as a real "comer" even before his breakthrough in 1958. His annual progression was as follows: 14.40 in 1955, 15.10 in 1956, 15.61 in 1957. A pulled tendon slowed him down in 1959, but he was back in stride the following year. He made history in the Polish Championships at Olsztyn on 5 August 1960, when in the first round of the final he compiled a ratio of 6.00, 5.02 and 6.01 for a new world record of 17.03, aided by a legal wind of 1.0 m/s. And he was said to have lost several centimetres due to an imperfect landing! Schmidt went on to win the Olympic title in Rome with 16.81, then the second best performance of his career. Vladimir Goryayev (16.63) and Vitold Kreer (16.43), both of USSR, relegated to fourth place Ira Davis, who could nevertheless rejoice for having set a new US record (16.41).

SHOT PUT:
O'Brien, the maestro

The first man who came dangerously close to Torrance's record (17.40) was Alfred Blozis (born at Garfield, New Jersey, on 5 January 1919; 1.98 m./109 kg.). The prize picture of an athlete, between 1940 and 1942 he had nine marks over 17 m., his longest being 17.22 on 15 June 1941 in New York. He excelled also as a discus thrower and in 1942 he topped the World Year List in this event (53.00), as well as in the shot (17.15).
In the same year he reached 17.61 with the iron ball during an indoor exhibition in New York. World War II not only deprived him of an Olympic chance but of his life as well: this former Georgetown student died on the Western front at the age of twenty-six.
Torrance's successor on the IAAF record book was a surprise to most experts, not so much because he

was black (men of that race had already figured prominently in the event, Bill Watson being the best example) but because of his relatively unimpressive frame. The man in question was Charles Fonville (born at Birmingham, Alabama on 27 April 1927; 1.88 m./88 kg.). He looked like a characteristic sprinter and in fact he was an "even time" 100 y. dashman, good going for a shot putter. He improved from 16.01 at nineteen to 16.73 at twenty - marks which then seemed well-nigh incredible for a youth of his age. On 17 April 1948 at Lawrence, Kansas, he shattered Torrance's world record with a mighty toss of 17.68. Unfortunately, he aggravated an old injury to his lower spine shortly before the London Games. At the US Olympic Tryouts in Evanston he made a gallant effort and managed a put of 16.49 but fini-

1941
1960

Parry O'Brien (USA), who set new milestones in shot put history. He was also a leading discus thrower.

shed no higher than fourth behind Jim Delaney (16.81), Wilbur Thompson and Jim Fuchs! Following an operation, Fonville tried again two years later but could not reproduce his best form. Meanwhile, Wilbur ("Moose") Thompson had won the 1948 Olympic title with a personal best of 17.12, while Delaney (16.68) and Fuchs (16.42) made it a clean sweep for Uncle Sam - with nearly one metre to spare vis-à-vis the fourth place man. The pattern of the speedy, explosive shot putter introduced by Fonville was perfected by the London bronze medallist, Jim Fuchs (born at Chicago on 6 December 1927; 1.87 m./101 kg.). At seventeen-plus he was Illinois High School champion in the 100 y. and was listed at 9.9 in the American Interscholastic Honour Roll. As a shot putter he improved from 15.15 in 1947 to 16.67 in 1948.

On 28 July 1949 at Oslo he broke the world record with a 17.79 toss. In 1950 he improved on his mark several times and wound up with 17.95 at Eskilstuna, Sweden, on 22 August. Using the width of the circle to full advantage with a fast action of the legs and a pronounced inclination of the trunk, he had a longer channel on which to apply pressure to the iron ball. His win streak was up to an unprecedented eighty-eight when

---

Inversely proportional

Since the earliest days of the sport, athletic performances have shown a steady and almost continuous upward trend. To keep abreast of ever improving times and distances over a long period of time is an impossible task even for the greatest of champions. A case in point is that of Parry O'Brien, the maestro of modern shot putting, who was responsible for the greatest advancement in the annals of the event. Although he continued to improve till the age of 34, he finally found himself on the losing side in his struggle against ever improving standards. His Olympic story well reflects the situation: he won in 1952 with 17.41 and in 1956 with 18.57, but dropped to second in 1960 with 19.11 and to fourth in 1964 with 19.20. In other words: ever better marks for inversely proportional placings. He was the first man to break the 18 m. and 19 m. barriers, but when he finally reached 19.69 in 1966, his lifetime best, he found himself no better than seventh on the All Time World List. A sad albeit inevitable lesson for the perfectionist he always was.

---

defeat came to him - on the eve of the 1952 Olympics in Helsinki. He injured his right hand and in the Games event he had to be content with third place (17.06) behind his compatriots Parry O'Brien (17.41) and Darrow Hooper (17.39). Fuchs' decline coincided, as it often happens, with the advent of a new champion, who was to outshine all his predecessors in efficiency of form and brilliance of performances - Parry O'Brien (born at Santa Monica, California, on 28 January 1932; 1.90 m./111 kg.). This man set a record of consistency and durability that still stands among the greatest in the history of athletics. His achievements can be summarized as follows:

(1) Won Olympic gold medal in Helsinki and Melbourne, silver in Rome;

(2) Advanced world's shot put record from 18.00 at Fresno on 9 May 1953 to 19.30 at Albuquerque, New Mexico, on 1 August 1959. He was the first man to break the 60-foot (18.29) barrier, with a toss of 18.42 at Los Angeles on 8 May 1954;

(3) Undefeated in 116 consecutive shot put contests from June 1952 till June 1956. First in "Track & Field News" World Ranking seven times (1952-56 and 1958-59), second twice (1957 and '60), and third twice (1961 and '66);

(4) Won AAU shot put title eight times (1951-55 and 1958-60);

(5) Was for many years a leading discus thrower, with top mark of 60.00 in 1965, and won the AAU title in 1955.

O'Brien was an outstanding performer in High School, with best of 17.61 with the 12 lb. shot in 1949. He developed an essential innovation in shot put form. At the start of his action, he faced directly back of the circle with his right foot pointing backwards, then used the latter as a pivot and made a 180° turn to release the shot at the opposite end of the circle, from the inner edge of the toe-board. This dynamic form called for great speed and co-ordination. O'Brien, a 10.8 metric sprinter, never ceased to perfect his style. He was one of the first shot putters to extensivley use weight training as a means for conditioning his body, a practice that was introduced a few years earlier by Otis Chandler, another leading shot putter (17.48 in 1950). (Chandler later became editor of the "Los Angeles Times" and as such he was instrumental for the organization of the 1964 USA vs USSR dual meet at Los Angeles).

At the Melbourne Olympics in 1956, O'Brien won at 18.57 from Bill Nieder (18.18) and Jirí Skobla of Czechoslovakia (17.65). Four years later, things took a different turn. The man who took over was Bill Nieder (born at Hempstead, New York, on 10 August 1933;

1.90 m./102 kg.). A great prospect in High School, Nieder severely damaged his right knee playing football and suffered from restricted movement for the major part of his career. After playing second fiddle to O'Brien for years, he topped a World Year List for the first time in 1957 with an 18.95 toss. But Parry was quick to regain the leadership and it was only in 1960 that Nieder finally came into his own. On 2 April of that year, at Austin, Texas, he got one off to 19.99, a new world record. And on 12 August at Walnut, California, he made history (in the eyes of metric minded observers, that is) with a great 20.06. In between these meets, however, Nieder had finished no better than fourth at the all-important US Olympic Trials, behind Dallas Long, O'Brien and Dave Davis. Later in the summer, Davis was hampered by an injured wrist and began to lose form, while Nieder improved to the above-mentioned record distance. The latter was finally selected for the trip to Rome, and Davis remained at home. But one more obstacle awaited Nieder on the way to that coveted gold medal, namely old warrior Parry O'Brien, fully determined to make it three in a row. The great battle was on 31 August. Going into the fifth round, O'Brien was the leader with 19.11, with Dallas Long (18.88) and Nieder (18.77) trailing. On his next-to-last try, Nieder did himself justice with 19.68 - and that won the gold medal for him. Long improved to 19.01, thus finishing a close third. (Nieder had been reported at 20.44 in training only a few days before the Rome final).

Dallas Long (born at Pine Bluff, Arkansas, on 13 June 1940; 1.93 m./118 kg.) could point to a meteoric rise. In 1958, after raising the interscholastic record to 21.10 with the 12 lb. (5.44 Kg.) implement, he made his début with the senior shot and reached 18.60, good enough to move to no. 3 on the All Time World List! Early in 1959 he wrested the world record from O'Brien with 19.25. From then on, he, Parry and Bill Nieder were involved in a ding-dong battle which in 1960 was finally won by Nieder. Meanwhile, however, Long had raised the world record to 19.67, only to lose it to Nieder a few days later.

In the four editions of the Olympics between 1948 and 1960, the Americans won eleven out of twelve medals at stake, the only European interference being that of Jiří Skobla, with his above-mentioned third place in 1956. In the early post-war years, Europe's best shot putters were Gunnar Huseby, a burly Icelander who won the continental title twice (1946 and '50, the latter with 16.74), and Heino Lipp, a versatile Estonian representing USSR, who did 16.98 in 1951. For some reason, Lipp was never allowed to take part in major international meets abroad. Further progress, markwise, was assured by Jiří Skobla of Czechoslovakia (born at Prague on 16 April 1930; 1.86 m./115 kg.), who was European champion in 1954 (17.20) and showed great consistency and reliability. He kept improving for many years, winding up with 18.52 in 1963, aged thirty-three. By then, however, he was no longer no. 1 in Europe ... Another talented performer was Arthur Rowe of Britain. European champion in 1958 (17.78), he went to the Rome Olympics as a possible medal contender but disappointed his fans, failing to survive the qualifying round.

He found partial consolation later in the year, namely on 16 October at Berlin, when he brought the European record to 19.11.

Another leading shot putter in those years was Silvano Meconi of Italy, who held the European record for a short time in 1959 and eventually wound up with 18.82 in 1960. Unfortunately, he was the type of man who would be at his best in low-fire competitions.

DISCUS THROW:
The Imperishable Society, from Consolini to Oerter

The first and only black athlete to own a world's discus record is Archie Harris of USA, a student from Indiana University who had his best year in 1941, when he capped a fine series of marks with 53.25 at Palo Alto, California, on 20 June, thereby wresting the global mark from Willy Schröder of Germany. Harris, who was also a better-than-average shot putter (15.68), had little time to rejoice though: on 26 October of the same year, at Giuriati ground in Milan, an Italian stalwart by the name of Adolfo Consolini threw the platter 53.34. That was the first world record by an Italian in the throwing events: it occurred in the morning hours of a cold, humid day, on Consolini's sixth and last trial. This man (born at Costermano near Verona on 5 January 1917; 1.80 m./105 kg.) was to prove a most durable performer: his long career stretched from 1937, when he threw 41.77, till 1969, when he managed 43.94, aged fifty-two. He died on 20 December 1969 at Milan, a few months after his last competition. The milestones in the athletic venture of this modest and extremely reliable champion can be summarized as follows:

(1) Bettered world record three times, with 53.34 in 1941, 54.23 in 1946, and 55.33 on 10 October 1948, always in Milan, the first two at the small Giuriati ground and the last at the Arena;

1941
1960

Adolfo Consolini (Italy), one of the most durable stalwarts in discus annals.

Fortune Gordien (USA) seen in a 190 ft. discus throw at Pasadena, California, in 1953. In a later try he will break the world record with 194 ft. 6 in. (59.28 m).

(2) Four times a competitor in the Olympics: first in London with 52.78, second in Helsinki with 53.78, sixth in Melbourne with 52.21, and seventeenth in Rome with 52.44;

(3) Bettered the European record six times between October 1941 and December 1955. He was less than one month short of his 39th birthday when he achieved his last continental record - 56.98 at Bellinzona on 11 December 1955. A few weeks earlier he had got one off to 57.41 during an exhibition at Vanzaghello;

(4) European champion three times, with 53.23 in 1946, 53.75 in 1950, and 53.44 in 1954. His appearances in this meet stretched over a period of twenty years, from his début in 1938 (fifth) till his farewell appearance in 1958 (sixth);

(5) Undefeated in European competition from September 1951 till June 1955;

(6) In over thirty years of athletic activity he took part in something like 400 discus competitions, exceeding 50 m. in over three-fourths of them.

Apart from occasional diversions in the shot put ring (best mark, 14.81), Consolini was a specialist in the strictest sense of the word. This squat-shouldered Hercules had a sound but conservative form. He relied on co-ordination of movements rather than speed. For a number of years he had a nemesis in his compatriot Giuseppe ("Beppe") Tosi, who surpassed his great rival in bulk (1.93 m./119 kg.) if not in brilliance. Tosi was second to Consolini at the 1948 Olympics in London (51.78) as well as in three editions of the European Championships (1946-50-54). Although less dedicated to the task than his compatriot, Tosi was at least Consolini's equal in competitive ability. His best, 54.80 in 1948, was a short-lived European record.

During Consolini's long European reign, America produced many fine discus throwers. Bob Fitch, a 1.88 m./100 kg. powder-ball from Minnesota University, was one of the nation's leading specialists as early as in 1941, when he did 49.52. He improved to 50.85 in 1942, then he lost several years of athletic activity owing to the war. Back in the circle by 1946, he took good advice from coach Jim Kelly: using his left shoulder and his upper body to the fullest advantage, he developed great centrifugal force, and on 8 June 1946, at Minneapolis, he broke Consolini's world record with a throw of 54.93. The following year he had a succcessful European "tournée" and beat Consolini in an international meet at Prague. Then he retired, aged 28, and thus missed the 1948 Olympics. The gap was, however, filled by another Jim Kelly protégé, Fortune Gordien (born at Spokane, Washington, on 9 September

1922; 1.84 m./104 kg.), an eccentric yet most durable performer. "Fortch" began in 1940 but the state of the world caused him to delay his "explosion" several years. He made the big jump between 1946 and 1947, when he improved from 49.19 to 54.64, which distance placed him first in the World List of the pre-Olympic year. In 1948 he threw 54.54 but managed only third (50.77) behind Consolini and Tosi at the London Games. He resumed his advance in 1949, when in the first meet of another European "tournée", at Lisbon on 9 July, he produced a sensational 56.46. Before the end of his tour he had brought the record to 56.97. Gordien had his greatest year in 1953, when he bettered 57 m. on several occasions and wound up with an eye-catching 59.28 at Pasadena, California, on 22 August. But he continued to disappoint his fans in Olympic competition: fourth in 1952 and second in 1956. In 1960, aged thirty-eight, he still managed 57.25. Surprisingly enough, in the long period of their sway he and Consolini met only four times, with the Italian prevailing three-to-one.

At the Helsinki Olympics in 1952, victory went to Sim Iness, a 22-year-old giant (1.98 m./109 kg.) from the University of Southern California, who topped a fine field with 55.03. The following year he set a new world record of 57.93 at the NCAA Championships in Lincoln, reportedly "with a mouth full of broken and missing teeth and a system upset by continuing doses of codeine" following an accident a few days earlier, when a flying discus smashed him squarely in the mouth. This exceptional talent retired at the end of that season, aged twenty-three. No matter how good his achievements, he was to remain a great "might-have-been". The next four editions of the Olympics (1956 through 1968) were to glorify the greatest competitor in the history of discus throwing - Alfred Oerter (born at Astoria, New York, on 19 September 1936; 1.92 m./106 kg.). He was spotted as a coming "Great" in 1954, when he threw the 3 lb. 9 oz. (1.61 kg.) High School discus 56.15, a new American Interscholastic record. From then on he never ceased to improve.

He went to the 1956 Olympics in Melbourne with good credentials, yet most observers favoured veterans Gordien and Consolini. "Al" upset his rivals with an opening throw of 56.36, a new Olympic as well as personal record, a "killer" that eventually won gold for the 20-year-old novice.

Gordien was second (54.81) and another American, Des Koch, was third (54.40), while Consolini, hampered by a cut in his right hand, had to be content with sixth place.

Gordien's record (59.28) was to resist all assaults till 1959, when Edmund Piatkowski of Poland brought the mark back to Europe with 59.91. This was curiously equalled by Rink Babka, another US giant (1.95 m./121 kg.), in 1960.

By the time of the Rome Olympics, however, Oerter was again the top man. Babka was the early leader with 58.02, but Oerter passed him with his next-to-last trial with a new personal record of 59.18! Dick Cochran was third (57.16) for another US sweep, while Piatkowski wound up in fifth place (55.12).

HAMMER THROW:
Russian dawn

German hammer men continued to dominate the picture throughout the early Forties, no matter if activity was at a low ebb owing to the war. Their best performer in those years was Karl Storch, who in 1943 had a top mark of 58.94, a few centimetres short of the world record.

Another outstanding performer was Bertie Healion, who could aptly be described as "the last of the Irish Whales". He too came close to Blask's world record with a throw of 58.80 in 1943.

In the early post-war years, with the Germans banned from international competition, a new leader emerged in the person of Imre Németh of Hungary (born at Kassa - today's Kosice in Czechoslovakia - on 23 September 1917; 1.84 m./82 kg.). Hungary was a fresh addition to the map of hammer throwing: as late as in 1939, her national record was below 48 m. Németh was by and large a self-taught man, no matter if he carefully studied films of the Christmann school. He had no imposing figure according to the standards of the event, but he used his relatively slender frame to obtain the maximum possible speed. He exceeded 55 m. for the first time in 1943, continuing to improve gradually; and on 14 July 1948, during a pre-Olympic rehearsal at the Hungarian training camp of Tata, he beat Blask's world record by a fractional margin with a 59.02 throw. In the Olympic arena, with the Germans not competing and Healion by then a "pro", Németh won with 56.07.

He revised the world record on two more occasions: 59.57 in 1949 and 59.88 in 1950. Early in 1952 another Hungarian, barely twenty years of age, began to loom as a major threat to Németh. This youngster, who did more than anyone else to destroy the fallacy that hammer throwing was a pastime for middle-aged men, was József Csermák. He became the first man to top 60 m. and did so in winning the

Olympic title at Helsinki on 24 July 1952 with a 60.34 throw. Karl Storch of Germany, a veteran of thirty-nine who had been waiting for an Olympic chance all his life, produced a fine series but finally had to settle with 58.86 and second place, ahead of Imre Németh (57.74).

By that time, a new power was ready to enter the picture: USSR. Like the Germans in pre-war years, the Russians spotted this difficult event as good hunting ground for men having a methodical approach. The USSR hammer record was first brought to a good international standard in 1938, when Sergey Lyakhov reached 53.08. In post-war years, Aleksandr Kanaki was one of Németh's chief rivals and achieved a distance of 58.59 in 1949.

Al Oerter (USA) a fourtime winner of the discus in the Olympics, a record of records.

Just like Lyakhov, he could point to a long career as an all-round weightman, and at one time he had done well in the decathlon too (6595 pts under the 1934 scoring table). The man who really set the world on fire was, however, Mikhail Krivonosov (born at Krichev, Byelorussia, on 1 May 1929; 1.89 m./105 kg.). The prize picture of an athlete who in all probability could have been equally great in other events, Krivonosov came to the fore with giant strides, improving from 42.91 in 1950 to 51.60 in 1951 and finally 60.51 in 1952. This fine athlete gave the full measure of his class at the 1954 European Championships.

Defending champion Sverre Strandli of Norway, a big man with a childish face, who then held the world record (62.36 in 1953), was regarded as the most likely winner of the title. But on 29 August, at Bern's Neufeld stadium, Krivonosov "killed" his Northern opponent with a record throw of 63.34, which was backed up by an unnecessary yet highly significant 63.25. Strandli was second at 61.07, while Csermák, receiving the very same shock he had inflicted to others at Helsinki two years earlier, was third (59.72).

Before the end of that year, another Russian surprisingly got one off to 64.05 in a meet at Baku. Stanislav Nyenashev was the name, and he was merely twenty! Only 1.70 m. tall, he was one of the first hammer throwers to use four turns, a technique which for many years failed to catch on. But Nyenashev never managed to do himself justice on big occasions.

The coming-of-age of Russian hammer throwers as an ensemble was emphasized by the results of a meet held at Nalchik, Caucasus, on 25 April 1956, when eleven men from that country beat 59 m. and the winner, Mikhail Krivonosov, raised the world record to 65.85. One may wonder what had happened in the meantime in the hammer cages of America, the country of choice of Flanagan, McGrath and Ryan.

The Americans had in fact put the event on their "black list", holding it in relatively few meets, and generally outside the stadium. The colleges in particular ignored the hammer throw almost completely.

The flame was kept alive by a tiny group of enthusiasts in a small section of the East. In the late Forties a man from this exclusive set, Sam Felton, became involved in the study of European methods. In the course of time he added considerably to the knowledge of his fellow Americans.

While Felton himself, being a man of average physical power, had to be content with fourth place in the 1948 Olympics and a top mark of 57.18 in 1950, others were able to go farther.

1941 1960

First to improve on Ryan's time-honoured US record was Martin Engel, who in 1953 got one off to 59.55. But the man who put USA in the orbit of the world's leading hammer throwers was Harold Connolly (born at Somerville, Massachusetts, on 1 August 1931; 1.83 m./106 kg.). During a visit to Germany, he received useful hints from Christmann and Storch. Adding a lot of study of his own, he improved from 55.40 in 1954 to an excellent 63.88 in 1955. Curiously enough, the first American to come up with a world record throw was not Connolly, but Clifford Blair, who had a solitary day of glory in July 1956, with a surprising 65.95. This mark was ratified as an American record but never made the IAAF book. Things really began to happen later in 1956, when Krivonosov and Connolly engaged in a ding-dong battle for world supremacy. Performing several thousands of miles apart, they took turns in bettering the world record, with the following sequence: Krivonosov 66.38 (Minsk, 8 July), Connolly 66.71 (Boston, 3 October), Krivonosov 67.32 (Tashkent, 22 October), Connolly 68.54 (Los Angeles, 2 November). The stage was set for a showdown at the Melbourne Olympics. In the meet that counted most, the two heroes fell somewhat below expectations, for the vicious circle or the tremendous pressure of the occasion. Connolly won from his Russian rival by a narrow margin, 63.19 to 63.03. Krivonosov (who was also a good discus thrower: 51.22) lost form in subsequent years, but Connolly continued to improve on his world record, with 68.68 in 1958 and 70.33 on 12 August 1960 at Walnut, California. His series in the latter meet was as follows: 68.58 - 66.00 - 70.33 - 65.79 - 68.12 - 68.83. Connolly, who had a short, withered arm, was then married to the 1956 Olympic discus champion, Olga Fikotová, formerly of Czechoslovakia. A few weeks after his historic 70-plus record, he suffered an unexpected defeat at the Rome Olympics, when he had to be content with eighth place (63.59). Victory went to Vasiliy Rudenkov, a Russian left-hander, with 67.10. Gyula Zsivótzky of Hungary was second (65.79), ahead of Tadeusz Rut of Poland (65.64), the 1958 European champion.

Lengthy pioneering job

The pioneer of Russian ball-and-chain experts was Aleksandr Pyotrovich Chistyakov - a recordman in longevity. Born in 1881, he became interested in sport as a teen-ager and turned to hammer throwing in 1911. The following year he set the inaugural Russian record: 25.91. By 1916 he had improved to 38.74. Then came the October Revolution and the new governing body of Russian sport decided to cancel all records set before 1918. Thus Chistyakov had to start all over again from scratch. By 1925 his "new" national record was no better than 37.26. Then he lost it to Sergey Lyakhov. But in 1928 the forty-seven-year-old Chistyakov recaptured the record with a 39.08 effort. In later years the old warrior inevitably had to give way to Lyakhov, 25 years his junior. At fifty-seven, Chistyakov still managed to exceed 34 m. In the meantime, he had attained national reputation in a new role, that of movie actor, starring in thirty-odd Russian pictures.

I know, however, of other "imperishable" hammer throwers who have done much better than Chistyakov in quality of performance, if not in terms of mere durability. A good example is Karl Hein of Germany, the 1936 Olympic champion, who did 53.00 in 1964, aged fifty-six - "merely" 5.77 m. short of his lifetime best, dating from 1938.

Vasiliy Rudenkov (USSR), winner of the hammer throw at the 1960 Olympics in Rome.

JAVELIN THROW:
The Held "glider"

The Russo-Finnish war and then World War II severely hampered the further development of such throwers as Nikkanen, Erkki Autonen (76.36 in 1939) and Matti Mikkola (75.61 in 1940). Even so, Finland still provided the winner at the first post-war Olympics in 1948. Tapio Rautavaara, who had a personal best of 75.47 (1945), won in London with a 69.77 throw. This fine athlete later became a well-known folk singer and actor. At the 1950 European Championships in Brussels, Toivo Hyytiäinen clinched the last major victory for Finland by annexing the continental crown with 71.26. In 1954 he succeeded Yrjö Nikkanen as national record holder with a throw of 78.98, but by then other countries had taken over the leadership. American javelin throwers had been inadequate and inconsistent for years, yet it may be of interest to record a prophecy made by Matti Järvinen after viewing some of America's best javelin men in 1932: "Within a reasonable time the Yanks will take to their heart the fine art of javelin throwing ... Then top results will be in numbers of three figures". This prophecy was to come true, or just about, half a century later, yet for many years there were experts, especially in Europe, ready to endorse the famous quotation of Dean Cromwell, one of America's greatest coaches: "About the best thing that can be said about the American javelin throwing form is this: Don't use it". In post-war years, however, Americans began to have their share of honours. Dr. Steve Seymour (né Seymour Cohen) broke the ice by finishing second to Rautavaara at the 1948 Olympics in London. He could point to a personal best of 75.84 (1947). But the man who gave new impetus to the American (and world) javelin fraternity was Franklin ("Bud") Held (born at Los Angeles on 25 October 1927; 1.85 m./75 kg.). His best as a collegian was 71.13 in 1950, but the following year he impressed Scandinavian experts when he beat some of the best Nordic throwers at Stockholm with a smooth 76.11 effort. At the 1952 Olympics in Helsinki he was hampered by a sore shoulder and finished an undistinguished ninth. His teammates Cyrus Young and Bill Miller more than filled the gap by taking first and second place, with 73.78 and 72.46 respectively. To the Finns this was indeed a bad blow, in no way softened by Toivo Hyytiäinen's bronze medal throw (71.89). Young and Miller had plenty of raw talent but never matched the knowledge of Held on the finer points of technique. Miller was also a good decathlon man as well as a 2.03 high jumper.

After lengthy experimentation, in which he treasured the advice given him by his father and his brother, Held devised a new type of javelin which had some of the characteristics of a glider. This was achieved after studying a wide range of implements old and new and seeking the best possible distribution of weights and measures within the limits set by IAAF rules. The shorter and lighter metal point would sometimes cause the javelin to land flat, but this deficiency was remedied, at least in part, in later models. Quite predictably, Held himself was first to take full advantage of the improved situation. On 8 August 1953 at Pasadena, California, he became history's first 80-metre man with a sensational 80.41 effort. The record throw came in round 3, after Held had come close to Nikkanen's mark with a 78.35 throw in round 2.

In Europe, the centre of gravity of javelin power was gradually moving away from Finland. The first 80-metre man among continentals was Janusz Sidlo of Poland (born at Szopienice on 19 June 1933; 1.82 m./87 kg.). A born javelin talent if ever there was one, he emerged at eighteen with a mark of 67.88. In the fall of 1953 he improved by almost 9 m. in two weeks and finally reached 80.15 on 2 October at Jena for a new European record. Sidlo's surprising effort was made from a grass runway and with a conventional metal javelin. That was the first spark of what turned out to be a long and stupendous career. Sidlo was European champion twice, with 76.35 in 1954 and 80.18 in 1958. (He was to win one more medal in .... 1969, when he finished third with 82.90). Meanwhile, Held had brought the world record to 81.75, at Modesto in 1955. A reply from Europe came the following year, when Soini Nikkinen threw a Finnish birch javelin 83.56 in a small meet held at Kuhmoinen, in the country of the countless lakes. This was, however, just a flash in the pan. Janusz Sidlo fought back bravely: only six days later, at Milan, he broke Nikkinen's mark with an 83.66 throw. But later in the season Sidlo himself was to find a very tough rival in Egil Danielsen of Norway. Unlike the Pole, who was to grace javelin runways for many more years, the Norwegian earned most of his fame in one superlative season - 1956. After achieving an impressive series of marks in Europe (notably including a near record mark of 83.57), the 23-year-old Danielsen went "Down Under" for the Olympics, and in Melbourne he stunned experts, moving from sixth to first in the crucial stage of the competition with a "killer" of 85.71, a new world record. The bewildered Sidlo was second with 79.98, ahead of Viktor Tsibulenko of USSR (79.50).

Danielsen offered further proof of his powers and in 1958 he finished second to Sidlo at the European Championships in Stockholm. Then his enthusiasm gradually declined.

Of course, many of these marks were made with the "Held javelin", or derivatives thereof. The "inventor" himself had bad luck though. In the summer of 1956 an injury put him out of the Olympic team at the time of the US Tryouts. In September he reached his lifetime best, 82.29, but under the rigid AAU selective system there was no opening for him and so he could not join the Melbourne-bound team. Even so, Held had at least succeeded in stirring the apathy of his compatriots. A few years later USA presented a duo of outstanding even if somewhat unpredictable javelin throwers: Al Cantello and Bill Alley. The former had a peculiar style: in unleashing the javelin he made a spectacular dive, landing on all fours just in front of the scratch line. In the spring of 1959, at the age of twenty-eight, he gained about ten metres on his previous best by getting one off to 86.04. This was at Compton, California, and Cantello's surprising effort cracked Danielsen's world record. Alley, one of the biggest javelin men seen until then (1.90 m./101 kg.) was a precocious talent who did 83.48 in 1960, when he also had an 86.46 effort nullified because of a sloping ground. (Under IAAF rules, the maximum allowance for the overall inclination of the field in the throwing direction shall not exceed 1:1000). In the meantime, the "Held" javelin and its derivatives were creating a problem for the IAAF. It was only a short time before the Rome Olympics, however, that the international body decided to put its house in oreder, labelling only two types as official for the Games, the traditional Finnish wood (beetle) javelin, and the Swedish metal javelin (the latter had been used by Danielsen in his record throw at Melbourne). The "Held" javelin was posthumously outlawed, and such a decision obviously upset the plans of many leading throwers. Not surprisingly, the winner of the 1960 Olympic title was an old javelin hand, who had been throwing for years with more or less conventional models. The man was Viktor Tsibulenko of USSR, 30, who was making his third appearance in the Olympics, after placing fourth in 1952 and third in 1956.

Under unfavourable weather conditions, he used a moment of lull before a rainstorm to produce the longest throw of his career - 84.64. And that turned out to be the gold medal throw. No matter if Janusz Sidlo had done better in the qualifying round, with 85.14. But in the final the Pole was among those who for one reason or another failed to do themselves justice. He wound up a disappointing eighth (76.46), while Cantello was an even more disappointing tenth (74.70).

DECATHLON:
A golden boy

For many years experts thought of the decathlon as an event only for mature men. The first serious blow to this conception was administered by a boy of seventeen years and eight months who won the 1948 Olympic crown in London. This boy was Robert Mathias (born at Tulare, California, on 17 November 1930; 1.90 m./88 kg.). A precocious lad by all physical standards, he was in the third decathlon of his career. Under unfavourable conditions, he emerged as the winner of a long-drawn-out contest with 7139 pts (1934 scoring table). When everything was over, the exhausted young man said: "Never again". But after a cooling-off period he was back at it. At the 1950 AAU Championship, which appropriately enough was held in his native town of Tulare, he succeeded Morris as world record holder with 8042 pts (7287 under 1985 table). Two years later, at Helsinki, he won his second Olympic gold medal with his lifetime best - 7887 pts under the new scoring table introduced in 1950 (7592 under 1985 table). Endowed with all the requisites of a great all-round performer, Mathias had a sort of natural aversion for one or two events. He was at his best in the discus (52.83) and in the "high" hurdles (13.8). He retired at twenty-two, certainly without exploring the depth of his potentialities.

Prior to 1952 black Americans had shown little inclination for the ten-event grind, the only notable exception being Bill Watson (6814 pts in 1940, as per 1934 scoring table). In the Fifties Milton Campbell definitely broke the ice. At twenty-one he was second to Mathias in the 1952 Olympics. Four years later he won the Olympic title with a sound score of 7937 pts (1950 table). He was relatively weak in the field events. But he was supreme in the "highs": in 1957 he became a co-holder of the world's 120 y. hurdles record with a time of 13.4! Almost at the same time another and even greater talent appeared on the American scene: Rafer Johnson (born at Hillsboro, Texas, on 18 August 1935; 1.90 m./91 kg.). This fine athlete achieved a world record score of 7985 pts (7608 under 1985 table) in the fourth decathlon of his career in 1955! Clearly in the best tradition of Bausch, Morris and Mathias. At the 1956 Olympics a bad knee kept him down to 7587 digits, not good enough against Milton Campbell but quite sufficient to earn a silver medal. In the same year he ran the "highs" in 13.8 and long jumped 7.76. In 1957 he ran the metric century in 10.3. Europe continued to lose to

1941
1960

Egil Danielsen (Norway) reached his peak at the 1956 Olympics in Melbourne, when he struck gold with a new world record of 85.71. Continued with declining interest till the early Sixties.

America in Olympic contests and yet had good decathlon men in numbers. Going back a few years, I would like to mention Heino Lipp of USSR, an Estonian who scored 7110 pts in 1948 but could not participate in the London Olympics. Several years later, USSR had an even greater talent, who proved luckier than Lipp. The man in question was Vasiliy Kuznyetsov (born at Kalikino on 7 February 1932; 1.85 m./83 kg.), who after years of hard but intelligent work achieved a high degree of efficiency in practically every event. He was European champion three times (6749 pts in 1954, 7865 pts in 1958, and 8026 pts in 1962), a feat previously achieved only by Adolfo Consolini in the discus. He was a bronze medallist in the Olympics on two occasions (1956 and 1960). The Russian, a well co-ordinated and powerful athlete, was the first man to excel 8000 pts under the 1950 scoring table. He did the trick at Krasnodar on 17 and 18 May 1958, with a score of 8014 pts (7653 pts under 1985 table). A few months later, in the first USSR vs USA dual meet in Moscow, he was pitted against Rafer Johnson. The American had by then switched concentration on the weight events, showing tremendous progress with such marks as 52.06 in the discus, 74.33 in the javelin, and 16.75 in the shot put. In the Moscow tussle the decision did in fact come in the next-to-last event, the javelin, in which Johnson, with a 72.59 throw, built up a commanding lead and laid the ultimate foundations for his record-shattering score: 8302 pts (7789 under 1985 table).

Kuznyetsov was second with 7897 pts. In 1959, while Johnson was momentarily sidelined with injuries sustained in a car accident, Kuznyetsov had his greatest year. On 16 and 17 May in Moscow, he recaptured the world record with 8357 pts (7839 under 1985 table). Then he showed his prowess watched by thousands of American eyes at Philadelphia, totalling 8350 digits in the face of almost unbearable weather conditions. It may be of interest to note that in the 1959 USSR List, Kuznyetsov ranked prominently in no less than six events, as follows (= tie):

100 m.	10.5 (=13th)
110 m. hurdles	14.4 (=5th)
pole vault	4.30 (=16th)
long jump	7.40 (13th)
discus	52.00 (11th)
javelin	72.79 (15th)

By 1960, however, Johnson was back in stride, better than ever before. What is more, he found new incentive in his own backyard, since one of his UCLA teammates had begun to shape up as an all-round man of tremendous potential. This man was Yang Chuan-kwang of Nationalist China (born at Taitung, Taiwan, on 10 July 1933; 1.80 m./80 kg.). Asia had never had a prominent decathlon man, and Yang created a sensation by improving, between 1954 and 1958, from 5454 to 7363 pts. The Athletic Federation of Nationalist China helped him enrol at the University of California at Los Angeles (UCLA), Rafer Johnson's school. Needless to say, the dedicated Yang soon derived great benefits from his daily training sessions with Johnson. The two teammates had met for the first time at the 1956 Oympics in Melbourne, with Johnson finishing second and Yang eighth. They met again at the 1958 AAU Championship at Palmyra, New Jersey, and Johnson won less comfortably than expected, 7754 to 7625. The following year Yang won the AAU title, with Johnson not competing, at 7549 pts and later raised his personal best to 7835 pts.

In the Olympic year 1960, Johnson and Yang had two great duels. The first round was at Eugene, Oregon, on 8 and 9 July. Aided by an elevated rubber-asphalt runway which yielded excellent marks in the long jump (Yang 7.75,Johnson 7.55), the two men got off to a great start. At the end of the two-day struggle Johnson recaptured the world record with a score of 8683 pts (7982 pts under 1985 table), and Yang too beat Kuznyetsov's listed mark with 8426 pts.

At the Rome Olympics, the compact Chinese came dangerously close to beating his college mate. In the hectic atmosphere of the Stadio Olimpico, Johnson finally emerged the winner by a scant margin - 8392 to 8334. Kuznyetsov, who had been hampered by an injury earlier in the season, was third with 7809 pts. When the pressure was off, a triumphant but exhausted Johnson was quoted as saying: "Victory obliterates fatigue, but I never want to go through that again - never". Unlike Mathias, Johnson kept his promise. His short and splendid career thus stretched over the length of an "Olympiad". Just like Morris, Mathias and Yang, he was to appear in several movies. And he was seen by millions of TV-viewers the world over the day Sen. Robert Kennedy was assassinated in Los Angeles in 1968. Rafer, a rabid Kennedy supporter, was standing next to him that night.

RELAYS - 4x100 m.
Speedy Americans, well-tuned Russians

After World War II some time elapsed before the high standards of the Thirties could be equalled or surpassed. At the London Olympics (1948) USA won hands down in 40.6. (At first, the Americans were disqualified for a change supposedly "out of bounds", but after viewing a film of the race the Jury of Appeal decided to reinstate them).

Four years later, at Helsinki, the long reigning champions met unexpected resistance from a new opponent - USSR. Such distinguished sprinters as Dean Smith, Harrison Dillard, Lindy Remigino and Andy Stanfield had to give all they had to finish a couple of metres ahead of their Soviet rivals (Boris Tokaryev, Lev Kalyayev, Levan Sanadze and Vladimir Sukharyev), who were clearly inferior in aggregate speed. The times were 40.1 and 40.3 respectively, Hungary being a fairly close third in 40.5. On that occasion the baton passing of Russians and Hungarians came in for a great deal of praise. Their lead-off man started with the baton in his right hand and, keeping to the inner section of his lane, he handed over to the second man, who took the baton from the outside, with his left hand. Near the end of his leg, the second man moved towards the outer section of his lane, thus allowing the third man to take the baton with his right hand. This procedure, repeated till the last change, was useful in that no man had to change the baton from hand to hand, an operation which often causes a runner to break his rhythm. The new method, since then adopted in many countries, is certainly economical but rather complex and implies a lot of preparatory work in order to be executed with mastery.Russian sprinters, relatively unimpressive in terms of pure blazing speed, owe much of their success in relay racing to their swift baton changes. In 1954-55 the centre of American relay power moved from California to Texas. It fell to a college quartet representing the Lone Star State to lower the 4x110 y. relay record to a nifty 40.2. This was in 1955, and a year later another team from the University of Texas lowered the mark to 40.1. In USA it often happens that college runners who can train together for the better part of a year turn out to be more efficient than internationals with a higher aggregate speed who usually get to know each other only a few weeks before a major commitment.

The European 4x100 m. record from pre-war days (40.1 by Germany) was finally equalled in October 1956, when Italy's national team did just that during a dual meet with France in Florence. Only twenty-four hours later, at Köln, Germany again became the sole owner of the record with 40.0. Both marks were posted on 500 m. tracks, hence on courses including only one turn. In the Melbourne Olympics, however, the teams that battled for top honours were again those from USA and USSR. In the final the Americans had two mediocre passes, but the explosive start of little Ira Murchison (1.62 m. tall), the breathtaking flight of Leamon King, the ability of Thane Baker as a curve runner, and the powerful finish of Bobby Morrow more than sufficed to give Uncle Sam another victory in the record time of 39.5. The Russians, with Boris Tokaryev, Vladimir Sukharyev, Leonid Bartenyev, and Yuriy Konovalov, again surpassed themselves, lowering the European record to 39.8.

Germany just held off Italy for third place (both 40.3). An automatic timer caught the first four teams in 39.59, 39.92, 40.34 and 40.43. In the four-year span between the Melbourne and the Rome Olympics, American college teams really provided some fireworks. In 1957 both the University of Texas and Abilene Christian University clocked 39.9 for the 4x110 y. relay around one turn.

In 1959, spectators at the California Relays in Modesto were treated to a dramatic three-way battle, won by the University of Texas in 39.6, still over the quarter mile route, while San Jose State College and Abilene Christian were second and third (39.7 and 39.8 respectively). At the 1958 European Championships in Stockholm, Germany barely held off a rejuvenated British quartet in the 4x100 m. relay, both teams returning 40.2. Only five days later, at Köln, a partly renovated German team consisting of a would-be 8-metre long jumper, Manfred Steinbach, a future world record breaker in the "high" hurdles, Martin Lauer, and two "pure" sprinters, Heinz Fütterer and Manfred Germar, used a one-turn course to good advantage and equalled the world record for the metric distance with 39.5.

In the Rome Olympics (1960) the Germans rose to the stature of the traditional masters from across the Atlantic, and the duel that followed was a fascinating one. Bernd Cullmann, Armin Hary, Walter Mahlendorf and Martin Lauer returned a record equalling 39.5 in the first qualifying round, while the Americans, with Frank Budd, Ray Norton, Stone Johnson and Dave Sime clocked 39.7 in another heat. In the semi-finals the two teams, running in different races, were content with seemingly effortless 39.7 clockings. It was by then obvious that USA, no matter if clearly superior in aggregate speed, could not afford to throw anything away with less than adequate changes.

In the final (8 September), their second-leg man, Norton, had a burning desire to avenge the defeats he had suffered in the individual races. He was pitted against Armin Hary, who had earlier won the 100 m. Ostensibly over-eager, Norton put himself in motion too early and thus received the baton from Budd beyond the boundaries of the exchange zone. The blunder was clear to spectators and runners, and the Germans, although beaten by the better part of a metre at the end of the journey, immediately started celebrating their "victory". And victory it was, because the American team was disqualified. The time for the "de jure" winners was 39.5, while the Americans, thanks chiefly to Dave Sime's strong finish, were unofficially timed in 39.4. An automatic timer gave 39.59 for USA and 39.66 for Germany. USSR was second in 40.1 and Great Britain (who, judging from a film of the race, appeared to have passed the baton outside the safety zone in the first change-over) barely beat Italy for third, with 40.2 for both.

4x400 m. Jamaica's day of glory

One of the most famous races involving college teams took place at Los Angeles on 17 June 1941. It was over 4x440 y. and the duel unfolded between the University of California (Berkeley) and the University of Southern California (Los Angeles). The former built up a substantial lead in the lead-off leg and was never headed, no matter if the men from USC - then the no.1 power in US collegiate athletics - finally managed to close the gap almost entirely.

Joy and sorrow

In the days when athletics was far from being a "pro" sport it could well happen that the rivalry between two champions lasted the length of a season, no more. That is what happened in 1941 with Grover Klemmer and Hubie Kerns, then battling for the mantle of America's no. 1 quarter-miler. More than their head-to-head tussles in individual races, California oldtimers remember their fight in the last leg of a memorable 4x440 y. relay race at the Los Angeles Coliseum in June of that year. Klemmer, 20, had a lead of nearly 3 metres on Kerns, 21, at the change-over. In such cases, when the contention is between two men of comparable value, the one who happens to trail the leader has the advantage of being able to time his effort accordingly, and possibly shoot ahead of his rival in the closing stage. That is what Kerns managed to do, but only 99 %. At the end Klemmer was still centimetres ahead, and thus earned for his team victory and world record. Maxwell Stiles, a California track writer who saw the race, noted that on that day young Klemmer fought against three Shadows. One was Kerns, the other was Time - and Klemmer had the upper hand with both. But, in Stiles' own words, "the third Shadow he did not see. It was the last shadow a man ever knows, yet whose presence he rarely even suspects". Five minutes after he had won the race, Klemmer was told that his father had died of a heart attack. Cal coach Brutus Hamilton had got the sad news a few hours earlier from the boy's mother, who bravely asked him not to tell Grover until after the meet.

The time for both teams was 3:09.4, a new world record. (Although the time for the non-winning team, taken on only one watch, was not ratified). The fastest legs were returned by Cliff Bourland and Hubert Kerns (both 45.8), the last two men of the "Trojan" (USC) quartet, but Cal's anchor man, Grover Klemmer, grimly held on (46.1) to finally save the day by a few centimeters. In intrinsic value, the record time was about equal to the 4x400 m. record (3:08.2) set by Carr & Co. at the 1932 Olympics on the same (Coliseum) track. To find a higher note in the history of the four-lap relay we must jump to the legendary Olympic final of 1952 in Helsinki.

On that occasion Jamaica had the rare privilege of being able to field three phenoms like Herb McKenley, George Rhoden and Arthur Wint, plus a 9.5 100 y. sprinter and better-than-average quarter-miler like Leslie Laing. Three of these men had grown up athletically in the "cauldron" of US college meets, and the fourth, Wint, had reached world prominence while residing in England. The Americans intended to counteract the menace from the Caribbean island with a team consisting of Ollie Matson, Eugene Cole, Charles Moore, and Mal Whitfield.

In fact, the fight was as close as could be wished. The story of the dramatic race is best told by the following splits, taken by unofficial timers of wide experience:

	Jamaica		USA
Wint	46.8	Matson	46.7
Laing	47.0	Cole	45.5
McKenley	44.6	Moore	46.3
Rhoden	45.5	Whitfield	45.5
	3:03.9		3:04.0

Both teams thus pulverized the 20-year-old world record set by Carr & Co. (3:08.2) at the 1932 Olympics. The average per man was a revolutionary 46.0. (The automatic timer caught Jamaica in 3:04.04 and USA in 3:04.19). McKenley's sizzling third leg left an indelible impression on all those who, like me, were lucky enough to see the race. He made shambles of a 47.0 quarter-miler like Moore, the Olympic 400 m. hurdles champion. Germany, with Hans Geister, Günther Steines, Heinz Ulzheimer and Karl-Friedrich Haas, was third in 3:06.6, a new European record. After the memorable Helsinki race it was generally felt that the record set by the Jamaicans would have a fairly long life. In fact it withstood all assaults for eight years. In 1956 the Americans revised the world record for the 4x440 y. relay when Charles Jenkins, Lonnie Spurrier, Tom Courtney and Lou Jones ran 3:07.3 in a pre-Olympic meet at Los Angeles. In Melbourne USA won practically unopposed in 3:04.8 with Jones, J.W.Mashburn, Jenkins and Courtney. The Australians surpassed themselves by winning the silver medal in 3:06.2. Jamaica's winning ways were partly resumed at the 1959 Pan-American Games in Chicago, when the Caribbean island contributed three men to the West Indies team that won the 4x400 m. relay from USA, 3:05.3 to 3:05.8. The three men were Mal and Mel Spence, twins, and George Kerr. The fourth man, Basil Ince, was from Trinidad. But at the 1960 Olympics in Rome the menace to American supremacy was provided by Germany, then having a vintage year in the 400 m. Otis Davis and Karl Kaufmann, who had finished

1941
1960

Jamaican follies

The Caribbean area is known athletically speaking as "tierra de relámpagos" (land of lightning), i.e. a fertile soil for the growth of the so-called "merchants of speed". Of all the islands in the area, Jamaica can point to the richest tradition. Her magic moment occurred at the 1952 Olympics in Helsinki, when Arthur Wint, Leslie Laing, Herb McKenley and George Rhoden won a memorable 4x400 m. race, beating USA and the world record as well. Outside the National Stadium in Kingston there is now a statue which is said to be a "composite" of the 1952 heroes. In fact, their victory created quite a stir in the island discovered by Columbus. In their valuable book "Herb McKenley Olympic Star", Errol Townshend and Jimmy Carnegie relate that many islanders went out of their way in celebrating. The Governor had decreed a national holiday, "but after the day of jubilation came the day of reckoning. Overjoyed Jamaicans were brought to court charged with breaches of the liquor laws. Their plea? "Helsinki, Your Honour". The judge smiled and passed sporting sentences". Meanwhile, in far-away Helsinki, McKenley & Co. were having celebrations of their own. A few hours after the historic race, team coach Joe Yancey and the happy record breakers invited the Duke of Edinburgh to share with them the glory of victory. "They had the foresight to stash away the whisky but not to procure drinking glasses. But they had a toothbrush tumbler. Cheerfully, the Duke drank his gig from it".

one-two in the individual 400 m. race, were again pitted against each other - in the anchor leg. By then the Americans had built up a sizable lead and the gallant Kaufmann found himself unable to close the gap. USA won in world record time, 3:02.2, and Germany also bettered the listed mark in finishing second in 3:02.7. (The automatic timer gave 3:02.37 and 3:02.84 respectively). Splits were as follows: USA - Jack Yerman 46.2, Earl Young 45.6, Glenn Davis 45.4, Otis Davis 45.0; Germany - Hans-Joachim Reske 47.0, Manfred Kinder 44.9, Johannes Kaiser 45.9, Karl Kaufmann 44.9. For once the Americans had the edge in the changes; otherwise the fight would have been even closer than it was. The West Indies team, with George Kerr in the anchor leg (45.4), was third in 3:04.0, almost duplicating the time that had earned glory for McKenley &Co. at Helsinki in 1952.

WALKS:
Sundry stalwarts

Almost parallel to her boom in middle distance running, during the Forties Sweden enjoyed a similarly bright period in race walking, chiefly thanks to John Mikaelsson, John Ljunggren and Werner Hardmo. The last named was lavish in producing world records over a wide range of English and metric distances, but failed to do himself justice in big-time competition. At the 1946 European Championships in Oslo he was disqualified in the 10 km. event, and the same thing happened to him at the 1948 Olympics in London. His countrymen Mikaelsson and Ljunggren had solid credentials though. In the 1946 meet at Oslo, the former won the 10 km. event with almost one minute to spare on Fritz Schwab of Switzerland, a son of Arthur Tell Schwab, Olympic silver medallist in the 50 km. at Berlin in 1936. Mikaelsson duplicated his victory, over the same distance, at the London Olympics, and again at Helsinki in 1952, when he achieved a new Olympic record of 45:02.8. The tenacious Fritz Schwab had his day of glory at the 1950 European Championships in Brussels, and on that occasion the indestructible Mikaelsson had to be content with third place. It should be added that this great Swede was officially credited with a high number of world record performances, plus several others which did not make the IAAF book. Notable among his achievements against the clock was a 1:32:28.4 for 20 km. at Växjö in 1942. Ljunggren, a miracle in terms of durability, was at his best in the long grind event, the 50 km. At this distance he remained in the front ranks for many years. At the European Championships his record was simply amazing: first in 1946, second in 1950, fourth in 1954, ninth in 1958 and fifth in 1962, aged forty-three! He won the Olympic gold medal in 1948 with 4:41:52, leaving the next man over 6 minutes behind. He went down to ninth in 1952 but then rose to third in 1956 and second in 1960, when he finished only a few seconds behind the winner, Don Thompson of Britain (4:25:30.0). He closed his great career as an Olympian in 1964, when he finished sixteenth - alas with a time almost 13 minutes faster than his winning effort of 1948 in London! It should be added that in the 1956 Games he also took fourth place in the 20 km. This imperishable, slender (1.78 m./59 kg.) walker set several world records, including one of 4:29:58.0 for 50 km. at Fristad in 1953. Ljunggren's decline virtually coincided with the end of Sweden's golden age. In the early Fifties other race walking powers had emerged, notably including a brand new one, USSR, and two which could point to a glorious past, Britain and Italy. The first Russian to win a major international competition was Vladimir Ukhov, first in the 50 km. (4:22:11.2) in the 1954 European Championships at Bern. At the Melbourne Olympics two years later, another Russian, Leonid Spirin, won the 20 km., which from then on replaced the 10 km., a precarious venture vis-à-vis the ever present issue "proper walking vs. blatant lifting". Russia's winning ways continued with Yevgeniy Maskinskov, first in the 50 km. at the 1958 European Championships in 4:17:15.4. But the most distinguished performer of the Soviet school was Vladimir Golubnichiy (born at Sumi, Ukraine, on 2 June 1936; 1.79 m./78 kg.). His swinging gait and his stamina carried him to the first of his many world records when he was merely nineteen: 1:30:02.8 for 20 km. at Kiev in 1955. Then, over a period stretching from 1956 till 1974, he took part in seven major (Olympic or European) title races and managed to win medals in all of them! His breakthrough as a competitor occurred at the Rome Olympics (1960), when he braved the dangers of a hot, humid climate to win the 20 km. from a crack field in 1:34:07.2. His later deeds will be related in the chapter on the period 1961-1980. Britain's great tradition was brilliantly upheld by Stanley Vickers, winner of the 20 km. at the 1958 European Championships in Stockholm. This gallant walker, at 1.85 m. one of the tallest in the business, came home in 1:33:09, with almost two minutes to spare on Leonid Spirin. Czechoslovakia also had a prominent walker, Josef Dolezal, who was well in his thirties when he coupled his many record performances with a victory in the 10 km. at the 1954 European Championships in Bern.

Last but not least among the leading powers of race walking during those years was Italy. The first great post-war walker from the peninsula was Giuseppe ("Pino") Dordoni, still remembered by experts as one of the purest stylists ever seen. The fact that he did not join the ranks of prolific record breakers can in no way detract from his stature. If there is a branch in athletics where competitive achievements outweigh, easily and by far, record performances made in "cold" attempts, that is race walking. And Dordoni was usually at his best in the races that counted most. He made his début in the Olympics in 1948, finishing ninth in the 10 km. at twenty-two, then a "green" age for a top-class walker. Two years later, at the European Championships in Brussels, he moved to the 50 km. and won in impressive fashion (4:40:42.6), beating the likes of Ljunggren and Dolezal. His greatest success was at the 1952 Olympics in Helsinki, when he emerged after a wise race to win the 50 km. in 4:28:07.8, a new Olympic record. Dolezal was second, over 2 minutes behind. And Harold Whitlock of Britain, the 1936 Olympic champion, managed to finish eleventh at the venerable age of forty-nine! In later years Dordoni had to be content with lesser placings, yet he continued to be a factor through the 1960 Olympics. His decline virtually coincided with the advent of another Italian, Abdon Pamich (born at Fiume - now Rijeka in Yugoslavia - on 13 October 1933; 1.83 m./74 kg.), who was to become the most consistently great long distance walker of all time. An international over a period of twenty years (1954-1973), he took part in five editions of the Olympic Games. Like his countryman, sprinter Pietro Mennea, he hit gold at his third attempt, a rare example of tenacity finally rewarded. At the age of twenty-one, Pamich placed seventh in the 50 km. at the 1954 European Championships. Two years later he was fourth over the same distance and eleventh in the 20 km. at the Melbourne Olympics. He entered the medal sphere at the 1958 European Championships in Stockholm, finishing second in the 50 km., less than one minute behind Maskinskov. The sturdy Italian hoped to hit gold in the 1960 Olympics, held in his home country, but in the Rome event he had to be content with a bronze medal. His rendezvous with the most coveted of honours was only delayed four years, as will be related later on.

Throughout the period 1941-60, Europe thus had a virtual monopoly in race walking honours. The only notable exception was registered at the 1956

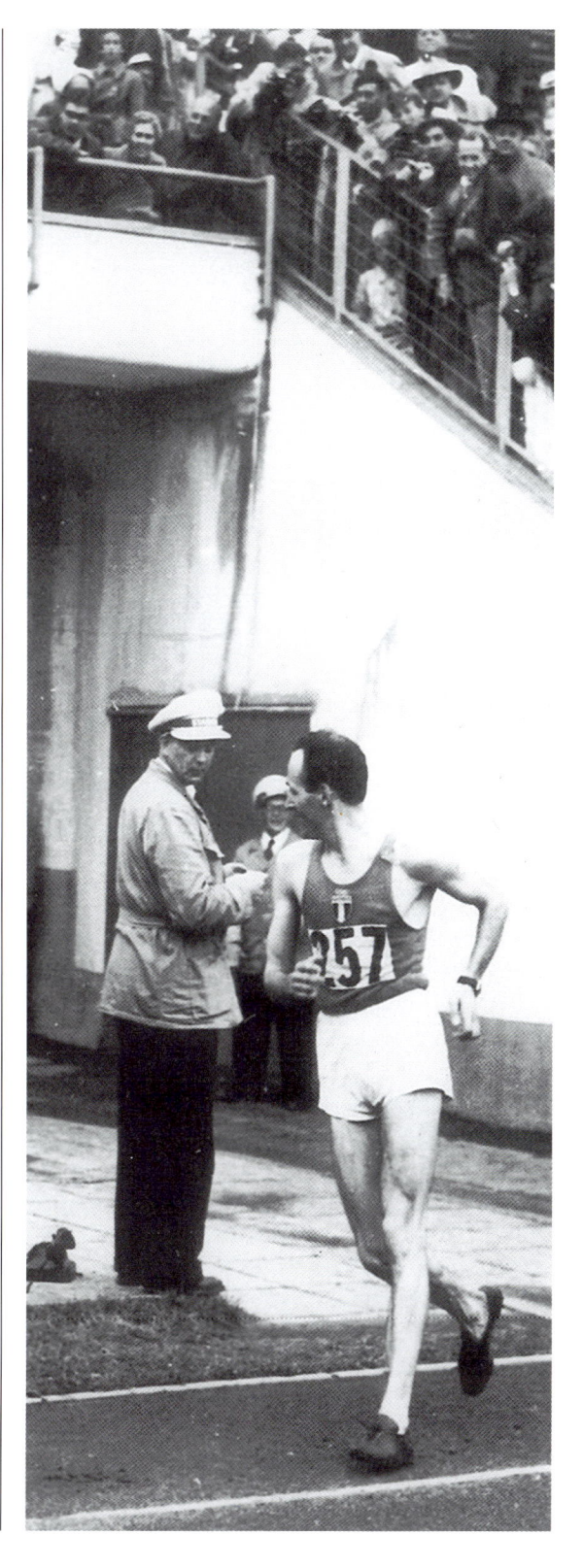

1941
1960

Giuseppe Dordoni (Italy), winner of the 50 km. walk at the 1952 Olympics in Helsinki.

Olympics in Melbourne, when Norman Read won the 50 km. in 4:30:42.8.

Born in England, he had settled down in Australia. Having in vain tried to be accepted in the Olympic team of either of those countries, he finally managed to gain selection in the New Zealand team.

His victory for the All blacks must have suggested second thoughts to those who had not believed in him! Read, who finished fifth in the 20 km. four years later in Rome, is not usually counted among the "Greats" of race walking, yet he will be remembered for providing one of the most stunning upsets in Olympic history.

1961 1980

CHAMPIONS AND RECORDS GALORE. POLITICAL INTERFERENCES. AFRICA ENTERS THE PICTURE

SPRINTS - 100 & 200 METRES: Hayes et al, speed demons galore

In running events, and particularly in the sprints, this period was characterized by three main factors, two of which were relevant to technical innovations and the third one connected with a shift in the balance of powers, race-wise at least. The first factor concerned the adoption at the international level of automatic electrical timing in hundredths-of-a-second. According to IAAF rules, this is to be assured with "equipment which is started automatically by the starter's gun and which records the finish time automatically". Something of the kind had been experimented in major Games as early as in 1932 (Los Angeles Olympics), but only as an aid to official manual timing, mainly to verify and possibly correct place differentials. Starting with the 1968 Olympics in Mexico City, automatic timing became official, thus replacing the traditional timing method assured by the fallible human element. In inverted roles, the latter was to be used merely as a back-up in case of malfunction of the electrical apparatus. At the Mexico Olympics the IAAF allowed a 0.05 sec. bonus to compensate for the reaction time, and marks thus obtained were rounded off to the tenth. The era of automatic timing without adjustments began with the Munich Olympics (1972).

It is commonly accepted that hand times are faster than automatic ones. This is probably due to the fact that timers (stationed alongside the finish line) tend to anticipate a runner's finish, rather than allow for the same delay as is caused by reaction to the flash of the starter's gun (obviously fired 100 or more metres away from the timers' stand). Experiments made during the Munich Olympics (1972) revealed an average plus of 0.24 sec. in the case of a 100 m. race timed automatically. Under this assumption, a "manual" 10.3 should be regarded as the theoretical equivalent of 10.54 with auto timing. However, it would be dangerous to take this as a fully reliable guideline, since hand timing practices vary from one country to another, sometimes even within the same country. In some areas, timers are so trained that their verdicts equate rather consistently with automatic times; in other areas, the difference may be as great as three tenths of a second, if not more.

In any case, it is generally conceded that the introduction of automatic timing has resulted in clearly more reliable verdicts, especially in the short races where the relative magnitude of error under hand timing was obviously greater.

The second relevant factor concerned tracks. Towards the end of the Sixties, conventional cinder tracks were gradually replaced by surfaces in synthetic materials. These so-called "all-weather tracks" (generally known under their trade name of "Tartan") soon proved more consistent and faster than the old cinder ones. The advantages derived from this innovation were certainly great, although obviously difficult, not to say impossible, to evaluate in actual fractions of time.

The third factor regarded the growing impact of

black sprinters, who during this period gradually outshone their white colleagues. Of course there had been a black victor in the Olympics as early as in 1932 (Eddie Tolan), but in the second half of the Sixties the trend became more and more evident, so much in fact that the eight finalists in the 100 m. of the Mexico Olympics (1968) were all black! This change has been particularly felt in USA, since time immemorial the richest reservoir of sprint talent. Since Bobby Morrow's 100/200 m. double at Melbourne (1956) and Dave Sime's second place in the 100m. in Rome (1960), no white sprinter from USA has ever won a medal in an Olympic sprint final! As an eye-witness to the 1976 and 1980 US Olympic Trials in Eugene, Oregon, I noticed that non-black sprinters were reduced to a negligible minority even in terms of quantity, and none of them would usually advance beyond the semi-finals. If one considers that in 1980 whites accounted for 83 % of the US population and blacks for 12 %, it seems reasonable to assume that "Caucasians" attending colleges and universities had by then begun to stay away from the sprints, obviously"scared" by the prowess of their black brothers. The best specimens of the white race in this department have recently come from Europe: after Hary and Berruti, the greatest menace to black supremacy was provided during the Seventies by Borzov, Mennea and Wells.

As it was, it fell to black Americans to stage a counter-attack after the bitter defeats suffered by Uncle Sam in the 1960 Olympics. First to lead the "vengeance parade" was solid Frank Budd. A year after finishing fifth in the 100 m. in Rome, this compact sprinter sped to a new world record of 9.2 in the 100 y. of the AAU Championships at New York on 24 June 1961. (An automatic Bulova timer caught him in 9.36). Shortly afterwards, two exceptional talents came to the fore: Bob Hayes and Henry Carr, great physical specimens both but rather different from each other. Hayes (born at Jacksonville, Florida, on 20 December 1942; 1.82 m./86 kg.) was essentially a power runner, endowed with a tremendous pick-up which made him almost unbeatable in the century. He ran the furlong on relatively rare occasions yet proved capable of challenging the world's best even at that distance. In 1961 he emerged practically from nowhere to chalk up times of 9.3 and 20.1 (straight course) for the English distances. In the next three years he was unquestionably the world's fastest 100 y./100 m. man. Between 1963 and 1964 he was caught in 9.1 for the 100 y. on four occasions, but for some reason only one of these clockings was ratified as a world record by the IAAF, namely his 9.1 in winning the AAU title on a rubberized asphalt track at St. Louis on 21 June 1963, aided by a legal wind of 0.85 m/s. Undefeated in the century in 1963-64, he went to the Tokyo Olympics as an odds-on favourite. The opposition notably included Enrique Figuerola, a stocky little fellow from Cuba, fourth in the 100 m. of the Rome Olympics and a 10.1 man; and Harry Jerome of Canada, who could point to a couple of 9.2 clockings in the 100 y. (both in 1962) and was thirsty for revenge after his unlucky show in 1960. Horacio Esteves of Venezuela, an Olympic semi-finalist in 1960 at the age of nineteen, ran history's third official 10-flat at Caracas on 15 August 1964, but an "ill-timed" injury kept him away from the Tokyo Olympics.

But when the chips were down, nobody was able to make an impression on the formidable Hayes. On the Tokyo Olympic track - which was to remain the last "conventional" surface used in the Olympics - he lost no time in laying his cards on the table: in his semi-final of the 100 m. he sped to a blistering 9.9, aided by a wind of 5.3 m/s. (The actual automatic time was 9.91). In the final, later in the day (15 October), he and Figuerola were off well, but then Hayes "exploded"and soon gained a full one-metre lead, which he increased to about 2 m. at the end of the race. One commentator described his margin of victory as "almost insulting to an Olympic final field". His official time was announced as a record equalling 10.0. In fact, his actual time was an automatic 10.06, which made his effort clearly superior in intrinsic value to all previous 10-flat marks returned with hand timing. Figuerola just nipped Jerome for second and both were officially credited with 10.2 (auto times, 10.25 and 10.27 respectively). The aiding wind was an allowable 1.1 m/s.

Hayes' competitive record between 1962 and 1964, notably including three wins in the 100 y. at the AAU Championships, was such as to make him a strong candidate for the title of World's Fastest Human of All Time, notwithstanding the achievements of Owens, Morrow and others. If we consider that his 10.06 was achieved on a conventional track and in a soft pole lane, one could venture the opinion that such a man has not been outshone by the speed demons of the Eighties.

While Hayes was ruling the roost in the century, his compatriot Henry Carr was treating likewise the world's best 200 m. men. Like Jesse Owens, this powerful yet smooth runner came from the "Deep South" (born at Montgomery, Alabama, on 27 November 1942; 1.90 m./84 kg.) and, like Owens, he emerged as a "speed demon" in the Middle West, namely at Detroit, capital of the automobile.

Consequently and inevitably, he was defined "the

fastest Car(r) ever to come out of Detroit". At nineteen he ran the English distances in 9.5, 20.6 (straight track) and 47.8. By then, Americans had abandoned their traditional 220 y. straightaway in favour of the Olympic (one turn) course. Results were quick to follow. After his High School days in the Middle West, Carr moved to a college in Arizona. In 1963, at Tempe, he ran 220 y. round a turn in a record shattering 20.3, and on 4 April 1964, still at Tempe, he improved to 20.2, aided by a wind of 0.5 m/s. On the eve of the Tokyo Games the only man who looked capable of giving him something to think about was Paul Drayton, a 20.4 performer in the 220 y. round a turn.

In the Tokyo final (17 October), Carr was not to be denied. Running in the favourable lane 8, against a wind of 0.8 m/s in the stretch, he disposed of his rivals as he pleased to win in 20.3 (actual auto time, 20.36) from Drayton, 20.5, and Edwin Roberts of Trinidad, 20.6 (or 20.58 and 20.63 respectively). Defending champion Livio Berruti of Italy was fifth in 20.8 (20.83). The last named had ostensibly "taken ten" after his 1960 victory in Rome, yet his Tokyo race in the unfavourable lane 1 amounted to one of his best efforts ever. Clock-wise at least, Henry Carr outshone the great Herb McKenley as a "complete" sprinter. In addition to 9.3 (100 y.), 10.2 (100 m.) and 20.2 (220 y.) in the "pure" sprints, he had a significant 45.4 in the 400 m.

In the late Sixties, good "merchants of speed" could be found in several parts of the world. Enrique Figuerola had revived a Cuban tradition born in the Twenties with José Barrientos (after whom is named Cuba's best known meet). On the way to his third Olympiad, Figuerola posted a record-equalling 10.0. at Budapest in 1967. Even Asia had some notable sprinters, like Hideo Iijima of Japan (10.1 in 1964) and Chen Chia-chuan of China, who in 1965 at Chungking (Chongqing in the Pinyin phonetic alphabet) was credited with 10.0 in the 100 m., a mark the IAAF could not take into consideration, since China was not a member of the international body at that time. In Europe, France had a promising sprinter hailing from Guadeloupe, Roger Bambuck, who in 1966 won the 200 m. at the European Championships in Budapest, thereby becoming the first black athlete to win a European title. (In the late Eighties, Bambuck was to become Minister of Sports and recreation in the French Government).

About halfway between the Tokyo and the Mexico Olympics, two exceptional talents came to the fore in USA: Jim Hines and Tommie Smith. The former

1961
1980

Olympic 100 metre final in Tokyo (1964). From left to right: M. Pender (USA), tied for 6th; T. Robinson (Bahamas), 8th; W. Maniak (Poland), 4th; H. Jerome (Canada), 3rd; G. Kone (Ivory Coast), tied for 6th; E. Figuerola (Cuba), 2nd; H. Schumann (Germany), 5th; and Bob Hayes (USA), 1st in 10.0, equalling the world record.

Tommie "Jet" Smith (USA), one of the All Time "Greats" in the 200 m.

(born at Dumas, Arkansas, on 10 September 1946; 1.83 m./81 kg.) was a 9.4 100 y. performer at eighteen. He was coached at Texas Southern by former Olympic sprint champion Bobby Morrow. Although hampered for some time by a serious false start problem, he eventually developed into a top-class sprinter. In 1967 he "exploded" with record equalling performances in both 100 y. (9.1 at Houston) and 100 m. (10.0 at Modesto). In the longer race he was extended by Willie Turner, who was also timed in 10.0. Shortly afterwards, another up-and-coming star, Charles Greene, took advantage of the rarefied atmosphere of Provo, Utah (1387 m.) to clock 9.1 for the 100 y. The automatic timer caught Greene in 9.21, which was to remain the fastest clocking ever registered for the time-honoured English distance. In 1976, all Imperial distances, except the mile, were dropped from the list of world records.

Tommie Smith (born at Acworth, Texas, on 5 June 1944; 1.90 m./84 kg.) is still regarded as one of the most talented sprinters in the annals of track. In terms of sustained speed he was probably the greatest of all. At twenty he was capable of 21.0 (200 m.) and 46.5 (440 y.). Like Carr, he could have discovered new worlds in the one-lap event, but for some reason in his adult years he generally stayed away from this distance, save for one serious head-to-head confrontation with Lee Evans in 1967 (more on this later). But Smith was instrumental in raising 200 m. running to a new dimension. He began to astound experts in 1966, while a student at San Jose State under Bud Winter, a dedicated, ebullient coach. On 7 May of that year, at San Jose, "Tommie Jet", as he was called, was credited with an incredible 19.5 for 220 y. straightaway, implying an average speed of 37.139 km. per hour. A truly superlative effort, even if favoured by a wind of 1.9 m/s in the stretch and sanctioned by somewhat controversial readings (watches showed 19.4, 19.5 and 19.6 at 200 m., 19.5, 19.5 and 19.6 at 220 y.). Later in the season, on 11 June at Sacramento, Smith ran the same distance round a turn in 20.0 (wind nil), virtually the first sub-20 secs. effort if converted to its 200 m. equivalent.

1968 was a memorable year in the domain of sprinting. The highlights were provided by the AAU Championships and the Mexico Olympics. In the former, held on 20 June at Sacramento on a conventional yet very fast track, Jim Hines got the ball rolling with a sensational 9.8 in the first heat of the 100 m., aided by an illegal wind of 2.8 m/s. In the first "semi" the wind was down to 0.8 m/s and Hines was able to chalk up history's first sub-10 secs. performance under legal conditions. His 9.9 had the support of an impressive auto time, 10.03. Ronnie Ray Smith finished about a metre behind Hines yet received the same official time (and a more truthful auto time, 10.14). In the other "semi", Charles Greene matched Hines' 9.9, with a wind of 0.9 m/s. The final offered a close fight between Greene and Hines, with the former winning by a scant margin and both credited with a wind- assisted 10.0. Next came Lennox Miller of Jamaica, Roger Bambuck of France and Ronnie Ray Smith in that order, all in 10.1. In one of the "semis" the Frenchman had been credited with 10.0 for a new European record. Really a mind-blowing day for sprint enthusiasts!

In the 200 m. the fireworks were provided by the US Olympic Trials, held at Echo Summit on 12 September.

That mountain site (altitude, 2250 m.) assured US technicians that conditions would be similar to those that were to be expected at Mexico City. John Carlos, an imposing figure who in 1967 had run the English distances in 9.4 and 20.3, had his Day of Days and won the 200 m. in 19.7 (auto time, 19.92), handing the great Tommie Smith (20.0/20.18) one of his rare defeats. The assisting wind (1.9 m/s) was within the allowable limit, yet Carlos' mark could not be submitted to the IAAF since he (and Smith) had used multi- spike "brush" shoes. The rules state that each shoe may have six spikes up front and two in the heel at the maximum. Smith ran in lane 1, while Carlos was in lane 4. In the Olympics, the rarefied atmosphere of Mexico City (altitude, 2200 m.) caused an even greater "explosion" in sprint standards. The prelims produced a host of fast times. In the final (14 October) eight men lined up at the start, and for the first time in Olympic annals all of them were black. Little Mel Pender of USA was fastest off the blocks, but Hines soon began his long, hard drive, and built up a lead. From then on he was never headed. Greene was expected to be his toughest rival, but in the closing stage he sensed a pull in his hamstring, eased up a little before resuming high speed, alas too late. He had to give way to Lennox Miller for second place. Aided by a rather negligible wind (0.3 m/s), Hines was credited with 9.95 - history's first sub-10 secs. mark with auto timing. Place winners were Miller (10.04), Greene (10.07), Pablo Montes of Cuba (10.14) and Bambuck (10.15). The Frenchman had done better (10.11) in a semi-final.

The 200 m. crown was awarded on 16 October. Tommie Smith was limping badly after his "semi", but two hours later he showed up for the final, "wrapped from the waist to the lower edge of his running shorts". In the heat of competition, however, he never seemed to be bothered. He was in lane 3, with his most feared rival, Carlos, just ahead of him in lane 4. The latter was out to duplicate his Echo Summit trick and got off like a bullet. At the half-way mark he led Smith by a metre, but when "Tommie Jet" got into high gear it was really no contest. He drew away with supreme ease with 60 m. to go. About 15 m. before the finish, Smith threw both arms up in a victory gesture: that cost him precious fractions of time, yet he managed to finish in a record- breaking 19.8 (auto time, 19.83; wind + 0.9 m/s). Meanwhile Carlos, probably suffering the effects of his hyper-fast getaway, lost second place to little known Peter Norman, an Australian who had come to the Games with a personal best of 20.5. Both were officially credited with 20.0, their auto times being 20.06 and 20.10 respectively. Next came Edwin Roberts of Trinidad (20.3) and Bambuck (20.5).

Before the final, Smith and Carlos badly wanted to mount the victory dais also for another reason. Like Lee Evans and a few other black Americans, they had adhered to the project of Prof. Harry Edwards, a sociologist who advocated using the Olympic "limelight" (to be seen by millions of TV viewers around the world) to demonstrate in favour of their "Olympic Project for Human Rights". Smith and Carlos thus appeared on the dais wearing black gloves, black socks and no shoes (symbols of black poverty) and saluted with clenched fists. Such a show, widely discussed in USA and elsewhere, obviously created a split in the US team, even among black athletes.

1961
1980

Valeriy Borzov (USSR) in a relay race. The only European sprinter to score the 100/200 m. double in the Olympics (Munich, 1972).

Don Quarrie (Jamaica), a durable and highly competitive sprinter.

The majority seemed to disapprove the idea of using the Olympic arena for what was after all a political demonstration. The two demonstrators were expelled from the Games Village by the US Olympic Committee. After the revolutionary results of Echo Summit and Mexico City, many observers came to the conclusion that the problem of record marks made at high altitude certainly deserved consideration. They felt that it would be advisable to separate such "inflated" marks from those made at or near sea level - as it was done in other sports. Jean Creuzé, a French student of statistics and aerodynamics, calculated that the effect of rarefied atmosphere at Mexico City was such as to equate, over a 100 m. course, to that of an assisting wind of 1.2 m/s. Considering that in the 100 m. Hines was aided by a negligible breeze of 0.3 m/s, then his 9.95 would have been legal even in the (theoretical) "double account" of altitude and wind (1.2 + 0.3 = 1.5). But in other cases, including for instance several triple jump efforts aided by a wind of 2.0 m/s, the advantage would have excelled the allowable limit. The problem of setting a borderline in terms of altitude is of course a difficult one, which may partly explain why the IAAF (as of 1990) has not pronounced judgment on the matter. The Association of Track & Field Statisticians (ATFS) has tentatively set 1000 m. as the borderline to distinguish between altitude and non-altitude marks, namely in the following events: 100, 200, 400 m. flat, 110 and 400 m. hurdles, long jump, triple jump, 4x100 and 4x400 m. relays - which could roughly be described as the domain of "short-lived" (mostly anaerobic) efforts. In its World Year Lists, the ATFS denotes marks made at altitudes over 1000 m. with an "A", but does not keep them separate from other marks. To wind up the tale on the Mexico Olympics, I may add that the banning of South Africa from the Games had resulted in the non-participation of Paul Nash, a 21-year-old sprinter who in the 1968 Zurich meet had done 10.0 and 20.1 in the space of 50 minutes. Towards the end of 1968, the European Junior Games held at Leipzig revealed a bright new prospect from USSR, Valeriy Borzov, who scored an impressive double with 10.4 and 21.0. A few weeks later, just before turning nineteen, he was down to 10.2 in the century. This man (born at Sambor, Ukraine, on 20 October 1949; 1.82 m./82 kg.) was to become one of the greatest sprinters of the Seventies, and probably the greatest ever in European annals. A compact runner if ever there was one, he had no weak points: a very fast starter, cool and poised in every phase of the race, he ran like a well-oiled machine from start to finish. He added to his natural gifts through years of hard and systematic work, mostly under the tutelage of Valentin Petrovskiy, a physiologist. In 1969 Borzov won the European 100 m. title in Athens (10.4) and in subsequent years he began to take the measure of his American rivals, beating them twice in the 100 m. of the USSR vs USA dual meet: at Leningrad in 1970 (10.4) and at Berkeley in 1971 (10.5). Hines and Smith had by then retired from the scene, and their successors were not in the same class. Borzov went on to score a fine double at the 1971 European Championships in Helsinki, with times of 10.27 and 20.30.

Americans gave signs of rejuvenation at their Olympic Trials in Eugene, Oregon, on 1 July 1972, when Eddie Hart, 23, equalled the "manual" world record for the 100 m., 9.9, in windless conditions. Rey Robinson, 20, a close second, was also timed in 9.9, while Robert Taylor was third in 10.0. These marks lacked the support of auto-timing though.

In the meantime two "gems" had appeared elsewhere in the world, both destined to fear no foes in terms of durability. They were Don Quarrie of Jamaica and Pietro Mennea of Italy. The former (born at Kingston on 25 February 1951; 1.73 m./70 Kg.) qualified for the Mexico Olympics as a teen-ager, but an injury stopped him on the eve of the Games. In later years he improved rapidly and in 1970 he was able to score a significant double (10.24 and 20.56, the former wind assisted) at the British Commonwealth Games in Edinburgh. He reached the top on 3 August 1971 at the Pan American Games in Cali (altitude, 1046 m.), when he came dangerously close to Tommie Smith's 200 m. record with a sparkling 19.86, aided by a legal wind of 0.9 m/s. A short man, the Jamaican showed an amazingly fast leg work. He grew up athletically in US collegiate ranks, and soon proved a tough competitor for everybody. Mennea (born at Barletta on 28 June 1952; 1.79 m./68 kg.) also emerged as a teen-ager, finishing fifth in the 200 m. at the 1970 European Junior Championships. He worked for many years with coach Carlo Vittori, a former Italian sprint champion (10.6 in the 100 m.). Mennea was very selective in choosing his commitments throughout the season and knew how to concentrate on major Games. This may have been not the last reason of his longevity as a top-class sprinter. Very soon he showed a preference for the 200 m., and in 1971 he placed sixth in this event at the European Championships in Helsinki with a new personal best of 20.88 (Borzov won in 20.30, as previously related). In June 1972 he and Borzov met at Milan, this time over 100 m., and the Ukrainian won by a scant margin as both equalled the European record (10.0). The next day, with Borzov not in the race, Mennea took the 200 m. in 20.2, equalling the European "manual" record set by Borzov himself at Moscow in 1971.

A man who looked capable of playing a prominent role in the Munich Games was Jean-Louis Ravelomanantsoa of Madagascar. After finishing eighth in the 100 m. at the Mexico Olympics, he made steady progress and in 1971 he compiled a fine set of 100 m. performances, including a 10.0 at Helsinki, enough to earn position no.2 in "Track & Field News" World Ranking, behind Borzov. Unfortunately he was hampered by a poor physical condition at Munich and thus failed to survive the 100 m. "semis".

A missed rendezvous

What happened to Eddie Hart and Rey Robinson at the 1972 Olympics in Munich certainly has right of place in the chapter of track's strangest memorabilia. On the eve of the Games these young US sprinters ranked among the favourites for the 100 m. crown, were it only for their record-equalling 9.9 marks at the US Olympic Trials early in July. In the Olympic arena they easily won their heats in the morning of 31 August, thus qualifying for the quarter-finals, which in their opinion (and that of US team coach Stan Wright) were to take place at 6 p.m. the same day - rather than 4 p.m. as indicated in the official timetable. (As it later transpired, Wright had been using a 15-month old schedule issued by the US Olympic Committee).

According to "Track & Field News", things went like this. Around 4 p.m., Hart and Robinson were in the ABC building just outside the Olympic Village, in the company of third US qualifier Robert Taylor. Fully relaxed, they were viewing on a TV set some races being run off at the Olympic stadium. "Hey, what's that? A re-run of the heats this morning?" asked one. "No, that's live", was the reply. "Happening right now. That's our race!" Before one could say (Jack) Robinson they were rushed to the Olympic Stadium, half a mile away, in an ABC car.

But by the time they arrived, both Robinson's and Hart's races had been run, and only Taylor was alive. The lucky escaper warmed up in a hurry, then lined up at the start of his quarter-final, with Borzov and others. With his adrenalin running high, he finished right behind Borzov (10.07) in 10.16, his best auto time ever! (In the final the next day Taylor was again second to Borzov).

Coach Stan Wright admitted it was entirely his fault if two co-holders of the 100 m. world record missed the rendezvous of their life. From the looks of things, Hart could have been a hard nut to crack for anyone, possibly including Borzov, but in my opinion the Soviet athlete would have won anyhow. As for Robinson, 20, he appeared to be limping after winning his heat in the morning.

1961
1980

201

At Munich, Valeriy Borzov left no doubts as to the identity of the World's Fastest Human anno 1972. In the 100 m. he was partly favoured by a strange incident (the Hart-Robinson case, dealt with in an aside). Yet the Ukrainian looked perfect in all his appearances. After lowering the European "automatic" record to 10.07 in the prelims, he won the final (1 September) in fine style from Robert Taylor of USA, 10.14 to 10.24. Lennox Miller, the powerful Jamaican, again won a medal (10.33), ahead of little Aleksandr Kornelyuk of USSR (10.36), a very fast starter. Incidentally, in Munich there was a machine known as "Startkontrolle" which verified the reaction time (to the starter's gun) of every sprinter. In the various rounds of the 100 m. the lowest differential, 0.12 sec., was provided by Borzov and Kornelyuk.

In the 200 m. final (4 September) Borzov's superiority was if possible even more apparent. After a perfect journey, he threw his arms in the air before crossing the line - in 20.00, a new European record and the fastest "auto" time ever at or near sea level (Munich: 520 m.), and in windless conditions. Larry Black of USA ran an excellent race in lane 1 to take second place in 20.19, ahead of Pietro Mennea (20.30) and another American, Larry Burton (20.37).

Borzov never fully regained the splendid condition he had exhibited at Munich. In subsequent years he mostly concentrated on the 100 m. At the 1974 European Championships in Rome he won from Mennea, 10.27 to 10.34. A very fast starter, Borzov won no less than seven European indoor titles at 50/60 m., between 1970 and 1977. He usually stayed away from the 200 m. and never again tried the 400 m., a distance he had run in 47.6 at the age of twenty.

In the Munich Games, Don Quarrie was stopped by a pulled muscle in the next-to-last round of the 200 m. But he was stubborn enough to overcome - he would have a third and a fourth Olympic chance .... During the Seventies he won seven AAU titles, two in the century and three in the furlong. His most serious rival in those years was Steve Williams, a magnificent US sprinter who amassed a lot of classy marks and won many important races but simply had no luck in Olympic years: in 1972 and again in 1976, he was stopped by injuries on the threshold of the Olympics. His physical prowess was not always accompanied by an adequate singleness of purpose. In 1973 at Fresno he equalled the world's 100 y. record (9.1) and the following year, at Westwood, he matched the 100 m. mark (9.9). In 1975-76 he amassed three more 9.9's and was once timed in 9.8 at Eugene, but on that occasion hand timing was only used unofficially, and the "auto" time for him was 10.19. Still at Eugene, on 7 June 1975, he was narrowly edged by Don Quarrie in the 220 y. and both were credited with a record-shattering 19.9. The early Seventies also featured a number of "meteoric" figures, like Ivory Crockett, a lithe American, AAU 100 y. champion twice, who on 11 May 1974 at Knoxville, Tennessee, ran history's first official 9.0 for the 100 y.(wind nil); like Dr. Delano Meriwether, who at the age of twenty-eight took time out from his medical duties to win the 1971 AAU 100 y. title in 9.0, aided by a wind over the limit; or like Houston McTear, an explosive starter

Pietro Mennea (Italy) setting a new world's 200 m. record (19.72) at the Universiade in Mexico City, 1979.

who in 1975, aged eighteen, equalled Crockett's 100 y. mark (9.0) in a High School meet. In 1976 he qualified for the US Olympic team but at the crucial moment he was stopped by an injury. In 1977 he fared well in several European meets, notably with a 10.13 for the 100 m. at Köln.

In 1975 (apart from Quarrie's and Williams' feats, previously related) one of the highlights was offered by the Zurich meet, which had by then risen to the no.1 rank among European Invitationals. In the 100 m., Steve Riddick of USA beat his rival and friend Steve Williams, 10.05 to 10.08, while Borzov was third (10.16). Exceptional times in view of the adverse wind (1.2 m/s). In the same year, Borzov barely held off Mennea in the 100 m. of the European Cup at Nice (both 10.40), then lost to the Italian for the first time in the 200 m., 20.61 to 20.42. These two had ruled the roost also at the 1974 European Championships the year before, with Borzov winning the 100 m. as related above, and the Italian taking the 200 m. title comfortably (20.60). New stars came to the fore on the eve of the 1976 Olympics in Montreal. At the US Olympic Trials in Eugene, 19-year-old Harvey Glance won the 100 m. in 10.11; in the 200 m., Millard Hampton won from an 18-year-old lad, Dwayne Evans, 20.10 to 20.22. Meanwhile, the Caribbean area was ready to field two gems in the persons of Don Quarrie of Jamaica and Hasely Crawford of Trinidad. The latter had made the 100 m. final in 1972, pulling up lame after a few strides. In later years this solid but somewhat unpredictable sprinter fared well on both sides of the Atlantic. At the Montreal Olympics, athletes competed in a huge stadium, which looked like a giant concrete mushroom. Its massive curving walls arched out to produce a wondrous roof which kept all snug and dry. Only an oval hole at the top kept the whole thing from being an indoor facility, which would have been unacceptable under IAAF rule 148/4b ("The record must be made out of doors"). Few Games, if any, were ever exempt from the wind factor as those held in Montreal. In the sprints, Central America simply K.O.'d USA and Europe. In the 100 m. final (24 July), mighty Crawford of Trinidad nosed out his Jamaican rival Don Quarrie, 10.06 to 10.07, while Borzov was third in 10.14, curiously the same time that had earned him a gold medal four years earlier. With Harvey Glance no better than fourth (10.19), USA failed to win a medal - for the first time since 1928. In the 200 m. (26 July), Quarrie's tenacity was finally rewarded: after a perfect race he went home the winner in 20.22, beating the US duo of Hampton and Evans (20.29 and 20.43 respectively), while Pietro Mennea, in the uncomfortable lane 1, was a disappointing fourth (20.54).

In 1977 the unlucky Steve Williams won the one and only major international honour of his career when he barely beat Eugen Ray of East Germany, 10.13 to 10.15, in the 100 m. of the inaugural World Cup at Düsseldorf. Silvio Leonard took third place (10.19), well ahead of Mennea (10.37). The Italian partly made amends for this bad blow by finishing centimetres behind Clancy Edwards of USA in a hotly contested 200 m. (both 20.17).

1978 saw the emergence of a not-so-green Scotsman, Allan Wells (born at Edinburgh on 3 May 1952; 1.83 m./77 kg). It is rather unusual for a sprinter to reach world class at twenty-six. Until then, in fact, Wells had done no better than 10.55 and 21.10 (and 7.32 in the long jump). So it was only in 1978, after working harder than ever under the guidance of a former "pro" sprinter, Wilson Young, that Wells finally made the grade at the international level. After setting a British 100 m. record of 10.15 in his native city, he went to Edmonton, Canada, to compete in the Commonwealth Games. In that important meet he held his own against Don Quarrie, barely losing to the Jamaican in the 100 m., 10.07 to 10.03 (wind-assisted), then winning the 200 m. in 20.12 ("windy" again), after Quarrie was stopped by an injury in the prelims.

In 1978 Mennea enjoyed the first of three nearly perfect seasons. His best work in terms of quality and quantity was at the European Championships in Prague. He won the 100 m. in 10.27 (after a 10.19 heat), beating the likes of Ray, Wells and Borzov, who was by then plagued by tendon troubles; then he won the 200 m. hands down in 20.16. In the space of six days, counting individual and relay events (prelims and finals), he made ten appearances, and in his last effort he ran a leg of the 4x400 m. relay in 44.4. His potential for the one-lap event had become apparent in 1977, when he did 45.87 outdoors, and was confirmed early in 1978, when he won the European Indoor title. But, like many top-class sprinters, he disliked the "longest dash" and subsequently forgot about it.

Other superlative sprinters of 1978 were Silvio Leonard of Cuba (10.08 and 20.06) and Clancy Edwards of USA (10.07 and 20.03). Also worthy of note was Eddie Hart's comeback. Six years after experiencing disappointment in Munich, he ran the metric century in 10.07 at high altitude but failed to make an impact in major competitions.

Clock-wise at least, Mennea reached his peak in 1979. His main target for the season was the Universiade to be held at Mexico City in September - his not-so-secret aim was to break Tommie Smith's famous 200 m. world record (19.83), made on the same track eleven years earlier. While preparing for

Michael Larrabee (USA) captures the 400 metre crown in the 1964 Olympics, time 45.1. Others from left: W. Mottley (Trinidad), 2nd; U. Williams (USA), 5th; and R. Brightwell (GB), 4th. A. Badenski (Poland), not in the picture, was 3rd.

that event with a great singleness of purpose, he rounded into form gradually. In August he had mixed fortunes in the European Cup at Turin, barely winning the 100 m. in 10.15 from Marian Woronin of Poland (10.16) and Allan Wells (10.19), and losing to the Scotsman in the 200 m., 20.31 to 20.29 (wind-assisted). Mennea went to Mexico early, and thus had plenty of time to acclimatize to the rarefied atmosphere. The benefits soon became apparent when in tune-up races held on consecutive days (3-4 September) he first returned a "manual" 19.8 for the 200 m., then 10.01 for the 100 m., thus beating Borzov's European record. In the Universiade proper he chose to concentrate on the 200 m. and produced the following series, on three consecutive days (10-12 September): 19.96 (heat), 20.04 (semi-final), and a record-shattering 19.72 (final). In the decisive race he was in his beloved lane 4, which in Italian meets had been "his" for years, almost by divine right. Aided by a 1.8 m/s wind down the stretch, he ran a beautiful race, finally winning as he pleased from Leszek Dunecki of Poland, who came home in 20.24, a personal best. It was a race aided by favourable conditions throughout: all the eight finalists but one chalked up new personal bests. The lonely exception was Otis Melvin of USA, who had improved on his PB in a semi-final! The average gain per man vis-à-vis previous bests at or near sea level was an eye-catching 0.38 secs. Having done better than "Tommie Jet" Smith under similar conditions, Mennea could now claim a record of substance. Mennea and Wells had stayed away from the World Cup, held at Montreal a few weeks earlier. Under the strictly "aseptic" conditions evidenced by the 1976 Olympics, James Sanford, a heavily muscled American, won the 100 m. from Silvio Leonard, 10.17 to 10.26, and the Cuban took the 200 m. in 20.34.

The Olympic Games of 1980 suffered heavily as a result of new inroads by international politics into sport. USA and other countries of the non-Communist world decided to boycott the Moscow event. The protest, led by US president Jimmy Carter, was over the invasion of Afghanistan by Soviet troops in 1979. A sad affair, four years after the African boycott of the Montreal Games. In some Western countries, notably including Britain and Italy, national Olympic committees refused to follow the line taken by their Governments and sent teams to Moscow. Outstanding among the absentees were USA, West Germany, Japan and Kenya. Quite understandably, the absence of US sprinters altered the picture in the sprint department, although it should be noted that 1980 did not look exactly like a vintage year for Uncle Sam's dashmen. At their Olympic Trials (run off only as a symbolic gesture), 19-year-old Stanley Floyd won the 100 m. from Harvey Glance, 10.26 to 10.27. Fourth in this race was another teenager, bound to be heard from in subsequent years: Carl Lewis. Had USA taken part in the Moscow Games, he would have run the 4x100 m. relay. James Butler topped the 200 m. field in 20.49.

Valeriy Borzov, by then in his thirties, tried to qualify for his third Olympic venture, but recurrent ankle problems (he had been operated on not long ago) prevented him from taking part. In Moscow, Allan Wells showed he was ready by running a quarter-final of the 100 m. in 10.11, his best ever. In a semi-final, Quarrie and Mennea had their gloomiest day ever and failed to survive. In the decisive race Wells had to give all he had to narrowly edge consistent Silvio Leonard, with both returning 10.25. Petar Petrov of Bulgaria was third in 10.39. To everybody's surprise, Mennea and Quarrie were back in good form by the time the 200 m. final was run. The Italian was in lane 8, with Allan Wells right behind in lane 7. Quarrie was in lane 4, and Leonard in the pole lane. Wells went out fast, too fast perhaps, and led by nearly 2 metres mid-way in the race. Then Mennea began to close the gap, collared his rival in the last stretch of track and beat him, 20.19 to 20.21. Quarrie was a solid third (20.29), just ahead of Leonard (20.30). The three medal winners averaged just over 28 years in age. Mennea had reportedly trained rather inconsistently before going to Moscow, probably as a result of contradictory reports about the participation of Italy in the Moscow Games. He eventually reached his best-ever form in post-Olympic meets: between 5 August and 27 September he competed in eight 200 m. races all over the world (Italy, Belgium, Japan and China), winning them all and averaging a phenomenal 20.07. His fastest time, 19.96, was achieved in his native town of Barletta. Having won a gold and a silver in the Olympics, Allan Wells certainly deserved a place of honour among Europe's best ever. Only Borzov, among continentals, had done better than the Scotsman in the Olympics. In post-Games meets Wells showed slightly decli-ning form and lost 1-to-2 in direct clashes with young Stanley Floyd of USA in the 100 m.

400 METRES - Mexico summit: Evans vs. James

1961 1980

All Time Lists for the one-lap event are among the "noblest" a statistician can ever dream of: at this distance, most if not all leading marks invariably occur in major international meets. Let's take the Olympic Games, 1960 through 1980, as an example: all those who won 400 m. gold medals in this period achieved the distinction by posting the fastest "auto" time of their career!

In 1961 a bright new prospect appeared in Britain: Adrian Metcalfe, a nineteen-year-old lad with a powerful physical build, who ran 400 m. in 45.7. A great start, no doubt, but for some reason that was to remain his best ever.

In 1962 major titles went to George Kerr of Jamaica at the British Commonwealth Games (440 y. in 46.74) and Robbie Brightwell of Britain at the European Championships (400 m. in 45.9). Then, in a college meet held at Tempe, Arizona, in the spring of 1963, Adolph Plummer of USA surprised a lot of people with a record-breaking "quarter" of 44.9 (220 y. fractions, 21.7 and 23.2). It was not a "cold" race though: Plummer was extended by Ulis Williams, who finished second in 45.6.

As the Tokyo Olympics drew near, a mature runner came to the fore in USA. This man was Mike Larrabee (born at Los Angeles on 2 December 1933; 1.85 m./79 kg.). After emerging in 1957 (46.5 in the 440 y.), he had shown in-and-out form for years. It was only in 1964 that he hit the form of his lifetime. At the US Olympic Trials in Los Angeles on 12 September he ran a wise race to equal the world's 400 m. record, 44.9 (fractions, 22.4 and 22.5), narrowly edging Ulis Williams (45.0). In the Olympic final at Tokyo, Larrabee was again the man who in the closing stage "decelerated the least". He moved from fifth to first in the last 100 m. and hit gold in 45.15, beating Wendell Mottley of Trinidad (45.24), Andrzej Badenski of Poland (45.64) and Robbie Brightwell (45.75). Mottley reached the top of his condition two years later at the British Commonwealth Games in Kingston, when he won the "quarter" in 45.08. Still in 1966, a new man destined to make history appeared on the ever changing American scene: Lee Evans (born at Madera, California, on 25 February 1947; 1.80 m./79 kg). Endowed with plenty of speed (20.4 in the 200 m.), he was especially redoubtable for his staying power in the conclusive stage of the race. As a teen-ager he improved from 48.2 in 1964 to 46.9 in

Alberto Juantorena (Cuba), who scored a unique 400/800 m. double at the 1976 Olympics in Montreal.

1965 (both in the 440 y.). He reached national class in 1966 with 45.2 at the metric distance. By then he was a hard man to beat. One of his rare defeats occurred at the hands of a ... non-specialist by the name of Tommie Smith. It happened on 20 May 1967 at San Jose in a "hot" 440 y. race. Curiously enough, Smith the supreme sprinter chose to "sit" behind his rival in the early stages. Evans thus led him at 110 y. (10.9 to 11.0) and 220 y. (21.5 to 21.7). Smith came into his own when Evans began to fade. Positions were thus reversed at the 330 y. mark (33.5 to 33.8). Then Smith increased his lead further and won a comfortable victory - 44.8 to 45.3. To his world's quarter-mile record Smith was able to add the metric mark (44.5) as well. That was to remain his only notable inroad into top-class quarter miling - with no regret, I suppose, on the part of the so-called specialists.

The year 1968 was marked by two notable events: the coming- of-age of synthetic tracks and the first ever Olympics at high altitude, i.e. in a rarefied atmosphere. These factors resulted in a big boost for athletic standards, especially in events belonging in the anaerobic sphere. The Americans decided to hold their Olympic Trials at Echo Summit, California, amidst the towering pines of the El Dorado National Forest. This mountain site (altitude, 2250 m.) enjoyed atmospheric conditions essentially similar to those that were to be expected at the Olympics in Mexico City. On 14 September, Evans and his new rival Larry James engaged in a fierce 400 m. battle, which saw the former emerge the winner - 44.06 to 44.19. Same as in the case of Carlos' record run in the 200 m. held in the same meet, Evans' record time could not be submitted for approval, since he (and James too) had used "brush shoes" not compatible with international rules. Ron Freeman (44.62) and Vince Matthews (44.86), third and fourth respectively, made this the fastest race ever. But more was to come later in the year.

The double advantage of a Tartan track and rarefied atmosphere became even more apparent at Mexico City. Some runners from outside the Euro-American sphere were hardly familiar with such factors, yet they showed notable gains vis-à-vis their best times at or near sea level. Sub-46 secs. times were ten a dime from the earliest rounds. In a semi-final Martin Jellinghaus of West Germany chalked up the fastest auto time ever by a European: 45.06. In the final the following day (18 October) Evans was less cautious than usual. Running in lane 6, he went out very fast: 10.4 at 100 m., 21.1 at 200 m. He slowed down a bit in the third fraction round the curve (32.2 at 300 m.) and in the stretch he suffered quite a bit, yet managed to hold off his great rival Larry James. Clock-wise, results were revolutionary: 43.86 for Evans and 43.97 for James. (These were the actual auto times, officially adjusted to 43.8 and 43.9). Ron Freeman was third (44.41), ahead of Amadou Gakou of Senegal (45.01) and Jellinghaus (45.33). It should be noted that the African runner had gone to Mexico with a seasonal best of 46.7, achieved at Font-Romeu, France (altitude, 1800 m.) and a sea-level best of 47.6! Evans' 100 m. fractions (10.4, 10.7, 11.1, 11.7) - apparently taken by a Russian coach ... - could be considered as a masterpiece in terms of gradual deceleration, and the general feeling of experts after the race was that Evans' record would stand for a long time.

Back to sea level, things took a less spectacular turn. In 1969 at Knoxville, Tennessee, Curtis Mills of USA lowered the world record for the quarter mile to 44.7 (fractions, 21.7 and 23.0), beating Evans (45.1). Mills' actual auto time was 44.93. Two years later at Eugene another American, John Smith, ran the same distance in 44.5 (fractions, 22.1 and 22.4) after a close fight with Wayne Collett (44.7). How these marks compared in intrinsic value with Evans' Mexican record, that was not easy to say, but conservative observers rated the advantage of altitude (around 2000 m.) as worth about 0.4 secs. in the 400 m.

Although steadily outclassed by USA in decisive moments, Europe continued to have good 400 m. men. One of these was Marcello Fiasconaro, a fine athletic specimen born in South Africa of an Italian father. He turned from rugby to athletics in November 1970 and in his official début he ran the 400 m. in 48.5. He was down to 46.5 before the end of the year. At the same time he revealed good staying power with a 1:51.0 800 m. These promising marks, relayed to European magazines by Harry Beinart, the dean of South African statisticians, caught the eye of FIDAL, the Italian athletics federation. Within a few months, Fiasconaro was gained to the cause of his father's native country. After improving to 45.5 in one of his first appearances in Italy, he went to Helsinki to compete in the European Championships. Jan Werner of Poland, the 1969 champion (45.75), was expected to be his main rival, but a 19-year-old Briton, David Jenkins, a 46.4 man on paper, rose to the occasion and upset both favourites. Jenkins got off like a bullet and led the field at the half-way mark with a sizzling 21.3. Fiasconaro (22.0) lagged far behind at that stage, but when Jenkins began to fade the Italian novice from South Africa all but closed the gap. Jenkins salvaged first place by centimetres. Both were officially credited with 45.5 (actual auto times, 45.45 and 45.49), and Werner was a close third in 45.6 (45.56).

At the Munich Olympics (1972) the Helsinki heroes failed to live up to expectations though. Fiasconaro was hampered by a foot injury and did not compete; and Jenkins was eliminated in the penultimate round. But the Americans were, of course, ready for any challenge. At their Olympic Trials (Eugene, 9 July) the great Evans was shunted to an uncomfortable fourth place (45.1) in a tough 400 m. race won by Wayne Collett (44.1, hand time) from John Smith (44.3) and Vince Matthews (44.9). Also eliminated was Fred Newhouse, who had run a sizzling 44.2 in the prelims. Matthews, who had been near the top for several years, had his Day of Days at the right time - in the Olympic final at Munich. He won in 44.66 from Collett (44.80). With Smith unable to finish because of an injury, third place went to Julius Sang of Kenya (44.92), who held off his compatriot Charles Asati (45.13). Fifth and best of the Europeans was Horst-Rüdiger Schlöske of West Germany (45.31).

Among those who failed to make the Olympic final was a Cuban who in later years was to earn the nickname "El caballo", thanks to his imposing stature and his muscular power. His full name was Alberto Juantorena Danger (born at Santiago de Cuba on 21 November 1950; 1.88 m./84 kg.). A basketball player in his youth, he turned to track in 1971 and before the end of the season he could point to a significant 48.2 for 400 m. The following year he

1961
1980

Anxieties of another sort

The name of David Jenkins, the onetime golden boy of British quarter-miling (who in the opinion of experts had failed to maximize his potential) hit the headlines again not so long ago, alas in connection with a sad affair. By then residing in USA, in December 1988 he was sentenced by a US Federal Court in San Diego to a seven-year prison term for masterminding a steroid smuggling (into California from Mexico) and distribution ring. The sentence also included five years on probation and a $750,000 fine. In his rebuke to Jenkins (who had pleaded guilty), Judge Lawrence Irving said: "You had it all - brains, education, apparently among the top 10 % academically of the British population, and a fantastic God-given athletic ability. Then greed entered and the whole thing went down the toilet".

Several weeks later, prisoner Jenkins was interviewed by a reporter from TF1 (first channel of the French TV), former pole vaulter Jean-Michel Bellot. By then fully conscious of his mistakes, Jenkins was quoted as saying: "Anxiety of the sort you can experience before an Olympic final is nothing if compared with the anxiety that assails whomsoever is about to listen to a sentence likely to have a great impact on the rest of his life." Jenkins also admitted having cheated as an athlete, first by accepting money under the table when amateurism was still the rule, then by taking drugs to boost his athletic performance in 1975 (incidentally the year of his fastest race ever).

Less than a year later, the US press announced that Jenkins' seven-year term had been reduced to the ten months he had already served. Of course he still had to serve a five-year probation. However, US Federal authorities dropped deportation proceedings and allowed him to remain in USA.

had his first taste of the Olympics: in Munich he did 45.94 in a heat, then failed to make the final by a tantalizing 0.5. He won his first international honour at the 1973 World University Games in Moscow with a sound 45.36, beating David Jenkins among others. In 1974 he led the World List with a "manual" 44.7. He suffered an unexpected defeat at the 1975 Pan-American Games in Mexico City, at the hands of Ron Ray of USA, 44.80 to 44.45. (The winner of this race never again rose to such heights).

Another unhappy loser in the 1972 Games was Karl Honz of West Germany, who earlier in the year on the same track had set a European record of 44.70. In the Olympic final he had to be content with an eighth place in 45.68. In later years he fought back bravely though. In 1974 he won the European title in Rome from a classy field in 45.04, while Jenkins was a distant second in 45.67. To tell the truth, Jenkins had failed to live up to his early promise of 1971. But in 1975 he surprised a lot of people by winning what for a European 400 m. man must surely rank as the rarest of honours: an AAU title. He did this at Eugene with a lifetime best of 44.93, winning from Fred Newhouse (45.22). But thereby hangs a tale, dealt with in the preceding aside.

1976 was Juantorena's golden year. In talking to Western journalists the Cuban would sometimes indulge in irony: "My second family name, Danger, is meant for Americans". From the start of the Olympic season it became apparent that he aimed at killing two (American?) birds with one stone: he was in fact alternating 400 and 800 m. So much in fact that some observers began to suspect that he was perhaps dreaming of a double until then never achieved in Olympic history... His best pre-Olympic marks in the one-lap department were as follows: 44.7 in April, 44.70 in June and 44.3 at Mexico City on 3 July. His sojourn in the rarefied atmosphere of Mexico in the weeks preceding the main rendezvous of the year was to prove beneficial.

In the meantime, Americans appeared to be a bit less redoubtable than usual. Maxie Parks took the AAU 400 m. title in 44.82, then needed no better than 45.58 to win the Trial race from Fred Newhouse (45.76). In Mont-real the 400 m. came after the 800 m. (won by Juantorena in a record-shattering 1:43.50). The big Cuban went through the prelims with a minimum effort. Some observers feared he might be tired by the time the final - his seventh race in just as many days - came about. An American friend of mine did not share this opinion: "Our men - he said - have only two chances against Juantorena: one if he breaks his right leg, the other if he breaks his left leg". In the decisive race Juantorena was in lane 2. Never a fast starter, he trailed Fred Newhouse, lane 4, for the greater part of the journey. The American blazed the first half in 21.5 and reached the 300 m. in 32.1. By then Juantorena (32.3) was drawing near, and in the stretch his superior power eventually won the day. He finished in 44.26, the fastest auto time ever registered at or near sea level. Newhouse, who at 1.75 m. was 13 centimetres shorter than his rival, was a brilliant second in 44.40. Another American, Herman Frazier, took third place in 44.95. Fons Brydenbach of Belgium, fourth in 45.04, fared better than David Jenkins, who finished seventh (45.57).

Juantorena was the world's no.1 man for two more years. In 1977 he suffered a narrow and unexpected defeat at the hands of Seymour Newman of Jamaica, 45.67 to 45.66, but shortly afterwards he made amends with a nice 44.79 in the America Trials for the World Cup. In the Cup itself, at Düsseldorf, the 400 m. was curiously run twice. The first race - won by Volker Beck of East Germany in 45.79, with Juantorena third (45.83) - was annulled following a protest by Cuba and USA, which claimed that their representatives (Juantorena and Robert Taylor) had been unable to hear the starter's gun due to noise from an overhead jet and a nearby clicking movie camera. Although looked upon by some observers as rather controversial, the appeal stood and a re-run was scheduled for the next day. Beck, better known as a specialist of the "intermediates", achieved his fastest ever (45.50), but found it insufficient against Juantorena, who won in 45.36.

At the 1978 Central American Games, held at Medellin, Colombia (altitude, 1450 m.), Juantorena posted the second fastest time of his career, 44.27. This was virtually his third venture in rarefied atmosphere, after his races at Mexico City in 1975 and '76, and it is interesting to note that in no one of them was he able to improve his sea-level best from the Montreal Olympics (44.26). Still in 1978, the European Championship title was won by Franz-Peter Hofmeister of West Germany (45.73), a former sprinter who seven years earlier had finished second to Borzov in the 200 m. of another European title meet. The pre-Olympic year 1979 found Juantorena in poor physical condition and probably on the verge of decline. For the first time since Glenn Davis' days the no.1 man of the year in the 400 m. flat was a specialist of the "intermediates", reliable Harald Schmid of West Germany, who did 44.92 and 44.98. He eventually returned to his first love in the World Cup at Montreal, where the flat race was won by Kasheef Hassan of Sudan in 45.39.

In 1980 the Olympic final at Moscow was obviously

devalued by the absence of athletes from boycotting countries such as USA, West Germany and Kenya.(At their "symbolic" Trials, the Americans had shown a low profile, with Bill Green the winner in 45.85).

Even so, the Moscow final (30 July) yielded excellent results. Viktor Markin of USSR surprised a lot of foreign guests as he went home the winner in 44.60, a new European record. The other medals went to Rick Mitchell of Australia (44.84) and Frank Schaffer of East Germany (44.87). Defending champion Juantorena, returning to the wars after surgery the previous fall, was short on condition, yet he managed to finish fourth in 45.09. The surprise winner (born at Oktyabrsk, Novosibirsk, on 23 February 1957; 1.83m./73 kg.) had a pre-1980 best of 47.20, yet he could point to interesting sprint marks (10.4 and 21.1). He had begun to look promising shortly before the Games with a 45.33 effort.

The Golden Gala event in Rome, six days after the Moscow final, brought together Markin and some of the most notable Olympic absentees. Harald Schmid topped them all in 45.17. Billy Konchellah of Kenya was second (45.55), while Markin was only third (46.02). Like many other Russians that year, he peaked perfectly at the right time, apparently losing form shortly afterwards.

MIDDLE DISTANCES - 800 METRES: Prodigy for "El Caballo" in Montreal

Peter Snell of New Zealand, surprise winner of the Olympic 800 m. crown in Rome, lost no time in confirming his athletic stature. Still in 1960, before returning home, he was timed in 1:44.8 during an 880 y. relay leg in London. Early in 1961 he repeatedly beat Roger Moens in meets held in New Zealand, thus serving indication that his Rome victory was no fluke. Snell's best day as a half-miler, clock-wise at least, was on 3 February 1962 at Christchurch. A week after setting a world's one-mile record, the Kiwi ace completed a historic double with a superb 1:45.1. He not only broke Courtney's 880 y. record by a huge margin (1.7 secs.) but succeeded Moens as holder of the 800 m. record by a similar margin with a scintillating 1:44.3. The early pace in this race was set by Barry Robinson, a 47.0 one-lap man, who ran the first half in 50.7, with Snell not far behind (51.0). Notwithstanding this hot early pace, Snell had enough staying power to cover the second half in 54.1. Statistician P.N. Heidenström gave Snell's 220 y. fractions as follows: 24.8, 26.2, 25.9, 28.2. It should be noted that the Kiwi had never ducked under 22 secs. in his (rare) attempts over 220 y.

In later years Snell favoured the mile rather than the "half", yet he returned to the shorter distance from time to time, e.g. at the 1962 Commonwealth Games in Perth, when he won a close decision from George Kerr, 1:47.6 to 1:47.7. By 1964 Lydiard's pupil was so well trained and so self-confident that he decided to put his eggs in two baskets in view of the Tokyo Olympics. No one had been able to achieve the 800/1500 m. double in the Games since the days of Albert Hill (1920). With this giant task in mind, Snell increased his training "ration" and covered 1628 km. in the space of ten weeks - an average of about 23 km. per day, more than a half marathon! In the Tokyo Games he ran six races in the space of a week, with the following sequence: 800 m. 1:49.0, 1:46.9, 1:45.1; 1500 m. 3:46.8, 3:38.8, 3:38.1. And he went through this ordeal in superb style, finally scoring the coveted double. In the 800 m. final he launched his attack in the backstretch of the second lap, then easily held off Bill Crothers of Canada, 1:45.1 to 1:45.6, while Wilson Kiprugut won the bronze medal for Kenya, narrowly beating George Kerr (both 1:45.9). Snell's 200 m. fractions: 25.1,

1961
1980

Genesis of the Kenyan wave

The bronze medal won by Wilson Kiprugut in the 800 m. of the Tokyo Olympics (1964) was the first ever by a Kenyan athlete in the quadrennial Games. The first of a collection which in the course of about a quarter century was to amount to 24 pieces - 10 gold, 8 silver and 6 bronze. All this was achieved despite the fact that Kenya stayed away from two editions of the Games (1976 and '80) for political implications. And all these medals came from track events.

A strange coincidence comes to mind: Kiprugut's bronze in Tokyo came less than a year after the declaration of Kenya's independence. Curiously enough, in Kalenjin the name of the Tokyo medallist stands for "born during a famine". Kenya has since become the no.1 reservoir of Africa's distance runners. In the 1990 World Lists, the East African country had five of the top ten in the 800 m. and in the steeplechase! What will the future bring? Well, an indirect clue may be found in the fact that the population of Kenya has nearly doubled in the past quarter century.

Peter Snell (New Zealand), to this day the last middle distance runner to score an 800/1500 m. double in the Olympics (Tokyo, 1964).

27.7, 26.6, 25.7. Snell had reached the peak of his athletic prowess between 24 and 26 years of age, thanks to his powerful build and a very intensive training programme. Great was therefore the surprise of experts when his world's half-mile record was beaten by a 19-year-old newcomer! This dramatic development unfolded on 10 June 1966 at Terre Haute, Indiana, and the lad who turned the trick was an American, James Ronald Ryun (born at Wichita, Kansas, on 29 April 1947; 1.88 m./75 kg.).

Stamped as a prodigy since his earliest athletic ventures, he was until then regarded as a miler, although his coach Bob Timmons maintained that the 880 y. was his best event. Ryun's fastest "half" was 1:50.3, but he had done much better in a relay (1:47.7). In the Terre Haute race he trailed a wise "hare", John Tillman, in the first half (52.9), then forged ahead and negotiated the second half in a crescendo, for a final time of 1:44.9. His 220 y. fractions were as follows: 26.2, 27.1 (53.3), 26.1, 25.5. The faster second half (51.6) seemed, and was, quite unusual for a record race at this distance. Ryun was not timed at 800 m., otherwise he might as well have earned the metric record, or a share of it. Two weeks later, at Los Angeles, Ryun showed that he could do well even in a more competitive atmosphere, when he won the 880 y. from a crack field in 1:46.2, again with a faster second half (52.9). Roger Moens still held the European 800 m. record, but he lost it later in 1966, when 21-year-old Franz-Josef Kemper of West Germany duplicated Ryun's tactics at Hannover with fractions of 53.0 and 51.9 for a final time of 1:44.9. In competitive terms the most brilliant European of that period was Manfred Matuschewski of East Germany, who won the European Championship title twice, with 1:50.5 at Belgrade in 1962 and 1:45.9 at Budapest in 1966, in the latter race after a big fight with Kemper (1:46.0). For his narrow victories in tight finishes, Matuschewski went down in European track history as the "Millimetre -Läufer" (in German the latter word stands for runner).

The 1968 track season was, of course, highlighted by the Mexico Olympics. Before the Games there was wide speculation about the possible effects of altitude in relation to the 800 m. and most observers feared that they might be slightly on the negative side. But times recorded in the Games largely belied this impression. Same as in 1960 and '64, the winner of the two-lap event again came from Oceania. This time the man in question was an Aussie, Ralph Doubell (born on 11 February 1945, 1.80 m./65 kg.), who was incidentally the only white man to emerge victorious in a flat running event at Mexico City. He was a surprise to many, although he had won the event at the Universiade in Tokyo the year before, nosing out European record holder Franz-Josef Kemper (time for both: 1:46.7). Wilson Kiprugut of Kenya, the bronze medallist of the 1964 Games, was expected to be at home in the rarefied atmosphere of the Mexican capital, having spent the better part of his life under similar atmospheric conditions. In fact, he was bold enough to set a scorching pace: 24.1 (200 m.), 51.0 (400 m.), 1:17.8 (600 m.), at which stage Doubell was his nearest pursuer (1:18.5). The Aussie champion surged in the stretch, passed his rival with less than 40 m. to go and finished in 1:44.3, thus matching Snell's world record. The gallant Kiprugut was second in 1:44.5. (Actual auto times for the first two, 1:44.40 and 1:44.57). Tom Farrell of USA was third in 1:45.4. Best of the Europeans was Walter Adams of West Germany, fourth (1:45.8). Next came a 19-year-old Czech, Jozef Plachy (1:45.9). Young Plachy was to rank no.1 in the world in 1969, thanks to a fine set of marks, highlighted by a runaway victory in the first America vs. Europe dual meet at Montreal. On this occasion he posted a fast 1:45.4, beating among others Dieter Fromm of East Germany. The latter, however, managed to turn the tables on Plachy at the European title meet in Athens, 1:45.9 to 1:46.2.

Until then USSR had never been a factor in top-class middle distance running. The first exception was provided by a sprightly Ukrainian, Yevgeniy Arzhanov (born on 9 February 1948 at Kalush, 1.79 m./73 kg.), who was a world leader for two seasons, 1970 and '71. After finishing fourth at the 1969 European Championships, he improved to 1:45.5 in 1970, then won the continental title at Helsinki in 1971 (1:45.6), beating Fromm (1:46.0) and Andy Carter of Britain (1:46.2). By that time, interesting news came from South Africa about two up-and-coming runners, Dick Broberg and Danie Malan, who had done 1:44.7 and 1:45.1 respectively in a race at Stellenbosch. But the Springboks were, of course, banned from the Olympics ....

The Americans regained the top in 1972. At their Olympic Trials in Eugene, Oregon, the two-lap event - run off on 1 July - was truly dramatic. Jim Ryun, holder of the world's half-mile record, took the lead in the backstretch of the second lap and tried to mow down his rivals by running the third 200 m. fraction in a murderous 24.8. But he was the chief victim of such a burst of speed: in a wild stretch battle he regressed from first to fourth and his 1:45.2 left him out of the Olympic team! (However, he earned a berth in the 1500 m. a few days later). The race was won by Dave Wottle in a record equalling 1:44.3, while Rick Wohlhuter (1:45.0) and Ken Swenson (1:45.1) earned the remaining berths. Wottle's splits were as follows: 26.0, 26.8, 25.0, 26.5. Hence, halves of 52.8 and 51.5. Ryun was thus beaten at his own game.

Wottle (born at Canton, Ohio, on 7 August 1950; 1.83 m./65 kg.) had earned a reputation as a "big kicker" as early as in 1970, when he ate up 4 m. of Marty Liquori's 7 m.-lead in the final straight of the NCAA Championship mile. Prior to 1972, however, he had done no better than 1:47.8 in the two-lap event. Even after his "explosion" at the Trials, few experts, if any, would have bet on him against the experienced Arzhanov, undefeated in international competition since the summer of 1969. The Ukrainian had just overcome the effects of an injury to lower his personal best to 1:45.3.

The Olympic final came as the third 800 m. round in just as many days. Two Kenyans, Mike Boit and Robert Ouko, set the pace in the early goings (400 m. in 52.3). At the bell Arzhanov was sixth and Wottle, easily recognizable because of his customary golf cap, was lying eighth and last. The Ukrainian attacked with 300 m. to go and was in the lead at 600 m. (1:19.2). At that crucial stage the group was tightly bunched and Wottle (1:19.7), although still closing up the rear, was starting his bid. Then he began to pass runner after runner, looking like a champion scratch man overtaking a crew of handicappers. Doing all his passing on the outside, Wottle caught Arzhanov in the last stretch of land and went through the tape in his usual form, while Arzhanov, who only a few seconds earlier felt he had the race nailed, made a desperate lunge at the tape and fell across the finish line. To no avail though, because Wottle was there three hundredths of a second earlier, 1:45.86 to 1:45.89. Boit was a close third (1:46.01), followed by Franz-Josef Kemper (1:46.50) and Ouko (1:46.53). Wottle had run an extremely even race, with 200 m. fractions of 26.4, 26.9 (53.3), 26.3 and 26.3. Cool and poised throughout the race, during the victory ceremony he was visibly moved, to the point of forgetting to take off his famous cap. (He later apologized for that). Arzhanov sadly commented: "It is very disappointing to lose in the very last stride by the length of your nose".

Missing from the Munich race - in addition to Jim Ryun - was Pekka Vasala of Finland, who had chosen to concentrate on the 1500 m. During 1972 the Finn showed great prowess in the two-lap event, with times of 1:44.5 and 1:44.6. As for Rick Wohlhuter, America's second string, he was eliminated in a heat, in the strangest possible way: while cutting to the pole, he tripped on himself and fell. ("I tripped on a sun beam", he said, with commendable humor). He made a gallant attempt to recover, but failed to qualify by a narrow margin. He began to make amends on 27 May 1973 at Los Angeles, when he lowered the world's half-mile record to 1:44.6, with even-paced halves (52.3 and 52.3). In this race he won from South Africa's Danie Malan (1:45.1). Acting as "hare" on this occasion was Mark Winzenried, who in that capacity was to become the Boysen of the Seventies. (Like the Norwegian, Mark was of course a very good runner, with a personal best of 1:45.69). In 1973 Marcello Fiasconaro of Italy (via South

1961
1980

Luciano Susanj (Yugoslavia), a superb winner of the 800 m. at the 1974 European Championships in Rome.

Africa) joined the select group of top-class half-milers. A silver medallist in the 400 m. at the 1971 European Championships, in 1972 he ran the two-lap event in 1:47.7 under unfavourable weather conditions. He rose to the top ranks the following year in a series of close battles with Danie Malan in South Africa. After losing the first three rounds, "March" turned the tables on his rival twice, with times of 1:45.2 and 1:44.7. On the latter occasion he closed his day's work with a 46.1 400 m. The fruits of his intensive training under coach Stewart Banner became evident for all to see in the Italy vs. Czechoslovakia dual meet at Milan on 27 June. (The old Arena had by then a regular 400 m. track). Starting in the pole lane, Fiasconaro led literally from start to finish, a very unusual occurrence in record-shattering 800 m. efforts - because his final time, 1:43.7, was in fact a new world record. His 200 m. fractions were as follows: 25.0, 26.2 (51.2), 25.3, 27.2. Jozef Plachy was second in 1:45.7. Later in the season, the fresh world record holder had two negative experiences though. In a dual meet with USA at Turin he was outsprinted by Rick Wohlhuter in the final stage, 1:45.8 to 1:45.3; then, in a semifinal of the European Cup at Oslo he was disqualified for two false starts - a very rare occurrence in middle distance races. Wohlhuter (born on 23 December 1948 at St.Charles, Illinois; 1.75 m./59 kg.) had his best-ever season in 1974. On 8 June at Eugene he improved on his 880 y. record with 1:44.1 (fractions, 51.0 and 53.1). He was not timed officially at 800 m., and that saved Fiasconaro's record. Later in the season, the American came dangerously close to that metric mark several times, doing 1:43.9 in the AAU meet, 1:44.03 in a dual meet with USSR and 1:43.91 at Stockholm. 1974 also offered two major title races. In the Commonwealth Games at Auckland, John Kipkurgat of Kenya won in 1:43.90, while at the European Championships in Rome it was the turn of Luciano Susanj of Yugoslavia, who simply "murdered" a crack field with a scorching stretch drive to win in 1:44.07, while an 18-year-old Briton, Steve Ovett, was second in 1:45.76. Fiasconaro, although hampered by a sore foot, led for the major part of the journey (50.1 at 400 m.) before fading to sixth in the stretch.

In the meantime Mike Boit, the Munich bronze medallist, continued to improve, with 1:44.18 in 1974 and 1:43.79 in 1975. The latter auto time, made at Zurich, may have been intrinsically faster than Fiasconaro's hand-timed world record, but the IAAF still failed to distinguish between the two timing systems at distances over 400 m. In his younger days Boit (born on 6 January 1949 at Lessos; 1.83 m./66 kg.) had been coached by Alex Stewart and Bruce Tulloh. He went to the 1972 Olympics as a virtual novice, although credited with such times as 1:47.0 and 3:37.4. And he made the final in both events, finishing third in the 800 m. and fourth in the 1500 m. Four years later, as a mature top-class man, he loomed as a great prospect for the Montreal Games. But at the very last moment most of the African countries, including Kenya, decided to boycott the Montreal event as a protest against the participation of New Zealand, in their eyes guilty of entertaining sports (rugby) relations with banned South Africa. This decision was obviously a bad blow for all those who had trained assiduously for years, with the big event on their mind. And Boit was surely among the saddest. ("I really couldn't believe what I heard", he was quoted as saying). This unpleasant development coincided with Alberto Juantorena's inroad in the two-lap department. The great Cuban had tried the 800 m. in 1973 (1:49.8) but it was only in 1976 that he began to give this event a truly serious thought. In preparing for Montreal he ran the distance in seven meets, his fastest time being 1:44.9, good enough to entertain a secret hope - landing an unprecedented 400/800 m. double in the Games. The Olympic final (25 July) came as the third 800 m. round in the space of 50 hours. Juantorena, never a fast starter, had an unimpressive getaway. Then he gradually moved up, and at the bell he was alongside leader Sri Ram Singh of India (50.85). The Cuban shot into the lead in the next-to-last curve, and from then on he was never headed. First Rick Wohlhuter, then Ivo Van Damme of Belgium tried to draw level with him but failed. Juantorena went home a superb winner in 1:43.50, a new world record. He covered the second lap in 52.6, the last 200 m. in 26.5 and the last 100 m. in a sizzling 11.9. (Four years earlier in Munich, Wottle was timed in 11.8 for the last century, off a much slower pace). For a virtual newcomer to the event, that surely was not bad! The solid Van Damme was second (1:43.86), beating the likes of Wohlhuter (1:44.12), Willi Wülbeck of West Germany (1:45.26), Steve Ovett of Britain (1:45.44), European champion Susanj (1:45.75) and the gallant Singh (1:45.77).

Poor Mike Boit sought partial consolation in European post- Olympic meets. His furor resulted in two superlative performances: 1:43.90 at Zurich on 18 August and 1:43.57 at Berlin two days later. He beat Olympic medallists Van Damme and Wohlhuter, but Juantorena was not there. In 1977, the Kenyan and the Cuban finally met, not once but twice. Not surprisingly, the long-awaited first round took place in the famous "Weltklasse" meet in Zurich on 24 August. Juantorena came to the rendezvous with the credential of a fresh prowess - a record run at the Universiade in Sofia only three days earlier! He had achieved the honour after leading virtually from gun to tape, with fractions of 51.4 and 52.0 and a final time of 1:43.4 (actual auto time, 1:43.44). In Zurich, another Kenyan by the name of Sammy Kipkurgat tried to take the sting out of a supposedly tired Juantorena with a fast early pace - to no avail. At the bell "El Caballo" was actually in front (49.6). Boit drew level with him in the backstretch, but that was all he could do. Juantorena was clearly the stronger man and finally won by a decisive margin, 1:43.64 to 1:44.64. The second round took place in the World Cup at Düsseldorf on 2 September. This was a race of rare beauty. Imagine two great runners battling round the final lap, never more than one metre apart. Same as in the 1976 Olympic final, Sri Ram Singh of India led at the bell (52.3), and again had to give way to Juantorena round the next-to-last curve. This time Boit waited till the homestretch to launch his attack. A "pure" middle distance runner who had never ducked under 46 secs. in the 400 m., he was renewing his challenge off the vantage point of a wiser early pace. After all, the real testing ground in middle (and long) distance running is endurance to speed rather than basic speed. Except that Juantorena was wonderfully equipped to mould the two concepts into one: with 10 m. to go he began to inch his way ahead and finally earned a close decision, 1:44.04 to 1:44.14.

Juantorena's power began to decline in 1978, with the emergence of physical problems. "Stress fracture" is a term often used nowadays to denote damage caused by an overdose of intensive training and competition. As it happens, Juantorena's decline coincided with the rise of two British stars who were to leave indelible imprints in the annals of middle distance running. The men in question were Stephen James Ovett (born on 9 October 1955 at Brighton; 1.83 m./70 kg.) and Sebastian Newbold Coe (born on 29 September 1956 at Chiswick; 1.77 m./54 kg.), known in British athletic circles simply as Steve and Seb. Apart from a great talent for the sport, they seemed to have little else in common. Steve was extrovert and outspoken, while Seb appeared to be quiet and reserved. The former looked more like the power runner in the traditional British sense, while the latter had a silken stride and a turn of speed likely to bewitch any track enthusiast. The British popular press went to work on these differences and depicted the two characters in the play as decidedly antithetic - the right ingredient to foster a strong rivalry, on and off the track. Ovett was first to emerge at the international level, with a victory in the 800 m. at the 1973 European Junior Championships in Duisburg. In a hectic finish, he won in 1:47.53 from Willi Wülbeck of West Germany (1:47.57), while Ivo Van Damme of Belgium was fourth (1:48.16). Here was a junior race that introduced not one but three champions of the future! As a two-lapper, Ovett went on to finish second in the 1974 European Championships and fifth in the 1976 Olympics, as previously related. Coe first ducked under 1:50 in

1961
1980

Three French wizards of the middle distances. From left to right, Michel Jazy, Jules Ladoumègue and "timer" Séra Martin.

1976 with 1:47.7. Early in 1977 he was sharp enough to win his first major title at the European Indoor Championships in San Sebastian: time, 1:46.54. Later in the year, outdoors, he improved to 1:44.95. Although living and operating in the same area, Steve and Seb met on surprisingly few occasions while in their prime. This obviously led several observers to conclude that they tended to avoid each other. Not infrequently, they would appear in the same meet, only to run in different races. The first unavoidable crossroads was Prague 1978, when both vied for the European 800 m. crown. Strangely enough, the first major round of their rivalry went to a third party - 21-year-old Olaf Beyer of East Germany. For once, Coe threw caution to the wind by blasting the first 400 m. in 49.32. Beyer was by then second (49.6) and Ovett third (50.0). Entering the homestretch, Coe was still in the lead, one metre up on Ovett and 3 m. ahead of Beyer. Then Ovett forged ahead and most observers thought he had the race won. But the unexpected Beyer was not done yet. And his final bid was too much even for Steve. The German won in 1:43.84 from Ovett (1:44.09) and Coe (1:44.76). Beyer, who had a pre-1978 best of 1:46.1, never again rose to such spectacular heights. Coe made amends for his suicidal Prague tactics with a phenomenal race at Oslo's Bislett stadium on 5 July 1979, when he astounded experts by clipping over a second off Juantorena's world record with a startling 1:42.33. The Briton led throughout the second lap and won by the proverbial block from Evans White of USA (1:45.75). Coe's 200 m. fractions - 24.6, 26.0 (50.6), 24.8, 26.9 - clearly reflected his progress in terms of staying power. The next unavoidable crossroads for Steve and Seb was Moscow - for the 1980 Olympics. And they were expected to meet in both 800 and 1500 m. The shorter event came first, and in the final Coe appeared to be far removed from his Prague tactics of 1978 - too far perhaps. He lagged behind throughout the first lap, running in lanes 2 and 3. At the bell the tightly bunched field was led by Agberto Guymaraes of Brazil in 54.3, while Ovett (54.6) and Coe (54.7) still lagged behind. After that, a spirited second lap was surely on the cards. Nikolay Kirov of USSR was first to set the world on fire: he shot ahead and led the field down the backstretch and round the last curve, with Ovett in his wake, and Coe still desperately behind. Then Ovett passed the Russian and began his long drive for home. Coe too was in high gear by then, but he could make little or no impression on his compatriot. Steve thus won in superb style in 1:45.40, while Coe (1:45.85) shunted Kirov (1:45.94) to third place. Ovett's last lap was a phenomenal 50.8, as opposed to Coe's 51.2. The world record holder was a shade faster than his rival only in the last 100 m. (12.1 vs. 12.2). Among those who missed the Olympics as members of boycotting countries was Don Paige of USA, who won the 800 m. at the "symbolic" Trials in 1:44.53. In a post-Olympic meet at Viareggio he scored a narrow victory over Coe, 1:45.04 to 1:45.07.

1500 METRES: Wizards from four continents

When the inimitable Elliott decided to leave the athletic arena, few experts thought that he would soon have a worthy successor. Chris Brasher of Britain, by then a member of the Fourth Estate, said that a man like Herb Elliott could only have come from a country such as Australia. In his view, Herb's uninhibited approach well reflected the geographical and psychological situation of the continent he came from. Lo and behold - Elliott's successor was a runner from Down Under, precisely a New Zealander. This man was Peter Snell, whose deeds as a two-lap runner have been recounted in the previous chapter. It was only in 1962 that Snell began to give the mile a serious thought. On New Year's Day he ran a casual 4:01.3 - not good enough to prepare the world for what was to follow on 27 January at Wanganui. Running on a 352 m. grass track, Snell took the lead at the half-way mark (2:00.6), but then let British distance champion Bruce Tulloh get out in front for a while. It was only with 300 m. to go that the Kiwi decided to "abandon the studied relaxation" (as he said later). He thus completed the second half in 1:53.8 for a final time of 3:54.4 - one tenth under Elliott's world record. Tulloh was second in 3:59.3. Snell's "quarters" were as follows: 60.7, 59.9, 59.0, 54.8. He was timed in 3:39.3 at 1500 m., so he covered the last 109.35 m. in 15.1.

Snell dominated the 1500 m./mile scene for three years (1962-64). As a rule he would win his races with a fantastic burst of speed in the closing stage. He could follow any pace and then prove superior in any stretch drive. In 1963 at Modesto, California, he covered the final 109.35 m. separating the 1500 m. from the mile in 14.0 (3:40.9 - 3:54.9). As previously related, he crowned his great career with a superb 800/1500 m. double at the Tokyo Olympics (1964). It is curious to note that he formally made his début in the 1500 m. on that momentous occasion, since all his previous efforts had been over the longer English route, i.e. one mile. In the final, his sixth race in the space of eight days, he covered the last 300 m. in 38.6 and won in 3:38.1 from Josef Odlozil of Czechoslovakia and John Davies, another Kiwi, who finished second and third respectively (both 3:39.6).

Before the end of the year the three Tokyo medallists met once more, namely at Auckland on 17 November. Snell set out to break his own 1-mile record, on the same fast cinder track at Western Springs Stadium. This time he had an entirely different strategy. He followed a pace-setter through scorching "quarters" of 56.4 and 57.7 (1:54.1), well ahead of Odlozil and Davies. By then his legs were understandably "crying for relief" (as he said later), yet he managed to go through "quarters" of 60.2 and 59.8 for a final time of 3:54.1, three tenths under his previous record. He passed 1500 m. in 3:37.6 and covered the last agonizing 109.35 m. in 16.5. In what looked like a "B" race, Josef Odlozil held off John Davies for second place, 3:56.4 to 3:56.8. After Snell's superb 1964 season, many fans around the world again regretted that he and Herb Elliott - both born in 1938 - had never "locked horns" over the 1-mile route when each was in his prime. They had in fact met once, at Dublin in 1960, long before Snell began to specialize in the mile, and Elliott had won easily in 3:57.0, with the Kiwi no better than fifth in 4:01.5. ("In the last lap I found I had no life at all", said Snell after the race). The only honour still missing in Snell's collection was by then the world record for the 1500 m. He planned to capture it during his farewell tour of the Northern Hemisphere in 1965. But he was injured in April and had trouble recovering. That was the beginning of his downfall. Long travels and frequent competitions when he was far from fit caused him to lose several times. The saddest moment was in connection with a mile race at Vancouver: affected by gastritis earlier in the day, he dropped to dead last in 4:15.4, a performance for which he felt bound to apologize over the public address system. "It will no doubt take a long time to get over the shame of having run last", he said.

Missing from the 1500 m. cast at the Tokyo Olympics was Michel Jazy of France, the silver medallist of 1960, then rated Europe's no.1 man. He had opted for the 5000 m., causing slanderous tongues to say that he had a "Snell complex". Jazy probably remains to this day the finest 1500 m./mile specimen ever to come out of a Latin country. Born on 13 June 1936 at Oignies, Pas-de-Calais, of Polish parents, he lost his father while very young, and thus went through difficult years, until he found - through the medium of Gaston Meyer, France's best known track writer - a part-time job as a printer with the famous sports daily "L'Equipe". Such an arrangement allowed him to devote part of his time to training, which he did mostly in the forest of Marly, under the guidance of his coach, René Frassinelli. A medium size runner (1.75 m./65 kg.) endowed with good basic speed, Jazy was in the sub-3:50 region as early as in 1956. That was the year of his first Olympic experience: at Melbourne, however, he was eliminated in the first round of the 1500 m. As pre-

1961
1980

1972 Olympics in Munich. Pekka Vasala (Finland) no.226, on his way to winning the 1500 metres in 3:36.33 from Kip Keino (Kenya) no.576, R. Dixon (NZ), partly covered by Keino; M. Boit (Kenya); and B. Foster (GB).

viously related, he did much better in Rome four years later. He reached the top of his condition between 1962 and 1966. During his busy 1962 season he set new world records for such non-Olympic distances as the 2000 m. (5:01.5) and the 3000 m. (7:49.2), and in addition ran the 800 m. in 1:47.1 and the 1500 m. in 3:38.3. He crowned all this with his first major title, winning the 1500 m. at the European Championships in Belgrade (3:40.9). Two years later, at the Tokyo Olympics, he had a frustrating experience, regressing from first to fourth in the very last stage of the 5000 m. He eventually overcame his Olympic reverse with a superb season in 1965, at twenty-nine years of age, when he compiled a great collection of marks at distances ranging from 1500 to 5000 m. On 9 June, at Rennes, he took the world's 1-mile record with a scintillating 3:53.6. As in all his record attempts, he was aided once more by competent pace-setters. At Rennes, one of these was Jean Wadoux, who in later years became one of Europe's best at both 1500 and 5000 m. After 440 y. fractions of 57.3, 59.2 and 60.9, Jazy moved into the lead and negotiated the last "quarter" in a fast 56.2, after passing the 1500 m. mark in 3:38.4. Gérard Vervoort was a well beaten second (3:59.9). As a metric-minded man, Jazy obviously wanted to annex the world's 1500 m. record too, but this was to remain an elusive target for him: best he could do was 3:36.3, a European record, at Sochaux on 25 June 1966. Jim Ryun's precocious virtues as a champion runner have been extolled in the chapter devoted to the 800 m. But his most famous deeds were to occur in the 1500 m./mile department. Before going into them, I would like to mention that shortly before his arrival on the American scene there had been several fine US milers: Jim Beatty, Dyrol Burleson (twice a finalist in the Olympic 1500 m.: sixth in 1960 and fifth in 1964), Tom O'Hara and Jim Grelle. This revival was partly brought about by such good coaches as Mihály Iglói, the tutor of Hungary's middle distance cream in the Fifties, and Bill Bowerman. But Jim Ryun was, of course, another class. Seemingly cool and detached, he was burnt by strong inner feelings which gave him a unique drive. Between 15 and 19 years of age his training "pensum" amounted to something like 4000 working hours, in all probability an unprecedented load for a boy of that age. Translated into 1-mile times, the results were startling, to say the least - from 5:38 in September 1962 to a world record of 3:51.3 in 1966! In the middle of this ascension he gained a berth in the US team for the Tokyo Olympics, but being indisposed and possibly past his peak for the season, he could not go beyond the semi-finals of the 1500 m. In 1965 he improved by a wide margin, winning the AAU 1-mile title in 3:55.3. The Kansas wonder "exploded" in 1966. Following a near miss (3:53.7) in his first attack against Jazy's 1-mile record at Compton on 4 June, Ryun hit the target in splendid fashion at Berkeley on 17 July. After trailing other runners through "quarters" of 57.9, 57.6 and 59.8, he moved into the lead and ran the last lap in a fast 56.0 for a final reward of 3:51.3 - 2.3 secs. under Jazy's world record! His 1500 m. time enroute was 3:36.1. Cary Weisiger, one of America's best milers, was hopelessly outclassed in second place (3:58.0). Later in the season Ryun collected a US 2-mile record with an 8:25.2 effort. Bob Timmons' dedicated pupil gave further proof of his phenomenal talent in 1967. On 23 June at Bakersfield, California, he won his third AAU 1-mile title, cutting two tenths off his record time with a nifty 3:51.1. He achieved his goal in a revolutionary way, moving into the lead at the gun and running all the rest of the race "on his own"! After three even-paced "quarters" (59.0, 59.9, 59.7), he had enough left for a superb last lap: 52.5. Once again, his rivals were left far behind, with Jim Grelle runner-up in 3:56.1. No time was taken for Jim at 1500 m., so there was at least one more target to aim at. The occasion was offered by the USA vs. British Commonwealth dual at Los Angeles on 8 July, when Ryun met for the first time the man who was to become his fiercest rival - Kipchoge Keino of Kenya. The latter had excellent credentials, notably including a 3:53.4 mile in London in 1966. The Los Angeles race was run in hot weather conditions, at 1.40 p.m. The 27-year-old Kenyan was never one to fool around with slow paces, and so he tried to take the sting out of his young rival with 400 m. fractions of 60.5, 55.5 and 57.5. But Ryun forged ahead in the last lap and covered the last 300 m. in 39.6. That was too much even for Keino and the Kansas boy won in 3:33.1 - a ludicrous 2.5 secs. under Herb Elliott's world record. Keino was second in 3:37.2. Ryun emerged from the test greater than ever, and with his "worst headache ever". The 20-year-old American closed his great season with a triumphal European tour. He beat Keino again in a mile race in London (3:56.0 to 3:57.4), then thrashed West Germany's best, Bodo Tümmler and Harald Norpoth, in a memorable 1500 m. race at Düsseldorf. He ran away from his rivals with less than one lap to go to win in 3:38.2. Splits attributed to him by some sources (last 400 m. in 50.6, last 300 m. in 36.4) looked almost too good to be true, but it is a fact that his frenzied spurt left Tümmler, the 1966 European champion, 4.1 secs. behind!

Hezekiah Kipchoge Keino (born on 17 January 1940 at Kipsamo, Nandi Hills; 1.78 m./66 kg.) had lost his mother at the age of four. Under the urge of circumstances he matured so rapidly that at ten he was experienced enough to tend a flock of goats all by himself. Rumour has it that he ran the first serious race of his life when he came face to face with a leopard which was eating a goat. He surely had other adventures uncommon to most runners from other parts of the world. He went to school at twelve and in his second year he finished fourth in a cross-country race. His father had won senior races at long distances and so he encouraged his offspring to train on their home-made track. Kipchoge made his official début at sixteen: fifth in a 3-mile race. He began to train seriously at nineteen, when he joined the Police. His best times in 1959 were 4:38 (mile) and 16:17 (3 miles), not much to brag about if compared with marks made at the same age by luckier Jim Ryun. Three years later, however, Keino was good enough to earn selection in the Kenya team for the British Commonwealth Games in Perth. He finished eleventh in the 3 miles in 13:50.0, and also ran the mile in 4:07.0, but failed to make the final.

In 1964 Keino - who by then had a family and a house - went to Tokyo for his first Olympic adventure. He finished a brilliant fifth in the 5000 m. (13:50.4), but was eliminated in a semi-final of the 1500 m., although he ran a creditable 3:41.9. He attributed his failure at the shorter distance to his mistake in running with the others at a tactical pace. He resolved that in the future he would always set his own pace. In 1965 he joined the élite, and like the overwhelming majority of African runners he achieved his best times overseas. He set two world records: 7:39.5 for 3000 m. at Hälsingborg, Sweden, and 13:24.2 for 5000 m. at Auckland. He made further progress in the mile too, even though in December he was twice beaten by Jürgen May of East Germany in New Zealand: 3:54.9 to 3:53.8 at Wanganui, and 3:54.4 to 3:54.1 at Auckland four

1961
1980

Jim Ryun (USA), the most precocious talent in middle distance annals.

217

days later. Keino awaited the Mexico Olympics (1968) with great confidence. He had to take advantage of his body's uncommon ability to utilize oxygen, developed from a lifetime of activity at high altitude. His pre-Olympic tests included a 3:55.5 mile at Kisumu (altitude 2285 m.). In the meantime Jim Ryun had qualified for the Games with a 3:49.0 for 1500 m. at Echo Summit, not a fast time for him, even if rescued in part by a 50.6 for the last 400 m. In Europe, Bodo Tümmler ran the fastest mile of the year, 3:53.8, at Karlskrona, Sweden.

At Mexico City the indefatigable Keino competed in three events - 10,000, 5000 and 1500 m.! Counting heats and finals, he ran six races in eight days. The three rounds of the 1500 m. came last, yet it was in this event that he offered his "chef- d'oeuvre". In the early goings of the decisive race he was aided by his countryman Ben Jipcho, who covered the first 400 m. in 56.0, with Keino (56.6) not very far and Ryun (58.5) near the rear of the pack. Keino took over in the second lap and went on at …. sea-level pace: 800 m. in 1:55.3, 1200 m. in 2:53.4, at which stage he had about 7 m. on Tümmler, while Harald Norpoth and Ryun (2:56.0) lagged farther back. In the last 300 m. Ryun moved past Norpoth and Tümmler but could make no impression on Keino, who actually increased his lead and won in 3:34.91. Ryun was a distant second (3:37.89), while Tümmler (3:39.08) took the bronze, well ahead of Norpoth (3:42.57). Keino was certainly great on that occasion, yet several experts felt he could have run faster without the hard runs of previous days. Keino "took ten" in 1969, a year that saw the emergence of two new figures - Marty Liquori of USA and Francesco Arese of Italy. The former, twelfth and last in the Mexico final at nineteen, showed vast improvement in 1969. At the NCAA meet he pulled an upset by beating Ryun in the mile, 3:57.7 to 3:59.3. It must be said that after his bitter disappointment at Mexico City, Ryun never again rose to his splendid form of 1966-67, even though he would occasionally resurge and run a fast race. He had physical problems now and then, and nobody would ever know to what extent his phenomenal efforts at a relatively unripe age had affected the rest of his career. Arese, a tall Italian, had a wide range. In his best years (1970-72) he compiled the following series of marks: 1:46.6 (800 m.), 2:16.9 (1000 m.), 3:36.3 (1500 m.), 13:40.0 (5000 m.) and 28:27.0 (10,000 m.). In the Mexico Olympics he was eliminated in the semi-finals of the 1500 m., but the following year he rose to new heights, finishing a fairly close second to Liquori, 3:37.6 to 3:37.2, in the Europe vs. America dual meet at Stuttgart. Arese reached his peak in 1971. On 1 July at Milan he and Liquori were again pitted against each other in a floodlight meet and the American earned a close decision, 3:36.1 to 3:36.3, after both had run the last 300 m. in 39.5. Later in the season, Arese won the European title at Helsinki in 3:38.4, beating Henryk Szordykowski of Poland (3:38.7) and Brendan Foster of Britain (3:39.2).

Earlier in 1971, on 16 May at Philadelphia, Liquori and Ryun had offered one of the most thrilling 1-mile races ever seen in American outdoor meets. After a relatively slow start (2:03.3 at 880 y.), Liquori negotiated the second half in a great 1:51.3 and went home the winner in 3:54.6, with Ryun 0.2 sec. back. At the end of the year, Liquori ranked first in "Track & Field News" World Ranking. But the Olympic year that followed was a sad one for both Liquori and Ryun. The former injured his left heel early in the year, tried to recover but by May he knew that his Olympic hopes had gone down the tubes. Ryun had ups and downs, yet qualified for the Games. Late in July a fast mile at Toronto, 3:52.8, seemed to project him as one of the top favourites for the Games. But his third Olympic experience was, if possible, even more frustrating than the previous two. In the fourth heat of the 1500 m., he was involved in a"traffic accident". He and Billy Fordjour of Ghana fell, and Fordjour's knee struck Ryun's throat. The world record holder suffered a concussion of the Adam's Apple. By the time he was back in stride the field was 100 m. away. He made a desperate attempt but he had no chance. After crossing the finish line a dejected ninth (3:51.52) he was met by Kipchoge Keino, who tried to console him. But Ryun

Dave Wottle beating Rick Wohlhuter in the 800 m. at the US Olympic Trials of 1972. The winner tied the world record (1:44.3).

was inconsolable: he was to go down in history as possibly the greatest of mile talents, but for some reason unable to do himself justice in the Olympic arena. Shortly before the Games, a new bright prospect had come to the fore in Europe. Half a century after the glorious days of Paavo Nurmi, Finland again had a middle distance runner able to challenge the rest of the world. The man in question was Pekka Vasala (born on 17 April 1948 at Helsinki; 1.83 m./65 kg.). Known in his mother country as Mr. Unpredictable, this ascetic looking man had improved from 3:41.0 in 1970 to 3:38.6 in 1971, and 3:36.8 a few weeks before the Games. And he could point to a significant 1:44.5 for the 800 m. He seemed far better than the man who only a year ago had finished a dismal ninth in the European title race at Helsinki. In the Olympic final (10 September), defending champion Kipchoge Keino found the initial pace too slow for his taste (2:01.4 at 800 m.), and so he took the lead and injected a third 400 m. in 55.1. But in spite of that Vasala was still in his wake, and in the homestretch the bearded Finn moved past the Kenyan to win majestically in 3:36.33. Keino was second in 3:36.81, followed by Rod Dixon of New Zealand (3:37.46) and Mike Boit of Kenya (3:38.41). Vasala's last 400 m. in 53.5 was good, but his last 800 m., forced to 1:49.0 by Keino, was simply fantastic. As for Keino, it should be added that six days earlier he had won a gold medal in the steeplechase. And shortly before the Games he had lowered his 800 m. best to 1:46.41.

Kenya continued to be the choice flower-bed in Africa's garden, but not the only one. In 1973 the track world came to know a man from Tanzania, Filbert Bayi (born on 23 June 1953 in a village near Arusha, at the foot of the Kilimanjaro; 1.83 m./59 kg.), who emphasized a tactic used by others on occasion but generally frowned upon by the majority of "wise" runners. He would move into the lead early and force the pace in an attempt to leave the opposition far behind. Near the end, when fatigue began to tell, he would simply strive to live on his savings the rest of the way. In his international début, at the Munich Olympics, he probably did not have enough confidence to resort to his strategy, yet he looked good with times like 8:41.4 in the steeplechase and 3:45.4 in the 1500 m. But he failed to make the finals. By 1973 he felt ready to impose his rule though, and results were startling, the best of all being a 3:34.6 in the 1500 m. at Helsinki, after going through the rounds in 53.6, 1:51.6 and 2:52.2. In this race he beat the likes of Dave Wottle, the 1972 Olympic champion in the 800 m., and Ben Jipcho (3:36.2 and 3:36.6 respectively). Later in the season, Bayi lost a couple of times to Ben Jipcho. One of these races was a mile, at Stockholm, and a tired Bayi ran against medical advice: even so he led till 60 m. from home, finally losing to the Kenyan, 3:52.86 to 3:52.17.

The 1974 season opened with a bang, a sensational 1500 m. race at the British Commonwealth Games at Christchurch, New Zealand, on 2 February. By no means scared in the presence of a crack field, Bayi ran his usual "crazy" race, passing 400 m. in 54.4 and 800 m. in 1:51.8, at which stage he led by more than 12 m. At 1200 m. in a sizzling 2:50.3, he needed a last 300 m. in 42.7 to break Ryun's world record. By then his lead had narrowed and Rod Dixon, Ben Jipcho and John Walker were closing in on him. But Bayi gallantly held on and finished in 3:32.16, a new world record by nearly a second (later ratified as 3:32.2). In his wake all place winners set new personal and/or national records: Walker 3:32.52, Jipcho 3:33.16, Dixon 3:33.89, Graham Crouch of Australia 3:34.22, Mike Boit 3:36.84, Brendan Foster 3:37.64. It was by far the fastest race ever run. Foster broke the British record and finished only seventh. Crouch, well-beaten in fifth place, lowered Herb Elliott's national record by 1.4 secs. Jipcho virtually matched Ryun's hand-timed world record, and yet finished only third. Walker

1961
1980

Filbert Bayi (Tanzania) on his way to victory in the 1500 m. at the 1974 Commonwealth Games in Christchurch. John Walker (NZ), no. 483, finished second.

219

improved on his previous best by 5.5 secs., broke the world record and lost.

Walker (born on 12 January 1952 at Papakura; 1.85 m./82 kg.), an exuberant Kiwi with blond flowing hair, was to become the most durable top-class miler of all time. As late as in 1990, aged thirty-eight, he was able to run the 1500m. in 3:37.43 and the mile in 3:55.19. By mid-August of 1990 he could claim an imposing tally of sub-4 min. miles: one hundred and thirty! Walker's placings in the annual World Ranking of "Track & Field News" have been as follows:
- 1974: 1st; 1975: 1st; 1976: 1st; 1977: 3rd: 1980: 5th; 1981: 6th; 1982: 4th; 1983: 9th; 1984: 6th; 1986: 10th. This enthusiastic and indefatigable runner has been a star attraction for European and American crowds for many years.

At the 1974 British Commonwealth Games, Walker had won a bronze medal in the 800 m. (1:44.9) four days before his great race in the 1500 m. Later in the season, in Europe, he turned the tables on his Christchurch conqueror Filbert Bayi, beating him by a decisive margin in a 1500 m. race at Helsinki, 3:33.89 to 3:37.20. Rod Dixon, Walker's inseparable travel companion, was third in 3:38.85.

By comparison, Europeans were far less brilliant in those years. The 1974 continental title in Rome was won by Klaus-Peter Justus of East Germany (3:40.6), who emerged from a closely bunched field in the closing stage of an otherwise dull race. The year 1975 was featured by sterling performances in the mile. First to make the headlines was Filbert Bayi, at Kingston, Jamaica, on 17 May. Once again, he imposed his bold tactics and was never headed. After uneven "quarters" (56.9, 59.7, 58.7, 55.7), he finished in 3:51.0, one tenth faster than Ryun's world record. Marty Liquori, by then back in stride, was a magnificent second in 3:52.2, his best ever. Then came Eamonn Coghlan of Ireland (3:53.3) and Rick Wohlhuter of USA (3:53.8). It should be noted that Bayi was faster than Liquori even in the final lap, 55.7 to 56.0. The Tanzanian by then held the world records for both 1500 m. and mile, but he lost the latter on 12 August at Göteborg, when John Walker broke the 3:50 barrier with a great 3:49.4 - a gain of exactly ten seconds vis-à-vis Roger Bannister's first sub-4 min. mile in 1954. Walker - who a few days earlier had run a couple of sub-23 200 m.'s in training - followed Göran Säwemark of Sweden in the first half (56.3, 59.9), then moved into the lead and increased the pace. Two more "quarters" in 57.3 and 55.9 earned him the world record by a sound 1.6 secs. margin. Enroute he was timed in 3:34.3 for the 1500 m. Ken Hall of Australia was second in 3:55.2. Walker crowned a near perfect 3-year spell with an Olympic victory at Montreal in 1976. The final of the 1500 m. (third round in just as many days) was featured by a slow starting pace (62.48). Maybe it was fear of Walker which influenced most of the contenders. They probably thought he would be less overpowering with a slow pace. In the central part of the race Eamonn Coghlan increased the pace, although not enough (2:03.15, 3:01.23). The battle began with 300 m. to go and Walker sprinted first, with Coghlan and Rick Wohlhuter in his wake. Ivo Van Damme of Belgium, fifth when the sprint began, used his speed (he was a 46.4 400 m. man) to pass Coghlan on the curve, gaining on Walker. But the Kiwi had enough left to decelerate less than his rivals in the final stage. A 13.2 in the last 100 m. carried him across the finish in 3:39.17, just ahead of Van Damme (3:39.27), Paul- Heinz Wellmann of West Germany (3:39.33), Coghlan (3:39.51), Frank Clement of Britain (3:39.65) and Wohlhuter (3:40.64). It was the closest finish in the history of the event, and Walker needed 52.7 for the last 400 m. and 25.4 for the last 200 m. to earn a narrow victory. Van Damme thus won his second silver medal in a week, having previously finished second in the 800 m. At twenty-two he looked like the greatest prospect in European history, but on 29 December the track world was shocked to hear that he was killed in a traffic accident in southern France. One of the biggest invitational meets of the European season, held annually at Brussels, is named after him. Among those who missed the Montreal Olympics because of a last minute boycott by African countries

John Walker (NZ), first from left, heading for home in his victorious 1500 m. at the Montreal Olympics (1976).

was of course the holder of the world's 1500 m. record, Filbert Bayi. Fortunately, he was to have another chance in 1980, which he used in another event, the steeplechase. Walker had an emergency appendectomy in October, but at the beginning of 1977 he was his usual self again. And by the end of the year he topped the World Year List in both 1500 m. (3:32.72) and mile (3:52.0). Yet something unusual happened to this great warrior: in the 1500 m of the World Cup at Düsseldorf he dropped out of the race in the last lap. Then he said: "I'm completely exhausted. No excuses. I got boxed, I was beaten and I quit. I have never done it before and I don't think I'll ever do it again".

The race was won by Britain's rising star Steve Ovett, who was by then making a career of sensational finishes. He did 3:34.46 to win from Thomas Wessinghage (3:35.98) and Jürgen Straub of East Germany (3:37.52).

Ovett was to remain undefeated in the 1500 m./mile department from May 1977 till August 1980 - 45 consecutive wins, a fabulous achievement in this time and age. This powerful runner usually relied on his "big kick" to carry him through in close finishes, but he was also prepared to take upon himself the burden of forcing the pace earlier, when he deemed it necessary. In 1978 he won the European 1500 m. title at Prague in 3:35.59, beating Coghlan (3:36.57), David Moorcroft of Britain (3:36.70) and Thomas Wessinghage (3:37.19). Ovett's finish was amazing: last 400 m. in 53.2, last 300 m. in 38.5, last 200 m. in 24.8 - the best ever recorded until then in a race so fast. Three weeks earlier, namely on 12 August at the British Commonwealth Games at Edmonton, Canada, there had been a 1500 m. race far more dramatic, in which Bayi played a prominent role. A light rain fell before the race, and Bayi blamed it for bringing on a touch of his malaria. Even so, he was as bold as ever and forced the pace (57.7, 1:55,2, 2:53.9), well ahead of the pack. But in the closing stage he faced strong British opposition and with 40 m. to go he had to give way to David Moorcroft, who beat him by a narrow margin, 3:35.48 to 3:35.59. Two other Britons, John Robson (3:35.60), third, and Frank Clement (3:35.66), fourth, made this one of the greatest finishes in history. Wilson Waigwa of Kenya was fifth in 3:37.49.

The years 1979 and 1980 were dominated by the famous British duo Ovett/Coe. At the end of 1978, the latter had no better than 3:42.67 in the 1500 m., but the following year he showed amazing progress and chalked up superlative performances. After his world's 800 m. record at Oslo on 5 July, he returned to the magic Bislett track and on 17 July he collected the mile record. In this race Coe trailed two

1961
1980

Steve Ovett (GB), left, and Mike Boit (Kenya) at the 1981 World Cup in Rome.

The three musketeers of British middle distance running in the Olympic 1500 m. final at Los Angeles (1984). From left, Steve Ovett, Steve Cram and Sebastian Coe, the eventual winner.

Americans, Steve Lacy and Steve Scott, for the greater part of the race (57.0 at 440 y., 1:54.5 at 880 y.), then went smoothly past Scott and led at three-quarters in 2:53.4. He caught a new European record (3:32.8) at 1500 m., then continued to increase his lead and won in 3:48.95, shattering Walker's world mark. Scott was second (3:51.11), followed by his compatriot Craig Masback (3:52.02), Coghlan (3:52.45), Robson (3:52.74) and John Walker (3:52.85), who thus witnessed the fall of his record from the track. That was a cast definitely worthy of an Olympic final. On 15 August Coe was in Zurich, where he picked up another world record - his third in five weeks. The race was over the "metric mile" and Coe did 3:32.03 (officially ratified as 3:32.1). Sammy Koskei of Kenya set a faster pace than Coe wanted, yet he stayed close, passing 400 m. in 54.3. Peter Coe, Seb's father/coach, was shouting at him to slow down. Seb complied to some extent, taking the lead shortly before the 800 m., which he passed in 1:53.2. Driven by his courage and the rhythmic clapping of 26,000 spectators, Coe injected another 400 m. in 57.6, then laboured through the last 300 m. in 41.3. "I will never forget that draining run to the finish", he said", and added: "Physically it had been hard, but the mental exhaustion was total". Craig Masback was second in this race in 3:36.97.

During that eventful season Ovett and Coe had never met. But the following year proposed a rendez-vous neither of the two champions wished to avoid: the Moscow Olympics. In pre-Olympic weeks Ovett treated himself to a unique "hors-d'oeuvre": two world records! On 1 July, on Oslo's Bislett track, he ran a mile in 3:48.8. Now beardless and sporting his customary red shirt with the label 'USSR', Ovett followed his countryman Dave Warren initially through laps in 55.7 and 58.1, then took the lead and reached three-quarters in 2:51.0, 2.4 secs. faster than Coe's pace at Zurich the year before. Steve was by then very tired, yet he struggled home and finally prevailed over his invisible opponent by the narrowest of margins - if he did, because his record was hand-timed, as opposed to Coe's auto-timed 3:48.95 of 1979. But the IAAF made no distinction between the two timing systems and for all official purposes Steve thus succeeded Seb as record holder. Second in this race was a 20-year-old Briton, Steve Cram (3:53.8). A name to remember.

Ovett returned to Oslo on 15 July with the declared purpose of breaking another Coe record, Seb's 3:32.1 for the 1500 m. On this occasion he equalled his rival's time, officially at least - because his actual auto time, 3:32.09, was a shade slower than Coe's 3:32.03. A "hare" failed to produce a fast pace and Ovett ran only 57.8 in the first lap. Then Steve Scott, America's premier miler, took over and increased the pace (1:53.6, 2:50.6). His job done, the American dropped out, and Ovett ran the last 300 m. in 41.5. He won from Thomas Wessinghage (3:33.16) and the ever present John Walker (3:33.31).

Prior to the Games, Coe went to Italy, where he trained hard for his double commitment in Moscow. What happened in round 1 of the Ovett vs Coe Olympic feud has been related in the chapter devoted to the 800 m. Ovett's victory in that event had come as a surprise to many, since Coe was believed to be the better two-lap runner, just as Ovett was believed to be the better 1500 m. man. The Moscow verdicts contradicted both these assumptions. In the 1500 m. Coe was eager for revenge, and he got it. The final came as the sixth race in a week for both him and Ovett, and just like in the 800 m. of the 1978 European Championships, a third party interfered in what was supposed to be an all-English affair. This man was Jürgen Straub of East Germany, a former steeplechaser. He led the operations, rather slowly at first (61.6, 2:04.9), then at a much faster pace (2:59.1 at 1200 m.). The two Britons closed on him down the homestretch, but only Coe had enough left to decisively forge ahead with a final 100 m. in 12.1, exactly the same as in the 800 m. final six days earlier, except that this time it was a winning effort! Coe came home an exhausted but happy victor in 3:38.40, followed by the tenacious Straub in 3:38.80, while Ovett, third in 3:38.99, saw the end of his fabulous winning streak. The Moscow Games thus failed to conclusively answer the question: who was the world's no.1 middle distance ace? But then the "draw" was acceptable for both Steve and Seb. They could peacefully continue to avoid each other for a long time to come, with or without the consent of meet promoters. Ovett, however, wanted to have one more happy day before the year was out. The occasion was offered by a post-Olympic meet in Koblenz on 27 August, when Steve met his rival and friend Dr.Thomas Wessinghage in a 1500 m. race. As a West German, Wessinghage had been obliged to stay away from the Moscow Olympics, so he was understandably anxious to make amends, at least in part, with a very fast run. As was the custom any time "a world record was in the air", the meet director had provided a "hare", who ran 55.6 and 1:53.0, closely trailed by Ovett and Wessinghage. The latter took over at 1000 m. and reached 1200 m. in 2:50.7, followed by Ovett and Harald Hudak, an injury-prone West German who had failed to live up to his early promise (3:36.1 at the age of 20 in 1977). Surprisingly, Hudak moved close to Ovett going into the last curve. For a moment it looked like a three-way affair, but then Ovett produced his patented "kick" and went away the winner in 3:31.36, a new world record. Yet he had to dispense with his usual wave to the roaring crowd, because Wessinghage was close. The German finished in 3:31.58, while Hudak was third in 3:31.96, he too under the listed world record jointly held by Seb and Steve! Hudak was a surprise to many, but then the history of middle distance running offers many examples of athletes who occasionally surpassed themselves when extended by superior rivals.

LONG DISTANCES - 5000 & 10,000 Metres: Two great doubles for the man from Myrskylä

1961 1980

The early Sixties brought a revival in American distance running. Uncle Sam's boys had played a minor role in this department for years - virtually since Ralph Hill's famous fight with Lauri Lehtinen in the 5000 m. of the 1932 Olympics. The teachings of Fred Wilt, himself a former distance runner, and the practical influence of Mihály Iglói helped several men to rise to international class. In 1962 Jim Beatty, an Iglói protégé, set a world's 2-mile record of 8:29.8, and also ran 5000 m. in 13:45.0. Two years later, Bob Schul and Billy Mills were to astound the track world at the Tokyo Olympics. Schul, a former steeplechaser (8:47.8 in 1961) and a sub-4 min. miler, had fresh credentials like a world record in the 2 miles (8:26.4 in August 1964) and the season's fastest time at 5000 m., 13:38.0. Mills, a 7/16 Sioux Indian, descendant of a war chief, was a virtual unknown on the international scene in the summer of 1964, his fastest 10,000 m. time being no better than 29:10.4.

In Europe, Pyotr Bolotnikov of USSR had another great season in 1962, when he lowered his own 10,000 m. world record to 28:18.2 at Moscow on 11 August, and won the European title at Belgrade in 28:54.0. He was thirty-two by then, and this was his swan song. Still in the Belgrade meet, Bruce Tulloh of Britain, renowned for his habit of running barefoot, won the 5000 m. title in 14:00.6. On the eve of the 1964 Olympics the leading European contender in the 5000 m. was Michel Jazy of France, who elected to run that distance in preference to the 1500 m. Yet the most interesting candidate appeared to be Ron Clarke of Australia (born on 21 February 1937 at Melbourne; 1.83 m./74 kg.). Younger brother of Jack, a football player of national prominence, Ron also played that game as a youth (Australian Rules Football being "almost a religion in Victoria, and nowhere more than in the Clarke family"). He was introduced to athletics by Franz Stampfl, who had coached Bannister, among others. His natural talent became apparent early in 1956, when he ran a mile in 4:06.8, a world Junior (under 20) best and a feat which incidentally assured him a peculiar début on the international scene: as carrier of the torch around the track on the inaugural day of the 1956 Olympics in Melbourne, hence in the presence of a large crowd.

After that episode, however, several years went by before the track world could hear Clarke's name again. His progress was slow and inconclusive. His feelings by the end of 1960 can be gathered from a later confession (in his book "The Unforgiving Minute", written in co-operation with Alan Trengove): "I was nearly twenty-four and I estimated I had another six years or so in which I could take part in top-class sport and many, many more in which top sport would be impracticable. Should I waste those six years? It seemed that so many sportsmen later rued their early retirement. You have only one life and it's futile looking back upon it and regretting that you didn't do something when you were capable of doing it". That was when he decided to move from purely recreational sport to a more methodical approach, implying intensive, systematic training. He joined a bunch of dedicated runners known as the "Caulfield Mob" or alternatively as the "Ferny Creek Gang", from places in Melbourne where they usually trained. Ron began to have two training sessions per day, before and after his office hours as an accountant. At last he was out to discover his true potential. Unconsciously perhaps, he was giving vent to a thought once expressed by a man of letters from France, Antoine Blondin: "The athlete is a man who has decided to broaden the walls of his prison". No matter how hard their work, Ron and his companions trained in an atmosphere of friendly togetherness. Years of intensive training turned the gifted Ron Clarke into the most efficient running machine ever seen until then. Late in 1962 he made his real international début at the British Commonwealth Games in Perth, placing second to Murray Halberg of New Zealand in the 3 miles. Time, 13:35.92. His record breaking spree began in December 1963, and in the space of five years he broke eighteen world records, at distances ranging from 2 miles to the 1-hour run. The list is given in the adjoining table. Clarke was never frightened by the prospect of having to take upon himself the burden of setting a "hot" pace. By his courage and his example he extended many of his rivals around the world to marks they had never dreamt of. This resulted in a general advance of distance running standards. Vis-à-vis pre-Clarke world records he gained 18 secs. in the 5000 m. and nearly 39 secs. in the 10,000 m.! The Oslo race of 1965 in which he broke the 28-min. barrier in the 10,000 m. must probably be considered his "chef-d'oeuvre". His kilometre fractions were as follows: 2:41.5, 2:43.5, 2:46, 2:47, 2:47, 2:48, 2:50, 2:50, 2:46, 2:40.4 (An auto timing device, used as a back-up, gave him a final time of 27:39.89). Great was the astonishment of spectators when the announcer said that Clarke had covered the first 5000 m. in 13:45.0, a new stadium record for that distance! When the race was over, somebody noted that "in theory" Clarke would have lapped the great Zátopek, whose best 10,000 m. time was

Clarke's World Records

Melbourne, 18 December 1963	6 miles	27:17.8	
	10,000 m.	28:15.5	*
Melbourne, 3 December 1964	3 miles	13:07.5	*
Hobart, 16 January 1965	5000 m.	13:34.7	*
Auckland, 1 February 1965	5000 m.	13:33.6	
Mentone, Vic., 3 March 1965	10 miles	47:12.7	*
Los Angeles, 4 June 1965	3 miles	13:00.4	
	5000 m.	13:25.7	*
Turku, 16 June 1965	10,000 m. (&)	28:14.0	
London, 10 July 1965	3 miles	12:52.4	
Oslo, 14 July 1965	6 miles	26:47.0	
	10,000 m.	27:39.4	
Geelong, 27 October 1965	20,000 m.	59:22.7	*
	20,232 m.	1 hour	
Stockholm, 5 July 1966	3 miles	12:50.4	
	5000 m.	13:16.6	
Västerås, 27 June 1967	2 miles	8:19.8	
London, 24 August 1968	2 miles	8:19.6	

* Officially rounded off to the nearest fifth above in accordance with IAAF rule. & Not ratified by the IAAF.

28:54.2. To which Clarke intelligently and modestly retorted: "Some day somebody will lap me!" (As of the end of 1990, nobody has come close to doing that...). The following year, in Stockholm, Clarke achieved his 13:16.6 for the 5000 m. with the following kilometre fractions: 2:40.4, 2:36.2, 2:40.8, 2:41.6, 2:37.6. Yet this great champion never won an Olympic gold medal. At the Tokyo Games (1964) he entered the 10,000 m. event as reigning world record holder and no.1 favourite, but in the end things took a different turn. On a track wet from the morning rains, 38 runners lined up at the start. In the decisive stage, the three leaders - Clarke, Mohamed Gammoudi of Tunisia and Billy Mills of USA - had to find their way through lapped runners. In a hectic sprint, Mills upset his more famous rivals and won in 28:24.4 from Gammoudi (28:24.8) and Clarke (28:25.8). The Australian estimated that in view of the difficult conditions his time was probably worth no less than his world record of the previous year (28:15.5). The final of the 5000 m., four days later, was run in a pelting rain and it was so dark that the stadium lights were on. The finish was, if possible, even more hectic than in the 10,000m. Michel Jazy started his bid at the bell, built up a lead, but mid-way in the homestretch he had nothing more to offer and within a few seconds he regressed from first to fourth. Bob Schul of USA won in 13:48.8, after covering the last 300 m. in a fantastic 38.7. Harald Norpoth of West Germany (13:49.6), Bill Dellinger of USA and Jazy (both 13:49.8) followed in that order. Clarke was very disappointing: ninth in 13:58.0. Two days earlier, in a heat, he had posted a seemingly effortless 13:48.4 ...

Kipchoge Keino, fifth in the Olympic 5000 m. in 13:50.4, was to become one of Clarke's most serious rivals. As related in the previous chapter, in 1965 the Kenyan set new world records for 3000 m. (7:39.5) and 5000 m. (13:24.2). But at the Helsinki World Games, on 30 June, both Keino and Clarke were outsprinted by a revived Jazy, who set a new European record, 13:27.6. Keino (13:28.2) beat Clarke (13:29.4) for second place. In 1966 at Budapest Jazy won the European title, beating Harald Norpoth, 13:42.8 to 13:44.0. In the same meet Jürgen Haase of East Germany won the 10,000 m. in 28:26.0. He was a medium-size, compact runner, and had an excellent finish. Norpoth was very much the opposite, so tall and slender as to appear emaciated, but his long sustained drive made him a dangerous man in the closing stage of a race. In 1966 he succeeded Jazy as holder of the European 5000 m. record with 13:24.8. Another great European in those years was Gaston Roelants of Belgium, who for a long time had the steeplechase as his first love. But he also gained the European 10,000 m. record in 1965 with 28:10.6. The following year, at Leuven, he set new world marks for the 20,000 m. (58:06.2) and the 1-hour run (20,664 m.), which performances amounted to running 50 laps of a 400m. track at an average speed of less than 70 secs. per lap. Following the triumphal days of Schul and Mills in Tokyo, the American "wave" strangely subsided, apart from an exciting 6-mile race at the 1965 AAU Championships in San Diego, won by Billy Mills in 27:11.5 from 21-year-old Gerry Lindgren (27:11.6). These times were under Clarke's world record, but the Aussie was to take over again, and by a huge margin, a few weeks later.

En passant I may mention that Jim Ryun once tried the 5000 m. during his 1967 European tour, finishing in 13:47.8.

1961 1980

Thereby hangs a tale

Ron Clarke played a very important role in the evolution of distance running standards during the Sixties. He operated at a time when competition at the international level was considerably stiffer than in the days of Paavo Nurmi or even in those of Emil Zátopek. But unlike his great predecessors, who coupled world records with great Olympic victories, Clarke never had the supreme satisfaction of winning a gold medal in the Olympics or, for that matter, in the British Commonwealth Games. The altitude of Mexico City probably deprived him of his best chance in 1968, when he appeared to be in excellent form. But even on other occasions, at or near sea level, he was for some reason unable to impose throughout the race that kind of sustained pace which had carried him to so many world records in competitions of lesser international renown.

Many years after his retirement, he was diagnosed as having a heart disorder (for which he was successfully operated on), an inborn anomaly which, according to some, would have made it almost impossible for him to withstand sudden changes of rhythm in a race, while not preventing him from sustaining long periods of running at a (more or less) steady pace. But then the annals of track contain many examples of great athletes who for some reason were not "equal to themselves" in "hot" competitions. In the opinion of most students of sport, this is chiefly due to psychological factors.

Heat of the 10,000 m. at the 1980 Olympics in Moscow. Werner Schildhauer (East Germany) leading from Lasse Viren (Finland).

At the 1968 Olympics in Mexico City, African runners had the lion's share. High altitude, to which most of them were accustomed from childhood, may have played into their hands to some extent, but as we now know their impact was to be strongly felt even in subsequent (sea-level) editions of the Games. So Mexico was simply the dawn of the African Era. Even so, it is a fact that the rarefied atmosphere of the Mexican capital put Ron Clarke, Jürgen Haase and other sea-level runners at a disadvantage. Only a few weeks before the Games, in Scandinavia, the Australian had beaten Gammoudi, Keino and Temu, precisely the three men who were to prove supreme at Mexico City. In the Olympic races, Clarke was sixth in the 10,000 m., then fifth in the 5000 m.

More dramatic was Haase's downfall: in the 10,000 m. the European champion finished no better than fifteenth. The winner at this distance was Naftali Temu of Kenya in 29:27.40, with Mamo Wolde of Ethiopia second (29:27.75) and Mohamed Gammoudi of Tunisia third (29:34.2). Such relatively slow times obviously told the tale about the negative effects of altitude in long distance events. Four days later, Gammoudi won the 5000 m. in 14:05.01, after a bitter fight with Kipchoge Keino (14:05.16), while Temu was third (14:06.41). Unlike Ethiopians and Kenyans, the 30-year-old Gammoudi was not familiar with high altitude, even though he had spent some time at the French training centre of Font-Romeu (1800 m.) in the Pyrenees shortly before the Games. He won with a terrifying last lap: 54.8. Temu, a little 23-year-old runner, had become internationally famous two years earlier, beating Clarke in the 6 miles of the British Commonwealth Games at Kingston. Clarke was certainly supreme as a record breaker, but failed to do himself justice when major international titles were at stake. In the Olympics he had to be content with a bronze medal (Tokyo, 1964). In the British Commonwealth Games (1962, '66 and '70) he won two silver medals in the 3 miles/5000 m. and again two silvers in the 6 miles/10,000 m.

In 1969-70, while Clarke's decline began to take shape, a most prominent figure was Scotland's Ian Stewart, who won two important titles, both in the 5000 m.: at the 1969 European Championships in Athens (13:44.8) and at the 1970 British Commonwealth Games in Edinburgh (13:22.8). In the latter race Keino and Clarke finished third and fifth respectively. In the same Edinburgh meet another Scotsman, Lachie Stewart (he and Ian were no relatives), beat Clarke - "my inspiration", as he said later - in the 10,000 m., 28:11.71 to 28:13.44. In the meantime Jürgen Haase had resurged from his Olympic demise in 1969 to win his second European title for the 10,000 m. (28:41.6).

The Finns, onetime rulers of long distance running, rose from years of indifferent performances to resume their winning ways in 1971-72. First to break the ice was Juha Väätäinen, who scored a widely acclaimed double at the 1971 European Championships in Helsinki. He brought the home crowd to its feet with a 54.0 last lap to win the 10,000 m. in 27:52.8 from Jürgen Haase (27:53.4), then he outsprinted Jean Wadoux of France and Harald Norpoth in a 13:32.6 5000 m. This bearded Finn, vaguely reminiscent of Santa Claus, was thirty and his breakthrough came towards the end of a troubled career. A year later he was not even Finland's best, for in the meantime another talent had risen to spectacular heights to rule over Suomi and the world as well. This man was Lasse Artturi Viren (born on 22 July 1949 at Myrskylä, 1.80 m./61 kg.). A cool, reserved and ascetic looking man, Viren was to achieve something no distance runner before or after has ever achieved: a 5000/10,000 double in two editions of the Olympic Games! Yet, curiously enough, he was ironically referred to as "a man who could win only in the Olympics". A slightly distorted appraisal no doubt, yet it is a fact that between his glories in Munich (1972) and Montreal (1976) he had many indifferent if not downright poor performances, and suffered many defeats. His "art" consisted in concentrating with great singleness of purpose on Olympic tasks. A book written by his coach Rolf Haikkola in co-operation with Pentti Vuorio, a noted track writer ("Lasse Viren, kullatut sekunnit" i.e. golden seconds), contains a summary of Viren's training loads in the years of his build-up for the Munich Olympics. Each figure relates to a twelve-month period stretching from October till September of the following year.

1967-68	1940 km.
1968-69	2967 km.
1969-70	3728 km.
1970-71	5332 km.
1971-72	7348 km.

Details of Viren's monthly loads in the period 1971-72 are also available: they range from a minimum of 392 km. in October '71 to a maximum of 844 km. in February '72, after which his "ration" decreased, save for a rise to 676 km. in August '72, on the eve of the Games. Viren's average for that period was 612 km. per month, slightly more than 20 km. per day. For the greater part it was "endurance training of the best quality". Even apart from what he did in Munich, 1972 was Viren's best year. During that season he set three world records (the entire tally of his career): 8:14.0 for 2 miles at Stockholm, shortly before the Games; 27:38.35 for 10,000 m. at Munich; and 13:16.4 for 5000 m. at Helsinki on 14 September. His 10,000 m. record at Munich came under peculiar circumstances certainly deserving a detailed account. At 4500 m. there was a collision, and in no time two men lay flat - Viren on the track, Mohamed Gammoudi on the green infield. The Finn lost only three seconds before getting to his feet and setting out after the pack, 10 m. away. And it took him little more than a half minute to catch everyone but the leader, Dave Bedford. Gammoudi, however, was so badly affected that he was late to recover. He tried to close the huge gap, but soon found he had

no chance and was forced to retire. Meanwhile Bedford was leading the field at the mid-way point in 13:44.0. But the Briton lost contact at 7000 m., leaving five men to battle it out for victory. Viren, apparantly unaffected by his earlier mishap, proved the strongest of them all. He moved down everybody with his progressive acceleration: last kilometre in 2:29.2, last 800 m. in 1:56.4, last 400 m. in 56.4. He finished a superb winner in 27:38.35, a new world record (which was ratified as 27:38.4). Emiel Puttemans of Belgium was second (27:39.58), followed by Miruts Yifter of Ethiopia (27:40.96) and Mariano Haro of Spain (27:48.14). A week later Viren annexed the 5000 m. title in 13:26.42, beat-

1961
1980

Dave Bedford (GB) set a world's 10,000 m. record in 1973.

227

ing a revived Gammoudi (13:27.33) and Ian Stewart (13:27.61) in a hectic finish. Puttemans was fifth, behind Steve Prefontaine of USA. This race was featured by a slow early pace and a spirited finish: Viren covered the last kilometre in 2:26.2, the last 800 m. in 1:56.0 and the last 400 m. in 56.0. Viren was only the fourth man in history to achieve such a great double, after Kolehmainen, Zátopek and Kuts.

Puttemans, a light-footed runner with a galloping stride, closed his 1972 account with two world records: 7:37.6 for 3000 m. at Aarhus on 14 September, and 13:13.0 for 5000 m. at Brussels on 20 September. The latter was a memorable day for Belgian athletics: in the same meet Gaston Roelants bettered his own world record for the 1-hour run, covering 20,784 m. Britain's Dave Bedford, a long-haired runner all arms and legs, caused a revolution in the philosophy of British distance running by laying the stress on quantity of work. His "condition" allowed him to produce wonderful times, generally in races he could more easily keep under control, but he failed to do himself justice on big occasions. On 13 July 1973 in London

---

Blood doping vs. reindeer milk

Lasse Viren was a very busy man during the last week of July 1976 in Montreal. Besides covering 72-plus kilometres in competition, he had to go through an IOC hearing on the subject of shoes, and answer all sorts of questions from members of the so-called Fourth Estate. Some papers had given vent to rumours according to which he was suspected of having resorted to blood transfusions in the weeks preceding the Montreal Olympics. (A process wherein blood is taken from an athlete and added again later so as to increase the number of red blood cells). According to some, such a "booster" could explain the difference between his generally indifferent marks earlier in the season and his exploits in Montreal. When a journalist asked him about this, Viren calmly replied: "I run 8000 kilometres a year. That is enough for me". Later, in a more ironical vein, he said that his secret weapon was reindeer milk. "We drink it daily. The only trouble is that you go bald". It was only a joke, but some papers apparently took the story very seriously. Unknowingly, Viren had publicized another product.

---

he shaved almost 8 secs. off Viren's 10,000 m. record with 27:30.80, his 5000 m. fractions being 13:39.4 and 13:51.4, i.e. the very opposite of Lasse Viren's pattern. Much more reliable as a competitor was Brendan Foster, another Briton who in the 5000 m. of the 1974 European Championships in Rome ran away from the opposition early and won in 13:17.21, leaving Manfred Kuschmann of East Germany (13:23.93) and Viren (13:24.57) far behind. Earlier in the year, at the British Commonwealth Games at Christchurch, Foster had finished a close second to Ben Jipcho, 13:14.6 to 13:14.4, over the same distance. Foster, also a leading 1500 m. man, was one of those rare runners who can set a "hot" pace and still hold their own in any stretch drive. Still in 1974, he achieved a world record of 7:35.1 for the 3000 m. Winner of the 10,000 m. at the European Championships in Rome on a hot day was Kuschmann, who barely edged Tony Simmons of Britain, 28:25.76 to 28:25.80. The most notable newsitem of 1975 was a sad one: the death of America's finest distance runner, Steve Prefontaine, in a traffic accident. Aged 24, "Pre" - as he was called by his fans - was coming home from yet another victory on his favourite track at Eugene, Oregon. A native of that state, he was immensely popular. His generosity led him to give all he had in any race, and he could point to such times as 13:22.2 (5000 m.) and 27:43.6 (10,000 m.), and was a 3:54.6 miler.

The African boycott greatly devalued the distance events of the 1976 Olympics in Montreal. Miruts Yifter in particular was badly missed. At the decisive moment the world of track saw the "real" Viren again. In the 10,000 m. he K.O.'d tenacious Carlos Lopes of Portugal, 27:40.38 to 27:45.17, after covering the second half in a sizzling 13:31.5. Brendan Foster was third in 27:54.92. When the race was over, Viren ran a lap, holding his spike shoes in the air. In times of growing commercialism, his gesture led someone to suspect that he wanted to publicize that particular footwear in the eyes of millions of tele-viewers. Which, of course, could make him a "professional". The day before the 5000 m. final there was an IOC hearing, during which Viren was asked if that gesture wasn't perhaps a commercial trick. The Finn explained that he got blisters during the race; when the battle was over, he took off his shoes to avoid further pain. No action was taken against him, and the next day Viren lined up at the start of the 5000 m., apparently as cool and unruffled as ever. This time he was up against two great milers, Dick Quax and Rod Dixon of New Zealand. True to his favourite strategy, Viren used progressive acceleration in the closing stage to "devitalize" them. He ran the last 1600 m. in 4:05.2, the last 800

1961 1980

Rono's eighty-days record spree (1978)

Berkeley, 8 April	5000 m.	13:08.4
Seattle, 13 May	3000 m. St.	8:05.4
Vienna, 11 June	10,000 m.	27:22.4
Oslo, 27 June	3000 m.	7:32.1

m. in 1:57.5 and the last 400 m. in 55.4. That sufficed to carry him home the victor in 13:24.76, ahead of Quax (13:25.16), Klaus-Peter Hildenbrand of West Germany (13:25.38), Dixon (13:25.50) and Foster (13:26.19). This was on 30 July. The following day Viren was bold, or crazy, enough to line up at the start of the marathon - his official début at the classic distance! He finished fifth, understandably exhausted, in 2:13:11. This feat passed almost unnoticed in the world press, but in view of the circumstances it was certainly on a par with his greatest deeds. Earlier in 1976 there had been another world record, namely on 1 May at Papendal, when Jos Hermens of Holland covered 20,944 m. in one hour. During his long journey, to avoid boredom and keep himself alive, he listened to rock music from a mini-stereo radio that was part of his equipment.

In 1977 a shooting star appeared in the firmament of top-class distance running: Samson Kimobwa of Kenya, then a 22-year-old student at Washington State University. From a previous best of 28:10.3 for the 10,000 m., he suddenly blossomed to a world record performance of 27:30.47 (ratified as 27:30.5) and did so in one of Europe's noblest meets, the World Games at Helsinki, on 30 June. His compatriot Mike Musyoki (27:41.92) and Franco Fava of Italy (27:42.65) finished second and third respectively. As a result of his sudden rise to fame, Kimobwa was submerged by invitations to appear in practically every corner of Europe. He accepted most of them and such an overdose of competitive efforts, obviously intertwined with long trips, resulted in his losing his golden form in a relatively short time. A more durable performer was Dick Quax of New Zealand, who had his greatest day on 5 July 1977 at Stockholm, when he lowered the world's 5000 m. record to 13:12.86 (officially ratified as 13:12.9).

On a strictly competitive side the best was offered by Marty Liquori and Miruts Yifter. The latter (born on 15 May 1944 in a village of Tigré; 1.62 m./53 kg.), a sturdy little runner, had first made the headlines in 1971, during the USA vs. Africa dual meet at Durham, N.C. On the first day, in the 5000 m., he started his finishing sprint in what he thought was the last lap, whereas it was in fact the next-to-last. When told about his blunder, Yifter was so tired that he had to give way to Steve Prefontaine of USA, who sprinted at the right time and won. But Yifter came back the next day to win the 10,000 m. At the 1972 Olympics in Munich, Yifter finished third in the 10,000 m., then missed his heat of the 5000 m., reaching the starting line when the race was well underway! There were contradictory versions on this episode (far less publicized in the press than the Hart-Robinson case I have alluded to in the chapter devoted to the sprints).

Yifter finally came into his own at the inaugural World Cup at Düsseldorf in 1977, when his tremendous turn of speed 250-to-300 m. from home earned him two smashing victories, first in the 10,000 m. (28:32.3), then in a hard-fought 5000 m. (13:13.82) against Marty Liquori (13:15.06).

In 1978 there was a man who stood head and shoulders above the rest: Henry Rono (born on 12 February 1952 at Kaprirsang, Nandi Hills; 1.70 m./63 kg.). Like many of his countrymen, this heavily muscled Kenyan grew up in the mountains. A US scholarship took him to Washington State University, where he joined other Kenyan distance men, under the tutelage of coach John Chaplin. By the end of 1977 he could point to such times as 13:22.1 and

1972 Olympics in Munich. Lasse Virén (Finland) no.228, leading a great 5.000 metre field in the closing stage. He won in 13.26.42. Others from left are: M. Gamoudi (Tunisia) 2nd; I. Stewart (GB), partly covered, 3rd; E. Puttemans (Belgium), 5th; and S. Prefontaine (USA), 4th.

229

27:37.8. What he did in 1978 belongs in the most exclusive chapter of athletic memorabilia. Between January and November he took part in fifty-odd competitions - on track and road, indoors and out - in many parts of the world. Not surprisingly, he was exhausted by the time this self-imposed torture came to an end in a road race held on a cold winter day at Madison, Wisconsin, where he wound up 237th in a field of 241. But history is bound to remember, preferably and justly, the four world records he set in the space of eighty days, as listed in a separate table.

Rono thus became the first distance runner to own world records for flat and barrier events at the same time. In contrast to Viren, who used to apply his progressive acceleration in the closing stage of the race, Rono would go all out from the start, then try to maintain his rhythm till the end. Such was his condition in 1978 that he could sometimes produce a final acceleration even after a fast, gruelling race. In his 5000 m. at Berkeley he covered the last 3000 m. in 7:49.6 and the last 1000 m. in 2:33.7. In his 10,000 m. at Vienna he negotiated the first half in 13:48.2 and the second in 13:34.2. In his 3000 m. at Oslo he ran the last kilometre in 2:27.4. While spreading himself thin in countless races, Rono still managed to win 11 out of 12 in the 5000 m., 5 out of 5 in the 10,000 m. and 10 out of 12 in the steeplechase!

The 1978 European Championships, held at Prague, projected into the limelight two Europeans, Martti Vainio of Finland and Venanzio Ortis of Italy. The former, a tall (1.92 m.) 28-year-old fighter, beat the latter in the 10,000 m. at the end of a hair-raising duel, 27:30.99 to 27:31.48. Six days later the 23-year-old Ortis nosed out a closely bunched field to win the 5000 m. in 13:28.57 (Vainio was sixth). While the Finn continued to be a factor for several years after that, his younger rival from Italy, hampered by injuries, never rose to such heights again.

In his golden year (1978) Rono had won two titles at the British Commonwealth Games in Edmonton: 5000 m. and steeplechase. In 1979, while the Kenyan began to show declining form, another African replaced him as

Henry Rono (Kenya) set 4 world records at 4 different distance events in 1978, his banner year.

Run for tea

Throughout the summer of 1978, track observers wondered what special "motor" was in Henry Rono's mind and muscles that allowed him to sustain such a unique series of Herculean labours. Even after setting four world records in the space of eighty days, the 26-year-old Kenyan continued to compete all over Europe with relentless energy, always with great performances. His chief aim was known only to close friends: Henry wanted to earn the money that was needed to enlarge his tea plantation at Kapsabet, cared for by his mother during his trips abroad.

It would not be exact to say that Rono showed unmistakable signs of greatness only in 1978, but it is a fact that in subsequent years he lacked consistency and was able to rise to his former stature only on rare occasions.

Maybe he paid a price for his super-work of 1978. He belame an alcohol addict, a problem that certainly did not help him in shaping his activity, on and off the track. He made the headlines again in the mid-Eighties, mostly in connection with his social problems. In brief, I would say that Henry Rono was an athletic genius, ruined to a notable extent by dissipation.

the world's no.1 distance runner. This man was Miruts Yifter, the "ageless" Ethiopian, as he was called because of controversial information about his year of birth (commonly accepted as 1944 by the Association of Track & Field Statisticians). In the World Cup at Montreal he duplicated his double of 1977, with 27:53.07 in the 10,000 m. (last 200 m. in 25.5) and 13:35.9 in the 5000 m. This most tenacious athlete finally achieved Olympic fame at Moscow in 1980, that is eight years after his bitter-sweet experience at Munich and four years after missing Montreal altogether. Unfortunately, Kenya happened to be on the boycotters' side this time too - for different political implications. Henry Rono thus missed his second (and last) Olympic chance. After a promising 27:31.68 in the 10,000 m. early in the season, he had fallen far below decent form.

Yifter was clearly the class of the field in Moscow. He won the 10,000 m. in 27:42.69 from an unexpected Finn, Kaarlo Maaninka (27:44.28). Mohammed Kedir, third (27:44.64), and Tolossa Kotu, fourth (27:46.47), made this a memorable day for Ethiopia. Defending champion Lasse Viren was with the leading pack till the last lap, but in the backstretch he had to give way to Yifter et al. He finished fifth (27:50.46). The race was run under difficult conditions, the temperature being around 30 °C. Viren, a Northerner, said: "Near the end of the race I felt like I was breathing fire". Even so, the irrepressible Yifter managed to run the last lap in 54.4! When the race was over, he injected a malicious remark: "I was in better form in Montreal (1976) than I have been here". Five days later, Yifter won the 5000 m. in 13:20.91, after a close battle with Suleiman Nyambui of Tanzania (13:21.60), while Maaninka (13:22.00) shunted to fourth place Eamonn Coghlan of Ireland (13:22.74), better known as holder of the world's indoor record for the mile. Here too Yifter was the fastest finisher: 54.9 for the last 400 m., as opposed to Nyambui's 55.5.

Moscow results definitely confirmed the gains of African distance men at the expense of their European colleagues. Even though Kenya was not in the run, Africans took four of the six medals at stake in 5000 and 10,000 m. The surprise man of the Games, Kaarlo Maaninka of Finland, had gone there as a virtual outsider, his only notable mark being a 13:25.0 in the 5000 m. Some track observers were still raving about his Moscow heroics several years later, when he admitted having resorted to "blood doping" to enhance his performance shortly before the 1980 Games. His confession apparently came as part of a spiritual re-consideration of his athletic venture. It could be argued that other athletes in other parts of the world may have gone through similar experiences, still with no urge towards confession.

MARATHON - Cierpinski follows in Bikila's footsteps

After his great victory in the 1960 Olympic marathon, Abebe Bikila remained a dominant figure for several years. Between the Rome and the Tokyo Olympics he ran six marathons and won them all except one, at Boston in 1963, when he had to be content with fifth place. In 1964 an appendectomy left him just six weeks to recover in time for the Tokyo Olympics. But on D-Day he proved ready and better than ever. He became the first man in history to successfully defend an Olympic marathon title, and did so with a sterling performance: 2:12:11.2, best-on-record up to that time. He left the runner-up, Basil Heatley of Britain, over 4 minutes behind. Bikila, now wearing shoes, had the following 10,000 m. fractions: 30:14, 30:44,

Harakiri

There is probably no country in the world where the marathon is as popular as in Japan. In the Empire of the Rising Sun this event is looked upon almost as a religion. That is possibly the only way an alien can explain the "Tsuburaya case". The Olympic marathon at Tokyo in 1964 was watched by an estimated half a million people. Tsuburaya, then 24, ran a great race and entered the stadium in second place (while winner Abebe Bikila, who had finished four minutes earlier, delighted the crowd with stretching exercises, a "cooling off" operation), closely followed by Britain's Basil Heatley. Going into the last curve, the latter spurted and finally shunted Tsuburaya to third place (2:16:19.2 to 2:16:22.8). Tsuburaya's bronze was the only medal won by Japanese athletes in those Games, yet he found it extremely hard to get over the fact that he had been "humiliated" by a rival in the presence of a huge home crowd. In 1967 he severely injured his right Achilles tendon. On 9 January 1968, while a 2nd Lieutenant at the national military Physical Training School, he committed suicide. He left a note saying: "I can't run anymore". One sports critic said Tsuburaya's suicide was a protest against the trend - common in Japan, as well as anywhere else in the world - to emphasize only victory and to ignore the human individual.

1961
1980

31:52 and 32:20. He was slower than in Rome (1960) only in the last 2195 m. (7:41.2)

Throughout his career, Abebe Bikila seldom tried the track events. One of his rare excursions in this domain was at Berlin in 1962, when he ran the 10,000 m. in 29:00.8 in losing to his compatriot Mamo Wolde (28:55.6) Then even Bikila's marathon record was surpassed. It happened in the classic Windsor-to-Chiswick race in 1965, when Morio Shigematsu of Japan ran the distance in 2:12:00, partly aided by a tailwind, a far from negligible factor on one-way courses such as the Polytechnic Harriers' event. On 3 December 1967 a more shocking news-item was relayed to the rest of the world from Japan. The Fukuoka marathon had by then become Japan's biggest event, and even observers from abroad regarded it as a sort of unofficial world championship. On that occasion an Australian, Derek Clayton, astounded everybody by recording 2:09:36.4. This talented runner (born on 17 November 1942 at Barrow-in-Furness, Lancashire; 1.88 m./73 kg.) had settled in Australia at twenty-one and at Fukuoka he was running his fifth marathon. His début over this distance dated from 1965, when he did 2:22:12, also a winning effort. At Fukuoka he clipped nearly 9 minutes off his previous best. His 10,000 m. fractions were: 29:57, 30:02, 30:33, 31:44. His time for the last 2195 m. was 7:20.4. Conditions were downright favourable, as shown by place times too: Seiichiro Sasaki of Japan was second in 2:11:17, he too under the previous record, and David McKenzie of New Zealand was third in 2:12:25.8.

Clayton's "explosion" obviously brought forth the question: what was the "secret" of this splendid Australian "machine"? Looking for an answer, some observers inevitably referred to a super-quantity of work. In fact, his training load amounted to a weekly average of 225 km., with an occasional "peak" of 322 km. (= 200 miles). On the other hand it may be assumed that his recurrent leg injuries in later years (needing surgery at times) were in some way connected with such an overdose of training. Two months before the Mexico Olympics (1968) he developed an ailment to his right knee. This circumstance, coupled with the problem of altitude, made it impossible for him to place higher than seventh in the Olympic race. Another "victim" on that occasion was Bikila himself. Not fully recovered from an injury sustained in Spain the year before, he was obliged to retire after 17 km. Yet the Olympic title did not leave Ethiopia, because Mamo Wolde finally had his long awaited day of glory. This light-footed runner (born on 12 June 1932 at Jirgalem; 1.72 m./53 kg.) had made his début in the Olympic arena twelve years earlier in Melbourne, finishing an undistinguished last in heats of the 800 and 1500 m. As a marathon runner he was in evidence as early as in 1964, when he finished a mere 0.4 sec. behind Abebe Bikila (2:16:19.2 to 2:16:18.8) in a pre-Olympic test at Addis Ababa. That was a remarkable performance, under high altitude conditions. In Tokyo he dropped out of the marathon but finished fourth in the 10,000 m. Even in Mexico City he ran both events: a week after winning a silver medal in the 10,000 m., Mamo succeeded Bikila as marathon champion in 2:20:26.4, with more than 3 minutes to spare on Kenji Kimihara of Japan. Clayton was obviously thirsty for revenge, and the following year, on 30 May at Antwerp, he came up with another record performance: 2:08:33.6. His 10,000 m. fractions showed great consistency: 30:06, 30:24, 30:26, 30:59, plus 6:38.6 for the last 2195 m. Once again, a Japanese was second: Akio Usami (2:11:27.8). Almost inevitably, there were Doubting Thomases who found it hard to believe in the authenticity of Clayton's mark.

Waldemar Cierpinski (East Germany) emulated Abebe Bikila as a twotime winner of the Olympic marathon (1976 and 1980).

There were in fact allegations that the course at Antwerp was under distance, but this was never categorically proven and the mark remained in the books as a best-on-record performance until 1981, when it was finally beaten. Clayton continued to run for several more years, but for some reason he was invariably disappointing on big occasions: he dropped out of two Commonwealth Games marathons (1970 and '74) and placed no higher than thirteenth at the Munich Olympics (1972).

In those years Europe had at least three top-class marathoners: Ron Hill of Britain, Karel Lismont and Gaston Roelants of Belgium. The Briton was a portent even in terms of longevity: during his career, which stretched over two decades, he belonged to the élite of marathon runners for at least seven years (1969-75). European champion at Athens in 1969 and Commonwealth champion at Edinburgh in 1970 (2:09:28), he was not so lucky in his Olympic adventures: the best he could do was a sixth place in Munich (1972). A textile chemist, he contributed to the evolution of marathon running in sundry fields of research, e.g. by advocating carbohydrate loading in preparation for competitive efforts, and designing a new range of running equipment. Lismont also had a long career. He was European champion in 1971 and won Olympic medals in Munich (silver) and Montreal (bronze). His compatriot Gaston Roelants turned to the marathon after a successful career in the steeplechase. He figured prominently in three editions of the European Championships: second in 1969, fifth in '71 and third in '74. The Munich Olympic race crowned an American, Frank Shorter, who had turned to the marathon after an honourable career in the track events. A onetime 4:06.4 miler, Shorter struck gold in his sixth marathon, incidentally in the German city where he had first seen the light 25 years earlier. He won in 2:12:19.8 from Lismont and Mamo Wolde, the defending champion. The 40-year-old Ethiopian thus closed in brilliant fashion his long Olympic adventure - started sixteen years earlier. Ian Thompson of Britain was the no.1 man in 1974, scoring a fine double: Commonwealth champion at Christchurch in January (2:09:12) and European champion in Rome seven months later (2:13:18.8).

But he was to join the legion of those who never had a lucky rendezvous with the Olympics. In 1976 he finished no better than seventh at the British Trials, and thus missed Montreal; four years later, in the Moscow Games, he did not finish.

Abebe Bikila's memorable one-two (Rome-Tokyo) in the Olympics was regarded by many as an exploit not likely to be duplicated soon. But athletic events can be as unpredictable as anything in life, and between 1976 and 1980 the track world saw a man move into the footsteps of the great Ethiopian (who had passed away in 1973, after spending the last four years of his life under the dire stress of an almost complete paralysis, the sad aftermath of a car accident). This man was Waldemar Cierpinski of East Germany (born at Neugattersleben on 3 August 1950; 1.70 m./59 kg.). Earlier in his career he had been an above-average steeplechaser (8:32.4 in 1974).

The Olympic competition of 1976 was only his fifth marathon and he turned it into a feast, winning from defending champion Frank Shorter, 2:09:55 to 2:10:45.7. His career record was in a way similar to that of Lasse Viren, inasmuch as he too failed to do anything of note in the years between Montreal and Moscow, apart perhaps from a fourth place in the marathon of the 1978 European Championships. But he rounded into form again shortly before the Moscow Olympics (1980). At the Games the event offered a great mass finish, with the first four in the space of 62 seconds. Cierpinski used a creditable 33.4 in the last 200 m. to emerge the winner in 2:11:03, closely followed by Gerard Nijboer of Holland (2:11:20) and Satimkul Dzhumanazarov of USSR (2:11:35).

Cierpinski followed up with a sixth place at the 1982 European Championships and crowned his excellent career with a bronze medal at the 1983 World Championships in Helsinki.

HURDLES - 110 m.: Euro-American feuds

A great talent whose potentialities surely remained untapped was Jerry Tarr of USA, a tall hurdler who in 1962 ran the "highs" in 13.3, the "lows" around a turn in 22.8 and the "intermediates" in 50.3, all over English distances. Soon after this he was attracted by a "pro" sport and the world of track never heard from him again. Much more consistent was the career record of Hayes Jones (born at Starksville, Mississippi, on 4 August 1938; 1.80 m./76 kg.), an agile man who emerged early, running the "highs" in 13.7 at nineteen. A very fast starter and an excellent sprinter (9.4 for the 100 y., just like Harrison Dillard), he was virtually unbeatable in the short indoor races: between 1959 and 1964 he compiled an undercover record of 55 consecutive wins.

His best in the 60 y. hurdles, a popular indoor event, was 6.8. Outdoors he probably had his greatest day, clock-wise at least, at the 1963 AAU Championships in St.Louis, when he ran the 120 y. hurdles in 13.5 (heat), 13.5 (semi-final) and 13.4 (final, auto-time

13.60), all on the same day, 21 June. The track used on that occasion was a new rubber-asphalt surface. In 1964 Jones duplicated his 13.4 over the slightly longer metric distance and won the Olympic title at Tokyo in 13.6 (actual auto time, 13.67). There were three Italians in the Tokyo final. One of them, Eddy Ottoz (born at Mandelieu, Haute Savoie, on 3 June 1944; 1.79 m./68 kg.) was to be Europe's no.1 man for the next five years. Like most of Italy's best hurdlers in those years he was a pupil of Sandro Calvesi (who was to become his father-in-law). Eddy showed early promise, with 14.9 at eighteen. In 1964 he improved rapidly and went to Tokyo with a personal best of 13.8. In the Games he did intrinsically better, with an auto time of 13.84, finishing fourth behind two Americans, Jones and Blaine Lindgren (13.74) and a Russian, Anatoliy Mikhailov (13.78). Ottoz was European champion twice, with 13.7 at Budapest in 1966 and 13.5 at Athens in '69. On the latter occasion he defeated David Hemery of Britain (13.7), who in 1968 had won a memorable 400 m. hurdles race at the Mexico Olympics. Although by no means impressive in physical build, Ottoz was endowed with great suppleness. He was at his best in the short indoor races, with three wins over 50 or 60 m. hurdles at the European Indoor Games (1966-68). In 1967, during a "tournée" in USA, he won 3 out of 7 races against the mighty American hurdlers. The next great American in the "highs" was Willie Davenport (born at Troy, Alabama, on 8 June 1943; 1.85 m./84 kg.). His career is inextricably tied with an Olympic saga: after competing in four editions of the summer Games as a trackman, in 1980 he represented his country in the Winter Games at Lake Placid, N.Y., in the 4-man bobsled. According to US historian Bill Mallon, only three other Americans have ever managed to compete in both sets (summer/winter) of Games. In the fall of 1964 Davenport seemed ready for major conquests, having beaten Hayes Jones in a close duel (13.6 for both) at the US Olympic Trials. But at Tokyo he was stopped by an injury in the semifinals. The next opportunity obviously came four years later in Mexico City, and Davenport seized it: after leading from start to finish, he won in 13.33 from another American, Erv Hall (13.42), while Eddy Ottoz took third place (13.46, best auto time ever by a European). Davenport was sturdy enough to star in two more editions of the Games: fourth in Munich and third in Montreal, aged 33. A unique longevity for a US specialist of the "highs". The "manual" world record, 13.2, set by Martin Lauer in 1959 and equalled by Lee Calhoun in '60, eluded the efforts of the world's leading hurdlers for several years. It was equalled again by Earl McCullouch at Minneapolis in 1967, and by Davenport himself at Zurich in 1969. For a better clocking one had to wait till the advent of a new phenomenon, Rodney Milburn (born at Opelousas, Louisiana, on 18 May 1950; 1.83 m./79

Rod Milburn (USA), Olympic champion and world record holder in the "high" hurdles (1972).

Retarded burst

A few months after his Olympic triumph in Montreal, Guy Drut announced his retirement from track. He said he was "sick and tired of the hypocrisy surrounding the world of "shamateurism". He explained that it was by then common practice for leading athletes to receive money "under the table": appearance money handed them by meet promoters ranged from $700 to $3000 per meet (Drut put himself in the "medium" range). The French champion was good enough to admit, alas tardily, that he too had been part of that hypocrisy. But he had done so only because he wanted to compete in the Olympic Games and win a gold medal. Predictably enough, first the French Athletic Federation (FFA), then the IAAF banned him from the amateur ranks "for life". This was at best a "retarded burst": the powers that be simply drove out a man who had already decided to leave the arena. In fact, it was not a retroactive sentence, and Drut was allowed to keep his records and his medals. P.S. Drut was reinstated a few years later and in 1980, aged thirty, he ran the 110 m. hurdles in 13.85.

kg.). Although he had no precise credentials as a sprinter, coaches maintained that he excelled most if not all his predecessors in hurdle- clearance time. If Davenport, always a strong finisher, was essentially "the man of the last three hurdles", Milburn appeared practically perfect from start to finish. He did 13.7 at nineteen, and two years later, on 25 June 1971, he reached the top at the AAU Championships in Eugene, when he was timed in 13.0 for the English distance, with an aiding but just legal wind of 1.95 m/s. This was a hand time, actually 12.94 in hundredths of a second, and "old" Davenport was runner-up in 13.3. By the summer of 1972 Milburn could point to 27 consecutive wins, but his lucky streak was broken at the US Olympic Trials in Eugene, when he knocked down the seventh hurdle and hit the tenth and last. Even so, he managed to earn a berth on the team by finishing third in 13.6 - the same time given to the men who finished fourth, fifth and sixth! (only one tenth covered the first six, the winner being Thomas Hill in 13.5). It is a fact that no athletic competition at national level has ever provided the thrills usually offered by the US Olympic Trials.

Milburn was back in stride by the time of the Munich Olympics. In the final he was off well and retained his lead till the end. He won in 13.24, a new world record with automatic timing. Second place went to Guy Drut of France with 13.34, a placing last achieved by a European in 1936 (Don Finlay, runner- up in the Berlin Games). This imposing Frenchman (born at Oignies, Pas-de-Calais, on 6 December 1950; 1.88 m./74 kg.) was the rightful heir of Eddy Ottoz and for some time he had been advised by Ottoz's coach, Sandro Calvesi. Drut was obviously more powerful than his Italian colleague. Between 1970 and 1976 his versatility was to yield such marks as 10.5 (100 m.), 5.20 (pole vault), 7.56 (long jump) and 7424 pts (decathlon). In his best event, the 110 m. hurdles, Drut emerged at nineteen with 13.85. Two years later, in 1971, he was down to 13.56. After winning a silver medal in Munich, he continued to improve. He was European champion in 1974 (13.40) and eventually reached the top of the world in 1975. In the meantime, Milburn had another great season in 1973, when he duplicated his 13.0 for the English distance, and did 13.1 twice over 110 m. hurdles in Europe, first at Zurich, then at Siena, all with aiding but legal winds. In 1974 he joined the "pro" group of Mike O'Hara.

Drut had at least three remarkable performances in 1975: a European automatic record of 13.28 (Saint-Etienne, 29 June), then hand times of 13.1 (Saint-Maur, 23 July) and 13.0 (Berlin, 22 August). On the last occasion he was aided by a wind of 1.78 m/s. and won from Charlie Foster of USA (13.2). This was incidentally the last manual world record ratified by the IAAF. At the Montreal Olympics (1976) the most serious threat to him came not from USA but from Cuba, in the person of 22-year-old Alejandro Casañas, who in 1975 had been credited with 13.44. The Frenchman took the lead early and never relinquished it, even though Casañas gave him a good run for his money. Times, 13.30 and 13.33. Veteran Willie Davenport was third (13.38), ahead of Charlie Foster (13.41).

Alejandro Casañas (born at Guanabacoa, Havana, on 29 January 1954; 1.88 m./79 kg.) was the first top-class hurdler to come out of Cuba, known until then as a reservoir of sprint talent. He had plenty of speed, by the way: in 1976 he was credited with 10.1 in the 100 m. In the "highs" he improved by leaps and bounds, from 14.6 at sixteen to 13.3 at eighteen. He could have played a prominent role in the Munich Olympics, but was laid low by an injury. As previously related, he was a close second four years later in Montreal. Clock-wise, the Cuban reached his peak in the Universiade at Sofia on 21 August 1977, when he had a record-shattering 13.21, aided by a wind of 0.6 m/s. But a few days later, in the first World Cup at Düsseldorf, he suffered an unexpected defeat at the hands of Thomas Munkelt of East Germany, 13.50 to 13.41. Munkelt, a consistent performer and an excellent competitor, went on to win the 1978 European title with 13.54.

The Americans were less brilliant than usual for some time, but eventually regained the top with Renaldo Nehemiah (born on 24 March 1959 at Newark, New Jersey; 1.87 m./71 kg.). A tremendously gifted ath-

1961
1980

Thomas Hill (USA), left, and Guy Drut (France) in a semi-final of the 110 m. hurdles at the Munich Olympics (1972).

David Hemery (GB), lane 6, on his way to winning the 400 metre hurdles at the 1968 Olympics in Mexico City. Others from left are: J. Sherwood (GB), 3rd; R. Whitney (USA), 6th; V. Skomorokhov (USSR), 5th; R. Frinolli (Ita), 8th; G. Vanderstock (USA), 4th; G. Hennige (Ger), 2nd; R. Schubert (Ger), 7th. The winner set a new world record of 48.1 (actual time 48.12).

lete, "Skeets" (as he was known since infancy for his "pretty short crawl") had a precise target from the beginning: beat 13 seconds. He began by doing just that in the High School ranks, over 39 in. (99 cm.) hurdles, with a US interscholastic record of 12.9 in 1977. Before the end of that year he had tried the senior (106 cm.) hurdles as well, with a promising 13.89. The following year he had his breakthrough with a series of brilliant performances, topped by a nifty 13.23 at Zurich. True, his countryman Greg Foster had done a shade better (13.22) earlier in the season, but in head-to-head confrontations "Skeets" won 4 out of 5 from Foster and thus ranked no.1 in "Track & Field News" World Ranking. In 1979 Nehemiah got off to a great start: on 14 April at San Jose he succeeded Casañas as world record holder with 13.16. And on 6 May at Westwood he faced Casañas himself. The Cuban had an incredibly fast start, but by the third hurdle Nehemiah had made up the disadvantage, and from then on he drew steadily away to win by a clear margin, 13.00 to 13.23. The aiding wind was a legal 0.9 m/s, and "Skeets" thus collected his second world record. He suffered only one defeat in 1979 (to Dedy Cooper in a relatively slow race at Zurich), but in the biggest meet of the year, the World Cup at Montreal, he had to fight pretty hard to vanquish the redoubtable Munkelt, 13.39 to 13.42, while Casañas was a close third (13.44).

Nehemiah was the world's no.1 man for two more years, but the US boycott of the Moscow Olympics prevented him from winning the most coveted title. Yet his seasonal record in 1980 was well nigh immaculate: only one defeat, and the fastest time of the year, 13.21. Casañas went to the Moscow Olympics fully determined to avenge his narrow loss of 1976 in Montreal, but after a good start he knocked down the first two hurdles. That was his doom: despite his strong finish he just failed to catch Thomas Munkelt, who won by a hair's breadth, 13.39 to 13.40. Aleksandr Puchkov of USSR was third (13.44). The Cuban ace thus had the sad privilege of emulating Jack Davis of USA, who in the Fifties had missed gold twice, by 0.09 in 1952 and 0.03 in 1956. Casañas' doom was sanctioned by even more tantalizing margins: 0.03 in 1976 and 0.01 in 1980. Of course, the absence of Nehemiah and Greg Foster considerably reduced the significance of the Moscow event.

400 METRES HURDLES - The golden days of Hemery and Akii-Bua - Moses, the one and only

Salvatore Morale of Italy was to join the ranks of those champions who reached their peak in non-Olympic years. After barely missing the Rome Olympic final at twenty-two, this powerful hurdler ranked no.1 in the world for two years. In 1961 he obtained two European hurdle records in Rome with 49.7 (400 m.) and 50.1 (440 y.). He made the world headlines at the 1962 European Championships in Belgrade: after a seemingly effortless 50.0 "semi" on 13 September, he equalled Glenn Davis' world mark (49.2) the next day, winning the final by a huge margin from Jörg Neumann (50.3) and Helmut Janz (50.5), both of West Germany.

As per tradition, the American reservoir yielded new figures on the eve of the Tokyo Olympics (1964). One of these was Bill Hardin, a son of the 1936 Olympic champion in the same event. He surpassed his father Glenn clock-wise, 49.8 to 50.6, and showed ability also in the 100 y. (9.7) and the "highs" (13.9). But he was in turn overtaken by Warren "Rex" Cawley (born at Detroit on 6 July 1940; 1.83 m./75 kg.), who had first emerged as a junior in 1959 with a hurdle series of 13.9, 23.0 and 51.5 (440 y.). But the 1960 Olympic Trials caught him still unripe and he finished seventh in 50.6. He rose to greater heights at the 1963 NCAA Championships in Albuquerque (altitude, 1507 m.), when in the space of three days he compiled a fantastic series: 47.2, 46.0 and 46.1 in the 440 y. flat; 52.3, 51.5 and 49.6 in the 440 y. hurdles. As a tri-

1961 1980

"I am one of 43"

Putting one's native country on the map of international athletics is probably the highest honour an athlete can ever dream of. Such a wonderful thing happened at the 1972 Olympics in Munich to John Akii-Bua. This enormously gifted athlete came from Uganda, a country with no athletic traditions worthy of the name. He was a Lango, a tribe of Nilotes from the north of Uganda. Talking about his "large family" during the post-race press conference in Munich, he said: "I am one of 43. My father had eight wives. There are 29 of the 43 children still living. Nineteen were boys". John was not the first athlete in the family. An elder brother, Lawrence Ogwang, had finished sixth in the triple jump at the British Commonwealth Games in 1954. Other boys in the family were also active athletes. John showed promise from the beginning and by the time he went to the Munich Games he was a well established quantity in the "intermediates". Yet only one out of six "experts" questioned by "Track & Field News" shortly before the Games picked him as a likely winner (that one was Jan Popper of Czechoslovakia). Running in lane 1, Akii-Bua was simply amazing. The fact that he strode thirteens till the fifth hurdle, then fourteens till the ninth, and fifteens between ninth and tenth was a further tribute to his staying power. After his triumph in Munich, Akii-Bua was involved in the political turmoil affecting his native country under the harsh rule of Gen. Idi Amin Dada, a former heavy-weight boxer. As a Lango, John was among those who met disgrace. But he managed to escape and took his family to West Germany. Yet his vicissitudes were not over, and he had ups and downs. In 1975 he ran a good 48.67, but the following year he was kept away from the Montreal Olympics as a result of the African boycott, a few weeks after he had shown excellent form with a personal best of 45.82 in the 400 m. flat. Another four years went by before he got another Olympic chance: in 1980 he went to Moscow, aged almost 31, but failed to advance beyond the "semis". His name was thus committed to history as that of a superlative performer whose potentialities were presumably exploited only in part.

bute to his staying power it should further be noted that the two finals were in the same afternoon. The following year he earned his berth on the Olympic team with a new world record for the 400 m. hurdles: 49.1 at Los Angeles on 13 September. Hardin (49.8) and Jay Luck (50.4) were the other qualifiers.

By that time Italy had found another good prospect in Roberto Frinolli. Although less powerful than Morale, he was an excellent stylist, near perfect except perhaps in the last 50 m., at which stage he would generally begin to fade. A few weeks before the Tokyo Olympics he ran an impressive 49.6 in Rome, beating Morale (50.1). In the Games final the two Italians drew the favourable outside lanes, with Frinolli in 7 and Morale in 8. Their most serious rival, Cawley, was right behind them in lane 6, while John Cooper of Britain was in 4. The Italians were in the lead till the fifth hurdle, then Cawley decisively drew away and from then on he was never threatened. Frinolli began to fade after the ninth hurdle, while Cooper and Morale staged a fierce fight for second. Cawley won in 49.6 and the Briton had his best-ever mark in narowly edging Morale (both 50.1), while Frinolli had to be content with sixth.

Frinolli eventually rose from the ashes of his Tokyo debacle and in 1966 he won the European title at Budapest in 49.8, holding on well against the fast closing Gerd Lossdörfer of West Germany (50.3). Frinolli went through the season undefeated and closed with a 49.7 performance at Mexico City, venue of the next Olympics. In 1967 he was outshone by Ron Whitney of USA, who wound up as seasonal

Roberto Frinolli (Italy), twice an Olympic finalist in the 400 metre hurdles, as well as European champion (1966). Now coach of Fabrizio Mori, 1999 world champion in the same event.

237

leader with 49.3. The American actually came from half-mile stock (1:48.6 in 1963).

In the year of the Mexico Olympics British traditions were revived by David Hemery (born at Cirencester on 18 July 1944; 1.86 m./75 kg.). In talking about this magnificent hurdler, one could perhaps paraphrase what was once said about Winston Churchill: "a fine Anglo-American product". In the case of the great politician the concept was linked with genetic factors. In Hemery's case, it was a question of having lived, trained and competed in USA for a large part of his active career. Already prominent as a junior, he first made the headlines in 1966, winning the British Commonwealth title in the high hurdles (14.1). In the same year he ran the 440 y. hurdles in 51.8. In preparing for the Mexico Olympics he decided to concentrate on the "intermediates". Competing for Boston University, he won the 1968 NCAA title in 49.8, beating Boyd Gittins and Geoff Vanderstock, who were to qualify for the US Olympic team later in the season. Hemery then went to London, where he improved to 49.6. He was ready to sting.

John Akii-Bua put Uganda on the map of world athletics by winning the 400 m. hurdles at the 1972 Olympics with a record-smashing 47.82.

Taking advantage of the high altitude of Echo Summit, Geoff Vanderstock won the 400 m. hurdles at the US Trials on 11 September with a record-smashing 48.8 (auto-time, 48.94), beating Gittins (49.1) and Whitney (49.4). At Mexico City the advantages of the rarefied atmosphere became apparent since the earliest rounds. There were sub-50 secs. marks galore, with personal and national records falling like autumn leaves. In the final (15 October) Frinolli was as fast as usual in the early stages but soon had to give way to Hemery (lane 2). The Englishman was unofficially timed in 23.3 at the half-way mark. Such was his stamina that he gallantly survived for a 24.8 second half. He thus smashed the world record with 48.1 (actual auto-time, 48.12). His rivals, although hopelessly beaten, still posted excellent times: Gerhard Hennige of West Germany was second in 49.02, followed by John Sherwood of Britain (49.03), Vanderstock (49.07), Vyacheslav Skomorokhov of USSR (49.12), Whitney (49.27), Rainer Schubert of West Germany (49.30) and Frinolli (50.13). Hemery strode thirteens till the sixth hurdle, then used fifteens till the tenth and last. He provided a splendid example of the champion who can surpass himself on the big occasion.

The double effect of high altitude and new Tartan tracks obviously caused a major reshuffle in the All Time World List: at the end of 1968, nine of the ten best performances listed had been made at high altitude, the lonely exception being Rex Cawley's 49.1, made at Los Angeles in 1964. It was inevitable that the following seasons, with most if not all the major competitions being held at or near sea level, would seem anti-climactic. In 1969 Vyacheslav Skomorokhov won the European title at Athens in 49.7, beating Olympic bronze medallist John Sherwood (50.1). At the 1970 NCAA Championships in Des Moines, Iowa, Ralph Mann lowered the world record for the English distance to 48.8, defeating Wayne Collett (49.2). The latter knew relatively little about hurdling technique, but he was a very fast man on the flat (he would do 44.1 in 1972). There is no telling what he could have done if he had taken the time and effort to specialize in the "intermediates".

The 1971 European Championships at Helsinki saw another fast runner on the flat, Jean-Claude Nallet of France, win the 400 m. hurdles in 49.15. And he had done better the year before with 48.6, plus 45.1 on the flat route.

The hero of the 1972 Olympics in Munich came from Uganda, an athletically unheralded country, if ever there was one. He was John Akii-Bua (born at Kampala on 3 December 1949; 1.82 m./77 kg.). An active athlete since the age of eighteen, by 1970 he was good enough to place fourth in the 400 m. hurdles at the British Commonwealth Games in Edinburgh, his time being 51.14 (John Sherwood won in 50.03). He really hit the headlines in the USA vs. Africa dual meet at Durham in 1971, when he sped to an eye-catching 49.0. On the eve of the Munich Olympics, however, most experts would favour Ralph Mann or defending champion David Hemery, i.e. the representatives of countries which could point to a great tradition. In the Olympic final (2 September) Hemery was in lane 5 and Mann in 6, while Akii-Bua was in the unfavourable pole lane. The Englishman went into an early lead and set a furious pace, even faster than his record run in Mexico City. At 200 m. he was unofficially timed in 22.8, but Mann and Akii-Bua were still in contention (both 23.0). Then Hemery began to fade and Akii-Bua took the lead right after the eighth hurdle. From then on the man from Uganda appeared to be unassailable. He covered the second half of the race in 24.8 and thus succeeded Hemery both as Olympic champion and world record holder. His auto-time was 47.82. Mann barely edged Hemery for second, 48.51 to 48.52, while Jim Seymour of USA found his excellent 48.64 only good for fourth place. Maybe Hemery went out a bit too fast, yet it could be argued that his 48.52 under near-sea-level conditions (Munich, 520 m.) was probably comparable, in intrinsic value, with his 48.12 at Mexico City.

> ### "My mistake. I won't do it again"
>
> Besides being a superlative athlete, Edwin Moses is a very proud man. As such he seeks perfection in whatever he attempts. This may have been not the last reason of his continued success. In 1976, as a virtual novice in the 400 m. hurdles, Moses lost only four races. The following year he lost just one: at Berlin on 26 August, when he tripped over the penultimate hurdle and had to give way to Harald Schmid of West Germany, who thus beat the Olympic champion, 49.07 to 49.29. When the race was over, Moses was quoted as saying: "I made a mistake. I won't do it again". Could anybody have guessed, there and then, that Moses would live up to his promise for the next ten years and compile a wondrous win streak of 122 consecutive victories (counting heats and finals) ?! In fact, he remained undefeated in the "intermediates" from the fall of 1977 till 4 June 1987, when Defeat knocked at his door again.

The 1974 European Championships in Rome pitted Alan Pascoe of Britain, who had made a name for himself in the "highs", against defending champion Jean-Claude Nallet of France. After a bitter fight they finished in that order, 48.82 to 48.94. In the same year, at Turin, Jim Bolding of USA lowered the world's 440 y. hurdles record to 48.7. The American, who had earlier done 48.1 for the metric distance, looked like a cinch to represent his country in the Montreal Olympics. But in 1976 things were to take a different turn ....At the dawn of the Olympic season a new man entered the picture, one who would eventually outshine everything and everybody. The man was Edward Corley ("Edwin") Moses (born at Dayton, Ohio, on 31 August 1955; 1.86 m./73 kg.). As late as in 1975, nobody looked upon him as a potential Olympian, let alone a gold medal prospect. In interscholastic competition he had done well in the "highs" and in the flat races, his one and only try in the "intermediates" resulting in a 52.0 over 440 y. hurdles - incidentally made in a heat (he did not run the final). Yet he chose to concentrate on that event in 1976. His breakthrough was ultra-rapid: he began with 50.1 in March, a non-winning effort, then improved to 49.8 in April and to 48.8 in May. Then came a splendid victory at the US Olympic Trials, where he clocked 48.30 to defeat Quentin Wheeler (48.65) and Mike Shine (49.33). As for Jim Bolding, he went out too fast, leading at the fifth hurdle (21.1) but fading in the crucial stage, to finish a disappointing fourth (49.55). Moses crowned his meteoric rise with a superb performance in the Montreal Olympics. In the final (25 July) he annihilated the opposition. After a fast first half (23.1) he was strong enough to negotiate the second in 24.5. His final reward was an auto-time of 47.63, a new world record. Mike Shine, a former high hurdles specialist, was second (48.69), followed by Yevgeniy Gavrilyenko of USSR (49.45). Experts began to wonder what was the "secret" of the new champion, who had reached the top of the world in his first full season in the event. Moses was above average in height and had unusually long legs. He used his seven-league "boots" to stride thirteens all the way, something nobody had been able to do until then. This allowed him to dominate anybody in the second half of the race. He combined great muscular power with good basic speed. In the course of his career he would be credited with 45.60 for the 400 m. flat and 13.64, plus a "manual" 13.5, for the 110 m. hurdles, at the latter distance beating Alejandro Casañas, among others.Following his phenomenal breakthrough in 1976, Moses dominated the 400 m. hurdles picture for many years to come - as no one had ever done in the history of the event. Up to the end of 1980 he improved on the world record three times: after his 47.63 in the Montreal Olympics, he did 47.45 on 11 June 1977 at Los Angeles, then 47.13 on 3 July 1980 at Milan, each time beating his nearest pursuer by more than one second! He was an easy winner in two World Cup races as well, with 47.58 at Düsseldorf in 1977 and 47.53 at Montreal in '79. On the eve of 1980 Moses loomed as an odds-on favourite for the Olympic gold medal. But then came the US boycott of the Moscow Games and he was ruled out. The same thing happened to Harald Schmid of West Germany. The latter had won the European title in 1978 with 48.51. Schmid had one of his greatest days in the final of the European Cup at Turin on 4 August 1979, when in the space of an hour he won the 400 m. hurdles in 47.85, a new European record, then the 400 m. flat in 45.31. When it was all over he revealed that he had decided to run both events a few days earlier, after a 1:14 time trial in the 600 m. "That told me I could handle the double". (Fastest official mark for the 600 m. at the time was Lee Evans' 1:14.3, made at Echo Summit in 1968).

The resulting sub-par race of the Moscow Olympics was won by Volker Beck of East Germany in 48.70, with Vasiliy Arkhipyenko of USSR a fairly close second in 48.86.

STEEPLECHASE - Gärderud: better late than never

The Sixties were a happy time for Soviet steeplechasers. In 1961, Grigoriy Taran got the ball rolling with a new world record of 8:31.2, achieved during a quadrangular meet at Kiev. But Olympic champion Zdzislaw Krzyszkowiak lost little time in recapturing the record: on 10 August 1961, at Walcz, he did 8:30.4, with uneven kilometre fractions (2:48.0, 2:57.0, 2:45.4). That was virtually the last cry of the great Polish warrior. His decline coincided with the advent of Gaston Roelants of Belgium (born at Opvelp on 5 February 1937; 1.74 m./58 kg.), a versatile runner who could do well at various distances, on the track and the road as well (he scored four victories in the International Cross-country Championships). As a steeplechaser Roelants began to distinguish himself with a fourth place at the 1960 Olympics (8:47.86). Two years later he won the European title at Belgrade in 8:32.6. His strategy consisted in drawing away from his rivals early. That's what he did on that occasion and the result was rewarding: his nearest pursuer, Zoltan Vamos of Romania, an excellent 1500m. man, finished far behind in 8:37.6. Roelants succeeded Krzyszkowiak as world record holder on 7 September 1963 at Leuven, breaking the 8:30 barrier with 8:29.6 (kilometre fractions: 2:45.9, 2:51.5, 2:52.2).

The Tokyo Olympics yielded excellent steeplechase performances: nine of the ten finalists improved on their personal bests, either in the prelims or in the decisive race. A remarkable record, if one considers that in other events such improvements would normally occur for one athlete out of three. Roelants K.O.'d the opposition early, then held on bravely till the end to win in 8:30.8. Maurice Herriott of Britain came from behind to take second place in 8:32.4. The indefatigable Roelants had another great year in 1965, when he combined a series of brilliant performances on the flat route with a new steeplechase record of 8:26.4. This was at Brussels on 7 August, with kilometre fractions of 2:47.4, 2:51.4 and 2:47.6. A fantastic solo race: Roelants won by nearly one minute! By then, however, new forces had emerged from the USSR reservoir. In that group was a runner endowed with a great turn of speed, Viktor Kudinskiy, who between 1964 and '65 improved from 8:48.2 to 8:31.0. In the 1966 European Championships at Budapest the self-confident Roelants used his patented tactics and soon built up a big lead. At the bell he still had about 15 m. on the Russian duo Kudinskiy/Kuryan. Then the Belgian began to fade and Kudinskiy began to close the gap. The final blow to the reigning champion was administered over the last water jump, where Roelants, for years the undisputed master of the event, had to surrender to his rival, who went home an easy victor in 8:26.6. Anatoliy Kuryan came up fast to nip the exhausted Roelants for second, 8:28.0 to 8:28.8. A few weeks later, at Mexico City, Roelants found partial consolation, downing the fresh European champion, 8:58.6 to 9:54.2. On that occasion the Russian obviously felt the "twinge" of high altitude more than his rival and on top of that he fell on a hurdle in the first lap, losing ground early. High altitude was a factor likely to upset everything and everybody: this was amply confirmed at the 1968 Olympics, still in Mexico City. Contrary to what happened in the sprints, the rarefied atmosphere was detrimental to runners in "aerobic" events such as the long distances, particularly to those who were not familiar with such conditions. In the steeplechase final, athletes who came from the Kenya mountains captured the first two places, with virtually unknown

Amos Biwott winning from Benjamin Kogo, 8:51.0 to 8:51.6. It was an ominous day for the highly touted Europeans: Roelants was seventh (after his usual bold start) and Kudinskiy dropped out. The honour of the "men from the plains" was saved by George Young of USA and Kerry O'Brien of Australia, third and fourth respectively (8:51.8 and 8:52.0).

Biwott, barely 21, was of course a major sensation. A Kenyan insider estimated that prior to the Olympics "he had not run six steeplechases in his life". His best going into the Games was an indifferent 8:44.8 in placing second to Kogo in the East African Championships at Dar-es-Salaam in August. When the season was over, that mark earned Biwott a tie for 75th in the 1968 World List! His style was, if possible, even more extraordinary than his achievements. At the water jump he would sail high in the air and past the puddle to land on the same foot with which he had stepped on the barrier! An absentee from the Games was Jouko Kuha of Finland, who on 17 July at Stockholm had lowered the world record to 8:24.2, with kilometre fractions in 2:51.0, 2:52.0 and 2:41.2. This rather inconsistent performer was taken ill shortly before the Games and could not make it to Mexico.

Europeans eventually regained the top, clockwise at least, in 1969. At the USSR Championships in Kiev, Vladimir Dudin shaved two seconds off Kuha's world record with 8:22.2, at the end of a close battle with Aleksandr Morozov (8:23.4). But in the meet of the year, the European Championships in Athens, the new record holder was upset by sturdy Mikhail Zhelev of Bulgaria, who won in 8:25.0 from Morozov and Dudin.

There were upsets even in 1970. Kerry O'Brien of Australia won the first round when he set a new world mark of 8:21.98 (ratified as 8:22.0) at Berlin on 4 July, but in the British Commonwealth Games at Edinburgh he met misfortune. While moving into the lead at the penultimate water jump he hit the top of the barrier and plunged sideways into the water. Victory went to another Aussie, Tony Manning, in 8:26.2. Olympic champion Biwott brought his personal best to 8:30.8 but had to be content with a bronze medal.

At the 1971 European Championships in Helsinki, former world record holder Vladimir Dudin set the pace for the greater part of the journey but dropped to ninth in the end. Jean-Paul Villain of France won in 8:25.2. Right behind Dudin in tenth place was a Swede who would be heard from in the following years: Anders Gärderud (born at Stockholm on 28 August 1946; 1.86 m./70 kg.). Ever since he emerged as a teen-ager, somebody in "gamla Sverige" (old Sweden) had branded him as "the new Hägg". As often as not, such predictions fail to come true, due to the many and partly invisible obstacles which may prevent a gifted youngster from living up to his early promise. For many years to come, Gärderud was in fact to remain in the limbo of good but partly unfulfilled talents, until ... something happened (better late than never). He had first caught the eye of international observers in the 1500 m. steeplechase of the European Junior Games at Warsaw in 1964. On that occasion he boldly ran away from his opponents right after the start. After two laps he led by nearly 100 m.! He had to give up the greater part of that lead in the closing stages, yet won handily in 4:08.0. The following year he ran the same distance in 4:00.6. As a senior, however, he disappointed his fans on several occasions, e.g. in the Olympics of 1968 and '72, and the European Championships of 1966 and '71, in flat races as well as in the steeplechase.

In 1972 the Kenyans went to the Munich Olympics fully determined to prove that their triumph of four years earlier in Mexico was not a mere gift of the high altitude. In their ranks was Kipchoge Keino, winner of a memorable 1500 m. at Mexico City. He knew relatively little about the steeplechase and by the end of 1971 his best in the barrier event was an indifferent 9:00.4. But in pre-Olympic weeks he worked hard on technique. He learnt quickly, and in the Munich final he edged his compatriot Benjamin Jipcho, supposedly a more refined steeplechaser, to win in 8:23.64! Jipcho barely held off Tapio Kantanen of Finland in the battle for second, 8:24.62 to 8:24.66. Defending champion Biwott showed improved form and in the prelims he lowered his personal best to 8:23.73. But in the final he could do no better than sixth. Anders Gärderud was his usual disappointing self at Munich, failing to make the final. But he fought back bravely in an international meet at Helsinki on 14 September. Pitted against Olympic bronze medallist Tapio Kantanen, he ran a great race and won in record time, 8:20.7 (ratified as 8:20.8), with Kantanen a close second in 8:21.0. The kilometre fractions were 2:47.6, 2:51.3 and a sizzling 2:41.8.

1973 was the golden year of Benjamin Wabura Jipcho (born in the region of Mount Elgon on 1 March 1943; 1.78 m./72 kg.). Athletically speaking he could be defined "a man of parts". He showed the best of his talent at the age of thirty, with such marks as 3:36.6 (1500 m.), 3:52.17 (mile - beating Filbert Bayi) and 13:30.0 (5000 m.). He was at his best in the steeplechase, revising the world record on three occasions. He began with 8:20.69 at the African Games at Lagos, Nigeria, in January, but this mark could not be ratified, since the water jump fell short of requirements in terms of size. The Nigerian hosts were very sorry for this, and among those who apologized to Jipcho was Gen.

1961
1980

Gowon, head of the military government. A few months later, Jipcho did himself justice at Helsinki, on 19 June, with 8:19.8. Late in the evening, in his hotel at Otaniemi he received a congratulatory cable from Gen. Gowon himself ... Jipcho did even better on 27 June, still in Helsinki, with a masterpiece of progressive acceleration: 2:48.0, 2:45.0 and 2:41.0, for a final time of 8:14.0 (actual auto-time, 8:13.91). Former world record holder Anders Gärderud was also in the race and finished a distant second in 8:21.2. Jipcho seemed capable of getting closer to the 8-min. barrier, but after an easy victory in the British Commonwealth Games early in 1974 (8:20.8) he decided to join Mike O'Hara's "pro" group in the States. In the meantime, new figures had appeared on the European scene. Outstanding among them was Bronislaw Malinowski of Poland (born at Nowe on 4 June 1951; 1.81 m./70 kg.). Although not as good as Gärderud in basic speed, he had that staying power which is a must for any ambitious steeplechaser. And he was above all a great competitor. Another good European in those years was Franco Fava of Italy, a generous performer if ever there was one, at all times ready to do his best in any race and against any rival. Equally good on the flat route and in the barrier event, he occasionally had to cope with another "enemy", tachycardia, which forced him to a stop - but he would invariably resume his run a few seconds later. He was one of the chief characters in the dramatic play of the 1974 European Championships in Rome. In this race Gärderud finally showed a competitive fire and barely lost to Malinowski in a hectic finish - 8:15.41 to 8:15.04. Michael Karst of West Germany edged Fava for third, 8:17.91 to 8:18.85. Gärderud came into his own in 1975, aged 29. He bettered the world record twice within a week: 8:10.4 at Oslo on 25 June and 8:09.70 (ratified as 8:09.8) at Stockholm on 1 July. In the former race he won from a young East German, Frank Baumgartl (8:18.4) and had kilometre fractions of 2:47.0, 2:43.0 and 2:40.4; in the latter race he decisively beat his old rival Malinowski (8:12.62) with another wonderful example of progressive acceleration: 2:47.4, 2:41.4 and 2:40.9. But the most dramatic act in the Gärderud vs. Malinowski feud was yet to come. It occurred in the final of the 1976 Olympics at Montreal, on 28 July. And what a race it was! A first half in 4:06.5 was followed by a second in 4:01.5! In the closing stage, old rivals Gärderud and Malinowski were not alone: fighting it out with them, somewhat unexpectedly, was 21-year-old Frank Baumgartl of East Germany, whose personal best, 8:17.6, dated from 1975. The young German and Gärderud were virtually even at the last barrier, with Malinowski close on their heels. While the experienced Swede cleared safey and cleanly, Baumgartl probably reached a little too much for his frame (1.74 m./60 kg.), cleared with his lead leg but hit the barrier with the knee of his trail leg - and fell. Gärderud, finally expressing the best of his great talent, went on to win in record time, 8:08.02 (ratified as 8:08.0), while Malinowski was second in 8:09.11. Baumgartl recovered well enough to close with a sprint, finishing third in 8:10.36. Next came Tapio Kantanen (8:12.60) and Michael Karst (8:20.14). New personal records for all but Karst. Quite predictably, some observers wondered what Baumgartl could have done if ... The German himself was gracious enough not to indulge in such idle speculation: "The simple fact is that Anders won this race", he said. Although his first reaction on the track was incredibly quick and efficient, the physical damage to his knee was such that it took him a long time to recover - and he was never his real self again. The kilometre fractions of the Olympic race were: 2:43.57, 2:45.50, 2:38.95. Gärderud thus closed a generally frustrating career with a perfect stroke. He built his ultimate success through years of serious application, and using his basic speed to full advantage. His best times on the flat route were 1:47.2 (800 m.), 3:36.73 (1500 m.), 3:54.45 (mile) and 13:17.59 (5000 m.).

Another runner endowed with great speed but with relatively little know-how as a steeplechaser astounded the barrier fraternity in 1978. This man was Henry Rono of Kenya, whose deeds in flat events have already been recounted. He had actually tried the steeplechase in the early years of his career. In 1976 he won a trial race for the Montreal Olympics in 8:29.0, but then African countries boycotted the Games and he could give no further proof of his real value. In his "Year of Years", 1978, he returned to the steeplechase with renewed vigour and on 13 May at Seattle he created a sensation by breaking Gärderud's world record with 8:05.4. This was virtually a solo race and Rono had even-paced fractions of 2:42.0, 2:42.8 and 2:40.6. A few weeks later, at Oslo, he broke the world record for 3000 m. flat in 7:32.1. As a result, his flat/hurdles differential was as high as 33.3. As such it compared unfavourably with those of Gärderud (8:08.02 - 7:47.8 = 20.2) and Malinowski (8:09.11 - 7:42.4 = 26.7). Although not a "specialist", Rono still managed to win 10 of his 12 steeplechase races during 1978!

Just like Gärderud, Malinowski achieved the highest honours towards the end of his career. He was the world's no.1 man in 1979, although he did not run the event in the World Cup at Montreal, where the race was won by... another Rono, first name Kiprotich, in 8:25.97. But then the "boycott game" kept both Rono's away from the 1980 Olympics in Moscow.

1961 1980

Malinowski's chief rival was Filbert Bayi of Tanzania, former holder of the world records for the 1500 m. and the mile. The latter was considered a virtual novice to the barrier event, but he had tried it in international competition as early as in 1972 at the Munich Olympics, when he was eliminated in a heat with 8:41.4. And a few weeks before the Games he had caused a surprise at Stockholm, vis-à-vis Malinowski. The Pole was leading when he stumbled on the last barrier and fell. Bayi went on to win in 8:17.98.

In the Olympic final Bayi was bold enough to run à la Bayi, thus re-editing the front running tactics which had generally paid dividends for him in the 1500 m/mile department. He went out very fast, with kilometre fractions of 2:38.8 and 2:41.5. With one kilometre to go he led Malinowski by 5.3 secs. But the strong Pole began to close the gap with three laps to go. And finally caught an exhausted Bayi on Heartbreak Hill, the last water jump. The Pole passed his rival - who had obviously underestimated the "hurdle factor" - and won easily in 8:09.70, after negotiating the last kilometre in 2:44.1. Bayi still won the one and only Olympic medal of his career in 8:12.48, while Eshetu Tura of Ethiopia was third in 8:13.57. Another notable absentee in Moscow was Mariano Scartezzini of Italy, who as a soldier of a NATO country had not been allowed to make the trip. In 1979 he had won the event in the final of the European Cup in 8:22.74. Shortly after the Moscow Olympics, in Rome, he did 8:12.5 in finishing second to another Moscow absentee, Kiprotich Rono of Kenya (8:12.0). And three days later, in London, Scartezzini beat Malinowski, 8:16.26 to 8:18.33.

JUMPS -
High Jump: From Brumel to the "Wizard of Foz"

After the Rome Olympics, Valeriy Brumel soon proved the most talented of the Soviets who had upset John Thomas in the Eternal City. Brumel (born at Tolbuzino, Siberia, on 14 April 1942; 1.85 m./77 kg.) was a high jump "addict" since the age of fourteen, when he cleared 1.40. His progress since then had been remarkably quick: 1.76 in 1957, 1.95 in '58, 2.01 in '59, 2.20 in '60. He rose to world record heights for the first time in an indoor meet at Leningrad on 28 January 1961, when he cleared 2.25. This was well above Thomas' official world record, but the mark, made from a dirt take-off, could not be ratified, since the IAAF continued to ignore anything that happened "under a roof".

But Brumel lost little time in meeting the demand even under outdoor conditions. He succeeded Thomas as world record holder on 18 June 1961 in Moscow with 2.236 (ratified as 2.23). In the same year he had two more record performances: 2.243 (ratified as 2.24) on 16 July in Moscow and 2.25 during the Universiade at Sofia on 31 August.

Brumel dominated the high jump scene for five years, 1961 through 1965. His matchless straddle allowed him to better the world record on three more occasions: 2.26 at Palo Alto, California, on 22 July 1962, 2.27 in Moscow on 29 September 1962 and 2.28 (his lifetime best, on third try) in Moscow on 21 July 1963. A clear indication of his competitive ability is provided by the fact that three of his six world records occurred in connection with USSR vs. USA dual meets, a confrontation which was given tremendous publicity at the time. He won the 1962 European title with 2.21 and two years later, in Tokyo, he won the Olympic gold medal. On the latter occasion he again faced his old rival John Thomas. It was a close duel, and Brumel felt the pressure as never before. After both had cleared 2.18 and failed at 2.20, the Russian got the nod on the fewer misses rule. John Rambo, a young American who stood 2 m. in his socks, took third place with 2.16.

In the fall of 1965 a motor accident put a premature end to the career of the phenomenal Brumel, then twenty-three. (the story is told in the adjoining aside). What he had done during his five-year reign was of course largely sufficient to earn him a special niche

Valeriy Brumel (USSR), a great exponent of the "dive straddle". He brought the world's high jump record to 2.28.

in the Hall of Fame of athletics. Few adepts of the straddle, if any, had brought that style to such a degree of near perfection. Brumel's assets notably included a fast approach run (he once did 10.5 for the 100 m.) and great strength in the left (take-off) leg. The latter virtually acted as a pole in converting propulsive force from horizontal to vertical. Brumel offered glimpses of great talent even as a long jumper (7.65 in 1961). Next to the incomparable Brumel, one of the most interesting figures during the Sixties was Ni Chi-chin of China (under Pinyin, the new phonetic alphabet adopted in 1979, his name is spelled Ni Zhiqin). Curiously enough, he and Brumel were "astrological twins", sharing the same birthdate: Ni was born in South-Western Fukien on 14 April 1942, and was strikingly similar to the Russian even in build, being 1.84 m. tall and weighing 82 kg. The Chinese was credited with 2.05 at eighteen. In 1961 he made a tour of Eastern Europe, taking lessons from Russian jumpers. After undergoing ankle surgery, he rose to world class in 1966, clearing 2.27 at the Games of the New Emerging Forces, held at Phnom-Penh. After another accident, he made the world headlines on 8 November 1970 at Changsha with a 2.29 jump, one centimetre over Brumel's official record. But in those days the People's Republic of China was not a member of the IAAF and so Ni's mark could not be ratified.

In the meantime there had been new technical developments which in a relatively short time were to have a great impact on the evolution of the event. The man behind this "revolution" was an American, Richard ("Dick") Fosbury (born at Portland, Oregon, on 6 March 1947; 1.93 m./83 kg.). He began with the old scissors style, clearing 1.625 at fifteen. He then reasoned that he might do better by simply ... "lying down". In fact, he lowered the centre of gravity by laying out on his back. His new technique included a curved run-up, which placed him side-on to the bar. Then he rotated his body and crossed the bar head first, legs last before landing on his shoulders. By the time Fosbury entered Oregon State University in 1965, he could point to a personal best of 2.007. But then his new coach Bernie Wagner, one of America's best known technicians, asked him to try the roll, straddle version. Fosbury regarded the conventional style as rather complicated, yet agreed to try - but eventually returned to his own style six months later, with the intelligent Wagner entirely on his side. Progress followed quickly and in 1967 Fosbury cleared 2.102. By then his story was reminiscent of another one which had occurred, still on West Coast high jump pits, some fifty-odd years earlier.... The new style came to be known as the "Fosbury Flop". In a lighter vein, the inventor was nicknamed "The Wizard of Foz", a free rendering of the title of a famous book for children by L. F. Baum. As it usually happens whenever a revolution breaks out, the new "invention" was looked upon with marked scepticism by several observers - especially in Europe. Chances are that the "breakthrough" of the new jumping form would have been delayed rather considerably if the inventor had not carried his style to victory in the noblest of competitions, the Olympic Games, a spectacle relayed to millions of TV-viewers around the world. 1968 was easily Fosbury's best year, yet his pre-Olympic season was not exceptional. He went to Mexico with a personal best of 2.21, curiously achieved in placing third at the US Olympic Trials behind Ed Caruthers and Reynaldo Brown, who cleared the same height but had fewer misses. But in the Olympic final he made no mistakes and finally topped a crack field with 2.24, a new Olympic record. Two "conven-

"Second attempt"

Brumel's athletic adventure came to an abrupt stop in October 1965 as a result of a motor accident. He was riding on the back of a motorcycle driven by a personal friend (actually a champion in this sport). The vehicle went out of control and hit a tree. Brumel's right leg was pinned under the machine and both men were still unconscious when help arrived. Brumel underwent surgery for two simple fractures below the knee and one multiple fracture of the ankle. Undamaged was his left (take-off) leg, ironically the one that had given him some problems recently. (He went no higher than 2.21 in 1965). That was the beginning of a long Odyssey. Several other operations followed and Brumel was in a cast for nearly three years. Then he spent many tantalizing hours in rehabilitation exercises. In the summer of 1969 he was able to resume competition. He managed 2.00, then 2.06, but his tortured leg did not respond adequately and his comeback, already miraculous, ended there and then. A few years later, a theatrical work bearing the significant title "Second attempt" reached the stage. It was inspired by Brumel's untiring efforts to regain his former physical prowess and was chiefly a tribute paid to his main "saviour", Prof. G.A.Ilizarov, who for a number of years had given him medical and psychological assistance.

tional" jumpers finished second and third: Caruthers and Valentin Gavrilov of USSR, with 2.22 and 2.20 respectively. Fosbury's "winning product" was sweeping the board in America. At the same time it began to catch the imagination of young jumpers in other parts of the world as well - and most of them were quick to adopt it. In Europe, however, established performers and coaches generally remained faithful to the "conventional" (straddle) style. Valentin Gavrilov of USSR won the European title at Athens in 1969 with 2.17. The first continental jumper to achieve fine results with the "Flop" was István Major of Hungary, who was at his best indoors and had a top mark of 2.24. Fosbury had a fairly good season in 1969, then disappeared from the scene. He joined the Mike O'Hara "pro" group in 1973, with limited success. Curiously enough, he never won the AAU title (he was second in 1969). Brumel's official successor as world record holder was an American exponent of the straddle, Pat Matzdorf. On 3 July 1971 at Berkeley, during a triangular meet USA-USSR-"World All Stars", he cleared 2.29 on his third attempt. Just like Fosbury, he had just one great season. But four years later he managed 2.24 ... with the "Flop". For many years he was to remain the only jumper credited with top-class marks with both styles.

The first European to win a continental outdoor title using the "Flop" was Kestutis Sapka of USSR, a Lithuanian who won at Helsinki in 1971 with 2.20. But in the 1972 Olympics in Munich the adepts of the straddle regained the top with Jüri Tarmak of USSR, who won the gold medal with 2.23, and Stefan Junge of East Germany, second with 2.21. The bronze medal, still at 2.21, was won by an American Flopper, Dwight Stones, barely eighteen and a half at the time. Stones, an American of Swedish extraction (born at Los Angeles on 6 December 1953; 1.95 m./81 kg.), had adopted the Flop early, overcoming a fear which was quite common in those days: the "danger factor" in landing head and shoulders first on sawdust pits. (This was to disappear only with the advent of synthetic materials). He made rapid progress: 1.918 in 1969, 2.007 in '70, 2.171 in '71 and 2.21 in winning the event at the US Olympic Trials in '72. On 11 July 1973 at Munich he captured the world record at the unripe age of 19 years and seven months, clearing 2.30 on his third attempt. That was his eighteenth jump of the afternoon, and it is curious to note that in some of his jumps at the lower heights he used the straddle! In 1976 Stones bettered the world record on two more occasions: 2.31 on 5 June and 2.32 on 4 August, both at Philadelphia's time honoured Franklin Field. In between these happy days, how-

> **Fruits of a rivalry**
>
> It does not happen everyday that three athletes from as many different countries, after meeting on the steps of an Olympic dais, may decide to join efforts and produce a book on their "art". This unusual circumstance materialized with Jacek Wszola of Poland, Greg Joy of Canada and Dwight Stones of USA, who finished in that order in the Olympic high jump final at Montreal.
> The book came out in 1983, under the inevitable title: "High Jump". The driving force behind this project was Dr. David Martin of Georgia State University, Atlanta, noted physiologist and track statistician as well as a close friend of the three champions.
> The book is a fine compendium of high jump technique, told through the experiences and reflections of three dedicated Floppers.

ever, he had a gloomy one in Montreal's Olympic arena. That was in fact a rainy day and Stones, who relied on speed so much, found himself unable to do better than 2.21, the same height he had cleared in his bright Olympic debut four years earlier - and again worth a bronze medal. Gold went to his rival and friend Jacek Wszola of Poland, who cleared 2.25, a great achievement under such conditions. Greg Joy of Canada was second at 2.23. Stones, a

1961
1980

Jacek Wszola (Poland) won the Olympic high jump title (1976) shortly before turning 20.

Wladyslaw Kozakiewicz (Poland), winner of a hotly contested pole vault competition at the 1980 Olympics in Moscow with a record shattering 5.78.

very consistent jumper, ranked no.1 in "Track & Field News" World Ranking for four consecutive years (1973-76). Early in the Seventies the "Flop" gradually conquered Europe as well. After his victory in the 1971 European Championships, Kestutis Sapka came close to successfully defending his title in Rome in 1974. On that occasion he was second with 2.25, the same height cleared by Jesper Törring of Denmark, who won on the fewer misses rule. USSR and East Germany were at any rate the last strongholds of the straddle. The former produced another great exponent of that jumping form with Vladimir Yashchenko (born at Zaporozhe, Ukraine, on 12 January 1959; 1.93 m./84 kg.). A truly gifted athlete, "Volodya" jumped 2.03 at fifteen. Three years later, on 3 July 1977, he cleared a bar set at 2.33, thus breaking Stones' world record. This happened at Richmond, Virginia, during a USA vs. USSR Junior match, and the feat of the 18-year-old Ukrainian, who had a previous best of 2.26 indoors, greatly impressed US experts. Yashchenko went on to clear 2.35 in the European Indoor Championships at Milan on 12 March 1978. And later in the same year, namely on 16 June at Tbilisi, he raised the official outdoor mark to 2.34. These results came as the sum total of great talent and plenty of hard work, possibly too hard for a boy of his age. The wear and tear of hyper-intensive training soon began to tell. Yashchenko managed to annex the 1978 European title in Prague with 2.30, but that was to remain his last cry. Stress fractures put a premature end to his meteoric career. Another "great" among latter-day straddle jumpers was Rolf Beilschmidt of East Germany, a consistent performer who achieved his best, 2.31, in the 1977 European Cup. Another interesting jumper in those years was Franklin Jacobs of USA, a Flopper who on 27 January 1978 in New York set an indoor record of 2.32 - 59 cm. above his head! This "differential" is still the greatest on record for jumpers who have done 2.30 or better. Jacobs' most notable victory was in the 1979 World Cup at Montreal, when he beat Jacek Wszola (both 2.27).

Wszola (born at Warsaw on 30 December 1956; 1.94 m./71 kg.) has been one of the most gifted and consistent jumpers of the modern era. He was for years Stones' most serious rival in international competition. Wszola, he too a Flopper, won his gold medal at Montreal before turning 20. Four years later, namely on 25 May 1980 at Eberstadt, he succeeded Yashchenko as world record holder with 2.35. (By the way, this German city was to become the Mecca of élite high jumpers, who would gather there every year for a High Jump Festival. Eberstadt has no stadium worthy of the name, only a high jump installation - and spectators gather around it to supply a warm atmosphere). Among the men beaten by Wszola at Eberstadt was a 19-year-old German, Dietmar Mögenburg, who gave the Pole an indirect "reply" within 24 hours. In a meet at Rehlingen on 26 May, Mögenburg cleared 2.35, thus equalling the ultra-fresh world record. As a West German, however, young Mögenburg had to stay away from the Moscow Olympics, just like the Americans. Defending champion Jacek Wszola thus loomed as an odds-on favourite. In the Olympic final the Pole cleared 2.31, yet found his effort good only for a silver medal (with Jörg Freimuth of East Germany third at the same height on the misses rule). The upset winner was a 21-year-old East German, Gerd Wessig, who on that day (1 August) achieved the seemingly impossible, improving on his pre-Games record (2.30) three times, with 2.31, 2.33 and finally 2.36 on his second attempt for the first men's high jump world record ever in the long history of the Games! Wessig, a Flopper who stood 2.01 in height, celebrated with a complete backward somersault! Yet he was to remain the phenomenon of a single day. In the following years recurrent injuries, and possibly other factors as well, kept him well below his Moscow "plafond".

POLE VAULT -
The fibreglass revolution

The year 1961 marked the advent of a new pole which was to revolutionize the standards of the event. It came to be known as the fibreglass pole. Implements made of such material had been experimented in USA since the early Fifties and one was actually used by Georgios Roubanis of Greece when he placed third in the 1956 Olympic final at Melbourne. According to Dr. Richard Ganslen, a former vaulter (NCAA champion in 1939 with 4.39, using a bamboo pole) and a keen student of vaulting materials and technique, experiments with flexible poles of a substantially similar nature had been made by Nikolay Ozolin in USSR as early as in 1928.

Such were the qualities of the new pole that 15-foot (4.57) or better vaults soon became commonplace occurrences. The relatively rigid metal poles used in early post-war years had yielded only minor advantages vis-à-vis the best bamboo models of previous years. Fibreglass brought about the most exciting change in the history of the event. Its main value lay in its flexion at take-off. It also permitted a higher (by 30/40 cms.) hand grip on the pole, and aided upward momentum during the push-up. Above all, the new pole had a great tensile strength. Given all these advantages, it would be unfair to compare marks made from 1961 onwards with those of the bamboo and/or metal era. Even so, I do not agree with those observers who claim that if bamboo poles were still in use today, the world record would still belong to the great Corny Warmerdam. Such a view obviously ignores or underestimates other important factors which have contributed to the evolution of this event, such as superior conditioning methods and the ever stiffer competition prevailing at the international level.

At any rate, fibreglass poles caused a real earthquake: between 1961 and 1980 the world record, which on the eve of the new era belonged to "Tarzan" Bragg with 4.80, was bettered forty-odd times (counting official marks plus a few others which were never ratified). By the end of 1980 the "ceiling" was up to 5.78, an improvement of nearly one metre in twenty years! Progress was great even in "depth", as can be seen from the following table, showing the marks of the first and fiftieth performers in the World Year Lists for 1960, virtually the last year of the Metal Era, 1961-64, i.e. the years of transition, 1970 and 1980.

	1st	50th
1960	4.80	4.45
1961	4.83	4.47
1962	4.94	4.56
1963	5.20	4.65
1964	5.28	4.75
1970	5.49	5.03
1980	5.78	5.40

No other athletic event had ever offered such an upward trend in a similarly short period of time.

1961
1980

Wolfgang Nordwig (East Germany) won the pole vault title at the 1972 Olympics, breaking a US monopoly dating from 1896.

The first vaulter to set a world record with fibreglass was George Davies of USA: 4.83 on 20 May 1961 at Boulder, Colorado. Shortly afterwards there was a European interlude thanks to Pentti Nikula of Finland (born at Somero on 3 February 1939; 1.79 m./67 kg.). On 22 June 1962 at Kauhava he broke a 35-year-old US monopoly by capturing the world record with a 4.94 effort. And he was also the first man to break the 5-metre barrier, alas under unofficial conditions. This was during an indoor meet at Pajulahti on 2 February 1963, when he cleared 5.00, 5.05 and 5.10 in close succession. Later in the same year, on 5 May at Pori, he cleared 5.00 outdoors, but this earned him only a European record because in the intervening time the Americans had fought back successfully. For official purposes, history's first 5-metre vaulter was Brian Sternberg of USA (born at Seattle, Washington, on 21 June 1943; 1.85 m./76 kg.), who cleared 5 metres even a few weeks before turning twenty, on 27 April 1963 at Philadelphia. In the following weeks, Sternberg and his compatriot John Pennel took turns in bettering the record. A few weeks after improving to 5.08, however, Sternberg was put off the track by a hideous accident. It happened during a training session on the trampoline. While attempting to perform a double back somersault, he lost control and instead of landing on his feet he came down on the back of his neck and shoulders. He suffered dislocation of cervical vertebrae, with damage to the spinal cord. Despite surgical treatment, he was to remain paralyzed from his neck down. Quite revealing of Sternberg's modesty was his comment after clearing 5.08: "I don't attach much importance to records made with the fibreglass pole. Cornelius Warmerdam still is the greatest".

Progress with the "catapult pole" - as Don Bragg chose to call it - continued at relentless speed. By the end of 1963 John Pennel had upped the world record to 5.20.

At the Tokyo Olympics (1964) the US first string, Fred Hansen, the newest world record holder at 5.28, was put to a hard test by three Germans. After a 9-hour struggle he finally emerged the winner with 5.10. Wolfgang Reinhardt (5.05) and Klaus Lehnertz (5.00), both of West Germany, followed in that order, while Manfred Preussger of East Germany, who also cleared 5.00, had to be content with fourth place. Even though fibreglass poles were particularly favoured by young vaulters, there were some established performers from the Metal Era who managed to convert to the new implement with remarkable success. Foremost in this group were Ron Morris of USA, the 1960 Olympic silver medallist, who improved from 4.70 (metal) to 5.03 (fibreglass), and Manfred Preussger of East Germany (from 4.65 to 5.15). The most prominent role in the record breaking spree was played by Robert Seagren of USA (born at Pomona, California, on 17 October 1946; 1.83 m./79 kg.). A "son of fibreglass", he bettered the world record time and again, beginning with 5.32 in 1966 and winding up with 5.63 in 1972! He won the 1968 Olympic title at Mexico City, exactly one day before turning twenty, with 5.40. It was a hard fought event and Seagren won on fewer misses from Claus Schiprowski of West Germany and Wolfgang Nordwig of East Germany, who also cleared 5.40 and were classified in that order. It was clear that Europeans were finally able to talk on even terms with America's best.

Pentti Nikula had won the 1962 European title with 4.80. Then came Nordwig, who scored three consecutive victories, with 5.10 in 1966, 5.30 in '69 and 5.35 in '71. This fine athlete (born at Siegmar, Chemnitz, on 27 August 1943; 1.84 m./72 kg.) was a great competitor. In 1970 he bettered the world record twice, with 5.45 and 5.46, but was exceeded

Bob Beamon (USA) in his famous "jump into the XXI century": 8.90 at the 1968 Olympics in Mexico City.

towards the end of the season by Christos Papanikolaou of Greece, who at Athens on 24 October treated his countrymen to a rare sight with a 5.49 clearance.

A memorable event occurred at the 1972 Olympics in Munich. After sixteen consecutive victories (1896 through 1968), American vaulters had to leave the highest step of the Olympic dais to a foreigner, the reliable Wolfgang Nordwig. Unfortunately, this event was preceded and partly clouded by a bitter controversy. Manufacturers had never ceased to devise new types of fibreglass poles and the latest models were definitely better than those used at the dawn of the new era. The newest ones had been used for months on both sides of the Atlantic and it was with one of them that Seagren raised the world record to 5.63 at the US Olympic Trials at Eugene on 2 July. The IAAF displayed a certain degree of inconsistency by first banning the new poles from the Olympics on 25 July, re-admitting them on 27 August and finally banning them for good on 30 August, i.e. two days before the qualifying round. This meant that Seagren and several others were compelled to abandon the poles they had been using throughout the major part of the season. It was rumoured that Nordwig too had tried the latest models, only to discard them in pre-Olympic weeks. Be as it may, Nordwig had his greatest day on 2 September in Munich and won the gold medal at 5.50, his lifetime best. Seagren was second (5.40), ahead of another American, Jan Johnson (5.35). Among those who fell by the wayside chiefly as a result of the pole controversy were two of the best Europeans, Kjell Isaksson of Sweden and Renato Dionisi of Italy. Both failed to make the final, a bitter pill especially for Isaksson, who earlier in the season had bettered the world record several times, up to 5.55 (plus an unratified 5.59), before finally losing it to Seagren. Despite his class and longevity, the Swede had to be content with two silver medals in the European Championships (1969 and '71). Dionisi won the event in the Europe vs America dual meet in 1969 and a European indoor title in 1973. His lifetime best was 5.45.

The great Nordwig decided to step out after his Munich victory. From that time onwards three vaulting "schools" began to fight it out for supremacy in Europe: France, Poland and USSR. The combined effect of their efforts was that USA finally had to relinquish its leadership of the event. At the 1974 European Championships in Rome victory went to Vladimir Kishkun of USSR with 5.35. In the Olympic year 1976 the Americans were predictably thirsty for revenge. In the meantime they had recaptured the world record with Dave Roberts, who did 5.65 in 1975. What followed in the early stages of 1976 seemed to confirm that US vaulters were back in lane 1. The record was revised again, first by Earl Bell, 5.67, then by Roberts himself, who won at the US Olympic Trials at Eugene on 22 June with 5.70. But the Montreal Olympic event gave partly unexpected results. The battle was featured by a lot of "poker strategy", with leading contenders passing this or that height in order to keep down the number of their trials in the light of a final countback of trials and failures, which would be decisive in breaking ties. Three men cleared 5.50 and Tadeusz Slusarski of Poland won "on points" from Antti Kalliomäki of Finland and world record holder Roberts. The French "school" made spectacular advances under the stimulus of two dedicated coaches, Jean-Claude Perrin and Maurice Houvion (the latter was a former national record hold-

1961
1980

Ralph Boston (USA), a dominant figure in the long jump during the Sixties.

er with 4.87 in 1963). The first Frenchman to be crowned world record holder, seventy-five years after the legendary Fernand Gonder, was Thierry Vigneron, who mastered 5.75 at Colombes on 1 June 1980. Then came Philippe Houvion, a son of the above-mentioned Maurice, who raised the mark to 5.77, two weeks before the Moscow Olympics.

With the Americans not in the game as a result of the boycott, the Olympic final loomed as a three-side affair involving USSR, France and Poland. Victory went to Wladyslaw Kozakiewicz of Poland (born at Solyechniki, USSR, on 8 December 1953; 1.87 m./84 kg.), a sturdy vaulter who could point to a long, gradual progress, from 2.00 at the age of twelve till 5.02 at nineteen. Earlier in 1980 he had raised the world record to 5.72, before the French took over. In Moscow (30 July) he won in the face of a seemingly hostile Russian crowd, mastering a height of 5.78. This was the first time since 1920 that an Olympic gold medal was won with a world record effort. Konstantin Volkov of USSR and defending champion Tadeusz Slusarski of Poland tied for second at 5.65, while Philippe Houvion was fourth, still with 5.65.

LONG JUMP - Beamon: "Tell me I am not dreaming"

After the 1960 Olympics in Rome, Ralph Boston and Igor Ter-Ovanesyan dominated the long jump scene for a long time. They took turns in beating the world record. A feud the like of which was not to be found in the history of the event. In the last sixty years, that is prior to Boston's breakthrough, only eight men had made the IAAF record book in the long jump. The ding-dong battle between Ralph and Igor was marked by the following record performances:

- Modesto, 27 May 1961: Boston 8.24
- Moscow, 16 July 1961: Boston 8.28
  (Ter-Ovanesyan 2nd with 8.01)
- Yereva, 10 June 1962: Ter-Ovanesyan 8.31
- Kingston, 15 August 1964: Boston 8.31
- Los Angeles, 12 September 1964: Boston 8.34
- Modesto, 29 May 1965: Boston 8.35
- Mexico City, 19 October 1967:
  Ter-Ovanesyan 8.35.

Boston, extraordinary in his consistency in the 8-metre-plus range, was first in "Track & Field News" World Ranking for eight straight years (1960-67), a superlative feat. Ter-Ovanesyan also showed great consistency and set a record in longevity, figuring in said Ranking for fifteen straight years, 1957 through 1971, although he was ranked first only once, in 1969. A marvel of durability in an event which taxes physical and mental resources like few others in athletics.

Boston had one of his greatest days at the 1964 US Olympic Trials in Los Angeles, when he compiled the following series: 8.49 (wind +2.6 m/s, hence illegal) - 8.21 - 8.34 (world record, wind +1.0 m/s) - 8.11 - 8.14 - pass. The following year at Modesto, on what he called "the fastest runway in the world", he had another great series: foul - 8.15 - 8.26 - 8.24 - 8.06 - 8.35 (world record, wind 0.0 m/s). It was a windy day and before taking his last jump Boston stationed his rival and friend Gayle Hopkins (he too an 8-metre-plus man) at the wind gauge. Boston stood at the end of the runway and waited for Hopkins to give the "hi-sign". This enabled the champion to take off in a windless moment. The result was a new world record. Ter-Ovanesyan was somewhat prone to injuries, hence more cautious in spreading himself. He was a technical marvel and had a great competitive heart. He had his best day, mark-wise at least, in a pre-Olympic meet at Mexico City in 1967, when he put together the following series: 8.33 - 7.97 - foul - 8.35 (equalling Boston's world record; wind 0.0 m/s) - 8.17 - 8.16. Among those who offered congratulations was Jesse Owens, visibly impressed by Ter's technical prowess. His comment: "I was lucky to do 8.13 with an almost primitive form".

From 1963 onwards the two great rivals got tough competition from a sturdy Welshman, Lynn Davies (born at Nantymoel near Bridgend, Glamorgan, on 20 May 1942; 1.85 m./76 kg.). He was a talented sprinter, with such marks as 9.5 and 21.2 over the English distances. On that basic asset he built a remarkable condition, especially through weight training. He thus improved from 7.14 in 1961 to 7.72 in '62. The latter mark earned him a fourth place at the British Commonwealth Games in Perth, the winner being Mike Ahey of Ghana with a wind-assisted 8.05. Davies was a great fighter and as such he offered his masterpiece in the 1964 Olympics in Tokyo, on a cold, rainy day, when he took the lead on his penultimate jump with 8.07. Boston replied with 8.03 on his last try but had to be content with silver, while Ter-Ovanesyan won the bronze with 7.99. In later years Davies continued to be a threat to both Boston and Ter-Ovanesyan, even though he was a bit behind them in general standard of performance. Ter-Ovanesyan won his second European title at Belgrade in 1962 with a wind-assisted 8.19, but four years later in Budapest he lost to the irrepressible Davies, 7.88 to 7.98. But Ter was indestructible and he came back in fine style at Athens in 1969 to beat Davies,

8.17 to 8.07, thus winning his third European title. In the meantime, however, the world of sport in general and the long jump fraternity in particular had been shocked by what appeared to be a "super-natural" event - a leap of eight metres ninety centimetres! It happened in the Olympic final at Mexico City on 18 October 1968. The man who turned that incredible trick was an American, Robert Beamon (born at Jamaica, New York on 29 August 1946; 1.90 m./75 kg.). A great natural talent if ever there was one, Beamon scaled the heights rapidly, improving from 7.80 in 1966 to 8.11 in '67. A 9.5 100 y. sprinter, he was acknowledged to possess tremendous potential. Boston was once quoted as saying: "Beamon has terrific abdominal strength, and just as amazing strength in his hamstrings. He can hold his legs up forever". Before going to Mexico, Beamon had a great season in USA: undefeated, he beat Boston six times. His best pre-Olympic marks were 8.33 in the AAU meet at Sacramento and a wind-assisted 8.39 in the US Olympic Trials at Echo Summit, hence in rarefied atmosphere. As destiny would have it, in Mexico he had his most difficult hour during the qualifying rounds in the morning of 17 October. After fouling on his first two tries, he decided to have a "safety jump" in his third and last - he took off with about 30 cms. to spare and hit the sand at 8.19! That was certainly an alarm bell for his rivals, no matter if Boston had qualified majestically on his first jump with a new Olympic record of 8.27. Even so, the track world was hardly prepared for what happened in the early afternoon of 18 October. Yet there was an "insider" like Ralph Boston who said: "I'm always nervous when Beamon goes down the runway, because I know that some day he might put all his great talent together in one big jump". The final started at 3.40 p.m. in cool temperature, following a rain shower. In the opening round, the first three jumpers fouled. Then came Beamon's turn. As Tom McNab, noted British coach and commentator, put it, "Beamon attacked the runway with incredible ferocity and seemed to leap as if from a trampoline". In fact, he hit the board with great precision and took off from his right foot (his shoe had six spikes). A 1.956 m. high jumper, in his flight he reached a peak which was estimated as 1.78 m. He landed well beyond the operational range of a special Cantabrian device which was used for measuring jumps. Judges thus had to resort to a conventional steel tape. Finally, the official announcement came: 8.90. There was an aiding wind, which was officially given as 2.0 m/s, the maximum allowable under IAAF rules. The listed world record, jointly held by Boston and Ter-Ovanesyan, was thus eclipsed by a giant margin - 55 cms! When he realized the immensity of his feat, Beamon exclaimed: "Tell me I am not dreaming". Still in that momentous first round, Charlie Mays, the third US string and an 8.01 man, had a narrow foul, said to be worth 8.61. Then it started raining - as Ter-Ovanesyan was taking his first jump. He managed 8.12, and shortly after that Boston did 8.16. But that was all the "Big Two" could do for the day. Beamon's phenomenal jump was bound to have a paralyzing effect on all his rivals. Yet it is curious to note that a "lesser light" such as Klaus Beer of East Germany surpassed himself in round 2 to clinch the silver medal with 8.19, his best ever. In his fifth try Boston himself had a foul which was said to be worth 8.48. He finally had to be content with a bronze medal - still a remarkable achievement, after his gold in 1960 and his silver in '64. Ter-Ovanesyan was fourth. Under better weather conditions somebody could have bridged at least part of the gulf separating Beamon from his nearest rival - 71 cms.! But this is of course idle speculation. When it was all over, experts began to search for details which might

Post-miracle atmosphere

No athletic performance in modern history has ever evoked such strong feelings as Bob Beamon's famous leap of 8.90 at the 1968 Olympics in Mexico City. When it happened, somebody called it "a jump into the XXI century". (This definition was valid till 1991 ....)
In the inner circle of Beamon's closest rivals, the best comment probably came from witty Ralph Boston: "Fourteen years of jumping in the sand is a long time, and now I gotta find something else to do". Beamon himself retired soon afterwards. I recall his appearance in the Europe vs. America dual meet at Stuttgart in 1969 - more for the tail-coat and derby hat he was sporting upon entering the stadium than for his show in the competition itself (he was fourth and last with 7.75). As far as athletics was concerned, by then he had no incentives. And in his heart of hearts he probably felt he would never come close to his "miracle jump".
As for his colleagues in the long jump fraternity, they soon learnt that it would be extremely difficult to come reasonably close to Beamon's mark, let alone excel it. In 1980, at the dawn of the Lewis Era, the second best jumper of all time was in statistical books with 8.54, still light years away from Beamon's world record flag.

explain Beamon's explosion or at least make it more "digestible" for common mortals. High altitude and wind assistance were obviously taken into account immediately. Dr. Donald H. Potts, a noted US mathematician and statistician, estimated that "the two elements gave him (Beamon) about 4 % advantage over dead calm sea-level conditions", which would make his record worth about 8.56 under normal conditions, still a fantastic improvement vis-à-vis all previous efforts. (And it would obviously be worth more than that if the wind "bonus", legal under under IAAF rules, was not obliterated).

After Beamon's fantastic achievement, long jump standards inevitably returned to "normal". And experts learnt to appreciate what was happening without necessarily referring to that "impossible" world record. In 1970, Sepp Schwarz of West Germany earned wide acclaim when he equalled Ter-Ovanesyan's European record (8.35) during a dual meet with USA at Stuttgart. And hardly anybody showed dismay when Max Klauss of East Germany won the 1971 European title in Helsinki with 7.92, almost one metre shy of "The Jump". The evergreen Ter-Ovanesyan was a close second with 7.91, thus collecting his fifth medal in just as many appearances in the European title meet. Lynn Davies was fourth. The 1972 Olympics in Munich crowned the youngest champion in the history of the event: Randy Williams of USA (born at Fresno on 23 August 1953; 1.75 m./72 kg.), who jumped 8.34 in the qualifying rounds, then won the final with 8.24, a few weeks after turning nineteen. Hans Baumgartner of West Germany edged Arnie Robinson of USA for the silver medal, 8.18 to 8.03. The best jumpers of the Seventies generally resisted the temptation of trying their luck in high altitude sites, even though most experts agreed that Beamon's record seemed virtually unassailable under sea-level conditions. One of the best jumpers in the early Seventies was Valeriy Podluzhniy of USSR, who won the 1974 European title in Rome with 8.12, beating Nenad Stekic of Yugoslavia (8.05). Podluzhniy, who had an excellent technique, compiled an amazing series at Munich in the fall of 1971: six valid jumps between 8.17 and 8.00, with an average of 8.09. Stekic, a rather unpredictable jumper, had his great day on 25 July 1975 at Montreal, when he used a wind of 1.95 m/s to reach 8.45, a new European record. The big jump came on his first try, after which he was content with 7.97 and a wind-aided 7.99. At the 1978 European Championships in Prague the winner was Jacques Rousseau of France, who beat Stekic in a close battle, 8.18 to 8.12. The Yugoslav never won a major title, yet continued to jump well for many years, and at 39 he was still capable of marks close to the 8-metre line. The 1976 Olympic title in Montreal was won by Clarence ("Arnie") Robinson (born at San Diego on 7 April 1948; 1.88 m./75 kg.), who did 8.35 in perfectly windless conditions, a feat for which he was lauded by spectator Bob Beamon. Defending champion Randy Williams was second with 8.11, and Frank Wartenberg of East Germany was third (8.02). Robinson, a very consistent jumper, also won the 1977 World Cup event, at Düsseldorf, with 8.19. USA also had a man who was to outshine everybody in terms of durability - Larry Myricks (born at Clinton, Mississippi, on 10 March 1956; 1.88 m./77 kg.). A most reliable performer, Myricks missed his rendezvous with Luck on important occasions. After improving from 7.83 in 1975 to 8.09 early in '76, Myricks began to loom as a possible medallist for the Montreal Games. At the US Olympic Trials he finished second to Arnie Robinson, 8.26 to 8.37 (both wind-aided). In Montreal he qualified for the final, but in warming up for the decisive test he broke an ankle. After a one-year lay-off, Myricks came back more determined than ever and in 1979 he moved to the no.1 position. His brightest victory that year occurred, of all places in the world, in Montreal. It was the final of the World Cup and Myricks won on his last jump with 8.52, wresting the lead from Lutz Dombrowski of East Germany (8.27). But then came 1980 and Myricks again faced an "adverse wind": the US boycott kept him away from the Moscow Olympics. The gold medal went to Dombrowski (born at Karl-Marx-Stadt, now Chemnitz, on 25 June 1959; 1.87 m./87 kg.), who won with his best-ever mark, 8.54, with a legal wind of 0.9 m/s. That was also the second longest jump in history. The no man's land separating Beamon from the rest of the world was gradually getting narrower. With Americans and West Germans not in the meet, the other medals went to Frank Paschek of East Germany (8.21) and Valeriy Podluzhniy of USSR (8.18). Dombrowski, a fast, powerful jumper, was later handicapped by recurrent injuries.

TRIPLE JUMP - Nearly four of a kind for Saneyev

Józef Schmidt of Poland, history's first 17-metre man, although occasionally hampered by muscular ailments, had a long and noble career. He was a good sprinter (10.4 for the 100 m.) and an excellent long jumper (7.84, plus a wind-aided 7.96). Form-wise, he showed a low trajectory in the hop and step, then regained height in the third leap, which thus resembled a full-fledged long jump. Always a great competitor, he won his second European title at Belgrade in 1962 with 16.55, beating Vladimir Goryayev (16.39) and former world record holder Olyeg Fyedoseyev (16.24), both of USSR.

In 1964 Schmidt, then 29, had to undergo knee surgery a few months before the Tokyo Olympics. His one and only mark prior to the Games, 15.81 in Rome, gave scarce indications about the extent of his recovery. But a couple of weeks later, in Tokyo, the Pole was his real self again and successfully defended his title with 16.85, a new Olympic record. The Russians again had to be content with silver and bronze, which went to Fyedoseyev (16.58) and Viktor Kravchenko (16.57) respectively. Schmidt thus joined Meyer Prinstein and A.F.da Silva as a two-time winner of the triple jump in the Games. In 1965, however, the Polish champion had another accident, and the following year, at Budapest, he did no better than fifth in the European title meet. Victory went to Georgi Stoikovski of Bulgaria at 16.67, with Hans-Jürgen Rückborn of East Germany second, one centimetre back. Schmidt fought back bravely and in 1967 he jumped 16.84. But the wave of progress had brought other jumpers closer and closer to the 17-metre line. One of these was Giuseppe Gentile, Italy's first triple jumper of international calibre. Tall and powerful although somewhat prone to injuries, he was a 16.32 man on the eve of the Olympic year 1968. A good combination of long jumper/triple jumper, he began to loom as an Olympic prospect in August 1968 with new national records of 7.91 and 16.74 on consecutive days. Yet there was a Finn, Pertti Pousi, who did even better, with 8.04 and 17.00, he too on consecutive days. Another serious candidate for Olympic honours was Viktor Saneyev, a Georgian representing USSR who had done 16.67 in 1967 and 16.87 in July 1968. Hardly anybody talked about Nelson Prudencio of Brazil, whose pre-Olympic best was a "mere" 16.30.

In the cauldron of Estadio Olimpico at Mexico City, Pousi was eliminated in the qualifying round (16 October), but Gentile rose to the occasion with a stunning world record, 17.10, achieved in windless conditions at 11.10 in the morning. The double effect of a Tartan runway and a rarefied atmosphere was by then evident, yet the final on the following day went above expectations. Within less than two hours, Gentile's fresh world mark was bettered four times! The dramatic sequence was as follows:

3.15 p.m. - Gentile 17.22 (wind nil)
4.05 p.m. - Saneyev 17.23 (wind +2.0)
5.00 p.m. - Prudencio 17.27 (wind +2.0)
5.05 p.m. - Saneyev 17.39 (wind +2.0)

Saneyev thus won from Prudencio and Gentile. Other place winners, "inspired" by the thin air, also surpassed themselves: 4.Art Walker (USA) 17.12w, 5.Nikolay Dudkin (USSR) 17.09w; 6.Phil May (Australia) 17.02; 7.Schmidt (Poland) 16.89. Markwise, the defending champion had done better than in his winning ventures of 1960 and '64 ... But it was obvious that conditions prevailing in Mexico City could hardly be compared with those of previous Games. After his bitter-sweet experience in Mexico, Giuseppe Gentile continued to be hampered by injuries now and then and could do no better than 16.72. The world at large was to see him again in 1970, when he played Jason to the Medea of Maria Callas in the movie "Medea".

1961
1980

Viktor Saneyev (USSR) won three golds and a silver in the triple jump at the Olympic Games (1968 through 1980).

253

Far more impressive was the career record of Viktor Saneyev (born at Sukhumi, Georgia, on 3 October 1945; 1.88 m./80 kg.). He eventually became the most durable top-class performer in the history of the event. This Georgian was an athlete of multiform capabilities, credited with such marks as 10.5 (100 m.), 7.90 (long jump) and 1.90 (high jump). He chose to concentrate on the triple jump in 1963, when he did 14.88. Four years later he was good enough to beat some of the best continental triple jumpers in the final of the European Cup at Kiev with 16.67. From then on he reigned supreme for several years, collecting three golds and a silver in the Olympic Games, two golds and two silvers in the European Championships. On 5 August 1971, during the Pan-American Games at Cali, Colombia (altitude, 1046 m.), a 19-year-old Cuban, Pedro Pérez Duenas, created a sensation with a new world record of 17.40 (wind +0.5 m/s), leaving Nelson Prudencio of Brazil far behind (16.82). Pérez had a great series: 16.92 - 17.40 - 14.92 - 17.04 - 17.12 - 17.19. A great improvement vis-à-vis his pre-Games best, 16.86. That was to remain, easily and by far, Pérez's greatest day. In later years injuries prevented him from rising to similar heights again. Saneyev annexed his first European title at Athens in 1969 with a "windy" 17.34, leaving his nearest opponent almost half a metre behind. Early in the Seventies the Georgian jumper had a fine rival in Jörg Drehmel of East Germany. At the 1971 European Championships in Helsinki, Drehmel edged his great opponent, 17.16 to 17.10 (both wind-assisted), but Saneyev fought back successfully in the Munich Olympics the following year, finally keeping Drehmel at bay by a narrow margin, 17.35 to 17.31. It should be noted, however, that in his winning effort Saneyev was aided by a wind slightly over the limit (2.2 m/s), whereas Drehmel reached his best distance with a legal wind (1.5 m/s). These are the inevitable vagaries of field event competitions, but on occasion they can play a significant, if not decisive, role. Third place went to Nelson Prudencio (17.05). Saneyev closed his 1972 account on a high note, recapturing the world record with 17.44 in a meet held in his native town, Sukhumi, on 17 October. He did this without the benefit of thin air and against a wind of 0.5 m/s.

The indefatigable Saneyev went on to win his second European title at Rome in 1974 with 17.23. But as the Montreal Olympics drew near he found a new challenger in João Carlos de Oliveira of Brazil (born at Pindamanhangaba near São Paulo on 28 May 1954; 1.86 m./76 kg.). This exceptional athlete had

João Carlos de Oliveira, the latest "pearl" in the Brazilian collection of triple jumpers.

> **Magic coincidence**
>
> At the 1968 Olympics the thin air of Mexico City (altitude, 2250 m.) obviously caused a revolution in the standards of anaerobic events, i.e. those implying relatively short-lived efforts. Beyond this, however, foreign observers were sometimes intrigued by wind readings announced in connection with record performances. During the Games (men's and women's events)there were no less than twelve world records affecting events in which a wind reading was required. Well, in five cases out of twelve - 41 % - the official wind reading was 2.0 m/s (favourable), exactly the maximum allowed by the rule. In the remaining seven cases, the wind ranged from 0.0 to 1.8 m/s (favourable). Stupendous, to say the least, was the coincidence that occurred in the triple jump final, with three world record marks spaced over one hour and all blessed with a wind of exactly +2.0 m/s !

first bettered 16 m. in 1974 with 16.34. The following year he went to Mexico City to compete in the Pan-American Games, and astounded the athletics world. He began by beating Arnie Robinson of USA in the long jump, 8.13 to 7.94, and two days later (15 October) he uncorked a triple jump of 17.89, thus excelling Saneyev's world record by 45 cms. And unlike Beamon in his miracle long jump in the same stadium seven years earlier, the Brazilian received no help from the wind. The record came in the second round. For the rest João had two fouls and three passes. Tommy Haynes of USA was second with 17.20. But the fresh record holder was hampered by sciatica in the spring of 1976 and the Olympic rendezvous in Montreal found him short on condition and he had to be content with the bronze medal (16.90). The irrepressible Saneyev was again the winner, this time at 17.29, while James Butts of USA was second with 17.18, a lifetime best, curiously achieved in perfect coincidence with the crack of the starter's pistol in getting a race off. Former world record holder Pedro Pérez Duenas was fourth (16.81).

João Carlos de Oliveira took partial consolation with a nice string of victories in the World Cup, his marks being 16.68 at Düsseldorf in 1977, 17.02 at Montreal in '79, and 17.37 in Rome in '81. Meanwhile, the great Saneyev was battling with ankle injuries. Despite several operations he could not regain his condition of old, yet stayed in line and at the 1978 European Championships in Prague he missed his third gold by a trifle in losing to Milos Srejovic of Yugoslavia, 16.93 to 16.94.

Despite his physical ailments, Saneyev still entertained a dream for 1980: match Al Oerter's stupendous record of four consecutive victories in the same event in the Olympics. In the Games final Saneyev, wearing a bandage below his right knee, managed an excellent 17.24, but had to bow to his compatriot Jaak Uudmäe, an Estonian who won with the mark of his lifetime, 17.35. João Carlos de Oliveira, the pre-meet favourite of many, was only third at 17.22. It should be said, however, that strange things happened that day. Some very good efforts by João and Australia's Ian Campbell (fifth with 16.72), which in the opinion of foreign observers seemed to excel Uudmäe's winning mark, were inexplicably ruled fouls by Soviet judges. Officials apparently contended that in Campbell's best jump the athlete's left foot had dragged along the runway during his step phase, but films failed to prove their point in a convincing manner. (In 1990 the following sentence was added to IAAF rules concerning the triple jump: "It shall not be considered a failure if the competitor, while jumping, touches the ground with the "sleeping leg").

SHOT PUT - Rotation style: early conquests

1961 1980

Arthur Rowe eventually overcame his post-Rome dejection and in 1961 he had his best ever season, raising the European record to 19.56. British fans expected him to do himself justice in the 1962 European Championships, but in July of that year he signed a professional rugby contract. This turned out to be a short-lived affair and the dynamic but unpredictable Rowe had time to regret his decision. (If born twenty years later, he could have been reinstated as an amateur athlete - as it happened to hurdler Renaldo Nehemiah in the mid-Eighties). Another leading European of those days, Silvano Meconi of Italy, never managed to excel in big-time competition, although he would occasionally do notable things, mark-wise at least (e.g. 18.62 in winning his event at the Six-Nations meet at Colombes in 1961).

In terms of consistency and reliability, the best European of that period was Vilmos Varju (born at Gyula on 10 June 1937; 1.90 m./115 kg.), a thickset Magyar who began to loom as a serious prospect in July 1960, when he did 18.67. But a few days later, during an "impromptu" soccer match, he fractured the fibula of his right leg, and thus had to stay away from the Rome Olympics. Varju came back in fine style two years later, winning the European title at Belgrade with 19.02. After losing to Bill Nieder in the final stages of the 1960 season, Dallas Long continued to improve and on 18 May 1962 at Los Angeles he bettered Nieder's world record with a 20.08 toss. Second in that event at 19.78 was Gary Gubner, a heavily muscled man who later proved just as good if not better in weight lifting, a sport in which he won a silver medal in the heavy-weight class at the 1965 World Championships. The Tokyo Olympics (1964) came at the right time for Long but a bit too early for a new phenomenon, Randy Matson. In pre-Olympic weeks Long bettered his own world record several times, with a top mark of 20.68 in the USA vs USSR dual meet at Los Angeles on 25 July. And shortly before leaving for Tokyo the 19-year-old Matson improved to 19.95. With this duo, flanked by old warrior Parry O'Brien, USA appeared to be as safe as ever. In the fourth round of the Olympic final Matson caused quite a stir by taking the lead with 20.20, but Long lost no time in replying with a 20.33 effort - the eventual winner. For once there was no US sweep though: Vilmos Varju won the bronze medal with 19.39. The 32-

year-old Parry O'Brien took fourth place with 19.20, ironically his best mark in four Olympic appearances but also the only one that failed to earn him a medal. After his victory in Tokyo, Long closed his brilliant career as the reigning Olympic champion and world record holder. 1965 was the first year of the Matson era. This colossus from the Lone Star State (born at Kilgore, Texas, on 5 March 1945; 1.99 m./118 kg.) had a dedication for the sport that almost equalled that of Parry O'Brien, and a physical build the like of which the shot put world had never seen since the distant days of Ralph Rose. He made his début with the senior shot at eighteen - with 18.44. The following year he was up to 20.20, the toss that earned him a silver medal in the Tokyo Olympics. By then a student at Texas Agricultural and Mechanical University at College Station, Matson was ready to take over. Intensive weight training helped him reach a new dimension and in 1965 he bettered the world record three times in the space of a month: 20.70 at College Station on 9 April, 21.05 at Austin on 30 April, and 21.52 again at College Station on 8 May. Matson was also a top-class discus thrower and on 8 April 1967, at College Station, he had a unique double: 21.47 in the shot and 65.16 in the discus, the latter being a personal best. Still on the campus of his university, on 22 April of the same year, he put the shot 21.78 for his fourth and last world record.

In the 1965 World List Matson led his nearest rival, Neal Steinhauer, by 2.18 m. But the very same Steinhauer rose to become a threat even for the big Texan. He credited an intensive programme of body building for his astounding progress, from 17.59 in 1964 to 21.01 in 1967, a year in which he managed to win 2 out of 10 from Matson. But in 1968 Steinhauer was sidelined with an injury at a crucial stage of the season and could not make the Olympic team. At Mexico City the Texas giant won, should I say inevitably, with a toss of 20.54 (after doing 20.68 in the qualifying rounds). The other medals went to George Woods of USA (20.12) and Eduard Gushchin of USSR (20.09). Even after his Olympic victory, Matson continued to be a factor for several years but never regained his 1967 vein. In "Track & Field News" World Ranking he was second in 1964, first for the next four years, then fifth in '69, again first in '70, second in '71 and sixth in '72.

Ever since policeman Hans Woellke won the Olympic

A dragon with (too) many heads

In the mid-Sixties rumour had it that strong men were intent on becoming ever stronger by resorting to substances which could easily be classified as drugs. This was said to be particularly true of athletes operating in the weight events. The drugs in question were supposed to belong, chiefly if not entirely, to the family of anabolic steroids, synthetized male sex hormones which can enhance muscle growth and aid the athlete's ability to take on heavier training loads. In those days the IAAF rule on doping was confined to a few lines saying that the use of drugs "with the intention of increasing athletic efficiency by their stimulating action upon muscles or nerves, or by paralyzing the sense of fatigue, was strongly deprecated not only on moral grounds but because of their danger to health". But it was only in the early Seventies that this general formula was replaced by a precise list of forbidden substances comprising five main groups: 1) psychomotor stimulant drugs, 2) sympathomimetic amines, 3) miscellaneous central nervous system stimulants, 4) narcotic analgesics, 5) anabolic steroids. Anti-doping controls began to be carried out at major international championships. The first athlete to be disqualified for failing to pass a doping test was Eduard de Noorlander of Holland, after finishing sixth in the decathlon at the 1969 European Championships in Athens. This development led many athletes to stop taking drugs, notably including anabolic steroids, a few weeks before a major event, relying on the widespread knowledge that the tests had a limited retrospective action. As a result it would be impossible to say how things actually stood in relation to this or that record holder. The greatest shot putter of the Sixties, Randy Matson, was always adamant in claiming that he had never used drugs, and many observers were inclined to believe him, considering that nature had endowed him with a physical build well above athletic averages.

Following the "Johnson case" (1988 Olympics) the IAAF introduced new doping rules which dealt with the problem under many new aspects. Doping controls were extended to include random tests likely to be conducted at any time of the year, even in training camps. Tests became mandatory for the approval of all world records, no matter where made. Parallel to harsher rules, however, human ingenuity developed new ways and means of effacing traces of drug consumption ... As of **year 2000** it seems reasonable to admit that the Doping Dragon has more heads than the IAAF can ever hope to cut off.

1961 1980

shot put title in 1936, Germany had apparently ceased to produce top-class shot putters. Towards the end of the Sixties, East Germany's throwers began to remedy the situation. Dieter Hoffmann was fourth at the 1968 Olympics in Mexico City with 20.00, and the following year East Germans made a clean sweep at the 1969 European Championships in Athens, with Hoffmann winning at 20.12 from his countrymen Hans-Joachim Rothenburg and Hans-Peter Gies. Their bonanza continued in the 1971 edition of that meet, held at Helsinki, when Hartmut Briesenick won with 21.08 from Rothenburg, while Wladyslaw Komar of Poland took the bronze medal.

The 1972 Olympic final in Munich was a nip-and-tuck affair, only four centimetres separating first from fourth! Result: 1.Komar 21.18, 2.George Woods (USA) 21.17, 3.Briesenick 21.14, 4.Gies 21.14. Then came two Americans who were to be heard from again later on: 5.Feuerbach 21.01, 6.Oldfield 20.91. There was a heated argument following Woods' sixth and last throw. Although the issue appeared to be controversial, consensus was that Woods' iron ball struck at the base of the flag marking Komar's best distance (21.18), which was also an Olympic record. After that the flag lay flat on the ground with a bend in the shaft. Woods felt he should receive another throw, on the assumption that the flight of his shot was somehow impeded, but officials did not share his view. They measured the throw at 21.05, and Woods had to be content with his previous effort of 21.17, only good enough for silver. In terms of physical build, Al Feuerbach was the least conspicuous of the Munich finalists, being "only" 1.85 m. tall, but in the opinion of knowledgeable observers he was the one with the most efficient technique. He used this to further advantage and on 5 May 1973, at San Jose, he got one off to 21.82, four centimetres beyond Matson's six-year-old world record. A year later, during an international meet at Malmö, Feuerbach set a record of sorts, totalling 37.05 in a two-hands event (21.38 right, 15.67 left). First to break the 22 m. barrier was the massive (1.88 m./131 kg.) George Woods, who reached 22.02 in an indoor meet at Inglewood, Los Angeles, on 8 February 1974. But then undercover marks continued to be ignored by the IAAF.

One of the most prominent figures in the Seventies was another American, Brian Oldfield (born at Elgin, Illinois, on 1 June 1945; 1.95 m./120 kg.). The ebullient type of athlete, he reached 20.97 with the O'Brien technique in 1972 and was sixth in the Munich Olympic final, as related above. By then, however, he had begun to play with a new technique, which came to be known as the rotation style. In this form the athlete basically uses the same general leg movements as those adopted by discus throwers. From the starting position, the athlete pivots on the foot opposite the throwing arm and rotates anti-clockwise if he is right-handed and clockwise if he is left-handed, and does a glide that brings him into a landing position very similar to that of the O'Brien technique. Advantages and disadvantages of this style are still a matter of discussion among coaches. The "discus style" probably gives the implement a higher initial speed, but some throwers may have trouble in staying in the ring. Oldfield worked hard for three years to perfect his new technique and results were finally rewarding: in 1975 he did 21.87 and 22.11 indoors, then had his greatest day in an outdoor meet at El Paso on 10 May, with 21.94 on his second throw, 22.25 on his fifth and an astounding 22.86 on his last. His comment, vaguely reminiscent of flamboyant rhetoric, was: "I decided to stop trying to break the record by a few inches each time ... I figured if I did what I knew I could do, the record would be eternalized - at least until I break it again". However, these marks were made in "pro" meets, that is outside the sphere of jurisdiction of the AAU, and as such could not be ratified. Some members of the shot fraternity, notably including O'Brien, aired sceptical views about the authenticity of Oldfield's feats. However, Brian was a tremendously gifted athlete (in 1975 he also threw the discus 62.26) and several years later he gave doubters some food for thought. In 1980, after he was reinstated in the amateur ranks, he won the US Championship title (incidentally the first meet staged by the new Federation, TAC) with 21.82. The following year he raised the US record to 22.02, and in 1984 he did 22.19 at the age of thirty-nine!

There is at any rate an incontrovertible fact: the rotation style was not invented by Brian Oldfield. According to an article which appeared in 1973 in "Yessis Review of Soviet Sports", Russian coach Viktor Alekseyev (former national record holder in the javelin, with 69.68 in 1947) experimented such a style with young shot putters as early as in the Fifties. And it was an Alekseyev pupil, Aleksandr Barishnikov, to first use it in a major international meet - the 1972 Olympics in Munich, when Barishnikov did 18.65 but failed to advance to the final.

Barishnikov (born at Khli near Khabarovsk on 11 November 1948; 1.99 m./122 kg.) caught the eye of international observers at the 1974 European Championships in Rome, when he placed fourth at 20.13, while Hartmut Briesenick of East Germany successfully defended his title with a winning toss of 20.50. A few days earlier, in Moscow, the big Russian had set a new European record of 21.70.

Early in 1976, Feuerbach's world record was beaten in a "cold" meet at Honolulu, when Terry Albritton got one off to 21.85. But a few months later, in the US Olympic Trials at Eugene, the new record holder did no better than 20.42 and failed to earn a berth on the Montreal-bound team. Feuerbach won at 21.12, beating Woods by 2 cm. On 10 July at Colombes, Barishnikov became the first adept of the rotation technique to earn an official world record with a toss of 22.00. That was not the end of upsets though. In the Olympic final, the Russian had to be content with a bronze medal, while Feuerbach and Woods were no better than fourth and seventh respectively. At the end of a close battle, young Udo Beyer of East Germany won at 21.05 from Yevgeniy Mironov of USSR (21.03) and Barishnikov (21.00).

Beyer (born at Eisenhüttenstadt on 9 August 1955; 1.95 m./125 kg.) proved to be a durable performer. He had first made the headlines in 1973, winning his event at the European Junior Championships in Duisburg with 19.65. After his upset victory in the 1976 Olympics, he confirmed his class on several occasions: in 1977 he won the World Cup event with 21.74, and on 6 July 1978, at Göteborg, he succeeded Barishnikov as record holder with 22.15. His winning streak continued at the 1978 European Championships (21.08) and in the 1979 World Cup (20.45), but was finally interrupted at the 1980 Olympics in Moscow, when he had to be content with a bronze medal (21.06). Victory went to an unheralded Russian, Vladimir Kiselyov, who did 21.35 - a typical once-in-a-lifetime feat, because Kiselyov never came close to such heights again. Barishnikov was second with 21.08.

DISCUS THROW -
"Too concerned about his injury to worry about anything else"
(That's how Oerter beat four world record holders)

The first man to hurl a discus beyond the 60-metre line was Jay Silvester of USA (born at Tremonton, Utah, on 27 August 1937; 1.89 m./104 kg.). It happened on 11 August 1961 at Frankfort/Main, when he threw the platter 60.56. (As will be related in detail later in this chapter, he was also the first man to better 70 m., albeit unofficially, ten years later). A dedicated thrower, Silvester had no luck in his Olympic ventures. In 1960 he was fourth at the US Olympic Trials and thus failed to make it to Rome. After that initial failure, he competed in four editions of the Olympics, placing fourth in 1964, fifth in '68, second in '72 and eighth in '76!

The history of athletics shows that conventional barriers, once broken, may soon become commonplace affairs. Only five days after Silvester's first 60-metre-plus throw, Edmund Piatkowski of Poland came dangerously close to the new record with a 60.47 effort. Silvester heard the alarm and four days later, on 20 August, he improved to 60.72 at the CISM Games in Brussels. If Silvester was essentially a man for records, his compatriot Al Oerter was above all a supreme competitor. Yet Oerter too had his share of record achievements, and in the eyes of America he had the supreme honour of breaking the 200-foot (60.96) barrier: this happened at Los Angeles on 18 May 1962, when he did 61.10, beating Silvester, among others. Less than a month later, Vladimir Trusenyov became the first thrower from USSR to set a world discus record: 61.64 at Leningrad on 4 June. But Oerter lost little time in fighting back, reaching 62.45 in a dual meet with Poland at Chicago on 1 July. The two-time Olympic champion revised the world record

Randy Matson (USA), Olympic champion and world record holder in the put. Was also a leading discus thrower.

two more times, with 62.62 (Walnut, 27 April 1963) and 62.94 (again at Walnut, 25 April 1964).

By the time he went to the Tokyo Olympics, however, Oerter had a very serious rival in Ludvík Danek of Czechoslovakia (born at Horice, Northern Bohemia, on 6 January 1937; 1.93 m./103 kg.), a man who came to the fore after several years of slow, gradual progress. The Czech made the big jump in 1963, when he reached 60.97. Early in 1964 he came close to Oerter's world record with 62.45, then made it with plenty to spare with a 64.55 throw at Turnov on 2 August. If Danek's condition was splendid, Oerter's certainly wasn't. The reigning Olympic champion had a dislocated cervical vertebra which obliged him to wear a home-made neck brace. His condition got even worse as the Tokyo Games drew near. Wrote Cordner Nelson, Editor of "Track & Field News": "Worst of all, Oerter had torn cartilages in his lower rib cage which hurt so much he had to quit exercising for six days before his event. He was heavily taped and his right side was periodically packed in ice to prevent internal haemorrhaging. Doctors advised him not to throw; he needed six weeks of rest - they said - to heal his wounds. His first practice throw doubled him up in pain. He said: I was thinking of dropping out". But to Oerter the Games were too important to consider quitting. In Tokyo he wore no neck brace, since the pain from that injury was nothing compared with his new problem.

The discus is an event in which experience and nervous tension play a truly dominant role. Oerter had the former and did not fear the latter. Somebody wrote that "he was too concerned about his condition to worry about anything else". Then came D Day and Oerter surprised many people, including himself, by qualifying with 60.54, a new Olympic record! It became apparent that tension would henceforth be in the nerves and arms of his opponents. Danek, who was said to have got one off to 66 m. in training a few days earlier, took the lead in round 4 of the final with 60.52. But in the next round the irrepressible Oerter counter-attacked with a 61.00 effort, and that settled the issue. Danek, a dejected second, was followed by Americans Dave Weill (59.49) and Jay Silvester (59.09). The field included five men who at one time or another had been world record holders: Oerter, Silvester, Danek, Piatkowski (seventh) and Trusenyov (eighth). Oerter won his gold medal by beating the other four!

In the four-year period between Tokyo and Mexico City, Oerter had a somewhat curtailed activity, healing his wounds and building his strength up. Even so, in 1966 he beat Danek at Modesto, 63.22 (a personal best) to 62.73. But the Czech managed to better his own world record twice: 65.22 at Sokolov on 12 October 1965, and 66.07 at Long Beach on 7 June 1966. The latter, however, could not be ratified: there was only one registered judge on hand, and as often as not throws were marked by the competitors themselves!

Jay Silvester had his best season in 1968. He improved on Danek's world record twice, first with 66.54 at Modesto on 25 May, then with 68.40 at Reno on 18 September, aided in the latter case by a good quartering wind. He went to the Mexico Olympics with a 6-1 score vis-à-vis Al Oerter. This seemed to put Al in a difficult, not to say hopeless, position, but

1961
1980

Ludvík Danek (Czechoslovakia), a master in longevity among discus throwers.

259

Ricky Bruch (Sweden), a co-holder of the world record in the discus (68.40 in 1972). (courtesy Å. Lager, Ulricehamn).

in the Olympic arena the great warrior again turned the tables on his most serious rival. No longer hampered by physical problems, between round 3 and round 6 the 32-year-old Oerter uncorked the three longest throws of his career, in the following order: 64.78, 64.74, 64.04. All of these were clearly superior to the best effort of the opposition. Lothar Milde of East Germany was second (63.08), followed by Danek (62.92), Hartmut Losch of East Germany (62.12) and Silvester (61.78), who spoiled an almost flawless seasonal record. Oerter thus won his fourth Olympic gold medal, twelve years after his upset victory in Melbourne. Ironically enough, this looked like the easiest of them all! As Silvester once said: "When you throw against Oerter, you don't expect to win. You just hope". Ludvík Danek, the never-say-die type of athlete, continued with dogged determination and reaped the best fruits towards the end of his long career. In 1971 he went to the European Championships for the fourth time. Prior to that he had placed ninth at Belgrade in 1962 (winner, Trusenyov, 57.11), fifth at Budapest in '66 (winner, Detlef Thorith of East Germany, 57.42), and fourth at Athens in '69 (winner, Hartmut Losch, 61.82). Danek's day finally came at Helsinki in '71, when he won at 63.90, with more than 2 metres to spare.

Still in 1971, Silvester resumed his record breaking spree, bettering 70 m. on two occasions: 70.38 at Lancaster, California, on 16 May, and 70.04 at Ystad, Sweden, on 10 June. Yet neither mark could be ratified. The former occurred in a "picnic" meet held in the Antelope Valley under informal conditions and with the benefit of strong quartering winds. The latter was in a Swedish meet officially registered as a national affair, and Silvester, competing as a guest of his rival and friend Ricky Bruch, was technically a "non-scorer". Bruch himself threw 67.92. Formalities apart, statisticians rightly considered Silvester's mark at Ystad as history's first acceptable 70-metre effort.

The above-mentioned Bruch, one of the most colourful and controversial figures ever to grace (or disgrace) an athletic field, matched Silvester's official world record, 68.40, on 5 July 1972 at Stockholm, beating veteran Ludvík Danek by more than 3 metres. Bruch had bitter-sweet experiences in major meets: eighth in the Mexico Olympics, second in '69 and ninth in '71 at the European Championships. He spent the best of his time and energies in "cold" local affairs, mostly at Malmö, where everything was fixed in such a way as to offer him the best possible conditions for record efforts, even to the point of choosing among different circles the one most favourably exposed to quartering winds. Year in and year out, Bruch would appear in a great number of such "meets". Chances are that in the long run this may have negatively affected his mental approach towards "hot" competitions.

Danek fulfilled his wildest dream at the 1972 Olympics in Munich, aged 35. To make this a really exciting drama, he won on his sixth and last throw with a 64.40 effort, wresting the lead from a bewildered and once more dejected Jay Silvester (63.50), while Bruch was third (63.40), ahead of John Powell of USA (62.82). Even after that great victory, Danek did not let up. At the 1974 European Championships in Rome he won a silver medal at 62.76, behind Pentti Kahma of Finland (63.62) and ahead of Bruch (62.00). He closed his long and glorious career with a ninth place at the 1976 Olympics.

In the meantime, a new generation of throwers had come to the fore. On 14 March 1975 at Stellenbosch, a South African standing 2.02 m. in his socks, John Van Reenen, had a field day: after throwing 68.06 in an invitational event, he had another competition arranged by officials for his own benefit, and in this one he exceeded the world record with 68.48. This mark was ratified by the IAAF, since South Africa - although banned from the Olympics - had not until then been ousted from the international body (this happened a few months later). Still in 1975, namely on 4 May at Long Beach, John Powell brought the record back to USA with a 69.08 throw.

By the time of the Montreal Olympics (1976), however, two new figures towered above the rest: Mac Wilkins of USA and Wolfgang Schmidt of East Germany. The American (born at Eugene on 15 November 1950; 1.93 m./115 kg.) was a great all-round thrower. In the course of his career he put together the following series: 21.06 (shot, indoors), 70.98 (discus), 63.66 (hammer) and 78.44 (javelin). The man with the flowing beard was obviously at his best in the discus: in 1975 he was pretty close to the élite with 66.78, and in the pre-Olympic weeks of 1976 he really set the world on fire. He succeeded Powell as record holder in April with 69.18, then had a great day at San Jose on 1 May, when his first three tries resulted in just as many improvements on his own world record: 69.80, 70.24, 70.86. John Powell was second with 67.16.

Wolfgang Schmidt (born at Berlin on 16 January 1954; 1.99 m./110 kg.) was to have a long and very troubled career. His name first appeared in the world press in connection with the 1973 European Junior Championships at Duisburg, where he won the discus (58.16) and was second to his compatriot Udo Beyer in the shot (18.54). In the spring of 1976 he captured the European discus record with 68.60. In the Montreal Olympics he was Wilkins' most serious rival. The American led the qualifiers with a mighty 68.28, a new Olympic record. In the final he found things a bit more difficult but finally won with 67.50, while Schmidt was second (66.22), ahead of John Powell (65.70).

In the following years, Schmidt and Wilkins met again on several occasions and the German had the upper hand in two editions of the World Cup: 67.14 to 66.64 at Düsseldorf in 1977, 66.02 to 64.92 at Montreal in '79. And on 9 August 1978 at Berlin, Schmidt wrested the global mark from his American rival and friend with 71.16. Even after that, Wilkins was confidently looking forward to defending his Olympic title in 1980. He had an excellent season, with 68.68 at the Olympic Trials and a new personal best of 70.98 at the World Games in Helsinki. As an American, however, he had to stay away from the Moscow event. In the Olympic final, Schmidt was hampered by a bad ankle and wound up in fourth place with 65.64. Viktor Rashchupkin of USSR, who in pre-meet predictions was at best considered an outsider, joined the group of Russians who had the luckiest day of their life in those Games and won with 66.64, a new personal best. The other medals went to Imrich Bugar of Czechoslovakia (66.38) and Luis Mariano Delis of Cuba (66.32). The last-named, one of the few black athletes ever to emerge in the top ranks of this event, thought his last throw was worth more than the

1961
1980

The peerless Oerter (Part 2)

After his fourth Olympic victory (Mexico City, 1968) Al Oerter had one more season of curtailed activity, then decided to leave the discus circle to concentrate on his family life and his job as a computer engineer. For eight years the world of athletics never heard about him again, save for occasional rumours about a possible comeback for the 1972 and 1976 Olympics. Until 1977, when he returned to action and amazed the track world with 60-metre-plus efforts. In 1979 he improved to 67.46, almost 3 metres over his personal best in Part 1 of his career! On 31 May 1980, at Wichita, Kansas, he caught a good breeze and reached 69.46. In the meantime, the Rest of the World had not stood still, yet that mark placed the 44-year-old Oerter fifth in the World All Time List as of the end of 1980. In the same year he competed in the US Olympic Trials at Eugene and finished fourth with 65.56, behind Wilkins (68.68), Powell and Ben Plucknett. Of course, the Trials had only a symbolic value, since USA had decided to stay away from the Moscow Olympics. Al's many admirers liked to believe that if the Trials had counted as real Trials he would have placed at least third .... In Part 2 of his career Oerter often trained really hard, probably harder than he had done in his younger days. He worked with the weights and also took advantage of finer technical points he had learned of late. But it was quite obvious that his mental approach had changed to some extent. He no longer had the "voracious appetite" that characterized him in Part 1 of his career. Even so, he went on for several more years, and as late as in 1988, aged 52, he managed a throw of 58.44, which ranked him no. 167 in the World List of that year, published in the ATFS Annual.

distance he was credited with, 66.32. According to "Track & Field News", he "was certainly robbed of the silver, perhaps the gold" due to a faulty measurement. In his excellent book "The 1980 Olympics - Track and Field", Finnish journalist Tapio Pekola said Delis' last throw was worth "about 67 metres".

Even apart from the wondrous feats of "old-timers", things had been moving swiftly during the Sixties. An interesting newsitem was offered by Silvano Simeon, the man who succeeded Adolfo Consolini as Italian record holder. By 1967 this fine athlete had improved to 61.72 and in the same year he competed in the America vs. Europe dual meet at Montreal, finishing second to Danek, 60.46 to 60.99. But in 1968 he had to undergo surgery in USA to eliminate a serious heart problem (narrowing of the descending aorta). Believe it or not, he staged a comeback and in 1976, aged thirty-one, he reached 65.10. By then, however, the élite of the event was far ahead ....

HAMMER THROW - Russia's richest flower-bed

Vasiliy Rudenkov of USSR, the 1960 Olympic champion, never entered the list of world record holders, yet he proved a reliable competitor on big occasions. By comparison, Harold Connolly of USA showed greater potential but had ups and downs as a competitor. On 21 July 1962, during the USA vs USSR dual meet at Palo Alto, he had a splendid series, the shortest of six valid throws being 68.58 and the longest 70.67, a new world record. Incidentally, the meet was attended by a crowd of 153,000 for the two days, the largest in US track history. Still in 1962, Gyula Zsivótzky of Hungary won the European title at 69.64 and came close to Connolly's mark with a 70.42 effort.

The 1964 Olympics in Tokyo saw another Russian on top: Romuald Klim (born at Khvoyevo near Minsk on 25 May 1933; 1.85 m./102 kg.), one of the coolest competitors ever seen in hammer cages. Like many other Russians of those days, he reached the top after many years of slow but steady progress. In Tokyo he won with a throw of 69.74. Zsivótzky, who in the winter had undergone two abdominal operations, was an excellent second at 69.09, ahead of 19-year-old Uwe Beyer of West Germany, whose 68.09 was a new world junior record. Connolly had thrown over 70 m. again in a pre-Olympic meet in California, but in the Games he was very disappointing: sixth with 66.65. In the following years, Klim proved a portent in terms of consistency and reliability. He won the 1966 European title at Budapest with 70.02, with Zsivótzky again second (68.62). Connolly continued to have long throws now and then and in 1965 he twice bettered his own world record, first with 71.06, then with 71.26, the latter at Walnut on 20 June. But the last word for the year came from Zsivótzky, who on 4 September at Debrecen became the third Hungarian to set a world hammer record with a mighty 73.75 (officially ratified as 73.74 in compliance with a new rule whereby measurements in the long throws - discus, hammer, javelin - had to be taken in even centimetres). Before the meet he had a warm-up throw of "about 76 m.". Such differences are quite common: they can be explained with the nervous tension that prevails in the competition proper, and/or the looseness with which unofficial throws are often measured.

Zsivótzky did it again three years later, shortly before the Mexico Olympics: in a meet at Budapest on 14 September he improved by the narrowest of margins, to 73.77 (ratified as 73.76). Even after that, however, most observers thought he would continue to play second fiddle to Klim on big occasions. But in the Olympic final the trend was finally reversed. Klim threw 73.28 in round 4, but the Hungarian was quick to answer in round 5 with 73.36. A narrow but most significant victory. Lázár Lovász of Hungary and Takeo Sugawara of Japan both threw 69.78, and the former clinched the bronze on the strength of second-best throw. By then, however, USSR was firmly established as the no.1 hammer power in terms of both quality and quantity. Good coaching and useful training clinics, usually held at Sochi on the Black Sea, gave the best men a chance to maximize their potential under favourable conditions. The always redoubtable Klim finally made the record book in an international meet at Budapest on 15 June 1969, when he scored an easy victory over his compatriot Anatoliy Bondarchuk and Zsivótzky with a 74.52 throw. Later in the year, at the European Championships in Athens, Bondarchuk turned the tables on Klim with a new record performance, 74.68 to 72.74. The new champion (born at Staro-Konstantinovka on 31 May 1940; 1.83 m./112 kg.) did even better before the end of the season, reaching 75.48 in a meet at Rovno. A rather unusual circumstance: this record was made shortly before noon.

Germans from both West and East provided the only notable opposition to the powerful Russian cohort, and occasionally had their share of success, e.g. at the 1971 European Championships in Helsinki, when Uwe Beyer (West) and Reinhard Theimer (East) finished one-two in that order, ahead of Bondarchuk and Klim. Beyer won at 72.36. Fifth place went to

1961 1980

another West German, Walter Schmidt, who only a few days later, at Lahr, beat Bondarchuk's world record with 76.41 (ratified as 76.40). This was a "cold" meet in the strictest sense of the word: the guy who finished second did no better than 40.05.
At the Munich Olympics (1972), the Russians again took over and struck gold with the reliable Bondarchuk (75.50), who won from Jochen Sachse of East Germany (74.96) and Vasiliy Khmyelevskiy of USSR (74.04), while Uwe Beyer was fourth (71.52) and the 35-year-old Zsivótzky fifth (71.38). Record holder Schmidt did not compete.
Hyper-intensive training and the refinement of technique allowed the record breaking spree to continue almost unabated. In 1974, Reinhard Theimer of East Germany threw 76.60 at Leipzig on 4 July. But the Russians regained lane 1 later in the season, when Aleksey Spiridonov reached 76.66 in an international meet at Munich on 11 September. A few days earlier, Spiridonov had won the European title in Rome, beating Jochen Sachse of East Germany by a narrow margin, 74.20 to 74.00, while Theimer was a distant third.
In the long run, however, the most valid figure of the German school was Karl-Hans Riehm (born at Konz near Trier on 31 May 1951; 1.87 m./118 kg.). Well co-ordinated in every phase of the exercise, this West German athlete bettered 70 m. at twenty and two years later he improved to 73.98. Early in 1975 he did 75.29, then went wild on 19 May at Rehlingen, where he achieved the seemingly impossible, a series of six valid throws all over the listed world record: 76.70 - 77.56 - 77.10 - 78,50 - 77.16 - 77.28. Second in that memorable event was Schmidt (74.56). Said the jovial Riehm: "Everything went just right today, but I think the record will be broken again pretty soon". And he mentioned Schmidt among his possible successors. The latter was regarded by his own coach as "an unstable soul" for his tendency to suffer when competitive pressure was on. Following his record throw of 1971 (76.40), Schmidt had recurrent muscular ailments which kept him away from the 1972 Olympics. When he finally recovered, he decided to train harder than ever (a close observer once described his training loads as "not human"). Then came his happiest day, 14 August 1975, when he surpassed Riehm's recent world record with 79.30. The meet, held at Frankfort/Main, was labelled "Werfer Tag" (Throwers' Day), but in actual fact Schmidt was the only competent thrower in the circle, the second place man doing no better than 44.14. At any rate, that was to remain a solitary firework. Schmidt continued to be disappointing in big meets. In 1977 he was suspended by DLV, West Germany's athletics federation, for doping abuse.
In 1973 the athletics world heard for the first time the name of the man who was to become the greatest hammer thrower of modern times, Yuriy Syedikh (born at Novocherkassk near Rostov on 11 June 1955; 1.85 m./102 kg.). That was when Syedikh won the European Junior championship title at Duisburg with 67.32. The following year he beat 70 m. and in 1975 he joined the élite with 75.00. He was coached by former world record holder Anatoliy Bondarchuk, who was still active in the hammer circle. In 1976 the pupil excelled his teacher, first with an early season throw of 78.86, then by beating him in the Olympic final at Montreal.
Syedikh won at 77.52 from Aleksey Spiridonov (76.08) and Bondarchuk (75.48), who shunted Riehm (75.46) to fourth by the narrowest of margins and thus made it a clean sweep for the Russian school. That was the first in a long series of major honours for the impeccable Syedikh. He began to be known in the hammer fraternity as a cool competitor and a master technician. His coach once listed as main features of Yuriy's technique his "keeping ideally straight arms throughout the (three) turns and an excellent balance in all support phases", and his realization that "the hammer head, not the body of the athlete, is the leading link in the thrower/hammer system". For some reason, Syedikh was generally if not always at his best in even years. 1977 was no exception to the rule: at the inaugural World Cup in Düsseldorf he was no better than fourth as Riehm narrowly won from Jochen Sachse of East Germany, 75.64 to 75.40. The 80-metre barrier was broken on 9 July 1978 in Moscow by a 31-year-old Russian, Boris Zaichuk, who reached 80.14 on his first try. A relatively unheralded performer, he was the easternmost talent of the Russian school, hailing from Tokmak in Kirghizia, only 300 km. away from the Chinese border. Fifteen years of hard work, with slow but steady progress, eventually landed him in the record holders' society. Yet he always remained in the shadow of the Big Guns. His record was bettered a few weeks later by Karl-Hans Riehm, who got one off to 80.32 on 6 August at Heidenheim. The most important test of the year, the European Championships in Prague, provided a virtual photo finish, with Syedikh (77.28) narrowly edging Roland Steuk of East Germany (77.24) and Riehm (77.02), while Zaichuk was sixth (75.62). In the meantime, another figure had emerged from the cohort of Soviet ball-and-chain adepts: Sergey Litvinov (born at Tsukarov, Krasnodar region, on 23 January 1958; 1.80 m./95 kg.). At the tender age of 17 this most

promising athlete finished third at the European Junior Championships in Athens with 64.44. Rather inconspicuous in physical build, he could generate tremendous speed. At twenty-one he entered the big game with a bang, thrashing Riehm in the World Cup at Montreal, 78.70 to 75.88. (It should be noticed that Syedikh was having one of his low-profile odd-year seasons, apparently meant to allow him a spell of physical and mental relaxation). It was soon noticed that Litvinov was using four turns in the circle, instead of three as did Syedikh and most of the other leading throwers. More on this in the adjoining aside.
1980 was a momentous year for Russian hammer throwers. Prior to the Moscow Olympics, the world record was bettered four times. It all began in a tune-up meet at Leselidze on 16 May, when Syedikh got the ball rolling with a throw of 80.38, only to be overtaken fifteen minutes later by Jüri Tamm, who got one off to 80.46. Another twenty minutes later, the irrepressible Syedikh was back in the lead with 80.64. On 24 May at Sochi there came Litvinov, who threw 81.66, beating Zaichuk, Syedikh and Tamm. Syedikh eventually regained full control of the situation in the Meet of the Year, the Olympic final (31 July). His first throw was a real "killer": 81.80, a new world record. His compatriots had "no answer" to that, yet they made it a clean sweep for Russia, with Litvinov second (80.64) and Tamm third (78.96). Steuk of East Germany was fourth (77.54). As a representative of West Germany, Riehm could not compete in Moscow. If present, he might have posed a problem to his Russian colleagues. He was in excellent form in those days, and he proved it in post-Olympic meets, beating Syedikh twice (by narrow margins), Litvinov and Tamm once each.

JAVELIN THROW - The golden years of Janis Lusis

Italy had never played a prominent role in javelin throwing, but athletics is an individual sport, so anything can happen sooner or later, virtually anywhere. The bright exception came early in the Sixties with Carlo Lievore. A powerful thrower, he had learned some of the finer points of technique from his elder brother Giovanni, who was sixth in the 1956 Olympics at Melbourne and threw 80.72 two years later. In 1960 Carlo was one of the world's leading men with 83.60, but sustained an injury three weeks before the Olympics and in Rome he could do no better than ninth. His lucky day came on 1 June 1961 at Milan, when he sent his "Held" metal javelin well beyond the boundaries of the field - to 86.74, a new world record. Later in the season he supplied supporting evidence with a throw of 84.30. Be it for his proneness to injuries or other reasons, he never won a major honour. At the 1962 European Championships in Belgrade he bettered 80 m. in the qualifying rounds but dropped to sixth in the final.
The IAAF had by then decided to approve the "Held javelin", were it only in a modified version vis-à-vis original models. There can be no doubt that the aerodynamic properties of this type of javelin have accounted to a large extent for the advancement of standards.
A most unpredicatble thrower was Terje Pedersen of Norway (born at Oslo on 9 February 1943; 1.93

Three or four turns?

One of the main items of discussion in hammer circles during the late Seventies concerned the number of turns taken by leading throwers before unleashing the implement - three or four.
Anatoliy Bondarchuk, one of the world's leading authorities on the subject, once wrote ("Track Technique", fall 1978): "It is the opinion of the author that three turns are at the moment more efficient and still open for many avenues of improvement. Four turns can be recommended only to athletes who are unable to reach maximum velocity with three turns, and are capable of controlling the extra speed by changing the throwing rhythm and developing specific speed. Although the three-turn technique enables throwers to reach the 75/80 m. range without difficulty, it is possible that four or more turns will be used by future hammer throwers, provided they have considerably more specific speed than the top performers of today".
This was written in 1978, when Syedikh, the best "interpreter" of the three-turn technique, was ruling the roost, and Litvinov was just coming up. The latter, a pupil of I.Timashkov, was to become the best exponent of the four-turn style. However, several years of hard work were necessary before he could reach fully satisfactory results. Four turns were to become more frequent towards the end of the Eighties.

m./93 kg.). This gifted athlete reached 60 m. at fifteen, 76.76 m. at seventeen and 83.90 at twenty. 1964 was his greatest year, but with joy and sorrow strangely intertwined. An inconsistent performer if ever there was one, his seasonal record ranged from a dismal 63.53 at Copenhagen, placing seventh, to a world record of 91.72 at Oslo. This dental student succeeded Lievore on 1 July at Oslo with 87.12. Whoever thought this was just a lucky accident had reason to reconsider when he got one off to 91.72, still at Oslo's Bislett stadium, on 2 September. The latter distance had the power of impressing both the metric and the English world, since it exceeded 90 metres and 300 feet as well. Just like Yrjö Nikkanen twenty-six years earlier, Pedersen emerged from that monumental record throw with a pain in his back and had to pass his remaining trials, "putting off the first 100 m. throw to a later time", as he smartly said. Unfortunately, Pedersen had no time for jokes at the Tokyo Olympics, where he was ushered out after three unimpressive throws (61.39, 66.78, 72.10) in the qualifying round. In the final the gold medal went to Pauli Nevala of Finland at 82.66, the place winners being Gergely Kulcsár of Hungary (82.32) and Janis Lusis of USSR (80.57), while Janusz Sidlo was fourth (80.17). The Finn, a sturdy competitor, had topped the 1963 World List with 86.33. In terms of consistency and longevity, Janusz Sidlo must be ranked among the greatest ever in throwing events. He appeared among the top ten in "Track & Field News" World Ranking for eighteen straight years (1953-70)! He was first five times (1954, 1957-60), second six times (1953, 1955-56, 1963-64 and 1966), and third once (1961). As irony and the ruthless law of progress would have it, his poorest placing (tenth) was in 1970, when he did 86.22 - his lifetime best. In subsequent years his interest inevitably waned, and so did his condition, yet he still managed 53.68 at the age of fity. If compared with such a fantastic record, his harvest in major Games was good but not exceptional: he was European champion twice (1954 and '58) but in the Olympics he had to be content with a silver medal (1956). A better competitive record was shown by Janis Lusis, a Latvian representing USSR (born at Jelgava, Latvia, on 19 May 1939; 1.80 m./84 kg.). He won Olympic medals three times: bronze in 1964, gold in '68 and silver in '72, when he was beaten by 2 cms. He set an all-time record for number of wins in a single event at the European Championships: four - with 82.04 at Belgrade in 1962, 84.48 at Budapest in '66, 91.52 at Athens in '69, and 90.68 at Helsinki in '71. Lusis was a most versatile athlete: he scored 7483 pts. in the decathlon, then did 11.2 (100 m.), 15.5 (110 m. hurdles), 1.92 (high jump), 3.80 (pole vault), 7.23 (long jump), 15.16 (shot) and 41.18 (discus). In his parade event he made "Track & Field News" World Ranking for thirteen straight years. True, Janusz Sidlo could point to a higher score (18), but Lusis' record was definitely more impressive in terms of quality, including no less than 9 first places, as shown in the adjoining table. Lusis set his first world record in the Temple of javelin throwing, Finland, namely at Saarijärvi on 23 June 1968, with 91.98. Later in the year he won the gold medal in the Olympic final at Mexico City with a solid 90.10, beating Jorma Kinnunen of Finland (88.58) and Gergely Kulcsár of Hungary (87.06).

Kinnunen, a sturdy little man, was a very active thrower. In the summer months he would take many hours off his job as a carpenter to compete all over Finland at relentless rhythm. He had his big day on

1961
1980

Gyula Zsivótzky (Hungary), a two-time Olympic silver medallist in the hammer throw. Held the world record with 73.76 (1968).

265

18 June 1969 at Tampere (Matti Järvinen's native town), when he got one off to 92.70, a new world record. On that occasion he won from Pauli Nevala (84.30). The latter (born at Pohja on 30 November 1940; 1.78 m./82 kg.) never figured in the list of world record holders, yet he was a very good competitor, generally more reliable than Kinnunen. At twenty-one he had caused quite a stir with an 84-plus throw. After that, eight years went by before he could finally better 90 m. with a 91.40 throw. In the same year (1969) he was Lusis' most serious rival at the European Championships in Athens. The Latvian opened with a "killer", 91.52, and Nevala answered with an honourable but not adequate 89.58. Kinnunen was a disappointing tenth. Two years later, at Helsinki, Lusis successfully defended his title. On this occasion he had no opposition worthy of the name and won by more than 5 metres with 90.68.

By then an odds-on favourite for the 1972 Olympic crown, Lusis added further credibility to his claim on 6 July of that year at Stockholm, when he got one off to 93.80 on his opening throw. At the Munich Olympics, however, the great Lusis was administered a bitter pill. A few days before the competition, Klaus Wolfermann of West Germany had thrown 90.10 in a tune-up meet at small Poststadion in Munich. In the opening round of the Olympic final Lusis took the lead with 88.88, but in round 4 Wolfermann came close with 88.40. That really ignited the home crowd. In the next round the bearded German sent the javelin flying - it was thunder in the stadium by the time the implement landed well beyond the 90-metre line, to a new Olympic and West German record of 90.48. Lusis, with only one throw left, was obviously in a tight corner, yet he reacted as only a great champion could do. He said to himself: "This must go over 90 metres". It did, but the distance, measured amidst the anguish of the predominantly German crowd, turned out to be 90.46, i.e. insufficient by the narrowest margin (2 cm.) allowed by IAAF rules for the "long throws" (discus, hammer, javelin). In the interview room, Wolfermann and Lusis were invited to sign their names on a special blackboard reserved for Olympic VIP's, and the runner-up wrote under his name the figures 93.80, his current world record, as if pointing to a target for Wolfermann's future. The quiet German got the message and on 5 May 1973 at Leverkusen he threw 94.08.

Lusis - His roaring years			
Year	Age	Best mark	Rank
1962	(23)	86.04	1.
1963	(24)	83.65	1.
1964	(25)	82.59	5.
1965	(26)	86.56	1.
1966	(27)	85.70	1.
1967	(28)	90.98	1.
1968	(29)	91.98*	1.
1969	(30)	91.52	1.
1970	(31)	88.02	6.
1971	(32)	90.68	1.
1972	(33)	93.80*	1.
1973	(34)	91.32	2.
1974	(35)	84.08	7.

* World Record
(Lusis did 81.01 in 1961 and 86.32 in '76, at 37)

"Gutta cavat lapidem"

In the annals of athletics there are many instances of members of the same family who figured prominently in the Olympics, at different times or even in the same edition of the Games. As of now, however, there is only one instance of a gold medal transmitted, so to speak, from father to son. It belongs to the Némeths of Hungary. Miklós Németh probably became an athletics addict under the influence of his father, Imre, who in early post-war years had been Olympic champion and world record holder in the hammer. As befits an independent thinker, however, young Miklós shied away from the heavy ball-and-chain and opted for the volatile javelin. But his career was for many years one of unfulfilled promises. Although he reached excellent distances soon (87.20 at twenty-one), his results on big occasions were by comparison unsatisfactory. Best he could do was fifth in the European Championships in '66 and seventh in the Olympics in '72. Miklós obviously did not like to be referred to as a "steady loser". Nor did his father, who in the meantime had become a leading sport authority as well as a Member of Parliament. When just about everybody had given up on Hungary's onetime boy-wonder, Miklós fought back. He was almost thirty when he finally did himself justice with a perfect stroke, winning the most coveted of titles with a world record throw.

The Finns had obviously lost their onetime monopoly, yet remained a noble set in the javelin fraternity, and occasionally they would send others a "reminder". As it happened in the 1974 European Championships in Rome, when the consistent Hannu Siitonen won with 89.58. Lusis, by then 35, was sixth at 83.06, 30 cm. behind Klaus Wolfermann.

An even greater upset occurred at the 1976 Olympics in Montreal on 26 July, when Miklós Németh of Hungary (born at Budapest on 23 October 1946; 1.83 m./88 kg.) came up with a world record of 94.58 in the opening round of the final: a real "killer", if ever there was one. Hannu Siitonen was second (87.92) and Gheorghe Megelea of Romania caused another surprise by finishing third (87.16). The indestructible Lusis was eighth.

Winner of the javelin in the inaugural edition of the World Cup (Düsseldorf, 1977) was Michael Wessing of West Germany, who did 87.46, beating Németh among others. The German went on to annex the European title at Prague in 1978 with 89.12. Wolfgang Hanisch of East Germany was second at Düsseldorf and third at Prague. His turn came the following year at Montreal, when he won the World Cup event with 86.48.

But the man who relieved Németh of his world record was another Hungarian, stocky Ferenc Paragi. He caused quite a stir when he sent his javelin 96.72 on his first attempt during a Throwers' meet at Tata on 23 April 1980. In doing so the 27-year-old Hungarian improved on his previous best by nearly four and a half metres. Another fine throw (96.20) later in the season seemed to project him as an odds-on favourite for the Moscow Olympics. In fact, he looked good as he led the qualifiers with 88.76, but in the final he lost contact with his real self and had to settle for tenth at 79.52. It should be added that this massive thrower was plagued by injuries for the greater part of his career. Unfortunately, the Moscow event gave rise to controversy when a judge ruled valid Dainis Kula's throw (88.88) in round 3 of the final, which enabled the USSR representative (who had fouled twice in his previous attempts) to advance to the last three rounds at the expense of Aimo Aho of Finland. In the opinion of neutral observers, Kula's javelin landed tail first. As such the throw should have been ruled a foul, in accordance with IAAF rule 186/5/b ("No throw shall be valid in which the tip of the metal head does not strike the ground before any other part of the javelin"). After passing unscathed through that crucial point, Kula showed his gratefulness for the "gift" by getting one off to 91.20, a throw that eventually gave him the gold medal. His teammate Aleksandr Makarov was second (89.64) and Wolfgang Hanisch of East Germany took third place (86.72). Kula a was at any rate an excellent thrower. After his victory in Moscow he ranked among the best in the world for three more years. As a Latvian, however, he was at best a pale replica of the great Janis Lusis, he too a Latvian.

1961
1980

Janis Lusis (USSR), one of the greatest javelin throwers of all time.

Early "killers"

The javelin is a light, volatile implement, but throwing it to record distances is a demanding job for anyone. Exertion on the muscles of the throwing arm and the psycho-physical tension that goes with it are so great that as often as not even the greatest of champions must be content with one or two long throws per meet. In this event a consistent series of six long throws is a rarity. Not surprisingly, record marks prevalently occur in the early rounds of the competition, i.e. when the thrower is at his best in terms of freshness. Between 1961 and 1984 the world record was bettered eleven times. Four of these record throws occurred in round 1, six in round 2 and only one in round 5.

DECATHLON - Euro-American feud

In 1961 Rafer Johnson's world record was beaten by his countryman Phil Mulkey, a 28-year-old outsider who amassed 8709 pts (8049 under 1985 Table) in a District AAU meet at Memphis. One reporter said that he was so exhausted after the 1500 m. that he was unable to walk for 30 minutes. And his pulse was up to 210, as compared with his normal rate of 42. Due to a technicality, however, his score never made the IAAF book. Still in 1961, Vasiliy Kuznyetsov was dethroned as European record holder by his countryman Yuriy Kutyenko, who was credited with a score of 8361 pts at Kiev. This 29-year-old veteran had placed fourth at the 1954 European Championships and in the 1960 Olympics. A kidney disease kept him away from the 1962 European Championships in Belgrade, where Kuznyetsov won the continental title for the third time after a fierce battle with Werner von Moltke of West Germany. At the end only four points (8026 - 8022) separated them, a virtual photo finish in decathlon terms. A margin of dubious significance, if one considers that they ran in different heats in three of the four track events, notably including the last one. In fact, Kuznyetsov had the advantage of running the 1500 m. in a later heat, so he knew exactly what he needed to emerge the winner vis-à-vis von Moltke: a time of 4:41.3. He did 4:41.0! When the battle was over, Count von Moltke behaved as the gentleman he was, shaking hands with his great rival. Nowadays the decathlon rule says that in the 1500 m. "one group (i.e. heat) should preferably contain the leading competitors at the end of nine events". As a result, the final issue is decided in a head-to-head competition. Yang Chuan-kwang, one of the heroes of the 1960 Olympic decathlon, rose to the status of world record holder in the spring of 1963 at Walnut, California, when he amassed 9121 pts (8009 under 1985 Table). His series notably included a 4.84 in the pole vault. However, Rooney Magnusson of Sweden, a keen student of decathlon marks, says that Yang actually got points (1515) for a 4.82 vault, since the Scoring Table in use at the time did not extend beyond that mark, centimetre-wise! (The fibreglass era had just begun....). At the 1962 IAAF Congress in Belgrade a new table had been introduced, which generally yielded lower ratings. For example, Yang's world record score (9121) was reduced to 8089 pts. The Tokyo Olympics (1964) marked the decline of both Yang and Kuznyetsov, who could do no better than fifth and seventh respectively. Willi Holdorf of West Germany won with 7887 pts from Rein Aun of USSR (7842) and Hans-Joachim Walde (7809). Werner von Moltke staged a brilliant comeback in 1966 and won the European title at Budapest with 7740 pts. His teammates Jörg Mattheis, second, and Horst Beyer, third, made it a clean sweep for West Germany. Chief "mentor" of the West German multiple-event school was coach Friedel Schirmer, who in his younger days had been a good decathlon man (eighth in the 1952 Olympics). Americans were back in the picture in the late Sixties with two powerful athletes, Bill Toomey and Russ Hodge. The former (born at Philadelphia on 10 January 1939; 1.86 m./88 kg.) excelled in the 400 m. and the long jump, while the latter was primarily a good thrower. At the 1966 AAU decathlon championship, held at Salina, Kansas, both exceeded Yang's world record, with Toomey the winner at 8234 pts and Hodge second at 8130. However, contradictory evidence on wind assistance in the long jump and the high hurdles prevented ratification. Three weeks later, at Los Angeles, the two met again and finished in inverse order: Hodge 8230, Toomey 8219. The winning score (which would convert to 8119 under the 1985 Table) made the IAAF book.

By then West Germany had a bright new prospect in well-built Kurt Bendlin (born at Thorn, East Prussia, on 22 May 1943; 1.83 m./87 kg.). He was brought up near Eutin, birthplace of Hans-Heinrich Sievert, Germany's first world class man in the decathlon. That coincidence probably inspired young Bendlin to use his heavy muscles to good advantage in the 10-event grind. Unfortunately, he was hampered for the greater part of his career by what the Germans call "Verletzungsmisere", the plague of injuries. In the spring of 1967, at Heidelberg, Bendlin put together a total of 8319 pts (8234 under 1985 Table) for a new world record. He had a uniform series of marks, notably including 10.6 (100 m.), 47.9 (400 m.), 74.85 (javelin) and 4:19.4 (1500 m.). The last mark in particular told a lot about the new conditioning methods of decathlon champions: until then no world record breaker had ever done better than 4:30.0 in the tenth and last event.

The hottest chapter of the USA vs West Germany feud unfolded at the Mexico Olympics (1968). Bill Toomey finally emerged the winner with 8193 pts, while Walde shunted Bendlin to third, 8111 to 8064. The American had a crucial moment in the pole vault, where he needed three tries to master the initial height (3.60), but went on to clear 4.20. Bendlin had a bad elbow, yet managed 75.42 in the javelin, possibly his best event. After that, the German was second, fairly close on Toomey's heels (7708 to 7764). But Toomey won the last tussle over 1500 m. Here

1961
1980

Nikolay Avilov (USSR), Olympic decathlon champion in 1972.

Bendlin did so poorly that he had to give way to Walde for the silver medal. Generally speaking, Toomey was able to take full advantage in short-lived efforts favoured by high altitude, notably with a 45.6 in the 400 m.

Toomey had his best season in 1969, when he completed nine decathlons in the space of six months - and won them all. In the very last of the series, a record attempt at Los Angeles in December, he got off to a Blitz-Start with 10.3 in the 100 m. and 7.76 in the long jump, and finally bettered Bendlin's score with 8417 pts (8309 under 1985 Table). That was the finishing touch. A week later he celebrated by marrying Mary Bignal Rand of Britain, the 1964 Olympic long jump champion, herself a great all-round performer.

After Toomey's retirement, Europe regained control of the situation. Joachim Kirst of East Germany won the continental title twice, with 8041 pts in 1969 and 8196 pts in '71. At the 1972 Olympics in Munich, a man towered above the rest with a superlative series of marks. He was Nikolay Avilov of USSR (born at Odessa, Ukraine, on 6 August 1948; 1.91 m./90 kg.), who had caught the eye of expert observers at the 1968 Olympics in Mexico City, placing fourth with 7909 pts at the age of twenty. At Munich he piled up a grand total of 8454 pts (8467 under 1985 Table), leaving his countryman Leonid Litvinyenko (8035) more than 400 pts behind. Scores of 8000 pts or better were fairly frequent by then, yet the demand of such efforts, with the hard training that went with them, was becoming apparent through an increasing series of injuries. Avilov himself had to pay his toll, and in 1974 he had to stay away from the European Championships in Rome. The title went to Ryszard Skowronek of Poland (8207 pts).

Virtually the first American to show uniform strength in most if not all events was Bruce Jenner (born at Mt.Kisco, New York, on 28 October 1949; 1.88 m./88 kg.). Over a three-year period (1974-76) he competed in thirteen decathlons and lost only once, at the 1975 AAU Championship, when he failed to master the opening height in the pole vault. A few weeks after that failure he broke Avilov's world record with 8524 pts (8420 under 1985 Table). That was at Eugene, Oregon, known since the early Seventies as the new Mecca of America's track. Again at Eugene, during the 1976 US Olympic Trials, Jenner improved to 8538 pts (8454 under 1985 Table).His escalation culminated in a great victory at the Montreal Olympics the following month, when he won the gold medal with his best-ever score, 8618 pts (8634 under 1985 Table). This was a great competition, with Guido Kratschmer of West Germany second (8411)

and Avilov third (8369). It was on that occasion that eagle-eyed experts began to rave about an 18- year-old Briton, who finished 18th with 7330 pts. He was Francis Morgan ("Daley") Thompson (born in London on 30 July 1958 of a Nigerian father and Scottish mother; 1.86 m./84 kg.). In spite of his age, at Montreal he was competing in his sixth decathlon, having made his début in 1975 with a score of 6523 pts. Later in '76 he improved to 7905 (with manual timing in the running events). The following year he captured the World Junior record with 8124 pts and won the European Junior title at Donyetsk. Since his earliest days in the sport he proved a phenomenal competitor. Ever ready for a wise-crack off the field, he became tremendously serious when engaged in the 10-event grind against strong opponents. His determination was simply ferocious. And he would always rise to the occasion when a serious challenge was on. In 1978 he won the British Commonwealth title at Edmonton with 8467 pts, notable among his marks being a wind-aided 8.11 in the long jump. Only three weeks later he finished second to Aleksandr Grebenyuk of USSR at the European Championships in Prague, 8289 to 8340. After that he would be untouchable for several years to come.

When Jenner retired after his victory at Montreal, Americans began to take the back seat to Europe. Yet they had some good men in the late Seventies, like Fred Dixon and Bob Coffman. But USA, like West Germany, boycotted the 1980 Moscow Olympics. In those Games the Russians surpassed themselves in a good many events, but in the decathlon they had to bow to Daley Thompson. The Briton had started his 1980 account with a bang, breaking the world record in the traditional "decathlon festival" at Götzis, Austria, in May, with a score of 8622 pts (8648 under 1985 Table).In the Olympics he won with 8495 pts from two Russians, Yuriy Kutsenko (8331) and Sergey Zhelanov (8135).

In the intervening time, however, Thompson's record had been eclipsed at Bernhausen by Guido Kratschmer, who compiled 8649 pts (8667 under 1985 Table).

RELAYS - 4x100 m.
Hayes:
"Just give it to me close"

The third USSR vs USA dual meet, held in Moscow on 15 July 1961, offered among other things a superlative sprint relay. An American team with

1961 1980

Hayes Jones, Frank Budd, Charles Frazier and Paul Drayton lowered the world record to 39.1. Even more surprising perhaps was the time of the USSR team, 39.4, since Edvin Ozolin, Nikolay Politiko, Yuriy Konovalov and Leonid Bartenyev were good but not exceptional sprinters, at any rate hardly capable of beating 10.4 in the century under competitive conditions. A year later, at the European Championships in Belgrade, the Russians inexplicably flopped, failing to make the final. West Germany, with Manfred Germar in the anchor leg, nipped Poland for the title (both 39.5).

A new IAAF rule introduced in 1960 made the full-lap (i.e. two turns) course mandatory for any record set in the sprint relay. Shortly before the Tokyo Olympics (1964), however, this disadvantage was counter-balanced by a liberalization in another sense: "Members of a team other than the first runner may commence running not more than 10 m. outside the take-over zone" (obviously with the exchange still occurring inside said zone). The advantages of this innovation first became apparent in the France vs Italy dual meet at Annecy in 1964, when both teams broke the European record, with the French winning by one tenth in 39.2.

At the Tokyo Olympics the customary US victory hung in the balance till the last exchange. Anchor leg man Bob Hayes, the "World's Fastest Human", had instructed his teammates before the race in simple language: "Just give it to me close". But Paul Drayton, Gerry Ashworth and Dick Stebbins were far from flawless in their "stick-work" (US track jargon for baton passing) and by the time Hayes received the baton the team was only fourth, about 3 m. behind France, the leader. But within a few seconds the large crowd was treated to a rare spectacle of explosive speed: the phenomenal Hayes not only closed the 3-metre gap but finally won by a similar margin, giving his team the gold medal and a new world record: 39.0 (auto-time 39.06). Poland (39.3), France (39.3) and Jamaica (39.4) came next in that order (auto-times: 39.36, 39.36, 39.49).

France's European record (39.2) was matched by Poland and USSR in 1965 and again by France in '66. The French were very good in those years. They won the European title at Budapest in '66 (39.4) and the following year, on 22 July at Ostrava, a team consisting of Marc Berger, Jocelyn Delecour, Claude Piquemal and Roger Bambuck gave France a new European record of 38.9. This was not a global record though, because a few weeks earlier, namely on 17 June at Provo (altitude, 1387 m.), a University of Southern California team with Earl McCullouch, Fred Kuller, O.J.Simpson and Jamaican Lennox Miller was clocked in 38.6 for the 4x110 y. relay. An interesting entry was of course "O.J.", a 9.4 100 y. man who was to become an all-time Great in American football. Still in 1967, the French foursome Berger-Delecour-Piquemal-Bambuck represented Europe in the dual meet with America at Montreal, and did an excellent job, winning in 39.1.

The Mexico Olympics (1968) offered a host of fast times. Jamaica, with Erroll Stewart, Michael Fray, Clinton Forbes and Lennox Miller, got the ball rolling with two record-breaking performances, 38.6 in a heat and 38.3 in a "semi" (auto-times, 38.65 and 38.39). In the final, however, USA was again on top, when Charles Greene, Melvin Pender, Ronnie Ray Smith and Jim Hines chalked up a new world mark of 38.2 (auto-time 38.24). No surprise: these men were all credited with 10-flat or better in the metric century! Cuba (38.3), France (38.4) and Jamaica (38.4) followed in that order (auto-times, 38.40, 38.42 and 38.47).

The sprint relay of the 1971 European Championships in Helsinki turned out to be a comedy of errors. West Germany failed to finish after fouling up the second exchange, East Germany and France were disqualified for changing outside the zone. Czechoslovakia was at any rate a worthy winner in 39.3.

At the Munich Olympics (1972) the Americans were obviously thirsty for revenge by the time the sprint relay came up. The incredible Hart-Robinson case in the 100 m. had obviously caused quite a stir, and US coach Stan Wright in particular, chosen by the media as the chief "culprit", was in search of relief. He got it when Larry Black, Robert Taylor, Gerald Tinker and Eddie Hart ran a near perfect race and went home the winners in 38.2, equalling the world record (However, the auto-time, 38.19, was better than the 38.24 credited to the US team at Mexico City in '68). USSR, with Valeriy Borzov in the anchor leg, was second in 38.50, ahead of West Germany (38.79).

France was back in stride at the 1974 European Championships in Rome, having by then replaced her famous quartet of the late Sixties, and won in 38.69, beating an Italian team anchored by Pietro Mennea (38.88).

The 1976 Olympic final in Montreal was remarkable in at least one way: for the first time since 1952 the winning team failed to break or tie the world record! USA won in 38.33, with Harvey Glance, Johnny Jones, Millard Hampton and Steve Riddick, well ahead of East Germany (38.66) and USSR (38.78). Tha Americans made amends for the "lost" world record in the 1977 World Cup at Düsseldorf, when

Bill Collins, Steve Riddick, Cliff Wiley and Steve Williams improved to 38.03, "passing about as well as any American national team ever has", as one commentator put it. East Germany was second (38.57).

In the next three years (1978-80) there were no major deeds in the sprint relay department. Poland won at the 1978 European Championships at Prague in 38.58. In the second World Cup, at Montreal in 1979, a US team lost to the Americas (two Brazilians and two Cubans), 38.77 to 38.70. Later in the same year an Italian team anchored by Pietro Mennea, then at his very best, did 38.42 in the Universiade at Mexico City, and thus equalled the European record set on the same track during the 1968 Olympics by a French foursome. USA was not present at the Moscow Olympics (1980). This no doubt made things easier for the Russians.

However, the hosts ran a near perfect race with Vladimir Muravyov, Nikolay Sidorov, Aleksandr Aksinin and Andrey Prokofyev, and lowered the European record to 38.26, beating a strong Polish team (38.33), while France was third (38.53). A few days earlier, Prokofyev had placed fourth in the "high" hurdles in 13.49.

4x400 METRES: From the first sub-3 to the Mexican epic of Evans & Co.

As per tradition, the world record (3:02.2) set by the Americans at the Rome Olympics (1960) lived the space of an Olympiad. In other words, it fell at Tokyo in 1964, when another US foursome won the Olympic crown in 3:00.7. The anchor leg man was Henry Carr, who had previously won the 200 m. He was pitted against Wendell Mottley of Trinidad and Robbie Brightwell of Britain, second and fourth respectively in the individual 400 m. event.

The American offered a glimpse of his great potential in the one-lap department, excelling his rivals with a 44.5 leg. He thus completed the excellent work previously accomplished by his teammates Ollan Cassell (46.0), Mike Larrabee (44.8) and Ulis Williams (45.4). Great Britain was second in 3:01.6, a new European record (Brightwell 44.8), and Trinidad a close third in 3:01.7 (Mottley 45.0).

History's first sub-3 min. clocking materialized in a "cold" race - an anomalous occurrence in relation to the history of the 1600 m. relay. It happened at Los Angeles on 24 July 1966, when a US national team ran the distance in 2:59.6 (manual timing), an average of 44.9 per man. The splits were as follows: Bob Frey 46.3, Lee Evans 44.5, Tommie Smith 43.8, Theron Lewis 45.0. Just as in Tokyo two years earlier, the fastest leg was by a "non-specialist", Tommie "Jet" Smith, who was to deliver a more intelligible message a year later, when he set a new world record for the individual 400 m. event (44.5). An Australian team finished a distant second in 3:13.5.

At the 1968 Olympics the rarefied atmosphere of Mexico City inspired another US quartet to an even greater performance, which at the end of 1990 still has to be bettered (although equalled in 1988). The mark, 2:56.1 (auto-time, 2:56.16), came as a result of the following efforts: Vince Matthews 45.0, Ron Freeman 43.2, Larry James 43.8, Lee Evans 44.1. Freeman's leg is still the fastest ever recorded at the metric distance, but it should be noted that in a meet held at Baton Rouge in 1973 another American, Maurice Peoples, was timed in 43.4 (splits, 21.5 and 21.9) in the last leg of a 4x440 y. relay, incidentally for a college team that finished no better than third. In the Mexico race Evans & Co. were up against a good team from Kenya (Charles Asati, Hezekiah Nyamau, Naftali Bon, Daniel Rudisha) who finished second in 2:59.64. In a close battle for the bronze West Germany barely nipped Poland, 3:00.57 to 3:00.58 (officially, both were credited with a new European record at 3:00.5).

Performances recorded by the winning teams at the European Championships during the Sixties were good but not exceptional: West Germany 3:05.8 at Belgrade in 1962, Poland 3:04.5 at Budapest in '66, and France 3:02.3 at Athens in '69.

At the 1972 Olympics in Munich the Americans "committed suicide". John Smith was injured; Wayne Collett and Vince Matthews were barred by the IOC "from all future Olympic competition" following their misbehaviour during the victory ceremony of the 400 m. "The surest gold medal prospect in the Games", namely the US 4x400 m. relay team, thus had to stay away because of "insufficient man power". Kenya seized the opportunity to give Africa its first gold medal in an Olympic relay. Asati (45.5), Nyamau (45.5), Robert Ouko (45.3) and Julius Sang (43.5) chalked up a final time of 2:59.83. Great Britain was second in 3:00.46, ahead of France (3:00.65) and West Germany (3:00.88).

The Americans regained control at the Montreal Olympics four years later with the best sea-level time recorded until then, 2:58.65, after doing 2:59.52 in a heat! The winning team consisted of Herman Frazier (45.3), Benny Brown (44.6), Fred Newhouse

(43.8) and Maxie Parks (45.0). With Kenya on the boycotters' side, the other medals went to Poland (3:01.48) and West Germany (3:01.98).

The axiom that a US 1600 m. relay team could only be beaten by self-default was confirmed during the 1977 World Cup at Düsseldorf, when the US anchor man, Maxie Parks, pulled a hamstring while leading down the backstretch and had to give up. West Germany won in 3:01.34. During the Seventies, West Germany and Britain dominated the scene at the European Championships, the former winning at Helsinki in 1971 (3:02.94) and at Prague in '78 (3:02.03) and the latter winning at Rome in '74 (3:03.3). The second World Cup, held at Montreal in '79, offered a close feud between USA and Europe, who finished in that order (3:00.70 and 3:00.80 respectively).

In 1980, the nth chapter of the perverse boycott "game" kept USA, Kenya and West Germany away from the Moscow Olympics. USSR emerged the winner in a final of depleted significance with Remigius Valiulis (45.7), Mikhail Linge (45.4), Nikolay Chernyetskiy (44.8) and Viktor Markin (45.2), their final time being 3:01.08. East Germany was a close second in 3:01.26, while Italy, anchored by Pietro Mennea (45.2) took the bronze in 3:04.3.

When the IAAF removed the English distances (except the mile) from the record book, the 4x440 y. relay was inevitably discontinued, even in the States. The last world record ratified by the IAAF for the 1-mile relay was a 3:02.4 made by a US team (Ronnie Ray, Robert Taylor, Maurice Peoples and Stan Vinson) at Durham in 1975.

WALKS - ¡Viva México!

The year 1961 saw the inaugural edition of an IAAF walking team competition which came to be known as the Lugano Trophy, so named after the Swiss town which was its first venue. Points were awarded for the first three walkers to finish from teams of four at both 20 and 50 km., and finally totalled to determine the team positions. The competition was originally confined to European teams, the first participant from the rest of the world being USA in 1967. From 1977 the event has been officially labelled as IAAF World Race Walking Cup. Held biennially, the event is regarded with great respect by the walking fraternity. It gives adepts of this branch of athletics a chance to cement rivalries, and friendships as well, in an atmosphere all their own.

1961
1980

The greatest walkers of the early Sixties were Ken Matthews of Britain (born at Birmingham on 21 June 1934; 1.85 m./78 kg.) and Abdon Pamich of Italy, whose early career has been briefly reviewed in a previous chapter. The Englishman was at his best in the 20 km. He had his only major mishap at the 1960 Olympics in Rome, where he set a fast pace and led for 8 km. before the joint effect of heat and fatigue took its toll and forced him to drop out. But in the following years he earned a reputation as a "giant killer". He won the 20 km. event in the first two editions of the Lugano Trophy (1961 and '63) and at the 1962 European Championships in Belgrade (1:35:54.8). And he fought back bravely in the Olympics, winning the gold medal at Tokyo in 1964, at the age of thirty, in 1:29:34.0.

Pamich was an extremely serious, dedicated athlete. Essentially a 50 km. specialist, he won his first international honour at the Lugano Trophy in 1961, with 4:25:38.0. On 19 November of the same year, in Rome, he broke two world records, covering 30 miles (48.28 km.) in 4:04:56.8 and 50 km. in 4:14:02.4. After winning his event at the 1962 European Championships in Belgrade, he had his greatest day at the Tokyo Olympics in '64, when he emerged the winner in a close battle with Paul Nihill, a Briton of Irish descent. At the end the two were separated by no more than 18.8 seconds, Pamich taking the gold in 4:11:12.4. The Italian's lucky streak continued till '66, when he won his second European title at Budapest.

Two years later, at the Mexico Olympics, he was hampered by gastroenteritis and had to drop out. At the 1969 European Championships in Athens he returned to the 20 km. event, placing sixth. His swan song coincided with his fifth and last appearance in the Olympics, at Munich in 1972, when he was disqualified during the 50 km. event while lying fifteenth. An international for Italian colours from 1954 to 1973, during this period his total mileage, including training and competition, amounted to nearly four round-the-world trips. In 1968 British expert Mel Watman referred to him as "the most consistently great long distance walker of all time". Pamich's rightful heir as king of long distance walkers was Christoph Höhne of East Germany (born at Borsdorf on 12 February 1941; 1.71 m./62 kg.). Just like Pamich, he won two gold medals at the European Championships, his times being 4:13:32.8 at Athens in 1969 and a "revolutionary" 3:59:05.6 at Rome in '74. And he was second to Venyamin Soldatyenko of USSR (4:02:22.0) at Helsinki in '71. In 1965 he broke Pamich's world record for the 50 km. on track with 4:10:51.8, and improved on this

Abdon Pamich (Italy), one of the All Time "Greats" in long distance walking.

mark at Berlin four years later with 4:08:05.0.

Vladimir Golubnichiy of USSR, whose début in the international ranks was dealt with in a previous chapter, had a very long career. Following his victory in the 20 km. at Rome in 1960, he won bronze at Tokyo in '64, and again gold at Mexico City in '68, narrowly escaping the frenzied finish of José Pedraza of Mexico - 1:33:58.4 to 1:34:00.0. He competed in two more editions of the Olympics, making it five altogether, just like Pamich. In 1972, at Munich, he was second in the 20 km., close behind Peter Frenkel of East Germany, and in '76, at Montreal, he managed to finish seventh - at the age of forty. He had a remarkable record in the European Championships as well: third in 1962, second in '66 and finally first in '74 at Rome, always in the 20 km. The Eternal City curiously marked the beginning and the end of his sway.

Other good Soviet walkers of this period were Gennadiy Agapov, who in 1969 set a new world record for the 20 km. (1:26:45.8), and Venyamin Soldatyenko, 1971 European champion in the 50 km., a distance for which he also held the world's track record (4:03:42.6 in '72). The East German school also had a fair number of top-notch performers. The above mentioned Peter Frenkel twice bettered the world's 20 km. record, first with 1:25:50.0, then 1:25:19.4. On the latter occasion (Erfurt, 1972) he was curiously bracketed in a tie for first with his countryman Hans-Georg Reimann, who thus shared the record. The tie was broken, so to speak, at the Munich Olympics a few weeks later, when Frenkel won in 1:26:42.4, while Reimann had to be content with third place. Another East German, Peter Selzer, succeeded Höhne as holder of the world's 50 km. track record with 4:04:19.8 (1971).

West Germany's most famous walker was Bernd Kannenberg (born at Königsberg on 20 August 1942; 1.76 m./75 kg.), a soldier who managed to hold at the same time the world records for 20 and 50 km., with 1:24:45.0 (1974) and 3:56:51.4 (1975) respectively. The latter, history's first sub-4-hour mark on the track, was achieved at Nerviano, Italy. The greatest achievement of his career was in any case his victory in the 50 km. at the Munich Olympics, three days after dropping out in the 20 km. event. At the longer distance he won from Soldatyenko, 3:56:11.6 to 3:58:24.0.

However, the most important event of the Seventies was the advent of a new power - Mexico. Of course, the world had received a signal at the 1968 Olympics in Mexico, when José Pedraza finished a close second in the 20 km., as related above. But the message was probably misunderstood, due to the fact that Pedraza's style left much to be desired in terms of correct walking. Sceptics began to have second thoughts when Daniel Bautista won Mexico's first Olympic gold at the 1976 Games in Montreal, dominating the 20 km. field in 1:24:40.6. In subsequent years, Bautista twice won his event in the Lugano Trophy and also bettered the world record a couple of times, his ultimate being 1:20:06.8 at Montreal in 1979. He was the "chef de file" in a group of up-and-coming Mexican walkers coached by Jerzy Hausleber, an instructor of Polish descent. Most of their training was done at high altitudes, curiously a reflex of what the "gazelles" from Kenya and Ethiopia had previously achieved under similar conditions in the running events.

In the meantime, neutral observers were obliged to admit that questionable stylistic developments were discrediting the walking world, producing as they did almost farcical performances, notably in the short-distance events. In major competitions, judges did their best to cope with the problem, but sometimes tended towards compromise, and their verdicts gave rise to controversy.

Another great Mexican walker was Raúl González, who was generally at his best in the 50 km. grind. He was responsible for spectacular advances in the record department, first with 3:52:23.5 in 1978, then with an astounding 3:41:38.4 at Fana, Norway, in 1979. However, the '50' was not included in the programme of the 1976 Olympics in Montreal, a controversial decision which damaged González and many others. The Mexican thus decided to compete in the 20 km. He finished fifth. Four years later, at the Moscow Olympics, he tried both 20 and 50 km. and to the surprise of many he did better at the shorter distance (sixth). In his parade event he finished an undistinguished seventeenth. González had a habit of going out very fast, and at times he would tie up in the closing stages. At the Lugano Trophy he won the 50 km. in 1977 but dropped to fourth in '79, after leading by more than 5 minutes at one stage. But, as will be seen in the next chapter, his greatest day was yet to come.

Jorge Llopart gave Spain her first-ever gold medal in the European Championships when he won the 50 km. at Prague in 1978 with 3:53:29.9. After that, he was looked upon as a strong favourite for the 1980 Olympic crown, but in Moscow he had to bow to Hartwig Gauder of East Germany, 3:51:25.0 to 3:49:24.0.

The Italian tradition was revived by Maurizio Damilano, a strongly determined Piedmontese who grew up in a family of walking addicts. He was sixth in the 20 km. at the 1978 European Championships in Prague, but in the 1979 Lugano Trophy he was disqualified in the same event. At the 1980 Olympics in Moscow the wheel of fortune turned in his favour: with less than 2 km. to go Bautista and Anatoliy Solomin of USSR, who were ahead of him, ran afoul of the judges and were disqualified. Damilano went on to win in 1:23:36.5.

1961
1980

1981 1999

WORLD CHAMPIONSHIPS IN ATHLETICS. SUPERSTARS: LEWIS AND BUBKA. A DRAGON CALLED DOPING

SPRINTS: From the Lewis vs. Ben Johnson saga to the last of the century's "fastest humans", Maurice Greene. Michael Johnson's superb 19.32 in the 200 m - the record of records?

The international athletics calendar has been growing steadily throughout the Eighties and Nineties, notably as regards invitation meets. Beginning with 1985, the most important ones were made part of the Grand Prix IAAF/Mobil, after the name of the sponsoring company that made it possible for the IAAF to award prizes to leading athletes. In 1998 the leading Grand Prix meets joined to form the IAAF Golden League, which offered a jackpot of $ 1 million to be divided among all of his or her Golden League events. IAAF President Primo Nebiolo thought that the next philosophy behind the reform would reinforce the concept of prize money while attempting to discontinue the trend of over-inflated appearance fees. Events, held in alternate order through the years, are usually seven for men and five for women. The inaugural edition of the World Athletics Championships, organized by the IAAF, was held at Helsinki in 1983. The second edition followed four years later in Rome. Beginning with Tokyo 1991 it became a biennial event, occurring the year before and the year after the Olympic Games. Given the wealth of major Games between 1981 and 1999 I deem it advisable to give at the beginning of each section a summary of the main results (medal winners) for the following events: OG = Olympic Games; WC = World Championships; WCup = World Cup; EC = European Championships.

1981 - WCup, Rome. 100 m (4 Sep) (Wind +0.2): 1.Wells (Eur/GB) 10.20, 2.Obeng (Afr/Gha) 10.21, 3.Emmelmann (EG) 10.31, ... 9.C.Lewis (USA) 10.96 (injured); 200 m (6 Sep) (+0.1): 1.Lattany (USA) 20.21, 2.Wells 20.53, 3.Emmelmann 20.57.

1982 - EC, Athens. 100 m (7 Sep) (-0.8): 1.Emmelmann 10.25, 2.Pavoni (Ita) 10.25, 3.Woronin (Pol) 10.28; 200 m (9 Sep) (-0.6): 1.Prenzler (EG) 20.46, 2.Sharp (GB) 20.47, 3.Emmelmann 20.60.

1983 - WC, Helsinki. 100 m (8 Aug) (-0.3): 1.C.Lewis 10.07, 2.C.Smith (USA) 10.21, 3.King (USA) 10.24; 200 m (14 Aug) (+1.1): 1.C.Smith 20.14, 2.Quow (USA) 20.41, 3.Mennea (Ita) 20.51.

1984 - OG, Los Angeles. 100 m (4 Aug) (+0.2): 1.C.Lewis 9.99, 2.Graddy (USA) 10.19, 3.Johnson (Can) 10.22; 200 m (8 Aug) (-0.9): 1.C.Lewis 19.80 (10.23 + 9.57), 2.Baptiste (USA) 19.96, 3.Jefferson (USA) 20.26.

1985 - WCup, Canberra. 100 m (4 Oct) (-0.4): 1.Johnson 10.00, 2.Imoh (Afr/Nig) 10.11, 3.Emmelmann 10.17; 200 m (6 Oct) (+0.5): 1.R.C.da Silva (Ame/Bra) 20.44, 2. Emmelmann 20.51, 3.Clark (Oce/Aus) 20.78. (Baptiste/USA, 1st in 20.38, was disqualfied for running out of lane).

277

1986 - EC, Stuttgart. 100 m (27 Aug) (-0.1): 1.Christie (GB) 10.15, 2.Bringmann (EG) 10.20, 3.Marie-Rose (Fra) 10.21; 200 m (29 Aug) (0.0): 1.Krilov (USSR) 20.52, 2.Evers (WG) 20.75, 3.Fyodoriv (USRR) 20.84.
1987 - WC, Rome. 100 m (30 Aug) (+1.0): 1.C. Lewis 9.93, 2.Stewart (Jam) 10.08, 3.L.Christie 10.14. B. Johnson (Can) won in 9.83 (WR) but was posthumously disqualified by the IAAF, following his own admission on drug abuse in 1989; 200 m (3 Sep) (-0.4): 1.C.Smith 20.16 (10.63 + 9.53), 2.Quénéhervé (Fra) 20.16 (10.57 + 9.59), 3.Regis (GB) 20.18.
1988 - OG, Seoul. 100 m (24 Sep) (+1.1): 1.C.Lewis 9.92 (World Record), 2.Christie 9.97, 3.C.Smith 9.99; Johnson (Can), 1st in 9.79, was disqualified for doping abuse, and his world record was not ratified; 200 m (28 Sep) (+1.7): 1.DeLoach (USA) 19.75 (10.27 + 9.48), 2.C.Lewis 19.79 (10.24 + 9.55), 3.R.C.da Silva (Bra) 20.04.
1989 - WCup, Barcelona. 100 m (8 Sep) (+0.5): 1.Christie 10.10, 2.Burrell (USA) 10.15, 3.Sangouma (Eur/Fra) 10.17; 200 m (10 Sep) (+1.9): 1.R.C.daSilva 20.00, 2.Heard (USA) 20.36, 3.Adeniken (Afr/Nig) 20.38.
1990 - EC, Split. 100 m (28 Aug) (+2.2): 1.Christie 10.00w, 2.Sangouma 10.04w, 3.Regis 10.07w; 200 m (30 Aug) (0.0): 1.Regis 20.11, 2.Trouabal (Fra) 20.31, 3.Christie 20.33.
1991 - WC, Tokyo. 100m (25 Aug) (+1.2): 1.C.Lewis (USA) 9.86 (World Record), 2.Burrell (USA) 9.88, 3.Mitchell (USA) 9.91; 200m (27 Aug) (-3.4) : 1.M.Johnson (USA) 20.01 (10.21+9.80), 2.Fredericks (Nam) 20.34, 3.Mahorn (Can) 20.49.
1992 - OG, Barcelona. 100m (1 Aug) (+0.5) : 1.Christie 9.96, 2.Fredericks 10.02, 3.Mitchell 10.04; 200m (6 Aug) (-1.0) 1.Marsh (USA) 20.01, 2.Fredericks 20.13, 3.Bates (USA) 20.38; WCup, Habana. 100m (25 Sep) (+0.3) 1.Christie 10.21, 2.Adeniken (Afr/Nig) 10.26, 3.C.Smith (USA) 10.33; 200m (27 Sep) (+0.5) 1.R.da Silva (Ame/Bra) 20.56, 2.Christie 20.72, 3.J.Williams (USA) 20.75.
1993 - WC, Stuttgart. 100m (15 Aug) (+0.3) 1.Christie 9.87, 2.Cason (USA) 9.92, 3.Mitchell 9.99; 200m (20 Aug) (+0.3) 1.Fredericks 19.85, 2.Regis (GB) 19.94, 3.C.Lewis 19.99.
1994 - EC, Athens. 100m (8 Aug) (-0.5) 1.Christie 10.14, 2.Moen (Nor) 10.20, 3.Porkhomovskiy (Rus) 10.31; 200m (11 Aug) (-0.1) 1.Moen 20.30, 2.Dologodin (Ukr) 20.47, 3.Stevens (Bel) 20.68; WCup, London. 100m (9 Sep) (-0.3) 1.Christie 10.21, 2.Adeniken 10.25, 3.Mansoor (Asi/Qat) 10.31; 200m (11 Sep) (-1.4) 1.Regis 20.45, 2.Fredericks 20.55, 3.Moen (Eur/Nor) 20.72.
1995 - WC, Göteborg. 100m (6 Aug) (+1.0) 1.Bailey (Can) 9.97, 2.Surin (Can) 10.03, 3.Boldon (Tri) 10.03; 200m (11Aug) (+0.5) 1.M.Johnson (USA) 19.79, 2.Fredericks 20.12, 3.J.Williams (USA) 20.18.
1996 - OG, Atlanta. 100m (27 Jul) (+0.7) 1.Bailey 9.84 (World Record), 2.Fredericks 9.89, 3.Boldon 9.90; 200m (1 Aug) (+0.4) 1.M.Johnson 19.32 (10.12+9.20) (World Record), 2.Fredericks 19.68, 3.Boldon 19.80.
1997 - WC, Athens. 100m (3 Aug) (+0.2) 1.M.Greene (USA) 9.86, 2.Bailey 9.91, 3.Montgomery 9.94; 200m (8 Aug) (+2.3) 1.Boldon 20.04w, 2.Fredericks 20.23w, 3.C.da Silva (Bra) 20.26w.
1998 - EC, Budapest. 100m (19 Aug) (+0.3) 1.Campbell (GB) 10.04, 2.Chambers (GB) 10.10, 3.Papadias (Gre) 10.17; 200m (21Aug) (-1.0) 1.D.Walker (GB) 20.53, 2.Turner (GB) 20.64, 3.Golding (GB) 20.72; WCup, Johannesburg. 100m (11 Sep) (-0.2) 1.Thompson (Ame/Bar) 9.87, 2.Ogunkoya (Afr/Nig) 9.92, 3.Chambers (GB) 10.03; 200m (13 Sep) (+1.3) 1.Fredericks 19.97, 2.Bradley (USA) 20.38, 3.Douglas (Eur/Hol) 20.40.
1999 - WC, Sevilla. 100m (22 Aug) (+0.2) 1.M.Greene 9.80, 2.Surin 9.84, 3.Chambers 9.97; 200m (27 Aug) (+1.2) 1.M.Greene 19.90, 2.C.da Silva 20.00, 3.Obikwelu (Nig) 20.11.

Two sprinters were head and shoulders above the rest during the Eighties: Carl Lewis of USA and Ben Johnson of Canada. The former has been great, versatile and most durable as a top-notch performer in the 100, 200 m (and long jump); the latter has been simply phenomenal as a single-event (100 m) man. Frederick Carlton ("Carl") Lewis (born at Birmingham, Alabama, on 1 July 1961; 1.88 m./79 kg.) collected a record number of medals between 1983 and 1996 - eight golds, one silver and one bronze in the World Championships; nine golds and one silver in the Olympic Games. In 1984, at Los Angeles, he equalled Jesse Owens' legendary feat from the 1936 Olympics, winning four gold medals, - in exactly the same events as the "Ebony Antelope": 100, 200 m., long jump and 4x100 m. relay. A unique series, especially if one considers that in order to qualify for these meets he had to pass every time through the "Caudine Forks" of the US Olympic Trials (or the US Championships), a test which as often as not was just as hard as the Olympic Games or the World Championships themselves. In my opinion, such honours amply suffice to stamp Carl Lewis as the "Athlete of the Eighties", and certainly one of the greatest of all time. Clock-wise; the man who was once dubbed "Figlio del vento" (Son of the Wind) by

Italian newsman Franco Arturi, can point to the following series of marks: - 100 m: fifteen legitimate marks between 9.86 (official world record) and 9.99; twelve marks between 9.78 and 9.99 with the aid of winds exceeding 2 m/s. - 200 m: ten legitimate marks between 19.75 and 19.99. - 4x100 m. relay: twelve marks between 37.40 and 37.99, always as anchor man. Tall and statuesque, Lewis is not considered a great starter, yet he held at one time the world's indoor record for the 60 y. (6.02 at Dallas in 1983). His pickup midway in the race is undoubtedly his main "atout". Always a reliable competitor on big occasions, he has diligently followed the advice given him by coach Tom Tellez. Comparing him as an athlete with Jesse Owens (who like Carl came from Alabama) would amount to a near absurdity, since so many things have changed in athletics during the half century that separated them. Each won four Olympic gold medals at the age of 23 (Owens in Berlin 1936 and Lewis in Los Angeles 1984) in exactly the same events: 100, 200 m, long jump and 4x100m relay. But such striking similarities end here: on his return from Berlin Owens found that medals and records could not be converted into money - that is, along the amateur path of his time. Having a family to support he was forced to quit school and athletics as well, in search of financially more rewarding paths. Lewis, however, happened to operate at a time when it was finally possible for a top-class athlete to be a self-avowed professional. So he was able to continue for many more years. Outside the track he was advised by an intelligent manager, Joe Douglas, and thus appeared to be ever conscious of the "image" he was likely to offer, even to the point of occasionally losing something in terms of spontaneity. Ben Johnson (born at Falmouth, Jamaica, on 30 December 1961; 1.80 m./75 kg.) has been Lewis' fiercest rival in the 100 m. Although not so precocious as his American rival, he managed to run the century in 10.25 shortly before turning twenty. He reached the top in 1985. As of the end of 1991, he and Lewis have met 18 times in the 100 m. (including heats), and Lewis leads 11 to 7. It should be noted, however, that Johnson won most of their latest duels, notably including the two "matches of the century", at the 1987 World Championships in Rome (9.83 to 9.93) and in the 1988 Olympics in Seoul (9.79 to 9.92). However, Johnson's record marks on these occasions have since been cancelled by the IAAF, following his

1981
1999

> ### Thorny question
>
> The widely publicized "Johnson affair" caused the IAAF to revise its doping rules, making them stricter and far-reaching. Doping controls have been intensified and now extend to random out-of-competition tests conducted in training camps. Johnson's belated confession was probably instrumental in the addition of the following paragraph (Rule 55/6): "An admission may be made either orally or in a verifiable manner or in writing. For the purpose of these Rules, a statement is not to be regarded as an admission where it was made more than six years after the facts to which it relates". In fact, Ben Johnson was deprived not only of the world record he set at Seoul, where he proved "positive" to a forbidden substance, but also of the one he set the year before in Rome, where in the admission of competent officials he had proven "negative" to the test conducted after the race. As a result, this retroactivity seems at best debatable. It amounts to an indirect admission, on the part of the IAAF, that control techniques used at the 1987 World Championships were far from faultless. Such a suspicion could easily be extended to other medal winners in that meet or, for that matter, any previous championship meet. If methods used at the time were inadequate, I see little or no utility in trying to "correct the past" on the strength of lone admissions or confessions. It is far more important to concentrate on enforcing the "law" at the present time - as uniformly as possible.

Ben Johnson (Canada).

disqualification for doping abuse. It happened after the Seoul final, when he proved "positive" at the doping control, with traces of an anabolic steroid named Stanozolol. Late in 1988 the Canadian Government decided to start an investigation on doping abuses in Canadian sports. The "Dubin Inquiry", as it was called after Charles Dubin, the judge presiding over it, inevitably involved Johnson and his clan. Prior to the athlete's testimony, his physician Dr. Mario ("Jamie") Astaphan and his coach Charlie Francis, as well as some athletes, made clear admissions which were later confirmed by Johnson himself. He admitted that he had used steroids, testosterone and human growth hormone, since 1981, following the advice of his "mentors". After his tearful confession, he said: "I did wrong, but I was confused at the time". He then urged young athletes to stay away from drugs. In the fall of 1988 the IAAF suspended Johnson for two years. Nobody can say to what extent Johnson derived benefits from his long use of drugs. One may wonder if the "patrimony" thus accumulated would still be extant (at least in part) in his muscles. Always a powerful sprinter, he looked strong in every phase of the race, particularly in his reaction to the gun (0.109 in the 1987 race in Rome, vs. 0.196 for Lewis) and his early acceleration. He was slightly inferior to Lewis in only one phase, the last 30 m. In the 1987 race in Rome he led the American 7.23 to 7.36 at 70 m. and 9.83 to 9.93 at the end, thus losing 0.03 in the last 30 m. Same difference at Seoul in 1988, when he led Lewis 7.17 to 7.33 at 70 m. and 9.79 to 9.92 at the end. Johnson's early acceleration was best reflected in the record (since cancelled) he set for the 60 m. at the 1987 World Indoor Championships at Indianapolis: 6.41. On the other hand, he did not like the 200 m., a distance he ran on rare occasions. His best was 20.41 in 1985 (plus a wind-aided 20.37 in '82). In 1991, being again eligible, he tried to make a comeback but turned out to be only the shadow of himself. In a widely publicized re-match with Carl Lewis at Villeneuve-d'Ascq, the Canadian finished a disappointing 7th in the 100 m. (10.46) as Lewis himself (10.20) was second to Dennis Mitchell (10.09). It was the first meeting between Carl and Ben since Seoul '88 and possibly the richest in the history of the sport (they reportedly would split $500,000) but results obviously looked ridiculous vis-à-vis the ballyhoo made in previous weeks about the affair .... In 1992 "Big Ben" managed to do 10.16 but at the Barcelona Olympics he did not go beyond the semi-finals. What is even worse, early in 1993 he again tested positive,

Final of the 100 m. at the 1991 World Championships in Tokyo. From l. to r. D. Mitchell, 3rd, Carl Lewis, 1st with a new world record (9.86), L. Christie, 4th and L. Burrell, 2nd.

this time to testosterone, and the IAAF banned him for life. In later years he made repeated attempts to be reinstated - to no avail. A sad end to a sad story. There have been other great sprinters in the Eighties, no matter if they were outshone by the formidable duo in decisive moments. In this respect I would like to single out two Americans, Calvin Smith and Joe DeLoach. The former (born at Bolton, Mississippi, on 8 January 1961; 1.78 m./64 kg.) won the 200 m. in two editions of the World Championships, 1983 and '87, in the absence of Lewis, that's true. Always a good competitor, Smith was at one time holder of the world's 100 m. record with a 9.93 made at Air Force Academy, Colorado (altitude, 2194 m.) in 1983. DeLoach (born on 5 June 1967 at Bay City, Texas; 1.84 m./75 kg.) had his greatest season in 1988, when he beat Lewis, his teammate at Santa Monica Track Club, in the 200 m. of the Seoul Olympics. Also outstanding in his best moments was Kirk Baptiste, runner-up to Lewis in the 200 m. of the Los Angeles Olympics in 19.96. Still in 1984 he ran the 300 m. in 31.70, best time on record at that seldom run distance. In Europe the early Eighties saw the latest successes of Pietro Mennea and Allan Wells. In 1983 they finished third and fourth respectively, merely 0.01 apart, in the 200 m. of the World Championships. In 1984 the Italian, then 32, managed to finish seventh at Los Angeles in his fourth Olympic 200 m. final - an all-time record for a sprinter. He made a second comeback in 1987 and the following year he represented Italy for the fifth time in the Olympics, were it only to the extent of running a heat of the 200 m. Mennea could not be described as an All-time Great in the truest sense of the word, but he was certainly one of the most durable champions in the annals of sprinting. Frank Emmelmann of East Germany never reached spectacular heights, yet he was a consistently good performer in the early Eighties. Linford Christie of Britain (born at St. Andrews, Jamaica, on 2 April 1960; 1.89 m./77 Kg.) was really what is usually described as a late comer. By the end of 1985, aged 25, his best was 10.33. Then he decided to give it a truly serious try, spurred on by his coach, Ron Roddan. And he began to live up to his great potential. In 1986 he won the European 100 m. title and rose to new heights with a seasonal best of 10.04. In 1988 he went on to post the first sub-10 sec. performance by a European - 9.97 in finishing second to Carl Lewis in the above-mentioned Olympic final at Seoul (following Johnson's disqualification). He has been Europe's best 100 m. man for almost a decade, winning the continental title three times and posting the first legal sub-10 sec. performance by a European - 9.97 in finishing second to Lewis in the Seoul Olympics. In those Games he also placed fourth in the 200 m. with his best-ever time, 20.09. In 1989-90, with Ben Johnson under suspension and Carl Lewis "taking ten", or just about, the leading figures were Raymond Stewart of Jamaica and Leroy Burrell of USA. The former had his best year in 1991, with a 100 m. best of 9.96. The latter (born at Philadelphia on 21 February 1967; 1.80 m./82 kg.) grew to world class in the shadow of Carl Lewis, mainly as his teammate at Santa Monica Track Club. At the end of 1990 this powerful sprinter could point to legitimate times of 9.94 and 9.96 (twice) in the 100 m. and 20.14 in the 200 m. At the latter distance, one he does not particularly like, he traded wins with Michael Johnson in 1990, once recording a wind-blown 19.61. Like Lewis, Burrell also excels as a long jumper: 8.37 in 1989. Latest in the line of superlative US sprinters is Michael Johnson (born at Dallas on 13 September 1967; 1.83 m./77 kg.). Injury-prone in his early years, he had his first full season in top-class international competition in 1990, when he developed into one of the greatest 200/400 m. performers in history. During the Nineties the world's 100 m. record was bettered on five occasions, always in important meets. Burrell got the ball rolling on 14 June 1991 at the US Championships held at Downing Stadium on Randall's Island, New York. Aided by a wind of 1.9 m/s, hence close to the maximum allowable limit, he sped to 9.90 beating his famous clubmate Carl Lewis (9.93) and Dennis Mitchell (10.00). But Carl, by then 30, still had one bolt in reserve and he shot it on the most important occasion - the World Championships at Tokyo on 25 August. The race was aptly described as the greatest of all time - 6 athletes beating 10 sec. and the first two under the listed world mark. Burrell was ahead of Lewis for the greater part of the race but in the closing stage Carl came on like a whirlwind to win by 0.02 in 9.86, with an aiding wind of 1.2 m/s. Lewis ran the first half in 5.61 (Burrell 5.55) and the second in a nifty 4.25, reaching his top speed between 70 and 80 m. - 0.83. Mitchell, third in 9.91, was fastest off the blocks, actually too fast, with a reaction time of 0.090 which was under the false-start limit set for the automatic recall of the athletes (0.100). At that moment, however, the starter was not wearing the headphones which would have given a high-pitched ring in his ears. So there was no recall: with the starter being, according to the IAAF rule, the sole and final judge, Mitchell got away with it, to the detriment of Linford Christie, 4th in 9.92, whose reaction time was a fast but legal 0.126. Lewis, seldom a supreme starter, showed a fair 0.140. His great victory came

1981
1999

281

eight years after his first world title (Helsinki '83) and surely fortified his claim to be considered the greatest 100 m. man of modern times. No "dashman" had ever been so prominent for so long. Tokyo '91 was Lewis's latest cry in the event. In subsequent years he never again ducked under 10 seconds, if not with a wind over the limit.

Linford Christie achieved top honours even later than Lewis. He won the Olympic 100 m. title in 1992 and confirmed his new status as "fastest human" in the 1993 World Championships when he sped to 9.87, aided by a negligible wind (+ 0.3), and thus missed Lewis's world record by 0.01. The American, by then past his peak mentally if not physically, was fourth in 10.02. In the 1992 Olympics at Barcelona the 200 m. was won by Michael Marsh, a teammate of Lewis at Santa Monica Track Club. In a semi-final this 25-year-old American produced a magnificent 19.73, easing off at the end of the race. That lengthened the life of Pietro Mennea's world record (19.72 in 1979). In the final a headwind of 1.0 m/s down the stretch limited Marsh to 20.01 as he won rather comfortably from the ever-present Frank Fredericks.

Leroy Burrell, hampered by injuries now and then, resurrected for a record breaking 9.85 in a Grand Prix meet at Lausanne on 6 July 1994. Aided by a wind of 1.2 m/s he won easily from Davidson Ezinwa of Nigeria and the ever present Dennis Mitchell (9.99 both). For Burrell this was a bright sparkle in an otherwise checkered season as well as the last of an exciting but uneven career.

Frank Fredericks of Namibia (born at Windhoek on 2 October 1967, 1.80 m./73 Kg.) can point to a career of amazing consistency. As a 100/200 m. man he has been near the top throughout the Nineties, winning medals in most of the major meets, particularly at his favorite distance, the 200 m. His long quest for gold was finally gratified in 1993 when he won the 200 m. in 19.85 at the World Championships in Stuttgart. Third in this race was Carl Lewis, who thereby picked up the last medal of his career in the sprint department.

Canada had by then discovered Ben Johnson's "vindicator" in the person of Donovan Bailey (born at Manchester, Jamaica, on 16 December 1967; 1.83 m./82 Kg.). Like "Big Ben", he came from Jamaica, the cradle of so many "speed demons". He emigrated to Canada in 1981 and did not break 11 sec. until he was 23 (10.42 in 1991). He reached world class in 1994 with 10.03. The following year he succeeded Christie as world champion and in 1996 he confirmed his leadership with a brilliant victory at the Atlanta Olympics, when he captured the world record with 9.84 (wind +0.7). After which the powerful, buoyant Canadian allowed himself a cigar to celebrate! There were no Americans on the podium at Atlanta (the same thing happened at the Göteborg Worlds in 1995), a bitter pill to swallow for the hosts in view of their superb tradition. Bailey was the slowest of the finalists off the marks (0.174), but soon picked up speed at a tremendous rate. According to Swatch Timing he reached his peak at 60 m. travelling at a speed of 12.1 m/s. Veteran Linford Christie was disqualified for two false starts, his reaction time for the second offence being 0.086. A bitter adieu to the front stage for a man who had beaten all age records by becoming world champion for the second time at the age of 33.

1997 saw a partial turnover in the highest ranks of the sprint. It fell to two protégés of coach John Smith (former holder of the world record for 440 yards: 44.5 in 1971) to turn the tide: Maurice Greene of USA (born at Kansas City on 23 July 1974; 1.76 m./75 Kg.) and Ato Boldon of Trinidad (born at Port-of-Spain on 30 December 1973; 1.76 m./75 Kg.). The latter was a well-established star by then, having won bronze medals at the 1995 World Championships (100 m.) and the 1996 Olympics (100 and 200 m.). Greene could point to a 10.08 when he moved from Kansas to California to join the John Smith squad in September 1996. The new "school" really worked wonders: he had an impressive season in 1997, with 8 clockings in the sub-10 sec. department in the 100 m. He also came on as a major force in the 200 m. (19.86). Boldon too made further progress and actually mastered his teammate in most of their duels. They took care of the sprints at the World Championships in Athens with Greene winning the 100 in 9.86 from defending champion Donovan Bailey and Boldon beating Fredericks in a wind-blown 200 in 20.04.

Such a tremendous couple, keen rivals on the track and close friends in every-day life, continued to rule the roost in 1998, but Boldon happened to be bogged down with an injury the subsequent year, after an impressive debut. At Athens on 16 June they had their hottest duel and Greene emerged the winner in 9.79 (wind +0.1 m/s), with Boldon second in 9.86. By official standards this was a new world record by 0.05, yet close followers of the sport well remembered that eleven years ago in Seoul another man had been credited with exactly the same time before sinking into official oblivion following a disqualification .... Later in the afternoon Boldon turned the tables on his friend, still over-elated, in the 200 - 19.86 to 20.03. Boldon was subsequently sidelined with an injury, which made it impossible for him to appear at the 1999 World Championships in Sevilla. Here Greene won the 100 in 9.80 and the 200 in 19.90, thus becoming the first sprinter to score such a double in the not-so-long history of the Worlds. When it was all over the powerful man dropped to one knee, a hand over his face - and shed tears of joy.

Throughout the Nineties the outstanding figure in the 200 m. was Michael Johnson, no matter if he seemed to have a somewhat deeper affection for the 400 m. Yet he won his first major title at the shorter distance, during the 1991 World Championships in Tokyo (20.01). Between May 1990 and June 1992 he had a sequence of 32 successive wins, which was finally broken by Frank Fredericks, usually his strongest rival. At the 1992 Olympics in Barcelona the American was unable to do himself justice due to an illness. It was not until 1995, aged 28, that he felt so strong as to try for a 200/400 m. double in top-class competition - an unprecedented trick in the history of "global" (Olympics/Worlds) competition. At the World Championships in Göteborg he first took the 400 in 43.39, then the 200 in 19.79, leaving arch rival Frank Fredericks 0.33 behind. The following year he wanted to turn that magic trick before an American crowd at the 1996 Olympics in Atlanta. He got a chance to test the new track there during the US Championships and Olympic Trials. First he won the 400 in 43.44, then on 23 June he finally broke Pietro Mennea's 17-year-old world record with a sound 19.66 (wind +1.7 m/s), leaving his nearest rival 0.37 behind. In the meantime he and his agent lobbied for a change in the timetable of the Atlanta Olympics. The IAAF finally decided to give MJ a helping hand by avoiding an overlapping of competition in the two events. At the Games the 400 again came first and Johnson won hands down in 43.49. Then on 1 August he chalked up what may well be remembered as the "Record of Records" of the 20th century - 19.32 for 200 m. The ever-present Fredericks ran his best ever race, yet he was left an awesome 0.36 behind. At the halfway mark Johnson, lane 3, had a narrow lead vis-à-vis his rival - 10.12 to 10.14 - and even Ato Boldon, then a budding star, was not too far behind (10.18).Then Johnson really pulled out all the stops and covered the second half in a wondrous 9.20, literally destroying the opposition. Just before the finish MJ felt a twinge in his lower right hamstring. In crossing the line he glanced to his left at the clock, frozen at a historic reading. A while later he strapped an ice bag to his aching hamstring and ran a lap of honour to the chorus of "You're unbelievable". In 1997 he was pitted against Donovan Bailey, the winner of the Olympic 100 m., in what was a self-avowed professional show at Toronto on 1 June.

A multi-national company guaranteed $ 500,000 to each of the two, plus another $ 1 million to the winner! The race, held indoors, was at the odd distance of 150 m. The Canadian soon built up a lead, 5.74 to 5.83 at 50 m., 10.24 to10.63 at 100 m. Johnson, usually a great curve runner, was beaten at his own game for once. But he was limping by then and had to call it quits with a damaged quadriceps. Bailey went on to win unopposed in 14.99. Outdoors the fastest time ever was a 14.97 by Linford Christie at Sheffield in 1994, beating Donovan Bailey among others. Back in 1983 at Cassino, Pietro Mennea achieved a hand-timed 14.8. On the whole, the Toronto affair, featured by an inadequate organisation and a concert of blabbering mouths before and after the race, was not an enlightening show for athletics. Johnson recovered just in time for the summer season, during which he concentrated on the 400 m. - just as he did in 1998-99. Having conquered the world in the 200 m., his target was now the elusive record for the one-lap event.

1981
1999

Donovan Bailey (Canada), right, with teammate Robert Esmie after their victory in the 4x100 m. relay at the 1996 Olympics.

After Linford Christie's retirement in the summer of 1997, Britain retained continental supremacy thanks to a cohort of young sprinters. At the 1998 European Championships in Budapest they won no less than five of the six medals at stake, with Darren Campbell first (10.04) and Dwain Chambers second in the 100 m., Doug Walker, Doug Turner and Julian Golding finishing 1-2-3 in that order in the 200 m. Walker, the only white man in the group, did 20.53. Since Jesse Owens's days, the world's 100 m. record has progressed by roughly six tenths, whereas for the 200 m. record the advancement has been roughly 1.5 sec. The latest IAAF Scoring Table rates Michael Johnson's 19.32 as worth 1335 pints, while it gives no more than 1294 for Maurice Greene's 9.79. But then scoring tables, even the best of them, are shaky instruments. Be as it may, the "ultimates" of human possibilities in the sprints are just as unpredictable in 2000 as they were in Owens's time.

Maurice Greene (USA), currently regarded as the "World's Fastest Human".

Inferiority Complex?

At the end of 1999 thirty sprinters had bettered 10 sec. in the metric century, since time immemorial the "blue ribbon" event of athletics. All of them were Negroes. The first white man to do the trick is still round the corner... The fastest clocking by a "paleface" dates from 1984: 10.00 by Marian Woronin of Poland. One has to go back twenty or more years to find the likes of Borzov, Wells and Mennea, white sprinters from Europe who were able to hold their own against their black counterparts. In USA the memories of men like Bobby Morrow and Dave Sime were even farther behind in time. In 1976 I was in Eugene to witness the US Olympic Trials and from the very first rounds of the sprints I happened to notice that whites were indeed a rarity. In recent years only one "paleface" from that country, Kevin Little, has been able to play a decent role in international competition - world indoor champion for 200 m. in 1997 and sixth over the same distance at the 1999 World outdoor Championships. In the meantime USA continued to win medals, drawing exclusively from the inexhaustible reservoir of its black minority (13% of the total US population). Some people feel that blacks dominate the sprints - as well as the middle and long distances - because they are inherently better physical specimens. Most scientists who study the subject, however, reject this simplistic reasoning. It may be appropriate to say that whites, especially in USA but not only there, are no longer trying as hard as they could.

400 METRES:
Four 100 m. fractions averaging 10.795

1981 - WCup, Rome (5 Sep): 1.Wiley (USA) 44.88, 2.Zuliani (Ita) 45.26, 3.Cameron (Ame/Jam) 45.27.
1982 - EC, Athens (9 Sep): 1.Weber (WG) 44.72, 2.Knebel (EG) 45.29, 3.Markin (USSR) 45.30.
1983 - WC, Helsinki (10 Aug): 1.Cameron 45.05, 2.Franks (USA) 45.22, 3.Nix (USA) 45.24.
1984 - OG, Los Angeles (8 Aug): 1.Babers (USA) 44.27 (21.7 + 22.6), 2.Tiacoh (Ivory Coast) 44.54, 3.A.McKay (USA) 44.71.

1981 1999

1985 - WCup, Canberra (5 Oct): 1.Franks 44.47, 2.Schönlebe (EG) 44.72, 3.Egbunike (Afr/Nig) 44.99.
1986 - EC, Stuttgart (29 Aug): 1.Black (GB) 44.59, 2.Schönlebe 44.63, 3.Schersing (EG) 44.85.
1987 - WC, Rome (3 Sep): 1.Schönlebe 44.33 (21.40 + 22.93), 2.Egbunike 44.56, 3.B.Reynolds (USA) 44.80.
1988 - OG, Seoul (28 Sep): 1.S.Lewis (USA) 43.87 (21.41 + 22.46), 2.B.Reynolds 43.93 (21.68 + 22.25), 3.D.Everett (USA) 44.09.
1989 - WCup, Barcelona (9 Sep): 1.Hernández (Ame/Cub) 44.58, 2.Carlowitz (EG) 44.86, 3.Tiacoh 44.97.
1990 - EC, Split (30 Aug): 1.Black 45.08, 2.Schönlebe 45.13, 3.Carlowitz 45.27.
1991 - WC, Tokyo (29 Aug): 1. Pettigrew (USA) 44.57, 2. Black 44.62, 3. Danny Everett (USA 44.63.
1992 - OG, Barcelona (5 Aug): 1. Watts (USA) 43.50, 2. S.Lewis (USA) 44.21, 3. S. Kitur (Ken) 44.24, WCup, Habana (26 Sep): 1. Bada (Afr/Nig) 44.99, 2. Richardson (GB) 45.86, 3. C.Jenkins (USA) 46.10.
1993 - WC, Stuttgart (17 Aug): 1. M.Johnson (USA) 43.65 (21.65 + 22.00), 2. Reynolds 44.13, 3. S. Kitur 44.54.
1994 - EC, Helsinki (11 Aug): 1. Ladejo (GB) 45.09, 2. Black 45.20, 3. Rusterholz (Swz) 45.96; WCup, London (10 Sep): 1. Pettigrew 45.26, 2. Ladejo 45.44, 3. Sena (Ame/Bra) 45.67.
1995 - WC, Göteborg (9 Aug): 1. M.Johnson 43.39 (21.26 + 22.13), 2. Reynolds 44.22, 3. Haughton (Jam) 44.56.
1996 - OG, Atlanta (29 Jul): 1. M. Johnson 43.49 (21.22 + 22.27), 2. Black 44.41, 3. D. Kamoga (Uga) 44.53.
1997 - WC, Athens (5 Aug): 1. M.Johnson 44.12 (21.64 + 22.48), 2. D.Kamoga 44.37, 3. T.Washington (USA) 44.39.
1998 - EC, Budapest (21 Aug): 1. I.Thomas (GB) 44.52, 2. Mackowiak (Pol) 45.04, 3. Richardson 45.14; WCup, Johannesburg (12 Sep): 1. I.Thomas 45.33, 2.E. Young (USA) 45.37, 3. McIntosh (Ame/Bah) 45.45.
1999 - WC, Sevilla (26 Aug): 1. M.Johnson 43.18, World Record, (21.22 + 21.96), 2. Parrela (Bra) 44.29, 3. Cárdenas (Mex) 44.31.

The incredible record set by Lee Evans at the 1968 Olympics in Mexico City, 43.86, withstood all assaults for twenty years. In the intervening time, most if not all championship races were obviously held at or near sea level, and this circumstance contributed to the longevity of Evans' mark, at least to some extent. In the early Eighties one of the men who could have threatened the record was Alonzo Babers of USA, the 1984 Olympic champion, but he had a relatively short career. Towards the end of the decade, sub-45 secs. performances became more and more frequent: a signal that the page was about to be turned. The man most likely to do the job was identified in 1987: Harry ("Butch") Reynolds (born at Akron, Ohio, on 8 August 1964; 1.93 m./84 kg.), a sort of Arthur Wint "using fuel of the Eighties". This strongly built American was endowed with plenty of speed and stamina, but appeared to be prone to injuries. At twenty he ran the 400 m. in 45.47, but two years had to go by before he could slightly improve, to 45.36. His breakthrough occurred in 1987, when he posted such times as 44.10, 44.13 and 44.15 - the fastest ever made under sea-level conditions. The 1988 US Olympic Trials (Indianapolis, 20 July) coincided with his first serious assault on Evans' record. He was spurred on by two young runners from UCLA, Danny Everett and 19-year-old Steve Lewis. The last-named had done 44.11 in a semi-final two days earlier - a world junior record achieved thanks to, or in spite of, a 20.8 first half. In the final Reynolds was in lane 6, while Everett was in 4 and Lewis in 7. With 100 m. to go Lewis (31.9) had a slight lead over the other two (both 32.0), but in the stretch Reynolds was the strongest man. He went home the winner in 43.93, with Everett a close second (43.98) and Lewis third (44.37). The winner had the following 100 m. splits: 10.6, 10.6, 10.8, 11.9. The 44 secs. barrier was thus broken even at sea level, by two men in the same race. Reynolds hit the target a few weeks later under favourable conditions, namely on 17 August at Zurich (altitude, 410 m.). Running in lane 4, he stayed away from the suicidal tactics of Innocent Egbunike of Nigeria (21.4 to 20.9), came into his own in the cru-

Butch Reynolds (USA) in his happiest moment, setting a world's 400 m. record of 43.29 (Zürich 1988).

cial part of the race and finished an impressive winner in 43.29. He thus broke Evans' 20-year-old record by a solid 0.57 sec., averaging 10.82 for each 100 m. section! His actual 100 m. splits were 11.2, 10.2, 10.7 and 11.2. Everett was a well beaten second (44.20), followed by Lewis (44.26), while Egbunike finished sixth (44.97). In spite of these superlative efforts, Reynolds failed to do himself justice in the meets that counted most - the 1987 World Championships in Rome and the 1988 Olympics in Seoul. On the former occasion he was hampered by intestinal problems and had to be content with third place. In Seoul he ran what seemed to be a wise race, only to be excelled by Lewis' bolder approach. Their intermediate times aptly tell the story:

Lewis (lane 6):
11.26, 10.15 (21.41), 10.72, 11.74 = 43.87
Reynolds (lane 3):
11.29, 10.39 (21.68), 10.90, 11.35 = 43.93

Everett was third (44.09) and Darren Clark of Australia fourth (44.55). The Aussie star had posted his best-ever time, 44.38, in a semi-final two days earlier - such was the price of partial glory anno 1988! Lewis (born in Los Angeles on 16 May 1969; 1.88 m./84 kg.), a phenomenal talent who was capable of 46.50 at seventeen, thus chose the ideal occasion to turn the tables on the two men -Reynolds and Everett - who had been his masters throughout pre-Olympic weeks. The best European one-lap specialists of this period were Thomas Schönlebe of East Germany and Roger Black of Britain. The former (born at Frauenstein on 6 August 1965; 1.85 m./71 kg.) was usually at his best on big occasions. He had his greatest day at the 1987 World Championships in Rome, where he upset Egbunike and Reynolds to win in 44.33, a new European record. After three excellent seasons (1985-87), an injury forced him to slow down in 1988. In the Seoul Olympics he ran 44.90 but failed to make the final. In another semi-final, Susumu Takano of Japan had exactly the same time, an Asian record, and the same dire destiny. Both went into statistical books as "the fastest non-qualifiers ever". Black (born at Portsmouth on 31 March 1966; 1.90 m./83 kg.) won the European title twice (1986 and '90), each time beating Schönlebe by a narrow margin. An operation (stress fracture in left ankle) caused him to stay away from the Seoul Olympics. Other leading 400 m. men of the Eighties were Erwin Skamrahl (44.50 in '83) and Hartmut Weber of West Germany, Gabriel Tiacoh of the Ivory Coast (44.30 in '86), Mohamed Al Malky of Oman (44.56 in '88) and Roberto Hernández of Cuba (44.14 in '90), Juantorena's successor as Cuban record holder. In 1990 a new man came to the fore and astounded experts for his skill in both 200 and 400 m. This man was Michael Johnson of USA and his fastest times, 19.85 and 44.21, amounted to the best combination ever at these distances. Although basically regarded as a 200 m. man, he beat the likes of Everett, Reynolds and Hernández in the one-lap event with consummate ease, and surprised many people by usually negotiating the first half in about 22 secs. or slightly less, belying to some extent his origin as "pure sprinter". In the last two years (1989-90) Reynolds was partly hampered by injuries and could do no better than 44.22. What is even worse, in the fall of 1990 he was found "positive" to a forbidden substance (Nandrolone, an anabolic steroid) during a test conducted at Monaco and was handed a two-year suspension. More or less at the same time, Darren Clark of Australia, the man who finished fourth in the last two Olympic finals (1984 and '88), announced his retirement from track. He said he was forced to this decision by frustration over fighting a losing battle against "drug-fuelled robots". Be as it may, a world's 400 m. record that is the equivalent of four consecutive 100 m.'s in 10.82, can only suggest that in this department the future inevitably belongs to top-notch sprinters.

Early in the Nineties two Americans enjoyed brief spells as kings of the one-lap event: Antonio Pettigrew who won at the 1991 World Championships, and Quincy Watts, a magnificent victor at the 1992 Olympics. The latter (born at Detroit on 19 June 1970; 1.90 m./88 Kg.) was a great talent whose versatility shone also in basketball and football. In 1991 he qualified for the team that was to represent USA at the Worlds in Tokyo, but found himself in poor form on the eve of the great rendezvous and decided to cede his spot to a teammate. He reportedly did so to concentrate on the relay, which was later in the week - and ran a great second leg, 43.4. The following year Watts was in a class by himself and won the Olympic title in 43.50, leaving his nearest rival 0.71 behind. That was the second fastest time on record. John Smith, who had been coaching Watts during the summers, ironically commented: "The amazing thing is, he still doesn't know how to run the race yet". If that was that, it could be said in the same vein that he never really learnt, because Watts never regained his '92 form.

From 1993 onwards there was a dominant figure in the one-lap department: Michael Johnson. He won the 1996 Olympic title and four consecutive World Championship titles (1993, '95, '97 and '99). As previously related, he usually alternated this event with the 200 m. And he managed to score a double at the 1995 World Championships and the 1996 Olympics - an achievement never before attained in high-level competition. The detailed story of his labours on these occasions was as follow:

1995 World Championships (Göteborg)

400 m	45.49	Heat	5/8
	45.15	Q-F	6/8
	44.91	S-F	7/8
	43.39	Final	9/8
200 m	20.57 (+0.2)	Heat	10/8
	20.35 (+0.1)	Q-F	10/8
	20.01 (+0.3)	S-F	11/8
	19.79 (+0.5)	Final	11/8

1996 Olympic Games (Atlanta)

400 m	45.80	Heat	26/7
	44.62	Q-F	27/7
	44.59	S-F	28/7
	43.49	Final	29/7
200 m	20.55 (-0.6)	Heat	31/7
	20.37 (-0.7)	Q-F	31/7
	20.27 (+0.3)	S-F	1/8
	* 19.32 (+0.4)	Final	1/8

*World Record

At Stuttgart in 1993 and Göteborg in 1995, Johnson won from world record holder Butch Reynolds by margins of 0.48 and 0.83 respectively. At the 1996 Olympics he left runner-up Roger Black an awesome 0.92 behind. The following year at Athens the great MJ, just recovering from an injury, had to be content with a "cheaper" margin: 0.25 vis-à-vis Davis Kamoga of Uganda. But for all his splendour MJ entered the 1999 season, aged 32, without that world record he had chased for so long. On his Day of Days, back in 1988 in Zurich, Butch Reynolds had been clocked in 43.29, which was to remain 0.62 better than his second fastest time. MJ had mastered his rival steadily in head-to-head competition, yet Butch's mark remained an elusive target. Johnson's long quest was finally crowned with success at the 1999 World Championships in Sevilla. This time he had only the 400 in mind and the shape of things to come became evident when he ran a semi-final in 43.95, easing up some 50 m. before the finish.... Two days later he lined up at the start of the final as confident and relaxed as in his best moments. Running in lane 5, he let others go as crazy as they pleased in the early stage while he, easily the fastest sprinter in the field, wisely bided his time.

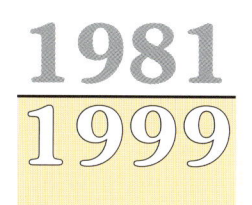

1981
1999

Michael Johnson (USA), right, in one of his rare defeats - to Frank Fredericks (Namibia) in a 200 m. race, 19.85 to 19.82 (Oslo 1996).

The film of the race for the first four was as follows:

	100m	200m	300m	400m
M. Johnson (USA)	11.10	21.22 (10.12)	31.66 (10.44)	43.18 (11.52)
S.C.Parrela (Bra)	11.12	21.13 (10.01)	32.10 (10.97)	44.29 (12.19)
A.Cárdenas (Mex)	10.99	21.19 (10.20)	32.11 (10.92)	44.31 (12.20)
J.Young (USA)	11.16	21.33 (10.17)	31.95 (10.62)	44.36 (12.41)

MJ thus fulfilled his dream with halves of 21.22 and 21.96. The latest IAAF scoring table gives 1293 points for a performance of 43.18 in the 400, far fewer than those allotted to MJ's fabulous 200 m. record, 19.32 (1335 pts) but just about as many as those alloted for Maurice Greene's 9.79 in the 100 m. (1294 pts). Be as it may, 43.18 is the equivalent of four consecutive 100 m.'s in 10.795. MJ is the most complete sprinter the world has ever seen. In addition to his world records for 200 and 400 m. he can point to a personal best of 10.09 (1994) in the 100 m., a distance he tried on relatively few occasions. Before his advent, only one man had ever had a similar "double" in terms of world records: Tommie Smith, who in 1967 was holder of the 220 y. and 440 y. marks with 20.0 and 44.8 respectively.

Britain has been the no. 1 European power in this event throughout the Nineties. Roger Black crowned a great career with a silver medal at the 1996 Olympics. Earlier in the same year he ran the 400 m. in 44.37. He and the likes of Iwan Thomas (44.36 in '97), Mark Richardson (44.37 in '98), David Grindley (44.47 in '92) have all failed by narrow margins in their attempt to surpass the European record, still held by Thomas Schönlebe of Germany with 44.33 (1987).

The best time on record for the seldom run 300 m. is 31.48 by Danny Everett of USA at Jerez de la Frontera on 3 September 1990. This came as a result of a torrid duel with Roberto Hernández of Cuba, who was given the same time. Four years later at Salamanca MJ made a casual try and was credited with 31.56.

MIDDLE DISTANCES
800 Metres: Coe's magic night in Florence - Kipketer, the supreme ruler.

1981 - WCup, Rome (4 Sep): 1.Coe (Eur/GB) 1:46.16 (last 200 m. in 25.1), 2.J.Robinson (USA) 1:47.31, 3.Wagenknecht (EG) 1:47.49.
1982 - EC, Athens (8 Sep): 1.Ferner (WG) 1:46.33, 2.Coe 1:46.68, 3.Härkönen (Fin) 1:46.90.
1983 - WC, Helsinki (9 Aug): 1.Wülbeck (WG) 1:43.65 (51.3 + 52.4), 2.Druppers (Hol) 1:44.20, 3.Cruz (Bra) 1:44.27.
1984 - OG, Los Angeles (6 Aug): 1.Cruz 1:43.00 (51.2 + 51.8), 2.Coe 1:43.64, 3.E.Jones (USA) 1:43.83.
1985 - WCup, Canberra (4 Oct): 1.Koskei (Ken) 1:45.14, 2.Kalinkin (USSR) 1:45.72, 3,.Guymaraes (Ame/Bra) 1:45.80.
1986 - EC, Stuttgart (28 Aug): 1.Coe 1:44.50 (52.7 + 51.8), 2.McKean (GB) 1:44.61, 3.Cram (GB) 1:44.88.
1987 - WC, Rome (1 Sep): 1.Konchellah (Ken) 1:43.06 (last 200 m. in 26.21), 2.P.Elliott (GB) 1:43.41, 3.Barbosa (Bra) 1:43.76.
1988 - OG, Seoul (26 Sep): 1.Ereng (Ken) 1:43.45 (51.07 + 52.38), 2.Cruz 1:43.90, 3.Aouita (Mor) 1:44.06.
1989 - WCup, Barcelona (8 Sep): 1.McKean 1:44.95, 2.Herold (EG) 1:45.04, 3.Kiprotich (Afr/Ken) 1:45.08.
1990 - EC, Split (29 Aug): 1.McKean 1:44.76, 2.Sharpe (GB) 1:45.59, 3.Piekarski (Pol) 1:45.76.
1991 - WC, Tokyo (27 Aug): 1. B.Konchellah 1:43.99, 2. Barbosa 1:44.24, 3. M.Everett (USA) 1:44.67.
1992 - OG, Barcelona (5 Aug): 1. W.Tanui (Ken) 1:43.66, 2. Kiprotich (Ken) 1:43.70, 3. J.Gray (USA) 1:43.97; WCup, Habana (25 Sep): 1. Sharpe (GB) 1:46.06, 2. W.Tanui 1:46.14, 3. Benvenuti (Eur/Ita) 1:46.53.
1993 - WC, Stuttgart (17 Aug): 1. Ruto (Ken) 1:44.71, 2. D'Urso (Ita) 1:44.86, 3. B.Konchellah 1:44.89.
1994 - EC, Helsinki (14 Aug): 1. Benvenuti 1:46.12, 2. Rodal (Nor) 1:46.53, 3. de Teresa (Spa) 1:46.57; WCup, London (9 Sep): 1. M.Everett 1:46.02, 2. W.Tanui 1:46.84, 3. Winrow (GB) 1:47.16.
1995 - WC, Göteborg (8 Aug): 1. Kipketer (Den) 1:45.08, 2. Hatungimana (Bur) 1:45.64, 3. Rodal 1:45.68.
1996 - OG, Atlanta (31 Jul): 1. Rodal 1:42.58, 2. Sepeng (SA) 1:42.74, 3. Onyancha (Ken) 1:42.79.

1981
1999

1997 - WC, Athens (8 Aug): 1. Kipketer 1:43.38, 2. Tellez (Cub) 1:44.00, 3. Kenah (USA) 1:44.25.
1998 - EC, Budapest (23 Aug): 1. Schumann (Ger) 1:44.89, 2. Bucher (Swz) 1:45.04, 3. Vydra (Cze) 1:45.23; WCup, Johannesburg (11 Sep): 1; Schumann 1:48.66, 2. M.Everett 1:48.73, 3. Tellez 1:48.92.
1999 - WC, Sevilla (2 Sep): 1. Kipketer 1:43.30, 2. Sepeng 1:43.32, 3. Said-Guerni (Alg) 1:44.18.

Sebastian Coe had a superlative season in 1981. In the two-lap department he offered his chef-d'oeuvre on 10 June at Florence's Stadio Comunale. The race was run at 11 p.m., by which time the heat of a sultry summer day had let up considerably. Eight runners toed the line and long-striding Billy Konchellah of Kenya led the field at the break for the pole. He covered the first 400 m. in 49.7, with Coe alongside him. The Englishman took over round the penultimate turn. What he did after that clearly showed that he was determined "to put the record out of sight". Even though no one was breathing down his neck, he ran an inspired race to the end, tying up a little only in the last 30 m. A malfunction in the automatic photo finish system forced the judges to determine the time on the strength of verdicts given by two parallel photo-cells with writing apparatus. These gave Coe 1:41.727 and 1:41.724, so the official time rounded to the hundredth-of-a-second above was 1:41.73. For all practical purposes, a third system was available - manual timing. Watches read 1:41.6, 1:41.7, 1:41.6. Coe's 200 m. splits were estimated thus: 24.4, 25.3, 25.3 and 26.7. Dragan Zivotic of Yugoslavia was a distant second in 1:47.42. In later years, Coe often referred to his Florence record as the most precious gem in his collection. Joaquim Carvalho Cruz of Brazil (born at Taguatinga, Brasilia, on 12 March 1963; 1.88 m./77 kg.), easily the greatest middle distance ace in South American history, was at his peak during the 1984 Olympics in Los Angeles, when in the space of 73 hours he had the following series: 1:45.66 (heat), 1:44.84 (quarter-final), 1:43.82 (semi-final) and 1:43.00 (final), beating Coe (1:43.64) in the decisive race. After the Games, Cruz repeatedly tried to smash Coe's record, without success. However, his best clocking, 1:41.77 at Köln on 26 August, being an automatic time, was probably as good as Coe's Florence effort in intrinsic value. Curiously enough, his 400 m. splits in this race (49.7 + 52.1) were strikingly similar to Coe's. But he had a strong opponent in Sammy Koskei of Kenya, whose time on that occasion, 1:42.28, still stands as an African record. Proneness to injuries severely hampered Cruz in subsequent years, yet he managed to rise again and in 1988 he finished second to Paul Ereng in the Olympic final at Seoul.

At other distances the Brazilian can point to such times as 47.17 (400 m.) and 3:34.63 (1500 m.), which compare unfavourably with Coe's 46.87 and 3:29.77. Kenya was to become the world's no.1 power in this event, to the point of owning five of the top ten performances in the 1990 World List. Billy Konchellah, the 1987 world champion, and Paul Ereng, the 1988 Olympic champion, both emerged as 400 m. men, with times of 45.38 and 45.6 respectively. Ereng (born at Trans-Nzoia on 22 August 1967; 1.86 m./72 kg.) is a Turkana who discovered the 800 m. early in 1988, while attending the University of Virginia (USA). He made rapid progress, yet his road to Seoul was a tortuous one. After losing quite a few races in Europe, he had a close call at the Kenya Olympic Trials, when he nearly committed suicide (49.0 in the first 400 m.) and

Joaquim Cruz (Brazil), the 1984 Olympic champion in the 800 m.

289

barely salvaged third place in a hectic finish. In the Olympics, however, this long-legged runner looked well nigh unbeatable and won in 1:43.45. Early in 1989 he bettered Coe's world indoor record with 1:44.84. This was at the World Indoor Championships in Budapest and Ereng moved from fourth to first in the last lap (200 m.), a stupendous achievement under indoor conditions. Other leading European runners of the Eighties were Willi Wülbeck and Hans-Peter Ferner of West Germany, Steve Cram, Tom McKean and Peter Elliott of Britain, all of whom won important honours in major Games.

The "African wave" reached greater heights during the Nineties, when 800 m. medals awarded in major Games (Olympic/World) were so divided among continents: Africa 10, Europe 6, North America 3, Central and South America 1 each. Europe's figure is somewhat deceiving if one considers that 50% of the medals on its count were brought home by a Kenia-born Dane, Wilson Kipketer. Since the early years of the decade Kenya in particular showed a tremendous turnover, supplying ever new winners in major Games: Billy Konchellah (1991 Worlds), William Tanui (1992 Olympics) and unsung Paul Ruto (1993 Worlds). The most amazing of the three was undoubtedly Billy Konchellah (born at Kilgoris on 20 October 1961, 1.88 m./74 Kg.), a fine runner from the Masai tribe who throughout his career often had to fight with poor health, notably tuberculosis and asthma, yet managed to come back time and again. As a youth he was credited with a hand-timed 21.2 for 200 m. and 45.38 for 400 m. As previously related, in 1981 he acted as "hare" in Seb Coe's world record race in Florence (1:41.73). Who could ever predict then that he would one day become a world champion himself? Konchellah joined the élite by finishing fourth in 1:44.03, a personal best, in the 1984 Olympic final at Los Angeles. His frequent bouts with poor health kept him away from the Olympics of 1988 and '92,

Wilson Kipketer (Denmark) lowering the world's 800 m. record to 1:41.24 (Zürich 1997). A few days later at Köln he improved to 1:41.11.

Turn it upside down and you'll read the future

Even among rabid track nuts not many are likely to remember Desta Asgedom of Ethiopia, who won the 800 m. in 1:46.35 (and was third in the 1500 m.) at the 1990 World Junior Championships in Plovdiv, Bulgaria. More familiar may be the name of Jonah Birir of Kenya, who was second in that race (1:46.61), two years after winning the same title at Sudbury, Canada. He later developed into an excellent 1500 m. man. In 1992 he did 3:33.36 and was second in the World Cup race at Habana. As for the third man of the Plovdiv race, Norberto Tellez of Cuba (1:47.33), he really fulfilled his boyhood dreams (or just about) as he succeeded the great Alberto Juantorena as Cuban record holder with 1:42.85 (1996) and finished second in the 1997 World Championships - barred from gold by one Wilson Kipketer of Denmark, who seven years earlier had finished a little noticed fourth (1:48.13) in the ominous Plovdiv race, running in the colours of his native country, Kenya. A few days later a plane of the Balkan Air Lines had taken young Kipketer to Copenhagen in the company of Ove Björn Kraft, president of a Danish club (KIF), who had spotted the boy as a real comer during a sojourn at St. Patrick's High School in Iten, Kenya (altitude, 2300 m.), where he lived and trained under the tutelage of Brother Colm O'Connell, a dedicated Irishman. The Danish talent scout took over to Copenhagen another young runner, Robert Kiplagat, better known now under his new Danish name, Andersen (3:31.17 for 1500 m. in 1997). An account of the 1990 race in Plovdiv tells us that "Kipketer was hopelessly outpaced in the decisive stage". But never say die.

1981 1999

but he had better luck with the World Championships, winning in Rome '87 with what was to remain his best-ever time, 1:43.06, and again in Tokyo '91. He had a strong finishing kick but at Stuttgart in 1993 he failed in his try for a third world title when he moved too late and had to be content with third place - in spite of a 52.6 second lap. A few years later his younger brother Patrick tried to follow in his footsteps and amazingly bettered the family record with 1:42.98 in 1997, namely in the wake of a record breaker whose feats will soon be recounted. Earlier in the same year Patrick Konchellah had placed fourth in the World Championships in Athens.

The greatest of them all, however, was a smiling yet reserved man from the Nandi tribe - Wilson Kipketer (born at Kapchemoiywo on 12 December 1970; 1.72 m./62 Kg.) who won three consecutive world titles (1995, '97 and '99), all in the colours of Denmark, his country of election. He also succeeded Seb Coe as world record holder. As related in detail in the adjoining aside, he made a rather unobtrusive international debut at the 1990 World Junior Championships in Plovdiv, Bulgaria, finishing a little noticed fourth in 1:48.13. At the time his year of birth was listed as 1968. If the currently accepted version (1970) is correct, then he was over-age at the time of the Plovdiv meet, the only major one in which he represented his native country. He emigrated to Denmark right after those championships and the rest of his career thus unfolded in Europe. Even though he obtained the Danish citizenship only after 7 years residence there, he was allowed to run for Denmark in the World Championships - but not in the Olympic Games, in which he is expected to make his debut at Sydney in 2000. Working under a Polish coach, Slawomir Nowak, he made amazing progress, reaching his peak in 1997. The shape of things to come became evident in March of that year, when he broke the world undercover record twice at the World Indoor Championships held in Paris, with 1:43.96 in a heat (7 March) and 1:42.67 in the final (9 March). In between the two races, on 8 March, he took a rest of sorts with an easy 1:48.49 semi-final .... Apart from the fact that he became the first man to set a world 800 m. record in a heat, what makes such performances even more remarkable is the "tactics" he used - he took an early lead and never relinquished it, thus negotiating four laps (of a 200 m. indoor track, i.e. eight curves) all in splendid isolation! In the final he won by more than 3 seconds. By then the track world expected great things from him in the outdoor season, well remembering that in the autumn of 1996 in Rieti he had come dangerously close to Coe's world mark with 1:41.83. In the summer of 1997 he lived up to expectations. He began by equalling the record, 1:41.73, at Stockholm on 7 July. Then he lowered it to 1:41.24 at Zurich on 13 August, in a fantastic meet that saw this and two other world records fall in the space of about 100 minutes! The finishing touch was given on 24 August at Köln: 1:41.11. It was here that Patrick Konchellah ran 1:42.98 in finishing second. In all of these races Kipketer followed a "hare" in the first lap, then forged ahead. A study of his 200 and 400 m. splits makes interesting reading:

200m	400m	600m	800m	2nd Half
Indoors - *Paris, 7.3.97*				
24.96	50.77 (25.81)	1:17.23 (26.46)	1:43.96 (26.73)	53.19
Indoors - *Paris, 9.3.97*				
24.22	50.22 (26.00)	1:16.49 (26.27)	1:42.67 (26.18)	52.45
Outdoors - *Stockholm, 7.7.97*				
24.0	49.6 (25.6)	1:16.3 (26.7)	1:41.73 (25.5)	52.1
Outdoors - *Zurich, 13.8.97*				
23.2	48.3 (25.1)	1:14.5 (26.2)	1:41.24 (26.7)	52.9
Outdoors - *Köln, 24.8.97*				
23.8	49.3 (25.5)	1:14.6 (25.3)	1:41.11 (26.5)	51.8

A heavy bout of malaria and later pneumonia curtailed his activity in 1998 and put an end to his win streak of 33 consecutive victories (including heats) over the period May '96-August '98. But he made a fine comeback in 1999 with another faultless season. Strangely enough, he was truly extended only in the World Championships at Sevilla, where he beat Hezekiel Sepeng of South Africa in a frenzied finish - 1:43.30 to 1:43.32. He has never done anything of real note at other distances and his personal bests of 46.85 for 400 m. and 3:42.80 for 1500 m. certainly look like a pale reflection of his potential in terms of speed + endurance. "March" Fiasconaro, the South Africa-born Italian who once held the world's 800 m. record (1:43.7 in 1973) was recently quoted as saying: "The more I look at Kipketer's flowing style the more I admire his incredible stamina. By comparison I was only a dilettante".

Kipketer's current rivals lag 1-to-2 seconds behind him in terms of best marks. Scandinavia recently had a good runner in Vebjörn Rodal of Norway, who won the 1996 Olympic title in 1:42.58 - in the absence of Kipketer, that's true. As for age records, the man who beat them all is Johnny Gray of USA. He won a bronze medal in the Olympics at 32 (Barcelona '92) and was still a 1:45 man at 39. A front runner par excellence, he can point to 26 sub-1:44.00 performances.

291

1500 METRES/1 MILE:
The British oligarchy Coe-Ovett-Cram. Then North Africa takes over: from Aouita to Morceli and his long reign, down to El Guerrouj's sterling records.

1981 - WCup, Rome (5 Sep): 1.Ovett (Eur/GB) 3:34.95, 2.Walker (Oce/NZ) 3:35.49, 3.O.Beyer (EG) 3:35.58.
1982 - EC, Athens (11 Sep): 1.Cram (GB) 3:36.49, 2.Kirov (USSR) 3:36.99, 3.Abascal (Spa) 3:37.04.
1983 - WC, Helsinki (14 August): 1.Cram 3:41.59, 2.Scott (USA) 3:41.87, 3.Aouita (Mor) 3:42.02.
1984 - OG, Los Angeles (11 August): 1.Coe 3:32.53 (last 300 m. in 39.3), 2.Cram 3:33.40, 3.Abascal 3:34.30.
1985 - WCup, Canberra (5 Oct): 1.Khalifa (Afr/Sud) 3:41.16, 2.O.Beyer 3:41.26, 3.Lotaryev (USSR) 3:41.92.
1986 - EC, Stuttgart (31 Aug): 1.Cram 3:41.09 (last 400 m. in 50.9, last 200 m. in 25.0), 2.Coe 3:41.67, 3.Kulker (Hol) 3:42.11.
1987 - WC, Rome (6 Sep): 1.Bile (Som) 3:36.80 (last 800 m. in 1:46.0, last 400 m. in 51.4), 2.González (Spa) 3:38.03, 3.Spivey (USA) 3:38.82.
1988 - OG, Seoul (1 October): 1.P.Rono (Ken) 3:35.96 (last 300 m. in 39.27), 2.P.Elliott (GB) 3:36.15, 3.Herold (EG) 3:36.21.
1989 - WCup, Barcelona (9 Sep): 1.Bile 3:35.56, 2.Coe 3:35.79, 3.Herold 3:35.87.
1990 - EC, Split (1 Sep): 1.Herold 3:38.25, 2.Di Napoli (Ita) 3:38.60, 3.Silva (Por) 3:38.73.
1991 - WC, Tokyo (1 Sep) : 1.Morceli 3:32.84, 2.Kirochi (Ken) 3:34.84, 3.Fuhlbrügge (Ger) 3.35.28.
1992 - OG, Barcelona (8 Aug) : 1.Cacho (Spa) 3:40.12, 2.El Basir (Mor) 3:40.62, 3.Suleiman (Qat) 3:40.69; WCup, Habana (26 Sep): 1.Suleiman (Asi/Qat) 3:38.37, 2.J. Birir (Afr/ken) 3:40.25, 3.Fairbrother (GB) 3:40.30.
1993 - WC, Stuttgart (22 Aug) : 1.Morceli 3:34.24, 2.Cacho 3:35.56, 3.Bile (Som) 3:35.96.
1994 - EC, Helsinki (9 Aug) : 1.Cacho 3:35.27, 2.Viciosa (Spa) 3:36.01, 3.Zorko (Cro) 3:36.88; WCup, London (10 Sep) : 1.Morceli 3:34.70, 2.Stenzel (Ger) 3:40.04, 3.Suleiman 3:40.52.
1995 - WC, Göteborg (13 Aug) : 1.Morceli 3:33.73, 2.El Guerrouj (Mor) 3:35.28, 3.Niyongabo (Bur) 3:35.56.
1996 - OG, Atlanta (3 Aug) : 1.Morceli 3:35.78, 2.Cacho 3:36.40, 3.Kipkorir (Ken) 3:36.72.
1997 - WC, Athens (6 Aug) : 1.El Guerrouj 3:35.83, 2.Cacho 3:36.63, 3.Estévez (Spa) 3:37.26.
1998 - EC, Budapest (20 Aug) : 1.Estévez 3:41.31, 2.R. Silva (Por) 3:41.84, 3.Cacho 3:42.13; WCup, Johannesburg (12 Sep) : 1.Rotich (Ken) 3:40.87, 2.R. Silva 3:40.95, 3.Whiteman (GB) 3:40.99.
1999 - WC, Sevilla (24 Aug) : 1.El Guerrouj 3:27.65, 2.Ngeny (Ken) 3:28.73, 3.Estévez 3:30.57.

1981 was a memorable year in the Coe-Ovett saga. The two English champions had the world's one-mile record as their bone of contention, but for some reason they never faced each other in a direct clash. Coe was first to strike, on 19 August in Zurich. He took the lead with 300 m. to go and chalked up a final time of 3:48.53 (quarters: 56.5, 57.7, 58.2, 56.2). He won from Mike Boit (3:49.74), Steve Cram (3:49.95) and John Walker (3:50.12). Ovett answered exactly a week later at Koblenz. Originally, the programme included only a 1500 m. event, but Ovett - who had made history and friends there in 1980 - talked organizers into adding a 1-mile race for his (their) own benefit. The 1500 m. race was won by Steve Scott of USA in 3:31.96. About ten minutes later, Ovett lined up for the mile. Useful "hares" helped him go through quarters in 56.6, 57.9, 57.0. He was on his own in the last quarter, which he negotiated in 56.9. That gave him a slight but decisive edge vis-à-vis Seb, his ghost - 3:48.40. Craig Masback of USA was second in 3:54.14. Yet even this record was short-lived, because Coe fought back ... two days later, at Brussels, in the IAAF Golden Mile. He went into the lead with 500 m. to go and finished in 3:47.33 (quarters: 55.3, 58.1, 58.8, 55.2). Even though the pace, set by the usual "hares", could hardly be described as uniform, Seb managed to run the last 100 m. in 13.2. Mike Boit was again second (3:49.45). In subsequent years the Big Two were bothered by recurrent injuries and ailments, but they fought back and on occasion they still managed to offer further proof of their true stature. By then, however, mother Anglia had a new standout in Steve Cram (born at Gateshead on 14 October 1960; 1.86 m./69 kg.), who in 1980 had gone to the Moscow Olympics as a newcomer, placing eighth in the 1500 m. final. A beautiful "mover" with an imperial stride, Cram was supreme for several years, until recurrent injuries began to slow him down. In the "metric mile" he won the 1982 European and Commonwealth titles and in 1983 he beat a crack field at the World Championships in a relatively slow race enlivened by a hectic finish. Still in 1983, the world's 1500 m. record was bettered on two occasions, first by Sydney Maree, a South Africa-born American who did 3:31.24 in a framed handicap at Köln on 28 August, then by Ovett, who did 3:30.77 at Rieti, Italy, on 4 September. Chief pace-setter in both races was David Mack of USA, a top-ranking 800 m. man. In Rieti he passed the 800 m. in a fast 1:51.67, with Ovett in his wake. The Briton reached 1200 m. in 2:49.14, then crowned his effort successfully with 41.63 in the last 300 m. In 1983 Coe had a disastrous bout with toxoplasmosis, and in the spring of 1984 Cram developed Achilles tendon problems. On the eve of the Los Angeles Olympics neither looked like a "sure-fire bet". Ovett had bronchial trouble during the Games and dropped out of the 1500 m. final. When the chips were down, Coe ran a masterful race and his strong finish (last 300 m. in 39.3) carried him home the victor, well ahead of Cram. The latter had his best-ever season the following year. By then he had a new rival, Said Aouita of Morocco (born at Kenitra on 2 November 1959; 1.75 m./58 kg.), who first came to the fore while living in France and matured to world class after moving to Italy. He ran 3:32.54 in 1983, but in the following year he decided to concentrate on the 5000 m. for the Los Angeles Games (he won the gold in impressive fashion). His one and only major clash with Steve Cram occurred on 16 July 1985 in Nice. True to his customary tactics, the Briton launched his attack with a lap to go and soon built up a substantial lead. Aouita fought back with 300 m. to go, closed the gap steadily - but not entirely. He finished faster than Cram (39.6 vs. 40.0 in the last 300 m., 13.0 vs. 13.5 in the last 100 m.), but the end found him 0.04 behind his rival. Results: 1.Cram 3:29.67, 2.Aouita 3:29.71, 3.José Luis González (Spain) 3:30.99, 4.Steve Scott (USA) 3:31.76. The 3:30 barrier was thus broken by two men in the same race. Reflection on progress: it took 27 years to advance from the first sub-3:50 to the first sub-3:40, and another 28 years to improve to the first sub-3:30. Cram ran another superlative race

1981
1999

Sebastian Coe (Great Britain) winning the 1500 metres at the 1984 Olympics in Los Angeles.

"This is no longer life or death for me"

As it happens to most human beings, the life of a champion is as often as not a mixture of joy and sorrow. Sebastian Coe had his share of both, always to a remarkable degree. The first man to win the 1500 m. in two (official) editions of the Olympic Games, a record-breaker in several middle distance events and, last but not least, a divine runner to watch in his best moments, Coe had more than one serious bout with ailments and injuries. He saw the end of the line at the 1990 Commonwealth Games in Auckland, when he finished sixth in the 800 m. (As it transpired, he had been suffering from a respiratory infection). His post-race comment was: "I feel like a boxer who looks great in the gym but as soon as he enters the ring gets knocked out. But then this is no longer life or death for me".

293

eleven days later at Oslo's Bislett Stadium, the Mecca of middle and long distance runners. He was up against the likes of Coe, González and Scott, but even such luminaries were outshone by Cram's last lap, a 53.2 "killer". The pace was set first by James Mays of USA, then by Mike Hillardt of Australia, with "quarters"in 57.4, 57.3 and 58.5. Cram took over right after the bell and K.O.'d his rivals with a long, sustained drive. His final time, 3:46.32, shaved 1.01 sec. off Coe's 1-mile world record. González was a magnificent second in 3:47.79, followed by Coe (3:49.22) and Scott (3:49.93). For Coe it was the first time he had ever lost in a record-setting race. Cram was timed in 3:32.29 at 1500 m., so he covered the last 109.35 m. in a sizzling 14.03. Here again the March of Progress spoke in lofty terms: a gain of 13 seconds vis-à-vis Bannister's first sub-4 min. mile thirty-one years earlier.

Said Aouita (Morocco) breaking the 13 min. barrier in the 5000 metres: 12:58.30 in Rome (1987).

After his narrow defeat to Cram at Nice, Aouita had a great win streak. Between July 1985 and September 1987 he won 44 consecutive races at distances ranging from 800 to 10,000 m. His lucky streak came to an end at the hands of Alessandro Lambruschini of Italy in an event Aouita was not familiar with, the 3000 m. steeplechase (8:21.92 to 8:19.72) in the Mediterranean Games at Lakafia. Aouita seized the world's 1500 m. record on 23 August 1985 at Berlin with 3:29.46, after covering the last 800m. in 1:50.0 and the last 400 m. in 54.5. Sydney Maree was second in 3:32.90. No runner past or present can match Aouita's series of marks in the range 800-10,000m. Here it is: - 1:43.86 (800 m.), 2:15.16 (1000 m.), 3:29.46 (1500 m. WR), 3:46.76 (mile), 4:50.81 (2000 m. WR), 7:29.45 (3000 m., WR), 8:13.45 (2 miles, WR), 12:58.39 (5000 m. WR), 27:26.11 (10,000 m.). Aouita at his best is a near perfect running machine: he can stand any pace and win with any tactics. His turn of speed in the crucial stage of a race is simply phenomenal. Another great African runner of recent years is Abdi Bile of Somalia (born at Las Anod on 28 December 1962; 1.85 m./75 kg.), who had his greatest moment at the 1987 World Championships in Rome, when he won the 1500 m. in 3:36.80 with a mind-boggling finish: last 1000m. in 2:16.6, last 800 m. in 1:46.0 and last 400 m. in 51.4. In 1988 an injury kept him away from the Seoul Olympics. With Aouita concentrating on the 800m. and Cram far from his best form, the 1500 m. crown in Seoul went to Peter Rono of Kenya, a "single-day" great, if ever there was one. In Britain a man like Peter Elliott, credited with such times as 1:42.97 (800 m.) and 3:32.69 (1500 m.), had to fight hard for years to earn a place in the sun in the face of the Coe-Ovett-Cram oligarchy. Other good European runners at the dawn of the Nineties were Jens-Peter Herold of East Germany and Genny Di Napoli of Italy.

Africa's supremacy was further enhanced throughout the Nineties, when athletes from that continent won 13 of the 21 medals awarded in the 1500 m. in major (World/Olympic) Games, providing the winner in 6 cases out of 7. In the wake of Said Aouita, the great Moroccan star of the Eighties, it fell to a couple of men from the same area - called "Maghreb" by Arabs - to enlighten the decade with their performances: Noureddine Morceli of Algeria and Hicham El Guerrouj of Morocco. They re-wrote the record book and swept the board on the occasions that counted most. In Europe the center of gravity of middle distance power moved towards the South, with Spain replacing Great Britain as the leading country.

1981
1999

Noureddine Morceli (born at Ténès on 28 February 1970: 1.72 m./62 Kg.) came to athletics in the wake of his elder brother Abderrahmane, who was a middle distance man of international caliber: fourth in the 1977 World Cup 1500 and credited with 3:36.26 (1500 m., 1977) and 3:54.63 (mile, 1983). He later acted as coach and adviser to Noureddine, who lost little time in revealing a great talent. At 18 he made his international debut in the 1988 World Junior Championships at Sudbury, Canada. Entering the final lap of the 1500 m. he led by 10 m. from defending champion Wilfred Kirochi of Kenya, but the latter had a strong recovery and finally won, 3:46.52 to 3:46.93. Third place went to Fermin Cacho of Spain (3:47.31) - another hint of things to come. Morceli progressed by leaps and bounds and was the world's no.1 man in 1990. He was awarded that position in the famous Ranking of "Track & Field News" magazine. And he retained the leadership till 1996 included for the longest reign ever in the 1500 m./1 mile department. In 1990 he won the Grand Prix final and lowered his 1500 m. best to 3:32.60. The following year he won his first major title at the World Championships in Tokyo, turning the tables on Kirochi, 3:32.84 to 3:34.84. In 1992 he was held back by an injury early in the season and ran a poor race in the Barcelona Olympics (7th in 3:41.70). However, he fully recovered to chalk up his first world record at Rieti on 6 September: 3:28.86 for 1500 m. During his long reign Morceli won 3 World Championship titles (1991, '93 and '95) but had to wait till 1996 to take his first Olympic crown. Between 1992 and '96 he had a winning streak of 45 consecutive victories at 1500 m./1 mile. Again at Rieti, on 12 September 1993, he had succeeded Steve Cram as holder of the world's 1 mile record with a scintillating 3:44.39, leaving the nearest man over 11 secs. behind. Always a great "finisseur", the Algerian covered the last 109.35 m. separating the 1500 from the mile in 14.82. His 440 y. splits were estimated as 54.9, 57.7, 57.3 and 54.5. After following a couple of "hares" he took the lead with a little more than a lap to go. He uttered his last word for the 1500 m. at Nice on 12 July 1995. He availed himself of "hares", as was by then the custom in all Grand Prix meets (one of them was his younger brother Ali), then took the lead by 1000 m. and finished in 3:27.37. His 400 m. fractions were 55.0, 56.3, 55.7, his last 200 m. 40.4. Morceli's record breaking spree also covered 2000 m. (4:47.88 in 1995) and 3000 m. (7:25.11 in 1994). He was once quoted as saying: "Perhaps I don't give the impression that I'm hurting out there on the track. But that is because I am animated by an interior force which covers my suffering". Yet those who knew him well regarded him as "a tremendous worker". His range was not as impressive as that of Said Aouita, but he could point to such marks as 1:44.79 in the 800 m. (1991) and 13:03.85 in the 5000 m. (1994). In the latter race he outshone such distance aces as Fita Bayissa (Ethiopia) and Khalid Skah (Morocco) with a punishing 52.2 last lap.

But even the great Morceli was to see his record marks surpassed pretty soon. The "answer" came from nearby Morocco in the person of Hicham El Guerrouj (born at Berkane on 14 September 1974; 1.76 m./58 Kg.). Prior to 1994 his best for 1500 m. was reportedly no better than 3:51, so he created a sensation when he ran 3:33.61 in July of that year at Nice, in the wake of two other Africans. However, keen followers of the sport remembered a previous achievement, namely the gallant race he had run at the World Junior Championships in Seoul two years earlier, when he finished third in the 5000 m. behind two runners who, like him, would make the headlines later on, Haile Gebrselassie and Ismail Kirui. El Guerrouj did

Noureddine Morceli (Algeria) had a long reign as "king" of the milers. Here he wins the 1500 m. crown at the 1996 Olympics.

295

13:46.79 in that race. But from 1994 on his attention was focussed on the 1500, which was to remain his parade distance. He was a distant second to Morceli in the 1995 World Championships. Then he drew closer by the time of the Atlanta Olympic final. Going towards the bell the young Moroccan challenged the great Morceli. There was an infinitesimal contact between Morceli's heel and El Guerrouj's knee. Victim of the clash was the younger man, who fell. "I was starting to accelerate" said Morceli after the race, "otherwise I may have gone down too". The Algerian went on to outsprint Fermin Cacho for victory (3:35.78 ro 3:36.40) while El Guerrouj, sadly disappointed, wound up 12th and last in 3:40.75. Nobody will ever know how things would have gone if Hicham had not fallen. Be as it may, the shape of things to come became evident a few weeks later when El Guerrouj put an end to Morceli's 4-year win streak, beating him (3:38.80 to 3:39.69) in the final of the Grand Prix at Milan. The champion was reportedly feeling the effects of a recent 'flu, yet he showed wisdom by saying: "I've dominated the 1500 for many years .... I wouldn't be surprised if he (El Guerrouj) were to do the same for some years to come". That was a good prediction. In subsequent years Morceli showed declining condition and interest: evidently such a long reign as his ought to demand a price, physically and mentally. On the contrary, El Guerrouj was just gathering momentum. He went on to annex World Championship titles in 1997 and '99 and also succeeded Morceli as holder of world records fo 1500 m. and 1 mile.

Like his predecessor he could stand any pace and was second to none in finishing speed. It was only in 1999 that he found a worthy challenger in a new "pearl" from Kenya - Noah Ngeny (born at Uasin Gishu on 2 November 1978; 1.82 m./68 Kg.). In his international debut at the 1996 World Junior Championships this powerful lad met all sorts of mishaps and finished eighth in 3:42.44. In the year that followed he improved to 3:32.91, best ever by a junior; in 1998 he was down to 3:30.34. His 1999 season was phenomenal - he spread himself thin in a high number of fast races, notably with six sub-3:30 clockings in just over 2 months! He seriously challenged El Guerrouj in a mile race at Rome's Golden Gala on 7 July. The stage for the birth of a memorable record was set with the collaboration of two de-luxe "hares", Robert Kibet and William Tanui, who had personal bests of 1:43.66

Hicham El Guerrouj (Morocco) jubilant after setting a new world record for the 1500 m. : 3:26.00 (Rome 1998).

and 1:43.30 respectively for 800 m. - and the latter had actually won a gold medal in that event at the 1992 Olympics! El Guerrouj took over with one lap to go, with young Ngeny hot on his heels. What followed was one of the fiercest battles ever seen over this classic distance, "A Mile For The Ages", as one observer put it. At times Ngeny looked capable of passing his rival, but the Moroccan held on grimly and finally won the day - 3:43.13 to 3:43.40, both inside Morceli's world record (3:44.39 in 1993). Swedish statistician A. Lennart Julin, an excellent video-analyst, supplied the following splits:

400m	800m	1200m	1500m	1 Mile
El Guerrouj				
55.2	1:51.2	2:47.0	3:28.2	3:43.13
Ngeny				
55.6	1:51.6	2:47.3	3:28.6	3:43.40

When two men run so close to each other all the way, the one who manages to remain in front till the end must obviously be the better runner. This was confirmed when the two locked horns again at the World Championships in Sevilla on 24 August. El Guerrouj had been kept to a relatively reserved season due to a hemorrhoid condition (he underwent surgery later in the year) yet he had things well under control and beat Ngeny again, 3:27.65 to 3:28.73. The young Kenyan was perhaps less impressive than in the mile race in Rome, yet he proved to have enough left for another major feat at Rieti on 5 September when he cancelled the last vestige of a Europe-born athlete in the world record list by succeeding Seb Coe as holder of the 1000 m. record with 2:11.96. Coe's record mark, 2:12.18, was made in Oslo, 1981. Such is the wealth of distance records broken in recent years in Rieti that this Central Italian town may henceforth be hailed as "the Oslo of the South". In that race Ngeny followed his countryman David Kiptoo for about 700 metres then finished the job in a masterful way. His splits: 49.9 (400 m.) and 1:44.62 (800 m.). There is no doubt that young Ngeny has all it takes for a stellar career, especially if he will avoid overwork in choosing his competitions, a danger which proved ruinous for other gifted Kenyans.

European milers had to be content with crumbs during the Nineties, in contrast with what had happened in the preceding decade with the likes of Coe, Ovett and Cram. The only European who had his share of glory was Fermin Cacho (born at Agreda, Soria on 16 February 1969; 1.75 m./65 Kg.) He had his greatest day at the 1992 Olympics in Barcelona, when he brought the home crowd to its feet with a frenzied 50.5 last lap to win the title after a tactical race (3:40.12). As previously recounted, Morceli was not well on that occasion and ran a poor race. Of course Cacho had to surrender to the great Algerian on several other occasions. A great "finisseur", the Spaniard had his best day clock-wise at Zurich on 13 August 1997, when he conquered the European 1500 m. record with 3:28.95, barely losing to Hicham El Guerrouj (3:28.91) at the end of a hair-raising battle. Another good Spanish runner is Reyes Estévez, European champion in 1998 and a bronze medallist at the World Championships in 1999. Of course men like J.M. Abascal and J.L. González had already shown the way during the Eighties, but it should be remembered that Spain had no traditions in the past. It was only in 1954 that the national 1500 m. record began to be expressed with a sub-4 min. mark.

1981
1999

Fermin Cacho (Spain) outsprints a strong 1500 m. field at the 1992 Olympics.

LONG DISTANCES - 5000 and 10,000 metres: Africa "über alles". Gebrselassie, supreme in everything but "doubles".

1981 - WCup, Rome, 5000 m. (6 Sep): 1.Coghlan (Eur/Ire) 14:08.39, 2.Kunze (EG) 14:08.54, 3.Fontanella (Ita) 14:09.06; 10,000 m. (4 Sep): 1.Schildhauer (EG) 27:38.43, 2.Kedir (Afr/Eth) 27:39.44, 3.Salazar (USA) 27:40.69.
1982 - EC, Athens, 5000 m. (11 Sep): 1.Wessinghage (WG) 13:28.90, 2.Schildhauer 13:30.03, 3.Moorcroft (GB) 13:30.42; 10,000 m. (6 Sep): 1.Cova (Ita) 27:41.03, 2.Schildhauer 27:41.21, 3.Vainio (Finland) 27:42.51.
1983 - WC, Helsinki, 5000 m. (14 Aug): 1.Coghlan 13:28.53, 2.Schildhauer 13:30.20, 3.Vainio 13:30.34; 10,000 m. (9 Aug): 1.Cova 28:01.04, 2.Schildhauer 28:01.18, 3.Kunze 28:01.26.
1984 - OG, Los Angeles, 5000 m. (11 Aug): 1.Aouita (Mor) 13:05.59, 2.Ryffel (Switz) 13:07.54, 3.Leitao (Por) 13:09.20; 10,000 m. (6 Aug): 1.Cova 27:47.54, 2.McLeod (GB) 28:06.22, 3.Musyoki (Ken) 28:06.46. Vainio, 2nd in 27:51.10, was disqualified for doping abuse.
1985 - WCup, Canberra, 5000 m. (6 Oct): 1.Padilla (USA) 14:04.11, 2.Mei (Eur/Ita) 14:05.99, 3.Bulti (Eth) 14:07.17; 10,000 m. (4 Oct): 1.Bulti 29:22.96, 2.Porter (USA) 29:23.02, 3.Schildhauer 29:25.63.
1986 - EC, Stuttgart, 5000 m. (31 Aug): 1.Buckner (GB) 13:10.15, 2.Mei 13:11.57, 3.Hutchings (GB) 13:12.88; 10,000 m. (26 Aug): 1.Mei 27:56.79, 2.Cova 27:57.93, 3.Antibo (Ita) 28:00.25.
1987 - WC, Rome, 5000 m. (6 Sep): 1.Aouita 13:26.44, 2.Dom.Castro (Por) 13:27.59, 3.Buckner 13:27.74; 10,000 m. (30 Aug): 1.P.Kipkoech (Ken) 27:38.63, 2.Panetta (Ita) 27:48.98, 3.Kunze 28:50.37.
1988 - OG, Seoul, 5000 m. (1 Oct): 1.Ngugi (Ken) 13:11.70, 2.Baumann (WG) 13:15.52, 3.Kunze 13:15.73; 10,000 m. (26 Sep): 1.Brahim Boutayeb (Mor) 27:21.46, 2.Antibo 27:23.55, 3.Kimeli (Ken) 27:25.16.
1989 - WCup, Barcelona, 5000 m. (10 Sep): 1.Aouita 13:23.14, 2.Doherty (Eur/Ire) 13:25.39, 3.Carreira (Spa) 13:25.94; 10,000 m. (8 Sep): 1.Antibo 28:05.26, 2.Abebe (Afr/Eth) 28:06.43, 3.Prieto (Spa) 28:07.42.
1990 - EC, Split, 5000 m. (1 Sep): 1.Antibo 13:22.00, 2.Staines (GB) 13:22.45, 3.Majusiak (Pol) 13:22.92; 10,000 m. (27 Aug): 1.Antibo 27:41.27, 2.Nakkim (Nor) 28:04.04, 3.Mei 28:04.46.
1991 - WC, Tokyo, 5000 m. (1 Sep): 1. Ondieki (Ken) 13:14.45, 2. Bayissa (Eth) 13:16.64, 3. B.Boutayeb (Mor) 13:22.70; 10,000 m. (26 Aug): 1. M.Tanui (Ken) 27:38.74, 2. Chelimo (Ken) 27:39.41, 3. Skah (Mor) 27:41.74.
1992 - OG, Barcelona, 5000 m. (8 Aug): 1. Baumann (Ger) 13:12.52, 2. Bitok (Ken) 13:12.71, 3. Bayissa 13:13.03; 10,000 m. (3 Aug): 1. Skah 27:46.70, 2. Chelimo (Ken) 27:47.72, 3. Abebe (Eth) 28:00.07; WCup, Habana, 5000 m. (27 Sep): 1. Bayissa 13:41.23, 2. Barrios (Ame/Mex) 13:50.95, 3. Farmer (USA) 14:02.90; 10,000 m. (25 Sep): 1. Abebe 28:44.38, 2. Serrano (Eur/Spa) 28:54.38, 3. Dasko (Eun/Rus) 29:00.26.
1993 - WC, Stuttgart, 5000 m. (16 Aug): 1. Kirui (Ken) 13:02.75, 2. Gebrselassie (Eth) 13:03.17, 3. Bayissa 13:05.40; 10,000 m. (22 Aug): 1. Gebrselassie 27:46.02, 2. M. Tanui 27:46.54, 3. Chelimo 28:06.02.
1994 - EC, Helsinki, 5000 m. (14 Aug): 1. Baumann 13:36.93, 2. Denmark (GB) 13:37.50, 3. Antón (Spa) 13:38.04; 10,000 m. (7 Aug): 1. Antón 28:06.03, 2. Rousseau (Bel) 28:06.63, 3. Franke (Ger) 28:07.95; WCup, London, 5000 m. (11 Sep): 1. Lahlafi (Afr/Mor) 13:27.96, 2. Nuttall (GB) 13:32.47, 3. Bremer (Ger) 13:33.57; 10,000 m. (9 Sep): 1. Skah 27:38.74, 2. Silio (Ame/Arg) 28:16.54, 3. Denmark 28:20.65.
1995 - WC, Göteborg, 5000 m. (13 Aug): 1. Kirui 13:16.77, 2. Boulami (Mor) 13:17.15, 3. S.Kororia (Ken) 13:17.59; 10,000 m. (8 Aug): 1. Gebrselassie 27:12.95, 2. Skah 27:14.53, 3. Tergat (Ken) 27:14.70.
1996 - OG, Atlanta, 5000 m. (3 Aug): 1. Niyongabo (Bur) 13:07.96, 2. Bitok 13:08.16, 3. Boulami 13:08.37; 10,000 m. (29 Jul): 1. Gebrselassie 27:07.34, 2. Tergat 27.08.17, 3. Hissou (Mor) 27:24.67.
1997 - WC, Athens, 5000 m. (10 Aug): 1. Komen (Ken) 13:07.38, 2. Boulami 13:09.34, 3. Nyariki (Ken) 13:11.09; 10,000 m. (6 Aug): 1. Gebrselassie 27:24.58, 2. Tergat 27:25.62, 3. Hissou 27:28.67.
1998 - EC, Budapest, 5000 m. (22 Aug): 1. Viciosa (Spa) 13:37.46, 2. Pancorbo (Spa) 13:38.03, 3. Carroll (Ire) 13:38.15; 10,000 m. (18 Aug): 1. Pinto (Por) 27:48.62, 2. Baumann 27:56.75, 3. Franke 27:59.90; WC, Johannesburg, 3000 m. (13 Sep): 1. Baumann 7:56.24, 2. Viciosa 7:56.47, 3. Nyariki 7:59.46; 5000 m. (11 Sep): 1. Komen 13:46.57, 2. Creighton (Oce/Aus) 13:53.66, 3. Baumann 13:58.40.

1981 1999

1999 - WC, Sevilla, 5000 m. (28 Aug) : 1. Hissou 12.58.13, 2. B.Limo (Ken) 12.58.72, 3. Mourhit (Bel) 12.58.80; 10,000 m. (24 Aug): 1. Gebrselassie 27:57.27, 2. Tergat 27:58.56, 3. Mezegebu (Eth) 27:59.15.

After his memorable but exorbitant season in 1978, Henry Rono lost form and soon disappeared from the top ranks, but for occasional outbursts, the most notable of which occurred in 1981, when in the space of four days he had the following series of 5000 m. marks: - Rieti, 9 September: 3rd in 13:12.47 (behind Hansjörg Kunze of East Germany, 13:10.40, a new European record, and Valeriy Abramov of USSR, 13.11.99). - London, 11 September: 1st in 13:12.34. - Knarvik, Norway, 13 September: 1st in 13:06.20, a new world record. In this race he was helped by several "hares", notably including Steve Cram, yet he ran with apparent "wisdom", his 1000 m. fractions being 2:38.5, 2:38.5, 2:38.0, 2:38.0 and 2:33.2. Several world-class milers tried the 5000 m. during the early Eighties, and three of them achieved excellent results. Eamonn Coghlan of Ireland, the king of indoor milers and a famous "big kicker", won the event at the 1983 World Championships in Helsinki. Thomas Wessinghage of West Germany won the 1982 European title in Athens. David Moorcroft of Britain went so far as to succeed Henry Rono as world record holder with an amazing 13:00.41 at Oslo on 7 July 1982. What was even more surprising, Moorcroft, a 3:49.34 miler, led from 800 m. onwards, with 1000 m. fractions of 2:38.0, 2:34.6, 2:37.6, 2:38.5 and a scorching 2:31.7. Scandinavia, and Finland in particular, had been for many years the power-house of European distance running, but in the Eighties the centre of gravity of continental power in this department was to be found at the Southern end of the continent - in Italy and, to a lesser extent, Portugal. First to break the ice among Italians was Venanzio Ortis, who won a gold and a silver at the 1978 European Championships in Prague. But his glory was short-lived. To carry on in a louder tone there came a few years later Alberto Cova (born at Inverigo near Como on 1 December 1958; 1.72 m./53 kg.), whose great finishing kick proved decisive in the 10,000 m. on three important occasions - the 1982 European Championships in Athens, the 1983 World Championships in Helsinki and the 1984 Olympics in Los Angeles. (During the Eighties, only three other Europeans have managed to score such a triple - pole vaulter Sergey Bubka, triple jumper Khristo Markov and decathlon man Daley Thompson). Cova's chief "victim" was tall Werner Schildhauer of East Germany, who was beaten by a few hundredths-of-a-second at Athens and also at Helsinki. In the Los Angeles race the Italian followed Martti Vainio of Finland for the major part of the

---

The accountant

Alberto Cova is a neat guy. His dark hair and moustache are neatly trimmed, and his blue shirt, even at the finish line, seems fresh from the laundry. Being an accountant, he is meticulous. His running form is one of the neatest, most economical ever seen, short and quick, with no discernible wasted motion. He also has a neat tactic for disposing of his rivals. He buries them in the homestretch.
(Cordner Nelson in "Track & Field News", September 1984).

Daniel Komen (Kenya) a talented but inconsistent performer, here winning a 5000 m. race in 12:48.98 (Rome 1997).

race, then shot ahead in the middle of the last curve to earn a runaway victory. (Vainio finished second but was later disqualified for doping abuse). In this race Cova covered the first half in 14:20.6 and the second in an impressive 13:27.0. Cova never seemed to care about fast times. Paradoxically enough, he never held the Italian record for the 10,000 m. His best-ever times - 13:10.06 in the 5000 m., an Italian record, and 27:37.59 in the 10,000 m. - were in losing efforts. He was a master tactician who would always be at his best when big honours were at stake. In the 1985 European Cup in Moscow he won a 5000/10,000 m. double. During the Eighties other excellent distance runners blossomed in Italy, and Cova found competition in his own country. Francesco Panetta, for some time Cova's club-mate, was primarily at his best in the steeplechase, but he did well also on the flat, especially in the 10,000 m., finishing second at the 1987 World Championships in Rome. Stefano Mei, a tall, long striding runner, handed Cova his first defeat in a major championship race. This was in the 1986 European Championships at Stuttgart, when Mei won the 10,000 m. beating Cova at his own game, with a long sprint (last 400 m. in 55.3). Salvatore Antibo finished third to give Italy a clean sweep - the first ever by any country in a track event at the European Championships (Two days later, the British proved good imitators by finishing one-two-three in the 800 m. with Coe, McKean and Cram). Portugal had a peculiar runner in Fernando Mamede, a man who could do excellent things against the clock but invariably failed when the pressure was on. He emerged as a middle distance runner in 1974, when he did 1:47.47 in a heat of the 800 m. at the European Championships in Rome (but failed to make the final). In subsequent years he moved to the longer distances. Clock-wise, his "chef d'oeuvre" was on 2 July 1984 in Stockholm, when in a sort of framed handicap he lowered the world's 10,000 m. record to 27:13.81, with "halves" in 13:45.40 and 13:28.41. His countryman Carlos Lopes was a fairly close second in 27:17.48. A few weeks later, at the Los Angeles Olympics, Mamede looked unaggressive from the beginning and midway in the race he dropped out - after what to most observers appeared to be a leisurely first half (14:20.6 for the leader). As a commentator put it, somewhat ironically: "Mamede swung out across the track and ran into the exit tunnel. His speed in the tunnel indicated an urgent need to go". The Portuguese ace performed indifferently in several other championship races. For his inability to do himself justice on big occasions he was almost a case apart, more so than Ron Clarke or even Dave Bedford. Towards the end of the Eighties, the leadership in distance running passed from Europe to Africa. The outstanding figure of the new "African wave" was Said Aouita of Morocco. His feats in general and as a 1500 m./1 mile runner in particular have been related in a previous chapter. In the 5000 m. he was superlative in terms of records and honours won. On 27 July 1985 at Oslo he shaved one hundredth-of-a-second off Moorcroft's world record with 13:00.40. The Moroccan led from 3000 m. onwards, and his finishing speed brought the crowd to its feet - last kilometre in 2:28.24, last 400 m. in 54.44. But he did even better on 22 July 1987 in Rome, when he broke the 13 min. barrier with a scintillating 12:58.39. It was an "All-Africa festival", with young Brahim Boutayeb of Morocco and Fethi Baccouche of Tunisia setting the stage for Said's

Alberto Cova (Italy) winning the 5000 m. at the 1984 Olympics in Los Angeles.

historic mark in the first three kilometres. Then Aouita took over and completed the work in a superlative manner. His kilometre fractions: 2:35.6, 2:37.7, 2:33.2, 2:39.6, 2:32.3. At the end of such a race he still had enough left for a 57.4 last lap. Sydney Maree was a distant second in 13:24.97. Aouita had been virtually unbeatable at this distance. His victories at the 1984 Olympics and the 1987 World Championships looked surprisingly easy to expert observers. Africa's rise was amply confirmed in the major competitions of the late Eighties. At the 1987 World Championships in Rome, Paul Kipkoech of Kenya won the 10,000 m. in 27:38.63, with more than 10 seconds to spare. The following year at the Seoul Olympics, another Kenyan, John Ngugi, moved upfront towards the end of the first kilometre with a 57.8 lap, ran away from the field and finally won in 13:11.70. In the 10,000 m., Africa took first and third place, with Brahim Boutayeb of Morocco (27:21.46) and Kipkemboi Kimeli of Kenya. Ngugi (born at Nyahururu on 10 May 1962; 1.78 m./62 kg.) had earned a reputation with three victories in the World Cross Country Championships (1986-88), to which he added one more in 1989. A Kikuyu, he has a galloping stride which at first sight seems rather unsuited for hard battles on the track. In fact, his competitive record is not impressive, apart from his victory at Seoul. Moulay Brahim Boutayeb of Morocco (born at Khemisset on 15 August 1967; 1.78 m./61 kg.) made a giant leap in one year, improving on his 10,000 m. best from 28:40.34 in 1987 to 27:21.46 in '88. A Mexican with a high reputation as a road runner, Arturo Barrios (born at Mexico City on 12 December 1963; 1.74 m./60 kg.), took advantage of a well planned race at Berlin on 18 August 1989 to capture the world's 10,000 m. record with 27:08.23 (first half in 13:32.5, second half all on his own in 13:35.7). In major championship races at this distance, Barrios can claim a fourth place at the 1987 World Championships and a fifth at the 1988 Olympics. Italians won 3 medals out of 6 in the distance events of the 1990 European Championships in Split. Salvatore Antibo (born at Altofonte near Palermo on 7 February 1962; 1.70 m./52 kg.) crowned years of steady progress with two smashing victories. First he won the 10,000 m. with nearly 23 seconds to spare, after running away from the field in the early stages. Then, in the 5000 m., he overcame the effects of a fall right at the start and outsprinted his rivals in a hectic finish.

African distance runners really ruled the roost in the last decade of the 20th century. Suffice it to say that they won 40 of the 42 medals awarded for the 5000 and 10,000 m. in major (Olympic/World) games. The lonely exceptions to the African rule were Dieter Baumann of Germany (gold in the 5000 at the 1992 Olympics) and Mohammed Mourhit of Belgium (bronze in the 5000 at the 1999 World Championships). The latter, mind you, was born in Morocco and became a Belgian citizen in 1997 ... Kenya had the lion's share, winning almost half of said medals (19 out of 42) but it fell to Ethiopia to provide the superman of the decade and possibly the greatest distance runner of the modern era - Haile Gebrselassie (born at Asela in the Arssi province on 18 April 1973; 1.64 m./53 Kg.). He grew up as the eighth of ten kids. As a boy he was reportedly excited when he heard on the radio about Miruts Yifter's wins at the 1980 Olympics in Moscow. Like many other East African youngsters he began to practice athletics in a police club. For the

1981
1999

Haile Gebrselassie (Ethiopia), the greatest distance runner of our time, seen here in his 10,000 m. victory at the 1999 World Championships.

Two aces from Africa, currently the cradle of the world's finest distance runners: Richard Chelimo (left) and Paul Tergat of Kenya.

outer world he came to the fore with a bang - a double victory at the 1992 World Junior Championships in Seoul, with times of 28:03.99 (10,000 m.) and 13:36.06 (5000 m.) on consecutive days. Oddly enough, this was to remain his only major "double" in international competitions. Even though he was to conquer world records at distances ranging from 3000 to 10,000 m., he has so far failed to emulate Kolehmainen, Zátopek, Kuts, Viren and Yifter in scoring 5000/10,000 m. doubles. Incidentally, that 5000 m. race of 1992 in Seoul was truly a portent of things to come: "Gebr" won from Ismael Kirui of Kenya (13:36.11) in a very close finish, while Hicham El Guerrouj of Morocco was a distant third (13:46.79),

both of whom later became world conquerors in their own right. A year later Gebrselassie made his international debut in the senior division at the 1993 World Championships in Stuttgart. In the 5000 m. he was involved in another hair raising finish with Kirui, who managed to turn the tables on him, 13:02.75 to 13:03.17. In the 10,000 m. six days later there was yet another Kenya vs. Ethiopia feud, the characters in the play being Gebrselassie and Moses Tanui, the defending champion. At the bell the Kenyan kicked hard but was stepped on by Gebrselassie so that his left shoe was flipped off. The stout Kenyan led into the last turn but he had to surrender to Gebrselassie's finishing kick (54.98 for the last 400 m.). The Ethiopian won, 27:46.02 to 27:46.54. The idea of emulating his boyhood hero, Miruts Yifter, entered his mind again in 1996, year of the Atlanta Olympics. In those Games he won the 10,000 m. with much pain, after suffering severe blisters from the hard track. Then he decided to withdraw from the 5000 m. "The prospect of three rounds of 5000 after two sessions of 10,000 on that hard track was too much", he said. Two weeks later Gebrselassie arrived in Zurich "just married and bold enough to combine track business with his honeymoon". But his feet were still aching and he lost badly to Daniel Komen of Kenya in the 5000 m. - 12:52.70 to 12:45.09. From then on "Gebr" invariably opted for the '10' in major championship meets.

1981 1999

Nowadays leading distance men are tempted by invitational meets, in which races are planned for record purposes, with the intervention of "hares". Prize money makes such races particularly alluring and worthwhile.

In fact Gebrselassie has been a great collector of world records, all achieved in invitational meets: 4 in the 5000 m. and 3 in the 10,000 m. The Dutch town of Hengelo, where he usually spends the summer months in the house of his manager and counselor, Jos Hermens (former holder of the 1-hour world record), has been his favorite playing ground. His record marks for the two Olympic distances follow:

1994:
5000 m. in 12:56.96 (Hengelo, 4 June)

1995:
10,000 m. in 26:43.53 (Hengelo, 5 June) and 5000 m. in 12:44.39 (Zurich, 16 August)

1997:
10,000 m. in 26:31.32 (Oslo, 4 July) and 5000 m. in 12:41.86 (Zurich, 13 August)

1998:
10,000 m. in 26:22.75 (Hengelo, 1 June) and 5000 m. in 12:39.36 (Helsinki, 13 June)

The last two were the current world records at the end of 1999. In the Hengelo race he followed three de-luxe "hares" - his countrymen Worku Bikila, Million Wolde and Assefa Mezegebu - who in turns "paved" the way up to 6000 m., then he went on alone. He ran the first half in 13:11.7 (which would have been a world record for 5000 m. until 1978!) and the second half in 13:11.1. His last km. was 2:31.2, his last 400 m. 58.0. In the 5000 m. race at Helsinki he took the lead midway in the race and had km. fractions of 2:34.8, 2:31.6, 2:32.9, 2:32.8 and 2:27.3. He thus covered the last 2000 m. in 5:00.1! The fleetness of foot of this little but very great runner never ceased to amaze experts. At one time he also had the best-on-record mark for 2 miles (8:07.46 in 1995 and 8:01.08 in 1997), a distance which is no longer on the IAAF list.

Gebrselassie's fiercest rival in the 3000/5000 m. department has been Daniel Komen of Kenya (born at Elgeiyo Marakwet on 17 May 1976; 1.70 m./55 Kg.), a tremendously gifted athlete, recently coached by Moses Kiptanui, the great steeplechaser. In his youth he was a high jumper and soccer goalkeeper but a precocious distance runner too. At 17 he ran the 5000 m. in 13:58.30. The following year he won a great doble at the World Junior Championships at Lisbon: 10,000 m. in 28:29.74, then 5000 m. 13:45.37. In 1995 he ducked under 13 minutes in the 5000 with 12:56.15 and a year later, after no fewer than three narrow misses, he conquered his first world record, to this day considered one of the greatest, if not the greatest, in the distance department: 3000 m. in 7:20.67. This was at Rieti on 1 September. After running in the wake of "hare" John Kosgei for 2000 m., he bettered Noureddine Morceli's world record by more than 4 secs. His kilometer frctions were 2:26.5, 2:26.9 and 2:27.3.

This pace was better than running two successive sub-4 min. miles, and in fact he did just that in a 2-mile race at Hechtel on 19 July 1997 with a time of 7:58.61. His actual 1-mile fractions were 3:59.8 and 3:58.8, the latter being faster than Roger Bannister's historic sub-4 for one mile in 1954.

Komen won the 5000 m. at the World Championships, still in 1997. Since then, however, he has shown uneven form, losing to lesser lights on several occasions. Prior to him, another Kenyan had

Salah Hissou (Marocco).

earned his share of glory: Ismael Kirui (born at Marakwet on 20 February 1975, 1.60 m./54 Kg.), who won two 5000 m. titles at the World Championships (1993 and '95), once beating the great Gebrselassie, as related above.

Other great African runners of recent years were Yobes Ondieki and Paul Tergat of Kenya, Venuste Niyongabo of Burundi and Salah Hissou of Morocco. Of these Tergat is perhaps the greatest talent. He is at his best as a harrier, having won the IAAF World Cross Country title for five successive years (1995-99). The leading European of the Nineties in the 5000 m. was Dieter Baumann of Germany (born at Blaustein on 9 February 1965; 1;78 m./64 Kg.). He had his most glorious day at the 1992 Olympics in Barcelona when he won the 5000 m. from Paul Bitok of Kenya and Fita Bayissa of Ethiopia. In subsequent years he had to be content with lesser placings on several occasions. In 1997 he became Europe's first sub-13 min. man as he did 12:54.70 in the famous Weltklasse meet in Zurich, finishing behind four Africans. He is married with Isabell (née Hozang), who is also his coach. Late in 1999 he proved positive to Nandrolone in a doping test and thereby became quite a "case" in German athletic circles, very sensitive to that subject, especially after the publication of Brigitte Berendonk's book "Doping" in 1991. This book, by now a classic, deals with the "state vices" in the former German Democratic Republic but also with the "private vices" of the German Federal Republic.

Rob de Castella (Australia), marathon winner in the inaugural edition of the World Championships (1983).

Family Race

In 1998 the most invincible of present-day distance runners, Haile Gebrselassie, became the subject of a film bearing the title "Endurance". The American troupe that made it was in Asela, the native place of the Ethiopian champion, for several months. His entire family provided the cast. As he said to Hannah Wallace: "My nephew plays me when I was a child; my cousin is my father as a young man, my sister plays my mother and my father plays himself. Everyone did very well. The movie starts in 1980 when as a boy I heard about the famous Ethiopian runner Miruts Yifter's wins at the Moscow Olympics". In the Amharic language Haile Gebrselassie means "Strength of the Holy Trinity". That was actually the name of the last Emperor (Negus) of Ethiopia, minus "Gebre" (holy).

MARATHON - A boundless planet

1981 - EurCup, Agen (13 September): 1.Magnani (Ita) 2:13:29, 2.Cierpinski (EG) 2:15:44, 3.Persson (Swe) 2:15:45.
1982 - EC, Athens (12 September): 1.Nijboer (Hol) 2:15:16, 2.Parmentier (Bel) 2:15:51, 3.Lismont (Bel) 2:16:04.
1983 - WC, Helsinki (14 August): 1.De Castella (Aus) 2:10:03, 2.Balcha (Eth) 2:10:27, 3.Cierpinski 2:10:37.
1984 - OG, Los Angeles (12 Aug): 1.Lopes (Por) 2:09:21, 2.Treacy (Ire) 2:09:56, 3.Spedding (GB) 2:09:58.
1985 - WCup, Hiroshima (14 Apr): 1.Salah (Dji) 2:08:09, 2.Nakayama (Jap) 2:08:15, 3.Robleh (Dji) 2:08:26.
1986 - EC, Stuttgart (30 Aug): 1.Bordin (Ita) 2:10:54, 2.Pizzolato (Ita) 2:10:57, 3.Steffny (WG) 2:11:30.
1987 - WCup, Seoul (12 Apr): 1.Salah 2:10:55, 2.Kodama (Jap) 2:11:23, 3.Bettiol (Ita) 2:11:28; WC, Rome (6 Sep): 1.Wakiihuri (Ken) 2:11:48, 2.Salah 2:12:30, 3.Bordin 2:12:40.
1988 - OG, Seoul (2 Oct): 1.Bordin 2:10:32, 2.Wakiihuri 2:10:47, 3.Salah 2:10:59.
1989 - WCup, Milan (16 April): 1.Mataferia Zeleke (Eth) 2:10:28, 2.Nedi (Eth) 2:10:36, 3.Poli (Ita) 2:10:49.

1981 1999

1990 - EC, Split (1 Sep): 1.Bordin 2:14:02, 2.Poli 2:14:55, 3.Chauvelier (Fra) 2:15:20.
1991 - WCup, London (21 April): 1. Tolstikov (USSR) 2:09.17, 2. Matias (Por) 2:10.21, 3. Huruk (Pol) 2:10.21; WC, Tokyo (1 September): 1. Taniguchi (Jap) 2:14.57, 2. A. Salah (Dji) 2:15.26, 3. Spence (USA) 2:15.36.
1992 - OG, Barcelona (9 August): 1. Hwang Young-Jo (Kor) 2:13.23, 2. Morishita (Jap) 2:13.45, 3. Freigang (Ger) 2:14.00.
1993 - WC, Stuttgart (14 August): 1. Plaatjes (USA) 2:13.57, 2. Swartbooi (Nam) 2:14.11, 3. Van Vlaanderen (Hol) 2:15.12; WCup, San Sebastian (31 Oct): 1. Nerurkar (GB) 2:10.03, 2. Bernardini (Ita) 2:10.12, 3. Gemechu (Eth) 2:10.16.
1994 - EC, Helsinki (14 August): 1. Fiz (Spa) 2:10.31, 2. D.Garcia (Spa) 2:10.46, 3.Juzdado (Spa) 2:11.18.
1995 - WCup, Athens (9 April): 1. Wakiihuri (Ken) 2:12.01, 2. Sunada (Jap) 2:13.16, 3. Milesi (Ita) 2:13.23; WC, Göteborg (12 August): 1. Fiz 2:11.41, 2. Cerón (Mex) 2:12.13, 3. L. dos Santos (Bra) 2:12.49.
1996 - OG, Atlanta (4 August): 1. Thugwane (SA) 2:12.36, 2. Lee Bong-ju (Kor) 2:12.39, 3. Wainaina (Ken) 2:12.44.
1997 - WC, Athens (10 August): 1. Antón (Spa) 2:13.16, 2. Fiz 2:13.21, 3. Moneghetti (Aus) 2:14.16.
1998 - EC, Budapest (22 August): 1. Baldini (Ita) 2:12.01, 2. Goffi (Ita) 2:12.11, 3. Modica (Ita) 2:12.53.
1999 - WC, Sevilla (28 August): 1 Antón 2:13.36, 3. Modica 2:14.03, 3. N. Sato (Jap) 2:14.07.

Marathon running has lately developed into a planet apart in the world of athletics. And a boundless one, because no other event can boast such a cosmopolitan cast, such a world-wide theatre of operations or such a wealth of prize money. The results given above, relevant to World, Olympic or European championship events, plus World Marathon Cup (first edition in 1985) give only a pale idea of what happened in this planet over the last ten years.

In the fall of 1981, Alberto Salazar of USA won the New York ("Big Apple") marathon in 2:08:13, a best-on-record mark which was later removed from the lists when, upon verification, the course turned out to be 148 m. short. The IAAF still carries no official world records for the marathon, yet in recent years it began to show concern about the correctness of marathon courses. Now there is an Association of International Marathons (AIMS), to which most of the major world marathons belong. It has competent measurers who verify the legitimacy of courses regarding distance. As a rule a certified course should be anything between 42,195 m. and 42,237 m. Even apart from length, course conditions can vary considerably. Point-to-point courses may have generally favourable terrain or wind conditions. Performances made on out-and-back courses, as used in international championship races, have a greater significance. Still in 1981, at Fukuoka, Rob de Castella of Australia came close to Salazar's mark with 2:08:18, on a certified course. The Aussie star had a remarkable career. His successor as holder of the best-on-record performance was Steve Jones of Britain, a Royal Air Force technician who did 2:08:05 at Chicago in 1984. One who could point to a fine record in terms of both honours and fast times was Carlos Lopes of Portugal (born at Viseu on 18 February 1947; 1.67 m./56 kg.). Eight years after placing second to Lasse Viren in the Olympic 10,000 m. at Montreal, this little, tenacious performer struck gold in the 1984 Olympic marathon at Los Angeles. A year later, at Rotterdam, he set a new best-on-record mark of 2:07:12. This mark was bettered by Belayneh Dinsamo of Ethiopia, who on 17 April 1988 did 2:06:50 on the fast Rotterdam course, after a great battle with the better known Ahmed Salah of Djibouti (2:07:07). Dinsamo, then a 23-year-old Police lieutenant, ran at a surprisingly even pace throughout, with 10 km. fractions of 30:05, 30:07, 30:01, 30:07, and 6:30 for the last 2195 m. In other words, four consecutive 10,000

Carlos Lopes (Portugal) after his victory in the 1984 Olympic marathon.

m., all in the region of Paavo Nurmi's onetime record for that distance! Among other excellent marathon runners of recent years I may single out Gelindo Bordin of Italy and Douglas Wakiihuri of Kenya. The former (born at Longare near Vicenza on 2 April 1959; 1.80 m./65 kg.) was a solid performer who could claim an Olympic title (1988) and two European titles (1986 and '90). In 1990 he became the first men's Olympic champion to win the Boston marathon, i.e. the oldest non-Olympic classic. Wakiihuri (born at Mombasa on 26 September 1963; 1.86 m./65 kg.), a Kikuyu, went to Japan in 1983 to train under Kiyoshi Nakamura. He won the world title in 1987, beating Bordin among others, but a year later at the Seoul Olympics he had to be content with second place, fifteen seconds behind Bordin. Other prominent runners were Steve Moneghetti of Australia, Juma Ikangaa of Tanzania and Abebe Mekonnen of Ethiopia.

The Nineties strengthened the status of the marathon as a planet of its own, by far the richest market in the world of athletics. Important races continued to grow in number. By the end of the decade the ATFS Annual counted over 120 international competitions in a year, most of them endowed with more or less alluring prizes. Such invitational races inevitably grew at the expense of traditional championship events (Olympics, World Championships, World Cup, the last two merged into one in '97). Generally speaking, the high-water marks of marathoning are three. The first in April, with such classics as London, Rotterdam and Boston, highly valued competitions in every respect.

The second coincides with the major championship races, usually held in the summer months. The third is in autumn, with such classics as Berlin, Chicago, New York and Fukuoka, all very important. Considering that top runners usually run no more than two big races a year, they are inevitably obliged to make a choice. In recent years the preference of the majority went to the "classics", which offer the double advantage of being held in moderate climatic conditions and offering lucrative prizes. As a result, the traditional championship races are often diluted by the absence of the so-called big money crowd. In fact, most if not all the fastest times of recent years were returned in invitational races.

Belayneh Dinsamo's 2:06.50 (1988) stood as the best performance on record for ten years. It fell to a relatively little known Brazilian to succeed him. The man in question was Ronaldo da Silva (born at Descoberto on 7 June 1970; 1.67 m./55 Kg.). In his second marathon he astounded observers with a time of 2:06.05 at Berlin on 20 September 1998. It was the first marathon run at a speed of over 20 Km. per hour. In other words, he ran at faster than 30 minutes 10 Km-speed for 42,195 metres - one may remember that it was not until 1939 that any man ran just one 10 Km. at that pace! Another amazing detail: after a somewhat ordinary 1:04.42 in the first half, the Brazilian ran the second half in 1:01.23!

Yet his mark was bettered only a year later when Khalid Khannouchi of Morocco ran the distance in 2:05.42 at Chicago on 24 October 1999. This man (born at Meknès on 22 December 1971; ....) lives in USA, where he is coached by his wife Sandra, an American citizen who originally came from the Dominican Republic. After showing excellent form at shorter distances in the lucrative circus of US road races, Khannouchi made his marathon debut at Chicago in 1997, winning from a classy field in 2:07.10, barely twenty seconds outside the best-on-record mark, then held by Belayneh Dinsamo. A year later, still at Chicago, he was shunted to second by Ondoro Osoro of Kenya (2:06.54) yet finished in 2:07.19. The record race of 1999 was barely his third official try at the distance and like the previous two it was at Chicago. He too ran a second half (1:02.35) faster than the first (1:03.07). At the end of his labours he was greeted by his wife and burst into tears of joy. He received $ 165,000 for his win, including a "World

Gelindo Bordin (Italy) scored wins in the two oldest marathon classics of modern times, Olympics (1988) and (here) Boston (1990).

record" bonus. As of now he has three of the 25 fastest marathon times on record but still has to appear in a major championship (Olympic/World) race.

The standard of performances has improved by leaps and bounds in recent years. In 1991, only 7 men ran the distance in less than 2:10.00. The same limit was surpassed by 16 men in 1995 and by .... 55 in 1999! In terms of major championship titles won during the Nineties the most successful couple came from Spain: Martin Fiz and Abel Antón. The former (born at Vitoria on 3 March 1963; 1.69 m./53 Kg.) ran his first marathon in 1993 and can now point to 8 wins in a total of 16 races at the distance. He won the European title in 1994 and became world champion the following year. Anton (born at Ojoel, Soria on 24 October 1962; 1.79 m./61 Kg.) had a long career at shorter distances before trying the marathon. His first major win was at the 1994 European Championships in Helsinki, where he outsprinted a strong field in the 10,000 m. and later placed third in the 5000 m. He was 34 by the time he made his marathon debut at Berlin in 1996: first in 2:09.15. He went on to win over that distance at the 1997 World Championships, nosing out his arch rival Fiz in the closing stage. And he successfully defended his title at Sevilla in 1999. He can now point to a brilliant career record as a marathoner: 5 wins out of 9 races. Clock-wise, he and Fiz lag behind a lot of runners, with personal bests of 2:07.57 and 2:08.05 respectively.

Practically every continent had its share of glory during the Nineties. Asia provided the winner at the 1991 World Championships (Hiromi Taniguchi of Japan) and the 1992 Olympics (Hwang Young-jo of Korea), North America had its turn at the 1993 World Championships (South Africa-born Mark Plaatjes of USA). Africa has a lot of prominent runners but can point to only one major victory: Josiah Thugwane of South Africa at the 1996 Olympics in Atlanta.

The IAAF recently devoted attention to the half marathon and the ever growing international calendar now includes an annual world championship at that distance (21,097 metres). The inaugural edition was held at Tyneside, England, in 1992 and the race was won by Benson Masya of Kenya in 60:24. Africa provided the winner in 6 of the 8 editions held as at the end of 1999. The best time on record was made in an invitational event at Milan on 4 April 1998 by Paul Tergat of Kenya with 59:17.

Most of the big marathons now attract very large fields, with hundreds of professional runners and several thousand amateurs as well. Dr. David Martin, the most acute and knowledgeable student of road running, had this to say in the 1998 ATFS Annual: "The new trend" of marathoning seems to be the idea of mixing tourism with training. There is now a marathon in every world capital as well as the remotest destinations (Antarctica, and the base of Mount Everest to name only two). Road racing and road running are bringing cultures together like no other social force in modern times".

1981
1999

Abel Antón (Spain), left, won the marathon at the 1997 World Championships in Athens aged 35 and did it again before a home crowd at Sevilla two years later.

Hiromi Taniguchi (Japan) brought the home crowd to its feet as he won the marathon at the 1991 World Championships in Tokyo.

110 METRES HURDLES - Nehemiah opens the sub-13 Club.

1981 - WCup, Rome (6 Sep) (-0.2): 1.G.Foster (USA) 13.32, 2.Casañas (Cub) 13.36, 3.Ivan (Eur/CSR) 13.66.
1982 - EC, Athens (11 Sep) (-0.9): 1.Munkelt (EG) 13.41, 2.Prokofyev (USSR) 13.46, 3.Bryggare (Fin) 13.60.
1983 - WC, Helsinki (13 Aug) (+1.3): 1.G.Foster 13.42, 2.Bryggare 13.46, 3.Gault (USA) 13.48.
1984 - OG, Los Angeles (6 Aug) (-0.4): 1.Kingdom (USA) 13.20, 2.G.Foster 13.23, 3.Bryggare 13.40.
1985 - WCup, Canberra (6 Oct) (+3.1): 1.Campbell (USA) 13.35, 2.Usov (USSR) 13.62, 3.Naumann (EG) 13.76.
1986 - EC, Stuttgart (30 Aug) (+2.0): 1.Caristan (Fra) 13.20, 2.Bryggare 13.42, 3.Sala (Spa) 13.50.
1987 - WC, Rome (3 Sep) (+0.5): 1.G.Foster 13.21, 2.Ridgeon (GB) 13.29, 3.Jackson (GB) 13.38.
1988 - OG, Seoul (26 Sep) (+1.5): 1.Kingdom 12.98, 2.Jackson 13.28, 3.Campbell 13.38.
1989 - WCup, Barcelona (10 Sep) (+2.6): 1.Kingdom 12.87, 2.Jackson 12.95, 3.Valle (Ame/Cub) 13.21.
1990 - EC, Split (31 Aug) (+0.2): 1.Jackson 13.18, 2.Jarrett (GB) 13.21, 3.Koszewski (WG) 13.50.
1991 - WC, Tokyo (29 Aug) (+0.7) : 1.G. Foster 13.06, 2.Pierce (USA) 13.06, 3.Jarrett (GB) 13.25.
1992 - OG, Barcelona (3 Aug) (+0.8) : 1.McKoy (Can) 13.12, 2.Dees (USA) 13.24, 3.Pierce 13.26; WCup, Habana (26 Sep) (+0.3) : 1.C.Jackson (GB) 13.07, 2.Usov (EUN/Uzb) 13.55, 3.Valle (Ame/Cub) 13.69.
1993 - WC, Stuttgart (20 Aug) (+0.5) : 1.Jackson 12.91 (World Record), 2.Jarrett 13.00, 3.Pierce 13.06.
1994 - EC, Helsinki (12 Sep) (+1.1) : 1.Jackson 13.08, 2.Schwarthoff (Ger) 13.16, 3.Jarrett 13.23; WCup, London (11 Sep) (-1.6) : 1.Jarrett 13.23, 2.A. Johnson (USA) 13.29, 3.Valle 13.45.
1995 - WC, Göteborg (12 Aug) (-0.1) : 1.Johnson 13.00, 2.Jarrett 13.04, 3.Kingdom (USA) 13.19.
1996 - OG, Atlanta (29 Jul) (+0.6) : 1.Johnson 12.95, 2.Crear (USA) 13.09, 3.Schwarthoff 13.17.
1997 - WC, Athens (7 Aug) (0.0) : 1.Johnson 12.93, 2.Jackson 13.05, 3.Kovac (Svk) 13.18.
1998 - EC, Budapest (22 Aug) (+1.5) : 1.Jackson 13.02, Balzer (Ger) 13.12, 3.Korving (Hol) 13.20; WCup, Johannesburg (25 Aug) (+1.0) : 1.Balzer 13.10, 2.Jackson 13.11, 3.A. Garcia (Ame/Cub) 13.14.
1999 - WC, Sevilla (25 Aug) (+1.0) : 1.Jackson 13.04, 2.Garcia 13.07, 3.Ross (USA) 13.12.

Renaldo Nehemiah (USA), first to break the 13 sec. barrier in the "high" hurdles (12.93 in 1981).

Renaldo Nehemiah had his best year in 1981, when his rivalry with Greg Foster came to fever pitch at the Weltklasse meet in Zurich on 19 August. Nehemiah gained a very slight lead over the first two hurdles, only to lose much of it a bit later. But for their opposite lead-leg styles, the two ran in perfect unison the rest of the way, never more than half a metre apart. Nehemiah finally edged his rival, 12.93 to 13.03. "Skeets" thus chalked up history's first sub-13 secs. mark, with a slight adverse wind (0.2 m/s). (Two years earlier, at Kingston, he was credited with a "manual" time of 12.8). Nehemiah closed his European campaign with 13.07, 13.04 and 13.07. After a successful indoor season early in 1982, he

1981 1999

signed a contract to play "pro" football with the San Francisco Forty-Niners. This automatically excluded him from the "amateur" track family. His four-year venture in the gridiron brought him money, some success (his team won a Superbowl) and lots of injuries. In retrospect, he once described the whole experience as "painful". By 1986 he was eager to come back to his first love. In the meantime, things had changed considerably in the atmosphere of world athletics: after keeping him on the waiting list for a while, the IAAF reinstated him in the "amateur" ranks. His second career began in August 1986 at Viareggio, Italy, where he chalked up a promising 13.48. Later tries were less satisfactory though. He had difficulties in re-adapting to the world of track, and injuries hampered him more than somewhat. He showed great determination though. He did 13.43 in 1988, 13.20 in '89 and 13.22 in '90. At thirty-one, he was once more close to the top ... yet most observers failed to recognize the man once credited with 10.24 and 20.37 in the sprints, 19.4 and 44.3 in relay stints and 7.60 in the long jump. Greg Foster (born at Maywood, Illinois, on 4 August 1958; 1.90 m./84 kg.) had a troubled career in more than one way and in the opinion of some observers he never maximized his potential, yet he was great enough to win the "highs" in three editions of the World Championships (1983, '87 and '91) and place second in the 1984 Olympics. At or near the top for over a decade, Foster may be regarded as the fastest sprinter (10.28 and 20.20 in 1979) in the hurdles department since "Bones" Dillard. But the man who succeeded Nehemiah as world record holder was big Roger Kingdom (born at Vienna, Georgia, on 26 August 1962; 1.85 m./91 kg.). Remarkably enough, this heavily muscled man achieved that distinction after winning the "highs" in two editions of the Olympics (1984 and '88), a trick previously turned by only one man, Lee Calhoun. Kingdom entered the sub-13 secs. club in August 1988 when he did 12.97 at Sestriere (altitude, 2050 m.). Then he ran 12.98 to win his second Olympic gold medal at Seoul. He finally hit the target at Zurich on 16 August 1989, when the photo-finish apparatus caught him in 12.913 - officially ratified as 12.92, i.e. one hundredth-of-a-second under Nehemiah's mark. In this race Kingdom had a worthy rival in Colin Jackson of Britain, who was second in 13.12. The wind (-0.10 m/s) was negligible. Although not a copy-book stylist as was Nehemiah in his best years, Kingdom had a muscular power that made him well-nigh unbeatable in the closing stages. It should be noted that the Zurich Letzigrund had previously seen four other world record marks in the high hurdles:

Lauer in 1959, Davenport in '69, Milburn in '73 and Nehemiah in '81. Colin Jackson (born at Cardiff on 18 February 1967; 1.82 m./73 kg.), a Briton of Jamaican descent, has been a dominant figure on the European scene since 1988. This fine stylist was on several occasions Kingdom's toughest rival as well. In 1990 he lowered the European record to 13.08 in winning the Commonwealth title at Auckland. He also had a wind-aided 12.95, as well as a significant 10.29 in the 100 m. flat. Even prior to his advent, Europe had several world-class hurdlers during the Eighties: Thomas Munkelt of East Germany, Arto Bryggare of Finland, both very good competitors, then Stéphane Caristan of France and Jonathan Ridgeon of Britain, both with curtailed careers on account of injuries.

Greg Foster (USA) won the 110 m. Hurdles in three editions of the World Championships (1987, '91 and '93).

Roger Kingdom (USA) winning the 110 m. hurdles in a wind-aided 12.87 at the 1989 World Cup in Barcelona, shortly after a torrential rain.

Colin Jackson remained at or near the top throughout the Nineties, no matter if he had his share of injuries, notably including a double knee cartilage operation in the autumn of 1995. Britain had waited a long time for the appearance of a man likely to honour the remote tradition of Don Finlay, her pre-war ace. Such a hurdler finally appeared in the person of this streamlined Welshman, who eventually went further than his predecessor, winning two golds, a silver and a bronze at the World Championships over a period of twelve years (1987-99). On one of these occasions, namely at Stuttgart in 1993, he went so far as to capture the world record with a splendid 12.91 in a race with little wind (+0.5) and after a quick but normal getaway (reaction time: 0.122). He thus became the first Briton to hold a world record in the "highs" since time immemorial - more exactly since 1865, when namesake Clement Jackson went over ten rigid barriers to clock 16.0 for 120 yards hurdles! Colin has been rather unlucky in the Olympics: after finishing second at Seoul in 1988, aged 21, he was held back by an injury in the 1992 final at Barcelona (seventh) and was no better than fourth at Atlanta in 1996. He will probably have his last chance at Sydney in 2000 .... Besides being a fine stylist, Jackson has a quick acceleration, as evidenced by what he has been able to do in the short indoor races. He is the current holder of the world record for 60 metres hurdles: 7.30 at Sindelfingen on 6 March 1994. In the same year he won a most unusual double at the European Indoor Championships: 60 metres flat (6.49) -60 metres hurdles (7.41). He had a winning streak of 44 hurdle races from August 1993 to February 1995. The man who put an end to this wondrous series, and by the narrowest of margins - 7.42 for both over 60 metres hurdles - was Allen Johnson of USA (born in Washington, D.C. on 1 March 1971; 1.78 m./70 Kg.), a most versatile athlete who could claim such marks as 8.14 in the long jump indoors ('93), 2.105 in the high jump and 14.83 in the triple jump (both in '89). He gave the utmost measure of his speed on the flat when he ran the 200 metres in 20.26 ('97). But he was of course at his very best in the "highs". He won 3 "global" titles in just as many consecutive years: Worlds ('95), Olympics ('96) and Worlds again ('97). Johnson has been unlucky in his quest for a world record though. In 1996 he was timed in 12.92 - merely 0.01 off Colin Jackson's mark - on two occasions. He can point to 7 of the 18 sub-13 (legitimate) marks registered as at the end of 1999. Colin Jackson has 5, Roger Kingdom 3, Renaldo Nehemiah, Jack Pierce and Mark Crear 1 each.

In the 1996 Olympic final Johnson toppled no less than eight of the ten hurdles he found on his way. According to "Track & Field News", the hurdle-bashing American" thus provoked many perplexed Olympics-only fans - a species largely diffused in USA, but also in other countries - to ask if he wouldn't be disqualified". Of course, this is no longer the case nowadays: IAAF rule 163/8 states that "the knocking down of hurdles shall not result in disqualification nor prevent a record being made".

USA is no longer able to score "clean sweeps" in

Colin Jackson (Great Britain) has been in the top ranks of the 110 m. hurdles for many years.

Underrated challenger

It is in the nature of things that defeat may one day knock at the door of any champion, no matter how great. It happened to Emil Zátopek in 1954, when he was beaten for the first time in a 10,000 m. race, after thirty-eight consecutive wins. And to many others in the annals of track and field. Moses' turn came in June 1987 at Madrid, at the hands of a compatriot ten years his junior, Danny Harris. Spanish daily "El Pais" revealed that the Madrid organizers paid Moses a cheque of 2 million pesetas as appearance money. And they paid Harris, the challenger, only 250,000 pesetas. The latter did himself justice in the best possible way, destroying the myth of Moses' invincibility.

major competitions, as it happened in the Olympics between 1948 and 1960, yet remains the no. 1 producer of talents. Next to Johnson I may mention Jack Pierce, who at the 1991 World Championships in Tokyo lost to his countryman Greg Foster by a few millimetres. Both were timed in 13.06. Even after watching slow-motion replays on the giant stadium screen, the two rivals were not sure of the outcome. This finally turned out to be in favour of Foster, who thus won his third world title. Another excellent hurdler is Mark Crear, who competed at the Atlanta Olympics only two weeks after suffering a broken arm and yet managed to finish second to Allen Johnson in 13.09. Canada had a fine hurdler in fast starting Mark McKoy, an Olympic champion in 1992. Cuba's Anier Garcia was a close second to Colin Jackson at the 1999 World Championships. In Britain, Tony Jarrett usually played second fiddle to Jackson, but his great comethrough ability allowed him to win medals on several occasions. Germany, with the likes of Florian Schwarthoff, Falk Balzer and others is currently Europe's no. 2 power.

1981
1999

Modern but hardly perfect

It happened during an indoor meet at Stuttgart on 7 February 1999, when Falk Balzer of Germany won the 60 metres hurdles in 7.34 (second fastest time ever), beating Colin Jackson of Britain (7.39), the very holder of the world record (7.30 in 1994). Balzer, known as a quick starter, was just too fast on that occasion. He took a blatant false start, yet there was no recall, reportedly because of the lack of an electronic apparatus capable of recording reaction times. However, Balzer's fault was crystal clear and the "author" himself apologized with Jackson. Following a protest by the manager of the Briton, the race was annulled. There was talk of a possible re-run, but this did not materialize. Keen observers of track doings recalled that twice before in important meets Jackson had been the (chief) victim of someone jumping the gun. Such occasions were as follows:
- World Indoor Championships in Toronto, 1993 - 60 metres hurdles: 1.Mark McKoy (Canada) 7.43, 2.Jackson 7.43. The winner had a reaction time of "only" 0.05 (Jackson 0.15).
- World Cup in Johannesburg, 1998 - 110 metres hurdles: 1.Balzer (Germany) 13.10, 2.Jackson 13.11. The German had an incredible reaction time of 0.03 (Jackson 0.15).
Contrary to what was to happen at Stuttgart in 1999, in such cases there was an apparatus recording reaction times, but for some reason the starters did not wear headphones and so they could not hear the acoustic signal emitted when the apparatus detects a false start. In observance to IAAF rule 162/10, this happens when the reaction time is less than 100/1000ths (0.100) of a second. In controversial cases, however, the starter will have the last word in deciding whether to accept the results or not. Both in Toronto and Johannesburg the wrong decision was made and results stood.
Modern technology can give us perfect (or near perfect) verdicts, yet there is always room for errors whenever human beings enter the picture, one way or another.

---

400 Metres Hurdles - From "King" Moses to Young, the first sub-47 performer.

1981 - WCup, Rome (4 Sep): 1.Moses (USA) 47.37, 2.Beck (EG) 49.16, 3.Schulting (Eur/Hol) 49.69.
1982 - EC, Athens (8 Sep): 1.Schmid (WG) 47.48, 2.Yatsevich (USSR) 48.60, 3.U.Ackermann (EG) 48.64.
1983 - WC, Helsinki (9 Aug): 1.Moses 47.50, 2.Schmid 48.61, 3.Kharlov (USSR) 49.03.
1984 - OG, Los Angeles (5 Aug): 1.Moses 47.75, 2.Harris (USA) 48.13, 3.Schmid 48.19.
1985 - WCup, Canberra (4 Oct): 1.Phillips (USA) 48.42, 2.Vasilyev (USSR) 48.61, 3.Schmid 48.83.
1986 - EC, Stuttgart (28 Aug): 1.Schmid 48.65, 2.Vasilyev 48.76, 3.Nylander (Swe) 49.38.
1987 - WC, Rome (1 Sep): 1.Moses 47.46, 2.Harris 47.48, 3.Schmid 47.48.
1988 - OG, Seoul (25 Sep): 1.Phillips 47.19, 2.Dia Ba (Sen) 47.23, 3.Moses 47.56.
1989 - WCup, Barcelona (8 Sep): 1.Patrick (USA) 48.74, 2.Amike (Afr/Nig) 49.24, 3.Akabusi (GB) 49.42.
1990 - EC, Split (29 Aug): 1.Akabusi 47.92, 2.Nylander 48.43, 3.Wallenlind (Swe) 48.52.
1991 - WC, Tokyo (27 August): 1. Matete (Zambia) 47.64, 2. Graham (Jam) 47.74, 3. Akabusi (GB) 47.86.

1992 - OG, Barcelona (6 August): 1 Young (USA) 46.78 World Record, 2. Graham 47.66, 3. Akabusi 47.82; WCup, Habana (25 September): 1. Matete 48.88, 2. Ridgeon (GB) 49.01, 3. Diagana (Fra) 49.34.
1993 - WC, Stuttgart (19 August): 1. Young 47.18, 2. Matete 47.60, 3. Graham 47.62.
1994 - EC, Helsinki (10 August): 1. Tverdokhlyeb (Ukr) 48.06, 2. Nylander (Swe) 48.22, 3. Diagana 48.23; WCup, London (9 September): 1. Matete (Afr/Zam) 48.77, 2. Tverdokhlyeb (Eur/Ukr) 49.26, 3. de Araujo (Ame/Bra) 49.62.
1995 - WC, Göteborg (10 August): 1. Adkins (USA) 47.98, 2. Matete 48.03, 3. Diagana 48.14.
1996 - OG, Atlanta (1 August): 1. Adkins 47.54, 2. Matete 47.78, 3. C.Davis (USA) 47.96.
1997 - WC, Athens (4 August): 1. Diagana 47.70, 2. Herbert (SA) 47.86, 3. Bronson (USA) 47.88.
1998 - EC, Budapest (20 August): 1. Januszewski (Pol) 48.17, 2. Mashchenko (Rus) 48.25, 3. Mori (Ita) 48.71; WCup, Johannesburg (11 September): 1. Matete 48.08, 2. Al-Nubi (Asi/Qat) 48.17, 3 Morgan (Ame/Jam) 48.40.
1999 - WC, Sevilla (27 August): 1. Mori 47.72, 2. Diagana 48.12, 3. Schelbert (Swz) 48.13.

Edwin Moses (USA), lane 3, in his last major victory in the 400 m. hurdles at the 1987 World Championships in Rome, nosing out H. Schmid (Germany), centre, and D. Harris (USA), left, all bracketed in two hundredths of a second (47.46, 47.48).

Throughout the major part of the Eighties, the incomparable Edwin Moses continued to be head and shoulders above the rest of the 400 m. hurdles fraternity. Considering what he did between 1976, the year of his breakthrough, and 1987, when he won his last major title, one can easily rank him as the greatest ever in the history of the event. He set his fourth and last world record on his twenty-eighth birthday, on 31 August 1983 at Koblenz, with 47.02. On paper he had two worthy rivals in his compatriot Andre Phillips and Harald Schmid of West Germany. The former remained in contention till the seventh hurdle, then had to give way to the "maestro". Phillips was second in 48.26 and Schmid only fourth. British journalist Dave Cocksedge caught Moses' touch-down splits on the ten hurdles as follows: 5.9, 9.4 (3.5), 13.1 (3.7), 17.0 (3.9), 20.9 (3.9), 24.8 (3.9), 28.9 (4.1), 32.9 (4.0), 37.3 (4.4), 41.7 (4.4), plus 5.4 for the last 40 m. An even-pace journey, with a slight deceleration in the closing stage, as is the rule in most if not all one-lap races, be they with or without hurdles. Moses' winning streak in his parade event stretched to 122 (including heats), a wondrous series achieved over a period of ten years, 1977-87. He finally went down to defeat on 4 June 1987 at Madrid against his younger countryman Danny Harris. The two matched strides for the greater part of the race, until Moses hit the last hurdle squarely with his lead foot. Harris won, 47.56 to 47.69.

After his first "faux pas" in ten years, Edwin Moses immediately decided to fight back. He did so in splendid manner, still in 1987, winning a hair-raising confrontation with Harris and Harald Schmid of West Germany at the World Championships in Rome. The three finished in that order, their times being 47.46, 47.48 and 47.48 respectively. The Old Lion won another hot battle at the 1988 US Olympic Trials in Indianapolis, when he did 47.37 to finish ahead of Andre Phillips (47.58), Kevin Young (47.72) and Danny Harris (47.75). The last-named thus earned the dubious honour of being the fastest non-qualifier of all time. After that, most prognosticators were picking Moses as the top favourite for the Seoul Olympics. Andre Phillips, for several years Edwin's underdog, rose to the occasion with a superlative effort and won the gold medal with 47.19, a new Olympic record. Quite unexpectedly, his toughest rival in that race was not Moses, third in 47.56, but Amadou Dia Ba of Senegal, who came dangerously close to Phillips in a rousing finish, taking the silver in 47.23 - 0.80 secs. under his previous best. Phillips, a versatile runner, could point to such times as 44.71 in the 400 m. flat and 13.25 in the 110 m. hurdles. At the latter distance he came close to making the 1988 US Olympic team! Dia Ba, known until then as a good but not exceptional performer, lost the race virtually at the start: his reaction time to the starter's gun was 0.22, as opposed to Phillips' 0.15. In terms of actual running time, the Senegalese was 0.03 faster than his rival. Harald Schmid (born at Hanau on 29 September 1957; 1.87 m./82 kg.) was for many years a steady loser in his duels with Moses, but remained easily and by far Europe's no.1 man. He won the continental 400 m. hurdles title three times (1978, '82 and '86). His best was 47.48, in '82 and again in '87. In flat events he had times of 10.3, 20.68, 44.92 and 1:44.83.

One of the men who lagged behind "King" Moses in the latter part of his career was Kevin Young (born in Los Angeles on 16 September 1966; 1.93 m./82 Kg.). He began as an all-around hurdler with marks of 14.12 and 51.09 as a junior in 1985, when he also did 7.09 in the long jump. Then he opted for the 400 metre hurdles and in 1986 he was third at the US Championships and lowered his best to 48.77, enough to earn 10th place in "Track & Field News" World Ranking. He improved to 5th in 1987 and to 3rd in 1988, when as related above he did 47.72 at the US Olympic Trials and placed fourth in the Seoul Olympics. When Moses stepped out, Young quickly rose to the rank of no. 1 in the 1989 World Ranking. By then he had begun to experiment with a new rythm. Being, at 1.93, taller than most of his rivals, he ran 13 strides between hurdles all the way. Because of his long legs, 12 steps would sometimes creep into his usual 13-step rythm. 1992 was his banner year. His coach was John Smith, former world record holder for 440 yards flat (44.5 in 1971), who was shaping up as a great "guru" in the domain of short-distance training. On the eve of the 1992 Olympics in Barcelona, "Track & Field News" quoted Smith as saying: "I wanted to give Kevin one last aerobic test before we did some specific race training. He ran 1:14.4 for 600 metres and came back 20 minutes later with a 20.8 in the 200. I knew then something magical was going to happen. I couldn't

Kevin Young (USA) succeeding Moses as world record holder in the 400 m. hurdles: 46.78 at the Barcelona Olympics (1992).

1981
1999

directly translate these times over to the hurdles, but I figured it meant something faster than 47.02 (Moses' world record)". Kevin himself was more precise: all over his room at the Olympic village he put up signs reading: 46.89. That seemed a lofty target to those who remembered that his best up to then was 47.72, made four years earlier.

Yet reality was to outshine dreams. In his semi-final Young lowered his best to 47.63, finishing a relaxed second to Winthrop Graham, who lowered the Jamaican record to 47.62. In the final, the following day (6 August), Young drew lane 4 and was flanked by Graham in 3 and Kriss Akabusi of Britain in 5. Young began to forge ahead at the fourth hurdle, but as usual it was around the last turn that he built up the major part of his lead. His stride pattern was 13-13-12-12-13-13-13-13-13.

Despite striking the last hurdle with his left foot and raising his arms skywards a few strides from the finish, he won by almost a second from Graham. His wondrous time - 46.78 - put an end to Edwin Moses' reign as world record holder. This happened in 1992, sixty years after another American, Ben Eastman, had first broken the 47-second barrier on a flat course. Graham (47.66) shunted Akabusi (47.82, a new British record) to third. In 1993 Young confirmed his superiority with a brillant victory at the World Championships in Stuttgart with 47.18, his second best time. He never again approached his superb form of 1992. An operation on his left knee in 1995 was followed by yet another attempt to resurrect. He was brave enough to do 49.50 in 1997 and 48.77 in 1998. Young, whose best on the flat course was an excellent 45.11 (1992), thus outshone Moses' record but not his fame. Not all record-breakers are necessarily greater than their predecessors. Even in terms of sub-48 secs. performances, Moses stayed well ahead of Young - 45 to 23.

USA had another good specialist in the Nineties, Derrick Adkins (born in Brooklyn, N.Y. on 2 July 1970; 1.88 m./80 Kg.), whose register included a 10.48 for 100 metres. He won at the 1995 World Championships (47.98) and in the 1996 Olympics (47.54, equalling his personal best, made at Lausanne the year before).

In other countries the most prominent performer of the decade was undoubtedly Samuel Matete of Zambia (born at Chingola on 7 July 1968; 1.83 n./77 Kg.). In 1991 he became the first athlete from his country to win a world title in athletics as he nosed out Winthrop Graham in Tokyo, 47.64 to 47.74. At the time he was attending Auburn University in USA and that was to remain his best season. In the "Weltklasse" meet in Zurich he went down to 47.10, his fastest time. He stayed at or near the top for many more years, winning silver medals at the 1993 and '95 World Championships and in the 1996 Olympics. With his yellow jersey he graced European meets for a long time and in 1999, aged 31, he ran the distance in 47.91.

An American, Bryan Bronson, had a near perfect season in 1998, clocking 47.03 - third best ever - and suffering only one defeat out of 20 races, alas on the most important occasion, the final of the Grand Prix series in Moscow, when he dropped from first to sixth in the last stretch of land. It was a costly defeat for he lost $ 250,000, which would have been his share of the jackpot allotted to those who had won their event in all meets of the series. (His failure enabled Hicham El Guerrouj, Haile Gebrselassie and on the distaff side Marion Jones, to win $ 330,000 each). What was perhaps even worse, in March

---

Nylander, a comethrough performer

The art of surpassing oneself in a major meet against stiff competition, exemplified by the ancient motto "Hic Rhodos, hic salta!", is the trademark of a true champion. A man who certainly deserved to be included in that noble breed was Sven Nylander, a tall Swedish runner who was a prominent figure in the 400 metre hurdles for many years. True, he never reached the top, yet he had the great merit of improving on his personal best in "hot" meets. He ducked under 50 secs. for the first time in the 1982 Swedish Championships at Piteå. From then on all his subsequent improvements happened in connection with big championship meets. The wondrous list is as follows:

49.88 (1)	Piteå (Swed.Ch)	15 Aug '82
49.64 (7)	Athens (Eur.Ch)	8 Sept '82
48.88 (1)	Houston (NCAA.Ch)	3 Jun '83
48.83 (2) s2	Stuttgart (Eur./Ch)	27 Aug '86
48.46 (3) s1	Rome (World Ch)	31 Aug '87
48.37 (4)	Rome (World Ch)	1 Sept '87
48.22 (2)	Helsinki (Eur. Ch)	10 Aug '94
48.21 (2)s1	Atlanta (Oly. Games)	31 Jul '96
47.98 (4)	Atlanta (Oly. Games)	1 Aug '96

In terms of honours the best he could do in global (World/Olympic) meets was fourth - 4 times! But he did win 3 medals (2 silver, 1 bronze) in the European Championships. Truly a sturdy performer, if ever there was one.

1999 he was suspended by the IAAF for proving positive ("an abnormal steroid concentration") in a doping test at the Golden Gala in Rome ... 8 months before. The delay was explained with the necessity of waiting for a full medical report from Bronson himself, who said he "had some medical problem".

In Europe the outstanding performers of recent years were Stéphane Diagana of France and Fabrizio Mori of Italy. The former, fast enough to clock 45.18 on the flat route, won at the 1997 World Championships in 47.70, after lowering the European record to 47.37 in 1995. Mori rose slowly but gradually: after reaching the semi-finals in three editions of the World Championships (1991, '93 and '95) and placing fourth in 1997, he finally rose to the top in 1999, winning at Sevilla in 47.72, his best time ever. As often as not he was the man "who decelerated the least" in the crucial closing stages.

3000 Metres Steeplechase - The sub-8 min. Club: the great Kiptanui and his pupils, an all-Kenyan affair.

1981 - WCup, Rome (5 Sep): 1.Maminski (Eur/Pol) 8:19.89, 2.Scartezzini (Ita) 8:19.93, 3.Shintaku (Asi/Jap) 8:23.64. H.Marsh (USA), 1st in 8:19.31, was disqualified for running round the water jump.
1982 - EC, Athens (10 Sep): 1.Ilg (WG) 8:18.52, 2.Maminski 8:19.22, 3.Ramón (Spa) 8:20.48.
1983 - WC, Helsinki (12 Aug): 1.Ilg 8:15.06, 2.Maminski 8:17.03, 3.Reitz (GB) 8:17.75.
1984 - OG, Los Angeles (10 Aug): 1.J.Korir (Ken) 8:11.80, 2.Mahmoud (Fra) 8:13.31, 3.Diemer (USA) 8:14.06.
1985 - WCup, Canberra (5 Oct): 1.Kariuki (Afr/Ken) 8:39.51, 2.Marsh 8:39.55, 3.Fell (Ame/Can) 8:40.30.
1986 - EC, Stuttgart (29 Aug): 1.Melzer (EG) 8:16.65, 2.Panetta (Ita) 8:16.85, 3.Ilg 8:16.92.
1987 - WC, Rome (5 Sep): 1.Panetta 8:08.57, 2 Melzer 8:10.32, 3.Van Dijck (Bel) 8:12.18.
1988 - OG, Seoul (30 Sep): 1.Kariuki 8:05.51, 2.P.Koech (Ken) 8:06.79, 3.Rowland (GB) 8:07.96.
1989 - WCup, Barcelona (9 Sep): 1.Kariuki 8:20.84, 2.Lambruschini (Ita) 8:21.75, 3.Melzer 8:23.21.
1990 - EC, Split (30 Aug): 1.Panetta 8:12.66, 2.Rowland 8:13.27, 3.Lambruschini 8:15.82.
1991 - WC, Tokyo (31 August): 1. Kiptanui (Ken) 8:12.59, 2. Sang (Ken) 8:13.44, 3. Brahmi (Alg) 8:15.54.
1992 - OG, Barcelona (7 August): 1. M.Birir (Ken) 8:08.84, 2. Sang 8:09.55, 3. Mutwol (Ken) 8:10.74; WCup, Habana (26 September): 1. Barkutwo (Afr/Ken) 8:26.81, 2. Van Dijck (Eur/Bel) 8:32.06, 3. Creighton (Oce/Aus) 8:33.79.
1993 - WC, Stuttgart (21 August): 1. Kiptanui 8:06.36, 2. Sang 8:07.53, 3. Lambruschini (Ita) 8:08.78.
1994 - EC, Helsinki (12 August): 1. Lambruschini 8:28.68, 2. Carosi (Ita) 8:29.81, 3. Van Dijck 8:30.93; WCup, London (10 September): 1. Kiptanui (Afr/Ken) 8:28.28, 2. Al-Asmari (Asi/KSA) 8:35.74, 3. Lambruschini (Eur/Ita) 8:40.34.
1995 - WC, Göteborg (11 August): 1. Kiptanui 8:04.16, 2. C. Kosgei (Ken) 8:09.30, 3. Al-Asmari 8:12.95.
1996 - OG, Atlanta (2 August): 1. J.Keter (Ken) 8:07.12, 2. Kiptanui 8:08.33, 3. Lambruschini 8:11.28.
1997 - WC, Athens (6 August): 1. Boit-Kipketer (Ken) 8:05.84, 2. Kiptanui 8:06.04, 3. Barmasai (Ken) 8:06.04.
1998 - EC, Helsinki (23 August): 1. Kallabis (Ger) 8:13.10, 2. Lambruschini 8:16.70, 3. Svenöy (Nor) 8:18.97; WCup, Johannesburg (12 September): 1. Kallabis 8:31.25, 2. Barmasai 8:31.85, 3. Al-Asmari 8:39.69.
1999 - WC, Sevilla (23 August): 1. C. Kosgei 8:11.76, 2. Boit-Kipketer 8:12.09, 3. Ezzine (Mor) 8:12.73.

Clock-wise, the Eighties saw little or no progress in steeplechase standards. Towards the end of the decade Kenya was firmly established as the no.1 power, with Italy a good second. Outstanding among the Europeans were Boguslaw Maminski of Poland, Patriz Ilg of West Germany, Hagen Melzer of East Germany and Joseph Mahmoud of France. The last-named still held the continental record at the end of 1999 with 8:07.62 ('84). Best of all, however, was Francesco Panetta of Italy (born at Siderno near Reggio Calabria on 10 January 1963; 1.75 m./64 kg.). Although a teammate of "big kicker" Alberto Cova for several years, he showed an entirely different approach: a front runner by inspiration and habit, he would invariably try to take the sting out of his rivals with a sustained pace. His tactics paid dividends on two important occasions, in the 1987 World Championships and the 1990 European

315

Championships. Kenyan runners have recently added lustre to the tradition of Kogo, Biwott, Keino and Jipcho. Olympic crowns went to Julius Korir at Los Angeles and Julius Kariuki at Seoul. And it was eventually a Kenyan who succeeded Henry Rono, another Kenyan, as world record holder. The man for this job was Peter Koech (born at Kiliburani on 18 February 1958; 1.80 m./67 kg.), who on 3 July 1989 at Stockholm beat his countryman Patrick Sang in a close battle, 8:05.35 to 8:06.03. (Rono's listed record was a "manual" 8:05.4). Koech's 1000 m. fractions were 2:43.35, 2:43.25 and 2:38.75; his "halves", 4:06.53 and 3:58.82. A slightly slower time had been credited in 1988 at Seoul to Julius Kariuki (born at Nyahururu on 12 June 1961; 1.81 m./62 kg.), who in the opinion of most experts seemed to be the best talent of them all. But in subsequent years he failed to improve further.

Throughout the Nineties the growing impact of Kenyan steeplechasers was best epitomized by their astounding success in major (World/Olympic) championships. They won 16 of the 21 medals (i.e. 79%) at stake, actually supplying winner and runner-up in each and every case and leaving to the rest of the world only 5 bronze medals! At the end of 1999 the World All Time List for this event shows 12 Kenyans on top - seldom if ever in recent decades has any country dominated an event in such an outrageous manner.

The most phenomenal performer in the annals of this event is Moses Kiptanui (born at Elgeyo Marakwet on 1 October 1970; 1.75 m./60 Kg.), who used his great basic speed to good advantage and re-wrote the record book in the steeplechase - and in the flat events as well. In 1989 he ran the barrier event in 8:46.6, good enough to find a place among the top 20 in the Kenyan Year List. Internationally he emerged from virtual obscurity to win the 1500 metres in 3:38.32 at the 1990 World Junior Championships in Plovdiv. Foreign observers who wondered how he had made the grade so quickly were simply told that "he had been running since the age of 3".... He was then listed with a date of birth in 1971 but he later admitted that he was a year older. In 1991 he made a sensation by winning the 3000 metre steeplechase at the World Championships in Tokyo, a title he was to defend successfully in 1993 and '95. The following year a knee injury held him back to 4th at the Kenyan Trials and so he failed to qualify for the Barcelona Olympics. The men who beat him - Matthew Birir, Patrick Sang and William Mutwol - went on to make a clean sweep for Kenya in the Games, finishing in that order. But Kiptanui took revenge in post-Olympic meets: he not only beat the Barcelona medallists easily but achieved a unique double with two world records in the space of three days: 7:28.96 for 3000 metres flat (Köln, 16 August) and 8:02.08 for 3000 metre steeplechase (Zurich, 19 August). Before the end of that month he also ran the 5000 in 13:00.93, missing Said Aouita's world record by a little more than 2 seconds. Kiptanui probably had his best year in 1995, when he opened up with a 5000 metre world record - 12:55.30 in Rome, 8 June. Then at Zurich on 16 August he became the first sub-8 performer in the annals of the steeplechase with a time of 7:59.18. To his credit he requested that meet organizers NOT provide any "hares". He was well clear of the pack as he reached 1000 metres (2:41.25). The second kilometre was covered at basically the same pace (2:40.95 for 5:22.20 at 2000 m.). Then he struggled gallantly and managed to negotiate the last kilometre in a fast 2:36.98. He thus finished in 7:59.18, well ahead of Gideon Chirchir (8:06.77) and three other Kenyans.

Moses Kiptanui (Kenya), the most important figure of recent years in the steeplechase.

Kiptanui's booty included $ 50,000 in cash and a 1-kilo ingot of gold. The 8-min. barrier had been first broken on the flat route by Gaston Reiff of Belgium in 1949, with 7:58.8..... Up to then nobody else had ducked under 8:05 in the steeplechase. Only two days after his great race in Zurich, the amazing Kiptanui once again astounded track observers with a time of 7:28.04 for 3000 metres flat (Köln, 18 August). By then, however, the world record belonged to Noureddine Morceli of Algeria (7:25.11 in 1994). Kiptanui was again hampered by an injury in 1996 and had to be content with second at the Atlanta Olympics behind his countryman Joseph Keter (8:08.33 to 8:07.12). He was runner-up again at the 1997 World Championships in Athens, this time to Wilson Boit-Kipketer, another Kenyan of course (8:06.04 to 8:05.84).

A few days later (Zurich, 13 August) Boit-Kipketer broke Kiptanui's world record by a scanty margin with 7:59.08, winning from Bernard Barmasai (8:00.35) and Kiptanui himself (8:00.78). This fantastic Kenyan saga reached the highest pitch at Köln on 24 August when Barmasai beat the old master at the end of a furious battle — 7:55.72 to 7:56.16 — and thus conquered the world record. In this race there was a "hare", who led the field in the first kilometre (2:38.19), closely followed by Barmasai and Kiptanui. Then the two main characters in the play took over, with Kiptanui in the lead. The second kilometre was run in 2:42.30 (2000 m. in 5:20.49). Off the final barrier Barmasai launched his attack and sprinted past his great rival. The time for the last kilometre was a sizzling 2:35.23. Kiptanui thus posted his fastest time ever - in a losing effort. Barmasai (born at Keiyo on 6 May 1974; 1.73 m./55 Kg.) had come from nowhere to run 8:14.18 in 1994. The following year he won the event at the African Games and did 8:08.56. He failed to advance in the Olympic year 1996, but he more than made amends for that in 1997. The Köln race was an all-Kenya affair, with 7 runners from that country among the top 10 finishers! Barmasai thus became the third Kenyan to hold the world record in the space of ten days! Boit-Kipketer could not compete in Köln due to an injury. In 1998 Kiptanui suffered a ruptured Achilles tendon at the Goodwill Games: a slight misstep ended his season prematurely. The following year he was back in harness but could do no better than 8:09.23. His countrymen Barmasai and Christopher Kosgei split honours, with the former winning at the World Championships in Sevilla and the latter having the lion's share in Grand Prix meets.

Best of the non-Kenyans in the Nineties was Alessandro Lambruschini of Italy, who won bronze

Relaxation, Kenyan style

"Kenyans have an amazing ability to relax most of the day; they do not need to be occupied as so many Westerners do. Wilson Musto, one of the Kenyans currently winning many European road races, had a day schedule while training in Sweden which included going back to bed after breakfast and the morning run, rising for lunch before retreating to bed once again, taking an afternoon run, eating dinner, then returning to bed!!"

The above observations were made by Toby Tanser, an acute judge of Kenya's running world. He spent several months in that country and summarized his experiences in a very enlightening book, "Train Hard, Win Easy" (Tafnews Press, 1997).

1981
1999

Bernard Barmasai (Kenya) holds the current world record for the 3000 m. steeplechase: 7:55.72 in 1997.

medals at the 1993 World Championships and in the 1996 Olympics, on the former occasion with his best time ever - 8:08.78. In both races he finished behind a Kenyan duo and shunted to fourth the third Kenyan string Matthew Birir, the Olympic champion of 1992. On the whole Europeans appeared to be on the downgrade though: at the end of 1999 most of the top marks on the All Time List for the "Old Continent" dated from the Seventies/Eighties, and Lambruschini with his 8:08.78 ranked no higher than fifth.

JUMPS - High Jump: 2.50 is for tomorrow

1981 - WCup, Rome (6 Sep): 1.Peacock (USA) 2.28, 2.Nagel (Eur/WG) 2.26, 3.Freimuth (EG) 2.24.
1982 - EC, Athens (11 Sep): 1.Mögenburg (WG) 2.30, 2.Trzepizur (Pol) 2.27, 3.Nagel 2.24.
1983 - WC, Helsinki (13 Aug): 1.Avdeyenko (USSR) 2.32, 2.Peacock 2.32, 3.Zhu Jianhua (Asi/Chn) 2.29.
1984 - OG, Los Angeles (11 Aug): 1.Mögenburg 2.35, 2.Sjöberg (Swe) 2.33, 3.Zhu Jianhua 2.31.

Zhu Jianhua (China) held the world record for the high jump: 2.39 in 1984.

1985 - WCup, Canberra (6 Oct): 1.Sjöberg 2.31, 2.Howard (USA) 2.28, 3.Sotomayor (Ame/Cub) 2.28.
1986 - EC, Stuttgart (31 Aug): 1.Paklin (USSR) 2.34, 2.Malchenko (USSR) 2.31, 3.Thränhardt (WG) 2.31.
1987 - WC, Rome (6 Sep): 1.Sjöberg 2.38, 2.(tie) Avdeyenko and Paklin, both 2.38.
1988 - OG, Seoul (25 Sep): 1.Avdeyenko 2.38, 2.Conway (USA) 2.36, 3.(tie) Povarnitsin (USSR) and Sjöberg (Swe), both 2.36.
1989 - WCup, Barcelona (10 Sep): 1.Sjöberg 2.34, 2.Grant (GB) 2.31, 3.Sotomayor 2.25.
1990 - EC, Split (1 Sep): 1.Topic (Yug) 2.34, 2.Yemelin (USSR) 2.34, 3.Dakov (Bu!) 2.34.
1991 - WC, Tokyo (1 Sep): 1.Austin (USA) 2.38, 2.Sotomayor 2.36, 3.Conway 2.36.
1992 - OG, Barcelona (2 Aug): 1.Sotomayor 2.34, 2.Sjöberg 2.34, 3.(tie) Conway, Forsyth (Aus), Partyka (Pol) 2.34. WCup, Habana (27 Sep): 1.Sergiyenko (EUN/Ukr) 2.29, 2.Sotomayor (Ame/Cub) 2.26, 3.Reilly (GB) 2.26.
1993 - WC, Stuttgart (22 Aug): 1.Sotomayor 2.40, 2.Partyka 2.37, 3.S.Smith (GB) 2.37.
1994 - EC, Helsinki (9 Aug): 1.Hoen (Nor) 2.35, 2.(tie) Partyka and S.Smith 2.33; WCup, London (11 Sep): 1.Sotomayor 2.40, 2.Forsyth 2.28, 3.S.Smith 2.28.
1995 - WC, Göteborg (8 Aug): 1.Kemp (Bah) 2.37, 2.Sotomayor 2.37, 3.Partyka 2.35, 4.(tie) S.Smith and Hoen 2.35.
1996 - OG, Atlanta (28 July): 1.Austin 2.39, 2.Partyka 2.37, 3.S.Smith 2.35.
1997 - WC, Athens (6 Aug): 1.Sotomayor 2.37, 2.Partyka 2.35, 3.Forsyth 2.35.
1998 - EC, Budapest (21 Aug): 1.Partyka 2.34, 2.Grant (GB) 2.34, 3.Klyugin (Rus) 2.32, 4.Buss (Ger) 2.32; WCup, Johannesburg (13 Sep): 1.Austin 2.31, 2.Sotomayor 2.28, 3.Klyugin (Eur/Rus) 2.28.
1999 - WC, Sevilla (23 Aug): 1.Voronin (Rus) 2.37, 2.Boswell (Can) 2.35, 3.Buss 2.32, 4.Topic (Yug) 2.32.

By the early Eighties the "Flop" had taken over as the ruling style. At the top the most notable leap forward was assured by a Chinese, Zhu Jianhua (born at Shanghai on 29 May 1963; 1.96 m./74 kg.). The most populated country on earth had already had a top-notch high jumper, Ni Zhiqin (whose 2.29 in 1970 was not ratified as a world record because at the time the Chinese People's Republic was not a member of the IAAF), yet there was no relation between him and his successor of the early Eighties. Ni was one of the last "straddlers", while Zhu soon developed into a fine "Flopper",

1981 1999

mastering 2.13 at sixteen. Still as a junior, in 1982, he jumped 2.33. He improved on the world record three times: 2.37 at Beijing and 2.38 at Shanghai in 1983 and finally 2.39 on 10 June 1984 at Eberstadt, during the traditional high jump festival held every year in that West German town. In this meet Zhu won from West Germans Carlo Thränhardt and Dietmar Mögenburg (both 2.36, a new European record) and Sweden's Patrik Sjöberg (2.33). However, Zhu was a temperamental athlete and as such he failed to reproduce his best form in the two major tests of his career. He thus had to be content with bronze medals at the 1983 World Championships at Helsinki and in the 1984 Olympics at Los Angeles. Winner in the former meet was a Russian who came out of nowhere to top a crack field with 2.32. He was Gennadiy Avdeyenko (born at Odessa on 4 November 1963; 2.02 m./82 kg.) and his name was to be heard time and again in the following years, were it only ... on occasions that mattered. Winner at Los Angeles in 1984 was Dietmar Mögenburg (born at Leverkusen on 15 August 1961; 2.01 m./78 kg.). His early breakthrough as a junior was related in a previous chapter. As time went on he developed into a most reliable competitor. He won the Olympic gold medal with 2.35 from Sjöberg (2.33) and Zhu (2.31). Veteran Dwight Stones of USA, in his third Olympic adventure, jumped higher than ever before in the Games yet finished no better than fourth (2.31). On 11 August 1985 a newsitem from USSR stunned the athletics world: in a regional meet at Donyetsk, a virtual unknown named Rudolf Povarnitsin had mastered a height of 2.40, a new world record. The surprise was due to the fact that prior to his magic day Povarnitsin had done no better than 2.26! He was a tall (2.01 m.) youngster, born 23 years ago at Votkinsk in the Udmurtsk Republic - the same birthplace of composer Pyotr Ilich Tchaikovskiy. At Donyetsk he improved on his personal best four times in quick succession, with 2.29, 2.32, 2.35 and 2.40! That was to remain easily and by far his happiest day. He was a factor in major meets only once, when he earned a tie for third at the 1988 Olympics in Seoul. A more consistent competitor was his countryman Igor Paklin, who raised the world record to 2.41 at the Universiade in Kobe on 4 September 1985 and was crowned European champion the following year at Stuttgart. In times of relative poverty for Scandinavian athletics, Sweden had an outstanding man in Patrik Sjöberg (born at Göteborg on 5 January 1965; 2.00 m./82 kg.), who proved a tough competitor on many occasions and won his good share of honours, notably including a world title at Rome in 1987. Earlier in the same year, on 30 June at Stockholm, he succeeded Paklin as world record holder with 2.42. The latest record-breaker is Javier Sotomayor of Cuba (born at Limonar, Matanzas province, on 13 October 1967; 1.95 m./82 kg.). A pupil of José Godoy, he reached spectacular heights very early: 2.00 at fifteen, 2.33 at seventeen and a world record 2.43 at Salamanca, Spain, on 8 September 1988 - incidentally the first world record set on Spanish soil. With Cuba boycotting the Seoul Olympics, he was unable to meet the world's best in that meet. He made partial amends at the 1989 World Indoor Championships at Budapest, where he won with 2.43.

Later that year, on 29 July at San Juan, Puerto Rico, he reached a milestone of great international appeal. On the eve of the event, Puerto Rican TV had launched an urgent appeal: "Vengan a ver el primer ser umano saltar ocho pies" (Come and see the first human being jump over 8 feet). "Soto" did not let them down. After his first two jumps (2.20 and 2.30) he was the only man left in the contest and thus able to fully concentrate on exalted heights. He cleared 2.35 and 2.40 in swift succession. At 22.20 hrs the bar was set at 2.44, one centimetre above his own world record. He brushed the bar off in his first attempt before clearing it on his second. By doing so he captured the imagination of the world of sport in a twofold manner. First, that metric height was a shade (actually, 1.5 mm.) over 8 English feet. Secondly, it happened to be just the height of the crossbar in the world's most popular sport - soccer.

Patrik Sjöberg (Sweden), world high jump champion in 1987, seen here in the 1995 edition at Göteborg - by then past his peak, he finished 6th.

319

But history often reminds us that the difference between one man's sucess and another's failure can be infinitesimal. The previous week in New York "Soto" was defeated by his arch rival Patrik Sjöberg, 2.34 to 2.37. After which he sat and watched the long-haired Swede narrowly miss at 8 feet not once but three times!The two men had hot duels in the early Nineties too, the closest being in the 1992 Olympics at Barcelona. On that occasion spectators were treated to the greatest "blanket finish" in the history of the event. Five men cleared 2.34 and none could go higher. Sotomayor, as the only one to master that height on his first try, won and thus fulfilled his dream. Sjöberg was second, while Hollis Conway (USA), Tim Forsyth (Australia) and Artur Partyka (Poland) tied for third, all with 2.34.

Both Sotomayor and Sjöberg, no matter how gifted in terms of talent, fought with the Moloch of Injuries for the greater part of their careers. In 1990 the Swede was quoted as saying: "It is too much for me. I have lost the touch. it is too hard training and then getting injured all the time". Yet he struggled on for several more years before calling it quits. Sotomayor averaged two injuries per year, some of them requiring surgery, between 1987 and '91. In a book dedicated to him, he was quoted as saying: "The physical and mental stress characterizing modern competition at the highest level entails great dangers, "los atletas constantemente estan jugando con fuego" (athletes are constantly playing with fire). Despite his frequent injuries, always affecting his take-off (left) leg, he managed to

Javier Sotomayor (Cuba), the first man to conquer 8 feet (2.44) and 2.45 m. in the hight jump.

resurrect time and again. In the Nineties he added considerably to his collection of laurels with two wins and two seconds in the World Championships and, as related above, his gold in the '92 Olympics.

He also managed to improve on his world record. On 27 July 1993 he returned to Salamanca, the ancient city in West-Central Spain where he had set his first global record in 1988 and upped his mark to 2.45.His work on that occasion was confined to 5 jumps: he cleared 2.23, 2.32 and 2.38 all on first tries, then he needed a pair at the record height. On his second the bar quivered but remained on the pegs. Troy Kemp of Bahamas was a distant second with 2.26. When it was all over, "Soto" indulged in a brief discussion of future possibilities in his event. He felt that up-and-coming jumpers could aim at heights in the range 2.46/2.48 but added that the event's next big barrier - 2.50 - was way off, "At any rate, he said, it's nothing I'm planning on". Throughout the Nineties, the Cuban constantly remained at or near the top, notwithstanding his injury problems. At the 1999 Pan American Championships in Winnipeg, aged 32, he fell foul of a doping control as traces of cocaine were detected in his urine sample. He was deprived of the title he had won (at 2.30). Supported by the Cuban State and press, he denied using cocaine and said he was simply "the victim of sabotage". At the time of writing the IAAF still has to pronounce final judgment on this case.

The no.1 American throughout the greater part of the Nineties was Charles Austin (born on 19 December 1967 at Bay City, Texas; 1.84 m./77 Kg.), a consistent performer who won a world title in 1991, beating Sotomayor (2.38 to 2.36), and triumphed at the Atlanta Olympics in 1996 (2.39), after overcoming the effects of a serious injury. The above-mentioned Troy Kemp of Bahamas had his day of glory at the 1995 World Championships, winning from "Soto" at 2.37 (for both). In Europe, the most consistent performer of the decade was Artur Partyka of Poland (born on 25 July 1969 at Stalowa Wola; 1.92 m. /71 kg.), who won silver medals in the 1996 Olympics as well as in the '93 and '97 World Championships, and bronze in the 1992 Olympics and the '95 World Championships. Son of an Algerian father and a Polish mother, he had a superb competitive record, even though he never went higher than 2.38. Steve Smith of Great Britain, a bronze medallist in the 1993 World Chjampionships and in the '96 Olympics, has been another excellent competitor.

As at the end of 1999 there have been 32 marks at 2.40 or higher. Sotomayor had 21, i.e. 65.6% of the total. The phenomenal "hausse" of the Eighties, when the world record was raised from 2.35 to 2.44, has been followed by a standstill in the most recent years. No jumper has gone over 2.40 in the last four seasons (1996-99). The "hausse" was due only in part to the "Flop". Hyper-intensive training was another factor. The top ten in the World All Time List at the end of 1999 average 1.93 in height, the extremes being Rudolf Povarnitsin and Dietmar Mögenburg (both 2.01) and at the other end Hollis Conway (1.83). That may be the best clue towards future progress.

POLE VAULT - Sergey, the Czar

1981 - WCup, Rome (5 September): 1.Volkov (USSR) 5.70, 2.Bellot (Eur/Fra) 5.55, 3.Olson (USA) 5.50.
1982 - EC, Athens (9 Sep): 1.Krupskiy (USSR) 5.60, 2.Polyakov (USSR) 5.60, 3.Tarev (Bul) 5.60.
1983 - WC, Helsinki (14 Aug): 1.S.Bubka (USSR) 5.70, 2.Volkov 5.60, 3.Tarev 5.60.
1984 - OG, Los Angeles (8 Aug): 1.Quinon (Fra) 5.75, 2.Tully (USA) 5.65, 3.(tie) Bell (USA) and Vigneron (Fra), both 5.60.
1985 - WCup, Canberra (5 Oct): 1.S.Bubka 5.85, 2.Collet (Eur/Fra) 5.60, 3.Bright (USA) 5.40.
1986 - EC, Stuttgart (29 Aug): 1.S.Bubka 5.85, 2.V.Bubka (USSR) 5.75, 3.Collet 5.75.
1987 - WC, Rome (5 Sep): 1.S.Bubka 5.85, 2.Vigneron 5.80, 3.Gataullin (USSR) 5.80.
1988 - OG, Seoul (28 Sep): 1.S.Bubka 5.90, 2.Gataullin 5.85, 3.Yegorov (USSR) 5.80.
1989 - WCup, Barcelona (9 Sep): 1.Collet (Eur/Fra) 5.75, 2.Bright 5.70, 3.Langhammer (EG) 5.55.
1990 - EC, Split (30 Aug): 1.Gataullin 5.85, 2.Yegorov 5.75, 3.Fehringer (Aut) 5.75.
1991 - WC, Tokyo (29 Aug): 1. Bubka 5.95, 2. Bagyula (Hun) 5.90, 3. Tarasov (USSR) 5.85, 4. Gataullin (USSR) 5.85.
1992 - OG, Barcelona (7 Aug): 1. Tarasov 5.80, 2. Trandenkov (Rus) 5.80, 3. Garcia (Spa) 5.75, 4. Tarpenning (USA) 5.75; WCup, Habana (26 Sep): 1. Potapovich (Eun/Kaz) 5.60, 2. Collet (Eur/Fra) 5.40, 3. Brits (Afr/SA) 5.30, 4. Takei (Asi/Jap) 5.30.
1993 - WC, Stuttgart (19 Aug): 1. Bubka (Ukr) 6.00, 2. Yegorov (Kaz) 5.90, 3. (tie) Tarasov (Rus) and Trandenkov (Rus) 5.80, 5. Huffman (USA) 5.80, 6. Petushinskiy (Rus) 5.80.
1994 - EC, Helsinki (11 Aug): 1. Gataullin (Rus) 6.00, 2. Trandenkov 5.90, 3. Galfione (Fra) 5.85; WCup, London (10 Sep): 1. Brits (Afr/SA) 5.90, 2. Galfione (Eur/Fra) 5,75, 3. (tie) Manzano (Ame/Cub) and Tiwontschik (Ger) 5.40, 5. Huffman 5.40, 6. Yegorov (Ais/Kaz) 5.40.
1995 - WC, Göteborg (11 Aug): 1. Bubka 5.92, 2. Tarasov 5.86, 3. Galfione 5.86.
1996 - OG, Atlanta (2 Aug): 1. Galfione 5.92, 2. Trandenkov 5.92, 3. Tiwontschik 5.92.
1997 - WC, Athens (10 Aug): 1. Bubka 6.01, 2. Tarasov 5.96, 3. Starkey (USA) 5.91.
1998 - EC, Budapest (22 Aug): 1. Tarasov 5.81, 2. Lobinger (Ger) 5.81, 3. Galfione 5.76, 4. Ecker (Ger) 5.76; WCup, Johannesburg (12 Sep): 1. Tarasov (Eur/Rus) 5.85, 2. Lobinger 5.80, 3. Hartwig (USA) 5.70.
1999 - WC, Sevilla (26 Aug): 1. Tarasov 6.02, 2. Markov (Aus) 5.90, 3. Averbukh (Isr) 5.80.

Vaulting standards continued to go up incessantly throughout the Eighties. Between 1981 and '89 the world record was bettered 14 times, in a debate involving two countries - France and USSR. The best exponent of the French school was Thierry Vigneron (born in Paris on 9 March 1960; 1.81 m./73 kg.), who achieved three record performances, the last of which being 5.91 at Rome in 1984, strangely enough in an event he did not win, because ten minutes later Sergey Bubka of USSR cleared 5.94. Another Frenchman, Pierre Quinon (born at Lyon on 20 February 1962; 1.80 m./74 kg.) had earlier held the world record with 5.82 (1983). He eventually became his country's first Olympic gold medallist when he beat the best Americans and Vigneron, at Los Angeles in 1984. The absence of the Russians did of course play in his favour. One in particular, Sergey Bubka (born at Voroshilovgrad on 4 December 1963; 1.83 m./80 kg.) was by then considered the undisputed master of the art. He made his début on the international scene at the 1981 European Junior Championships, tying for seventh with 5 metres even. Only two years later he was selected at the last moment to represent USSR at the World Championships in Helsinki. He surprised a lot of people by outlasting his older and more experienced rivals in a nerve-wrecking competition. He finally won at 5.70, and that was the beginning of a long reign. What "czar" Sergey has done from 1983 onwards entitles him to be considered as the greatest vaulter of our time and probably of all time, without wishing in any way to detract from the achievements of "Dutch" Warmerdam, the king of the Bamboo Era. Here is a summary of Bubka's feats:
1) Seventeen world outdoor records: 5.85, 5.88, 5.90 and 5.94 in '85, 6.00 in '85, 6.01 in '86, 6.03 in '87, 6.05 and 6.06 in '88, 6.07, 6.08, 6.09

and 6.10 in '91, 6.11, 6.12 and 6.13 in '92 and 6.14 in '94. Eighteen world indoor records, the last one being 6.15 in '93. And he was the most "cosmopolitan" of record breakers in choosing the sites for his record performances: 27 in Europe, 5 in Asia and 3 in North America.

2) Apart from the 1984 Olympics in Los Angeles, from which he had to stay anway as the citizen of a boycotting country, he has won every major honour at stake. Outdoors he was world champions 6 times in a row, from 1983 up to and including 1997! He was European champion in 1986. Indoors he was world champion 4 times. He became history's first 6-metre man on 13 July 1985 at Stade Jean-Bouin in Paris, when he cleared exactly that height on his third attempt. At record heights he uses a grip of 5.10 (or slightly higher). His coach Vitaliy Petrov once timed him in 0.978 secs. (with a digital watch) for the last 10 m. of his run - a speed of 36 km. per hour. Bubka's most serious challenger emerged in his own country in the person of Rodion Gataullin (born at Tashkent on 23 November 1965; 1.89 m./78 kg.), who first beat the "czar" in the final of the Grand Prix IAAF/Mobil in 1988. But Bubka turned the tables on his challenger in the Seoul Olympics.

By 1990, however, Gataullin was ready to take over and did in fact defeat Bubka at the European Championships in Split. Taller and slimmer than his great rival, Gataullin was once credited with 14.4 in the 110 m. hurdles. He became history's second 6-metre man during the 1989 indoor season (6.00 at Leningrad, then 6.02 at Gomel) and later in the season, at Tokyo, he turned the trick outdoors as well, with exactly 6 metres At the dawn of the Nineties, USSR dominated the pole vault scene just as did USA thirty and more years ago. Suffice it to say that in 1990 five Russians credited with marks in the range 5.85/5.80 were not rated good enough to make the USSR team for the European Championships in Split! France had by then a good vaulter in Philippe Collet, a stocky little man who did 5.94 indoors in 1990, reportedly after "steadying the bar with his hands", thus saving an otherwise doomed jump. This "technique" is known as "Volzing" in USA, after the name of the vaulter (Dave Volz) who had been using it most frequently in recent years.

There was no provision in the rule book for any attempt aimed at "corriger la fortune", as the French say. The prevailing idea probably was that one could

Maksim Tarasov (Russia) succeeded "Czar" Sergey Bubka as world's pole vault champion in 1999.

hardly do such refined "handiwork" while up in the air. Yet similar practices had been occasionally used in the past. My friend Prof. Luciano Fracchia of Asti, Italy, owner of a fantastic collection of films on athletic competitions, tells me that such a phenomenon was clearly discernible during the 1980 Olympic final in Moscow. But it was only in 1998 that the IAAF added a new clause to rule 172/6, reading as follows: "A competitor fails if ..... during the vault he replaces deliberately with his hands or fingers a bar which is about to fall off the supports". The man most instrumental for causing such a change was Jeff Hartwig, the first American to conquer 6 metres (6.00, then 6.01 in 1998, and 6.02 in '99), who had apparently perfected his "Volzing technique" to an admirable degree. At the 1999 World Indoor Championships in Maebashi, Japan, the new rule was in force and Hartwig conformed to it and finished second with 5.95. Ironically enough, victory went to Jean Galfione of France who went over 6.00, a personal best, steadying the bar with his left hand. A protest from the U.S. delegation was denied by the Jury of Appeal.

Sergey Bubka was forced to assume a low profile in 1989-90, mostly on account of injuries. But he was back in harness by 1991. He not only regained the top but managed to maintain it for ... seven more seasons (1991-97). After which he could claim the longest reign as no. 1 in "Track & Field News" World Ranking - 13 "victories" (1983-88 and 1991-97). In undercover competition his top efforts were in 1993: 6.14 at Liévin on 13 February and 6.15 in his backyard at Donyetsk on 21 February. On the latter occasion he took seven jumps in all, clearing 5.70 first time, 5.90 and 6.15 third time. Outdoors his top effort was at Sestriere, a mountain resort in North-Western Italy (altitude 2,050 m.) on 31 July 1994. Once again his work was clear-cut: he needed two attempts at 5.70 then went over 5.90 and 6.14 always on his first attempt, using a perfect tailwind. By doing so he became the first athlete to win a shiny red Ferrari, the prize awarded to athletes who would break a global mark in that meet. During the Nineties, the dismantling of the USSR led Bubka, by then a full-time professional, to expatriate. He settled down in Berlin for a while, then took residence in Monaco with his wife Lilyana and sons Vitaliy and Sergey Jr. Now and then he would visit his native Ukraine, mostly in connection with the Donyetsk indoor meet, of which he soon became the central figure. As a competitor, "Czar Sergey" continued to reign supreme. In the Olympic Games he was not so lucky: after a hard won victory at Seoul in 1988, he went unplaced (no height) at Barcelona in 1992. Then Achilles tendon trouble kept him away from the Atlanta final in 1996.

While the "czar" was on the throne his main rivals continued to improve, slowly but steadily. However, no one scaled "Bubka heights".

As at the end of 1999 no more than 9 men had conquered the once magic 6-metre barrier. The best of them was Maksim Tarasov of Russia 'born on 2 December 1970 at Yaroslavl; 1.94 m./80 kg.) Outstanding since his schoolboy days (5.60 at 18, 5.80 at 19) he inevitably played second fiddle to the "czar" for a long while, yet took advantage of Bubka's unlucky day at Barcelona to win an Olympic gold medal (1992). At the World Championship this blond, very consistent vaulter collected medals galore: bronze in 1991 and '93, silver in 1995 and '97, and finally struck gold at Sevilla in 1999 with 6.02, the best mark on record in major championship competition. The best exponent of the French tradition is now Jean Galfione, who won the Olympic title at Atlanta in 1996. In 1999 he scaled 6 metres even in an indoor meet.

1981
1999

> ### "It looked as if the clock was running faster than usual"
>
> Even a superstar like Sergey Bubka has often experienced the difference between "cold" meets in a friendly atmosphere, ideal for record attempts, and "hot" competition in major championship meets governed by stricter rules. In the latter type of meet his best ever is 6.01 (1997 World Championships).
> His failure at the Barcelona Olympics in 1992 was thus recounted in "Track & Field News": " Having been spoiled on the international circuit by accommodating judges, (at Barcelona) Bubka was constantly rushed for time as the strictly enforced 2-minute limit (for every try) was not long enough for him to catch a usable runup without a headwind. On his first attempt at 5.70 he was forced to go with only two seconds remaining on the clock. His second attempt, also a failure, was similar. He took his third attempt at 5.75, so as to have more time to prepare, but he balked on his run and when he went again he was not in a position to make a complete vault as the pole he had selected was too soft for the speed he generated, now with a slight tailwind. After that final failure he admitted that nerves were a problem. To me it looked like the clock was running faster than usual, he said".

LONG JUMP
Lewis is the greatest, but Powell conquers Fort Beamon

1981 - WCup, Rome (4 Sep): 1.Lewis (USA) 8.15, 2.Honey (Oce/Aus) 8.11, 3.Abbyasov (USSR) 7.95.
1982 - EC, Athens (9 Sep): 1.Dombrowski (EG) 8.41 (wind +2.9), 2.Corgos (Spa) 8.19, 3.Leitner (CSR) 8.08.
1983 - WC, Helsinki (10 Aug): 1.Lewis 8.55, 2.Grimes (USA) 8.29, 3.Conley (USA) 8.12.
1984 - OG, Los Angeles (6 Aug): 1.Lewis 8.54, 2.Honey 8.24, 3.Evangelisti (Ita) 8.24.
1985 - WCup, Canberra (5 Oct): 1.Conley 8.20, 2.Emmiyan (USSR) 8.09, 3.Szalma (Hun) 8.09.
1986 - EC, Stuttgart (29 Aug): 1.Emmiyan 8.41, 2.Layevskiy (USSR) 8.01, 3.Evangelisti 7.92.
1987 - WC, Rome (5 Sep): 1.Lewis 8.67, 2.Emmiyan 8.53, 3.Myricks (USA) 8.33.
1988 - WC, Seoul (26 Sep): 1.Lewis 8.72, 2.Powell (USA) 8.49, 3.Myricks 8.27.
1989 - WCup, Barcelona (8 Sep): 1.Myricks 8.29, 2.Alli (Afr/Nig) 8.00, 3.Faulkner (GB) 7.84.
1990 - EC, Split (30 Aug): 1.Haaf (WG) 8.25, 2.A.Hernández (Spa) 8.15, 3.Maas (Hol) 8.00. Bilac (Yug), 3rd with 8.09, was disqualified for doping abuse.
1991 - WC, Tokyo (30 Aug): 1. Powell 8.95 (+0.3) WR, 2. Lewis 8.91w (+2.9), 3. Myricks 8.42.
1992 - OG, Barcelona (6 Aug): 1. Lewis 8.67, 2. Powell 8.64, 3. J.Greene (USA) 8.34; WCup, Habana (25 Sep): 1. Pedroso (Cub) 7.97, 2. McKee (USA) 7.89, 3. Chen Zunrong (Asi/Chi) 7.84.
1993 - WC, Stuttgart (20 Aug): 1. Powell 8.59, 2. Tarasenko (Rus) 8.16, 3. Kirilenko (Ukr) 8.15.
1994 - EC, Helsinki (10 Aug): 1. Mladenov (Bul) 8.09, 2. Gombala (Cze) 8.04, 3. Koukodimos (Gre) 8.01; WCup, London (9 Sep): 1. Salle (GB) 8.10, 2. D. de Souza (Ame/Bra) 7.96, 3. Bentley (USA) 7.93.
1995 - WC, Göteborg (12 Aug): 1. Pedroso 8.70, 2. Beckford (Jam) 8.30, 3. Powell 8.29.
1996 - OG, Atlanta (29 Jul): 1. Lewis 8.50, 2. Beckford 8.29, 3. J.Greene 8.24.
1997 - WC, Athens (5 Aug): 1. Pedroso 8.42, 2. Walder (USA) 8.38, 3. Sosunov (Rus) 8.18.
1998 - EC, Budapest (19 Aug): 1. Sosunov 8.28, 2. Tarus (Rum) 8.21, 3. Dachev (Bul) 8.06; WCup, Johannesburg (11 Sep): 1. Pedroso 8.37, 2. Taurima (Oce/Aus) 8.32, 3. Moursal (Afr/Egy) 8.26.
1999 - WC, Sevilla (28 Aug): 1. Pedroso 8.56, Lamela (Spa) 8.40, 3. Cankar (Slo) 8.36.

Relativity of the absolute

As a superlative performer in three events - 100, 200 m. and long jump - over a period of ten years, Carl Lewis has excellent credentials to be considered the greatest athlete of our time, if not of all time. Yet he never owned a world record for any of these events until his non-winning 9.92 for the century in the 1988 Olympic final became a "de facto" world record, following the disqualification of Ben Johnson, winner of that race in 9.79. Prior to that Lewis had made the IAAF record book only as a member of American 4x100 m. relay teams. This incredible "fast" could largely be explained by the fact that in his heyday Lewis was up against "altitude-inflated" records such as Calvin Smith's 9.93, Pietro Mennea's 19.72 and Bob Beamon's 8.90. It stands to Lewis' honour that he never tried to have a meet organized for his benefit at Mexico City or some other high-altitude site. As a true champion, he always vied for honours, national and international, rather than records. For all his greatness, Bob Beamon had only one jump over 8.50 in the whole of his life. Lewis had 30 (counting legitimate marks only). This clearly answers the question as to the greatest long jumper of our time. After all, even a world record commonly regarded as "the absolute" may sometimes reflect only a relative value.

From 1981 onwards Carl Lewis dominated the long jump scene as no one else had ever done before. His early years in the sport were recounted in connection with the sprints. His deeds as a long jumper have been, if possible, even more impressive. At sixteen he jumped 7.26 while at Willingboro High School in New Jersey. Only two years later, in 1979, he was good enough to place third at the Pan-American Games in San Juan, Puerto Rico, with a leap of 8.13, curiously the same distance achieved by Jesse Owens in his "Day of Days" at Ann Arbor in 1935. Lewis suffered his last defeat on 27 February 1981 at the US Indoor Championships in New York, when Larry Myricks beat him, 8.13 to 8.08. Since then he has gone unscathed through 64 long jump competitions, spaced over ten seasons. Lewis has often said that the long jump remains his first love. Most of his wins have been by wide margins, yet he had a close call now and then, e.g. at the 1988 US Olympic

Trials in Indianapolis, when his arch rival Larry Myricks took the lead in round 3 with his best-ever jump, 8.74. Only two minutes later, Lewis answered with 8.76 and thus settled the issue. In spite of his overwhelming superiority over such a long period of time, Lewis still had to succeed in his quest for a new world record.

Beamon's famous 8.90 continued to be an elusive target. Carl did 8.79 on two occasions: on 19 June 1983 at Indianapolis and on 27 January 1984 indoors at New York - the latter was still the "undercover" record at the end of 1999. In an outdoor meet at Indianapolis on 24 July 1982 Lewis had a hairline foul which in the opinion of expert observers was definitely worth "9 metres-plus". Larry Myricks was Lewis' chief rival for more then ten years. Between 1976 and 1994 he put together a mammoth series of classy marks: 269 over 8 metres! He still tops Lewis in quantity, but not in quality.

By comparison, however, Myricks' competitive record at the international level is relatively "thin".

He won a bronze at the 1987 World Championships and another bronze at the 1988 Olympics. Besides being a regular loser vis-à-vis Lewis, he lost to lesser lights on several important occasions. Unfortunately, Myricks' monumental career record was tarnished when the IAAF announced that he was found "positive" to a forbidden stimulant on three different occasions during the 1990 indoor season. He was originally disqualified for life but the ban was later shortened to 1 year. The outstanding figures of the decade on the European scene were Lutz Dombrowski of East Germany and Robert Emmiyan of USSR. After his victory at the 1980 Olympics, the German continued to be a factor for several years, although hampered by injuries from time to time. He won the 1982 European title but had to stay away from the 1984 Olympics in Los Angeles, his country being in the boycotters' camp. Emmiyan (born at Leninakan, Armenia, on 16 February 1965; 1.78 m./69) is a fine adept of the "hang" style. A precocious talent, he mastered 8 metres at the tender age of eighteen. Three years later, during the Goodwill Games in Moscow, he captured the European record with a leap of 8.61, beating Larry Myricks (8.41). Born and brought up in a mountainous area, he had his longest jump on 22 May 1987 at Tsakhkadzor (altitude, 1980 m.), when he offered a replica of the Beamon classic with a stupendous 8.86, aided by a legal wind of 1.85 m/s. He continued with 8.65 and 8.53, then decided to call it a day. His 8.86 was the closest approach to Bob Beamon's legendary world record. As irony would have it, a few days later Emmiyan went down to Turin for the Italy vs USSR match and lost to Giovanni Evangelisti, 8.09 to 8.10. Later in the year, the Armenian did himself justice by finishing second to Carl Lewis at the World Championships in Rome. In later years injuries made things more difficult for him. But he was lucky in one way: he happened to be in Moscow for medical treatment the day a terrific earthquake hit Armenia in December 1988. The loss of his father and extensive damage to his hometown, Leninakan, obviously affected him in more than one way. Several months later he was back in stride, but seemed to lack his former consistency. Mark-wise, his high altitude/sea level differential is "merely" 25 cms. (8.86 - 8.61), as opposed to 57 cm. for Bob Beamon (8.90 - 8.33).

1981
1999

Larry Myricks (USA), winner of the long jump at the 1979 World Cup in Montreal.

325

At the end of the greatest long jump battle in history, Mike Powell (USA) consoles teammate Carl Lewis after beating him and the world record in Tokyo (1991), 8.95 to 8.91w.

Meanwhile, another excellent prospect had emerged from the rich reservoir of the U.S. long jump fraternity - Mike Powell (born on 10 November 1963 at Philadelphia; 1.88 m./77 kg.). Basket was for some time his first love but later on he turned his attention to athletics, and the long jump in particular. As destiny would have it, the joyous and talented Mike found himself chasing Carl Lewis instead of Michael Jordan, his hero ... He first conquered 8 metres in 1983 (8.06). The following year he was sixth at the U.S. Olympic Trials. During the Los Angeles Games he used to drive a bus taking the Swedish team to the Coliseum. But he continued to make progress, first under the tutelage of John Smith, then under coach Randy Huntington. By 1988 he was ready to challenge everybody but Lewis. In the Seoul Olympics he managed to shunt Larry Myricks to third - 8.49 to 8.27 - but finished well behind Lewis (8.72), who captured his second Olympic gold in the event, an unprecedented exploit. Powell reached the top, statistically at least, in 1990, when his 8.66 was the best mark of the season. But Lewis continued to be untouchable in head-to-head confrontations. By then "King Carl" was confining his long jumping to a couple of meets per season. In 1991 he and Powell met twice and both tussles were real thrillers. At the national championships, serving as Trials for the World title meet in

---

A sad story

Giovanni Evangelisti has been one of Europe's best long jumpers for many years, winning medals in important competitions such as the Olympics (bronze in 1984), the World Indoor Championships (bronze in '87), the European Championships (bronze in '86) and the European Indoor Championships (bronze in 1982 and '88, silver in '87). On another occasion, the 1987 World Championships held at Rome's Stadio Olimpico, he received a bronze medal which did not belong to him. His sixth and last jump was lengthened by at least half a metre and made 8.38 by ill-advised judges, probably affected by ill-conceived patriotism. The fake 8.38 that was flashed on the electronic scoreboard raised Evangelisti from fourth (at 8.19) to third, ahead of Larry Myricks of USA (8.33). But many spectators seated on Tribuna Tevere, alongside the long jump runway, immediately sensed the "error".

The rumour that something was wrong persisted for several days after the meet, until an Italian TV channel came up with a computer analysis of videotapes of the event which left little or no doubt about the misconduct of Italian judges. At first the IAAF confirmed the "official" results, even though Evangelisti himself publicly announced that he wanted to get rid of a medal that was not his. In the meantime the Italian Olympic Committee had started an investigation, which eventually clarified the misbehaviour of the judges, who were consequently ousted from federation ranks. The report also hinted to "negligence" on the part of higher officials in dealing with the case.

This caused the IAAF to finally revise its stand on the matter: Evangelisti's fake mark was removed from official results, and the bronze medal was awarded to Larry Myricks. This sad story inevitably damaged the image of Italian athletics.

True, the history of the sport shows quite a few cases of marks which were "inflated" by incompetent or ill-advised officials (some of these cases are related in this book), yet there is no doubt that the "Evangelisti affair" is entitled to a choice place in track's "Museum of Errors".

Ivan Pedroso (Cuba), a threetime winner of the long jump at the world championships (1995, '97 and '99).

Tokyo, Lewis won by the narrowest of margins, 8.64 to 8.63. The wind readings in such jumps (+1.7 and +0.6 respectively) gave Lewis a certain advantage. After that close call, Lewis could claim 15 straight wins over Powell in an 8-year span (1983-91) but the latter felt more confident than ever... Then came the World Championships in Tokyo. In the qualifyng round (29 August) Powell advanced with 8.19 on first try. Lewis needed two: after a "monster" foul of about 8.80, he qualified with 8.56.

The final the following day offered the most exciting and dramatic competition in the long history of the event. Powell jumped ahead of Lewis and opened with a cautious 7.85. Lewis, looking sharper than ever, answered with 8.68. In round 2 Powell improved to 8.54 and Lewis fouled. In round 3 Powell did 8.29 and Lewis replied with a superb 8.83, his longest jump ever but windy (+2.3). Powell began to look dangerous in the next round with a foul of about 8.76. Then Lewis landed just beyond Bob Beamon's world record flag, but his 8.91 was spoiled by an aiding wind (+2.9). In round 5 Powell had a dream jump: he made a near-perfect take-off and had a fantastic landing, getting maximum extension. A wondrous figure - 8.95 - was flashed on the board. The wind was a mere +0.3 and Fort Beamon thus fell after resisting all attacks for 23 years. Lewis reacted as only a great champion could be expected to do under such circumstances. He closed with his best legal jumps ever, 8.87 (-0.2) and 8.84 (+1.7), but that was not enough for the day. With his fantastic series (four jumps in the range 8.83/8.91) he probably qualified as the Greatest Loser in athletic history. Powell closed with a foul. When it was all over he really let himself go, running crazily across the infield and startling a seemingly cold Japanese judge with a bearhug. He had killed two birds with a stone, breaking the most famous of athletic records and beating arch rival Lewis for the first time! From then on all his clashes with Carl were touch-and-go affairs. Between 1992 and '96 they met six more times and Powell edged Lewis 4 to 2. But the old lion had the upper hand on the occasions that counted most, the Olympics of 1992 and '96. In the former, at Barcelona, Lewis beat Powell by 3 cms - 8.67 to 8.64. At Atlanta four years later, Lewis needed only one good jump (8.50) to clinch his fourth Olympic gold in the event. He thus equalled Al Oerter's record for victories in the same event. The American discus thrower had turned the trick between 1956 and '68. Powell entered the Atlanta competition with a frail groin muscle and could do only 8.17 for fifth place. On his last try, a heart-rending foul, he aggravated his condition dramatically. At the end of their saga, Lewis retained a big lead

(17 to 5) in head-to-head confrontations. A P.S. about Powell's world record jump at Tokyo: scientific analysis revealed that he had actually jumped 8.98 as the toe-to-plasticine distance was measured at 3 cms. Another great jumper of the Nineties was Ivan Pedroso (born on 17 December 1972 at Ciudad Habana; 1.72 m./66 kg.), a Cuban who in the latter part of the decade wrested the lead form U.S. long jumpers. He emerged at the 1990 World Junior Championships in Plovdiv, Bulgaria, finishing fourth with 7.81 at the unripe age of 17 years 8 months. Two years later he joined the élite of the event with 8.53 (and a wind-aided 8.79) and placed fourth in the Barcelona Olympics, well behind a U.S. trio. He won his first major title at the 1993 World Indoor Championships. Outdoors he rose to no. 1 at the 1995 World Championships in Göteborg with an excellent 8.70. At the end of 1999 he could claim 3 world titles outdoors (1995, '97 and '99) and 4 indoors (1993, '95, '97 and '99), a truly imposing tally. This man of medium build is endowed with a very fine technique. Hamstring surgery spoiled his 1996 season and he could do no better than 12th at the Atlanta Olympics. His personal best is 8.71 (1995). In a meet at Sestriere (altitude 2050 m.) on 29 July 1995 he was credited with a great 8.96, one centimetre over Mike Powell's world record. At first the wind reading was given as legal (+1.2), but there were allegations of interference by an Italian coach standing right in front of the anemometre, especially, if not exclusively, during Pedroso's jumps.

When the competition was over it emerged that only 4 out of a total of 60 jumps had been wind-legal, and three of those four were by Pedroso, who had the following sries: f - 8.89 (+2.4) - f - 7.80 (+1.0) - 8.30 (+1.0) - 8.96 (+1.2). FIDAL, the Italian Athletics Federation, badly burnt by the Evangelisti long jump scandal of 1987 (as related in an aside earlier in this book), decided that it would not submit Pedroso's 8.96 to the IAAF for ratification, being convinced that without the interference of the man blocking the anemometre the wind reading would have been well over the allowable limit (2 m/s), as it was in the over-whelming majority of the other jumps. Notwithstanding these circumstances, it is generally felt that Pedroso remains capable of 9-metre jumps - especially with the aid of altitude.

In Europe there has been no worthy successor for Armenian Robert Emmiyan. The best prospect seems to be Yago Lamela of Spain, who did 8.56 in 1999, both indoors and out, and was second to Pedroso in the World Championships at Sevilla. An excellent comethrough performer, as often as not he reaches his best form in the last round of the competition.

TRIPLE JUMP
Edwards breaks barriers for all tastes: 18 metres and 60 feet.

1981 - WCup, Rome (5 Sep): 1.J.C.de Oliveira (Ame/Bra) 17.37, 2.Zou Zhenxian (Asi/Chn) 17.34, 3.Banks (USA) 17.04.
1982 - EC, Athens (10 Sep): 1.Connor (GB) 17.29, 2.Grishchenkov (USSR) 17.15, 3.Bakosi (Hun) 17.04.
1983 - WC, Helsinki (8 Aug): 1.Hoffmann (Pol) 17.42, 2.Banks 17.18, 3.Agbebaku (Nig) 17.18.
1984 - OG, Los Angeles (4 Aug): 1.Joyner (USA) 17.26 (+2.1), 2.Conley (USA) 17.18, 3.Connor 16.87.
1985 - WCup, Canberra (4 Oct): 1.Banks 17.58, 2.Protsenko (USSR) 17.47, 3.Markov (Bul) 17.13.
1986 - EC, Stuttgart (30 Aug): 1.Markov 17.66, 2.Bruziks (USSR) 17.33, 3.Protsenko 17.28.
1987 - WC, Rome (31 Aug): 1.Markov 17.92, 2.Conley 17.67, 3.Sakirkin (USSR) 17.43.
1988 - OG, Seoul (24 Sep): 1.Markov 17.61, 2.Lapshin (USSR) 17.52, 3.Kovalyenko (USSR) 17.42.
1989 - WCup, Barcelona (9 Sep): 1.Conley 17.49, 2.Inozyemtsev (USSR) 17.31, 3.J.Edwards (GB) 17.28.
1990 - EC, Split (31 Aug): 1.Voloshin (USSR) 17.74, 2.Markov 17.43, 3.Lapshin 17.34.
1991 - WC, Tokyo (26 Aug): 1. Harrison (USA) 17.78, 2. Voloshin 17.75, 3. Conley 17.62.
1992 - OG, Barcelona (3 Aug): 1. Conley 18.17w (+2.1), 2. Simpkins (USA) 17.60, 3. Rutherford (Bah) 17.36; WCup, Habana (28 Sep): 1. Edwards 17.34, 2. Rutherford (Ame/Bah) 17.06, 3. Rabenala (Afr/Mad) 17.03.
1993 - WC, Stuttgart (16 Aug): 1. Conley 17.86, 2. Voloshin (Rus) 17.65, 3. Edwards 17.44.
1994 - EC, Helsinki (13 Aug): 1. Kapustin (Rus) 17.62, 2. Hélan (Fra) 17.55, 3. Bruziks (Lat) 17.20; WCup, London (10 Sep): 1. Quesada (Ame/Cub) 17.61, 2. Golley (GB) 17.06, 3. Sakirkin (Asi/Kaz) 16.81.
1995 - WC, Göteborg (7 Aug): 1. Edwards 18.29 (+1.3) WR, 2. Wellman (Ber) 17.62w, 3. Romain (Dmn) 17.59w.
1996 - OG, Atlanta (27 Jul): 1. Harrison 18.09, 2. Edwards 17.88, 3. Quesada 17.44.
1997 - WC, Athens (8 Aug): 1. Quesada 17.85, 2. Edwards 17.69, 3. Urrutia (Cub) 17.64.

1998 - EC, Budapest (23 Aug): 1. Edwards 17.99, 2. Kapustin 17.45, 3. Dimitrov (Bul) 17.26w; WCup, Johannesburg (12 Sep): 1. Friedek (Ger) 17.42, 2. Kapustin (Eur/Rus) 17.32, 3. Quesada (Ame/Cub) 17.25.
1999 - WC, Sevilla (25 Aug): 1. Friedek 17.59, 2. Dimitrov 17.49, 3. Edwards 17.48.

A few weeks after his third victory in the World Cup (1981) João Carlos de Oliveira was involved in a traffic accident and suffered heavy fractures, finally necessitating the amputation of his right leg. A sad end to a great career. Few triple jumpers, if any, have ever had João's natural gifts. He was a 10.1 sprinter and an 8.36 long jumper. His successor as world record holder was Willie Banks of USA (born at Travis Air Force Base, California, on 11 March 1956; 1.90 m/77 kg.). He grew up as an athlete alternating long jump and triple jump in High School and then at UCLA, once bringing his college to a widely acclaimed victory in a dual meet with crosstown rival USC. In 1981 he topped the World List in the triple jump with 17.56 and long jumped 8.11. Then he alternated ups and downs, like placing second in the triple jump at the 1983 World Championships and only sixth at the 1984 Olympics. He finally came into his own on 16 June 1985, when he won a hot triple jump battle at the US Championships with a record-shattering 17.97, aided by a legal wind of 1.47 m/s. He won from Mike Conley (17.71), Charles Simpkins (17.52) and 1984 Olympic champion Al Joyner (17.46). Banks became popular, especially in Europe, for his ability in captivating crowds, encouraging them to clap him before and during his jumps to an accelerating tempo. At the 1988 US Olympic Trials, still on Indianapolis' "magic carpet", he jumped 18.20, history's longest effort, no matter if nullified by a 5.2 m/s wind. Charles Simpkins was second at 17.93, also wind-assisted. But later in the year, at the Seoul Olympics, Banks had to be content with sixth, same as in Los Angeles four years earlier. On a strictly competitive basis the most successful triple jumper of the post-Saneyev era was long-haired Khristo Markov of Bulgaria (born at Dimitrovgrad on 27 January 1965; 1.84 m./78 kg.). Between 1986 and '88 he scored a perfect triple, annexing European, World and Olympic titles. His lifetime best and European record, 17.92, was made on one of these occasions, on 31 August 1987 in Rome. Markov excelled also as a long jumper: 8.23 indoors in 1985.

By then another American had appeared on the scene, Mike Conley (born in Chicago on 5 October 1962; 1.85 m./78 kg), a man who was to develop into the best long jump/triple jump artist ever seen.

At 19 he had personal bests of 7.46 and 15.80, but a year later he made astounding progress, with 8.19 and 17.01. In 1983 he qualified for the inaugural World Championships in both events. At Helsinki he was fourth in the triple jump (17.13) and two days later he won a bronze medal in the long jump (8.12) behind his countrymen Carl Lewis and Jason Grimes. Beginning with 1984, however, he found that the triple jump was his best hunting ground. At the U.S. Olympic Trials he was a dismal seventh in the long jump but won the triple jump with 17.50, a new personal best. In the latter event he had an excellent season and was no. 1 in "Track & Field News" World Ranking, alas with a flaw - in the Olympic final at Los Angeles he lost to his teammate Al Joyner, 17.18 (-0.4) to 17.26w (+2.1). Conley had gone farther in the qualifiying round with 17.36 (+0.8), but on his first jump of the final he sprained an ankle. Usually a comethrough performer, he braved pain to the extent of producing a jump of about 17.65 on his final effort, a foul. He did not know, then, that he would take sweet revenge eight years later ... In the meantime, he had another bitter experience at the 1988 Olympic Trials, when he failed to qualify - fourth in the triple jump and fifth in the long jump. He had better luck in the World Championships: second in 1987 and third in 1991. He had his brightest day at the 1992 Olympics in Barcelona when he reached 17.63 in round 2 and improved to a great 18.17 on his favored try, the last. He did win the crown he had been dreaming of for years, but a baffling wind (+2.1)

1981
1999

Jonathan Edwards (Great Britain) on his greatest day, after setting a new world triple jump record (18.29) at Göteborg in 1995.

nullified his performance for record purposes. He was easily no. 1 in his profession though, a status he confirmed a year later when he won at the World Championships in Stuttgart (17.86). His ability in often reaching his best distance on his last trial was simply amazing - throughout his career he had ten legal efforts in the range 17.87/17.67 and <u>seven</u> of these were achieved in the sixth round!

The 18-metre barrier continued to be an elusive target for triple jumpers. The man who finally turned the trick was Jonathan Edwards (born in London on 10 May 1966; 1.81 m./70 kg). For all its glory in the annals of the sport, Britain had a rather meager tradition here. Her first Olympic medal was a bronze by Keith Connor in the 1984 Olympics. A vicar's son and himself a committed Christian, prior to 1993 Edwards would not compete on Sunday, which caused him to bypass the 1991 World Championships, where the qualifying round was scheduled for that very day. He later changed his mind as he thought he should at any time "honour God for the gift of athletic ability" he had given him. Edwards, who had first bettered 17 metres in 1989, reaped the first major reward for his hard and meticulous training by placing third at the 1993 World Championships with 17.44, a personal best. He had his greatest season in 1995. In June/July he bettered 18 metres four times, always with the aid of a wind over the limit: 18.43 (+2.4) and 18.39 (+3.7) in the European Cup at Villeneuve-d'Ascq on 25 June; 18.03 (+2.9) at Gateshead on 2 July; and 18.08 (+2.5) at Sheffield on 23 July. Shortly before the last meet, however, he managed to succeed Willie Banks as world record holder with a legal 17.98 (+1.8) at Salamanca on 18 July. At the World Championships in Göteborg he had his Day of Days (7 August), breaking barriers for everybody's taste: 18 metres, for the major part of the world, and 60 feet (18.28), for nostalgic lovers of the English measuring system. His series was as follows: 18.16 (+1.3), 18.29 (+1.3), p, p, 17.49, p. He thus bettered Banks' ten-year-old world record twice and won the world title by an awesome margin: 67 cms. Later in the same month (London, 27 August) he had another mark of 18.00 (+1.3). The breakdown of his best performances was as follows:

After the Göteborg final he was quoted as saying: "My edge at the moment is that I have very good foot speed on the ground. My last phase (jump) is very long because of the speed I maintain".

He surely maximized his potential to a great extent. His other personal bests (10.48 in the 100 m. and 7.41 in the long jump) look rather deceptive in that respect. Edwards and his "choirboy smile" graced European crowds for several more years although he never duplicated his magic moments of 1995, save perhaps for a mark of 18.01 at Oslo in 1998. At the 1996 Olympics in Atlanta he had to bow to Kerry "Kenny" Harrison (born at Milwaukee on 13 February 1965; 1.78 m./77 kg.). This rather unpredictable American had first reached the top in 1990 with 17.93, then very close to Banks' U.S. and world record. The following year he won at the World Championships in Tokyo with 17.78. He re-emerged in the summer of 1996 after a layoff of 15 months due to "numerous injuries". His comeback at the U.S. Olympic Trials was sensational. In his one and only try he flew to 18.01, aided by a generous wind (+3.7) - good enough for an easy victory over veteran Mike Conley (17.57). In the Olympics he was again scarce in quantity but superb in quality. He had only two valid jumps: 17.99 and 18.09, both legal and superior to Banks' U.S. record. Jonathan Edwards had to be content with 17.88 and second place. Harrison was also a good long jumper: 8.17 indoors, way back in 1986. The last two world champions of the Nineties were Yoel Quesada of Cuba in 1997 and Charles-Michael Friedek of Germany in 1999. The former was a boy prodigy in his younger days, with 17.13 at 18 and 17.23 at 19. His best so far is 17.85, the mark that won a world title for him at Athens in 1997.

THROWS - Shot Put: Big deeds galore (amid a cat-and-mouse game)

1981 - WCup, Rome (4 Sep): 1.Beyer (EG) 21.40, 2.Mironov (USSR) 20.34, 3.Laut (USA) 19.90.
1982 - EC, Athens (9 Sep): 1.Beyer 21.50,

	Hop	Step	Jump	
Villeneuve d'Ascq, 25 June '95	6.50w	5.60w	6.33w	= 18.43w
Göteborg, 7 August '95	6.05	5.22	7.02	= 18.29

2.Bojars (USSR) 20.81, 3.Machura (CSR) 20.59.
1983 - WC, Helsinki (7 Aug): 1.Sarul (Pol) 21.39, 2.Timmermann (EG) 21.16, 3.Machura 20.98.
1984 - OG, Los Angeles (11 Aug): 1.Andrei (Ita) 21.26, 2.Carter (USA) 21.09, 3.Laut 20.97.
1985 - WCup, Canberra (5 Oct): 1.Timmermann 22.00, 2.Smirnov (USSR) 21.72, 3.Andrei 21.14.
1986 - EC, Stuttgart (28 Aug): 1.Günthör (Swi) 22.22, 2.Timmermann 21.84, 3.Beyer 20.74.
1987 - WC, Rome (29 Aug): 1.Günthör 22.23, 2.Andrei 21.88, 3.Brenner (USA) 21.75.
1988 - OG, Seoul (23 Sep): 1.Timmermann 22.47, 2.Barnes (USA) 22.39, 3.Günthör 21.99.
1989 - WCup, Barcelona (8 Sep): 1.Timmermann 21.68, 2.Günthör 21.40, 3.Barnes 21.10.
1990 - EC, Split (29 Aug): 1.Timmermann 21.32, 2.Buder (EG) 21.01, 3.Andersen (Nor) 20.71. Likho (USSR), 3rd with 20.81, was disqualified for doping abuse.
1991 - WC, Tokyo (31 Aug): 1. Günthör 21.67, 2. Nilsen (Nor) 20.75, 3. Klimyenko (USSR) 20.34. Andersen (Nor), 2nd with 20.81, was disqualified for doping abuse.
1992 - OG, Barcelona (31 Jul): 1. Stulce (USA) 21.70, 2. Doehring (USA) 20.96, 3. Likho (EUN) 20.94; WCup, Habana (25 Sep): 1. Stulce 21.34, 2. Nikolayev (EUN/Rus) 20.14, 3. Günthör (Eur/Swi) 19.75.
1993 - WC, Stuttgart (21 Aug): 1. Günthör 21.97, 2. Barnes (USA) 21.80, 3. Bagach (Ukr) 20.40. Stulce, 3rd with 20.94, was disqualified for doping abuse.
1994 - EC, Helsinki (13 Aug): 1. Klimyenko (Ukr) 20.78, 2. Bagach 20.34, 3. Virastyuk (Eur/Ukr) 19.59; WCup, London (9 Sep): 1. C.J.Hunter (USA) 19.92, 2. Klimyenko (Eur/Ukr) 19.16, 3. Ireland (Oce/NZ) 18.93.
1995 - WC, Göteborg (9 Aug): 1. Godina (USA) 21.47, 2. Halvari (Fin) 20.93, 3. Barnes 20.41.
1996 - OG, Atlanta (26 Jul): 1. Barnes 21.62, 2. Godina 20.79, 3. Bagach 20.75.
1997 - WC, Athens (2 Aug): 1 Godina 21.44, 2. Buder (Ger) 21.24, 3. Hunter 20.33. Bagach, 1st with 21.47, was disqualifed fo doping abuse.
1998 - EC, Budapest (18 Aug): 1. Bagach 21.17, 2. Buder 20.98, 3. Byelonog (Ukr) 20.92; WCup, Johannesburg (11 Sep): 1. Godina 21.48, 2. Bagach 20.45, 3. Buder 20.42.
1999 - WC, Sevilla (21 Aug): 1. Hunter 21.79, 2. Buder 21.42, 3. Bagach 21.26.
The rotation or discus style, launched in the Seventies by Barishnikov and Oldfield, failed to sweep the board in the following decade. It caught on in the States, but not in Europe. In fact, three of the four men who bettered the world record between 1981 and 1990 were adepts of the conventional (O'Brien) style. Udo Beyer and Ulf Timmermann of East Germany took turns in breaking the global mark. The former reached 22.22 at Los Angeles on 25 June 1983 but was succeeded by his younger countryman, who got one off to 22.62 at Berlin on 22 September 1985. The massive Beyer successfully fought back on 20 August 1986, still in Berlin, where he reached a lifetime best of 22.64. An Italian interference followed in 1987, when Alessandro Andrei produced an incredible series at Viareggio on 12 August, averaging 22.62 on six valid throws, the longest one being 22.91. Three years earlier, at Los Angeles, Andrei had won the Olympic title (in the absence of East Germans and Russians), so he was definitely a top-notch performer. Even so, that Viareggio throw was (and still is) 74 cm. beyond his second best ever. This gave rise to suspicions about the regularity of circle and landing area on that particular occasion. The Italian Athletic Federation was adamant in rejecting such rumours, and the mark was ratified by the IAAF. The following month Andrei was second at the World Championships in Rome with 21.88, his best ever in hot competition, but still 1.03 m. shy of his fresh world record. A "loss" of that magnitude in passing from a cold to a hot competition was not unique after all. In 1986 Udo Beyer did 20.74 at the European Championships only eight days after his record 22.64 at Berlin, thus "losing" 1.90 m. In fact, the main item of discussion in and around throwing circles during the Eighties was the so-called "drug war". It was common knowledge that many athletes stopped taking anabolic steroids a few weeks before a major event, knowing that the tests conducted on such occasions had only a limited retrospective action. Even so, "positive" cases emerged now and then, probably due to errors on the part of athletes either in "timing" the perverse hide-and-seek game or in "predicting" how their body would react. Be as it may, the list of leading shot putters who were suspended for doping abuse is a rather impressive one, including such men as Yevgeniy Mironov of USSR, an Olympic silver medallist in 1976, Remigius Machura of Czechoslovakia and Augie Wolf of USA (the last-named for refusing a test). More recently, along with intensified and more sophisticated doping tests, there have been such "victims" as Vyacheslav Likho of USSR and, last but by no means least, Randy Barnes of USA. On the European front, the two most reliable performers of the late Eighties were Ulf Timmermann of East Germany and Werner Günthör of Switzerland. The former (born at Berlin on 1 November 1962; 1.94 m./120 kg.) has the

best competitive record among active throwers. Mark-wise, he had his field day on 22 May 1988 at Khania on the island of Crete, when he succeeded Andrei as world record holder with 23.06. His series also included three 22-metre-plus efforts and two fouls. Udo Beyer was second with 21.58. Günthör (born at Utwil on 11 July1961; 2.00 m./126 Kg.), physically one of the most impressive throwers ever seen in a shot put circle, failed to produce record performances but was very reliable in meets that really counted. He won European titles indoors and out and was the 1987 world champion.

A problem in his back brought him to a halt in 1990. Latest in the line of record breakers is Randy Barnes (born at Charleston, West Virginia, on 16 June 1966; 1.94 m./132 kg.), an exponent of the rotation style. Brought up as an athlete at Texas A & M (Randy Matson's alma mater), he improved from 18.56 in 1985 to 21.88 in '86. At the Seoul Olympics he challenged world record holder Ulf Timmermann. The latter was his usual consistent self and led at the end of round 5 with 22.29, followed by Günthör (21.99) and Barnes (21.31). On his sixth and last trial the American "exploded" with a 22.39 toss and wrested the lead from Timmermann. But a few minutes later the German "answered" with 22.47 and settled the issue in his favour. Barnes took indirect revenge on 20 May 1990 at Westwood, when he wrested the world record from Timmermann with a 23.12 toss. For once he had an impressive series too, averaging 22.52 with six valid throws. Six days later, at San Jose, he did 23.10 in his one and only valid throw. He met disgrace after a summer meet in Malmö, where he was found "positive" to methyltestosterone, an anabolic steroid. He was consequently suspended by the IAAF for two years.

In 1989 the world body had announced that it would begin random, out-of-competition testing for steroids and related masking agents on a global basis. The new policy turned out to be a good deterrent - that's how the majority of experts interpreted the landslide in the number of 20.00-or-better performers in the World Year Lists, which was as follows:

1982 - 47	1991 - 23
1983 - 64	1992 - 35
1984 - 66	1993 - 30
1985 - 54	1994 - 27
1986 - 61	1995 - 21
1987 - 56	1996 - 24
1988 - 53	1997 - 25
1989 - 37	1998 - 36
1990 - 36	1999 - 28

Even so, the cat-and-mouse game went on relentlessly.

Ulf Timmermann (East Germany) won a great shot put battle at the 1988 Olympics in Seoul.

1981 1999

On several occasions during the Nineties, at least one of the medal winners at the World Championships turned positive at the doping test and was disqualified. While the storm was raging, Werner Günthör, the massive Swiss, continued to show remarkable consistency. In 1991 he successfully defended the world title he had won four years earlier. And in 1993 he made it three in a row. In between these triumphs, however, he had a bitter experience at the 1992 Olympics in Barcelona. For once he could not stand the mental pressure - always great in this event - and wound up fourth with 20.91. Curiously enough, all his conquerors on that occasion - Mike Stulce, Jim Doehring and Vyacheslav Likho - had served drugs bans in the past. World record holder Randy Barnes returned to the warpath after his two-year suspension. Although unable to reproduce his form of 1990, he finished a fairly close second to Günthör (21.80 to 21.97) at the 1993 World Championships. He dropped to 20.41 and third in the 1995 edition but rose to the occasion before a home crowd at the 1996 Olympics in Atlanta. After the penultimate round he was only sixth with 20.44, while his countryman John Godina was leading at 20.79. In his final effort the unpredictable Randy exploded with a mighty 21.62. "That was the competition to end all competitions", as he said later. The 30-year-old American could tell a strange tale, reading like this: how I missed Olympic gold in 1988 with a last round effort of 22.39 and how I won it eight years later with "merely" 21.62, still in the last round. The ups-and-downs that had characterized his career were not over though: in March 1998 he again failed a drug test and was suspended. But in U.S.A. he could be replaced with other excellent performers. In terms of consistency one of the very best was John Godina (born at Fort Sill, Oklahoma, on 31 May 1972; 1.93 m./129 kg.). He can point to two World Championship titles, won in 1995 and '97. On the latter occasion he was lucky in more than one way. At the American Trials he was only fourth, but to his rescue came a new IAAF rule which assured a "wild card" entry to all defending champions. In the World Championship final he was narrowly edged by Aleksandr Bagach of Ukraine (21.44 to 21.47) but his rival failed the drug test and was disqualified. Godina also finished fifth in the discus. In this day and age it is not easy to figure among the world's best in two throwing events, Thanks to his best marks - 22.02 and 69.91 - Godina ranks as the best shot/discus artist of all time. Yet he too fell below expectations on one important occasion: at the 1999 World Championships in Sevilla he had to be content with 20.35 and seventh place. That was also the occasion of the first victory of a Negro shotputter in a global competition. The man in question was C.J. Hunter (born in Washington, D.C., on 14 December 1968; 1.86 m./135 kg.), a massive athlete who chose such a momentous event to improve on his personal best by no less than 35 cms. with 21.79 - on his last try. Hunter was by then the husband of the famous Marion Jones. At Sevilla each won a world title (she in the 100 m.) - one day apart. Possibly the best European of recent years was Aleksandr Bagach (born at Matusov on 21 November 1966; 1.94 m./135 kg.), a prominent figure on the international circuit for almost a decade. He collected medals in all major competitions: bronze in the 1996 Olympics as well as in the 1993 and '99 World Championships; silver in the 1994 and '98 European Championships. Like Randy Barnes, he had a troubled career. After placing third in his event at the 1989 European Cup, he was disqualified for a positive drugs test, and thereby caused a sensation as his demise cost the USSR a place

Werner Günthör (Switzerland), a threetime world champion in the shot put (1987, '91 and '93).

in the ensuing World Cup. Eight years later in Athens he suffered another blow - as related above.

As at the end of 1999 there have been eighty 22-metre-or-better performances, seventy of which made before 1990! As for the ten remaining marks, 5 were made in 1990 - all by Randy Barnes, including his world record of 23.12 - and only 5 between 1991 and '99.

Finally it should be recorded that by the end of the century the "rotation style" had practically taken over, even though adepts of the conventional (O'Brien) style were still numerous.

DISCUS THROW: Neubrandenburg, windy Paradise

1981 - WCup, Rome (5 Sep): 1.Lemme (EG) 66.38, 2.Delis (Ame/Cub) 66.26, 3.Bugár (Eur/CSR) 64.34.
1982 - EC, Athens (11 Sep): 1.Bugár 66.64, 2.Duginyets (USSR) 65.60, 3.Warnemünde (EG) 64.20.
1983 - WC, Helsinki (14 Aug): 1.Bugár 67.72, 2.Delis 67.36, 3.Valent (CSR) 66.08.
1984 - OG, Los Angeles (10 Aug): 1.Danneberg (WG) 66.60, 2.Wilkins (USA) 66.30, 3.Powell (USA) 65.46.
1985 - WCup, Canberra (4 Oct): 1.Kolnootchenko (USSR) 69.08, 2.Schult (EG) 68.30, 3.Delis 67.60.
1986 - EC, Stuttgart (31 Aug): 1.Ubartas (USSR) 67.08, 2.Kolnootchenko 67.02, 3.Kidikas (USSR) 66.32.
1987 - WC, Rome (4 Sep): 1.Schult 68.74, 2.Powell 66.22, 3.Delis 66.02.
1988 - OG, Seoul (1 Oct): 1.Schult 68.82, 2.Ubartas 67.48, 3.Danneberg 67.38.
1989 - WCup, Barcelona (9 Sep): 1.Schult 67.12, 2.Delis 66.72, 3.Danneberg (Eur/WG) 65.30.
1990 - EC, Split (1 Sep): 1.Schult 64.58, 2.de Bruin (Hol) 64.46, 3.Schmidt (WG) 64.10.
1991 - WC, Tokyo (27 Aug): 1. Riedel (Ger) 66.20, 2. de Bruin (Hol) 65.82, 3. Horváth (Hun) 65.32.
1992 - OG, Barcelona (5 Aug): 1. Ubartas (Lit) 65.12, 2. Schult (Ger) 64.94, 3. Moya (Cub) 64.12; WCup, Habana (26 Sep): 1. Washington (USA) 64.86, 2. Moya (Ame/Cub) 63.66, 3. Yu Wenge (Asi/Chi) 63.06.
1993 - WC, Stuttgart (17 Aug): 1. Riedel 67.72, 2. Shevchenko (Rus) 66.90, 3. Schult 66.12.
1994 - EC, Helsinki (14 Aug): 1. Dubrovshchik (Bye) 64.78, 2. Shevchenko (Rus) 64.56, 3. Schult 64.18; WCup, London (10 Sep): 1. Dubrovschchik (Eur/Bye) 64.54, 2. Elizalde (Ame/Cub) 61.50, 3. Olukoju (Nig) 60.22.
1995 - WC, Göteborg (11 Aug): 1. Riedel 68.76, 2. Dubrovshhik 65.98, 3. Kaptyukh (Bye) 65.88.
1996 - OG, Atlanta (31 Jul): 1. Riedel 69.40, 2. Dubrovschchik 66.60, 3. Kaptyukh 65.80.

Randy Barnes (USA), world record holder in the shot put (23.12 in 1990). He barely lost an Olympic title with 22.39 in 1988 but came back to win 8 years later with .....21.62.

1997 - WC, Athens (10 Aug): 1. Riedel 68.54, 2. Alekna (Lit) 66.70, 3. Schult 66.14.
1998 - EC, Budapest (23 Aug): 1. Riedel 67.07, 2. Schult 66.69, 3. Alekna 66.46; WCup, Johannesburg (12 Sep): 1. Alekna (Eur/Lit) 69.66, 2. Riedel 67.47, 3. Kruger (Afr/SA) 65.73.
1999 - WC, Sevilla (24 Aug): 1. Washington (USA) 69.08, 2. Schult 68.18, 3. Riedel 68.09.

Among athletes suspended in recent years for doping offences, discus throwers cannot be said to have taken the back seat. The list includes such internationally prominent athletes as Knut Hjeltnes of Norway, Velko Velev of Bulgaria, Hein-Direck Neu of West Germany, Markku Tuokko of Finland, Luis Mariano Delis of Cuba and Ben Plucknett of USA. The last named (born at Beatrice, Nebraska, on 13 April 1954; 2.01 m./147 kg) was a world leader at the time of his disqualification in 1981. In January of that year he failed a doping test conducted during the Pan Pacific Games at Christchurch, but the result was announced only several months later - after he had broken the world record twice with throws of 71.20 at Modesto on 16 May and 72.34 at Stockholm on 7 July. These marks were not ratified by the IAAF, but curiously made the US record book. After his reinstatement, in 1983, Plucknett threw 71.32. That was no longer good for a world record though: a few days earlier, on 29 May 1983 in Moscow, Yuriy Dumchev of USSR had got one off to 71.86. The American never competed in the Olympics: at the Trials he was seventh in 1976, third in '80 (when USA did not send a team to Moscow ...), tenth in '84 and fourth in '88. Even apart from the advantages some throwers may at times derive from the use of anabolic steroids, the discus remains an unpredictable event. Few other events show such a marked drop in standards when the men move from "cold" to "hot" meets. If we consider major championship meets held between 1981 and '90, the longest throw on record is no better than 69.08 (by Georgiy Kolnootchenko of USSR in the 1985 World Cup at Canberra). One possible reason for this may be found in the fact that big stadia are so constructed as to reduce the influence of the wind factor. Be as it may, discus records continue to occur in minor meets - when the pressure is off and Aeolus is more likely to be among the guests. The latest and biggest record throw was at Neubrandenburg on 6 June 1986, when Jürgen Schult of East Germany got one off to 74.08 on his fourth trial, exactly 2.22 m. over Dumchev's listed record and 4.34 m. over Schult's previous best! On a field open to the winds, that phenomenal throw - the only notable one in a series otherwise including an opener of 67.20, three fouls and one pass - was reportedly favoured "by the right kind of ventilation". Schult himself said: "Don't expect me to do it again soon". In fact, his second best as of the end of 1999 is 70.46. Even so, the German (born at Neuhaus, Hagenow, on 11 May 1960; 1.93 m./110 kg.) is an excellent competitor. He can point to victories in all major Games held in recent years, his longest throw in the series being 68.82 at the Seoul Olympics in 1988. Other excellent throwers of the Eighties were Imrich Bugár of Czechoslovakia, Rolf Danneberg of West Germany and Romas Ubartas of USSR. Veterans are still doing fine in this event. In 1984, John Powell of USA and Ricky Bruch of Sweden, then 37 and 38 respectively, achieved a lifetime best of 71.26. Former world record holder Wolfgang Schmidt had quite a story to tell. In the early Eighties he fell foul of the authorities in his native country, East Germany, and was imprisoned on charges of non-alignment. He spent fourteen months in jail, first at Bautzen, then at Frankfurt/Oder. He was finally allowed to go to West Germany, where he made a fine return to competition, to the point of topping the 1989 World List with 70.92, at the age of 35.

Shortly after the dismantling of the German Democratic Republic (1990) many secrets about the state-controlled doping practices of that country were finally unveiled. The most circumstantial evidence was supplied by Brigitte Berendonk in her book "Doping, von der Forschung zum Betrug" (Doping, from research to cheat), in which Jürgen Schult, the world record holder, figured in a list of regular consumers of anabolic steroids. The list, with details on drugs, doses, etc., included other world record holders like Udo Beyer, Ulf Timmermann (shot) and Uwe Hohn, (javelin). The athletes in question tried to deny such allegations and found indirect help in the circumstance that the "powers that be" of international athletics could not condemn retroactively anyone who, like them, had passed unscathed through tests conducted in connection with major international meets. The D.L.V. (by then the all-German Federation) tried in vain to inject the idea that all world records set before 1990 could be cancelled ...

Be as it may, Schult continued to rank among the world's best discus throwers for many more years, no matter if his longest throw during that decade was no better than 69.04 (1992), as opposed to his world record of 74.08 (1986). His record in the World Championships has been truly remarkable: he was a finalist in all editions held between 1983 and 1999, his placings being as follows:

1983 - 5th	**1995** - 5th
1987 - 1st	**1997** - 3rd
1991 - 6th	**1999** - 2nd
1993 - 3rd	

However, the no. 1 discus thrower of the Nineties was another German, Lars Riedel (born on 28 June 1967 at Zwickau; 1.99 m./110 kg.). He too came from the G.D.R. but, being seven years younger than Schult, he reached top levels only after the unification of the "two Germanies". A magnificent technician, this impressive giant won four consecutive World Championship titles (1991, '93, '95 and '97). In particular, he achieved the rare feat of winning global (World or Olympic) crowns in three consecutive years (1995, '96 and '97). His victory at the 1996 Olympics in Atlanta was by an awesome margin: 2.80 metres - the widest in Olympic annals since 1912. And this was after fouling on his first two tries in the final! A man of deeds rather than words, he was once quoted as saying: "There is no secret recipe to winning in big championships". His reign came to a halt at the 1999 World Championships in Sevilla. Hampered by injury earlier in the year, the German giant was not at his best. Going into the last round of the final he was second to his old rival and friend Jürgen Schult, 68.09 to 68.18. Right there, however, both were upset by another veteran, Anthony Washington of U.S.A., who on his last try moved from fourth to first with 69.08. Washington (born on 16 January 1966 at Glasgow, Montana; 1.86 m./109 Kg.) had been a prominent thrower for years, his highest international honour being a victory in the 1992 World Cup at Habana. Then he was fourth in the 1996 Olympics. His comethrough performance at Sevilla was the sort of throw "when it matters" his closest supporters had long been waiting for. Up to then he had given his best in relatively "cold" meets. In 1996 at Salinas, California, he got one off to 71.14, his personal record so far. His victory at Sevilla made him the first Negro to win a global discus title. (A target Luis Mariano Delis of Cuba could have reached at the 1980 Olympics in Moscow but for some hideous circumstances, as related earlier in this book). Other excellent European throwers of recent years have mostly come from Eastern Europe: Romas Ubartas, the 1992 Olympic champion, and Virgilijus Alekna, both of Lithuania, and Vladimir Dubrovshchik of Byelarus. Occasionally they have been able to beat the two German stalwarts, who remain, however, the kings of the event. Riedel can so far point to three 70 metre plus marks, his best being 71.50 in 1997. He averages 69.91 on his top ten marks, as opposed to Schult's 69.77.

Unfortunately, discus throwers can claim a record of sorts: 12 of the 50 best performers of all time as at the end of 1999 have been suspended for doping offences, at one time or other.

Lars Riedel (Germany), a fourtime world champion in the discus throw (1991, '93, '95 and '97).

Right: Anthony Washington (USA), the first Negro to win a world title in the discus throw (1999).

HAMMER THROW:
The Syedikh - Litvinov Saga

1981 - WCup, Rome (5 Sep): 1.Syedikh (USSR) 77.42, 2.Riehm (WG) 75.60, 3.Urlando (Ita) 71.92.
1982 - EC, Athens (10 Sep): 1.Syedikh 81.66, 2.Nikulin (USSR) 79.44, 3.Litvinov (USSR) 78.66.
1983 - WC, Helsinki (9 Aug): 1.Litvinov 82.68, 2.Syedikh 80.94, 3.Kwasny (Pol) 79.42.
1984 - OG, Los Angeles (6 Aug): 1.Tiainen (Fin) 78.08, 2.Riehm 77.98, 3.Ploghaus (WG) 76.68.
1985 - WCup, Canberra (5 Oct): 1.Tamm (USSR) 82.12, 2.Rodehau (EG) 78.44, 3.Logan (USA) 76.68.
1986 - EC, Stuttgart (30 Aug): 1.Syedikh 86.74 (WR), 2.Litvinov 85.74, 3.Nikulin 82.00.
1987 - WC, Rome (1 Sep): 1.Litvinov 83.06, 2.Tamm 80.84, 3.Haber (EG) 80.76.
1988 - OG, Seoul (26 Sep): 1.Litvinov 84.80, 2.Syedikh 83.76, 3.Tamm 81.16.
1989 - WCup, Barcelona (9 Sep): 1.Weis (Eur/WG) 77.68, 2.Deal (USA) 76.38, 3.Haber 76.28.
1990 - EC, Split (31 Aug): 1.Astapkovich (USSR) 84.14, 2.Gécsek (Hun) 80.14, 3.Nikulin 80.02.
1991 - WC, Tokyo (25 Aug): 1.Syedikh 81.70, 2.Astapkovich 80.94, 3.Weis 80.44.
1992 - OG, Barcelona (2 Aug): 1.Abduvaliyev (EUN/Tjk) 82.54, 2.Astapkovich (EUN/Bye) 81.96, 3.Nikulin (EUN/Rus) 81.38. WCup, Habana (26 Sep): 1.Gécsek (Eur/Hun) 80.44, 2.Nikulin 78.28, 3.Deal (USA) 77.08.
1993 - WC, Stuttgart (15 Aug) : 1.Abduvaliyev (Tjk) 81.64, 2.Astapkovich (Bye) 79.88, 3.Gécsek 79.54.
1994 - EC, Helsinki (11 Aug) : 1.Sidorenko (Rus) 81.10, 2.Astapkovich 80.40, 3.Weis 78.48; WCup, London (10 Sep) : 1.Abduvaliyev (Asi/Tjk) 81.72, 2. Deal (USA) 81.14, 3.Weis (Ger) 80.32.
1995 - WC, Göteborg (6 Aug) : 1.Abduvaliyev 81.56, 2.Astapkovich 81.10, 3.Gécsek 80.98.
1996 - OG, Atlanta (28 Jul) : 1.Kiss (Hun) 81.24, 2.Deal 81.12, 3.Krikun (Ukr) 80.02.
1997 - WC, Athens (3 Aug) : 1.Weis 81.78, 2.Skvaruk (Ukr) 81.46, 3.Sidorenko 80.76.
1998 - EC, Budapest (19 Aug) : 1.Gécsek 82.87, 2.Kiss 81.26, 3.Kobs (Ger) 80.13; WCup, Johannesburg (12 Sep) : 1.Gécsek (Eur/Hun) 82.68, 2.Weis (Ger) 80.13, 3.Abduvaliyev (Asi/Uzb) 79.40.
1999 - WC, Sevilla (22 Aug) : 1.Kobs 80.24, 2.Németh (Hun) 79.05, 3.Piskunov (Ukr) 79.03.

The dominance of USSR hammer throwers continued throughout the Eighties and not even the results of the 1984 Olympics can be said to have been an exception to the rule, since the Russians had to stay away from that meet. This made it a lot easier for Juha Tiainen of Finland to clinch the gold medal. The most famous man in the field, Karl-Hans Riehm of West Germany, finished 10 cm. behind in second place and thereby missed the chance of his lifetime. Yuriy Syedikh and Sergey Litvinov were the outstanding figures of the Eighties. They took turns in beating the world record and also in winning titles. It should be noted that effective 1 May 1981 the minimum and maximum lengths allowed for the diameter of the hammer head were increased to 110 mm. and 130 mm. (from 102 and 120 mm.). This aimed at reducing the length of hammer results, mainly as a safety measure when the throws landed outside the sector. German experts said this change would cut approximately one and a half metres off an 80 m. throw made with a pre-1981 hammer. In the opinion of Yuriy Syedikh, however, such a pessimism was ill-founded. He said throwers would adapt to the change

1981 1999

Yuriy Syedikh (USSR) for many years the leading hammer thrower, still holds the world record with 86.74 (1986).

in a relatively short time, after which the upward trend would start again. First to prove him right was his arch rival Sergey Litvinov, who raised the world record to 83.98 in 1982, then to 84.14 in '83, always in Moscow. But Syedikh obviously wanted to have his share in the demonstration. The occasion was offered by a "pilgrimage" to the mother country of hammer throwing, Ireland. It happened on 3 July 1984 at Cork, in a head-to-head confrontation between him and Litvinov. Syedikh settled the issue at the start with a mighty throw of 86.34. In round 2 Litvinov also exceeded the previous record with 85.20, but that was all he could do. The descendants of Flanagan, McGrath, Ryan and O'Callaghan must have looked at such explosive throwing with admiration ....

The last two rounds of the Syedikh vs. Litvinov battle for the world record unfolded in 1986. And the former, a superlative competitor, won both times. During the USSR vs. East Germany dual meet at Tallinn on 22 June, Syedikh started with 86.00, then improved to 86.66, thus improving his own record. Litvinov had to be content with 84.36. The feud rose to fever pitch at the European Championships in Stuttgart on 30 August, when the two champions had the following series: Syedikh: 83.94 - 85.28 - 85.46 - 86.74 - 86.68 - 86.62 Litvinov: 85.74 - 81.60 - foul - foul - 82.12 - 80.44 Litvinov thus remained in the lead till round 4, when Syedikh went wild and offered the finest exhibition of throwing efficiency ever seen in a hammer circle.

Sergey Litvinov (USSR), the 1988 Olympic hammer champion, still ranks no. 2 in the All Time List with 86.04 (1986).

His average for six valid throws was 85.78, i.e. better than Litvinov's longest effort! Said the happy winner: "I knew that Sergey (Litvinov) had thrown 87.30 in training. That certainly stimulated me." Igor Nikulin, third with 82.00, made it a clean sweep for USSR, yet passed almost unnoticed. Syedikh allowed himself a low-key season in 1987, but was on the warpath again the following year. Yet he had to play second fiddle to his arch rival Litvinov at the Seoul Olympics. By 1989 both had to give way to the younger generation, but still remained pretty close to the top. Late in 1990 Syedikh took a coaching job in France, while continuing to be an active thrower. Best of the new men to come out of the Soviet reservoir is Igor Astapkovich (born at Minsk on 4 January 1963; 1.91 m./118 kg.), who won the 1990 European title at Split with 84.14, his best to date. In the "Track & Field News" World Ranking for 1990 there were no less than eight Russians among the top ten, namely in positions 1, 2, 3, 4, 5, 7, 9 and 10. Germany and, to a lesser degree, Bulgaria and Hungary, were the only countries likely to provide a worthy challenger now and then.

After the disintegration of the USSR, athletes from that vast Euro-Asian area combined for the last time to form a unified team (EUN) in 1992, in connection with the Barcelona Olympics.

Starting with 1993, however, they began to represent their respective republics. At first this new state of affairs seemed to offer wider possibilities, notably in the hammer throw, once the pride and joy of USSR. When it came to global championships, republics such as Russia, Ukraine and Byelarus were theoretically able to field a total of 9 hammer throwers, instead of 3 as before. But in the long run factors of a negative kind also emerged, such as lack of a centralized training programme. As time wenty by, disadvantages seemed to outweigh advantages. This is reflected in a comparison of positions earned by hammer throwers of the former USSR area among the top 8 finalists at World Championships held six years apart:

1993 (Stuttgart) - 1-2-4-5-6-7
1999 (Sevilla) - 3-5-8

The above-mentioned Igor Astapkovich continued to rank among the best in the world for the major part of the Nineties. After his victory in the 1990 European Championships, however, he failed to do himself justice on the occasions that mattered most. For five years in a row (1991-95) he finished second in <u>all</u> major championship meets he contested. He opened this bitter-sweet series at the 1991 World Championships in Tokyo, where he had to bow to the great Yuriy Syedikh, who won the last major honour of his fabulous career. Beginning with 1992, Astapkovich found his "bête noire' in Andrey Abduvaliyev (born on 30 June 1966 in Leningrad; 1.86 m. / 112 Kg.) This pupil of former world record holder Anatoliy Bondarchuk lived for the greater part of his career in Dushanbe (the former Stalinabad), capital of Tadzhikistan, hence in Asia. In the early years of his international activity he had mixed fortunes. But he came into his own in 1992, when he began to appear as a great comethrough performer. During the season he met Igor Astapkovich 9 times, losing always except once, in the Olympic final at Barcelona! This was the first major "war of nerves" between the two stalwarts, and Abduvaliyev duplicated his victory at the World Chamionships in 1993, and again in 1995. On the latter occasion Astapkovich led up to the last round, when the devilish Andrey turned the tables on him. The unlucky runner-up smiled and said: "I must be the record holder for 2nd places in big championships". He really was: when Abduvaliyev, by then citizen of an Asian Republic, became ineligible for the 1994 European Championships in Helsinki, Astapkovich finally seemed to have things going his way. But in the Finnish rendezvous he was again shunted to his beloved (?) second place by Vasiliy Sidorenko of Russia! Amazingly enough, Astapkovich continued to beat Abduvaliyev in the majority of their encounters in meets of lesser renown ....

In the latter part of the Nineties the balance of powers in the ball-and-chain event shifted in favour of Hungarian and German throwers, i.e. the representatives of two countries that could point to a great tradition. Balázs Kiss, a powerful Hungarian who attended the famous University of Southern California, won the Olympic crown at Atlanta in 1996, nosing out by 12 cms. (81.24 to 81.12) Lance Deal of USA, who thus became the first American to win a medal in this event since 1956. Another Hungarian, Tibor Gécsek, turned the tables on Kiss at the 1998 European Championships. The last two world titles, however, went to a couple of strong Germans: Heinz Weis (Athens, 1997) and Karsten Kobs (Sevilla, 1999).

In relation to doping offences, hammer throwers seem to be "less affected" than their colleagues in shot and discus. Only 4 of the top 50 performers of all time as at the end of 1999 had been suspended for failing a test. But in this tiny group we find Tibor Gécsek, who turned positive in 1995 and was inflicted a 4-year ban. The IAAF later reduced such suspensions to 2 years, and late in 1997 Gécsek returned to competition. In 1998 he surprised a lot of people by smashing his 10-year-old personal best (81.68 in 1988) to win the European title! Later in the season he reached 83.68. Be as it may, throughout the Nineties the standard of the top men remained well below that of the Syedikh-Litvinov saga of 1986.

JAVELIN THROW - Implements become less expansive

1981 - WCup, Rome (4 Sep): 1.Kula (USSR) 89.74, 2.Michel (EG) 89.38, 3.Sinersaari (Eur/Fin) 83.26.
1982 - EC, Athens (7 Sep): 1.Hohn (EG) 91.34, 2.Puuste (USSR) 89.56, 3.Michel 89.32.
1983 - WC, Helsinki (12 Aug): 1.Michel 89.48, 2.Petranoff (USA) 85.60, 3.Kula 85.58.
1984 - OG, Los Angeles (5 Aug): 1.Härkönen (Fin) 86.76, 2.Ottley (GB) 85.74, 3.Eldebrink (Swe) 83.72.
1985 - WCup, Canberra (6 Oct): 1.Hohn 96.96, 2.Puuste 87.40, 3.Petranoff 87.34. "New" javelin introduced 1 April 1986.
1986 - EC, Stuttgart (27 Aug): 1.Tafelmeier (WG) 84.76, 2.Michel 81.90, 3.Yevsyukov (USSR) 81.80.
1987 - WC, Rome (30 Aug): 1.Räty (Fin) 83.54, 2.Yevsyukov 82.52, 3.Zelezny (CSR) 82.20.
1988 - OG, Seoul (25 Sep): 1.Korjus (Fin) 84.28, 2.Zelezny 84.12, 3.Räty 83.26.
1989 - WCup, Barcelona (10 Sep): 1.Backley (GB) 85.90, 2.Mizoguchi (Asi/Jap) 82.56, 3.Hadwich (EG) 80.30.
1990 - EC, Split (28 Aug): 1.Backley 87.30, 2.Zaitsev (USSR) 83.30, 3.Bodén (Swe) 82.66.
1991 - WC, Tokyo (26 Aug): 1. Kinnunen (Fin) 90.82, 2. Räty (Fin) 88.12, 3. Sasimovich (USSR) 87.08.
1992 - OG, Barcelona (8 Aug): 1. Zelezny (Cze) 89.66, 2. Räty 86.60, 3. Backley 83.38; WCup, Habana (27 Sep): 1. Zelezny (Eur/Cze) 88.26, 2. Petranoff (Afr/SA) 79.90, 3. Sasimovich (Eur/Rus) 78.40.
1993 - WC, Stuttgart (16 Aug): 1. Zelezny 85.98, 2. Kinnunen 84.78, 3. Hill (GB) 82.96.
1994 - EC, Helsinki (8 Aug): 1. Backley 85.20, 2. Räty 82.90, 3. Zelezny 82.58; WCup, London (11 Sep): 1. Backley 85.02, 2. Hecht (Ger) 84.36, 3. Lovegrove (Oce/NZ) 82.28.
1995 - WC, Göteborg (13 Aug): 1. Zelezny 89.58, 2. Backley 86.30, 3. Henry (Ger) 86.08.
1996 - OG, Atlanta (3 Aug): 1. Zelezny 88.16, 2.

1981
1999

339

Backley 87.44, 3 Räty 86.98.
1997 - WC, Athens (5 Aug): 1. Corbett (SA) 88.40, 2. Backley 86.80, 3. Gatsioudis (Gre) 86.64.
1998 - EC, Budapest (23 Aug): 1. Backley 89.72, 2. Hill 86.92, 3. Hecht 86.63; WCup, Johannesburg (13 Sep): 1. Backley 88.71, 2. Makarov (Eur/Rus) 86.96, 3. Hecht 84.92.
1999 - WC, Sevilla (29 Aug): 1. Parviainen (Fin) 89.52, 2. Gatsioudis 89.18, 3. Zelezny 87.67.

Javelin manufacturers never ceased to study ways and means of improving the "sailing" qualities of implements, obviously within the rules laid down by the IAAF. With leading throwers generally taller and stronger than their predecessors, record performances rose to such an extent that IAAF legislators rightly began to worry about the safety of spectators, especially in medium-size stadia. First to go to "extreme lengths" mark-wise was Tom Petranoff of USA (born at Aurora, Illinois, on 8 April 1958; 1.87 m./98 kg.). He first reached international class in 1980, when he threw 85.44 and just failed to make the "symbolic" US Olympic team. His "high noon" was on 15 May 1983 on the UCLA campus at Westwood, when exactly at that time of the day he got one off to 99.72, eclipsing Ferenc Paragi's world record by exactly 3 metres. The three-figure record prophesied by Matti Järvinen half a century earlier was about to become reality. The man who turned the trick was a young giant from East Germany, Uwe Hohn (born at Rheinsberg on 16 July 1962; 1.98 m./112 kg.). He got started in his international career with a bang, winning the 1981 European Junior title with 86.56. The following year he won the continental senior title at Athens with 91.34. Hohn, coached by Wolfgang Skibba, a former hammer thrower, had his greatest year in 1984, even though he had to stay away from the Los Angeles Olympics. His quest for a new global mark began on 25 May at Potsdam, when he came dangerously close to Petranoff's mark with a 99.52 throw. On a rainy day in July, at Berlin's Sportforum, he did 97.12. A few days later, namely on 20 July, he was at it again, this time at Friedrich-Ludwig-Jahn Sportpark, still in Berlin. The public somehow sensed that a historic record was in the air and chanted: "Heute wollen wir die 100 Meter sehen!" (Today we want to see a 100 m. throw"). After an opener of 89.80, Hohn stepped up, put everything together and produced a throw of unimaginable dimensions. He must have been the first to realize that it was extra good, because he threw both arms over his head while the javelin was still flying. For the first time in athletic history, a throwing implement went beyond the 100 m. line, landing at 104.80, i.e. more than 5 metres over Petranoff's record mark. The elated Hohn passed his four remaining trials. His countryman Detlef Michel, a world champion only a year earlier, was hopelessly outclassed as he finished second with 92.48. Hohn was the no.1 man even in 1985, when he won the World Cup event at Canberra with nearly ten metres to spare vis-à-vis the runner-up. Then something developed to disrupt this phenomenal throwing machine. Maybe an overdose of hard training caused him serious problems in the vertebral region, something not even repeated surgery managed to offset. He was thus lost for athletics at twenty-three. In commenting on his pupil's master throw, Wolfgang Skibba reportedly said: "There is still room in the stadia for further improvement!". But IAAF officials obviously had different views. They

Uwe Hohn (East Germany) threw the "Held" javelin 104.80 in 1984 - the longest throw in history led IAAF legislators to adopt a less "expansive" implement.

feared that 100-m-plus throws might become commonplace within a few years. If so, the javelin could be a deadly implement within the confines of an enclosed stadium. The IAAF thus decided to introduce a modified javelin, in which the maximum distance from the tip of the metal head to the centre of gravity was reduced from 1.10 to 1.06 m. This correction lessened the "sailing" qualities of the implement. In addition to that, javelins so constructed would be sure to land head first as prescribed by the rules. The "gliders" used by Petranoff, Hohn et al often caused controversy as they tended to land flat. As a result of this modification, which became effective on 1 April 1986, the clock of javelin history was put back several years. Initially, the drop in standard of performance was almost dramatic: the 50th best performer in the 1985 World List ("old" javelin) had 84.70; the 50th best performer of 1986 ("new" javelin) had 77.38! At the very top the difference was, of course, greater: the leader of 1985, Hohn, had 96.96, his counterpart of 1986, Klaus Tafelmeier of West Germany, had 85.74. In later years the gap was reduced, somewhat slowly but gradually. The "loss" was obviously more noticeable for veterans who had been using the old javelin throughout their career. Up-and-coming youngsters, able to use the new implement virtually from the start, were generally quicker in getting used to it. Remarkably enough, the IAAF decided to open a new Record Book for marks made with the new implement. Klaus Tafelmeier was among those who tried the new javelin even before it became "official". In 1985 he threw 78.62, a "record" which was bettered by several men in '86. But the first mark to be ratified as the inaugural world record belonged to Tafelmeier: 85.74 at Como, Italy, on 21 September 1986. Czechoslovakia, a country that had never been a factor in the history of the event, entered the picture in 1987, when Jan Zelezny (born at Mladá Boleslav on 16 June 1966; 1.86 m./77 kg.) threw 87.66 at Nitra on 31 May. Surprisingly enough, the new record withstood all assaults for three years. In the intervening time it was threatened only once: that was when Kazuhiro Mizoguchi of Japan threw 87.60 at San Jose in 1989. Things began to move again in 1990, when the global mark was bettered four times in the space of just as many months. Patrik Bodén, a Swede attending the University of Texas, got the ball rolling with an 89.10 throw at Austin on 24 March. Then came Steve Backley of Britain and reached 89.58 at Stockholm on 2 July, beating Bodén among others. In the meantime, a new type of javelin conceived by former Olympic champion Miklós Németh of Hungary and featuring a lift-imparting rough section behind the grip, began to appear on the market. In fact, it had been approved by the IAAF at Barcelona in the fall of 1989. Using a "Németh" javelin, Jan Zelezny recaptured the world record at Oslo on 14 July with 89.66. Only six days later, in London, there was a showdown between him and Backley. The Englishman used his customary implement in the first two rounds, then decided to face his rival with the same "weapon". "There were three Némeths available - said Backley afterwards - but I chose to pick up the one Zelezny was using". The result of this move was positive: 89.20, then a new world record of 90.98! Zelezny was a distant second at 85.84. The Németh javelin was not allowed at the European Championships

1981 1999

Not fluent in "javelin speaking"

Javelin throwing has been the pride and joy of Finnish athletics since time immemorial. In this event no other country can claim a record even remotely comparable with that of Suomi. Finnish ranking lists have age classes down to 9-year-olds, where the national record for the 400-gramme javelin is 44.90 by Kimmo Kinnunen (he was to become a world champion in 1991). A notable exception to the rule in Eduard Hämäläinen, a great decathlon man but by no means a javelin artist. Thereby hangs a tale: his Finnish grandfather was deported to Siberia in 1917 when Finland was under Russian rule. Eduard was born in Karaganda, Kazakhstan, in 1969. His family later settled in Byelarus, where the boy inherited his love for athletics in general and the multiple events in particular from his father, Pavel, a good decathlon man in his younger days. Eduard eventually developed into a versatile talent. He represented Byelarus for several years but after moving to Finland he became eligible to represent the country of his ancestors in 1997. In major competitions he can point to an amazing sequence of silver medals: in the World Championships of 1993, '95 and '97 and in the European Championships of 1998!
Strangely enough for a Finn, the javelin has never been his forte. In 1998 at Budapest he was on his way to winning the European decathlon title when Erki Nool of Estonia turned the tables on him in the javelin - 70.65 to 55.34! And his personal record is "only" 61.88.

later in 1990, allegedly because the new implement had been on the "market" for less than 18 months. And there were rumours that the very latest Némeths appeared to be somewhat different from the model approved by the IAAF in 1989. With all throwers using conventional spears, Backley won the European title comfortably with 87.30. Zelezny failed to qualify for the final. The Englishman (born at Sidcup on 12 February 1969; 1.96 m./97 kg.) is the latest and most brilliant product of a British "school" which has recently had such excellent throwers as David Ottley, a silver medallist at the 1984 Olympics, Mick Hill and Roald Bradstock. Backley, a sports science student at Loughborough University, did 79.50 at nineteen, then ranked no.1 in the world in 1989 and '90.

Seppo Räty of Finland, after scoring an upset victory at the 1987 World Championships, had his best season in 1991, when he twice bettered Steve Backley's world record - first with 91.98 at Shizuoka, Japan, on 6 May, then with an imposing 96.96 in a Finnish meet at Punkalaidum on 2 June. At that point, however, there had been a further development with the latest "Németh javelin". Although made under the new specifications, it had behind the grip a series of serrations which served to make the javelin fly further.

This contravened the new (1986) rules, but it could not be legislated against until the IAAF Congress of August 1991 in Tokyo. Consequently, records made by Zelezny (89.66 in 1990), Backley (90.98 in 1990) and Räty (the above-mentioned marks of 1991), which had been approved, were subsequently deleted. Backley's 89.58 of 1990, made in Stockholm, was listed as the accepted world record. It fell to the Briton himself to break the 90-metre barrier under acceptable conditions: 91.46 at North Shore, Auckland, on 25 January 1992. However, this long and somewhat hideous "chassé-croisé" offered one more chapter when Jan Zelezny, by then representing the Czech Republic, got one off to 94.74 at Oslo on 4 July 1992. As it turned out, this was made with yet another "Németh javelin", which had an additional piece of metal inside the normally hollow spear to help stabilize the javelin in flight. It was banned by the IAAF and Zelezny's Oslo mark was not ratified. The great Czech did himself justice the following year: at Pietersburg, South Africa, on 6 April, he did 95.54 on his first try, thus obliterating Backley's world record by a huge margin. He had an even better day at Sheffield on 29 August, producing the following series: 87.06 - 95.34 - <u>95.66</u> - foul - 89.02 - pass. Mick Hill of Britain, who was a distant second with

Seppo Räty, one of the latest heirs of a great Finnish javelin tradition.

85.62, had this to say about Zelezny's record throw of 95.66: "It was awesome - a privilege to see it. I thought he was going to throw 100 metres, With the old javelin, it would have gone 115 metres". That throw, as it often happens for javelin records, came with the aid of a strong tailwind. Zelezny said: "It's not impossible that a 100 metre throw may again materialize". He had to wait 3 years to see his dream come ... closer. On 25 May 1996 at Jena he got one off to 98.48. Inspired by the presence of a good German duo - Raymond Hecht and Boris Henry - he had the following series: 87.76 - 92.88 - 98.48 - 91.44 - foul - 87.88, with a stupendous average of 91.69 for his five valid throws. Hecht was second with 90.06 and Henry third with 86.94.

Even apart from record performances, Zelezny was the dominant figure of the Nineties also as a competitor. He won four global titles - two in the World Championships (1993 and '95) and two in the Olympic Games (1992 and '96). Oddly enough, he was unlucky in the European Championships, in which he reached the podium only once (bronze in 1994). Over a period of seven years (1991-97) he won 91 of 109 competitions, a stupendous record in an event governed by a volatile implement. Serious injuries bogged him down now and then.

In 1998 there were fears that he might never compete again. Yet he recovered well enough to place third in the 1999 World Championships. Steve Backley was clearly outshone by the Czech wonder

1981
1999

Steve Backley, the first British male thrower to set a world record: 89.58 with the javelin in 1990.

Jan Zelezny (Czech Rep.), the greatest javelin ace of the Nineties and a two - time winner in both Olympics (1992 and '96) and World Championships (1993 and '95).

but continued to be his usual consistent self. He won silver medals in the World Championships twice and in the 1996 Olympics. He excelled Zelezny in at least one respect: he won three successive titles in the European Championships (1990-94-98), which in this event are the equivalent of a world championship, or just about. The great Finnish tradition was honoured in 1999 by 25-year-old Aki Parviainen, who won the world title at Sevilla shortly after reaching 93.09 in a Finnish meet - a distance excelled only by Zelezny with the new javelin.

A major upset occurred at the 1997 World Championships in Athens, the chief character in the play being Marius Corbett, a giant from South Africa. He had revealed unique comethrough qualities at the 1994 World Junior Championships, winning with a personal best of 77.98. Early in 1997 he improved to 83.40. No matter how good, this mark barely sufficed to rank him 19th among throwers entering the World Championships. But in Sevilla he delivered yet another thunderbolt when he got one off to 88.40 in the second round of the final. No one of his rivals was able to answer that and Corbett became the most surprising winner in the history of the event at such levels. In 1998 he confirmed his devilish ability in meets that mattered by winning at the Commonwealth Games with a new personal best of 88.75. A year later at the World Championships in Sevilla he finally met disappointment by failing to reach the final.

By the end of the century, the general standard remained well below that of the early Eighties. In 1998 the 50th best performer in the year list had 79.52; in 1999 the 50th best thrower had 79.56.

DECATHLON - Thompson ... O'Brien ... Dvorák - and 9000 is just round the corner.

1982 - EC, Athens (7/8 Sep): 1.Thompson (GB) 8743 pts. WR; 2.Hingsen 8517 pts, 3.Stark (EG) 8433 pts.
1983 - WC, Helsinki (12/13 Aug): 1.Thompson 8666 pts., 2.Hingsen 8561 pts., 3.Wentz (WG) 8478 pts.
1984 - OG, Los Angeles (8/9 Aug): 1.Thompson 8798 pts. equals WR; 2.Hingsen 8673 pts., 3.Wentz 8412 pts. New scoring table adopted in 1985
1986 - EC, Stuttgart (27/28 Aug): 1.Thompson 8811 pts., 2.Hingsen 8730 pts., 3.Wentz 8676 pts.
1987 - WC, Rome (3/4 Sep): 1.Voss 8680 pts., 2.Wentz 8461 pts., 3.Tarnovyetskiy (USSR) 8375 pts.
1988 - OG, Seoul (28/29 Sep): 1.Schenk (EG) 8488 pts., 2.Voss 8399 pts., 3.Steen (Can) 8328 pts.
1990 - EC, Split (28/29 Aug): 1.Plaziat 8574 pts., 2.Szabó (Hun) 8436 pts., 3.Schenk 8433 pts.
1991 - WC, Tokyo (29/30 Aug): 1. O'Brien (USA) 8812 pts., 2. Smith (Can) 8549 pts., 3. Schenk (Ger) 8394 pts.
1992 - OG, Barcelona (5/6 Aug): 1. Zmelik (Cze) 8611 pts., 2. Peñalver (Spa) 8412 pts., 3. D.Johnson (USA) 8309 pts.
1993 - WC, Stuttgart (19/20 Aug): 1. O'Brien 8817 pts., 2. Hämäläinen (Bye) 8724 pts., 3. Meier (Ger) 8548 pts.
1994 9- EC, Helsinki (12/13 Aug): 1. Blondel (Fra) 8453 pts., 2. Dagård (Swe) 8362 pts., 3. Lobodin (Ukr) 8201 pts.
1995 - WC, Göteborg (6/7 Aug): 1. O'Brien 8695 pts., 2. Hämäläinen 8489 pts., 3. Smith 8419 pts.
1996 - OG, Atlanta (31 Jul/1 Aug): 1. O'Brien 8824 pts., 2. Busemann (Ger) 8706 pts., 3. Dvorák (Cze) 8664 pts.
1997 - WC, Athens (5/6 Aug): 1. Dvorák 8837 pts., 2. Hämäläinen (Fin) 8730 pts., 3. Busemann 8652 pts.
1998 - EC, Budapest (19/20 Aug): 1. Nool (Est) 8667 pts., 2. Hämäläinen (Fin) 8587 pts., 3. Lobodin 8571 pts.
1999 - WC, Sevilla (24/25 Aug): 1. Dvorák 8744 pts., 2. Macey (GB) 8556 pts., 3. Huffins (USA) 8547 pts.

Daley Thompson was the undisputed king of the 10-event grind up to and including 1986, thereby setting a new record in terms of longevity at the highest level. After losing to Aleksandr Grebenyuk at the 1978 European Championships, he won all there was to win and never lost an important test. Between 1977 and 1988 he appeared in "Track & Field News" World Ranking eight times: 1st in 1980, '82, '83, '84 and '86, 3rd in '78, 4th in '77 and 5th in '88. (In the four remaining years he simply chose to "hibernate"). Jürgen Hingsen of West Germany (born at Duisburg on 25 January 1958; 2.00 m./102 kg.) was a foil and often a victim of the talents of the great Briton. In their head-to-head confrontations the big German always ended on the losing side. Yet they took turns in bettering the world record. As the perverse game of ever-changing tables would have it, in 1985 a new scoring system came into force. It is therefore necessary to detail Thompson's and Hingsen's record efforts under both the 1962/77 table (A), under which they were officially calculated, and that

A	B	
8704	8730	Thompson (Götzis, 22/23 May '82)
8723	8741	Hingsen (Ulm, 14/15 Aug '82)
8743	8774	Thompson (Athens, 7/8 Sep '82)
8779	8825	Hingsen (Bernhausen, 4/5 Jun '83)
8798	8832	Hingsen (Mannheim, 8/9 Jun '84)
8798	8847	Thompson (Los Angeles, 8/9 Aug '84)

of '85 (B), still in use at the present time (see adjoining table): Thompson's score at the Los Angeles Olympics was originally given as 8797 pts., which caused him to miss Hingsen's world record by one tantalizing point. In 1986 a thorough study of the photo finish led the IAAF to correct Thompson's time for the 110 m. hurdles from 14.34 to 14.33. This posthumously raised his total to 8798, equal to Hingsen's previous effort. By then, however, a new scoring table had come into force which made Thompson's Los Angeles marks worth 8847 pts. He thus became the sole owner of the record. His marks on that occasion were as follows: - 10.44 (100 m.), 8.01 (long jump), 15.72 (shot put), 2.03 (high jump), 46.97 (400 m.); 14.33 (110 m. hurdles), 46.56 (discus), 5.00 (pole vault), 65.24 (javelin), 4:35.00 (1500 m.) Hingsen once managed to do 2.18 in the high jump, a wondrous achievement for a man weighing over one hundred kilograms. He was probably second to Thompson only in sheer competitive ability. The Briton, famous for his irreverent humour, was once quoted as saying: "Too bad such a handsome and strong man like him (Hingsen) is doomed to lose to an ugly duckling like me". Jokes apart, a story of countless hours of work and toil lies behind the super scores of this day and age. This is no longer the time when a decathlon man could win medals simply by capitalizing on his skill in two or three events. The world class man must now be technically efficient in each and every one of the ten labours. In his usual vein, Thompson once put it this way: "The decathlon champion? He's like a man who has ten lovers and must do justice to all of them".

Thompson gave the last measure of his competitive ability at the 1988 Olympics in Seoul. After a long lay-off and while still hampered by injuries, he finished fourth, less than 200 points behind winner Christian Schenk of East Germany. On the same occasion his arch rival Hingsen had the gloomiest day of his career. In the opening event, the 100 m., he was disqualified for three false starts. (That's the rule in the decathlon, as opposed to two in individual running events).

Most German commentators were very harsh in judging his mishap. Poor Hingsen, who had gone to Seoul short on condition as a result of a recent injury, was so affected by this aftermath that for some time the hideous memory of those false starts reportedly haunted him even in his dreams.

A gifted American, Dan O'Brien (born on 18 July 1966 at Portland; 1.89 m./84 kg.) was Thompson's rightful heir. The son of a black American father and a half-Finnish mother, he was adopted at the age of two by a white couple from Oregon, Jim and Virginia O'Brien. Although he revealed talent early, it was only in 1988 that he earnestly began to get his act together as a major decathlon prospect with a score of 7891 pts. After that he continued to improve steadily and climbed to the top by 1991, when he qualified for the World Championships with a sensational 8844, only three ponts shy of Thompson's

Jürgen Hingsen (Germany) held the world's decathlon record but was a foil and often a victim of the devilish competitive talent of his arch rival, Britain's Daley Thompson.

Dan O'Brien (USA), Olympic decathlon champion in 1996 as well as a threetime winner in the World Championships (1991, '93 and '95).

world record. However, his 10.23 in the 100 metres was before the wind gauge became available and his 13.95 in the 110 metre hurdles the next day was aided by a wind of 4.2 m/s, just over the deca-legal limit. Two months later, at the World Championships in Tokyo, he showed his great competitive "élan", winning with almost 300 pts. to spare with a fine score of 8812. 1992 was a year of bitter-sweet experiences, even though it ended on a high note.

At the U.S. Olympic Trials he met disaster in the 8th event, the pole vault, often a tricky passage for a decathlon man - he failed at his initial height, 4.80, and finished a poor 11th with 7856 pts. Of course he was blamed by some observers for choosing such a relatively high setting as it was figured that he would have made the team rather comfortably by clearing ... 2.80 (the third and last qualifier amassed a total of 8163 pts). Dan consequently missed the Barcelona Olympics and the quadrennial title went to Robert Zmelik of the Czech Reublic with 8611 pts. The American suffered a foot injury just before the Games but recovered well enough to set a new world record of 8891 pts. at Talence on 4/5 September. His marks were as follows: 10.43 (100 m.), 8.08 (long jump), 16.69 (shot put), 2.07 (high jump), 48.51 (400 m.), 13.98 (110 m. hurdles), 48.56 (discus throw), 5.00 (pole vault), 62.58 (javelin throw) and 4:42.10 (1500 m). Olympic champion Zmelik was a distant second with 8344 pts. That was to remain O'Brien's top score, yet he went on to add three more global titles to his collection with victories at the World Championships (1993 and '95) and the 1996 Olympics. A very strong 1st day man, O'Brien has his forte in the long jump (8.08) and the 110 metre hurdles (13.47) and his relative weakness in the 1500 metres. Unbeaten in 11 successive decathlons over a period of six years (1992-98), he can point to five 8800-plus scores. Injuries have kept him low of late and his successor appeared, sooner than he and several others would have thought, in the person of Tomás Dvorák of the Czech Republic (born on 11 May 1972 at Gottwaldov, now Zlín; 1.86 m./85 kg.). At the international level this Czech soldier had been growing steadily throughout the O'Brien era. In 1991, aged 19, he was second in the European Junior Championships with a personal best of 7748 pts. In 1993 he made his first appearance in the World Championships and finished tenth. Then he improved to fifth in the 1995 edition. He finally made the grade at the 1996 Olympics in Atlanta, setting new personal bests in four events and winning an unexpected bronze medal with 8664 pts., his highest score up to then. In 1997 he won his first major title at the World Championships in Athens with yet another personal record - 8837 pts. O'Brien, sidelined with an injury, was not there. A partial setback for Dvorák came in 1998 when he finished no better than third at the Goodwill Games with 8428 pts., while O'Brien feted his comeback with a clear victory (8755 pts.).

In 1999, with the American again sidelined with injury, Dvorák had a perfect season: four victories with such scores as 8738 (Götzis), 8994 (world record, European Cup), 8744 (World Championships) and 8690 (Talence). He succeeded O'Brien as world record holder at Prague on 3 and 4 July with the following marks: 10.54 (100 m.), 7.90 (long jump), 16.78 (shot put), 2.04 (high jump), 48.08 (400 m.), 13.73 (110 m. hurdles), 48.33 (discus throw), 4.90 (pole vault), 72.32 (javelin throw) and 4:37.20 (1500 m). His coach Zderek Vana was once quoted as saying that his pupil's forte consisted in having no real weaknesses. Yet, despite his record, he still has to beat O'Brien in a head-to-head confrontation.

RELAYS - 4x100 METRES: An average at 9.35 per man

1981 - WCup, Rome (5 Sep): 1.Eur/Pol (Zwolinski, Licznerski, Dunecki, Woronin) 38.73, 2.EG 38.79, 3.USA 38.85.

1982 - EC, Athens (11 Sep): 1.USSR (Sokolov, Aksinin, Prokofyev, Sidorov) 38.60, 2.EG 38.71, 3.WG 38.71.

1983 - WC, Helsinki (10 Aug): 1.USA (King, Gault, C.Smith, C.Lewis) 37.86, WR, 2.Italy 38.37, 3.USSR 38.41.

1984 - OG, Los Angeles (11 Aug): 1.USA (Graddy, Brown, C.Smith, C.Lewis) 37.83, WR, 2.Jamaica 38.62, 3.Canada 38.70.

1985 - WCup, Canberra (5 Oct): 1.USA (Glance, Baptiste, C.Smith, Evans) 38.10, 2.Americas 38.31, 3.USSR 38.35.

1986 - EC, Stuttgart (31 Aug): 1.USSR (Yevgenyev, Yushmanov, Muravyov, Brizgin) 38.29, 2.EG 38.64, 3.GB 38.71.

1987 - WC, Rome (6 Sep): 1.USA (McRae, L.McNeill, Glance, C.Lewis) 37.90, 2.USSR 38.02, 3.Jamaica 38.41.

1988 - OG, Seoul (1 Oct): 1.USSR (Brizgin, Krilov, Muravyov, Savin) 38.19, 2.GB 38.28, 3.France 38.40.

1989 - WCup, Barcelona (9 Sep): 1.USA (Cason, Council, Dees, Watkins) 38.29, 2.GB 38.34, 3.Eur/Fra 38.47.

1990 - EC, Split (1 Sep): 1.France (Morinière, Sangouma, Trouabal, Marie-Rose) 37.79, WR, 2.GB 37.98, 3.Italy 38.39.

1991 - WC, Tokyo (1 Sep): 1. USA (Cason, Burrell, Mitchell, C. Lewis) 37.50, WR, 2. France 37.87, 3. GB 38.09.

1992 - OG, Barcelona (8 Aug): 1. USA (Marsh, Burrell, Mitchell, C. Lewis) 37.40, WR, 2. Nigeria 37.98, 3. Cuba 38.00; WCup, Habana (26 Sep): 1. USA (Bridgewater, Braunskill, C. Smith, J. Williams) 38.48, 2. Americas 38.51, 3. Africa 39.08.

1993 - WC, Stuttgart (22 Aug): 1. USA (Drummond, Cason, Mitchell, Burrell) 37.48 (the same foursome equalled the WR, 37.40, in a semi-final on 21 Aug), 2. GB 37.77, 3. Canada 37.83.

1994 - EC, Helsinki (13 Aug): 1. France (Lomba, Sangouma, Trouabal, Perrot) 38.57, 2. Ukraine 38.98, 3. Italy 38.99; WCup, London (10 Sep): 1. GB (Braithwaite, Jarrett, Regis, Christie) 38.46, 2. Africa 38.97, 3. USA 39.33.

1995 - WC, Göteborg (13 Aug): 1. Canada (Esmie,

1981
1999

Tomás Dvorák (Czech Rep.) came close to 9000 pts. in raising the world's decathlon record to 8994 in 1999.

Gilbert, Surin, Bailey) 38.31, 2. Australia 38.50, 3. Italy 39.07.
1996 - OG, Atlanta (3 Aug): 1. Canada (Esmie, Gilbert, Surin, Bailey) 37.69, 2. USA 38.05, 3. Brazil 38.41.
1997 - WC, Athens (10 Aug): 1. Canada (Esmie, Gilbert, Surin, Bailey) 37.86, 2. Nigeria 38.07, 3. GB 38.14.
1998 - EC, Budapest (23 Aug): 1. GB (Condon, Campbell, Walker, Golding) 38.52, 2. France 38.87, 3. Poland 38.98; WCup, Johannesburg (12 Sep): 1. GB (Condon, Devonish, Golding, Chambers) 38.09, 2. USA 38.25, 3. Africa 38.29.
1999 - WC, Sevilla (29 Aug): 1. USA (Drummond, Montgomery, B. Lewis, M. Greene) 37.59, 2. GB 37.73, 3. Nigeria 37.91.

As of the end of 1989 the 38-secs. barrier had been broken on four occasions, always by US teams that had Carl Lewis as anchor leg man. The breakthrough was at the 1983 World Championships in Helsinki, where a team consisting of Emmit King, Willie Gault, Calvin Smith and Lewis was clocked in 37.86. "King Carl" was timed in 8.98. The following year, at Los Angeles, another US team - Sam Graddy, Ron Brown, Smith and Lewis - did even better with 37.83, and Lewis' split was 8.94. However, Carl's fastest (anchor) leg was registered three years later at the World Championships in Rome: 8.86, even though the final time for the team was "only" 37.90. The year 1990 brought a new touch. For the first time since 1960, a European team wrested the world record from USA. It happened at the European Championships in Split, when two teams ducked under 38 secs., with France lowering the world record to 37.79 and Britain second in 37.98. On the basis of their best 100 m. marks in individual races, the four Frenchmen -Max Morinière, Daniel Sangouma, Jean-Charles Trouabal and Bruno Marie-Rose - had an aggregate of 40.65, as opposed to 40.05 for their American predecessors of 1984 (Graddy, Brown, Smith, Lewis). Surprisingly enough, French baton passing was far from perfect on at least two occasions. A few weeks earlier, at Barcelona, a Santa Monica Track Club foursome with a speed aggregate of 40.07 - Mark Witherspoon, Floyd Heard, Leroy Burrell, Carl Lewis - had done no better than 37.93.

U.S. sprinters reclaimed "their" world record in 1991. It took them two shots to make the target: at Monaco on 3 August, Michael Marsh, Leroy Burrell, Floyd Heard and Carl Lewis, representing the Santa Monica Track Club, equalled the mark set by the French the year before (37.79); four days later, at the famous "Weltklasse" meet in Zurich, a U.S. national team with Marsh, Burrell, Dennis Mitchell and Lewis lowered the record to 37.67. The French national team was in both these races: at Monaco they were disqualified for a faulty pass in the early stages and in Zurich, with exactly the same men of the 1990 race at Split, they finished in 38.39. At the World Championships in Tokyo the two teams wound up in the same order and U.S.A., with Andre Cason, Burrell, Mitchell and Lewis, was timed in 37.50, WR, while the French, worthy rivals, finished second in 37.87. The incomparable Lewis made his <u>sixth</u> and last appearance in a record breaking (or tying) team over a period of 9 years (1983-1992) at the Barcelona Olympics of 1992, where he masterfully completed the work of Marsh, Burrell and Mitchell with a fantastic anchor leg ("caught by some watches in 8.8" as per "Track & Field News") to achieve a wondrous 37.40. Nigeria was second in 37.98, a new African record. But in 1993 Uncle Sam's boys showed that they could run fast even without Lewis. At the World Championships in Stuttgart a foursome consisting of Jon Drummond, Cason, Mitchell and Burrell equalled the world record (37.40) in a semi-final and went on to win the final the following day in 37.48. Their strongest rivals on this occasion were the British (Colin Jackson, Tony Jarrett, John Regis and Linford Christie), who captured the European record with 37.77. Canada was third in 37.83 - a prelude to what was to follow in subsequent years. A well-oiled team consisting of Robert Esmie, Glenroy Gilbert, Bruny Surin and Donovan Bailey really swept the board for the Maple Leaf, winning global titles at Göteborg ('95 Worlds), Atlanta ('96 Olympics) and Athens ('97 Worlds)! Never before had a sprint relay team from a country other than U.S.A. dominated the scene with such consistency. It should be noted, however, that both in 1995 and 1997 the U.S. team failed to make the finals as a result of missed handoffs in the prelims. In the Olympic final at Atlanta in 1996 they were in the race yet lost to the Canadians by a sound margin - 38.05 to 37.69. It was only at the 1999 World Championships in Sevilla that the Americans, with 100 metre world record holder Maurice Greene in the anchor leg, regained the top in 37.59 after a big fight with a British team consisting of Jason Gardener, Darren Campbell, Marlon Devonish, Dwain Chambers, who lowered the European record to 37.73. The "nouvelle vague" of British sprinters of the post-Christie era looms as a major threat to Americans in years to come. Considering that the baton passing of the latter has often been far from faultless, one may conclude that there is room for improvement in the sprint relay, no matter if the current world record (37.40) implies an average of 9.35 per man!

4x400 METRES - Mexico mark bettered 24 years later

1981 - WCup, Rome (6 Sep): 1.USA (McCoy, Wiley, W.Smith, Darden) 2:59.12, 2.Europe 3:01.47, 3.Americas 3:02.01.
1982 - EC, Athens (11 Sep): 1.WG (Skamrahl, Schmid, Giessing, Weber) 3:00.51, 2.GB 3:00.68, 3.USSR 3:00.80.
1983 - WC, Helsinki (14 Aug): 1.USSR (Lovachev, Troshilo, Chernyetskiy, Markin) 3:00.79, 2.WG 3:01.83, 3.GB 3:03.53.
1984 - OG, Los Angeles (11 Aug): 1.USA (Nix, Armstead, Babers, McKay) 2:57.91, 2.GB 2:59.13, 3.Nigeria 2:59.32.
1985 - WCup, Canberra (6 Oct): 1.USA (McCoy, Phillips, Armstead, Franks) 3:00.71, 2.EG 3:00.82, 3.Oce/Aus 3:01.35.
1986 - EC, Stuttgart (31 Aug): 1.GB (Redmond, Akabusi, Whittle, Black) 2:59.84, 2.WG 3:00.17, 3.USSR 3:00.47.
1987 - WC, Rome (6 Sep): 1.USA (D.Everett, Haley, McKay, B.Reynolds) 2:57.29, 2.GB 2:58.86, 3.Cuba 2:59.16.
1988 - OG, Seoul (1 Oct): 1.USA (D.Everett, S.Lewis, Robinzine, B.Reynolds) 2:56.16, equals WR, 2.Jamaica 3:00.30, 3.WG 3:00.56.
1989 - WCup, Barcelona (10 Sep): 1.Americas (Martinez/Cub, Burnett/Jam, S.Menezes/Bra, Hernández/Cub) 3:00.65, 2.USA 3:00.99, 3.Africa 3:01.88.
1990 - EC, Split (1 Sep): 1.GB (Sanders, Akabusi, Regis, Black) 2:58.22, 2.WG 3:00.64, 3.EG 3:01.51.
1991 - WC, Tokyo (1 Sep): 1. GB (Black, Redmond, Regis, Akabusi) 2:57.53, 2. U.S.A. 2:57.57, 3. Jamaica 3:00.10.
1992 - OG, Barcelona (8 Aug): 1. USA (Valmon, Watts, M. Johnson, S. Lewis) 2:55.74, WR, 2. Cuba 2:59.51, 3. GB 2:59.73; WCup, Habana (27 Sep): 1. Africa (Lahlou/Mor., Matete/Zam., Kemboi/Ken., Bada/Nig.) 3:02.14, 2; Americas 3:02.95, 3. GB 3:03.95.
1993 - WC, Stuttgart (22 Aug): 1. USA (Valmon, Watts, Reynolds, M. Johnson) 2:54.29, WR, 2. Kenya 2:59.82, 3. Germany 2:59.99.
1994 - EC, Helsinki (14 Aug): 1. GB (McKenzie, Whittle, Black, Ladejo) 2:59.13, 2. France 3:01.11, 3. Russia 3:03.10; WCup, London (11 Sep): 1. GB (McKenzie, Ladejo, Baulch, Black) 3:01.34, 2. Africa 3:02.66, 3. Europe 3:03.26.
1995 - WC, Göteborg (13 Aug): 1. USA (Ramsey, Mills, Reynolds, M. Johnson) 2:57.32, 2. Jamaica 2:59.88, 3. Nigeria 3:03.18.
1996 - OG, Atlanta (3 Aug): 1. USA (L. Smith, A. Harrison, Mills, Maybank) 2:55.99, 2. GB 2:56.60, 3. Jamaica 2:59.42.
1997 - WC, Athens (10 Aug): 1. USA (Young, Pettigrew, C. Jones, Washington) 2:56.47, 2. GB 2:56.65, 3. Jamaica 2:56.75.
1998 - EC, Budapest (23 Aug): 1. GB (Hylton, Baulch, Thomas, Richardson) 2:58.68, 2. Poland 2:58.88, 3. Spain 3:02.47; WCup, Johannesburg (13 Sep): 1. USA (Everett, Pettigrew, Woody, Young) 2:59.28, 2. GB 2:59.71, 3. Americas 2:59.77.
1999 - WC, Sevilla (29 Aug): 1. USA (Jer. Davis, Pettigrew, Taylor, M. Johnson) 2:56.45, 2. Poland 2:58.91, 3. Jamaica 2:59.34.

The phenomenal record set by Lee Evans & Co. at the 1968 Olympics at Mexico City (2:56.16) withstood all assaults for twenty years - to be finally matched to the hundredth-of-a-second by another US team! As per tradition, it happened at another Olympic celebration, the 1988 Games at Seoul. The men, with their official splits, were: Danny Everett 43.79, Steve Lewis 43.69, Kevin Robinzine 44.74, Butch Reynolds 43.94. Of course, the 1968 mark had been favoured to some extent by the high altitude of Mexico City. In fact, it took three sub-44 secs. men to match that record under normal (sea level) conditions. Earlier in the season, at Zurich, anchor leg man Butch Reynolds had in fact succeeded Evans as world record holder for the individual 400 m. with an almost incredible 43.29. Still, the Seoul race was hardly a competitive test in the strict sense of the word: the Americans won by more than 4 seconds. Europe's first sub 3-min. performance was achieved at the 1984 Olympics, when Britain trailed USA in second place with 2:59.13. The splits were as follows: Kriss Akabusi 45.87, Garry Cook 44.74, Todd Bennett 44.17, Phil Brown 44.35. Three years later, at the World Championships in Rome, another British team lowered the continental record to 2:58.86, still in the wake of a victorious US quartet. The latest link in a great British tradition was provided at the 1990 European Championships in Split, when Paul Sanders (45.85), Kriss Akabusi (44.48), John Regis (43.93) and Roger Black (43.96) turned in a remarkable 2:58.22. Especially worthy of note was the split of John Regis, a "pure" sprinter who earlier in the meet had finished third in the 100 m. and first in the 200 m.

Britons finally succeeded in turning the tables on their American rivals: it happened at the 1991 World Championships in Tokyo, when a team consisting of Black, Derek Redmond, Regis and Akabusi won against Andrew Valmon, Quincy Watts, Danny Everett and Antonio Pettigrew. It was an exciting ding-dong battle all the way. The Americans gained a sizable lead in the second leg, thanks to Watts' great 43.4, but lost it in the closing stage when Akabusi, a 400 metre hurdles specialist, nosed out Pettigrew by a hair's breadth. Final times: 2:57.53 and 2:57.57. In subsequent years the Americans resumed their winning ways though. At the 1992 Olympics in Barcelona, a foursome made of Valmon, Watts, Michael Johnson and Steve Lewis broke a 24-year-old record with a scintillating 2:55.74, finishing well ahead of Cuba (2:59.51) and Britain (2:59.73). Unofficial splits for the winners, in the order given above, were: 44.5, 43.1, 44.7 and 43.4. All this despite the fact that Johnson, "with his health still in question, ran a controlled race"! But he was feeling much better a year later at the World Championships in Stuttgart, where he ran the anchor leg in 42.94 (unofficial 200 metre splits: 20.8 and 22.1). Prior to him, Valmon (44.5), Watts (43.6) and Reynolds (43.23) had set the stage for a record performance and the final result was 2:54.29. Kenya was a distant second (2:59.82).

One had to wait till 1996 and the Atlanta Olympics to see the Americans hardly pressed - and Britain was again the challenger. Michael Johnson was not in the race: he was put to rest by a slight muscle injury suffered at the end of his historic 200 metre race (19.32) two days earlier. The picture of the race is reflected in the following set of splits: USA - LaMont Smith 44.62, Alvin Harrison 43.84, Derek Mills 43.66, Anthuan Maybank 43.87 - 2:55.99; Great Britain - Iwan Thomas 44.92, Jamie Baulch 44.19, Mark Richardson 43.62, Roger Black 43.87 - 2:56.60 (European record). An even closer battle followed a year later at the 1997 World Championships in Athens, with the Americans again edging their British "cousins" - 2:56.47 to 2:56.65. Toward the end of the Nineties, however, Johnson gave U.S. teams a helping hand on two important occasions. On 22 July 1998 at Uniondale, N.Y., a team consisting of Jerome Young (44.3), Pettigrew (43.2), Tyree Washington (43.5) and Johnson (43.2) set a new world record of 2:54.20 - an average of 43.55 per man! A year later, at the World Championships in Sevilla, Jerome Davis, Pettigrew, Angelo Taylor and Johnson gave U.S.A. another victory in 2:56.45. On both occasions there was a "new" runner-up, Poland (2:58.00 at Uniondale and 2:58.91 at Sevilla). As at the end of 1999 twelve countries had fielded sub-3 min. relay teams.

WALKS - 20 km. Walkers moving at 15 km.-per-hour

1981 -WCup, Valencia (3 Oct): 1.Canto (Mex) 1:23:52, 2.Wieser (EG) 1:24:12, 3.Pezzatini (Ita) 1:24:24.
1982 - EC, Athens (7 Sep): 1.Marin (Spa) 1:23:43, 2.Pribilinec (CSR) 1:25:55, 3.Blazek (CSR) 1:26:13.
1983 - WC, Helsinki (7 Aug): 1.Canto 1:20:49, 2.Pribilinec 1:20:59, 3.Yevsyukov (USSR) 1:21:08. - WCup, Bergen (24 Sep): 1.Pribilinec 1:19:30, 2.Canto 1:19:41, 3.Solomin (USSR) 1:19:43.
1984 - OG, Los Angeles (3 Aug): 1.Canto 1:23:13, 2.R.González (Mex) 1:23:20, 3.M.Damilano (Ita) 1:23:26.
1985 - WCup, Douglas, Isle of Man (29 Sep): 1.Marin 1:21:42, 2.M.Damilano 1:21:43, 3.Mostovik (USSR) 1:22:01.
1986 - EC, Stuttgart (27 Aug): 1.Pribilinec 1:21:15, 2.M.Damilano 1:21:17, 3.Prieto (Spa) 1:21:36.
1987 - WCup, New York (3 May): 1.C.Mercenario (Mex) 1:19:24, 2.Mostovik 1:19:32, 3.Gorshkov (USSR) 1:20:04. - WC, Rome (30 Aug): 1.M.Damilano 1:20:45, 2.Pribilinec 1:21:07, 3.Marin 1:21:24.
1988 - OG, Seoul (23 Sep): 1.Pribilinec 1:19:57, 2.Weigel (EG) 1:20:00, 3.M.Damilano 1:20:14.
1989 - WCup, Hospitalet (27 May): 1.Kostyukyevich (USSR) 1:20:21, 2.Shchennikov (USSR) 1:20:34, 3.Misyulya (USSR) 1:20:47.
1990 - EC, Split (28 Aug): 1.Blazek 1:22:05, 2.D. Plaza (Spa) 1:22:22, 3.Toutain (Fra) 1:23:22.
1991 - WCup, San José, CA (1 June): 1. Shchennikov (USSR) 1:20:43, 2. Canto (Mex) 1:20:46, 3. Toutain (Fra) 1:20:56; WC, Tokyo (24 Aug): 1. Damilano 1:19:37, 2. Shchennikov 1:19:46, 3. Misyulya (USSR) 1:20:22.
1992 - OG, Barcelona (31 Jul): 1. D. Plaza (Spa) 1:21:45, 2. LeBlanc (Can) 1:22:25, 3. De Benedictis (Ita) 1:23:11.
1993 - WCup, Monterrey, Mex (24 April): 1. D. Garcia (Mex) 1:24:26, 2. Massana (Spa) 1:24:32, 3. Cruz (Mex) 1:24:37; WC, Stuttgart (15 Aug): 1. Massana 1:22:31, 2. De Benedictis 1:23:06, 3. D.Plaza 1:23:18.

1981 / **1999**

1994 - EC, Helsinki (8 Aug): 1. Shchennikov (Russia) 1:18:45, 2. Misyulya (Bye) 1:19:22, 3. Massana 1:20:33.
1995 - WCup, Beijing (29 Apr): 1. Li Zewen (Chi) 1:19:44, 2. Shchennikov 1:19:58, 3. Segura (Mex) 1:20:32; WC, Göteborg (6 Aug): 1. Didoni (Ita) 1:19:59, 2. Massana 1:20:23, 3. Misyulya 1:20:48.
1996 - OG, Atlanta (26 Jul): 1. Pérez (Ecu) 1:20:07, 2. Markov (Rus) 1:20:16, 3. Segura 1:20:23.
1997 - WCup, Podebrady (19 Apr): 1. Pérez 1:18:24, 2.Garcia 1:18:27, 3. Markov (Rus) 1:18:30; WC, Athens (2 Aug): 1. D.Garcia 1:21:43, 2. Shchennikov 1:21:53, 3. Khmyelnitskiy (Bye) 1:22:01.
1998 - EC, Budapest (18 Aug): 1. Markov 1:21:10, 2. Fadejevs (Lat) 1:21:29, 3. Fernández (Spa) 1:21:39.
1999 - WCup, Mézidon-Canon (1 May): 1. Segura 1:20:20, 2. Yu Guohui (Chi) 1:20:21, 3. Andreyev (Rus) 1:20:29; WC, Sevilla (21 Aug): 1. Markov 1:23:34, 2. Pérez 1:24:19, 3. D.Garcia 1:24:31.

The masters of speed walking during the Eighties were Ernesto Canto of Mexico, Maurizio Damilano of Italy and Jozef Pribilinec of Czechoslovakia. The first named (born on 18 October 1959; 1.70 m./59 kg.) won the 20 km. event at the inaugural World Championships and a year later he duplicated his victory at the Los Angeles Olympics. In between these important wins, he had a field day at Fana (Bergen) on 5 May 1984, when he lowered the world track record to 1:18:39.9 - a speed of 15,254 km. per hour! Maurizio Damilano (born at Scarnafigi near Cuneo on 6 April 1957; 1.83 m./70 kg.) remained at or near the top for many years, following his victory at the 1980 Olympics in Moscow.
Like most walkers, he occasionally had a gloomy day e.g. at the 1982 European Championships in Athens, where he was disqualified with less than a mile to go, while in the lead. His happiest day came at the 1987 World Championships in Rome, when he topped the 20,000 m. field again, seven years after his success in Moscow. He tried the 50 km. event as well, chalking up a fast 3:46:51 in 1990. Jozef Pribilinec (born at Kremnica on 6 July 1960; 1.68 m./66 kg.) has been a most consistent performer in recent years, compiling a magnificent record in major competitions. The inevitable flaw occurred in the 1985 IAAF World Race Walking Cup, at the Lugano Trophy in 1985, when he was disqualified after finishing first. .
Such mishaps are of course more frequent at this relatively short distance. Typical in this respect is what happened to Daniel Garcia of Mexico: twice disqualified at the World Championships (1993 and '95), he finally won the title in 1997, and was third in '99.
One of the most consistent performers of the Nineties was Mikhail Shchennikov of Russia (born on 24 December 1967 at Sverdlovsk; 1.82 m./70 kg.). He won medals in several editions of the World Championships and the World Cup but had to be content with lesser placings in the Olympic Games. But he found the way to this most coveted podium when he moved to 50 km. in 1996: in his second race at this distance he won a silver medal at Atlanta. Russia, Mexico, Spain and Italy were the leading powers at the 20 km. distance throughout the last

Maurizio Damilano (Italy), one of the greatest walkers in the 20 Km. event.

decade of the century. The great Maurizio Damilano added one more gold medal to his collection when he won the world championship title at Tokyo in 1991. The world track record at the end of 1999 belonged to Bernardo Segura of Mexico with 1:17:25.6, made on the magic Fana track near Bergen on 7 May 1994.

However, the most sensational event of the Nineties was in all probability the victory of Jefferson Pérez of Ecuador at the 1996 Olympics in Atlanta. His gold was Ecuador's first Olympic medal at any sport. Pérez (born on 1 July 1974 at Cuenca; 1.74 m./59Kg.) was by no means an unknown though, having won at the World Junior Championships in 1992. His success at the Atlanta Games understandably had a tremendous impact in Ecuador. Postal authorities issued a stamp with his picture and a stadium in his native town of Cuenca (at 2600 m. altitude) was named after him. Jefferson himself fulfilled a religious vow by walking from Quito, the capital city, to Cuenca along the Pan-American Freeway, a distance of 459 kilometres over a mountainous route, in 16 days, an average of 28.68 km. per day. In 1997 Pérez showed that his Olympic victory was no fluke by winning the World Cup race at Podebrady, Czech Republic, and taking second at the World Championships in Sevilla.

50 Km.
Iron men galore

1981 - WCup, Valencia (4 Oct): 1.R.González (Mex) 3:48:30, 2.Gauder (EG) 3:52.18, 3.Bellucci (Ita) 3:54:57.
1982 - EC, Athens (10 Sep): 1.Salonen (Fin) 3:55:29, 2.Marin (Spa) 3:59:18, 3.Gustafsson (Swe) 4:01:21.
1983 - WC, Helsinki (12 Aug): 1.Weigel (EG) 3:43:08, 2.Marin 3:46.42, 3.Jung (USSR) 3:49:03. - WCup, Bergen (25 Sep): 1.R.González 3:45:37, 2.Jung 3:48:26, 3.Dorovskikh (USSR) 3:49:47.
1984 - OG, Los Angeles (11 Aug): 1.R.González 3:47:26, 2.Gustafsson 3:53:19, 3.Bellucci 3:53:45.
1985 - WCup, Douglas, Isle of Man (28 Sep): 1.Gauder 3:47:31, 2.Perlov (USSR) 3:49:23, 3.Noack (EG) 3:56:53.
1986 - EC, Stuttgart (31 Aug): 1.Gauder 3:40:55, 2.Ivanyenko (USSR) 3:41:54, 3.Suntsov (USSR) 3:43:38.
1987 - WCup, New York (2 May): 1.Weigel 3:42:26, 2.Gauder 3:42:52, 3.Meisch (EG) 3:43:14. - WC, Rome (5 Sep): 1.Gauder 3:40:53, 2.Weigel 3:41:30, 3.Ivanyenko 3:44:02.
1988 - OG, Seoul (30 Sep): 1.Ivanyenko 3:38:29, 2.Weigel 3:38:56, 3.Gauder 3:39:45.
1989 - WCup, Hospitalet (28 May): 1.Baker (Aus) 3:43:13, 2.Perlov 3:44:12, 3.Vezhel (USSR) 3:44:50.
1990 - EC, Split (31 Aug): 1. Perlov 3:54:36, 2.Gummelt (EG) 3:56:33, 3.Gauder 4:00:48.
1991 - WCup, San José, CA. (2 Jun): 1. Mercenario (Mex) 3:42:03, 2. Baker (Aus) 3:46:36, 3. Weigel (Ger) 3:47:50; WC, Tokyo (31 Aug): 1. Potashov (USSR) 3:53:09, 2. Perlov (USSR) 3:53;09, 3. Gauder (Ger) 3:55:14.
1992 - OG, Barcelona (7 Aug): 1. Perlov 3:50:13, 2. Mercenario 3:52:09, 3. Weigel 3:53:45.
1993 - WCup, Monterrey, Mex. (25 Apr): 1. Mercenario 3:50:28, 2. J.A. Garcia (Spa) 3:52:44, 3. Sánchez (Mex) 3:54:15; WC, Stuttgart (21 Aug): 1. J.A. Garcia 3:41:41, 2. Kononen (Fin) 3:42:02, 3. Spitsin (Rus) 3:42:50.
1994 - EC, Helsinki (13 Aug): 1. Spitsin 3:41:07, 2. Toutain (Fra) 3:43:52, 3. Perricelli (Ita) 3:43:55.
1995 - WCup, Beijing (30 Apr): 1. Zhao Yongshen (Chi) 3:41:20, 2. J.A. Garcia 3:51:54, 3. Kononen 3:42:50; WC, Göteborg (10 Aug): 1. Kononen 3:43:42, 2. Perricelli 3:45:11, 3. Korzeniowski (Pol) 3:45:57.
1996 - OG, Atlanta (2 Aug): 1. Korzeniowski 3:43:30, 2. Shchennikov (Rus) 3:43:46, 3. Massana (Spa) 3:44:19.
1997 - WCup, Podebrady (20 Apr): 1. J.A. Garcia 3:39:54, 2. Ishutkin (Rus) 3:40:12, 3. Kononen 3:41:09; WC, Athens (7 Aug): 1. Korzeniowski 3:44:46, 2. J.A. Garcia 3:44:59, 3. Rodriguez (Mex) 3:48:30.
1998 - EC, Budapest (21 Aug): 1. Korzeniowski 3:43:51, 2. Kononen 3:44:29, 3. Plotnikov (Rus) 3:45:53.
1999 - WCup, Mézidon-Canon (2 May): 1. Koryepanov (Kzk) 3:39:22, 2. Lipiec (Pol) 3:40:08, 3. Matyukhin (Rus) 3:40:13; WC, Sevilla (25 Aug): 1. Skurigin (Rus) 3:44:23, 2. Brugnetti (Ita) 3:47:54, 3. Matyukhin 3:48:18.

Mexican veteran Raúl González (born on 29 February 1952; 1.75 m./65 kg.) had his long delayed rendezvous with Olympic glory at Los Angeles in 1984, when at the age of thirty-two he won silver in the 20 km., then gold in the 50 km. His world track record of 3:41:38.4 from 1979 was still unmatched at the end of the decade. Outstanding among the iron men of recent years in the long walk were two East Germans, Hartwig Gauder and Ronald Weigel. The former (born at Vaihingen on 10

1981
1999

Mikhail Shchennikov (Russia) was at his best in the 20 Km. walk but also managed to win an Olympic silver medal when he moved to the 50 Km. event in 1996.

November 1954; 1.86 m./70 kg.) was actually born in West Germany, but his family moved to the East when he was five.

This architectural student belongs to that very select group of champions who have won World, Olympic and European titles, plus his good share of honours in the Lugano Trophy. Weigel (born at Hildburghausen on 8 August 1959; 1.76 m./61 kg.), a student of journalism, won gold in the 50 km. at the 1983 World Championships and two silver medals, in 20 and 50 km., at the 1988 Olympics. Commenting on his Seoul race in the longer event, he said: "I had problems with my legs. When I tried to go faster, I got two red cards.I had to slow down and be content with second". The race was won by Vyacheslav Ivanyenko, who thereby notched the first Olympic gold medal for USSR in the history of the event.

Something unusual occurred at the 1991 World Championships in Tokyo, the characters in the play being two Russians, Aleksandr Potashov and Andrey Perlov. Earlier in the year, in the World Cup race at San José, California, both had been disqualified. In Tokyo they reached the closing stage with a safe margin vis-à-vis their nearest pursuer, so they decided it would be better to finish together rather than take chances in trying to kill each other. So they crossed the line, arms around each other, hoping for a .... tie. But officials proved unsympathetic and eventually decided that Potashov was first and Perlov second, as per video evidence. The two vowed to cut their medals in half as two Japanese vaulters, Shuhei Nishida and Sueo Oe, had done (for second and third) at the 1936 Olympics in Berlin. Perlov did himself justice in the most proper sense by winning a gold medal at the Barcelona Games a year later. Russia, Mexico and Spain continued to be the major powers here too, but two other countries also had their share: Poland with Robert Korzeniowski (born on 30 July 1968 at Lubaczów; 1.68 m./60Kg.), who won at the 1996 Olympics in Atlanta and at the 1997 World Championships in Athens; and Finland with Valentin Kononen (born on 7 March 1969 at Helsinki; 1.81 m./68 Kg), who won at the 1995 World Championships in Göteborg. A walker of lesser renown, Thierry Toutain of France, set a world track record of 3:40:57.9 at Héricourt on 29 September 1996. On the road the best time on record at the end of the Nineties belonged to the above-mentioned Andrey Perlov with a time of 3:37:41, made at Leningrad on 5 August 1989.

1900
1940

FROM EARLY WHISPERS TO THE MONTECARLO "PREMIÈRE"

The Vassar pioneers: "Nimble, supple, vivacious girls run and jump"

Historians seem generally inclined to believe that women's athletics originated a long long time ago, though perhaps in forms rather different from those prevailing in the sport of our days. It is a known fact that in Egypt women engaged in gymnastics and acrobatics since the early days of the Middle Kingdom, about 2000 B.C. In ancient Greece married women were not allowed to attend the celebrated men's games, under pain of punishment that extended to the death penalty. The veto did not apply to unmarried girls though. Yet, contrary to a widespread "lieu commun", women had athletic competitions of their own, held at Olympia every four years, entirely separate from the men's games. The festival was in honour of Hera, wife of Zeus, and was in fact named Heraia. The girls were divided into three age groups and ran over a distance of 500 Olympic feet, equal to 160.22 m. The girls ran with their hair unbound, and wearing a short "chiton" which left their right shoulder uncovered to the breast. Above all this there was of course the myth of Atalanta, the swift-footed huntress who was often taken as a symbol of females engaged in sports activities. In ancient times, however, even illustrious men had mental reservations about the participation of women in sports. Unfortunately, this prejudice subsisted even in the early days of modern athletics. It was vaguely explained with the "differences" between the sexes, but in reality it stemmed from the role traditionally reserved to women in the social life of most if not all civilizations, a role which made it difficult for them to engage in sport as independent individuals. There are, however, Teutonic legends which occasionally refer to women's sports. British historians refer to two handicap races in a meeting held in Dublin in 1891 as "the first of known timed track performances". What is generally considered as the earliest organized women's meet of modern times took place at Vassar College, USA, on 9 November 1895, when a group of "nimble, supple and vivacious girls" engaged in running and jumping events, under unfavourable weather conditions. Vassar College, a private school for women founded in 1861 by Matthew Vassar, was located at Poughkeepsie in the state of New York. Vassar's first "Field Day" for women was what we would now describe as an exclusive affair. Said a paper of the time: "Every effort was made to have the programme carried through without publicity. The oval field is admirably adapted to secure the girls from undesired spectators, being surrounded by a thick evergreen hedge, about 12 feet (3.65 m.) high. Orders were given to exclude reporters and also all masculine visitors". In the vivid description of "The Sun" the girls wore "divided skirts and white sweaters, loose enough to disguise every curve of the body, but which did not hide the broad, well-developed shoulders of the athletes. Black stockings and rubber-soled canvas shoes without heels completed the costumes. The young women wore no hats. They scorned mackintoshes and umbrellas, although by 11

A "Great illustration of physical culture" anno 1877, announcing the feat of an American "Lady Pedestrienne".

a.m. the rain settled into a downpour". There were five events on the programme, plus a basketball competition. Under the careful supervision of women officials, the following marks were recorded: - 100 y. Miss Vassar (a niece of the college's founder) 16.0 (after a 15 1/4 heat); long jump, Miss Baker 3.48; 120 y. Hurdles, Miss Thallon 25.0 (after a 24 3/4 heat); high jump, Miss Brownell 1.22; 220 y. Miss Haight 36 1/4. The second Vassar "Field Day", held early in 1896, yielded partially better results, e.g. 3.58 by Miss Booth in the long jump, 22 1/2 by Miss Barbour in the 120 y. hurdles and 15.0 by Miss Wilkinson in the 100 y. On that occasion college boys had "a peep at the Field Day fun". By 1903 the march of progress was such that one Agnes Wood managed 30 2/5 in the 220 y. and 1.276 in the high jump. The revivers of the modern Olympics did not have progressive views on the subject of women participating in sports events, Pierre de Coubertin himself being no exception. Yet, in addition to USA, other English speaking countries such as Britain, Australia, New Zealand and South Africa held women's meets since the first decade of the XX century. However, the real boost came from France, more exactly from a fervent "suffragette" named Alice Milliat, who in 1917 founded the "Fédération Féminine Sportive de France". Two years later, her request to have women events included in the Olympic programme was refused by the IOC. The tenacious French pioneer and her associates went ahead by themselves and decided to organize the first multi-national women's meet. This was held in the Principauté de Monaco from 24 to 31 March 1921 and was essentially an Anglo-French festival. The programme included eleven events. Mary Lines of England, aged 27 but reportedly in her first year of competition, had the lion's share. She won the 60 m. in 8 1/5, the 250 m. in 36 3/5, the long jump at 4.70 and anchored two victorious British relay teams. Just for good measure, she also placed second in the 800 m.! Curiously enough, the programme included shot put and javelin both hands. Later in 1921, Madame Milliat and her associates founded the "Fédération Sportive Féminine Internationale" (FSFI). Six countries were represented: France, Britain, Czechoslovakia, Italy, Spain and USA. Madame Milliat was elected President of the newly born organization, which held the inugural Women's World Games at Stade Pershing, Paris, on 20 August 1922. The whole programme, eleven events (partly with preliminary rounds), was completed in one day. The meet was witnessed by 20,000 spectators! The winners:
- 60 m. Marie Mejzliková (Czechoslovakia) 7 3/5;

100 y. Nora Callebout (GB) 12.0 (Mejzliková did 11 2/5, a new world record, in a heat); 300 m. Mary Lines (GB) 44 4/5 (Alice Cast, GB, did 44.0 in a heat); 1000 m. Lucie Bréard (Fra) 3:12.0; 4x110 y. Relay, Great Britain 51 4/5; 100 y. hurdles, Camille Sabie (USA) 14 2/5; high jump, Hilda Hatt (GB) 1.46; long jump, Mary Lines 5.06; Standing long jump, Sabie 2.485; shot put, both-hands, Lucille Godbold (USA) 20.22; javelin, both-hands, Francesca Pianzola (Switzerland) 43.24.

The FSFI held on and organized three more editions of the World Games: Göteborg (1926), Prague (1930) and London (1934), by which time the number of countries involved was up to nineteen. The programme in London consisted of 12 events, including a pentathlon. In the meantime, however, the ostracism of the powers that be of men's sports had come to a predictable and just end: in 1926 the CIO finally took notice of the serious purposes that animated Madame Milliat and her associates and voted (12 to 5) to include women's events in the Olympics. The occasion for this historic event were the Games of 1928 in Amsterdam. The women's programme was thin though, consisting of only five events: 100 and 800 m., high jump, discus and 4x100 m. relay. It must be said that this début was saluted with mixed feelings by the press in general, then a virtual monopoly of the male sex. There were witty remarks too, e.g. by a Swedish paper which carried a picture showing a woman athlete in training, with the caption: "Eva tränar för A'dam" (Eve training for A'dam, an obvious contraction of Amsterdam). The Amsterdam events yielded three new world records: 2:16 4/5 in the 800 m. by Lina Radke-Batschauer of Germany, 39.62 in the discus by Halina Konopacka of Poland, and 48 2/5 by Canada in the 4x100 m. relay. The remaining titles went to Elizabeth Robinson of USA (12 1/5 in the 100 m.) and Ethel Catherwood of Canada (1.59 in the high jump). The last-named was to marry Harold Osborn of USA, he too a high jump (and decathlon) champion in the 1924 Olympics. The breach opened at Amsterdam inevitably led to a happy conclusion, which came about in 1936, when the FSFI merged with the IAAF, thus ensuring that men's and women's athletics would at last have one and the same governing body. The early days of women's athletics were not a bed of roses though. One serious problem was gender identity. The lack of

1900
1940

One of the earliest "Field Days" for women at Vassar College circa 1900. A hurdle race.

sex tests made it possible for people posing as women to chalk up sensational records, the most striking examples being a 2:12 4/5 for the 800 m. by Zdenka Koubková of Czechoslovakia at the 1934 World Games in London and a 1.70 high jump by Dora Ratjen of Germany at the 1938 European Championships. Following protests from delegations representing other competitors in these events, both were subjected to sex controls and found to be ineligible for women's sport. In connection with Ratjen's disqualification by the IAAF, the German weekly "Der Leichtathlet" published a communiqué from the main body of German sport which said: "Severe instructions have been imparted to make sure that no similar cases will henceforth occur in National-socialist Germany". Notwithstanding such (relatively few) incidents, international competitions held in the years between the two World Wars certainly provided a notable impetus for the development of women's athletics. I will now try to single out the outstanding performers of that period in the various branches of the sport. In the sprints the no.1 star was a tall, sturdy American, Helen Stephens (born at Fulton, Missouri, on 3 February 1918; 1.82 m./70 kg.). In only three years of track activity she ran over 100 races and was never beaten. The "Missouri Tornado" had unratified times of 10.4 in the 100 y. (Toronto, 1935), 11.5 in the 100 m. (Memphis and Dresden, both in 1936) and 23.2 in the 220 y. straightaway (Toronto, 1935). At the Berlin Olympics she won the 100 m., anchored the victorious US team in the 4x100 m. relay -

Finish of a sprint race at Vassar College.

and was ninth in the discus. In the individual sprint race she beat the redoubtable Stanislawa Walasiewicz of Poland, 11.5 to 11.7 (wind-aided). Walesiewicz (born at Wierzchownia on 3 April 1911; 1.62 m./54 kg.) was unparalleled in terms of athletic longevity. Erich Kamper, a noted track writer and historian, recently discovered that at birth she was actually named Stefania, although the athletics world always knew her as Stanislawa. She continued to represent her native country in international competition even after she emigrated to USA and took the name Stella Walsh. Her masculine appearance gave rise to perplexity in some quarters. Unfortunately, suspicions were confirmed in 1980, when she was shot dead while accidentally involved in a robbery outside a grocery store. An autopsy revealed a situation certainly not compatible with participation in women's sports. This and other similar cases of physical ambiguity were likely to make the identification of sex difficult in the early days of the century, when medical knowledge was far from today's sophisticated levels. At any rate, it is difficult for a track observer to adequately value Walasiewicz's results in the light of women's athletics. Her best official times were 11.6 in the 100 m. (Berlin, 1937) and 23.6 in the 200 m. (Warsaw, 1935). The latter was made on a course which upon remeasurement turned out to be 12 cm. short, a truly insignificant amount in a 200 m. race timed in tenths of a second. She also had an unratified 6.12 in the long jump (Cleveland, 1939).

Distance running was long regarded as taboo for women. But here too Madame Milliat and her followers acted as ice breakers. The meet held at Monaco in 1921 included an 800 m. race, which was won by Lucie Bréard of France in 2:30 1/5. At the inaugural Women's World Games (1922) Bréard won the 1000 m. in 3:12.0. In subsequent editions times became faster and faster, till the above-mentioned 2:12 4/5 by Koubkova in London (1934). In view of the subsequent disqualification of the Czech runner, victory should revert to Martha Wretman of Sweden, second in a time estimated as 2:13 4/5. Curiously enough, in these World Games there was no 400 m. event. At the Amsterdam Olympics (1928) the 800 m. gave rise to heated controversy, partly due to an unwise time schedule which called for heats and final to be held on concecutive days. At the end of the decisive race some competitors were clearly exhausted. Competent observers valued their condition as "no worse" than what sometimes occurred to men after similar efforts, but conservatives within the IOC and the IAAF obviously thought differently and decided that the 800 m. would no longer be part of the women's programme. (The event

1900-1940

would reappear in 1960 ...). Winner of the Amsterdam race was Lina Radke-Batschauer of Germany in 2:16 4/5, a new world record. Kinue Hitomi, a Japanese all-rounder, was second in 2:17 3/5. The German looked surprisingly fresh at the end of the gruelling race. In pre-Olympic weeks she had been training with her husband on the beach at Zandvoort, Northern Holland. By 1940 the country with the highest standard in the 400 and 800 m. was USSR, then not a member of the IAAF. At the longer distance the best time was 2:15.3 by Yevdokiya Vasilyeva (1938) and Kseniya Shilo (1940). In the early days of women's athletics the paucity of competition made it relatively easy for the best talents to shine in more than one event. Typical in this respect was Mildred Didrikson of USA (born at Port Arthur, Texas, on 26 June 1911; 1.69 m./46 kg.). "Babe", as she was called, had a rather short career in athletics, yet conquered virtually all there was to conquer. At the 1932 AAU Championships, which also served as Olympic Tryouts, she competed in eight events in the space of two-and-one-half hours! She won 80 m. hurdles, shot, javelin and baseball throw, tied for first in the high jump with Jean Shiley, was fourth in the discus and failed to make the final in the 100 m. and the 220 y. She won the team title for Employers' Casualty AA of Dallas all by herself! At the Los Angeles Olympics she won the javelin with 43.86, the 80 m. hurdles in 11.7, a new world record, and was second to Jean Shiley in the high jump. In the last two events she probably had a mixture of good and bad luck. In the hurdles race her winning margin over Evelyne Hall (also timed in 11.7) was at best infinitesimal. Malicious observers went so far as to say that with Babe being so famous it was hard for the judges to rule against her. In the high jump, Babe and Shiley cleared 1.65 for a new world record, then failed at 1.68. In a jump-off at 1.67, both girls cleared first time. At that stage, however, the judges declared Didrikson's jump illegal because she dived over the bar head first, which was against the rule in those days. She told the judges she had been using the same style all afternoon, but they retorted: "If you were diving before, we didn't see it. We just saw it this time". Didrikson,, who married "pro" wrestler George Zaharias in 1938, was until then the only woman to have won Olympic medals on the track as well as on the field. She excelled in several other sports, notably including golf, in which she won the US Open title three times, the last one in the comeback of her life, after undergoing surgery for cancer. She died in 1956, at the age of forty-five.

The only hurdle event in use as of 1940 was the 80 m., with eight hurdles, 2 ft 6 in. (76.2 cm) high. Outstanding among early champions was Ruth Engelhard of Germany, who won the 1934 world title in 11.6. This time was equalled in a semi-final of the Berlin Olympics in 1936 by Trebisonda ("Ondina") Valla of Italy, who went on to win the final the next day. This was a highly competitive race, with the first four sharing the same time, 11.7. The "Zielzeitkamera", used as back-up evidence to

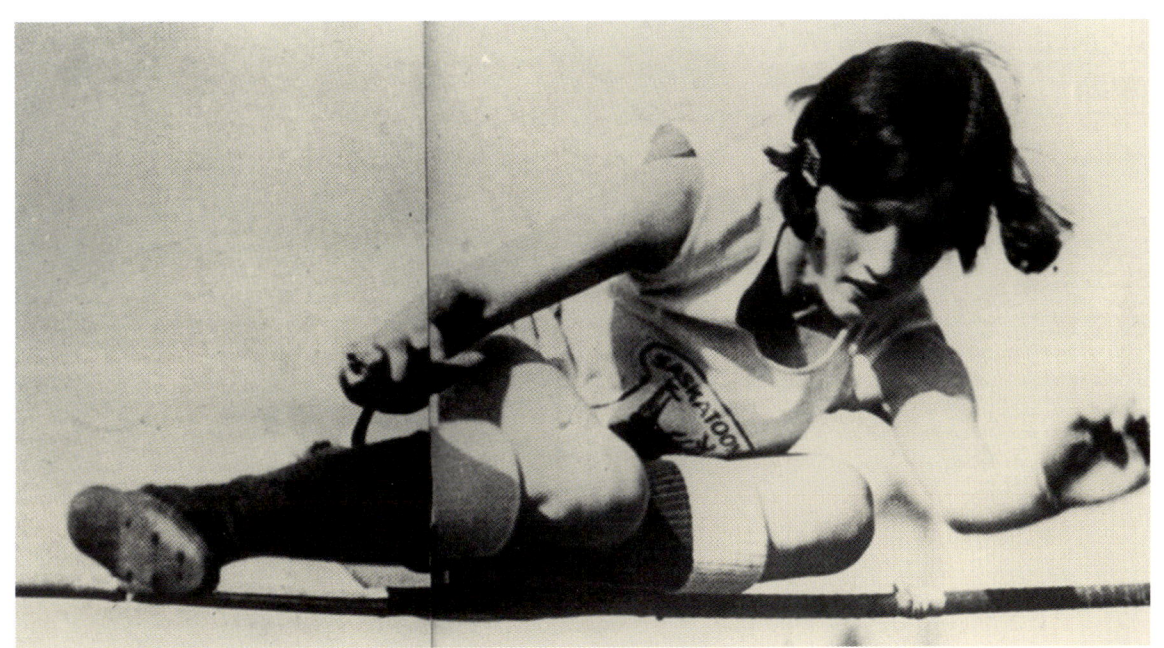

Ethel Catherwood (Canada), know as "the Saskatoon Lily", became an Olympic high jump champion at 18 years of age.

Gisela Mauermayer (Germany), world record holder in shot and discus in the Thirties.

verify placings, gave the following times: - 1.Valla 11.748, 2.Anni Steuer (Germany) 11.809, 3.Elizabeth Taylor (Canada) 11.811, 4.Claudia Testoni (Italy) 11.818. Testoni made further progress in subsequent years. In 1938 she won the European title and the following year she lowered the world record to 11.3, a time she achieved on two occasions (Garmisch-Partenkirchen and Dresden), thrashing the leading Germans. Still in 1939, Testoni did 12.0 for the 100 m. flat, which time ranked her equal third in the World Year List! Another versatile performer was Kinue Hitomi of Japan (born on 1 January 1908), who in the late Twenties held world records for 100 m. (12.2), 200 m. (24.7, on a straight course), 400 m. (59.0) and long jump (5.98). At the Amsterdam Olympics (1928) a restricted programme obliged her to confine her efforts to 100 and ..800 m. She failed to make the final in the former, but finished second in the latter. Hitomi won no less than eight medals in two editions of the World Games (1926 and 1930) in such events as 60 m., 100 y., running and standing long jump, discus, javelin and pentathlon. During a Japan vs Germany dual meet at Keijo (now Seoul) in 1929 she had a wind-aided long jump of 6.075. She died in 1931, aged twenty-three. First to be credited with an official 6-metre-plus mark in the long jump was Christel Schulz of Germany, who did 6.12 in the ISTAF meet at Berlin in 1939, winning from Fanny Koen of Holland (5.97), about whom more will be said later. Schulz was only eighteen at the time and could point to an amazing progress: her best the year before was

Age riddles

Even in this time and age track statisticians are sometimes confronted with controversial information about the age of certain athletes, particularly those born in Africa. Age riddles were of course met even more frequently in days long gone by. Mildred "Babe" Didrikson, regarded by many as the greatest sportswoman America has ever had (25 lines of text in the "Encyclopaedia Britannica", 1963 edition), appears to be a case in point. On entry lists of the 1932 Olympics in Los Angeles (where she won two golds and a silver) she apparently gave her birthyear as 1913.
Later on, other sources gave the year as 1914, a version accepted by "Britannica" itself and to be found also on a Texas state historical marker near her gravesite. In his excellent book "Track's Greatest Women", Jon Hendershott reveals that Didrikson was actually born on 26 June 1911, as per three sources: 1) The headstone above her grave; 2) a baptismal certificate, and 3) a family Bible. He also found that her family name was Didriksen (she was the daughter of Norwegian immigrants). but "Babe", as a fervent patriot, chose to write it as Didrikson. Minor details, of course, which do not change history. They just reveal certain tendencies sometimes prevailing in human nature.

1900
1940

Yevdokiya Vasilyeva (USSR), one of the pioneers in women's distance running. Set unofficial world records for 800, 1000, 1500 and 2000 metres.

5.41! In later years, under the restricted programme imposed by wartime conditions, she continued to do well (6.04 in 1942) but never again rose to her 1939 heights. The outstanding figure in the throwing events was another German, Gisela Mauermayer (born at Munich on 24 November 1913; 1.72 m./70 kg.), who held the world record in the shot (14.38 at Warsaw in 1934), the discus (48.31 at Berlin in '36) and the pentathlon (418 pts. at Stuttgart in '38, under German Table then in use; equal to 4391 pts. under 1954 IAAF Table). At the Berlin Olympics (1936) the programme included only one of these events, the discus, which Mauermayer won at 47.63. At the outbreak of World War II, however, USSR could claim a better discus record for Nina Dumbadze (born at Tbilisi on 23 January 1919; 1.78 m./82 kg.), a plump Georgian who in 1939 did 49.11 at Moscow, then 49.54 in her native town of Tbilisi, marks which could not be submitted to the IAAF, since USSR was not affiliated to the international body. However, the powerful Dumbadze successfully defied the red tape of bureaucracy by staying in the ring till 1945 (when USSR finally joined the IAAF) and after, as will be recounted in another chapter. At the end of 1940 the world record for the javelin throw was held by Nan Gindele of USA, who had done 46.74 in a pre-Olympic meet at Chicago in 1932. This girl placed no higher than fifth at the Los Angeles Games. In 1938 a better throw, 47.80, was achieved by Erika Matthes of Germany, but this mark was not put forward for ratification, officially because of a "slight following wind" but actually because of doubtful gender status. In the domain of multi-event competitions the earliest experiments were made with a pentathlon, a two-day affair which consisted of the following events: first day - shot put, long jump; second day - 100 m., high jump, javelin. The above-mentioned record score by Mauermayer (418 pts., German Table) was made with the following marks: 13.07 (shot), 5.62 (long jump), 12.4 (100 m.), 1.56 (high jump) and 36.90 (javelin). Germany, the undisputed no. 1 power in women's athletics at the outbreak of World War II, also held the world record for the 4x100 m. relay: 46.4, made in a heat at the Berlin Olympics (1936) by Emmy Albus, Käthe Krauss, Marie Dollinger and Ilse Dörffeldt.

In the final the Germans were leading by a clear margin when they missed connection on the last change and dropped the baton. The two unlucky girls were in tears and the huge crowd was silent when Helen Stephens brought USA to victory in 46.9. A rematch between the two teams took place at Wuppertal a few days later. The German girls won at the end of a big fight, 46.6 to 46.7.

1941 1970

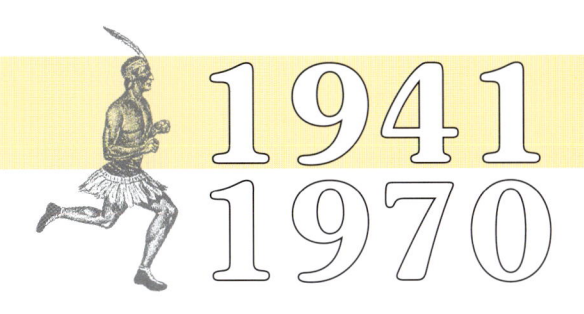

THE FIRST QUEEN COMES FROM HOLLAND

SPRINTS - Fanny et al.

Francina ("Fanny") Blankers née Koen (born in Amsterdam on 26 April 1918; 1.75 m./63 kg.) was the first "queen" of modern athletics in a truly international perspective. Through her smashing victories, her many records and, last but not least, her unassuming behaviour, she put women's athletics in a new dimension.

A most versatile talent, she emerged as a teen-ager, in 1935, with a 2:29.0 in the 800 m., her first national record. At the Berlin Olympics (1936) young Fanny was sixth in the high jump and contributed to Holland's fifth place in the sprint relay. She achieved her first world record at Amsterdam in 1938: 11.0 in the 100 y., a record tying effort.

In 1940 she married her coach Jan Blankers, a former triple jumper of international calibre (14.69 in winning the 1933 AAA title in London). The following year, Jan Jr. was born. Mummy stayed away from track only the minimum necessary and in 1942, still at Amsterdam, she tied Testoni's world record for the 80 m. hurdles (11.3). In 1943 she conquered two more global marks, with 1.71 in the high jump at Amsterdam and 6.25 in the long jump at Leiden. In 1946, shortly after the birth of her second child - a daughter named Fanny - she was bold enough to compete in four events at the European Championships in Oslo, and good enough to win two gold medals, in the 80 m. hurdles and the sprint relay. She earned worldwide fame at the 1948 Olympics in London, where she won four golds: 100

The incomparable Fanny Blankers-Koen (Holland), as a runaway winner in the 200 metres at the London Olympics (1948).

363

m. (11.9), 200 m. (24.4), 80 m. hurdles (11.2) and the 4x100 m. relay (47.5), all this at the age of thirty. Hailed in the international press as a female version of Owens (who had won the same number of gold medals twelve years earlier in Berlin), she was treated to a large parade upon her return to Amsterdam. Mildly bemused, she kept saying: "All I did was win some foot races". She won a "few" more in the years that followed. Between 1938 and 1951 she collected world records in seven events. In addition to those already mentioned, she had the following others: 10.8 in the 100 y. (Amsterdam, 1948), 24.2 in the 220 y. (Brescia, '50), 11.0 in the 80 m. hurdles (Amsterdam, '48) and 4691 pts. in the pentathlon (Amsterdam, '51). In three editions of the European Championships (1938, '46 and '50) she collected eight medals, including five golds. Australia had some superlative athletes in the early Fifties. Marjorie Jackson won 100 and 200 m. (11.5 and 23.7) at the 1952 Olympics in Helsinki and Betty Cuthbert did likewise four years later in Melbourne. The blonde Cuthbert (born at Merrylands, near Sydney, on 20 April 1938; 1.69 m./57 kg.), then eighteen, brought the huge home crowd to its feet, first with her victories in the individual events (11.5 and 23.4), then by anchoring the victorious Australian 4x100 m. relay team in world record time (44.5). After some less rewarding years, she made history again at Tokyo in 1964, when she won the first-ever Olympic 400 m. title in 52.0. Shirley Strickland de la Hunty (born at Guildford, Western Australia, on 18 July 1925) collected seven Olympic medals, with gold in the 80 m. hurdles twice (1952 and '56) and in the sprint relay ('56). It should be added that in the 200 m. of the London Games of 1948 she should have been placed third and not fourth, a mistake revealed many years later when a photo finish print was finally discovered. This would raise her medal tally to eight.

Wilma Rudolph (USA), who won three gold medals at the 1960 Olympics in Rome.

During the Rome Olympics (1960) the world of sports was moved to enthusiasm by Wilma Rudolph of USA (born at Clarksville, Tennessee, on 23 June 1940; 1.81 m./60 kg.), a sprinter who combined speed and grace to an extraordinary degree. The 20th of 22 children born into an underprivileged family, Wilma contracted paralysis in her left leg as an infant and was unable to walk normally until she was ten. She first tried sprinting two years later and in 1956 she had her first taste of the Olympics, at the tender age of sixteen! Eliminated in the prelims of the 200 m., she won a bronze medal in the 4x100 m. relay. In Rome, four years later, she was at her glorious best. She won both sprints as she pleased, with a wind-aided 11.0 in the 100 m. and 24.0 in the 200 m., then anchored the US sprint relay to victory in 44.5 (after lowering the world record to 44.4 in a heat). She held the global records for both metric sprints with times of 11.2 (Stuttgart, 1961) and 22.9 (Corpus Christi, Texas, '60). She left the arena at twenty-two, even earlier than Jesse Owens. She was a cool competitor and as such she was called "The great frozen face". Wilma's likeness stands in Madame Tussaud's Wax Museum in London. Not so famous but still a two-time winner of the 100 m. in the Olympics - an exploit until then unmatched by either women or men - was another American, Wyomia Tyus (born at Griffin, Georgia on 29 August 1945; 1.70 m./61 kg.). At the Tokyo Olympics (1964) this sprightly speedster equalled Rudolph's world record in a quarter-final of the 100 m. (11.2), then won the final in 11.4 (adverse wind, 1.3 m/s), beating Edith McGuire of USA and Ewa Klobukowska of Poland. (The last named was to be declared ineligible for women's competitions in 1967). Tyus, then 19, also won a silver medal in the sprint relay, behind a Polish team anchored by Klobukowska. Four years later, at Mexico City, Tyus took advantage of the rarefied atmosphere to set a new world record of 11 flat (auto-time 11.08) in successfully defending her crown (aiding wind, 1.2 m/s). In this race she beat another American, Barbara Ferrell, as well as Poland's Irena Szewinska. Tyus won the third and last gold of her career in anchoring the US sprint relay team to a new world record of 42.8 (auto-time, 42.88). Irena Szewinska née Kirszenstein (born at Leningrad of Polish parents on 24 May 1946; 1.76 m./63 kg.) has excellent credentials to be rated among the greatest athletes of our time, if not the greatest. She participated in five editions of the Olympics (Tokyo '64 through Moscow '80) and won seven medals, including three golds. At Tokyo, aged 18, she astounded experts by finishing second in the 200 m. in 23.1, a European record, and in the long jump, with 6.60, a Polish record. She crowned her sensational début with a victory in the 4x100 m. relay. She thus revealed from the beginning what was to be her main trait over the years: a unique ability to excel herself under pressure. At the Mexico Games (1968) she won the 200 m. with a new world record, 22.5 (auto-time 22.58), aided by a maximum permissible wind of 2.0 m/s. Prior to that she had placed third in the 100 m. On Christmas Day 1967 she had married Janusz Szewinski. Early in 1970 they had a son, Andrzej. Irena's feats in the Seventies obviously belong in the next chapter. A great star, especially in the years 1969-70, was Chi Cheng (born at Hsinchu on 15 March 1944; 1.72 m./62 kg.), a charming Chinese from Taiwan who must rate as the greatest Asian athlete seen so far in the second half of the century. At the Mexico Olympics (1968) she won a bronze medal in the 80 m. hurdles and placed seventh in the 100 m. flat. In the two following seasons she won 153 out of her 154 competitions, losing only to Barbara Ferrell at 100 y. in a close and disputed decision. Her range covered flat events up to and including 440 y., hurdles, long jump and relays. She set Asian records galore and made the IAAF world record book in all sprint and hurdle events, her best being as follows (all in 1970): 10.0 in the 100 yards at Portland, 11.0 in the 100 m. at Vienna, 22.4 in the 200 m. and 12.8 in the 100 m. hurdles, both at Munich on the same day. This wonderful athlete was advised by her husband-coach Vince Reel of USA, a good low hurdler in the days of Jesse Owens. In subsequent years Chi's career was severely curtailed by injuries. It should be noted that in 1969 the 100 m. had replaced the 80 m. in the hurdles department. The new event comprised ten flights of 2 ft. 9 in. (84 cm.) hurdles.

MIDDLE DISTANCES - Rome reopens Olympic tale

The 800 m. was included in the programme of the European Championships at Bern in 1954, the earliest winner being Nina Otkalenko of USSR (2:08.8). The two-lap event reappeared in the Olympics at Rome in 1960, thirty-two years after the widely discussed Amsterdam opener. (Strangely enough, the 400 m. was to remain on the waiting list till 1964). The Rome event was won by Lyudmila Shevtsova née Lisyenko, a 22-year-old Russian who did 2:04.3, matching her own world record, set in Moscow earlier in the season. The Russians also acted as ice-breakers in the 400 m., their best performer being the nimble Maria Itkina, who did 53.6 at Moscow in 1957 and 53.4 at the European Championships in

1962. By the time the event appeared in the Olympics, in 1964, victory went to a "pure" sprinter, Betty Cuthbert of Australia, as related above.

More or less at that time Asia had a great but somewhat mysterious performer in Shin Geum Dan of North Korea, who was credited with several world records, only one of which made the IAAF book, 51.9 in the 400 m. (Pyongyang, 1962). In 1963 she did 1:59.1 (800 m.) and 51.4 (400 m.) on consecutive days at Djakarta, but the meet (GANEFO = Games of the new emerging forces) was not recognized by the IAAF. Even her ultimate bests, 51.2 and 1:58.0, both at Pyongyang in 1964, remained unratified.

One of the most dramatic races of those years was the 400 m. event at the 1969 European Championships in Athens, where two supple French women, Nicole Duclos and Colette Besson, battled all the way to finish inches apart in that order, both with a new world record of 51.7. The auto-timer saw a slight difference though: Duclos 51.72, Besson 51.74. The latter had struck gold at the Mexico Olympics the year before (52.0), in a close contest with Lillian Board of Britain, a charming athlete who was to die in 1970, at the age of twenty-two. At the end of 1970 the world record for the one-lap event belonged to Marilyn Neufville of Jamaica: 51.0 (actually 51.02) in the Commonwealth Games of that year at Edinburgh. This record was made with grossly unequal halves: 23.8 and 27.2. By the same time the global mark for the 800 m. was 2:00.5 by Vera Nikolic of Yugoslavia (London, 1968).

LONG DISTANCES - Toward new frontiers

Toward the end of the Sixties there was a growing number of women athletes who had enough staying power to endure prolonged efforts in running. Outstanding among these was Paola Cacchi née Pigni (born at Milan on 30 December 1945; 1.70 m./63 kg.). She started as a medium class sprinter, then moved up gradually toward the longer distances. In 1969 she broke the world's 1500 m. record with 4:12.4, outpacing Maria Gommers of Holland in a hot test at Milan.

In 1973, at Viareggio, she achieved the first sub-4:30 mile with a time of 4:29.5. A keen student of problems connected with distance running, she also operated in partly unexplored ground, chalking up best-on-record performances such as 9:09.2 for 3000 m. (Formia, 1972) and 15:53.6 for 5000 m. (Milan, '69), distances until then not included in the IAAF record book. She even tried the marathon. In this respect, however, one should perhaps remember the old adage: "There is nothing really new under the sun".

As early as in 1896 there were unconfirmed reports that a Greek woman named Melpomene took part in the marathon of the inaugural Olympics and finished in about 4:30.

Some sources, however, are inclined to regard this merely as a piece of "modern" mythology.

Going down to facts, in 1926 a British runner named Violet Piercy covered the classic Polytechnic

Boston: clandestine passengers on board

Modern athletics faithfully reflects the tendencies of ancient Greece in at least one important detail, namely in keeping women's events separate from those of the other sex. This "rule" is still in force in track and field events.

The first step toward the removal of this restriction must be credited to the marathon world. It happened in the Boston marathon of 1966, when Roberta Gibb managed to join the group of male runners as an uninvited guest and finished the race in 3:21:40 - an estimated time, since she did not figure among official entries. She did it again the following year, with another woman following in her footsteps - Kathrine Switzer.

The former went on more or less undisturbed and finished in 3:27:17, while the latter, listed on the registration sheet as K. Switzer and given entry number 261, did not appear for the pre-race physical examination and therefore entered as a "clandestine passenger". But she was soon spotted as an "anomalous fish" by one of the race officials.

The man tried to push her to the side of the road and out of the race. To Kathrine's rescue there came her boyfriend, who was more effective in pushing the official out of the way. Switzer finished with an estimated time of 4:20:02. The official view was that international rules barred "mixed" races. It was at any rate a case of "alea jacta est", in the sense that a decisive step had been taken. This widely publicized episode opened the way to "mixed" marathon races, at Boston and in other parts of the world. Switzer, after earning distinction as a marathon runner (2:51:37 at Boston in 1975), inevitably and justly became a zealous promoter of long distance races for women.

Harriers' marathon course in 3:40:22, most probably in a solo time trial. The best-on-record time at the end of 1970 was 3:02:53, achieved early that year on a standard course at Seaside, Oregon, by a 16-year-old American, Caroline Walker.

Getting back to track events, the world records at the end of 1970 were 4:10.7 for 1500 m. by Jaroslava Jehlicková of Czechoslovakia (1969 European Championships, Athens) and 4:36.8 for the mile by Maria Gommers of Holland at Leicester, also in '69.

1941
1970

Grete Waitz (Norway), centre, competing in a "mixed" marathon race.

HURDLES - Longer course, higher hurdles

The last world record holder for the 80 m. hurdles was Vyera Korsakova of USSR: 10.2 at Riga in 1968. She was only 1.64 m. tall, a height which did not represent a handicap for such a short race, run over 76 cm. hurdles. In earlier years USSR had a more distinguished performer in Irina Press (born at Kharkov on 10 March 1939; 1.68 m./65 kg.), the younger of two famous sisters and certainly one of the most versatile talents seen up to that time. She won the 80 m. hurdles twice in the Olympics (1960 and '64) and lowered the world record to 10.3 (1965). She retired shortly before the 1966 European Championships in Budapest, officially on account of a knee injury. Some Western reporters suspected a connection between her decision and the introduction of sex tests by the IAAF (her sister Tamara retired at the same time).

The 100 m. hurdles, with ten flights of 84 cm. hurdles, was obviously a test calling for greater athletic ability. Among established stars of the 80 m. who did not suffer the transition unduly I would like to single out Karin Balzer née Richert of East Germany (born at Magdeburg on 5 June 1938; 1.71 m./64 kg.), who at different times held the world record for both 80 m. (10.5 in 1964) and 100 m. (12.7 in '70). She was an Olympic champion at the shorter distance in 1964, and eight years later she won a bronze medal at the longer one. At the European Championships she earned silver in 1962, then gold three times in a row ('66-69-71).

JUMPS - Iolanda's Empire

As previously related, the versatile Fanny Blankers-Koen offered glimpses of her potential even in this department, with world records of 1.71 (high jump) and 6.25 (long jump), both in 1943. But track events were and always remained her prime love. A high jumper who managed to outlast the war period and still retain top form was Dorothy Tyler née Odam of Britain (born at Stockwell, London, on 14 March 1920; 1.68 m./52 kg.). She blossomed to world class as a teen-ager and in 1936 she won a silver medal at the Berlin Olympics, matching the height of Ibolya Csák of Hungary (1.60), who cleared 1.62 in a jump-off to win the gold. Twelve years later Dorothy - by then Mrs. Tyler and the mother of two - was second at the London Olympics, again matching the height of the winner, Alice Coachman of USA, 1.68. The American won on the fewer misses count, a new criterion adopted in the meantime. Under the same criterion the Briton, and not Csák, would have won at Berlin in 1936.

If there has ever been an athlete who towered head and shoulders above her contemporaries for a seemingly endless time this was certainly Iolanda Balas (born at Timisoara on 12 December 1936; 1.85 m./72 kg.), a Romanian who set fourteen world records in the high jump, starting with 1.75 at

Iolanda Balas (Romania) ruled over the high jump sorority for many years.

Alice Coachman: first ebony gold

In the men's ranks, the first black to win an Olympic gold medal in an individual event was William DeHart Hubbard of USA (long jump, 1924). In the ranks of the fair sex such a "first" belongs to another American, Alice Coachman (born at Albany, Georgia, on 9 November 1923; 1.70 m./57 kg.), who won the high jump at the 1948 Olympics in London with a personal best of 1.68.

During her career she won 25 AAU titles, indoors and out, ten of which in the outdoor high jump (1939-48). She won the first of these titles before turning sixteen. At the 1943 AAU Championships in Cleveland she finished a close second to Stella Walsh in the 100 m., with an estimated 11.7.

Budapest in 1956 and ending with 1.91 at Sofia on 16 July '61. She made her Olympic début at Melbourne in 1956: although already a world record holder, she had to be content with a fifth place. The winner, Mildred McDaniel of USA, wrested the record from her with a 1.76 clearance. Iolanda's revenge was sweet and long lasting: after that defeat, she went unscathed through all her high jump competitions for over ten years, compiling a wondrous streak of 140 consecutive victories, an all-time record in modern athletics. She finally lost again in June 1967, while hampered by an injury. Balas was well above average in height (1.85 m.) on the yardstick of her time. She could not adapt to either the Western Roll or the Straddle, so she used a modified version of the scissors. She was coached by Ion Söter, a former high jumper of international class (2.055 in 1956) who later became her husband. Balas won her event twice in both the Olympics (1960 and '64) and the European Championships (1958 and '62). By the time she raised the world record to her career best of 1.91 she had a 13 cm. lead vis-à-vis the second best performer of all time! Her reign was long, happy, and somewhat tedious. She herself once put it this way: "Sometimes it was hard to compete; there was no opposition for me". The first athlete to exceed six and a half metres in the long jump was Tatyana Shchelkanova of USSR: 6.53 at Leipzig in 1962. Two performers who managed the perfect trick, i.e. conquering Olympic gold and world record at the same time, were Mary Rand of Britain, 6.76 at Tokyo in 1964, and Viorica Viscopoleanu of Romania, who took advantage of the rarefied atmosphere of Mexico City to reach 6.82 in 1968. Even better, and without the benefit of thin air, was Heide Rosendahl of West Germany (born at Hückeswagen on 14 February 1947; 1.74 m./66 kg.) who did 6.84 at the 1970 Universiade in Turin. This performance, achieved on the last try, partly softened the disappointment she had experienced a few minutes earlier when an instrinsically better jump worth about 6.90 was declared a foul. But Heide's chief glory was yet to come.

THROWS - Under Russian rule

Being virtually the only major power actively interested in this branch of women's athletics, USSR had taken control of the throwing events since the earliest post-war years. Results came accordingly. In the shot the pre-war best of Gisela Mauermayer (14.38)

was bettered time and again and by 1970 the world record was up to ... 20.43. Three Russians made history with the 4-kilo iron ball. Their names and best distances follow: Galina Zibina, 16.76 at Tashkent in 1956; Tamara Press, 18.59 at Kassel in '65; and Nadyezhda Chizhova, who first broke the 20-metre barrier in the summer of '69 and improved to 20.43 at the European Championships later in the same year. The most celebrated of the three was Tamara Press (born at Kharkov on 10 May 1937; 1.80 m./94 kg.), who was a dominant force also in the discus, her latest world record being 59.70 at Moscow in 1965. The massive Tamara retired from the scene in 1966, along with sister Irina. I have already hinted to Nina Dumbadze's early years in the discus circle.

1941
1970

Mary Rand (GB), first in the long jump and second in the pentathlon at the 1964 Olympics in Tokyo.

369

Heide Rosendahl (West Germany) first in the long jump and second in the pentathlon at the 1972 Olympics in Munich. She also anchored the victorious 4x100 m. relay team.

This statuesque Soviet athlete had a very long career. In 1946, when USSR finally entered international competition, she won the European title at Oslo. A few days later she broke the 50-metre barrier for the first time with a 50.50 throw at Sarpsborg, Norway. But it was only in 1948, i.e. almost a decade after her first record-breaking performance, that her name finally reached IAAF books, with a 53.25 throw made at Moscow that year. However, USSR chose to stay away from the London Olympics and Dumbadze thus had to wait till 1952 for her first and only chance. And at Helsinki, aged thirty-three, she had to be content with a bronze medal.

Even so, the Georgian lioness roared once more later in 1952, when in her native town of Tbilisi she outshone all previous records with 57.04, a mark that resisted all assaults for eight years.

The 50-metre barrier in the javelin was conquered by Klavdiya Mayuchaya of USSR: 50.32 at Moscow in 1947, a mark which did not make the IAAF book.

At the 1952 Olympics in Helsinki the Russians expected to reap their first gold medal in this event, but they were upset by Dana Zátopková of Czechoslovakia, wife of the famous Emil Zátopek.

The two were in fact "astrological twins", i.e. born on the same day, 19 September 1922. She came to life as Dana Ingrová at Tryskat, six hours after Emil's birth at Koprivnice.

And, lo and behold, they struck Olympic gold on the same day, 24 July 1952, when Emil won the 5000 m. and Dana followed with a victory in the javelin with 50.47. She was at one time holder of the world record with 55.73 (Prague, 1958).

Elvira Ozolina of USSR, she too the wife of a famous athlete (Janis Lusis), was first to surpass 60 m. with the javelin: 61.38 at Kiev in 1964.

Something unusual happened at the Tokyo Olympics two months later: Yelena Gorchakova raised the world mark to 62.40 in the qualifying rounds, but in the final a few hours later she "lost" more than 5 m. and had to be content with third place as Mihaela Penes of Romania won with 60.54. Ozolina, the 1960 champion, was fifth.

1941
1970

From throwing circles to the piano

The transition from a throwing circle to the key-board of a piano seems to be an unusual one in the life of a woman thrower. Micheline Ostermeyer of France supplied a nice exception. This versatile woman (born at Berck-sur-Mer, Pas-de-Calais, on 23 December 1922; 1.79 m./73 kg.) lived in North Africa in her early years and became an athlete in the ranks of a Tunis club. She later returned to France and made her international début at the 1946 European Championships in Oslo, placing second in the shot put.

The climax of her career was at the 1948 Olympics in London, where she won gold medals in shot (13.75) and discus (41.92) and bronze in the high jump (1.61).

Without wishing to detract from her merits, it is obvious that such a rich harvest was partly made possible by the absence from those Games of USSR and Germany, then the leading powers in throwing circles.

At the 1950 European Championships in Brussels, with the Russians in the game, Ostermeyer won bronze medals in shot and hurdles and was fourth in the discus. By then, however, she was devoting the better part of her time to the piano. She eventually won the first prize at the Conservatoire de Paris and developed into an excellent concert pianist.

PENTATHLON -
Shaky tables

In post-war years the pentathlon schedule was revised to comprise shot put, high jump and 200 m. on the first day, 80 m. hurdles and long jump on the second day. Compared with the past, two running events instead of one, and no javelin.

The first official record holder was Fanny Blankers-Koen, who in 1951 at Amsterdam put together the following marks: 11.50 (shot), 1.60 (high jump), 24.4 (200 m.), 11.4 (80 m. hurdles) and 5.88 (long jump), for a total score of 4692 pts.

That was the beginning of a new era, in which Russian athletes were to play a prominent role. The schedule was changed once more in 1961, with the 80 m. hurdles advanced to the first day and the 200 m. postponed to the second.

Under the new sequence the highest score was achieved by Irina Press at the 1964 Olympics in Tokyo: 10.7 (80 m. hurdles), 17.16 (shot), 1.63 (high jump), 6.24 (long jump) and 24.7 (200 m.), for a score of 5246 pts. In 1969 the hurdle distance was changed to 100 m.

Best in this era, alas very brief, was Burglinde Pollak of East Germany, with 5406 pts at Erfurt in 1970, her marks being 13.3, 15.57, 1.75, 6.20 and 23.8.

RELAYS - Aussies, Yanks sparkle

Same as in the men's department, relay records were invariably the result of highly competitive races. In this respect, the Olympics furnished the ideal occasion. At the 1948 Games in London, Holland used her anchor leg runner Fanny Blankers-Koen to good advantage and won from Australia by a narrow margin, 47.5 to 47.6.

But to witness the fall of the world record (46.4 by Germany in 1936) one had to wait till the 1952 Olympics in Helsinki, when an Australian team consisting of Shirley Strickland, Verna Johnston, Winsome Cripps and Marjorie Jackson did 46.1 in a heat. In the decisive race the Aussies led till the last exchange, when tragedy struck them. In the words of a witty reporter, "the shapely knee of incoming Winsome Cripps knocked the baton from Marjorie Jackson's grasp".

The latter was as fast as lightning in retrieving the baton, yet by the time she got underway other teams had an unsurmountable lead. USA won from Germany in a tight finish, both clocking 45.9 (auto-times, 46.14 and 46.18). And Australia was fifth in 46.6. The Aussies had to wait till the 1956 Olympics for a sweet revenge.

Running before a huge home crowd at Melbourne, a team consisting of Strickland, Norma Croker, Fleur Mellor and Betty Cuthbert made no mistakes and won in record time, 44.5 (auto-time, 44.65).

Winners of the sprint relay in the following editions of the Games were USA in Rome (44.5, after lowering the record to 44.4 in a heat), Poland in Tokyo (43.6, auto-time 43.69) and USA again at Mexico City, where Barbara Ferrell, Margaret Bailes, Mildrette Netter and Wyomia Tyus sped to a nifty 42.8 (auto-time, 42.88).

It should be added that Poland's victory at Tokyo was tainted by the subsequent disqualification of Ewa Klobukowska, the anchor leg runner, who as previously related was declared ineligible for women's competition.

Micheline Ostermeyer (France), who won shot and discus at the 1948 Olympics in London.

GREAT ACHIEVEMENTS AND SOME PROBLEMS. STARS FROM ALL CORNERS OF THE GLOBE

SPRINTS:
German dynasty, Ashford, then Hurricane "Flo-Jo"

The dominant figure of the sprints at the Munich Olympics (1972) was muscular Renate Stecher née Meissner of East Germany (born at Süptitz near Torgau on 12 May 1950; 1.70 m./69 kg.), who won the 100 m. in 11.07 and the 200 m. in 22.40, both times from Raelene Boyle of Australia, who was a serious challenger especially at the longer distance (22.45). The solidly built Stecher was branded as a female version of Valeriy Borzov, who on the same occasion scored a similar double in the men's sprints. Clock-wise, the German conquered new world records in 1973, with hand times of 10.9 (Ostrava, 7 June) and 10.8 (Dresden, 20 July) in the century, and 22.1 (Dresden, 21 July) in the 200 m., always with a wind close to the permissible limit.

At the 1976 Olympics in Montreal she won silver in the 100 m. and bronze in the 200 m. Very few sprinters, male or female, have ever managed to shine to such an extent in two editions of the Olympics. Stecher was coached by Horst-Dieter Hille, who in the following years tutored other prominent speedsters such as Marlies Göhr and Bärbel Eckert.

The latter was at her best in the 200 m. She won the Olympic title twice, with 22.37 at Montreal in 1976 and 22.03 at Moscow in '80, in the latter case under her married name, Wöckel.

Marlies Göhr née Oelsner (born at Gera on 21 March 1958; 1.65 m./54 kg.) must be rated as one of the most durable sprinters seen so far in female ranks. A small but ever consistent and reliable "powerhouse", she made her Olympic début at Montreal, aged eighteen, winning gold with East Germany's sprint relay and placing eighth in the 100 m. In subsequent editions of the Games she was not particularly lucky though.

At Moscow in 1980 she was nosed out by Lyudmila Kondratyeva of USSR in a close 100 m. finish, 11.07 to 11.06, and in 1984 she had to stay away from the Los Angeles Games when East Germany sided with boycotting countries.

At Seoul in 1988 she was nursing an injury and failed to make the 100 m. final by three hundredths of a second. But she was able to win two more medals in the sprint relay: gold in 1980 and silver in '88. Marlies probably had her brightest day when she won the century in 10.97 at the 1983 World Championships in Helsinki.

Prior to that she had achieved the first sub-11 secs. mark with automatic timing: 10.88 at Dresden on 1 July 1977, with an aiding wind of 2.0 m/s. She improved to 10.81 at Berlin on 8 Ju-ne 1983 in an exciting duel with Marita Koch (10.83), with an aiding breeze of 1.7 m/s. She did not like the 200 m., yet she managed a nifty 21.74 in winning the national title in 1984. Another excellent sprinter of the East German school was Silke Gladisch, who was coached by Wolfgang Meier. She was at her peak in the 1987 World Championships in Rome, where she scored a fine double with 10.90 and 21.74. For several years the only serious threat to East German supremacy came from Evelyn Ashford of USA (born at

Shreveport, Louisiana on 15 April 1957; 1.65 m./52 kg.). With her tiny build and her great competitive ability she evoked the paraphrase: "Dynamite comes in small boxes". She had several tussles with leading East German sprinters, particularly with Marlies Göhr. In one of these, on 22 August 1984 at Zurich, Ashford won in record time, 10.76 to 10.84, aided by a 1.7 m/s wind. Marlies had a quicker getaway, but Evelyn countered with an irresistible finish. This duel was awaited with great interest since Göhr had missed the Los Angeles Games, where Ashford won the 100 m. comfortably in 10.97. The American did not run the 200 m. too frequently, yet she proved her class even at this distance, e.g. at the 1979 World Cup in Montreal, where she convincingly beat world record holder Marita Koch, 21.83 to 22.02, and also won the 100 m. from Göhr, 11.06 to 11.17.

Ashford's saddest day came in the 1983 World Championships at Helsinki, where she pulled up lame midway in the 100 m., while trying to catch the leading Göhr. In the spring of 1985 she and husband Ray Washington, a basketball player, had a baby, Raina Ashley, who soon became mum's inseparable companion during meets at home and abroad. As late as in 1990, Ashford was still able to perform well at international levels.

Marlies Göhr (East Germany) as anchor leg runner in the victorious 4x100 m. relay team at the 1985 World Cup. Time, 41.37, still standing as a world record.

At the Los Angeles Olympics (1984) America had another great performer in Valerie Brisco-Hooks, who won the 200 m. (21.81) and the 400 m. (48.83), an unprecedented double. Of course, Marita Koch of East Germany and Jarmila Kratochvílová of Czechoslovakia were not there, and the American actually lost to them in post-Olympic meets.

All the above feats were outshone in 1988 by a phenomenal Florence Griffith (born at Los Angeles on 21 December 1959; 1.70 m./59 kg.), whose exploits gave track nuts all over the world plenty of food for discussion, more perhaps than any others in the history of women's athletics. "Flo-Jo", as she was called, was able to run the sprints in 11.51 and 23.55 at twenty-one. Her progress in subsequent years was gradual and steady, with 10.99 and 22.04 in 1984, when she won a silver medal in the 200 m. at the Los Angeles Olympics; then 10.96 and 21.96 in 1987, when she won silver again at the longer distance in the World Championships, shortly before marrying Al Joyner, the 1984 Olympic triple jump champion. Even so, her fame by the end of 1987 curiously rested more on her highly styled beauty and eccentricity, e.g. in sporting 10 cm. fingernails and flashy bodysuits, than on her valuable athletic skill.

But during the winter 1987/88 she made a great leap forward, a most unusual one in a sprinter approaching her thirties. In 1988 she made history chiefly in two important meets, the US Olympic Trials at Indianapolis and the Olympic Games in Seoul.

Times and wind readings aptly tell the tale (she won all these races):

	1988 US Olympic Trials			
100 m.	10.60w	(+3.2)	Heat	16/7
	*10.49	(0.0)	Q-F	16/7
	10.70	(+1.6)	S-F	17/7
	10.61	(+1.2)	Final	17/7
200 m.	21.96	(+0.6)	Heat	22/7
	21.77	(-0.1)	Q-F	22/7
	21.90w	(+2.4)	S-F	23/7
	21.85	(+1.3)	Final	23/7
	1988 Olympic Games			
100 m.	10.88	(+1.0)	Heat	24/9
	10.62	(+1.0)	Q-F	24/9
	10.70w	(+2.6)	S-F	25/9
	10.54w	(+3.0)	Final	25/9
200 m.	22.51	(+0.7)	Heat	28/9
	21.76	(+0.7)	Q-F	28/9
	*21.56	(+1.7)	S-F	29/9
	*21.34	(+1.3)	Final	29/9
* World Record.				

That 10.49 in a quarter-final at the Trials created quite a stir, being an improvement of 0.27 sec. vis-à-vis Evelyn Ashord's listed world record. Several eye-witnesses questioned the wind reading (officially "nil"), noting that in the men's triple jump, going on virtually alongside, at the same time and in the same running direction, there were only 3 legal readings out of 46, notably including a 4.3 m/s on the board as the 10.49 race began. However, wind gauge operators and the company they worked for firmly confirmed the correctness of the verdict, and Griffith's time made the IAAF book. Apart from that incredible mark, she could point to such clockings as 10.61 and 10.62, both made under undisputably correct conditions. They still represent a remarkable progress vis-à-vis Ashford's previous record (10.76). Then what "Flo-Jo" did at Seoul, especially in the 200 m., largely suffices to confirm that she had reached a new dimension. East German coach Horst-Dieter Hille, certainly not a partisan source, studied the Seoul races carefully and came to the conclusion that "Flo-Jo" had the speed of an excellent male sprinter in all but the first 10 m. and the last 10 m. Griffith won by unusually wide margins: 0.29 on Ashford in the 100 m. and 0.38 on Grace Jackson of Jamaica in the 200 m. And each time she had a radiant smile on her face well before coming home the winner! Of course, many observers wondered how a sprinter pretty close to the age of thirty could improve by as much as 0.47 (100 m.) and 0.62 (200 m.) in one year. "Strength work and repeated videotape study of the starts of the fastest humans of all" was the reply given by "Flo-Jo" and her coach Bob Kersee. Some commentators, obviously influenced by the Ben Johnson "case" which unfolded at the same time, were inclined to suspect that drugs may have entered the picture even in Griffith's case, somehow or other. But no light had gone up when she was subjected to tests, in the States and in Seoul. Under such conditions, the dictum "honni soit qui mal y pense" seems to be in order. Be as it may, the Doubting Thomases seemingly gained new vigour when "Flo-Jo" announced her retirement from track shortly after the Seoul Games. Genuine track fans simply regretted that she would no longer have a chance to give the 400 m. a truly serious try. (The 1983 NCAA champion at that distance, Griffith was once quoted as saying: "I especially like the 400 m. because it is the most challenging event").

1971
1999

Evelyn Ashford (USA) winning the 100 m. at the 1984 Olympics in Los Angeles.

As destiny would have it, the life of the fastest woman of modern times was to pass away almost as rapidly as her most memorable races. On 21 September 1998 the track world was struck by the news that Delorez Florence Griffith had passed away in her sleep while at home in Mission Viejo, California - three months before turning 39. An autopsy revealed that her death was due to "suffocation following an epileptic seizure". She had a congenital brain abnormality known as a "cavernous angioma". Dr. Richard Fukumoto, chief of forensic medicine at the Orange County Coroner's Office, incidentally remarked that said "abnormality never has been associated with steroids or any other drugs".

Florence Griffith (USA) in her most glorious week (1988 Olympics), here winning the 100 m.

As at the end of the Nineties no female sprinter had come reasonably close to the records set by the flamboyant "Flo-Jo". The fastest times returned in the last decade of the century were 10.65 for 100 m. and 21.62 for 200 m., both by Marion Jones of USA in the altitude (1,748 m.) of Johannesburg in 1998. This tremendously gifted athlete (born on 12 October 1975 at Los Angeles; 1.78 m./68 Kg.) began to show tremendous promise at a very early age. In the summer of 1991, before turning 16, she astounded experts by placing 4th in the 200 m. (22.76) at the national championships, narrowly missing selection for the World Championships in Tokyo. A year later she came close to making the U.S. Olympic team at the national trials, finishing 5th in the 100 and 4th in the 200. Her best times that year (1992) were 11.14 and 22.58. By then, however, she turned her attention to basketball, in which she progressed to the point of winning the NCAA title, playing point guard on the North Carolina team. In 1995 she suffered fractures of the left foot twice, after which she decided to forget about contact sports and returned to athletics. It took her a while to regain top form, but in 1997 she joined the world class with times such as 10.76 and 21.76 as well as 6.93 in the long jump. At the World Championships of that year in Athens she won the 100 in 10.83 but was only 10th in the long jump, in which her technique still left much to be desired. Her 1998 season was stupendous: she won 34 individual events in a row before bowing to Heike Drechsler of Germany in the long jump at the World Cup in Johannesburg (7.00 to 7.07). Earlier in the same meet, however, she had won 100 and 200 metres, as related earlier. Her times on that occasion (10.65 and 21.62) earned her position no. 2 in the All Time World Lists. At the end of that fabulous season she married shot putter C. J. Hunter. She was expected to go from strength to strength in 1999. At the World Championships in Sevilla she won the 100 in 10.70 - very good time at sea level and with no wind (-0.1). (Her husband had got the ball rolling the day before by capturing the men's shot put with a new personal best). Then she suffered a crushing defeat in the long jump, finishing third. Disaster came in a semifinal of the 200 metres when great pains in her lower back forced her to stop about halfway down the homestretch. Hopefully, the track world has not seen the best of Marion Jones yet. Coach Bob Kersee once expressed the belief that she could run 10.50/21.00 in the sprints and reach 25 feet (7.62) in the long jump. To all other sprinters, however, Flo-Jo's records continued to appear "out of this world". Merlene Ottey of Jamaica, for example, has been in the front row for almost two decades, always showing great consistency, yet she had to be content with 10.74 (at 36 years of age) and 21.64. This magnificent specimen of "beauty in motion" (born on 10 May 1960 at Cold Spring, Hanover, Jamaica; 1.73 m./59 Kg.) collected 14 medals in the World Championships and 7 in the Olympic Games over a period stretching from 1980 to 1997 - for a grand total of 21, one notch more than the great Carl Lewis in the men's department. However, her tally of golds was limited to three, all at the Worlds - twice in the 200 (1993 and '95) and once in the 4x100 relay (1991). She lost two major 100 m. titles by tantalizing margins measured in a few thousandths of a second, both times to her "bête noire" Gail Devers of USA: at the 1993 Worlds (time for both, 10.82) and at the 1996 Olympics (both 10.94). Her long and bittersweet career probably came to a sad end in 1999, when she failed a drugs test.

"An act of God"

Marion Jones went to the 1999 World Championships in Sevilla with the declared aim of winning four gold medals (100, 200, long jump and 4x100). As related above, defeat in the long jump and then injury in a 200 m. semi shattered her dreams. About the latter, "Track & Field News" made the following remarks: "Perhaps it was the cumulative and dehydrating effect of gearing up again and again on 100° (F)-degree Sevilla days for rounds and finals in three events. Or maybe it was the hard track or her awkward landing in the long jump. Maybe it was simply what the insurance companies call "an act of God". Or maybe, I dare say, her dream of winning four golds was simply put off till the 2000 Olympics in Sydney. In this respect, the overconfident Marion was quoted as saying that for Sydney she has five golds in mind, thus including the longer (4x400 m.) relay as well. Not a bad dream, considering that the likes of Jesse Owens and Carl Lewis in their prime won "only" four golds in the department of the (supposedly) stronger sex.
By the way, Marion's mother hailed from Belize and the girl herself had a dual nationality for some time before opting for the USA. I may here advance a somewhat irreverent reflection: Marion's bests in the sprints (10.65 and 21.62) excel the Belize records in the male department (10.96 and 21.72).

Another American, Gail Devers (born on 19 November 1966 at Seattle; 1.60 m.52 kg.) may well be regarded as the fastest ever woman sprinter-hurdler, a female version of Harrison Dillard. A serious thyroid disorder caused her to miss competition in 1989-90 and she was pretty close to have a foot amputated. Yet she braved ill fortune and eventually blossomed into a dynamic short-distance marvel. She reached her peak at the 1993 World Championships in Stuttgart, where she won the 100 metres flat in 10.82 (by a hair's breadth, or less, from Ottey) and the 100 metres hurdles in 12.46.

The no. 1 European sprinter of the Nineties was in all probability Irina Privalova of Russia. She was at the peak of her versatitlity in the 1994 World Cup in London when on three successive days she was second to Ottey in the 200, won the 100 and finally the 400, this last in her second try at the distance. She held the European 100 m. record with 10.77 (1994) and has a 200 m. best of 21.87 (1995).

Irena Szewinska's deeds in the sprints have already been recounted. The Polish marvel was great even in the Seventies, when she set world records for 200 m. (22.21 at Potsdam in '74) and 400 m. (49.28 at the Montreal Olympics in '76). In the one-lap event she had been the first to break the 50 secs. barrier at Warsaw in '74, when splits of 11.8, 11.1 (22.9), 12.8 and 14.2 carried her home an exhausted but glorious conqueror in 49.9. As late as in 1977, at the age of 31, she scored a great double in the

1971
1999

Merlene Ottey (Jamaica), a most durable performer in topclass female sprinting, here winning a 100 m. race from G. Devers (USA) in the Grand Prix final at Milano in 1996.

World Cup at Düsseldorf, winning the 200 m. from Bärbel Eckert, 22.72 to 23.02, and the 400 m. from Marita Koch, 49.52 to 49.76. At the European Championships, between 1966 and 1978, this charming and indefatigable woman collected ten medals, half of them gold. During her career she was also capable of 56.62 in the 400 m. hurdles, 1.68 in the high jump, 6.67 in the long jump and 4705 pts in the pentathlon. How could she manage to do so much for so long? An American observer probably found the answer when he wrote: "Irena thrives on the joy, the beauty and the exhilaration of sport". Another incomparable athlete was Marita Koch of East Germany (born at Wismar on 18 February 1957; 1.71 m./63 kg.). She was the first woman to duck under 22 secs. in the 200 m.: 21.71 on 10 June 1979 at Karl-Marx-Stadt - Chemnitz until 1953 and again from 1990 onwards - and matched this mark at Potsdam in 1984. She made history in an even more remarkable way in the 400 m. After wresting the world record from Szewinska at Leipzig in 1978 with a time of 49.19, she improved on several occasions, her ultimate effort being a great 47.60 in the World Cup at Canberra on 6 October 1985. In this race she had a worthy opponent in Olga Vladikina (later Brizgina) of USSR, yet she led from the start and was never headed. Coach Wolfgang Meier (who later became her husband) caught the following 100 m. splits for Marita: 10.9, 11.5 (22.4), 11.7, 13.5. Certainly one of the finest exploits in the history of women's athletics. Vladikina was second in 48.27. Koch won the 400 m. at the 1980 Olympics and the 200 m. at the 1983 World Championships. After Szewinska's retirement from track she found a serious challenger in Jarmila Kratochvílová of Czechoslovakia, a solidly built athlete who beat the German in the 400 m. of the 1981 World Cup in Rome, 48.61 to 49.27, and even held the world record for some time with a remarkable 47.99 effort (halves, 23.1 and 24.9) at Helsinki in 1983. Shortly before the devastating advent of "Flo-Jo" Griffith, East Germany had one more great talent in Heike Drechsler née Daute (born at Gera on 16 December 1964; 1.80 m./70 kg.), a rare combination of sprinter/long jumper who in 1986 twice equalled Koch's 200 m. record (21.71). The second mark was at the European Championships in Stuttgart on a cold, wet day, and with an 0.8 adverse wind in the stretch. About fifteen minutes earlier, Vladimir Krilov of USSR had won the men's title over the same distance in 20.52. Seldom if ever had such an important international championship offered a differential as narrow as that (1.19 sec.) between the sexes in the 200 m.! More will be said about Drechsler in connection with the long jump.

Marita Koch's world record for the 400 metres (47.60 in 1985) was to remain an elusive target throughout the Nineties. The nearest approach was by Marie-José Pérec of France (born on 9 May 1968 at Basse Terre, Guadeloupe; 1.80 m./60 kg.), who ran the distance in 48.25 in winning the Olympic title at Atlanta in 1996. This earned her position no. 3 in the All Time World List behind two stars of the Eighties, Koch and Jarmila Kratochvilová. Pérec's first major international test had a bittersweet savour: she was disqualified for running out of lane after winning the 1989 World Cup 400 m. in 50.30. She won her first world title at Tokyo two years later in 49.13 and duplicated her victory at the Olympic Games in 1992, improving to 48.83. A gifted but somewhat lazy performer for several years, she began to come close to her potential when she went to America and joined coach John Smith's powerful

Irena Szewinska (Poland), one of the most versatile talents in the annals of women athletics.

sprint squad. She once said of her American coach (a former world record holder for the quarter-mile): "He puts the bar very far - a variation of the bar very high". Hard work was to pay more and more dividends for Pérec. After winning her second 400 m. world title in 1995, she went for an arduous 200-400 double at the Atlanta Olympics in 1996. Another woman, Valerie Brisco-Hooks of USA, had turned that trick at the 1984 Games in Los Angeles, but in the absence of potentially dangerous rivals from boycotting Eastern European countries. Pérec did it in more convincing circumstances. On 29 July she won the 400 in 48.25 and on 1 August she took the 200 after overhauling a somewhat bewildered Ottey in the closing stage - 22.12 to 22.24. Pérec could by then be regarded as one of the greatest all-around sprinters with such times as 10.96 ('91), 21.99 ('93) and 48.25 ('96). Back in 1992, after her first Olympic victory, she had dismissed Koch's 400 m. world record as "beyond reach and biologically aided". Implicitly, she referred to the fact that drugs tests were less frequent and less effective pior to 1989, i.e. until the introduction of "random tests". After her 48.25 in the Atlanta Games she began to see the world record as "a distant possibility". Unfortunalely, a stress fracture of the shin and then a virus illness have virtually kept her away from competition in the last two years.

By the end of the century the world's leadership in the one-lap event had passed to Cathy Freeman (born on 16 February 1973 at Mackay, Queensland; 1.64 m./52 kg.). Clock-wise she has reached her peak so far in placing second to Pérec at the 1996 Olympics in 48.63. In the absence of the French star, Freeman went on to win world titles in 1997 (49.77) and '99 (49.67). She was incidentally the first Aboriginal to represent Australia in the Olympic Games, as well as the first world champion.

1971
1999

Marita Koch (East Germany) still holds the world record for the 1-lap event (47.60 in 1985).

MIDDLE DISTANCES - The seven labours of Jarmila

The first official sub-2 min. mark in the 800 m. was credited to Hildegard Falck of West Germany: 1:58.5 at Stuttgart in 1971. The following year at Munich she won the Olympic title in a tight finish with 1:58.6. That was the beginning of a new era. To give the event a new dimension there came a nimble but tenacious Russian, Tatyana Kazankina (born at Petrovsk in the Saratov region on 17 December 1951; 1.61 m./48 kg.), a feather-weight runner with a fantastic aggregate of speed and stamina. At the 1976 Olympics in Montreal this seemingly frail woman achieved a great double, winning the 800 m. in world record time (1:54.94) and then the 1500 m. (4:05.48). Four years later another Russian, Nadyezhda Olizarenko, came up with a fractionally faster time for the 800 m.: 1:54.85 during an international meet in Moscow. The following month Olizarenko, 27, went on to capture the Olympic title on the same track in a startling 1:53.43, with halves of 56.2 and 57.3. But the last word was to come from Jarmila Kratochvílová of Czechoslovakia (born at Golcuv Jenikov on 26 January 1951; 1.70 m./64 kg.). I have already referred to her exploits in the 400 m., but she was just as good if not better in the two-lap event. 1983 was her greatest year. On 26 July in Munich she lowered the world record to 1:53.28 in what was virtually a solo effort (halves, 56.1 and 57.2), a time still unmatched as of the end of 1990. The following month, at the World Championships in Helsinki, Jarmila went through what must be rated as the hardest "tour de force" ever sustained by a woman in topclass competition. Between 7 and 10 August she went through "Seven Labours", namely three 800 m. rounds and four 400 m. rounds, perversely intertwined in the time schedule. The crucial point was on the third day, 9 August, with the 400 m. semi-final and the 800 m. final only 35 minutes apart. She overcame ... and her winning time in the latter race was a brilliant 1:54.68. (The following day she won the 400 m. crown in 47.99, a new world record). Retrospectively, she described the Helsinki schedule as "a cruel combination". After years of intensive weight training, Kratochvílová was strength personified, but not the type of woman likely to please aesthetes (of the other sex). One of her Western European rivals came up with bitter comments on her physical aspect, to which Jarmila retorted: "If she wants to produce performances like mine, she will have to have sacrificed some of her good looks". It should be noted that Kratochvílová had bests of 11.09 and 21.97 for the sprint distances.

In subsequent years the 800 m. record of the Czech "powerhouse" remained virtually unchallenged. Sigrun Wodars of East Germany showed great consistency as she won the event at the 1987 World Championships (1:55.26) and the 1988 Olympics (1:56.10), with her compatriot Christine Wachtel in the runner-up position both times. The season 1989 belonged to a solidly built Cuban, Ana Fidelia Quirot, who ruled the roost in both 400 m. and 800 m., as her compatriot Alberto Juantorena once used to do in the men's ranks. In the key event of that year, the World Cup in Barcelona, Quirot convincingly beat Wodars in the 800m., 1:54.44 to 1:55.70. The most recent years have seen a marked drop in stand-

Jarmila Kratochvilová (Czechoslovakia), holder of the world's 800 m. record, 1:53.28 in 1983.

ard of performance at both 400 and 800 m. The best times recorded at these distances in 1990 were 49.50 by Grit Breuer of East Germany (a World Junior record) and 1:55.87 by Wodars respectively. Many observers tend to regard the intensified anti-doping campaign of the IAAF as one of the chief reasons for such a slow-down.

Throughout the Nineties things did not change much, standard-wise, in the two-lap event. But there was a most remarkable outburst in the 1500 metres, as part of a trend affecting all distance events up to and including the 10,000. This was at the hands of a couple of young Chinese runners and curiously turned out to be short-lived.

During this period no one came close to Jarmila Kratochvilová's 800 metres record, the fastest time being a 1:54.82 by Ana Fidelia Quirot at Köln in 1997, still 0.38 short of her personal best dating from the 1989 World Cup. This strong runner (born on 23 March 1963 at Palma Soriano, Santiago de Cuba; 1.65 m./59 kg) saw her career seriously imperilled early in 1993, following a horrid accident in her home. She was burnt over a third of her body when a bottle of cleaning fluid exploded. She was seven months pregnant at the time: doctors induced labour and she gave birth to a daughter, who died a few days later due to the premature birth. Even so, Quirot managed to make a gallant recovery - to the point of winning the 800 metres in two editions of the World Championships (1995 and '97), securing a silver medal at the 1996 Olympics and, as related above, coming close to her personal best! Her arch rival through the greater part of the Nineties was a staunch performer from Mozambique, Maria Lurdes Mutola (born on 27 October 1972 at Maputo; 1.62 m./61 kg.) She was a good soccer player as a teenager but showed great promise in athletics as well, with such times as 54.8 (400 m.) and 2:04.36 (800 m.) just before turning 16. The latter was in placing seventh in a heat at the Seoul Olympics, where she had the honour of carrying the national flag. A double victory (800 and 1500 m.) at the 1990 African Championships earned her a scholarship to train in

1971
1999

Odd comparison

Tatyana Kazankina's latest 1500 m. world record (3:52.47 at Zurich in 1980) brought back to the memory of statisticians a similar time achieved in the male ranks by one Paavo Nurmi at Helsinki in 1924: 3:52.6, then a world record.

This thought gave rise to an idea, probably irreverent to both parties involved, that of comparing the intermediate times of the two historic races. Here they are:

	Nurmi (1924)	Kazankina (1980)
400 m.	57.3	58.3
800 m.	2:01.0	2:04.5
1200 m.	3:06.0	3:07.1
1500 m.	3:52.6	3:52.47

The long lapse of time separating these achievements, with the countless changes that have occurred in the world of track in all these years, may be considered a heavier factor than the sex difference itself. Otherwise it would be hard to explain how Kazankina could have bettered Nurmi by over a second in the last 300 m.

In Nurmi's defence one could of course say that his 1500 m. was only the first of his two labours at Helsinki on that distant day in 1924. About an hour later he ran the 5000 m, achieving another world record (14:28.2). Bearing in mind what was to follow, maybe he did not go all out in the first race.

Ana Fidelia Quirot (Cuba) leading from Svyetlana Masterkova (USSR) in an 800 m. race at Nice in 1991. They finished 1st and 3rd respectively.

Qu Yunxia (China) lowered the world's 1500 m. record to a great 3:50.46 during the Chinese "Revolution" of 1993.

the United States through the Olympic Solidarity Committee. She attended a high school in Oregon and in 1991 she astounded experts by placing fourth in the 800 meters at the World Championships in Tokyo in 1:57.63, a World Junior record. She has been a regular medal winner in major championship meets ever since, reaching the top at the 1993 World Championships in Stuttgart (first in 1:55.43), where she left the runner-up almost 2 seconds behind. She and Quirot were upset by a European at the 1996 Olympics in Atlanta, their castigator being Svyetlana Masterkova of Russia (born on 17 January 1968 at Achinsk, Siberia; 1.72 m. 59 kg.). Using her finishing kick to good advantage, Masterkova won both middle distance events in Atlanta: on 29 July she took the 800 metres in 1:57.73 from Quirot (1:58.11) and Mutola (1.58.71); on 3 August she won the 1500 in 4:00.83 from a budding new star, Gabriela Szabo of Romania (4:01.54). Later in the year Masterkova crowned her brilliant season with two world records for non-Olympic distances: 4:12.56 for the mile (Zurich, 14 August) and 2:28.98 for 1000 metres (Brussels, 23 August).

The 1500 m. event was first included in the Olympic programme at Munich in 1972. Not surprisingly, the "première" was featured by a record breaking spree. Lyudmila Bragina of USSR (born at Sverdlovsk on 24 July 1943; 1.65 m./57 kg.) improved on her own global mark - 4:06.9 earlier in the same year - three times in a row: 4:06.47 (heat), 4:05.07 (semi-final) and 4:01.38 (final). The races were on 4, 7 and 9 September. Bragina won the decisive test from Gunhild Hoffmeister of East Germany (4:02.83) and Paola Pigni-Cacchi of Italy (4:02.85). Then came a runner who really put the record "out of sight", Russia's Tatyana Kazankina. Her doings in the two-lap department have been recounted, but it was at the "metric mile" that she earned most of her glory. As a competitor she won the Olympic 1500 m. title twice (1976 and '80). As a record breaker she succeeded Bragina at Podolsk in 1976 with a nifty 3:56.0. In 1980 she improved to 3:55.0 during the Znamenskiy Memorial Meet in Moscow, then offered her "chef d'oeuvre" in the Weltklasse meet at Zurich on 13 August with a superb 3:52.47.

Unfortunately, she made the headlines in a different way four years later in connection with an international meet in Paris, when she refused to take a drug test, reportedly on the advice of the official heading the USSR delegation. As per international rules she was suspended from track activities for 18 months. A sad end to an otherwise splendid career. (She returned to action in 1986 with generally indifferent results). In the ten years that have elapsed since Kazankina's 3:52.47 in Zurich only two women have ducked under 3:55 in the 1500 m.: Olga Dvirna of USSR, who did 3:54.23 at Kiev in 1982, and Paula Ivan of Romania, who clocked 3:53.96 to win the Olympic title at Seoul in 1988. The dramatic drop in standard of performance at this distance is best focussed through a comparison between the first and tenth best performers in the World Lists of 1980 and 1990.

	1st	10th
1980	3:52.47	3:59.82
1990	3:58.69	4:04.56

The above figures certainly give food for thought.

In 1993 the 1500 metre sorority was shocked by the above-mentioned Chinese "earhtquake". In the province of Liaoning, in the North of the vast Asian country, there was a coach by the name of Ma Junren who was known for his harsh training methods. He began to tutor a group of young female runners early in the Eighties. More on him and his training ways will be told in connection with the long distance events. The best product of the so-called "Ma's Army" in the 1500 metres was unquestionably Qu Yunxia (born on 25 December 1972 in the Liaoning province; 1.70 m./58 Kg.). Internationally she came to the fore when not yet 18 as she won the 1500 metres in 4:13.67 and placed sixth in the 800 at the 1990 World Championships in Plovdiv, Bulgaria. Two years later she mounted the podium at the 1992 Olympics in Barcelona by finishing third (3:57.08) in the 1500 metres. 1993 was her banner year. The shape of things to come became apparent at the World Championships in Stuttgart, where the Chinese phalanx won medals galore. This included a clean sweep in the 3000 metres, won by Qu in 8:28.71 from Zhang Linli and Zhang Lirong, after covering the last 400 in 59.22. Qu stayed away from the 1500, which went to another Chinese, Liu Dong, in 4:00.50, beating such prominent runners as Sonia O'Sullivan of Ireland and defending champion Hassiba Boulmerka of Algeria. Liu, not yet 20, ran the last lap in 57.48. She was to make the news again in 1994, when she was expelled from Ma Junren's training squad because she refused to have her hair cut short and break up with her boyfriend, sprinter Cui Hui. Even after these victories, what followed at China's National Games in September surpassed all expectations. In this meet Ma's girls really let themselves go. Qu vied for honours in three events - 800, 1500 and 3000 metres. Counting prelims and finals, she ran five races in just as many days! On 9 September she was second to Liu Dong in the 800 metres - 1:56.24 to 1:55.54. On 11 September she ran the race of her life, winning the 1500 metres with a new world record, 3:50.46 - an awesome 2.01 sec. under Tatyana Kazankina's 13-year-old world record! A time that would have sufficed for a world record in the men's department as late as 1930. Strangely enough, the girl commissioned to act as hare in this race was none other than world champion Liu Dong, who led the field through 57.1 (400 m.) and 2:00.7 (800 m.) then stepped off the track. Qu ran the third lap in 64.5 (1200 m. in 3:05.2), having in her wake another fresh world champion (10,000 m.), Wang Junxia. After a dingdong battle in the last 300, Qu emerged the winner, but her rival (3:51.92) also managed to better Kazankina's record. Seven women ducked under 4 minutes in this fantastic race. The girl who finished seventh, 17-year-old Wang Yuan, set a World Junior record of 3:59.81. The following day Qu was at work in a heat of the 3000 metres, finishing second to arch rival Wang Junxia - 8:12.27 to 8:12.19, both under the ultra-fresh world record set in heat 1 by Zhang Linli (8:22.06).

On 13 September the indefatigable Qu was again second to Wang in the final as both massacred the world record with 8:12.18 and 8:06.11 respectively. Qu thus had the unique experience of ducking under listed world marks three times in just as many days, actually winning only once! What amazed Western experts most was the ultra-rapid rate of recovery exhibited by Ma's girls. But such Chinese "flames" were to disappear just as rapidly as they had appeared. Qu, for example, performed indifferently in 1994-96. It was only in 1997 that the rest of the world received news of a new "earthquake" of lesser proportions, served by Ma with a different cast. In the 1500 metres the leading character was Jiang Bo, who in China's National Games at Shanghai (18 October) chalked up a great 3:50.98, second fastest time on record, winning from Lang Yinglai (3:51.34). Poor Qu Yunxia was only eighth in 3:57.83, after doing 3:55.38 in a heat the day before. For Jiang Bo, 20, it was a giant step forward, considering that her pre-1997 best was 4:11.76 (1995).

More prominent in terms of international honours is the career record of Algeria's Hassiba Boulmerka (born on 10 July 1968 at Constantine; 1.65 m./57 Kg.). In 1991 she became the first African woman to win a world title as she took the 1500 metres in Tokyo in 4:02.21. The following year she annexed an Olympic title in Barcelona with 3:55.30, winning from Lyudmila Rogachova of Russia (3:56.91) and Qu Yunxia (3:57.08). The winner's time was to remain the fastest of the Nineties in global championship competition and was 5 sec. under her previous best. Boulmerka did it again at the 1995 World Championships (4:02.42).

The general standstill throughout the last decade of the century is reflected in a comparison between the first and the tenth best performers in the World Year Lists of 1990 and 1999:

	1st	10th
1990	3:58.69	4:04.56
1999	3:59.31	4:03.14

1971
1999

LONG DISTANCES - No-woman's land? No longer!

Mary Decker (USA) was consoled by husband Richard Slaney after a "traffic accident" in the 3000 m. of the 1984 Olympics in Los Angeles.

Among athletes who have recently excelled in both 1500 and 3000 m. it is fairly easy to single out the likes of Mary Decker Slaney of USA and Tatyana Samolyenko of USSR, were it only for the fact that both have scored such a double in the World Championships. Decker did it at Helsinki in 1983, with 4:00.90 and 8:34.62, while Samolyenko turned the trick four years later in Rome with 3:58.56 and 8:38.73. Apart from that, they differed from each other in more than one way. Decker (born at Flemington, New Jersey, on 4 August 1958; 1.68 m./49 kg.; married to distance runner Ron Tabb, then to British discus thrower Richard Slaney) was an advocate of front running tactics and remained faithful to her philosophy throughout her career. Samolyenko née Khamitova (born at Sekretarka, Orenburg on 12 August 1961; 1.66 m./57 kg.) was essentially a "big kicker", hence the type of runner who likes to "kill" the opposition with a strong finish, after trailing others for the greater part of a race. As truly great runners, however, both were generally capable of holding their own under any circumstance. Decker emerged very early. At fifteen she astounded the track world with such times as 2:02.43 in the 800 m. and 4:25.7 in the 1500 m. Unfortunately her career was dogged by an incredible series of injuries, some of which necessitated surgery. But she would always fight back with great determination. Besides winning those world titles at Helsinki, she made the IAAF world record book on several occasions, at distances ranging from 1 mile (best: 4:16.21 at Zurich in 1985) to 10,000 m. (31:35.3 at Eugene in 1982). As a competitor she had her saddest moment at the 1984 Olympics in Los Angeles. She was obviously one of America's biggest hopes, but midway in the 3000 m. she collided with Zola Budd of Britain and fell, sustaining a hip injury. Her personal bests for the standard distances are 1:56.90 and 3:57.12.

The charming Samolyenko tried to duplicate her Rome double of 1987 at the Seoul Olympics the following year. She began with a sound victory in the 3000 m., outsprinting Paula Ivan of Romania, 8:26.53 to 8:27.15. But six days later she was outpaced by Ivan in the 1500 m. and had to be content with a bronze medal. Paula Ivan née Ilie (born at Heresti on 20 July 1963; 1.70 m./55 kg.) really had her Day of Days on that occasion. In what was a splendid solo effort she led from gun to tape, with intermediate times of 62.52 (400 m.), 2:05.76 (800 m.), and 3:08.25 (1200 m.). She won by more than six seconds and her final time, 3:53.96, was the second fastest ever. However, she was well behind Kazankina's 1980 pace after the first lap (62.52 vs 58.3) and that eventually cost her the record. In 1989 the Romanian gained the 1-mile record at Nice with a 4:15.61 clocking, after passing the 1500 m. in 3:59.23 - a differential of 16.38 for the last 109.35 m.

In earlier years, Bragina and Kazankina had largely contributed to the advancement of the 3000 m. record, the former with 8:27.12 at College Park, Maryland, in 1976; the latter with 8:22.62 at Leningrad on 26 August 1984, a mark that still stands. It should be noted that no global record has been set at standard distances (800, 1500, 3000 m.) in the last six years. This regression is counterbalanced to some extent by woman's advances in the long distance department. Here the range of the fair sex is now the same as that of the men, comprising the marathon as well. The 3000 m. event was included in the programme of the inaugural World Championships in 1983, and the following year it was contested at the Los Angeles Olympics. Similarly, the 10,000 m. entered the picture at the 1987 World Championships and the following year it appeared in the Olympics as well. Curiously enough, the 5000 m. is still not part of major international championships. The undisputed ruler of women's distance running in what was virtually the infant stage of the branch was a Norwegian, Ingrid Kristiansen née Christensen (born at Trondheim on 21 March 1956; 1.69 m./50 kg.). As befits a good Scandinavian, her first approach to sport was through cross-country skiing, which she practised with good results. But it was athletics that soon captured her heart and soul. She eventually became the first woman to hold world records at 5000 m., 10,000 m. and marathon. She first ducked under 15 minutes in the 5000 m. at Oslo in 1984, with a time of 14:58.89. The following year she lost the record to Zola Budd but fought back in 1986, when she achieved a startling 14:37.33 at Stockholm with kilometre fractions of 2:52.9, 2:55.1, 2:57.5, 2:58.4 and 2:43.5. She was a barrier-breaker in the 10,000 m. too, with 30:59.42 in 1985 and 30:13.74 in '86, both times at Oslo. On the latter occasion she was on her own after 2800 m. and had halves of 15:11.33 and 15:02.41. Her main honours were at the 1986 European Championships and the 1987 World Championships, each time with a smashing victory in the 10,000 m. On both occasions she "disappeared early" and was never headed. More will be said about her feats in the marathon. Zola Budd

1971 1999

Imperfect application

As destiny would have it, Zola Budd, one of the most precocious distance runners of our time, came to life in South Africa, a country the IOC and the IAAF had banned from the international sporting family since the late Sixties on account of its policy of Apartheid. In order to have access to international competition, Zola used her English parentage (father) to good advantage and managed to obtain British citizenship at the age of eighteen. A similar "trick" had been successful for March Fiasconaro (destination, Italy) and, through a long and troubled journey, even for Sydney Maree (destination, USA). In Zola's case the manoeuvre was made possible with the help of British conservative circles. In the end, however, it was successful only to a limited extent. Once in England, the "gazelle" from South Africa became the subject of a heated political controversy. Pressed by countries from black Africa and the Communist bloc, the IAAF finally sided with Zola's enemies, i.e. with those who objected to her presence in international games. Following a brief international career, notably featured by two wins in the World Cross Country Championships (1985 and '86), Zola was obliged to return to her native country. The position of both IOC and IAAF was, of course, in keeping with Article 1 of the Olympic Charter, which states that no discrimination shall be admitted against any country or individual on racial, religious or political grounds. In my opinion, the discrimination against South Africa - which obviously damages the black majority of that country no less than its white minority - could have been accepted as logical only if the IOC and the IAAF had applied the same principle with all the countries which, one way or another, transgress Article 1 of the Olympic Charter. Political discriminations, for example, have long been the order of the day wherever there is a constitution that virtually sanctions the one-party rule. In the field of sport there are many examples of discrimination against individuals on political grounds. Most famous is the case of Wolfgang Schmidt of East Germany, a former world record holder in the discus (71.16 in 1978). He was imprisoned, basically for political non-alignment, and spent fourteen months in captivity, first at Bautzen, then at Frankfort/Oder. He fully regained his rights as a sportsman only after East German authorities allowed him to emigrate to West Germany, whose colours he has since represented in international competition. (Following the unification of Germany, he was rehabilitated even by East German track authorities ...) Of course I realize that a complete, consistent application of Article 1 would involve many countries, notably including most of those which have led the campaign against South Africa. This would undoubtedly cause a major split in the international athletic family. In the face of such a danger, the IOC and the IAAF seem to favour compromise, i.e. an imperfect application of the Olympic rule.

of South Africa and Britain was one of the pioneers in the advancement of women's distance running. A precocious talent if ever there was one, in 1985 she captured the world record for the 5000 m., defeating the great Kristiansen in London, 14:48.07 to 14:57.43. Budd was only nineteen at the time and there was no telling what she could do in the following years. But a perverse political intermezzo (discussed in the previous aside) put a premature end to her international career.

Spearhead of the "Chinese Revolution" of 1993 in the long distances was Wang Junxia (born on 9 January 1973 at Jiapigou, a village in the Jilin province; 1.60 m./45 kg). According to a story which appeared in "China Sport", "as a little girl she was small, thin and weak. But she was not what she seemed ... rather like the ugly duckling who turned out to be not a duck at all, but a beautiful swan". Her parents were advised to steer her towards sport. Miao Zhigong, her first PE teacher, soon discovered that she had great qualities as a runner. These began to fully develop when she joined Ma Junren's squad in 1991. Her first known mark dates from that year - 4:17.18 for 1500 metres. By 1992 she was ready for action at international levels and at the World Junior Championships in Seoul she outpaced a strong field in the closing stages of the 10,000 metres to win in 32:29.90. In doing so she left behind future stars like Gete Wami of Ethiopia, Sally Barsosio and Lydia Cheromei of Kenya. The historic 1993 season started on a high note for "Ma's Army". On 4 April Wang, barely 20, emerged the winner in a marathon held at Tianjin in the phenomenal time of 2:24.07. Qu Yunxia was runner-up in 2:24.32. Both were apparently at their first competitive attempt over that distance! Wang covered the first half in 74:58 and the second in an unheard of 69:09. Western experts were obviously astonished and expressed doubts as to the actual distance .... ("Not quite a marathon" wrote "Track & Field News"). But much more was to follow. Wang won two titles at the Chinese Championships in June: 10,000 metres (31:08.42) and 3000 metres (8:27.68), with Qu second in the latter (8:29.30). Yet the Chinese phalanx was awaited at the World Championships in Stuttgart with mixed feelings. Ma decided to play it safe, limiting the field of action for everybody to just one event. Wise tactics no doubt, as Chinese athletes generally lacked international experience. In Stuttgart they were content to apply the pressure in the closing stages and such a strategy surely paid dividends. Ma's girls won 5 of the 6 medals at stake in the long distances. As related above, Qu and two others scored a clean sweep in the 3000 metres. Wang won the 10,000 with ease in 30:49.30, a time which raised her to no. 2 behind Ingrid Kristiansen in the All TIme List. Zhong Huandi was second (31:12.55) and Sally Barsosio of Kenya was third (31:15.38). This last, said to be only 15, was originally disqualified for cutting across an opponent (Elana Meyer of South Africa, who finally dropped out), but was later reinstated, as "no official second warning had been issued". Wang's second half (15:05.66) was considerably faster than the first (15:43.64). It was obvious that Wang and her teammates had several seconds tucked up their sleeves. The world records held by Tatyana Kazankina (8.22.62 for 3000 metres) and Ingrid Kristiansen (30:13.74 for 10,000 metres) were 9 and 7 years old respectively and it seemed reasonable to assume that they were ripe to fall. But hardly anybody could imagine

Wang Junxia (China) winning the 10.000 m. at the 1993 World Championships. Later in the same year she lowered the world record to a superb 29:31.78.

that they would be massacred. The story regarding the 3000 has been told already. In the 10,000 Wang lowered Kristiansen's mark by an awesome margin (41.96 secs) with an incredible 29:31.78. Zhong Huandi, at 26 the veteran of "Ma's Army", led for 7,000 metres, closely followed by Wang. The first half was covered in a fast 15:05.69, yet things really began to move when Wang took the lead with 3 km. to go. Thanks to her phenomenal endurance to speed the time for the second 5000 was a thrilling 14:26.09, actually faster than the official world record for that distance! Particularly impressive was Wang's time for the last 3000 metres - 8:17.47, i.e. well below Kazankina's world record from 1984. Zhong Huandi was second in 30:13.37, a fraction under Kristiansen's mark. Zhang Lirong finished third in 31:09.25. Needless to say, the news from Beijing created quite a stir in the rest of the world. Speculations ran high as to possible performance-enhancing drugs. But the chairman of the IAAF Medical Commission, Dr. Arne Ljungqvist of Sweden (a 2.01 high jumper back in 1952) said: "There is no such doping available that would all of a sudden make you run one minute faster in the 10,000. They're pretty good runners, that's my conclusion". An Italian medical expert, Dr. Enrico Arcelli, said: "It's altogether possible that the Chinese may use a substance existing in herbs, something deeply rooted in their traditional medicine. Such a substance may not only produce a performance-enhancing effect but above all act as an anti-stress medium likely to speed up recovery from physical exertion".

Ingrid Kristiansen (Norwey), a great pioneer in women's long distance running.

Gabriela Szabo (Romania), whose terrific finish earned her quite a few victories in the Golden League in 1998/99.

To add to the mystery, Ma's girls had indifferent seasons in the years that followed. The new world record holder for 3 and 10 kilometres actually left Ma's squad in 1995 and chose to prepare for the 1996 Olympics with a new coach. At Atlanta she was bold enough to try for a 5000/10,000 double. (By the way, the 5000 had replaced the 3000 as standard distance since the 1995 World Championships in Göteborg). The Chinese girl was confronted with tremendous odds though: very warm weather, a hard track and a time schedule in which heats for the two events happened to be perversely intertwined. She tried to save energies in the prelims with 15:24.28 for the 5000 on 26 July and 32:36.53 for the 10,000 on 27 July. She won the final of the shorter distance on 28 July in 14:59.88, after a 67.5 last lap. After that she had four full days for rest, yet she was outsprinted in the closing stage of the 10,000 by Fernanda Ribeiro of Portugal - 31:02.58 to 31:01.63. This was reportedly Wang's first defeat at the distance after 13 consecutive victories over a 4 years period (1992-96).

Shortly afterwards she was said to suffer from neurasthenia causing her insomnia and making it painful for her to run. Almost inevitably, the illness was blamed on her intense training over the past five years. Late in 1997 she tried to stage a comeback, alas with indifferent results.

In his own country Ma Junren was involved in controversies and even had health problems for some time. Yet the track world was to hear from him again in 1997, when he came up with a new generation of young runners. Once again, the fireworks were reserved for China's National Games, this time at Shanghai. The outburst of 1993 had spared at least one world record, that of Ingrid Kristiansen for 5000 metres (14:37.33 in 1986). This was bettered by Fernanda Ribeiro of Portugal with a time of 14:36.45 at Hechtel on 22 July 1995. The Shanghai outburst of October 1997 yielded the same pattern exhibited four years earlier at Beijing - the record was bettered in the prelims and again in the final. On 21 October Dong Yanmei did 14:31.27 in a heat, just ahead of Jiang Bo (14:31.30). Positions ware reversed in the final two days later as Jiang won in 14:28.09 from Dong (14:29.82). Dong Yanmei (born on 16 February 1977 at Xuengdong in the Liaoning province; 1.66 m./ 51 kg) had shown great promise in 1995, with times of 15:11.80 and 32:04.42. In the 1997 meet at Shanghai she really spread herself thin, with five races in the space of six days.

In addition to her 5000 metre record, she ran 3:55.07 for the 1500 and 30:38.09 for the 10,000. As if this was not enough, merely three days after the last of her Shanghai labours she won a marathon at Dalian in 2:28.09! A year later, however, the two Chinese girls had a sad aftermath. They went to Uniondale, New York, to compete in the Goodwill Games. Opposed to runners who had far inferior credentials, clock-wise at least, they had dismal returns. In a 5000 metre race, won by Olga Yegorova of Russia in 15:53.05, Dong was fourth in 16:00.56 and Jiang was ninth in 16:17.32. In a 10,000 metre race won by Tegla Loroupe of Kenya, a great marathon runner, in 32:15.44, Dong was third in 32:59.85 and Jiang again ninth in 35:43.13.

Ma's Thorny Road

No coach of modern times has been sung and praised, but also criticized and even vituperated, like Ma Junren. However, everybody seems to agree at least on one point: the boom of women distance runners in China - first in 1993, and again in '97 - was chiefly if not entirely his merit. Even in his own country Ma has been valued from different angles, as it became apparent from a series of articles published in "China Sport" magazine early in 1994. This "Iron Man" was born on 28 October 1944 at Qinjia Village, Shenyang, in Liaoning province, as the third of eight children in a family of poor farmers. His life was described in the above-mentioned articles by Deng Xuezheng as "A Thorny Path to Success". Ma went through harsh experiences first as a hard working teen-ager then as a soldier. In 1968 he lost his mother, who committed suicide by jumping into a well. In 1971 he became a PE instructor at a middle school in Ansham, some 20 Km. away from his home. Then he began to coach young girls, some of whom went on to distinguish themselves at national levels.

Ma really put his protégées to hard work, so much in fact that a colleague of his ridiculed his training methods as "helping the shoots grow by pulling them upwards". Authoritarian and at times cocky in temperament, he was known for his uncompromising ways. Surely the training load to which his pupils were subjected must have exceeded all known methods until then used in women's athletics. Each year he took his runners on five or six trips to a training centre at high altitude, where he combined an intense mixture of speed work and aerobic training. His pupils spent the better part of the year away from home, training up to 300 Km. per week. No wonder Wang, Qu and the rest could do just as well in the middle distances as in the marathon. There was little room left for their private life. But then Ma himself was ready to sacrifice anything for their sake. Indeed he "felt very sorry for having taken little care of his family, for being neither a good husband to his wife nor a good father to his two children, nor a good son to his old father".

In Europe, the outstanding distance runners of the Nineties were the above-mentioned Fernanda Ribeiro of Portugal, who won a world title in the 10,000 metres (31:04.99) in 1995, a year before her above-mentioned victory over Wang Junxia in the Atlanta Olympics; Sonia O'Sullivan of Ireland, a longtime campaigner who had her brightest moment in 1995, when she won the 5000 metres at the World Championships (14:46.47); and more recently the tiny Gabriela Szabo of Romania, who used her strong finishing kick to good advantage to win the 5,000 metres in two editions of the World Championships (1997 and '99). Szabo can point to times such as 3:56.97 (1500 m.), 8:24.31 (3000 m.) and a new European record of 14:31.48 (5,000 m.) all in 1998. Through her many victories in the IAAF Golden League in '99 she also set new records in the prize money department.

Africa has lately produced several outstanding runners: Derartu Tulu and Gete Wami of Ethiopia, who won global titles in the 10,000 metres (1992 and '99 respectively). Even Sally Barsosio, the Kenyan teen-ager who had caused havoc in the 10,000 metre race of the 1993 World Championships, returned in fine style to annexe a world title over the same distance in 1997.

MARATHON -
Van Aaken's theory

No other branch of women's athletics has recently shown such a dramatic progress as the marathon. The 42.195 km. distance was in chronological terms the last discovery made by the fair sex. Since the early Sixties magazines concerned with distance running had given publicity to the theory of a West German physiologist, Dr. Ernst Van Aaken, who claimed that women had the ideal physical and mental prerequisites to excel in the long-grind department. And he predicted that at such distances Eve would come close to men's standards more quickly than in other branches of the sport. He noted that the smaller sweat losses among women during a race reduced the stress of dehydration. Furthermore, women have a generally slower pace and weigh less, all of which reduces susceptibility to fatigue. One of the pioneers of marathon running was such a noted track ace as Paola Pigni-Cacchi, who on the last day of 1971, in Rome, covered the distance on a one-way course in 3:00:43. That was a best-on-record mark for Europe, but earlier in the same year the global mark had been brought to 2:46:30 by a 28-year-old

1971
1999

Australian named Adrienne Beames. That startling achievement came on a cold, wet Southern Hemisphere winter day, 31 August, at Werribee, Victoria, on an out-and-back course, "shaped much like a question mark". And somebody said that Beames owed her feat to a hard "100 miles (160 km.) per week training ration". That was only the beginning. Nine years later, the best-on record performance was down to an amazing 2:25:41! That performance was authored by a Norwegian teacher, Grete Waitz née Andersen (born at Oslo on 10 October 1953; 1.72 m./54 kg.) in the most widely publicized of modern marathons, the "Big Apple" affair in New York, on 26 October 1980. As Grete Andersen she had been a good track performer, winning a bronze medal in the 1500 m. at the 1974 European Championships. Asked if she intended to move up to the 3000 m., she then replied: "No. I've raced the distance once and thought it far too long". However, she had great staying power but only a moderate speed, and this circumstance eventually obliged her to move up ... In 1978, as Grete Waitz, she won another bronze medal at the European Championships, this time over 3000 m. This was still disappointing, in view of the fact that she owned the world record for that distance with 8:45.4 (1976). And later in 1978 she made her marathon debut - in the New York classic! The result was a runaway victory in 2:32:30, leaving her nearest pursuer more than 9 minutes behind. For the nimble yet sturdy Grete that was the first in a chain of nine victories in the New York event. The last one came in 1988, when she was thirty-five. Yet she ran her fastest ever marathon elsewhere, namely in London: 2:24:54 in 1986. The only flaw in her superb record at this distance is the lack of an Olympic gold medal. At the 1984 Olympics in Los Angeles she ran 2:26:18 but had to be content with silver behind Joan Benoit of USA, who went home in a splendid 2:24:51.4. This remains to this day the most competitive of all high class marathons, since third place went to Rosa Mota of Portugal and fourth to Ingrid Kristiansen of Norway, two runners who in later years were to follow in Waitz's footsteps as queens of the marathon. At her best, Benoit (born at Portland, Maine, on 16 May 1957; 1.60 m./47 kg.) was certainly supreme, her record including a 2:21:21 at Chicago in 1985 and a 2:22:43 at Boston in '83. But her career was curtailed by injuries and her overall international record suffered accordingly. The tiny Rosa Mota (born at Foz do Douro on 29 June 1958; 1.57 m./45 kg.) can claim three victories at the European Championships (1982, '86 and '90). No other marathon runner, male or female, has been able to score such a triple over a period of eight years in major international championships. Mota also won world (1987) and Olympic titles (1988), thus achieving another unprecedented triple. "Rosinha de Portugal", as she is affectionately called in her native country, must be rated as the most successful competitor of all, her carnet also including victories in various classics, such as Rotterdam, Chicago, Tokyo, Boston and Osaka. Clock-wise, the best effort up to 1998 was credited to Ingrid Kristiansen: 2:21:06 in winning the London marathon on 21 April 1985. On that occasion the

Rosa Mota (Portugal), possibly the greatest competitor in the annals of the women's marathon, here winning the 1988 Olympic title.

29-year-old Norwegian intended to become the first woman to run under 2:20. For much of the distance she motored along on a sub-2:20 pace, but finally had to slow down and settle for something less than that. She found partial consolation in the fact that she received the equivalent of $78,000 for winning the race and setting a world record. Kristiansen had 10 km. fractions of 32:52, 33:38, 32:48 and 34:00 and covered the last 2,195 m. in 7:48. I may recall that in the men's ranks a time better than Kristiansen's record was not achieved until 1952. The "historical gap" between the sexes is definitely narrower here than in most if not all other events. In major championship competition Kristiansen has been less brilliant though. She was third at the 1982 European Championships and fourth, as related above, in the 1984 Olympic race. A runner who has been consistently close to the top for years is Laura Fogli of Italy. Between 1981 and 1989 she placed among the top four in no less than eight editions of the New York marathon, her best being a second to Waitz in 1983. She was twice runner-up to Mota in the European Championships (1982 and '86). She picked up her fastest time, 2:27:49, in placing sixth in the 1988 Olympic marathon at Seoul.

Rosa Mota crowned her incredible career with a victory in the 1991 World Cup Marathon in London, time 2:26.14. After which she was quoted as saying, in a very wise vein: "For me the marathon always is a fight against my opponents, not the clock. The courses and weather are so different that nothing really is comparable. It's impossible to judge the value of a performance, so for me all that matters is winning". When she decided to close her account, after ten years of marathoning (1982-92), she could point to 14 wins out of a total of 21 races at that distance.

For the rest of the Nineties there was no woman capable of matching the competitive record of "Rosinha de Portugal". Clock-wise, however, there was a steady progress, as evidenced by the marks of the 1st, 10th and 50th best performers in World Year Lists:

	1st	10th	50th
1985	2:21:06	2:28:38	2:35:27
1990	2:25:24	2:28:56	2:33:19
1995	2:25:11	2:28:00	2:31:48
1999	2:20:43	2:25:29	2:29:20

Ingrid Kristiansen's best-on-record mark (2:21:06 in 1985) was bettered twice during the Nineties, both times by a tiny runner from Kenya, Tegla Loroupe (born on 9 May 1973 at Kapsait, West Pokot District; 1.53 m. / 40 Kg). In the early years of her career she concentrated on cross-country and track events, particularly the 10,000 metres, finishing fourth over this distance at the 1993 World Championships. For her debut in the marathon she chose the most celebrated of "windows" - New York's "Big Apple" classic. This was on 6 November 1994 and she made an immense impact on the marathon world with a sound victory in 2:27:37. That was the starting point of a new and most profitable career. As at the end of 1999 she can claim three victories at Rotterdam, two in New York and one in Berlin. Only the oldest classic in the world, Boston, continues to elude her - the best she could do was second in 1996. Yet, for all her victories in classics, she has never tried this distance in global (Olympic/World) championships. In such meets she usually opted for the 10,000 metres, making the podium twice at the World Championships (1995 and '99). On the latter occasion she lowered her personal best to 30:32.13. Her record performances in the marathon have occurred on two of the fastest courses available in the "business": Rotterdam and Berlin. Her 10 Km. splits follow:

	Rotterdam, 19 April '98	Berlin, 26 September '99
10,000 m	33:09	32:32
20,000 m	1:06:25 (33:16)	1:06:04 (33:32)
30,000 m	1:39:59 (33:34)	1:40:38 (34:34)
40,000 m	2:13:30 (33:31)	2:13:33 (32:55)
42,195 m	2:20:47 (7:17)	2:20:43 (7:10)

In both races, however, she had the advantage of "personalized pacing". In Rotterdam she was paced and shielded by a couple of Kenyan male colleagues. In Berlin she was accompanied until 40 km. by three Kenyan men from the stable of her German manager, Volker Wagner. In the opinion of most observers, these men partly served as a "windshield" to Loroupe. In her own opinion, however, they simply protected her "from other people stepping on my heels and pushing", as it often happens in mixed races as are most if not all the classics. On each occasion, Loroupe netted well over $ 100,000 in prize money.

The fastest time so far recorded in races for women only is 2:21:47 by Naoko Takahashi of Japan in the Asian Games at Bangkok on 6 December 1998, on a point-to-point course. The fastest time for an out-and-back course is 2:22:12 by Eri Yamaguchi of Japan at Tokyo on 22 November 1999.

Championship honours were divided during the

Nineties among runners of different areas of the world, with a clear advantage for Asia: at the World Championships, Japan supplied the winner twice, with Junko Asari in 1993 (2:30:03) and Hiromi Suzuki in 1997 (2:29:48); North Korea's Jong Song-ok won in 1999 (2:26:59). Wanda Panfil won for Poland in 1991 (2:29:53) and Manuela Machado for Portugal in 1995 (2:25.39). The two Olympic crowns of the decade went to Valentina Yegorova of Russia in 1992 (2:32:41) and Fatuma Roba of Ethiopia in 1996 (2:26:05).

The fastest time ever in global championships is Joan Benoit's 2:24:52 in winning the highly competitive Olympic marathon of 1984 in Los Angeles.

Tegla Loroupe (Kenya) holds the best-on-record time for the marathon: 2:20:43 in 1999.

HURDLES - One-lap event is on the map

Karin Balzer of East Germany retained her no.1 position in the 100 m. hurdles even in 1971, winning her third European title and lowering the world record to 12.6. This durable performer was coached by husband Karl-Heinz, 17 years her senior, who in his younger days had been East Germany's first 4-metre pole vaulter (1952). Balzer's successor as queen of the "highs" was her compatriot Annelie Ehrhardt née Jahns (born at Ohrsleben on 18 June 1950; 1.66 m./58 kg.), who in spite of her inconspicuous build won the 1972 Olympic title in Munich with 12.59 (the first auto-timed world record). The following year at Dresden she chalked up the last manual record, 12.3. Less reliable in bigtime competition but very prolific as a record breaker was Grazyna Rabsztyn of Poland (born at Wroclaw on 20 September 1952; 1.72 m./63 kg.). Her ultimate effort, 12.36 at Warsaw in 1980, was remarkable in view of her good but not exceptional speed, 11.42 on the flat route. She could thus point to a hurdles/flat differential of merely 0.94. But she would sometimes have trouble when the pressure was on. She was fifth twice in Olympic finals (1976 and '80) and performed indifferently at the European Championships. She did win her event in two editions of the World Cup (1977 and '79) though.

Two Bulgarians, Yordanka Donkova and Ginka Zagorcheva, were the dominant figures of the event during the late Eighties. The former (born at Yana, Sofia, on 28 September 1961; 1.77 m./67 kg.) lost three fingers on her right hand in an accident at the age of five. As a junior she was good enough to make the Olympic semi-finals at Moscow in 1980 but had to wait till 1986 to win her first major title, at the European Championships in Stuttgart. She went on to win Olympic gold at Seoul in 1988. She beat the world record several times, her best effort being 12.21 at Stara Zagora on 20 August 1988. Since she had a 100 m. flat best of 11.27, her hurdles/flat differential equalled that of Grazyna Rabsztyn - 0.94. Zagorcheva (born at Rakovski, Plovdiv, on 12 April 1958; 1.75 m./67 kg.) was in a class with Donkova on occasions. She had her best year in 1987, when she won the event at the World Championships in Rome and lowered the world record to 12.25 in an international meet at Drama. But an injury severely hampered her in 1988 and she failed to survive the first round at the Seoul Olympics. She excels Donkova in at least one respect: her hurdles/flat differential is as low as 0.87 (12.25/11.38).

Dominant figures of the Nineties in the high hurdles were Lyudmila Narozhilenko (later Engquist) and Gail Devers, who between them won most if not all the global (Olympic/World) titles awarded during that period. The former, a Russian (née Leonova on 21 April 1964 at Tambov; 1.74 m./66 kg) came to prominence under her first married name, Narozhilenko. She came forward nicely but had no luck in her first major experience, the 1988 Olympics at Seoul: in a semi-final, running with a heavily-taped leg, she fell at the last barrier and did not finish. Three years later she came into her own and won at the World Championships in Tokyo, after a hot duel with an American, Gail Devers - 12.59 to 12.63. In 1992 she started on a high note with a new personal best of 12.26, 0.05 off Donkova's world record, in an international meet at Sevilla on 6 June. This was to remain the fastest time recorded in the Nineties. In her second Olympic experience, at Barcelona, she was unlucky again as an injury stopped her in the next-to-last round. Early in 1993 she met disaster of another kind by failing a drug test in an indoor meet at Liévin. She was sentenced by the IAAF to a 4-year suspension. By then divorced, she maintained that her vitamin supplement had been spiked by her husband. Later a Russian court lifted this ban and in December 1995 the IAAF reinstated her under a so-called "exceptional circumstances" rule. In the meantime she had moved to Sweden, where she married her manager, Johan Engquist. She was granted Swedish citizenship just a few weeks before the Atlanta Olympics. Running for her new yellow-blue colours, she made a great comeback, winning the most coveted of titles in 12.58 and beating among others her arch rival Devers. Engquist did it again at the 1997 World Championships in Athens (time, 12.50). Two years later it was revealed that she was suffering from breast cancer. In the spring of 1999 she had her right breast removed. About four months later she stunned the track world when she showed up at an international meet in Stockholm and won her event in 12.68. The indomitable woman, by then 35, went on to win a bronze medal at the World Championships in Sevilla. It was, in her own words, "a near miracle".

Gail Devers, whose deeds as a sprinter have already been recounted, has been just as great as a hurdler. She can point to 3 world titles (1993, '95 and '99). On the last occasion, at Sevilla, she achieved a lifetime best, 12.37, winning from Glory Alozie of Nigeria (12.44) and the gallant Engquist (12.47). Devers has been unlucky in the Olympics as far as the hurdles are concerned. In the final at Barcelona in 1992 she led till the last hurdle but the sole of her lead foot slammed into the bar. She stumbled forward but somehow managed to sprawl across the finish line in — 12.75. Victory went to a Greek outsider, Paraskevi Patolidou, who ran the race of her life, 12.64. LaVonna Martin of USA (12.69) and world record holder Yordanka Donkova of Bulgaria (12.70) came next and Linda Tolbert of USA barely nosed out Devers for fourth, sharing her time. Four years later, at Atlanta, Devers had to be content with fourth in the race won by Engquist.

On the whole, the top marks of the Nineties were generally slower than those returned during the preceding decade.

1971
1999

Yordanka Donkova (Bulgaria), whose 12.21 for the 100 m. hurdles from 1988 was still a world record at the dawn of 2000.

The 400 m. hurdles event was added to the IAAF record book in 1974. The barriers are 76 cm. high, as opposed to 91 cm. in the men's event. First official record holder was Poland's Krystyna Kacperczyk: 56.51 at Augsburg in 1974. The first major title was awarded at the 1978 European Championships in Prague and was won by Tatyana Zelentsova of USSR in 54.89. The event was included in the programme of the inaugural World Championships at Helsinki (1983) and victory again went to a Russian, Yekaterina Fesenko, in 54.14. The first Olympic title, at Los Angeles in 1984, was won by Nawal El Moutawakil of Morocco in 54.61. Then a 22-year-old student at Iowa State University (USA), she was the smallest runner in the field, and her victory literally put Morocco on the map of world athletics. (Three days later, the North African country was to win another gold medal with Said Aouita). Of course it must be said that here, as in many other events, the absence of East Germany and USSR no doubt altered the overall picture. One of the most consistent performers of recent years was Sabine Busch of East Germany (born at Erfurt on 21 November 1962; 1.77 m./66 kg.), who won at the 1987 World Championships in Rome. Possibly the fastest of them all on the flat route (49.24), she lowered the world record to 53.55 at Berlin in 1985 and eventually reached a career best of 53.24 in 1987. As a result, her hurdles/flat differential was as high as 4.0 secs. In the meantime, however, the record had gone Russia's way, thanks to Marina Styepanova née Makeyeva (born at Meglovo on 1 May 1950; 1.70 m./60 kg.). She was a "late comer" in the strictest sense of the word, having bettered 60 secs. for the first time at the age of twenty-seven. She was down to 54.78 at twenty-nine and eventually reached the top in 1986, aged thirty-six, when she lowered the world record to 53.32 in winning the European title at Stuttgart. She thus became the oldest woman ever to set a global mark in a standard event. Later in 1986, namely on 17 September at Tashkent, she did even better with 52.94. Curiously enough, this was in a preliminary round of the Spartakiade for Under-23 runners and the "old lady" was allowed to compete "vnye konkursa", i.e. as a guest. With a 400 m. flat best of 51.25, she could point to a differential as low as 1.69. The latest crop of good 400 m. hurdles specialists

Lyudmila Narozhilenko-Engquist, a born Russian, gained the Swedish citizenship just in time to become that country's first female Olympic champion as she won the world's 100 m. hurdles title in 1996.

notably included Debbie Flintoff-King of Australia, winner of the 1988 Olympic title in 53.17, and Sandra Farmer-Patrick of USA, who did 53.37 in 1989. The latter is married to David Patrick, a 47.75 performer in the same event, male division.

Sally Gunnell of Great Britain (born on 29 July 1966 at Chigwell; 1.67 m./56 kg.) was the most brilliant performer in the 400 metre hurdles during the early Nineties. In 1988 she switched from the high hurdles to the longer event and improved so rapidly that she managed to finish fifth in 54.03 in the Olympic final at Seoul. Then things turned out to be more difficult, yet she won a silver medal at the 1991 World Championships, finishing 0.05 behind Tatyana Lyedovskaya (53.11) of Byelarus. Gunnell, a fine technician, was at her best in 1992/93. She won at the Barcelona Olympics in 53.23, beating the consistent Sandra Farmer-Patrick of USA (53.69). The flamboyant American and her British rival were re-matched a year later at the World Championships in Stuttgart. Both bettered Marina Styepanova's world record (52.94) and the British girl was again the winner, this time by a narrow margin - 52.74 to 52.79. In subsequent years Gunnell was hampered by foot injuries and the Americans took over, with new talents. Kim Batten (born on 29 March 1969 at McRae, Georgia; 1.70 m./57 kg) and Tonja Buford-Bailey (born on 13 December 1970 at Dayton, Ohio; 1.76 m./62 kg) offered a thrilling duel at the World Championships in Göteborg on 11 August 1995. There was never more than a few centimetres separating them and Batten just won with a desperate lunge - 52.61 to 52.62. They not only bettered Gunnell's world record but also improved on their previous best by more than a second. Deon Hemmings of Jamaica was third in 53.48. The Jamaican turned the tables on the two Americans at the 1996 Olympics in Atlanta, beating them on their home ground in 52.82. Batten was second (53.08) and Buford-Bailey third (53.22).

In the latter part of the Nineties honours went to Nezha Bidouane of Morocco and Daimi Pernia of Cuba. The former was crowned world champion at Athens in 1997 (52.97) and the latter at Sevilla in 1999 (52.89). Batten's world record survived all onslaughts, yet this remains a "fresh" event and further progress is to be expected in the near future.

1971
1999

Sally Gunnell (Great Britain), lane 4, winning the 400 m. hurdles in world record time, 52.74, at the 1993 World Championships.

JUMPS - High Jump: Rosemarie opens 2-Metre Club

Iolanda Balas' last world record (1.91 in 1961) remained unbeaten for ten years, in spite of the fact that in the meantime the majority of élite high jumpers had adopted the more efficient Straddle style. Iolanda's successor finally arrived in the person of Ilona Gusenbauer of Austria, who mastered 1.92 at Vienna in 1971. The 1972 Olympic final in Munich was featured by a major upset: a 16-year-old West German, Ulrike Meyfarth (born at Frankfort/Main on 4 May 1956; 1.86 m./71 kg.) outjumped a bunch of seasoned performers, including Gusenbauer, and struck gold with a record equalling 1.92, thereby becoming the youngest individual event winner in Olympic history. A fantastic achievement for a girl whose pre-1972 best was 1.80, although it should be noted that at that stage of her development Ulrike stood 1.84 - well above the average height of élite jumpers in those days. This exploit had a curious aftermath: years of utter mediocrity for the precocious Ulrike, including a tie for second (at 1.80!) in the 1973 European Junior Championships and a dismal 1.78 at the 1976 Olympics in Montreal, where she failed to qualify for the final. It was only in 1978 that she finally improved on her 1972 mark with 1.95. That was the beginning of a new career for the tall German. More on this later. The first woman to conquer the 2-metre barrier was a fine straddle jumper from East Germany, Rosemarie Ackermann née Witschas (born at Lohsa on 4 April 1952 1.75 m./59 kg.). At twenty she made the Olympic final in Munich, placing seventh at 1.85. Two years later she produced her first world record (1.94), then kept improving steadily, in the process winning European (1974) and Olympic (1976) titles. On 26 August 1977 at Berlin she made history by clearing 2.00 on her first attempt. Woman's breakthrough at such a height thus came sixty-five years after George Horine's pristine 2-metre effort in the male ranks. By 1978 Ackermann had a worthy rival in Sara Simeoni of Italy (born at Rivoli Veronese on 19 April 1953; 1.77 m./60 kg.), one of the greatest competitors in the annals of women's athletics. Sara had her first major clash with life at twelve, when she applied for the "corps de ballet" at the Arena, Verona's famous open-air theatre. The recruiter turned her down on the grounds that she had big feet and was a bit too tall for her age. But the girl was able to use those "big feet" to good advantage in another walk of life - and eventually became the "prima ballerina" of high jumping. To achieve that goal she had to work and toil for twelve years, starting from the day of her début in 1966, when she cleared 1.25 using a most rudimen-

Sara Simeoni (Italy) won high jump medals in three editions of the Olympics, striking gold in 1980.

tary style. She improved steadily year after year, passing from the scissors to the Flop. As regards the latter style, it should be said that it was put on the map of women's athletics by Debbie Brill, a Canadian who first used it as a teen-ager, more or less at the time Dick Fosbury introduced it in the male ranks. To preserve her identity, Debbie chose to call it "Brill Bend". She had a long but somewhat troubled career, with a personal best of 1.99 (indoors) in 1982.

Simeoni made the great leap forward between 1977 and 1978, when she improved by 8 cm. - from 1.93 to a record smashing 2.01. She achieved the latter height during an international meet at Brescia on 4 August 1978. That set the stage for a great showdown with Ackermann at the European Championships in Prague four weeks later. (Until then, the German had always had the upper hand in her clashes with the Italian).

The Prague event was a see-saw battle, which Sara won by equalling her fresh world record, while Ackermann had to be content with 1.99 and second place. The Italian cleared the winning height on her second try. As an eyewitness, I still remember that Ackermann made it too ... except that the bar fell seconds later, while she was standing in the pit with arms raised. In few events, if any, can the difference between success and failure be as infinitesimal as in a high jump contest. Simeoni had a unique ability in excelling herself under pressure, Between 1971 and '78 she did just that at every major international meet, as one can see from the following chart (PB = personal best):

	Result	Pre-meet PB	Diff. cm.
1971 Euro. Ch.	1.78 (9.)	1.76	+2
1972 Olympics	1.85 (6.)	1.80	+5
1974 Euro. Ch.	1.89 (3.)	1.86	+3
1976 Olympics	1.91 (2.)	1.90	+1
1978 Euro. Ch.	2.01 (1.)	2.01	=

In 1979 Sara and Rosi split, 1-1. By then, however, the German was plagued by recurrent tendon problems. Not even repeated surgery was able to put an end to her torment. At the 1980 Olympics in Moscow, jumping with a wrap just under the knee of her take-off leg, she had to be content with a fourth place at 1.91. Simeoni won at 1.97. Soon after that glorious day, she too began to suffer the effects of countless hours of intensive training. While her great German rival said farewell to the sport, the Italian struggled on for several more years. After many ups and downs, she offered one more glimpse of her competitive élan at Los Angeles in 1984. In what was her fourth Olympic venture, she cleared 2.00 - a height she had last mastered six years earlier. But that sufficed only for a silver medal. The winner? Lo and behold, the athlete who had first won the title as a teen-ager at Munich in 1972 - Ulrike Meyfarth.

1971
1999

Ulrike Meyfarth (Germany), a twotime winner of the Olympic high jump title - twelve years apart (1972 and '84).

This time she cleared 2.02. If Simeoni was great in winning her third Olympic medal, an unprecedented feat in this event, Meyfarth was simply amazing in duplicating her Munich victory twelve years later! In fact, she had returned to top form in 1982, winning the European title at Athens and breaking Simeoni's world record with 2.02. The following year she battled with a new star, Tamara Bikova of USSR, for world supremacy. The Russian (born at Azov, Rostov region, on 21 December 1958; 1.79 m./62 kg.) had the upper hand at the World Championships in Helsinki, 2.01 to 1.99. A week later, in the European Cup at Crystal Palace, London, both raised the world record to 2.03, with the German winning on the countback. But Bikova had the last word for the year when she cleared 2.04 at Pisa four days after the London battle. The Russian improved to 2.05 at Kiev on 22 June 1984, but her country chose to boycott the Los Angeles Games and so she had to stay away from the big feast. This great athlete had made her first appearance in the Olympics in 1980, placing ninth with 1.88. She was tenacious enough to go on for several more years, winning silver at the 1987 World Championships and bronze at the 1988 Olympics.

The most recent holders of the world record have come from Bulgaria: Lyudmila Andonova and Stefka Kostadinova. The former, daughter of a Bulgarian father and a Russian mother, reached her peak in 1984, a year after giving birth to a daughter. At Berlin on 20 July she shattered Bikova's fresh mark with a 2.07 clearance. As a Bulgarian she was of course among the unlucky athletes who missed the Los Angeles Olympics. In 1985 tragedy struck her in a more serious way when she was found "positive" to a stimulant (amphetamine) during a doping test. She was consequently suspended by the IAAF. When she returned to action, in 1987, she was merely a shadow of her former self. Kostadinova (born at Plovdiv on 25 March 1965; 1.80 m./60 kg.) had a more solid career. A precocious talent, she cleared 2 metres for the first time at nineteen. Two years later, in 1986, she matched Andonova's record at Sofia. And only a few days later, still at Sofia, she jumped 2.08. In 1987 she crowned a near perfect season with a victory at the World Championships in Rome, where she raised the record to 2.09, winning a tough duel with Bikova (2.04). Kostadinova's seasonal record in 1987 stands as the greatest ever in the annals of the event. Between 21 January and 26 September she had 32 competitions, indoors and out, and lost only three. Her average for the year was a hair over 2.00! In athletics, however, the balance of powers can change anytime anywhere, and at the 1988 Olympics in Seoul the Bulgarian unexpectedly lost to Louise Ritter, a 30-year-old American. Both cleared 2.01 in the competition proper, then failed at 2.03. But Ritter mastered 2.03 in a jump-off, equalling her personal best, while Kostadinova failed again. That settled the issue and added to the long list of Olympic upsets.

Stefka Kostadinova (Bulgaria), holder of the world's high jump record with 2.09 (1987).

The American, who prior to 1988 had been a good but not exceptional jumper (her highest honour being a bronze at the 1983 World Championships), certainly timed her peak condition perfectly. The Seoul event was at any rate a turning point in Kostadinova's career. Subsequently plagued by a knee injury, she has been unable to reproduce her 1987 form. Winner of the World Cup event at Barcelona in 1989 was Silvia Costa of Cuba, who chose the occasion to raise her lifetime best to 2.04.

The only jumper who came fairly close to Stefka Kostadinova's world record (2.09 in 1987) during the Nineties was Heike Henkel of Germany (born Redetzky on 5 May 1964 at Kiel; 1.82 m./ 63 kg). A gifted athlete no doubt, yet she had been active for more than ten years when she mastered two metres for the first time, in 1989. But only two years later she reached the top, winning at the World Championships in Tokyo with 2.05, with 7 centimetres to spare vis-à-vis Yelena Yelesina of USSR, who was second. Henkel had her best ever mark in an indoor meet at Karlsruhe in 1992 - 2.07.

Later in the same year she was crowned Olympic champion at Barcelona with 2.02. She thus succeeded Ulrike Meyfarth as Germany's high jump queen both mark-wise and in honours. She gave birth to a son in 1994, after which she repeatedly attempted a comeback, but persistent injuries hampered her and she never regained top form.

World record holder Kostadinova had a longer spell at the top. She too gave birth to a son, in 1995, yet a few months later she won her second world title at Göteborg with a 2.01 clearance. In 1996 she went on to annexe her first Olympic title at Atlanta with 2.05 - a great achievement, 10 years after her first world record performance.

This was in fact one of the highest "summits" ever, with Niki Bakogianni of Greece a surprise second at 2.03 and Inga Babakova of Ukraine third at 2.01. The imperishable Kostadinova won her last major title at the 1997 World Indoor Championships. Incidentally, this was her fifth victory in the annals of the undercover championships as opposed to two outdoor titles. As it happened to many great high jumpers, the wear and tear of training and competition with the resulting injuries finally put an end to Kostadinova's incredible career.

There has been a relative standstill in high jump standards of late. The last two world titles were won at 1.99, by Hanne Haugland of Norway in 1997 and by Inga Babakova of Ukraine in 1999. The latter has won medals in most if not all the major championships from 1991 to date.

POLE VAULT: Emma, the trail blazer; Stacy, the first world champion.

The most spectacular of jumping events was added to the women's international programme only towards the end of the 20th century. In certain countries, however, the excercise of vaulting for height was practised long before then. The remotest trace is offered by statistician Dave Carey, who credits the earliest US "record" to Ruth Spencer of Lake Erie College: 1.73 in 1911. In the years between the two World Wars pole vaulting had a certain number of practitioners in Germany and USSR. The best known mark for the first half of the century is 2.53 by Zoya Romanova, a Russian, in 1935. Sometime during the Eighties the most active explorer of women's talent in this event was China. It fell to Zhang Chunzhen to first clear a height of exactly 4 metres (1991). Another Chinese woman, Sun Caiyun, went up to 4.23 outdoors (1995) and 4.28 indoors (1996), alas after suffering a 3-month ban through a positive test for stimulants in 1994. In the meantime, however, the lead had been taken by an Australian, Emma George (born on 1 November 1974 at Beechworth, Victoria; 1.72 m./64 kg).

1971
1999

Emma George (Australia), a trail blazer in the evolution of the women's pole vault.

Stacy Dragila (USA), the first outdoor world champion (1999) in the women's pole vault.

As a teen-ager she was a trapeze artist in the Flying Fruit Flies Circus for several years. Her early interest in athletics was for the sprints and the long jump. Late in 1994 she entered her first pole vault competition, clearing 2.55. That was the start of a meteoric rise. Exactly a year later, on 30 November 1995 in Melbourne, she set the first of a long series of world records with 4.25. That was incidentally the year when the IAAF began to ratify record performances. George acted as a trail blazer to an ever growing number of women who in various parts of the world had taken up the event. As she went higher and higher, she adopted the approved Sergey Bubka manner, improving by one centimetre at a time. A barrier which over half a century ago had captured the imagination of men, namely 15 feet (4.57), was mastered by George on 20 February 1998 at Auckland. On that occasion she exhibited a change in her technique, jumping off 12 steps instead of her regular 16. "I didn't think it would be possible", she said. "To do this off my shorter run is just fantastic for me". Later in the same year she did 4.58, then 4.59. With her 17th world record, at Sydney on 20 February 1999, she conquered another barrier, more significant in the eyes of the metric-minded world - 4.60. In terms of competitive ability, however, she was clearly outshone by an American, Stacy Dragila (née Mikaelsen on 25 March 1971 at Auburn, California; 1.72 m./63 kg). In fact, Dragila had been at work a bit longer than her Aussie rival, but her progress was slower. Yet, when the IAAF decided to award the first major title at the 1997 World Indoor Championships in Paris, Dragila beat George, 4.40 to 4.35.

Wrote "Track & Field News": "Emma George forgot one of the elemental rules of vaulting - it doesn't matter how high you jump, it's how high you jump when the bar gets high. In fact, the Aussie star produced some spectacular clearances at lower heights, but when push came to shove, she couldn't clear the bar. And surprising Stacy Dragila could". This was confirmed time and again in subsequent seasons. George just could not do herself justice in hot competitions.

At the 1999 World Championships in Sevilla, on 21 August, George was the shadow of herself: just back from injury after a disastrous European campaign, she merely managed 4.15 and finished unplaced. Anzhela Balakhonova of Ukraine held the lead for a long time, but when the bar was raised to 4.60, Dragila turned the tables on her, going over on her second try. The American thus equalled George's world record and became the first world's outdoor champion in the history of the event. Balakhonova was second at 4.55 and Tatiana Grigorieva, a born Russian now competing for Australia, was third at 4.45.

As at the end of 1999, nine vaulters had gone 4.50 or higher. Quite predictably, the years that lie ahead will see plenty of further progress. It is altogether possible to envisage marks in the 4.80-region for a not-too-distant future.

LONG JUMP:
Lithuanian breaks 7-metre barrier

I have already hinted to the all-round ability of Heide Rosendahl. The daughter of a good discus thrower, she showed great promise as a junior, winning a silver medal in the pentathlon at the 1966 European Championships in Budapest. The long jump was her parade event. After capturing the world record in 1970 (6.84), she annexed the Olympic crown at Munich in 1972, edging Diana Yorgova of Bulgaria in a close contest, 6.78 to 6.77. Those Games were in fact the high-water mark in Heide's career. She also won a silver medal in the pentathlon and capped an unforgettable week with a fantastic anchor leg in the sprint relay, winning gold for West Germany. Her successor as world record holder in the long jump was Angela Voigt of East Germany, who did 6.92 at Dresden in 1976. Only a few days later, still at Dresden, she was beaten by her compatriot Siegrun Siegl, who wrested the record from her with a 6.99 effort. Voigt eventually won the rubber race at the Montreal Olympics with 6.72, while Siegl was only fourth. (The latter won the pentathlon in a photo finish decision a few days later).

The elusive 7-metre barrier was broken in 1978 by a Lithuanian representing USSR, Wilma Bardauskiene née Augustinaviciute (born at Pakruojis, Lithuania, on 15 June 1953; 1.72 m./61 kg.). She emerged as a topnotch performer at twenty-four with 6.82. On 18 August 1978 at Kishinyov she mastered 7 metres not once but three times: 7.07 (wind +1.9), 7.07 (wind over limit) and 7.06. At the European Championships in Prague, eleven days later, she improved on her record mark in the qualifying round with 7.09, then won the title with 6.88. With such marks as 11.2 in the 100 m. and 1.68 in the high jump, she certainly had a great potential. An expert like Igor Ter-Ovanesyan once described her as "7.50 stuff". But like so many other great athletes of our time she had to pay a heavy tribute to the Moloch of Injuries. A stress fracture severely hampered her in 1980 and she was unable to qualify for the Moscow Olympics. That was the end of her career. As it often happens when a conventional barrier finally crumbles, other jumpers soon entered 7-metre territory. The 1980 Olympic event in Moscow offered a hot battle, at the end of which a jump of 6.95 only sufficed for fourth place. Winner of a tight contest was Tatyana Kolpakova of USSR at 7.06, with Brigitte Wujak of East Germany and Tatyana Skachko of USSR filling the next positions with 7.04 and 7.01 respectively. In the early Eighties, two Romanians took turns in beating the world record. On 1 August 1982 Anisoara Stanciu née Cusmir succeeded Bardauskiene during the Romanian Championships at Bucharest with a 7.15 effort, but five minutes later she was outshone by Valeria Ionescu, who went 7.20 and thereby clinched title and record. But Stanciu had the last word in this "internal struggle" when she reached 7.27, then 7.43, still at Bucharest, on 4 June 1983. At the World Championships in Helsinki, later in the year, both Romanians had to bow to a talented East German, Heike Daute, who won with 7.27. The following year, at the Los Angeles Olympics, Romania was the only Eastern European country to enter. Stanciu and Ionescu seized the opportunity and finished one-two in that order (6.96 and 6.81 respectively). Heike Drechsler (née Daute on 16 December 1964 at Gera; 1.81 m./68 kg)) eventually put an end to the Romanian intermezzo in 1985, when she reached 7.44 at Berlin. The following year she did 7.45 twice,

1971
1999

Heike Drechsler (Germany), for many years a topclass long jumper. In her early years she was also a leading sprinter, equalling the world's 200 m. record in 1986 with 21.71.

401

first at Tallinn on 21 June then at Dresden on 3 July. By then also a co-holder of the world's 200 m. record (21.71), she excelled all her predecessors in basic speed. She won a great double in these events at the European Championships in Stuttgart, later in 1986, with 21.71 and 7.27. However, even the talented Drechsler was to find a tough nut to crack - tough enough to beat her in both the 1987 World Championships and the 1988 Olympics. The woman in question was Jackie Joyner-Kersee of USA (born at East St.Louis, Illinois, on 3 March 1962; 1.78 m./70 kg.), who gradually developed into the greatest all-rounder in the annals of women's athletics. This agile but solidly built American, sister of triple jumper Al Joyner (the 1984 Olympic champion), married her coach Bob Kersee in 1986. The long jump was her best event. She first landed in 7-metre territory at twenty-three and by 1987 she was able to challenge all comers. She equalled Drechsler's world record, 7.45, during the Pan-American Games at Indianapolis on 13 August 1987. The following month she had her first major clash with Drechsler at the World Championships in Rome, where she defeated the German, 7.36 to 7.13. In fairness to Drechsler, it should be added that she injured her left knee midway in the competition and was unable to take her remaining jumps. She finished only third, close behind Yelena Byelovskaya of USSR (7.14). But Joyner won the re-match at the Seoul Olympics the following year, edging Drechsler again, 7.40 to 7.22.

The current world record holder is Galina Chistyakova of USSR (born at Izmail, Ukraine, on 26 July 1962; 1.69 m./54 kg.). At twenty-two she managed 7.29, while no faster than 11.6 as a sprinter. She broke the world mark held by Drechsler and Joyner during the Znamenskiy Memorial meet at Leningrad on 11 June 1988, landing at 7.52 (wind +1.4 m/s). Prior to that, however, she had to take the back seat vis-à-vis Joyner and Drechsler, placing fifth at the 1987 World Championships and third at the 1988 Olympics. She is married to a world class triple jumper, Aleksandr Beskrovniy (17.53 in 1983). The most recent years have also seen the dawn of the triple jump, fair sex version. The first to beat 14 m. was Li Huirong of China, with 14.04 in 1987. In 1989 the event appeared for the first time in the programme of a big international meet. It happened in the Dagens Nyheter Games at Stockholm on 3 July and Galina Chistyakova seized the opportunity to raise the world's best to 14.52. But the latest word to this day belongs to Li Huirong, who did 14.54 at Sapporo on 25 August 1990.

Throughout the Nineties Galina Chistyakova's world record (7.52 in 1988) withstood all assaults - like many other record marks established in the decade we may recall as the "Smoky Eighties". Begrimed with smoke, yes, were it only in the sense that drugs tests left much to be desired at the time in terms of both frequency and effectiveness. However, one jumper managed to menace Chistyakova's record, namely Heike Drechsler,

Galina Chistyakova (USSR) holds the current women's world record for the long jump - 7.52 in 1988.

who did 7.63 at Sestriere on 31 July 1994, an effort which was nullified by an aiding wind of 2.1 m/s - over the allowable limit by an infinitesimal margin. However, if we consider that Sestriere, an Italian ski resort, is located 2,050 metres above sea level, then we may conclude that in intrinsic value Drechsler's 7.63 was surely no better than several other marks in the range 7.52/7.48, made with legal winds at or near sea level. That notably includes a mark of 7.48 made by Drechsler herself at Lausanne on 8 July 1992 with an aiding wind of merely 0.4 m/s.

As a top-class athlete Drechsler managed to survive the downfall of the GDR Communist regime better than most other champions of that country, whose names - just like hers - appear on several occasions with circumstantial evidence in Brigitte Berendonk's book "Doping". In the Nineties she definitely preferred the long jump to her other love, the sprints, and although failing in her repeated efforts to break Chistyakova's record she performed at 7.20-plus levels more consistently than any other jumper. After giving birth to a son in 1989, she returned to action and barely lost to her arch rival Jackie Joyner-Kersee, 7.29 to 7.32, at the 1991 World Championships in Tokyo. She regained the top a year later at the Barcelona Olympics with 7.14, winning from Inessa Kravets (7.12) and Joyner-Kersee (7.07). She won yet another world title at Stuttgart in 1993 (7.11) - ten years after her first victory in Helsinki. In later years injuries, necessitating surgery on both Achilles tendons, hampered her more than somewhat. After finishing fourth at the 1997 World Championships, she nonetheless managed to resist rust, so to say, and in 1999, at 35, she still jumped 6.91. Jackie Joyner-Kersee, the versatile American, also remained at or near the top for a long time. She actually reached her lifetime best in 1994 - 7.49 twice, first in New York then at Sestriere.

That still ranks as second best ever, after Chistyakova's record. The American won her second world title in 1991 (7.32) and was third in two editions of the Olympic Games (1992 and '96).

The most consistent medal-winner in the latter part of the Nineties was Fiona May (born on 12 December 1969 at Slough, England; 1.82 m./61 kg). In the early part of her career she competed in the colours of her native country Great Britain. Following marriage with an Italian athlete, Gianni Iapichino (national record holder in the pole vault with 5.70), she became eligible to represent Italy from 1994 onwards. This tall, streamlined girl showed great promise as a youngster, winning a world junior title in 1988. Then, after years of a relative standstill, she blossomed again under Italian colours. At the World Championships she collected a first in 1995 (6.98 with a wind over the limit), a third in 1997 and a second in 1999. In the Atlanta Olympics (1996) she was second to Chioma Ajunwa of Nigeria, 7.02 to 7.12. For all her competitive achievements she has a personal best of "merely" 7.11 (1998), plus a wind-aided 7.23 at Sestriere (1995).

The above-mentioned Ajunwa returned to competition after a 4-year drugs ban in June 1996, just in time to become Nigeria's first Olympic champion in the Atlanta Games. The remaining world titles of the decade went to Lyudmila Galkina of Russia (Athens 1997, with a personal best of 7.05) and to Niurka Montalvo (Sevilla 1999). The latter had finished second to May in the 1995 meet, competing for her native country, Cuba. She turned the tables on May four years later, 7.06 to 6.94. In the meantime she too had changed nationality through marriage and represented Spain in the Sevilla meet. Her winning leap was as close to being a foul as one could ever imagine. (Runner-up May obviously had a slightly different opinion...)

Potentially the greatest prospect by the end of the century was Marion Jones, the great American sprinter. As a long jumper she still has technical flaws, yet she did 7.31 in 1998 - the best mark of the last five years. After finishing no better than tenth at the 1997 World Championships she rose to third at Sevilla in 1999. Close observers of her training deeds rate her as "7.60 stuff".

1971
1999

Fiona May (Italy), a British-born long jumper, was a steady collector of medals, including a world title (1995), toward the end of the century.

403

TRIPLE JUMP -
Kravets really put it on the map

The triple jump is among the latest additions to the standard programme of women's athletics, which by the end of the 20th century very nearly coincided with that of the men, save for the steeplechase, the last fortress still to be conquered by Eve's descendants. Although adopted by the IAAF only in recent years, this event has a history which goes back to the end of the 19th century. American statisticians have unearthed a mark of 6.72 made by Mary Ayer of Bryn Mawr College (Pennsylvania) in 1899. In later decades, the event was competed in more or less regularly in USA, Japan, USSR and China, among others. Leading long jumpers would occasionally try it, e.g. Kinue Hitomi of Japan, who did 11.62 in 1926. The event really began to blossom in the Eighties and the last unofficial world record was credited to Galina Chistyakova: 14.52 in 1989. The IAAF book was opened the following year and Li Huirong of China, 24, became the first official holder of the world record - 14.54 at Sapporo on 25 August 1990.

The triple jump was first included in the programme of the World Championships in 1993 and the inaugural title on 21 August went to a Russian, Anna Biryukova (born on 27 September 1967 at Sverdlovsk; 1.74 m./58 Kg.), who chose the occasion to break the 15-metre barrier with 15.09. She was a good but not exceptional long jumper (6.89 in 1990). In fact, she had failed to qualify for the final of that event a few days earlier. Then came the woman who really put the event on the map: Inessa Kravets (née Shulyak on 5 October 1966 at Dnyepropetrovsk; 1.78 m. / 58 kg.). She was a top-class performer in the long jump, with a personal best of 7.37 plus a second place in the Olympics, both in 1992. In fact, she had been one of Biryukova's predecessors as holder of the triple jump record too (14.95 in 1991). At the 1995 World Championships in Göteborg she had a poor day in the long jump, finishing no better than tenth. She was thirsty for revenge and on 10 August she made history in the triple jump. Three days earlier she had watched Jonathan Edwards sail to a world record of 18.29 in the men's event. The Ukrainian girl very much wanted to emulate him. But she had a poor start, fouling her first two tries, apparently because she "found the runway so fast that she had increased the length of her usual runup". After that she badly needed a "safe" jump, still good enough to make the top 8 who were allowed to go on.

Here again she misjudged things, but in a different way for she "exploded" with a mighty 15.50 - 41 centimetres beyond Biryukova's world record! The wind was a legal + 0.9 m/s. Later in round 3 Biryukova reacted with a gallant 15.08 and in round 5 Iva Prandzheva of Bulgaria took second place with 15.18. Kravets' last three tries were anti-climatictic: foul, pass, 14.55. She amazingly described her world record as "an imperfect jump". The following year she annexed the Olympic title as well, with 15.33. Kravets, who back in 1993 had been inflicted a 3-month drugs ban for stimulants, had an operation in 1997 on a serious right thigh injury. Her above-mentioned marks of 15.50 and 15.33 were still the longest on record by the end of 1999. The last world champions of the century were Sárka Kaspárková of the Czech Republic in 1997 (15.20) and Paraskevi Tsiamita of Greece in 1999 (14.88, after doing 15.07 in the qualifying round).

Inessa Kravets (Ukraine), an excellent long jumper who reached the top when she turned to a new event, the triple jump.

THROWS - Shot Put:
Big advance
(on shaky ground),
then a long standstill

The name of Nadyezhda Chizhova of USSR (born at Usolye-Sibirskoye, Irkutsk region, on 29 September 1945; 1.74 m./90 kg.) appears in the evolution of the world's shot put record no less than ten times. Starting with 18.67 in 1968, she improved steadily year after year and chalked up her last record on 29 September 1973 at Varna with a toss of 21.45. She was the first woman to exceed both 20 m. and 21 m. She won three medals in the Olympics: bronze in 1968, gold in '72 and silver in '76. And she won the European title four times (1966, '69, '71, '74), a record in its kind. Far less brilliant was the competitive record of Helena Fibingerová of Czechoslovakia (born at Vicemerice on 13 July 1949; 1.79 m./99 kg.), who was a prolific record breaker but seldom did herself full justice in major championship meets. She succeeded Chizhova as record holder in 1974 with 21.57, then lost and regained the honour time and again, till 1977, when she reached 22.32. She had an even better mark indoors, 22.50, still in 1977. At the dawn of 1983, aged thirty-four, she could claim a bronze medal in the Olympics (1976), two silver and a bronze in the European Championships, and three seconds in the World Cup -but no golds. To rescue her there came, exactly in 1983, the inaugural edition of the World Championships. By then she had lost the world record to Ilona Slupianek of East Germany, her "bête noire". Judging from what happened in the early rounds, that 12th of August 1983 looked like another "ordinary" day in the life of the plump, affable Czech. With only one round to go she was no better than fourth, but on her sixth and last trial she tossed the iron ball 21.05 for the victory of her life! Following that great comethrough performance, she was in ecstasy for a long time, shedding tears, jumping and throwing kisses in the air and bear-hugging startled shot officials! Ilona Slupianek née Schoknecht of East Germany (born at Demmin on 24 September 1956; 1.80 m./85 kg.) was a real stalwart and as such she dominated the event for a long time. She had a "traffic accident" early in her international career, in 1977, when she was found "positive" to an anabolic steroid in a doping test conducted during the final of the European Cup, after she had won her event at 21.20. She was suspended by the IAAF but the ban was short-lived and in 1978 the world of sport was stunned and partly dismayed when she was allowed to compete in the European Championships at Prague. She duly won the title, with a toss of 21.41. Her best days still lay ahead though: in 1980 she broke the world record twice in the space of nine days, with 22.36 at Celje, Yugoslavia, and 22.45 at Potsdam. She crowned that season with a smashing victory at the Moscow Olympics, where she did 22.41 and left the runner-up almost a full metre behind!

USSR eventually regained the leadership with Natalya Lisovskaya (born at Alegazy, Bashkir Republic, on 16 July 1962; 1.86 m./100 kg.), who did 22.53 at Sochi in 1984. Three years later, at the Znamenskiy Memorial meet in Moscow, on 14 June, she improved to 22.63. She went on to collect the world title in Rome with 21.24. The following year she did 22.55 at the national championships in

1971
1999

Natalya Lisovskaya (USSR) can point to a world record of 22.63 in the shot put (1987), a distance which seems to be a distant cry under present-day standards.

405

Tallinn, her second best ever, then won the Olympic title hands down, with 22.24. In 1990 her standard dropped rather abruptly, curiously enough in conjunction with the intensification of the IAAF anti-drug campaign. At the European Championships in Split she was defeated by a 20-year-old East German, Astrid Kumbernuss, 20.06 to 20.38. Remarkably enough, the Asian Games held the same year at Beijing yielded better results as Xinmei Sui and Zhihong Huang, both of China, did 20.55 and 20.46 respectively. At the end of the season, Sui and Huang led the 1990 World List with 21.66 and 21.52 respectively. This was no major surprise though, because there had been earlier signs of China's coming of age, notably in 1988, when the 29-year-old Li Meisu threw 21.76 for a new Asian record, then won a bronze medal at the Seoul Olympics; and again in 1989, when the above-mentioned Huang won the World Cup event at Barcelona with 20.73, while Lisovskaya finished no better than fourth. With the doping ghost always round the corner, the shot put sorority obviously rests on shaky ground.

The problem of records made in the "Smoky Eighties" reaches paroxysmal proportions in events like shot and discus, where stereoids play a leading rôle in accelerating the growth of muscular power. The best shot put mark made in the last ten years is 21.69 by Vita Pavlish of Ukraine in 1998; the second best is 21.66 by Sui Xinmei of China in 1990. Lo and behold: at different times both were disqualified for doping offences - Sui for 2 years, after winning at the 1991 World Student Games in Sheffield, Pavlish also for 2 years, after winning at the 1999 World Indoor Championships in Maebashi (losing in the process a $ 50,000 first prize as well). Ironically and sadly enough, a few weeks later it was announced that Irina Korzhanenko of Russia, who was promoted to champion after the disqualification of Pavlish, had also failed a drugs test. Consequently, Korzhanenko was inflicted a similar ban. Hopes that steroid abuse among women throwers was on the decline were thus dashed again. Even so, the downfall of standards vis-à-vis the Eighties is clear enough to prove that the anti-doping campaign has been effective to some extent.

On the basis of competitive ability, two shotputters were particularly outstanding during the Nineties - Huang Zhihong of China and Astrid Kumbernuss of Germany, who between them won most of the global titles awarded in such a period of time. The former (born on 7 May 1965 at Zhejiang, Lanxy county; 1.74 m./100 kg) came forward gradually and never achieved near-record performances, but she was hard to beat in meets that counted most. She reached the top at the 1991 World Championships in Tokyo, winning with 20.83 ahead of world record holder Natalya Lisovskaya (20.29) and Svyetlana Krivelyova (20.16), both of Russia. Krivelyova turned the tables on her Chinese rival at the 1992 Olympics in Barcelona (21.06, a personal best, to 20.47) but the plump Huang resumed her winning ways at the 1993 World Championships in Stuttgart, beating Krivelyova, 20.57 to 19.97. Sixth in that event was an up-and-coming German, Astrid Kumbernuss (19.42). In the second half of the Nineties Kumbernuss was the dominant figure of the event, while Huang - who lived for some time in Britain and then in Holland - appeared to be on the downgrade. At the 1995 World Championships in Göteborg she was no match for the rising German, who won by more than 1 metre, 21.22 to 20.04. The Chinese champion had a lifetime best of 21.52 (1990).

Astrid Kumbernuss (born on 5 February 1970 at Grevensmühlen, then in the GDR; 1.86 m. / 89 Kg) first made the grade as a discus thrower, placing second in that event at the 1988 World Junior Championships in Sudbury. In the same year she threw the platter 66.60, which was to remain her best ever. She had been practising the shot as well, and in the Nineties this eventually became her parade event. Powerful and technically proficient, she won three World Championship titles in a row - in 1995 (21.22), 1977 (20.71) and 1999 (19.85). She also took the 1996 Olympic title (20.56). Kumbernuss was at her best in 1995/96, when she amassed a series of 53 consecutive wins, a streak that came to

Huang Zhihong (China), a consistent medal winner in important shot put competitions.

an end at the 1997 World Indoor Champioships in Paris: just recovering from injury, she was narrowly edged by Vita Pavlish, 19.92 to 20.00. Later in the year, at the outdoor Worlds in Athens, Kumbernuss and Pavlish engaged in another close battle, with the German finally on top by a narrow margin (20.71 to 20.66). On that occasion Huang Zhihong, by then 32, was fourth. Kumbernuss has a personal best of 21.22, made at the 1995 Worlds, as related above. This just suffices to place her 22nd in the All Time World List. But honours obviously rate above statistical rankings.

DISCUS THROW:
East Germany rules the winds

First to hurl the 1 kg. discus beyond 70 m. was muscular Faina Myelnik of USSR (born at Bakota, Khmyelnitskiy region, on 9 June 1945; 1.72 m./88 kg.), who turned the trick on 20 August 1975 at Zurich with a 70.20 throw. The following year, in one of Russia's traditional tune-up meets at Sochi, a Black Sea resort, she improved to 70.50. She won the Olympic title in 1972 and was European champion twice (1971 and '74). East Germany had a tough competitor in Evelin Jahl née Schlaak (born at Annaberg on 28 March 1956; 1.79 m./84 kg.), who won the Olympic title twice (1976 and '80) and bettered the world record twice, with a best of 71.50 in 1980. Another thrower who would always do well when it counted was Martina Hellmann née Opitz (born at Leipzig on 12 December 1960; 1.78 m./76 kg.), a two-time world champion (1983 and '87) and winner of the 1988 Olympic title. Although she never "interfered" in the record breaking spree, she invariably had the upper hand against record holders in championship meets. Current world record holder is another East German, Gabriele Reinsch (born at Cottbus on 23 September 1963; 1.85 m./88 kg.). She emerged early, placing second in the shot put and sixth in the discus at the 1981 European Junior Championships. Her best with the discus at the end of 1987 was 67.18, so she caused quite a stir when in June 1988 she improved to 73.42. And more was to follow soon: on 9 July, at Neubrandenburg, she whirled the platter an impressive 76.80, a new world record. But things took an entirely different turn at the Seoul Olympics later in the season: here Reinsch could do no better than 67.26 and placed a disappointing seventh, far behind her compatriots Hellmann and Diana Gansky, who finished one-two in that order. A note concerning Neubrandenburg: this town in Mecklenburg has a stadium (Jahn Stadion) where winds often play a prominent role. As of the end of 1999, no less than 7 of the 30 longest throws of all time in the women's discus had been made there! Latest in the line of East Germany's discus aces is Ilke Wyludda (born at Leipzig on 28 March 1969; 1.85 m./97 kg.). A prodigy as a junior, she placed fourth at the 1987 World Championships. The following year she threw 74.40 for a new World Junior record, but was not selected for East Germany's Olympic team. In 1989 she improved to 74.56 and was clearly the world's no.1 thrower. The following year she won the European title at Split. She is also a good shot putter (20.23).

In recent years even discus throwers have been unable to come close to the standard of the Eighties. Xiao Yanling of China accounted for the longest throw of the decade with 71.68. That was in March 1992 and a few weeks later she ran into trouble following a positive drug test. She was disqualified for 4

Ilke Wyludda (Germany), Olympic discus champion in 1996.

1971
1999

years. And her top mark was more than 5 metres shy of Gabriele Reinsch's world record! But then 70-plus marks are now a rarity, especially in major international tests. In fact there were only two in global (Olympic/World) competitions held during the Nineties: 71.02 by Tsvetanka Khristova of Bulgaria at the 1991 World Championships, and 70.06 by Maritza Martén of Cuba at the 1992 Olympics. The former was an outstanding performer over a long period of time (1982/92) but she too failed a drugs test in 1993 and was disqualified for 4 years. She made a low-key comeback in 1997. One of the most interesting performers of the decade was Ilke Wyludda of Germany. Taller than most of the leading throwers, she won the title of world junior champion twice, in 1986 and '88. As a senior she was second in the World Championships in 1991 and again in '95. She had her most glorious day at the 1996 Olympics in Atlanta, where she won with 69.66, leaving her nearest opponent more than 3 metres behind. She had a streak of 41 successive victories between 1989 and '91. Another German, Franka Dietzsch, was also prominent throughout most of the Nineties, finally clinching a global title in 1999 at Sevilla (68.14). That was her fifth appearance in the World Championships.

An interesting case was offered by Beatrice Faumuiná of New Zealand. Her parents hailed from Western Samoa and she became the first Polynesian to win a global title, at the 1997 World Championships in Athens. She did it the hard way though, after fouling her first two heaves in the qualifying round, and fouling again her first two in the final! In both cases she remedied just in time with her third try. In the final it was that third throw (66.82) that eventually led her to make history.

HAMMER THROW:
Pioneering efforts

The hammer throw was officially added to the IAAF list of world records at the beginning of 1995. As it had been done for shot, discus and javelin, here too it was decided to have a lighter implement vis-à-vis the one in use for men, namely 4 Kg. instead of 7,260 Kg. Length of hammer and diameter of head are fractionally inferior too.

The pre-history of the event, so to say, was not really much. Ekkehard zur Megede and Richard Hymans, both members of the ATFS, give a mark of 17.03 by Lucinda Moles of Spain in 1931 as the earliest of records. But it was not until the Eighties that somebody really got to work seriously. Not surprisingly, USSR was the first country to "fall in love" with the ball-and-chain event, no doubt as a reflection of their proficiency in the men's department. The IAAF retroactively ratified as first official world record a throw of 66.84 by Olga Kuzyenkova of Russia, made on 23 February 1994 at Adler, a resort on the Black Sea that had been for many years the favorite winter training centre of USSR hammer throwers. Until now, two women have been head and shoulders above the rest. One is Kuzyenkova (born on 4 October 1970 at Smolensk; 1.76 m./70 kg) and the other is a Romanian, Mihaela Melinte (born on 27 March 1975 at Bacau; 1.70 m./84 kg). Between them, they have accounted for the overwhelming majority of world record performances in the pioneering stage of the event. The Russian was first over 70 metres - 70.78 at Smolensk on 11 June 1997. However, this mark could not be ratified as there was no doping test. But a few days later, on 22 June in Munich, she got one off to 73.10 in winning the event at the European Cup. Melinte was second with 69.76, and that was to remain her last defeat at the hands of her Russian rival. The stocky, dark-haired Romanian clearly outshone Kuzyenkova in 1998 and '99, defeating her 8-0 in direct clashes. What's more, Melinte had the upper hand in all major meets. At the 1998 European Championships in Budapest, Kuzyenkova was still in the lead with two rounds to go, but Melinte finally forged ahead to win by a safe margin - 71.17 to 69.28. In 1999 the first world title was awarded in Sevilla and the Romanian again won from the Russian - 75.20 to 72.56. The feud was closer in the record department: Kuzyenkova had the last word for 1998 with 73.80 (Togliatti, 15 May), to which Melinte was able to respond with no better than 73.14, in a different meet. The Romanian regained the lead in 1999 with marks of 75.97 and 76.07, the latter at Rüdlingen, on 29 August. In between these record perfomances, Kuzyenkova brought her personal best to 74.30.

JAVELIN THROW:
The Felke-Whitbread feud

A stalwart in women's javelin annals was Ruth Fuchs née Gamm of East Germany (born at Egeln near Wanzleben on 14 December 1946; 1.69 m./65 kg.). She bettered the world record six times, starting with 65.06 at Potsdam in 1972 and ending up with 69.96 at Split in 1980. She was a two-time winner in both the Olympic Games (1972 and '76) and the

European Championships (1974 and '78). The conventional 70 m. barrier fell to a little known performer, Tatyana Biryulina of USSR, who came practically from nowhere to reach 70.08 at Podolsk on 12 July 1980. Like many other record-breakers, however, she "melted" in the hot atmosphere of the Moscow Olympics, finishing sixth at 65.08. On the same occasion even the fabulous Fuchs met a debacle: eighth at 63.94. The event was won by Maria Caridad Colón of Cuba at 68.40. The happy winner, aged twenty-two, became the first black woman to win an Olympic gold medal in a throwing event. In 1984, at Los Angeles, she was eventually succeeded as Olympic queen by another black marvel, Tessa Sanderson of Britain, who won with 69.56. Of course it should be remembered that USSR, East Germany and Cuba stayed away from the Californian rendezvous. Several countries have lately contributed to the advancement of records in this event. Bulgaria showed a meteor named Antoaneta Todorova, who produced a world record of 71.88 at the age of eighteen at the 1981 European Cup in Zagreb. After such an explosive start the rest of her career was utterly disappointing. Greece had her golden year in 1982, when Anna Verouli won the European title and Sofia Sakorafa broke the world record at Khania, Crete, with 74.20. Finland, a master country in men's javelin ranks, had a splendid performer in Tiina Lillak. In June 1983, at Tampere, she raised the world record to 74.76. Later in the season, at the World Championships in Helsinki, she brought a huge home crowd to its feet by clinching the gold medal on her last trial with a 70.82 throw. Fatima Whitbread, a Briton of Cypriot descent (born at Hackney, London, on 3 March 1961; 1.67 m./77 kg.), crowned twelve years of continuous improvement in 1986, when she conquered the world record with a 77.44 throw in the qualifying round of the European Championships at Stuttgart. This startling performance occurred at an unusual time of the day, as records go - 9.19 a.m. "A bit too early to understand all this", said the happy Fatima. The following day, in the final, she obliged with a throw of 76.32 and clinched the continental title. The following year, in Rome, she annexed the world title with another excellent mark, 76.64. On both these important occasions she beat the redoubtable Petra Felke of East Germany, who in 1985 had made the IAAF world record book with 75.40. Felke (born at Saalfeld on 30 July 1959; 1.72 m./63 kg.) had in any case recaptured the record in July 1987 at Leipzig with an impressive 78.90. The following year the sturdy German went to the Seoul Olympics with a very impressive credential: a world record of

1971
1999

Fatima Whitbread (Great Britain), world javelin champion in 1987, a year after setting a world record (77.44) in the qualifying rounds of the European Championships, held early in the morning.

409

80.00, made at Potsdam on 9 September. In the Games she finally turned the tables on Whitbread, 74.68 to 70.32. Towards the end of the century the downfall of standards in the javelin was even greater than in shot and discus. Petra Felke-Meier's world record (80.00 in 1988) remained a distant cry. The German herself, who between 1984 and 1991 was said to have won 103 out of her 119 competitions, headed a world year list for the last time in 1990 with 73.08. In the years that followed no one bettered 73 metres. Effective 1 April 1999 the IAAF introduced a new javelin with a modified centre of gravity likely to ensure that the implement would land point first. As will be remembered, a similar trick had been devised several years before for the men's javelin. According to some observers, such a change would result in a loss of 3/4 metres at top levels. (Marks made in 1999 suggest that the loss may not be so great).

Petra Felke-Meier (East Germany), holder of the world javelin record with the "old" implement (80.00 in 1988).

The most consistent performer of the Nineties was Elsa Katrine "Trine" Hattestad (née Solberg on 18 April 1966 at Lörenskog; 1.73 m./76 kg). This colourful and versatile woman was in her youth a clever goal scorer in Norwegian second division handball. In athletics she made her first appearance in the Olympics at Los Angeles under her maiden name of Solberg, aged 18, and finished fifth. It was only in her fourth appearance (Atlanta 1996) that she finally reached the podium, as third. Her record in the World Championships is far more impressive: first in 1993 (69.18) and 1997 (68.78), third in 1999. She can claim the longest throw of the past nine years, 72.12 in 1993, as well as the longest (but unratified) throw with the new javelin - 68.19 at Fana on 28 July 1999. Amid all this, she gave birth to two sons in 1990 and '95 and braved a storm of a vicious kind in 1989, when she was suspended for a supposed doping offence. However, she protested her innocence and after discoveries of variances in the results of tests, she was reinstated and successfully sued Norges Fri-Idrettsforbund for $ 50,000 loss of earnings!

There's plenty of strength in those lovely arms

To many observers the throwing events look like one branch of athletics in which women will seldom, if ever, come reasonably close to men's standards. Woman's smaller muscular frame is obviously a serious handicap in such events, more perhaps than in most other sections of the sport. Of course, throwing implements used by women are lighter than those in use in the men's division, yet there is a table, worked out almost thirty years ago by Dr. Fernando Amado of Portugal, which allows a comparison between marks made with implements of different weight.
Here is how current women's world records (listed first) convert vis-à-vis marks made with men's implements:
Shot   22.63 (4 kg) = c:a 16.50   (7.260 kg)
Discus   76.80 (1 kg) = c:a 52.00   (2 kg)
Javelin   80.00 (600 gr)= c:a 68.50   (800 gr)
As one can see, the distances reached by the likes of Lisovskaya, Reinsch and Felke correspond, more or less, to the top marks registered in the men's department a little more than half a century ago. A further proof that woman has in her arms all it takes to do herself justice.

Another prominent thrower was Natalya Shikolenko of Byelarus, who was a close second to Silke Renk of Germany, 68.26 to 68.34, in the 1992 Olympics, after leading until the last round. The following year she was third in the World Championships, just ahead of her younger sister Tatyana, and finally won in 1995 (67.56). Tatyana, who first represented Byelarus, then Russia from 1996 onwards, was second in the 1999 World Championships behind Mirela Manjani-Tzelili of Greece, 66.37 to 67.09. The latter mark is the new official world record.

The other global titles awarded in the Nineties went to Xu Demei of China, who upset world record holder Felke-Meier in a close contest in 1991 (68.78 to 68.68); and to Heli Rantanen of Finland, who gave her javelin-mad country the first women's title in the Olympics (67.94 in 1996).

PENTATHLON / HEPTATHLON

Joyner in the limelight

One of the fiercest battles in pentathlon competition took place at the Munich Olympics in 1972. The chief characters in the play were Mary Peters of Britain (born at Halewood, Lancashire, on 6 July 1939; 1.73 m./71 kg.) and Heide Rosendahl of West Germany. The former had been a pentathlon addict for 17 years but on those two days in Munich she really surpassed herself. With Rosendahl also in top form - as previously related in connection with the long jump - the contest ended in a photo finish decision. Both broke the world record (4775 pts by Burglinde Pollak of East Germany in 1970) and Peters won, 4801 to 4791. In the last event on the programme, the 200 m., Rosendahl went home first in 22.96, while Peters was fourth in 24.08. One could therefore say that Rosendahl formally held the world record for 1.12 secs.! In all probability there had never been such a short-lived global record. But one with a shorter "life span" was to follow in 1980.... At the Montreal Olympics (1976) the pentathlon offered an even closer decision: two girls from East Germany, Siegrun Siegl and Christine Laser, finished with the same score, 4745 pts. The gold medal was awarded to Siegl, who had excelled her rival in 3 out of 5 events. Burglinde Pollak made it a clean sweep for East Germany, trailing her teammates only five points behind! When combined events competitions yield such close verdicts, one is inevitably tempted to doubt the significance of the final result, resting as it does on the vagaries of a shaky scoring table. Beginning with 1977 the pentathlon was contested in one day, the sequence of events being as follows: 100 m. hurdles, shot, high jump, long jump, 800m. This was to be the last version and the ultimate record was set during the 1980 Olympics in Moscow. Here the Russians, led by Nadyezhda Tkachenko (born at Kremenchug, Poltava region, on 19 September 1948; 1.65 m./70 kg.), monopolized honours. The thick-set Tkachenko was back after an 18-month suspension, having been disqualified for drug abuse at the 1978 European Championships in Prague (a contest she had won). In Moscow she won with 5083 pts., with the following marks: 13.29 (100 m. hurdles), 16.84 (shot), 1.84 (high jump), 6.73 (long jump) and 2:05.2 (800 m.). Olga Rukavishnikova (4937 pts) and Olga Kuragina (4875 pts) also bettered the previous record, held by Kuragina (4856 pts earlier in 1980). In the last event, the 800 m., the three Russians finished in the following order: Kuragina 2:03.6, Rukavishnikova 2:04.8, Tkachenko 2:05.2. As a result, the eventual place winners formally held the world record for a short while, Rukavishnikova for merely 0.4 sec., a record in its kind. Tkachenko owed her victory, chiefly if not entirely, to her superior mark in the shot put (16.84). Rukavishnikova actually beat her in 3 events out of 5, and even bronze medallist Kuragina excelled Tkachenko in 3 events and was tied with her in a fourth.

In 1981 the pentathlon was replaced by the heptathlon, in recognition of the fact that women had by then acquired a high degree of staying power. The seven events were to be held on two consecutive days, as follows: 1st day - 100 m. hurdles, high jump, shot, 200 m.; 2nd day - long jump, javelin, 800 m. The first official world record was set by Ramona Neubert of East Germany: 6716 pts at Kiev in 1981. Two years later, at Moscow, she was up to 6836 pts and in the same year she won at the World Championships in Helsinki (6714 pts). However, the first star of the heptathlon came from America, in the person of the ultra-dynamic Jackie Joyner-Kersee, whom I have introduced in the chapter devoted to the long jump. She was the first woman to top 7000 pts. She did so at the Goodwill Games in Moscow on 6 and 7 July 1986, when she piled up 7148 pts with the following marks: 12.85 (100 m. hurdles), 1.88 (high jump), 14.76 (shot), 23.00 (200 m.), 7.01 (long jump), 49.86 (javelin), 2:10.02 (800 m.). She was to exceed 7000 pts four more times and her highest score was at the 1988 Olympics in Seoul -7291 pts, with the following marks: 12.69 (100 m. hurdles), 1.86 (high jump), 15.80 (shot), 22.56 (200 m.), 7.27 (long jump),45.66 (javelin),

2:08.51 (800 m.). She was clearly in a league of her own, her victory margin over second place winner Sabine John of East Germany being 394 pts ! The year before, in Rome, she had won the World Championship title by an even more ludicrous margin: 564 pts (7128 / 6564). Runner-up in Rome was Larisa Nikitina of USSR, who in 1989 at Bryansk became the second 7000-plus performer with a score of 7007 pts. On that occasion she used a wind of 4.0 m/s (the maximum allowed in multi-event competitions) to reach 6.73 in the long jump.

The incomparable Jackie Joyner-Kersee continued to be a dominant force well into the Nineties, even though she was hampered by injuries now and then. One such case occurred at the 1991 World Championships in Tokyo. After 3 events she was clearly in the lead and well on her way to achieving a high score when a hamstring pull in the 200 metres forced her to drop out. That put an end to a wondrous series of 14 consecutive heptathlon victories (1985-91). She came back in fine style at the 1992 Olympics in Barcelona, where she won easily with 7044 pts, which was to remain the highest score of the Nineties. And she was on top again at the World Championships in Stuttgart a year later, even though her winning margin over Sabine Braun of Germany was pretty narrow - 6837 to 6797 pts. That was Jackie's seventh global (Olympic/World) title in the period 1987-1993 on the long jump/heptathlon axis. This phenomenal athlete, no doubt among the very greatest in the history of women's athletics, throve for years in the atmosphere of a sport-loving family. Her brother Al was an Olympic champion in the triple jump in 1984 and her sister-in-law, Florence Griffith-Joyner, made history in the sprints. Then, as previously related, she married her coach, Bob Kersee, a former sprinter.

No other athlete has been able to come close to Joyner-Kersee's top scores in recent years. A most durable performer was Sabine Braun (born on 19 June 1965 at Essen; 1.74 m. / 62 kg) who over a period of fifteen years competed in four editions of the Olympic Games and six editions of the World Championships. In the former her best was a third place in 1992, but in the latter she won the title twice, in 1991 (6672 pts) and 1997 (6739 pts) and was second once (1993).

Another stalwart of the last decade of the century was Ghada Shouaa of Syria (born on 10 September 1972 at Mahrda; 1.87 m. / 61 kg). A basketball international in 1989-90, she came to the fore by winning several events at the Pan-Arab Games in the early Nineties and eventually reached world class under coach Kim Bukhantsev, a former USSR discus thrower of international caliber. She put her country on the map of athletics by winning at the 1995 World Championships in Göteborg (6651 pts). The following year she retained her leadership at the Atlanta Olympics with 6780 pts, leaving her nearest opponent more than 200 digits behind. Her highest score is 6942 pts. made earlier in 1996 at Götzis, an Austrian town that has been for many years the springtime rendezvous of multiple event buffs from sundry corners of the globe. This tall, streamlined Syrian was laid to rest for the better part of two years (1997-98) by a severe back injury. Yet she made a gallant comeback at the 1999 World Championships in Sevilla, finishing third with 6500 pts behind Eunice Barber of France (6861 pts), a native of Sierra Leone, and Denise Lewis of Britain (6724 pts).

Early in 1999, when the IAAF introduced a javelin with a different technical specification, the question arose whether Joyner-Kersee's heptathlon record (7291 pts in 1988) should be removed from the books or not. There was a debate on the subject but

Jackie Joyner-Kersee (USA), the greatest of all in the multiple events, was also a topclass long jumper.

it was finally decided that the existing record should remain. The point was well summarized by Bob Hersh, a US member of the IAAF technical committee: "The javelin is only one event of seven, and the revision of the implement is not so significant as to warrant the creation of a new heptathlon record and the deletion of the existing record".

RELAYS - Russo-German-American symphony

The East German school continued to dominate the picture in the sprint relay, providing the winning foursome in two Olympics - at Montreal (42.55) and Mocow (41.60, a new world record), and in the 1983 World Championships (41.76). The teams, coached by Horst-Dieter Hille, invariably displayed great cohesion and had an excellent anchor leg runner in little Marlies Göhr. The current world record, 41.37, was set in the 1985 World Cup at Canberra by a team consisting of Silke Gladisch, Sabine Rieger, Ingrid Auerswald and Göhr. In recent years the strongest opposition has come from USA. The Americans won the 1984 Olympic title at Los Angeles (41.65), with East Germany not in the race. Four years later, at the Seoul Olympics, a US team with Alice Brown, Sheila Echols, "Flo-Jo" Griffith and Evelyn Ashford beat the redoubtable East Germans, 41.98 to 42.09. The world record set by the GDR girls in 1985 (41.37) withstood all assaults even in the Nineties. The closest approach occurred at the 1997 World Championships in Athens, where a US quartet consisting of Chryste Gaines, Marion Jones, Inger Miller and Gail Devers sped to a nifty 41.47, second best

1971
1999

Ghada Shouaa (Syria) put her country on the map of athletics by winning the heptathlon at the 1995 World Championships. She did it again at the Atlanta Olympics in 1996.

413

ever, for a comfortable victory over an Ottey-less Jamaican team (42.10). As per tradition, the Americans had been practising in that lineup for a relatively short time and their passes ranged from "safe" to "conservative". For sheer excitement, however, the greatest battle of the decade had unfolded four years earlier at the World Championships in Stuttgart. The feud between Russia (Olga Bogoslovskaya, Galina Malchugina, Natalya Voronova, Irina Privalova) and USA (Michelle Finn, Gwen Torrence, Wenda Vereen, Gail Devers) was as close as a sprint race could ever be. Naked eyes just could not tell who had won. Russia was finally declared the winner and both teams were credited with 41.49. Devers, whose impact as anchor leg runner was almost as great as that of Carl Lewis in the men's department, said the race had been decided by the handoffs. An obvious conclusion, no doubt.

Even so, USA won 4 of the 7 global titles awarded in the Nineties, while Jamaica, Russia and Bahamas took one each.

East Germany's runners have played a decisive role even in the 4x400 m. relay. This event was included in the Olympic programme at Munich in 1972 and the winners were Dagmar Käsling, Rita Kühne, Helga Seidler and Monika Zehrt, who earned the gold medal for East Germany in 3:22.95. East Germany duly duplicated at Montreal four years later, again in world record time, 3:19.23. Their ultimate to date is 3:15.92 (Erfurt, 1984), with a team consisting of Gesine Walther, Sabine Busch, Dagmar Rübsam and Marita Koch. This mark stood as a world record till the 1988 Olympics in Seoul, where USSR and USA engaged in a hot duel and finished in that order, with times of 3:15.17 and 3:15.51. The splits tell the story of the dramatic race:

USSR (3:15.17)

Tatyana Lyedovskaya	50.12
Olga Nazarova	47.82
Maria Pinigina	49.43
Olga Brizgina	47.80

USA (3:15.51)

Denean Howard	49.82
Diane Dixon	49.17
Valerie Brisco	48.44
Florence Griffith	48.08

Griffith's anchor leg was remarkable, coming as it did only 40 minutes after her victorious race in the sprint relay. This was her eleventh labour in the space of a week, and the only non-winning one!

The 4x400 metre relay was yet another event where the world record (3:15.17 by USSR in 1988) remained unapproached in the last decade of the century. The fastest time of the Nineties was 3:16.71 by a US team at the 1993 World Championships in Stuttgart - the fourth best on record. Splits were as follows: Gwen Torrence 49.0, Maicel Malone 49.4, Natasha Kaiser-Brown 49.5, Jearl Miles 48.8. Russia, with Irina Privalova timed in 48.5 for the anchor leg, was second in 3:18.38.

During the decade, USSR/Russia and USA each had 3 wins in global championships, and Germany had one.

WALKS -
Fleet-footed gals

The earliest race walking records for women to appear in IAAF books were 22:50.0 for 5000 m. by Aleksandra Dyeverinskaya of USSR and 47:58.2 for 10,000 m. by Anne Jansson of Sweden, both made in 1981. Since then, big advances have been registered in this domain, but it is only fair to admit that some records are of dubious significance due to different interpretations of what constitutes fair walking in the days of "lifting". Performances made in solo efforts during local or national meets obviously seem less credible than those recorded in major international games, yet even the latter have been questioned on occasion. Some of the major indoor meets have adopted ultra-short walking events, which often border on farce. The most prolific record breaker of recent years, little Kerry Saxby of Australia (born at Ballina, New South Wales, on 2 June 1961; 1.63 m./57 kg.) has had her share of trouble, e.g.in the 3000 m. of the 1987 World Indoor Championships in Indianapolis, where she was disqualified with 400 m. to go. Later in the same year she had to be content with second behind Irina Strachkova of USSR in the 10,000 m. at the World Outdoor Championships in Rome. Saxby won her first international title at the 1989 World Indoor Championships in Budapest, beating the redoubtable Beate Anders of East Germany in the 3000 m. in a record shattering 12:01.65. Early in 1990, at Sydney, Saxby was credited with another world record, this time over 5000 m.: 20:17.19. Later in the season, at the Goodwill Games in Seattle, she had to settle for second behind Nadyezhda Ryashkina of USSR in a hot 10,000 m. The times were the fastest on record: Ryashkina 41:56.23, Saxby 41:57.22. But even Ryashkina had her day of sorrow before the season was out. This was in the 10,000 m. of the European Championships at Split. After repeated warnings, she incurred the final wrath of a judge with 2000 m. to go, while leading. . She initially ignored the ruling, but she met the firm and somewhat rude opposition of the judge and finally had to give up. TV viewers around the world saw her as she sat alone on the sidewalk crying her eyes out. Victory went to Anna Rita Sidoti, a diminutive Italian.

Even in the last decade of the century important competitions were featured as often as not by disqualifications for incorrect walking. In a few cases the fatal (third) red card happened to be notified after the "culprit" had crossed the finish line. Some of the leading stars had mixed fortunes in this respect. Like, for example, Alina Ivanova of Russia. She won the 10 Km. event at the 1991 World Championships in Tokyo (time, 42:57). A year later, at the Barcelona Olympics, she again crossed the finish line first only to pick up a post-race disqualification. In a thrilling finish she had simply thrown caution to the wind .... Chen Yueling of China was the official winner (44:32) ahead of another Russian, Yelena Nikolayeva. That was not all: Ileana Salvador of Italy, who came next, was also disqualified, so that another Chinese, Li Chunxiu, had the unique experience of winning a bronze medal after crossing the line as fifth.

The above-mentioned Nikolayeva was one of the most consistent performers of the decade. She was place winner in most of the vital competitions, including the IAAF World Cup, and had her most glorious day at the 1996 Olympics in Atlanta, where she won with a fast 41:49, a new Olympic record. She can claim a world record of 41:04 on road, made at Sochi on 20 April 1996. The fastest time on a track course is still Nadyezhda Ryashkina's 41:56:23 (1990).

Finland had a bright star in Sari Essayah, the daughter of a Finnish mother and a Moroccan father. Her rendezvous with glory was at the 1993 World Championships in Stuttgart, where she won in 42:59. Italy is still one of the leading powers. Ileana Salvador and Elisabetta Perrone were place winners on several occasions, but were outshone by a sprightly little genius, Anna Rita Sidoti, who at 1.50 was declared the "smallest ever world champion" when she won at Athens in 1997 (42:55.49). In 1998 she won her second gold at the European Championships, eight years after the first.

In connection with the 1999 World Championships in Sevilla the 10 Km. event was replaced by a longer one, double in length. Easily the best performer of the year was Liu Hongyu of China, a walker from the Liaoning province, cradle of many distance runners as well.

She scored a notable double, winning the IAAF World Cup race at Mézidon on 2 May in a fast 1:27:32, and the World Championship title at Sevilla in 1:30:50, barely ahead of her teammate Wang Yan (1:30:52). A Russian veteran, Nadyezhda Ryashkina, had previously set a new world record of 1:27:30 (Adler, 7 February). By then 33, she could point to a long career, rich in fast times but rather indifferent in terms of international honours. Similar to that of another veteran, Australia's Kerry Saxby-Junna, 39, who nonetheless finished a brilliant third in the World Championship race at Sevilla, twelve years after placing second over 10 Km. in Rome.

1971
1999

Anna Rita Sidoti (Italy), the smallest but also one of the greatest walkers in the 10 Km. event.

Flashes of lightning on the way to Sydney
Highlights of the 2000 athletic season
(up to the end of June)

The "pièce de résistance" of the 2000 athletic season will be the Sydney Olympics, the second ever held in Australia and, for that matter, in the Southern Hemisphere. The Games will take place from 22 September to 1 October.
What follows is a brief summary of the most notable performances made by the first half of the year. At the time of writing the list of forthcoming events notably includes the US Olympic Trials at Sacramento, California, and the African Championships at Algiers.
In the latter, alas, organizers will have to reckon with a high number of notable absentees, mostly leading distance runners whose eyes are principally focussed on the circus of European Grand Prix meets.

MEN

Sprinter Ato Boldon of Trinidad, who was bogged down with an injury in the crucial stage of the 1999 season, appears to be on the comeback trail. At Lausanne on 5 July he scored a fine 100/200 metre double with times of 9.95 and 19.97. Incidentally, he holds the record for the fastest one-day double at these distances: 9.90 and 19.77 at Stuttgart on 13 July 1997. However, the best 100 metre time of the year so far belongs to his rival and friend Maurice Greene of USA, who sped to 9.91 at Osaka on 13 May, fine running with a slightly adverse wind (0.4 m/s). But Greene had ups and downs in European meets and will be hard pressed at the US Olympic Trials in both 100 and 200 metres. At the longer distance he will meet the incomparable Michael Johnson, who is looking for a 200/400 double there – and in the Sydney Olympics as well. Early in the year MJ had a brief but scintillating South African campaign. After a 19.71 in the 200 metres (Pietersburg, 18 March), he went on to clock a superb 30.85 for the 300 metres at Pretoria on 24 March, easily and by far the fastest time ever recorded over this distance. The altitude factor (Pretoria is 1400 m. above sea level) may have helped him somewhat, yet he ran a very impressive race, with 100-metre fractions of 10.68, 9.43 (200 in 20.11) and 10.74. The runner-up finished almost 2 seconds behind. Johnson wound up his tour with a "manual" 43.9 for the 400 metres at sea level (Cape Town, 31 March).

2000

The main feature of the middle distance events was a hot 800 metre duel between André Bucher of Switzerland and Djabir Said-Guerni of Algeria in the Lausanne meet of 5 July. Spurred on by the home crowd, the Swiss beat the bronze medallist of the 1999 World Championships – 1:43.12 to 1:43.32. World record holder Wilson Kipketer is eagerly looking forward to his first Olympic experience. By now a Danish citizen, he opened his 2000 account with a new world indoor record for the kilometre: 2:14.96.

Noah Ngeny of Kenya is living up to his promises but we still wonder whether his schedule in big meets isn't perhaps too heavy. Within a week he ran 1000 metres in 2:15.53 (Athens, 28 June), 1500 metres in 3:29.99 at the Golden Gala in Rome (30 June) and then in 3:31.61 (Lausanne, 5 July). And this will be a long season, especially for athletes operating in the Northern Hemisphere. Algeria seems to have a possible successor to the great Morceli in the 22-year-old Ali Saidi Sief. He had shown great potential in 1999 with such times as 3:30.91 (1500 m.) and 7:36.97 (3000 m.). In the opening stage of the Olympic season he amazed experts with impressive victories over strong Kenyan rivals, his top marks being 7:27.67 in the 3000 metres (Paris, 23 June) and 12:50.86 in the 5000 (Rome, 30 June). The latter earned him position no.5 in the All Time List. In his wake runner-up Sammy Kipketer of Kenya did 12:54.07 - a fantastic time for a young man who will turn 19 by the time of the Sydney Olympics. Paul Tergat and Richard Limo, 20, came next in 12:55.18 and 12:58.70 respectively. The undisputed king of distance runners, Ethiopia's Haile Gebrselassie, recently announced that he will confine himself to the 10,000 metre event for the Olympics – just as he has done in all recent editions of "global" meets..

Antonio Pinto of Portugal, 34, won the famous London marathon (16 April) in 2:06.36, the best time on record for a European. He can point to a long career, the highlight of which on the track was a victory in the 10,000 metres at the 1998 European Championships. His record as a marathoner is rather impressive, including 3 victories in the London classic and one in Berlin. But he still has to do himself justice in "global" championships. As befits a marathon ace of the present age, he has excellent credentials in the middle distances too (3:39.25 in the 1500 m.).

In an Olympic perspective both hurdle events appear to be quite open. The reigning world champion over 400 metre hurdles, Fabrizio Mori of Italy, is at present far removed from his best form. He lost several races. Eric Thomas of USA and Llewellyn Herbert of South Africa can already point to sub-48 secs. marks - 47.97 and 47.98 respectively, made in different races. The steeplechase remains Kenya's favorite hunting ground. The Moroccan duo Ali Ezzine/Brahim Boulami (8:03.57 and 8:03.82 respectively) looms as the main danger.

Late in June an IAAF Arbitration Panel banned Javier Sotomayor of Cuba from competition until 30 July 2001. This was in relation to a doping offence (cocaine) committed on 31 July 1999 during the Pan-American Games at Winnipeg. Backed up by Cuba's political and sport authorities he had always denied the charge. When the final judgment was divulged, the holder of the world's high jump record vowed to return in time for the 2001 World Championships, scheduled for early August of that year in Edmonton, Canada. While awaiting the verdict, he had jumped 2.36 in an exhibition at Camagüey early in the year. In the meantime, the rest of the high jump fraternity continues to struggle in the sub-2.40 region, the best mark of the year so far being 2.38 indoors by Matt Hemingway of USA, a distant relative of novelist Ernest Hemingway, the 1954 Nobel prize winner in literature.

Pole vault king Sergey Bubka returned to competition after a long layoff and two operations. Not surprisingly, he has difficulties in trying to regain top condition. Best he could do indoors was 5.60 and even his outdoor debut was a low-key affair. Jeff Hartwig raised his US record to 6.03 (Jonesboro, 14 June) and looms as the no.1 threat for the hyper-consistent Maksim Tarasov. Long jump ace Ivan Pedroso (8.65 at Jena on 3 June) appears to be well-nigh invincible, whereas Jonathan Edwards, the king of triple jumpers, is struggling to regain top form.

Shot put standards appear to be on the rise again. Mika Halvari of Finland did 22.09 indoors. Four others were in the 21.86/21.60 region in the early stages of the season and C.J. Hunter of USA seems to be the most consistent. Virgilijus Alekna of Lithuania joined the exclusive 70 Metre Club in the discus with a fine 70.39 (Tartu, 11

P.S. On 2 August the IAAF Council reduced this suspension from 2 years to 1 year, so he will be eligible for the Sydney Olympics

June) and won early season confrontations with such stalwarts as Lars Riedel and Jürgen Schult of Germany. In the hammer Gilles Dupray of France, 30, created a sensation by bringing his country's record to 82.38 (Chelles, 21 June). Obviously, he will have to confirm his new status against the well established stars.

From the look of things, javelin throwers should have a hot season. Kostas Gatsioudis, the consistent Greek, won a big fight at Kuortane, Finland, on 24 June, beating local hero Aki Parviainen, 91.69 to 90.97. But both must reckon with a resurging Jan Zelezny, who bettered 90 metres in a couple of meets (90.59 and 90.56).

World decathlon champion Tomás Dvorák opened his Olympic season with an inspiring score in the traditional springtime rendez-vous at Götzis (3/4 June) – 8900 points, second best ever. Roman Sebrle, also of the Czech Republic, and Erki Nool of Estonia were second and third respectively with 8757 and 8742. Former world record holder Dan O'Brien, who had knee surgery last summer, hopes to be on the comeback trail by the time the US Olympic Trials roll around.

Very fast times were returned in the Russian walking championships held in Moscow on a road course. On 19 May Roman Rasskazov covered 20 Km. in 1:17:46, equalling the best time on record on the road. Two days later Valeriy Spitsin set a new world record of 3:37:26 for 50 Km.

WOMEN

Marion Jones, back in stride and aiming for 5 gold medals in the Olympics (100, 200 metres, long jump, 4x100 and 4x400 metre relays), had mixed fortunes in the early stages of the 2000 season. She did well in the running events, with 10.84 (100 m.) and 49.59 (400 m.), the latter being a new personal record. But she was her usual inconsistent self in the long jump, suffering several defeats and going no farther than 6.97. However, season's leader Fiona May of Italy has no better than 7.09 so far, so everything can happen ...

Jamaican veteran Merlene Ottey, 40, had been accused of a doping offence last year (nandrolone) but an IAAF Arbitration panel recently found that the testing laboratory had not taken into account factors regarding the specific gravity of the sample, which did not actually exceed the threshold recommended under IOC rules. Consequently, she was cleared and can now look forward to her sixth Olympiad!

Three new world records were established in the first half of the year. Stacy Dragila did 4.62 in the pole vault (Phoenix, 27 May). The American had mastered the same height a couple of months earlier in an indoor meet. She went even higher at Santa Barbara on 11 June as she cleared 4.70 on her final attempt to win a $50,000 payoff. However, the mark cannot be ratified because it was made on an elevated wooden runway built on the sand of Leadbetter Beach. Trine Hattestad of Norway upped the world mark for the new javelin to 68.22 (Rome, 30 June). Of course, this is still a distant cry vis-à-vis Petra Felke's 80.00 of 1988 with the old javelin, since the importance of new specifications is not to be overestimated.

Tatyana Gudkova of Russia set a new world's best of 1:25:18 (Moscow, 19 May) for the 20 Km. walk. In this road race four other women ducked under the previous record, 1:27:30 ! Mel Watman, the great British expert, noted that the winner's time was bettered by only one man in his country last year!

At a meeting in Paris on April 2, the IAAF Council decided that "in the interest of the athletes during an Olympic year" the Golden League Jackpot (50 kg. of gold bars worth $500,000, instead of the previous $1 million) would be made easier to win in 2000. It will now be shared among those athletes, men and women, who win 5 Golden League events in total, as against the 7 victories required until last year.

STATISTICS

LEADING TRACK AND FIELD PERFORMANCES THROUGH THE YEARS

MEN

100 METRES (AND 100 YARDS)

End of 1900 (hand timing)
100 YARDS (= 91.44 m.)
9 3/4	L. Cary (USA)	1891
9 4/5	V. Schifferstein (USA)	1888
9 4/5	J. Owen (USA)	1890
9 4/5	W. Macpherson (AUS)	1891
9 4/5	J. Hempton (NZ)	1892
9 4/5	C. Stage (USA)	1893
9 4/5	C. Bradley (GB)	1895
9 4/5	A. Downer (GB)	1895
9 4/5	B. Wefers (USA)	1895
9 4/5	J. Rush (USA)	1897
9 4/5	J. Maybury (USA)	1897
9 4/5	A. Duffey (USA)	1900

100 METRES
10 3/4	L. Cary (USA)	1891

End of 1920 (hand timing)
100 YARDS
9 3/5	A. Duffey (USA)	1902
9 3/5	D. Kelly (USA)	1906
9 3/5	A. Robinson (USA)	1913
9 3/5	D. Lippincott (USA)	1913
9 3/5	H. Drew (USA)	1914

100 METRES
10 1/2	E. Ketterer (Germany)	1911
10 1/2	R. Rau (Germany)	1911
10 1/2	E. Kern (Germany)	1912

End of 1940 (hand timing)
100 YARDS
9.4	G. Simpson (USA)	1929
9.4	F. Wykoff (USA)	1930
9.4	H. Meier (USA)	1930
9.4	D. Joubert (SAF)	1931
9.4	J. Owens (USA)	1933
9.4	R. Metcalfe (USA)	1933
9.4	G. Anderson (USA)	1934
9.4	C. Jeffrey (USA)	1940

100 METRES
10 1/5	C. Paddock (USA)	1921
10.2	R. Metcalfe (USA)	1932
10.2	J. Owens (USA)	1936

End of 1960 (hand timing)
100 YARDS
9.3	M. Patton (USA)	1948
9.3	H. Hogan (AUS)	1954
9.3	J. Golliday (USA)	1955
9.3	L. King (USA)	1956
9.3	D. Sime (USA)	1956
9.3	B. Morrow (USA)	1957
9.3	L. Murchison (USA)	1957
9.3	R. Norton (USA)	1958
9.3	W. Woodhouse (USA)	1959
9.3	R. Cook (USA)	1959

100 METRES
10.0	A. Hary (W. Ger.)	1960
10.0	H. Jerome (Canada)	1960
10.1	L. LaBeach (Panama)	1950
10.1	W. Williams (USA)	1956
10.1	I. Murchison (USA)	1956
10.1	L. King (USA)	1956
10.1	R. Norton (USA)	1959
10.1	C. Tidwell (USA)	1960
10.1	D. Sime (USA)	1960

End of 1980 (automatic timing)
100 YARDS
9.21	C. Greene (USA)	1967

Note - This event was removed from the World Record list in 1976, along with all other English distances, except the Mile.

100 METRES
9.95	J. Hines (USA)	1968
9.98	S. Leonard (Cuba)	1977
10.01	P. Mennea (Italy)	1979
10.02	C. Greene (USA)	1968
10.02	J. Sanford (USA)	1980
10.04	L. Miller (Jamaica)	1968
10.05	S. Riddick (USA)	1975
10.06	R. Hayes (USA)	1964
10.06	H. Crawford (Trinidad)	1976
10.07	V. Borzov (USSR)	1972
10.07	D. Quarrie (Jamaica)	1976
10.07	C. Edwards (USA)	1978
10.07	E. Hart (USA)	1978
10.07	S. Williams (USA)	1978
10.07	M. Roberson (USA)	1979
10.07	S. Floyd (USA)	1980

End of 1999 (automatic timing)
100 METRES
9.79	M. Greene (USA)	1999
9.84	D. Bailey (Canada)	1996
9.84	B. Surin (Canada)	1999
9.85	L. Burrell (USA)	1994
9.86	C. Lewis (USA)	1991
9.86	F. Fredericks (Namibia)	1996
9.86	A. Boldon (Trinidad)	1998
9.87	L. Christie (GB)	1993
9.87	O. Thompson (Barbados)	1998
9.91	D. Mitchell (USA)	1991

Disqualified for doping abuse:
9.79	B. Johnson (Canada)	1988

200 METRES (AND 220 YARDS)

End of 1900 (hand timing)
220 YARDS (= 201.17 m)
Half-to-full turn:
21 2/5	J. Maybury (USA)	1897
21 4/5	B. Wefers (USA)	1896

Straight course:
21 1/5	B. Wefers (USA)	1896

End of 1920 (hand timing)
220 YARDS
Half-to-full turn:
21 1/5	W. Applegarth (GB)	1914

Straight course:
20 4/5	A. Robinson (USA)	1913
21 1/5	B. Wefers (USA)	1896
21 1/5	D. Kelly (USA)	1906
21 1/5	R. Craig (USA)	1910
21 1/5	D. Lippincott (USA)	1913
21 1/5	H. Drew (USA)	1914
21 1/5	G. Parker (USA)	1914

End of 1940 (hand timing)
200 METRES
(* 220 yards time less 0.1)
Half-to-full turn:
20.5*	J. Carlton (Australia)	1932
20.6	R. Metcalfe (USA)	1933
20.7	J. Owens (USA)	1936
20.8	M. Robinson (USA)	1936
20.8	B. Johnson (USA)	1937
20.9	J. Weiershauser (USA)	1937
20.9	P. Walker (USA)	1938

Straight course:
20.2*	J. Owens (USA)	1935
20.3*	R. Metcalfe (USA)	1933

20.4*	R. Locke (USA)	1926
20.4*	H. Wallender (USA)	1935
20.4	H. Davis (USA)	1940

End of 1960 (hand timing)
200 METRES
(*220 yards time less 0.1)
Half-to-full turn:

20.4*	P. Radford (GB)	1960
20.5*	J. Carlton (Australia)	1932
20.5*	A. Stanfield (USA)	1951
20.5*	R. Norton (USA)	1960
20.5	S. Johnson (USA)	1960
20.5	L. Berruti (Italy)	1960
20.6	R. Metcalfe (USA)	1933
20.6*	T. Baker (USA)	1956
20.6	B. Morrow (USA)	1956
20.6*	E. Collymore (USA)	1958
20.6	M. Germar (W. Ger.)	1958
20.6*	W. Woodhouse (USA)	1959
20.6	S. Plaza (Mexico)	1960
20.6*	S. Antao (Ghana)	1960
20.6	M. Foik (Poland)	1960
20.6	L. Carney (USA)	1960

Straight course:

19.9*	D. Sime (USA)	1956
20.0*	M. Agostini (Trinidad)	1956
20.0*	R. Norton (USA)	1960
20.1*	M. Patton (USA)	1949
20.1	E. Jefferys (SAF)	1960

End of 1980 (automatic timing)
200 METRES
(*220 yards time less 0.1)
Half-to-full turn:

19.72	P. Mennea (Italy)	1979
19.83	T. Smith (USA)	1968
19.86	D. Quarrie (Jamaica)	1971
19.92	J. Carlos (USA)	1968
20.00	V. Borzov (USSR)	1972
20.03	C. Edwards (USA)	1978
20.06	P. Norman (Australia)	1968
20.06	S. Leonard (Cuba)	1978
20.07	J. Mallard (USA)	1979
20.08	La M. King (USA)	1980

Straight course (hand timing):

19.4*	T. Smith (USA)	1966

Note: Straight course races at 200 m./220 y. were discontinued towards the end of the Sixties.

End of 1999 (automatic timing)
200 METRES
(*220 yards time less 0.1)
Half-to-full turn:

19.32	M. Johnson (USA)	1996
19.68	F. Fredericks (Namibia)	1996
19.72	P. Mennea (Italy)	1979
19.73	M. Marsh (USA)	1992
19.75	C. Lewis (USA)	1983
19.75	J. DeLoach (USA)	1988
19.77	A. Boldon (Trinidad)	1997

19.83	T. Smith (USA)	1968
19.84	F. Obikwelu (Nigeria)	1999
19.86	D. Quarrie (Jamaica)	1971
19.86	M. Greene (USA)	1997

Straight course (hand timing):

19.4*	T. Smith (USA)	1966

400 METRES (AND 440 YARDS)

End of 1900 (hand timing)
440 YARDS (= 402.34 m.)

47 4/5	M. Long (USA)	1900
48 1/2	H.C. L. Tindall (GB)	1889
48 1/2	E. Bredin (GB)	1895
48 3/4	L. Myers (USA)	1881
48 4/5	T. Burke (USA)	1896
49.0	R.L. Whitley (USA)	1894
49.0e	G. Jordan (GB)	1895
49.0	P. Blignaut (SAF)	1897

Straight course:

47.0	M. Long (USA)	1900
47 2/5	W. Downs (USA)	1890
47 3/4	W. Baker (USA)	1886

e = estimated time

End of 1920 (hand timing)
440 YARDS

47 2/5	J.E. Meredith (USA)	1916
47 2/5	B. Dismond (USA)	1916
47 3/5	F. Shea (USA)	1918
47 4/5	M. Long (USA)	1900
48.0	C. Reidpath (USA)	1912
48.0	W. Wilcox (USA)	1915
48 1/5	H. Hillman (USA)	1908
48 1/5	J. Taylor (USA)	1908
48 1/5e	V. Wilkie (USA)	1915

e = estimated time
Straight course:

47.0	M. Long (USA)	1900
47.0 w	F. Sloman (USA)	1915
47.0 w	J.E. Meredith (USA)	1915
47 2/5	W. Downs (USA)	1890

w = assisting wind

End of 1940 (hand timing)
400 METRES
(*440 yards time less 0.3)

46.0	R. Harbig (Germany)	1939
46.1*	B. Eastman (USA)	1932
46.1	A. Williams (USA)	1936
46.2	W. Carr (USA)	1932
46.3	J. LuValle (USA)	1936
46.3*	R. Malott (USA)	1938
46.4	H. Smallwood (USA)	1936
46.4*	C. Belcher (USA)	1940
46.5*	G. Hardin (USA)	1934
46.5	H. Cagle (USA)	1936
46.5	L. Orr (Canada)	1940

End of 1960 (hand timing)
400 METRES
(*440 yards time less 0.3)

44.9	O. Davis (USA)	1960
44.9	K. Kaufmann (W. Ger.)	1960
45.2	L. Jones (USA)	1956
45.4*	G. Davis (USA)	1958
45.5*	J. Lea (USA)	1956
45.5*	E. Southern (USA)	1958
45.5	M. Spence (SAF)	1960
45.6	M. Singh (India)	1960
45.7*	H. McKenley (Jamaica)	1948
45.7	T. Woods (USA)	1960
45.7*	G. Kerr (Jamaica)	1960
45.7	E. Young (USA)	1960

Straight course:

44.7* w	H. McKenley (Jamaica)	1947

w = assisting wind

End of 1980 (automatic timing)
400 METRES

43.86	L. Evans (USA)	1968
43.97	L. James (USA)	1968
44.26	A. Juantorena (Cuba)	1976
44.40	F. Newhouse (USA)	1976
44.41	R. Freeman (USA)	1968
44.45	R. Ray (USA)	1975
44.60	J. Smith (USA)	1971
44.60	V. Markin (USSR)	1980
44.66	V. Matthews (USA)	1972
44.70	K. Honz (W. Ger.)	1972

End of 1999 (automatic timing)
400 METRES

43.18	M. Johnson (USA)	1999
43.29	B. Reynolds (USA) +	1988
43.50	Q. Watts (USA)	1992
43.81	D. Everett (USA)	1992
43.86	L. Evans (USA)	1968
43.87	S. Lewis (USA)	1988
43.97	L. James (USA)	1968
44.09	A. Harrison (USA)	1996
44.09	J. Young (USA)	1998
44.13	D. Mills (USA)	1995

+ Disqualified for doping abuse (1990)

800 METRES (AND 880 YARDS)

End of 1900 (hand timing)
880 YARDS (= 804.67 m)

1:53 2/5	C. Kilpatrick (USA)	1895
1:54 2/5	E. Hollister (USA)	1897
1:54 1/2	W. Dohm (USA)	1891
1:54 3/5	F. Cross (GB)	1888
1:55.0	E. Bredin (GB)	1895
1:55 2/5	L. Myers (USA)	1884
1:55 2/5	F. Horan (GB)	1895
1:55 3/5	A. Tysoe (GB)	1897

End of 1920 (hand timing)
800 METRES
(* 880 yards time less 0.7)
1:51.5*	J.E. Meredith (USA)	1916
1:51.8*	V. Windnagle (USA)	1916
1:52.0	M. Sheppard (USA)	1912
1:52.0	I. Davenport (USA)	1912
1:52.1*	E. Lunghi (Italy)	1909
1:52.5*e	F. Riley (USA)	1909
1:52.5*	D. Scott (USA)	1916
1:52.7*	C. Kilpatrick (USA)	1895
1:52.7	M. Brock (Canada)	1912
1:52.7*	D. Caldwell (USA)	1914
1:52.8*e	G. Brown (USA)	1914
1:52.9*	L. Campbell (USA)	1915
1:52.9*e	W. Bingham (USA)	1916

e = estimated time

End of 1940 (hand timing)
800 METRES
(* 880 yards time less 0.7); + 798.48 m. time plus 0.2)
1:46.6	R. Harbig (Germany)	1939
1:48.0+	J. Woodruff (USA)	1937
1:48.4	S. Wooderson (GB)	1938
1:48.9*	E. Robinson (USA)	1937
1:49.0	M. Lanzi (Italy)	1939
1:49.0	P. Moore (USA)	1940
1:49.1*	B. Eastman (USA)	1934
1:49.2	E. Burrowes (USA)	1940
1:49.5	C. Kane (USA)	1940
1:49.7	T. Hampson (GB)	1932
1:49.7	G. Cunningham (USA)	1936

End of 1960 (hand timing)
800 METRES
(* 880 yards time less 0,7)
1:45.7	R. Moens (Belgium)	1955
1:45.8	T. Courtney (USA)	1957
1:45.9	A. Boysen (Norway)	1955
1:46.2	P. Schmidt (W. Ger.)	1959
1:46.3	P. Snell (NZ)	1960
1:46.4	G. Kerr (Jamaica)	1960
1:46.5*	D. Bowden (USA)	1957
1:46.5	S. Lewandowski (Pol.)	1959
1:46.6	R. Harbig (Germany)	1939
1:46.6	D. Johnson (GB)	1957
1:46.6*	H. Elliott (Australia)	1958
1:46.6	E. Cunliffe (USA)	1960

End of 1980 (automatic timing)
800 METRES
(h= hand timing;
* 880 yards time less 0.7)
1.42.33	S. Coe (GB)	1979
1.43.4*h	R. Wohlhuter (USA)	1974
1.43.44	A. Juantorena (Cuba)	1977
1.43.57	M. Boit (Kenya)	1976
1.43.7 h	M. Fiasconaro (Italy)	1973
1.43.84	O. Beyer (E. Ger.)	1978
1.43.85	J. Kipkurgat (Kenya)	1974
1.43.86	I. Van Damme (Belgium)	1976
1.43.9h	J. Marajo (France)	1979
1.44.07	L. Susanj (Yugoslavia)	1974

End of 1999 (automatic timing)
800 METRES
1:41.11	W. Kipketer (Denmark)	1997
1:41.73°	S. Coe (GB)	1981
1:41.77	J. Cruz (Brazil)	1984
1:42.28	S. Koskei (Kenya)	1984
1:42.58	V. Rodal (Norway)	1996
1:42.60	J. Gray (USA)	1985
1:42.62	P. Ndururi (Kenya)	1997
1:42.69	H. Sepeng (SAF)	1999
1:42.69	J. Kimutai (Kenya)	1999
1:42.79	F. Onyancha (Kenya)	1996

° photo-electric cell time.

1500 METRES (and 1 Mile)

End of 1900 (hand timing)
1500 METRES
4:06 1/5	C. Bennett (GB)	1900

1 MILE (= 1609.35 m)
4:15 3/5	T. Conneff (USA)	1895
4:17.0	F. Bacon (GB)	1895
4:17 1/5	H. Welsh (GB)	1898
4:18 2/5	W. George (GB)	1884
4:18 1/2e	W. Snook (GB)	1884
4:19 1/5	H. Wade (GB)	1892
4:19 3/5e	W. Lutyens (GB)	1895
4:20 e	J. Kibblewhite (GB)	1887

End of 1920 (hand timing)
1500 METRES
3:54.7	J. Zander (Sweden)	1917
3:55 4/5	A. Kiviat (USA)	1912
3:56 2/5e	N. Taber (USA)	1912
3:56.8	A. Strode-Jackson (GB)	1912
3:57.2	J.P. Jones (USA)	1912
3:57.6	Ernst Wide (Sweden)	1912
3:59.3	S. Lundgren (Sweden)	1920
3:59 4/5	H. Wilson (GB)	1908

Indoors:
3:57.0	J. Ray (USA)	1920

e = estimated time

1 MILE
4:12 3/5	N. Taber (USA)	1915
4:14 2/5	J.P. Jones (USA)	1913
4:14 2/5	J. Ray (USA)	1919
4:15.0	V. Windnagle (USA)	1916
4:15.0	E. Fall (USA)	1919
4:15 3/5	T. Conneff (USA)	1895
4:15 3/5	A. Kiviat (USA)	1912
4:16 4/5	J. Binks (GB)	1902
4:16.8	J. Zander (Sweden)	1918
4:16 4/5	A. Hill (GB)	1919

Indoors:
4:16.0	J. Overton (USA)	1917

End of 1940 (hand timing)
1500 METRES
3:47.8	J. Lovelock (NZ)	1936
3:47.9	W. Mehl (USA)	1940
3:48.2	G. Cunningham (USA)	1940
3:48.6	M. Szabó (Hungary)	1937
3:48.7	S. Wooderson (GB)	1938
3:48.7	P. Moore (USA)	1940
3:48.7	H.Jonsson-Kälarne (SWE)	1940
3:48.8	W. Bonthron (USA)	1934
3:48.8	A. Andersson (Sweden)	1939
3:48.8	G. Hägg (Sweden)	1940
3:49.0	L. Beccali (Italy)	1933
3:49.0	A. Jansson (Sweden)	1940

1 MILE
4:06.4	S. Wooderson (GB)	1937
4:06.7	G. Cunningham (USA)	1934
4:07.2	A. San Romani (USA)	1937
4:07.2	D. Lash (USA)	1937
4:07.6	J. Lovelock (NZ)	1933
4:08.3	L. Zamperini (USA)	1938
4:08.3	C. Fenske (USA)	1940
4:08.7	B. Rideout (USA)	1940
4:08.7	W. Bonthron (USA)	1933
4.08.8	H.Jonsson-Kälarne(SWE)	1937

Indoors:
4:04.4	G. Cunningham (USA)	1938
4:07.4	C. Fenske (USA)	1940
4:07.9	L. Zamperini (USA)	1940
4:08.2	G. Venzke (USA)	1940
4:09.0	L. Beccali (Italy)	1937

End of 1960 (hand timing)
1500 METRES
3:35.6	H. Elliott (Australia)	1960
3:38.1	S. Jungwirth (Czech.)	1957
3:38.4	M. Jazy (France)	1960
3:38.6	D. Waern (Sweden)	1960
3:38.7	S. Valentin (E. Ger.)	1960
3:38.8	M. Halberg (NZ)	1958
3:38.8	I. Rózsavölgyi (Hungary)	1960
3:39.8	A. Hamarsland (Norway)	1958
3:40.2	O. Salsola (Finland)	1957
3:40.2	O. Salonen (Finland)	1957

1 MILE
3:54.5	H. Elliott (Australia)	1958
3:55.9	M. Lincoln (Australia)	1958
3:56.5	S. Valentin (E. Ger.)	1959
3:57.2	D. Ibbotson (GB)	1957
3:57.5	R. Delany (Ireland)	1958
3:57.5	M. Halberg (NZ)	1958
3:57.9	J. Landy (Australia)	1954
3:58.0	J. Beatty (USA)	1960
3:58.5	D. Waern (Sweden)	1957
3:58.6	J. Bailey (Australia)	1956
3:58.6	A. Thomas (Australia)	1958
3:58.6	D. Burleson (USA)	1960

End of 1980 (automatic timing)
1500 METRES (h = hand timing)
3:31.36	S. Ovett (GB)	1980

3:31.58	T. Wessinghage (W. Ger.)	1980
3:31.96	H. Hudak (W. Ger.)	1980
3:32.03	S. Coe (GB)	1979
3:32.16	F. Bayi (Tanzania)	1974
3:32.4 h	J. Walker (NZ)	1975
3:33.1 h	J. Ryun (USA)	1967
3:33.16	B. Jipcho (Kenya)	1974
3:33.33	S. Scott (USA)	1980
3:33.68	J. Straub (E. Ger.)	1979

1 MILE

3:48.8 h	S. Ovett (GB)	1980
3:48.95	S. Coe (GB)	1979
3:49.4 h	J. Walker (NZ)	1975
3:50.56	T. Wessinghage (W. Ger.)	1979
3:51.0 h	F. Bayi (Tanzania)	1975
3:51.1 h	J. Ryun (USA)	1967
3:51.11	S. Scott (USA)	1979
3:52.0 h	B. Jipcho (Kenya)	1973
3:52.02	C. Masback (USA)	1979
3:52.2 h	M. Liquori (USA)	1975

End of 1999 (automatic timing)
1500 METRES

3:26.00	H. El Guerrouj (Morocco)	1998
3:27.37	N. Morceli (Algeria)	1995
3:28.6+	N. Ngeny (Kenya)	1999
3:28.95	F. Cacho (Spain)	1997
3:29.18	V. Niyongabo (Burundi)	1997
3:29.46	S. Aouita (Morocco)	1985
3:29.46	D. Komen (Kenya)	1997
3:29.67	S. Cram (GB)	1985
3:29.77	S. Maree (USA)	1985
3:29.77	S. Coe (GB)	1986

+ During 1-mile race.

1 MILE

3:43.13	H. El Guerrouj (Morocco)	1999
3:43.40	N. Ngeny (Kenya)	1999
3:44.39	N. Morceli (Algeria)	1993
3:46.32	S. Cram (GB)	1985
3:46.38	D. Komen (Kenya)	1997
3:46.70	V. Niyongabo (Burundi)	1997
3:46.76	S. Aouita (Morocco)	1987
3:47.33	S. Coe (GB)	1981
3:47.65	L. Rotich (Kenya)	1997
3:47.69	S. Scott (USA)	1982

5000 METRES (and 3 Miles)

End of 1900 (hand timing)
3 MILES (= 4828.04 m)

14.24.0	S. Thomas (GB)	1893
14:25.0e	E. C. Willers (GB)	1893
14:27 2/5	F. Crossland (GB)	1896
14:27 3/5	F. Bacon (GB)	1894

e = estimated time

5000 METRES

15:29 1/5	C. Bennett (GB)	1900

End of 1920 (hand timing)
3 MILES

14:17 1/5	A. Shrubb (GB)	1904

5000 METRES

14:36.6	H. Kolehmainen (Fin)	1912
14:36.7	J. Bouin (Fra)	1912
14:45.0°	C. Hunter (USA)	1920
14:51.0	E. Backman (Sweden)	1919
14:54.3	R. Falk (Sweden)	1919
14:55 3/5	J. Guillemot (Fra)	1920
14:57.5	J. Zander (Sweden)	1918
14:59.1	A. Halstvedt (Norway)	1919
15:00.0	P. Nurmi (Fin)	1920
15:01.2	A. Robertson (GB)	1908

° = Doubtful distance
(probably one lap short, although ratified as a US record by the AAU).

End of 1940 (hand timing)
3 MILES

13:42.4	T. Mäki (Fin)	1939

5000 METRES

14:08.8	T. Mäki (Fin)	1939
14:16.2	K. Pekuri (Fin)	1939
14:16.9	L. Lehtinen (Fin)	1932
14:18.3	V. Iso-Hollo (Fin)	1932
14:18.8	H. Jonsson (Sweden)	1939
14:20.6	B. Hellström (Sweden)	1940
14:21.2	T. Kurki (Fin)	1939
14:22.0	I. Salminen (Fin)	1939
14:22.2	G. Höckert (Fin)	1936
14:22.4	V. Tuominen (Fin)	1940

End of 1960 (hand timing)
3 MILES

13:10.8	A. Thomas (Aus)	1958

5000 METRES

13:35.0	V. Kuts (USSR)	1957
13:36.8	G. Pirle (GB)	1956
13:38.1	P. Bolotnikov (USSR)	1960
13:40.6	S. Iharos (Hungary)	1955
13:42.4	F. Janke (E. Ger.)	1959
13:43.4	M. Halberg (NZ)	1960
13:44.4	K. Zimny (Poland)	1959
13:44.6	H. Grodotzki (E. Ger.)	1960
13:47.6	J. Kovács (Hungary)	1959
13:47.8	S. Eldon (GB)	1959

End of 1980 (automatic timing)
3 MILES (h = hand timing)

12:47.8h	E. Puttemans (Belgium)	1972

5000 METRES (h = hand timing)

13:08.4 h	H. Rono (Kenya)	1978
13:12.29	S. Nyambui (Tanzania)	1979
13:12.86	D. Quax (NZ)	1977
13:13.0 h	E. Puttemans (Belgium)	1972
13:13.32	M. Ryffel (Switz.)	1979
13:13.69	K-P. Hildenbrand (W. Ger.)	1976
13:13.82	M. Yifter (Eth.)	1977
13:13.88	K. Fleschen (W. Ger.)	1977
13:14.4	B. Jipcho (Kenya)	1974
13:14.54	P. Weigt (W. Ger.)	1977
13:14.6	B. Foster (GB)	1974

End of 1999 (automatic timing)
5000 METRES

12:39.36	H. Gebrselassie (Eth)	1998
12:39.74	D. Komen (Kenya)	1997
12:49.87	P. Tergat (Kenya)	1997
12:50.80	S. Hissou (Morocco)	1996
12:53.41	K. Boulami (Morocco)	1997
12:53.72	P. Mosima (Kenya)	1996
12:53.84	A. Mezegebu (Eth)	1998
12:54.70	D. Baumann (Germ)	1997
12:54.85	M. Kiptanui (Kenya)	1996
12:55.86	B. Limo (Kenya)	1999

10,000 METRES (and 6 Miles)

End of 1900 (hand timing)
6 MILES (= 9656.07 m.)

30:17.4/5	S. Thomas (GB)	1892
30:19.4/5	F. Bacon (GB)	1895
30:21.1/2	W. George (GB)	1884

10,000 METRES

31:40.0*	W. George (GB)	1884

* 6 1/4 miles (= 10,058.41 m.) time.

End of 1920 (hand timing)
6 MILES

29:51 3/5	J. Bouin (Fra)	1911

10,000 METRES

30:58 4/5	J. Bouin (Fra)	1911
31:02 2/5	A. Shrubb (GB)	1904
31:13.7	E. Backman (Sweden)	1918
31:20.8	H. Kolehmainen (Fin)	1912
31:30.0	G. Peterson (Sweden)	1910
31:40.0*	W. George (GB)	1884
31:43 3/5	W. Kramer (USA)	1912
31:45 4/5	P. Nurmi (Fin)	1920
31:47 1/5	J. Guillemot (Fra)	1920
31:50 4/5	J. Wilson (GB)	1920

* 6 1/4 miles (= 10.058.41 m.) time

End of 1940 (hand timing)
6 MILES

28:55.6	T. Mäki (Fin)	1939

10,000 METRES

29:52.6	T. Mäki (Fin)	1939
30:05.5	J. Salminen (Fin)	1937
30:06.1	P. Nurmi (Fin)	1924
30:06.6	M. Syring (Germ)	1940
30:07.6	V. Tuominen (Fin)	1939
30:10.6	K. Pekuri (Fin)	1939
30:11.4	J. Kusocinski (Pol)	1932
30:12.6	V. Iso-Hollo (Fin)	1932
30:15.0	L. Lehtinen (Fin)	1937
30:15.6	A. Askola (Fin)	1936

End of 1960 (hand timing)
6 MILES

27:43.8	S. Iharos (Hungary)	1956

10,000 METRES

28:18.8	P. Bolotnikov (USSR)	1960

28:30.4	V. Kuts (USSR)	1956
28:37.0	H. Grodotzki (E. Ger.)	1960
28:38.2	D. Power (Aus)	1960
28:39.6	A. Desyatchikov (USSR)	1960
28:42.8	S. Iharos (Hun)	1956
28:48.0	M. Halberg (NZ)	1960
28:50.2	M. Truex (USA)	1960
28:52.4	J. Kovács (Hun)	1956
28:52.4	Z. Krzyszkowiak (Pol)	1960

End of 1980 (automatic timing)
(h = hand timing)
6 MILES

26:47.0 h	R. Clarke (Aus)	1965

10,000 METRES

27:22.4 h	H. Rono (Kenya)	1978
27:29.16	C. Virgin (USA)	1980
27:29.3 h	B. Foster (GB)	1978
27:30.47	S. Kimobwa (Kenya)	1977
27:30.80	D. Bedford (GB)	1973
27:30.99	M. Vainio (Fin)	1978
27:31.48	V. Ortis (Italy)	1978
27:31.50	A. Antipov (USSR)	1978
27:36.27	D. Black (GB)	1978
27:36.64	G. Tebroke (Hol)	1978

End of 1999 (automatic timing)
10,000 METRES

26:22.75	H. Gebrselassie (Eth)	1998
26:27.85	P. Tergat (Kenya)	1997
26:36.26	Paul Koech (Kenya)	1997
26:38.08	S. Hissou (Morocco)	1996
26:51.49	C. Kamathi (Kenya)	1999
26:52.23	W. Sigei (Kenya)	1994
26:52.30	M. Mourhit (Belgium)	1999
26:58.38	Y. Ondieki (Kenya)	1993
27:06.44	W. Bikila (Eth)	1995
27:06.45	H. Jifar (Eth)	1999

110 METRES (and 120 yards) Hurdles

End of 1900 (hand timing)
120 YARDS (= 109.73 m.) Hurdles

15 1/5	A. Kraenzlein (USA)	1898
15 2/5	S. Chase (USA)	1895
15 3/5	E. Dyer (USA)	1895
15 3/5e	G. Shaw (GB)	1895
15 3/5	E. Morgan (USA)	1897
15 3/5	F. B. Fox (USA)	1899

e= estimated time
110 Metres Hurdles

15 2/5	A. Kraenzlein (USA)	1900

End of 1920 (hand timing)
110 Metres (y= 120 yards) Hurdles

14 2/5y	E. Thomson (Can)	1920
14 3/5y	R. Simpson (USA)	1916
14 4/5y	F. Kelly (USA)	1916
15.0	F. Smithson (USA)	1908
15.0	H. Barron (USA)	1920
15.0y	T. Shideler (USA)	1904
15.0y	A. Shaw (USA)	1908
15.0y	F. Murray (USA)	1916
15.0y	H. Wilson (NZ)	1920
15.0y	F. Yount (USA)	1920

End of 1940 (hand timing)
110 Metres (y= 120 yards) Hurdles

13.7	F. Towns (USA)	1936
13.7y	F. Wolcott (USA)	1940
13.8y	B. Gatewood (USA)	1940
13.9y	E. Dugger (USA)	1940
14.0	H. Lidman (Sweden)	1940
14.0y	R. Osgood (USA)	1937
14.0y	T. Lavery (SAF)	1938
14.0y	P. Owens (USA)	1940
14.1	J. Batiste (USA)	1940
14.1y	J. Keller (USA)	1933
14.1y	R. Staley (USA)	1936

End of 1960 (hand timing)
110 Metres (y= 120 yards) Hurdles

13.2	M. Lauer (W. Ger.)	1959
13.2	L. Calhoun (USA)	1960
13.4	J. Davis (USA)	1956
13.4	W. May (USA)	1960
13.4y	M. Campbell (USA)	1957
13.4y	E. Gilbert (USA)	1957
13.5	R. Attlesey (USA)	1950
13.5	H. Jones (USA)	1960
13.6	W. Stevens (USA)	1957
13.6	A. Robinson (USA)	1958
13.6	A. Mikhailov (USSR)	1960
13.6y	H. Dillard (USA)	1948

End of 1980 (automatic timing)
110 Metres Hurdles

13.00	R. Nehemiah (USA)	1979
13.21	A. Casañas (Cuba)	1977
13.22	G. Foster (USA)	1978
13.24	R. Milburn (USA)	1972
13.28	G. Drut (Fra)	1975
13.33	W. Davenport (USA)	1968
13.34	D. Cooper (USA)	1980
13.37	T. Munkelt (E. Ger.)	1977
13.38	E. Hall (USA)	1968
13.38	J. Wilson (USA)	1975

End of 1999 (automatic timing)
110 METRES HURDLES

12.91	C. Jackson (GB)	1993
12.92	R. Kingdom (USA)	1989
12.92	A. Johnson (USA)	1996
12.93	R. Nehemiah (USA)	1981
12.94	J. Pierce (USA)	1996
12.98	M. Crear (USA)	1999
13.00	T. Jarrett (GB)	1993
13.01	L. Wade (USA)	1999
13.03	G. Foster (USA)	1981
13.03	R. Torian (USA)	1998

400 METRES (and 440 yards) Hurdles

End of 1900 (hand timing)
400 Metres Hurdles
(* 440 yards time less 0.3)

56.9*	G. Shaw (GB)	1891
57.5*	T. Donovan (Ireland)	1896
57.5*	A. Trafford (GB)	1899
57 3/5	J. Tewksbury (USA)	1900

End of 1920 (hand timing)
400 Metres Hurdles
(*440 yards time less 0.3)

53.9*	J. Norton (USA)	1920
54.0	F. Loomis (USA)	1920
54.3*	W. Meanix (USA)	1915
54.5*	W. Hummel (USA)	1916
54.5*	F. Smart (USA)	1917
54.7*e	C.A. Hoenish (USA)	1916
54.7*e	R. Ferguson (USA)	1916
54.7e	A. Desch (USA)	1920
54.8e	G. André (Fra)	1920
55.0	C. Bacon (USA)	1908

Straight course:

52.3*	W. Meanix (USA)	1915
53.2*e	E. Lighter (USA)	1915
53.2*e	H. Goelitz (USA)	1915
53.3*	A.F. Muenter (USA)	1916
53.7*e	S. House (USA)	1916

e = estimated time

End of 1940 (hand timing)
400 METRES Hurdles

50.6	G. Hardin (USA)	1934
51.6	Joe Patterson (USA)	1936
51.6	F.W. Hölling (Germ.)	1939
51.6	C. McBain (USA)	1940
51.7	R. Tisdall (Ireland)	1932
51.7	D. Schofield (USA)	1936
51.9	R. Cochran (USA)	1939
52.0	F.M. Taylor (USA)	1928
52.0	R. Simmons (USA)	1939
52.0	G. Glaw (Germ.)	1939

End of 1960 (hand timing)
400 METRES Hurdles
(*440 yards time less 0.3)

49.0*	G. Potgieter (So. Afr.)	1960
49.2	G. Davis (USA)	1958
49.6	C. Cushman (USA)	1960
49.7	E. Southern (USA)	1956
49.7	R. Howard (USA)	1960
49.8*	Don Styron (USA)	1960
49.9	H. Janz (W. Ger.)	1960
50.2	J. Culbreath (USA)	1957
50.3*	D. Lean (Aus)	1958
50.4	Y. Lituyev (USSR)	1953

End of 1980 (hand timing)
400 METRES Hurdles

47.13	E. Moses (USA)	1980

47.82	J. Akii-Bua (Uganda)	1972
47.85	H. Schmid (W.Ger.)	1979
48.12	D. Hemery (GB)	1968
48.35	V. Arkhipyenko (USSR)	1979
48.39	Q. Wheeler (USA)	1979
48.44	H. Schulting (Hol)	1979
48.48	J. Walker (USA)	1979
48.51	R. Mann (USA)	1972
48.55	J. Bolding (USA)	1975
48.55	T. Andrews (USA)	1976

End of 1999 (automatic timing)
400 METRES HURDLES

46.78	K. Young (USA)	1992
47.02	E. Moses (USA)	1983
47.03	B. Bronson (USA)	1998
47.10	S. Matete (Zambia)	1991
47.19	A. Phillips (USA)	1988
47.23	A. Dia Ba (Senegal)	1988
47.37	S. Diagana (France)	1995
47.38	D. Harris (USA)	1991
47.48	H. Schmid (Germ.)	1982
47.54	D. Adkins (USA)	1995

3000 METRES Steeplechase

End of 1940 (hand timing)

9:03.8	V. Iso-Hollo (Fin)	1936
9:05.2	N. Ollander (Sweden)	1940
9:06.8	K. Tuominen (Fin)	1936
9:06.8	L. Kaindl (Germ)	1939
9:07.0	L. Larsson (Sweden)	1940
9:07.2	A. Dompert (Germ)	1936
9:07.4	K. Pekuri (Fin)	1939
9:08.2	H. Manning (USA)	1936
9:09.0	M. Matilainen (Fin)	1936
9:09.2	A. Lindblad (Fin)	1938

End of 1960 (hand timing)

8:31.4	Z. Krzyszkowiak (Pol)	1960
8:32.0	J. Chromik (Pol)	1958
8:32.4	N. Sokolov (USSR)	1960
8:34.0	H. Buhl (E. Ger.)	1960
8:35.6	S. Rozsnyói (Hun)	1956
8:35.6	S. Rzhishchin (USSR)	1958
8:37.4	H. Hüneke (W. Ger.)	1958
8:37.4	A. Konov (USSR)	1960
8:37.4	V. Yevdokimov (USSR)	1960
8:40.6	S. Ponomaryov (USSR)	1958
8:40.6	A. Simon (Hun.)	1960

End of 1980 (automatic timing)

8:05.4h	H. Rono (Kenya)	1978
8:08.02	A. Gärderud (Sweden)	1976
8:09.11	B. Malinowski (Pol)	1976
8:10.36	F. Baumgartl (E. Ger.)	1976
8:12.0h	K. Rono (Kenya)	1980
8:12.48	F. Bayi (Tanzania)	1980
8:12.5h	M. Scartezzini (Italy)	1980
8:12.60	T. Kantanen (Fin)	1976

| 8:13.57 | E. Tura (Eth.) | 1980 |
| 8:13.91 | B. Jipcho (Kenya) | 1973 |

h= hand timing.

End of 1999 (automatic timing)

7:55.72	B. Barmasai (Kenya)	1997
7:56.16	M. Kiptanui (Kenya)	1997
7:59.08	W. Boit Kipketer (Kenya)	1997
8:03.41	P. Sang (Kenya)	1997
8:03.89	J. Kosgei (Kenya)	1997
8:05.01	E. Barngetuny (Kenya)	1995
8:05.35	Peter Koech (Kenya)	1989
8:05.37	P. Barkutwo (Kenya)	1992
8:05.4 h	H. Rono (Kenya)	1978
8:05.43	C. Kosgei (Kenya)	1999

h = hand timing

HIGH JUMP (* Indoors)

End of 1900

1.972	M. Sweeney (USA)	1895
1.965	G. Rowdon (GB)	1890
1.949	P. Leahy (Ire)	1898
1.943	J. Ryan (Ire)	1895
1.930	W. Page (USA)	1887
1.918	I. Baxter (USA)	1900
1.905	J. Winsor (USA)	1897
1.899	P. Davin (Ire)	1880
1.899	M. O'Brien (Ire)	1893

End of 1920

2.029	C. Larsen (USA)	1917
2.014	E. Beeson (USA)	1914
2.007	G. Horine (USA)	1912
1.972	M. Sweeney (USA)	1895
1.969	W. Oler (USA)	1915
1.965	G. Rowdon (GB)	1890
1.956	T. Carroll (Ire)	1913
1.956	A. Richards (USA)	1915
1.949	Pat Leahy (Ire)	1898
1.949	F. Maker (USA)	1916

End of 1940

2.09	M. Walker (USA)	1937
2.076	C. Johnson (USA)	1936
2.076	D. Albritton (USA)	1936
2.070	W. Marty (USA)	1934
2.067	L. Steers (USA)	1940
2.067	J. Wilson (USA)	1940
2.064*	E. Burke (USA)	1937
2.054*	G. Cruter (USA)	1936
2.045*	G. Spitz (USA)	1932
2.04	K. Kotkas (Fin)	1936
2.038	H. Osborn (USA)	1924
2.038	D. Boydston (USA)	1940
2.038	J. Williamson (USA)	1940

End of 1960

| 2.229 | J. Thomas (USA) | 1960 |
| 2.20 | V. Brumel (USSR) | 1960 |

2.16 +	Y. Styepanov (USSR)	1957
2.16	R. Shavlakadze (USSR)	1960
2.15	C. Dumas (USA)	1956
2.15 +	V. Sitkin (USSR)	1957
2.15	V. Bolshov (USSR)	1960
2.14 +	I. Kashkarov (USSR)	1957
2.134	J. Faust (USA)	1960
2.13	S. Pettersson (Sweden)	1960

+ with a built-up shoe

End of 1980

2.36	G. Wessig (E. Ger.)	1980
2.35*	V. Yashchenko (USSR)	1978
2.35	J. Wszola (Pol)	1980
2.35	D. Mögenburg (W. Ger.)	1980
2.32	D. Stones (USA)	1976
2.32*	F. Jacobs (USA)	1978
2.31	R. Beilschmidt (E. Ger.)	1977
2.31*	G. Joy (Can)	1978
2.31	C. Thränhardt (W. Ger.)	1980
2.31	J. Freimuth (E. Ger.)	1980

End of 1999

2.45	J. Sotomayor (Cuba)	1993
2.42	P. Sjöberg (Sweden)	1987
2.42*	C. Thränhardt (Germ.)	1988
2.41	I. Paklin (USSR)	1985
2.40	R. Povarnitsin (USSR)	1985
2.40	S. Matei (Romania)	1990
2.40*	H. Conway (USA)	1991
2.40	C. Austin (USA)	1991
2.39	Zhu Jianhua (China)	1984
2.39*	D. Mögenburg (Germ.)	1985
2.39*	R. Sonn (Germ.)	1991

POLE VAULT (* Indoors)

End of 1900
(cedar, hickory, fir or white ash poles)

3.62	R. Clapp (USA)	1898
3.55	B. Johnson (USA)	1900
3.51	J.L. Hurlburt (USA)	1898
3.50	C. Dvorak (USA)	1900

"Climbing" technique:

3.58	R. Dickinson (GB)	1891
3.57	T. Ray (GB)	1888
3.57	L. Stones (GB)	1889

End of 1920
(bamboo poles)

4.09	F. Foss (USA)	1920
4.02	M. Wright (USA)	1912
3.98	R. Gardner (USA)	1912
3.98	E. Myers (USA)	1920
3.98	E. Jenne (USA)	1920
3.97	R. Spearow (USA)	1919
3.96	S. Wagoner (USA)	1913
3.95	H. Babcock (USA)	1912
3.93	L. Scott (USA)	1910
3.92	P. Graham (USA)	1916

3.91	W. Newstetter (USA)	1915
3.91	E. Knourek (USA)	1920

End of 1940
(bamboo poles)

4.60	C. Warmerdam (USA)	1940
4.54	W. Sefton (USA)	1937
4.54	E. Meadows (USA)	1937
4.47	K Dills (USA)	1940
4.46	G. Varoff (USA)	1937
4.44	L. Day (USA)	1938
4.39	K. Brown (USA)	1935
4.39	R. Ganslen (USA)	1939
4.38	G. Smith (USA)	1940
4.37	W. Graber (USA)	1932
4.37	A. Haller (USA)	1936
4.37	J. Mauger (USA)	1937
4.37	R. Hansen (USA)	1939

End of 1960
(metal poles)

4.82	R. Gutowski (USA)	1957
4.81*	D. Bragg (USA)	1959
4.78* +	C. Warmerdam (USA)	1943
4.75*	J. D. Martin (USA)	1960
4.72*	R. Richards (USA)	1957
4.70	A. Dooley (USA)	1959
4.70	J. Graham (USA)	1959
4.70	R. Morris (USA)	1960
4.65*	D. Laz (USA)	1952
4.65	M. Schwartz (USA)	1959
4.65	D. Clark (USA)	1960
4.65	H. Wadsworth (USA)	1960
4.65	J. Krasovskis (USSR)	1960
4.65	M. Preussger (E. Ger.)	1960

+ = bamboo pole.

End of 1980
(fibre-glass poles)

5.78	W. Kozakiewicz (Pol)	1980
5.77	P. Houvion (Fra)	1980
5.75	T. Vigneron (Fra)	1980
5.71	M. Tully (USA)	1978
5.70	D. Roberts (USA)	1976
5.70	J.M. Bellot (Fra)	1980
5.70	K. Volkov (USSR)	1980
5.70	S. Ferreira (Fra)	1980
5.69	L. Jessee (USA)	1980
5.67	E. Bell (USA)	1976
5.67	B. Olson (USA)	1980

End of 1999
(fibre-glass poles)

6.15*	S. Bubka (Ukraine)	1993
6.05	M. Tarasov (Russia)	1999
6.03	O. Brits (South Africa)	1995
6.02*	R. Gataullin (USSR)	1989
6.02	J. Hartwig (USA)	1999
6.01	I. Trandenkov (Russia)	1996
6.00	T. Lobinger (Germ.)	1997
6.00	D. Markov (Byelarus)	1998
6.00*	J. Galfione (France)	1999
5.98	L. Johnson (USA)	1996

LONG JUMP

End of 1900

7.51	P. O'Connor (Ire)	1900
7.50	M. Prinstein (USA)	1900
7.43	A. Kraenzlein (USA)	1899
7.32	W. Newburn (Ire)	1898
7.21	J. Mooney (Ire)	1894
7.20	M. Roseingreve (Ire)	1896
7.17	C. Reber (USA)	1891
7.17	C. Fry (GB)	1893
7.17	P. Remington (USA)	1898
7.16	D. Shanahan (Ire)	1896

End of 1920

7.61	P. O'Connor (Ire)	1901
7.60	A. Gutterson (USA)	1912
7.57	T. Ahearne (Ire)	1908
7.51	S. Butler (USA)	1920
7.50	M. Prinstein (USA)	1900
7.48	F. Irons (USA)	1908
7.43	A. Kraenzlein USA)	1899
7.37	D. Kelly (USA)	1906
7.35	P. Stiles (USA)	1915
7.34	C. Johnson (USA)	1919

End of 1940

8.13	J. Owens (USA)	1935
8.00	E. Peacock (USA)	1935
7.98	C. Nambu (Japan)	1931
7.93	S. Cator (Haiti)	1928
7.91	R. Clark (USA)	1936
7.90	E. Hamm (USA)	1928
7.90	L. Long (Germ)	1937
7.89	W.De H.Hubbard (USA)	1925
7.88	K. King (USA)	1937
7.84	A. Olson (USA)	1935

End of 1960

8.21	R. Boston (USA)	1960
8.13	J. Owens (USA)	1935
8.11	I. Roberson (USA)	1960
8.10	G. Bell (USA)	1957
8.07	W. Steele (USA)	1947
8.04	I.Ter-Ovanesyan (USSR)	1960
8.03	R. Range (USA)	1955
8.01	J. Bennett (USA)	1955
8.00	E. Peacock (USA)	1935
8.00	G. Brown (USA)	1952
8.00	M. Herman (USA)	1960
8.00	M. Steinbach (W. Ger.)	1960

End of 1980

8.90	R. Beamon (USA)	1968
8.54	L. Dombrowski (E. Ger.)	1980
8.52	L. Myricks (USA)	1979
8.45	N. Stekic (Yugo)	1975
8.36	J. C. de Oliveira (Bra)	1979
8.36	F. Paschek (E. Ger.)	1980
8.35	R. Boston (USA)	1965
8.35	I.Ter-Ovanesyan (USSR)	1967
8.35	J. Schwarz (W. Ger.)	1970
8.35	A. Robinson (USA)	1976

End of 1999

8.95	M. Powell (USA)	1991
8.90	R. Beamon (USA)	1968
8.87	C. Lewis (USA)	1991
8.86	R. Emmiyan (USSR)	1987
8.74	L. Myricks (USA)	1988
8.74	E. Walder (USA)	1994
8.71	I. Pedroso (Cuba)	1995
8.63	K.Streete-Thompson (USA)	1994
8.62	J. Beckford (Jamaica)	1997
8.56*	Y. Lamela (Spain)	1999

Note - Myricks was disqualified for doping abuse in 1990.

TRIPLE JUMP

End of 1900
(+ Presumably "two hops and a jump")

15.26+	M. Roseingreve (Ire)	1895
15.25+	D. Shanahan (Ire)	1888
15.17+	P. Looney (Ire)	1888
15.11+	J. Purcell (Ire)	1887
15.11+	T. Kiely (Ire)	1892
15.08+	J. O'Sullivan (Ire)	1890
15.08+	Pat Leahy (Ire)	1897
14.99+	W. McManus (Aus)	1893
14.94+	J. Connolly (USA)	1896
14.93+	W. Campion (Ire)	1898
14.78	E. Bloss (USA)	1893

End of 1920
(+ Presumably "two hops and a jump")

15.52	D. Ahearn (USA)	1911
15.34+	J. Breshnihan (Ire)	1906
15.30	V. Tuulos (Fin)	1919
15.26+	M. Roseingreve (Ire)	1895
15.25+	D. Shanahan (Ire)	1888
15.17+	P. Looney (Ire)	1888
15.16+	P. Kirwan (Ire)	1910
15.15+	Pat Leahy (Ire)	1901
15.11+	J. Purcell (Ire)	1887
15.11+	T. Kiely (Ire)	1892

D. Ahearn also did 15.66 (1911) with two hops and a jump.

End of 1940

16.00	N. Tajima (Japan)	1936
15.86	K. Togami (Japan)	1937
15.82	K. Oshima (Japan)	1934
15.78	J. Metcalfe (Aus)	1935
15.75	M. Harada (Japan)	1934
15.72	C. Nambu (Japan)	1932
15.70	L. Miller (Aus)	1939

15.68	Genken Kim (Japan)	1940
15.64	B. Dickinson (Aus)	1935
15.58	M. Oda (Japan)	1931

End of 1960
17.03	J. Schmidt (Pol)	1960
16.70	O. Fyedoseyev (USSR)	1959
16.70	V. Einarsson (Iceland)	1960
16.63	D. Goryayev (USSR)	1960
16.59	O. Ryakhovskiy (USSR)	1958
16.56	A. F. da Silva (Bra)	1955
16.49	V. Kreyer (USSR)	1960
16.48	M. Kogake (Japan)	1956
16.46	L. Shcherbakov (USSR)	1956
16.44	R. Malcherczyk (Pol)	1959

End of 1980
17.89	J. C. de Oliveira (Bra)	1975
17.44	V. Saneyev (USSR)	1972
17.40	P. Pérez Dueña (Cuba)	1971
17.35	J. Uudmäe (USSR)	1980
17.31	J. Drehmel (E. Ger.)	1972
17.29	G. Valyukyevich (USSR)	1979
17.27	N. Prudencio (Bra)	1968
17.24	J. Butts (USA)	1978
17.23	W. Banks (USA)	1979
17.22	G. Gentile (Italy)	1968

End of 1999
18.29	J. Edwards (GB)	1995
18.09	K. Harrison (USA)	1996
17.97	W. Banks (USA)	1985
17.92	K. Markov (Bulgaria)	1987
17.92	J. Beckford (Jamaica)	1995
17.90	V. Inozyemtsev (USSR)	1990
17.89	J.C.de Oliveira (Bra.)	1975
17.87	M. Conley (USA)	1987
17.86	C. Simpkins (USA)	1985
17.85	Y. Quesada (Cuba)	1997

SHOT PUT (* Indoors)

End of 1900
(+ from a 2.13 m. square)
14.75	G. Gray (Can)	1898
14.68+	D. Horgan (Ire)	1897
14.10	R. Sheldon (USA)	1900
13.73	W. Coe (USA)	1900
13.67+	J. O'Brien (Ire)	1885
13.48	F. Beck (USA)	1900
13.45	W. Hickock (USA)	1895
13.32	J. McCracken (USA)	1898

End of 1920
(+ from a 2.13 m. square)
15.54	R. Rose (USA)	1909
15.34	P. McDonald (USA)	1912
15.08	W. Coe (USA)	1905
14.93	A. Mucks (USA)	1915
14.90	R. Beatty (USA)	1912
14.88+	D. Horgan (Ire)	1904

14.86	E. Niklander (Fin)	1913
14.81	V. Pörhölä (Fin)	1920
14.75	G. Gray (Can)	1898
14.70	J. Horner (USA)	1911

End of 1940
17.40	J. Torrance (USA)	1934
17.08	A. Blozis (USA)	1940
17.04	E. Hackney (USA)	1939
16.86	S. Anderson (USA)	1940
16.70	J. Lyman (USA)	1934
16.62	W. Watson (USA)	1939
16.60	H. Woellke (Germ)	1936
16.60	H. Trippe (Germ)	1940
16.49	G. Stöck (Germ)	1939
16.45	L. Williams (USA)	1939

End of 1960
20.06	W. Nieder (USA)	1960
19.67	D. Long (USA)	1960
19.33	P. O'Brien (USA)	1960
19.11	D. Davis (USA)	1960
19.11	A. Rowe (GB)	1960
18.88	V. Ovsepyan (USSR)	1960
18.82	S. Meconi (Italy)	1960
18.67	V. Varju (Hun)	1960
18.60	Z. Nagy (Hun)	1960
18.53	C. Butt (USA)	1959
18.53	J. Silvester (USA)	1960

End of 1980
22.15	U. Beyer (E. Ger.)	1978
22.02*	G. Woods (USA)	1974
22.00	A. Barishnikov (USSR)	1976
21.85	T. Albritton (USA)	1976
21.82	A. Feuerbach (USA)	1973
21.82	B. Oldfield (USA)	1980
21.78	R. Matson (USA)	1967
21.69	R. Ståhlberg (Fin)	1979
21.68	G. Capes (GB)	1980
21.67	H. Briesenick (E. Ger.)	1973

End of 1999
23.12	R. Barnes (USA) +	1990
23.06	U. Timmermann (E. Ger.)	1988
22.91	A. Andrei (Italy)	1987
22.86	B. Oldfield (USA)	1975
22.75	W. Günthör (Switz.)	1988
22.64	U. Beyer (E. Ger.)	1986
22.52	J. Brenner (USA)	1987
22.24	S. Smirnov (USSR)	1986
22.10	S. Gavryushin (USSR)	1986
22.09	S. Kasnauskas (USSR)	1984

+ Disqualified for doping abuse (1990)

DISCUS THROW

End of 1900
+ 2.13 m. circle.
" 2.50 m. square.
| 36.19+ | C. Henneman (USA) | 1897 |

36.04"	R. Bauer (Hun)	1900
35.25"	F. Janda-Suk (Bohemia)	1900
34.74+	R. Sheldon (USA)	1900

End of 1920
(2.50 m. circle, as per rule still in force)
48.27	A. Taipale (Fin)	1913
47.58	J. Duncan (USA)	1912
47.29	A. Mucks (USA)	1916
47.18	E. Niklander (Fin)	1916
45.84	S. Toldi (Hun)	1914
45.77	O. Zallhagen (Sweden)	1916
45.54	R. Ujlaky (Hun)	1913
45.28	K. Ambrozy (Hun)	1914
44.84	V. Järvinen (Fin)	1909
44.62	A. Pope (USA)	1920

End of 1940
53.10	W. Schröder (Germ)	1935
53.08	K. Carpenter (USA)	1936
53.02	H. Andersson (Sweden)	1935
52.54	P. Fox (USA)	1939
52.25	G. Dunn (USA)	1936
51.73	P. Jessup (USA)	1930
51.72	G. Bergh (Sweden)	1936
51.57	R. Sörlie (Nor)	1937
51.53	J. Wotapek (Aut/Germ)	1939
51.49	G. Oberweger (Italy)	1938

End of 1960
59.91	E. Piatkowski (Pol)	1959
59.91	R. Babka (USA)	1960
59.28	F. Gordien (USA)	1953
59.18	A. Oerter (USA)	1960
59.03	J. Szécsényi (Hun)	1959
58.36	R. Cochran (USA)	1960
58.28	J. Ellis (USA)	1957
58.19	J. Silvester (USA)	1960
58.08	J. Wade (USA)	1960
57.93	S. Iness (USA)	1953

End of 1980
71.16	W. Schmidt (E. Ger.)	1978
70.98	M. Wilkins (USA)	1980
70.38	J. Silvester (USA)	1971
69.50	K. Hjeltnes (Nor)	1979
69.46	A. Oerter (USA)	1980
69.40	A. Swarts (USA)	1979
69.26	K. Stadel (USA)	1979
69.08	J. Powell (USA)	1975
68.48	J. Van Reenen (So. Afr.)	1975
68.40	R. Bruch (Sweden)	1972

Note - Disqualified for doping abuse: Hjeltnes in 1977 and Swarts in 1986.

End of 1999
74.08	J. Schult (E. Ger.)	1986
71.86	Y. Dumchev (USSR)	1983
71.50	L. Riedel (Germ.)	1997
71.32	B. Plucknett (USA)	1983
71.26	J. Powell (USA)	1984

71.26	R. Bruch (Sweden)	1984
71.26	I. Bugar (Czech.)	1985
71.18	A. Burns (USA)	1983
71.16	W. Schmidt (E. Ger.)	1978
71.14	A. Washington (USA)	1996

Disqualified for doping abuse (1981):
| 72.34 | B. Plucknett (USA) | 1981 |

HAMMER THROW

End of 1900
51.61	J. Flanagan (USA)	1900
50.30	A. Plaw (USA)	1900
46.83	J. McCracken (USA)	1898
45.21	J. C. Coffey (USA)	1899
45.13	T. Hare (USA)	1900
44.45	C. Chadwick (USA)	1899
44.21	J. Mitchel (USA)	1892
44.08	L. Boynton (USA)	1900

End of 1920
57.77	P. Ryan (USA)	1913
57.10	M. McGrath (USA)	1911
56.18	J. Flanagan (USA)	1909
54.11	C. Walsh (USA)	1911
53.79	H. Bailey (USA)	1915
53.59	K. Shattuck (USA)	1913
52.88	L. Talbott (USA)	1910
52.52	C. Childs (USA)	1912
51.95	A. Plaw (USA)	1904
51.89	S. Gillis (USA)	1908

End of 1940
59.56	P. O'Callaghan (Ire)	1937
59.00	E. Blask (Germ)	1938
58.77	K. Hein (Germ)	1938
58.67	U. Veirilä (Fin)	1939
58.52	K. Storch (Germ)	1939
57.77	P. Ryan (USA)	1913
57.28	O. Lutz (Germ)	1938
57.10	M. McGrath (USA)	1911
56.87	S. Mayer (Germ)	1938
56.18	J. Flanagan (USA)	1909

End of 1960
70.33	H. Connolly (USA)	1960
69.53	G. Zsivótzky (Hun)	1960
68.73	V. Rudenkov (USSR)	1960
67.32	M. Krivonosov (USSR)	1956
67.23	A. Hall (USA)	1958
66.83	T. Rut (Pol)	1960
66.66	F. Tkachev (USSR)	1958
66.53	A. Samotsvyetov (USSR)	1960
66.52	A. Baltovskiy (USSR)	1960
66.52	Yuriy Nikulin (USSR)	1960

End of 1980
81.80	Y. Syedikh (USSR)	1980
81.66	S. Litvinov (USSR)	1980
80.80	K. H. Riehm (W. Ger.)	1980
80.48	B. Zaichuk (USSR)	1980
80.46	J. Tamm (USSR)	1980
80.34	Igor Nikulin (USSR)	1980
79.16	M. Hüning (W. Ger.)	1979
78.94	D. Gerstenberg (E. Ger.)	1980
78.62	A. Spiridonov (USSR)	1976
78.58	A. Kozlov (USSR)	1980

Disqualified for doping abuse (1977):
| 79.30 | W. Schmidt (W. Ger.) | 1975 |

End of 1999
86.74	Y. Syedikh (USSR)	1986
86.04	S. Litvinov (USSR)	1986
84.62	I. Astapkovich (Byel.)	1992
84.48	I. Nikulin (USSR)	1990
84.40	J. Tamm (USSR)	1984
83.68	T. Gécsek (Hungary) +	1998
83.46	A. Abduvalyev (USSR)	1990
83.40	R. Haber (E. Ger.)	1988
83.04	H. Weis (Germ.)	1997
83.00	B. Kiss (Hungary)	1998

+ Disqualified for doping abuse (1996)

JAVELIN THROW

End of 1900
| 49.32 | E. Lemming (Sweden) | 1899 |

End of 1920
66.10	J. Myyrä (Fin)	1919
64.64	P. Johansson (Fin)	1919
64.35	U. Peltonen (Fin)	1916
62.67	G. Lindström (Sweden)	1920
62.39	J. Saaristo (Fin)	1920
62.39	A. Klumberg (Est)	1920
62.32	E. Lemming (Sweden)	1912
62.20	H. Lilliér (Sweden)	1919
61.81	Y. Häckner (Sweden)	1917
60.88	J. Halme (Fin)	1914

End of 1940
78.70	Y. Nikkanen (Fin)	1938
77.23	M. Järvinen (Fin)	1936
76.36	E. Autonen (Fin)	1939
75.93	G. Sule (Est)	1938
75.61	M. Mikkola (Fin)	1940
75.10	L. Atterwall (Sweden)	1937
73.96	G. Stöck (Germ)	1935
73.40	G. Weimann (Germ)	1933
73.27	E. Lokajski (Pol.)	1936
72.78	J. Várszegi (Hun)	1938

End of 1960
86.04	A. Cantello (USA)	1959
85.71	E. Danielsen (Nor)	1956
85.56	J. Sidlo (Pol)	1959
84.90	V. Kuznyetsov (USSR)	1958
84.64	V. Tsibulenko (USSR)	1960
83.60	C. Lievore (Italy)	1960
83.56	S. Nikkinen (Fin)	1956
83.48	W. Alley (USA)	1960
83.37	J. Kopyto (Pol)	1957
83.02	M. Macquet (Fra)	1960

End of 1980
96.72	F. Paragi (Hun)	1980
94.58	M. Németh (Hun)	1976
94.22	M. Wessing (W. Ger.)	1978
94.08	K. Wolfermann (W. Ger.)	1973
93.90	H. Siitonen (Fin)	1973
93.84	P. Sinersaari (Fin)	1979
93.80	J. Lusis (USSR)	1972
93.54	S. Hovinen (Fin)	1976
92.74	A. Puranen (Fin)	1979
92.72	H. Schreiber (W. Ger.)	1979

End of 1985
104.80	U. Hohn (E. Ger.)	1984
99.72	T. Petranoff (USA)	1983
96.72	F. Paragi (Hun)	1980
96.72	D. Michel (E. Ger.)	1983
95.80	R. Roggy (USA)	1982
95.10	B. Crouser (USA)	1985
94.58	M. Németh (Hun)	1976
94.22	M. Wessing (W. Ger.)	1978
94.20	H. Puuste (USSR)	1983
94.08	K. Wolfermann (W. Ger.)	1973

End of 1999
(New javelin introduced in 1986)
98.48	J. Zelezny (Czech.)	1996
93.09	A. Parviainen (Finland)	1999
92.60	R. Hecht (Germ.)	1995
91.46	S. Backley (GB)	1992
90.60	S. Räty (Finland)	1992
90.44	B. Henry (Germ.)	1997
89.93	S. Makarov (Russia)	1999
89.84	K. Gatsioudis (Greece)	1999
89.16	T. Petranoff (USA)	1991
89.10	P. Bodén (Sweden)	1990

Javelins with roughened tails (now banned by the IAAF):
| 96.96 | S. Räty (Finland) | 1991 |
| 90.82 | K. Kinnunen (Finland) | 1991 |

DECATHLON

End of 1920
(1920 scoring table)
7751.06+	J. Thorpe (USA)	1912
7363.625	A. Klumberg (Est)	1920
7218.985	E. Nilsson (Sweden)	1920
7191.755	B. Ohlson (Sweden)	1920
7125.25	H. Lövland (Nor)	1919
7062.60+	H. Wieslander (Sweden)	1912

+ Over 3 days.
Thorpe's score under 1985 table: 6564.

End of 1940
(1934 scoring table)
| 7900 | G. Morris (USA) | 1936 |

7824	H. H. Sievert (Germ)	1934
7601	R. Clark (USA)	1936
7523	W. Watson (USA)	1940
7396	J. Bausch (USA)	1932
7378	A. Järvinen (Fin)	1930
7337	O. Bexell (Sweden)	1937
7281	J. Parker (USA)	1936
7277	J. Mortensen (USA)	1931
7267	F. Müller (Germ)	1939

Morris' score under 1985 table: 7254.

End of 1960
(1950 Scoring Table)

8683	R. Johnson (USA)	1960
8426	Y. Chuan-Kwang (Taiwan)	1960
8357	V. Kuznyetson (USSR)	1959
8176	D. Edström (USA)	1960
7989	Y. Kutyenko (USSR)	1958
7955	M. Lauer (W. Ger.)	1959
7937	M. Campbell (USA)	1956
7887	R. Mathias (USA)	1952
7652	P. Mulkey (USA)	1960
7598	U. Palu (USSR)	1960

Johnson's score under 1985 table: 7982

End of 1980
(1977 Scoring table - automatic timing)

8649	G. Kratschmer (W. Ger.)	1980
8622	D. Thompson (GB)	1980
8617	B. Jenner (USA)	1976
8480	S. Stark (E. Ger.)	1980
8478h	A. Grebenyuk (USSR)	1977
8456	N. Avilov (USSR)	1972
8417h	W. Toomey (USA)	1969
8407	J. Hingsen (W.Ger.)	1980
8390	F. Dixon (USA)	1977
8331	Y. Kutsenko (USSR)	1980

h= hand timing
Kratschmer's score under 1985 table: 8667.

End of 1999
(1985 Scoring table - automatic timing)

8994	T. Dvorák (Czech.)	1999
8891	D. O'Brien (USA)	1992
8847	D. Thompson (GB)	1984
8832	J. Hingsen (W. Ger.)	1984
8792	U. Freimuth (E. Ger.)	1984
8762	S. Wentz (W. Ger.)	1983
8735	E. Hämäläinen (Finland)	1994
8727w	D. Johnson (USA)	1992
8709	A. Apaichev (USSR)	1984
8706	F. Busemann (Germ.)	1996

w = wind-assisted in the long jump

MARATHON

End of 1920
2:32:35.8 H. Kolehmainen (Fin) 1920

End of 1940
2:26:42	Kee Chung Sohn (Jap/Korea)	1935
2:26:44	Y. Ikenaka (Jap)	1935
2:27:29.6	E. Brown (USA)	1940
2:27:49	F. Suzuki (Jap)	1935
2:28:18	J. Kelley (USA)	1940
2:28:28.6	J. Côté (Can)	1940
2:29:01.8	A. Michelsen (USA)	1925
2:29:55	S. Nakamura (Jap)	1935
2:30:27.6	P. Dengis (USA)	1938
2:30:38	M. Dias (Port)	1937

End of 1960
2:15:16.2	Abebe Bikila (Eth)	1960
2:15:17	S. Popov (USSR)	1958
2:15:41.6	Rhadi ben Abdesselem (Morocco)	1960
2:17:18.2	B. Magee (NZ)	1960
2:17:39.4	J. Peters (GB)	1954
2:18:04.8	P. Kotila (Fin)	1956
2:18:15.6	D. O'Gorman (GB)	1960
2:18:51	E. Oksanen (Fin)	1955
2:18:56.4	V. Karvonen (Fin)	1956
2:19:06	P. Kantorek (Czecho.)	1959
2:19:06	A. Keily (GB)	1960

End of 1980
2:08:33.6	D. Clayton (Aus)	1969
2:09:01	G. Nijboer (Hol)	1980
2:09:05.6	Shigeru Soh (Japan)	1978
2:09:12	I. Thompson (GB)	1974
2:09:27	W. Rodgers (USA)	1979
2:09:28	R. Hill (GB)	1970
2:09:45	T. Seko (Japan)	1980
2:09:49	Takeshi Soh (Japan)	1980
2:09:55	W. Cierpinski (E. Ger.)	1976
2:10:00	M. Smet (Bel)	1979

End of 1999
2:05:42	K. Khannouchi (Morocco)	1999
2:06:05	R. da Costa (Bra)	1998
2:06:16	M. Tanui (Kenya)	1999
2:06:33	G. Thys (South Africa)	1999
2:06:44	J. Kiprono (Kenya)	1999
2:06:47	F. Kiprop (Kenya)	1999
2:06:49	T. Jifar (Eth.)	1999
2:06:50	B. Dinsamo (Eth.)	1988
2:06:50	W. Kiplagat (Kenya)	1999
2:06:54	O. Osoro (Kenya)	1998

NOTE - There are no official records for the marathon.

LEADING TRACK AND FIELD PERFORMANCES THROUGH THE YEARS
WOMEN (▼ Doubtful gender identity)

100 METRES (and 100 Yards)

End of 1940 (hand timing)
100 YARDS
10.4	H. Stephens (USA)	1935
10.5 ▼	S. Walasiewicz (Pol)	1938

100 METRES
11.5	H. Stephens (USA)	1936
11.6 ▼	S. Walasiewicz (Pol)	1936
11.8	K. Krauss (Germ)	1935
11.8	M. Dollinger (Germ)	1935

End of 1970 (hand timing)
100 YARDS
10.0 Chi Cheng (Taiwan) 1970

10.3	M. Mathews (Aus)	1958
10.3	W. Tyus (USA)	1965

100 METRES
11.0 *	W. Tyus (USA)	1968
11.0	Chi Cheng (Taiwan)	1970
11.0	R. Meissner (Stecher)(E. Ger.)	1970
11.1	I. Kirszenstein (Szewinska)(Pol)	1965
11.1	B. Ferrell (USA)	1967
11.1	L. Samotyesova (USSR)	1968
11.1	M. Bailes (USA)	1968
11.1	R. Boyle (Aus)	1968

Declared ineligible for women's competitions in 1967:
11.1 E. Klobukowska (Pol) 1965

* automatic time: 11.08

End of 1999 (automatic timing)
100 METRES
10.49	F. Griffith-Joyner (USA)	1988
10.65	M. Jones (USA)	1998
10.73	C. Arron (France)	1998
10.74	M. Ottey (Jamaica)	1996
10.76	E. Ashford (USA)	1984
10.77	I. Privalova (Russia)	1994
10.78	D. Sowell (USA)	1989
10.79	Li Xuemei (China)	1997
10.79	I. Miller (USA)	1999
10.81	M. Göhr (E. Ger.)	1983

200 METRES (and 220 Yards)

End of 1940
(hand timing; *220 yards time less 0.1)

23.8 ▼	S. Walasiewicz (Pol)	1938
24.1	H. Stephens (USA)	1936
24.4 *	D. Norman (Aus)	1938
24.4	K. Krauss (Germ)	1938
24.6	T. Schuurman (Hol)	1933
24.6	F. Koen (Hol)	1938
24.6 *	J. Bennie (So. Afr.)	1938

Made over 199.88 m.:
23.6 ▼	S. Walasiewicz (Pol)	1935

Straight course:
23.1*	H. Stephens (USA)	1935

End of 1970
(hand timing; *220 yards time less 0.1)

22.4	Chi Cheng (Taiwan)	1970
22.5''	I. Szewinska (Pol)	1968
22.7	R. Boyle (Aus)	1968
22.7	R.Meissner (Stecher) (E. Ger)	1970
22.8 *	M. Burvill (Aus)	1964
22.8	B. Ferrell (USA)	1968
22.8	J. Lamy (Aus)	1968
22.9	W. Rudolph (USA)	1960
22.9	M. Bailes (USA)	1968

'' automatic time: 22.58

End of 1999 (automatic timing)

21.34	F. Griffith-Joyner (USA)	1988
21.62	M. Jones (USA)	1998
21.64	M. Ottey (Jamaica)	1991
21.71	M. Koch (E. Ger.)	1979
21.71	H. Drechsler (E. Ger.)	1986
21.72	G. Jackson (Jamaica)	1988
21.72	G. Torrence (USA)	1992
21.74	M. Göhr (E. Ger.)	1984
21.74	S. Gladisch (E. Ger.)	1987
21.75	J. Cuthbert (Jamaica)	1992

400 METRES (and 440 Yards)

End of 1940
(hand timing; *440 Yards time less 0.3)

56.5* ▼	N. Halstead (GB)	1932
57.6 ▼	S. Walasiewicz (Pol)	1935
57.7	V. Pizhurina (USSR)	1938

End of 1970
(hand timing; *440 Yards time less 0.3)

51.0''	M. Neufville (Jam)	1970
51.2	Shin Geum Dan (No. Korea)	1964
51.7	N. Duclos (Fra)	1969
51.7	C. Besson (Fra)	1969
52.0	B. Cuthbert (Aus)	1964
52.1*	J. Pollock (Aus)	1965
52.1	L. Board (GB)	1968
52.1	K. Hammond (USA)	1969
52.2	A. Packer (GB)	1964
52.2	N. Pyechenkina (USSR)	1968
52.2*	Chi Cheng (Taiwan)	1970

'' automatic time: 51.02

End of 1999
(automatic timing)

47.60	M. Koch (E. Ger.)	1985
47.99	J. Kratochvilova (Czech)	1983
48.25	M-J. Pérec (France)	1996
48.27	O. Vladikina (Brizgina) (USSR)	1985
48.59	T. Kocembova (Czech)	1983
48.63	C. Freeman (Australia)	1996
48.83	V. Brisco (USA)	1984
49.05	C. Cheeseborough (USA)	1984
49.10	F. Ogunkoya (Nigeria)	1996
49.11	O. Nazarova (USSR) +	1988

+ disqualified for doping abuse (1996)

800 METRES (and 880 Yards)

End of 1940
(hand timing; *880 yards time less 0.8)

2:15.3	Y. Vasilyeva (USSR)	1938
2:15.3	K. Shilo (USSR)	1940
2:15.6 ▼	N. Halstead (GB)	1935
2:15.9	A. Basenko (USSR)	1940

Estimated times:
2:13.8	M. Wretman (Sweden)	1934
2:14.2	G. Lunn (GB)	1934

Declared inieligble for women's competitions in 1935:
2:12.8	Z. Koubková (Czecho)	1934

End of 1970
(hand timing; *880 yards time less 0.8)

1:58.0	Shin Geum Dan (N.Korea)	1964
2:00.5	V. Nikolic (Yugo)	1968
2:00.9	M. Manning (USA)	1968
2:01.0	J. Pollock (Aus)	1967
2:01.1	A. Packer (GB)	1964
2:01.2*	D. Willis (Aus)	1962
2:01.4*	M. Chamberlain (NZ)	1962
2:01.4	L. Board (GB)	1969
2:01.8	I. Silai (Rom)	1968
2:01.8	G. Hoffmeister (E. Ger.)	1970

End of 1999 (automatic timing)

1:53.28	J.Kratochvilova (Czech)	1983
1:53.43	N. Olizarenko USSR)	1980
1:54.44	A.F. Quirot (Cuba)	1989
1:54.81	O. Mineyeva (USSR)	1980
1:54.94	T. Kazankina (USSR) +	1976
1:55.05	D. Melinte (Romania)	1982
1:55.19	M.L. Mutola (Mozam.)	1994
1:55.26	S. Wodars (E. Ger.)	1987
1:55.32	C. Wachtel (E. Ger.)	1987
1:55.42	N. Shtereva (Bulgaria)	1976

+ Disqualified for doping abuse (1984)

1500 METRES

End of 1970 (hand timing)

4:10.7	J. Jehličková (Czecho)	1969
4:11.9	M. Gommers (Hol)	1969
4:12.0	P. Pigni (Italy)	1969
4:12.2	K. Burneleit (E. Ger.)	1970
4:13.0	I. Keizer (Hol)	1970
4:13.0	E. Tittel (W. Ger.)	1970

End of 1999 (automatic timing)

3:50.46	Qu Yunxia (China)	1993
3:50.98	Jiang Bo (China)	1997
3:51.34	Lang Yinglai (China)	1997
3:51.92	Wang Junxia (China)	1993
3:52.47	T. Kazankina (USSR) +	1980
3:53.91	Yin Lili (China)	1997
3:53.96	P. Ivan (Romania)	1988
3:53.97	Lan Lixin (China)	1997
3:54.23	O. Dvirna (USSR)	1982
3:54.52	Zhang Ling (China)	1997

+ Disqualified for doping abuse (1984)

1 MILE (= 1609.35 m.)

End of 1970 (hand timing)

4:36.8	M. Gommers (Hol)	1969
4:37.0	A. Smith (GB)	1967

End of 1999 (automatic timing)

4:12.56	S. Masterkova (Russia)	1996
4:15.61	P. Ivan (Rom.)	1989
4:15.8 h	N. Artyomova (USSR) +	1984
4:16.71	M. Decker-Slaney (USA)	1985
4:17.25	S. O'Sullivan (Ireland)	1994

h = hand timing
+ Disqualified for doping abuse (1992)

3000 METRES

End of 1970 (hand timing)

9:38.0	P. Pigni (Italy)	1969
9:43.4	A. O'Brien (Ire)	1970

End of 1999 (automatic timing)

8:06.11	Wang Junxia (China)	1993
8:12.18	Qu Yunxia (China)	1993
8:16.50	Zhang Linli (China)	1993
8:19.78	Ma Liyan (China)	1993
8:21.64	S. O'Sullivan (Ireland)	1994
8:21.84	Zhang Lirong (China)	1993
8:22.62	T. Kazankina (USSR) +	1984
8:24.31	G. Szabo (Rom)	1998
8:25.83	M. Decker-Slaney (USA)	1985
8:26.48	Z. Ouaziz (Morocco)	1999

+ Disqualified for doping abuse (1984)

5000 METRES

End of 1970 (hand timing)
15:53.6   P. Pigni (Italy)   1969

End of 1999 (automatic timing)
14:28.09 Jiang Bo (China)   1997
14:29.82 Dong Yanmei (CHina)   1997
14:31.48 G. Szabo (Rom)   1998
14:32.08 Z. Ouaziz (Morocco)   1998
14:32.33 Liu Shixiang (China)   1997
14:36.08 G. Wami (Eth)   1998
14:36.45 F. Ribeiro (Por)   1995
14:37.33 I. Kristiansen (Nor)   1986
14:39.96 Yin Lili (China)   1997
14:41.40 S. O'Sullivan (Ireland)   1995

10,000 METRES

End of 1970 (hand timing)
35:30.5   P. Pigni (Italy)   1970

End of 1999 (automatic timing)
29:31.78 Wang Junxia (China)   1993
30:13.37 Zhong Huandi (China)   1993
30:13.74 I. Kristiansen (Nor.)   1986
30:24.56 G. Wami (Eth)   1999
30:27.13 P. Radcliffe (GB)   1999
30:32.03 T. Loroupe (Kenya)   1999
30:38.09 Dong Yanmei (China)   1997
30:39.41 Lan Lixin (China)   1997
30:39.98 Yin Lili (China)   1997
30:47.22 Dong Zhaoxia (China)   1997

80 METRES HURDLES

End of 1940 (hand timing)
11.3   C. Testoni (Italy)   1939
11.4   E. Biess (Germ)   1940
11.5   S. Dempe (Germ)   1939
11.5   A. Spitzweg (Germ)   1939
11.6   R. Engelhard (Germ)   1934
11.6   B. Burke (So. Afr.)   1937
11.6   L. Peter (Germ)   1939
11.6   T. Valla (Italy)   1940

End of 1968 (hand timing)
10.2   V. Korsakova (USSR)   1968
10.3   I. Press (USSR)   1965
10.3   M. Caird (Aus)   1968
10.4   P. Kilborn (Aus)   1965
10.4   G. Zarubina (USSR)   1968
10.4   T. Talisheva (USSR)   1968
10.4   Chi Cheng (Taiwan)   1968

100 METRES HURDLES
(introduced in international competitions in 1969)

End of 1970 (hand timing)
12.7   K. Balzer (E. Ger.)   1970
12.7   T. Sukniewicz (Pol)   1970
12.8   Chi Cheng (Taiwan)   1970
12.9   A. Jahns (Ehrhardt) (E. Ger.)   1970
12.9   V. Bufanu (Rom)   1970
13.0   B. Podeswa (E. Ger.)   1970

End of 1999 (automatic timing)
12.21   Y. Donkova (Bulg.)   1988
12.25   G. Zagorcheva (Bul.)   1987
12.26   L. Narozhilenko (Russia)   1992
12.36   G. Rabsztyn (Pol.)   1980
12.37   G. Devers (USA)   1999
12.39   V. Komisova (USSR)   1980
12.39   N. Grigoryeva (Ukr.) +   1991
12.42   B. Jahn (E. Ger.)   1983
12.43   L. Kalek-Langer (Pol.)   1984
12.44   G.Uibel-Siebert (E.Ger.)   1987
12.44   O. Shishigina (Kaz.)   1995
12.44   G. Alozie (Nigeria)   1998
+Disqualified for doping abuse (1992)

400 METRES HURDLES
(Introduced in international competitions in 1974)

End of 1999 (automatic timing)
52.61   K. Batten (USA)   1995
52.62   T.Buford-Bailey (USA)   1995
52.74   S. Gunnell (GB)   1993
52.79   S. Farmer-Patrick (USA)   1993
52.82   D. Hemmings (Jamaica)   1996
52.89   D. Pernia (Cuba)   1999
52.90   N. Bidouane (Morocco)   1999
52.94   M. Styepanova (USSR)   1986
53.11   T. Lyedovskaya (Byel.)   1991
53.17   D. Flintoff-King (Aus)   1988

HIGH JUMP

End of 1940
1.66   D. Odam (GB)   1939
1.651   E. Van Heerden (So. Afr.)   1940
1.65   J. Shiley (USA)   1932
1.65   M. Didrikson (USA)   1932
1.64   I. Csák (Hun)   1938
1.64   N. Van Balen-Blanken (Hol)   1938
1.64   F. Solms (Germ)   1938
1.63   E. Kaun (Germ)   1939
1.63   I. Pfenning (Switz)   1940
1.63   F. Koen (Blankers) (Hol)   1940
Declared ineligible for women's competitions in 1938:
1.70   D. Ratjen (Germ)   1938

End of 1970
1.91   I. Balas (Rom)   1961
1.87   R. Schmidt (E. Ger.)   1968
1.87   A. Lazaryeva (USSR)   1970
1.86   S. Hrepevnik (Yugo)   1970
1.85   M. Hübnerová (Czecho)   1970
1.85   I. Gusenbauer (Aut)   1970
1.85   C. Popescu (Rom)   1970
1.84   M. Komka (Hun)   1970
1.835   M. Brown (Aus)   1964
1.835   D. Brill (Can)   1970

End of 1999
(* indoors)
2.09   S. Kostadinova (Bulg.)   1987
2.07   L. Andonova (Bulg.) +   1984
2.07*   H. Henkel (Germ.)   1992
2.05   T. Bikova (USSR)   1984
2.05   I. Babakova (Ukr.)   1995
2.04   S. Costa (Cuba)   1989
2.04*   A. Astafei (Germ.)   1995
2.04   H. Cloete (South Africa)   1999
2.03   U. Meyfarth (W. Ger.)   1983
2.03   L. Ritter (USA)   1988
2.03   T. Motkova (Russia)   1995
2.03   N. Bakoyiánni (Greece)   1996
2.03   V. Veneva (Bulg.)   1998
2.03*   M. Dinescu (Rom.)   1999
+ = Andonova was disqualified for doping abuse in 1985

POLE VAULT

End of 1970
2.59   D. Bragg (USA)   1952
2.59   B. Walker (USA)   1969

End of 1999
(*Indoors)
4.60   E. George (Aus.)   1999
4.60   S. Dragila (USA)   1999
4.56*   N. Humbert (Germ.)   1999
4.55   A. Balakhonova (Ukr.)   1999
4.51   D. Bártová (Czech.)   1998
4.51*   S. Szabó (Hungary)   1999
4.50*   M. Mueller (USA)   1999
4.50*   N. Rishich (Germ.)   1999
4.50   T. Grigoryeva (Aus)   1999
4.46*   K. Suttle (USA)   1999
4.46   Y. Belyakova (Russia)   1999

LONG JUMP (* Indoors)

End of 1940
6.12   C. Schulz (Germ)   1939
6.09 ▼   S. Walasiewicz (Pol)   1937
6.07   E. Junghanns (Germ)   1938
5.98   K. Hitomi (Japan)   1928
5.97   F. Koen (Blankers) (Hol)   1939
5.91   S. Grieme (Germ)   1931
5.89   T. Göppner (Germ)   1935
5.88   I. Praetz (Germ)   1938
5.88   G. Jahn-Voss (Germ)   1939
5.88   E. Boeck (Germ)   1939

End of 1970
6.84   H. Rosendahl (W. Ger.)   1970
6.82   V. Viscopoleanu (Rom)   1968

6.76	M. Rand (GB)	1964
6.73	T. Shchelkanova (USSR)	1966
6.73	I. Mickler (Becker) (W. Ger.)	1970
6.73	S. Sherwood (GB)	1970
6.67	I. Szewinska (Pol)	1968
6.66	T. Talisheva (USSR)	1968
6.65	M. Herbst (E. Ger.)	1970
6.64	S. Ammann (Switz.)	1969

End of 1999
7.52	G. Chistyakova (USSR)	1988
7.49	J. Joyner-Kersee (USA)	1994
7.48	H. Drechsler (E. Ger.)	1988
7.43	A. Cusmir-Stanciu (Rom.)	1983
7.39	Y. Byelevskaya (USSR)	1987
7.37	I. Kravets (Ukr.)	1992
7.31	Y. Kokonova (USSR)	1985
7.31	M. Jones (USA)	1998
7.26	M. Maggi (Bra)	1999
7.24	L. Berezhnaya (Ukr.)	1991

TRIPLE JUMP (*Indoors)

End of 1970
11.66	R. Yamaguchi (Japan)	1939

End of 1999
15.50	I. Kravets (Ukr.)	1995
15.20	S. Kaspárková Czech	1997
15.18	I. Prandzheva (Bulg.) +	1995
15.16	R. Mateescu (Rom)	1997
15.16*	A. Hansen (GB)	1998
15.09	A. Biryukova (Russia)	1993
15.09	I. Lasovskaya (Russia)	1997
15.07	P. Tsiamita (Greece)	1999
15.03*	I. Chen (Russia)	1995
14.98	S. Bozhanova (Bul)+	1994

+ Disqualified for doping abuse: Prandzheva in 1996; Bozhanova in 1994.

SHOT PUT (* Indoors)

End of 1940
14.38	G. Mauermayer (Germ)	1934
14.09	H. Schröder (Germ)	1938
13.70	G. Heublein (Germ)	1931
13.62	T. Sevryukova (USSR)	1936
13.52	H. Wessel (Germ)	1938
13.21	W. Flakowicz (Pol)	1938
13.19	Z. Borisova (USSR)	1939
13.16	A. Andreyeva (USSR)	1939
13.07	Trudy Mauermayer (Germ)	1939
12.99	F. Kojima (Japan)	1939

Declared ineligible for women's competitions:
13.40	S. Pekarová (Czecho)	1935

End of 1970
20.43	N. Chizhova (USSR)	1969
20.10	M. Gummel (E. Ger.)	1969
18.94	A. Ivanova (USSR)	1970
18.78	M. Lange (E. Ger.)	1968
18.63	H. Friedel (E. Ger.)	1970
18.59	T. Press (USSR)	1965
18.21	V. Korablyeva (USSR)	1970
18.18	I. Solontsova (USSR)	1970
18.12	I. Friedrich (E. Ger.)	1970
18.05	I. Khristova (Bulg)	1970

End of 1999
22.63	N. Lisovskaya (USSR)	1987
22.50*	H. Fibingerová (Czecho)	1977
22.45	I. Slupianek (E. Ger.) +	1980
22.19	C. Losch (W. Ger.)	1987
21.89	I. Khristova (Bulg)	1976
21.86	M. Adam (E. Ger.)	1979
21.76	Li Meisu (China)	1988
21.73	N. Akhrimyenko (USSR)	1988
21.69	V. Pavlish (Ukr) +	1998
21.66	Sui Xinmei (China) +	1990

Disqualified for doping abuse: Slupianek in 1977, Sui Xinmei in 1991 and Pavlish in 1999.

DISCUS THROW

End of 1940
49.54	N. Dumbadze (USSR)	1939
48.31	G. Mauermayer (Germ)	1936
46.22	J. Wajsówna (Pol)	1936
44.38	B. Lundström (Sweden)	1938
44.33	H. Sommer (Germ)	1938
43.59	A. Hagemann (Germ)	1936
43.58	P. Mollenhauer (Germ)	1939
43.35	L. Gabric (Italy)	1939
43.28	Z. Sinitskaya (USSR)	1939
42.72	G. Turova (USSR)	1938

Declared ineligible for women's competitions:
43.47	E. Volkhausen (Germ)	1938

End of 1970
63.96	L. Westermann (W. Ger.)	1969
63.66	K. Illgen (USSR)	1970
62.54	T. Danilova (USSR)	1970
61.80	F. Myelnik (USSR)	1970
61.64	C. Spielberg (E. Ger.)	1968
61.32	L. Muravyova (USSR)	1970
61.26	G. Hinzmann (E. Ger.)	1970
60.70	I. Solontsova (USSR)	1970
60.00	J. Kleiber (Hun)	1970
59.80	A. Popova (USSR)	1968

End of 1999
76.80	G. Reinsch (E. Ger.)	1988
74.56	Z. Silhavá (Czecho) +	1984
74.56	I. Wyludda (E. Ger.)	1989
74.08	D. Gansky (E. Ger.)	1987
73.84	D. Costian (Rom) +	1988
73.36	I. Meszynski (E. Ger.)	1984
73.28	G. Savinkova (USSR)	1984
73.22	T. Khristova (Bulg) +	1987
73.10	G. Beyer (E. Ger.)	1984
72.92	M. Hellmann (E. Ger.)	1987

+ Disqualified for doping abuse: Silhavá in 1985, Costian in 1986, Khristova in 1993.

HAMMER THROW

End of 1970
22.85	M. Moles (Spain)	1932

End of 1999
76.07	M. Melinte (Rom.)	1999
74.30	O. Kuzyenkova (Russia)	1999
72.09	T. Konstantinova (Russia)	1999
70.16	D. Ellerbe (USA)	1999
68.40	B. Achilles (Germ.)	1999
68.27	L. Gubkina (Byel.)	1999
68.21	S. Sudak (Byel.)	1999
68.11	M. Montebrun (France)	1999
67.64	K. Divós (Hungary)	1999
67.48	A. Davidova (Russia)	1996

JAVELIN THROW

End of 1940
47.80 ▼	E. Matthes (Germ)	1938
46.74	N. Gindele (USA)	1932
46.27	L. Krüger (Germ)	1939
45.88	K. Laptyeva (USSR)	1939
45.74	L. Gelius (Germ)	1938
45.71	H. Bauma (Aut)	1936
45.50	I. Plank (Germ)	1940
45.18	O. Fleischer (Germ)	1936
44.82	S. Pastoors (Germ)	1938
44.64	E. Braumüller (Germ)	1932

Declared ineligible for women's competitions:
47.17	E. Volkhausen (Germ)	1938

End of 1970
62.40	Y. Gorchakova (USSR)	1964
61.77	P. Rivers (Aus)	1970
61.44	D. Jaworska (Pol)	1970
61.38	E. Ozolina (USSR)	1964
60.68	M. Penes (Rom)	1967
60.60	R. Fuchs (E. Ger.)	1970
60.58	A. Ranky (Hun)	1969
60.55	B. Friedrich (USA)	1967
59.86	A. Koloska (W. Ger.)	1969
59.82	R. Bair (USA)	1967

End of 1998
80.00	P. Felke (E. Ger.)	1988
77.44	F. Whitbread (GB)	1986
74.76	T. Lillak (Fin)	1983
74.20	S. Sakorafa (Gre)	1982
73.58	T. Sanderson (GB)	1983
72.70	A. Verouli (Gre) +	1984
72.16	A. Kempe-Zollkau (E.Ger.)	1984
72.12	T. Hattestad (Nor)	1993

71.88	A. Todorova (Bulg)	1981
71.82	I. Leal (Cuba)	1985

+ Disqualified for doping abuse in 1984

New Javelin introduced in 1999

68.19	T. Hattestad (Nor.)	1999
67.09	M.Tzelili-Manjani (Greece)	1999
66.91	T. Damaske (Germ.)	1999
66.49	O. Menéndez (Cuba)	1999
66.37	T. Shikolenko (Russia)	1999

PENTATHLON

End of 1970

(Order of events - 1st Day:
100 m. hurdles, shot, high jump;
2nd Day: long jump, 200 m.
1954 Scoring Table).

5406	B. Pollak (E. Ger.)	1970
5398	H. Rosendahl (W. Ger.)	1970
5352	L. Prokop (Aut)	1969
5282	I. Mickler (Becker)(W.Ger.)	1970
5215	M. Herbst (E. Ger.)	1970
5148	M. Peters (GB)	1970

Note - Pollak's score under 1971 table: 4775

End of 1980

(Order of events, all in one day: 100 m. hurdles, shot, high jump, long jump, 800 m. 1971 Scoring table.

5083	N. Tkachenko (USSR)	1980
4937	O.Rukavishnikova (USSR)	1980
4875	O. Kuragina (USSR)	1980
4834	Y. Smirnova (USSR)	1979
4823	E. Wilms (W. Ger.)	1977
4768	D. Konihowski (Can)	1978
4735	N. Alyoshina (USSR)	1980

HEPTATHLON

Introduced in 1981.
Order of events -
1st Day: 100 m. hurdles, high jump, shot, 200 m.;
2nd Day: long jump, javelin, 800 m.
1985 Scoring table.

End of 1999

7291	J. Joyner-Kersee (USA)	1988
7007	L. Nikitina (USSR) +	1989
6985	S. Braun (Germ.)	1992
6946	S. Paetz (E. Ger.)	1984
6942	G. Shouaa (Syria)	1996
6935	R. Neubert (E. Ger.)	1983
6861	E. Barber (France)	1999
6859	N. Shubenkova (USSR)	1984
6858	A.Vater-Behmer (E. Ger)	1988
6845	I. Byelova (Russia) +	1992

+ Disqualified for doping abuse:
Nikitina in 1990, Byelova in 1993.

MARATHON

End of 1970

3:02.53	C. Walker (USA)	1970

End of 1999

2:20:43	T. Loroupe (Kenya)	1999
2:21:06	I. Kristiansen (Nor)	1985
2:21:21	J. Benoit (USA)	1985
2:21:45	U. Pippig (Germ.)	1994
2:21:47	N. Takahashi (Japan)	1998
2:22:12	E. Yamaguchi (Japan)	1999
2:22:23	C. McKiernan (Ireland)	1998
2:23:21	F. Roba (Eth.)	1998
2:23:22	J. Chepchumba (Kenya)	1999
2:23:24	L. Simon-Slavuteanu (Rom.)	1999

Note - There are no official records for the marathon.

BIBLIOGRAPHY

Berendonk, B. "Doping, von der Forschung zum Betrug" Rowohlt Sport, 1992.
Cumming, J. "Runners & Walkers, A Nineteenth Century Sports Chronicle", Regnery Gateway, Chicago, 1981.
Doherty, K. "Track & Field Omnibook", Tafnews Press, Los Altos, California, 1980.
Greenberg, S. "The Guinness Book of Olympics - Facts and Feats", Guinness Superlatives Limited, Enfield, Middlesex, 1983.
Gynn, R. "The Guinness Book of the Marathon", Guinness Superlatives Limited, Enfield, Middlesex, 1984.
Hannus, M. "Yleisurheilu - Tuhat tähteä", WSOY, Helsinki, 1983.
Hendershott, J. "Track's Greatest Women", Tafnews Press, Los Altos, California, 1987.
Khinchuk, L.L. and Mikhailova, G.I. "Lyogkaya Atletika v SSSR", Fizkultura i Sport, Moskva, 1951.
Lovesey, P. "The Official Centenary History of the AAA", Guinness Superlatives Limited, Enfield, Middlesex, 1979.
Mallon, B. and Buchanan, I. "Quest for Gold, the Encyclopedia of American Olympians", Leisure Press, New York, 1984.
Martini, M. "Da Bargossi a Mennea", FIDAL, Roma, 1988.
Matthews, P. "The Guinness Book of Athletics - Facts and Feats", Guinness Superlatives Limited, Enfield, Middlesex, 1982.
Mengoni, L. "World & National Leaders in Track & Field Athletics 1860-1972", ATFS, 1973.
Misángyi, O. "Az Ujkori Atletika Története" - Budapest, 1932.
Nelson, C. "Track's Greatest Champions", Tafnews Press, Los Altos, California, 1986.
Nelson, C. and Quercetani, R.L. "The Milers", Tafnews Press, Los Altos, California, 1985.
"Nordisk Familjeboks Sportlexikon" A. Sohlman & Co., Stockholm, 1946.
Parienté, R. "La fabuleuse histoire de l'athlétisme", Editions ODIL, Paris, 1978.
Richardson, H.A. "Archie's Little Black Book", Rich-Burn Company, Los Angeles, 1953.
Shearman, M. "Athletics and Football", Longmans, Green and Co., London, 1888.
Wilt, F. "How They Train" Tafnews Press, Los Altos, California, 1973.
zur Megede, E. and Hymans R. "Progression of World Best Performances and Official IAAF World Records", International Athletic Foundation, Monaco (Principauté), 1987.

And many almanacs, year-books, periodicals and newspapers from many parts of the world.

INDEX MEN

Aaltonen, W. (Finland) 95
Abascal, J.M. (Spain) 292, 297
Abbyasov, S. (USSR) 324
Abduvaliyev, A. (USSR) 337, 339, 427
Abebe Addis (Ethiopia) 298
Abebe Bikila (Ethiopia) 159, 162, 231, 232, 233, 428
Åberg, O. (Sweden) 149
Ablowich, E. (USA) 124
Abrahams, H. (GB) 44, 57, 71, 72, 74, 80, 111, 113, 123, 136
Abramov, V. (USSR) 299
Achilles, 15
Ackermann, U. (E. Ger.) 311
Adams, P. (USA) 63
Adams, W. (W. Ger.) 211
Adeniken, O. (Nigeria) 278
Adkins, D. (USA) 312, 314, 424
Agapov, G. (USSR) 274
Agbebaku, A. (Nigeria) 328
Agostini, M. (Trinidad) 132, 133, 134, 420
Ahearn, D. (USA) 62, 63, 114, 425
Ahearne, T. (GB) 61, 62, 425
Ahey, M. (Ghana) 250
Åhman, A. (Sweden) 177
Aho, A. (Finland) 267
Airoldi, C. (Italy) 27
Akabusi, K. (GB) 311, 312, 314, 349, 350
Akii-Bua, J. (Uganda) 236, 237, 238, 239, 424
Aksinin, A. (USSR) 272, 347
Al Malky, M. (Oman) 286
Al-Asmari, S. (Saudi Arabia) 315
Albritton, D. (USA) 107, 111, 424
Albritton, T. (USA) 258, 426
Alderman, F. (USA) 124
Alekna, V. (Lithuania) 335, 336, 417
Alekseyev, V. (USSR) 257
Allen, S. (USA) 100
Alley, W. (USA) 187, 427
Alli, Y. (Nigeria) 324
Al-Nubi, M. (Qatar) 312

Altimani, F. (Italy) 70
Amado, F. (Portugal) 410
Ambrozy, K. (Hungary) 426
Amike, H. (Nigeria) 311
Amin, Dada, I. (Uga) 237
Andersen, O. (Finland) 105
Andersen, G. (Norway) 331
Anderson, G. (USA) 77, 419
Anderson, J. (USA) 118
Anderson, Stanley (USA) 426
Anderson, Stephen (USA) 99
Anderson, W. (USA) 167
Andersson (Arbin), Harald (Sweden) 22
Andersson, A. (Sweden) 14, 93, 145, 146, 147, 148, 149, 156, 171, 421
Andersson, Harald (Sweden) 118, 119, 426
André, G. (France) 57, 58, 59, 423
Andrei, A. (Italy) 331, 332, 426
Andrews, T. (USA) 424
Andreyev, V. (Russia) 351
Antao, S. (Ghana) 420
Antibo, S. (Italy) 298, 300, 301
Antipov, A. (USSR) 423
Antón, A. (Spain) 298, 305, 307
Aouita, S. (Morocco) 288, 292, 293, 294, 295, 298, 300, 301, 316, 394, 422
Apaichev, A. (USSR) 428
Applegarth, W. (GB) 44, 45, 68, 419
Arcelli, E. (Italy) 387
Archer, J. (GB) 129
d'Arcy, V. (GB) 68
Arese, F. (Italy) 218
Arifon, J-C. (France) 166
Aristotle, 11
Arkhipyenko, V. (USSR) 240, 424
Armstead, R. (USA) 349
Arri, V. (Italy) 56
Arturi, F. (Italy) 279
Arzhanov, Y. (USSR) 211

Asakuma, Y. (Japan) 106
Asati, C. (Kenya) 207, 272
Asgedom, D. (Ethiopia) 290
Ashenfelter, H. (USA) 169
Ashworth, G. (USA) 271
Askola, A. (Finland) 95, 96, 422
Astaphan, M. "Jamie" (St. Kitts) 280
Astapkovich, I. (USSR/Bye) 337, 338, 339, 427
Atkinson, S. (South Africa) 99
Atterwall, L. (Sweden) 123, 427
Attlesey, R. (USA) 163, 164, 423
Ault, R. (USA) 166
Aun, R. (USSR) 268
Austin, C. (USA) 318, 320, 424
Autonen, E. (Finland) 186, 427
Avdeyenko, G. (USSR) 318, 319
Averbukh, A. (Israel) 321
Avery, G. (Australia) 177
Avilov, N. (USSR) 269, 270, 428
Babcock, H. (USA) 60, 424
Babers, A. (USA) 284, 285, 349
Babka, R. (USA) 183, 426
Baccouche, F. (Algeria) 300
Backley, S. (GB) 339, 340, 341, 342, 343, 427
Backman, E. (Sweden) 422
Bacon, C. (USA) 57, 423
Bacon, F. (GB) 28, 48, 421, 422
Bada, S. (Nigeria) 285, 349
Badenski, A. (Poland) 204, 205
Bagach, A. (Ukraine) 331, 333
Bagyula, I. (Hungary) 321
Bailey, H. (USA) 427
Bailey J. (Australia) 152, 153, 421
Bailey, D. (Canada) 278, 282, 283, 348, 419
Baird, G. (USA) 124
Baker, B.H. (GB) 105
Baker, P.J. (Noel-Baker) (GB) 49, 50, 52
Baker, S. (Australia) 352
Baker, T. (USA) 131, 132, 133, 134, 189, 420

433

Baker, Wendell (USA) 24, 420
Baker, William (USA) 79, 80
Bakosi, B. (Hungary) 328
Balcha, K. (Ethiopia) 304
Baldini, S. (Italy) 305
Ball, J. (Canada) 80
Bally, E. (France) 131
Baltovskiy, A. (USSR) 427
Balzer, F. (Germany) 308, 311
Balzer, K-H. (E. Ger.) 392
Bambuck, R. (France) 197, 198, 199, 271
Banks, W. (USA) 328, 329, 330, 426
Banner, S. (South Africa) 212
Bannister, R. (GB) 146, 148, 149, 150, 151, 152, 153, 154, 161, 170, 220, 223, 294, 303
Baptiste, K. (USA) 277, 281, 347
Barbosa, J.L. (Brazil) 288
Barbuti, R. (USA) 80, 124
Barclay-Allardice, R. (GB) 39
Barishnikov, A. (USSR) 257, 258, 331, 426
Barkutwo, P. (Kenya) 315, 424
Bärlund, S. (Finland) 117
Barmasai, B. (Kenya) 315, 317, 424
Barnard, A. (USA) 163, 167
Barnes, L. (USA) 108, 109
Barnes, R. (USA) 331, 332, 333, 334, 426
Barngetuny, E. (Kenya) 424
Barrientos, J. (Cuba) 197
Barrios, A. (Mexico) 298, 301
Barron, H. (USA) 423
Barsi, L. (Hungary) 89
Bartenyev, L. (USSR) 189, 271
Barthel, J. (Luxemburg) 16, 149
Bates, M. (USA) 278
Batiste, J. (USA) 162, 423
Bauer, R. (Hungary) 36, 426
Baulch, J. (GB) 349, 350
Baum, L. F. (USA) 244
Baumann, D. (Germany) 298, 299, 301, 304, 422
Baumgartl, F. (E. Ger.) 242, 424
Baumgartner, H. (W. Ger.) 252
Bausch, J. (USA) 123, 187, 428
Bautista, D. (Mexico) 275
Baxter, H. (USA) 32
Baxter, I. (USA) 32, 33, 424
Bayi, F. (Tanzania) 219, 220, 221, 241, 243, 422, 424
Bayissa, F. (Ethiopia) 295, 298, 304
Beamon, R. (USA) 248, 250, 251, 252, 255, 324, 325, 327, 425

Beard, P. (USA) 99, 100
Beatty, J. (USA) 216, 223, 421
Beatty, R. (USA) 426
Beccali, L. (Italy) 85, 86, 88, 89, 90, 91, 93, 421
Beck, F. (USA) 426
Beck, V. (E. Ger.) 208, 240, 311
Beckford, J. (Jamaica) 324, 425, 426
Bedford, D. (GB) 227, 228, 300, 423
Beer, K. (E. Ger.) 251
Beeson, E. (USA) 59, 60, 424
Beetham, C. (USA) 85, 86
Beilschmidt, R. (E. Ger.) 246, 424
Beinart, H. (South Africa) 207
Belcher, C. (USA) 420
Bell, E. (USA) 249, 321, 425
Bell, G. (USA) 176, 425
Bellini, M. (Italy) 87, 88
Bellot, J-M. (France) 207, 321, 425
Bellucci, A. (Italy) 352
Belokas, S. (Greece) 28
Bendlin, K. (W. Ger.) 268, 270
Bennett, C. (GB) 27, 421, 422
Bennett, J. (USA) 176, 425
Bennett, L. "Deerfoot" (USA) 27, 28
Bennett, T. (GB) 349
Bentley, D. (USA) 324
Benvenuti, A. (Italy) 288
Berger, C. (Holland) 75, 77
Berger, M. (France) 271
Bergh, G. (Sweden) 426
Berlin, I. (USA) 57
Bernardini, S. (Italy) 305
Berruti, L. (Italy) 135, 136, 196, 197, 420
Bertini, R. (Italy) 97
Beskrovniy, A. (USSR) 402
Bettiol, S. (Italy) 304
Bexell, O. (Sweden) 428
Beyer, O. (E. Ger.) 214, 292, 300, 421
Beyer, H. (W. Ger.) 268
Beyer, Udo (E. Ger.) 258, 261, 330, 331, 332, 335, 426
Beyer, Uwe (W. Ger.) 262, 263
Biffle, J. (USA) 176
Bikila, W. (Ethiopia) 303, 423
Bilac, B. (Yugoslavia) 324
Bile, A. (Somalia) 292, 294
Bingham, N.W. (USA) 39
Bingham, W. (USA) 421
Binks, J. (GB) 47, 48, 51, 421
Birir, J. (Kenya) 290, 292
Birir, M. (Kenya) 315, 316, 318
Bitok, P. (Kenya) 298, 304
Biwott, A. (Kenya) 241, 316

Black, D. (GB) 423
Black, L. (USA) 202, 271
Black, R. (GB) 285, 286, 287, 288, 349, 350
Blair, C. (USA) 185
Blake, A. (USA) 28
Blankers, J. (Holland) 363
Blask, E. (Germany) 121, 183, 427
Blazek, P. (Czechosl.) 350
Blignaut, P. (South Africa) 420
Blondel, A. (France) 344
Blondin, A. (France) 224
Bloss, E. (USA) 35, 425
Blozis, A. (USA) 179, 426
Bodén, P. (Sweden) 339, 341, 427
Bodosi, M. (Hungary) 106
Bogrow, H. (USA) 137
Boisset, R. (France) 82
Boit, M. (Kenya) 211, 212, 213, 216, 219, 221, 292, 421
Boit-Kipketer, W. (Kenya) 315, 317, 424
Bojars, J. (USSR) 331
Bolding, J. (USA) 239, 424
Boldon, A. (Trinidad) 278, 282, 283, 416, 419, 420
Bolinder, A. (Sweden) 171
Bolotnikov, P. (USSR) 159, 160, 223, 422
Bolshov, V. (USSR) 173, 424
Bon, N. (Kenya) 272
Bondarchuk, A. (USSR) 262, 263, 264, 339
Bonhag, G. (USA) 70
Bonthron, W. (USA) 90, 91, 92, 93, 421
Boone, G. (USA) 77
Borah, C. (USA) 71
Borchmeyer, E. (Germany) 75, 77, 124
Borck, H. (USA) 86
Bordin, G. (Italy) 304, 305, 306
Borzov V. (USSR) 15, 196, 199, 200, 201, 202, 203, 204, 205, 208, 271, 284, 373, 419, 420
Boston, R. (USA) 177, 249, 250, 251, 425
Boswell, M. (Canada) 318
Bouillé, A. (France) 30, 53
Bouin, J. (France) 49, 52, 53, 94, 422
Boulami, B. (Marocco) 417
Boulami, K. (Morocco) 298, 422
Bourland, C. (USA) 129, 131, 137, 191
Boutayeb, B. (Morocco) 298, 300, 301
Bowden, D. (USA) 421
Bowerman, W. (USA) 216
Bowman, C. (USA) 74
Boydston, D. (USA) 424
Boynton, L. (USA) 427

Boysen, A. (Norway) 143, 144, 211, 421
Bradley, C. (GB) 21, 22, 419
Bradley, G. (USA) 278
Bradstock, R. (GB) 342
Bragg, A. (USA) 130, 131, 133
Bragg, D. (USA) 175, 176, 247, 248, 425
Brahmi, A. (Algeria) 315
Braithwaite, D. (GB) 347
Brandscheit, H. (Germany) 87, 88
Brasher, C. (GB) 150, 170, 215
Braun, H. (Germany) 46, 47, 48, 49
Braunskill, K. (USA) 347
Bréal, M. (France) 28
Bredin, E. (GB) 24, 420
Bremer, M. (Germany) 298
Brenner, J. (USA) 331, 426
Breshnihan, J. (Ireland) 35, 425
Bresnahan, G. T. (USA) 73
Bridgewater, B. (USA) 347
Briesenick, H. (E. Ger.) 257, 426
Bright, T. (USA) 321
Brightwell, R. (GB) 142, 204, 205, 272
Bringmann, S. (E. Ger.) 278
Brits, O. (South Africa) 321, 425
Brix, H. (USA) 116
Brizgin, V. (USSR) 347
Broberg, D. (South Africa) 211
Brock, M. (Canada) 48, 421
Bronson, B. (USA) 312, 314, 315, 424
Brooks, M.J. (GB) 31
Brown, B. (USA) 272
Brown, E. (USA) 428
Brown, George I (USA) 421
Brown, George II (USA) 425
Brown, Godfrey (GB) 22, 23, 82, 125, 139
Brown, K. (USA) 109, 425
Brown, P. (GB) 349
Brown, R. (USA) 244, 347, 348
Bruch, R. (Sweden) 260, 335, 426, 427
Brugnetti, I. (Italy) 352
Brumel, V. (USSR) 173, 243, 244, 245, 424
Brunetto, L.A. (Argentina) 114
Bruziks, M. (USSR/Latvia) 328
Brydenbach, F. (Belgium) 208
Bryggare, A. (Finland) 308, 309
Bubka, S. (USSR) 9, 277, 299, 321, 322, 323, 400, 417, 425
Bubka, V. (USSR) 321
Bucher, A. (Switzerland) 289, 417
Buckner, J. (GB) 298
Budd, F. (USA) 135, 136, 190, 196, 271
Buder, O-S. (E.Ger./Germany) 331
Bugar, I. (Czechosl.) 261, 334, 335, 427
Buhl, H. (E. Ger) 424

Bukhantsev, K. (USSR) 412
Bulanchik, Y. (USSR) 163, 164
Bulatov, V. (USSR) 176
Bulti, W. (Ethiopia) 298
Burke, E. (USA) 107, 424
Burke, T. (USA) 21, 22, 24, 39, 420
Burleson, D. (USA) 216, 421
Burnett, H. (Jamaica) 349
Burns, A. (USA) 427
Burrell, L. (USA) 278, 280, 281, 282, 347, 348, 419
Burrowes, E. (USA) 421
Burton, L. (USA) 202
Bury, T. (GB) 21
Busemann, F. (Germany) 344, 428
Buss, M. (Germany) 318
Butler, G. (GB) 79
Butler, J. (USA) 205
Butler, S. (USA) 61, 425
Butt, C. (USA) 426
Butts, J. (USA) 255, 426
Byelonog, Y. (Ukraine) 331
Byléhn, E. (Sweden) 83
Cabrera, D. (Argentina) 160
Cacho, F. (Spain) 292, 296, 297, 422
Cagle, H. (USA) 125, 420
Caldwell, D. (USA) 48, 421
Calhoun, L. (USA) 164, 165, 234, 309, 423
Calvesi, A. (Italy) 234, 235
Cameron, B. (Jamaica) 284
Campbell, A. "Tonie" (USA) 308
Campbell, D. (GB) 278, 284, 348
Campbell, I. (Australia) 255
Campbell, J. (USA) 137
Campbell, L. (USA) 421
Campbell, M. (USA) 187, 423, 428
Campion, W. (Ireland) 425
Cankar, G. (Slovenia) 324
Cantello, A. (USA) 187, 427
Canto, E. (Mexico) 350, 351
Capes, G. (GB) 426
Cárdenas, A. (Mexico) 285, 288
Carey, D. (USA) 399
Caristan, S. (France) 308, 309
Carli, E. (Italy) 54, 55
Carlos, J. (USA) 199, 206, 420
Carlowitz, J. (E. Ger.) 285
Carlton, J. (Australia) 73, 419, 420
Carnegie, J. (Jamaica) 191
Carney, L. (USA) 135, 136, 420
Carosi, A. (Italy) 315
Carpenter, J. (USA) 46
Carpenter, K. (USA) 119, 426
Carr, E.W. "Slip" (Australia) 73

Carr, H. (USA) 196, 197, 198, 272
Carr, S. (USA) 109
Carr, W. (USA) 79, 80, 81, 84, 124, 138, 141, 191, 420
Carreira, J.L. (Spain) 298
Carroll, M. (Ireland) 298
Carroll, T. (Ireland) 105, 424
Carter, A. (GB) 211
Carter, J. (USA) 204
Carter, M. (USA) 331
Cartmell, N. (USA) 43, 44, 68
Caruso, E. (Italy) 57
Caruthers, E. (USA) 244, 245
Carvajal, F. (Cuba) 55
Cary, L. (USA) 21, 419
Casañas, A. (Cuba) 235, 236, 239, 308, 423
Casey, L. (USA) 114
Cason, A. (USA) 278, 347, 348
Cassell, O. (USA) 272
Castro, Domingos (Portugal) 298
Cator, S. (Haiti) 112, 113, 425
Cawley, W. (USA) 236, 237, 238
Cecil (Lord Burghley), D. (GB) 13, 102, 103, 125
Ceron, D. (Mexico) 305
Cerutty, P. (Australia) 150, 151, 152, 153, 154
Chadwick, C. (USA) 427
Chalkokondylis, A. (Greece) 21
Chambers, D. (GB) 278, 284, 348
Chambers, J. (GB) 40
Champion, E. (France) 30
Chandler, O. (USA) 180
Chaplin, J. (USA) 229
Charleston, I. (GB) 80
Chase, S. (USA) 423
Chataway, C. (GB) 150, 152, 158, 159
Chauvelier, D. (France) 305
Chekhov, A. (Russia) 9
Chelimo, R. (Kenya) 298, 302
Chen Chia-chuan (China) 197
Chen Zunrong (China) 324
Chernyetskiy, N. (USSR) 273, 349
Childs, C. (USA) 427
Chinnery, W. (GB) 26
Chirchir, G. (Kenya) 316
Chistyakov, A. (USSR) 185
Christie, L. (GB) 278, 280, 281, 282, 284, 347, 348, 419
Christmann, J. (Germany) 119, 121, 185
Chromik, J. (Poland) 160, 169, 170, 424
Churchill, W.S. (GB) 238
Cierpinski, W. (E. Ger.) 231, 232, 233, 304, 428

Clapp, R. (USA) 32, 424
Clark, D. (Australia) 277, 286
Clark, D. (USA) 425
Clark, Ellery (USA) 32, 33
Clark, Ernest (USA) 125
Clark, R. (USA) 113, 425, 428
Clarke, J. (Australia) 223
Clarke, L. (USA) 124
Clarke, R. (Australia) 223, 224, 225, 226, 300, 423
Clayton, D. (Australia) 232, 233, 428
Clement, F. (GB) 220, 221
Cloughen, R. (USA) 44
Coaffee, C. (Canada) 72
Cochran, C. (USA) 124
Cochran, Richard (USA) 183, 426
Cochran, Roy (USA) 104, 164, 166, 167, 423
Cocksedge, D. (GB) 312
Coe, P. (GB) 222
Coe, S. (GB) 16, 213, 214, 221, 222, 223, 288, 289, 290, 291, 292, 293, 294, 297, 300, 421, 422
Coe, W. (USA) 36, 63, 426
Coffey, J.C. (USA) 427
Coffman, R. (USA) 270
Coghlan, E. (Ireland) 220, 221, 222, 231, 298, 299
Cole, E. (USA) 139, 191
Collet, P. (France) 321, 322
Collett, W. (USA) 207, 238, 272
Collins, W. (USA) 272
Collymore, E. (USA) 420
Comstock, B. (USA) 30
Condon, A. (GB) 348
Conley, M. (USA) 324, 328, 329, 330, 426
Conneff, T. (USA) 26, 27, 48, 49, 421
Connolly, H. (USA) 185, 262, 427
Connolly, J. (USA) 34, 35, 425
Connor, K. (GB) 328, 330
Consolini, A. (Italy) 119, 181, 182, 183, 188, 262
Conway, H. (USA) 318, 320, 321, 424
Conwell, E. (USA) 129
Cook, E. (USA) 60
Cook, G. (GB) 349
Cook, R. (USA) 419
Cooper, Dedy (USA) 236, 423
Cooper, Don (USA) 174
Cooper, J. (GB) 237
Cope, P. (USA) 100
Corbett, M. (South Africa) 340, 344
Corgos, A. (Spain) 324

Cornes, J. (GB) 90, 93
Coroebus of Elis, 11
Corson, J. (USA) 117
Corts, R. (Germany) 124
Côté, G. (Canada) 160, 428
Coubertin, P. de (France) 12, 13, 15, 56, 356
Council, D. (USA) 347
Courtney, T. (USA) 143, 144, 145, 191, 209, 421
Coutinho da Silva, H. (Brazil) 178
Cova, A. (Italy) 298, 299, 300, 315
Craig, R. (USA) 43, 44, 45, 419
Cram, S. (GB) 16, 222, 288, 290, 292, 293, 294, 295, 297, 299, 300, 422
Crawford, H. (Trinidad) 203, 419
Crear, M. (USA) 308, 310, 311, 423
Creighton, S. (Australia) 298, 315
Creuzé, J. (France) 200
Crockett, I. (USA) 202, 203
Cromwell, D. (USA) 106, 107, 109, 186
Croome, A. (GB) 31
Cross, B. (GB) 72
Cross, F. (GB) 25, 420
Crossland, F. (GB) 422
Crothers, W. (Canada) 209
Crouch, G. (Australia) 219
Crouser, B. (USA) 427
Crowley, F. (USA) 90
Cruter, G. (USA) 107, 424
Cruz, Ignacio (Mexico) 350
Cruz, J.C. (Brazil) 288, 289, 421
Cruz, R. (Puerto Rico) 176
Csermák, J. (Hungary) 183, 184
Cuhel, F. (USA) 102
Cui Hui (China) 383
Culbreath, J. (USA) 167, 168, 423
Cullmann, B. (W. Ger.) 190
Cumming, J. (USA) 20, 39, 40
Cummings, W. (GB) 26
Cunliffe, E. (USA) 421
Cunningham, G. (USA) 85, 86, 90, 91, 92, 93, 147, 421
Curtis, T. (USA) 21, 31
Curtis, W.B. (USA) 12, 19, 20, 22, 25
Curtius, E. (Germany) 64
Cushman, C. (USA) 168, 423
Dachev, P. (Bulgaria) 324
da Costa, R. (Brazil) 428
Dagård, H. (Sweden) 344
Dahl, R. (Sweden) 172
Dakov, G. (Bulgaria) 318
Dalins, J. (Latvia) 125, 126
Daly, J. (Ireland) 34
Damilano, M. (Italy) 275, 350, 351, 352

Danek, L. (Czechosl.) 259, 260, 262
Danielsen, E. (Norway) 186, 187, 188, 427
Danneberg, R. (Germany) 334, 335
Darden, T. (USA) 349
da Silva, Claudinei Q. (Brazil) 278
da Silva, Robson C. (Brazil) 277, 278
da Silva, Ronaldo (Brazil) 306
Dasko, M. (Russia) 298
Davenport, I. (USA) 48, 421
Davenport, W. (USA) 234, 235, 423
Davidson, E. (Australia) 73
Davies, G. (USA) 248
Davies, J. (N. Z.) 215
Davies, L. (GB) 250, 252
Davin, P. (Ireland) 33, 424
Davis, C. (USA) 312
Davis, D. (USA) 181, 426
Davis, G. (USA) 140, 141, 167, 192, 208, 236, 420, 423
Davis, H. (USA) 127, 128, 420
Davis, I. (USA) 179
Davis, J. (USA) 163, 164, 165, 167, 168, 236, 423
Davis, Jerome (USA) 349, 350
Davis, O. (USA) 141, 142, 191, 192, 420
Davis, W. (USA) 170, 171
Day, L. (USA) 425
de Araújo, E. (Brazil) 312
De Benedictis, G. (Italy) 350
De Bruin, E. (Holland) 334
De Castella, R. (Australia) 304, 305
Deal, L. (USA) 337, 339
Dees, T. (USA) 308, 347
Delaney, J. (USA) 180
Delany, R. (Ireland) 152, 153, 154, 421
Delecour, J. (France) 135, 271
Delis, L.M. (Cuba) 118, 261, 262, 334, 335, 336
Dellinger, W. (USA) 225
DeLoach, J. (USA) 278, 281, 420
DeMar, C. (USA) 97, 98
Demuynck, L. (Belgium) 143
Deng Xuezheng (China) 389
Dengis, P. (USA) 428
Denisenko, P. (USSR) 175
Denmark, R. (GB) 298
de Noorlander, E. (Holland) 256
de Oliveira, J.C. (Brazil) 254, 255, 328, 329, 425, 426
de Ré, E. (Belgium) 22
Desch, A. (USA) 57, 423
de Souza, D. (Brazil) 324
Desyatchikov, A. (USSR) 423
de Teresa, T. (Spain) 288

Devonish, A. (Venezuela) 178
Devonish, M. (GB) 348
Dia Ba, A. (Senegal) 311, 313, 424
Diack, L. (Senegal) 14
Diagana, S. (France) 312, 315, 424
Dias, M. (Portugal) 428
Dickinson, B. (Australia) 115, 426
Dickinson, R. (GB) 32, 424
Didoni, M. (Italy) 351
Diebolt, A. (USA) 137
Diemer, B. (USA) 315
Dillard, H. (USA) 128, 129, 162, 163,
    164, 167, 189, 233,
    309, 377, 423
Dills, K. (USA) 425
Dimitrov, R. (Bulgaria) 329
Di Napoli, G. (Italy) 292, 294
Dinsamo, B. (Ethiopia) 305, 306, 428
Dionisi, R. (Italy) 249
Disley, J. (GB) 169
Dismond, B. (USA) 47, 82, 420
Dixon, C. (USA) 162, 163, 167
Dixon, F. (USA) 270, 428
Dixon, R. (N. Z.) 216, 219, 220, 228, 229
Dobermann, R. (Germany) 113
Dodds, G. (USA) 147
Doehring, J. (USA) 331, 333
Doherty, J. (Ireland) 298
Doherty, J.K. (USA) 25, 76, 174
Dohm, W. (USA) 420
Dohrow, G. (W. Ger.) 149
Dole, N. (USA) 60
Dolezal, J. (Czechosl.) 192, 193
Dologodin, V. (Ukraine) 278
Dombrowski, L. (E. Ger.) 252, 324, 325, 425
Dompert, A. (Germany) 105, 424
Donaldson, J. (Australia) 45
Donovan, T. (Ireland) 423
Dooley, Andrew (USA) 76
Dooley, Aubrey (USA) 425
Dordoni, G. (Italy) 193
Dorovskikh, V. (USSR) 352
dos Santos, L.A. (Brazil) 305
Doubell, R. (Australia) 210
Douda, F. (Czechosl.) 116, 117
Douglas, J. (USA) 279
Douglas, Troy (Holland) 278
Downer, A. (GB) 20, 22, 419
Downs, W. (USA) 24, 420
Doyle, A.C. (GB) 57
Drake, L. (Australia) 73
Draper, F. (USA) 77, 124
Dray, W. (USA) 60, 109
Drayton, P. (USA) 197, 271

Drehmel, J. (E. Ger.) 254, 426
Drew, H. (USA) 44, 45, 419
Drummond, J. (USA) 347, 348
Druppers, R. (Holland) 288
Drut, G. (France) 234, 235, 423
Dubin, C. (Canada) 280
Dubrovshchik, V. (Byelarus) 334, 336
Dudin, V. (USSR) 241
Dudkin, N. (USSR) 253
Duffey, A. (USA) 22, 31, 41, 42, 43, 419
Dugger, E. (USA) 423
Duginyets, I. (USSR) 334
Dumas, C. (USA) 171, 173, 424
Dumchev, Y. (USSR) 335, 426
Duncan, J. (USA) 65, 426
Dunecki, L. (Poland) 204, 347
Dunn, D. (USA) 77
Dunn, G. (USA) 119, 426
Dupray, G. (France) 418
Duquesne, L. (France) 105
D'Urso, G. (Italy) 288
Dvorak, C. (USA) 33, 60, 424
Dvorák, T. (Czech R.) 344, 346, 347,
    418, 428
Dyachkov, V. (USSR) 110, 173
Dyer, E. (USA) 423
Dyer, H. (USA) 124
Dzhumanazarov, S. (USSR) 233
Eastman, B. (USA) 79, 80, 81, 84, 85,
    86, 124, 125, 136,
    314, 420, 421
Eby, E. (USA) 48
Ecker, D. (Germany) 321
Edmonds, W. (USA) 109
Edstrom, D. (USA) 428
Edström, J.S. (Sweden) 13
Edward, H. (GB) 46
Edwards, C. (USA) 203, 419, 420
Edwards, H. (USA) 199
Edwards, J. (GB) 328, 329, 330, 404,
    417, 426
Edwards, P. (Canada) 83, 84, 85, 86,
    90, 93
Egbunike, I. (Nigeria) 285, 286
Einarsson, V. (Iceland) 178, 179, 426
Ekelund, B. (Sweden) 60
El Basir, R. (Morocco) 292
El Guerrouj, H. (Morocco) 292, 294, 295,
    296, 297, 302,
    314, 422
Eldebrink, K. (Sweden) 339
Eldon, S. (GB) 422
Eldracher, E. (Germany) 74
Elizalde, A. (Cuba) 334

Ellerbe, M. (USA) 127
Elliott, H. (Australia) 94, 144, 145, 146,
    151, 152, 153, 154,
    215, 217, 219, 421
Elliott, L. (GB) 21
Elliott, P. (GB) 288, 290, 292, 294
Ellis, F.B. (USA) 38
Ellis, J. (USA) 426
El Mabrouk, P. (France) 149
Elmsäter (Pettersson), E. (Sweden) 168, 169
El Ouafi, B. (France) 97
Emmelmann, F. (E. Ger.) 277, 281
Emmiyan, R. (USSR) 324, 325, 328, 425
Enck, S. (USA) 83
Engdahl, N. (Sweden) 124
Engel, M. (USA) 185
Engelhard, H. (Germany) 82, 83
Engquist, J. (Sweden) 393
Ereng, P. (Kenya) 288, 289, 290
Ericsson, I. (Sweden) 149
Eriksson, H. (Sweden) 148, 149
Esmie, R. (Canada) 283, 347, 348
Esteves, H. (Venezuela) 196
Estévez, R. (Spain) 292, 297
Evangelisti, G. (Italy) 324, 325, 326, 328
Evans, D. (USA) 203, 347
Evans, L. (USA) 198, 199, 205, 206,
    207, 240, 272, 285,
    286, 420
Everett, D. (USA) 285, 286, 288, 349,
    350, 420
Everett, M. (USA) 288, 289, 349
Evers, J. (W. Ger.) 278
Ewell, N. "Barney" (USA) 127, 128,
    129, 131
Ewry, R. (USA) 61, 62
Ezinwa, D. (Nigeria) 282
Ezzine, A. (Morocco) 315, 417
Facelli, L. (Italy) 102, 103, 166
Fadejevs, A. (Latvia) 351
Fairbrother, S. (GB) 292
Falk, R. (Sweden) 422
Fall, E. (USA) 421
Farmer, J. (USA) 298
Farrell, T. (USA) 211
Fast, E. (Sweden) 30
Faulkner, S. (GB) 324
Faust, J. (USA) 173, 424
Fava, F. (Italy) 229, 242
Fehringer, H. (Austria) 321
Fell, G. (Canada) 315
Felton, S. (USA) 184
Fenske, C. (USA) 93, 421
Ferguson, R. (Canada) 151

Ferguson, R. (USA) 423
Fernándes Salvador, A. (Ecu) 130
Fernández, F.J. (Spain) 351
Ferner, H-P. (W. Ger.) 288, 290
Ferreira da Silva, A. (Brazil) 177, 178, 253, 426
Ferreira, S. (France) 425
Ferris, D. (USA) 104
Ferris, S. (GB) 97
Feuerbach, A. (USA) 257, 258, 426
Fiasconaro, M. (Italy) 207, 211, 212, 291, 385, 421
Figuerola, E. (Cuba) 136, 196, 197
Filiput, A. (Italy) 166
Finlay, D. (GB) 99, 100, 101, 163, 165, 235, 310
Fischer, L. (USA) 24
Fitch, A. (USA) 125
Fitch, H. (USA) 79
Fitch, R. (USA) 182
Fitzgerald, E. (Ireland) 62, 102
Fiz, M. (Spain) 305, 307
Flack, E. (Australia) 25, 27, 28, 29
Flanagan, J. (USA) 37, 42, 64, 65, 66, 184, 338, 427
Fleschen, K. (W. Ger) 422
Floyd, S. (USA) 205, 419
Foik, M. (Poland) 136, 420
Fontanella, V. (Italy) 298
Fonville, C. (USA) 179, 180
Forbes, C. (Jamaica) 271
Ford, M. (USA) 33
Fordjour, B. (Ghana) 218
Forsyth, T. (Australia) 318, 320
Fosbury, R. (USA) 244, 245, 397
Foss, F. (USA) 60, 424
Foster, B. (GB) 216, 218, 219, 228, 229, 422, 423
Foster, C. (USA) 235
Foster, G. (USA) 236, 308, 309, 311, 423
Fox (Levy), P. (USA) 119, 426
Fox, F.B. (USA) 423
Fracchia, L. (Italy) 323
Francis, C. (USA) 280
Francis, S. (USA) 117
Franke, S. (Germany) 298
Franks, M. (USA) 284, 285, 349
Frassinelli, R. (France) 215
Fray, M. (Jamaica) 271
Frazier, C. (USA) 271
Frazier, H. (USA) 208, 272
Fredericks, F. (Namibia) 278, 282, 283, 287, 419, 420
Freeman, R. (USA) 206, 272, 420

Freigang, S. (Germany) 305
Freimuth, J. (E. Ger.) 246, 318, 424
Freimuth, U. (E. Ger.) 428
Frenkel, P. (E. Ger.) 274
Frey, R. (USA) 272
Friedek, C-M. (Germany) 329, 330
Frigerio, U. (Italy) 70, 125
Frinolli, R. (Italy) 236, 237, 238
Fritz, W. (Canada) 125
Fromm. D. (E. Ger.) 211
Fry, C.B. (GB) 33, 425
Fuchs, J. (USA) 180
Fuhlbrügge, H. (Germany) 292
Fujii, M. (Japan) 41, 43
Fukumoto, R. (USA) 376
Fulton, J. (USA) 142
Fuqua, I. (USA) 124
Fütterer, H. (W. Ger.) 132, 133, 141, 190
Fyedoseyev, O. (USSR) 179, 253, 426
Fyodoriv, A. (USSR) 278
Gailly, E. (Belgium) 160
Gakou, A. (Senegal) 206
Galfione, J. (France) 321, 323, 425
Gammoudi, M. (Tunisia) 225, 226, 227, 228, 229
Ganslen, R. (USA) 247, 425
Garcelon, W.F. (USA) 39
Garcia, Anier (Cuba) 308, 311
Garcia, Daniel (Mexico) 350, 351
Garcia, Diego (Spain) 305
Garcia, Javier (Spain) 321
Garcia, Jesús Angel (Spain) 352
Garcia, W. (USA) 54
Gardener, J. (GB) 348
Gärderud, A. (Sweden) 240, 241, 242, 424
Gardner, R. (USA) 60, 424
Garrett, R. (USA) 35, 36
Gataullin, R. (USSR) 321, 322, 425
Gatewood, B. (USA) 101, 423
Gathers, J. (USA) 131
Gatsioudis, K. (Greece) 340, 418, 427
Gauder, H. (E. Ger.) 275, 352
Gault, W. (USA) 308, 347, 348
Gavrilov, V. (USSR) 245
Gavrilyenko, Y. (USSR) 239
Gavryushin, S. (USSR) 426
Gay, Roberts E.L. (GB) 47
Gebrselassie, H. (Ethiopia) 295, 298, 299, 301, 302, 303, 304, 314, 417, 422, 423
Gécsek, T. (Hungary) 337, 339, 427
Geister, H. (W. Ger.) 139, 191
Gemechu, K. (Ethiopia) 305

Genken Kim (Won Kwon-kim) (Jap/Korea) 177, 426
Gentile, G. (Italy) 253, 426
George, W. (GB) 20, 25, 26, 48, 50, 421, 422
Germar, M. (W. Ger.) 134, 141, 190, 271, 420
Gerner, D. (Germany) 177
Gerschler, W. (Germany) 87, 143, 149
Gerstenberg, D. (E. Ger.) 427
Geyelin, H.L. (USA) 38
Gies, H-P. (E. Ger.) 257
Giessing, T. (W. Ger.) 349
Gilbert, A. (USA) 60
Gilbert, E. (USA) 423
Gilbert, G. (Canada) 348
Gillis, S. (USA) 427
Gilmour, G. (N. Z.) 146
Gitsham, C. (South Africa) 56
Gittins, B. (USA) 238
Glance, H. (USA) 203, 205, 271, 347
Glaw, G. (Germany) 104, 423
Glover, E. (USA) 60
Godina, J. (USA) 331, 333
Godoy, J. (Cuba) 319
Goelitz, H. (USA) 423
Goffi, D. (Italy) 305
Golding, J. (GB) 278, 284, 348
Golley, J. (GB) 328
Golliday, J. (USA) 130, 133, 419
Golubnichiy, V. (USSR) 192, 274
Gombala, M. (Czech R.) 324
Gönczy, L. (Hungary) 58
Gonder, F. (France) 60, 250
González, J-L. (Spain) 292, 293, 294, 297
González, R. (Mexico) 275, 350, 352
Goodwin, G. (GB) 125
Gordien, F. (USA) 182, 183, 426
Gordon, E. (USA) 112
Gordon, J. (USA) 80
Gorno, R. (Argentina) 160
Gorshkov, A. (USSR) 350
Goryayev, D. (USSR) 426
Goryayev, V. (USSR) 179, 253
Gosper, K. (Australia) 140
Goulding, J. (Canada) 68, 70
Gourdin, E. (USA) 111
Gourdine, M. (USA) 176
Gouskos, M. (Grecia) 35
Gowon (Gen.), (Nigeria) 242
Graber, W. (USA) 109, 425
Grace, W.G. (GB) 30
Graddy, S. (USA) 277, 347, 348
Graham, G. (USA) 108, 175
Graham, J. (USA) 175, 425

Graham, P. (USA) 424
Graham, W. (Jamaica) 311, 312, 314
Granger, R. (Canada) 73
Grant, D. (GB) 318
Gray, G. (Canada) 34, 35, 426
Gray, J. (USA) 288, 291, 421
Grebenyuk, A. (USSR) 270, 344, 428
Green, T. (GB) 125
Green, W. (USA) 209
Greenberg, K. (USA) 42
Greene, C. (USA) 198, 199, 271, 419
Greene, J. (USA) 324
Greene, M. (USA) 277, 278, 282, 283, 284, 288, 348, 416, 419, 420
Grelle, J. (USA) 216, 217
Grieve, R. (USA) 76
Griffiths, C. (GB) 83
Grimes, J. (USA) 324, 329
Grindley, D. (GB) 288
Grishchenkov, V. (USSR) 328
Grodotzki, H. (E. Ger.) 160, 422, 423
Gubner, G. (USA) 255
Guillemot, J. (France) 53, 93, 422
Gummelt, B. (E. Ger.) 352
Günthör, W. (Switzerland) 331, 332, 333, 426
Gushchin, E. (USSR) 256
Gustafsson, B. (Sweden) 352
Gustafsson, R. (Sweden) 142, 147, 148
Gutowski, R. (USA) 175, 176, 425
Guts-Muths, J.C.F. (Germany) 32
Gutterson, A. (USA) 61, 425
Guymaraes, A. (Brazil) 214, 288
Gynn, R. (GB) 29
Haaf, D. (W. Ger.) 324
Haas, K-F. (W. Ger.) 138, 139, 140, 141, 191
Haase, J. (E. Ger.) 225, 226
Haber, R. (E. Ger.) 337, 427
Häckner, Y. (Sweden) 37, 66, 427
Hackney, E. (USA) 117, 426
Hadwich, V. (E. Ger.) 339
Hägg, G. (Sweden) 14, 93, 145, 146, 147, 148, 149, 150, 155, 156, 158, 171, 421
Hagström, G. (Sweden) 169
Hahn, A. (USA) 19, 42, 43, 44
Hahn, L. (USA) 83
Haikkola, R. (Finland) 227
Halberg, M. (N.Z.) 145, 153, 154, 159, 160, 224, 421, 422, 423
Haley, R. (USA) 349
Hall, A. (USA) 427
Hall, E. (USA) 234, 423

Hall, K. (Australia) 220
Haller, A. (USA) 425
Hallowell, N. (USA) 90
Hallows, N. (GB) 48
Halme, J. (Finland) 427
Halstvedt, A. (Norway) 422
Halswelle, W. (GB) 46
Halvari, M. (Finland) 331, 417
Hämäläinen, E. (Byel/Finl) 341, 344, 428
Hämäläinen, P. (Byelarus) 341
Hamarsland, A. (Norway) 421
Hamilton, B. (USA) 190
Hamilton, W. (USA) 68
Hamm, E. (USA) 112, 425
Hampson, T. (GB) 83, 84, 85, 89, 421
Hampton, M. (USA) 203, 271
Hanisch, W. (E. Ger.) 267
Hanner, F. (USA) 110
Hänni, P. (Switzerland) 77
Hannus, M. (Finland) 52
Hansen, F. (USA) 248
Hansen, R. (USA) 425
Hansenne, M. (France) 142
Harada, M. (Japan) 115, 116, 425
Harbig, R. (Germany) 79, 82, 83, 86, 87, 88, 125, 137, 139, 142, 143, 144, 149, 151, 420, 421
Hardin, G. (USA) 101, 103, 104, 125, 166, 167, 420, 423
Hardin, W. (USA) 174, 236, 237
Hardmo, W. (Sweden) 192
Hare, T. (USA) 427
Härkönen, A. (Finland) 339
Härkönen, J. (Finland) 288
Haro, M. (Spain) 227
Harper, E. (GB) 98
Harris, A. (USA) 181
Harris, Danny (USA) 310, 311, 312, 313, 424
Harris, Douglas (N. Z.) 142
Harris, E. (USA) 137
Harris, H.A. (GB) 33
Harrison, A. (USA) 349, 350, 420
Harrison, K. (USA) 328, 330, 426
Hart, E. (USA) 201, 202, 203, 229, 271, 419
Hartranft, G. (USA) 118
Hartwig, J. (USA) 321, 323, 417, 425
Hary, A. (W. Ger.) 134, 135, 136, 137, 190, 196, 419
Hassan, El Kashief (Sudan) 208
Hatungimana, A. (Burundi) 288
Haughton, G. (Jamaica) 285

Hausleber, J. (Poland) 275
Havel, J. (Bohemia) 39
Hawtrey, H. (GB) 48, 51
Hayes, J. (USA) 55, 57
Hayes, R. (USA) 195, 196, 197, 270, 271, 419
Haynes, T. (USA) 255
Healion, B. (Ireland) 183
Heard, F. (USA) 278, 348
Heatley, B. (GB) 231
Hecht, R. (Germany) 339, 340, 343, 427
Hefferon, C. (South Africa) 55
Heidenström, P.N. (N. Z.) 209
Hein, K. (Germany) 120, 121, 185, 427
Heino, V. (Finland) 155, 156, 157, 161
Hélan, S. (France) 328
Held, F. "Bud" (USA) 186, 187
Helffrich, A. (USA) 94, 124
Heljasz, Z. (Poland) 117
Hellsten, V. (Finland) 139, 140, 141
Hellström, B. (Sweden) 155, 422
Hemery, D. (GB) 234, 236, 238, 239, 424
Hemingway, E. (USA) 417
Hemingway, M. (USA) 417
Hempton, J. (N.Z.) 419
Hendershott, J. (USA) 360
Henneman, C. (USA) 36, 426
Hennige, G. (W. Ger.) 236, 238
Henry, B. (Germany) 339, 343, 427
Henry, W. (USA) 96
Herbert, J. (USA) 86, 137
Herbert, L. (South Africa) 312, 417
Herman, M. (USA) 425
Hermens, J. (Holland) 229, 303
Hernández, A. (Spain) 324
Hernández, R. (Cuba) 285, 286, 288, 349
Herodotus, 28
Herold, J-P. (E. Ger.) 288, 292, 294
Herriott, M. (GB) 240
Hersh, B. (USA) 413
Hewitt, F. (Australia) 25
Hewson, B. (GB) 152, 153, 155
Hickock W. (USA) 426
Hicks, T. (USA) 54
Hildenbrand, K-P. (W. Ger.) 229, 422
Hildreth, P. (GB) 165
Hill, A. (GB) 48, 50, 209, 421
Hill, G. (USA) 44
Hill, M. (GB) 339, 340, 342
Hill, Ralph (USA) 96, 223
Hill, Ron (GB) 233, 428
Hill, T. (USA) 235
Hillardt, M. (Australia) 294
Hille, H-D. (E. Ger.) 373, 375, 413

Hillman, H. (USA) 46, 57, 58, 420
Hines, J. (USA) 197, 198, 199, 200, 271, 419
Hingsen, J. (W. Ger.) 344, 345, 428
Hippias, 11
Hirschfeld, E. (Germany) 116, 117
Hissou, S. (Morocco) 298, 299, 303, 304, 422, 423
Hjeltnes, K. (Norway) 335, 426
Höckert, G. (Finland) 96, 422
Hodge, P. (GB) 58
Hodge, R. (USA) 268
Hoen, S. (Norway) 318
Hoenish, C.A. (USA) 423
Hoff, C. (Norway) 107, 108, 109, 110, 114
Hoffmann, D. (E. Ger.) 257
Hoffmann, F. (Germany) 22
Hoffmann, Z. (Poland) 328
Hoffmeister, H. (Germany) 118
Hofmeister, F-P. (W. Ger.) 208
Hogan, H. (Australia) 132, 134, 419
Hogenson, W. (USA) 43
Hogg, R. (GB) 34
Hohn, U. (E. Ger.) 335, 339, 340, 341, 427
Höhne, C. (E. Ger.) 273, 274
Holdorf, W. (W. Ger.) 268
Holland, J. (N.Z.) 166
Hölling, F-W. (Germany) 104, 166, 423
Hollister, E. (USA) 420
Holmes, C. (GB) 78
Homer, 37
Honey, G. (Australia) 324
Honz, K. (W. Ger.) 208, 420
Hooper, D. (USA) 180
Hopkins, G. (USA) 250
Horan, F. (GB) 25, 420
Horgan, D. (Ireland) 35, 36, 37, 63, 426
Horine, G. (USA) 58, 59, 60, 65, 105, 396, 424
Hornberger, G. (Germany) 124
Hornbostel, C. (USA) 85, 86
Horner, J. (USA) 426
Horton, D. (USA) 32
Horváth, A. (Hungary) 334
Houben, H. (Germany) 72, 73, 124
House, M. (USA) 423
Houser, C. (USA) 116, 117
Houvion, M. (France) 249
Houvion, P. (France) 250, 425
Hovinen, S. (Finland) 427
Howard, John (GB) 33
Howard, R. (USA) 168, 318, 423
Howells, H. (USA) 82
Hoyt, W. (USA) 32

Hubbard, W. DeHart (USA) 72, 111, 112, 368, 425
Hudak, H. (W. Ger.) 223, 422
Huffins, C. (USA) 344
Huffman, S. (USA) 321
Hulse, W. (USA) 147
Hummel, W. (USA) 423
Hüneke, H. (W. Ger.) 424
Hüning, M. (W. Ger.) 427
Hunter, C. (USA) 422
Hunter, C.J. (USA) 331, 333, 376, 417
Huntington, R. (USA) 326
Hurlburt, J.L. (USA) 424
Huruk, J. (Poland) 305
Huseby, G. (Iceland) 181
Hussey, F. (USA) 124
Hutchens, H. (GB) 20
Hutchings, T. (GB) 298
Hutson, G. (GB) 52
Hwang Young-jo (Korea) 305, 307
Hylton, M. (GB) 349
Hymans, R. (GB) 408
Hyytiäinen, T. (Finland) 186
Iapichino, G. (Italy) 403
Ibbotson, D. (GB) 153, 154, 159, 421
Iglói, M. (Hungary) 152, 159, 216, 223
Ignatyev, A. (USSR) 139, 140
Iharos, S. (Hungary) 16, 151, 152, 159, 422, 423
Iijma, H. (Japan) 197
Ikangaa, J. (Tanzania) 306
Ikenaka, Y. (Japan) 98, 428
Ilg, P. (W. Ger.) 315
Ilizarov, G.A. (USSR) 244
Ilyasov, Y. (USSR) 106
Imbach, J. (Switzerland) 79
Imoh, C. (Nigeria) 277
Ince, B. (Trinidad) 191
Iness, S. (USA) 183, 426
Inozyemtsev, V. (USSR) 328, 426
Ireland, C. (NZ) 331
Irons, F. (USA) 61, 425
Irving, L. (USA) 207
Isaksson, K. (Sweden) 249
Ishutkin, O. (Russia) 352
Iso-Hollo. V. (Finland) 95, 96, 105, 422, 424
Ivan, J. (Czechosl.) 308
Ivanyenko, V. (USSR) 352
Jack, T. (GB) 55
Jackson, Clement (GB) 30, 310
Jackson, Colin (GB) 308, 309, 310, 311, 348, 423
Jacobs, D. (GB) 68
Jacobs, F. (USA) 246, 424

James, L. (USA) 205, 206, 272, 420
Janda-Suk, F. (Bohemia) 36, 426
Janke, F. (E. Ger.) 422
Jansson (Spångert), A. (Sweden) 93, 421
Jansson, G. (Sweden) 161
Januszewski, P. (Poland) 312
Janz, H. (W. Ger.) 168, 236, 423
Jarrett, T. (GB) 308, 311, 347, 348, 423
Järvinen, A. (Finland) 65, 123, 428
Järvinen, K. (Finland) 65
Järvinen, M.H. (Finland) 65, 120, 121, 122, 123, 186, 266, 340, 427
Järvinen, V. (Finland) 64, 65, 426
Järvinen, Y. (Finland) 65
Jarvis, F. (USA) 22
Jazy, M. (France) 154, 214, 215, 216, 223, 225, 421
Jefferson, G. (USA) 109
Jefferson, T. (USA) 277
Jefferys, E. (South Africa) 136, 420
Jeffrey, C. (USA) 79, 125, 419
Jellinghaus, M. (W. Ger.) 206
Jenkins, Charles (USA) 140, 141, 191
Jenkins, Chip (USA) 285
Jenkins, D. (GB) 207, 208
Jenne, E. (USA) 424
Jenner, B. (USA) 270, 428
Jens, W. (Germany) 85
Jerome, H. (Canada) 135, 136, 196, 197, 419
Jessee, L. (USA) 425
Jessup, P. (USA) 118, 426
Jifar, H. (Ethiopia) 423, 428
Jipcho, B. (Kenya) 218, 219, 228, 241, 242, 316, 422, 424
Johansson, P. (Finland) 427
Johnson, Allen (USA) 308, 310, 423
Johnson, Bascom (USA) 424
Johnson, Ben (Canada) 256, 277, 278, 279, 280, 281, 282, 324, 375, 419
Johnson, Ben (USA) 79, 419
Johnson, Carl (USA) 425
Johnson, Cornelius (USA) 106, 107, 111, 424
Johnson, Dave (USA) 344, 428
Johnson, Derek (GB) 143, 144, 153, 421
Johnson, J. (USA) 249
Johnson, Lawrence (USA) 425
Johnson, Michael (USA) 277, 278, 281, 283, 284, 285, 286, 287, 288, 349, 350, 416, 420

Johnson, R. (USA) 187, 188, 189, 268, 428
Johnson, S. (USA) 135, 136, 190, 420
Johnstone, D. (GB) 34
Jonath, A. (Germany) 74, 75, 76, 77, 124
Jones, C. (USA) 349
Jones, E. (USA) 288
Jones, H. (USA) 165, 233, 234, 271, 423
Jones, J.P. (USA) 49, 50, 51, 421
Jones, Johnny (USA) 271
Jones, L. (USA) 139, 140, 141, 191, 420
Jones, R.T. (USA) 42
Jones, S. (GB) 305
Jones, S. (USA) 58
Jonsson (Kälarne), H. (Sweden) 14, 93, 96, 97, 146, 147, 148, 421, 422
Jordan, G. (GB) 24, 420
Jordan, M. (USA) 326
Jordan, P. (USA) 124
Joubert, D. (South Africa) 73, 74, 75, 76, 419
Joy, G. (Canada) 245, 424
Joye, P. (France) 104
Joyner, A. (USA) 328, 329, 374
Juantorena, A. (Cuba) 206, 207, 208, 209, 213, 214, 286, 290, 380, 420, 421
Julin, A.L. (Sweden) 297
Jung, S. (USSR) 352
Junge, S. (E. Ger.) 245
Jungwirth S. (Czechosl.) 151, 153, 154, 155, 421
Justus, K-P. (E. Ger.) 220
Juzdado, A. (Spain) 305
Kaas, E. (Norway) 110
Kahma, P. (Finland) 260
Kaindl, L. (Germany) 424
Kaiser, J. (W. Ger.) 192
Kalinkin, V. (USSR) 288
Kallabis, D. (Germany) 315
Kalliomäki, A. (Finland) 249
Kalyayev, L. (USSR) 189
Kamathi, C. (Kenya) 423
Kamoga, D. (Uganda) 285, 287
Kamper, E. (Austria) 358
Kanaki, A. (USSR) 184
Kane, C. (USA) 421
Kannenberg, B. (W. Ger.) 274
Kantanen, T. (Finland) 241, 242, 424
Kantorek, P. (Czechosl.) 428
Kaptyukh, V. (Byelarus) 334
Kapustin, D. (Russia) 328, 329
Karikko, P. (Finland) 53
Kariuki, J. (Kenya) 315, 316

Karst, M. (W. Ger.) 242
Karvonen, V. (Finland) 161, 428
Kashkarov, I. (USSR) 171, 172, 424
Kasnauskas, S. (USSR) 426
Kataja, E. (Finland) 174
Kaufmann, K. (W. Ger.) 141, 142, 191, 192, 420
Kazantsev, V. (USSR) 169
Kedir, M. (Ethiopia) 231, 298
Keily, A. (GB) 428
Keino, K. (Kenya) 216, 217, 218, 219, 225, 226, 241, 316
Kekkonen, U. (Finland) 94, 95
Keller, J. (France) 89
Keller, J. (USA) 100, 423
Kelley, J. (USA) 428
Kellner, G. (Hungary) 28, 29
Kelly, D. (USA) 43, 419, 425
Kelly, F. (USA) 57, 423
Kelly, J. (USA) 182
Kemboi, S. (Kenya) 349
Kemp, T. (Bahamas) 318, 320
Kemper, F-J. (W. Ger.) 210, 211
Kenah, R. (USA) 289
Kennedy, R. (USA) 189
Kern, E. (Germany) 44, 419
Kerns, H. (USA) 136, 137, 190, 191
Kerr, G. (Jamaica) 144, 145, 146, 191, 192, 205, 209, 420, 421
Kerr, R. (Canada) 44
Kersee, R. (USA) 375, 376, 412
Keter, J. (Kenya) 315
Ketterer, E. (Germany) 44, 45, 419
Khalifa, O. (Sudan) 292
Khannouchi, K. (Morocco) 306, 428
Kharlov, A. (USSR) 311
Khmyelevskiy, V. (USSR) 263
Khmyelnitskiy, M. (Byelarus) 351
Kibblewhite, J. (GB) 421
Kibet, R. (Kenya) 296
Kidikas, V. (USSR) 334
Kiely, T. (Ireland) 425
Kiesel, R. (USA) 124
Kilpatrick, C. (USA) 25, 420, 421
Kimeli, K. (Kenya) 298, 301
Kimihara, K. (Japan) 232
Kimobwa, S. (Kenya) 229, 423
Kimutai, J. (Ken) 421
Kinder, M. (W. Ger.) 142, 192
King, E. (USA) 277, 347, 348
King, K. (USA) 425
King, LaMonte (USA) 420
King, Leamon (USA) 133, 134, 189, 419
King, R. (USA) 106

Kingdom, R. (USA) 308, 309, 310, 423
Kinnunen, J. (Finland) 265, 266
Kinnunen, K. (Finland) 339, 341, 427
Kinsey, D. (USA) 99
Kipketer, S. (Kenya) 417
Kipketer, W. (Denmark) 288, 289, 290, 291, 417, 421
Kipkoech, P. (Kenya) 298, 301
Kipkorir, S. (Kenya) 292
Kipkurgat, J. (Kenya) 212, 421
Kipkurgat, S. (Kenya) 213
Kiplagat, W. (Kenya) 428
Kiplagat-Andersen, R. (Denmark) 290
Kiprono, J. (Kenya) 428
Kiprop, F. (Kenya) 428
Kiprotich, N. (Kenya) 288
Kiprugut, W. (Kenya) 209, 210, 211
Kiptanui, M. (Kenya) 303, 315, 316, 317, 422, 424
Kiptoo, D. (Kenya) 297
Kirby, G. (USA) 75
Kirilenko, V. (Ukraine) 324
Kirk, J. (USA) 166
Kirkpatrick, L. (USA) 100
Kirksey, M. (USA) 46, 69
Kirochi, W. (Kenya) 292, 295
Kirov, N. (USSR) 214, 292
Kirst, J. (E. Ger.) 270
Kirui, I. (Kenya) 295, 298, 302, 304
Kirwan, P. (Ireland) 425
Kiselyov, V. (USSR) 258
Kishkun, V. (USSR) 249
Kiss, B. (Hungary) 337, 339, 427
Kitur, S. (Kenya) 285
Kivi, A. (Finland) 117, 118
Kiviat, A. (USA) 49, 51, 91, 421
Klauss, M. (E. Ger.) 252
Klemmer, G. (USA) 136, 137, 190, 191
Klim, R. (USSR) 262
Klimyenko, A. (USSR/Ukr) 331
Klumberg (Kolmpere), A. (Esthonia) 123, 427
Klyugin, S. (Russia) 318
Knebel, A. (E. Ger.) 284
Knourek, E. (USA) 425
Kobs, K. (Germany) 337, 339
Koch, D. (USA) 183
Köchermann, E. (Germany) 113
Koczán (Kovács), M. (Hungary) 66
Kodama, T. (Japan) 304
Koech, Paul (Kenya) 423
Koech, Peter (Kenya) 315, 316, 424
Kogake, M. (Japan) 426
Kogo, B. (Kenya) 241, 316
Kök, N. (Turkey) 9

Kolehmainen, Johannes"Hannes" (Finland) 51, 53, 56, 59, 94, 157, 160, 228, 302, 422, 428
Kolehmainen, Taavetti"Tatu" (Finland) 52, 56
Kolehmainen, William"Viljami" (Finland) 52
Kolnootchenko, G. (USSR) 334, 335
Komar, W. (Poland) 257
Komen, D. (Kenya) 298, 299, 302, 303, 422
Konchellah, P. (Kenya) 291
Konchellah, W. (Kenya) 209, 288, 289, 290
Kone, G. (Ivory Coast) 197
Kononen, V. (Finland) 352, 354
Konov, A. (USSR) 424
Konovalov, Y. (USSR) 189, 271
Kopyto, J. (Poland) 427
Korir, J. (Kenya) 315, 316
Korjus, T. (Finland) 339
Kornelyuk, A. (USSR) 202
Körnig, H. (Germany) 72, 73, 124
Kororia, S. (Kenya) 298
Korving, R. (Holland) 308
Koryepanov, S. (Kazakstan) 352
Korzeniowski, R. (Poland) 352, 354
Kosgei, C. (Kenya) 315, 317, 424
Kosgei, John (Kenya) 303, 424
Koskei, S. (Kenya) 222, 288, 289, 421
Koski, M. (Finland) 53
Kostyukyevich, F. (USSR) 350
Koszewski, D. (W. Ger.) 308
Kotila, P. (Finland) 428
Kotkas, K. (Finland) 106, 107, 171, 424
Kotu, T. (Ethiopia) 231
Koukodimos, K. (Greece) 324
Kovac, J. (Slovakia) 308
Kovács, József I (Hungary) 104
Kovács, József II (Hungary) 158, 159, 422, 423
Kovalyenko, A. (USSR) 328
Kovtun, N. (USSR) 106, 172
Kozakiewicz, W. (Poland) 246, 250, 425
Kozlov, A. (USSR) 427
Kraenzlein, A. (USA) 31, 33, 57, 61, 423, 425
Kraft, O.B. (Denmark) 290
Kramer, W. (USA) 422
Krasovskis, J. (USSR) 176, 425
Kratschmer, G. (W. Ger.) 270, 428
Kravchenko, V. (USSR) 253
Kreek, A. (Estonia) 117
Kreer, V. (USSR) 178, 179, 426
Krenz, E. (USA) 118
Krikun, A. (Ukraine) 337
Krilov, V. (USSR) 278, 347, 378
Krivonosov, M. (USSR) 184, 185, 427

Kruger, F. (South Africa) 335
Krupskiy, A. (USSR) 321
Krzyszkowiak, Z. (Poland) 157, 160, 170, 240, 423, 424
Kucharski, K. (Poland) 86
Kuck, J. (USA) 116
Kudinskiy, V. (USSR) 240, 241
Kuha, J. (Finland) 241
Kula, D. (USSR) 267, 339
Kulcsár, G. (Hungary) 265
Kulker, H. (Holland) 292
Kuller, F. (USA) 271
Kunze, H. (E. Ger.) 298, 299
Kurki, T. (Finland) 422
Kuryan, A. (USSR) 240
Kuschmann, M. (E. Ger.) 228
Kusocinski, J. (Poland) 89, 95, 96, 422
Kuts, V. (USSR) 15, 155, 156, 158, 159, 160, 228, 302, 422, 423
Kutsenko, Y. (USSR) 270, 428
Kutyenko, Y. (USSR) 268, 428
Kuznyetsov, Vasili (USSR) 188, 189, 268, 428
Kuznyetsov, Vladimir (USSR) 427
Kwasny, Z. (Poland) 337
LaBeach, L. (Panama) 128, 129, 130, 131, 419
Laborde, H. (USA) 118
Lacy, S. (USA) 222
Ladejo, D. (GB) 285, 349
Ladoumègue, J. (France) 14, 89, 91, 214
Lahlafi, B. (Morocco) 298
Lahlou, B. (Morocco) 349
Laing, L. (Jamaica) 131, 191
Lambruschini, A. (Italy) 294, 315, 317, 318
Lamela, Y. (Spain) 324, 328, 425
Lamers, R. (Germany) 149
Lammers, G. (Germany) 73, 74, 75
Landon, R. (USA) 60
Landström, E. (Finland) 175, 176
Landy, J. (Australia) 146, 149, 150, 151, 152, 153, 154, 161, 421
Lane, J. (Ireland) 33
Lang. W. (GB) 26, 27, 28
Langhammer, U. (E. Ger.) 321
Lansky, J. (Czechosl.) 172
Lanzi, M. (Italy) 79, 82, 83, 85, 86, 87, 88, 137, 139, 142, 143, 151, 421
Lapshin, I. (USSR) 328
Larner, G. (GB) 70
Larrabee, M. (USA) 204, 205, 272
Larsen, E. (Norway) 170

Larsen, F. (Norway) 143
Larson, C. (USA) 60, 424
Larsson, L. (Sweden) 424
Larsson, R. (Sweden) 166
Larva, H. (Finland) 89, 90
Lash, D. (USA) 421
Lattany, M. (USA) 277
Lauer, M. (W. Ger.) 135, 164, 165, 190, 234, 309, 423, 428
Laut, D. (USA) 330, 331
Lavery, T. (South Africa) 100, 423
Lavrentis, G. (Greece) 28
Lawlor, J. (Ireland) 37
Lawrence, A. (Australia) 159
Layevskiy, S. (USSR) 324
Laz, Don (USA) 174, 175, 425
Laz, Doug (USA) 174
Lea, J. (USA) 139, 140, 420
Leahy, C. (Ireland) 42, 58, 59
Leahy, P. (Ireland) 424, 425
Lean, D. (Australia) 168, 423
LeBlanc, G. (Canada) 350
Leconey, A. (USA) 124
Lee Bong-ju (Korea) 305
LeGendre, R. (USA) 112
Legg, W. (South Africa) 75
Lehnertz, K. (W. Ger.) 248
Lehtinen, L. (Finland) 94, 95, 96, 223, 422
Leichum, W. (Germany) 113
Leitao, A. (Portugal) 298
Leitner, J. (Czechosl.) 324
Lemme, A. (E. Ger.) 334
Lemming, E. (Sweden) 37, 66, 427
Len Tau (South Africa) 54
Leonard, S. (Cuba) 203, 204, 205, 419, 420
Lermusiaux, A. (France) 28, 29
Lévêque, J. (France) 87
Lewandowski, S. (Poland) 421
Lewden, P. (France) 105
Lewis, B. (USA) 348
Lewis, C. (USA) 9, 205, 251, 277, 278, 279, 280, 281, 282, 324, 325, 326, 327, 329, 347, 348, 377, 414, 419, 420, 425
Lewis, S. (USA) 285, 286, 349, 350
Lewis, T. (USA) 272
Licznerski, Z. (Poland) 347
Liddell, E. (GB) 44, 79, 80, 81, 82
Lidman, H. (Sweden) 100, 101, 163, 164, 423
Liesche, H. (Germany) 59
Lievore, C. (Italy) 264, 265, 427
Lievore, G. (Italy) 264

Lightbody, J. (USA) 47, 49, 58
Lighter, E. (USA) 423
Likho, V. (USSR) 331, 333
Liljekvist, H. (Sweden) 142
Lilliér, H. (Sweden) 427
Limo, B. (Kenya) 299, 422
Limo, R. (Kenya) 417
Lincoln, M. (Australia) 153, 154, 421
Lind, C.J. (Sweden) 65, 119
Lindahl, J. (Sweden) 103
Lindberg, A. (Sweden) 110
Lindberg, E. (USA) 69
Lindberg, K. (Sweden) 44
Lindblad, A. (Finland) 424
Lindblom, G. (Sweden) 63
Lindgren, B. (USA) 234
Lindgren, G. (USA) 225
Lindhagen, S. (Sweden) 52
Lindström, G. (Sweden) 121, 427
Linge, M. (USSR) 273
Lipiec, T. (Poland) 352
Lipp, H. (USSR) 181, 188
Lippincott, D. (USA) 45, 419
Liquori, M. (USA) 211, 218, 220, 229, 422
Lismont, K. (Belgium) 233, 304
Little, K. (USA) 284
Lituyev, Y. (USSR) 166, 168, 423
Litvinov, S. (USSR) 263, 264, 337, 338, 339, 427
Litvinyenko, L. (USSR) 270
Li Zeven (China) 351
Ljunggren, J. (Sweden) 192, 193
Ljungqvist, A. (Sweden) 387
Llopart, J. (Spain) 275
Loaring, J. (Canada) 104
Lobinger, T. (Germany) 321, 425
Lobodin, L. (Ukraine) 344
Locke, R. (USA) 72, 73, 420
Loesch, M. (Switzerland) 13
Logan, J. (USA) 337
Lokajski, E. (Poland) 427
Lomba, H. (France) 347
London, J. (GB) 72, 75
Long, D. (USA) 181, 255, 426
Long, L. (Germany) 113, 425
Long, M. (USA) 24, 39, 47, 420
Longboat, T. (Canada) 55
Longfellow, H.W. (USA) 27
Loomis, F. (USA) 57, 423
Looney, P. (Ireland) 425
Lopes, C. (Portugal) 228, 300, 304, 305
Lord, F. (GB) 55
Lorger, S. (Yugoslavia) 165
Lorz, F. (USA) 54

Losch, H. (E. Ger.) 260
Lossdörfer, G. (W. Ger.) 237
Lossman, J. (Esthonia) 56
Lotaryev, I. (USSR) 292
Louis, S. (Greece) 27, 28, 29
Loukola, T. (Finland) 105
Lovachev, S. (USSR) 349
Lovász, L. (Hungary) 262
Lovegrove, G. (NZ) 339
Lovelock, J. (N. Z.) 88, 90, 91, 92, 93, 149, 421
Lövland, H. (Norway) 68, 427
Lowe, D. (GB) 83, 84, 88
Lucas, C. (USA) 63
Lucian, 28
Luck, J. (USA) 237
Lueg, W. (W. Ger.) 149
Lundberg, R. (Sweden) 175
Lundgren, S. (Sweden) 421
Lundqvist, E. (Sweden) 121, 122
Lunghi, E. (Italy) 47, 48, 50, 89, 91, 421
Lusis, J. (USSR) 264, 265, 266, 267, 371, 427
Lutyens, W. (GB) 421
Lutz, O. (Germany) 427
LuValle, J. (USA) 82, 125, 420
Lyakhov, S. (USSR) 184, 185
Lydiard, A. (N. Z.) 209
Lyman, J. (USA) 117, 426
Lyons, H.S. (USA) 39
Ma Junren (China) 383, 386, 387, 388, 389
Maaninka, K. (Finland) 231
Maas, F. (Holland) 324
MacDonald, O. (USA) 124
MacDonald, R. (N. Z.) 21
Macey, D. (GB) 344
Machura, R. (Czechosl.) 331
Macintosh, H. (GB) 68
Mack, D. (USA) 293
Mackowiack, R. (Poland) 285
Macpherson, W. (Australia) 419
Macquet, M. (France) 427
Maffei, A. (Italy) 113
Magee, B. (N. Z.) 162, 428
Magnani, M. (Italy) 304
Magnusson, R. (Sweden) 268
Mahlendorf, W. (W. Ger.) 190
Mahmoud, J. (France) 315
Mahorn, A. (Canada) 278
Major, I. (Hungary) 245
Majusiak, S. (Poland) 298
Makarov, A. (USSR) 267
Makarov, S. (Russia) 340, 427
Maker, F. (USA) 424

Mäki, T. (Finland) 96, 97, 155, 422
Malan, D. (South Africa) 211, 212
Malchenko, S. (USSR) 318
Malcherczyk, R. (Poland) 426
Malecek, K. (Bohemia) 39
Malinowski, B. (Poland) 242, 243, 424
Malkov, Y. (USSR) 106
Mallard, J. (USA) 420
Mallon, B. (USA) 34, 234
Malott, R. (USA) 82, 86, 420
Mamede, F. (Portugal) 300
Maminski, B. (Poland) 315
Maniak, W. (Poland) 197
Mann, R. (USA) 238, 239, 424
Manning, H. (USA) 424
Manning, T. (Australia) 241
Mansour, T. (Qatar) 278
Manzano, A. (Cuba) 321
Marajo, J. (France) 421
Maree, S. (USA) 293, 294, 301, 385, 422
Mariani, O. (Italy) 79
Marie, A-J. (France) 164
Marie-Rose, B. (France) 278, 347, 348
Marin, J. (Spain) 350, 352
Markin, V. (USSR) 209, 273, 284, 349, 420
Markov, D. (Byel/Australia) 321, 425
Markov, I. (Russia) 351
Markov, K. (Bulgaria) 299, 328, 329, 426
Marsh, H. (USA) 315
Marsh, M. (USA) 278, 282, 347, 348, 420
Marshall, G. (GB) 21
Martin, D. (USA) 29, 245, 307
Martin, J.D. (USA) 425
Martin, P. (Switzerland) 83, 84
Martin, S. (France) 83, 84, 89, 214
Martinez, L. (Cuba) 349
Marttelin, M. (Finland) 97
Marty, W. (USA) 107, 424
Masback, C. (USA) 222, 292, 422
Mashburn, J.W. (USA) 140, 191
Mashchenko, R. (Russia) 312
Mashiani, J. (South Africa) 54
Maskinskov, Y. (USSR) 192, 193
Massana, V. (Spain) 350, 351, 352
Masya, B. (Kenya) 307
Matei, S. (Romania) 424
Matete, S. (Zambia) 311, 312, 314, 349, 424
Mathias, R. (USA) 187, 189, 428
Matias, M. (Portugal) 305
Matilainen, M. (Finland) 424
Matson, O. (USA) 138, 139, 191
Matson, R. (USA) 255, 256, 257, 258, 332, 426
Mattheis, J. (W. Ger.) 268

Matthews, K. (GB) 273
Matthews, V. (USA) 206, 207, 272, 420
Matuschewski, M. (E. Ger.) 146, 210
Matyukhin, N. (Russia) 352
Matzdorf, P. (USA) 245
Mauger, J. (USA) 425
May, J. (E. Ger./W. Ger.) 217
May, P. (Australia) 253
May, W. (USA) 164, 165, 423
Maybank, A. (USA) 349, 350
Maybury, J. (USA) 419
Mayer, S. (Germany) 427
Mays, C. (USA) 251
McAllister, R. (USA) 73
McArthur, K. (South Africa) 55
McBain, C. (USA) 104, 423
McCorquodale, A. (GB) 128, 129
McCoy, W. (USA) 349
McCracken, J. (USA) 426, 427
McCullouch, E. (USA) 234, 271
McDermott, J. (USA) 29
McDonald, P. (USA) 62, 63, 426
McDonald-Bailey, E. (Trinidad) 128, 129, 130, 131
McGhee, J. (GB) 161
McGrath, M. (USA) 65, 66, 119, 184, 338, 427
McIntosh, T. (Bahamas) 285
McKay, A. (USA) 284, 349
McKean, T. (GB) 288, 290, 300
McKee, G. (USA) 324
McKenley, H. (Jamaica) 130, 131, 137, 138, 139, 140, 144, 191, 192, 197, 420
McKenzie, D. (GB) 349
McKenzie, D. (N. Z.) 232
McKoy, M. (Canada) 308, 311
McLeod, M. (GB) 298
McManus, W. (Australia) 425
McMillen, R. (USA) 149
McNab, T. (GB) 251
McNaughton, D. (Canada) 106
McNeill, L. (USA) 347
McRae, L. (USA) 347
McTear, H. (USA) 202
McWhirter, R. (GB) 150
Meadows, E. (USA) 109, 110, 425
Meanix, W. (USA) 57, 423
Meconi, S. (Italy) 181, 255, 426
Megelea, G. (Romania) 267
Mehl, W. (USA) 93, 421
Mei, S. (Italy) 298, 300
Meier, A. "Gus" (USA) 100

Meier, H. (USA) 419
Meier, Paul (Germany) 344
Meier, W. (E. Ger.) 373, 378
Meisch, D. (E. Ger.) 352
Mekonnen, A. (Ethiopia) 306
Melvin, O. (USA) 204
Melzer, H. (E. Ger.) 315
Menezes, S. (Brazil) 349
Mennea, P. (Italy) 193, 196, 201, 202, 203, 204, 205, 271, 272, 273, 277, 281, 282, 283, 284, 324, 419, 420
Mercenario, C. (Mexico) 350, 352
Meredith, J.E. "Ted" (USA) 23, 46, 47, 48, 69, 79, 80, 420, 421
Meriwether, D. (USA) 202
Merrill, S.M. (USA) 39
Metcalfe, A. (GB) 205
Metcalfe, John "Jack" (Australia) 115, 425
Metcalfe, R. (USA) 74, 75, 76, 77, 78, 79, 124, 419, 420
Metzner, A. (Germany) 81
Meyer, A. (USA) 45
Meyer, G. (France) 215
Mezegebu, Assefa (Ethiopia) 299, 303, 422
Miao Zhigong (China) 386
Michel, D. (E. Ger.) 339, 340, 427
Michelsen, A. (USA) 98, 428
Mickelsson, P. (Finland) 94
Mihalic, F. (Yugoslavia) 161
Mikaelsson, J. (Sweden) 192
Mikhailov, A. (USSR) 165, 234, 423
Mikkola, M. (Finland) 186, 427
Milburn, R. (USA) 234, 235, 309, 423
Milde, L. (E. Ger.) 260
Milesi, D. (Italy) 305
Milkha Singh (India) 141, 142, 420
Miller, Lennox (Jamaica) 198, 199, 202, 271, 419
Miller, Lloyd (Australia) 425
Miller, W. I (USA) 109, 118
Miller, W. II (USA) 186
Mills, C. (USA) 206
Mills, D. (USA) 349, 350, 420
Mills, E. (GB) 27
Mills, W. (USA) 223, 225
Mimoun O'Kacha, A. (France) 157, 158, 161, 163
Mironov, Y. (USSR) 258, 330, 331
Misyulya, Y. (USSR) 350, 351
Mitchel, J. (USA) 37, 427
Mitchell, D. (USA) 278, 280, 281, 282, 347, 348, 419
Mitchell, R. (Australia) 209
Mizoguchi, K. (Japan) 339, 341
Mladenov, I. (Bulgaria) 324
Modica, V. (Italy) 305
Moen, G. (Norway) 278
Moens, R. (Belgium) 143, 144, 145, 146, 209, 210, 421
Mögenburg, D. (W. Ger.) 246, 318, 319, 321, 424
Moltke, W. Graf von (W. Ger.) 268
Moneghetti, S. (Australia) 305, 306
Monilaw, W.J. (USA) 77
Montes, P. (Cuba) 199
Monteverde, A. (USA) 53
Montgomery, T. (USA) 278, 348
Mooney, J. (Ireland) 425
Moorcroft, D. (GB) 221, 298, 299, 300
Moore, C. (USA) 166, 191
Moore, P. (USA) 88, 93, 421
Moore, T. (USA) 100
Morale, S. (Italy) 168, 236, 237
Morceli, Abderrahmane (Algeria) 295
Morceli, Ali (Algeria) 295
Morceli, Noureddine (Algeria) 292, 294, 295, 296, 297, 303, 317, 417, 422
Moreau, A. (USA) 100
Morel, R. (France) 89
Morgan, D. (Jamaica) 312
Morgan, E. (USA) 423
Mori, F. (Italy) 237, 312, 315, 417
Morinière, M. (France) 347, 348
Morishita, K. (Japan) 305
Morozov, A. (USSR) 241
Morris, G. (USA) 123, 187, 189, 427, 428
Morris, R. (USA) 176, 248, 425
Morris, S. (GB) 31
Morriss, J. (USA) 100
Morrow, B. (USA) 132, 133, 134, 135, 141, 189, 196, 198, 284, 419, 420
Mortensen, J. (USA) 428
Morton, J.W. (GB) 42, 43, 44
Moses, E. (USA) 236, 239, 240, 310, 311, 312, 313, 314, 423, 424
Mosima, P. (Kenya) 422
Mostert, J. (Belgium) 93
Mostovik, V. (USSR) 350
Mottley, W. (Trinidad) 204, 205, 272
Moulton, F. (USA) 43
Mourhit, M. (Belgium) 299, 301, 423
Moursal, H. (Egypt) 324

Moya, R. (Cuba) 334
Mucks, A. (USA) 426
Muenter, A.F. (USA) 423
Muinonen, V. (Finland) 98
Mulkey, P. (USA) 268, 428
Müller, F. (Germany) 428
Müller, H. (Switzerland) 135
Munkelt, T. (E. Ger.) 235, 236, 308, 309, 423
Murakoso, K. (Japan) 95, 96
Muravyov, V. (USSR) 272, 347
Murchison, I. (USA) 133, 134, 189, 419
Murchison, L. (USA) 69, 72, 74, 124
Murphy, M. (USA) 21
Murphy, T. (USA) 145
Murray, F. (USA) 423
Musto, W. (Kenya) 317
Musyoki, M. (Kenya) 229, 298
Mutwol, W. (Kenya) 315, 316
Myers, E. (USA) 424
Myers, L. (USA) 20, 22, 23, 24, 25, 26, 420
Myricks, L. (USA) 252, 324, 325, 326, 425
Myron, 36
Myyrä, J. (Finland) 66, 67, 121, 427
Nagel, G. (W. Ger.) 318
Nagy, Z. (Hungary) 426
Nai, D. (Italy) 90
Nakamura, K. (Japan) 306
Nakamura, S. (Japan) 428
Nakayama, T. (Japan) 304
Nakazawa, Y. (Japan) 109
Nakkim, A. (Norway) 298
Nallet, J-C. (France) 238, 239
Nambu, C. (Japan) 112, 115, 116, 425
Nan, S. (Japan) 98
Nankeville, W. (GB) 149
Nash, P. (South Africa) 200
Naumann, J. (E. Ger.) 308
Ndururi, P. (Kenya) 421
Nebiolo, P. (Italy) 9, 14, 277
Neckermann, K. (Germany) 79, 124
Nedi, D. (Ethiopia) 304
Nehemiah, R. (USA) 235, 236, 255, 308, 309, 310, 423
Nelson, C. (USA) 110, 259, 299
Nelson, F. (USA) 60
Németh, I. (Hungary) 183, 184, 266
Németh, M. (Hungary) 266, 267, 341, 342, 427
Németh, Z. (Hungary) 337
Nerurkar, R. (G.B.) 305
Neu, H-D. (W. Ger.) 335
Neumann, J. (W. Ger.) 168, 236
Nevala, P. (Finland) 265, 266

Newburn, W. (Ireland) 33, 425
Newhouse, F. (USA) 207, 208, 272, 420
Newman, S. (Jamaica) 208
Newstetter, W. (USA) 425
Ngeny, N. (Kenya) 292, 296, 297, 417, 422
Ngugi, J. (Kenya) 298, 301
Ni Chi-Chin (Zhiqin) (China) 244, 318
Nikolayev, S. (USSR/Russia) 331
Nicole, A. (Switzerland) 19
Nicolson, T. (GB) 119
Nieder, W. (USA) 180, 181, 255, 426
Nielsen, G. (Denmark) 143, 144, 151, 152
Nihill, P. (GB) 273
Niittymaa, V. (Finland) 118
Nijboer, G. (Holland) 233, 304, 428
Nikkanen, Y. (Finland) 122, 186, 265, 427
Nikkinen, S. (Finland) 186, 427
Niklander, E. (Finland) 65, 426
Nikula, P. (Finland) 248
Nikulin, I. (USSR/Russia) 337, 338, 427
Nikulin, Y. (USSR) 427
Nilsen, L.A. (Norway) 331
Nilsson, B. (Sweden) 171, 172
Nilsson, E. (Sweden) 427
Nishida, S. (Japan) 109, 110, 118, 354
Niskanen, O. (Sweden) 162
Nix, S. (USA) 284, 349
Niyongabo, V. (Burundi) 292, 298, 304, 422
Noack, A. (E. Ger.) 352
Noël, J. (France) 118
Nokes, M. (GB) 119
Nool, E. (Estonia) 341, 344, 418
Nordwig, W. (E. Ger.) 247, 248, 249
Norman, A.C.St. (South Africa) 68
Norman, P. (Australia) 199, 420
Norpoth, H. (W. Ger.) 217, 218, 225, 226
Norton, B. (USA) 44
Norton, J. (USA) 57, 423
Norton, R. (USA) 135, 136, 190, 419, 420
Nowak, S. (Poland) 291
Nurmi, P. (Finland) 14, 51, 53, 71, 88, 89, 92, 93, 94, 95, 96, 97, 104, 105, 125, 157, 219, 225, 306, 381, 422
Nuttal, James (GB) 25
Ny, E. (Sweden) 85, 91, 92
Nyamau, H. (Kenya) 272
Nyambui, S. (Tanzania) 231, 422
Nyariki, T. (Kenya) 298
Nyberg, E. (Sweden) 156
Nyenashev, S. (USSR) 184
Nylander, S. (Sweden) 311, 312, 314
Obeng, E. (Ghana) 277
Oberweger, G. (Italy) 119, 426
Obikwelu, F. (Nigeria) 278, 420

O'Brien, D. (USA) 344, 345, 346, 347, 418, 428
O'Brien, E. (USA) 125
O'Brien, J. (Ireland) 426
O'Brien, K. (Australia) 241
O'Brien, M. (Ireland) 424
O'Brien, P. (USA) 179, 180, 181, 255, 256, 257, 331, 334
O'Callaghan, P. (Ireland) 102, 119, 120, 121, 338, 427
O'Connell, C. (Ireland) 290
O'Connor, L. (Canada) 100
O'Connor, P. (Ireland) 61, 111, 113, 425
Oda, M. (Japan) 114, 115, 177, 426
Odlozil, J. (Czechosl.) 215
O'Donoghue, T. (Ireland) 35, 153
Oe, S. (Japan) 109, 110, 354
Oerter, A. (USA) 65, 181, 183, 184, 255, 258, 259, 260, 261, 327, 426
O'Gorman, D. (GB) 428
Ogunkoya, S. (Nigeria) 278
Ogwang, L. (Uga) 237
O'Hara, M. (USA) 13, 235, 242, 245
O'Hara, T. (USA) 216
Ohlson, B. (Sweden) 427
Oksanen, E. (Finland) 428
Olander, G. (Sweden) 146
Oldfield, B. (USA) 257, 331, 426
Oler, W. (USA) 424
Ollander, N. (Sweden) 424
Olson, A. (USA) 425
Olson, B. (USA) 321, 425
Olukojn, A. (Nigeria) 334
Ondieki, Y. (Kenya) 298, 304, 423
Onyancha, F. (Kenya) 288, 421
Orr, L. (Canada) 78, 83, 420
Ortis, V. (Italy) 230, 299, 423
Orton, G. (USA) 31
Osborn, H. (USA) 105, 106, 107, 108, 123, 357, 424
Osendarp, M. (Holland) 78, 79, 124
Osgood, R. (USA) 100, 423
Oshima, K. (Japan) 115, 116, 425
Osoro, O. (Kenya) 306, 428
O'Sullivan, J. (Ireland) 425
Ottley, D. (GB) 339, 342
Ottoz, E. (Italy) 234, 235
Ouko, R. (Kenya) 211, 272
Overton, J. (USA) 421
Ovett, S. (GB) 16, 212, 213, 214, 221, 222, 223, 292, 293, 294, 297, 421, 422
Ovsepyan, V. (USSR) 426

Owen, J. (USA) 21, 23, 141, 419
Owens, J.C. (USA) 71, 75, 76, 77, 78,
        79, 80, 101, 111,
        112, 113, 114, 124,
        129, 131, 141, 162,
        163, 167, 176, 177,
        196, 250, 278, 279,
        284, 324, 364, 365,
        377, 419, 425
Owens, P. (USA) 423
Ozolin, E. (USSR) 271
Ozolin, N. (USSR) 110, 175, 247
Packard, R. (USA) 78
Paddock, C. (USA) 42, 44, 45, 46, 69,
        71, 72, 74, 142, 419
Padilla, D. (USA) 298
Page, W.B. (USA) 32, 424
Pagliani, P. (Italy) 54
Paige, D. (USA) 214
Paklin, I. (USSR) 318, 319, 424
Palu, U. (USSR) 428
Pamich, A. (Italy) 193, 273, 274
Pancorbo, M. (Spain) 298
Panetta, F. (Italy) 298, 300, 315
Papadiamantopoulos, G. (Greece) 28, 29
Papadias, H. (Greece) 278
Papanikolau, C. (Greece) 249
Paragi, F. (Hungary) 267, 340, 427
Paraskevopoulos, P. (Greece) 36
Parker, G. (USA) 419
Parker, J. (USA) 428
Parks, M. (USA) 208, 273
Parmentier, H. (Belgium) 304
Parrela, S.C. (Brazil) 285, 288
Parsons, E. (USA) 47
Parsons, J. (GB) 33
Partyka, A. (Poland) 318, 320
Parviainen, Aki (Finland) 340, 344, 418, 427
Paschek, F. (E. Ger) 252, 425
Pascoe, A. (GB) 239
Paterson, A. (GB) 171
Patrick, D. (USA) 311, 395
Patterson, J. (USA) 104, 423
Patton, M. (USA) 45, 128, 129, 130, 131,
        132, 133, 419, 420
Paulen, A. (Holland) 13
Paulus, E. (Germany) 118
Pavoni, P. (Italy) 277
Peacock, E. (USA) 76, 77, 78, 112,
        113, 176, 425
Peacock, T. (USA) 318
Pearman, R. (USA) 144
Pedersen, N. (Den.) 70
Pedersen, T. (Norway) 264, 265

Pedraza, J. (Mexico) 274, 275
Pedrazzini, P. (Italy) 136
Pedroso, I. (Cuba) 324, 327, 328, 417, 425
Pekola, T. (Finland) 262
Pekuri, K. (Finland) 96, 222, 224
Pelham, A. (GB) 25
Peltonen, U. (Finland) 427
Peltzer, O. (Germany) 80, 83, 84, 85,
        88, 89, 92, 94
Peñalver, A. (Spain) 344
Pender, M. (USA) 197, 199, 271
Pennel, J. (USA) 248
Penttilä, E. (Finland) 121
Peoples, M. (USA) 272, 273
Peräsalo, V. (Finland) 106
Pérez Duénas, P (Cuba) 254, 255, 426
Pérez, J. (Ecuador) 351, 352
Perlov, A. (USSR) 352, 354
Perricelli, G. (Italy) 352
Perrin, J-C. (France) 249
Perrot, E. (France) 347
Persson, R. (Sweden) 147, 148
Persson, T. (Sweden) 304
Peters, J. (GB) 160, 161, 428
Petersen, H. (Den.) 60, 107
Peterson, G. (Sweden) 422
Petersson, W. (Sweden) 61
Petranoff, T. (USA) 339, 340, 341, 427
Petrov, P. (Bulgaria) 205
Petrov, V. (USSR) 322
Petrovski, V. (USSR) 200
Pettersson, Å. (Sweden) 148
Pettersson, Sten (Sweden) 99, 102, 103
Pettersson, Stig (Sweden) 171, 172,
        173, 424
Pettigrew, A. (USA) 285, 286, 349, 350
Petushinskiy, D. (Russia) 321
Pezzatini, A. (Italy) 350
Philip (Duke of Edinburgh) (GB) 191
Philippides, 28
Phillips, A. (USA) 311, 312, 313, 349, 424
Phillips, B. (GB) 9
Phillips, W.P. (GB) 21
Philpot, R. (GB) 23
Piatkowski, E. (Poland) 183, 258, 259, 426
Piekarski, P. (Poland) 288
Pierce, J. (USA) 308, 310, 311, 423
Pietri, D. (Italy) 54, 55, 56, 57, 160, 161
Pihkala, L. (Finland) 52
Pilgrim, P. (USA) 47
Pinto, A. (Portugal) 298, 417
Piquemal, C. (France) 271
Pirie, G. (GB) 158, 159, 422
Piskunov, V. (Ukraine) 337

Pizzolato, O. (Italy) 304
Plaatjes, M. (South Afr/USA) 305, 307
Plachy, J. (Czechosl.) 211, 212
Plaw, A. (USA) 427
Plaza, D. (Spain) 350
Plaza, M. (Chile) 97
Plaza, S. (Mexico) 420
Plaziat, C. (France) 344
Ploghaus, K. (W. Ger.) 337
Plotnikov, A. (Russia) 352
Plucknett, B. (USA) 261, 335, 426, 427
Plummer, A. (USA) 205
Plutarch, 28
Poage, G. (USA) 46
Podluzhniy, V. (USSR) 252
Pohl, B. (Bohemia) 39
Poli, G. (Italy) 304, 305
Politiko, N. (USSR) 271
Pollard, F. (USA) 100
Pollock, M. (USA) 77
Polyakov, V. (USSR) 321
Ponomaryov, S. (USSR) 424
Pope, A. (USA) 426
Popov, S. (USSR) 161, 162, 428
Popper, J. (Czechosl.) 237
Pörhölä, V. (Finland) 64, 120, 121, 426
Porkhomovskiy, A. (Rus/Israel) 278
Porritt, A. (N. Z.) 72, 74
Porter, C. (Australia) 171
Porter, H. (USA) 59
Porter, P. (USA) 298
Porter, W. (USA) 162
Postle, A. (Australia) 45
Potapovich, J. (Kazakstan) 321
Potashov, A. (USSR) 352, 354
Potgieter, G. (South Africa) 168, 423
Potts, D.H. (USA) 13, 127, 140, 252
Pousi, P. (Finland) 253
Povarnitsin, R. (USSR) 318, 319, 321, 424
Powell, F. (GB) 39
Powell, John (GB) 86
Powell, John (USA) 260, 261, 334,
        335, 426
Powell, M. (USA) 324, 326, 327, 328, 425
Power, D. (Australia) 160, 423
Prefontaine, S. (USA) 228, 229
Prenzler, O. (E. Ger.) 277
Preussger, M. (E. Ger.) 176, 248, 425
Pribilinec, J. (Czechosl.) 350, 351
Price, J. (GB) 55
Prieto, A. (Spain) 298
Prieto, M. (Spain) 350
Prinstein, M. (USA) 33, 35, 61, 62, 178,
        253, 425

Prokofyev, A. (USSR) 272, 308, 347
Protsenko, O. (USSR) 328
Prudencio, N. (Brazil) 253, 254, 426
Puchkov, A. (USSR) 236
Pugh, D. (GB) 139
Pujazon, R. (France) 169
Puranen, A. (Finland) 427
Purcell, J. (Ireland) 34, 35, 425
Purje, E. (Finland) 89, 90, 91, 94
Puttemans, E. (Belgium) 227, 228, 229, 422
Puuste, H. (USSR) 339, 427
Quarrie, D. (Jamaica) 200, 201, 202, 203, 205, 419, 420
Quax, T.J.L. "Dick" (N. Z.) 228, 229, 422
Quénéhervé, G. (France) 278
Quesada, Y. (Cuba) 328, 329, 330, 426
Quinon, P. (France) 321
Quow, E. (USA) 277
Rabenala, T. (Madagascar) 328
Raby, J. W. (GB) 40
Radford, P. (GB) 134, 136, 420
Rajasaari, O. (Finland) 116
Rambo, J. (USA) 243
Ramón, D. (Spain) 315
Rampling, G. (GB) 81, 125
Ramsey, M. (USA) 349
Range, R. (USA) 176, 425
Rangeley, W. (GB) 73
Rashchupkin, V. (USSR) 261
Rasskazov, R. (Russia) 418
Räty, S. (Finland) 339, 340, 342, 427
Rau, R. (Germany) 44, 45, 419
Rautavaara, T. (Finland) 186
Ravelomanantsoa, J-L. (Madagascar) 201
Rawson, M. (GB) 144
Ray, E. (E. Ger.) 203
Ray, J. (USA) 50, 88, 97, 421
Ray, R. (USA) 208, 273, 420
Ray, T. (GB) 32, 424
Rayevskiy, G. (USSR) 110
Read, N. (N. Z.) 194
Reber, C. (USA) 425
Rector, J. (USA) 44
Redmond, D. (GB) 349, 350
Reed, H.A. (GB) 23, 25
Reel, V. (USA) 365
Regis, J. (GB) 278, 347, 348, 349, 350
Regli, F. (Switzerland) 13
Reidpath, C. (USA) 46, 69, 420
Reiff, G. (Belgium) 149, 156, 157, 317
Reilly, B. (GB) 318
Reimann, H-G. (E. Ger.) 274
Reinhardt, W. (W. Ger.) 248
Reitz, C. (GB) 315

Remecz, J. (Hungary) 118
Remigino, L. (USA) 130, 131, 189
Remington, P. (USA) 425
Reske, H-J. (W. Ger.) 192
Revere, P. (USA) 29
Reynolds, H. "Butch" (USA) 285, 286, 287, 349, 350, 420
Rhadi, ben Abdesselem (Morocco) 162, 427
Rhoden, G. (Jamaica) 138, 139, 191
Rice, G. (USA) 147
Richard, R. (USA) 133
Richards, A. (USA) 59, 424
Richards, Robert I (USA) 174, 175, 425
Richards, Robert II (USA) 174
Richards, T. (GB) 160
Richards, W. (GB) 26
Richardson, H.A. (USA) 59
Richardson, M. (GB) 285, 288, 349, 350
Richtzenhain, K. (E. Ger.) 153
Riddick, S. (USA) 203, 271, 272, 419
Rideout, B. (USA) 93, 421
Ridgeon, J. (GB) 308, 309, 312
Riedel, L. (Germany) 334, 335, 336, 418, 426
Riehm, K-H. (W. Ger.) 263, 264, 337, 427
Riley, F. (USA) 76, 421
Rimmer, J. (GB) 31
Rinteenpää, O. (Finland) 169
Ritola, V. (Finland) 94, 97, 104, 105
Robbins, W. (USA) 46
Roberson, I. (USA) 177, 425
Roberson, M. (USA) 419
Roberts, D. (USA) 249, 425
Roberts, E. (Trinidad) 197, 199
Roberts, W. (GB) 82, 125, 139
Robertson, A. (GB) 52, 58, 422
Robertson, L. (USA) 48, 58, 81
Robinson, Albert (USA) 45, 419
Robinson, Ancel (USA) 423
Robinson, B. (N. Z.) 209
Robinson, C. "Arnie" (USA) 252, 255, 425
Robinson, E. (USA) 86, 88, 421
Robinson, J. (USA) 288
Robinson, M. (USA) 78, 419
Robinson, R. (USA) 201, 202, 229
Robinson, T. (USA) 197
Robinzine, K. (USA) 349
Robleh, D. (Djibouti) 304
Robson, J. (GB) 221, 222
Rochard, R. (France) 96
Rodal, V. (Norway) 288, 291, 421
Roddan, R. (GB) 281
Rodehau, G. (E. Ger.) 337

Rodgers, W. (USA) 428
Rodriguez, M. (Mexico) 352
Roelants, G. (Belgium) 225, 228, 233, 240, 241
Roggy, R. (USA) 427
Rokhlin, E. (USSR) 106
Romain, J. (Dominica/France) 328
Rono, H. (Kenya) 229, 230, 231, 242, 299, 316, 422, 423, 424
Rono, K. (Kenya) 242, 243, 424
Rono, P. (Kenya) 292, 294
Rose, R. (USA) 60, 62, 63, 64, 116, 256, 426
Roseingreve, M. (Ireland) 34, 425
Ross, D. (USA) 308
Rothenburg, H-J. (E. Ger.) 257
Rothert, H. (USA) 117
Rotich, L. (Kenya) 292, 422
Roubanis, G. (Greece) 175, 247
Roudny, J. (Czechosl.) 169
Rousseau, J. (France) 252
Rousseau, V. (Belgium) 298
Rowdon, G. (GB) 32, 424
Rowe, A. (GB) 181, 255, 426
Rowland, M. (GB) 315
Rózsavölgyi, I. (Hungary) 16, 152, 154, 159, 421
Rozsnyói, S. (Hungary) 169, 170, 424
Rückborn, H-J. (E. Ger.) 253
Rudd, B. (South Africa) 47, 48
Rudenkov, V. (USSR) 185, 262, 427
Rudisha, D. (Kenya) 272
Runge, J. (Germany) 47
Rush, J. (USA) 419
Russell, A. (GB) 58
Russell, H. (USA) 73
Rusterholz, M. (Switzerland) 285
Rut, T. (Poland) 185, 427
Rutherford, F. (Bahamas) 328
Ruto, P. (Kenya) 288, 290
Ryakhovskiy, O. (USSR) 179, 426
Ryan, J. (Ireland) 424
Ryan, P. (USA) 65, 66, 121, 184, 185, 338, 427
Rydbeck, E. (Sweden) 150
Ryffel, M. (Switzerland) 298, 422
Ryun, J. (USA) 210, 211, 212, 216, 217, 218, 219, 225, 422
Rzhishchin, S. (USSR) 170, 424
Saaristo, J. (Finland) 66, 427
Sachse, J. (E. Ger.) 263
Said-Guerni, D. (Algeria) 289, 417
Saidi Sief, A. (Algeria) 417

Saint-Yves, H. (France) 55
Sakirkin, O. (USSR/Kazak) 328
Sala, C. (Spain) 308
Salah, A. (Djibouti) 304, 305
Salazar, A. (USA) 298, 305
Saling, G. (USA) 99, 100
Salle, F. (GB) 324
Salminen, I. (Finland) 95, 96, 422
Salonen, O. (Finland) 421
Salonen, R. (Finland) 352
Salsola, O. (Finland) 154, 421
Saltikov, M. (USSR) 169
Samotsvyetov, A. (USSR) 427
Sanadze, L. (USSR) 189
Sánchez, G. (Mexico) 352
Sanders, P. (GB) 349
Saneyev, V. (USSR) 252, 253, 254, 255, 329, 426
Sanford, J. (USA) 204, 419
Sang, J. (Kenya) 207, 272
Sang, P. (Kenya) 315, 316, 424
Sangouma, D. (France) 278, 347, 348
San Romani, A. (USA) 92, 93, 421
Santee, W. (USA) 149, 151, 152
Sapka, K. (USSR) 245, 246
Sarialp, R. (Turkey) 177
Sarul, E. (Poland) 331
Sasaki, S. (Japan) 232
Sasimovich, V. (USSR/Russia) 339
Savin, V. (USSR) 347
Säwemark, G. (Sweden) 220
Sayer, L. (USA) 39
Scartezzini, M. (Italy) 243, 315, 424
Schade, H. (W. Ger.) 158
Schaffer, F. (E. Ger.) 209
Schärer, W. (Switzerland) 88
Scheele, H. (Germany) 104
Schelbert, M. (Switzerland) 312
Schenk, C. (E. Ger.) 344, 345
Schersing, M. (E. Ger.) 285
Scheuring, J. (Germany) 79, 124
Schifferstein, V. (USA) 419
Schildhauer, W. (E. Ger.) 226, 298, 299
Schiprowski, C. (W. Ger.) 248
Schirmer, F. (W. Ger.) 268
Schlöske, H-R. (W. Ger.) 207
Schmid, H. (W. Ger.) 208, 209, 239, 240, 311, 312, 313, 349, 424
Schmidt, E. (Den.) 21
Schmidt, J. (Poland) 178, 179, 252, 253, 426
Schmidt, P. (W. Ger.) 144, 145, 146, 421
Schmidt, Walter (W. Ger.) 263, 427

Schmidt, Wolfgang (E. Ger./W. Ger.) 261, 334, 335, 385, 426, 427
Schnepp, F. (Bohemia) 39
Schofield, D. (USA) 104, 423
Scholz, J. (USA) 44, 69, 71, 72, 73, 74
Schönlebe, T. (E. Ger.) 285, 286, 288
Schreiber, H. (W. Ger.) 427
Schröder, W. (Germany) 118, 119, 181, 426
Schubert, R. (W. Ger.) 236, 238
Schul, R. (USA) 223, 225
Schüller, J. (Germany) 73
Schult, J. (E. Ger.) 334, 335, 336, 418, 426
Schulting, H. (Holland) 311, 424
Schumann, H. (Germany) 197
Schumann, N. (Germany) 289
Schüttler, J. (W. Ger.) 135
Schwab, Arthur Tell (Switzerland) 126, 192
Schwab, Fritz (Switzerland) 192
Schwarthoff, F. (Germany) 308, 311
Schwartz, M. (USA) 425
Schwarz, J. "Sepp" (W. Ger.) 252, 425
Scipio Africanus, 11
Scott, C. (USA) 162, 163
Scott, D. (USA) 421
Scott, L. (USA) 424
Scott, S. (USA) 222, 292, 293, 294, 422
Seagren, R. (USA) 248, 249
Sebrle, R. (Czech. Rep.) 418
Sefton, W. (USA) 109, 110, 425
Segura, B. (Mexico) 351, 352
Seko, T. (Japan) 428
Selzer, P. (E. Ger.) 274
Sena, I. (Brazil) 285
Sepeng, H. (South Africa) 288, 289, 291, 421
Sergiyenko, Y. (Ukraine) 318
Serrano, A. (Spain) 298
Seward, G. (USA) 19, 20, 23
Sexton, L. (USA) 117
Seye, A. (France) 135, 136, 141
Seymour (Cohen), S. (USA) 186
Seymour, J. (USA) 239
Shanahan, D. (Ireland) 34, 35, 425
Shankle, J. (USA) 164
Sharp, C. (GB) 277
Sharpe, D. (GB) 288
Shattuck, K. (USA) 427
Shavlakadze, R. (USSR) 173, 424
Shaw, C. (USA) 125
Shaw, G. (GB) 31, 423
Shchennikov, M. (USSR) 350, 351, 352, 353
Shcherbakov, L. (USSR) 178, 426
Shea, F. (USA) 47, 420
Shearman, M. (GB) 12, 21, 22, 27, 30

Sheldon, R. (USA) 36, 426
Shelton, E. (USA) 171
Shenton, B. (GB) 131
Sheppard, M. (USA) 47, 48, 49, 68, 69, 154, 421
Sheridan, M. (USA) 38, 63, 64
Sherrill, C. (USA) 21
Sherwood, J. (GB) 236, 238, 239
Shevchenko, D. (Russia) 334
Shideler, T. (USA) 423
Shigematsu, M. (Japan) 232
Shine, M. (USA) 239
Shintaku, M. (Japan) 315
Shore, D. (South Africa) 83
Shorter, F. (USA) 233
Shrubb, A. (GB) 47, 51, 52, 422
Sidlo, J. (Poland) 186, 187, 265, 427
Sidorenko, V. (USSR) 337, 339
Sidorov, N. (USSR) 272, 347
Sievert, H.H. (Germany) 123, 268, 428
Sigei, W. (Kenya) 423
Siitonen, H. (Finland) 267, 427
Silio, A. (Argentina) 298
Silva, M. (Portugal) 292
Silva, R. (Portugal) 292
Silvester, J. (USA) 258, 259, 260, 426
Sime, D. (USA) 133, 135, 136, 190, 196, 284, 419, 420
Simeon, S. (Italy) 262
Simmons, A. (GB) 228
Simmons, R. (USA) 104, 423
Simon, A. (Hungary) 424
Simpkins, C. (USA) 328, 329, 426
Simpson, G. (USA) 73, 74, 75, 76, 419
Simpson, O.J. (USA) 271
Simpson, R. (USA) 57, 99, 129, 423
Sinersaari, P. (Finland) 339, 427
Sippala, M. (Finland) 122
Sir, J. (Hungary) 77
Sitkin, V. (USSR) 172, 424
Sjöberg, P. (Sweden) 318, 319, 320, 424
Sjöstedt, B. (Finland) 99
Sjöstrand, T. (Sweden) 169
Skah, K. (Morocco) 295, 298
Skamrahl, E. (W. Ger.) 286, 349
Skibba, W. (E. Ger.) 340
Skiöld, O. (Sweden) 119, 120
Skobla, J. (Czechosl.) 180, 181
Skomorokhov, V. (USSR) 236, 238
Skowronek, R. (Poland) 270
Skurigin, G. (Russia) 352
Skvaruk, A. (Ukraine) 337
Slaney, R. (GB) 384
Sloane. W.M. (USA) 22

Sloman, F. (USA) 47, 420
Slusarski, T. (Poland) 249, 250
Slykhuis, W. (Holland) 149, 156, 157
Smallwood, H. (USA) 82, 125, 420
Smart, F. (USA) 423
Smet, M. (Belgium) 428
Smirnov, S. (USSR) 331, 426
Smith, A. (USA) 27
Smith, C. (USA) 277, 281, 324, 347, 348
Smith, D. (USA) 131, 189
Smith, G. (USA) 174, 425
Smith, J. (USA) 206, 207, 272, 282, 286, 313, 326, 378, 420
Smith, L. (USA) 349, 350
Smith, M. (Canada) 344
Smith, R.R. (USA) 198, 271
Smith, Steve (GB) 318, 320
Smith, T. (USA) 197, 198, 199, 200, 201, 203, 204, 206, 272, 288, 420
Smith, W. (USA) 349
Smithson, F. (USA) 57, 58, 423
Snell, P. (N. Z.) 145, 146, 209, 210, 211, 215, 421
Snook, W. (GB) 421
Snyder, L. (USA) 76, 141
Söderström, B. (Sweden) 60
Soh, S. (Japan) 428
Soh, T. (Japan) 428
Sokolov, N. (USSR) 170, 347, 424
Sokolov, S. (USSR) 347
Soldatyenko, V. (USSR) 273, 274
Solomin, A. (USSR) 275, 350
Somodi, I. (Hungary) 59
Son, Kitei (Sohn Kee-Chung) (Jap./Korea) 98, 428
Sonn, R. (Germany) 424
Sörensen, N.H. (Denmark) 139, 142
Sörlie, R. (Norway) 426
Sosunov, K. (Russia) 324
Söter, I. (Romania) 369
Sotomayor, J. (Cuba) 318, 319, 320, 417, 424
Southern, E. (USA) 140, 141, 167, 168, 420, 423
Sowell, A. (USA) 144, 145
Spearow, R. (USA) 424
Spedding, C. (GB) 304
Spence, M. (South Africa) 140, 141, 142, 168, 420
Spence, Mal (Jamaica) 191
Spence, Mel (Jamaica) 191
Spence, Steve (USA) 305
Spencer, E. (USA) 80, 124

Spiegler, E. (Austria) 70
Spiridonov, A. (USSR) 263, 427
Spirin, L. (USSR) 192
Spitsin, V. (Russia) 352, 418
Spitz, G. (USA) 106, 107, 424
Spivey, J. (USA) 292
Spurrier, L. (USA) 144, 191
Srejovic, M. (Yugoslavia) 255
Sri Ram Singh (India) 213
Stadel, K. (USA) 426
Stadler, J. (USA) 46
Stage, C. (USA) 419
Ståhlberg, R. (Finland) 426
Staines, G. (GB) 298
Staley, R. (USA) 100, 423
Stallard, H.B. (GB) 83, 88
Stampfl, F. (Australia) 150, 154, 223
Stanfield, A. (USA) 130, 131, 132, 133, 134, 176, 189, 420
Stanley, L. (USA) 144
Stark, S. (E. Ger.) 344, 428
Starkey, D. (USA) 321
Stebbins, R. (USA) 271
Steele, W. (USA) 176, 425
Steen, D. (Canada) 344
Steers, L. (USA) 170, 424
Steffny, H. (W. Ger.) 304
Stein, P. (USSR) 173
Steinbach, M. (E. Ger./W. Ger.) 176, 177, 190, 425
Steines, G. (W. Ger.) 191
Steinhauer, N. (USA) 256
Stekic, N. (Yugoslavia) 252, 425
Stenroos, A. (Finland) 52, 97
Stenzel, R. (Germany) 292
Stephens, D. (Australia) 159
Stern, D. (USA) 40
Sternberg, B. (USA) 248
Steuk, R. (E. Ger.) 263, 264
Stevens, P. (Belgium) 278
Stevens, W. (USA) 423
Stevenson, W. (USA) 124
Stewart, A. (GB) 212
Stewart, E. (Jamaica) 271
Stewart, I. (GB) 226, 228, 229
Stewart, J. (USA) 107
Stewart, L. (GB) 226
Stewart, R. (Jamaica) 278, 281
Stewart, W. (USA) 170
Stiles, M. (USA) 68, 190
Stiles, P. (USA) 425
Stirling, A. (Argentina) 97
Stöck, G. (Germany) 117, 122, 123, 426, 427

Stoikovski, G. (Bulgaria) 253
Stoller, S. (USA) 77
Stones, D. (USA) 245, 246, 319
Stones, L. (GB) 424
Storch, K. (Germany) 121, 183, 184, 185, 427
Storskrubb, B. (Finland) 142, 166
Strand, L. (Sweden) 147, 148, 149
Strandberg, L. (Sweden) 78
Strandli, S. (Norway) 184
Straub, J. (E. Ger.) 221, 223, 422
Streete-Thompson, K. (Cayman I.) 425
Strode-Jackson, A. (GB) 49, 51, 421
Ström, K. (Norway) 116
Stulce, M. (USA) 331, 333
Sturgess, W. (GB) 40
Styepanov, Y (USSR) 106, 172, 173, 424
Styron, D. (USA) 423
Sugawara, T. (Japan) 262
Suh Yun Bok (Korea) 160
Sukharyev, V. (USSR) 189
Sule, G. (Esthonia) 123, 427
Suleiman, M. (Qatar) 292
Sullivan, J.E. (USA) 41, 42
Sunada, T. (Japan) 305
Sunde, O. (Norway) 66
Suntsov, V. (USSR) 352
Surin, B. (Canada) 278, 348, 419
Susanj, L. (Yugoslavia) 212, 213, 421
Suzuki, F. (Japan) 428
Svenöy, J. (Norway) 315
Svensson, E. (Sweden) 115, 116
Swartbooi, L. (Namibia) 305
Swarts, A. (USA) 426
Sweeney, M. (USA) 31, 32, 424
Swenson, K. (USA) 211
Syedikh, Y. (USSR) 263, 264, 337, 338, 339, 427
Syring, M. (Germany) 422
Szabó, D. (Hungary) 344
Szabó, M. (Hungary) 85, 92, 421
Szalma, L. (Hungary) 324
Szécsényi, J. (Hungary) 426
Szentgáli, L. (Hungary) 143
Szewinski, J. (Poland) 365
Szokolyi, A. (Hungary) 22
Szordykowski, H. (Poland) 218
Sztantics, G. (Hungary) 70
Tabb, R. (USA) 384
Taber, N. (USA) 49, 50, 51, 421
Tábori, L. (Hungary) 16, 152, 153, 159
Tacitus, 37
Tafelmeier, K. (W. Ger.) 339, 341
Taipale, A. (Finland) 65, 118, 426

Tajima, N. (Japan) 113, 115, 116, 177, 425
Takano, S. (Japan) 286
Takei, H. (Japan) 321
Talbott, L. (USA) 427
Talley, A. (USA) 77
Tamila, E. (Finlandia) 98
Tamm, J. (USSR) 264, 337, 427
Tanaka, H. (Japan) 106
Taniguchi, H. (Japan) 305, 307
Tanser, T. (GB) 317
Tanui, M. (Kenya) 298, 302, 428
Tanui, W. (Kenya) 288, 290, 296
Taran, G. (USSR) 240
Tarasenko, S. (Russia) 324
Tarasov, M. (USSR/Russia) 321, 322, 323, 417, 425
Tarev, A. (Bulgaria) 321
Tarmak, J. (USSR) 245
Tarnovyetskiy, P. (USSR) 344
Tarpenning, K. (USA) 321
Tarr, J. (USA) 233
Tarus, B. (Romania) 324
Taurima, J. (Australia) 324
Tauzin, H. (France) 31
Tavernari, E. (Italy) 89
Taylor, A. (USA) 350
Taylor, F.M. I (USA) 101, 102, 103, 104, 112, 124, 174, 423
Taylor, F.M. II "Buzz" (USA) 102, 174
Taylor, J. (USA) 46, 68, 420
Taylor, Robert I (USA) 82
Taylor, Robert II (USA) 201, 202, 271
Taylor, Robert, III (USA) 208, 273
Tchaikovskiy, P.I. (USSR) 319
Tebroke, G. (Holland) 423
Tegnér, T. (Sweden) 63
Telles da Conceição, J. (Brazil) 132, 171
Tellez, N. (Cuba) 289, 290
Tellez, T. (USA) 279
Templeton, R. "Dink" (USA) 80, 81
Temu, N. (Kenya) 226
Tergat, P. (Kenya) 298, 299, 302, 304, 307, 417, 422, 423
Ter-Ovanesyan, A. (USSR) 176
Ter-Ovanesyan, I. (USSR) 176, 177, 250, 251, 252, 401, 425
Tewanima, L. (USA) 52, 53, 68
Tewksbury, J.W. (USA) 31, 423
Théato, M. (France) 29, 30
Theimer, R. (E. Ger.) 262, 263
Theodoratus, G. (USA) 117
Theodosius, 11
Thom, W. (GB) 39

Thomas, A. (Australia) 153, 154, 159, 160, 421, 422
Thomas, E. (USA) 417
Thomas, Iwan (GB) 285, 288, 349, 350
Thomas, J. (USA) 170, 172, 173, 243, 424
Thomas, R. (GB) 91
Thomas, S. (GB) 28, 422
Thompson, D. (GB) 192
Thompson, F.M. "Daley" (GB) 270, 299, 344, 345, 428
Thompson, I. (GB) 233, 428
Thompson, O. (Barbados) 278, 419
Thompson, W. (USA) 180
Thomson, E. (Canada) 57, 99, 423
Thorith, D. (E. Ger.) 260
Thorpe, J. (USA) 53, 59, 67, 68, 123, 427
Thränhardt, C. (W. Ger.) 318, 319, 424
Threadgill, A. (USA) 107
Thugwane, J. (South Africa) 305, 307
Thurber, D. (USA) 107
Thys, G. (South Africa) 428
Tiacoh, G. (Ivory Coast) 284, 285, 286
Tiainen, J. (Finland) 337
Tidwell, C. (USA) 135, 136, 419
Tidwell, W. (USA) 144
Tillman, J. (USA) 210
Timashkov, I. (USSR) 264
Timmermann, U. (E. Ger.) 331, 332, 335, 426
Timmons, R. (USA) 210, 216
Tindall, H.C. Lenox (GB) 24, 420
Tinker, G. (USA) 271
Tisdall, R. (Ireland) 102, 103, 423
Tiwontschik, A. (Byel/Germany) 321
Tkachev, F. (USSR) 427
Togami, K. (Japan) 425
Toivonen, K. (Finland) 122
Tokaryev, B. (USSR) 132, 189
Tolan, E. (USA) 73, 74, 75, 76, 124, 196
Toldi, S. (Hungary) 426
Tolstikov, Y. (USSR) 305
Toomey, W. (USA) 268, 270, 428
Tootell, F. (USA) 119
Topic, D. (Yugoslavia) 318
Toppino, E. (USA) 124
Torian, R. (USA) 423
Toribio, S. (Philippines) 106
Torrance, J. (USA) 117, 179, 426
Törring, J. (Denmark) 246
Tosi, G. (Italy) 182, 183
Toutain, T. (France) 350, 352, 354
Towns, F. (USA) 99, 100, 101, 423
Townshend, E. (Jamaica) 191
Trafford, A. (GB) 423

Trandenkov, I. (Russia) 321, 425
Treacy, J. (Ireland) 304
Trengove, A. (Australia) 224
Trippe, H. (Germany) 117, 426
Triulzi, A. (Argentina) 101, 163
Troshilo, A. (USSR) 349
Trouabal, J-C. (France) 278, 347, 348
Truex, M. (USA) 423
Trusenyov, V. (USSR) 258, 259, 260
Trzepizur, J. (Poland) 318
Tsibulenko, V. (USSR) 186, 187, 427
Tsuburaya, K. (Japan) 231
Tsuda, S. (Japan) 97
Tulloh, B. (GB) 212, 215, 223
Tully, M. (USA) 321, 425
Tümmler, B. (W. Ger.) 217, 218
Tuokko, M. (Finland) 335
Tuominen, K. (Finland) 105, 424
Tuominen, V. (Finland) 422
Tura, E. (Ethiopia) 243, 424
Turner, D. (GB) 278, 284
Turner, W. (USA) 198
Tuttle, W.W. (USA) 73
Tuulos, V. (Finland) 63, 114, 116, 425
Tverdokhlyeb, O. (Ukraine) 312
Tysoe, A. (GB) 25, 420
Ubartas, R. (USSR) 334, 335, 336
Ujlaki, R. (Hungary) 426
Ukhov, V. (USSR) 192
Ulzheimer, H. (W. Ger.) 143, 191
Upcher, A. (GB) 23
Urlando, G. (Italy) 337
Urrutia, A. (Cuba) 328
Usami, A. (Japan) 232
Usov, S. (USSR) 308
Uudmäe, J. (USSR) 255, 426
Väätäinen, J. (Finland) 226
Vainio, M. (Finland) 230, 298, 299, 300, 423
Valent, G. (Czechosl.) 334
Valentin, S. (E. Ger.) 155, 421
Valiulis, R. (USSR) 273
Valkama, J. (Finland) 176, 177
Valle, E. (Cuba) 308
Valmon, A. (USA) 349, 350
Valyukyevich, G. (USSR) 426
Vamos, Z. (Romania) 240
Vana, Z. (Czech R.) 347
Van Aaken, E. (W. Ger.) 389
Van Damme, I. (Belgium) 213, 220, 421
Vanderstock, G. (USA) 236, 238
Van Dijck, W. (Belgium) 315
Van Lee, L. (France) 24
Van Osdel, R. (USA) 106
Van Reenen, J. (South Africa) 261, 426

Van Vlaanderen, B. (Holland) 305
Varju, V. (Hungary) 255, 426
Varoff, G. (USA) 109, 110, 111, 425
Várszegi, J. (Hungary) 427
Vasala, P. (Finland) 211, 216, 219
Vasilakos, C. (Greece) 28, 29
Vasilyev, A. (USSR) 311
Vassar, M. (USA) 355
Veirilä (Weidt), U. (Finland) 427
Velev, V. (Bulgaria) 335
Venzke, G. (USA) 90, 91, 92, 421
Vervoort, G. (France) 216
Vezhel, S. (USSR) 352
Viciosa, I. (Spain) 292, 298
Vickers, S. (GB) 192
Vigneron, T. (France) 250, 321, 425
Villain, J-P. (France) 241
Vinson, S. (USA) 273
Virastyuk, R. (Ukraine) 331
Viren, L. (Finland) 226, 227, 228, 229, 231, 233, 302, 305
Virgin, C. (USA) 423
Virtanen, L. (Finland) 95, 96, 97
Visser, H. (Holland) 176
Vittori, C. (Italy) 201
Voigt, E. (GB) 51
Volkov, K. (USSR) 250, 321, 425
Voloshin, L. (USSR) 328
Volz, D. (USA) 322
Voronin, V. (Russia) 318
Voss, T. (E. Ger.) 344
Vuorio, P. (Finland) 227
Vuorisalo, O. (Finland) 154
Vydra, L. (Czech R.) 289
Wade, H. (GB) 421
Wade, J. (USA) 426
Wade, L. (USA) 423
Wadoux, J. (France) 216, 226
Wadsworth, H. (USA) 425
Waern, D. (Sweden) 154, 421
Wagenknecht, D. (E. Ger.) 288
Wägli, C. (Switzerland) 145
Wagner, B. (USA) 244
Wagner, V. (Germany) 391
Wagoner, S. (USA) 424
Waigwa, W. (Kenya) 221
Wainaina, E. (Kenya) 305
Wakiihuri, D. (Kenya) 304, 305, 306
Walde, H-J. (W. Ger.) 268, 270
Walder, E. (USA) 324, 425
Walker, A. (USA) 253
Walker, D. (GB) 278, 284, 348
Walker, G. (USA) 166
Walker, James (USA) 424

Walker, John (N. Z.) 219, 220, 221, 222, 292, 422
Walker, M. (USA) 107, 170, 424
Walker, P. (USA) 77, 79, 419
Walker, R. (South Africa) 44, 45
Wallender, H. (USA) 77, 420
Wallenlind, N. (Sweden) 311
Walsh, C. (USA) 427
Ward, W. (USA) 113
Warmerdam, C. (USA) 110, 173, 174, 175, 247, 248, 321, 425
Warnemünde, W. (E. Ger.) 334
Warner, G. "Pop" (USA) 68
Warner, K. (USA) 124
Warngård, F. (Sweden) 121
Warren, D. (GB) 222
Wartenberg, F. (E. Ger.) 252
Washington, A. (USA) 334, 335, 336, 427
Washington, R. (USA) 374
Washington, T. (USA) 285, 349, 350
Watkins, W.L. "Slip" (USA) 347
Watkins, H. (GB) 28
Watman, M. (GB) 273, 418
Watson, W. (USA) 117, 179, 187, 426, 428
Watts, Q. (USA) 285, 286, 349, 350, 420
Webb, E. (GB) 70
Weber, H. (W. Ger.) 284, 286, 349
Webster, F.A.M. (GB) 41, 121
Wefers, B. (USA) 21, 22, 24, 39, 419
Weiershauser, J. (USA) 419
Weigel, R. (E. Ger.) 350, 352, 354
Weightman-Smith, G. (South Africa) 99
Weigt, P. (W. Ger.) 422
Weill, D. (USA) 259
Weimann, G. (Germany) 427
Weinberg, R. (Australia) 164
Weis, H. (W. Ger.) 337, 339, 427
Weisiger, C. (USA) 216
Wellman, B. (Bermudas) 328
Wellmann, P-H. (W. Ger.) 220
Wells, A. (GB) 196, 203, 204, 205, 277, 281, 284
Welsh, H. (GB) 421
Wennström, E. (Sweden) 99
Wentz, S. (W. Ger.) 344, 428
Werner, Charles "Chic" (USA) 169
Werner, J, (Poland) 207
Wessig, G. (E. Ger.) 247, 424
Wessing, M. (W. Ger.) 267, 427
Wessinghage, T. (W. Ger.) 221, 222, 223, 298, 299, 422
Westman, F. (Sweden) 146
Weston, E.P. (USA) 39, 40
Wharton, A. (GB) 21

Wheeler, Q. (USA) 239, 424
White, D. (Ceylon) 166
White, E. (USA) 214
White, J. (GB) 27, 28
White, M. (Philippines) 104
Whiteman, A. (GB) 292
Whitfield, M. (USA) 138, 139, 142, 143, 144, 191
Whitley, R.L. (USA) 420
Whitlock, H. (GB) 126, 193
Whitney, L. (USA) 62
Whitney, R. (USA) 236, 237, 238
Whittle, B. (GB) 349
Wide, Edvin (Sweden) 88, 89, 92, 94
Wide, Ernst (Sweden) 49, 51, 421
Wieser, R. (E. Ger.) 350
Wieslander, H. (Sweden) 67, 68, 427
Wilcox, W. (USA) 420
Wiley, C. (USA) 272, 284, 349
Wilkie, V. (USA) 420
Wilkins, M. (USA) 261, 334, 426
Wilkinson, R. (GB) 70
Willers, E.C. (GB) 422
Williams, A. (USA) 82, 83, 125, 420
Williams, H. (USA) 30
Williams, J. (USA) 278, 347
Williams, L. (USA) 426
Williams, P. (Canada) 72, 73, 74, 75
Williams, R. P. (USA) 43
Williams, Randy (USA) 252
Williams, S. (USA) 202, 203, 272, 419
Williams, U. (USA) 204, 205, 272
Williams, V. (USA) 80
Williams, W. (USA) 134, 419
Williamson, C. (USA) 125
Williamson, H. (USA) 85, 86
Williamson, J. (USA) 424
Wilmer, W. (USA) 21
Wilson, A. (Canada) 81, 84, 85
Wilson, Harold (GB) 48, 49, 421
Wilson, Harry (N.Z.) 423
Wilson, James (GB) 422
Wilson, Jerry (USA) 423
Wilson, John (USA) 424
Wilt, F. (USA) 51, 169, 223
Winder, P. (USA) 135
Windnagle, V. (USA) 48, 421
Winrow, C. (GB) 288
Winsor, J. (USA) 424
Wint, A. (Jamaica) 137, 138, 139, 142, 191, 285
Winter, A. (Australia) 114, 138
Winter, "Bud" (USA) 127, 198
Winter, J. (Australia) 170

Winter, P. (France) 118
Winzenried, M. (USA) 211
Wise, B. (GB) 30
Witherspoon, M. (USA) 348
Woellke, H. (Germany) 117, 256, 426
Wohlhuter, R. (USA) 211, 212, 213,
218, 220, 421
Wolcott, F. (USA) 99, 100, 101, 162, 423
Wolde Mamo (Ethiopia) 226, 232, 233
Wolde, Million, (Ethiopia) 303
Wolf, A. (USA) 331
Wolfermann, K. (W. Ger.) 266, 267, 427
Wolff, F. (GB) 125
Wood, C. (GB) 21
Wood, K. (GB) 153
Wooderson, Sydney (GB) 87, 88, 92, 93,
143, 155, 156, 421
Woodhouse, W. (USA) 419, 420
Woodring, A. (USA) 46
Woodruff, J. (USA) 83, 85, 86, 88, 421
Woods, G. (USA) 256, 257, 258, 426
Woods, T. (USA) 141, 420
Woody, J. (USA) 349
Workman, H. (GB) 47
Woronin, M. (Poland) 204, 277, 284, 347
Wotapek, J. (Austria) 426
Wottle, D. (USA) 211, 213, 218, 219
Wright, Duncan McL. (GB) 97
Wright, M. (USA) 60, 65, 109, 424
Wright, S. (USA) 201, 271
Wszola, J. (Poland) 245, 246, 424
Wülbeck, W. (W. Ger.) 213, 288, 290
Wyatt, H. (GB) 30, 31
Wykoff, F. (USA) 72, 73, 74, 75, 77,
78, 123, 124, 419
Yamada, K. (Japan) 97
Yancey, J. (USA) 191
Yang Chuan-Kwang (Taiwan) 188, 189,
268, 428
Yashchenko, V. (USSR) 246, 424
Yatsevich, A. (USSR) 311
Yegorov, G. (USSR) 321
Yemelin, A. (USSR) 318
Yerman, J. (USA) 141, 192
Yevdokimov, V. (USSR) 424
Yevgenyev, A. (USSR) 347
Yevsyukov, V. (USSR) 339
Yevsyukov, Y. (USSR) 350
Yifter, M. (Ethiopia) 227, 228, 229, 231,
302, 304, 422
Yoshioka, T. (Japan) 75, 76
Young, C. (USA) 186
Young, Earl (USA) 141, 142, 192, 420
Young, G. (USA) 241
Young, J. (USA) 285, 288, 349, 350, 420
Young, K. (USA) 312, 313, 314, 424
Young, R. (USA) 125
Young, W. (GB) 203
Yount, F. (USA) 423
Yrjölä, P. (Finland) 123, 125
Yu Guohui (China) 351
Yu Wenge (China) 334
Yulin, A. (USSR) 166
Yushmanov, N. (USSR) 347
Zabala, J.C. (Argentina) 97, 98, 160
Zagar, P. (USA) 119
Zaharias, G. (USA) 359
Zaichuk, B. (USSR) 263, 264, 427
Zaitsev, V. (USSR) 339
Zallhagen, O. (Sweden) 426
Zamperini, L. (USA) 421
Zander, J. (Sweden) 49, 50, 421, 422
Zátopek, E. (Czechosl.) 16, 127, 155, 156,
157, 158, 159,
160, 161, 162,
163, 224, 225,
228, 302, 310,
371
Zeleke Metaferia (Ethiopia) 304
Zelezny, J. (Czechosl.) 339, 340, 341,
342, 343, 344,
418, 427
Zhao Yongshen (China) 352
Zhelanov, S. (USSR) 270
Zhelev, M. (Bulgaria) 241
Zhu Jianhua (China) 318, 319, 424
Zimny, K. (Poland) 160, 422
Zivotic, D. (Yugoslavia) 289
Zmelik, R. (Czech R.) 38, 344, 346
Zorko, B. (Croatia) 292
Zou Zhenxian (China) 328
Zsivótzky, G. (Hungary) 185, 262, 263,
265, 427
Zuliani, M. (Italy) 284
zur Megede, E. (Germany) 408
Zwolinski, K. (Poland) 347

INDEX WOMEN

Surnames given in the following index are those under which the athletes were generally known at the peak of their career. In the case of married women their maiden name is given in parentheses.

Achilles, B. (Germany) 431
Ackermann (Witschas), R. (E. Ger.) 396, 397
Adam, M. (E. Ger.) 431
Ajunwa, C. (Nigeria) 403
Akhrimyenko, N. (USSR) 431
Albus, E. (Germany) 362
Alozie, G. (Nigeria) 393, 430
Alyoshina, N. (USSR) 432
Ammann, S. (Switzerland) 431
Anders, B. (E. Ger.) 414
Andonova (Zhecheva), L. (Bulgaria) 398, 430
Andreyeva, A. (USSR) 431
Arron, C. (France) 428
Artyomova, N. (USSR) 429
Asari, J. (Japan) 392
Ashford, E. (USA) 373, 374, 375, 413, 428
Astafei, A. (Germany) 430
Auerswald, I. (E. Ger.) 413
Ayer, M. (USA) 404
Babakova, I. (Ukraine) 399, 430
Bailes, M. (USA) 372, 428, 429
Bair, R. (USA) 431
Baker, E.L. (USA) 356
Bakogianni, N. (Greece) 399, 430
Balakhonova, A. (Ukraine) 400, 430
Balas, I. (Romania) 368, 369, 396, 430
Balzer, K. (E. Ger.) 368, 392, 430
Barber, E. (France) 412, 432
Barbour, K.H. (USA) 356
Bardauskiene (Augustinaviciute), W. (USSR) 401
Barsosio, S. (Kenya) 386, 389
Bártová, D. (Czech R.) 430
Basenko, A. (USSR) 429
Batten, K. (USA) 395, 430

Bauma, H. (Austria) 431
Baumann, (Hozang) I. (Germany) 304
Beames, A. (Australia) 390
Behmer, A. (E. Ger.) 432
Belyakova, Y. (Russia) 430
Bennie, J. (South Africa) 429
Benoit, J. (USA) 390, 392, 432
Berendonk, B. (Germany) 304, 335, 403
Berezhnaya, L. (USSR) 431
Besson, C. (France) 366, 429
Beyer, G. (E. Ger.) 431
Bidouane, N. (Morocco) 395, 430
Biess, E. (Germany) 430
Bikova, T. (USSR) 398, 430
Biryukova, A. (Russia) 404, 431
Biryulina, T. (USSR) 409
Blankers-Koen, F. (Holland) 360, 363, 368, 371, 372, 429, 430
Board, L. (GB) 366, 429
Boeck, E. (Germany) 430
Bogoslovskaya, O. (Russia) 414
Booth, (USA) 356
Borisova, Z. (USSR) 431
Boulmerka, H. (Algeria) 383
Boyle, R. (Australia) 373, 428, 429
Bozhanova, S. (Bulgaria) 431
Bragg, D. (USA) 430
Bragina, L. (USSR) 382, 384
Braumüller, E. (Germany) 431
Braun, S. (W. Ger.) 412, 432
Bréard, L. (France) 357, 358
Breuer, G. (E. Ger.) 381
Brill, D. (Canada) 397, 430
Brisco-Hooks, V. (USA) 374, 379, 414, 429
Brizgina (Vladikina), O. (USSR) 378, 414, 429
Brown, A. (USA) 413
Brown, M. (Australia) 430
Brownell, L.J. (USA) 356
Budd, Z. (South Africa) 384, 385, 386
Bufanu, V. (Romania) 430

Buford-Bailey, T. (USA) 395, 430
Burke, B. (South Africa) 430
Burneleit, K. (E. Ger.) 429
Burvill, M. (Australia) 429
Busch, S. (E. Ger.) 394, 414
Byelevskaya (Mityayeva), Y. (USSR) 402, 431
Byelova, I. (Russia) 432
Caird, M. (Australia) 430
Callas, M. (USA) 253
Callebout, N. (GB) 357
Cast, A. (GB) 357
Catherwood, E. (Canada) 105, 357, 359
Chamberlain, M. (N.Z.) 429
Cheeseborough, C. (USA) 429
Chen, I. (Russia) 431
Chen Yueling (China) 415
Chepchumba, J. (Kenya) 432
Cheromei, L. (Kenya) 386
Chi Cheng (Taiwan) 365, 428, 429, 430
Chistyakova, G. (USSR) 402, 403, 404, 431
Chizhova, N. (USSR) 369, 405, 431
Cloete, H. (South Africa) 430
Coachman, A. (USA) 368
Colón, M.C. (Cuba) 409
Costa, S. (Cuba) 399, 430
Costian, D. (Romania) 431
Cripps, W. (Australia) 372
Croker, N. (Australia) 372
Csák, I. (Hungary) 368, 430
Cusmir-Stanciu, A. (Romania) 401, 431
Cuthbert, B. (Australia) 364, 366, 372, 429
Damaske, T. (Germany) 432
Danilova, T. (USSR) 431
Davidova, A. (Russia) 431
Decker-Slaney, M. (USA) 384, 429
Dempe, S. (Germany) 430
Devers, G. (USA) 377, 393, 413, 414, 430
Didrikson, M. (USA) 359, 360, 430
Dietzsch, F. (Germany) 408
Dinescu, M. (Romania) 430
Divós, K. (Hungary) 431
Dixon, D. (USA) 414
Dollinger, M. (Germany) 362, 428

Dong Yanmei (China) 388, 430
Dong Zhaoxia (China) 430
Donkova, Y. (Bulgaria) 392, 393, 430
Dörffeldt, I. (Germany) 362
Dragila, S. (USA) 399, 400, 418, 430
Drechsler (Daute), H. (E.Ger.) 376, 378, 401, 402, 403, 429, 431
Duclos, N. (France) 366, 429
Dumbadze, N. (USSR) 362, 369, 371, 431
Dvirna, O. (USSR) 382, 429
Dyeverinskaya, A. (USSR) 414
Echols, S. (USA) 413
Eckert-Wöckel, B. (E.Ger.) 373, 378
Ehrhardt (Jahns), A. (E.Ger.) 392, 430
El Moutawakil, N. (Morocco) 394
Ellerbe, D. (USA) 431
Engelhard (Becker), R. (Germany) 359, 430
Essayah, S. (Finland) 415
Falck (Janze-Kimmich), H. (W. Ger.) 380
Farmer-Patrick, S. (USA) 395, 430
Faumuiná, B. (NZ) 408
Felke (Meier), P. (E.Ger.) 408, 409, 410, 411, 418, 431
Ferrell, B. (USA) 365, 372, 428, 429
Fesenko, Y. (USSR) 394
Fibingerová, H. (Czechosl.) 405, 431
Fikotová (Connolly), O. (Czechosl./USA) 185
Finn, M. (USA) 414
Flakowicz, W. (Poland) 431
Fleischer, O. (Germany) 431
Flintoff-King, D. (Australia) 395, 430
Fogli, L. (Italy) 391
Freeman, C. (Australia) 379, 429
Friedel, H. (E. Ger.) 431
Friedrich, B. (USA) 431
Friedrich, I. (E. Ger.) 431
Fuchs (Gamm), R. (E. Ger.) 408, 409, 431
Gabric, L. (Italy) 431
Gaines, C. (USA) 413
Galkina, L. (Russia) 403
Gansky (Sachse), D. (E. Ger.) 407, 431
Gelius, L. (Germany) 431
George, E. (Australia) 399, 400, 430
Gibb, R. (USA) 366
Gindele, N. (USA) 431
Gladisch-Möller, S. (E. Ger.) 373, 413, 429
Godbold, L. (USA) 357
Göhr (Oelsner), M (E. Ger.) 373, 374, 413, 428, 429
Gommers, M. (Holland) 366, 367, 429
Göppner, T. (Germany) 430
Gorchakova, Y. (USSR) 371, 431

Grieme, S. (Germany) 430
Griffith-Joyner, F. (USA) 374, 375, 376, 378, 412, 413, 414, 428, 429
Grigoryeva, N. (USSR/Ukr) 430
Grigoryeva, T. (Australia) 400, 430
Gubkina, L. (Byelarus) 431
Gudkova, T. (Russia) 418
Gummel (Helmbold), M. (E. Ger.) 395, 431
Gunnell, S. (GB) 395, 430
Gusenbauer, I. (Austria) 396, 430
Hagemann, A. (Germany) 431
Haight, H.l. (USA) 356
Hall, E. (USA) 359
Halstead, N. (GB) 429
Hammond, K. (USA) 429
Hansen, A. (GB) 431
Hatt, H. (GB) 357
Hattestad, T. (Norway) 410, 418, 431, 432
Haugland, H. (Norway) 399
Hemmings, D. (Jamaica) 395, 430
Henkel, H. (W. Ger.) 399, 430
Herbst, M. (E. Ger.) 431, 432
Heublein, G. (Germany) 431
Hinzmann, G. (E. Ger.) 431
Hitomi, K. (Japan) 359, 360, 404, 430
Hoffmeister, G. (E. Ger.) 382, 429
Howard, D. (USA) 414
Hrepevnik, S. (Yugoslavia) 430
Huang Zhihong (China) 406, 407
Hübnerová, M. (Czechosl.) 430
Humbert, N. (Germany) 430
Illgen, K. (E. Ger.) 431
Ionescu, V. (Romania) 401
Itkina, M. (USSR) 365
Ivan (Ilie), P. (Romania) 382, 384, 429
Ivanova, A. (Russia) 415, 431
Jackson, G. (Jamaica) 375, 429
Jackson, M. (Australia) 364, 372
Jahn, B. (E. Ger.) 430
Jahn-Voss, G. (Germany) 430
Jansson, A. (Sweden) 414
Jaworska, D. (Poland) 431
Jehličková, J. (Czechosl.) 367, 429
Jiang Bo (China) 383, 388, 429, 430
John, S. (E. Ger.) 412
Johnston, V. (Australia) 372
Jones, M. (USA) 333, 376, 377, 403, 413, 418, 428, 429, 431
Jong Song-ok (PRK) 392
Joyner-Kersee, J. (USA) 402, 403, 411, 412, 431, 432
Junghanns, E. (Germany) 430
Kacperczyk, K. (Poland) 394

Kaiser-Brown, N. (USA) 414
Kalek (Langer), L. (Poland) 430
Käsling, D. (E. Ger.) 414
Kaspárková, S. (Czech R.) 404, 431
Kaun, E. (Germany) 430
Kazankina, T. (USSR) 380, 381, 382, 383, 384, 386, 429
Keizer, I. (Holland) 429
Kempe-Zollkau, A. (E. Ger.) 431
Khristova, I. (Bulgaria) 431
Khristova, T. (Bulgaria) 408, 431
Kilborn-Ryan, P. (Australia) 430
Kleiber, J. (Hungary) 431
Klobukowska, E. (Poland) 365, 372, 428
Kocembová, I. (Czechosl.) 429
Koch, M. (E. Ger.) 373, 374, 378, 379, 414, 429
Kojima, F. (Japan) 431
Kokonova, Y. (USSR) 431
Koloska, A. (W. Ger.) 431
Kolpakova, T. (USSR) 401
Komisova (Nikitina), V. (USSR) 430
Komka, M. (Hungary) 430
Kondratyeva, L. (USSR) 373
Konikowski, D. (Canada) 432
Konopacká, H. (Czechosl.) 357
Konstantinova, T. (Russia) 431
Korablyeva, V. (USSR) 431
Korsakova, V. (USSR) 368, 430
Korzhanenko, I. (Russia) 406
Kostadinova, S. (Bulgaria) 398, 399, 430
Koubková, Z. (Czechosl.) 358, 429
Kratochvilová, J. (Czechosl.) 374, 378, 380, 381, 429
Krauss, K. (Germany) 362, 428, 429
Kravets I. (USSR/Ukr) 403, 404, 431
Kristiansen (Christensen), I. (Norway) 385, 386, 387, 388, 390, 391, 430, 432
Krivelyova, S. (Russia) 406
Krüger, L. (Germany) 431
Kühne, R. (E. Ger.) 414
Kumbernuss, A. (Germany) 406, 407
Kuragina, O. (USSR) 411, 432
Kuzyenkova, O. (Russia) 408, 431
Lamy, J. (Australia) 429
Lan Lixin (China) 429, 430
Lang Yinglai (China) 383, 429
Lange, M. (E. Ger.) 431
Laptyeva, K. (USSR) 431
Laser, C. (E. Ger.) 411
Lasovskaya, I. (Russia) 431
Lazaryeva, A. (USSR) 430
Leal, I. (Cuba) 432
Lewis, D. (GB) 412

Li Chunxiu (China) 415
Li Huirong (China) 402, 404
Li Meisu (China) 406, 431
Li Xuemei (China) 428
Lillak, T. (Finland) 409, 431
Lines, M. (GB) 356, 357
Lisovskaya, N. (USSR) 405, 406, 410, 431
Liu Dong (China) 383
Liu Hongju (China) 415
Liu Shixiang (China) 430
Loroupe, T. (Kenya) 388, 391, 392, 430, 432
Losch, C. (W. Ger.) 431
Lundström, B. (Sweden) 431
Lunn, G. (GB) 429
Lyedovskaya, T. (USSR) 395, 414, 430
Ma Liyan (China) 429
Machado, M. (Portugal) 392
Maggi, M. (Brazil) 431
Malchugina, G. (Russia) 414
Malone, M. (USA) 414
Manjani-Tzelili, M. (Greece) 411, 432
Manning-Jackson, M. (USA) 429
Marshall, M. (USA) 356
Martén, M. (Cuba) 408
Martin, L. (USA) 393
Masterkova, S. (Russia) 381, 382, 429
Mateescu, R. (Romania) 431
Mathews-Willard, M. (Australia) 132, 428
Matthes, E. (Germany) 362, 431
Mauermayer, G. (Germany) 360, 362, 369, 431
Mauermayer, T. (Germany) 431
May, F. (GB/Italy) 403, 418
Mayuchaya (Laptyeva), K. (USSR) 371
McDaniel, M. (USA) 369
McGuire, E. (USA) 365
McKiernan, C. (Ireland) 432
Mejzliková, M. (Czechosl.) 356, 357
Melinte, D. (Romania) 429
Melinte, M. (Romania) 408, 431
Mellor, F. (Australia) 372
Melpomene (Greece) 366
Menéndez, O. (Cuba) 432
Meszynski, I. (E. Ger.) 431
Meyer, E. (South Africa) 386
Meyfarth, U. (W. Ger.) 396, 397, 398, 399, 430
Mickler (Becker), I. (W. Ger.) 431, 432
Miles, J. (USA) 414
Miller, I. (USA) 413, 428
Milliat, A. (France) 13, 356, 357, 358
Mineyeva, O. (USSR) 429
Moles, L. (Spain) 408, 431

Mollenhauer, P. (Germany) 431
Montalvo, N. (Cuba/Spain) 403
Montebrun, M. (France) 431
Mota, R. (Portugal) 390, 391
Motkova, T. (Russia) 430
Mueller, M. (USA) 430
Muravyova, L. (USSR) 431
Mutola, M.L. (Mozambique) 381, 382, 429
Myelnik, F. (USSR) 407, 431
Narozhilenko-Engquist, L. (Russia/Sweden) 393, 394, 430
Nazarova, O. (USSR) 414, 429
Netter, M. (USA) 372
Neubert (Göhler), R. (E. Ger.) 411, 432
Neufville, M. (Jamaica) 366, 429
Nikolayeva, Y. (Russia) 415
Nikitina, L. (USSR) 412, 432
Nikolic, V. (Yugoslavia) 366, 429
Norman, D. (Australia) 429
O'Brien, A. (Ireland) 429
Odam-Tyler, D. (GB) 368, 430
Ogunkoya, F. (Nigeria) 429
Olizarenko (Mushta), N. (USSR) 380, 429
Opitz-Hellmann, M. (E. Ger.) 407, 431
Ostermeyer, M. (France) 371, 372
O'Sullivan, S. (Ireland) 383, 389, 429, 430
Otkalenko, N. (USSR) 365
Ottey, M. (Jamaica) 376, 377, 379, 414, 418, 428, 429
Ouaziz, Z. (Morocco) 429, 430
Ozolina, E. (USSR) 371, 431
Packer, A. (GB) 429
Paetz (Möbius), S. (E. Ger.) 432
Panfil, W. (Poland) 392
Pastoors, S. (Germany) 431
Patolidou, P. (Greece) 393
Pavlish, V. (Ukraine) 406, 407, 431
Pekarová, S. (Czechosl.) 431
Penes, M. (Romania) 371, 431
Pérec, M-J. (France) 378, 379, 429
Pernia, D. (Cuba) 395, 430
Perrone, E. (Italy) 415
Peter, L. (Germany) 430
Peters, M. (GB) 411, 432
Pfenning, I. (Switzerland) 430
Pianzola, F. (Switzerland) 357
Piercy, V. (GB) 366
Pigni-Cacchi, P. (Italy) 366, 382, 389, 429, 430
Pinigina (Kulchunova), M. (USSR) 414
Pippig, U. (Germany) 432
Pizhurina, V. (USSR) 429
Plank, I. (Germany) 431
Podeswa, B. (E. Ger.) 430

Pollak, B. (E. Ger.) 371, 411, 432
Pollock (Amoore), J. (Australia) 429
Popescu, C. (Romania) 430
Popova, A. (USSR) 431
Praetz, I. (Germany) 430
Prandzheva, I. (Bulgaria) 404, 431
Press, I. (USSR) 368, 369, 371, 430
Press, T. (USSR) 369, 431
Privalova, I. (Russia) 377, 414, 428
Prokop, L. (Austria) 432
Pyechenkina, N. (USSR) 429
Qu Yunxia (China) 382, 383, 386, 389, 429
Quirot, A.F. (Cuba) 380, 381, 382, 429
Rabsztyn, G. (Poland) 392, 430
Radcliffe, P. (GB) 430
Radke (Batschauer), L. (Germany) 357, 359
Rand (Bignal), M. (GB) 270, 369, 431
Ranky, A. (Hungary) 431
Rantanen, H. (Finland) 411
Ratjen, D. (Germany) 358, 430
Reinsch, G. (E. Ger.) 407, 408, 410, 431
Renk, S. (Germany) 411
Ribeiro, F. (Portugal) 388, 389, 430
Rieger, S. (E. Ger.) 413
Rishich, N. (Germany) 430
Ritter, L. (USA) 398, 430
Rivers, P. (Australia) 431
Roba, F. (Ethiopia) 392, 432
Robinson, E. (USA) 357
Rogachova, L. (Russia) 383
Romanova, Z. (USSR) 399
Rosendahl, H. (W. Ger.) 369, 370, 401, 411, 430, 432
Rübsam, D. (E. Ger.) 414
Rudolph, W. (USA) 364, 365, 429
Rukavishnikova, O. (USSR) 411, 432
Ryashkina, N. (USSR) 414, 415
Sabie, C. (USA) 357
Sakorafa, S. (Greece) 409, 431
Salvador, I. (Italy) 415
Samolyenko (Khamitova) (Dorovskikh) T. (USSR) 384
Samotyesova (Ignatyeva), L. (USSR) 428
Sanderson, T. (GB) 409, 431
Savinkova, G. (USSR) 431
Saxby, K. (Australia) 414, 415
Schlaak-Jahl, E. (E. Ger.) 407
Schmidt, R. (E. Ger.) 430
Schröder, H. (Germany) 431
Schulz, C. (Germany) 360, 430
Schuurman, T. (Holland) 429
Seidler, H. (E. Ger.) 414
Sevryukova, T. (USSR) 431
Shchelkanova, T. (USSR) 369, 431

Sherwood, S. (GB) 431
Shevtsova (Lisyenko), L. (USSR) 365
Shikolenko, N. (Byelarus) 411
Shikolenko, T. (Byel/Russia) 411, 432
Shiley, J. (USA) 359, 430
Shilo, K. (USSR) 359, 429
Shin Geum Dan (No. Korea) 366, 429
Shishigina, O. (Kazakstan) 430
Shouaa, G. (Syria) 412, 413, 432
Shtereva, N. (Bulgaria) 429
Shubenkova, N. (USSR) 432
Sidoti, A.R. (Italy) 415
Siegl (Thon) S. (E. Ger.) 401, 411
Silai, I. (Romania) 429
Silhavá, Z. (Czechosl.) 431
Simeoni, S. (Italy) 396, 397, 398
Simon-Slavuteanu, L. (Romania) 432
Sinitskaya, Z. (USSR) 431
Skachko, T. (USSR) 401
Slupianek (Schoknecht-Briesenick), I.
   (E. Ger.) 405, 431
Smirnova, Y. (USSR) 432
Smith, A. (GB) 429
Solms, G. Gräfin zu (Germany) 430
Solontsova, I. (USSR) 431
Sommer, H. (Germany) 431
Sowell, D. (USA) 428
Spencer, R. (USA) 399
Spielberg, C. (E. Ger.) 431
Spitzweg, A. (Germany) 430
Stecher (Meissner), R. (E. Ger.) 373, 428, 429
Stephens, H. (USA) 358, 362, 428, 429
Steuer, A. (Germany) 360
Strachkova, I. (USSR) 414
Strickland-de la Hunty, S. (Australia) 364, 372
Styepanova (Makeyeva), M. (USSR) 394, 395, 430
Sudak, S. (Byelarus) 431
Sui Xinmei (China) 431
Sukniewicz, T. (Poland) 430
Sun Caiyun (China) 399
Suttle, K. (USA) 430
Suzuki, H. (Japan) 392
Switzer, K. (USA) 366
Szabo, G. (Romania) 382, 388, 389, 429, 430
Szabó, Z. (Hungary) 430
Szewinska (Kirszenstein), I. (Poland) 365, 377, 378, 428, 429, 431
Takahashi, N. (Japan) 391, 432
Talisheva, T. (USSR) 430, 431
Taylor, E. (Canada) 360
Testoni, C. (Italy) 360, 363, 430
Thallon, I. (USA) 356
Tittel, E. (W. Ger.) 429

Tkachenko, N. (USSR) 411, 432
Todorova, A. (Bulgaria) 409, 432
Tolbert, L. (USA) 393
Torrence, G. (USA) 414, 429
Tsiamita, P. (Greece) 404, 431
Tulu, D. (Ethiopia) 389
Turova, G. (USSR) 431
Tyus, W. (USA) 365, 372, 428
Uibel (Kovarik-Siebert), G. (E. Ger.) 430
Valla, T. (Italy) 359, 360, 430
Van Heerden, E. (South Africa) 430
Van Balen Blanken, N. (Holland) 430
Vasilyeva, Y. (USSR) 359, 361, 429
Vassar, E.F. (USA) 356
Veneva, V. (Bulgaria) 430
Vereen, W. (USA) 414
Verouli, A. (Greece) 409, 431
Viscopoleanu, V. (Romania) 369, 430
Voigt (Schmalfeld), A. (E. Ger.) 401
Volkhausen, E. (Germany) 431
Voronova, N. (Russia) 414
Wachtel, C. (E. Ger.) 380, 429
Waitz (Andersen), G. (Norway) 367, 390, 391
Wajsówna, J. (Poland) 431
Walasiewicz - Walsh, S.
   (Poland) 358, 368, 428, 429, 430
Walker, B. (USA) 430
Walker, C. (USA) 367, 432
Wallace, H. (USA) 304
Walther, G. (E. Ger.) 414
Wami, G. (Ethiopia) 389, 430
Wang Junxia (China) 383, 386, 387, 388, 389, 429, 430
Wang Yan (China) 415
Wang Yuan (China) 383
Wessel, H. (Germany) 431
Westermann, L. (W. Ger.) 431
Whitbread, F. (GB) 408, 409, 431
Wilkinson, A.L. (USA) 356
Willis, D. (Australia) 429
Wilms, E. (W. Ger.) 432
Wodars (Ludwigs), S. (E. Ger.) 380, 429
Wood, A. (USA) 356
Wretman, M. (Sweden) 358, 429
Wujak, B. (E. Ger.) 401
Wyludda, I. (Germany) 407, 408, 431
Xiao Yanling (China) 407
Xinmei Sui, (China) 406
Xu Demei (China) 411
Yamaguchi, E. (Japan) 391, 432
Yamaguchi, R. (Japan) 431
Yegorova, O. (Russia) 388
Yegorova, V. (Russia) 392
Yelesina, Y. (USSR) 399

Yin Lili (China) 429, 430
Yorgova, D. (Bulgaria) 401
Zagorcheva, G. (Bulgaria) 392, 430
Zarubina, G. (USSR) 430
Zátopková (Ingrová), D. (Czechosl.) 371
Zehrt, M. (E. Ger.) 414
Zelentsova, T. (USSR) 394
Zhang Chunzhen (China) 399
Zhang Ling (China) 429
Zhang Linli (China) 383, 429
Zhang Lirong (China) 383, 387, 429
Zhong Huandi (China) 386, 387, 430
Zibina, G. (USSR) 369

Printed in Italy
August 2000